DATE DUE

For Reference

Not to be taken from this room

HISTORY OF U.S. POLITICAL PARTIES

HISTORY OF U.S. POLITICAL PARTIES

VOLUME IV
1945-1972
The Politics of Change

General Editor

Arthur M. Schlesinger, Jr.

Albert Schweitzer Professor in the Humanities
City University of New York

New York
CHELSEA HOUSE PUBLISHERS

Executive Editor: Leon Friedman
Managing Editor: Karyn G. Browne
Associate Editor: Jeanette Morrison
Assistant Editors: Michele Sacks, Betsy Nicolaus
Harold Steinberg. Chairman, Publisher.
Andrew Norman, President.
Susan Lusk, Vice President

Library of Congress Cataloging in Publication Data
Schlesinger, Arthur Meier, 1917—
    History of U.S. political parties.
    CONTENTS: v. 1. 1789-1860: from factions to
parties.—v. 2. 1860-1910: the gilded age of
politics.—v. 3. 1910-1945: from square deal to
New Deal. [etc.]
    1. Political parties—United States—History.
I. Title.
JK2261.S35   329'.02   72-8682
ISBN 0-87754-134-5

History of U.S. Political Parties

Volume I
1789-1860 From Factions to Parties

Volume II
1860-1910 The Gilded Age of Politics

Volume III
1910-1945 From Square Deal to New Deal

Volume IV
1945-1972 The Politics of Change

Contents

Volume IV
1945–1972 The Politics of Change

The Democratic Party, 1945-1960 *Davis R. B. Ross* 2673

Appendix

Democratic Platform of 1948 2711

Harry S. Truman, Acceptance Speech, July 13, 1948 2720

Harry S. Truman, Jefferson-Jackson
Day Dinner Address, March 29, 1952 2725

Democratic Platform of 1952 2732

Adlai E. Stevenson, Speech to New York
State Democratic Convention, August 28, 1952 2757

Paul Douglas, Speech to 1952 Democratic Convention 2762

Adlai E. Stevenson, "The American Vision,"
Speech at Columbia University, June 5, 1954 2772

Democratic Platform of 1956 2780

Adlai E. Stevenson, Speech at
Minneapolis, September 29, 1956 2814

Lyndon B. Johnson, Remarks to
Senate Democrats, January 7, 1959 2820

The Democratic Party, 1960-1972 *Richard Wade*. 2827

Appendix

Civil Rights Plank, Democratic
Platform of 1960, July 12, 1960 2869

John F. Kennedy, Acceptance
Speech, Los Angeles, July 15, 1960. 2871

John F. Kennedy, Speech to Houston
Ministerial Association, September 12, 1960 2876

Excerpts From the Great
Debates, September and October 1960 2879

Lyndon B. Johnson, "Let Us Con-
tinue" Address, November 27, 1963 2909

Lyndon B. Johnson, "Great Society" Speech, May 22, 1964 .. 2913

Lyndon B. Johnson, Message Requesting
Gulf of Tonkin Resolution, August 5, 1964 2917

Gulf of Tonkin Resolution, August 10, 1964 2920

Eugene McCarthy, Statement Announc-
ing His Candidacy, November 30, 1967 2922

Robert F. Kennedy, Statement
Announcing His Candidacy, March 16, 1968 2924

Lyndon B. Johnson, Address to
the Nation, Washington, March 31, 1968 2927

Robert F. Kennedy, Statement on the Assassina-
tion of Martin Luther King, Jr., April 4, 1968 2934

Hubert H. Humphrey, Speech
on American Cities, July 2, 1968 2935

Majority and Minority War
Planks, Democratic Platform of 1968 2942

Hubert H. Humphrey, Campaign
Speech on Vietnam, September 30, 1968 2945

"Mandate for Reform," McGovern Commission
Report on Delegate Selection, September, 1971 2952

O'Hara Commission Report on Rules, October, 1971 2965

The Republican Party, 1952-1972 Lee W. Huebner 2985

Appendix

Dwight D. Eisenhower, First
Inaugural Address, January 20, 1953 3057

Richard M. Nixon, Television
Address on "McCarthyism," March 13, 1954 3062

Arthur Larson, A Republican Looks at His Party, 1956 3069

Nelson A. Rockefeller, Statement on
Problems Facing the Republican Party and His
Withdrawal from the Presidential Race, June 8, 1960 3073

The "Treaty of Fifth Avenue," Rockefeller-
Nixon Pact on GOP Platform, July 23, 1960 3079

Barry Goldwater, "Grow Up, Conservatives," Address
to GOP Convention Withdrawing His Nomination, 1960 3083

Richard M. Nixon, Account of First
Television Debate with Senator Kennedy, 1960 3085

Dwight D. Eisenhower, Farewell Address, January 17, 1961 .. 3090

Nelson A. Rockefeller, Call for a United
Republican Party in 1964 Election, July 14, 1963 3095

William A. Scranton, Letter Attack-
ing Senator Goldwater, July 13, 1964 3100

Barry Goldwater, Acceptance Speech, July 17, 1964 3102

Richard M. Nixon, First Acceptance Speech, August 8, 1968 .. 3109

Richard M. Nixon, Inaugural Address, January 20, 1969 3118

Selected Speeches of Spiro T.
Agnew, October and November, 1969

    October 19, 1969, New Orleans, La.,
        Citizens Testimonial Dinner 3123

    October 30, 1969, Harrisburg, Pa.,
        Republican Dinner 3130

    November 13, 1969, Des Moines, Iowa,
        Midwest Regional Republican Committee Meeting ... 3135

    November 20, 1969, Montgomery, Alabama,
        Chamber of Commerce 3141

Richard M. Nixon, Vietnam Address, November 3, 1969..... 3147

Richard M. Nixon, Acceptance Speech, August 23, 1972 3156

The American Communist Party *Joseph R. Starobin* 3169

Appendix

Declaration of the American Delegation to the
Second Congress of the Comintern, Moscow, July 24, 1920 .. 3205

John Reed and Louis C. Fraina on "The National
and Colonial Question," Moscow, July 26, 1920.......... 3206

The Comintern on the Negro Question, 1928 3211

Joseph Stalin, Speech on the
American Communist Party, May 6, 1929 3213

Comintern Address to the
American Communist Party, 1929 3220

American Communist Party's Re-
sponse to Comintern Address, May 18, 1929 3227

Culture and the Crisis, 1932 3228

Georgi Dimitroff, "The United Front," August 2, 1935 3239

Documents on the Dissolution of the Comintern, 1943
    Proposal of the Presidium of the Executive Com-
    mittee of the Communist International for the Dis-
    solution of the Communist International, May 15, 1943 .. 3248
    The Letter of Joseph Stalin to Harold
    King, Reuter Correspondent, in Reply to
    a Question With Reference to the Dissolution
    of the Communist International, May 28, 1943 3250
    The Statement of Georgi Dimitroff, in
    Behalf of the Presidium of the Executive
    Committee of the Communist International, on the
    Approval by the Comintern Sections of the Proposal
    to Dissolve the Communist International, June 10, 1943.. 3251

Earl Browder, "The Changes in
Communist Organization," 1944...................... 3253

Jacques Duclos, Critique of Earl Browder, April, 1945 3257

American Communist Party
Draft Resolution, September 13, 1956 3274

The Progressive and States' Rights Parties of 1948
Leonard Dinnerstein 3309

Appendix

Henry A. Wallace, Speech on
Foreign Policy, September 12, 1946 3333

Henry A. Wallace, Broadcast An-
nouncing His Candidacy, December 29, 1947 3339

Henry A. Wallace, "Stand Up
and Be Counted," January 15, 1948 3343

Alfred Friendly, *Washington Post* Article, May 2, 1948 3351

Progressive Platform of 1948 3356

Henry A. Wallace, Acceptance
Speech, Philadelphia, July 24, 1948 3375

Henry A. Wallace, Campaign
Speech, New York, September 10, 1948 3383

Gov. Fielding Wright of Mississippi, State-
ment to Democratic Party Leaders, January, 1948 3399

Harry S. Truman, Civil Rights Message, February 2, 1948 3402

J. Strom Thurmond, Motion at Southern
Governors' Conference, February 7, 1948 3409

Southern Governors' Committee, Statement on Democratic Civil Rights Program, Washington, February 23, 1948 . . 3411

Southern Governors' Civil Rights Resolution, March 13, 1948   3413

Gov. Frank M. Dixon of Alabama, Keynote Address at
Southern Democratic Convention, Birmingham, July 17, 1948   3415

States' Rights Platform of 1948 3422

The American Independent Party *Marshall Frady* 3429

Appendix

American Independent Platform of 1968 3447

Press Interviews with George C.
Wallace, September and October 1968 3475

George C. Wallace, Speech at Madi-
son Square Garden, October 24, 1968 3491

Acknowledgements 3499

Index 3501

The Democratic Party
1945-1960

DAVIS R. B. ROSS is Associate Professor of History at Herbert H. Lehman College of the City University of New York. He is the author of *Preparing for Ulysses: Politics and Veterans during World War II* and has edited, with others, the six-volume *The Structure of American History*.

The Democratic Party 1945-1960

by *Davis R. B. Ross*

On April 14, 1945 a special train moved slowly into Washington's Union station bearing the body of Franklin D. Roosevelt. Moments before, a closed limousine had brought three men to the sad duty of meeting their former chief. Harry S. Truman, James F. Byrnes, and Henry A. Wallace—the major rivals for their party's 1944 vice presidential nomination—now on that Saturday morning stood unified in grief. The new president from Missouri, with shrewd instinct, had asked the South Carolinian Byrnes and the New Dealer Wallace to ride with him. Their presence together symbolized the nature of the Democratic party coalition that FDR had so carefully handcrafted. Conservative South, liberal North, and practical Border waited on that train platform. For not only had a great president of all the people died, but also a master politician.

And politics could not be excluded on this somber day. Later, as the three men drove toward the White House, Wallace and Byrnes chatted about Roosevelt's political blunder in 1938, when the president had unsuccessfully attempted to "purge" his party of anti-New Deal members. Both agreed that Democratic party unity had suffered. Little did either man know then that they would imperil that unity far more than FDR had, when they would personally lead major defections in 1948 and 1952. They could only sense, perhaps, that the dominant issues of postwar America—civil rights, Russo-American relations, internal security, economic expansion, political corruption, and national defense—would strain the delicate bonds that held the party together.

What kind of man had inherited Roosevelt's party leadership? Harry Truman liked to be thought of as an ordinary man. Plain speaking, unassuming, honest, he had the air of the average citizen. His pre-presidential years lend credence to this view. Born in 1884 in Lamar, Missouri, Truman was educated in public schools. He farmed his family acres until entering the army in 1917. He saw action in France as an artillery captain in the St. Milhiel and Meuse-Argonne offensives. After a brief, unsuccessful, but celebrated postwar stint as haberdashery store part-owner, Truman entered politics as a successful candidate for county judge in 1922. Defeated for reelection in 1924, he came back to win in 1926. Thenceforward voters kept him continuously in public office until 1953: United States senator in 1934, reelected in 1940; vice president in 1944; president in 1945, and elected to that office on his own in 1948.

He considered himself a good Democrat. He even remembered his father draping their home's weather vane with bunting to celebrate Grover Cleveland's 1892 victory. He had been a page at the party's Kansas City convention in 1900; for each election after 1906 he had been a Democratic clerk. Regularity of course did not mean blind obedience; he voted once for a Republican candidate for county marshal. Nonetheless in 1922 he possessed the prime requisites that Kansas City Democratic boss Tom Pendergast needed: as a farmer and veteran with an unblemished public record, Truman could assist the boss in maintaining party control. For the next nineteen years while Pendergast ruled Kansas City politics, the judge and later senator loyally sided with the boss. In 1941 when the machine was toppled by scandals, Truman refused to denounce Pendergast.

Some viewed this pattern of loyalty in unflattering terms. When he arrived in the Senate in 1934, a number of his colleagues—he remembers especially the old Progressives George Norris and Bronson Cutting—treated him as a hick politician. Shunning publicity, he proved to be a consistent backbench supporter of most New Deal programs. He stayed with the president until he voted to override FDR's 1936 veto of a veterans' bonus bill. Thereafter he could be counted on by the president's legislative managers. Yet Roosevelt overlooked this loyalty in 1940 when he covertly supported Truman's opponent in the Democratic primary; the emerging story of Pendergast corruption had made it expedient to ignore the incumbent.

Truman's 1940 senatorial campaign suggests he was no ordinary politician. Almost shunned by the national party leadership, bearing the full weight of a tottering Kansas City machine, a lesser man would have withdrawn or accepted the inevitable defeat quietly. Truman decided to run hard. He capitalized on his widespread connections made while serving as county judge. Slowly his perserverance won respect and, after his primary victory, the support of organized labor leaders like Alexander F. Whitney of the Brotherhood of Railroad Trainmen and, equally important, from the political chieftain of the St. Louis Democrats, Robert E. Hannegan.

The 1940 victory sent Truman back to Washington as his own man. He proceeded to show more signs of being a non-mediocre politician. In the Summer before the Pearl Harbor attack, Truman initiated a Senate probe of the then faltering preparedness effort. For the next three years he chaired the Senate Special Committee to Investigate the National Defense Program—the so-called Truman Committee—leading a deliberately low-keyed wartime inquiry into such matters as coal strikes, defense housing lags, defective airplanes, aluminum shortages, and rubber stockpiling. The hallmark of the committee and its chairman was thorough preparation and avoidance of newspaper headlines. Some observers concluded in 1945 that Truman, among civilians and aside from FDR, contributed most to the American victory. Few persons in Washington knew as much about the war effort and the nation's economy as the unobtrusive Missouri senator.

As vice president, Truman had little opportunity to serve an executive apprenticeship, let alone prepare for party leadership after April, 1945. In keeping with custom, national party machinery became his agent. The Democratic National Committee traditionally played a subordinate, perhaps even an obscured role with a vigorous Democratic president in power. Throughout much of the war, for example, the Democratic National Committee headquarters at the Mayflower Hotel was neglected. Frank Walker, Roosevelt's Postmaster General, rarely was in attendance; even the small staff had little to do. Sentiment alone dictated the keeping of such men as Charles Michelson, Herbert Hoover's bane, on the roll. The president had named Robert E. Hannegan to the post of chairman when Walker resigned in January, 1944. Hannegan had begun his political career as a Democratic committeeman in a St. Louis ward in 1934. His support of Truman in 1940 proved decisive in that campaign and Truman repaid the debt in 1941. Roosevelt offered him the post of Internal Revenue Collector for the eastern district of Missouri; in October, 1943 he moved up to the post of Internal Revenue commissioner in Washington and three-and-a-half months later he accepted the DNC chairmanship. In that position he returned the favor to Truman: in the intra-party high level discussions and pre-convention maneuvers in 1944, Hannegan helped steer the vice presidential choice to Truman.

With a congenial partner at the helm of the national party apparatus in 1945, Truman's task would be to keep in those portions of the New Deal coalition that had remained loyal throughout the war years, and to rebuild where he could those parts that had already begun to defect. The Roosevelt coalition after all was always shifting in its regional, class, racial, and ethnic composition. The pre-1933 Democratic party had been provincial and conservative in tone; it had relied mainly on southern rural and northern city Irish populations for support. Al Smith's 1928 presidential candidacy had netted the support of large numbers of Roman Catholics. By 1936, Roosevelt had completed Smith's foray by grafting onto the party Italians, Jews, Poles, and other new immigrant groups. Negroes, long loyal to the GOP, had turned Lincoln's picture to the wall by 1936 as they switched affiliation to the Democratic party. Big city machines in North and West, dispensing New Deal originated patronage and relief, helped keep these diverse ethnic, racial, and religious groups together. Organized labor, using LaFollette's 1924 Progressive campaign as a way station in its transition from Republican to Democratic politics, had also completed the step by 1936. Even farmers had been successfully wooed, largely through an enormously expanded national aid to agriculture. Middle class intellectuals, attracted by FDR's flair and openness to innovation, made up the last element of the coalition; not numerous, they nonetheless influenced party policymarking and publicity.

But the great 1936 victory had been a high water mark. The very thrust of the New Deal, appealing as it did to the disadvantaged, urban classes, increased the strains of intra-party competition. Organized labor became more prominent in party councils. The Congress of Industrial Organization's Political Action Committee (CIO-PAC) under Sidney Hillman's leadership since 1944, had become particularly visible, increasing the unease of southern conservatives. Roosevelt's own emphasis in 1940 on the New Deal goals of the four freedoms (freedom of information, of religion, of self-expression, and from fear) and his advocacy in 1944 of an "Economic Bill of Rights" (the right to jobs, food, recreation, clothing, homes, adequate health care, and education) had aroused conservative suspicions even more.

Thus in April, 1945, as Harry Truman peered ahead he could see little to cheer him about his party's future. Despite a Democratic victory in 1944 the trend seemed clear. In the House of Representatives the Democrats had lost ninety of their 333 seats from 1936 to 1945; in the Senate they had relinquished eighteen of seventy-five. The war had affected each of the Democratic party's constituent parts in ways that would make party unity difficult to achieve. War prosperity, if continued, would undercut the potent class appeal that had united Democrats in their struggle with the party of business. Organized labor had chafed throughout the war under the dual yoke of a no-strike pledge and the wage restraints of the "little steel" formula. At the same time its leaders had been emboldened by the prospects of continuing and widening their organizing drives in areas like the South ("Operation Dixie") where industrialization had spurted under war imperatives. Union membership had moved from 27.9 percent of the total United States nonagricultural work force in 1941 to 35.5 percent in 1945—the highest it was destined to reach in postwar United States history. The mixture of frustration from war restraints and of burgeoning hope about postwar advances, promised to widen the gulf between labor and the conservative wing of the party.

Black Americans had begun to enjoy new benefits, not least their improved chances of obtaining jobs in industrial employment. They would not quietly acquiesce to a rolling back of such gains as the war-born Fair Employment Practices Committee (1941). Indeed they would demand and expect that their struggle for equality be continued. Obviously this would strain the North-South party axis even more.

Cutting across class and regional lines would be a host of war-created urban problems. The long-term population shift from farm to city was dramatically accelerated during the defense and war period. By 1945, when Harry Truman came to party leadership, the old-time Democratic city machines had been seriously weakened. Leaders like Frank Hague of Jersey City, N.J.; Ed Crump of Memphis, Tennessee; James Curley of Boston; James Pendergast (Tom's nephew) or Kansas City, Missouri; and Ed Kelly of Chicago had either lost control or were in the process of doing so. More important, the exit from cities of younger men and women into military service and war industry jobs in other areas, combined with the large-scale influx of their replacements changed election precincts and districts in terms of race, ethnicity, and religion almost overnight. The older machines had too much to digest too rapidly. Also, the added burden of a swollen urban population created a housing crisis, as well as compounding the difficulty of controlling prices of other living necessities. Urban problems, never easy to solve, seemed even more intractable as a result of the war.

The non-southern agricultural portion of the New Deal coalition had, by 1945, already begun to swing back to the GOP. Roosevelt had lost the farm states of North and South Dakota, Kansas, Nebraska, Colorado, Iowa, and Indiana in 1940; joining them in 1944 were Wyoming, Wisconsin, and Ohio. As with labor and urban dwellers, farmers were concerned with war controls over prices; but as sellers they viewed price controls on meat and other foodstuffs differently. Insofar as the Democratic party became identified with efforts to keep a lid on food prices, its appeal to farmers was diminished.

Equally problematic was the stance of the liberal intellectuals within the party. Much had happened since the exciting days of the early New Deal. Even before the war the alliance between southern Democrats and conservative Republicans in Congress had frustrated the continuation of New Deal measures. The war had ended even more. The National Resources Planning Board, the National Youth Administration, the Farm Security Administration, among others, had been ambushed in 1943 by conservatives anxious to clip the wings of soaring presidential power. What might be called the third wave of liberal intellectuals—those who became identified with the New Deal after 1936—often became disengaged when they entered military service. It was not unusual for middle-level bureaucrats in the Office of Price Administration (who had been recruited from prewar New Deal agencies), for example, to don military garb. Once released in 1945 and 1946 they no longer had a home in the prewar agency, let alone with the temporary OPA. Even those who had served in civilian war agencies throughout the war, scampered to law practices or other pursuits after V-J Day.

But as unsettling as these parts of the war heritage were to Harry S. Truman, one legacy held out the hope of party unity. America's emerging role as the leading world power in the west sat easily with the party that since 1933 had promoted the cause of internationalism. To be sure some Democrats, particularly liberal intellectuals, feared that the new emphasis on fulfilling global responsibilities would deflect the nation from completing unfinished New Deal reform goals. As early as 1944, the *New Republic*, a leading liberal periodical associated with the Democratic party and the independent left, had warned FDR not to become distracted from domestic needs by his commitment to the proposed United Nations Organization. Allied with them within the party there stood a few stalwarts of prewar isolationism. But world leadership in time of peace might reasonably be expected to fuse the party, much as the requirements of war had done.

In fact the politics of reconversion and Truman's leadership sorely tested party unity most in the first two years of his administration. The party became torn over such key issues as labor-management controversies, price controls, and

Soviet-American relations. The president's often unsteady leadership helped to widen party divisions.

An early sign of party trouble came in the wake of Truman's noted "21-Point" address of September 6, 1945, calling for an expansion of peacetime welfare measures in health, housing, labor, farm, and other fields. The president had believed a major restatement of New Deal goals would provide a focus for the reconversion period and beyond. The first of the twenty-one proposals to be sent to Congress urged the creation of a permanent Fair Employment Practices Commission (FEPC). Moderately successful during the war, the FEPC had received a short lease on life in the Summer of 1945 when the administration secured a modest appropriation for it. The administration's bill for permanent status came up for debate in the Senate in February, 1946. The predictable southern filibuster, which FEPC supporters failed to end with a direct vote to impose cloture, killed the measure. The southern Democrats, who alone in the party had unanimously voted against the 1945 appropriation, were joined by seven others (primarily from the Mountain states) in beating back the cloture efforts. The southerners had been particularly angry that this had been the only administration measure ready at the outset of the Seventy-ninth Congress' second session. Senator Walter F. George (Ga.) rumbled: "If this is all that Harry Truman has to offer, God help the Democratic party in 1946 and 1948."

Robert Hannegan's ill-concealed preference for the liberal-labor wing of the party also caused trouble with southerners. With Truman's initial blessings Hannegan had assembled a new brain trust advisory group for the Democratic National Committee (DNC). The staff, which critics dubbed "Hannegan's Torpedoes," was made up of young lawyers who had originally been recruited to government service during the late New Deal and wartime periods. The DNC planning group, Hannegan vainly hoped, would develop a liberally inclined party strategy. Hannegan also openly courted the CIO-PAC and the independent urban voter. He cleared the way in 1945, for example, for the appointments of a CIO-PAC man to the United States Maritime Commission and a Negro lawyer to the United States Customs Court at New York. Hannegan's preferences, Truman's New Deal-type speeches, and Henry A. Wallace's statements in March, 1946 favoring a purge of party conservatives led the southern-dominated House caucus to stiffen its resolve to avert domination of the party by the liberal-labor wing. Hannegan's attempts to patch up matters proved fruitless. His illness and convalescence away from Washington during early 1946 blunted both his conciliatory and leadership roles.

Other domestic issues imperilled Democratic unity. Administration planners during the war had prophesized a sharp decline in economic activity in the immediate postwar period. They believed that with a rapid drop in military spending, total demand would fall off sharply, unemployment would rise, and, in the gloomiest prognosis, the Great Depression would resume. President Truman's 21-point message had included a full employment bill (ultimately passed in 1946), reflecting this concern about the resumption of hard times. As it turned out the economy moved in the opposite direction. Government spending did plummet; but pent-up consumer demand helped take up the slack. Wartime savings, numerous wage increases across the board in industries like steel and coal, began to cook up pressure on prices. Rather than facing a period of economic hardships, the nation was posed with the problem of maintaining stability in wages and prices.

Wage and price control measures of course had particular significance to Democrats. Such measures dramatically reversed the strategic role of the president (acting as party leader) from one of dispensing favors to one of withholding them. The test of party leadership would then call for a delicate balancing of restraints.

The wage issue emerged first. A rash of labor disputes broke out during 1945 and early 1946. In the short period between V-J Day and January, 1946 major strikes occured in electrical, oil, bituminous coal, northwest lumber, and auto industries. The president's desire in November, 1945 to "cool off" the situation, however, proved of little avail. Neither industry nor labor were willing to accept his formula of linking wage gains with price rise limitations. Meanwhile disputes continued unabated; more than a million workers in communications, electrical, meatpacking, and most important, steel industries walked off the job in January, 1946 alone.

The appeal to voluntarism having failed, Truman then proposed that Congress authorize fact-finding boards in labor disputes effecting the public interest. The conservative House majority rapidly converted this relatively modest proposal into a harsher anti-labor bill. The Case Bill was supported by almost forty-eight percent of the Democrats who had voted, despite strenuous efforts by House leadership. The South went almost entirely for the bill; only liberally-inclined members like Luther Patrick (Alabama) and Estes Kefauver (Tennessee) voted against it. Before the Senate could act, the Brotherhoods of Railroad Trainmen and Locomotive Engineers in April, 1946 rejected a wage settlement suggested by a fact-finding board; the unions prepared to walk out on May 18 (later changed to May 23) if their demands were rejected.

The president's response almost tore his party apart. Infuriated by the obdurate attitudes of the railway labor chieftains Alvanley Johnston of the Engineers and Alexander F. Whitney of the Trainmen, the president used his war powers to seize the railroads when the workers struck on May 23. Then he angrily denounced them on the 25th when they refused to accept the government's wage proposals. The president appeared before a joint session of Congress to ask for emergency power to draft the striking workers into military service. Shortly after beginning the talk, he was handed a note announcing the settlement of the dispute. Undaunted in his resolve, Truman completed his address, seemingly encouraging Congress to continue on its anti-labor course. The railroad workers had to capitulate. But they did so with real bitterness; Whitney vowed that his union would use its entire $47 million treasury to defeat Truman in 1948 if he chose to run for reelection.

Four days after Truman's speech Congress sent an amended version of the Case Bill to the president for approval. Those who had predicted that Truman would accept the Case Bill were proved wrong. In a lengthy veto message he asserted that the proposed legislation would not ease the settlement of labor disputes; at the same time he said that no legislation should be either anti- or pro-labor. The House failed by only five votes to overturn his veto. Again southern Democrats broke ranks as forty-five percent of the party members who voted refused to stand by the president.

Truman had triumphed. But the cost in party unity was high. The events on the labor front of late 1945 and throughout 1946 exposed an important vulnerability of the party. Southerners in Congress could and did unite against their urban colleagues of North and West. The president's seemingly erratic and intemperate reactions to strikers angered organized labor and liberals. Both usually provided willing workers at the precinct level to bring out the voters, the majority of whom nationally were registered Democrats. A reduction in the liberal-labor wing's zeal would seriously impair the party.

Attempts to control prices—the other half of a basic reconversion problem—compounded the party's difficulties. During the Autumn of 1945 the Truman administration had lifted most wartime controls. As food, housing, and clothing prices soared in December, 1945 and early January, 1946, Truman tried to reverse policy and have his price control authority augmented. On January 21, 1946 he asked Congress to extend his war powers, due to expire on June 30. He asserted that inflation was "our greatest immediate domestic problem;" without controls, he warned, "our country would face a national disaster." The struggle over price controls and subsidies (payments to producers in lieu of price increases) began in earnest.

Congress was in no mood to heed his entreaties. Although constituents from urban centers might implore their representatives to hold firm on prices, organized pressure groups found more sympathy. Thus beef cattle producers, food processors, and farmers generally had greater leverage than urban consumers. Controls and subsidies alike were repugnant to those who believed in a largely unrestricted, expanding market economy. Some, like the Maryland Democratic Congressman Dudle G. Roe believed that God had sanctioned the law of supply and demand. The Office of Price Administration (OPA) became the culprit in rising prices, giving opponents of bureaucracy—a safe political target—other reasons to oppose the noxious controls. Whatever the reason, Congress passed a control bill so riddled by crippling amendments that the president concluded he preferred inflation with no law to inflation with one. The House failed to override his veto by thirty-seven votes; as with the Case Bill, large numbers of Democrats (forty-five percent) deserted their leader. Congress then extended the executive's existing authority, but with restrictions that made the president's power almost meaningless.

The most dramatic result of the protracted struggle over controls was a serious beef shortage in the Fall of 1946, shortly before the congressional elections. Beef producers blamed the government controls for the sharply reduced supply of cattle for slaughter; OPA supporters argued that the producers themselves had gone on a "strike," forcing the shortage. The president, with little else he could do, lifted all controls on meat on October 14. Urban consumers, organized labor, and liberals were angered by the move.

Thus, on both wage and price fronts, the president had contributed to internal party friction. Conservatives were not mollified by Truman's appeal for stern emergency power over labor disputes in light of his veto of the Case Bill. Liberals saw him back and fill on price control despite his veto of the price control extension bill.

By Autumn 1946, the liberals had already started on the road that would lead some of them to a formal break in 1948. In retrospect much of the liberals' discontent seems to have flowed from a dissatisfaction over their party leader's style, rather than with the content of his policies. Enamored by FDR, it was hard to accept his successor without comparing the two men. An illuminating incident occurred in March, 1946 over an attempt by Truman to repay a political debt. He had nominated Edwin W. Pauley, a prominent Californian and past treasurer of the Democratic National Committee, to the position of Assistant Secretary of the Navy. To many this seemed a routine move to reward a big contributor. But not so to a suspicious long-time Bull Mooser, Harold L. Ickes, the Secretary of the Interior. Ickes smelled oil in the deal. Pauley was an independent oil producer and a vigorous advocate of state control over oil located under submerged offshore lands. Ickes feared not unreasonably that Pauley would exert a sinister influence on federal oil policy. The old curmudgeon waited until the Senate commenced formal hearings before he let loose with his condemnation. When he did, he in effect told the president "choose Pauley or me." Truman, under no obligation to Ickes, stuck by his friend. The damage had been done, however, and Pauley withdrew from consideration.

Ickes was not the only disgruntled liberal. During the Summer of 1946 Chester Bowles, head of the OPA, and Wilson Wyatt, the Housing Expediter, left the administration disillusioned over their failures to persuade Truman to embark on bolder price control programs.

More important that the defection of Ickes, Bowles, or Wyatt, was the explosion involving Henry A. Wallace in September, 1946. Shunted aside by party leaders in 1944 in favor of Truman, Wallace had become the self-professed carrier of the New Deal tradition. During the war Wallace had issued a steady flow of letters and speeches that set forth goals for a continuing, expanded postwar New Deal. By 1945 he had proclaimed that America, through private and public sectors, should provide for a minimum of sixty million jobs.

But this was Wallace's foreign policy views that raised difficulties in 1946. He believed that the United States should extend friendly accomodation to the Soviet Union. He assumed that he understood what course FDR would have adopted if he had lived. As Soviet-American relations began to grow troubled during late 1945 and early 1946, Wallace became uneasy. From his vantage point it appeared as if Harry Truman was surrounding himself with advisers who not only distrusted Soviet intentions, but also forced the Russians to fulfill the advisers' prophecies. Both the Secretary of State James F. Byrnes and the Ambassador to the Soviet Union Averell Harriman in fact urged a firm stance toward Russian postwar demands.

During the Summer of 1946 Wallace began to speak out in favor of peaceful accomodations with the Russians. The climactic break came as a result of his September 12, 1946 speech in New York City. Wallace criticized both the United States and Russian policy; but the anti-Russian portions tended to be subdued and, more important, largely ignored by press accounts of the speech. Even while Wallace spoke in New York, Byrnes was conferring with the Russians in Paris on the terms of the East European peace treaties. Byrnes wired Truman: "If it is not completely clear in your own mind that Mr. Wallace should be asked to refrain from criticising the foreign policy of the United States while he is a member of your cabinet I must ask you to accept my resignation immediately." Wallace asserted that he had gone over the speech with Truman paragraph by paragraph. Truman, responding to reporters' questions on the day of the speech said that he had cleared it. Two days later when pressed on the issue, Truman said he had approved of Wallace's right to make the address, but not the sentiment it conveyed.

Accompanied to the Paris Conference by the ranking members of the Senate Foreign Relations Committee—Tom Connally of Texas and Arthur Vandenburg of Michigan—Byrnes was not content. He continued his critique of Wallace; this plus a barrage of hostile editorial and mail opinion adverse to Wallace, pushed Truman to the decision that he must fire his Commerce Secretary. Firing Wallace was a clumsy way to extricate himself from a mess; it also encouraged third party adherents in the Democratic party's left wing. Wallace's address had been delivered to an Independent Citizens Committee of the Arts, Sciences, and Professions (ICCASP) and National Citizens Political Action Committee (NCPAC) sponsored political rally to support the New York State Democratic-American Labor party ticket in the 1946 Autumn elections. In the short run, dumping Wallace hardly made ICCASP or NCPAC members willing to increase their campaign exertions for administration candidates. At issue was not the detachment of a minor element of the Democratic party coalition. The NCPAC was an auxiliary publicity machine of the CIO-PAC; it, along with ICCASP and the anti-communist Union for Democratic Action (UDA) represented a considerable amount of the Democratic party's youth and glamor. Loss of NCPAC might presage loss of CIO-PAC and of labor generally. Loss of labor would cripple the party's ability to penetrate areas not served by the older Democratic party's city machines, such as Detroit, Los Angeles, and Philadelphia. The industrial unions were entry points to many urban communities; this could not be ignored by party strategists as they looked forward to the November, 1946 congressional elections and beyond them to the big year of 1948.

Wallace's dismissal also raised another difficulty for the party in the postwar period. His proposal for peaceful accommodation with the Soviet Union ran counter to a latent but growing anti-Communist feeling shared widely within the party. Anti-Communism in 1945 and 1946 extended from the conservative southerner John E. Rankin of Mississippi to James Loeb, the executive secretary of the UDA. The liberal-labor wing was particulary torn by the Communist question. Labor unions like the United Auto Workers (CIO) and United Electrical Workers (CIO) suffered from internal struggles over the role of Communists within their own ranks.

By late October, 1946 pollsters had picked up the tremors of voter discontent. High meat prices, food shortages, scarce housing, intraparty feuding over Communism—all pointed to a rocky election experience for Democrats. The GOP had a multitude of issues; the slogan "Had Enough? Vote Republican," summed them up. The Democrats were listless. Truman was asked to stay at home. Hannegan and other party leaders used recordings of FDR's speeches in a vain attempt to capitalize on the frayed New Deal memories that once had worked so well. Even the CIO-PAC, so energetic in 1944, moved about with no particular confidence as it worked selectively to punish incumbent congressmen for their anti-labor voting records.

The election returns jolted the party. It lost control of both Houses; in the Senate the Democrats lost twelve seats, in the House of Representatives, fifty-five. The GOP had made its most successful gains since 1920. Eleven Democratic senators had stood for reelection outside the safety of the deep South. Only four, Harley M. Kilgore (West Virginia), Joseph C. O'Mahoney (Wyoming), Ernest McFarland (Arizona), and Dennis Chavez (New Mexico) survived. Five other Democratic seats had been contested in North and West: Democrats captured only two, J. Howard McGrath (Rhode Island), and Herbert R. O'Conor (Maryland). The story was the same to the House. The party lost more than forty percent (57 of 138) of its non-Southern seats; the GOP lost but three of its own. The urban centered wing of the party lost heavily. The democracy in California, Illinois, Michigan, Missouri, New York, and Pennsylvania yielded up a combined total of thrity-three of its seventy-six seats to the GOP. All six of Philadelphia's Democratic congressmen lost; the party lost four of its nine in Chicago, five of seven in Los Angeles, five of twenty in New York City, two of five in Detroit, and so on. Particularly acute was the devastation to the liberal-labor faction. Liberal Democrats (defined by adherence in the past to liberal issues) lost seven of eight contests for the Senate, and thirty-seven of sixty-nine in the House.

Truman's reputation was very low. At one point during the campaign the DNC desperately had tried to bypass the president and to shake loose from the political potential of price control. It had passed a resolution directing Hannegan to discuss with the Decontrol Board "ways and means of increasing the meat supply available to the American people." Truman had dressed down both the DNC and Hannegan; the latter tore up the resolution. The incident underscored the fact that the president embarassed the party. The party's use of the Roosevelt speeches and the restraint placed upon the president's campaign activities were humiliating confirmations of Truman's low repute. After the election, Arkansas Democrat J. William Fulbright even proposed that Truman appoint a Republican Secretary of State, and then resign to allow the voters' will to be truly carried out. Only Dean Acheson, the Under Secretary of State, and a couple of newsmen were at hand to welcome the president back to Washington after he had cast his vote at Independence, Missouri. Now a minority party in Congress with a tarnished leader in the White House, the Democratic party saw a cheerless future leading to 1948.

Dismal prospects at least forced the presidential wing to develop a winning strategy, to refurbish Truman's image. The device hit upon—at first instinctively, then designedly—received its final form in late 1947 at the hands of Clark Clifford, the president's chief speech writer. He believed Truman should move to the left—become the champion of civil rights, of housing reform, of labor's rights—co-opt as many liberal programs as possible to halt the movement away from the party of its urban components. Clifford thought the South had little choice but to remain within the party; even if some did take a walk they would not seriously injure the president's chances to capture southern electoral votes. But the problems in the northern democracy, Clifford reasoned, were more dangerous. The northern dissidents had a willing third party leader around whom to rally in the person of Henry A. Wallace (who in fact became an avowed candidate in December, 1947). The big swing states of New York, Pennsylvania, Ohio, Michigan, and California had sizeable numbers of Democrats who might respond to Wallace's siren call.

From the very beginning of the Eightieth Congress' first session in January, 1947, Truman had begun to veer to the left. Despite the decimation of the pro-labor Congressmen, Truman locked horns with Republicans and conservative Democrats over the Taft-Hartley Act. The bill banned, among other provisions, the closed shop, jurisdictional strikes, secondary boycotts, mass picketing, and political campaign contributions by unions. Southerners in both Houses, with few exceptions, supported the bill. Truman's substitute measure, introduced by Senator James E. Murray (Montana) and ten others, lost in the Senate by the devastating vote of 19-73, with Democrats dividing 19-23.

To no one's surprise, Truman vetoed the act on June 20, 1947. His general statement summed up his objections:

> The bill taken as a whole would reverse the basic direction of our national labor policy, inject the Government into private economic affairs on an unprecedented scale, and conflict with important principles of our democratic society. Its provisions would cause more strikes, not fewer. It would contribute neither to industrial peace nor to economic stability and progress. It would be a dangerous stride in the direction of a totally managed economy. It contains seeds of discord which would plague this Nation for years to come.
>
> * * *
>
> I have concluded that the bill is a clear threat to the successful working of our democratic society.

Passage of the Taft-Hartley Act (the Labor-Management Relations Act of 1947) over Truman's veto had considerable political consequences for the Democratic party. In one way the act (despite its support by southerners) became an important rallying point for the party so torn by internal dissension. President Truman used it skillfully as a campaign issue while in office through 1953—and later, as the party's distinguished elder statesman. In his charges that the Eightieth Congress was a "do-nothing" body, the Taft-Hartley Act took on a central role: Republicans "did nothing" positively to aid labor, only "penalized" with the bill.

By the end of 1947, Truman had at least attained order in his own house. In September, 1947 he had replaced the ailing Hannegan with J. Howard McGrath, a newly elected senator from Rhode Island, as head of the DNC. The president also had achieved numerous gains in his "get tough" policy with international Communism in 1947. Soviet intransigence in the United Nations and pressure on Turkey brought forward the Truman Doctrine and Greek-Turkish aid in May. The Marshall Plan was unveiled at a Harvard University commencement exercise in June. These bipartisan moves enhanced Truman's image as a statesman. His veto of the Taft-Hartley Bill improved his standing with the liberal-labor wing.

Local elections in 1947—although mixed in results—cheered the Democrats. Special congressional elections had seen no continuance of the GOP 1946 sweep. On the state level, the only important election saw the victory in Kentucky of the former Congressman Earle C. Clements for governor. The Taft-Hartley Act was the chief issue in the election; Clements had voted against it, his GOP opponent had praised it. Clements' victory carried in a Democratic slate in Louisville, displacing twelve Republican aldermen. As usual, the local mayoralty campaigns showed no clear patterns. The old Edward J. Kelly machine in Chicago had entered a temporary decline when a Democratic-Independent, Martin Kennelly, won the mayor's seat. Kelly himself had been ousted as Democratic National Committeeman by the county committee, led by Kelly's protégé and successor, Colonel Jacob M. Arvey. Elsewhere the party did well in mayoralty races in Indiana, Massachusetts, Detroit, and Cleveland; the Republicans maintained or advanced their positions in Connecticut, New York, and Philadelphia.

The Clifford strategy became conscious policy in February, 1948 when Truman sent a special message to Congress on civil rights. He called for the enactment of items from a long menu, ranging from a permanent FEPC to statehood for Alaska and Hawaii. Again, as two years before, southerners were enraged that the civil rights question should be the first proposal to be thrust at Congress. Eugene E. Cox (Georgia) claimed that "Harlem is wielding more influence with the administration than the entire white South." Senator Tom Connally (Texas) thundered that the program was a "lynching of the Constitution." A House ad hoc group of seventy-four southerners pledged themselves to work with southern governors to defeat Truman's program. Although nothing came of his civil rights program in the Eightieth Congress, the strategy of attracting liberals was well underway.

At first, Clifford's strategy brought meager results. All that appeared to come of Truman's new stance was increased resistance by liberals and the urban machines to his candidacy for nomination. During the 1948 Spring, a "Draft Eisenhower" movement got underway. The popular commander of allied forces in Europe seemed a perfect candidate for desparate Democrats, convinced that Truman would lose in November. Although some southerners like Richard Russell and Harry F. Byrd supported the Draft-Eisenhower boomlet, the main impetus came from northern and western urban components of the party. City machine politicians like Colonel Jacob Arvey of Chicago-Cook county; Paul O'Dwyer of New York; Frank Hague of Jersey City; and FDR's eldest son James, in Los Angeles; and liberals like Senator Claude Pepper (Florida), Minneapolis Mayor Hubert H. Humphrey, and former OPA director, Leon Henderson, Chester Bowles—clung to the hope (at least until June) that Eisenhower would lead the party away from sure defeat. The more Truman wooed the liberals, it seemed, the more convinced they became of his inadequacies.

With Eisenhower refusing to run, Truman won on the first ballot at the Philadelphia convention, sweeping aside the token candidacy of Richard Russell. The president woke up the somnolent delegates with his 2:00 a.m. acceptance speech. He castigated the GOP for its "rich man's" stand on taxes, housing, and price controls. He called for the repeal of the Taft-Hartley law. Most dramatically he hurled a challenge at the "do-nothing" Eightieth Congress. He would bring Congress back into a special session on July 26 ("Turnip Day in Missouri") to complete all the unfinished business before it: anti-inflation legislation, social security extension, more public power projects, and a new immigration law that would not be "anti-Semitic" or "anti-Catholic" in intent. The speech overshadowed both the convention's sentimental choice of the Senate minority leader Alben Barkley (Kentucky) as the vice presidential candidate, and the walk-out of the Mississippi and Alabama delegations when the vigorous civil rights plank was adopted.

Emerging from Philadelphia, the party became saddled with potentially a serious issue: disclosures that alleged that Communists had held government positions under the New Deal and war administrations. From 1945 onward, congressional committees—particularly the House Un-American Activities Committee (HUAC)—had busily probed for evidence of Soviet affiliated Communist activity in the United States. Labor unions, the Hollywood motion picture industry, and the American Communist party itself had been investigated. Up to 1948 the focus had been extra-governmental.

But the probes turned inward in 1948. In July a confessed former Communist agent, Elizabeth Terrill Bentley, testified before HUAC that Lauchlin Currie, one of FDR's wartime assistants, and Harry Dexter White, formerly an assistant secretary of the treasury, had given information to a spy ring allegedly run by another treasury official, Nathan Gregory Silvermaster. Both Currie and White denied Bentley's allegations. In August, a second disclosure was more dramatic. Whittaker Chambers—a former Communist party member and, in 1948, a senior editor for *Time* magazine—accused nine governmental officials of participating in governmental spy rings. His most important target was Alger Hiss, one-time State Department adviser and currently president of the Carnegie Endowment for International Peace. Chambers' story was rejected in all its particulars by Hiss. A series of confrontations between the two men (some of which were arranged by an hitherto obscure HUAC member, Richard M. Nixon) became front page news during the Autumn, 1948 election campaign. President Truman had, as early as August 5 (two days after Chambers' first testimony), dismissed the disclosures as merely a "red herring" to distract attention from the fact that HUAC shunned hard work.

Truman, ignoring the subversion charges, waged a classic barnstorming campaign. He focused his attacks more on the "do-nothing" Congress than on his opponents, Republican Thomas E. Dewey, States' Rights Strom Thurmond, and Progressive Henry A. Wallace. The president travelled 31,000 miles, speaking at hundreds of railroad stops throughout the country. He used "give-em-hell" tactics whenever he could. After the Turnip session had ended without enacting Truman's program, the president pilloried it further: "When I called them back into session what did they do? Nothing. Nothing. That Congress never did anything the whole time it was in session." Stumping the nation, the president also told his listeners to vote the straight party ticket, as he did from a railroad car in Oklahoma: "Send Bob Kerr to the Senate, and send Tom Steed here to the House. If you do that in Oklahoma, and all over the United States, the Republicans won't have a chance to sabotage the people's programs in the next session."

As the campaign drew to a close, Truman appealed to ethnic and religious minorities, reminding them of the party's solicitude over the past fifteen years. The DNC's nationalities division, headed by Polish-American Michael Cieplinski, specialized in reaching in the nation's foreign language press. Fortunately for Democrats, Wallace's campaign crumbled as his party became associated more and more with Communists, helping to blunt its ethnic appeal. Polish-Americans, for example, would be slow to support such a party, given the post-1945 Russian actions in Poland. The Democratic party's 1948 platform, moreover, had mentioned the Poles specifically. A last minute radio speech by Eleanor Roosevelt—undoubtedly the party's favorite liberal—had been arranged by the DNC as a counter to Wallace's attempt to garner liberal votes. Truman's own speeches about United States support of Israel, aimed at New York's Jewish voters, capped the largely successful Democratic effort to contain the Progressives' drive. Truman could expect a traditionally strong urban-ethnic vote.

The 1948 election changed Truman from a has-been to a bringer of miracles. He later quipped, "before you offer to bury a good Democrat, you better be sure he is dead." Although he lost the industrial states of Pennsylvania, Indiana, New Jersey, Maryland, Michigan, and New York (the last three undoubtedly due to Wallace's candidacy), and the southern states of Alabama, Louisiana, Mississippi, and South Carolina (due to Thurmond's successes), Truman carried Massachusetts, the border states, the bulk of the southern states, the Midwest farm states, the Mountain states, and all but Oregon on the Pacific coast. He received 303 electoral votes to Dewey's 189 and Thurmond's 39; he gathered approximately 49.6 percent of the total popular vote, to Dewey's 45.1, and Thurmond's and Wallace's 2.4 each.

Besides vindicating the president, the voters returned Democrats to majority power in both Houses. A net gain of seventy-five seats in the House of Representatives gave the party a margin of ninety-two; in the Senate, Democrats won nine seats, moving them to a majority of twelve. Among the Senate victors there would be new faces and future leaders: Paul H. Douglas (Illinois), Lyndon Baines Johnson (Texas), and Estes Kefauver (Tennessee). Even in gubernatorial contests, Democrats did well, gaining a net of seven statehouses, bringing them a bulge of twelve. They wrested governorships from GOP hands in Massachusetts, Connecticut, Ohio, Indiana, Michigan, and Illinois.

A big winner for the Democrats was Adlai Ewing Stevenson, as governor of Illinois. Stevenson, a grandson and namesake of Grover Cleveland's second term vice president, had been in and out of national government service from early New Deal days through the war. He had wanted to run for the Senate, believing that his best talents were forensic rather than executive. Jacob Arvey, however, thought that the veteran Republican incumbent, C. Wayland Brooks, needed to be matched "wound for wound, deed for deed" in downstate Illinois. Paul H. Douglas, a World War II marine veteran and university professor, seemed better suited. Arvey offered the gubernatorial nomination to Stevenson. He then went on to win with the largest plurality in Illinois history, 572,067 votes, probably helping Truman to win the state, since the latter's margin was a mere 33.612.

The party's number one attraction remained Harry S. Truman. As he had done in 1945, the president launched a "Fair Deal" legislative program on January 5, 1949. The Fair Deal set ambitious goals. Truman asked for legislation to replace the hateful Taft-Hartley Law by a modified Wagner Act. The rest of the list included requests for laws to enact civil rights, to control inflation, to raise corporate taxes, to raise minimum wages, to broaden social security benefits, to strengthen anti-trust laws, to continue farm subsidies, to provide financial aid to education and housing, to set up a compulsory national health insurance system, and to protect national natural resources (especially undersea petroleum).

Although enjoying a nominal Democratic majority in the Eighty-first Congress, Truman fared poorly with these proposals. Congress did pass, to be sure, a slum clearance and public housing act on July 15, 1949. The legislation had been long aborning; for four years it had been a source of major domestic controversies. Formidable lobbying efforts lined up virtually every organized pressure group either for or against the bill. But victory for public housing adherents came when the administration held the House Democratic conservative vote against the bill to only eleven votes more than the liberal Republicans voting for it; the large non-southern liberal block then carried the bill's passage easily. The president also succeeded in obtaining limited minimum wage gains in 1949, when Congress agreed to the seventy-five cent per hour limit that Truman had requested. His last major success came with the adoption of a far-reaching reform of the social security system in 1950.

Still, Truman lost on federal aid to education, which ran against the rocks of powerful religious feelings. The House did pass FEPC and poll tax measures; but both languished in the Senate. Taft-Hartley remained on the books. A reorganization plan setting up a Health, Education, and Welfare cabinet-level post was rejected by the Senate in 1949 and by the House in 1950. Lastly, the administration's farm program, the Brannan plan, was rejected outright.

The Fair Deal had run out of steam by 1950. Worsening foreign affairs and a preoccupation with domestic subversion spelled the end of Truman's hopes for extensive domestic legislation. The Democratic party now was placed on the defensive. In foreign affairs, the year 1949 had opened with mixed returns: Truman proposed the famous Point Four (technical aid to developing countries) on January 20; two days later the Chinese Communists had seized Peking. The balancing of firm action and bad news continued during the year: the North Atlantic Treaty Organization was set up in April; Dean Acheson, the new Secretary of State, ruled out further aid to Nationalist Chinese forces in August. The Soviet Union lifted the Berlin blockade in September; but the Americans learned that the Russians had exploded their first atomic bomb that very month. From then on into 1950, events seemed unrelentingly bad: the Chinese Nationalists fled the mainland in December, 1949 and, most important, North Koreans crossed the 38th parallel on June 25, 1950.

Setbacks abroad were paced by disclosures of perfidy at home. Eleven top American Communists were convicted on October 14, 1949, after a nine-month trial, of advocating the violent overthrow of the United States government. On January 21, 1950, Alger Hiss was found guilty of perjury when he had said that he had not previously known Whittaker Chambers. An unknown Republican senator from Wisconsin, Joseph R. McCarthy, told a Wheeling, West Virginia, group in February, 1950 that he had a list of State Department employees who were known Communist sympathizers. The GOP demanded that Truman eat his "red herring."

Not less embarrassing were disclosures during 1949 and 1950 that influence peddlers—"5 percenters," so-called because of the fee they charged for obtaining government contracts and other favors—had been able to gain advantages at the behest of President Truman's close friend and air force aide, Brigadier General Harry Vaughan. Vaughan was accused of interceding on behalf of influence peddlers to obtain a permit for scarce building materials to be used for a race track, to seek molasses for a New Jersey firm, and to get clearance early in the postwar period for business trips to Europe on Army planes. The big headlines, however, involved deep freezes that had been given to Vaughan, to Mrs. Truman, to Chief Justice Fred M. Vinson, to Federal Reserve Governor James K. Vardaman, and to the president's secretary Matthew J. Connelly. A senate investigating committee chaired by Democrat Clyde R. Hoey (North Carolina), censured Vaughan. The president, true to form, stood by his friend.

Bad times were indeed in store for Democrats. Hints of electoral trouble for Truman and his supporters within the party came during the 1950 party primaries. Two key contests suggested that a definite period of reaction had set in. The first pitted the popular liberal incumbent senator of North Carolina Frank P. Graham against Willis Smith, a past president of the American Bar Association. Graham had won the first primary handily, missing the needed majority by a scant one percent. But during the last days of the runoff primary Graham's campaign was derailed by a brushfire of racial intolerance. Handout sheets warned voters: "White people, wake up before it is too late. . . . Graham favors mingling of the races." Although Smith disclaimed responsibility, the appeal stampeded the vote against Graham; he lost by 18,000 votes. Counties with large Negro populations which had gone for Graham the first time around (ensuring the coat-tail choice of local white candidates), predictably swung to Smith. More surprising were the large majorities that Smith gained in the prosperous middle-class white suburbs. Graham's defeat dealt a severe blow to the cause of southern liberalism.

Sharing Graham's fate was another southern liberal, Florida's incumbent Senator Claude Pepper. Although Pepper had served since 1936, his pronounced left-of-center position since 1945 had made him highly vulnerable. A well-organized and successful CIO drive to register Negro voters backfired when it triggered a larger outpouring of white voters against Pepper. He lost heavily, as had Graham, in the more prosperous, suburban areas around Florida cities. Although Truman may have been pleased to see one of his critics replaced, the successor, former Representative George A. Smathers had not supported the president in Congress and carried the animus over into the post-1950 period as senator.

The setbacks to liberalism within the party begun in the primaries continued in the regular elections. The Senate Majority Leader, Scott W. Lucas, lost his Illinois seat to the conservative Congressman Everett M. Dirksen. The record low Democratic turnout in Chicago spelled defeat for Lucas. His assistant whip in the Senate, Francis J. Myers of Pennsylvania, was beaten by the GOP governor, James H. Duff. A major loss occurred in California when Richard M. Nixon defeated liberal Congresswoman Helen Gahagan Douglas in a slugfest that revolved around charges that Mrs. Douglas was "soft on Communism." Still another loss came with the unseating of Senator Elbert D. Thomas of Utah by Wallace F. Bennett. The influence of Joseph R. McCarthy was felt in the close loss of conservative Democrat Millard R. Tydings to John M. Butler in Maryland. Tydings had led a Democratic attempt to label McCarthy as irresponsible for his Wheeling and subsequent speeches. Moreover, Robert A. Taft won a resounding victory despite the most-publicized and well-funded labor effort to defeat him. Other liberal Democratic losses came in gubernatorial contests in Connecticut, where Chester Bowles lost in his bid for reelection, and in California, where James Roosevelt went down to defeat. The loss of five Senate seats and thirty in the House did not change the party's majority position; but the administration's liberal wing was demoralized.

Elsewhere the 1950 elections had gone poorly even for party stalwarts. Frank Hague's Jersey City machine, defeated initially in 1949, did not revive in 1950. Hague's long tenure had ended; he was replaced by John Kenny. Across the river, Carmine DeSapio imperilled his one-year old control of Tammany Hall by backing the wrong candidate, Ferdinand Pecora, in the New York City mayoralty race, won by Vincent Impelliteri. In gubernatorial elections, the Republicans did well, picking up six statehouses for a new majority of two. In New York, Thomas Dewey continued his mastery in the state by winning with a solid 564,844 vote margin.

Shaken by the 1950 defeats, the party suffered even more during the next two years from the dual charges of being a haven for Communists and a harbor for corrupt politicians. The first charge flowed logically, if not with empirical proof, from the pre-1950 disclosures and was exploited skillfully by the Republicans. The second, a continuation of the five percenter probes, actually was promoted most actively by the Democrats themselves.

Two of the investigations, into income tax scandals and Reconstruction Finance Corporation (RFC) loans, implicated DNC chairman William M. Boyle, Jr., a Truman political aide, Donald S. Dawson, and an assistant attorney general, Theron Lamar Caudle. The most bizarre aspect of the Senate RFC hearings, chaired by J. William Fulbright, occurred when it became known that a White House secretarial assistant had received a mink coat from a fur company seeking a RFC loan. Fulbright called for an investigation of the general moral tone at the White House. Truman steadfastly supported both Dawson and Boyle; he called Fulbright's report asinine. When asked if the men around him lacked moral or ethical responsibility, the president retorted: "That is not true. Pointblank. Categorically. It is just *not* true."

True or not the disclosures continued. Another major congressional probe, the interstate crime hearings, were conducted by a party maverick, Senator Estes Kefauver (Tennessee). Kefauver had been a thriving Chatanooga lawyer prior to his successful campaign in the 1939 special House election; reelected to the House four times, he earned a reputation as a southern-border state liberal. In 1949, he won election to the

Senate, bucking the Memphis city boss Ed Crump. In that 1948 campaign Kefauver gained a folksy symbol. Boss Crump had placed a newspaper ad that likened Kefauver to a pet raccoon who cunningly tried to divert attention from where its foot was and what it was into. Kefauver countered: "I may be a pet coon . . . but I won't be Crump's. My coon has rings around his tail, but there are no rings around my nose." Thereupon Kefauver doffed a coonskin cap, which he wore for political campaign photographs. In the Senate he was shunned by the inner circle. Southerners distrusted him because of his liberal voting record and his studied air of independence; northerners often were offended by his folksy, neo-populistic attitude.

In 1950, Kefauver's Special Committee to Investigate Organized Crime in Interstate Commerce held hearings across the country. Sensational stories emerged from the hearing rooms, implicating political chieftains with the descendents of Capone mob and with other underworld figures. The Chicago hearings uncovered police graft; it was widely believed in the Democratic party that the revelations had contributed to Scott Lucas' defeat. The hearings were expanded in 1951. Television brought Americans face-to-face or, in the case of reputed crime boss Frank Costello, face-to-hands (since Costello refused to appear on camera) with the underworld. Former New York Democratic Mayor William O'Dwyer (then U.S. Ambassador to Mexico) received censure by the committee for allegedly allowing organized crime to flourish in Manhattan. Kefauver emerged from the hearings as an embattled crime-fighter and, as a consequence, a presidential contender. Truman and the Democratic party came out of the hearings badly bruised, carrying one more instance of the decline of public morality.

By early Spring 1952, Democrats groaned under the burden of issues accumulated during the Truman years. Truman himself had not yet declared that he would not run (he held off until March 29, 1952). His party colleagues either wanted to dump him or dissociate entirely from his record. Richardson Dilworth, Philadelphia's district attorney, newly elected in the hitherto GOP stronghold in 1951, declared that Pennsylvania would be lost to the Democrats if Truman headed the ticket in 1952. Southerners actively championed a "Dump Truman" movement. People like Byrd and Russell, who had remained at least nominally in the party in 1948, now vowed to wreck it if Truman became the candidate once again. Preferring Senator Robert Kerr (Oklahoma), Adlai E. Stevenson, or even Kefauver, to Truman, the southerners in March laid plans for a possible bolt in June. Texas Democrats wanted to repudiate Truman so badly that anyone associated with the president faced political defeat. Even so durable a fixture as Tom Connally, who had been in Washington as representative from 1917 to 1929 and senator since 1929, began to run for cover early in 1952. He sharply criticized a pending foreign aid bill (a big reversal since he himself had promoted the program after 1945 as chairman and ranking Democrat on the Foreign Relations Committee). He even objected to being photographed with Dean Acheson. When Truman announced he would not run for reelection—after he had been walloped by Kefauver in the New Hampshire primary—southerners expressed pleasure and many other Democrats sighed in relief.

The 1952 presidential primaries brought out the great strengths of Estes Kefauver. His approach was low-keyed: "My name is Estes Kefauver. I'm running for the presidential nomination, and I'd sure appreciate your help." In New Hampshire he had worked hard against the lethargic, overconfident patronage-dominated party regulars; at the same time he won the Wisconsin primaries practically unopposed. From March to June he captured or ran well in the twelve primaries he entered, scattering the party regulars before him. Along the way he picked up endorsements from Paul Douglas, James Roosevelt, Gael Sullivan, a DNC staff member, Joseph Clark and Richardson Dilworth of Philadelphia, and Claude Pepper. Nonetheless, his stock among the party chiefs remained low. Truman preferred almost any one to Kefauver. Since he believed that "all these primaries are just eyewash when the convention meets," he continued to ignore the Tennessean. Southerners and urban machine leaders had been offended by Kefauver's disregard of party interests. Polls of political "experts" disclosed that even as Kefauver won primary after primary, the belief that he would actually be nominated declined.

The political status of Adlai E. Stevenson remained the enigma for Democrats during the late Spring and early Summer. He steadfastly maintained that he desired only to run for reelection as Illinois governor; equally as firmly, he indicated that nothing short of a draft would bring him into the presidential picture. As governor he had compiled a record attractive to both conservatives and liberals. He had achieved some of his aims—chiefly a constitutional change, more funds for schools and unemployment compensation, and funds for highways. But his record had flaws as well. Like Truman, Stevenson found that his administration had its share of political corruption. Kefauver's committee, for example, had uncovered dubious connections between Stevenson's director of labor and former Capone officials. A major race riot in Cicero, Illinois during July, 1951 and a mine disaster at West Frankfurt five months later when 119 men lost their lives, demonstrated that his reputation as a leader in civil rights and mine safety—two emphases of his gubernatorial program—rested a great deal more on words than accomplishments. Lastly, the nationally publicized breakup of his twenty-one year marriage in 1949 had become a personal political liability. Nonetheless, he was the frontrunner in the preconvention period, even though he refused to say he was a candidate.

Stevenson, as the host governor at the Chicago Democratic National Convention that began July 21, 1952, welcomed delegates with a blend of wit and seriousness that was fast becoming a trademark. He ridiculed the claim made by the GOP—which had held its convention in the same hall just ten days earlier—that the preceding twenty years had been years of failure: "For almost a week pompous phrases marched over this landscape in search of an idea, and the only idea they found was that the two great decades of progress in peace, victory in war, and bold leadership in this anxious hour, were the misbegotten spawn of bungling, corruption, socialism, mismanagement, waste and worse. They captured, tied and dragged that idea in here and furiously beat it to death." Altering his tone, Stevenson then sounded the theme destined to dominate his rhetoric and to shape the ideals of youthful Democrats from 1952 forward. There would be no "superficial solutions. . . . Words are not deeds and there are no cheap and painless solutions to war, hunger, ignorance, fear and imperialist communism. . . . We dare not just look back to great yesterdays. We must look forward to great tomorrows." Hard work, sacrifice, patience, and reason would be the characteristics needed in a "world in the torment of transition from an age that has died to an age struggling to be born."

On a less lofty level, other speakers during the six hectic days heeded Truman's admonition that "there must be no betrayal of the New Deal and the Fair Deal." Senator Paul Douglas told the "truth" about the Korean War: a classic statement of the "domino" theory of international politics, Douglas valiantly attempted to convince television viewers that the Korean War was truly worth fighting—a feeling that had been eroded seriously by criticism over the limited nature of the war and by the bitter controversy that had developed with Truman's recall of General Douglas MacArthur on April 11, 1951.

As in 1948, the party was faced with a potential southern walkout. Liberals wished to bar delegations (such as the Texas "regulars" led by Governor Allan Shivers) composed of unrepentant Dixiecrats or of individuals who refused to pledge advance loyalty to the national party ticket. Failing to stop the seating of the Shivers-dominated Texas delegation in favor of the "loyalist" one led by former Congressman Maury Maverick, liberals came close to disbarring the Louisiana, South Carolina, and Virginia units from voting. A confusing parliamentary situation, however, was ultimately resolved in favor of the southerners by convention leaders anxious not to see a repeat of the 1948 division. All sides benefited. Southerners were not iron-bound to support the party's choice in advance, and liberals—like Hubert Humphrey (Minnesota)—could honestly report that they had put up a good fight. In 1952 this type of plastering over of differences seemed expedient.

The choice of a candidate actually turned out to be easier than expected. Kefauver led on the first two ballots, but the animosity of party leaders from all sections proved too formidable for him. Although probably not decisive, he hurt his chances of winning over tradition-bound party members when he broke a long taboo against professed candidates' appearing on the convention floor. After Averell Harriman and other favorite son candidates had withdrawn, Stevenson was nominated at the end of the third ballot. John J. Sparkman (Alabama) was tapped as Stevenson's running mate.

Once nominated and committed to a campaign that would "talk sense to the American people," Stevenson had to decide how closely he could associate himself with Harry Truman. It would be awkward; he could not repudiate the record nor accept the man. At the beginning of the campaign Stevenson held the proud president at arm's length. He surrounded himself with new faces, rather than with the old pros of the DNC and Truman's entourage. Stevenson's closest advisers were longtime Illinois associates William McCormick Blair, Jr., and Stephen A. Mitchell. Wilson W. Wyatt became his campaign manager; less well-known researchers, speech writers, and publicists like Arthur Schlesinger, jr., Newton Minow, W. Willard Wirtz, and John Bartlow Martin, all were serving their apprenticeships. Nonetheless, Truman, irritated with being shunted aside, was used more and more by Stevenson by the beginning of September.

Korea, corruption in government, internal Communism, and domestic economic questions became the dominant issues in 1952. Dwight D. Eisenhower, the GOP's choice over its sentimental favorite Robert A. Taft, had the clear advantage on each. Stevenson rarely left his defensive stance. A glimmer of a chance came on September 18. Reports said that Eisenhower's running mate, Richard M. Nixon, had been aided by an undisclosed personal fund, contributed to by wealthy California businessmen. Nixon's emotional response in the "Checkers" speech and stories that Stevenson had a private fund of his own (though used, it developed, to supplement the salaries of men in the Illinois state government), torpedoed this seemingly promising campaign issue for Democrats. Most decisive, perhaps, was Eisenhower's pledge on October 24 that he would go to Korea to end the unpopular war.

Eisenhower won in November by a landslide. Stevenson carried only nine states, all in the South or border areas. He lost such traditional Democratic states as Texas, Oklahoma, Florida, Virginia, and Tennessee. Eisenhower polled almost 34 million votes to Stevenson's 27 million; the electoral college returns were equally lopsided, 442 to 89. Stevenson's loss of the southern states continued a trend noticeable in the 1950 North Carolina and Florida primaries; the growing suburban vote moved against the Democrats. The continuation of the 1948 civil-rights plank convinced many southern democrats to respond to GOP overtures. The postwar rapid rise of southern Negro registration, mostly as Democrats—estimates showed a jump from 600,000 to 1,000,000 total Negro registrants from 1947 to 1952; as a percentage of voting-age blacks, from twelve to twenty—helped account for an unprecedented move away from the party.

Governor Shivers was quoted after the election that Ike's Texas victory was "an expression of independence that ought to strengthen the Democratic party and help bring those promoting the liberal-pinko type of party to their senses." James F. Byrnes, perhaps irked that his state had narrowly voted for Stevenson and forgetful of the Thurmond bolt in 1948, announced that "South Carolinians will no longer slavishly follow the national Democratic party. The white Democrats of this state have more in common with Republicans of the agricultural areas of the North than with Democratic organizations of the big cities."

Other factors, of course, influenced voters as well. Texans, for example, long upset by the Truman administration's successful delaying tactics in settling title claims for offshore oil, angrily had demanded Stevenson to take a stand in favor of the states. Governor Allen Shivers had journeyed to Springfield in August only to be greeted by Stevenson's abrupt refusal to repudiate Truman's stand that the offshore oil belonged to the nation. Eisenhower on the other hand indicated that he favored the Texan's position.

Eisenhower's great victory had not wiped out the Democratic party entirely. Widespread ticket splitting had shown that Ike's coattails—although long—could not carry unpopular GOP candidates with him. Massachusetts voters, for example, gave Eisenhower a 208,800 vote edge over Stevenson; but Representative John F. Kennedy beat Eisenhower's campaign manager Henry Cabot Lodge for the Senate seat by 70,737. Missourians chose Eisenhower by 29,599 and former Secretary of the Air

Force Stuart Symington by 150,353. Montana gave Ike 59.4 percent of the vote and Representative Mike Mansfield 51.1, to unseat GOP incumbent Zales N. Ecton. Washington went for Eisenhower by 54.3 percent, while Representative Henry M. Jackson swamped GOP Senator Harry P. Cain with 56.4 percent. Other Democratic Senate incumbents survived the Eisenhower landslide in generally Democratic states, like Kilgore (West Virginia) and Chavez (New Mexico): in Senate races in the southern states that Ike carried, Democrats had either no GOP opposition (Virginia, Florida, and Texas) or token resistance (Tennessee). But in marginal states, GOP candidates unseated such incumbents as the Senate majority leader, Ernest McFarland of Arizona (by Barry Goldwater), and Joseph C. O'Mahoney of Wyoming (by Frank A. Barrett). In both these states thumping majorities for Ike (58.3 for Arizona and 62.7 percent of the vote for Wyoming) clearly pulled Goldwater (with 51.3 percent) and Barrett (51.6 percent) into office.

The net effect in Senate races was a loss of two for the Democrats and loss of their Eighty-second Congress' slim majority. The House also went to the GOP, when the Democrats suffered a net loss of twenty-two seats, almost half in New York and Pennsylvania alone. The GOP's gubernatorial margin of two was increased to twelve. Despite the Republican failure to defeat Michigan's G. Mennen Williams and Ohio's Frank Lansche, they captured the former Democratic-held statehouses in Illinois, Indiana, Delaware, Massachusetts and Montana.

Out of power for the first time in twenty years, the Democratic party's cleavage into presidential and congressional arms became all the more visible. The congressional wing now had the advantage. The senior partner of the leadership was the former Speaker, Sam Rayburn (Mr. Sam), who now became House minority leader. Rayburn had come to the House forty years earlier, a witness to Woodrow Wilson's first inaugural. When Adolph J. Sabath, a venerable Democrat from Chicago who had served continuously since 1907, died two days after the 1952 election, Rayburn became the senior House member. His colleagues respected their dean, even though he tended to defer in the post-1953 period to his energetic junior partner, fellow Texan and Senate minority leader, Lyndon Baines Johnson.

Johnson's rise to party leadership had been rapid, a mixture of ability and chance. Elected in 1937 to the House, he ran for the Senate in 1948, winning the primary by the tiny margin of 87 votes. He had admired FDR and supported his New Deal programs. In the postwar years he often backed Truman, voting, for example, to uphold the president's veto of the 1946 price control bill. He did join the majority, however, to override the 1947 veto of the Taft-Hartley Bill. In the Senate, he moved with the increasingly conservative temper of Texas politics. Solicitous of his states's oil and natural gas interests, Johnson ably advocated state control of offshore oil and the exemption of natural gas producers from federal rate control. In 1949 he led the battle that denied confirmation as chairman of the Federal Trade Commission to Truman's liberal appointee, Leland Olds. His talents were recognized by his southern colleagues, particularly by Richard Russell of Georgia, the most respected southern Democrat. When Russell's choice as majority leader to replace Scott Lucas in 1951, Ernest McFarland lost his seat in 1952, Johnson was tapped to be minority leader. All except the more committed Senate members of the presidential wing of the party, such as Hubert H. Humphrey (Minnesota) and Herbert H. Lehman (New York), immediately pledged support to Johnson. When the newly elected Mike Mansfield (Montana), Albert Gore (Tennessee), and Stuart Symington (Missouri) fell into line shortly after the 1952 election, any hope by liberals to contest Johnson's selection collapsed.

The Johnson-Rayburn leadership quickly established the congressional wing's strategy in January, 1953. Johnson said: "We are now in the minority. I have never agreed with the statement that it is 'the business of the opposition to oppose.' I do not believe the American people have sent us here merely to obstruct." This view contradicted Adlai Stevenson's post-election comment that "the Democratic Party will take a position of positive and intelligent opposition." Even after Johnson's firm repudiation of the classic role of the opposition, Stevenson gamely continued the theme, albeit somewhat muffled: " ... the New Dealers have all left Washington to make way for the car dealers. ... Let us never be content merely to oppose. Let us always propose something better." But Stevenson departed on a five-month world tour in March, 1953.

Even if Stevenson had stayed to lead the loyal opposition, it is doubtful that he would have been heeded. The nation had had a long period of confrontations, of constant frictions. The Democratic party had been wracked by a decade of internal conflict. Johnson proposed to pour oil on the waters of intraparty dissension. "It is one of my deepest convictions," he told a reporter in January, 1953, "that there are more issues to hold Democrats together than there are differences to drive them apart. ... In the past few years, considerable attention has been centered upon one or two issues which split the Democratic party. They have been assigned an importance that is beyond justification." Johnson was a fitting party complement to the leadership that Dwight D. Eisenhower offered the nation. Neither man would quarrel with LBJ's favorite biblical quote, from Isaiah: "Come now, and let us reason together."

By the 1953 Summer, Democrats had fully recovered from the 1952 defeat. Most agreed with Johnson's strategy: allow the GOP to squabble among themselves; take potshots at Eisenhower's advisers (while withholding direct fire from the popular president himself, at least until after the 1954 elections); and review Ike's program, supporting him where they could—hoping thereby to gain voter confidence in the party's sense of responsibility. Democrats even began to criticize McCarthy more openly. Caution still ruled, of course, since McCarthy reputedly could wreak revenge against those who opposed him, as in the cases of Senators Millard Tydings (Maryland), and of William Benton (Connecticut), unseated in 1952. Still, when Republicans resuscitated the Harry Dexter White case in 1953, Democrats generally rallied to Truman's defense. Truman, refusing a demand by GOP Representative Harold H. Velde (Illinois) to appear before HUAC to discuss the White case, made one of the more eloquent and direct indictments of McCarthyism that appeared during the 1950's.

Confidence did seem justified in 1953 and early 1954. The DNC had been reorganized. A satirical publication, *The Democratic Digest* (formerly published by the DNC's Women's Division), became under the editorship of Clayton Fritchey, the bright, new vehicle to carry tales of GOP weaknesses and Democratic strengths. House special elections in 1953 gave Democrats encouragement; they won former GOP seats in Wisconsin and New Jersey. Meanwhile unemployment was rising, farm income was falling, and the Republicans seemed bent on wrecking such longtime New Deal vote-getting programs as public power and reclamation.

The 1954 congressional elections continued the swing. Democrats now controlled both Houses. In the Senate, the margin was but one seat; in the House twenty-nine. Johnson himself broke the hex on recent Democratic Senate party leaders when he won reelection; he now became majority leader. Hubert H. Humphrey won an impressive reelection victory in Minnesota. His Democratic-Farmer-Labor alliance, which he had forged as Minneapolis mayor from 1945 to 1949, had worked so well in 1954 that Orville Freeman was elected governor. Humphrey, an outspoken liberal, had started to tone down his criticism of conservatives. In the Senate he was beginning to be regarded even by southern leaders in a friendly way; Johnson particularly began to treat his younger colleague with affection.

The Democrats did particularly well in the 1954 governors' contests, winning nine from the GOP, including New York (W. Averell Harriman) and Connecticut (Abraham Ribicoff). The gubernatorial balance swung back to their favor by a new margin of six. Two victories brought special notice. Democrats in Pennsylvania took control at Harrisburg; the Philadelphia reform faction unified the Pennsylvania democracy: Joseph Clark and Richardson Dilworth, with Philadelphia regular Matthew McCloskey and Pittsburgh's machine boss David Lawrence, combined behind the winning candidacy of George M. Leader. The other surprise came in Maine, long a bastion of GOP orthodoxy. Dissension among Republicans, however, opened the door for a likeable Democratic lawyer, Edmund S. Muskie. Muskie, himself a Polish-American Catholic, welded together Maine's heterogeneous Democrats, a mixture of French Catholics and Yankee nonconformists. Maine, like New York, Minnesota, and Pennsylvania, had not had a Democratic governor in the postwar period.

Cheered by election returns in 1954, Democrats who desired national party unity nonetheless were troubled by the quality of the southern victories. In May, 1954, a unanimous Supreme Court handed down the famous *Brown* v. *The Board of Education of Topeka* decision. The immediate political consequences were the blunting of the Negroes' drive for voter registrations on the one hand (black voters' registration increased by only 200,000 between 1952 and 1956, much of that prior to 1954), and on the other, a perceptible hardening of the southern Democratic positions on racial and liberal issues generally. An example of the latter phenomenon came in the 1955 gubernatorial primaries in Mississippi. Each of the five candidates bitterly assailed the school desegregation decision. Lawyer Ross Barnett summed up the tone of all: "It is the darkest cloud which has been over us since Reconstruction. . . . We shall maintain segregation . . . as long as I am governor." Throughout the South, opposition to integration rose, perplexing national-minded Democrats. Not to support the court's decision would alienate northern urban voters, particularly Negroes who had flocked to the party banners even in Eisenhower's 1952 victory. To support it too vigorously had a dual southern implication: the South might bolt to a third party, as in

1948, or, more dangerously, continue to flow into the Republican presidential columns as it had in 1952.

Throughout 1955 party unity demanded moderation. When the Democrats chose Johnson as majority leader, a group of New and Fair Deal senators caused a brief flurry about the filibuster rule. No civil rights legislation could be brought out of the Senate, it was believed, until the rule was changed. But Johnson had laid conduits of moderation to the very core of the liberal bloc. Hubert Humphrey, who had rallied liberals in the past, now cautioned his colleagues against adopting a "devil theory of politics;" party unity was more important than achieving an anti-filibuster rule.

Yet quadrennial portents of party strife appeared on schedule in 1956. Civil rights legislation provided the focus as usual for intraparty quarrels. Eisenhower had proposed that Congress create a bipartisan Civil Rights Commission, a Civil Rights Division in the Justice Department, and an expansion of national enforcement powers over voting and other civil rights. The House passed such a bill in July, 1956—shortly after eighty-three southern Democrats had issued a "Southern Manifesto" urging rejection of the bill—with the Democrats divided almost evenly on regional lines. The bill did not reach the Senate floor.

Liberals were alarmed. Humphrey warned in February, 1956: "The Democratic party is spelling its longterm doom unless it does something. Our party ought to be the champion of equal rights—it's morally right and it's politically right." Clarence Mitchell, Washington director of the National Association for the Advancement of Colored People, echoed Humphrey's warning in March: "Tell those Democrats if they keep a stinking albatross like Senator [James O.] Eastland around their necks they can kiss our votes goodbye." Rumblings were heard from labor as well, when Walter Reuther at a UAW-CIO Education conference in April told Democrats: "that in 1956 you've got to make a choice—you cannot have Mr. Eastland and have us at the same time." These were not entirely idle threats. The party's funds were dangerously low for a presidential year; at one point in April, Paul M. Butler, the new national chairman, said there was only about $75,000 in the treasury. Since organized labor had shelled out at least $2 million over and above Democratic spending in 1952, the DNC had reason to be concerned about any signs of discontent in 1956.

The liberals' disaffection impinged on Adlai Stevenson's chances to win the party's nomination. Since his foreign tour in 1953, Stevenson had been an unavowed candidate. He had helped pay off the party's deficit with book sales of his collected speeches and with fund-raising talks. In three years he had become an unusually well-informed spokesman for the party's presidential wing, particularly on foreign and national defense policies. Some advisers urged him not to run in 1956 and suffer certain defeat; but Stevenson felt he could not use the party, then cast it aside when the timing did not seem right. This reasoning led him to adopt a moderate tone; party loyalty meant party unity. On civil rights he urged that the nation move slowly towards integration: rights could not be achieved by "troops or bayonets. We must proceed gradually, not upsetting habits or traditions that are older than the Republic."

Stevenson's moderation evoked coolness from liberals. During the early Spring, liberal periodicals expressed reservations about his candidacy. A sign of his difficulty came with the Minnesota primary in late March. He had entered the contest against an old foe, Estes Kefauver, expecting to win easily. Party leaders in Minnesota enthusiastically endorsed Stevenson; Humphrey's state machine, still euphoric over its 1954 victory, predicted that Stevenson would defeat Kefauver in most districts by a three to one margin. Kefauver's campaign seemed forlorn; while Stevenson made telling points on such matters as falling farm income, Kefauver stumbled along. But the Tennessean upset Stevenson, taking almost fifty-seven percent of the vote and capturing twenty-six to thirty delegates to the national convention.

Humiliation in Minnesota altered Stevenson's tactics. In defeat he said grimly, "I will try even harder. . . . It has just begun." Kefauver's jubilant campaign manager had not helped when he answered a query about the acceptability of Stevenson as Kefauver's vice presidential candidate, "I think it might be given serious consideration if he can demonstrate a greater capacity to get votes." Stevenson needed little prompting. He vowed to do just that in the upcoming Florida and California primaries.

The "new Stevenson" emerged most clearly in the California primary. California party leaders, like those in Minnesota and Florida, enthusiastically endorsed him. No longer complacent, Stevenson campaigned like a politician: he kissed babies with minimum obvious distaste, pumped peoples' hands, and made grammatical errors (he said he was under orders to make at least one a day). In Florida he appeared as a conservative; his chief support came from segregationist areas, forcing him to emphasize the moderation part of his civil rights stance. These tactics helped him to a narrow victory in Florida on May 29, and to a decisive one in California on June 5. Kefauver garnered a mere thirty-seven percent of California's vote. Stevenson captured all sixty-eight delegates. This, plus earlier losses in Washington, D.C. and in Oregon, ended Kefauver's bid. He withdrew in July, pledging his support for Stevenson, who now had virtually a clear road for the nomination. Only Harriman (who had received Truman's nod) barred his way.

The 1956 primary victories levied their toll on Stevenson. He did become a politician; but he also used up vital energy. Already weary at the conclusion of the primaries, he faced the stupendous effort of a full-scale presidential campaign—and that as an underdog. Four years later observers commented that Stevenson had never fully recovered from the bonewearying campaigns of 1956.

Stevenson entered the national convention with an insurmountable lead and won nomination on the first ballot. Then over the objections of Rayburn and Johnson, Stevenson told the delegates that "the selection of the vice presidential nominee should be made through the free processes of this convention." Conceived by Stevenson's advisers, who desired to contrast their party's "free choice" with the GOP's uncontested selection of Richard M. Nixon, the ploy also served to spare the candidate the unhappy task of choosing among the many contenders.

The decision thrust one of the leading contenders, John Fitzgerald Kennedy, into national prominence. Kennedy's Democratic party roots reached back into Boston's Irish ward politics, to both grandfathers, John ("Honey Fitz") Fitzgerald and Patrick Kennedy. His father, Joseph P. Kennedy, a friend and early backer of Franklin Roosevelt, had been a major contributor to party coffers during the entire postwar period. The young Kennedy had served in the Navy during the war; he had received the Navy and Marine Cross for bravery in a much-publicized PT boat action in the Pacific. After the war he had served briefly as a freelance reporter at the San Francisco United Nations conference in 1945 (where he may have seen Stevenson for the first time, since the latter was serving as the State Department's press officer). He entered the hurly-burly of politics in 1946, winning Boston's 11th congressional seat; he was graduated to the Senate in 1952, winning (as noted above) a notable victory in that Eisenhower year.

Kennedy's push for the vice presidential nomination in 1956 reintroduced the issue of Roman Catholicism, long believed to have cost Al Smith his bid for election in 1928. In the weeks prior to the convention John M. Bailey, a newly emergent national party leader from Connecticut, had circulated within party circles his analysis of the importance of the Roman Catholic vote in presidential elections. Bailey, hitching his wagon to Kennedy's rising political fortunes, argued that approximately seven percent of Eisenhower's 1952 national vote had come from normally Democratic Roman Catholics. Rather than injuring the party's chances, a Roman Catholic on the ticket would help draw defectors back into the fold. Since their strength was heavily concentrated in the industrial states—Bailey's estimates ranged from fifty percent (Massachusetts) to thirty-two percent (New York) to twenty percent (Ohio)—the appeal of a Roman Catholic on the ballot could not be ignored. Although some leaders disputed Bailey's conclusions (believing that the supposed gains would be offset by a like or greater number of losses), the party at least had begun to consider the possibilities.

Kennedy's bid failed, however; Estes Kefauver won on the second ballot, after Kennedy had come within 38½ votes of the required 686½. Kefauver's more potent appeal among farmers probably convinced delegates as much as any other issue. His folksy campaign style would complement Stevenson's which (despite its new look) still was heavily issue-oriented. The convention's choice of Kefauver did have liabilities. Deep southerners would not find in him a pro-segregation balancing force. Nor would it please Harry S. Truman, who had come to Chicago hoping to stop Stevenson; frustrated in that, he received another setback with Kefauver's victory.

The Stevenson-Kefauver campaign stressed themes that seemed to be ill-timed or out of tune with the nation's mood. With little apparent effect, they assailed Eisenhower's "absentee" leadership and Secretary of State John Foster Dulles' "nomadic" wanderings in foreign policy. Stevenson's proposals for a unilateral halt to hydrogen bomb testing and his controversial call to stop the draft were dismissed as irresponsible by Eisenhower. When Stevenson argued that the GOP had sacrificed national defense for budget-cutting considerations, Eisenhower's supporters pointed to their candidate's long military service as a more convincing expertise. In the international context of crises over the Suez Canal and an East European uprising in Hungary, the GOP could appeal to voters for a continuance of a steady hand at the helm. Republicans echoed Richard M. Nixon's hyperbolic assertion that "this is not the moment to replace the greatest Commander-in-chief America has ever had in war or peace with a jittery, inexperienced novice . . . who is utterly unqualified to make the great decisions demanded."

The Eisenhower-Nixon ticket won with the largest popular vote in history up to then; the plurality of 57.4 percent had been exceeded only by FDR in 1936. From his 1952 defeat, Stevenson managed only to regain Missouri for the Democrats; he lost Louisiana, Kentucky, and West Virginia—reducing his 1952 electoral count by sixteen. According to one authoritative estimate, Eisenhower cut into the Democratic Catholic vote more deeply than in 1952; for the first time a majority of Catholics had voted for a Republican candidate. Equally as ominous to some Democrats was a sizeable jump in the black vote for Eisenhower. Only sixty-four percent of Negro voters supported Stevenson in 1956, compared with an estimated seventy-nine percent in 1952. Eisenhower also did well in big cities, carrying such normally Democratic strongholds as Chicago and Jersey City, and others like Baltimore, Milwaukee, Los Angeles, and San Francisco.

The 1956 defeat of their national candidate had been expected by party professionals. They had hoped, however, that Eisenhower's coattails would be as short for congressional races as they had been in 1952. Such indeed was the case. For the first time in over a century an incumbent president failed to carry at least one branch of Congress. The Democratic party actually added two seats to its 232-203 majority in the House. With the switch of Senator Wayne Morse (Oregon)—from Republican to Independent (1952) to Democratic (1955)—the party now had a margin of two votes in the upper chamber. The 1952 ticket-splitting tendency of continued. Only one incumbent Democrat, Earle Clements (Kentucky), the keynoter at the national convention, was unseated. Thirteen Democratic candidates failed to dislodge GOP incumbents; but three succeeded—thirty-three year old Frank Church in Idaho, the unpredictable Governor Frank Lausche in Ohio, and Philadelphia's reform Mayor Joseph S. Clark in Pennsylvania. Even in the two contested seats with no incumbent in the race, the Democrats could claim a moral victory, since they carried one—former Truman aide John A. Carroll, in Colorado—and lost the other, in New York.

With continued control of Congress and a lame duck president, Democrats looked ahead to a promising future. The presidential wing had not been seriously damaged: the new Senators Carroll, Church, and Clark joined the dozen or so liberals that included the future presidential hopefuls, Humphrey and Kennedy. Moreover, for the first time in the postwar period the liberals institutionalized themselves within the party. Shortly after the election, Stevensonians announced through Paul M. Butler the establishment of the Democratic Advisory Council (DAC), an affiliate of the DNC. Its professed aim was to represent and to voice, on a continuing basis, the views of the rank-and-file Democrats who may or may not have been represented in either House of Congress.

Butler issued the call to join DAC to twenty Democrats: ten congressional chieftains, five state and local leaders, and five prominent at-large members. The congressional leaders responded slowly and negatively. Only Humphrey joined DAC at once. Much later, in 1960, Kennedy became a member. Johnson, Mansfield, and Smathers remained aloof. The House leaders—Rayburn, McCormack, Mike Kirwan (Ohio), Carl Albert (Oklahoma), and Edith Green (Oregon)—similarly refused to join. The state and local invitations brought prompt acceptances from governors Harriman

(New York) and Williams (Michigan). Raymond Tucker, mayor of St. Louis, also quickly accepted. Ernest McFarland, governor of Arizona, came in late and remained less than a year. Governor Luther Hodges (North Carolina), like former Governor John S. Battle (Virginia)—an at-large invitee—declined the honor. Three other at-large members—Stevenson, Truman, and Kefauver—were delighted to enlist. Eleanor Roosevelt agreed to serve as a "consultant," not wishing to affect her nonpartisan diplomatic status in the United Nations. Lastly, some members of the DNC became ex-officio members.

The DAC obviously represented the liberal, presidential wing of the party. Well-organized, the DAC withstood the ill-concealed animosity of congressional party leaders until its termination after Kennedy's 1960 victory. Committees chaired by such experts as Dean Acheson (foreign policy) and Harvard economist John Kenneth Galbraith (economic policy) wrote periodic liberal white papers. The DAC helped meet the critical problem of maintaining high visibility for its non-congressional policy while the party was out of power.

Meanwhile the vaunted domestic stability attributed to Eisenhower's "peace and prosperity" program began to crack, giving openings through which Democrats could attack. The sharpest, but shortest, postwar economic recession, beginning in August, 1957 and lasting through April, 1958, caught the administration unprepared. The rise in unemployment to a peak of 7.5 percent in April, 1958—by the close of 1958 almost 1.5 million workers had been unemployed for fifteen weeks or more (for the fourteen year period 1947-1960, the average was 640,000)—had political implications. The president's commitment to fiscal responsibility inclined the Republican response to one of riding out the recession, rather than actively promoting programs to offset the decline. This gave Democratic congressional leaders the chance to use their majority to force Eisenhower's hand. Although the president opposed ambitious counter-recession programs, he did reluctantly accept some emergency housing and highway measures. Eisenhower's inconsistency on budgetary questions (he actually became a leading critic of his own budget in 1957), moreover, encouraged Democrats in their probing for political weaknesses.

An offset to Eisenhower's fumblings on the budget came with his continued advocacy of civil rights legislation. In January, 1957 he had repeated his 1956 plea for federally protected civil rights, particularly voting rights. During the seven months following, Eisenhower persistently repeated his urging. Congress, for a variety of reasons (not least the increasing importance of the Negro vote), finally passed the first civil rights legislation in almost a century. The bill set up a Civil Rights Commission with general investigatory powers, authorized an additional assistant attorney general, provided for expansion of district court powers to hear civil rights cases, gave the attorney general power to initiate actions to protect voting rights, and empowered courts to hand down criminal contempt citations to violators of the statute.

The 1957 Civil Rights Act provided political capital to a curious combination. Eisenhower personally stood to gain by the act; Republicans could garner some reflection from his glory. Southern Democrats claimed a partial victory: they had succeeded in amending the bill to provide that jury trials be allowed in certain criminal contempt cases (raising the possibility that southern juries would still control the standards of enforcement). Liberals in both parties redeemed ancient pledges. Less noticeable at first was the role of Johnson. He had cajoled, wheedled, and strong-armed senators during the long struggle to bring forth the controversial bill. Concurrently, he subtly began to change his southern political identity—largely acquired from 1953 to 1956—to a western one, more suitable for national recognition.

Just five days before the president approved the Civil Rights Act, he had become embroiled in another conflict: the Little Rock, Arkansas, school crisis. The Democratic Governor Orval Lee Faubus had refused to permit the carrying out of a court-ordered desegregation of Little Rock's Central High School, using the national guard to bar entry to nine black students. When Faubus withdrew the troops, rioting erupted. Eisenhower then federalized the national guard and sent in paratroopers to escort the students. Any hope Republicans might have had of continuing their invasion of the Democratic South received a setback. Perversely, the Little Rock crisis aided Democrats. The international community was shocked by news photographs of marital escorts for students. The vision of declining American prestige, long a major theme of Adlai Stevenson, had a greater reality after Little Rock.

Prestige also was buffeted by the Soviet space exploits in October, 1957. Spinning in orbit, Sputnik reminded Americans of another Stevensonian theme: that America lagged behind the Soviet Union in national defense and scientific matters. "More bank for the buck"—an Eisenhower administration slogan to justify defense spending cutbacks (which had been endorsed by Democratic fiscal conservatives)—now seemed an expensive folly. Democrats, out of power, claimed that only if their wise counsel had been heeded, then national humiliation (the "missile gap") would have been spared.

Some of the political promise that lurked in the crumbling Eisenhower equilibrium appeared with the electoral success of William Proxmire in winning the Wisconsin Senate seat of Joseph R. McCarthy, who died in May, 1957. In November, New Jersey reelected Governor Robert B. Meyner by a thumping 200,000 vote majority. Disclosure of dubious financial relations of presidential assistant Sherman Adams with a New England textile manufacturer, Bernard Goldfine, provided more grist for the political mill. When the Democrats went on the campaign trail in 1958, they were on the right side of issues that had bedeviled their party in the Truman years. A faltering economy, a faltering president (Eisenhower suffered his third major illness when a stroke felled him in November, 1957 and restricted his activities thereafter until March, 1958), a corrupt administration, and a faltering international image formed a potent combination to attract voters.

The 1958 elections brought a landslide victory to the Democrats, the biggest triumph since FDR's smashing success of 1936. One of the biggest surprises came also as the earliest: Maine's Governor Edmund S. Muskie was elected to the Senate in September, the first Democrat ever to serve the state in that capacity. Muskie was succeeded by a Democrat; accompanying him to Washington were two Democratic Congressmen.

Delighted Democrats watched the November returns roll in. No less than nine incumbent GOP senators were defeated, twenty-six of thirty-four Democrats were elected or reelected. The party's majority in the House was increased from 235-200 to 282-153, with big gains in Indiana, Iowa, Ohio, and Connecticut. State governorship victories brought the Democrats to the lopsided edge of 34-14; the party won control of South Dakota, Wisconsin, and Nebraska—each of which had a GOP governor all during the postwar period.

Many of the victories clearly were individual triumphs. John F. Kennedy won reelection in Massachusetts with 73.6 percent of the vote, inundating his opponent by 874,000 votes. Other senatorial incumbents did even better in so-called contested elections: Mike Mansfield won 76.2 percent of the Montana vote and Albert Gore gathered 80.6 of Tennessee's vote. Still, although liberal forces in the Senate, for example, were augmented by such new men as Eugene McCarthy (Minnesota) and Harrison A. Williams, Jr. (New Jersey), the party's presidential wing suffered a blow in New York, where W. Averell Harriman lost decisively to Nelson A. Rockefeller in the gubernatorial contest.

The 1958 elections thus eliminated one Democratic party contender from the presidential sweepstakes. Otherwise, 1958 confirmed or encouraged hopeful candidates for the party's nod in 1960. Kennedy had been repairing ever since his unsuccessful bid for the vice presidency in 1956; his great victory endorsed that decision. Humphrey was strengthened by the continued success of his state organization, which had sent Eugene McCarthy—one of his close supporters—to Washington to serve as his colleague in the Senate. Stuart Symington had won reelection with 66.4 percent of Missouri's senatorial vote. In Texas, Ralph Yarborough, also had won a whopping victory by 79.5 percent, helping shore up Johnson's already strong state party base. In California, Edmund G. (Pat) Brown defeated Willian F. Knowland by over one million votes. In Michigan the perennially popular Governor G. Mennen Williams showed his durability in winning a sixth term, although with a lower plurality.

The heavy majority in Congress seemed to give an edge to the four prominent senators, especially to the majority leader. But the Democrats' legislative program successes were meager in 1959 and 1960 as Eisenhower, defying predictions that he would be an ineffective lame duck president, proved an able political manipulator. Along with Charles Halleck, the new House minority leader, Eisenhower revitalized the old GOP-conservative Democratic coalition against liberal spending programs like school construction, area redevelopment, and health aid for the aged.

The failure of school construction aid proved a bitter pill to Democrats. Few items had greater political potential. Eisenhower had proposed a general school aid program in 1959 that involved long-term inducements to local school districts for classroom construction. Northern Democrats (and presidential hopefuls) wished to add to the program direct grants to needy areas and aid for teachers' salaries. By May, 1960 they had succeeded in obtaining Senate endorsement of direct aid. But the House Rules Committee, dominated by the conservative coalition, refused to authorize a House-Senate conference to adjust differences between the two bodies. Failure at this stage seemed especially irritating since Democratic spokesmen had counted on Eisenhower's veto if the bill had passed, ensuring the party of a fine issue during the 1960 campaign.

A few legislative trophies had been achieved. The party overrode the president's veto of the federal employees' salary increase act of 1960—only the second time Congress had succeeded in ten attempts to override Eisenhower's vetoes. Democrats also added funds to the administration's defense budget requests for missile expenditures. Overall, however, the president had come off extraordinarily well despite the Democratic majorities.

As with the two preceding presidential election years, the Democratic primaries in 1960 had unusual significance. During the Spring the chief candidates were Humphrey, Kennedy and Johnson; in the background stood such men as Symington, Stevenson, Brown, Meyner, and G. Mennen Williams. Only the strategies of Humphrey and Kennedy, however, required entering the primaries. Johnson's major task was to avoid being tagged the "southern" nominee, the label he bore in 1956. His careful currying of western support, both among his Senate colleagues and state organizations, helped dissociate his image from the South. Not least significant was his ability to enlist an eastern wing that consisted of old New Deal and Truman men like Dean Acheson, Tommy Corcoran, and Oscar Chapman. With this kind of backing, a frontal collision with a popular eastern or midwestern liberal in the primaries would be unwise.

Both Kennedy and Humphrey needed primary successes to convince the party leaders that they should be given the presidential chance. Humphrey had to demonstrate that he could run well in the midwest where his labor support might turn Democratic votes into Republican ones (as in the celebrated case of labor's dismal crusade against Taft in 1950). Kennedy had two large tasks: to prove that his vote gathering appeal had other than New England and Roman Catholic dimensions, and that his youth would not be a liability.

Two primaries, Wisconsin and West Virginia, decided the issue. Although Wisconsin bordered Humphrey's home preserve, the state voters almost notorious independence tended to reduce the impact of the neighbor effect. Humphrey, moreover, had little money and only weekend staff support. Kennedy's campaign group organized Kennedy clubs throughout most of the state's districts. Kennedy won the primary, but by a smaller margin than expected, carrying only six of ten districts. Humphrey's relatively good showing was attributed to a Catholic-Protestant split, an ominous sign that Kennedy's religion would be a crippling liability in large areas of the country.

The showdown came in West Virginia. There the large majority of white Protestant Democrats would conclusively demonstrate whether a Roman Catholic could attract support. Humphrey, embittered by what he called "political payola" being used against him by the well-financed Kennedy machine, complained that he did not have "a daddy who can pay the bills." Kennedy dealt with the religious issue head on in the West Virginia campaign and answered Humphrey's charges with his own claims that his opponent had distorted the record. The Massachusetts senator carried West Virginia; the next day Humphrey withdrew from the race.

The path from West Virginia to his party's nomination in July had been carefully laid out by Kennedy's staff. His younger brother, Robert, served as campaign manager, sharing with Abraham Ribicoff of Connecticut the duties of floor chief at the convention itself. Another brother, Edward, with the help of Congressman Stewart L. Udall in Arizona, and of Byron White in Colorado, had chipped away at Johnson's western support. The Kennedy team also widened their candidate's eastern votes. John Bailey had reached across his Connecticut border into upstate New York, lining up Peter Crotty, the Erie County chairman. Joseph P. Kennedy had led expeditions into northern New Jersey and even into New York City itself, bringing onto the Kennedy bandwagon party leaders like the Bronx's Charles A. Buckley and Brooklyn's Eugene Keogh. When they had finished, the Kennedy team had outmaneuvered the slow moving and ineffective Tammany organization of Carmine DeSapio. In the midwest, Kennedy carefully courted the powerful Michigan party leadership, swinging C. Neil Staebler, state chairman, Governor Williams, and the UAW's Walter Reuther into his camp before the convention. Despite a last minute surge of sentiment for Stevenson, John F. Kennedy's four years of hard work, organization, talent, and money brought victory on the first ballot.

Kennedy's contribution to a growing Democratic party tradition of surprises came during the 1960 convention with his choice of Lyndon Baines Johnson as his running mate. Dispute still exists as to whether Kennedy seriously thought that Johnson would accept the offer—the proud Texan after all had been in the public eye in responsible positions far longer than Kennedy. But after the shock to liberals had worn off, the decision seemed wise. Johnson could strengthen the ticket in the South where Kennedy needed it most. The ticket did blend youth and experience, helping to offset some of the Republican barbs that contrasted the GOP's choice of Vice President Richard M. Nixon largely for his eight years service in an executive capacity.

Kennedy's acceptance speech coined a term the "New Frontier," to point out the challenges facing the United States: "I tell you the New Frontier is here, whether we seek it or not. Beyond that frontier are uncharted areas of science and space, unsolved problems of peace and war, unconquered pockets of ignorance and prejudice, unanswered questions of poverty and surplus."

The speech was reminiscent of Adlai Stevenson in 1952 and 1956. Although Kennedy and his men resented the older man's refusal to speak out in favor of the young senator during the pre-convention period, they owed far more to Stevenson than they would have admitted in 1960. His spirit had permeated the party's youth. The bright areas of Democratic energy during the 1950's had been animated by Stevenson: California's bastion of liberalism, with such leaders as Pat Brown, Jesse Unruh, and James Roosevelt; Minnesota's Humphrey, McCarthy, and Freeman; Michigan's Williams, Reuther, and Staebler; New Jersey's Meyner; Pennsylvania's Clark, Dilworth, and (surprisingly) Lawrence; and even the Massachusetts' Kennedy team. These men had begun their careers before Stevenson had reached national attention; but their ability to keep morale high during the eight years of the Eisenhower regime in part rested on Stevenson's inspiration. In a very practical sense, these were key states; Kennedy carried all but California, losing there by a slender margin of approximately 35,000 votes out of almost 6.5 million cast.

Kennedy bested Nixon at the polls in one of the closest elections in American history. Starting out as an underdog, Kennedy capitalized on the Republican involvement in continued international crises: the U-2 incident, the president's unhappy experiences in personal diplomacy (after auspicious beginnings), and the renewal of friction with China over offshore islands in the Formosa straits. Kennedy's expert handling of issues in the nationally televised debates with Nixon put to rest the assertion that he was ill-equipped for the presidency. With Johnson's help he held the South, carrying enough of the industrial states in the North and Midwest to eke out his narrow victory: a plurality in the popular vote of 112,803 out of more than 68.8 million votes cast. Kennedy received 49.7 percent of the vote–Nixon, 49.5 percent.

Kennedy's victory restored the presidency to Democratic control. When Kennedy stirred the nation with his inaugural address in January, 1961, Democrats could look back over almost sixteen years with a measure of pride. The crucial question of the durability of the Roosevelt coalition had been answered. That diverse combination had weathered the decade and a half of intraparty strife rather well. Virtually all the component parts remained intact in 1960 as they had been in 1945. Even the city bosses of an earlier age–Curley, Hague, Crump, Kelly–were supplanted by others who differed from their predecessors stylistically but not substantially: Richard Daley in Chicago, John Kenny in Jersey City, and Carmine DeSapio in New York.

The transitional period from war to peace had called forth leadership qualities in the combative Truman that few thought he possessed. But reflection about his long political career shows that the screening process of party recruitment had in fact brought a talented leader to the fore. Throughout the postwar period, the Democratic party continued to attract able young men. Defections in 1948 and 1952 merely masked the building process. One reason for the party's success lay in the extraordinary population mobility and increasing urban growth. Democrats had always welcomed the immigrant; even though the new migration was not from the Old World–but from the countryside–the party's traditions favored accomodation of the newly arrived.

The startling fact about the party in 1960 was not the stability of the coalition, but the youth and talent of its leaders. So energetic had they been that few areas of the country had not seen Democratic advances. Only Vermont, New Hampshire, Iowa, and North Dakota had a GOP governor throughout the period 1945-1960. Republicans in Wyoming and New Hampshire remained as those states' sole congressional representatives–all other states, including Vermont, had at least one Democrat as a congressman in the period 1945-1960. The farm states of Illinois, Indiana, Iowa, Kansas, Nebraska, Ohio, and Wisconsin had seen the largest surge of Democrats by 1960: from a total of twenty-one House members in the Seventy-ninth Congress to forty-five in the Eighty-sixth. The postwar period thus saw the increasing nationalizing of the Democratic party.

The New Frontier of Kennedy meant challenge for the nation. For the party it meant that a new generation of leaders had taken charge. They stood on the shoulders of those who had gone before–on the coalition-building genius of Franklin D. Roosevelt, on a record of great achievements in foreign and domestic policy under Harry S. Truman, and on an equally significant pointing of the way by Adlai E. Stevenson.

Appendix

DEMOCRATIC PLATFORM OF 1948

The Democratic Party adopts this platform in the conviction that the destiny of the United States is to provide leadership in the world toward a realization of the Four Freedoms.

We chart our future course as we charted our course under the leadership of Franklin D. Roosevelt and Harry S. Truman in the abiding belief that democracy—when dedicated to the service of all and not to a privileged few—proves it superiority over all other forms of government.

Our party record of the past is assurance of its policies and performance in the future.

Ours is the party which was entrusted with responsibility when twelve years of Republican neglect had blighted the hopes of mankind, had squandered the fruits of prosperity and had plunged us into the depths of depression and despair.

Ours is the party which rebuilt a shattered economy, rescued our banking system, revived our agriculture, reinvigorated our industry, gave labor strength and security, and led the American people to the broadest prosperity in our history.

Ours is the party which introduced the spirit of humanity into our law, as we outlawed child labor and the sweatshop, insured bank deposits, protected millions of home-owners and farmers from foreclosure, and established national social security.

Ours is the party under which this nation before Pearl Harbor gave aid and strength to those countries which were holding back the Nazi and Fascist tide.

Ours is the party which stood at the helm and led the nation to victory in the war.

Ours is the party which, during the war, prepared for peace so well that when peace came reconversion promptly led to the greatest production and employment in this nation's life.

Ours is the party under whose leadership farm owners' income in this nation increased from less than $2.5 billions in 1933 to more than $18 billions in 1947; independent business and professional income increased from less than $3 billions in 1933 to more than $22 billions in 1947; employees' earnings increased from $29 billions in 1933 to more than 128 billions in 1947; and employment grew from 39 million jobs in 1933 to a record of 60 million jobs in 1947.

Ours is the party under which the framework of the world organization for peace and justice was formulated and created.

Ours is the party under which were conceived the instruments for resisting Communist aggression and for rebuilding the economic strength of the democratic countries of Europe and Asia—the Truman Doctrine and the Marshall Plan. They are the materials with which we must build the peace.

Ours is the party which first proclaimed that the actions and policies of this nation in the foreign field are matters of national and not just party concern. We shall go forward on the course charted by President Roosevelt and President Truman and the other leaders of Democracy.

We reject the principle—which we have always rejected, but which the Republican 80th Congress enthusiastically accepted—that government exists for the benefit of the privileged few.

To serve the interests of all and not the few; to assure a world in which peace and justice can prevail; to achieve security, full production, and full employment—this is our platform.

OUR FOREIGN POLICY

We declared in 1944 that the imperative duty of the United States was to wage the war to final triumph and to join with the other United Nations in the establishment of an international organization for the prevention of aggression and maintenance of international peace and security.

Under Democratic leadership, those pledges were gloriously redeemed.

When the United States was treacherously and savagely attacked, our great Democratic President, Franklin D. Roosevelt, and a Democratic Congress preserved the nation's honor, and with high courage and with the invincible might of the American people, the challenge was accepted. Under his inspiring leadership, the nation created the greatest army that ever assembled under the flag, the mightiest air force, the most powerful navy on the globe, and the largest merchant marine in the world.

The nation's gallant sons on land, on sea, and in the air, ended the war in complete and overwhelming triumph. Armed aggression against peaceful peoples was resisted and crushed. Arrogant and powerful war lords were vanquished and forced to unconditional surrender.

Before the end of the war the Democratic administration turned to the task of establishing measures for peace and the prevention of aggression and the threat of another war. Under the leadership of a Democratic President and his Secretary of State, the United Nations was organized at San Francisco. The charter was ratified by an overwhelming vote of the Senate. We support the United Nations fully and we pledge our whole-hearted aid toward its growth and development. We will continue to lead the way toward curtailment of the use of the veto. We shall favor such amendments and modifications of the charter as experience may justify. We will continue our efforts toward the establishment of an international armed force to aid its authority. We advocate the grant of a loan to the United Nations recommended by the President, but denied by the Republican Congress, for the construction of the United Nations headquarters in this country.

We pledge our best endeavors to conclude treaties of peace with our former enemies. Already treaties have been made with Italy, Hungary, Bulgaria and Rumania. We shall strive to conclude treaties with the remaining enemy states, based on justice and with guarantees against the revival of aggression, and for the preservation of peace.

We advocate the maintenance of an adequate Army, Navy and Air Force to protect the nations's vital interests and to assure our security against aggression.

We advocate the effective international control of weapons of mass destruction, including the atomic bomb, and we approve continued and vigorous efforts within the United Nations to bring about the successful consummation of the proposals which our Government has advanced.

The adoption of these proposals would be a vital and most important step toward safe and effective world disarmament and world peace under a strengthened United Nations which would then truly constitute a more effective parliament of the world's peoples.

Under the leadership of a Democratic President, the United States has demonstrated its friendship for other peace-loving nations and its support of their freedom and independence. Under the Truman doctrine vital aid has been extended to China, to Greece, and to Turkey. Under the Marshall Plan generous sums have been provided for the relief and rehabilitation of European nations striving to rebuild their economy and to secure and strengthen their safety and freedom. The Republican leadership in the House of Representatives, by its votes in the 80th Congress, has shown its reluctance to provide funds to support this program, the greatest move for peace and recovery made since the end of World War II.

We pledge a sound, humanitarian administration of the Marshall Plan.

We pledge support not only for these principles—we pledge further that we will not withhold necessary funds by which these principles can be achieved. Therefore, we pledge that we will implement with appropriations the commitments which are made in this nation's foreign program.

We pledge ourselves to restore the Reciprocal Trade Agreements program formulated in 1934 by Secretary of State Cordell Hull and operated successfully for 14 years—until crippled by the Republican 80th Congress. Further, we strongly endorse our country's adherence to the International Trade Organization.

A great Democratic President established the Good Neighbor Policy toward the nations of the Western Hemisphere. The Act of Chapultepec was negotiated at Mexico City under Democratic leadership. It was carried forward in the Western Hemisphere defense pact concluded at Rio de Janeiro, which implemented the Monroe Doctrine and united the Western Hemisphere in behalf of peace.

We pledge continued economic cooperation with the countries of the Western Hemisphere. We pledge continued support of regional arrangements within the United Nations Charter, such as the Inter-American Regional Pact and the developing Western European Union.

President Truman, by granting immediate recognition to Israel, led the world in extending friendship and welcome to a people who have long sought and justly deserve freedom and independence.

We pledge full recognition to the State of Israel. We affirm our pride that the United States under the leadership of President Truman played a leading role in the adoption of the resolution of November 29, 1947, by the United Nations General Assembly for the creation of a Jewish State.

We approve the claims of the State of Israel to the boundaries set torth in the United Nations resolution of November 29th and consider that modifications thereof should be made only if fully acceptable to the State of Israel.

We look forward to the admission of the State of Israel to the United Nation: and its full participation in the international community of nations. We pledge appropriate aid to the State of Israel in developing its economy and resources.

We favor the revision of the arms embargo to accord to the State of Israel the right of self-defense. We pledge ourselves to work for the modification of any resolution of the United Nations to the extent that it may prevent any such revision.

We continue to support, within the framework of the United Nations, the internationalization of Jerusalem and the protection of the Holy Places in Palestine.

The United States has traditionally been in sympathy with the efforts of subjugated countries to attain their independence, and to establish a democratic form of government. Poland is an outstanding example. After a century and a half of subjugation, it was resurrected after the first World War by our great Democratic President, Woodrow Wilson. We look forward to development of these countries as prosperous, free, and democratic fellow members of the United Nations.

OUR DOMESTIC POLICIES

The Republican 80th Congress is directly responsible for the existing and ever increasing high cost of living. It cannot dodge that responsibility. Unless the Republican candidates are defeated in the approaching elections, their mistaken policies will impose greater hardships and suffering on large numbers of the American people. Adequate food, clothing and shelter—the bare necessities of life—are becoming too expensive for the average wage earner and the prospects are more frightening each day. The Republican 80th Congress has lacked the courage to face this vital problem.

We shall curb the Republican inflation. We shall put a halt to the disastrous price rises which have come as a result of the failure of the Republican 80th Congress to take effective action on President Truman's recommendations, setting forth a comprehensive program to control the high cost of living.

We shall enact comprehensive housing legislation, including provisions for slum clearance and low-rent housing projects initiated by local agencies. This nation is shamed by the failure of the Republican 80th Congress to pass the vitally needed general housing legislation as recommended by the President. Adequate housing will end the need for rent control. Until then, it must be continued.

We pledge the continued maintenance of those sound fiscal policies which under Democratic leadership have brought about a balanced budget and reduction of the public debt by $28 billion since the close of the war.

We favor the reduction of taxes, whenever it is possible to do so without unbalancing the nation's economy, by giving a full measure of relief to those millions of low-income families on whom the wartime burden of taxation fell most heavily. The form of tax reduction adopted by the Republican 80th Congress gave relief to those who need it least and ignored those who need it most.

We shall endeavor to remove tax inequities and to continue to reduce the public debt.

We are opposed to the imposition of a general federal sales tax.

We advocate the repeal of the Taft-Hartley Act. It was enacted by the Republican 80th Congress over the President's veto. That act was proposed with the promise that it would secure "the legitimate rights of both employees and employers in their relations affecting commerce." It has failed. The number of labor-management disputes has increased. The number of cases before the National Labor Relations Board has more than doubled since the Act was passed, and efficient and prompt administration is becoming more and more difficult. It has encouraged litigation in labor disputes and undermined the established American policy of collective bargaining. Recent decisions by the courts prove that the Act was so poorly drawn that its application is uncertain, and that it is probably, in some provisions, unconstitutional.

We advocate such legislation as is desirable to establish a just body of rules to assure free and effective collective bargaining, to determine, in the public interest, the rights of employees and employers, to reduce to a minimum their conflict of interests, and to enable unions to keep their membership free from communistic influences.

We urge that the Department of Labor be rebuilt and strengthened, restoring to it the units, including the Federal Mediation and Conciliation Service and the United States Employment Service, which properly belong to it, and which the Republican 80th Congress stripped from it over the veto of President Truman. We urge that the Department's facilities for collecting and disseminating economic information be expanded, and that a Labor Education Extension Service be established in the Department of Labor.

We favor the extension of the coverage of the Fair Labor Standards Act as recommended by President Truman, and the adoption of a minimum wage of at least 75 cents an hour in place of the present obsolete and inadequate minimum of 40 cents an hour.

We favor legislation assuring that the workers of our nation receive equal pay for equal work, regardless of sex.

We favor the extension of the Social Security program established under Democratic leadership, to provide additional protection against the hazards of old age, disability, disease or death. We believe that this program should include: Increases in old-age and survivors' insurance benefits by at least 50 percent, and reduction of the eligibility age for women from 65 to 60 years; extension of old-age and survivors' and unemployment insurance to all workers not now covered; insurance against loss of earnings on account of illness or disability; improved public assistance for the needy.

We favor the enactment of a national health program for expanded medical research, medical education, and hospitals and clinics.

We will continue our efforts to aid the blind and other handicapped persons to become self-supporting.

We will continue our efforts to expand maternal care, improve the health of the nation's children, and reduce juvenile delinquency.

We approve the purposes of the Mental Health Act and we favor such appropriations as may be necessary to make it effective.

We advocate federal aid for education administered by and under the control of the states. We vigorously support the authorization, which was so shockingly ignored by the Republican 80th Congress, for the appropriation of $300 million as a beginning of Federal aid to the states to assist them in meeting the present educational needs. We insist upon the right of every American child to obtain a good education.

The nation can never discharge its debt to its millions of war veterans. We pledge ourselves to the continuance and improvement of our national program of benefits for veterans and their families.

We are proud of the sound and comprehensive program conceived, developed and administered under Democratic leadership, including the GI Bill of Rights, which has proved beneficial to many millions.

The level of veterans' benefits must be constantly re-examined in the light of the decline in the purchasing power of the dollar brought about by inflation.

Employment and economic security must be afforded all veterans. We pledge a program of housing for veterans at prices they can afford to pay.

The disabled veteran must be provided with medical care and hospitalization of the highest possible standard.

We pledge our efforts to maintain continued farm prosperity, improvement of the standard of living and the working conditions of the farmer, and to preserve the family-size farm.

Specifically, we favor a permanent system of flexible price supports for agricultural products, to maintain farm income on a parity with farm operating costs; an intensified soil conservation program; an extended crop insurance program; improvement of methods of distributing agricultural products; development and maintenance of stable export markets; adequate financing for the school lunch program; the use of agricultural surpluses to improve the diet of low-income families in case of need; continued expansion of the rural electrification program; strengthening of all agricultural credit programs; intensified research to improve agricultural practices, and to find new uses for farm products.

We strongly urge the continuance of maximum farmer participation of all these programs.

We favor the repeal of the discriminatory taxes on the manufacture and sale of oleomargarine.

We will encourage farm cooperatives and oppose any revision of federal law designed to curtail their most effective functioning as a means of achieving economy, stability and security for American agriculture.

We favor provisions under which our fishery resources and industry will be afforded the benefits that will result from more scientific research and exploration.

We recognize the importance of small business in a sound American economy. It must be protected against unfair discrimination and monopoly, and be given equal opportunities with competing enterprises to expand its capital structure.

We favor non-discriminatory transportation charges and declare for the early correction of inequalities in such charges.

We pledge the continued full and unified regional development of the water, mineral, and other natural resources of the nation, recognizing that the progress already achieved under the initiative of the Democratic Party in the arid and semi-arid states of the West, as well as in the Tennessee Valley, is only an indication of still greater results which can be accomplished. Our natural resources are the heritage of all our people and must not be permitted to become the private preserves of monopoly.

The irrigation of arid land, the establishment of new, independent, competitive business and the stimulation of new industrial opportunities for all of our people depends upon the development and transmission of electric energy in accordance with the program and the projects so successfully launched under Democratic auspices during the past sixteen years.

We favor acceleration of the Federal Reclamation Program, the maximum beneficial use of water in the several states for irrigation and domestic supply. In this connection, we propose the establishment and maintenance of new family-size farms for veterans and others seeking settlement opportunities, the development of hydroelectric power and its widespread distribution over publicly owned transmission lines to assure benefits to the water users in financing irrigation projects, and to the power users for domestic and industrial purposes, with preference to public agencies and R.E.A. cooperatives.

These are the aims of the Democratic Party which in the future, as in the past, will place the interest of the people as individual citizens first.

We will continue to improve the navigable waterways and harbors of the nation.

We pledge to continue the policy initiated by the Democratic Party of adequate appropriations for flood control for the protection of life and property.

In addition to practicing false economy on flood control, the Republican-controlled 80th Congress was so cruel as even to deny emergency federal funds for the relief of individuals and municipalities victimized by recent great floods, tornadoes and other disasters.

We shall expand our programs for forestation, for the improvement of grazing lands, public and private, for the stockpiling of strategic minerals and the encouragement of a sound domestic mining industry. We shall carry forward experiments for the broader utilization of mineral resources in the highly beneficial manner already demonstrated in the program for the manufacture of synthetic liquid fuel from our vast deposits of coal and oil shale and from our agricultural resources.

We pledge an intensive enforcement of the antitrust laws, with adequate appropriations.

We advocate the strengthening of existing antitrust laws by closing the gaps which experience has shown have been used to promote concentration of economic power.

We pledge a positive program to promote competitive business and to foster the development of independent trade and commerce.

We support the right of free enterprise and the right of all persons to work together in cooperatives and other democratic associations for the purpose of carrying out any proper business operations free from any arbitrary and discriminatory restrictions.

The Democratic Party is responsible for the great civil rights gains made in recent years in eliminating unfair and illegal discrimination based on race, creed or color.

The Democratic Party commits itself to continuing its efforts to eradicate all racial, religious and economic discrimination.

We again state our belief that racial and religious minorities must have the right to live, the right to work, the right to vote, the full and equal protection of the laws, on a basis of equality with all citizens as guaranteed by the Constitution.

We highly commend President Harry S. Truman for his courageous stand on the issue of civil rights.

We call upon the Congress to support our President in guaranteeing these basic and fundamental American Principles: (1) the right of full and equal political participation; (2) the right to equal opportunity of employment; (3) the right of security of person; (4) and the right of equal treatment in the service and defense of our nation.

We pledge ourselves to legislation to admit a minimum of 400,000 displaced persons found eligible for United States citizenship without discrimination as to race or religion. We condemn the undemocratic action of the Republican 80th Congress in passing an inadequate and bigoted bill for this purpose, which law imposes unAmerican restrictions based on race and religion upon such admissions.

We urge immediate statehood for Hawaii and Alaska; immediate determination by the people of Puerto Rico as to their form of government and their ultimate status with respect to the United States; and the maximum degree of local self-government for the Virgin Islands, Guam and Samoa.

We recommend to Congress the submission of a constitutional amendment on equal rights for women.

We favor the extension of the right of suffrage to the people of the District of Columbia.

We pledge adherence to the principle of nonpartisan civilian administration of atomic energy, and the development of atomic energy for peaceful purposes through free scientific inquiry for the benefit of all the people.

We urge the vigorous promotion of world-wide freedom in the gathering and dissemination of news by press, radio, motion pictures, newsreels and television, with complete confidence that an informed people will determine wisely the course of domestic and foreign policy.

We believe the primary step toward the achievement of world-wide freedom is access by all peoples to the facts and the truth. To that end, we will encourage the greatest possible vigor on the part of the United Nations Commission on Human Rights and the United Nations Economic and Social Council to establish the foundations on which freedom can exist in every nation.

We deplore the repeated attempts of Republicans in the 80th Congress to impose thought control upon the American people and to encroach on the freedom of speech and press.

We pledge the early establishment of a national science foundation under principles which will guarantee the most effective utilization of public and private research facilities.

We will continue to maintain an adequate American merchant marine.

We condemn Communism and other forms of totalitarianism and their destructive activity overseas and at home. We shall continue to build firm defenses against Communism by strengthening the economic and social structure of our own democracy. We reiterate our pledge to expose and prosecute treasonable activities of anti-democratic and un-American organizations which would sap our strength, paralyze our will to defend ourselves, and destroy our unity, inciting race against race, class against class, and the people against free institutions.

We shall continue vigorously to enforce the laws against subversive activities, observing at all times the constitutional guarantees which protect free speech, the free press and honest political activity. We shall strengthen our laws against subversion to the full extent necessary, protecting at all times our traditional individual freedoms.

We recognize that the United States has become the principal protector of the free world. The free peoples of the world look to us for support in maintaining their freedoms. If we falter in our leadership, we may endanger the peace of the world—and we shall surely endanger the welfare of our own nation. For these reasons it is imperative that we maintain our military strength until world peace with justice is secure. Under the leadership of President Truman, our military departments have been united and our Government organization for the national defense greatly strengthened. We pledge to maintain adequate military strength, based on these improvements, sufficient to fulfill our responsibilities in occupation zones, defend our national interests, and to bolster those free nations resisting Communist aggression.

This is our platform. These are our principles. They form a political and economic policy which has guided our party and our nation.

The American people know these principles well. Under them, we have enjoyed greater security, greater prosperity, and more effective world leadership than ever before.

Under them and with the guidance of Divine Providence we can proceed to higher levels of prosperity and security; we can advance to a better life at home; we can continue our leadership in the world with ever-growing prospects for lasting peace.

HARRY S. TRUMAN, ACCEPTANCE SPEECH
Philadelphia, July 13, 1948

Thank you very much.

I am sorry that the microphones are in your way, but they have to be out of the way because I have to see what I am doing; because I always have to be able to see what I am doing.

I cannot tell you how very much I appreciate the honor which you have just conferred upon me. I shall continue to try to deserve it.

I accept the nomination, and I want to thank this Convention for its unanimous nomination of my good friend and colleague, Senator Barkley, of Kentucky. He is a great man and a great public servant. Senator Barkley and I will win this election and make those Republicans like it. Don't you forget that.

We will do that because they are wrong and we are right, and I will prove it to you in just a few minutes.

This Convention met to express the will and reaffirm the beliefs of the Democratic Party. There have been differences of opinion, and that is the democratic way. Those differences have been settled by a majority vote as they should be, and it is time for us to get together and beat the common enemy, and that is up to you.

We will be working together for victory in a great cause. Victory has become a habit of our Party, and it has been elected four times in succession; and I am convinced that it will be elected a fifth time next November.

The reason is that the people know the Democratic Party is the people's party, and the Republican Party is the party of special interests and it always has been and always will be.

The record of the Democratic Party is written in the accomplishments of the last ten years. I don't need to repeat them. They have been very ably placed before this Convention by the keynote speaker, the candidate for Vice President, and by the Permanent Chairman.

Confidence and security have been brought to the American people by the Democratic Party. Farm income has increased from less than $2.5 billion in 1932 to more than $18 billion in 1947. Never in the world were the farmers of any Republic or any Kingdom, or any other country as prosperous as the farmers of the United States and if they don't do their duty by the Democratic Party, they are the most ungrateful people in the world.

And what I have said to the farmer I will say again: They are the most ungrateful people in the world if they pass the Democratic Party by this year.

The wages and salaries in this country were $29 billion in 1933, and more than $128 billion in 1947. That is labor, and labor never had but one friend in politics, and that is the Democratic Party, and Franklin D. Roosevelt.

The total national income has increased from less than $40 billion in 1933 to $203 billion in 1947, the greatest in all of the history of the world.

These benefits have been spread to all of the people because it is the business of the Democratic Party to see that the people get a fair share of these things. This last worst 80th Congress proved just the opposite for the Republicans. The record on foreign policy of the Democratic Party is that the United States has been turned away permanently from isolationism and we have converted the greatest and best of the Republicans to our viewpoint on that subject.

The United States has to accept its full responsibility for leadership in international affairs. We have been the backers, and the people who organized and started the United Nations, first started under that great Democratic President Woodrow Wilson as the League of Nations. The League was sabotaged by the Republicans in 1920 and we must see that the United Nations continues a strong and going body so we can have ever-lasting peace in the world.

We have removed the trade barriers in the world which is the best asset we can have for peace. Those trade barriers must not be put back into operation again. We have started a foreign aid program which means the recovery of Europe and China and the Far East. We instituted the program for Greece and Turkey, and I will say to you that all of these things were done in a cooperative bi-partisan manner.

The Foreign Relations Committees of the Senate and House were taken into the full confidence of the President in every one of these moves, and don't let anybody tell you anything else.

As I have said time and time again, foreign policy should be the policy of the whole nation and not a policy of one Party or the other. Partisanship should stop at the water's edge, and I shall continue to preach that through this whole campaign.

I would like to say a word or two now about what I think the Republicans did here, and I will speak from actions and from history and from experience. The situation in 1932 was due to the policies of the Republican Party in control of the Government of the United States. The Republican Party, as I said a while ago, favors the privileged few and not the common, every-day man. Ever since its inception that Party has been under the control of special privilege, and they concretely proved it in the 80th Congress. They proved it by the things they did to the people and not for them. They proved it by the things they failed to do.

Now let us look at some of them, just a few. Time and again I demanded the extension of price control before it expired on June 30, 1946. I asked for that extension in September of 1945, in November 1945, in the message on the State of the Union in 1946, and that price control legislation did not come to my desk until June 30, 1946, on the day on which it was supposed to expire, and it was such a rotten bill that I could not sign it; and after that they sent me one just as bad, and I had to sign it because they quit and went home.

It was said when OPA died that prices would adjust themselves for the benefit of the country. They have adjusted themselves all right. They have gone all of the way off the chart in adjusting themselves at the expense of the consumer and for the benefit of the people that hold the goods.

I called a special session of Congress in November of 1947–November 17, 1947–and I set out a ten-point program for the welfare and benefit of this country, among other things stand-by price control.

I got nothing. Congress has still done nothing. Away back four and a half years ago, while I was in the Senate, we passed a housing bill in the Senate known as the Wagner-Ellender-Taft Bill. It was a bill to clear the slums in the big cities and to help erect low-rent housing.

That bill, as I said, passed the Senate four years ago. It died in the House. That bill was reintroduced in the 80th Congress as the Taft-Ellender-Wagner Bill,–the name was slightly changed–but it was practically the same bill and it passed the Senate. It was allowed to die in the House of Representatives.

The Banking and Currency Committee sat on that bill and it was finally forced out of the committee, and then the Rules Committee took charge, and it is still in the Rules Committee.

But despite that, that party in Philadelphia in that Convention that met there three weeks ago could not get that Housing Bill passed. They passed a bill they called a Housing Bill which is not worth the paper on which it is written.

In the field of labor, we needed moderate legislation to promote labor-management harmony, but Congress instead passed that so-called Taft-Hartley Act, which has disrupted labor-management relations, and will cause strife and bitterness for years to come, if it is not repealed, as the Democratic Platform says it ought to be repealed.

I tried to strengthen the Labor Department. The Republican platform of 1944 said if they were in power they would build up a strong Labor Department, and you know what they did to the Labor Department. They have simply torn it up.

There is one bureau left that is functioning, and they cut the appropriation on that so it cannot function properly. I recommended an increase in the minimum wage and what did I get? Nothing–absolutely nothing. I suggested that the schools in this country were crowded, with teachers underpaid, and that there was a shortage of teachers.

One of the greatest national needs is more and better schools. I urged Congress to provide $300 million to aid the states in relieving the present educational crisis. Congress did nothing about it. Time and again I have recommended improvements in the Social Security Law, including extending protection to those not now covered, increasing the benefits, reducing the eligible age of women from 65 to 60.

Congress studied the matter for two years and could not get time to extend benefits, but did get time to take Social Security benefits away from 750,000 people. They passed that over my veto. I have repeatedly asked the Congress to pass a health program. The nation suffers from lack of medical care. That situation can be remedied any time the Congress wants to act upon it.

Everybody knows that I recommended to the Congress a civil rights program. I did so because I believe it to be my duty under the Constitution.

Some of the members of my own Party disagree violently on this matter, but they stand up and do it openly. People can say where they stand, but the Republicans all tell where we stand, but the Republicans all profess to be for these measures but the 80th Congress failed to act. They had enough men, and they had cloture. There were enough people that would vote for cloture.

Everybody likes to have low taxes, but we must reduce the national debt in times of prosperity, and when tax relief can be given, it ought to go to those who need it most and not go to those who need it least, as the Republican rich-man tax bill did, as they did when they passed it over my veto on the third try.

The first one of these tax bills that they sent me was so rotten that they could not stomach it themselves. They finally did send one that was somewhat improved, but it still helps the rich and sticks the knife into the backs of the poor.

Now, the Republicans came here a few weeks ago and they wrote up a platform.

I hope you have all read that platform. They adopted a platform and that platform had a lot of promises and statements of what the Republican Party was for and what they would do if they were in power. They had promised to do in that platform a lot of things that I have been asking them to do, and that they had refused to do when they had the power.

The Republican platform cries about cruelly high prices. I have been trying to get them to do something about high prices ever since they met the first time. Now, listen to this one: This one is equally bad, and as cynical.

The Republican platform comes out for slum clearance and low-rental housing. I have been trying to get them to pass this housing bill ever since they met the first time and it is still resting in the Rules Committee.

The Republican platform talks about equality and opportunity and promotion of education. I have been trying to get Congress to do something about that ever since they came there, and that bill is at rest in the House of Representatives.

The Republican platform urges expanding and increasing Social Security benefits. Think of that. That is increasing social security benefit, and yet when they had the opportunity they took 750,000 people off the Social Security rolls. I wonder if they think they can fool the people of the United States with such poppy-cock as that.

There is a long list of test promises in the Republican platform, and if it weren't so late I would tell you about all of them.

I have discussed a number of these affairs of the Republican 80th Congress and every one of them is important. Two of them are of major concern to nearly every American family: the failure to do anything about high prices, and the failure to do anything about housing.

My duty as President requires that I use every means within my power to get the laws the people need on such important matters, and I am therefore calling this Congress back into session on the 26th of July. That is on the 26th day of July, which out in Missouri we call Turnip Day.

I am going to call that Congress back, and I am going to ask them to pass laws halting rising prices and to lower the housing prices, which they say that they are for in their platform. At the same time, I shall ask them to act upon other vitally needed measures, such as aid to education, which they say that they are for; a National Health Program; Civil Rights legislation, which they say that they are for; and increase in the minimum wage, which I doubt very much they are for; an extension of Social Security coverage and increased benefits, which they say they are for; the projects needed in our program to provide public power and cheap electricity. By indirection, this 80th Congress has tried to sabotage the power policy which the United States has pursued for 14 years.

That power lobby is just as bad as the real estate lobby which is sitting on the Housing Bill. I shall ask for adequate and decent laws for displaced persons instead of this anti-Semetic and anti-Catholic law which the 80th Congress passed.

Now, my friends, if there is any reality behind that Republican platform, we ought to get some action out of the short session of the 80th Congress, and they could do this job in 15 days if they wanted to do it, and still have time to go out in the country.

They are going to try to dodge their responsibility, and they are going to drag all of the red herrings they can across this campaign, but I am here to say to you that Senator Barkley and I are not going to let them get away with it.

Now, what that worst 80th Congress does in this special session will be the test. The American people will not decide by listening to mere words or by reading a mere platform. They will decide on the record, the record as it has been written, and in the record is the stark truth that the battle lines of 1948 are the same as they were back in 1932 when the Nation lay helpless and prostrate as a result of the Republican inaction.

In 1932 we were attacking the citadel of special privilege and greed, when we were fighting to drive the money-changers from the temple. Today in 1948 we are now the defenders of the strongholds of democracy and of equal opportunity. The haven of the ordinary people of this land, and not of the favorite classes or the powerful few.

The battle cry is just the same now as it was in 1932, and I paraphrase the words of Franklin D. Roosevelt and say as he issued the challenge in accepting the nomination in Chicago, "This is more than a political call to arms. Give me your help, not to win votes alone, but to win in this new crusade and keep America secure and safe for its own people."

Now, my friends, with the help of God, and the wholehearted push which you can put behind this campaign, we can save this country from a continuation of the 80th Congress and from misrule from now on.

I must have your help, you must get in and push and win this election. The country can't afford another Republican Congress.

HARRY S. TRUMAN
JEFFERSON-JACKSON DAY DINNER ADDRESS
March 29, 1952

Mr. Chairman, Mr. Vice President, Mr. Speaker, Mr. Chairman of the Democratic Committee, distinguished guests and fellow Democrats:

I am very happy to be here tonight.

This makes seven Jefferson-Jackson dinners that I have spoken to in the city of Washington. I hope to attend several more, in one capacity or another.

They have all been wonderful dinners. One of the things I like about the dinners is the fact that they are political meetings. I like political meetings, and I like politics.

Politics—good politics—is public service. There is no life or occupation in which a man can find a greater opportunity to serve his community or his country.

I have been in politics more than 30 years, and I know that nothing else could have given me greater satisfaction. I have had a career from precinct to President, and I am a little bit proud of that career.

I am sure all of you here tonight are very much interested in the presidential election this year.

In view of that fact, I thought I would give you a little analysis of the political situation as I see it.

The political situation in this country may look complicated, but you can find the key to it in a simple thing: The Republicans have been out of office for 20 long years—and they are desperate to get back in office so they can control the country again.

For 20 years the Republicans have been wandering in a political desert—like camels looking for an oasis. They don't drink the same thing that camels do, though. And if they don't find it pretty soon, the Republican Party may die out, altogether.

And you know, I would just hate to see that happen. I would like to help keep the Republican Party alive, if that is at all possible. So I am going to offer them a little advice about the error of their ways.

There are some very good reasons why the Republicans have been out of office so long and haven't been able to get back in control.

The first reason is that they were voted out in 1932 because they had brought the country to the brink of ruin.

In the 1920's the Republican administrations drew back in petrified isolation from our world responsibilities. They spent all their time trying to help the rich get richer, and paid no attention to the welfare of the workers and the

Public Papers of the Presidents, Harry S. Truman, 1952, Item 69, 220-25.

farmers. All in all, they paved the way for the biggest economic smashup this country has ever seen.

That is the reason the Republicans were thrown out of office in 1932 and one of the very good reasons why they have been kept out ever since. People don't want any more "Great Depressions."

The second reason why the Republicans have been out of office for 20 years is that the Democratic Party has been giving the country good government. Instead of trying to build up the prosperity of the favored few, and letting some of it trickle down to the rest, we have been working to raise the incomes of the vast majority of the people. And we have been steadily expanding the base for prosperity and freedom in this country. The people have kept right on reelecting Democrats because we have been serving them well and they know it.

The third reason the Republicans have been kept out of power for 20 years is because they have never been able to agree on a sensible program to put before the country. They have been on almost every side of every question, but they have seldom or never been on the right side.

In 1936 they said the New Deal was terrible and they were against it and all its works. And in the election that fall they just lost by a landslide.

In 1940 they admitted there might be some good in some parts of the New Deal, but they said you needed a Republican to run it. And they were overwhelmingly beaten again.

In 1944 the Republicans said the New Deal might have been good in its day, but it had gotten old and tired and it was no good any more. But the people didn't agree, and the Republicans were snowed under once more.

Now in 1948 they said—well, as a matter of fact, by 1948 they were so sure of winning that they really didn't bother to take a position on anything. And they got just exactly what they deserved—they got another good licking.

And by now the Republicans can't figure out what to do. Every day you hear a new Republican theory of how to win the election of 1952.

One theory they have is that they ought to come right out and say they are against all advances the country has made since 1932.

This is the kind of dinosaur school of Republican strategy. They want to go back to prehistoric times. Republicans of this school say: "Let's stop beating about the bush—and let's say what we really believe. Let's say we're against social security—and we're against the labor unions and good wages—and we're opposed to price supports for farmers—that we're against the Government doing anything for anybody except big business."

Now, I have a lot of sympathy for these Republicans. They have been hushed up for a long time. They would certainly be happier if they could tell the truth for once and campaign for what they really believe. It would be good for their souls. But it wouldn't be good for their party, or for the country either. This dinosaur school of Republican strategy would only get the dinosaur vote—and there are not many of them left, except over at the Smithsonian.

Next, there is the Republican theory that the Republicans can win if they oppose the foreign policy of the United States. They can't agree among themselves as to how they want to oppose it, but most of them want to oppose it somehow.

Some Republicans seem to think it would be popular to pull out of Korea, and to abandon Europe, and to let the United Nations go to smash. They reason this way: "The American people aren't very bright. Let's tell them they don't have to build up defenses, or serve in the Army, or strengthen our allies overseas. If they fall for that, then we Republicans will be in—and that's all that matters."

The trouble with the Republican theory is that the American people are a lot smarter than the Republicans who thought it up. The American people have learned a lot from two world wars and from the last 7 years of working to keep the peace. They know that as long as communism is loose in the world we must have allies and we must resist aggression. The American people are living in the atomic age, and they know that the ideas of the stone age won't work any more—if they ever did work.

And there is another group of Republicans who attack our foreign policy by advocating the "all-out" or "let's get it over with" theory. These are the Republicans who say they want to expand the fighting in Korea, and start dropping atomic bombs, and invite a new world war. They figure it's good politics to talk that way. They don't stop to count the cost. They think people don't understand that the hardest and bravest thing in the world is to work for peace—and not for war. But if war comes—and God forbid that it comes—if the showdown comes, these loud talkers would be the first people to run for the bomb shelters. And the voters know it.

None of these Republican theories of how to win the election holds much promise of success this year. All they show is that the platform that the Republicans write in Chicago in July will have to be a fearful and wonderful thing to cover all these different theories. It will have to be a bigger tent than the Ringling Brothers circus—and it will have to cover just about as many freaks. It has even become fashionable for the Republican candidates to saw themselves in half and put part on each side of the fence. That would fit under the tent, too.

The real Republican campaign is not going to be fought on the issues. The Republicans are going to wage a campaign of phony propaganda. They are going to try what we might call the "white is black" and the "black is white" strategy. The reasoning behind it is this: The Republicans know that the Nation is strong and prosperous, that we are building up defenses against communism, that the Democratic administration has worked for the good of the people. The only chance for the Republicans, therefore, is to make the people think the facts aren't so. The job for the Republicans is to make people believe that white is black and black is white.

This is a pretty difficult way to win an election. It wouldn't appeal to anybody but very desperate Republican politicians. But the Republicans have some reason for thinking it might succeed. They will have the support of most of the press, and most of the radio commentators. And they may have the professional poll-takers with them again—as they were in 1948. The Republicans, as always, will have a lot of money. They have slick advertising experts. And they don't have too many scruples about how they use them. Remember that carpetbagger from Chicago who got convicted for the way he elected a Republican Senator in Maryland in 1950? They will try that all over the country.

The Republicans are all set to try this "white is black" technique. And this is the way it will work. First of all, they will try to make people believe that everything the Government has done for the country is socialism. They will go to the people and say: "Did you see that social security check you received the other day—you thought that was good for you, didn't you? That's just too bad! That's nothing in the world but socialism. Did you see that new flood control dam the Government is building over there for the protection of your property? Sorry—that's awful socialism! That new hospital that they are building is socialism. Price supports, more socialism for the farmers! Minimum wage laws? Socialism for labor! Socialism is bad for you, my friend. Everybody knows that. And here you are, with your new car, and your home, and better opportunities for the kids, and a television set—you are just surrounded by socialism!"

Now the Republicans say, "That's a terrible thing, my friend, and the only way out of this sinkhole of socialism is to vote for the Republican ticket."

And if you do that, you will probably have a garage and no car, a crystal radio set and no television—and probably not even a garage to live in, but a secondhand tent out on the lawn. I don't believe people are going to be fooled into that condition, because they went through it once before.

Now, do you think they can sell that bill of goods? This country today has more freedom for all its people than any country in the history of the world. And all the efforts of all the Republican politicians can't convince the people that this is socialism.

The next part of this "white is black" campaign is to try to make people believe that the Democratic Party is in favor of communism. That is an even tougher job than selling the socialism nonsense, but the Republicans are desperate, so they are going to try it.

Of course, we have spent billions of dollars to build up our defenses against communism; we have created an alliance of the free nations against communism; we are helping them to arm against communism; we have met and halted communism in Greece and Turkey, in Berlin and Austria, in Italy and Iran, and the most important of all, in Korea. We have fought communism abroad. We have fought communism at home. We have an FBI and a Central Intelligence Agency defending us against spies and saboteurs. The Federal loyalty program keeps Communists out of Government.

That's the record, and how do the Republicans propose to get around it? Here's what they will try to do. They will go to the voters and say, "Did you know the Government was full of Communists?" And the voters say, "No. What makes you say that?" And then the Republicans explain that somebody named Joe Doakes works for the Government, and he has a cousin who sells shoelaces, or a ribbon clerk in a department store, and this cousin has a wife who wrote an article, before Joe married her, that was printed in a magazine that also printed an article in favor of Chinese Communists—and they will continue that ad lib. This may sound very silly, and it is. But some political fakers spend all their time trying to pull the wool over the people's eyes with this sort of nonsense.

The real test of anti-communism is whether we are willing to devote our resources and our strength to stopping Communist aggression and saving free people from its horrible tyranny. This kind of anti-communism takes money and courage—and not just a lot of talk. The next time you hear some of this loud anti-Communist talk from our Republican friends, ask them how they voted—ask them how they voted on aid to Greece, ask them how they voted on the Marshall plan, ask them how they voted on the mutual security program. The chances are they voted to cut or cripple these all-important measures against communism.

I say to you in all seriousness, beware of those who pretend to be so violently anti-Communist in this country, and at the same time vote to appease communism abroad. In my book, that is talking out of both sides of the mouth at once; and I don't think the American people are going to be taken in by it.

The next part of the Republican "white is black" campaign is to try to fool the voters into thinking that the Democratic Party is dishonest—that the Government is full of grafters and thieves and all kinds of assorted crooks. To hear them talk you wouldn't think that there was an honest man in Washington. And that includes some of them, too, maybe.

Now, I want to say something very important to you about this issue of morality in government.

I stand for honest government. I have worked for it. I have probably done more for it than any other President. I have done more than any other President to reorganize the Government on an efficient basis, and to extend the civil service merit system.

I hate corruption not only because it is bad in itself, but also because it is the deadly enemy of all things the Democratic Party has been doing all these years. I hate corruption everywhere, but I hate it most of all in a Democratic officeholder, because that is a betrayal of all that the Democratic Party stands for.

Here is the reason. To me, morality in government means more than a mere absence of wrongdoing. It means a government that is fair to all. I think it is just as immoral for the Congress to enact special tax favors into law as it is for a tax official to connive in a crooked tax return. It is just as immoral to use the lawmaking power of the Government to enrich the few at the expense of the many, as it is to steal money from the public treasury. That *is* stealing money from the public treasury.

All of us know, of course, about the scandals and corruption of the Republican officeholders in the 1920's. But to my mind the Veterans' Administration scandals, in those days, and the Teapot Dome steal, were no worse—no more immoral—than the tax laws of Andrew Mellon, or the attempt to sell Muscle Shoals to private owners. Legislation that favored the greed of monopoly and the trickery of Wall Street was a form of corruption that did the country four times as much harm as Teapot Dome ever did.

Private selfish interests are always trying to corrupt the Government in this way. Powerful financial groups are always trying to get favors for themselves.

Now, the Democratic administration has been fighting against these efforts to corrupt the powers of Government. We haven't always won, but we have never surrendered, and we never will.

For all these years, we have been fighting to use our natural resources for the benefit of the public, to develop our forests and our public oil reserves and our water power for the benefit of all, to raise the incomes of all our citizens, to protect the farmer and the worker against the power of monopoly.

And where have the Republicans been in this fight for morality in Government? Do they come out and vote with us to keep the special interests from robbing the public? Not at all. Most of them are on the other side.

It's the same thing when you come to the question of the conduct of Government officials. The Republicans make a great whoop and holler about the honesty of Federal employees, but they are usually the first to show up in a Government office asking for special favors for private interests, and in raising cain if they don't get them. These Republican gentlemen can't have it both ways—they can't be for morality on Tuesday and Thursday, and then be for special privileges for their clients on Monday, Wednesday, and Friday.

The press recently—for a wonder—has been giving some facts on this subject that have been very hard to get at.

I'm disgusted with these efforts to discredit and blacken the character and reputation of the whole Federal service. We have a higher percentage of Federal employees under civil service than ever before, and on the whole they are a finer, better type of men and women than we have ever had in the service before. It is just as much our duty to protect the innocent as it is to punish the guilty. If a man is accused, he ought to have his day in court, and I don't mean a kangaroo court, either.

I hate injustice just as much as I hate corruption.

Of course, we must always work to keep our Government clean. Our Democratic Senators and Congressmen have been working and I have been working to clean up bad conditions where they exist, and to devise procedures and systems to prevent them in the future. And I would like to have help in this fight from everybody, Democrats and Republicans alike. I have just got one reorganization plan through the Congress, and I am going to send up some more plans to the Congress soon—to put more of our Federal officials under civil service and out of politics. I would like to see how many of the Republicans vote for them.

I don't think the "black is white" campaign of the Republican Party is going to succeed. I think the voters are going to see through this holier-than-thou disguise that our Republican friends are putting on.

All the tricks of Republican propaganda cannot make the people forget that the Democratic Party has been working for their welfare.

We are working for the welfare of the farmer. We hold to the ideal that goes back to Jefferson, that a farmer should have the opportunity to own his farm, to share in the benefits of scientific progress, and to secure a fair income for his efforts.

The Democratic Party is working for the success of our free enterprise system. We have worked to prevent monopoly, to give the small businessman a fair chance, and to develop our natural resources for all the people, and not just for the favored few.

The Democratic Party is working for the welfare of labor. We have worked for good wages and hour legislation, for unemployment compensation, and for fair labor relations laws.

The Democratic Party is dedicated to the ideal that every family is entitled to fair opportunities for decent living conditions, to a chance to educate their children, to have good medical services, and reasonable provision for retirement. That is why we have worked for good social security laws, for better education and health services, for good housing, and for equal rights and opportunities for all our people, regardless of color, religion, or national origin.

Above all, the Democratic Party is working for peace on earth and goodwill among men. We believe that war is not inevitable, that peace can be won, that free men of all lands can find the way to live together in the world as good neighbors. That is why we have been willing to sacrifice to stop aggression, willing to send our money and our goods to help men in other countries stand up against tyranny, willing to fight in Korea to stop world war III before it begins. For if the bloody harvest of world war were to begin anew, most of us would never see a peaceful world again.

This is the record of the Democratic Party. It is a proud record, and an honorable record. It is a record of progress, of actions that are right because they are solidly founded on American ideals.

Whoever the Democrats nominate for President this year, he will have this record to run upon.

I shall not be a candidate for reelection. I have served my country long, and I think efficiently and honestly. I shall not accept a renomination. I do not feel that it is my duty to spend another 4 years in the White House.

We must always remember the things the Democratic Party has done, and the high ideals that have made it great. We must be true to its principles and keep it foremost in service of the people.

If we do that, we can be sure that there will be a Democratic President in the White House for the next 4 years.

DEMOCRATIC PLATFORM OF 1952

PREAMBLE

Our nation has entered into an age in which Divine Providence has permitted the genius of man to unlock the secret of the atom.

No system of government can survive the challenge of an atomic era unless its administration is committed to the stewardship of a trustee imbued with a democratic faith, a buoyant hope for the future, the charity of brotherhood, and the vision to translate these ideals into the realities of human government. The Government of the United States, administered by the Democratic Party, is today so entrusted.

The free choice of the Democratic Party by the people of America as the instrument to achieve that purpose will mean world peace with honor, national security based on collective pacts with other free nations, and a high level of human dignity. National survival demands that these goals be attained, and the endowments of the Democratic Party alone can assure their attainment.

For twenty years, under the dedicated guidance of Franklin Delano Roosevelt and Harry S. Truman, our country has moved steadily along the road which has led the United States of America to world leadership in the cause of freedom.

We will not retreat one inch along that road. Rather, it is our prayerful hope that the people, whom we have so faithfully served, will renew the mandate to continue our service and that Almighty God may grant us the wisdom to succeed.

TWENTY YEARS OF PROGRESS

Achieving Prosperity

An objective appraisal of the past record clearly demonstrates that the Democratic Party has been the chosen American instrument to achieve prosperity, build a stronger democracy, erect the structure of world peace, and continue on the path of progress.

Democratic Party policies and programs rescued American business from total collapse—from the fatal economic consequences of watered stock, unsound banks, useless and greedy holding companies, high tariff barriers, and predatory business practices, all of which prevailed under the last Republican administrations. Democratic policies have enabled the Federal Government to help all business, small and large, to achieve the highest rate of productivity, the widest domestic and world markets, and the largest profits in the history of the Nation.

The simple fact is that today there are more than four million operating business enterprises in this country, over one million more than existed in 1932. Corporate losses in that fateful year were over three billion dollars; in 1951, corporate profits, after taxes, reached the staggering total of eighteen billion.

Democratic policies and programs rescued American agriculture from the economic consequences of blight, drought, flood and storm, from oppressive and indiscriminate foreclosures, and from the ruinous conditions brought about by the bungling incompetence and neglect of the preceding twelve years of Republican maladministration. Economic stability, soil conservation, rural electrification, farm dwelling improvement, increased production and efficiency and more than sevenfold increase in cash income have been the return to farmers for their faith in the Democratic Party.

Democratic labor policies have rescued the wage earners in this country from mass unemployment and from sweatshop slavery at starvation wages. Under our Democratic administrations, decent hours, decent wages, and decent working conditions have become the rule rather than the exception.

Self organizations of labor unions and collective bargaining, both of which are the keystone to labor management, peace and prosperity, must be encouraged, for the good of all.

Unemployment is now less than 3 per cent of the labor force, compared with almost 25 per cent in 1932. Trade union membership has reached a total of 16 million, which is more than five times the total of 1932.

The welfare of all economic and social groups in our society has been promoted by the sound, progressive and humane policies of the Democratic Party.

Strengthening Democracy

We are convinced that lasting prosperity must be founded upon a healthy democratic society respectful of the rights of all people.

Under Democratic Party leadership more has been done in the past twenty years to enhance the sanctity of individual rights than ever before in our history. Racial and religious minorities have progressed further toward real equality than during the preceding 150 years.

Governmental services, Democratically administered, have been improved and extended. The efficiency, economy, and integration of Federal operations have been advocated and effectuated through sound programs and policies. Through cooperative programs of Federal aid, State and local governments have been encouraged and enabled to provide many more services.

The Democratic Party has been alert to the corroding and demoralizing effects of dishonesty and disloyalty in the public service. It has exposed and punished those who would corrupt the integrity of the public service, and it has always championed honesty and morality in government. The loyalty program of President Truman has served effectively to prevent infiltration by subversive elements and to protect honest and loyal public servants against unfounded and malicious attacks.

We commend the relentless and fearless actions of Congressional Committees which, under vigorous Democratic leadership, have exposed dereliction in public service, and we pledge our support to a continuance of such actions as conditions require them.

The administration of our government by the Democratic Party has been based upon principles of justice and equity, and upon the American tradition of fair play. Men who are elected to high political office are entrusted with high responsibilities. Slander, defamation of character, deception and dishonesty are as truly transgressions of God's commandments, when resorted to by men in public life, as they are for all other men.

Building Peace with Honor

The Democratic Party has worked constantly for peace—lasting peace, peace with honor, freedom, justice and security for all nations.

The return of the Democratic Party to power in 1933 marked the end of a tragic era of isolationism fostered by the Republican Administrations which had deliberately and callously rejected the golden opportunity created by Woodrow Wilson for collective action to secure the peace.

This folly contributed to the second World War. Victory in that war has presented the nations of the world a new opportunity which the Democratic Party is determined shall not be lost.

We have helped establish the instrumentalities through which the hope of mankind for universal world peace can be realized. Under Democratic leadership, our Nation has moved promptly and effectively to meet and repel the menace to world peace by Soviet imperialism.

Progress in the New Era

The Democratic Party believes that past progress is but a prelude to the human aspirations which may be realized in the future.

Under Democratic Party leadership, America has accepted each new challenge of history and has found practical solutions to meet and overcome them. This we have done without departing from the principles of our basic philosophy, that is, the destiny of man to achieve his earthly ends in the spirit of brotherhood.

A great Democrat—Franklin Delano Roosevelt—devised the programs of the New Deal to meet the pressing problems of the 1930s. Another great Democrat—Harry S. Truman—devised the programs of the Fair Deal to meet the complex problems of America in the 1940s. The Democratic Party is ready to face and solve the challenging problems of the 1950s. We dedicate ourselves to the magnificent work of these great Presidents and to mould and adapt their democratic principles to the new problems of the years ahead.

In this spirit we adopt and pledge ourselves to this, the Democratic platform of 1952:

OUR GOAL IS PEACE WITH HONOR

Peace with honor is the greatest of all our goals.

We pledge our unremitting efforts to avert another world war. We are determined that the people shall be spared that frightful agony.

We are convinced that peace and security can be safeguarded if America does not deviate from the practical and successful policies developed under Democratic leadership since the close of World War II. We will resolutely move ahead with the constructive task of promoting peace.

THE DEMOCRATIC PROGRAM FOR PEACE AND NATIONAL SECURITY

Supporting the United Nations

Under Democratic leadership, this country sponsored and helped create the United Nations and became a charter member and staunchly supports its aims.

We will continue our efforts to strengthen the United Nations, improve its institutions as experience requires, and foster its growth and development.

The Communist aggressor has been hurled back from South Korea. Thus, Korea has proved, once and for all, that the United Nations will resist aggression. We urge continued effort, by every honorable means, to bring about a fair and effective peace settlement in Korea in accordance with the principles of the United Nations' charter.

Strong National Defense

Our Nation has strengthened its national defenses against the menace of Soviet aggression.

The Democratic Party will continue to stand unequivocally for the strong, balanced defense forces for this country—land, sea and air. We will continue to support the expansion and maintenance of the military and civil defense forces required for our national security. We reject the defeatist view of those who say we cannot afford the expense and effort necessary to defend ourselves. We express our full confidence in the Joint Chiefs of Staff. We voice complete faith in the ability and valor of our armed forces, and pride in their accomplishments.

COLLECTIVE STRENGTH FOR THE FREE WORLD

We reject the ridiculous notions of those who would have the United States face the aggressors alone. That would be the most expensive—and the most dangerous—method of seeking security. This nation needs strong allies, around the world, making their maximum contribution to the common defense. They add their strength to ours in the defense of freedom.

The Truman Doctrine in 1947, the organization of hemisphere defense at Rio de Janeiro that same year, the Marshall Plan in 1948, the North Atlantic Treaty in 1949, the Point IV program, the resistance to Communist aggression in Korea, the Pacific

Security pacts in 1951, and the Mutual Security programs now under way—all stand as landmarks of America's progress in mobilizing the strength of the free world to keep the peace.

Encouraging European Unity

We encourage the economic and political unity of free Europe and the increasing solidarity of the nations of the North Atlantic Community.

We hail the Schuman Plan to pool the basic resources of industrial Western Europe, and the European Defense Community. We are proud of America's part in carrying these great projects forward, and we pledge our continuing support until they are established.

Support for Free Germany

We welcome the German Federal Republic into the company of free nations. We are determined that Germany shall remain free and continue as a good neighbor in the European community. We sympathize with the German people's wish for unity and will continue to do everything we can by peaceful means to overcome the Kremlin's obstruction of that rightful aim.

Support for the Victims of Soviet Imperialism

We will not abandon the once-free peoples of Central and Eastern Europe who suffer now under the Kremlin's tyranny in violation of the Soviet Union's most solemn pledges at Teheran, Yalta, and Potsdam. The United States should join other nations in formally declaring genocide to be an international crime in time of peace as well as war. This crime was exposed once more by the shocking revelations of Soviet guilt as disclosed in the report filed in Congress by the special committee investigating the Katyn Forest massacre. We look forward to the day when the liberties of Poland and the other oppressed Soviet satellites, including Czechoslovakia, Hungary, Rumania, Bulgaria, Albania, Lithuania, Estonia and Latvia and other nations in Asia under Soviet domination, will be restored to them and they can again take their rightful place in the community of free nations. We will carry forward and expand the vital and effective program of the "Voice of America" for penetration of the "Iron Curtain," bringing truth and hope to all the people subjugated by the Soviet Empire.

Support for the Nations of the Middle East

We seek to enlist the people of the Middle East to work with us and with each other in the development of the region, the lifting of health and living standards, and the attainment of peace. We favor the development of integrated security arrangements for the Middle East and other assistance to help safeguard the independence of the countries in the area.

We pledge continued assistance to Israel so that she may fulfill her humanitarian mission of providing shelter and sanctuary for her homeless Jewish refugees while strengthening her economic development.

We will continue to support the tripartite declaration of May 1950, to encourage Israel and the Arab States to settle their differences by direct negotiation, to maintain and protect the sanctity of the Holy Places and to permit free access to them.

We pledge aid to the Arab States to enable them to develop their economic resources and raise the living standards of their people. We support measures for the relief and reintegration of the Palestine refugees, and we pledge continued assistance to the reintegration program voted by the General Assembly of the United Nations in January 1952.

South Asia: A Testing Ground for Democracy

In the subcontinent of South Asia, we pledge continuing support for the great new countries of India and Pakistan in their efforts to create a better life for their people and build strong democratic governments to stand as bastions of liberty in Asia, secure against the threat of Communist subversion.

Collective Security in the Pacific

We welcome free Japan as a friendly neighbor and an ally in seeking security and progress for the whole Pacific area. America's security pacts with Japan and with the Philippines, Australia, and New Zealand are indispensable steps toward comprehensive mutual security arrangements in that area. Our military and economic assistance to the Nationalist Government of China on Formosa has strengthened that vital outpost of the free world, and will be continued.

Strengthening the Americas

In the Western Hemisphere, we pledge ourselves to continue the policy of the good neighbor. We will strive constantly to strengthen the bonds of friendship and cooperation with our Latin American allies who are joined with us in the defense of the Americas.

Disarmament Remains the Goal

The free world is rearming to secure the peace. Under Democratic leadership, America always stands prepared to join in a workable system for foolproof inspection and limitation of all armaments, including atomic weapons. This Nation has taken the leadership in proposing concrete, practical plans for such a system. We are determined to carry on the effort for real, effective disarmament.

We look forward to the day when a great share of the resources now devoted to the armaments program can be diverted into the channels of peaceful production to speed the progress of America and of the underdeveloped regions of the world.

Helping Other People to Help Themselves

Even though we cannot now disarm, we will go forward as rapidly as possible in developing the imaginative and farsighted concept of President Truman embodied in the Point IV program.

We will continue to encourage use of American skills and capital in helping the people of underdeveloped lands to combat disease, raise living standards, improve land tenure and develop industry and trade. The continuance of ever stronger and more vigorous Point IV programs—sponsored both by this country and the United Nations—is an indispensable element in creating a peaceful world.

Upholding the Principle of Self-Determination

In an era when the "satellite state" symbolizes both the tyranny of the aggressor nations and the extinction of liberty in small nations, the Democratic Party reasserts and reaffirms the Wilsonian principle of the right of national self-determination. It is part of the policy of the Democratic Party, therefore, to encourage and assist small nations and all peoples in the peaceful and orderly achievement of their legitimate aspirations toward political, geographical and ethnic integrity so that they may dwell in the family of sovereign nations with freedom and dignity.

Expanding World Trade

The Democratic Party has always stood for expanding trade among free nations. We reassert that stand today. We vigorously oppose any restrictive policies which would weaken the highly successful reciprocal trade program fathered by Cordell Hull.

Since 1934, the United States has taken the lead in fostering the expansion and liberalization of world trade.

Our own economy requires expanded export markets for our manufactured and agricultural products and a greater supply of essential imported raw materials. At the same time, our friends throughout the world will have opportunity to earn their own way to higher living standards with lessened dependence on our aid.

Progressive Immigration Policies

Solution of the problem of refugees from communism and over-population has become a permanent part of the foreign policy program of the Democratic Party. We pledge continued cooperation with other free nations to solve it.

We pledge continued aid to refugees from communism and the enactment of President Truman's proposals for legislation in this field. In this way we can give hope and courage to the victims of Soviet brutality and can carry on the humanitarian tradition of the Displaced Persons Act.

Subversive elements must be screened out and prevented from entering our land, but the gates must be left open for practical numbers of desirable persons from abroad whose immigration to this country provides an invigorating infusion into the stream of American life, as well as a significant contribution to the solution of the world refugee and over-population problems.

We pledge continuing revision of our immigration and naturalization laws to do away with any unjust and unfair practices against national groups which have contributed some of our best citizens. We will eliminate distinctions between nativeborn and naturalized citizens. We want no "second-class" citizens in free America.

OUR DOMESTIC POLICY

Economic Opportunity and Growth

The United States is today a land of boundless opportunity. Never before has it offered such a large measure of prosperity, security and hope for all its people.

Horizons of even greater abundance and opportunity lie before us under a Democratic Administration responsive to the will of the people.

The Democratic Administration has had a guiding principle since taking office 20 years ago: that the prosperity and growth of this Nation are indivisible. Every step we have taken to help the farmers has also helped the workers and business. Every improvement in the status of the worker has helped both farmers and business. Every expansion of business has provided more jobs for workers and greater demand for farm products.

A STABILIZED ECONOMY

Combatting Inflation

The Democratic Administration early recognized that defense production would limit the amount of goods in civilian markets, and subject our economy to heavy inflationary pressure. To prevent this from resulting in ruinous inflation, the Administration proposed pay-as-we-go taxation to keep the national debt as low as possible and to prevent excess money pressure on scarce goods and services.

Direct controls were also proposed to channel scarce materials into highly essential defense production, and to keep prices down.

In 1951 and 1952 Republican Congressmen demonstrated their attitude toward these necessary measures when they sponsored amendments which would have destroyed all controls.

Prices

We shall strive to redress the injury done to the American people—especially to white collar workers and fixed-income families—by the weakening amendments which the Republicans in Congress have forced into our anti-inflation laws.

We pledge continuance of workable controls so long as the emergency requires them. We pledge fair and impartial enforcement of controls and their removal as quickly as economic conditions allow.

Rents

We strongly urge continued federal rent control in critical defense areas and in the many other localities still suffering from a substantial shortage of adequate housing at reasonable prices.

Full Employment

The Democratic Administration prudently passed the Employment Act of 1946 declaring it to be national policy never again to permit large scale unemployment to stalk the land. We will assure the transition from defense production to peace-time production without the ravages of unemployment. We pledge ourselves at all times to the maintenance of maximum employment, production, and purchasing power in the American economy.

Integrity in Government Finances

We solemnly pledge the preservation of the financial strength of the Government. We have demonstrated our ability to maintain and enhance the nation's financial strength. In the six full fiscal years since V-J Day, our fiscal policy has produced a $4 billion budget surplus. We have reduced the public debt $17 billion from the postwar peak.

We have demonstrated our ability to make fiscal policy contribute in a positive way to economic growth and the maintenance of high-level employment. The policies which have been followed have given us the greatest prosperity in our history. Sustained economic expansion has provided the funds necessary to finance our defense and has still left our people with record high consumer incomes and business with a record volume of investment. Employment and personal incomes are at record levels. Never have Americans enjoyed a higher standard of living and saved more for contingencies and old age.

Federal Taxes

We believe in fair and equitable taxation. We oppose a Federal general sales tax. We adhere to the principle of ability to pay. We have enacted an emergency excess profits tax to prevent profiteering from the defense program and have vigorously attacked special tax privileges.

Tax Reductions

In the future, as in the past, we will hold firm to policies consistent with sound financing and continuing economic progress. As rapidly as defense requirements permit, we favor reducing taxes, especially for people with lower incomes. But we will not imperil our Nation's security by making reckless promises to reduce taxes. We deplore irresponsible assertions that national security can be achieved without paying for it.

Closing Tax Loopholes

Justice requires the elimination of tax loopholes which favor special groups. We pledge continued efforts to the elimination of remaining loopholes.

Government Expenditures

We believe in keeping government expenditures to the lowest practicable level. The great bulk of our national budget consists of obligations incurred for defense purposes. We pledge ourselves to a vigilant review of our expenditures in order to reduce them as much as possible.

THE AMERICAN FARMER AND AGRICULTURE

We know that national prosperity depends upon a vigorous, productive and expanding agriculture.

We take great pride in our Party's record of performance and in the impressive gains made by American agriculture in the last two decades. Under programs of Democratic Administrations the net agricultural income has increased from less than two billion dollars to almost fifteen billion dollars. These programs must be continued and improved.

Resource Conservation

The soil resources of our country have been conserved and strengthened through the Soil Conservation Service, the Agricultural Conservation Program, the Forestry and the Research programs, with their incentives to increased production through sound conservation farming. These programs have revolutionized American agriculture and must be continued and expanded. We will accelerate programs of upstream flood prevention, watershed protection, and soil, forest and water conservation in all parts of the country. These conservation measures are a national necessity; they are invaluable to our farmers, and add greatly to the welfare of all Americans and of generations yet unborn.

Grass Roots Administration

We will continue the widest possible farmer participation through referenda, farmer-elected committees, local soil conservation districts, and self-governing agencies in the conduct and administration of these truly democratic programs, initiated and developed under Democratic administrations.

Price Supports

Under the present farm program, our farmers have performed magnificently and have achieved unprecedented production. We applaud the recent Congressional action in setting aside the "sliding scale" for price support through 1954, and we will continue to protect the producers of basic agricultural commodities under the terms of a mandatory price support program at not less than ninety percent of parity. We continue to advocate practical methods for extending price supports to other storables and to the producers of perishable commodities, which account for three-fourths of all farm income.

Abundant Production

We will continue to assist farmers in providing abundant and stable supplies of agricultural commodities for the consumers at reasonable prices, and in assuring the farmer the opportunity to earn a fair return commensurate with that enjoyed by other segments of the American economy.

The agricultural adjustment programs encourage the production of abundant supplies while enabling producers to keep supply in line with consumer demand, preventing wide fluctuations and bringing stability to the agricultural income of the Nation. We pledge retention of such programs.

We pledge continued efforts to provide adequate storage facilities for grain and other farm products with sufficient capacity for needed reserves for defense, and other emergency requirements, in order to protect the integrity of the farm price support programs.

Research

We are justly proud of the outstanding achievements of our agricultural research. We favor a greatly expanded research and education program for American agriculture in order that both production and distribution may more effectively serve consumers and producers alike, and thus meet the needs of the modern world. We favor especial emphasis on the development of new crops and varieties, on crop and livestock disease and pest control, and on agricultural statistics and marketing services.

Marketing

We must find profitable markets for the products of our farms, and we should produce all that these markets will absorb. To this end we will continue our efforts to reduce trade barriers, both at home and abroad, to provide better marketing and inspection facilities, and to find new uses and outlets for our foods and fibers both in domestic and foreign markets.

Farm Credit

We have provided credit facilities for all agriculture, including means by which young men, veterans of military service, and farm tenants have been encouraged to become farmers and farm home-owners, and through which low-income farmers have been assisted in establishing selfsustaining and fully productive farm units. We will not waver in our efforts to provide such incentives.

Crop Insurance

Crop insurance to protect farmers against loss from destruction of their crops by natural causes has been created and developed under Democratic Administrations into a sound business operation. This program should be expanded as rapidly as experience justifies, in order that its benefits may be made available to every farmer.

Rural Electrification

Democratic Administrations have established the great Rural Electrification Program, which has brought light and power to the rural homes of our Nation. In 1935, only 10% of the farm homes of America had the benefits of electricity. Today 85% of our rural homes enjoy the benefits of electric light and power. We will continue to fight to make electricity available to all rural homes, with adequate facilities for the generation and transmission of power. Through the Rural Telephone Program, inaugurated by the Democratic 81st Congress, we will provide the opportunity for every farm home to have this modern essential service. We pledge support of these selfliquidating farm programs.

Cooperatives

We will continue to support the sound development and growth of bona fide farm cooperatives and to protect them from punitive taxation.

Defense Needs

We will continue to recognize agriculture as an essential defense industry, and to assist in providing all the necessary tools, machinery, fertilizer, and manpower needed by farmers in meeting production goals.

Family Farming

The family farm is the keystone of American agriculture. We will strive unceasingly to make the farm homes of our country healthier and happier places in which to live. We must see that our youth continues to find attractive opportunity in the field of agriculture.

The Republican Party platform is loud in its criticism of our great farm programs. We challenge Republicans and other enemies of farm progress to justify their opposition to the program now in operation, to oppose the improvements here proposed, or to advocate repeal of a single vital part of our program.

A FAIR DEAL FOR WORKERS

Good Incomes

There can be no national prosperity unless our working men and women continue to prosper and enjoy rising living standards. The rising productivity of American workers is a key to our unparalleled industrial progress. Good incomes for our workers are the secret of our great and growing consumer markets.

Labor-Management Relations

Good labor-management relations are essential to good incomes for wage earners and rising output from our factories. We believe that to the widest possible extent consistent with the public interest, management and labor should determine wage rates and conditions of employment through free collective bargaining.

Taft-Hartley Act

We strongly advocate the repeal of the Taft-Hartley Act.

The Taft-Hartley Act has been proved to be inadequate, unworkable, and unfair. It interferes in an arbitrary manner with collective bargaining, tipping the scales in favor of management against labor.

The Taft-Hartley Act has revived the injunction as a weapon against labor in industrial relations. The Act has arbitrarily forbidden traditional hiring practices which are desired by both management and labor in many industries. The Act has forced workers to act as strikebreakers against their fellow unionists. The Act has served to interfere with one of the most fundamental rights of American workers—the right to organize in unions of their own choosing.

We deplore the fact that the Taft-Hartley Act provides an inadequate and unfair means of meeting with national emergency situations. We advocate legislation that will enable the President to deal fairly and effectively with cases where a breakdown in collective bargaining seriously threatens the national safety or welfare.

In keeping with the progress of the times, and based on past experiences, a new legislative approach toward the entire labor management problem should be explored.

Fair Labor Standards

We pledge to continue our efforts so that government programs designed to establish improved fair labor standards shall prove a means of assuring minimum wages, hours and protection to workers, consistent with present-day progress.

Equal Pay for Equal Work

We believe in equal pay for equal work, regardless of sex, and we urge legislation to make that principle effective.

The Physically-Handicapped

We promise to further the program to afford employment opportunities both in government and in private industry for physically handicapped persons.

Migratory Workers

We advocate prompt improvement of employment conditions of migratory workers and increased protection of their safety and health.

STRENGTHENING FREE ENTERPRISE

The free enterprise system has flourished and prospered in America during these last twenty years as never before. This has been made possible by the purchasing power of all our people and we are determined that the broad base of our prosperity shall be maintained.

Small and Independent Business

Small and independent business is the backbone of American free enterprise. Upon its health depends the growth of the economic system whose competitive spirit has built this Nation's industrial strength and provided its workers and consumers with an incomparable high standard of living.

Independent business is the best offset to monopoly practices. The Government's role is to insure that independent business receives equally fair treatment with its competitors.

Congress has established the permanent Small Business Committee of the Senate and the Special Small Business Committee of the House, which have continued to render great service to this important segment of our economy. We favor continuance of both these committees with all the powers to investigate and report conditions, correct discriminations, and propose needed legislation.

We pledge ourselves to increased efforts to assure that small business be given equal opportunity to participate in Government contracts, and that a suitable proportion of the dollar volume of defense contracts be channeled into independent small business. The Small Defense Plants Administration, which our Party caused to be established should retain its independent status and be made a continuing agency, equipped with sufficient lending powers to assist qualified small business in securing defense contracts.

We urge the enactment of such laws as will provide favorable incentives to the establishment and survival of independent businesses, especially in the provision of tax incentives and access to equity or risk capital.

Enforcement of Anti-Trust Laws

Free competitive enterprise must remain free and competitive if the productive forces of this Nation are to remain strong. We are alarmed over the increasing concentration of economic power in the hands of a few.

We reaffirm our belief in the necessity of vigorous enforcement of the laws against trusts, combinations, and restraints of trade, which laws are vital to the safeguarding of the public interest and of small competitive business men against predatory monopolies. We will seek adequate appropriations for the Department of Justice and the Federal Trade Commission for vigorous investigation and for enforcement of the anti-trust laws. We support the right of all persons to work together in cooperatives and other democratic associations for the purpose of carrying out any proper business operations free from any arbitrary and discriminatory restrictions.

Protection of Investors and Consumers

We must avoid unnecessary business controls. But we cannot close our eyes to the special problems which require Government surveillance. The Government must continue its efforts to stop unfair selling practices which deceive investors, and unfair trade practices which deceive consumers.

Transportation

In the furtherance of national defense and commerce, we pledge continued Government support, on a sound financial basis, for further development of the Nation's transportation systems, land, sea and air. We endorse a policy of fostering the safest and most reliable air transportation system of the world. We favor fair, nondiscriminatory freight rates to encourage economic growth in all parts of the country.

Highways

In cooperation with State and local governmental units, we will continue to plan, coordinate, finance, and encourage the expansion of our road and highway network, including access roads, for the dual purposes of national defense and efficient motor transportation. We support expansion of farm-to-market roads.

Rivers and Harbors

We pledge continued development of our harbors and waterways.

Merchant Marine

We will continue to encourage and support an adequate Merchant Marine.

Yet, unless we redouble our conservation efforts we will become a "have-not" nation in some of the most important raw materials upon which depend our industries, agriculture, employment and high standard of living. This can be prevented by a well rounded and nation-wide conservation effort.

Land and Water Resources

We favor sound, progressive development of the Nation's land and water resources for flood control, navigation, irrigation, power, drainage, soil conservation and creation of new, small family-sized farms, with immediate action in critical areas.

We favor the acceleration of all such projects, including construction of transmission facilities to load centers for wider and more equitable distribution of electric energy at the lowest cost to the consumer with continuing preference to public agencies and REA Cooperatives.

The Democratic Party denounces all obstructionist devices designed to prevent or retard utilization of the Nation's power and water resources for the benefit of the people, their enterprises and interests.

The wise policy of the Democratic Party in encouraging multipurpose projects throughout the country is responsible for America's productive superiority over any nation in the world and is one of the greatest single factors leading toward the accomplishment of world peace. Without these projects our atomic weapons program could never have been achieved, and without additional such projects it cannot be expanded.

The Democratic Party is dedicated to a continuation of the natural resources development policy inaugurated and carried out under the administrations of Presidents Roosevelt and Truman, and to the extension of that policy to all parts of the Nation—North, South, East, Midwest, West and the territories to the end that the Nation and its people receive maximum benefits from these resources to which they have an inherent right.

The Democratic Party further pledges itself to protect these resources from destructive monopoly and exploitation.

River Basin Development

We pledge the continued full and unified regional development of the water, mineral and other natural resources of the nation, recognizing that the progress already achieved under the initiative of the Democratic Party in the arid and semi-arid States of the West, as well as in the Tennessee Valley, is only an indication of still greater results which can be accomplished.

Fertilizer Development

Great farming areas, particularly of the Midwest and West, are in acute need of low-cost commercial fertilizers. To meet this demand, we favor the opening of the Nation's phosphate rock deposits in the West, through prompt provision of sufficient low-cost hydro-electric power to develop this great resource.

Forests and Public Lands

We seek to establish and demonstrate such successful policies of forest and land management on Federal property as will materially assist State and private owners in this conservation efforts. Conservation of forest and range lands is vital to the strength and welfare of the Nation. Our forest and range lands must be protected and used wisely in order to produce a continuing supply of basic raw materials for industry; to reduce damaging floods; and to preserve the sources of priceless water. With adequate appropriations to carry out feasible projects, we pledge a program of forest protection, reforestation projects and sound practices of production and harvesting which will promote sustained yields of forest crops.

We propose to increase forest access roads in order to improve cutting practices on both public and private lands.

On the public land ranges we pledge continuance of effective conservation and use programs, including the extension of water pond construction and restoration of forage cover.

Arid Areas

In many areas of the Nation assistance is needed to provide water for irrigation, domestic and industrial purposes. We pledge that in working out programs for rational distribution of water from Federal sources we will aid in delivering this essential of life cheaply and abundantly.

Minerals and Fuels

The Nation's minerals and fuels are essential to the national defense and development of our country. We pledge the adoption of policies which will further encourage the exploration and development of additional reserves of our mineral resources. We subscribe to the principles of the Stockpiling Act and will lend our efforts to strengthening and expanding its provisions and those of the Defense Production Act to meet our military and civilian needs. Additional access roads should be constructed with Government aid. Our synthetic fuels, including monetary metals, research program should be constructed with Government aid. Our synthetic fuels, including monetary metals, research program should go forward. Laws to aid and assist these objectives will be advocated.

Domestic Fisheries

We favor increased research and exploration for conserving and better utilizing fishery resources; expanded research and education to promote new fishery products and uses and new markets; promotion of world trade in fish products; a public works and water policy providing adequate protection for domestic fishery resources; and treaties with other nations for conservation and better utilization of international fisheries.

Wildlife Recreations

In our highly complex civilization, outdoor recreation has become essential to the health and happiness of our people.

The Democratic Party has devoted its efforts to the preservation, restoration and increase of the bird, animal and fish life which abound in this Nation. State, local and private agencies have cooperated in this worthy endeavor. We have extended and vastly improved the parks, forests, beaches, streams, preserves and wilderness areas across the land.

To the 28,000,000 of our citizens who annually purchase fishing and hunting licenses, we pledge continued efforts to improve all recreational areas.

ATOMIC ENERGY

In the field of atomic energy, we pledge ourselves:

(1) to maintain vigorous and non-partisan civilian administrations, with adequate security safeguards;

(2) to promote the development of nuclear energy for peaceful purposes in the interests of America and mankind;

(3) to build all the atomic and hydrogen firepower needed to defend our country, deter aggression, and promote world peace;

(4) to exert every effort to bring about bonafide international control and inspection of all atomic weapons.

SOCIAL SECURITY

Our national system of social security, conceived and developed by the Democratic Party, needs to be extended and improved.

Old Age and Survivors Insurance

We favor further strengthening of old age and survivors insurance, through such improvements as increasing benefits, extending them to more people and lowering the retirement age for women.

We favor the complete elimination of the work clause for the reason that those contributing to the Social Security program should be permitted to draw benefits, upon reaching the age of eligibility, and still continue to work.

Unemployment Insurance

We favor a stronger system of unemployment insurance, with broader coverage and substantially increased benefits, including an allowance for dependents.

Public Assistance

We favor further improvements in public assistance programs for the blind, the disabled, the aged and children in order to help our less fortunate citizens meet the needs of daily living.

Private Plans

We favor and encourage the private endeavors of social agencies, mutual associations, insurance companies, industry-labor groups, and cooperative societies to provide against the basic hazards of life through mutually agreed upon benefit plans designed to complement our present social security program.

Needs of Our Aging Citizens

Our older citizens constitute an immense reservoir of skilled, mature judgment and ripened experience. We pledge ourselves to give full recognition to the right of our older citizens to lead a proud, productive and independent life throughout their years.

In addition to the fundamental improvements in Old Age and Survivors Insurance, which are outlined above, we pledge ourselves, in cooperation with the States and private industry, to encourage the employment of older workers. We commend the 82nd Congress for eliminating the age restriction on employment in the Federal Government.

Health

We will continue to work for better health for every American, especially our children. We pledge continued and wholehearted support for the campaign that modern medicine is waging against mental illness, cancer, heart disease and other diseases.

Research

We favor continued and vigorous support, from private and public sources, of research into the causes, prevention and cure of disease.

Medical Education

We advocate Federal aid for medical education to help overcome the growing shortages of doctors, nurses, and other trained health personnel.

Hospitals and Health Centers

We pledge continued support for Federal aid to hospital construction. We pledge increased Federal aid to promote public health through preventive programs and health services, especially in rural areas.

Cost of Medical Care

We also advocate a resolute attack on the heavy financial hazard of serious illness. We recognize that the costs of modern medical care have grown to be prohibitive for many millions of people. We commend President Truman for establishing the non-partisan Commission on the Health Needs of the Nation to seek an acceptable solution of this urgent problem.

Housing

We pledge ourselves to the fulfillment of the programs of private housing, public low-rent housing, slum clearance, urban redevelopment, farm housing and housing research as authorized by the Housing Act of 1949.

We deplore the efforts of special interests groups, which themselves have prospered through Government guarantees of housing mortgages, to destroy those programs adopted to assist families of low-income.

Additional Legislation

We pledge ourselves to enact additional legislation to promote housing required for defense workers, middle income families, aged persons and migratory farm laborers.

Veterans' Housing

We pledge ourselves to provide special housing aids to veterans and their families.

EDUCATION

Every American child, irrespective of color, national origin, economic status or place of residence should have every educational opportunity to develop his potentialities.

Local, State and Federal governments have shared responsibility to contribute appropriately to the pressing needs of our educational system. We urge that Federal contributions be made available to State and local units which adhere to basic minimum standards.

The Federal Government should not dictate nor control educational policy.

We pledge immediate consideration for those school systems which need further legislation to provide Federal aid for new school construction, teachers' salaries and school maintenance and repair.

We urge the adoption by appropriate legislative action of the proposals advocated by the President's Commission on Higher Education, including Federal scholarships.

We will continue to encourage the further development of vocational training which helps people acquire skills and technical knowledge so essential to production techniques.

Child Welfare

The future of America depends on adequate provision by Government for the needs of those of our children who cannot be cared for by their parents or private social agencies.

Maternity, Child Health and Welfare Services

The established national policy of aiding States and localities, through the Children's Bureau and other agencies, to insure needed maternity, child health and welfare services should be maintained and extended. Especially important are the detection and treatment of physical defects and diseases which, if untreated, are reflected in adult life in draft rejections and as handicapped workers. The Nation, as a whole, should provide maternity and health care for the wives, babies and pre-school children of those who serve in our armed forces.

School Lunches

We will enlarge the school lunch program which has done so much for millions of American school children and charitable institutions while at the same time benefiting producers.

Day Care Facilities

Since several million mothers must now be away from their children during the day, because they are engaged in defense work, facilities for adequate day care of these children should be provided and adequately financed.

Children of Migratory Workers

The Nation, as a whole, has a responsibility to support health, educational, and welfare services for the children of agricultural migratory workers who are now almost entirely without such services while their parents are engaged in producing essential crops.

Veterans

The Democratic Party is determined to advance the welfare of all the men and women who have seen service in the armed forces. We pledge ourselves to continue and improve our national program of benefits for veterans and their families, to provide the best possible medical care and hospitalization for the disabled veteran, and to help provide every veteran an opportunity to be a productive and responsible citizen with an assured place in the civilian community.

STRENGTHENING DEMOCRATIC GOVERNMENT

Streamlining the Federal Government

The public welfare demands that our government be efficiently and economically operated and that it be reorganized to meet changing needs. During the present Democratic Administration, more reorganization has been accomplished than by all its predecessors. We pledge our support to continuing reorganization wherever improvements can be made. Only constant effort by the Executive, the Congress, and the public will enable our Government to render the splendid service to which our citizens are entitled.

Improving the Postal Service

We pledge a continuing increase in the services of the United States Postal Service. Through efficient handling of mail, improved working conditions for postal employees, and more frequent services, the Democratic Party promises its efforts to provide the greatest communication system in the world for the American people.

Strengthening the Civil Service

Good government requires a Civil Service high in quality and prestige. We deplore and condemn smear attacks upon the character and reputations of our Federal workers. We will continue our fight against partisan political efforts to discredit the Federal service and undermine American principles of justice and fair play.

Under President Truman's leadership, the Federal Civil Service has been extended to include a greater proportion of positions than ever before. He has promoted a record number of career appointees to top level policy positions. We will continue to be guided by these enlightened policies, and we will continue our efforts to provide Federal service with adequate pay, sound retirement provisions, good working conditions, and an opportunity for advancement.

We will use every proper means to eliminate pressure by private interests seeking undeserved favors from the Government. We advocate the strongest penalties against those who try to exert improper influence, and against any who may yield to it.

Democracy in Federal Elections

We advocate new legislation to provide effective regulation and full disclosure of campaign expenditures in elections to Federal office, including political advertising from any source.

We recommend that Congress provide for a non-partisan study of possible improvements in the methods of nominating and electing Presidents and in the laws relating to Presidential succession. Special attention should be given to the problem of assuring the widest possible public participation in Presidential nominations.

Strengthening Basic Freedoms

We will continue to press strongly for worldwide freedom in the gathering and dissemination of news and for support to the work of the United Nations Commission on Human Rights in furthering this and other freedoms.

Equal Rights Amendment

We recommend and endorse for submission to the Congress a constitutional amendment providing equal rights for women.

Puerto Rico

Under Democratic Party leadership, a new status has been developed for Puerto Rico. This new status is based on mutual consent and common devotion to the United States, formalized in a new Puerto Rican Constitution. We welcome the dignity of the new Puerto Rican Commonwealth and pledge our support of the Commonwealth, its continued development and growth.

Alaska and Hawaii

By virtue of their strategic geographical locations, Alaska and Hawaii are vital bastions in the Pacific. These two territories have contributed greatly to the welfare and economic development of our country and have become integrated into our economic and social life. We, therefore, urge immediate statehood for these two territories.

Other Territories and Possessions

We favor increased self-government for the Virgin Islands and other outlying territories and the trust territory of the Pacific.

District of Columbia

We favor immediate home rule and ultimate national representation for the District of Columbia.

American Indians

We shall continue to use the powers of the Federal Government to advance the health, education and economic well-being of our American Indian citizens, without impairing their cultural traditions. We pledge our support to the cause of fair and equitable treatment in all matters essential to and desirable for their individual and tribal welfare.

The American Indian should be completely integrated into the social, economic and political life of the nation. To that end we shall move to secure the prompt final settlement of Indian claims and to remove restrictions on the rights of Indians individually and through their tribal councils to handle their own fiscal affairs.

We favor the repeal of all acts or regulations that deny to Indians rights or privileges held by citizens generally.

Constitutional Government

The Democratic Party has demonstrated its belief in the Constitution as a charter of individual freedom and an effective instrument for human progress. Democratic Administrations have placed upon the statute books during the last twenty years a multitude of measures which testify to our belief in the Jeffersonian principle of local control, even in general legislation involving nation-wide programs. Selective service, Social Security, Agricultural Adjustment, Low Rent Housing, Hospital, and many other legislative programs have placed major responsibilities in States and counties and provide fine examples of how benefits can be extended through Federal-State cooperation.

In the present world crisis with new requirements of Federal action for national security, and accompanying provision for public services and individual rights related to defense, constitutional principles must and will be closely followed. Our record and our clear commitments, in this platform, measure our strong faith in the ability of constitutional government to meet the needs of our times.

Improving Congressional Procedures

In order that the will of the American people may be expressed upon all legislative proposals, we urge that action be taken at the beginning of the 83rd Congress to improve Congressional procedures so that majority rule prevails and decisions can be made after reasonable debate without being blocked by a minority in either House.

Civil Rights

The Democratic Party is committed to support and advance the individual rights and liberties of all Americans.

Our country is founded on the proposition that all men are created equal. This means that all citizens are equal before the law and should enjoy equal political rights. They should have equal opportunities for education, for economic advancement, and for decent living conditions.

We will continue our efforts to eradicate discrimination based on race, religion or national origin.

We know this task requires action, not just in one section of the Nation, but in all sections. It requires the cooperative efforts of individual citizens and action by State and local governments. It also requires Federal action. The Federal Government must live up to the ideals of the Declaration of Independence and must exercise the powers vested in it by the Constitution.

We are proud of the progress that has been made in securing equality of treatment and opportunity in the Nation's armed forces and the civil service and all areas under Federal jurisdiction. The Department of Justice has taken an important part in successfully arguing in the courts for the elimination of many illegal discriminations, including those involving rights to own and use real property, to engage in gainful occupations and to enroll in publicly supported higher educational institutions. We are determined that the Federal Government shall continue such policies.

At the same time, we favor Federal legislation effectively to secure these rights to everyone: (1) the right to equal opportunity for employment; (2) the right to security of persons; (3) the right to full and equal participation in the Nation's political life, free from arbitrary restraints. We also favor legislation to perfect existing Federal civil rights statutes and to strengthen the administrative machinery for the protection of civil rights.

CONCLUSION

Under the guidance, protection, and help of Almighty God we shall succeed in bringing to the people of this Nation a better and more rewarding life and to the peoples of the entire world, new hope and a lasting, honorable peace.

ADLAI E. STEVENSON
SPEECH TO NEW YORK STATE DEMOCRATIC CONVENTION
August 28, 1952

New York City

Lest you think I entertain any ill feeling, let me say at the outset that I have forgiven my friend Averell Harriman and the New York delegates to the National Convention for what they did to me there!

It is with great pride that I come among you this evening as the nominee of the Democratic Party. I must add that I also come here with some trepidation, because even in Chicago we have to admit that New York is important—at least on election day!

I am a Democrat by inheritance—but I am also a Democrat by conviction. I believe in the progressive policies of the Democratic Party. I believe that they are the best policies for our country to follow, and I believe the people think so too, and that the Democratic Party will win again in November. And I expect to win running like a singed cat. The singeing hasn't been very painful so far.

There is one face I miss here this evening—your great Senator and my honored friend, Herbert Lehman. But I don't begrudge him one minute of his well-earned holiday in Europe. And I doubt if he begrudges me one minute of my campaign in the United States! For many years Senator Lehman has been one of the best and purest influences in our public life. And today he exerts in the Senate a moral authority and leadership comparable to that provided twenty years ago by George Norris.

We have a good time ahead of us this autumn. We have a good platform. A group of honest men got together in Chicago and made an honest attempt to grapple with the great problems of our day. They came out with good answers. I stand on that platform. And I don't feel the need—so understandably felt by my distinguished opponent—of having my campaign manager say that I will write my own platform.

We have a great Vice Presidential candidate. I hope you in New York will soon get to know him better. To me he is somehow the physical embodiment of the social and economic progress of the past two great decades of Democratic leadership.

John Sparkman was the son of a tenant farmer. He worked his way up from rural poverty to win an education, a law degree, and an outstanding position as a legislator. But John Sparkman has never forgotten his beginnings. It has been his ambition in life to make more freely available to other poor boys and girls the opportunities which only stubborn determination could win for himself.

He is a leading representative of the new liberalism which is changing the face and the folkways of the South. He has been the devoted champion of legislation promoting farm ownership, better housing, social security, the T.V.A., rural electrification, soil conservation, and crop insurance. None know the problems of the small businessman better than he, and his intimate knowledge of the revolutionary convulsions that torment our world has been accentuated by service on the United States Delegation to the United Nations Assembly. He has enlisted for life in the struggle to improve the economic lot and the security of all our people. I am very proud to have John Sparkman as my running mate. And I hope I can keep up with him.

We have, in addition, a Presidential candidate. Perhaps the less said about him the better. You know what we have done and tried to do in Illinois. I propose to outline in the next few weeks what I should like to do in the nation. Let me say now that I shall do my best to conserve our gains and to carry forward the great Democratic tradition of government in the service of all the people, the tradition of Franklin Roosevelt and Harry Truman.

The Republicans have been talking of late as if I was ashamed of the accomplishments in war and peace of the past twenty years which they, by some miraculous agility, both embrace and condemn at the same time. I have been tempted to say that I was proud to stand on that record, if only the General would move over and make room for me!

But it is not enough, it seems to me, just to stand on the successes of the past. The people know what *has* been done, and now they want to know what *will* be done. A party cannot live on laurel leaves. We remember what happened to Lot's wife. And the people whom we seek to govern, though prosperous and well, are sorely taxed and troubled by war and threats of war.

The transcendent problem before us and the great unfinished business of our generation is peace in the world. There is only one way to work for peace. It is not an easy way. There is no substitute for the long, complex and patient processes of building strength and unity in the free world—political strength, economic strength, military strength, and moral strength—the strength of a common faith that nations can be free and people can stand erect and unafraid.

I am disturbed by some of the Republican contributions to the foreign-policy debate. A Republican foreign-policy expert said the other day that the Democratic Party was interested only in Europe and regarded all other nations as "second-class expendables." This kind of statement is not simply absurd; it is also irresponsible and dangerous. And I hope that such excessive partisanship does not do irreparable damage to our country. Of course, we are interested in Europe. But if this country, and I mean Democrats and Republicans alike, stands for anything, it stands for freedom and against the expansion of communist dominion anywhere in the world. Does Mr. Dulles think that President Truman by his prompt and courageous decision of June 27, 1950, treated Korea like "a second-class expendable"? If he does not think so, he would serve his party and his country and our friends in Asia better by more candor and less claptrap.

I hope that the Republican leaders will permit us to discuss our somber foreign problems on the plane where they belong—not on the plane of demagoguery, but on the plane of serious, factual discussion, and in terms of alternatives that are real, rather than epithets that are false.

And we could well apply the same rule to the problems here at home. One of these I want to mention here tonight is civil rights.

The phrase civil rights means a number of concrete things. It means the right to be treated equally before the law. It means the right to equal opportunity for education, employment and decent living conditions. It means that none of these rights shall be denied because of race or color or creed. The history of freedom in our country has been the history of knocking down the barriers to equal rights. One after another they have fallen, and great names in our history record their collapse: the Virginia Statute of Religious Freedom, the Bill of Rights, the Emancipation Proclamation, the Woman's Suffrage Amendment, down to the 1947 Report of the President's Commission on Civil Rights.

The record of our progress is a proud one, but it is far from over. Brave and important tasks remain. We cannot rest until we honor in fact as well as word the plain language of the Declaration of Independence.

This is our goal. It requires far more than action by government. Laws are never as effective as habits. The fight for equal rights must go on every day in our own souls and consciences, in our schools and our churches and our homes, in our factories and our offices—as well as in our city councils, our state legislatures and our national Congress. In this discussion, of all discussions, let us not be self-righteous. Let us work for results, not just empty political advantage. We are dealing here with fundamental human rights, not just votes.

This is a job for the East, the North and the West, as well as for the South. I know. I have been a Governor of a great Northern state. I have had to stop outrages committed against peaceful and law-abiding minorities. I have twice proposed to my legislature a law setting up in our state an enforceable fair employment practices commission. I am proud to say that the Democrats in our legislature voted almost solidly for the bill. But I must report in simple truth that the bill was lost in Springfield, Illinois, because of virtually solid opposition from the party which claims descent from Abraham Lincoln. All the same, gratifying progress has been made in Illinois toward the elimination of job discrimination by the initiative of business itself. And I would be less than fair if I didn't acknowledge it gratefully.

In saying this is not a sectional problem, I do not mean to say that there is no particular problem in the South. Of course there is a problem in the South. In many respects, the problem is more serious there than elsewhere. But, just as it is chastening to realize our own failures and shortcomings in the North, so it is both just and hopeful to recognize and admit the great progress in the South. Things are taking place in the South today that would have seemed impossible only a few years ago. In the last two years alone ten state universities have admitted Negro students for the first time to their graduate and professional schools. And that is only one of many examples that could be cited of the wonders that are working in the South.

We can agree that the problem is nationwide; we can agree that good progress has been made; but I think we can also agree that unremitting effort is the cause of most of that progress, and that unremitting effort is the way to assure more progress in the future. Part of that effort must be legislative. The Democratic platform of 1952 states the goals of Federal legislation.

I have often affirmed my belief in strong state and local administration. I believe—with your own great Governors, Al Smith and Franklin Roosevelt and Herbert Lehman—that affirmative state government can rise to meet many pressing social problems, and can thereby arrest the trend toward overcentralized Federal power. In Illinois I have worked to make the state government responsive to the needs of the people so that it would not be necessary for them to turn to Washington for help. I like to think that people are becoming more and more conscious of the role of the states in the Federal system; more and more conscious that we will save more money by doing the jobs at home than by screaming about waste and extravagance in Washington.

In the case of equal opportunity for employment, I believe that it is not alone the duty but the enlightened interest of each state to develop its own positive employment practices program—a program adapted to local conditions, emphasizing education and conciliation, and providing for judicial enforcement. That is the kind of law I proposed in Illinois.

I think the time has come to talk sensibly about how we can make more rapid progress in this field rather than how we can make more votes. I think—indeed, I know—that there are leaders in the South who are just as anxious as we are to move ahead. But we must frankly recognize their local difficulties. We must recognize, too, that further government interference with free men, free markets, free ideas, is distasteful to many people of good will who dislike racial discrimination as much as we do.

This is not the time to discuss all these familiar obstacles. Let me only say that in a spirit of give and take, of tolerance and understanding, we can clean up this fire hazard in our basement faster and more effectively.

But our platform also favors Federal legislation—particularly, I assume, when states fail to act and inequalities of treatment persist. The problem, of course, is what kind of legislation.

Personally, I have been much impressed by a bill recently reported favorably by the Senate Labor Committee. Only three members opposed it, one of whom was Senator Richard Nixon. Both your New York Senators joined in sponsoring the bill.

It creates a Federal Commission and encourages it to stay out of any state with an effective commission; by the same token, however, it encourages the states to act because, if they do not, the national government has the power to do so. The bill requires the Federal Commission to undertake a nonpartisan and nationwide educational program, to proceed by persuasion as far as possible, and, in cases of complaints of violation, to proceed by very careful deliberation and full and fair hearings. Enforcement would be by order of a court, not an administrative body.

You know as well as I do that we have reached a sort of legislative stalemate in this field in the Congress. In so far as this is due to real, legitimate objections to the substance of the legislation, I think this Senate bill goes a very long way toward meeting such objections. It may be that it can be improved still further, especially in the direction of giving the states a reasonable time in which to act.

In so far as the present stalemate is due to misuse of the processes of deliberation and debate in Congress, the problem is somewhat different.

I believe firmly in the principle stated in our platform—the principle that majority rule shall prevail, after reasonable debate, in both houses of our Congress. And from my experience, with the practical workings of representative government, I would interpret "reasonable" very liberally, because majorities can be tyrannical too.

This principle of majority rule is important in a much broader area than that of civil rights—it is of vital importance, for example, in the field of foreign policy. One of the most famous of all filibusters occurred in 1917 in the debate over President Wilson's proposal to arm merchant ships for the protection of American lives and property against power-mad aggression. It is not inconceivable that a similar situation might occur today or tomorrow in the delicate state of our foreign relations. In these perilous times we cannot risk submerging our national purposes in a sea of interminable conversation.

The precise nature of the changes that should be made in the present rules of Congress, is, of course, a problem for the Congress itself, for each House, under our Constitution, makes its own rules for doing business. As President I could not make the decision, but I could and would use whatever influence I may have to encourage the Congress to shake off its shackles.

I would urge in these fields and in many others that affect national policy that all of us resolve to take a fresh look. There has been too much freezing of positions, too much emotion, too many dogmatic statements of irrevocable attitudes. We are dealing with human situations, with human emotions, with human intelligence; our purpose must be to reason together for the common betterment of us all; our interest must be, not in controversy, but in results.

This has been my attitude, and this will be my attitude. If there are those who disapprove, I will be sorry but not surprised. If there are those who approve, I bespeak their best efforts and pledge them mine, confident that in the long run results will be more eloquent than oratory.

I have been talking about methods. About goals there can, of course, be no disagreement. We believe in the equality of rights and the equality of opportunity for all Americans. In affirming this belief, the Democratic platform was but the mirror of our own conscience. We must continue this fight until it is won.

PAUL DOUGLAS
SPEECH TO 1952 DEMOCRATIC CONVENTION

Mr. Chairman, fellow Democrats and fellow Americans:

I shall speak about the Korean War. My purpose is to tell the truth and I shall try to speak in an objective spirit. For the full story of why we took up the challenge in Korea, what it has meant to us and to the free world, what the problems are which we have faced and the strengths and weaknesses of alternative lines of action has not been told. That is what I shall try to do and I shall speak to the American people themselves and not merely to the members of this Convention.

When, on June 27, 1950, the North Korean Communists under Russian prompting and direction invaded South Korea, the President of the United States had to make a fateful decision. He could have taken the immediately popular course. Mindful of the fact that American mothers have a natural horror of having their sons fight and die on foreign soil, he could have contented himself with a note of protest to the Communists but have refrained from sending our troops.

That is what many of his critics are now implying that he should have done. An eminent leader of the opposing party has for over a year been referring to the struggle in Korea as "Truman's War." By this he apparently means that either it was President Truman who got us into the war, or that he is responsible for its continuance. In either case, it is implied that Truman is the man who is to blame. Two weeks ago this charge was often repeated from this very platform by numerous Republicans and apparently it will be stressed as an issue this fall.

Let us consider this question and ask ourselves what would have happened had the President done what his critics now imply he should have done and refrained from sending our men to check the Communist attack?

First, make no mistake about it, Korea would have fallen in two or three days.

Second, I invite you to look at the map of Asia which is behind me and see what would have happened to Japan. The northernmost island of Japan is virtually touched by the Kuriles, which is a Russian possession. Korea, in turn, almost touches Japan on the South. Japan would then have been placed between the upper and lower jaws of communism and could not have continued as a free, democratic and non-Communist country. Sooner or later, it would have been forced into the Communist orbit and Russia would have taken over its 85 million people and its huge industrial plant.

But this would only have been the beginning. Look again at the map of Asia and note the peninsula which juts out from the south-east. Here are 150 million people of Malay stock divided into five promising but militarily weak countries. These countries are struggling to establish themselves as non-Communist democracies. But they have Communist fifth columns within them; and north of their borders, ready to strike, is a

Chinese Communist Army. Had we let the Communists get away with Korea, there is no doubt whatsoever but that this army would have moved in and the whole peninsula with its 150 million people would have been lost. With them would have gone all of the world's supply of natural rubber (which we still need for trucks and heavy vehicles), two-thirds of the world's supply of tin and great oil resources.

Moreover, Burma and Thailand are the "rice bowl" of Asia. They are the only areas on that continent which have surplus food and the rice which they export, alone, constitutes the balance which keeps India and Japan from starvation. With the Communists in possession of the Malay Peninsula, this food would have been shut off and India and Japan would have been starved into the Communist ranks. We would have lost all of Asia with its billion people. And if Asia were to fall, so would the Middle and Near East where two-thirds of the oil resources of the world are located.

Moreover, once the avalanche started in Asia, our allies in Western Europe would have lost heart and the trimmers and doubters would have moved over into the Communist camp. Just as it is true that if we lose Europe, we also lose Asia; so is it also true that if we lose Asia, we lose Europe. It is not a question of Europe first or Asia first. Both are necessary for each other and for us.

I know there are many who will dispute this latter statement and who sincerely believe our safety in no wise depends upon the fate of the rest of the world. Those people honestly believe that the United States can still live secure behind the Atlantic and Pacific Oceans, even though Asia, Africa and Europe were to fall into the hands of the enemy.

Certainly our first duty is to defend the United States. But could the defense of this country be secure if all the rest of the world, save North America and the northern tip of South America, were against us? They would have 2 billion people to our 250 million. Their industrial plant would be greater than ours. They would control the overwhelming proportion of the minerals and material resources of the world upon which increasingly our manufacturing and transportation depend.

The Communists do not subscribe to the doctrine of live and let live. They are out to conquer the world for they believe that there is an inevitable conflict between their world and ours. That conflict is not so much over economic systems as over freedom versus dictatorship; the sacred rights of the individual as against the steam roller of the police state, and of individual conscience aided by true religion against the centralized brute force of materialism.

In such a struggle and under such conditions, war would be inevitable. Moreover, it would be a war fought on our own soil against heavy odds and at terrible cost to ourselves.

Therefore, if we had allowed the Communists to take Korea, it would have started an avalanche which in all probability would have quickly imperiled our safety. The President was, therefore, acting to protect the security of the United States as well as of the free world when he sent our troops to check the Communist advance into Korea and when he got the United Nations to cooperate with us. As some of you know, I have had differences with the President. But perhaps this very fact permits me to say that in this instance, as in so many crucial situations, President Truman put the interests of our country ahead of personal and partisan advantage.

I have recently come across a statement which describes the moral rightness of the President's action more eloquently than I could ever hope to do:

> The decision of President Truman lighted into a flame a lamp of hope throughout Asia that was burning dimly toward extinction. It marked for the Far East the focal and turning point in this area struggling for freedom. It swept aside in one great monumental stroke all of the hypocrisy and the sophistry which has confused and deluded so many people distant from the actual scene.[1]

Now, I wonder if there is anyone here who can tell me from whose pen this rich prose flowed?

It came from the same pen which brought forth the keynote address which was delivered from this very spot two weeks ago tonight—none other than General of the Army Douglas MacArthur.

II

But it is objected that President Truman should have gained the consent of Congress before he acted. Perhaps he should have done so. But a quick decision had to be made and the delay of a day and possibly even of a few hours might have cost us Korea, Japan, Asia and the world. It is also true that the distinguished body in which I serve seldom lets any measure go through without prolonged debate and time was of the essence as the Communist troops rolled swiftly into South Korea.

The founding fathers who framed the Constitution understood the dangers of Congressional delay. The first draft of the Constitution in 1787 gave to Congress the sole power "to make war." But this was changed by a vote of seven States to two for the provision that Congress was to have the power "to declare war." This was done, as James Madison wrote in his notes, in order to leave "to the Executive the power to repel sudden attacks." It is also a matter of solemn record that the President met with the Congressional leaders of both parties and that aside from a comment or two there was no real protest from the floor of Congress. On the whole I do not think the President can be appreciably blamed for not asking for formal Congressional approval.

III

What then have been the results of the two years struggle? There are those who say that it has been "a futile war" and that the blood of our men has been shed in vain.

---

[1] Press release of General MacArthur, quoted in Congressional Record.

Certainly our losses have been heavy—18,000 killed, 82,000 wounded (most of whom have returned to duty) and 13,000 missing, most of whom we presume are prisoners. No one can or should minimize the human cost of these casualties.

I think I feel as deeply as any man can about these losses since my old division is one of those on the line and many of my friends and former comrades have been wounded or killed. But heavy as these losses have been, it has not been a futile war. For despite all the frustrations which have attended it, we, with the aid of our allies, have accomplished three important results.

First, we have prevented the Communists from taking over Korea and hence have checked the avalanche. Had the democracies stood together and taken similar firm action when Hitler marched his troops into the Rhineland in 1936, we might never have had to fight World War II.

Secondly, we have inflicted terrific losses of well over a million upon the Communist armies and we have demolished a large fraction of their best troops. These losses are beginning to make the Chinese people lose patience with their Communist government which sends their sons across the Yalu River to die on foreign soil in attacking friendly nations. And the Chinese are beginning to hate their Russian masters who treat them as catspaws by egging them on to their destruction while the Russians remain safe and sound in the background while stealing the Chinese province of Manchuria and all its wealth. The soil is therefore being prepared for a revolt of the Chinese peoples which may ultimately oust their Communist masters and make them free once more.

Thirdly, the two years have bought us time in which to prepare. In June 1950 we had only 1.4 million men under arms with only 12 under-strength infantry divisions and 46 air groups. Now we have 3.6 million men, and the equivalent of from 24 to 27 full strength divisions, and 96 air groups. Now we are on our way to 143 air groups and we have recommissioned nearly 500 naval vessels. Our strength is vastly greater than it was and so is that of our allies. Two years ago there were only a handful of divisions between Russia and the English Channel and the Communists could have gone through standing up. Today it would be far more difficult. Our allies, France, Great Britain, Italy, Greece, Turkey, the Low Countries, Norway and Denmark, are rearming and in from 18 to 24 months we hope to have from 40 to 50 divisions in the Western European Army with adequate supporting power in the air.

The purpose of this rearmament is not war, as the Communists charge. We will not wage a preventive war. Our purpose is instead to accumulate sufficient force to deter the Russians from attacking. The only weapon a police state respects is force and if we get enough of it, Stalin may beware of monkeying with the buzz saw of the free world.

If we can deter him for a few years from attacking, we may gain a long peace. For Stalin is over 70 years of age. He has lived a hard and cruel life; he cannot live forever and perhaps not for long. While it is un-Christian to wish for anyone's death, even Stalin's, still it may be proper to say if it should please the Lord to take him from us, we would be resigned to his loss. For when he dies, a struggle for power may break out between rivals within the Politburo which would convulse Russia and render it incapable of aggression for a long time. And once the Russian dictatorship starts breaking up, the ice will melt rapidly. For the subject peoples of the enslaved border states hate the Russian dictatorship and if given a chance will want to throw it off. Then the Baltic states, Poland, Czechoslovakia, Eastern Germany, Hungary, Bulgaria and Roumania may once again be free and the glacier of tyranny, which has threatened to overspread the earth will retreat back to its own lair.

It would of course be wrong to say that our policy is an ironclad guarantee of peace. Since the decision whether or not to attack will be Russia's and not ours to make, there can be no certainty as to what the rulers of the Kremlin will do. All we can say is that our policy of effective resistance to Communist aggression is not only the best but is indeed the only hope for peace in the world.

Our Republican friends are very loud in their denunciation of the conduct of the Korean War. But they are either silent or contradictory about what they would have us do in the future. Commonly, they say that either we should enlarge the war into China or get out of Korea, without letting us know which of these sharply opposite courses they would have us follow.

Two weeks ago, from this very platform, General MacArthur in effect advocated enlarging the Korean War into China. On the very next night, former President Hoover advocated giving up the use of appreciable land armies in order to reduce taxes and also retreating to island air bases. This could only have meant Korea as well as Europe.

We do not know which of these opposing policies the Republican Party and its candidates actually favor. Some of them have even said we should both go forward and backward at the same time. This of course is a manifest absurdity even for an opposition party to assume.

If the Republicans were to take power, they would have to choose. The American people are entitled to know which policy the Republicans really advocate so that the people can decide. There is an obligation upon our opposition to make their choice clear and not confuse the public by advocating contradictory policies.

May I briefly point out the grave errors which either one of these lines of action would involve.

First, for us to get out of Korea would be fatal. All the disasters which I have shown would follow from Communist occupation would occur and many others in addition. For it would be judged as a confession of military defeat and would strengthen Communist prestige while weakening ours. On the other hand to go into China would bog us down on the continent of Asia in a huge war against hordes of Chinese. This in all probability would also be fatal.

Now I know that our critics will say that this is not their intention and that all they want is for us to bomb the Chinese bases and supply lines in Manchuria. I know the appeal which such a proposal naturally makes both to those at the front and to us in the rear. It is possible that we may have to take such action in the future. But while I do not possess any inside information, I think I know why the Joint Chiefs of Staff have opposed it in the past. First, we would inevitably kill Chinese women and children by such bombing and the Communists would use this fact as a powerful propaganda weapon to inflame the darker-skinned races of Asia and to swing India and the Malays against us.

We should be careful not to play into their hands and allow them to turn this struggle for freedom into a race war.

Secondly, the opening of an all out aerial war might have unfortunate military consequences which those of us in the street cannot fully realize.

Finally, Russia and China have a treaty of mutual assistance under which each country agrees to come to the aid of the other if attacked by an ally of Japan. The Chinese have been unable to invoke this treaty because it is they who crossed the Yalu River into Korea to attack us on foreign soil. But if we were to bomb China, it would be difficult for Russia to refuse China's plea without gravely losing face.

If Russia then came directly to China's aid, our Joint Chiefs of Staff are afraid that we would then be involved in a war at the wrong time, in the wrong place and with the wrong enemy—namely, China instead of our real opponent, Russia. For we should not forget what every corporal knows, that when one's opponent initially attacks he is not usually making his main assault. The strategy of war is indeed parallel to the tactics of prize-fighting, to feint with one's left and then hit hard with one's right. It is quite possible, and in my judgment probable, that the Communist attack in Korea was intended as a feint. For the Russian reserves are still uncommitted and if we throw the main strength of our Army and Air Force into Korea and deplete our reserves, it would then be very easy for them to strike Europe with their full force and take it over.

Under these conditions, it would be as unwise to rush our reserves into Korea to effect a knockout there as it would for a boxer to put both hands to his stomach to parry a jab while leaving his jaw open for the knockout. The proper tactic, instead, as every second lieutenant quickly learns, is to engage in a holding action until the real intentions of the enemy have developed, and in the meantime to build up and conserve our reserves. This is good tactics on the company level and it is good strategy on the world stage.

There are those who hold that "in war there is no substitute for victory" and by victory they apparently mean a conquering of the enemy's land or a total annihilation of his forces.

Victory in this sense has not been a necessary goal for the wars America has fought. In the War with Spain, for example, we did not seek to conquer Spain itself, but properly contented ourselves with the specific objective we had set forth, namely, the freeing of Cuba. Likewise, in the current conflict, our objective is not to overrun the enemy's land, but to win the freedom and lasting security of Korea and to show the Communist leaders that further aggression will not go unpunished.

The Joint Chiefs, therefore, have remembered basic military principles which certain other military leaders seem to have forgotten.

To fight such a holding action requires much patience. It is one of the hardest tests which a military commander can go through. It is particularly difficult for a civilian population. But patience is absolutely necessary for both survival and success.

As a citizen-soldier I tried to learn the virtues of patience and came to realize that service in a holding action, whether it be on a small or large scale, was honorable and worthwhile. With understanding on the part of the American people, the virtues and merits of patience in this difficult struggle should become more evident and the tasks of the Joint Chiefs and of our Commander-in-Chief less difficult.

IV

We have of course suffered many frustrations during the war. I, for one, regret that our associates in the United Nations have not seen fit to carry more than approximately one-seventh of the load. But let us also remember that France has been engaged for years in a major war with Communist-led groups inside Indo-China which has cost it many lives, much money and has pinned down a large military force. And, that the British are having their troubles in Malaya. And when I get somewhat fed up with Englishmen who are apparently unable to understand the importance of the Korean struggle and who are captious in their criticism of those who are bearing the heat and burden of the battle, I remember that in World War I it took us three years and in World War II over two years before we realized that our fate was also involved with that of the free world. When unfair criticism is offered from abroad, I reflect that we are seeking not the world's love but the world's safety and our own as well.

The interminable armistice talks have also been frustrating. The issue which at the moment is in dispute is whether or not we shall return 125,000 prisoners who do not want to go back to the Communists. The Communists know the names of these men and if they are returned the Communists would shoot and torture them. President Truman might perhaps have brought peace by sending these men back. But since we had induced them to desert by promising them security of life, the President has properly felt that we should not break faith by sending these men to certain death. And he also knows that if we were to do such a thing, we would never get further desertions from the Iron Curtain countries and from the Communist ranks. For men would then be afraid to come over to us, lest we force them back to death when we got into a tight hole. Let us hope that the military do not try to overrule the wise and humane policies of the President.

V

But there is yet another charge which the Republicans make. It is that the present Administration invited the Communists to attack South Korea. Thus their platform declared:

> In South Korea, they (the present Administration) withdrew our occupation troops in the face of the aggressive, poised for action, Communist military strength on its northern border. They publicly announced that Korea was of no concern to us . . . With foresight, the Korean war would never have happened.

Let me take up the withdrawal of our troops from Korea.

There were three principal events leading up to the withdrawal which I think might interest this Convention.

In September 1947—when our military manpower had been drastically reduced by the demobilization demanded by the American people, and by politicians of both parties—the Joint Chiefs of Staff were asked about the effect upon our national security of withdrawing our occupation troops from Korea.

The Joint Chiefs replied that the United States had little strategic interest in maintaining our troops in Korea and that in the light of the severe shortage of military manpower we could well use those troops elsewhere.[2]

Now, who do you suppose was Chief of Staff of the Army when this military advice was given.

It was Dwight D. Eisenhower, standard-bearer of those who now charge us with withdrawing our troops and of bringing on the Korean War.

One month later, on the basis of this military advice, the United States proposed to the United Nations General Assembly a resolution calling for election in Korea and the *withdrawal of all forces at the earliest possible date*.

Now, who do you suppose it was who made this proposal for us and got it through the United Nations?

It was none other than John Foster Dulles—the man who wrote the foreign policy plank of the Republican platform, charging the Administration with withdrawing our troops from Korea.[3]

The withdrawal of troops began in 1948, under the responsibility of the Deputy Chief of Staff of the Army in charge of plans and operations.

And who do you think held that important post in 1948?

None other than General Albert C. Wedemeyer—who has now exercised his rights as a private citizen and has become a prominent member of the opposition party.

Then, following the elections in South Korea in 1948, we put before the United Nations another resolution, calling for the recognition of the Republic of Korea, and again asking for the withdrawal of all foreign occupation troops.

And who handled this resolution for us in the United Nations?[4]

---

[2] See "Supplemental Appropriations, 1951", Hearings before the Senate Appropriations Committee, 81st Congress, 2nd Session (August, 1950), p. 298:

Secretary Acheson: ". . . At that point the Secretary of State asked the Secretary of Defense to review the situation and see whether it was better to go ahead and try to get a united Korea by the withdrawal of all occupation forces, or whether there was any strategic reason for the United States in remaining in the South.

"That question was reviewed by the Joint Chiefs of Staff, and their opinion was sent to the Secretary of State by the Secretary of Defense. *It said that* it was in the interest of the United States to go forward with the interest of the United States to go forward with the creation of a united Korea and *that we had no strategic interest in occupying the South; that the best possible interest of the United States was to go ahead with the plan in the Cairo declaration* (for a United Korea). That was in September 1947. I think the date was September 26, 1947."

See also Foreign Affairs Outlines, No. 24, "The Fight Against Aggression in Korea", p. 4. (Department of State, Autumn, 1950).

[3] See proceedings, U. N. General Assembly, 1947.

[4] See proceedings, U. N. General Assembly, December, 1948.

Again, none other than that Republican platform drafter, John Foster Dulles.

At the end of 1948, the Russians announced the removal of all their troops in Korea, and began a propaganda barrage against the remaining American troops, who were then engaged in training a force of 114,000 South Korean soldiers. The President was, therefore, reluctant to withdraw the last of our troops in Korea until he had the assurances of our *top military commander* in the Far East that it would be entirely safe to do so. In the spring of 1949, he sought and received those assurances from that top military commander.[5]

Now, does anyone have a notion as to who our top military commander in the Far East was in 1949?

Of course, it was Douglas MacArthur, who only two weeks ago today so roundly attacked the Administration for its role in the Korean War and its prelude.

Let me now turn for a moment to the second aspect of the Republicans' charge—namely, that the Administration "publicly announced that Korea was of no concern to us." This is what I would call a "Republican history" and not "history of the Republic," for I think a review of the facts will show that if anyone showed a lack of concern for Korea, it was the Republican Party.

First of all, the Administration which has been charged with being "unconcerned" about the defense of Korea, actually gave to that republic over a hundred million dollars worth of military equipment and helped to train a South Korean Army before finally withdrawing all our troops.

In 1947, the Administration which is attacked for its "unconcern" for Korea also developed and recommended to the Republican 80th Congress a program of economic aid to help Korea become self-supporting by 1950.

That was when the Republican leadership began to demonstrate its own lack of foresight and of concern over the fate of Korea. They failed to even consider the Korean aid program during the entire 80th Congress.

The Administration again submitted its program of economic aid to the Congress in 1949. In January of 1950—only five months before the Communist attack—this program came to a vote in the House of Representatives. There the House Republicans greeted it with a magnificent demonstration of their concern for Korea. They voted against the Korean aid bill, 130 to 21.

---

[5] See "Supplemental Appropriations, 1951", Hearings before the Senate Appropriations Committee, 81st Congress, 2nd Session (August, 1950), pp. 298-99:

Secretary Acheson: ". . . This matter (of withdrawing the last of our troops from Korea) was reviewed two or three times in the early part of 1949, and finally by agreement, it was decided that the U.S. regimental combat team would be withdrawn when the Far East Commander reported that the Korean forces were equipped, trained and ready to take over.

That report was made sometime early in 1949 and withdrawal was finally completed on June 29, 1949."

See also Foreign Affairs Outlines, No. 24, "The Fight Against Aggression in Korea", p. 5 (Department of State, Autumn, 1950):

"*In view . . . of the judgment of the responsible American military representatives in the field* that the state of combat readiness of the Korean forces was such as to justify withdrawal of American forces, it was decided by the National Security Council, with the approval of the President, that preparation should be undertaken to permit completion of the withdrawal of U.S. occupation forces from Korea not later than June 30, 1949." (Italics added)

Despite the support of a heavy majority of the Democrats, the bill was defeated by a single vote. If one more House Republican—say, for example, the likeable Republican Vice Presidential nominee, Congressman Nixon—had voted for the bill instead of against it, the Korean aid bill would have passed.

In spite of this defeat the Administration refused to give up. It sent another bill to the House, this time with aid included also for the Republic of China, but the Republicans did little better. They voted nearly 3 to 1 to cut the aid to Korea by two-thirds, and then when the Democrats staved off this cut, they voted against all aid to Korea and China by a vote of 91 to 42—over 2 to 1. Remember, this is the party that purports to put Asia first.

Now many House Republicans will defend themselves by saying that these bills contained no *military* aid for Korea—just economic aid. Well, they had a chance to vote on military aid to Korea, too, as part of the entire military aid program in 1949. And if we interpret the words of their own platform by their votes they publicly announced that Korea was of no concern to them. 65 per cent of the House Republicans voted against this military aid program—including aid to Korea—in 1949, and 54 per cent of them voted against a continuation of that program—including $100 million in military aid to Korea—on March 31, 1950, *less than three months before the Communists launched their attack.*

"With foresight, the Korean War would never have happened," the Republicans say in their platform—a safe enough statement, and particularly safe in an election year.

Perhaps that war could have been avoided by foresight, no one can say. But the record clearly shows that it would not have been avoided by any foresight of the Republican Party in Congress; nor would it have been by any foresight of the Republican presidential nominee.

I have not mentioned these facts in order to belittle the character of the men whom I have quoted but only to set the record straight. I believe that the men in question are without exception able, and patriotic Americans. It is probable that under the heat and passion which all too often characterized political campaigns, they have now forgotten the full history of Korea. I have set these facts down therefore not in malice but so that the people, and indeed our Republican friends themselves, may have the full story and not a distorted version.

If mistakes were made prior to the invasion of Korea, Republicans shared in them equally with Democrats. Since the Communist attack, we have on the whole conducted ourselves well. I hope we may all go forward in united and militant resistance to Communist aggression and that we may help to forge a Far Eastern alliance of mutual assistance which will include Japan, the Philippines, Australia and New Zealand, Indonesia, the other free countries of Southeastern Asia and the world.

With the unity of the American people, let us go forward to the victory of democratic principles at home and abroad.

ADLAI E. STEVENSON, "THE AMERICAN VISION" SPEECH AT COLUMBIA UNIVERSITY
June 5, 1954

Dr. Russell, Mrs. Roosevelt, President Kirk, ladies and gentlemen:

Here at Columbia our country celebrates an institution that has had continuous existence and tradition for 200 years—an existence that goes back before there was a United States.

In recent days you have heard far wiser men than I enlarge upon this theme and I would be presumptuous indeed to lecture this distinguished audience about the nature of the university let alone the nature of Columbia. In fact I am presumptuous to be here at all, I am afraid.

One of the most curious and persistent myths of democratic society is that political figures have anything important or interesting to say, especially when they are out of office.

I was instructed to speak here about a half dozen different things and finally I was told to say whatever I pleased—and my desultory remarks could perhaps be very crudely entitled "Hooray for America" and "Look Out, America."

'Irrational Abuse of America'

I am a great believer in national humility, modesty, self-examination and self-criticism, and I have preached these virtues vigorously, although of course, I haven't practiced them. Of late I have been disturbed, as I am sure many of you have, by what seems to me to be the course at home and abroad of irrational criticism, abuse and mistrust of America, its conduct, its motives and its people.

I don't mean just the voices that have been raised, we thank God, in protest against our current deficiencies, against the attacks on academic freedom, the pressure for conformity, our failures abroad or the present wretched manifestations in Washington of our national neurosis.

Nor do I mean the wholesome and the continuous debate and self-examination that should and must go on among us and among Allies; the candid controversy that makes for good friends. Rather, I am talking of the malice, distemper and the new fashion of being cynical, sarcastic, skeptical, deprecating about America or fellow Americans in large groups and therefore about America.

New York Times, June 6, 1954.

What the Voices are Saying

There are rising voices here and abroad that forget that although America occasionally gags on a gnat, it also has some talent for swallowing tigers whole; voices that tell us that our national energy is spent, that our old values have decayed, that it is futile to try to restore them.

There are voices that say that at best we are as Rome; that once our bridges, our skyscrapers, our factories and our weapons fall before the iron law of decay, no trace will be left no great issues, no great cause to mark our past in universal history.

And there are voices that seem to say that we are as Carthage, that our vital principle is commerce, just commerce; our ethics, our politics, our imaginative faculties, they say, are all bent and twisted to serve our sovereign—commerce.

Other voices cry havoc, fear that America is not equal to the task; that communism is the way to the future—is irresistible, just as fascism was for them not so long ago.

Even novelists and poets seem to have been infected. Humanism passes as realism. The very excitement in a time of change and testing is suspect.

Now some of this talk may reflect a wholesome attitude here of self-criticism, if in a slightly fevered form. Some of it may even mark the reaction to the easy and the groundless optimism of the nineteenth century.

I don't know, but I do know that if we doubt ourselves we will persuade no one. If we doubt our mission in the world, we will do nothing to advance it. And if we are craven before the slanders that fill our ears we will secede from each other. But to view our present and our future with such sickly anxiety is to ignore the lessons and the achievements of our past.

Generations of Achievement

For the plain truth is that we here in America have written the greatest success story in human history. The plain truth is that on the record of performance we here in America have in a few years made socialism obsolete, shown that communism is nothing but a noisome stagnant pool of reaction.

And it wasn't merely in 1776, when King's College was a stripling, that America left its footprints on eternity. For in our lifetime, we, the seventh generation of free and independent Americans, have given a tidal force to the forward roll of what was set in motion by the first generation.

If we but lift our heads for a moment above this storm of criticism, of abuse, doubt and "un-American activities," and survey the past fifty years, I think you will say with me "Hooray for America!"

The first and most obvious thing we have to cheer about is our material progress. The miracle of American mass production is commonplace. And under our capitalist system we have increased our wealth to an extent almost unimaginable fifty years ago, at the turn of the century.

Now this increase in our wealth has of course greatly changed our country. The change for the sake of change—as I've tried with a notable lack of success to point out to my countrymen—isn't worthy of applause. What matters is not that we have changed but how we have changed.

Our national income is distributed far more equitably than it was at the turn of the century. As late as 1935-36 there were only about a million American families and unattached individuals, as they commonly say, with incomes of $5,000 or more, and 17,000,000 with incomes of less than $1,000. Fifteen years later, in 1950, these proportions were just about reversed, and even after allowing for inflation, the change is still dramatic.

It is not in terms of money and products that we can see most clearly the change that America has undergone. Rather it is in the attitude of the people and in the role of the Government. For we have succeeded not only in making our society prosperous but in keeping it fluid.

And, while this was easy enough in the days of the frontier, it seemed all but an idle dream by 1900. The frontier was closed; the homestead land was gone; women and children labored in dingy sweatshops, and robber barons plundered at will. Miners in company towns and immigrants compressed into filthy tenements were fast becoming a miserable proletariat.

Keys to a Great Transition

How could the roads of opportunity be kept open?

How, short of revolution, could we adjust modern capitalism to democratic ends? To many it seemed hopeless. Yet see what happened: the gap between rich and poor has been greatly narrowed without revolution; without socialism and without robbing A to give to B—although there may be some dissent to that downtown!

Our wealth has been mightily increased and better distributed. The rising tide has lifted all the boats.

How has this transformation been accomplished? By increasing productivity and by putting government to the service of the people. Woodrow Wilson, Theodore Roosevelt, Robert La Follette and so on, led a revolt of the American conscience, followed by the reforms under Franklin Roosevelt. They've altered the face of America.

The child labor laws, wage and hour laws, the anti-trust acts, banking legislation, rural electrification, soil conservation, social security, unemployment compensation, the graduated income tax, inheritance taxes—it may be too much to say that all this and more amounts to a bloodless revolution, but it certainly amounts to a transformation of our economic and social life.

Now why was all this done? Why did America adopt the concept of man's responsibility for his fellow man? Our decision that the well-being of the least of us is the responsibility of all of us was, of course, not merely an economic and a political decision; it was, at bottom, a moral decision. And it was not, as some are now saying in the nation's capital, all a sinister conspiracy of the great philanthropic foundations.

It rested upon the conviction that it's the duty of the Government to keep open to all the people the avenues of opportunity that stretched so broad and so far before us in the days of our frontier. It rested upon the conviction that the Government must safeguard the people against catastrophe not of their making.

Facing Challenges of Our Era

But this great decision has brought us face to face with vexing problems which have engaged your attention, as I understand it, during this past week—the problems of the conflict between freedom and security, between the individual and his social safeguards.

It seems to me there is something gallant about man's fight to become the master rather than the slave of nature; but there is something rather tragic about his struggle to keep himself free from the impositions of his own social creations.

Now it would be fatuous to claim that we are anywhere near solving this conflict, in my judgment, as it would be fatuous to say that because our material well-being increases year by year all must be well with America. It isn't.

Too many of our people still dwell in wretched slums or on worn-out land. Once again our top soil, our national skin, is blowing away out on the plains. Our schools and hospitals are overcrowded. so are our mental institutions and our prisons. Too many of our cities are wasting away from neglect. And how can we boast of our high estate when more than one of every ten citizens still do not enjoy fully equal opportunities?

Nonetheless our progress has been astonishing—more Americans are living better than ever before. The middle class, whose disappearance Marx so confidently predicted, has expanded as never before in the history of any other nation. And while the Communist conspirators fulminate about the cruel capitalists, the lackeys of Wall Street and the downtrodden masses, we have created a free society that promotes the general welfare of all far better, far more successfully than it has ever been promoted by any other system or social organization.

Briefly, I think America's record is terrific—if I may borrow a word from junior son. And it is my view that its performance abroad is even more spectacular.

Since the turn of the century we have successively and emphatically renounced first imperialism, then isolation, and finally our historical neutrality. We have transformed our foreign policy as completely as our domestic policy. Twice America has decisively topped the scales for freedom in a mighty global exertion.

Instead of isolation our policy is total involvement, instead of noncooperation we have been the prime mover in the United Nations; instead of neutrality we have organized the greatest defensive coalition in history. And in Korea we fought and bled almost alone for the United Nations and for collective security.

But this isn't all. In the process America has fathered three unprecedented ideas: Lend-lease for Hitler's intended victims in war, the Marshall Plan for Stalin's intended victims in peace, and Point 4 to help undeveloped areas. And to pay for it all Americans have borne a tax load, I mean a collected tax load, that is without counterpart save in Britain and that few beyond our borders appreciate.

Lifting Others and Ourselves

And what have we asked in return? Why have we done all of this? Some will say self-interest, and there is truth in that because communism follows the geography of human misery. Some will say magnanimity, and there is truth in that, too. For it would have been easy to go home as we did after the first war, or go it alone as some of our people have proposed.

Call it what you will; the point is to help others help themselves, to help make independence and democracy work, to share the burdens of the less fortunate, to raise the tide a little all around the world, lifting all of the boats with it, just as we have done here at home. It was bold and imaginative. It was wise and responsible, it was good for them and it was good for us. As Edmund Burke said: "Magnanimity is not seldom the truest wisdom."

Now, I have touched lightly, I know, on a vast subject and, while I emphatically approve and loudly cheer America's purposes abroad, past and present, I don't mean to imply for a moment that I approve any more than all of you do all of our foreign policies, past or present—especially present!

My purpose has been just to suggest the main outlines of a success story in which we can all take pride. As we look back to 1900 and look around us today the infinite evidence of our creative impulses and of our vast achievements ought to be heralded, not mocked.

We have heard the "least of these." We have enlarged our vision, opened our heart, and we have disciplined our strength. We have turned it into a servant of justice—justice not alone for ourselves, but justice for the worldwide commonwealth of free men and of free institutions.

Here, indeed, is a case where mankind has a right to knowledge and to the use thereof—the knowledge of what America has done, how America has spread out the decision-making process, within its many parts.

It is the knowledge of how we have committed 160,000,000 people to vast social projects, not by coercion, but by persuasion and consent, and by a balancing of the right of the one with the needs of the many.

I say it is a grand and glorious story. On the basis of the record we have outperformed any rival proposals of communism or of fascism; and America has nobly accepted her responsibility and proudly met her time for greatness in a troubled age.

Fear that Imperils Future

Why then all this abuse and criticism? Why then have we of late grown afraid of ourselves? Why have we of late acted as though the whole of this nation is a security risk? Why do you suppose we have given in to the bleatings of those who insist that it is dangerous for a man to have an idea? Why do we talk of saving ourselves by committing suicide—in the land of Jefferson?

So, having said: "Three cheers for America—you've done a great job of work," we have to add: "But look out America, your work has just begun; though you've nobly grasped the present you could meanly lose the future."

What's the matter with us anyhow? (Laughter) The usual diagnosis is ignorance and fear. Ignorance leads many to confuse ends with means, to act as though material progress were an end in itself rather than a means to great and noble ends. This, I suggest, is the peril of our hard-headed, pragmatic attitude that has helped us so much to achieve our vast social and economic transformation, for if we ever succumb to materialism the meaning will go out of America.

And ignorance begets fear—the most subversive force of all. If America ever loses confidence in herself, she will retain the confidence of no one, and she will lose her chance to be free, because the fearful are never free.

But I wonder if all of these alarming concerns are not America's surface symptoms of something even deeper; of a moral and human crisis in the Western world which might even be compared to the fourth, fifth and sixth-century crisis when the Roman Empire was transformed into feudalism and primitive Christianity, early Christianity, into the structure of the Catholic Church, or the crisis a thousand years later when the feudal world exploded and the individual emerged with new relationships to God, nature, to society.

I sometimes rather wonder if that sentence sounds as wise at Columbia as it did on the farm when I wrote it.

And now in our time in spite of our devotion to the ideas of religious and secular humanism, I wonder if we are in danger of falling into a spirit of materialism in which the aim of life is a never-ending increase of material comfort, and the result a moral and religious vacuum.

Is this leading, as lack of faith always must, to a deep sense of insecurity and a deterioration of reason? And I wonder, too, if today mass manipulation is not a greater danger than economic exploitation; if we are not in greater danger of becoming robots than slaves.

Humanism Versus Paganism

Since man cannot live by bread alone, is not the underlying crisis whether he is going to be inspired and motivated again by the ideas of the humanistic tradition of Western culture, or whether he falls for the new pagan religions, the worship of the state and a leader, as millions of believers in the Fascist and Soviet systems have already done.

That we are not invulnerable, that there is a moral and a human vacuum within us, is, I think demonstrated by many symptoms, of which McCarthyism—which has succeeded in frightening so many is only one.

But it is even more certain that there are millions who see or at least who dimly sense the danger, and who want to make life in its truly human meaning the main business of living; who want to express the humanistic tradition of reason and of human solidarity—who want to understand the truth and not be drawn into the mass manipulative influence of sentimentality and rationalization.

I venture to say that there are in the world many with a deep, intense longing for a vision of a better life not in the material, but in a spiritual sense; for love, for human solidarity. There is a hunger to hear a word of truth, a longing for an ideal, a readiness for sacrifice. Churchill's famous speech at the beginning of the war is an illustration and so is the totalitarians' appeal to emotional forces rather than to material interests.

But the conventional appeal seems to be so often to the better life in material terms. I wonder if people are not eager to hear about the better life in human terms.

And I think that deep down the ideas of independence, of individuality, of free initiative, represent the strongest appeals to Americans who want to think for themselves, who don't want to be automatons.

The question is, I suppose, whether the human and rational emotions can be aroused instead of the animal and irrational to which the totalitarians appeal. But fill the moral vacuum, the rational vacuum, we must; reconvert a population soaked in the spirit of materialism to the spirit of humanism we must, or bit by bit we too will take on the visage of our enemy, the neo-heathens.

The Answer Within Us

I have said to you that in my judgment America has accomplished miracles at home and abroad, but that despite all of this wisdom, this exertion, this goodness, the horror of our time in history is that things are worse than ever before. There is not peace; we are besieged, we are rattled. Perhaps we are even passing through one of the great crises of history when man must make another mighty choice.

Beset by all of these doubts and difficulties in which direction then do we look?

We look to ourselves—and we are not ashamed. We are proud of what freedom has wrought—the freedom to experiment, to inquire, to change, to invent. And we shall have to look exactly in the same directions to solve our problems now—to individual Americans, to their institutions, to their churches, to their governments, to their multifarious associations—and to all the free participants in the free life of a free people.

And we look, finally, to the free university whose function is the search for truth and its communication to succeeding generations. Only as that function is performed steadfastly, conscientiously and without interference does a university keep faith with the great humanist tradition of which it is a part.

For the university is the archive of the Western mind, it's the keeper of the Western culture, and the foundation of Western culture is freedom. Men may be born free; they cannot be born wise; and it is the duty of the university to make the free wise. The university is the guardian of our heritage, the teacher of our teachers. It's the dwelling place of the free mind.

More than 100 years ago William Ellery Channing defined the free mind this way:

> I call that mind free which jealously guards the intellectual rights and powers, which calls no man master, which does not content itself with a passive or hereditary faith, which opens itself to light whencesoever it may come, and which receives new truth as an angel from heaven.

I wonder, my friends, how many of us fulfill Channing's definition. And I wonder if that could be part of our trouble today.

Thank you.

DEMOCRATIC PLATFORM OF 1956

PREAMBLE

In the brief space of three and one-half years, the people of the United States have come to realize, with tragic consequences, that our National Government cannot be trusted to the hands of political amateurs, dominated by representatives of special privilege.

Four years ago they were beguiled, by empty promises and pledges, to elect as President a recent convert to Republicanism. Our people have now learned that the party of Lincoln has been made captive to big businessmen with small minds. They have found that they are now ruled by a Government which they did not elect, and to which they have not given their consent. Their awareness of this fact was demonstrated in 1954 when they returned control of the legislative machinery of the Federal Government to the 84th Democratic Congress.

From the wreckage of American world leadership under a Republican Administration, this great Democratic Congress has salvaged a portion of the world prestige our Nation enjoyed under the brilliant Administrations of Franklin Delano Roosevelt and Harry S. Truman.

Our Democratic 84th Congress made one of the greatest legislative records in the history of our country. It enacted an active program of progressive, humane legislation, which has repudiated the efforts of reactionary Republicanism to stall America's progress. When we return to the halls of Congress next January, and with a Democratic President in the White House, it will be the plan and purpose of our Party to complete restoration and rehabilitation of American leadership in world affairs. We pledge return of our National Government to its rightful owners, the people of the United States.

On the threshold of an atomic age, in mid-Twentieth Century, our beloved Nation needs the vision, vigor and vitality which can be infused into it only by a government under the Democratic Party.

We approach the forthcoming election with a firm purpose of effecting such infusion; and with the help and assistance of Divine Providence we shall endeavor to accomplish it. To the end that the people it has served so well may know our program for the return of America to the highway of progress, the Democratic Party herewith submits its platform for 1956.

I. FOREIGN POLICY AND NATIONAL DEFENSE

The Democratic Party affirms that world peace is a primary objective of human society. Peace is more than a suspension of shooting while frenzied and fearful nations stockpile armaments of annihilation.

Achievement of world peace requires political statesmanship and economic wisdom, international understanding and dynamic leadership. True peace is the tranquillity of ordered justice on a global scale. It may be destroyed without a shot being fired. It can be fostered and preserved only by the solid unity and common brotherhood of the peoples of the world in the cause of freedom.

The hopes and aspirations of the peoples of all nations for justice and peace depend largely upon the courageous and enlightened administration of the foreign and defense policies of the United States. We deplore the fact that the administration of both policies since 1953 has confused timidity with courage, and blindness with enlightenment.

THE REPUBLICAN RECORD OF CONFUSION AND COMPLACENCY IS THE PRESIDENT'S RESPONSIBILITY

The world's hopes for lasting peace depend upon the conduct of our foreign policy, a function which the Constitution vests in the President of the United States and one which has not been effectively exercised by President Eisenhower. Since 1953, responsibility for foreign affairs has been President Eisenhower's, his alone, and his in full.

In the past three years, his conduct of our policies has moved us into realms where we risk grave danger. He has failed to seek peace with determination, for his disarmament policy has failed to strike hard at the institution of war. His handling of the day-by-day problems of international affairs has unnecessarily and dangerously subjected the American people to the risk of atomic world war.

OUR GOVERNMENT LACKS LEADERSHIP

We need bold leadership, yet in the three years since Stalin's death, in the full year since President Eisenhower's meeting at the "summit," the Republican Administration has not offered a single concrete new idea to meet the new-style political and economic offensive of the Soviets, which represents, potentially, an even graver challenge than Stalin's use of force. President Eisenhower and his Secretary of State talk at cross-purposes, praising neutralism one day, condemning it the next. The Republicans seem unable either to make up their minds or to give us leadership, while the unity of the free world rapidly disintegrates.

We in America need to make our peaceful purpose clear beyond dispute in every corner of the world—yet Secretary Dulles brags of "brinks of war." We need a foreign policy which rises above jockeying for partisan position or advantage—yet, not in memory has there been so little bipartisanship in the administration of our policies, so little candor in their presentation to our people, so much pretending that things are better than they are.

THE REPUBLICAN BLUSTER AND BLUFF

Four years ago the Republican Party boasted of being able to produce a foreign policy which was to free the Communist satellites, unleash Chiang Kai-shek, repudiate the wartime agreements, and reverse the policy of containing Communist expansion.

Since 1953 they have done just the opposite, standing silent when the peoples rise in East Germany and Poland, and thereby weakening the positive Democratic policy of halting Communist expansion.

OUR FRIENDS LOSE FAITH IN US

Our friends abroad now doubt our sincerity. They have seen the solid assurance of collective security under a Democratic Administration give place to the uncertainties of personal diplomacy. They have seen the ties of our international alliances and friendship weakened by inept Republican maneuvering.

They have seen traditional action and boldness in foreign affairs evaporate into Republican complacency, retrenchment and empty posturing.

THE FAILURE ABROAD

Blustering without dynamic action will not alter the fact that the unity and strength of the free world have been drastically impaired. Witness the decline of NATO, the bitter tragedy of Cyprus, the withdrawal of French forces to North Africa, the uncertainty and dangers in the Middle East, an uncertain and insecure Germany, and resentment rising against United States leadership everywhere.

In Asia—in Burma, Ceylon, Indonesia, India—anti-Americanism grows apace, aggravated by the clumsy actions of our Government, and fanned by the inept utterances of our "statesmen."

In the Middle East, the Eisenhower Administration has dawdled and drifted. The results have been disastrous, and worse threatens. Only the good offices of the United Nations in maintaining peace between Israel and her neighbors conceal the diplomatic incapacities of the Republican Administration. The current crisis over Suez is a consequence of inept and vacillating Republican policy. Our Government's mistakes have placed us in a position in the Middle East which threatens the free world with a loss of power and prestige, potentially more dangerous than any we have suffered in the past decade.

THE FAILURE AT HOME

Political considerations of budget balancing and tax reduction now come before the wants of our national security and the needs of our Allies. The Republicans have slashed our own armed strength, weakened our capacity to deal with military threats, stifled our air force, starved our army and weakened our capacity to deal with aggression of any sort save by retreat or by the alternatives, "massive retaliation" and global atomic war. Yet, while our troubles mount, they tell us our prestige was never higher, they tell us we were never more secure.

THE CHALLENGE IS FOR DEMOCRACY TO MEET

The Democratic Party believes that "waging peace" is a monumental task to be performed honestly, forthrightly, with dedication and consistent effort.

The way to lasting peace is to forego bluster and bluff, to regain steadiness of purpose, to join again in faithful concert with the community of free nations, to look realistically at the challenging circumstances which confront us, to face them candidly and imaginatively, and to return to the Democratic policy of peace through strength.

This is a task for Democrats. This facing of new problems, this rising to new challenges, has been our Party's mission and its glory for three generations past. President Truman met and mastered Stalin's challenge a decade ago, with boldness, courage and imagination, and so will we turn to the challenge before us now, pressing the search for real and lasting peace. To This We Pledge:

Support for the United Nations

The United Nations is indispensable for the maintenance of world peace and for the settlement of controversies between nations small and large. We pledge our every effort to strengthen its usefulness and expand its role as guide and guardian of international security and peace. We deplore the Republicans' tendency to use the United Nations only when it suits them, ignoring or by-passing it whenever they please.

We pledge determined opposition to the admission of the Communist Chinese into the United Nations. They have proven their complete hostility to the purposes of this organization. We pledge continued support to Nationalist China.

Release of American Prisoners

We urge a continuing effort to effect the release of all Americans detained by Communist China.

Support for Effective Disarmament

In this atomic age, war threatens the very survival of civilization. To eliminate the danger of atomic war, a universal, effective and enforced disarmament system must be the goal of responsible men and women everywhere. So long as we lack enforceable international control of weapons, we must maintain armed strength to avoid war. But technological advances in the field of nuclear weapons make disarmament an even more urgent problem. Time and distance can never again protect any nation of the world. The Eisenhower Administration, despite its highly publicized proposals for aerial inspection, has made no progress toward this great objective. We pledge the Democratic Party to pursue vigorously this great goal of enforced disarmament in full awareness that irreparable injury, even total destruction, now threatens the human race.

Adequate Defense Forces

We reject the false Republican notion that this country can afford only a second-best defense. We stand for strong defense forces so clearly superior in modern weapons to those of any possible enemy that our armed strength will make an attack upon the free world unthinkable, and thus be a major force for world peace. The Republican Administration stands indicted for failing to recognize the necessity of proper living standards for the men and women of our armed forces and their families. We pledge ourselves to the betterment of the living conditions of the members of our armed services, to a needed increase in the so-called "fringe benefits."

Training for Defense

The Democratic Party pledges itself to a bold and imaginative program devised to utilize fully the brain power of America's youth, including its talent in the scientific and technical fields.

Scholarships and loan assistance and such other steps as may be determined desirable must be employed to secure this objective. This is solely in the interest of necessary and adequate national defense.

Strengthening Civil Defense

We believe that a strong, effective civil defense is a necessary part of national defense. Advances in nuclear weapons have made existing civil defense legislation and practices obsolete.

We pledge ourselves to establish a real program for protecting the civilian population and industry of our Nation in place of the present weak and ineffective program. We believe that this is essentially a Federal responsibility.

Collective Security Arrangements

The Democratic Party inaugurated and we strongly favor collective defense arrangements, such as NATO and the Organization of American States, within the framework of the United Nations. We realize, as the Republicans have not, that mutually recognized common interests can be flexibly adapted to the varied needs and aspirations of all countries concerned.

Winning the Productivity Race

The Republican Party has not grasped one of the dominant facts of mid-century—that the growth of productive power of the Communist states presents a challenge which cannot be evaded. The Democratic Party is confident that, through the freedom we enjoy, a vast increase in productive power of our Nation and our Allies will be achieved, and by their combined capacity they will surmount any challenge.

Economic Development Abroad

We believe that, in the cause of peace, America must support the efforts of under-developed countries on a cooperative basis to organize their own resources and to increase their own economic productivity, so that they may enjoy the higher living standards which science and modern industry make possible. We will give renewed strength to programs of economic and technical assistance. We support a multilateral approach to these programs, wherever possible, so that burdens are shared and resources pooled among all the economically developed countries with the capital and skills to help in this great task.

Further, while recognizing the relation of our national security to the role of the United States in international affairs, the Democratic Party believes the time has come for a realistic reappraisal of the American foreign aid program, particularly as to its extent and the conditions under which it should be continued. This reappraisal will determine the standards by which further aid shall be granted, keeping in mind America's prime objective of securing world peace.

Bringing the Truth to the World

The tools of truth and candor are even more important than economic tools. The Democratic Party believes that once our Government is purged of the confusion and complacency fostered by the Republican Administration a new image of America will emerge in the world: the image of a confident America dedicated to its traditional principles, eager to work with other peoples, honest in its pronouncements, and consistent in its policies.

Freedom for Captive Nations

We condemn the Republican Administration for its heartless record of broken prom-ises to the unfortunate victims of Communism. Candidate Eisenhower's 1952 pledges to "liberate" the captive peoples have been disavowed and dishonored.

We declare our deepest concern for the plight of the freedom-loving peoples of Central and Eastern Europe and of Asia, now under the yoke of Soviet dictatorship.

The United States, under Democratic leaders, has never recognized the forcible annexation of Lithuania, Latvia, and Estonia, or condoned the extension of the Kremlin's tyranny over Poland, Bulgaria, Rumania, Czechoslovakia, Hungary, Albania and other countries.

We look forward to the day when the liberties of all captive nations will be restored to them and they can again take their rightful place in the community of free nations.

We shall press before the United Nations the principle that Soviet Russia withdraw its troops from the capitve countries, so as to permit free, fair and unfettered elections in the subjugated areas, in compliance with the Atlantic Charter and other binding commitments.

Upholding the Principle of Self-Determination

We rededicate ourselves to the high principle of national self-determination, as enunciated by Woodrow Wilson, whose leadership brought freedom and independence to uncounted millions.

It is the policy of the Democratic Party, therefore, to encourage and assist small nations and all peoples, behind the Iron Curtain and outside, in the peaceful and orderly achievement of their legitimate aspirations toward political, geographical, and ethnic integrity, so that they may dwell in the family of sovereign nations with freedom and dignity. We are opposed to colonialism and Communist imperialism.

We shall endeavor to apply this principle to the desires of all peoples for self-determination.

Reciprocal Trade Among the Nations

The Democratic Party has always worked for expanding trade among free nations. Expanding world trade is necessary not only for our friends, but for ourselves; it is the way to meet America's growing need for industrial raw materials. We shall continue to support vigorously the Hull Reciprocal Trade Program.

Under Democratic Administrations, the operation of this Act was conducted in a manner that recognized equities for agriculture, industry and labor. Under the present Republican Administration, there has been a most flagrant disregard of these important segments of our economy resulting in serious economic injury to hundreds of thousands of Americans engaged in these pursuits. We pledge correction of these conditions.

Encouraging European Unity

Through the Marshall Plan, the European Economic Organization and NATO, the Democratic Party encouraged and supported efforts to achieve greater ecomomic and political unity among the free nations of Europe, and to increase the solidarity of the nations of the North Atlantic community. We will continue those efforts, taking into account the viewpoints and aspirations of different sectors of the European community, particularly in regard to practical proposals for the unification of Germany.

Peace and Justice in the Middle East

The Democratic Party stands for the maintenance of peace in the Middle East, which is essential to the well-being and progress of all its peoples.

We will urge Israel and the Arab States to settle their differences by peaceful means, and to maintain the sanctity of the Holy Places in the Holy Land and permit free access to them.

We will assist Israel to build a sound and viable economy for her people, so that she may fulfill her humanitarian mission of providing shelter and sanctuary for her homeless Jewish refugees while strengthening her national development.

We will assist the Arab States to develop their economic resources and raise the living standards of their people. The plight of the Arab refugees commands our continuing sympathy and concern. We will assist in carrying out large-scale projects for their resettlement in countries where there is room and opportunity for them.

We support the principle of free access to the Suez Canal under suitable international auspices. The present policies of the Eisenhower Administration in the Middle East are unnecessarily increasing the risk that war will break out in this area. To prevent war, to assure peace, we will faithfully carry out our country's pledge under the Tripartite Declaration of 1950 to oppose the use or threat of force and to take such action as may be necessary in the interest of peace, both within and outside the United Nations, to prevent any violation of the frontiers of any armistice lines.

The Democratic Party will act to redress the dangerous imbalance of arms in the area resulting from the shipment of Communist arms to Egypt, by selling or supplying defensive weapons to Israel, and will take such steps, including security guarantees, as may be required to deter aggression and war in the area.

We oppose, as contrary to American principles, the practice of any government which discriminates against American citizens on grounds of race or religion. We will not countenance any arrangement or treaty with any government which by its terms or in its practical application would sanction such practices.

Support for Free Asia

The people of Asia seek a new and freer life and they are in a commendable hurry to get it. They struggle against poverty, ill health and illiteracy. In the aftermath of war, China became a victim of Communist tyranny. But many new free nations have arisen in South and Southeast Asia. South Korea remains free, and the New Japan has abandoned her former imperial and aggressive ways. America's task and interest in Asia is to help the governments of free peoples demonstrate that they have improved living standards without yielding to Communist tyranny or domination by anyone. That task will be carried out under Democratic leadership.

Support of Our Good Neighbors to the South

In the Western Hemisphere the Democratic Party will restore the policy of the "good neighbor" which has been alternately neglected and abused by the Republican Administration. We pledge ourselves to fortify the defenses of the Americas. In this respect, we will intensify our cooperation with our neighboring republics to help them strengthen their economies, improve educational opportunities, and combat disease. We will strive to make the Western Hemisphere an inspiring example of what free peoples working together can accomplish.

Progressive Immigration Policies

America's long tradition of hospitality and asylum for those seeking freedom, opportunity, and escape from oppression, has been besmirched by the delays, failures and broken promises of the Republican Administration. The Democratic Party favors prompt revision of the immigration and nationality laws to eliminate unfair provisions under which admissions to this country depend upon quotas based upon the accident of national origin. Proper safeguards against subversive elements should be provided. Our immigration procedures must reflect the principles of our Bill of Rights.

We favor eliminating the provisions of law which charge displaced persons admitted to our shores against quotas for future years. Through such "mortgages" of future quotas, thousands of qualified persons are being forced to wait long years before they can hope for admission.

We also favor more liberal admission of relatives to eliminate the unnecessary tragedies of broken families.

We favor elimination of unnecessary distinctions between native-born and naturalized citizens. There should be no "second class" citizenship in the United States.

The administration of the Refugee Relief Act of 1953 has been a disgrace to our country. Rescue has been denied to innocent, defenseless and suffering people, the victims of war and the aftermath of wars. The purpose of the Act has been defeated by Republican mismanagement.

Victims of Communist Oppression

We will continue to support programs providing succor for escapees from behind the Iron Curtain, and bringing help to the victims of war and Communist oppression.

The Challenge of the Next Four Years

Today new challenges call for new ideas and new methods.

In the coming years, our great necessity will be to pull together as a people, with true nonpartisanship in foreign affairs under leaders informed, courageous and responsible.

We shall need to work closely with each other as Americans. If we here indict the Republican record, we acknowledge gratefully the efforts of individual

Republicans to achieve true bipartisanship. In this spirit an affirmative, cooperative policy can be developed. We shall need to work closely, also, with others all around the world. For there is much to do—to create once more the will and the power to transform the principles of the United Nations into a living reality; to awaken ourselves and others to the effort and sacrifice which alone can win justice and peace.

II. THE DOMESTIC POLICY—THE REPUBLICAN REACTION TO 20 YEARS OF PROGRESS

THE DEMOCRATIC BEQUEST

Twenty years of vivid Democratic accomplishments revived and reinforced our economic system, and wrote humanity upon the statute books. All this, the current Republican Administration inherited.

THE REPUBLICAN BRAND OF PROSPERITY

Substituting deceptive slogans and dismal deeds for the Democratic program, the Republicans have been telling the American people that "we are now more prosperous than ever before in peacetime." For the American farmer, the small businessman and the low-income worker, the old people living on a pittance, the young people seeking an American standard of education, and the minority groups seeking full employment opportunity at adequate wages, this tall tale of Republican prosperity has been an illusion.

The evil is slowly but surely infiltrating the entire economic system. Its fever signs are evidenced by soaring monopoly profits, while wages lag, farm income collapses, and small-business failures multiply at an alarming rate.

The first time-bomb of the Republican crusade against full prosperity for all was the hard-money policy. This has increased the debt burden on depressed farms, saddled heavier costs on small business, foisted higher interest charges on millions of homeowners (including veterans), pushed up unnecessarily the cost of consumer credit, and swelled the inordinate profits of a few lenders of money. It has wrought havoc with the bond market, with resulting financial loss to the ordinary owners of Government bonds.

The Republican tax policy has joined hands in an unholy alliance with the hard-money policy. Fantastic misrepresentation of the Government's budgetary position has been used to deny tax relief to low- and middle-income families, while tax concessions and handouts have been generously sprinkled among potential campaign contributors to Republican coffers. The disastrously reactionary farm program, the hardhearted resistance to adequate expansion of Social Security and other programs for human well-being, and favoritism in the award of Government contracts, all have watered the economic tree at the top and neglected its roots.

THE STUNTING OF OUR ECONOMIC PROGRESS

The Republicans say that employment and production are "higher" than ever before. The fact is that our over-all rate of growth has been crippled and stunted in contrast to its faster increase during the Democratic years from 1947 to 1953, after World War II.

With production lagging behind full capacity, unemployment has grown.

The Republican claim that this stunted prosperity is the price of peace is a distortion. National-security outlays have averaged a higher part of our total production during these Republican years than during 1947-53, and yet the annual growth in total production during these Republican years has been only about 60 percent as fast as in the preceding Democratic years. The progress of low-income families toward an American standard of living, rapid during the Democratic years, has ground to a stop under the Republicans.

Federal budgetary outlays for education and health, old-age assistance and child care, slum clearance and resource development, and all the other great needs of our people have been mercilessly slashed from an annual rate of more than $57 per capita under the Democrats to $33 per capita under the Republicans, a cut of 42 percent.

THE FAILURE OF THE REPUBLICAN BUDGET-BALANCERS

During the Republican fiscal years 1954-1957 as a whole, the deficits have averaged larger, and the surpluses smaller, than during the Democratic fiscal years 1947-1953, financial manipulation to the contrary notwithstanding.

DEMOCRATIC PRINCIPLES FOR FULL PROSPERITY FOR ALL:

(1) We repudiate the Republican stunting of our economic growth, and we reassert the principles of the Full Employment Act of 1946;

(2) We pledge ourselves to achieve an honest and realistic balance of the Federal Budget in a just and fully prosperous American economy;

(3) We pledge ourselves to equitable tax revisions and monetary policies designed to combine economic progress with economic justice. We condemn the Republican use of our revenue and money systems to benefit the few at the expense of the vast majority of our people;

(4) We pledge ourselves to work toward the reduction and elimination of poverty in America;

(5) We pledge ourselves to full parity of income and living standards for agriculture; to strike off the shackles which the Taft-Hartley law has unjustly imposed on labor; and to foster the more rapid growth of legitimate business enterprise by founding this growth upon the expanding consuming power of the people; and

(6) We pledge ourselves to expand world trade and to enlarge international economic cooperation, all toward the end of a more prosperous and more peaceful world.

DEMOCRATIC GOALS TO BE ACHIEVED DURING
FOUR YEARS OF PROGRESS

By adhering to these principles, we shall strive to attain by 1960 the following full prosperity objectives for all American families:

(1) A 500 billion dollar national economy in real terms;

(2) An increase of 20 percent or better in the average standard of living;

(3) An increase in the annual income of American families, with special emphasis on those whose incomes are below $2000;

(4) A determined drive toward parity of incomes and living standards for those engaged in the vital pursuit of agriculture;

(5) The addition of all necessary classrooms for our primary and secondary schools; the construction of needed new homes, with a proper proportion devoted to the rehousing of low- and middle-income families in urban and rural areas; the increase of benefits under the Old Age Assistance and Old Age Survivors Insurance Programs; a substantial expansion in hospital facilities and medical research; and a doubling of our programs for resource development and conservation; and

(6) National defense outlays based upon our national needs, not permitting false economy to jeopardize our very survival.

This country of ours, in the factory, in business and on the farm, is blessed with ever-increasing productive power. The Republicans have not permitted this potential abundance to be released for the mutual benefit of all. We reject this stunted Republican concept of America. We pledge ourselves to release the springs of abundance, to bring this abundance to all, and thus to fulfill the full promise of America.

These are our Democratic goals for the next four years. We set them forth in vivid contrast to Republican lip-service protestations that they, too, are for these goals. Their little deeds belie their large and hollow slogans. Our performance in the past gives validity to our goals for the future.

Our victory in 1956 will make way for the commencement of these four years of progress.

III. FREE ENTERPRISE

"Equal rights for all and special privileges for none," the tested Jeffersonian principle, remains today the only philosophy by which human rights can be preserved by government.

It is a sad fact in the history of the Republican Party that, under its control, our Government has always become an instrument of special privilege; not a government of the people, by the people, and for the people. We have had, instead, under Harding, Coolidge and Hoover, and now under Eisenhower, government of the many, by the few, and for the few.

We recognize monopolies and monopolistic practices as the real barriers between the people and their economic and political freedom. Monopolies act to stifle equality of opportunity and prevent the infusion of fresh blood into the lifestream of our economy. The Republican Administration has allowed giant corporate entities to dominate our economy. For example, forty thousand automobile dealers now know they were incapable of coping with these giants. They were, as the Democratic 84th Congress found, subjected to abuse and threatened with extinction. The result was the passage of the O'Mahoney-Celler bill giving the automobile dealers of America economic freedom. We enacted this law, and we pledge that it shall be retained upon the statute books as a monument to the Democratic Party's concern for small business.

We pledge ourselves to the restoration of truly competitive conditions in American industry. Affirmative action within the framework of American tradition will be taken to curb corporate mergers that would contribute to the growth of economic concentration.

SMALL AND INDEPENDENT BUSINESS

In contrast to the maladministration by the Republican Party of the Federal program to assist small and independent business, we pledge ourselves—

(1) To the strict and impartial enforcement of the laws originally fostered and strengthened by the Democratic Party and designed to prevent monopolies and other concentrations of economic and financial power; and to enact legislation to close loopholes in the laws prohibiting price discrimination;

(2) To tax relief for all small and independent businesses by fair and equitable adjustments in Federal taxation which will encourage business expansion, and to the realistic application of the principle of graduated taxation to such corporate income. An option should be provided to spread Federal estate taxes over a period of years when an estate consists principally of the equity capital of a closely held small business;

(3) To adoption of all practical means of making long- and short-term credit available to small and independent businessmen at reasonable rates;

(4) To the award of a substantially higher proportion of Government contracts to independent small businesses, and to the award of a far larger percentage of military procurement, by value, after competitive bids rather than by negotiation behind closed doors. We severely condemn Republican discrimination against small and independent business;

(5) To replacement of the weak and ineffective Republican conduct of the Small Business Administration, and its reconstitution as a vigorous, independent agency which will advocate the cause of small and independent businessmen, and render genuine assistance in fulfilling their needs and solving their problems. We condemn the Republican Administration for its failure to serve this important segment of our economy.

LAW ENFORCEMENT

We pledge ourselves to the fair and impartial administration of justice. The Republican Administration has degraded the great powers of law enforcement. It has not used them in the service of equal justice under law, but for concealment, coercion, persecution, political advantage and special interests.

MERCHANT MARINE

In the interest of our national security, and of the maintenance of American standards of wages and living, and in order that our waterborne overseas commerce shall not be unfairly discriminated against by low-cost foreign competition, we pledge our continued encouragement and support of a strong and adequate American Merchant Marine.

TRANSPORTATION

The public and national defense interests require the development and maintenance, under the competitive free enterprise system, of a strong, efficient and financially sound system of common-carrier transportation by water, highway, rail, and air, with each mode enabled, through sound and intelligent exercise of regulatory powers, to realize its inherent economic advantages and to reflect its full competitive capabilities. Public interest also requires, under reasonable standards, the admission of new licensees, where public convenience may be served, into the transport fields. We deplore the lack of enforcement of safety regulations for protection of life and property under the present Republican Administration, and pledge strict enforcement of such regulations.

HIGHWAYS

We commend the foresight of the Democratic 84th Congress for its enactment of the greatest program in history for expansion of our highway network, and we congratulate it upon its rejection of the unsound, unworkable, inadequate and unfair roads bill proposed by the present Republican Administration. In cooperation with state and local governments, we will continue the programs developed and fostered under prior Democratic Administrations for planning, coordinating, financing and encouraging the expansion of our national road and highway network so vital to defense and transportation in the motor age. We support expansion of farm-to-market roads.

RIVERS AND HARBORS

We pledge continued development of harbors and waterways as a vital segment of our transportation system. We denounce as capricious and arbitrary the Eisenhower pocket veto of the 1956 Rivers and Harbors bill, which heartlessly deprived the people in many sections of our country of vitally needed public works projects.

IV. A MAGNA CHARTA FOR LABOR

LABOR-MANAGEMENT RELATIONS

Harmonious labor-management relations are productive of good incomes for wage earners and conducive to rising output from our factories. We believe that, to the widest possible extent consistent with the public interest, management and labor should determine wage rates and conditions of employment through free collective bargaining.

The Taft-Hartley Act passed by the Republican-dominated 80th Congress seriously impaired this relationship as established in the Wagner National Labor Relations Act, enacted under the Roosevelt Administration. The Wagner Act protected, encouraged and guaranteed the rights of workers to organize, to join unions of their own choice, and to bargain collectively through these unions without coercion.

The vicious anti-union character of the Taft-Hartley Act was expressly recognized by Candidate Eisenhower during the 1952 election campaign.

At that time, he made a solemn promise to eliminate its unjust provisions and to enact a fair law. President Eisenhower and his Administration have failed utterly, however, to display any executive initiative or forcefulness toward keeping this pledge to the workers. He was further responsible for administratively amending Taft-Hartley into a more intensely anti-labor weapon by stacking the National Labor Relations Board with biased pro-management personnel who, by administrative decision, transformed the Act into a management weapon. One such decision removed millions of workers from the jurisdiction of the NLRB, which in many cases left them without protection of either State or Federal legislation.

We unequivocally advocate repeal of the Taft-Hartley Act. The Act must be repealed because State "right-to-work" laws have their genesis in its discriminatory anti-labor provisions.

It must be repealed because its restrictive provisions deny the principle that national legislation based on the commerce clause of the Constitution normally overrides conflicting State laws.

The Taft-Hartley Act has been proven to be inadequate, unworkable and unfair. It interferes in an arbitrary manner with collective bargaining, causing imbalance in the relationship between management and labor.

Upon return of our National Government to the Democratic Party, a new legislative approach toward the entire labor-management problem will be adopted, based on past experience and the principles of the Wagner National Labor Relations Act and the Norris-La Guardia Anti-Injunction Law.

FAIR LABOR STANDARDS

We commend the action of the Democratic 84th Congress which raised the minimum wage from 75 cents to $1.00 an hour despite the strenuous objection of President Eisenhower and the Republicans in Congress. However, the inadequacies of the minimum wage become apparent as the cost of living increases, and we feel it imperative to raise the minimum wage to at least $1.25 an hour, in order to approximate present-day needs more closely.

We further pledge as a matter of priority to extend full protection of the Fair Labor Standards Act to all workers in industry engaged in, or affecting, interstate commerce.

WALSH-HEALEY CONTRACTS ACT

We pledge revision and honest administration of the Walsh-Healey Act, to restore its effectiveness and usefulness as an instrument for maintaining fair standards of wages and hours for American workers.

EQUAL PAY FOR EQUAL WORK

We advocate legislation to provide equal pay for equal work, regardless of sex.

THE PHYSICALLY HANDICAPPED

The Democratic Party has always supported legislation to benefit the disabled worker. The physically handicapped have proved their value to Government and industry. We pledge our continued support of legislation to improve employment opportunities of physically handicapped persons.

MIGRATORY WORKERS

We shall support legislation providing for the protection and improvement of the general welfare of migratory workers.

JOBS FOR DEPRESSED AREAS

We pledge our Party to support legislation providing for an effective program to promote industry and create jobs in depressed industrial and rural areas so that such areas may be restored to economic stability.

V. AGRICULTURE

Sustained national prosperity is dependent upon a vigorous agricultural economy.

We condemn the defeatist attitude of the Eisenhower Administration in refusing to take effective action to assure the well-being of farm families. We condemn its fear of abundance, its lack of initiative in developing domestic markets, and its dismal failure to obtain for the American farmer his traditional and deserved share of the world market. Its extravagant expenditure of money intended for agricultural benefit, without either direction or results, is a national calamity.

The Eisenhower Administration has failed utterly to develop any programs to meet the desperate needs of farmers in the face of fantastic promises, and it has sabotaged the progressive programs inherited from prior Democratic Administrations by failing to administer them properly in the interest either of farmers or of the Nation as a whole.

Specifically, we denounce President Eisenhower's veto of the constructive legislation proposed and passed by the Democratic 84th Congress to reverse the alarming fall of farm prices and restore farmers to a position of first-class economic citizenship in the sharing of benefits from American productive ability.

We also condemn the Republican Administration for its abandonment of the true principles of soil conservation and for its destruction of the Soil Conservation Service. We pledge to support continued improvements in the soil bank program passed by the Democratic 84th Congress and originally opposed by President Eisenhower and Secretary Ezra Taft Benson. We deplore the diversion of this conservation program into a direct vote-buying scheme.

Farmers have had to struggle for three and one-half years while their net farm income has fallen more than one billion dollars a year. Their parity ratio, which under Democratic Administrations had been 100 percent or more during the eleven years prior to 1953, dropped to as low as 80 percent during the Eisenhower Administration, and the farmers' share of the consumers' food dollar shrank from 47 cents in 1952 to as low as only 38 cents. One stark fact stands out clearly for all to see—disastrously low farm prices and record high consumer prices vie with each other for the attention of responsible government. In a reduction of this incongruous spread lies the answer to some of the most vexing problems of agricultural economics.

In their courageous fight to save their homes and land, American farmers have gone deeper and deeper into debt. Last year farmers' mortgage indebtedness increased more than in any year in history with the exception of the year 1923.

The Democratic Party met similar situations forthrightly in the past with concrete remedial action. It takes legitimate pride in its consistent record of initiating and developing every constructive program designed to protect and conserve the human and natural resources so vital to our rural economy. These programs enabled consumers to obtain more abundant supplies of high-quality food and fiber at reasonable prices while maintaining adequate income for farmers and improving the level of family living in rural areas.

In order to regain the ground lost during the Eisenhower Administration, and in order better to serve both consumers and producers, the Democratic Party pledges continuous and vigorous support to the following policies:

Sponsor a positive and comprehensive program to conserve our soil, water and forest resources for future generations;

Promote programs which will protect and preserve the family-type farm as a bulwark of Americian life, and encourage farm-home ownership, including additional assistance to family farmers and young farmers in the form of specially designed credit and price-support programs, technical aid, and enlarged soil conservation allowances;

Maintain adequate reserves of agricultural commodities strategically situated, for national security purposes. Such stockpiles should be handled as necessary strategic reserves, so that farmers will not be penalized by depressed prices for their efficiency and diligence in producing abundance;

Promote international exchange of commodities by creating an International Food Reserve, fostering commodity agreements, and vigorously administering the Foreign Agricultural Trade Development and Assistance Act;

Undertake immediately by appropriate action to endeavor to regain the full 100 percent of parity the farmers received under the Democratic Administrations. We will achieve this by means of supports on basic commodities at 90 percent of parity and by means of commodity loans, direct purchases, direct payments to producers, marketing agreements and orders, production adjustments, or a combination of these, including legislation, to bring order and stability into the relationship between the producer, the processor and the consumer;

Develop practical measures for extending price supports to feed grains and other nonbasic storables and to the producers of perishable commodities such as meat, poultry, dairy products and the like;

Inaugurate a food-stamp or other supplemental food program administered by appropriate State or local agencies to insure that no needy family shall be denied an adequate and wholesome diet because of low income;

Continue and expand school lunch and special milk programs to meet the dietary needs of all school children;

Increase the distribution of food to public institutions and organizations and qualified private charitable agencies, and increase the distribution of food and fiber to needy people in other nations through recognized charitable and religious channels;

Devise and employ effective means to reduce the spread between producers' prices and consumers' costs, and improve market facilities and marketing practices;

Expand the program of agricultural research and education for better distribution, preservation and marketing of farm products to serve both producers and consumers, and promote increased industrial use of farm surpluses;

Provide for an increased reservoir of farm credit at lower rates, designed particularly to accommodate operators of small family-type farms, and extend crop insurance to maximum coverage and protection;

Return the administration of farm programs to farmer-elected committeemen, eliminate the deplorable political abuses in Federal employment in many agricultural counties as practiced by the Eisenhower Administration, and restore leadership to the administration of soil conservation districts;

Insure reliable and low-cost rural electric and telephone service;

Exercise authority in existing law relating to imports of price-supported agricultural commodities in raw, manufactured or processed form as part of our national policy to minimize damage to our domestic economy;

Encourage bona fide farm cooperatives which help farmers reduce the cost-price squeeze, and protect such cooperatives against punitive taxation;

Expand farm forestry marketing research and price reporting on timber products, and provide adequate credit designed to meet the needs of timber farmers; and

Enact a comprehensive farm program which, under intelligent and sympathetic Democratic administration, will make the rural homes of America better and healthier places in which to live.

VI. GENERAL WELFARE

The Democratic Party believes that America can and must adopt measures to assure every citizen an opportunity for a full, healthy and happy life. To this end, we pledge ourselves to the expansion and improvement of the great social welfare programs inaugurated under Democratic Administrations.

SOCIAL SECURITY

By lowering the retirement age for women and for disabled persons, the Democratic 84th Congress pioneered two great advances in Social Security, over the bitter opposition of the Eisenhower Administration. We shall continue our efforts to broaden and strengthen this program by increasing benefits to keep pace with improving standards of living; by raising the wage base upon which benefits depend; and by increasing benefits for each year of covered employment.

UNEMPLOYMENT INSURANCE

We shall continue to work for a stronger unemployment insurance system, with broader coverage and increased benefits consistent with rising earnings. We shall also work for the establishment of a floor to assure minimum level and duration of benefits, and fair eligibility rules.

WAGE LOSSES DUE TO ILLNESS

In 1946, a Democratic Congress enacted an insurance program to protect railroad workers against temporary wage losses due to short-term illnesses. Because this program has worked so effectively, we favor extending similar protection to other workers.

PUBLIC ASSISTANCE

We pledge improvements in the public assistance program even beyond those enacted by the Democratic 84th Congress, through increased aid for the aged, the blind, dependent children, the disabled and other needy persons who are not adequately protected by our contributory insurance programs.

ADDITIONAL NEEDS OF OUR SENIOR CITIZENS

To meet the needs of the 14 million Americans aged 65 or over, we pledge ourselves to seek means of assuring these citizens greater income through expanded opportunities for employment, vocational retraining and adult education; better housing and health services for the aged; rehabilitation of the physically and mentally disabled to restore them to independent, productive lives; and intensified medical and other research aimed both at lengthening life and making the longer life more truly livable.

HEALTH AND MEDICAL CARE

The strength of our Nation depends on the health of our people. The shortage of trained medical and health personnel and facilities has impaired American health standards and has increased the cost of hospital care beyond the financial capacities of most American families.

We pledge ourselves to initiate programs of Federal financial aid, without Federal controls, for medical education.

We pledge continuing and increased support for hospital construction programs, as well as increased Federal aid to public health services, particularly in rural areas.

MEDICAL RESEARCH

Mindful of the dramatic progress made by medical research in recent years, we shall continue to support vigorously all efforts, both public and private, to wage relentless war on diseases which afflict the bodies and minds of men. We commend the Democratic Party for its leadership in obtaining greater Congressional authorizations in this field.

HOUSING

We pledge our Party to immediate revival of the basic housing program enacted by the Democratic Congress in 1949, to expansion of this program as our population and resources grow, and to additional legislation to provide housing for middle-income families and aged persons. Aware of the financial burdens which press upon most American communities and prevent them from taking full advantage of Federal urban redevelopment and renewal programs we favor increasing the Federal share of the cost of these programs.

We reaffirm the goal expressed by a Democratic Congress in 1949 that every American family is entitled to a "decent home and a suitable living environment." The Republican Administration has sabotaged that goal by reducing the public housing program to a fraction of the Nation's need.

We pledge that the housing insurance and mortgage guarantee programs will be redirected in the interest of the home owner, and that the availability of low-interest housing credit will be kept consistent with the expanding housing needs of the Nation.

We favor providing aid to urban and suburban communities in better planning for their future development and redevelopment.

EDUCATION

Every American child, irrespective of race or national origin, economic status or place of residence, has full right under the law and the Constitution, without discrimination, to every educational opportunity for developing his potentialities.

We are now faced with shortages of educational facilities that threaten national security, economic prosperity and human well-being. The resources of our States and localities are already strained to the limit. Federal aid and action should be provided, within the traditional framework of State and local control.

We pledge the Democratic Party to the following:

(1) Legislation providing Federal financing to assist States and local communities to build schools, and to provide essential health and safety services for all school children;

(2) Better educational, health and welfare opportunities for children of migratory workers;

(3) Assistance to programs for training teachers of exceptional children;

(4) Programs providing for the training of teachers to meet the critical shortage in technical and scientific fields; and

(5) Expansion of the program of student, teacher and cultural exchange with other nations.

VOCATIONAL EDUCATION

We commend the 84th Congress for voting the maximum authorized funds for vocational education under the Smith-Hughes Act for the first time in the history of the Act. We pledge continuing and increased support of vocational training for youth and adults, including aid to the States and localities for area technical-vocational schools.

CHILD WELFARE

To keep pace with the growing need for child care and welfare, we pledge an expanded program of grants to the States. We pledge continued support of adequate day care centers to care for the children of the millions of American mothers who work to help support their families.

AID TO THE PHYSICALLY HANDICAPPED

There are today several million physically handicapped citizens, many of whom could become self-supporting if given the opportunity and training for rehabilitation. We pledge support to a vastly expanded rehabilitation program for these physically handicapped, including increased aid to the States, in contrast to the grossly inadequate action of the Republican Administration.

VII. FINANCIAL POLICY

TAX ADJUSTMENT

A fully expanding economy can yield enough tax revenues to meet the inescapable obligations of government, balance the Federal Budget, and lighten the tax burden. The immediate need is to correct the inequities in the tax structure which reflect the Republican determination to favor the few at the expense of the many. We favor realistic tax adjustments, giving first consideration to small independent business and the small individual taxpayer. Lower-income families need tax relief; only a Democratic victory will assure this. We favor an increase in the present personal tax exemption of $600 to a minimum of at least $800.

DEBT MANAGEMENT

The Republican debt management policy of higher interest rates serves only to benefit a few to the detriment of the general taxpayer, the small borrower, and the small and middle-class investor in Government bonds. We pledge ourselves to a vigilant review of our debt management policy in order to reduce interest rates in the service of our common welfare.

PROTECTION OF INVESTORS

Effective administration of the Federal securities laws has been undermined by Republican appointees with conflicting interests. Millions of investors who have bought securities with their savings are today without adequate protection. We favor vigorous administration and revision of the laws to provide investor safeguards for securities extensively traded in the over-the-counter market, for foreign securities distributed in the United States, and against proxy contest abuses.

VIII. GOVERNMENT OPERATIONS

The Democratic Party pledges that it will return the administration of our National Government to a sound, efficient, and honest basis.

CIVIL SERVICE AND FEDERAL EMPLOYEE RELATIONS

The Eisenhower Administration has failed either to understand or trust the Federal Employee. Its record in personnel management constitutes a grave indictment of policies reflecting prejudices and excessive partisanship to the detriment of employee morale.

Intelligent and sympathetic programs must be immediately undertaken to insure the re-establishment of the high morale and efficiency which were characteristic of the Federal worker during 20 years of Democratic Administrations.

To accomplish these objectives, we propose:

(1) Protection and extension of the merit system through the enactment of laws to specify the rights and responsibilities of workers;

(2) A more independent Civil Service Commission in order that it may provide the intelligent leadership essential in perfecting a proper Civil Service System;

(3) Promotion within the Federal Service under laws assuring advancement on merit and proven ability;

(4) Salary increases of a nature that will insure a truly competitive scale at all levels of employment;

(5) Recognition by law of the right of employee organizations to represent their members and to participate in the formulation and improvement of personnel policies and practices; and

(6) A fair and non-political loyalty program, by law, which will protect the Nation against subversion and the employee against unjust and un-American treatment.

RESTORING THE EFFICIENCY OF THE POSTAL SERVICE

The bungling policies of the Republican Administration have crippled and impaired the morale, efficiency and reputation of the U.S. Postal Service. Mail carriers and clerks and other Postal employees are compelled to work under intolerable conditions. Communication by mail and service by parcel post have been delayed and retarded with resulting hardships, business losses and inconveniences. A false concept of economy has impaired seriously the efficiency of the best communication system in the world.

We pledge ourselves to programs which will:

(1) Restore the principle that the Postal Service is a public service to be operated in the interest of improved business economy and better communication, as well as an aid to the dissemination of information and intelligence;

(2) Restore Postal employee morale through the strengthening of the merit system, with promotions by law rather than caprice or partisan politics, and payment of realistic salaries reflecting the benefits of an expanded economy;

(3) Establish a program of research and development on a scale adequate to insure the most modern and efficient handling of the mails; and

(4) Undertake modernization and construction of desperately needed Postal facilities designed to insure the finest Postal system in the world.

CONFLICT OF INTERESTS

Maladministration and selfish manipulation have characterized Federal Administration during the Eisenhower years. Taxpayers, paying billions of dollars each year to their Government, demand and must have the highest standards of honesty, integrity and efficiency as a minimum requirement of Federal Executive conduct. We pledge a strong merit system as a substitute for cynical policies of spoils and special favor which are now the rule of the day. We seek the constant improvement of the Federal Government apparatus to accomplish these ends.

Under certain conditions, we recognize the need for the employment of personnel without compensation in the Executive Branch of the Government. But the privileges extended these dollar-a-year men have resulted in grave abuses of power. Some of these representatives of large corporations have assumed a dual loyalty to the Government and to the corporations that pay them. These abuses under the Republican Administration have been scandalous. The Democratic Party proposes that any necessary use of non-compensated employees shall be made only after the most careful scrutiny and under the most rigidly prescribed safeguards to prevent any conflict of interests.

FREEDOM OF INFORMATION

During recent years there has developed a practice on the part of Federal agencies to delay and withhold information which is needed by Congress and the general public to make important decisions affecting their lives and destinies. We believe that this trend toward secrecy in Government should be reversed and that the Federal Government should return to its basic tradition of exchanging and promoting the freest flow of information possible in those unclassified areas where secrets involving weapons development and bona fide national security are not involved. We condemn the Eisenhower Administration for the excesses practiced in this vital area, and pledge the Democratic Party to reverse this tendency, substituting a rule of law for that of broad claims of executive privilege.

We reaffirm our position of 1952 "to press strongly for world-wide freedom in the gathering and dissemination of news." We shall press for free access to information throughout the world for our journalists and scholars.

CLEAN ELECTIONS

The shocking disclosures in the last Congress of attempts by selfish interests to exert improper influence on members of Congress have resulted in a Congressional investigation now under way. The Democratic Party pledges itself to provide effective regulation and full disclosure of campaign expenditures and contributions in elections to Federal offices.

EQUAL RIGHTS AMENDMENT

We of the Democratic Party recommend and indorse for submission to the Congress a Constitutional amendment providing equal rights for women.

VETERANS ADMINISTRATION

We are spending approximately 4-3/4 billion dollars per year on veterans' benefits. There are more than 22 million veterans in civil life today and approximately 4 million veterans or dependents of deceased veterans drawing direct cash benefits from the Veterans Administration. It is clear that a matter of such magnitude demands more prominence in the affairs of Government. We pledge that we will elevate the Veterans Administration to a place of dignity commensurate with its importance in national affairs.

We charge the present Administration with open hostility toward the veterans' hospital program as disclosed by its efforts to restrict severely that program in fiscal year 1954. We further charge the Administration with incompetence and gross neglect in the handling of veterans' benefits in the following particulars:

(1) The refusal to allow service connection for disabilities incurred in or aggravated by military service, and the unwarranted reduction of disability evaluations in cases where service connection has been allowed; and

(2) The failure to give proper protection to veterans purchasing homes under the VA home loan program both by inadequate supervision of the program and, in some instances, by active cooperation with unscrupulous builders, lenders and real estate brokers.

In recognition of the valiant efforts of those who served their Nation in its gravest hours, we pledge:

(1) Continuance of the Veterans Administration as an independent Federal agency handling veterans programs;

(2) Continued recognition of war veterans, with adequate compensation for the service-connected disabled and for the survivors of those who have passed away in service or from service incurred disabilities; and with pensions for disabled and distressed veterans, and for the dependents of those who have passed on, where they are in need or unable to provide for themselves;

(3) Maintenance of the Veterans Administration hospital system, with no impairment in the high quality of medical and hospital service;

(4) Priority of hospitalization for the service-connected disabled, and the privilege of hospital care when beds are available for the non-service-connected illness of veterans who are sick and without funds or unable to procure private hospitalization;

(5) Fair administration of veterans preference laws, and employment opportunities for handicapped and disabled veterans;

(6) Full hearings for war veterans filing valid applications with the review, corrective and settlement boards of the Federal Government; and

(7) Support for legislation to obtain an extension of the current law to enable veterans to obtain homes and farms through the continuance of the GI Loan Program.

STATEHOOD FOR ALASKA AND HAWAII

We condemn the Republican Administration for its utter disregard of the rights to statehood of both Alaska and Hawaii. These territories have contributed greatly to our national economic and cultural life and are vital to our defense. They are part of

America and should be recognized as such. We of the Democratic Party, therefore, pledge immediate Statehood for these two territories. We commend these territories for the action their people have taken in the adoption of constitutions which will become effective forthwith when they are admitted into the Union.

PUERTO RICO

The Democratic Party views with satisfaction the progress and growth achieved by Puerto Rico since its political organization as a Commonwealth under Democratic Party leadership. We pledge, once again, our continued support of the Commonwealth and its development and growth along lines of increasing responsibility and authority, keeping as functions of the Federal Government only such as are essential to the existence of the compact of association adopted by the Congress of the United States and the people of Puerto Rico.

The progress of Puerto Rico under Commonwealth status has been notable proof of the great benefits which flow from self-government and the good neighbor policy which under Democratic leadership this country has always followed.

VIRGIN ISLANDS

We favor increased self-government for the Virgin Islands to provide for an elected Governor and a Resident Commissioner in the Congress of the United States. We denounce the scandalous administration of the first Eisenhower-appointed Governor of the Virgin Islands.

OTHER TERRITORIES AND POSSESSIONS

We favor increased self-government for Guam, other outlying territories and the Trust Territory of the Pacific.

DISTRICT OF COLUMBIA

We favor immediate home rule and ultimate national representation for the District of Columbia.

AMERICAN INDIANS

Recognizing that all American Indians are citizens of the United States and of the States in which they reside, and acknowledging that the Federal Government has a unique legal and moral responsibility for Indians which is imposed by the Constitution and spelled out in treaties, statutes and court decisions, we pledge:

Prompt adoption of a Federal program to assist Indian tribes in the full development of their human and natural resources, and to advance the health, education and economic well-being of Indian citizens, preserving their traditions without impairing their cultural heritage;

No alteration of any treaty or other Federal-Indian contractual relationships without the free consent of the Indian tribes concerned; reversal of the present policies which are tending toward erosion of Indian rights, reduction of their economic base through alienation of their lands, and repudiation of Federal responsibility;

Prompt and expeditious settlement of Indian claims against the United States, with full recognition of the rights of both parties; and

Elimination of all impediments to full citizenship for American Indians.

GOVERNMENTAL BALANCE

The Democratic Party has upheld its belief in the Constitution as a charter of individual rights, an effective instrument for human progress. Democratic Administrations placed upon the statute books during their last 20 years a multitude of measures which testify to our belief in the Jeffersonian principle of local control even in general legislation involving Nation-wide programs. Selective Service, Social Security, agricultural adjustment, low-rent housing, hospital, and many other legislative programs have placed major responsibilities in States and counties, and provide fine examples of how benefits can be extended through Federal-State cooperation.

While we recognize the existence of honest differences of opinion as to the true location of the Constitutional line of demarcation between the Federal Government and the States, the Democratic Party expressly recognizes the vital importance of the respective States in our Federal Union. The Party of Jefferson and Jackson pledges itself to continued support of those sound principles of local government which will best serve the welfare of our people and the safety of our democratic rights.

IMPROVING CONGRESSIONAL PROCEDURES

In order that the will of the American people may be expressed upon all legislative proposals, we urge that action be taken at the beginning of the 85th Congress to improve Congressional procedures so that majority rule prevails and decisions can be made after reasonable debate without being blocked by a minority in either House.

IX. NATURAL RESOURCES

Our national economic strength and welfare depend primarily upon the development of our land, water, mineral and energy resources, with which this Nation has been abundantly blessed.

We pledge unstinting support to a full and integrated program of development, protection, management and conservation of all of our natural resources for all of the people.

The framework of time-tested conservation and mining policy is fixed in laws under which America has developed its natural resources for the general welfare.

The Democratic 84th Congress has remained steadfast to this traditional policy. It has built upon the tremendous conservation and development achievements of the Roosevelt and Truman Administrations by undertaking the greatest program of natural resources development ever assumed by any Congress in our Nation's history.

This constructive Democratic record, embracing all resources of land, water, energy and minerals, is in sharp contrast to the faithless performance of the Eisenhower Administration which has despoiled future generations of their heritage by utter failure to safeguard natural resources. Our people will long remember this betrayal of their heritage as symbolized by the infamous Dixon-Yates contract; the Al Sarena timber scheme; the low-level Hells Canyon Dams; and for its unreasonable resistance to authorizing the Niagara Project which would benefit so many millions in the State of New York and adjacent areas.

We condemn, and will continue to decry, this pillaging in our dwindling natural resource wealth through political manipulation and administrative subversion by the Eisenhower Administration. We pledge ourselves to halt this betrayal of the people's trust.

We shall devise for the American people a dynamic, far-reaching and progressive conservation program.

The Democratic Party proposes, and will strive to secure, this comprehensive resources program for America's future.

LAND

Our land will be preserved and improved for the present and future needs of our people, and not wastefully exploited to benefit special-interest groups.

SOIL CONSERVATION

In contrast to the wasteful neglect of the present Administration, soil conservation practices will be stimulated and intensified to reduce land deterioration under the vital Soil Conservation Service assistance program conceived and fostered by the Democratic Party.

NATIONAL PARKS, RECREATION AND WILDLIFE

We pledge adoption of an immediate and broad policy to mobilize the efforts of private and public agencies for protection of existing recreational areas, provision of new ones, and improvement of inadequate facilities. Slum conditions fostered by Republican neglect are intolerable to the tens of millions of American using our national parks and forests. Democratic Administration will end this shocking situation.

Fish and game habitats will be guarded against encroachment for commercial purposes. All river basin development plans will take into full consideration their effect upon fish, wildlife, national park and wilderness areas. The Fish and Wildlife Service must and will be returned to the career status from which it was removed by the political patronage policy of the present Administration.

Recreational facilities for the millions of field and stream sportsmen of America will be conserved and expanded.

FOREST AND GRAZING LANDS

Timber on Federal commercial forest lands will be harvested and managed on a sustained-yield basis.

We propose to increase forest access roads in order to improve cutting practices on both public and private lands.

Private owners of farm, forest and range lands need and must have financial and technical assistance so that all lands will be utilized to contribute more fully to the national welfare by production of food and fiber and protection of our watersheds. Any effort to transform grazing permits from a revocable license to a vested right will be rejected.

We will vigorously advocate Federally-financed forestation, upstream erosion control and flood control programs on our public range, timber lands and small drainage basins to protect our watersheds and double the rate of forage and commercial timber growth. We will promote cooperative programs with Government assistance to reduce timber losses from fire, insects, and disease.

Prospecting and mining on unreserved Federal lands will be encouraged, but surface areas not needed in mining will be safeguarded by appropriate legislation.

WATER

We pledge the resumption of rapid and orderly multiple-purpose river basin development throughout the country. This program will bring into reality the full potential benefits of flood control, irrigation and our domestic and municipal water supply from surface and underground waters. It will also materially aid low-cost power, navigation, recreation, fish and wildlife propagation and mineral development. We pledge our aid to the growing requirements of the semiarid Western States for an adequate water supply to meet the vital domestic, irrigation and industrial needs of the rapidly growing urban centers. Enhanced regional economies will strengthen the economy of the Nation as a whole.

We will take appropriate and vigorous steps to prevent comprehensive drainage basin development plans from being fragmented by single purpose projects. The conservation of water is essential to the life of the Nation. The Democratic Party pledges itself to conservation of water in the public interest.

The Democratic 84th Congress has taken a long step toward reducing the pollution of our rivers and streams. We pledge continuation and expansion of this program, vital to every citizen.

The program of obtaining a large new source of fresh water supply from salt water was begun by the Democratic Party, but has been allowed to lapse by the Eisenhower Republican Administration. It will be resumed and accelerated.

ENERGY

We pledge ourselves to carry forward, under national policy, aggressive programs to provide abundant supplies of low-cost energy, including continued research for the development of synthetic liquid fuel from coal, shale and agricultural products. These we must have to feed our insatiable industrial economy, to enable our workers to develop their skills and increase their productivity, to provide more jobs at higher wages, to meet the ever-mounting demands for domestic and farm uses, including the production of lower-cost farm fertilizers and lower-cost power to consumers.

We will carry forward increased and full production of hydroelectric power on our rivers and of steam generation for the Tennessee Valley Authority to meet its peacetime and defense requirements. Such self-liquidating projects must go forward in a rapid and orderly manner, with appropriate financing plans. Integrated regional transmission systems will enhance exchange of power and encourage diversified industrial development.

We shall once more rigorously enforce the anti-monopoly and public body preference clauses, including the Holding Company Act, administratively circumvented by the Eisenhower Republican Administration. We shall preserve and strengthen the public power competitive yardstick in power developments under TVA, REA, Bureau of Reclamation, Bonneville, Southeast and Southwest Power Administrations and other future projects, including atomic power plants, under a policy of the widest possible use of electric energy at the lowest possible cost.

MINERALS

The Republican Administration has seriously neglected and ignored one of the Nation's basic industries, metal mining. We recognize that a healthy mining industry is essential to the economy of the Nation, and therefore pledge immediate efforts toward the establishment of a realistic, long-range minerals policy. The Nation's minerals and fuels are essential to the safety, security and development of our country. We pledge the adoption of policies which will further encourage the exploration and development of additional reserves of our mineral resources.

DOMESTIC FISHERIES

We will undertake comprehensive scientific and economic research programs for the conservation and better utilization of, and new markets for, fishery products. We favor and will encourage reciprocal world trade in fish products.

We pledge ourselves to a public works and water policy providing adequate protection for domestic fishery resources.

We favor treaties with other nations for conservation and better utilization of international fisheries.

SCENIC RESOURCES

To the end that the scenic beauty of our land may be preserved and maintained for this and future generations to enjoy, we pledge accelerated support of educational programs to stimulate individual responsibility and pride in clean, attractive surroundings—from big cities to rural areas.

X. ATOMIC ENERGY

The atomic era came into being and was developed under Democratic Administrations.

The genius of American scientists, engineers and workmen, supported by the vision and courage of Franklin D. Roosevelt, made possible the splitting of the atom and the development of the first atomic bomb in time to end World War II.

With the ending of the war, the supremacy of America in atomic weapons was maintained under the leadership of President Truman, and the United States pushed ahead vigorously toward utilizing this new form of energy in peaceful pursuits, particularly in the field of medicine, agriculture and industry. By the end of the Truman Administration, the pre-eminence of the United States in the nuclear field was clearly established, and we were on the threshold of large-scale development of industrial nuclear energy at home and as an instrument of world peace.

The Eisenhower Administration promptly reversed the field and plunged the previously independent and nonpartisan Atomic Energy Commission into partisan politics. For example, President Eisenhower ordered the Commission to sign the scandalous Dixon-Yates contract. He was later forced to repudiate the same contract, after the exposure of the illegal activities of one of his own consultants with a secret office in the Bureau of the Budget.

The Republican Administration has followed the same pattern in the field of atomic energy that it has pursued in its treatment of other natural resources—lofty words, little action, but steady service to selfish interests. While the AEC and the special private interests consult and confer, the United States is lagging instead of leading in the world race for nuclear power, international prestige and world markets.

The Democrats in Congress believed that the national interest thus became imperiled, and they moved to meet the challenge both at home and abroad. They established a nonpartisan panel of eminent Americans to study the impact of the peaceful atom.

Following the comprehensive report of this panel, the Joint Congressional Committee on Atomic Energy held extensive hearings on bills to accelerate the atomic reactor demonstration program. Though the bills were reported unanimously from committee, the Republican members of Congress, under heavy pressure from the White House, insured the final defeat of this legislation in the Congress.

But the fight to bring nuclear power to the people has only begun. As the United States was first in the development of the atom as a weapon, so the United States must lead in bringing the blessings of the peaceful uses of nuclear energy to mankind.

Hence, the Democratic Party pledges itself:

(1) To restore nonpartisan administration of the vital atomic energy program and to expand and accelerate nuclear development by vigorous action;

(2) To accelerate the domestic civilian atomic power program by the construction of a variety of demonstration prototype reactors;

(3) To give reality—life and meaning—to the "Atoms for Peace" program. We will substitute deed for words;

(4) To increase the production of fissionable material for use in a stockpile for peacetime commitments at home and abroad, and for an ever-present reserve for weapons to guarantee freedom in the world;

(5) To conduct a comprehensive survey of radiation hazards from bomb tests and reactor operations, in order to determine what additional measures are required to protect existing and future generations from these invisible dangers; and

(6) To make the maximum contribution to the defense of our Nation and the free world through the development of a balanced and flexible stockpile of nuclear weapons, containing a sufficient number and variety to support our armed services in any contingency.

XI. CIVIL RIGHTS

The Democratic Party is committed to support and advance the individual rights and liberties of all Americans. Our country is founded on the proposition that all men are created equal. This means that all citizens are equal before the law and should enjoy all political rights. They should have equal opportunities for education, for economic advancement, and for decent living conditions.

We will continue our efforts to eradicate discrimination based on race, religion or national origin. We know this task requires action, not just in one section of the Nation, but in all sections. It requires the cooperative efforts of individual citizens, and action by State and local governments. It also requires Federal action. The Federal Government must live up to the ideals of the Declaration of Independence and must exercise the powers vested in it by the Constitution.

We are proud of the record of the Democratic Party in securing equality of treatment and opportunity in the nation's armed forces, the Civil Service, and in all areas under Federal jurisdiction. The Democratic Party pledges itself to continue its efforts to eliminate illegal discriminations of all kinds, in relation to (1) full rights to vote, (2) full rights to engage in gainful occupations, (3) full rights to enjoy security of the person, and (4) full rights to education in all publicly supported institutions.

Recent decisions of the Supreme Court of the United States relating to segregation in publicly supported schools and elsewhere have brought consequences of vast importance to our Nation as a whole and especially to communities directly affected. We reject all proposals for the use of force to interfere with the orderly determination of these matters by the courts.

The Democratic Party emphatically reaffirms its support of the historic principle that ours is a government of laws and not of men; it recognizes the Supreme Court of the United States as one of the three Constitutional and coordinate branches of the Federal Government, superior to and separate from any political party, the decisions of which are part of the law of the land. We condemn the efforts of the Republican Party to make it appear that this tribunal is a part of the Republican Party.

We condemn the Republican Administration's violation of the rights of Government employees by a heartless and unjustified confusing of "security" and "loyalty" for the sole purpose of political gain and regardless of consequences to individual victims and to the good name of the United States. We condemn the Republican Administration's misrepresentation of facts and violation of individual rights in a wicked and unprincipled attempt to degrade and destroy the Democratic Party, and to make political capital for the Republican Party.

ADLAI E. STEVENSON
SPEECH AT MINNEAPOLIS
September 29, 1956

Minnesota is the great overarching bridge between the old Midwest and the new Northwest, where people breathe freer and look higher and, somehow, the blood is quickened in the clean North air, where men are not afraid to speak their minds or vote their deep convictions. Up here in Minnesota men are never satisfied that things can't be better than they are.

Minnesota has always led the great traditions of protest in the upper Midwest— the protest against things that could be better.

In recent years across your Eastern border the heirs of the Wisconsin Progressives have found a home in the Democratic party; today to the west in North Dakota the Nonpartisan League is moving in with us, too.

Here in Minnesota the heirs of that same great tradition have fused their strength in the Democratic-Farmer-Labor party.

And two men who have helped to write the Democratic-Farmer-Labor story are its great leaders today—Hubert Humphrey and Orville Freeman.

These men—and the national leaders of the Democratic party down the years— had several things in common. They were not afraid of new ideas. They were not content to leave well enough alone. They had a passion for human life—they cared and, they cared deeply about people. And they tackled the people's problems with an enthusiasm that was boundless and unbeatable.

I want to talk to you tonight about the need for enthusiasm and new ideas in our national life.

Of course today the Republicans would have us feel all the problems are solved, that what we need is not enthusiasm and new ideas but caution, complacency and a passion not for the people but for things as they are.

Well, here is how things are for some of our people unfortunately.

Farmers and their wives and children are being forced to pack up and leave the farm—a good farm—and uproot their whole lives.

Men are being forced to sell the store on Main Street that for years has provided for their family and served their community well.

Too many of our older citizens are spending what ought to be the golden years in want and neglect.

Too many children are going to school in crowded ramshackle buildings with teachers that are only half-trained.

Millions of sick people can't afford to call a doctor.

Hundreds of thousands of our mental patients are consigned to disgraceful medieval institutions.

One family out of five must get by on less than $2,000 in times like these.

Millions of American citizens are still barred from schools and jobs and an equal chance merely because of their color.

In the city slums children are roaming the alleys behind the tenement buildings, and in some parts of our country poverty is converting farmland into a rural slum.

I say this is not right. And I say that only the Democratic party has the passion for human justice, the enthusiasm and determination and the new ideas, to drive want and suffering from all American homes, not just some of them.

But beyond this lies another goal—the goal of peace, and I want to say something about that tonight.

Like most Americans, I've read some of what that wise New England philosopher, Ralph Waldo Emerson, wrote. I fear I've forgotten a lot of what he said, but I've remembered this:

"Nothing great," Emerson said, "was ever achieved without enthusiasm." How true that is. As we look back over the centuries, we can see that nearly all the glorious achievements of mankind, nearly all the best things that characterize our society, sprang from the uncrushable enthusiasm of those who believed in the genius of man, and who believed in the possibility of doing the seemingly impossible. To these enthusiasts, whose optimism often exposed them to scorn and ridicule, we chiefly owe all the good things of our civilization.

This thought of Emerson's—this tribute to the power of man's ability to master his destiny—came to me again only recently when I heard the President's recent expression of views on war and peace—the area above all others where we need fresh and positive thinking.

I was distressed to see that the President not only had nothing new to suggest for the future but he seemed resentful over the efforts of others—including myself—to find some new and more hopeful answers to the problems of life and death that now confront us.

To be more specific, I have said before and I'll say it again that I, for one, am not content to accept the idea that there can be no end to compulsory military service. While I, like most others who have had intimate experience with our armed forces in war and peace, have felt that it was and is necessary, at the same time I have felt, and many others likewise, that the draft is a wasteful, inefficient, and often unfair way of maintaining our armed forces, and now it is fast becoming an obsolete way.

Let me make it perfectly clear that as long as danger confronts us, I believe we should have stronger, not weaker, defenses than we have now. Ever since Mr. Eisenhower became President we Democrats have fought hard to prevent the Administration from putting dollars ahead of defense. The Democrats in Congress forced the Administration to reverse itself and restore deep cuts in the strategic Air Force even during this last session of Congress.

But my point is that the draft does not necessarily mean a strong defense. Conditions change, and no conditions have changed more in our time than the conditions of warfare. Nothing is more hazardous in military policy than rigid adherence to obsolete ideas. France learned this in 1939; she crouched behind the

Maginot Line, which was designed for an earlier war, and German panzers overran France. The Maginot Line gave France a false—and fatal sense of security. We must not let Selective Service become our Maginot Line.

What I am suggesting is that we ought to take a fresh and open-minded look at the weapons revolution and the whole problem of recruiting and training military manpower. We may very well find that in the not far distant future we can abolish the draft and at the same time have a stronger defense and at lower cost.

Defense is now so complex, its demand for highly skilled and specialized manpower so great, that the old fashioned conscript army, in which many men serve short terms of duty, is becoming less and less suited to the needs of modern arms. And it is becoming more and more expensive.

Let me say right here in all frankness that I have no special pride, no conceit, in the suggestions that I have tried to advance. No one will be happier than I if others find better solutions.

Once we start exploring this possibility seriously many new ideas will be forthcoming; that is always the case when men turn their creative energies full time upon a problem. Right now I had hoped to do no more than get this kind of creative thinking started.

I am distressed that President Eisenhower should dismiss this objective out of hand. If anyone had proposed the abolition of the draft right now, today, the President's attitude would be understandable; indeed, I would share it. But I don't see how we can ever get anywhere against the rigid, negative position that we cannot even discuss the matter, or even look forward to a time when we can do away with compulsory military service. I say it's time we stopped frowning and started thinking about them.

I am even more distressed that this attitude on the part of Mr. Eisenhower carries over into the all-important problem of controlling the hydrogen bomb, for here we are talking about the actual survival of the human race itself.

The testing alone of these super bombs is considered by scientists to be dangerous to man; they speak of the danger of poisoning the atmosphere; they tell us that radioactive fall-out may do genetic damage with effects on unborn children which they are unable to estimate.

I think almost everyone will agree that some measure of universal disarmament—some means of taming the nuclear weapons—is the first order of business in the world today.

It is not enough to say, well, we have tried and failed to reach agreement with the Russians. It is not enough to throw up our hands and say it's no use to try this or that new approach. This is one time we cannot take no for an answer, for life itself depends on our ultimately finding the right yes.

Again, I have no foolish pride in my own ideas on this subject. But there must be a beginning, a starting point, a way to get off the dead center of disagreement, I have proposed a moratorium on the testing of more super H-bombs. If the Russians don't go along, well then at least the world will know we tried. And we will know if they don't because we can detect H-bomb explosions without inspection.

It may be that others will come forward with other ideas; indeed, I hope they do. But I say to you that in this field, as in many others, fresh and open-minded thinking is needed as never before—and in this field we may not have unlimited time to get the answers. We'd better start thinking now.

Furthermore, I do not see how we can ever hope to get the answers if fresh ideas, new proposals, new solutions, are not encouraged.

I was shocked when Mr. Eisenhower the other night brushed off my suggestion as a theatrical gesture. I don't believe that was worthy of the President of the United States. I have never questioned his sincerity on a matter that I am sure means more to both of us than anything else in the world—the matter of permenent peace—and I do not think he should have questioned mine.

All decent men and women everywhere hate war. We don't want our boys to be drafted and we don't want to live forever in the shadow of a radioactive mushroom cloud. And when I say "we," I mean Democrats and Republicans alike—I mean mankind everywhere.

Peace is not a partisan issue. Every American, Democrat and Republican alike, wants peace. There is no war party in this country; there is no peace party.

And the way to get started on the difficult road to disarmament and peace is not, I repeat, to scorn new ideas.

Just because this Administration has not been able to make any progress toward safe disarmament or even toward controlling H-bomb development, does not mean that such agreements are forever impossible. No matter which party wins in November, another supreme effort must be undertaken, and, if that fails, then another and another, for leaders must lead, and the conquest of this scourge is a more imperative goal of mankind than the conquest of the black plague in the Middle Ages.

I shall continue to concentrate my own attention on this problem, and I shall also do everything I can to encourage others to do likewise, for, as I have said, I know in my heart that Emerson was right when he said that "nothing great was ever achieved without enthusiasm."

And we saw it proved in our own time. For many years, you will recall, the world had dreamed of splitting the atom and releasing its boundless energy.

But most men despaired of ever making this dream come true. Had it not been for Franklin D. Roosevelt and his determination, the so-called impossible might still seem impossible. Then, as now, there were the skeptic, the defeatists, the non-enthusiasts who thought Roosevelt was off on a wild goose chase, who dubbed Oakridge his billion dollar folly. But he was not deterred.

He would not take no for an answer. Nuclear energy was finally placed at the disposal of man, and if we, who survived Franklin Roosevelt, show the will to control this energy that he showed in creating it, then it still may prove to be one of the greatest blessings of all time.

Franklin Roosevelt was not a physicist. He knew nothing about the hidden secrets of uranium. But he had to a supreme degree the first attributes of political leadership—that is, he had the enthusiastic will to act, and the genius for organizing great undertakings.

I, too, know little or nothing about the mechanics of the H-bomb. But I do know this: if man is capable of creating it, he also is capable of taming it. And nothing—including Presidential frowns—can make me believe otherwise.

My friends, this is not the first time the Republicans have dismissed or scorned Democratic efforts to make this a better world.

When Woodrow Wilson had his immortal dream of a League of Nations, the Republicans called it worse names than a "theatrical gesture"—yet American participation might have prevented a second World War.

Franklin Roosevelt proposed the United Nations. Yet even today many Republican leaders, even Senator Knowland, are still suspicious of it or positively hostile. The U.N. isn't perfect. Like most human institutions it probably never will be, and certainly not without the wholehearted support of America's leaders.

This negative, defeatist attitude among Republican leaders comes in an unbroken line down to the present. President Hoover's Fortress America concept is familar. Senator Taft's negative, isolationist views are still shared by many of his followers.

And the fact is that the Republican party has been so divided since the first war and the League of Nations fight that even to this day it cannot conduct a coherent, consistent foreign policy, and the purpose of foreign policy for the United States is peace. Time and again in the past four years we have seen allied unity abroad sacrificed to Republican unity at home.

This is not to suggest for a second that the Republican party is, therefore, the war party, or that the Democratic party is the party of peace. I have no patience with such blanket charges.

Both parties are dedicated to peace, but historically they differ on how to realize this great objective. I think it is fair to say that, generally speaking, the Republican way has been the narrow, nationalistic one of the low, limited horizon, while the Democratic way has been that of the wide horizon, dotted with the ships and sails of beckoning hope.

One way, of course, is just as patriotic as the other. But in my opinion the Democratic way has usually been more attuned to the changes, the challenge and surprise, of this everchanging world. And I think this is just as true today as it has ever been.

And I think our Democratic enthusiasm for new ideas can better solve our problems here at home, too. For on the record it is the Democratic party that has always made new gains for the good of all the people.

Ours is the party that stopped child labor and started the nation on an eight-hour day, invented Social Security and built the T.V.A. It was the Democratic party that rescued the farmer with the Triple-A in the great depression, curbed the excesses of the stock promoters, built housing for the people, and wrote the G.I. Bill of Rights, and I could go on and on.

I spoke a few minutes ago of the Democratic-Farmer-Labor story written here in Minnesota. We're going to tell a larger story, too, this year. Woodrow Wilson restrained the excesses of a new industrialism and met the challenge of the Kaiser; Franklin Roosevelt lifted the people from the slough of depression and beat down totalitarianism; Harry Truman made the great decision that lifted prostrate Europe and gave our nation leadership of the free in the world—and that is our story, written in the Twentieth Century here in blessed America.

I say there is yet much to be done. Great work lies ahead. I believe with all my heart and soul that this nation is about to enter a richer age than man has ever known. The question is: Shall we use our riches for all the people, or just for some of them? And, can we master the new machines, or must we serve them? And, can we put the atom to our peaceful use, or will it destroy us?

These are great questions, they require great answers, and those answers can come only from the strength and wisdom of you, the American people. And they will not be drawn forth by leadership that fails to lead, that frowns on new ideas. They will be drawn forth only by leadership that dares to try the new, that meets the crises of our times with unbeatable enthusiasm.

"Nothing great," I repeat, "was ever achieved without enthusiasm." Let us go forward in the spirit of you of Minnesota, never satisfied with things as they are, daring always to try the new, daring nobly and doing greatly, and so building a New America.

It is in this spirit that I come to you tonight. It is in this spirit that we will win in November.

LYNDON B. JOHNSON
REMARKS TO SENATE DEMOCRATS
January 7, 1959

We start today a new year and a new Congress.

We have met now to transact the necessary business of our party, but I feel it would be inappropriate to proceed without acknowledging the context in which we assemble.

For us, this is the starting of a new era.

We have been given great strength. In all the long history of the Senate, never has one party won so many seats at a single election as we have won. For this, we are grateful—and certainly we are proud. Yet, we realize that our strength has never been, and is not now, the strength of numbers.

Our strength is what we are, and what we prove ourselves to be. What we hold we have earned. What we keep will be no more than what we deserve.

That is our special challenge.

Our strength will be deserving in proportion as we use it for the interests of all. By this standard, we have won the public trust; by this means, we shall honor the trust we have won.

New strength has brought us to a new era. Yet, as we note this, we cannot fail to note that this is, in much the same terms, the beginning now of a new era for our Nation, for the world, and for all humankind.

Our Nation is at the edge of what can clearly be its greatest age of expansion, growth, and abundance. Among the nations of the earth, we see emerging the first beginnings of a new age. Our times are yielding daily new capabilities for man.

The capabilities of government must keep pace with the capabilities of the people it serves. For this we know with certainty. There is no expense of government more costly or more intolerable than the burden of laggard government.

That is the work to which we come.

It is our purpose to fashion greater capabilities for our Government from the growing capabilities of man.

As Americans, not as partisans, we must acknowledge this reality: The capabilities of our Nation and its people are, in many vital areas, now outrunning the capabilities of our Government.

There is between the people and their Government a deficit of vigor, a deficit of confidence, and a deficit of will.

Prudence requires that we bring these books into balance.

Congressional Record, 86th Cong., 1st sess., 1959, vol. 105, pt. 1, 586-87.

To do so, we must seek the cause rather than tilt at the symptom. The faults of men and the failings of the system must not be confused. The one will pass; the other must be removed.

Government, if it is to serve at all, must serve the future—not the present alone, and most certainly not the past.

Today the future is already the controlling fact of these times—and of the decisions we take here.

The advent of a 200 million population, a $500 billion national income, a trillion dollar economy are all near at hand.

Throughout our system, conservative men are already working with these facts.

Yet where men are responding to this future, their Government is not. The past is served—at penalty to the present and at the danger of default to the future.

It is against this danger of default that we must work.

Responsible government is responsive government. Our urgent duty—and our special opportunity—is to undertake the labors necessary to make the Government of our land responsive to the potential and the promise of the future.

What we can do now is subject to certain limits.

We have been given great strength, but not overriding strength. The executive arm of National Government remains under control of another party.

We have—by our majority here—an obligation to lead. We do not have authority to command. We have powers to advise and consent. We do not have powers to implement and accomplish.

These facts we appreciate, yet they do not matter for much beyond the confines of the Senate.

Our mandate is a mandate for confident and creative and constructive leadership—beginning now, not 2 years hence.

We shall honor the mandate.

Our opportunity—the great opportunity of this Senate—is to marshal the considerable resources of inquiry of the legislative branch to the task of defining for America new goals for the many new capabilities of its people, its economy, its technology and its national will.

We are clearly moving to a new age—an age of new standards, new accomplishments, and new potentials.

Against the promise of this new age, American industry and business is now pouring forth billions in research to discover new capabilities.

Government, though, is moving hardly at all.

Research is under way on instruments of national security but, beyond that, little is being done. Great minds of the Nation are not being mobilized to the challenges of self-government by free men. The intellect of the Nation is not being used where it is most needed. This failing imperils us, fully as much, I believe, as would a failure to pursue research in the more obvious realms of national security.

I speak only for myself, of course, but I believe this. I believe that we should, through the resources available to us in the legislative branch, undertake the rewarding work of turning our land into the campus of the West.

We are working with the future. We are working with a new dimension—the most challenging men have ever faced.

If we are to be competent even for the routine of tomorrow, we shall need vision in our preparations—and we shall need both boldness and freshness.

We do not have it now.

It is the indictment of those who presently hold the responsibility of the action arm of our leadership that in dynamic times they have exalted—and still exalt—the static.

Free men can afford much. They can never afford the price of inertia.

Today we must face this fact: We have led the free world through a time of sickness and convalescence, but we are faced now with a well and vital world. The test of our national character and capacity will be our ability to lead a well world by our vigor and purpose as we have led a sick world by our wealth and compassion.

We need new ideas in many fields. We need to forge new tools of government.

Our controls over the monetary system are now two world wars old.

Our budget processes were formed in another day.

Our tax structure is obsolescent.

Our Government is dedicated, in many areas, to programs for which the purpose is no longer pertinent.

If we are not to default the integrity of our free enterprise system, we must concentrate vigorous efforts on its future—rather than hold to easy concepts of its past.

We must not surrender to inflation.

We must not surrender to poverty.

We must not surrender to educational blight or medical mediocrity or social depression in any field of our society.

We must not abandon regions or cities or classes or ages to despair.

We must not allow the obsolescence of our ideas to foredoom vital segments of our enterprise.

We must not allow ourselves to forfeit the goals of equal standards of freedom, opportunity, and equality for want of boldness.

We certainly must not abdicate progress to the rule of tension and strife.

In a world reborn—facing the new youth of a new age and a new dimension of space—we must certainly not default the leadership of vigor to the totalitarians.

Fiscal solvency concerns us all. It is a first concern, for no course is honest without the courage of financial prudence. But we cannot afford to bankrupt the national conscience to serve the ends of political bookkeeping.

Moral integrity, as well as fiscal integrity, requires that we acknowledge deficits of will and deficits of effort and undertake a united search for responsible solutions to the problems of our times.

We, here in the Senate, have within the powers open to us under the Constitution a great opportunity to reach out across the land—into the universities and colleges, into private business, into labor, the professions, all walks of our national life—and ask great minds to come here to help us seek and search.

We can reach beyond our shores—to all the Western World and especially to our neighbor republics of this hemisphere—and ask others to share this labor with us.

We can bring men together to explore tomorrow's horizons for our land, our hemisphere, and the world.

From such explorations, we will find the facts and form the ideas with which we shall work the next decade to make government responsive to the potential of the future.

The world is in a race today that is more likely to be won by minds than missiles. We neglect this at our peril.

There is much that we must do and shall do in this session; yet, for our work, we do not come with a checklist in hand to attend only the pressing problems of the present.

We are—as are the people who sent us here—looking to the future.

We know that we shall win respect by our vision, not by our vendettas; by courage, not by carping.

Our first responsibility is responsibility itself.

The era is new. The promise is new. We work with new and growing capabilities. Yet our purpose remains unchanged. Always our party has been the party of confident men and we have drawn our strength from young and confident regions of a young and confident land.

Today there is a new youth and zest and confidence across all our land and we, in consequence, find ourselves here now as party of all the Nation.

New strength is ours. With that new strength we shall—by responsible service—add strength to our Nation, our world, and our times.

Bibliographical Note

The following are among the most significant books concerning the Democratic party from 1945 to 1960: Stuart Gerry Brown, *Conscience in Politics; Adlai E. Stevenson in the 1950's* (Syracuse, 1961); Angus Campbell, *et al.*, comps., *The Voter Decides* (Evanston, Ill., 1954); Kenneth Sydney Davis, *The Politics of Honor: A Biography of Adlai E. Stevenson* (New York, 1967); J. David Greenstone, *Labor in American Politics* (New York, 1969); Samuel Lubell, *The Future of American Politics*, 2d rev. ed. (Garden City, N.Y., 1956); Cabell Phillips, *The Truman Presidency; The History of a Triumphant Succession* (New York, 1966); Jack Redding, *Inside the Democratic Party* (Indianapolis and New York, 1958); Adlai E. Stevenson, *The New America* (New York, 1957); Harry S. Truman, *Memoirs by Harry S. Truman*, 2 vols. (Garden City, N.Y., 1955); H. Bradford Westerfield, *Foreign Policy and Party Politics, Pearl Harbor to Korea* (New Haven, 1955); Theodore H. White, *The Making of the President 1960* (New York, 1961).

The Democratic Party
1960-1972

RICHARD C. WADE is Professor of History at the City University of New York. He is the author of *The Urban Frontier; Slavery in the Cities;* and *Chicago: Growth of a Metropolis.* He served as Illinois chairman for Kennedy for President in 1968 and New York chairman for McGovern for President in 1972.

The Democratic Party 1960-1972

by *Richard C. Wade*

"Let the word go forth from this time and place, to friend and foe alike," the young president asserted on that crisp, cold yet sunny day, "that the torch has been passed to a new generation of Americans—born in this century, tempered by war, disciplined by a hard and bitter peace, proud of our ancient heritage." The decade began with the inauguration of a Democratic administration bearing the promise of "getting the country moving again." Richard Nixon, one of the dominating figures of the 1950's, had been defeated; the new president, after due deference to the elder statesmen of his party, surrounded himself with fresh faces and crackling energy. Though the precise outlines of the impending era were vague, everyone assumed it would be different from the Republican years of Dwight Eisenhower.

Yet the period ended with the reelection of Richard Nixon by an overwhelming margin, leaving the Democratic party badly divided and in great distemper. In between lay twelve of the most turbulent years in American history. The young president and his brother had been assassinated; the historic frustrations of the nation's black community had erupted into intermittent violence; American troops were engaged in a bitter and losing war in Southeast Asia; a new generation came of age in a spirit of mutiny if not revolution. Society seemed both receptive to and yet fearful of change. Almost a hundred years before, Walt Whitman had described the historical situation. "Society remains unformed, it sits still between things just ended in things just begun."

If the years of the 1960's had been dangerous and agitated for the country, it had been more so for the Democratic party. Indeed, as the majority party in the country, in control of the White House for eight of the twelve years, it became the center of the treacherous winds that swept across a baffled nation.

Though the Republicans occupied the White House, the Democratic party entered 1960 with formidable resources. Every poll demonstrated a commanding lead over the GOP both in commitment and enrollment. After a good off-year election in 1958, the party handily controlled Congress—66 to 34 in the Senate and 283 to 154 in the House. Moreover, thirty-three Democratic governors indicated its breadth of state support; and finding a Republican mayor in a large city remained a research project. To be sure, the unity among these parts was generally illusory, but the party's success reflected the ability to adjust to local and regional diversity. The Democratic party was, in short, the country's only national party.

Nor was the party short of effective leadership. Adlai Stevenson, despite two losses to President Eisenhower, remained the party's dominant figure. His grip on the reformers continued, and regulars had come to understand, with a few exceptions, that he posed no threat to their control. And the public, which had rejected him for the highest office, respected his integrity and intelligence and even came to appreciate his wit and urbanity. In Congress, Senator Lyndon Johnson of Texas exercised almost unique power. Perhaps the century's most skilled legislator, he managed to accommodate both a Republican president and enough liberals to pass a moderate program during two Eisenhower administrations. Proposals might begin with the executive, but when signed into law they bore the imprint of the Senate's majority leader.

But it was the new forces which were to dominate the presidential year. To be sure, Senator Hubert Humphrey was no newcomer to the national scene, but 1960 was his first serious entry into the presidential sweepstakes. He had entered the Senate as the voice of the new postwar liberalism. A reform mayor of Minneapolis and a founder of Americans for Democratic Action in 1947, he became the focus of the congressional left, the spokesman for the liberal agenda. Yet over the decade, his genial personality and pragmatic politics had moved him into the Senate clubhouse; by 1958, he was majority whip and an associate, if not confidant, of Lyndon Johnson. In addition, long service and endless lunches and dinners had provided a national base in the labor, Jewish and black communities. In 1960, the base was there for a presidential effort.

The most intriguing figure of all, however, was the young senator from Massachusetts. Just forty-two years old, handsome, wealthy and intelligent, John F. Kennedy was probably already better known to the voters than Hubert Humphrey. His own Massachusetts organization had already elected him twice to the Senate, in 1958 by the largest margin in the state's history. The national public first saw him nominate Adlai Stevenson at the 1956 convention and then almost win the vice presidential spot when the candidate threw open the choice of a running mate to the delegates. For four years, he was the darling of the media, which delighted in covering (though not always favorably) every move of the family and every speech of the senator. His major political handicap was his religion—no Catholic had ever been elected president of the United States.

Moreover, underneath the old party leadership the new people brought into politics by Adlai Stevenson began to surface. Amateur clubs became increasingly professional; the wonderful abandon of 1952 had become firm day-to-day politics for thousands. In some places, like Philadelphia, new forces succeeded; in others, they harassed established leaders engaging in numberless primaries for local and state offices. The national committee recognized this fresh current by appointing the Democratic Advisory Council to issue policy statements between presidential elections. Though boycotted by southerners and congressional leaders, the DAC provided a public forum from which to attack the administration while keeping alive the party platform of 1956.

In addition, beneath the leadership were layers of imposing strength. One source was the trade union movement. Born in its present structure in the depression and expanded during the war, it became a central element of the party. On every level, labor leaders sat on policy committees, influenced patronage, and helped select tickets. Indeed, in some states like Ohio and Michigan, the Democratic party became almost the political appendage of the labor movement. In turn, the unions provided a vast and somewhat cohesive voting bloc; they furnished the money to carry on increasingly expensive campaigns, and often gave the manpower needed for registration drives and election day activity. Some, like the United Auto Workers in Detroit or the Teamsters in St. Louis, built block organizations which functioned as surrogate parties.

Another source lay in the urban minorities, both black and white. The New Deal had made them Democratic for a generation. The whites had been the major beneficiaries of unemployment insurance, social security, minimum wages and wartime jobs. The Democratic attachment was deep and seemed secure; and it was constantly expressed in local, state and national elections. Black support dated from 1936 when the group abandoned its old GOP moorings and went over to Franklin Roosevelt. The Democratic party in the North and West generally welcomed the newly converted and throughout the 1940's and 1950's it earned their backing by pressing for civil rights legislation and appointing blacks to important and highly visible positions in government. Together these urban minorities constituted a comfortable majority in almost every American city of over 100,000 people.

With the retirement of the extraordinarily popular Republican president, this Democratic strength was reassuring, but the weaknesses of the party were also impressive. Most obvious, of course, was the steady deterioration of Democratic organizations across the country. The old apparatus built under the umbrella of New Deal victories was simply getting old. "Our district meetings look like a social security gathering," a ward leader confided to John Kennedy as he worked his way across upstate New York in search of support for his candidacy. One local election after another in the 1950's contained the obituary of a noted machine. Some gave way to concerted reform attacks; others, like old soldiers, did not die but just faded away.

The attrition could be explained easily enough. The machine had been built on the vulnerability of large numbers of people. When jobs were scarce, the organization could find them; when ethnic discrimination in the private sector limited opportunity, public office, no matter how modest, provided some remedy; when individual problems became overwhelming, the local machine could often be of service; and in a world of growing anonymity, membership and participation in the local organization gave identity and dignity. Postwar conditions altered this context. Continuing prosperity, at least by depression standards, furnished jobs in private enterprise; in large sectors of the country, unions, not the machine, controlled employment; the whole panoply of New Deal programs created a floor of security for those old or out of work; individuals increasingly sought meaningful relations within reform clubs, trade unions or private associations.

In addition, the focus of patronage power slowly drifted toward Washington, leaving local organizations with a dwindling share of public jobs. By 1960, successful urban organizations had replaced the old chewed cigars with a "new breed" of broker/boss who could manage the emerging forces; yet even there, the old capacity to turn out the huge New Deal majorities was steadily limited.

The problem was compounded by the rise of the suburbs. The cliché of the 1950's was the dominance of "urban America," which conjured up images of the spread of concrete tenements and high-rise apartments. In fact, nearly all urban growth took place on the outer edges. Between 1950 and 1960 the percentage of the metropolitan population jumped from 89 million to 113 million, or 26 percent. These areas had been as Republican historically as the cities had been Democratic since 1932. While commentators always noted with amusement the overwhelming machine vote in a low-income city ward, they seldom noted similar statistics in the affluent election districts in the suburbs. "Out here," a Lake Forest, Illinois, GOP leader observed smugly, "only the retainers and domestics vote Democratic." Dwight Eisenhower had drawn his support from the crabgrass roots of the suburbs; any Republican candidate could count on huge majorities from the same places.

The Democratic party also suffered some ethnic losses. The most significant was the slippage among Irish Catholics. On the surface, they clung to the positions of visible power—county, state and national chairmanship for example. But the problem was there. Many Irish had joined the trek to the suburbs and floated in the tranquil waters of Republicanism. Some became wealthy and began to vote their pocketbooks rather than their political past. Senator Joseph McCarthy provided an easy bridge to the GOP for conservative Democrats who could rationalize their switch on the higher grounds of ideology (if they could overlook the lower ground of tactics). The attrition was discernible everywhere, often breaking family tradition. When an elderly Irish father heard that one of his sons had voted Republican, he asked incredulously, "Does he still go to Mass?" This Irish apostasy was visible in voting returns; it could also be seen in the emergence of Italians in positions of party and public power. DeSapio in New York, DiSalle in Ohio, Pastore in Rhode Island were all beneficiaries of the relative decline of the Irish.

The year 1960 began with the announcement by John F. Kennedy that he would seek the nomination of the Democratic party for president of the United States. "In the past forty months," he said on January 2, "I have toured every state in the Union and I have talked to Democrats in all walks of life. My candidacy is therefore based on the conviction that I can win both the nomination and election." The rest of the statement was designed to answer the question of his youth; it did not mention his Catholicism.

The task ahead was formidable. Hubert Humphrey had already announced his candidacy; Stuart Symington was snuggling up to the old Truman faction; Lyndon Johnson's friends circulated on his behalf while the majority leader stuck to his job in the Senate. Kennedy was, despite careful courting of party leaders for four years, still an outsider. Indeed, he could count on virtually none of his Senate colleagues. Moreover, the bulk of delegates would be hand-picked by a few power brokers in state committee meetings or rigged conventions. And over it all brooded the "religious question." Could a Catholic be elected president? The only route lay through the primaries to test this nagging issue and find out whether the party was ready for a new direction.

The crucial contests were Wisconsin and West Virginia. In no sense did either represent a cross section of the voters, much less enrolled Democrats. Yet Humphrey and Kennedy forces found that the central battleground for the nomination rested in two states with a total of twenty electoral votes. Kennedy's assets were his newness, his money, and his organization; Humphrey relied on his liberal record, old loyalties and labor support. Though generally outmatched, Humphrey almost ambushed Kennedy in Wisconsin. The Massachusetts senator won fifty-six percent of the popular vote and six of ten congressional districts, but this was below the general expectation. Hence, West Virginia became the testing ground. Overwhelmingly Protestant, with no large cities and a large labor vote, it would decide the nominatability of the young Catholic candidate. The results were conclusive: a Kennedy sweep. In a tearful farewell to his workers seen on television across the country, Humphrey withdrew from the race. The road to Los Angeles was now clear.

Or nearly so. When the convention opened, old Stevenson supporters launched a drive to stop Kennedy. The former standard bearer, with the blessings of Eleanor Roosevelt, received a tumultuous ovation on the convention floor during an unannounced appearance. Over a hectic day the anti-Kennedy forces tried to put together enough votes to move to a second ballot. Though there was every evidence that Kennedy would be stronger after the initial count, his backers pressed hard for a first ballot decision. It came at the tail end of the alphabet; Wyoming put the young senator across. In the acceptance speech, the new candidate struck the theme of the election—and the next administration:

> . . . I think the American people expect more from us than cries of indignation and attack. The times are too grave, the challenge too urgent, the stakes too high to permit the customary passions of political debate. We are not here to curse the darkness, but to light the candle that can guide us through that darkness to a safe and sane future. As Winston

Churchill said on taking office some 20 years ago: if we open a quarrel between the present and the past we shall be in danger of losing the future ... Today our concern must be with that future. For the world is changing. The old era is ending. The old ways will not do. . . .

... The problems are not all solved and the battles are not all won—and we stand today on the edge of a New Frontier—the frontier of the 1960's—a frontier of unknown opportunities and perils—a frontier of unfulfilled hopes and threats.

Woodrow Wilson's New Freedom promised our nation a new political and economic framework. Franklin Roosevelt's New Deal promised security and succor to those in need. But the New Frontier of which I speak is not a set of promises—it is a set of challenges. It sums up, not what I intend to offer the American people, but what I intend to ask of them. It appeals to their pride, not their pocketbook—it holds out the promise of more sacrifice instead of more security.

Can a nation organized and governed such as ours endure? That is the real question. Have we the nerve and the will? Can we carry through in an age where we will witness not only new breakthroughs in weapons of destruction—but also a race for mastery of the sky and the rain, the ocean and the tides, the far side of space and the inside of men's minds. . . .

It has been a long road . . . to this crowded convention city. Now begins another long journey, taking me into your cities and homes all over America. Give me your help—give me your hand—your voice and your vote.

The campaign and the election revealed a good deal about the party and the electorate. The primaries and the convention had left deep scars. Established leaders had been beaten (some thought run over); Stevensonian liberals were lukewarm when not hostile; the black community was wary and uncertain; despite Johnson's presence on the ticket, the South felt abandoned. Kennedy immediately began replacing the divots. He centralized the campaign within the Democratic National Committee, thus avoiding the worst conflicts that had afflicted Stevenson's effort in 1956. The senator's brother, Robert, became the campaign manager, hence relieving the candidate of a major role in operational work. Connecticut State Chairman John Bailey was dispatched to cruise among the regulars, and a citizen's committee organized the disaffected liberals and black leaders as well as stimulating volunteer activity. By October, the party achieved a greater cohesion than in previous campaigns.

The platform was directed to the reestablishment of what some called the old "New Deal Coalition," a collection of farmers, working people, minorities, intellectuals, and the "urban masses." It was not long, however, before it was clear that 1960 was not 1936 or even 1948. A trip across the rural areas of Iowa, Illinois and Indiana demonstrated that the farmers who voted for Truman were not coming to Kennedy. The relative decline of city population meant that even good majorities would not be enough to win. But the crowds were big at the outer edges of the city and in the inner suburbs and around the cloverleafs that dot the expressways between the airports and downtown. Victory required penetrating the suburbs or at least reducing traditional Republican margins.

The last days of the campaign symbolized the importance of the suburban vote. The Republicans exhumed former President Dwight Eisenhower and had him work the fringes of Philadelphia and Cleveland. John F. Kennedy abandoned the traditional Madison Square Garden rally to campaign by helicopter in the suburbs around New York City and Philadelphia. In a peculiar sense, the shopping center had become the battle ground of contemporary politics. When the results were in Kennedy had won by 112,000 votes out of over 38,000,000 votes cast—two-tenths of one percent. An analysis of the suburbs showed that he was the first Democrat to break into those communities. In the large metropolitan areas outside of the South he had contrived either slight majorities or broke even in the inner suburbs, those which abutted on the cities. Nixon, however, swept the outer suburbs with characteristic GOP majorities.

This new metropolitan consensus furnished the Democratic party with the opportunity of a generation of political power. If it could hold the cities and win the tangential suburbs, it could maintain its position as the majority party. A growing suburban crisis was bound to cut into GOP strength and dwindling rural population would necessarily reduce its other historic source of support. The narrowness of Kennedy's victory concealed this new pattern. National pollsters also missed the significance of this change by continuing to divide the population by age, sex, religion, occupation, income, education and ethnic and racial background rather than by residence. Yet the division between the enlarged center and the periphery continued to be the fundamental fact of American politics in an urban age.

The Kennedy victory, however, no matter how slim, ended the Catholic question with regard to the presidency. Whether his religion helped or hurt his candidacy is still being debated, but it was clear that Catholicism was no bar to the White House. Yet the issue no doubt affected congressional races. The Democrats suffered a net loss of two seats in the Senate and twenty-one in the House. The resultant alignment—64 to 34 and 263 to 175—did not appear to be damaging, but in brute terms it meant that the southern Democratic-GOP coalition was still in business. Worse still, successful northern congressmen ran substantially ahead of the national ticket, thus reducing the leverage usually a part of the president's bargaining power with the legislative branch.

Despite this fragile victory, Kennedy moved ahead with audacity and style. He reached beyond conventional limits in assembling his cabinet and administration. He had his share of professional politicians, but those like Robert McNamara came from the business world, still others from the academy. But most characteristic were a breed of "New Frontiersmen" whom he had assembled along the route to the presidency. Most were young, at least by previous standards—all abounded in confidence and energy, all believed that it was possible to "get the country moving again." There was even a physical stereotype—the men were lean, with short cut hair, in conservative clothes (though always found in shirtsleeves while on the job) and the telephone appeared as almost an appendage of the shoulder; the women were chic when not glamorous and always socially active.

Kennedy brought new blood into the Democratic party, but did little to reorganize its structure. John Bailey, an accomplished pro, became chairman of the National Committee; patronage was formally dispensed after consultation with local leaders though usually to those who had helped the president. The Kennedy influence, however, was not reflected in a wholesale restructuring of the party that many had hoped for and others feared. The Kennedy apparatus was awesome when operating for one of the family, but it was not easily transferable. Indeed, no Kennedy has been able to unify the party in Massachusetts, and later Robert Kennedy as senator came to despair of ever getting peace, much less substantial agreement, among the warring factions of New York.

The off-year election of 1962 provided a convenient gauge of the Kennedy impact on the party and electorate. It was not so much the administration's record that was at stake. The Bay of Pigs remained an embarrassment, but the roll-back on steel prices, the admission of blacks to universities in Alabama and Mississippi, the Alliance for Progress and the Peace Corps were all pluses among certain voting segments. And in the midst of the campaign itself, the Cuban missile crisis magnified the presidency above the congressional races. Yet it was the Kennedy "style" that began to work its magic. For the first time since 1934 the incumbent party held even in the off year. The gain of four in the Senate more than compensated for the loss of the same number in the House.

These figures could be partly explained by the relatively weak showing of Democrats in 1960; the party simply had less to lose. But it was the kind of winning candidate that revealed most. Philip Hoff became the first Democratic governor in Vermont in 100 years, John King won the state house and Thomas McIntyre a seat in the Senate from New Hampshire. Birch Bayh and Gaylord Nelson replaced elderly Republicans in the Senate from Indiana and Wisconsin. Five new representatives made the black contingent in the House the largest since 1874. Ticket-splitting was unusually heavy, leading analysts to conclude that younger, more articulate candidates in both parties reflected the new taste and growing independency of the electorate. Yet a genuine Kennedy majority would have to await the 1964 election when the popularity of the president would offer long coattails to a covey of "new breed" Democrats.

The year included some promising events. A limited nuclear test ban treaty with the Soviet Union and a proposal for joint Soviet-American space exploration reduced somewhat the chill of the Cold War. The president's personal popularity remained high. But the best Democrats could do on the domestic scene was to produce programs that were cut down by conservatives in Congress; these new proposals would be the platform for 1964. Yet the most fundamental issues in American life surfaced in the same year. Black frustration and rage spilled over into mass demonstrations, calmed only by the responsiveness of the president and heroic responsibility of such black leaders as Martin Luther King. Even more troublesome was the dispatch of American advisors to South Vietnam where civil war threatened the precarious peace established in Geneva almost ten years before. President Kennedy, both concerned and frustrated, decided to take his case to the country in the Fall.

An early trip to the West found a warm response; the president returned refreshed and reassured. The trip had been billed as nonpolitical with the theme of conservation. An excursion in November was more clearly political—to put together the fragmented parts of the Texas Democratic party. Guerilla warfare between its conservatives and liberals had reduced it to a shambles and put in jeopardy the electoral votes which had helped Kennedy in 1960. The vice president had been compromised by his relationship with the New Frontier; only, it was argued, the president could provide the mucilage. John F. Kennedy had won the nomination in a bitter party-splitting campaign; his last days were spent assuaging its differences.

The trip to downtown Dallas was like so many others. Slim turnouts near the airports grew denser as the motorcade headed downtown. Around the cloverleafs and at the overpasses people congregated as they had seen the route in the newspaper. Local sponsors and advance men relaxed—the crowd was there. Then suddenly it was like no other trip. Shots cracked out—the president pitched forward. The limousines suddenly accelerated and headed for the hospital. In a few brief moments, the historical context of a generation had been altered.

The assassination of the president drew the country together in grief. In a morbid irony, it also united the Democratic party. Lyndon Johnson had been the embodiment of the party establishment; he was now the heir of the Kennedy legacy as well. In that spirit, he announced at the outset, "let us continue," an extension of JFK's motto, "let us begin." For a time, the New Frontiersmen stayed, more out of loyalty and trauma than belief in the new president. The period of transition moved slowly but harmoniously. Old divisions and personal rivalries were for a time embalmed in national mourning.

Moreover, Johnson moved quickly to demonstrate that his commitment went beyond mere rhetoric. In a blinding display of legislative virtuosity, the executive branch began to push through Congress most of the agenda of the previous three years. The focus was initially domestic, designed to handle the problems that had risen slowly to the surface in the preceding decade. At Ann Arbor, Michigan, in May, 1964, the president gave conceptual shape to the new administration. "In our time we have the opportunity to move not only toward the rich society and the powerful society but upward to the Great Society. The Great Society rests on abundance and liberty for all, demands an end to poverty and racial injustice to which we are committed in our time." The New Frontier officially gave way to the Great Society; the transition from Kennedy to Johnson was completed with the election of 1964.

Actually, President Kennedy had been coaxing a Goldwater candidacy in 1963, skillfully goading the Arizona senator farther to the right while appropriating a large section of the center for himself. His successor continued the strategy sensing that the combination of an extreme conservative candidate on the Republican ticket and a united Democratic party was certain to assure an easy victory. The only remaining question was the vice presidency. In a way, Robert F. Kennedy seemed the logical choice. A Johnson/Kennedy ticket would be even more formidable than the Kennedy/ Johnson team of 1960. A little juggling of the theme—"the Great Frontier" or "the New Society"—would tie the administrations together. The campaign could combine freshness and nostalgia; the national committee could even retire its old debts. But the two men had never been close, and the president had always been wary of RFK's aggressive ambitions. Looking for a tidy way to avoid this distasteful arrangement, he archly announced that cabinet members should be above politics and none should be considered for the spot. "I am sorry I took so many nice fellows over the side with me," the Attorney General quipped when he heard of the president's nifty footwork.

With nothing much to do, the party met in a place devoted to doing nothing, Atlantic City. The party prepared for a coronation rather than a nomination; indeed the timing coincided with the president's birthday. It was surely the dullest convention in memory. "Atlantic City is the *real* Bay of Pigs," moaned a reporter. Johnson tried to give the event a little suspense by toying with the leading vice presidential aspirants—Thomas Dodd of Connecticut, Hubert Humphrey and Eugene McCarthy, both from Minnesota. A credentials struggle between the Mississippi Freedom Democratic party and the regulars briefly broke the ennui while raising a fundamental issue which would agitate 1968. Finally, the president announced that Hubert Humphrey would be his running mate, a choice designed to reassure the liberals that the dumping of Robert Kennedy did not represent a move away from its progressive past. With the ticket in shape and the platform adopted, the convention listened to a night devoted to the memory of John F. Kennedy, highlighted by a brief but moving eulogy by the slain president's brother which tearfully ended with the words from "Romeo and Juliet":

> . . . and when he shall die,
> Take him and cut him out in little stars,
> And he will make the face of heaven so fine,
> That all the world will be in love with night,
> And pay no worship to the garish sun.

The platform of 1964 updated that of 1960. The previous promises were now "four years of unrelenting effort and unprecedented achievement." There were few new ideas; rather, the emphasis lay on broadening existing policies in order to "cross the New Frontier and enter upon the Great Society." The party declared that the "42 months of uninterrupted expansion under Kennedy/Johnson" had been the "largest and strongest peace time prosperity in modern history." The foreign policy planks dwelt on peace: "The world is closer to peace today than it was in 1960," the party asserted, "international Communism has lost its unity and momentum." The document also bore down heavily on GOP candidate Goldwater. "One rash act, one thoughtless decision, one unchecked reaction," it warned, "and cities could become smoldering ruins and farms parched wasteland." And, as for extremism, the platform denounced it "whether from the Right or Left, including the extreme tactics of such organizations as the Communist Party, the Ku Klux Klan and the John Birch Society."

The election itself was uneventful. However, it permitted the Texan to break out of his regional base and become a genuinely national figure. Presenting himself as a man of peace and a great unifier, he painted Goldwater into a narrow Republican corner. Everywhere the crowds were immense. In Providence, Rhode Island, a half million people turned out to "come down and hear the speakin'" in a town of 208,000. Local candidates jostled to get a piece of the coattails. Election night the results indicated that Lyndon Johnson had won one of the largest victories in presidential history. Not only did he rack up 61.1 percent of the popular vote, but in Congress Democrats picked up two Senate and thirty-eight House seats. In the electoral college, he lost only Arizona and five southern states. The Republican defoliation was even more apparent in state legislatures where Democrats now controlled thirty-three governor's mansions and, even more remarkably, both Houses in thirty-two of them. The election of 1964 was not merely a landslide; it was an earthquake.

Democratic euphoria in the wake of 1964 was understandable. Even political analysts speculated on the disappearance of the GOP; after all, had not the Whigs gone the same way? Yet historians knew that death notices of great parties were nearly always premature. After the disaster of 1912 when President William H. Taft had run third, the Republican party came within an eyelash of beating incumbent President Woodrow Wilson four years later; Hoover overwhelmed Alfred E. Smith in 1928, but a Democrat replaced him in the next election; after the Roosevelt landslide in 1936 Wendell Willkie put on a respectable show in 1940. The compensating forces of the system would inevitably operate to redress the imbalance very quickly. The suburban explosion provided the GOP with a solid base for a future campaign, and less obviously, within the war in Southeast Asia lay a danger to the country and to the party foreseen in 1964 by only a very few. Yet everything seemed so secure and serene in the afterglow of the election.

The Johnson/Humphrey ticket in 1964 not only easily won an electoral victory, but it also significantly altered the Democratic party. On the surface, it seemed a tidy blend of the old liberalism and the old establishment. But essentially it took the leadership away from the Kennedy people, who had often operated independently of the old apparatus, and gave it back to more orthodox forces. The president was, of course, preeminently a party man; indeed, some polls had shown him the state and local leaders' favorite in 1960. He moved easily amidst "the boys," enjoyed the rituals which JFK had found so tiresome and loved nothing so much as delivering a rousing partisan speech at a Jefferson-Jackson Day banquet. The vice president, scarred by his primary defeats at the hands of the Kennedy forces, was a veteran of the labor, black and Jewish circuit and relished the fact that he had kept organized liberalism safe for Democratic purposes.

John Bailey remained as national chairman, thus maintaining the continuity with the New Frontier. But on the local level patronage flowed into the old channels. Soon the president assembled a new "team" and the Kennedy appointments returned home, some to their private affairs; many moved into the emerging quasi-public sector of the system—the foundations, universities, law firms "with a conscience," or corporations with a social planning dimension. Those with political ambitions left Washington to carve out elective careers of their own. Robert Kennedy led the way by winning a Senate seat from New York; others headed for Congress or state legislatures, and a surprising number reflected JFK's growing interest in urban questions by running for councilman or mayor.

The Democratic party was now a mixture of Johnson power and Kennedy programs and, backed by nearly forty new northern Democratic congressmen swept in by the anti-Goldwater landslide, the combination did spectacularly in Congress. In 1965, it doubled the appropriations for poverty programs, passed the most extensive education bills in history, accepted Medicare, changed the long-standing immigration bill, and adopted the Voting Rights Act. Moreover, Congress began to address itself directly to the problems of cities, voting increasing sums for urban renewal and housing and taking the first steps to federalize air and water pollution control. To signal this new domestic direction and give credibility to his civil rights convictions, Johnson appointed the first Negro to serve in a presidential cabinet as Secretary of Housing and Urban Development.

But each new piece of legislation took its toll on the Johnson majority. While redeeming a promise to one group, the administration often alienated another. And since much of the new enactments benefitted central cities, whites increasingly equated the Great Society with black preference. This became especially marked when black frustration, not wholly abated by new attention and future promises, spilled over into violence in a dozen cities across the nation. By 1966, the electorate called a halt to new legislation by exhuming the presumably dead Republican party. The GOP picked up three seats in the Senate and forty-seven in the House. In terms of the old southern Democratic and Republican conservative coalition, the score was now 278 to 157 northern Democrats. Richard Nixon may have exaggerated when he called this the "sharpest rebuff of a President in a generation," but even the most optimistic Democrat admitted that the giddiness induced by the 1964 landslide was over.

More ominous for the party than the Republic resurgence in 1966 was the escalation of the war in Vietnam. In 1964 the president had campaigned on the pledge of "no wider war" in Southeast Asia, but as months went by, American involvement became deeper and deeper. By the Summer of 1967, over 450,000 troops had been committed to the conflict. Bombing began modestly, but it soon surpassed the proportions of Allied operations over Europe and Japan in World War II. At the outset, the president enjoyed widespread backing in what was understood as an effort to contain Chinese Communism by supporting South Vietnam, but as the war dragged on with no visible end this backing started to erode. By 1968, the evening TV "body count" included not just the large Viet Cong losses, but also American casualties reaching into five figures. As the debate developed, a bitterness seeped into American politics which afflicted the discussion of almost every issue, domestic as well as foreign.

The war was only the most obvious question facing the country and its dominant party. As dangerous and vexing was racial division. The searing resentment of black Americans against three centuries of slavery and second class citizenship had already erupted into rioting and bloodshed. Though it was the young who threw the rocks and pillaged the stores, every public opinion poll indicated that most older blacks identified themselves with the rioters, not with white society. And while the poor in the ghettoes hit the streets first, the children of successful blacks livened up college campuses. In the mid-1960's, black Americans tried to make it clear that they would settle for nothing less than the full measure of justice—and very soon if not immediately.

Another division threatening the social fabric was the widening gap between young and old. Of course, this tension had always been there, but two new conditions in the 1960's dangerously aggravated relations. The first stemmed from the postwar educational revolution which created a new class of college students and graduates. At the turn of the century only about five percent of the nation's youth went to college; by the 1960's, almost half went to some institution of higher learning. Neither parents nor universities were prepared for the social consequences of that change. Secondly, it was the youth who were asked to fight a war they had not made and increasingly opposed. Unable to vote, they resorted to mass demonstrations, harrassment and sit-ins to influence public policy. The rhetoric was usually extravagant but it was built on widespread alienation.

The relations between rich and poor also worsened in the decade. It was not, however, because there were more poor people than before. In fact, the proportionate numbers had never been so few. What made the issue so explosive was the country's affluence, not its want. In a nation enjoying unprecedented wealth, any need on a large scale seemed intolerable, even to the successful. Moreover, with the attendant publicity, the poor themselves came around to the belief that their misery sprang not from themselves but rather from external, often governmental, sources. And since a large number of the poor were black and young, this problem magnified other divisions in American society.

The debate on these national problems took place almost exclusively within the Democratic party. Bearing the responsibility of power, the administration became the storm center of each controversy and increasingly the president himself was caught up in the conflicting winds. The Republican party remained strangely immune and aloof. It had few poor, blacks or young to lose, and, with only occasional exceptions, GOP leaders were hawkish on the war. Hence, the turbulence of the entire nation centered on one party and its presidential choice in 1968.

At the outset it seemed that there would be no contest. President Johnson was in full control of the formal party machinery; he had the support of labor; and his domestic accomplishments seemed to protect his liberal flank. A few, like the youth leader Allard Lowenstein, toyed with the idea of a symbolic gesture of opposition to the war by running a peace candidate in the primaries. Senators Robert Kennedy and George McGovern turned down the invitation, the former because he thought it would look too much like a personal vendetta against Johnson, the South Dakotan because he had a hard fight for reelection in his own state. Finally, Eugene McCarthy agreed to make the race. Though a senator for nearly two decades, he had been overshadowed by his Minnesota colleagues, Hubert Humphrey and Orville Freeman. Nationally, most knew him for his eloquent nomination of Adlai Stevenson in 1960 at Los Angeles.

At first no one really was happy about the decision and even McCarthy seemed only to be going through the motions. Five weeks after the decision, Robert Kennedy said he did not think the candidacy would "further the cause of peace" and asserted his neutrality, adding that he expected Johnson to win. On January 30, he asserted that there were "no foreseeable circumstances" which would impel him to oppose the president. But soon the young people began to flock into New Hampshire and suddenly a campaign came into being. The cause began to shape the candidate: quickly it became clear there was a contest.

On March 14, McCarthy scored a stunning upset. Though he had not actually defeated Johnson, he had come within a few percentage points of doing so and had demonstrated the strength of anti-war sentiment, at least in New England. The results of New Hampshire had scarcely been recorded when Robert Kennedy shed his caution and announced he was "reassessing" his own position. A few days later his candidacy became official. Opposition to the president was now enhanced by the celebrated Kennedy mystique and the family's immense resources. Moreover, it took the campaign away from its simple anti-war focus by adding RFK's growing commitment to wide-scale social change at home.

The McCarthy and Kennedy candidacies presented Johnson with a formidable problem. To win renomination would take a gigantic effort and even then success was not assured. Meanwhile, the war and the prospects of another "long, hot summer" put the nation's problems on his desk every day. On March 31, on the eve of the Wisconsin primary, he stepped aside. In his announcement he alluded to a "divided nation" and expressed the hope that his action might bring an end of the war a little closer. New Hampshire had upset every conventional calculation; the Johnson withdrawal introduced a new measure of chaos into American politics.

From March to June, McCarthy and Kennedy fought for the nomination through the obstacle course of state primaries. Humphrey, Johnson's heir apparent, finessed most of them by waiting twenty-eight days to announce his candidacy. Kennedy won all the contested elections, except Oregon, but their broader significance rested in the fact that in each case the spokesmen for change defeated regular party figures. Whether it was Governor Roger Branigan in Indiana or Senator Humphrey in South Dakota, identification with the Johnson administration brought conclusive defeat at the polls.

Part of the Kennedy success stemmed from his prestige in the black community. Some of that popularity was inherited from his brother, but most of it he earned for himself. Not only had he supported the claim of Negroes to genuine equality in the face of the white backlash, but he had tried to do something about it in the Bedford-Stuyvesant project in New York City. RFK was, in short, the only significant white link to the nation's embittered blacks. This situation became even more obvious in April when the Reverend Martin Luther King was shot to death in Memphis by a white assassin. The Atlanta minister was easily the most powerful figure in black America. The most eloquent spokesman of nonviolence, he had led the successful integration of buses in Montgomery, Alabama, and, later, the freedom march on Washington in 1963. He was in Memphis on a characteristic mission—supporting underpaid public garbage collectors. Standing on the balcony of a motel, he was cruelly struck down by a shotgun blast.

Blacks around the country seethed in anger and frustration. Rioting broke out in several cities. Everywhere militants of both races who opposed Dr. King's nonviolence exploited the event as the inevitable result of intractable white racism. That midnight Robert Kennedy kept a campaign date before a crowd of young Negroes on a playground in Indianapolis. Explaining that he knew only too well their feelings at the moment, he counseled patience and understanding. A stunned and anxious nation breathed easier as calm returned and once again the funeral of a political leader brought people briefly together.

Two months later, he too was dead—and by an assassin's bullet. Once again, a saddened nation had lost one of its most promising leaders. In despair, the historian Arthur M. Schlesinger, jr. told a graduating class that "the United States has become the most frightening country on earth." The black community, already reeling under the shock of Dr. King's death, saw the remaining symbol of hope pulled away. For the anti-war young an election that had come so alive in the snows of New Hampshire died suddenly on a steaming night in Los Angeles. Everywhere a sullen gloom settled over the land.

What looked like a certain Kennedy nomination now clearly would go to Hubert Humphrey. McCarthy had been accumulating delegates along the primary trail as well as in the complicated caucuses and conventions of most states, but he was far short of the target. Yet this was 1968 and uncertainties remained for the vice president. Senator George McGovern entered the race when the Kennedy delegates, whom most expected would go to either of the leading candidates, refused to budge. He was the most legitimate "dove" in the Senate, having warned the nation of the consequences of the Vietnam policy as early as 1963. Moreover, he had served in the Kennedy administration and had been close to all the Kennedys for over a decade. It was a measure of the unpredictable year that a virtually unknown senator from South Dakota could be a serious force in the convention in only eighteen days. An abortive attempt to draft Senator Edward Kennedy further underlined Humphrey's problem in Chicago.

In addition, all the divisive issues of the day were fully aired and debated on the floor of the convention. The question of civil rights arose in the Credentials Committee where the seating of southern delegations involved racial discrimination. The Rules Committee confronted the "new politics" on the unit rule and the legitimacy of the selection procedures in most of the states. And, of course, the minority plank on Vietnam put the administration war policy to a vote. At every step the bitterness engendered by the long pre-convention campaign flowed through caucuses and committee meetings.

Outside the convention hall, things were even less orderly. Demonstrators and police clashed in a dozen places, turning the lakefront parks and back streets into a virtual battleground. What later came to be called the "Chicago riot" was surely the most fully covered event in American history, yet what happened remains the subject of continuing controversy. Whatever the ultimate judgment, the episode was a nagging reminder of the enormous strain which the events of 1968 placed on the democratic process. For the system depends on permitting dissent without disruption and maintaining order without repression. The balance has always been delicate; it broke down in August, 1968 in Chicago.

Everyone suffered–demonstrators and police included–but the major casualty was Hubert Humphrey. The candidate of the discredited administration and a divided party, he went into the election with staggering handicaps. Nixon, on the other hand, led a united GOP. Though he had been widely thought to be a divisive figure in his twenty years of public life, he now went to the people as the voice of moderation and reconciliation. The campaign of the major parties was without great interest. Only the extraordinary gaffes of Republican vice presidential candidate Spiro T. Agnew of Maryland and the general attractiveness of Edmund Muskie, Humphrey's running mate, provided the public with good copy.

But 1968 did not allow the election to end so calmly. A third candidate increasingly dominated the campaign. George Wallace, the former governor of Alabama, entered as the candidate of the American Independent party. In his own way, he too represented the alienation of the times. He appealed to a large number of those who, no less than blacks and young people, felt neglected by public policy. Southern whites, blue collar and skilled workers, the middle level clerks and small businessmen, the emergent immigrant groups, and those resenting the pressure of blacks and the young for greater power found in Wallace someone who, from their point of view, "told it like it was." To be sure Wallace was more a caricature of their attitude than an authentic spokesman. But lacking any other figure in whom they had confidence, they permitted Wallace to mount the most serious threat to the two party system in a generation. Indeed, it looked for a time that he might precipitate a constitutional crisis by throwing the election into the House of Representatives.

The election, however, ended in a burst of anticlimax. A late Humphrey surge cut Nixon's early margin to a fraction of one percent (43.4 percent to 42.7 percent); and Wallace though receiving 9,900,000 votes (13.5 percent) wound up as essentially a southern candidate. A year which had demanded new directions and change ended with a president-elect who had been around for twenty years and had never been associated with a fresh or new idea. Worse still, he had been early a hawk on the Vietnam war, received less than one vote out of ten among the blacks and had no connections with the restless young. All the issues which had made 1968 the most turbulent year in recent history lay untouched by the outcome of the election. The tide had risen but it had not turned.

The apparent closeness of the 1968 election obscured the real situation of the Democratic party. On the surface all that seemed necessary was time to let the old wounds heal and permit a Nixon administration to reunify the party. But the divisions were deep, and the loss of the White House removed the focus which had kept a tolerable peace since 1960. Fortunately, the convention had created vehicles for the orderly incorporation of new elements into the party structure. The primaries of 1968 had demonstrated the power not only of the war issue, but the broad extent of the reform surge. Indeed, within the convention the delegates had adopted a mandate for party change at the same time that the majority had voted down the "peace plank." Ironically, the long-term legacy of

1968 was not the attempt to end the war in Vietnam but to bring peace to the party.

In December, National Chairman Fred Harris appointed Senator George Mc-Govern as chairman of the Committee on Delegate Selection and Party Reforms and Congressman James O'Hara to head the committee to establish new rules for the internal conduct of the 1972 convention. The South Dakotan was chosen because he had been both an advocate of reforms and a skilled party organizer. O'Hara's credentials stemmed from his own well-known liberalism and his long concern with party affairs. The mandate for both commissions was broad though their authority was somewhat vague. Yet the historic significance was clear; for the first time the national committee of a major party would function as something beyond a holding company for fifty separate state organizations. The subtle movement from confederacy to national party had begun.

Senator McGovern's first act was to appoint Senator Harold Hughes of Iowa as vice chairman. As a McCarthy supporter, Hughes had made the first serious examination of the delegate selection process in 1968 and he continued to represent the interests of McCarthy followers for party change. His presence reassured proponents of the "new politics," just as the inclusion of many regulars, such as Will Davis of Texas, that the commission's work would draw on all elements of the party. Senator Edmund Muskie was represented by his national committeeman, George Mitchell; Vice President Hubert Humphrey could count on representative Donald Frazier of his home state; Adlai Stevenson III brought the voice of the large residual groups in the party which his father had inspired; Dr. Aaron Henry of Mississippi, Louis Martin of Chicago and Earl Graves of New York spoke for the deep interest in reform of the blacks while Albert A. Peña of Texas provided a Spanish-speaking perspective. David Mixner, a McCarthy delegate to the Chicago convention who had been injured in a confrontation with the police, argued the interests of the young. However, the women, who constituted half of the party, found representation in only three members.

Over the commission's deliberation hovered the forbidding clouds of 1968. The bitterness of anti-organization feeling, lodged deep in the staff, surfaced in the hearings throughout the country, although it was usually tempered by the cooperation of local party figures or important Democratic spokesmen. The principal concern was to make certain that the party did not suffer another 1968 in 1972. "Unless changes are made," Senator McGovern warned, "the next convention will make the last look like a Sunday school picnic by comparison." The remedy seemed clear; reform or continued disintegration. Indeed, much of the testimony related more to past disputes rather than future prospects. There was throughout a compensatory atmosphere, an attempt to atone for 1968. This fact accounts for some of the most significant provisions in the guidelines.

The controversy over internal procedures was easily resolved. The 1968 convention outlawed the unit rule. In one sharp stroke, this eliminated one of the most objectionable practices both in the selection of delegates and in voting on the floor. No longer would it be possible for a majority to bind the minority in caucuses and conventions; no longer could a full delegation vote the lesser numbers on the convention floor. Perhaps Texas was the best illustration of the changes. In 1968, Mc-Carthy groups had accumulated a significant number of delegates at conventions held in state senatorial districts. But that minority was wiped out at the congressional district level, and ultimately almost a third of the voters lost their influence in the process when all of Texas's votes responded to the wishes of the establishment (and conservative forces). Though some argued that the California "winner-take-all" primary violated the unit rule prohibition, there was no effort to restore this undemocratic device.

In pursuance of other convention decisions the McGovern Commission began its work with a series of hearings held across the country. Although some states and local chairmen were hostile, the meetings permitted an accumulation of testimony from diverse groups about the actual workings of the delegate selection process. While most of the testimony came from the practitioners of the "new politics," suggestions for reform came from some unexpected sources. For example, Mayor Richard J. Daley, presumably the symbol of the status quo, argued for a wider primary system, including a provision that no candidate could be placed in nomination who had not entered at least one third of the primaries. (This provision would have excluded Hubert Humphrey in 1968. "If we had known how weak he was, we would not have chosen him," the mayor said privately, "the primaries would have shown that.") Other witnesses advocated everything from a national primary to the abolition of conventions altogether.

But the bulk of the testimony revolved around the capriciousness of the delegate selection system. In some states, delegates were chosen the year of the convention, in others, they were chosen one or even two years before the convention year. In some places it was governed by statute, especially in primary states; in others, complicated caucus and convention practices were created under party rules; still other states used a mixture of these forms. Moreover, within each category, practices varied widely. Some illustrations will suggest the wide range. At one end was California, where the candidates established slates and ran statewide, the winner getting the entire delegation. In Wisconsin, delegates ran from congressional districts and the candidates garnered whatever they could from each unit. In Illinois, two delegates were selected from each congressional district, but a state party convention chose the remainder which amounted to over half of the total. Similar disparities existed in caucus and convention states. A state like Iowa had a three-tier system which began early in the year and lasted three months; Rhode Island did its business in one day. State legislatures vied with each other to make their primary (in New Hampshire's case) the first or (New York's) last. The Commission highlighted what presidential campaign staffs had learned the hard way since 1952.

In some states, the rules governing the creation of delegate slates were never written or could not be found; in others, both the rules and statutes were consistently violated; in most, a process had grown up with the sanction of tradition rather than of the law or formal party rules. The system, if it could be called that, was sustained largely because no one seemed interested in or willing to contest it. But beginning with the Mississippi challenge in 1948, each convention had to grapple with an increasing number of credentials fights. These struggles more and more dominated the public's assessment of the party and its conduct. And, on the state level, a fight at the national convention left scars that could not easily be healed. At the hearings, the McGovern commission listened to the re-runs of battles fought over the past decade. It was clear that the 1968 convention, whatever its other faults, had been correct in insisting on clear and fair, if not uniform, rules governing the selection of delegates.

The hearings also emphasized the trickery and chicanery which surrounded the whole process. Caucuses were often not publicized at all, or were held in unfamiliar places, sometimes even in the home of the county chairman or district committeeman. Slate making usually took place in the inner recesses of the party organization rather than on the floor of local conventions. Party money was spent to pit one set of Democrats against another; organizational power was turned against one faction or used to promote another. Leaders often manipulated the hours of voting or the location of booths. Election commissioners capriciously approved or invalidated petitions; arbitrary regulations favored party operatives over newcomers. Almost everywhere the pattern was clear; statutes, rules and traditions favored those who made them and transformed primary contests for delegates to the national convention into an obstacle course for the uninitiated.

What was not so quickly comprehended, however, was that in establishing convention guidelines the national party would force state parties to change their rules and open up their organizations to new elements. Though ostensibly covering only the selection of delegates every four years, the McGovern Commission forced state parties to establish and publicize rules governing their own practices. The new regulations covered the years between conventions and provided the legal framework for their everyday affairs. The establishment of national standards resulted in reforms all across the country and substantially altered the nature and composition of the party. Recalcitrant state organizations were certain to face not only exclusion from the convention but also court cases on other internal controversies as well. In seeking a fairer national convention, the McGovern Commission had reached into the conduct of every state party. "If you want a national Democratic party superceding state party sovereignty," Will Davis, the shrewd national committeeman from Texas asserted during one Commission session, "then let us say so." Dr. Aaron Henry, beleaguered for years in a liberal Mississippi compound quickly agreed, "We are the only people in my state who consistently support the national ticket. We cannot endorse racist, reactionary state candidates; either we are a part of a national party or we have to cease being Democrats."

Two central questions needed to be resolved: first, the procedures of selection should be made clear and fair; second was the assurance of a broader representation of those who felt aggrieved—especially the blacks, Spanish-speaking, women and youth. The former occasioned a great deal of work, but little controversy; the second contained problems of both the greatest magnitude and finest delicacy.

The apportionment guidelines caused trouble first because it required a definition of the word "Democrat." The issue could be easily stated: delegates to the national convention came from states, but should they be pro-rated according to the general population, party memberships, Democratic voters, or some combination of these factors? Since no one wanted the first option, the problem revolved around defining a Democrat. This had never been done before on a national level. Enrollment was early discarded because of the wide variations in practice throughout the country.

In addition, a large number of southern Democrats quite obviously had ceased voting for their presidential candidate long ago, and to reward them with extra delegates would sanction disloyalty. Others thought the best criterion was the last gubernatorial election, thus strengthening state organizations and in some instances permitting a later reading of party support in the off year. These devices were ultimately discarded in favor of calculating each state's share of the convention by a combination of all its population and the share of the total vote cast for the last presidential candidate. Though it seemed modest at the time, this decision marked another step away from state confederacy to a national party, since the national committee, not state organizations or statutes, now defined a "Democrat."

The proportionality plank harbored even greater difficulties and ultimately greater danger. Critics of the 1968 convention had pointed out that one of its problems was the unrepresentative character. Women, young people, blacks and Latins had few delegates, hence their special concerns—the war, civil rights and poverty— could not get a fair hearing. Moreover, it was argued that though these groups did not constitute a voting majority, they did comprise a disproportionate share of the party's supporters. The Commission was charged with finding ways to increase their representation in 1972. The members treaded warily through this mine field, knowing full well the notion smacked of quotas. Yet somehow the convention had to be made more representative of the party's constituent parts and those historically aggrieved. The phrase "reasonable relationship" to their share of the population was finally adopted even though Commission members insisted that no quota system was being established. Nonetheless, they had unwittingly placed a thorn in the party's side which was to irritate and fester in 1972.

Another part of the rules changes mandated at Chicago concerned the internal governance of the convention. There had always been charges of unfairness: the chairman's gavel was too quick or his hearing too slow, debate was inadequate, committee reports came too late for serious consideration, Wyoming delegates envied Alabama in the roll call. There was also a general backlash against the highjinks on the floor—the contrived demonstration, the jockeying for the attention of TV cameras, the swarm of non-delegate hangers-on, and somewhat paradoxically, excessive absenteeism. Convention practices had grown up with little attention or thought even without formal codification. The demand for reform was almost universal and the 1968 convention was happy to turn it over to what came to be known as the O'Hara Commission. Significantly, its 1972 printed report was entitled "call to order."

The bulk of the O'Hara recommendations were quickly accepted by the National Committee and later by the convention itself. Yet the most significant part of its report was put off until later. The Commission drew up a charter for the national party which was to be submitted to the delegates for adoption. The Rules Committee at Miami, however, recommended another look, and the convention (in some confusion to be sure) charged the DNC with the task of drawing up a new charter. But the original draft contained a provision which proposed a quiet revolution in the history of the party—a membership clause. Previously citizens became Democrats by enrolling in a state party or, more vaguely, by supporting candidates appearing on the Democratic line. The new charter provided a more precise definition—an authorized card. Out of the loose coalition of states, a national party was slowly emerging. More than delegate selection, more than the conduct of a convention, this movement signified a radical change in the country's two party system.

The elections of 1970 provided the first opportunity to see how deep the wounds of 1968 had been. The most sensational part of an otherwise lackluster campaign was the unleashing of Vice President Spiro Agnew on what he called "radic-libs"—established Democratic figures as Albert Gore, Edward Kennedy, Edmund Muskie, William Proxmire, and Harrison Williams. The president made an intemperate entrance into the contests in the last few days revealing, once again, that if you scratch the "new" Nixon you find the "old." While most of the targets survived a few did not. On the national level the party did less well than is customary for the "outs." A loss of two in the Senate and a gain of nine in the House was considerably lower than early predictions. But the appearance of some familiar names among the newcomers, Adlai Stevenson III from Illinois and John Tunney of California, softened even those blows.

The gubernatorial results furnished better reading. The Democrats picked up eleven state houses, the best record of either party since 1938. Inevitably in the larger states the new governors took on some national significance. Milton Schapp in Pennsylvania and John Gilligan of Ohio immediately drew attention because of the size of their states; and Dale Bumpers of Arkansas because he beat Winthrop Rockefeller and Reubin Askew because of his moderation in the conservative state of Florida. This control on the state level also had a long-range importance for the federal census, for the "one man—one vote" principle meant that redistricting would take place in these states under Democratic auspices.

But the election solved no internal party problems. The DNC still had a ten million dollar debt from the 1968 election, and the factionalism had been papered over but not removed. Most of the prominent leaders had now abandoned the war, but the platform of 1968 could not, of course, be repealed. Finally late in the year, Senator Fred Harris, the national chairman, resigned, saying he wanted to be "free of the constraints which apply to the job." No eager line of applicants for the post appeared. After three days of meetings the committee succeeded in drafting Lawrence O'Brien who had close ties to both the Kennedy and Humphrey camps. Moreover, he had privately and publicly committed himself to the reforms of both the McGovern and O'Hara Commissions ("they're my survival kit," he wryly observed).

The election of 1970 provided a favorable preview for the task of the new McGovern reforms. Senator Hubert Humphrey came back to the Senate from Minnesota—and back in the presidential sweepstakes. Senator Muskie enhanced his party and national standing by his cool, rational television statement on the eve of the congressional election. In addition, on the wide margins of the party stood a covey of new faces toying with the notion of seeking the presidential nomination. Senator Fred Harris of Oklahoma, who had made the original organization rounds as co-manager of the Humphrey effort in 1968, strengthened his position by his service as head of the National Democratic Committee. Senator Harold Hughes of Iowa offered both the credentials of a reformer and the most imposing speaking voice in the profession. Birch Bayh, Indiana's junior senator, brought youth and good labor connections to his ambitions. In the long run, of course, the most important prospect was George McGovern. His brief candidacy in 1968 had left a favorable impression and furnished him with a small but dedicated organization. Most of all, his chairmanship of the McGovern Commission gave him an intimate knowledge of the new regulations which would govern the selection of delegates.

Fittingly enough, the first candidate to announce for the nomination was the South Dakota senator. On January 18 he met the national press after a brief announcement in his home state. Explaining that his slim resources and relative obscurity required a long campaign, McGovern announced he would test the new regulations governing delegate selection. The logic behind his candidacy was that he was the only candidate (since Edward Kennedy insisted he would not run) who could pre-empt a fourth party on the left and at the same time be acceptable to the regulars. His own constituency was modest. His long opposition to the involvement in the Vietnam war made him pre-eminent in the anti-war movement; his association with the Kennedys made him the logical non-family inheritor of a potent if tragic legacy. Less known was an extraordinary personal self-confidence which made formidable obstacles look somehow manageable.

George McGovern never doubted the wisdom of the early announcement. But nearly everyone else thought it premature. Some newspapers even refused to assign reporters to what was certain to be a long—and for them—an expensive campaign. Politicians talked of over-exposure and voter apathy. A small staff was assembled and early mailings brought in a surprisingly large amount of money. Patiently a grassroots organization began to take shape, especially in the states with the most significant primaries.

McGovern's financing was as unconventional as the early announcement. He took his case to thousands, indeed perhaps a million, small contributors rather than relying on the traditional large donors (he had only a few of these anyway). Utilizing the techniques of mass mailing, he flooded the postal system with pleas to those who had given to liberal causes before or who had previously supported his attempts to end the war. Others responded to newspaper advertisements or numberless small gatherings and rallies. Ultimately he raised over $30 million, eighty percent of it from contributions averaging twenty-five dollars apiece. Moreover, he managed to run a twenty month campaign without accumulating a debt. This system, liberating a candidate from dependence on large givers or big labor, may do more in the future to open up the party than the McGovern Commission guidelines themselves.

The early supporters came from those who supported McCarthy and Kennedy and were attracted to a campaign which seemed like an extension of 1968. Most significant, however, was the simple fact that these activists were four years older, many had never held any position that was unconnected with politics. They were the "new pros." Too young to have become important in regular party affairs and too experienced after the 1968 campaign to begin at the bottom of established Democratic organizations, they sought a professional outlet for their careers. A McGovern campaign was tailor-made for this purpose: a chance to combine their residual idealism and career-oriented employment.

The South Dakotan's scenario (for that was the operative word of the year) was simple. As the chairman of the McGovern Commission, he was committed to the primary route. Since over twenty states now had primaries, he selected the historic corridor to the nomination—New Hampshire, Wisconsin, Massachusetts, Nebraska, Oregon, California, and New York. Anyone who won that set, it was calculated, could not be denied the nomination. It was anticipated that new primaries would be adopted, but the public would fix on those which had been traditional testing grounds. It was also assumed that though initially there would be a host of candidates, the real contest lay in two phases: McGovern v. Muskie at the outset; McGovern versus Humphrey at the end. The breaking point would be Wisconsin; after that the Maine senator would recede and the former vice president would come on strong. And in the end, Democrats across the country would choose the new over the old.

The press and the public were skeptical. Yet the only portion of the scenario that went awry was the prediction that McGovern would slowly rise in the polls as he became better known and as he racked up primary victories. Until California, he seldom scored better than five percent. Otherwise the plan moved ahead almost like clockwork. Hughes and Harris formally announced their candidacy; Bayh and his fellow Indiana senator Vance Hartke followed; Wilbur Mills of Arkansas let it be known he was available; Henry Jackson of Washington came in from the right and Mayor John Lindsay of New York, a converted Republican, entered from the left; McCarthy remained coy but fitfully active. Without any entrance fee, the presidential nomination became the largest political tournament in memory.

But the number of candidates was illusory and most were predicated on a deadlocked convention. But, the party had not gone beyond one ballot since 1952, and it was even less likely to do so now that the number of primaries had increased. The early favorite was the senator from Maine. He had been the most impressive figure of the 1968 campaign; he was a centrist, acceptable to large segments of the party; and he held a commanding lead over all the others in public opinion polls. His weaknesses— a low key but high-strung personality, a respectable but undistinguished legislative record, and early support of the war—seemed almost suited to the public mood. He quickly established a large national staff, shrewdly picking and choosing from the various factions of the party. Later, in a moment of inexplicable expansiveness, he announced he would enter all of the primaries.

Senator Humphrey's problems were difficult yet simpler. The viability of his campaign rested on the decline of Muskie. He already had a skeleton national staff and supporters who had been with him for nearly two decades. He remained the favorite of labor, Jews, blacks and a large portion of the regulars. And in the polls, his ratings always hovered between seventeen and twenty percent of declared Democrats. Moreover, by 1972 he had edged away from the Vietnam involvement and joined the doves in Senate resolutions. Yet his chance at the brass ring depended on Muskie stumbling along the primary route.

Wallace became more a factor in the Democratic primary process than had early been anticipated. Most analysts assumed he would enter scattered states as he had done before and then opt for a third party again. This seemed especially logical because Nixon became a competitor (despite rumors of deals) in Dixie through his "southern strategy," which seemed like a raid on Wallace's natural constituency. But over the decade, Wallacism, if not the personal following of the Alabama governor, had seeped into the North. Blue collar factory workers and white collar clerks, small businessmen and old people had adopted his public posture if not his programs. With his cry against Washington bureaucrats, permissive courts, and public officials, radical intellectuals, and big interests generally, he tapped the anxieties and fears of millions. He had not counted in the primaries of 1968; he played a central role in 1972.

In March, the scenario began to unfold. Muskie carried his neighboring state of New Hampshire but by much less than expected. The road show then hit Florida and Illinois both with a larger number of delegates than New Hampshire or Wisconsin combined. McGovern did badly in both, but had committed himself only modestly in each state. Indeed, he came in fifth in the first contest and won only 13 out of 181 delegates in the second. But the attention had been on other candidates. Wallace walked away with Florida and Muskie disposed of McCarthy in Illinois.

Wisconsin became the crucial test for Muskie and McGovern. It would be, too, for Mayor Lindsay, but no one had taken his ambitions for the top position seriously. ("You don't make a new parishioner Pope the first year," cracked an old line Democrat in March.) McGovern's campaign had centered on this state from the beginning and his organization had been carefully built for eighteen months. Muskie was spread too thinly, and allowed other candidates to pick up experienced operatives along the way. McGovern carried the state handily; Muskie and Lindsay were crushed. But Wallace, with virtually no campaigning at all, ran a strong second. For the senator from Maine, it was the end of the road; the only question remaining was the timing of the withdrawal. Lindsay dropped out immediately; he had received only seven percent of the vote in a liberal state.

Defeats in the primaries and unpromising prospects pulled most of the contenders from the pack. Then an assassin's bullet removed George Wallace. He was walking through a crowd of supporters in a Maryland shopping center when he was gunned down by a young man wearing a Wallace hat and sporting other campaign paraphernalia. Though not killed, he was hospitalized for weeks and paralyzed from the waist down. The nation was stunned by the attack which reminded the people once again of those grim days in 1963 and 1968. Violence clearly knew no ideological bounds; nor did the sympathy of the American public. In Michigan, ordinary voters gave him a sweeping victory in the primary and for weeks the country's most prominent leaders were photographed at his bedside. Most significantly, however, his disability cleared the way for a Nixon victory as his followers turned increasingly to the president.

Humphrey moved in to take up the slack in the narrowing field. Though Nebraska and Oregon came next, his attention was fixed on California, second largest delegation and a winner-take-all primary. If McGovern could be ambushed here, a deadlocked convention would probably turn to Humphrey. Though the bitterness had been increasing from primary to primary, the contests had been less divisive than 1968. But in California the old rivalries suddenly flared. A Humphrey-McGovern debate was inconclusive, but the Minnesotan's charge against McGovern's welfare and defense programs hurt, forcing the South Dakotan to the defensive. McGovern's comfortable edge slipped away; when the returns were in he had won by only five percent—and, though not mentioned at the time, he inherited a messy credentials fight that went raucously to the convention floor in Miami.

McGovern's problem was obscured by a resounding sweep in New York two weeks later. But the damage had been done. Humphrey had raised substantive issues which reflected the party's division. The attack on his opponent's "alternative budget" designed to save thirty billion dollars in defense spending was couched in "second-rate power" terms and subtly opened old Vietnam wounds. He had also caught McGovern with a proposal to replace present welfare programs by a "demigrant" of $1,000 a year for every man, woman, and child in the country. Humphrey harped on the program calling it reckless and impractical. Other Democrats had already accused the South Dakotan of being "soft" on the issues of marijuana, abortion, and amnesty. Later, those who made the charges would support him as candidate, but the momentum that had carried McGovern so spectacularly through the primaries was broken, never to be regained.

The Miami convention met to ratify the outcome of the primaries. McGovern was within a hundred votes of a first ballot victory thanks, in part, to a roving staff which engineered remarkable victories in the caucus and convention states against an apathetic or overconfident opposition. Yet a stop-McGovern movement formed around the defeated candidates, hoping for a deadlock and the emergence of a compromise candidate or perhaps Senator Edward Kennedy himself. Its only hope rested on a challenge in the California delegation where the Humphrey forces argued that the winner-take-all system was in effect a unit rule and thus violated the new guidelines. The Credentials Committee upheld this interpretation by a close vote. Stung, McGovern supporters then unseated fifty-nine Chicago delegates claiming they had been improperly slated.

The two challenges made the first night of the convention its liveliest. The California decision indicated who was in control. The passage of the minority plank gave McGovern back his full delegation and assured his nomination. The Chicago situation was stickier and involved an historical fracture of the party. The fifty-nine delegates were regulars from Chicago and included some of its most prominent leaders, one of whom was Mayor Richard J. Daley. The challengers were independents who had fought the Cook County organization for years. A strict interpretation of the rules would have seated neither side since both had violated the guidelines more than once. When the roll call came Daley and his slate were removed and the reformers took their place. The "new politics" had defeated the old, but those who stayed up until dawn to watch it on television knew that the cost of that victory was high.

The convention that began its deliberations the next day was in marked contrast to previous ones. The number of women had risen to nearly forty percent; young people accounted for another quarter; blacks and Puerto Ricans were represented above their share of the population, but below their portion of enrolled Democrats. In the New York delegation 250 of the 278 had never been to a convention before. Who was not there was significant, too. Governors, mayors, senators and congressmen accustomed to attendance, were reduced to onlookers, if they came at all. Labor leaders who used to be automatic delegates from the big industrial states watched the proceedings on television from hotel rooms. Those prominent in old ethnic politics— Irish, Italians, Slavs, etc.—complained about their "exclusion." Yet, under the O'Hara guidelines, the convention did its business in a serious and orderly fashion, not closing up shop each day until the early hours of the morning. A national poll later showed that sixty-seven percent of the voters had a positive opinion about the whole affair.

To some extent McGovern's nomination was an anticlimax. He had established his control over the convention the first night and it was never really challenged again. Indeed the Miami platform itself contained few surprises. It was basically an extension of the party's position since 1960. The Vietnam plank, to be sure, was stronger and crisper than before, but the others largely expanded early proposals. The section on crime was longer and more detailed; revenue sharing became more explicit; tax reform was elevated to a critical spot and the usual call for closing loopholes included more specific points. The new issues of amnesty, abortion and drugs achieved their importance more for the minority planks which failed than for positions embodied in the first document. Floor fights highlighted the growing concern over social issues previously outside political discussion and contributed to the general notion that the convention had been dominated by radical elements.

With the nomination assured, McGovern turned to the task of choosing a running mate. His first choice was Edward Kennedy who brought strong connections with labor, Catholics, and regulars as well as the formidable Kennedy personal following and resources. When the Massachusetts senator refused, the selection became something of a lottery. The criteria were clear: the vice president ought to be from a large state, preferably Catholic, and acceptable to labor and traditional party leaders. A long list was whittled down to a half dozen. At the last moment, McGovern announced that Senator Thomas Eagleton of Missouri was the man. Though unknown to even most of the delegates, he had all the credentials plus some others—he came from a border state; as a former attorney general he could handle the "law and order" issue; and he had demonstrated appeal to suburban voters. His comparative obscurity emboldened those supporting other candidates to go through the motions of nomination. McGovern's choice, of course, carried handily, but it was noteworthy that Cissy Farenthold, former candidate for governor of Texas, became the first serious woman contender for the vice presidency in the party's history.

The delegates had scarcely gone home when the bombshell exploded. Newspaper reporters discovered that Senator Eagleton had a history of "nervous exhaustion" and had been hospitalized three times. Once, at the Mayo Clinic in Minnesota, doctors used shock treatment as part of the therapy. Eagleton had not informed McGovern of these events at the time of the nomination. To avoid a sensational exposé by the press, Eagleton and McGovern called a joint press conference (appropriately, it turned out, at

Custer, South Dakota) to disclose the facts in an orderly and sober fashion. But nothing could minimize the impact. The news touched off a vigorous and prolonged debate on whether the Missouri senator possessed presidential temperament, whether, as it was put, he had the balance needed to make tough decisions in an atomic age. Most political leaders counseled withdrawal, even dumping if necessary; others observed that previous presidents had histories of depression and performed well in office. The central fact, however, was that few people were indifferent.

Senator McGovern, who had assembled his staff in South Dakota to plan his campaign, now faced the first public test since his nomination. Cautious and compassionate by nature, he first asked for all the relevant facts, consulted Eagleton's doctors, and conferred with nationally known medical experts. While this information was being assembled, he postponed the ultimate decision. Eagleton, on the other hand, determined to stay on the ticket, made several appearances around the country to drum up public support. Under persistent questioning, McGovern unwisely said he was still "one thousand percent" behind his running mate. This statement, designed to buy a little time, dogged the candidate for the rest of the campaign.

The national spotlight was now on the presidential nominee who was largely unknown to most voters outside the primary states. Privately angered because Eagleton had not told him before the selection, McGovern waited for public opinion to crystallize. It never did and the debate continued. Finally, the senator decided that whatever the merits of the case, the campaign would be dominated by a discussion of Eagleton's health rather than the greater issues facing the nation. Hence, he asked his running mate to step aside as a gesture of party unity and national reassurance. The vice presidential nominee was understandably reluctant, but at a joint conference in Washington he withdrew with dignity.

The damage had been done—the seven days shook the campaign and it would never be the same again. Though McGovern had acted deliberately and decently, it looked to many that he lacked decisiveness. Worse still, debate over the case only declined, it did not disappear. Even staff members, eager to escape blame, kept the question alive by contradictory statements about the conversation with Eagleton in the hectic hours before the final selection. Worse still, the intense round of campaign planning never took place and subsequent months had the air of improvisation rather than clear direction. "We could never get the train back on the track," a dejected McGovernite observed after it was all over.

Finding another nominee was not a simple matter. McGovern tried six other possibilities, including Senators Humphrey and Muskie, before deciding on Sargent Shriver. The irreverent charged he was getting a second string Kennedy, but Shriver had impressive credentials of his own. As former chairman of the School Board in Chicago, he had a first hand knowledge of the educational crisis; his tenure as the first Director of the Peace Corps had given him invaluable information about foreign affairs; as head of President Johnson's war on poverty he had pioneered in the difficult world of urban revival. In addition, he was known to be an excellent campaigner—articulate and energetic. When Eagleton was nominated, people rightfully asked "Tom Who?" That question could not be raised about Sargent Shriver. A hastily called meeting of the National Committee enthusiastically ratified McGovern's choice.

The whole delay, however, cost the Democratic campaign the advantage of an early convention. McGovern's first step was to reach out to those elements in the party he had defeated to get the nomination. Well publicized meetings with Lyndon Johnson, George Wallace, Richard J. Daley and southern governors demonstrated that he realized that to win he had to put together what the primaries had pulled apart. Overtures to the A.F.L.-C.I.O. high command were less successful and he finally had to rely on a Labor for McGovern Committee comprised of many of the largest and most effective unions but without the formal sanction usually accorded a Democratic presidential candidate. Indeed, George Meany exercised what can best be described as a malicious neutrality throughout, withholding from McGovern everthing except snide comments. With his campaign in deep trouble, the candidate spent most of his organizational activity in courting regular leaders.

This strategy, however, conflicted with the media campaign which increasingly dominated the entire effort. The theory was simple: the media had replaced the party as a communicator with the voters, therefore McGovern's central concern should be television coverage at the six and ten o'clock news spots. These required "visuals," a film clip showing the candidate at a hospital, factory, shopping center, etc. talking to ordinary people about their problems. Schedules increasingly were built around this media strategy requiring the candidate to fly from time zone to time zone to accommodate the demands of television. Thus, it was argued "millions of people are 'exposed' to the candidate" instead of the thousands who attend even the best organized rallies. On the last day of the campaign, McGovern flew from New York and wound up in South Dakota after having dropped down in Philadelphia, Wichita, and California in between, a fitting summary of the "new media politics."

The system, however, had two serious drawbacks. One was that it was designed to contrast with Nixon's expected conventional campaign and match the president in public interest. However, the Republican candidate never came out on the hustings. He remained at the White House or some retreat in California, Florida or Maryland on a calculated policy of disengagement. He would not debate his opponent; he refused to meet the press; he even stopped political correspondence. Under virtual house arrest by his managers, he remained aloof from the public and out of his opponent's reach. McGovern had counted on the biennial appearance of the "old" Nixon, feeling his own low key, rational style would make "character" a good issue. Instead, the voters read of an increasingly desperate Democratic candidate darting around the country while the president stayed put, tending to the nation's business.

A second problem was that the logistics of the media strategy increasingly isolated the candidate from the voters. Every morning the routine was first a "visual" and perhaps a press conference, then "wheels up" for a flight to another city where the sequence would be repeated for the local cameras. Each stop required the clumsy deboarding while the candidate waited for 200 reporters to get off the plane and be bused to the next "event." It was not unusual to be airborne for four or five hours with at least another four hours eaten up coming and going from airports to meetings. This left little time for conventional campaigning, street rallies, party lunches, or private conferences. At the end, the "people's candidate" was almost as isolated as the president. And the press, with nothing much else to do, took to writing damaging stories about internal staff differences. Moreover, because his chief advisers were always in the plane, McGovern became involved in endless distracting decisions and controversies. The authors of the strategy thought they would manipulate the media; it turned out that the camera molded the campaign.

Toward the end, after courting traditional Democratic sources, he returned to his original constituency. This meant, especially, a return to the peace issue which had first thrust the South Dakotan onto the national scene.

But this issue, too, eluded him. On October 26 Henry Kissinger, the president's negotiator with the North Vietnamese, called a press conference and announced that "peace was at hand." An arrangement had been made with the enemy which needed only "three or four days more" discussion before the settlement became final. Nixon had repeatedly claimed that the talks in Paris were so delicate that they could not become involved in a political campaign. Now, two weeks before the election, he appropriated the issue. McGovern never believed the optimism of the president and the press, yet he did not want to seem to inject a partisan note into the proceedings. Finally, he went on television for a half hour in an extraordinarily candid statement asserting that peace was not near at hand, the areas of difference between the parties concerned were still large, and he expected a resumption of bombing on an even larger scale. Yet the confidence of the voters rested with the White House.

By November it was clear that McGovern was hopelessly behind and the surge that brought Humphrey abreast of Nixon in 1968 was not developing. Though the crowds were large and enthusiastic, the polls persistently showed a spread of twenty or more points. The result on November 7 confirmed their analysis. The Democratic candidate was badly defeated. Nixon won over 60.8 percent of the popular vote and swept the electoral college. McGovern carried only Massachusetts and the District of Columbia. The Wallace vote had obviously moved to the president en masse, and the defection of the traditional white Democrats continued unabated. Only the blacks by a large margin and the young by a narrow one, remained firm. But, unlike the Goldwater route in 1964, state and local slates were largely immune from the presidential landslide.

The Nixon victory inevitably led to a search for an explanation and, in some circles, a scapegoat. Regular leaders, still smarting from the primary defeat, quickly blamed the "McGovern people" who presumably had excluded them from the convention in Miami and later from the campaign. Columnists tended to emphasize the broken momentum of the effort which began perhaps as early as the California primary and certainly became critical with the Eagleton episode in July. Others dwelt on staff problems that persistently plagued the Senator's entourage. Still others asserted that Nixon's tactics of isolation and aloofness prevented any contest much less a rational choice for the electorate.

Yet none of these analyses explained a more than twenty point difference between the candidates. No doubt the Eagleton affair cost millions of votes, the disaffections of the regulars accounted for some more, a better disciplined staff would at least have saved some embarrassment, and Nixon's strategy made a genuine choice difficult. Any one of these might have explained a close election, but not even the entire list accounts for the massive gap in the popular vote.

Rather what lay beneath the surface was a massive backlash against the tumultuous events of the 1960's. The Nixon years had not seen cities in flames or campuses in turmoil. Television screens no longer featured the violent rhetoric or ugly confrontation that dominated President Johnson's second term. Moreover, the war which discomfited even those who supported it had "wound down." Somehow voters believed that the country had returned to "normalcy." To be sure, underneath were all the vexing questions—race, injustice, war, and a new generation—but the daily upheavals of the previous years had disappeared. The tide which had swelled in 1968 had receded and though the wreckage lay in uncomfortable view across the beach, most Americans preferred to look beyond at a more tranquil sea.

President Nixon, of course, had little to do with the fact the tide was going out but he was the president and the public associated four years of relative social peace with the man who presided over it. This domestic judgment was reinforced in foreign affairs. Nixon's new *detente* with China and Russia, no matter how slight or fragile they might turn out to be, relieved international tensions and quieted American anxieties. Moreover, the Nixon campaign shrewdly capitalized on this uneasiness. By refusing to campaign conventionally, by substituting busing for direct discussion of civil rights, by replacing the debate about poverty with a restatement of the "work ethic," and by blaming much of the previous unrest on "permissiveness," he at once reassured people about the things that bothered them at the same time he appeared to be moderate rather than conservative. At the same time, voters equated the McGovern candidacy with the disturbing events of the 1960's. Among his followers were the blacks, chicanos, and young people who had been the rough cutting edge of previous demonstrations. Added to this was the emergence of militant feminism with its unsettling tactics and unpredictable consequences. It was to preserve the fragile tranquillity of the recent years that so many voters turned away from the Democratic candidate to vote for a man whose own political career had been involved in the most divisive events of the postwar period.

But the presidential result did not represent the appearance of a "new Republican majority," for the Democrats kept a strong control in both Houses of Congress. Liberals and conservatives alike returned to their seats. Moreover, new faces such as J. R. Biden of Delaware and William Hathaway of Maine replaced established GOP veterans in the Senate and well known Democratic liberals withstood strong challenges. There was little support in the congressional returns for those who argued 1972 was a repudiation of modern liberalism. Indeed, since many established committee leaders had retired or were defeated in the primaries, the Congress seemed to be slightly more liberal and substantially younger than its predecessor.

The disparity between Nixon's wide margin over McGovern and the Democratic success on the congressional level indicated that the voters were still nervous about the future even while they extended the president's leadership for another four years. This fact throws light on both the explanation of the presidential outcome and the prospects of the Democratic party. Obviously party reform had not inhibited, indeed may have enhanced, the effectiveness of the state and local organizations. The inability of the Republicans to capitalize on the Nixon landslide reflected GOP weakness as well as the residual strength of the Democratic party. Yet no optimistic analysis could conceal the deep problems facing the party.

Beneath the crisis was the nation's foremost problem—race. Like the question of the war, this fundamental issue was centered increasingly in the Democratic party. John Kennedy received the bulk of the black vote in 1960, though the percentage is in some dispute, with Gallup projecting as low as sixty percent and the *New York Times* estimating as high as eighty. At any rate, by 1968 the GOP share dropped below five percent, and was not much higher in 1972.

Moreover, the numbers of black voters continued to rise, especially in the South, which gave additional meaning to these percentages. Indeed, the 1970 census revealed that fifty-nine congressional districts were at least one-third black. Only six of them, all in the South, were represented by Republicans. In the major urban states nearly every Democratic senator or governor owes his seat in part to black voters. In addition, the number of black office-holders had risen dramatically to over 2,000. While this still grossly underrepresented the black population, it comprised a more permanent stake in the political process and a stronger, ever larger lever in the Democratic party. The 1972 convention in Miami had a larger black contingent than ever before, and the election of Basil Patterson as national vice chairman signalled further recognition.

The emergence of this black power, however, raised problems with the traditional white support enjoyed by the party since the New Deal. In the South, these new developments rocked the old established leadership and nearly every gain was made at the expense of the other Democrats. By 1972 the GOP picked up six congressional seats and were serious challengers for offices at other levels. And, of course, Nixon's southern strategy was built on the white backlash in Dixie. The urban areas were especially vulnerable in national elections where the suburbs around Miami, Atlanta, and Houston turned in large Republican majorities. Nor was there much chance that this trend would easily be reversed since it was built both on new suburbanization and old racial fear. Moreover, Democratic presidential candidates had learned to get along without the South for more than a generation.

More damaging was the attrition among the whites in northern metropolitan areas. The outer suburbs, of course, had always belonged to the GOP. But the rise of the blacks brought racial collisions in almost every large city. Most of this had nothing to do with the Democratic party itself but lay deep in the process of urban growth. As blacks moved into the heart of the city, they occupied areas which were being abandoned by other groups; and, what was more important, as their numbers mounted they pressed against more stable working class neighborhoods where families were less successful and lacked the resources to move further out to the edge of town or into the suburbs beyond. The shifting boundaries between the two became the battleground between the conflicting groups. Unscrupulous real estate agents, mindless governmental programs, and political manipulation fed the chaos and aggravated a continuously explosive situation. To the dismay of the party, almost always all the actors in the drama were Democrats.

It became fashionable among political analysts to identify the whites in this guerrilla warfare as "ethnics," by which were particularly meant the Irish, Italians, Jews, and Eastern Europeans. In some cities that was true, but this explanation also concealed the ugly racial basis of the confrontation. In places with a heavy immigrant history like Chicago, New York, Boston, or San Francisco, the whites involved met the "ethnic" definition. But even when there were no ethnics involved the process was similar. The blacks met the same resistance in the west end of Louisville where the residents were all Protestant and "native" as they did in Brooklyn's Jewish Borough Park. Atlanta's south side contained few with an immigrant past, but they were as spirited in defense of their turf as Bridgeport in Chicago. Finding ethnics in Dallas was difficult; yet the neighborhood abrasiveness was not less than Boston's north side. The simple, elemental, and inescapable fact is that race presented the Democratic party the same dilemma which had fractured it more than a hundred years ago. In unconscious irony, many polemicists and journalists called for a "New Populism," unaware that the Old Populism stumbled over the same problem.

This racial abrasiveness, however, heightened the sense of ethnicity among white minorities. Paradoxically, the movement emulated the techniques of black militancy. Groups established new organizations to raise the "ethnic consciousness" of various groups. Jews had always had an elaborate defense mechanism, but Irish-American or Italian-American societies now stepped up their activity and visibility while younger leaders formed additional committees. Journalists popularized the rediscovery of old roots, usually tying them to urban neighborhoods and political action. The emphasis moreover, was heavily on the working class remnants of immigrant groups living in the outer city or in industrial suburbs. "The mixed ethnic working class feels trapped between the blacks on the one side and middle-class suburbia on the other," wrote Monsignor Gino C. Baroni, head of the Center for Urban Ethnic Affairs, in a characteristic expression of the problem. Saul Alinsky defined the issue more elaborately. "They're oppressed by taxation, and inflation, poisoned by pollution, terrorized by urban crime, frightened by the new youth culture, baffled by the computerized world around them. They're losing their kids and losing their dreams. They're alienated, depersonalized, without any feeling of participation in the political process, and they feel rejected and hopeless—frozen and festering in apathy."

Monsignor Baroni further observed that "a lot of votes are up for grabs in 1972. Who gets them depends on whoever is going to respond, whoever doesn't take them for granted, whoever is fair with them." Just how many votes were involved was uncertain, though there are roughly fifty million first-through-fourth generation ethnic Americans. The largest group is English, Scottish and Welsh, accounting for 15.3 percent of the total. Germans are next largest with 12.7 percent but they are generally not included in the present ethnic revival. The census bureau in March, 1971 calculated that the Irish comprised 8 percent of the total population, Italians 4.3, Polish 2.4, Russian 1.1 and Spanish-speaking 4.4. The proportions are hence not large, but their concentration in fifty northeastern and midwestern cities as well as rural areas in the southwest gives them disproportionate political power.

The party's minority division had been the historic vehicle for carrying these votes. Broad in coverage and with roots in the hyphenated societies and the foreign language press, the committee managed to maintain formal connections with most of the important ethnic groups. By the 1960's, however, this emphasis was increasingly considered "old fashioned" or even demeaning. In 1972, Mrs. Jean Westwood went so far as to suggest the abandonment of these categories all together. Only then fierce objections of party leaders across the country salvaged the traditional concern and a new All-American Council was established to replace the old minorities division. The role of the blacks and Spanish-speaking representatives reflected the changing interests of each, blacks asked for their own separate operation and the Latins opted for incorporation.

Yet the problem lay deeper than organization. The urban ethnic neighborhoods continued to decline, and those that remained were largely older residents. In New York City alone, only eight percent of the Irish remained in town and over half of the Italians had joined the trek to the suburbs. The residual compounds faced continuous pressure of the blacks and the obsolescence of facilities. These neighborhoods might be the object of nostalgia and romanticism by journalists and intellectuals, but they provided an uncertain base for the Democratic party. As it rewarded Negroes and Puerto Ricans for their loyalty, white ethnics became more vulnerable to Republican blandishments. The move to the GOP was first discernible in local elections; but the apostasy soon spread to state and national contests.

In some places, white ethnics headed for Wallace rather than the GOP, but this transition was only open every four years. Senator McGovern, the beneficiary of the new forces in the party, vainly attempted to lure the blue collar workers back into the fold with a strong attack on the unjust tax structure, tough positions on narcotics pushers and a "G. I. Bill" for policemen as well as emphasis on the dangers of inflation and unemployment. But Nixon, sustained by the benevolent neutrality of George Meany and the construction trades, inherited eighty percent of the Wallace vote without visiting a single factory or addressing a single trade union meeting and without the endorsement of the Alabama governor. At the end of 1972, the "ethnic" or "blue collar" question went deeper into the ranks of the party than any time since the days of Franklin Roosevelt.

The full range of the party's problems of the 1970's can perhaps be best illustrated by looking at three big states: New York, California and Illinois, which are essential for a national Democratic revival in 1976 and 1980. While it is always possible to put together electoral majorities by juggling the states in any particular election, it is very difficult for any foreseeable Democratic presidential candidate to win without at least two of the three. This is not only true because of their size and location, but because Illinois and California especially are what analysts call "Barometer states"—those whose results most nearly reflect the national outcome. They also present three different organizational profiles which have their analogues across the country.

Indeed, New York's last two decades are in many ways the story of the national party. Beginning in the 1950's a reform movement generated power and influence against the traditional organization dominated by Tammany Hall. Even though the Tammany leader, Carmine DeSapio, was widely hailed as a "new breed" of boss and could claim some credit for electing Robert Wagner as mayor and Averill Harriman as governor, newer elements kept winning primaries and converts. The new and the old collided in Buffalo at the state convention in 1958 when DeSapio rammed through Frank Hogan as the candidate for senator, turning down former Secretary of the Air Force Thomas K. Finletter, the reformers' choice. It was a display of technical mastery which included at one point the hasty rearrangement of the agenda. But the price was high. Hogan was swamped in the general election and the poison of faction spread rapidly throughout the state.

Kennedy's election in 1960 obscured these divisions for a while because he was able to deal with a Charles Buckley, the old-line boss of the Bronx, as easily as with most of the reform faction. The election of Robert Kennedy to the Senate added a further respite. But underneath the disintegration continued. In 1961, Carmine DeSapio, who had opposed Kennedy before the 1960 convention was toppled, losing his race for district leader and hence his Tammany chairmanship. Historically, the party had always gone through a brief period of disorganization between the decline of one leader and the appearance of another. But this time, no new figure appeared who could manage much less harness the disparate forces. Regular county chairmen seldom agreed on major questions, and the reform movement became so large and successful that it, too, fell into disarray. Even the considerable organizational skills and immense public prestige of Senator Kennedy could not bring tolerable order.

As the decade wore on fragmentation increased and each year found new and often improbable alliances that lasted only through a single election (and occasionally not that long). Reformers usually won the primaries and then lost the general elections. Regulars kept alive by nimbly playing off one faction against another. By 1970, a new "system" had appeared built on permanent division. No one any longer looked around for a cohesive force; careers were built and decisions made on the expectation of continued factionalism. The possibility of future unity sent shudders down the spine of reformer and regular alike. The focus of New York Democratic leaders was so local and intensely personal that Senator McGovern could come into the state, appeal directly to enrolled voters and walk away with ninety-one percent of the delegates. (In fact, on the convention floor, the vote on the only ballot was 278 to 0, something not even Tammany Hall in its salad days could produce.)

The present low estate of New York's Democratic party is thus the harvest of two decades of internecine warfare. It was not created by the McGovern candidacy; indeed, 1972 was only an evanescent moment in the struggle. Nor does there seem to be any end in sight.

Regulars look upon a primary loss as somehow an affront to an institution of which they are the ordained custodians. They don't see the primary as an essential part of that institution, as the way the party is kept close to its members and the process by which its vital tissues are renewed. Though the sensible response to defeat would be accommodation with the winners, the usual reaction is "Don't get mad, get even." Resentment soon spills over to revenge, and the cry is raised: "Wait until next time."

Reformers, on the other hand, look upon a primary victory as a singular triumph of good over evil. They interpret the results as a mandate to exile the sinner, or, if he had once been a reformer, the fallen angel. The phrase "Cleaning the Augean stable" becomes an elevated codeword for a purge. Worse still, judgments in one election become a kind of permanent litmus test which, if correct, constitute a continuing passport to virtuous political society, or, if wrong, will place forever the mark of Cain on anyone who made an unforgivable decision. In short, the regulars don't know how to lose and the reformers don't know how to win.

To be sure, the long range future lies with reformers. The flood of new enrollees feel less tied to established party leadership and the older rank and file die off or retire to Florida and California. This ought to be small consolation to the victors, however, for as the party weakens, it becomes less worth controlling. Ticket-splitting deprives nominations of their historic significance, financial backers are reluctant to invest in risky campaigns; even the number of voters decline. As one witness asked plaintively at a hearing before the McGovern Commission three years ago: "What if we gave a reform party and nobody came?"

The disintegration of the New York party could be readily placed at the Buffalo convention in 1958. California's disorganization began as early as 1910 when Hiram Johnson brought Progressivism to state government. In breaking the grips of predatory monopolies, new devices were designed to place political decisions in the hands of the voters. Referendum and initiative put important reforms on the ballot rather than in the legislature, and a new primary system opened up both parties. Moreover, California developed a crossfiling system which permitted candidates to run in both party primaries. The result was a pervasive non-partisanship which became the hallmark of California's public life. Personality increasingly replaced conventional organization. The unpredictability of this "system" quickly earned the state the reputation as "the largest outdoor insane asylum in the world."

Into this persistent political instability in the 1960's was dropped every national issue. The growth of the black and brown population brought a severe racial crisis; indeed, in Watts the ghetto first erupted on a large scale; uncontrolled suburban expansion dominated the changing postwar population development; the Vietnam conflict produced both a war oriented economy and one of the largest anti-war movements in the nation. Student unrest spilled over into violence at Berkeley and became perhaps ugliest at San Francisco State. The environmental issue seemed best symbolized for a generation in the smog of Los Angeles and the consumption by fire of some of the most precious forest land in the nation. The question of poverty became nationally embodied in Cesar Chavez's campaign for rural migrant laborers. And it was in the kitchen corridor of Los Angeles's Ambassador Hotel where the assassination of Robert Kennedy laid bare again the senseless brutality of the times. In short, California was the nation writ large.

An orderly response to these swirling events would have challenged the strongest political system and the most effective party. But by 1970 the Democratic organization had fragmented so badly that one shrewd Californian observed that "if you dumped the thousand most prominent Democrats in the ocean, all you would lose is a thousand votes." The fact that the party held a three to two majority in registration over the GOP was of little consolation since it could seldom be translated into victory at the polls. While the Democrats held the two Senate seats in 1972, they had won the governorship only three times in the twentieth century. And no new compelling figure appeared on the horizon who could provide cohesive leadership to an atomized party.

One consequence of organizational weakness in California has been the rise of professional management firms as a substitute for the party. Beginning with William and Baxter in 1930's, these corporations handle campaigns for money without regard to ideology or permanent commitment. Delightfully non-partisan, they provide services once the province of political parties. Armed with computers, polling information, and a continuous reading of the California electorate, they could circulate petitions, handle the media, write and prepare speeches, contact the voter, and monitor the results. In the 1960's a change in the enrollment law ended the old system of cross-filing and hence furnished a modicum of party responsibility and integrity. Yet the organizational chaos was endemic; the real question was whether California represented the future of parties everywhere or was simply an historical sport.

In Illinois some of the same forces of disorganization were at work in the sixties but on a more modest scale. The central fact about the state party was its domination by the Cook County organization and its chairman, Richard J. Daley. Variously described as the last of the old bosses or the first of the new, Daley's great and persistent influence rested on combining the power of an elected mayor with party leadership. This simple fact explained why no independent base of any scale could develop within Democratic ranks. And if it did, the major figure was either co-opted or courteously helped to the House or Senate in Washington. Since no downstate aspirant could be elected to statewide office without Cook County voters, only sporadic mutinies occurred beyond the municipal boundaries.

Outsiders always believed Daley's power rested on a monolithic organization with legions who obeyed every command from their chief. Actually, the mayor has always presided over a factionalized party which he manages to hold together by shrewd manipulation, skillful use of patronage, and personal connections which reach across the political spectrum. His longevity resulted not from the arbitrary exercise of power but from his knowledge of its limitations. A dozen more or less cohesive groups had always engaged in continuous, if quiet, warfare within the party. Each was placated by office and attention; those too large or stubborn to move around were left alone so long as they didn't make public waves. Adept at infighting and in close contact with his constituency, Daley knew his party and his city like no one else.

Nonetheless, the Cook County organization was not immune from the forces shaping the national party. As early as 1966 the struggle between blacks and whites created an ugly confrontation in Cicero when Martin Luther King was stoned during a march into a white neighborhood. The political fallout hit Senator Paul Douglas when he was destroyed in white city wards he had carried handily three times before. In 1972 the black wards deserted the Democratic candidate for State's Attorney because of his brutality in handling the Black Panthers. Although Jesse Jackson's opposition attracted most national attention, Congressman Ralph Metcalfe's break with Daley over the police treatment of two constituents constituted a more important development of black leverage, if not independence, in Chicago politics. At any rate, the old coalition of black and white wards which had sustained the Cook County Democratic party for more than a generation was coming apart.

These new factions reinforced the traditional independent opposition to the Cook County organization. As early as 1941 liberals had formed the Independent Voters of Illinois as a vehicle for formal and continuous activity by irregulars. Though Democrats comprised the bulk of its membership, the IVI did in fact endorse Republicans for public office. The Committee on Illinois Government (CIG) was launched by a group of young Democrats who first tasted influence, if not power, in the Stevenson governorship between 1948 and 1952. Originally, CIG confined its attention to state affairs, but after Paul Douglas' defeat in 1966 it moved gradually into the battlefield of intra-party warfare. After the state convention, irregular groups, usually with a neighborhood base, popped up to take local offices away from the regulars. Then reform movements made marginal gains in the city council and state assembly, but their white, middle-class and professional base meant a limited general impact. Yet, when combined with black unrest and suburban growth, they contributed to paring down the overwhelming power of the Democratic machine.

All the divisive forces converged in Illinois in the election of 1972. In the primaries Daniel Walker, a Montgomery Ward vice president and the author of the famous "Walker Report" describing the trouble at the 1968 Democratic Convention as in great part a "public riot," challenged the entire state organization for the gubernatorial nomination. His opponent was himself a liberal; Paul Simon, a downstater and Lieutenant Governor, was a member of both IVI and CIG, a strong advocate of civil rights and popular in the suburbs. Yet he was the organization choice, making the Walker challenge, initially at least, one from the left. At the same time Edward Hanrahan, first designated then dumped as candidate for State's Attorney by the party, bore in from the right. In addition, McGovern, McCarthy, and Muskie all sought delegates for the national convention. In the melee that followed Walker and Hanrahan both won and the presidential primary produced the major credentials fight in Miami. Daley had never suffered such defeats on such a broad scale before.

But the mayor did not lose his resilience. He quickly accepted the ticket— McGovern, Walker, and Hanrahan—and put on a vigorous campaign. The outcome was mixed; Walker won, but the presidential and state's attorney candidates lost. The organization had been dented by 1972 but not destroyed. Indeed, what was most likely to defeat the Cook County Democratic Party was not new forces but the oldest—age. The mayor himself was sixty-nine; many of the key leaders were over sixty, the foot soldiers in the precincts were no longer energetic, and Chicago's young were no less independent than their peers elsewhere. It seemed unlikely that the heralded machine could last long beyond Daley's retirement or death; no leader presently active could be expected both to win the mayoralty and become county chairman as well. The seventies might indeed witness the "Last Hurrah" in its most visible stronghold.

The McGovern defeat produced a shattering impact on the Democratic National Committee. When it met on December 9, 1972, the formal agenda was already long: the selection of twenty-five at-large members and the appointment of a new commission to reexamine party rules. But it was apparent that the December 9th meeting would assess responsibility for the presidential debacle. The convenient target was Mrs. Jean Westwood, the first woman chairman of either party. A McGovern appointment, she symbolized what older elements in the party considered the excesses of reform. Initially, the opponents had no single candidate around which to rally. Lawrence O'Brien let it be known that he was available for a third term; Sargent Shriver, was willing; George Mitchell—a confidant of Senator Muskie and a former member of the McGovern Commission brought formidable credentials to his candidacy.

But the regulars quickly moved to Robert Strauss, a wealthy Texas businessman and former treasurer of the DNC. A former close associate of John Connally and backed by organized labor, he was as much a symbol of the old as Mrs. Westwood was of the new. During the Nixon years he had cut the party's debt in half and established cordial contacts with state and county chairmen all across the country, especially in the West and South. His first move was to line up the majority of Democratic governors at a conference in St. Louis. Most had favored some other candidate than McGovern during the primaries and few had been delegates. In addition, they represented a traditional resentment of governors over the Washington domination of party affairs. Their endorsement made Strauss a serious contender. Additional support came from Senate majority leader, Mike Mansfield, and House majority whip, Thomas "Tip" O'Neill. Senators McGovern and Kennedy, the dominant leaders of the party, remained along the sidelines. Strauss's crucial advantage, however, lay in the division of his opponents. Agreement among the liberals on any of the compromise candidates would have been decisive. Indeed, Mrs. Westwood beat back an attempt at ouster by 5 out of 205 votes before resigning. The margin of Strauss' victory and its sources revealed again the deep cleavage in the Democratic Party. By a margin of 1.5 votes the National Committee had replaced a "reform" chairman with a "regular" one, and all the old wounds began to drain again.

Worse still, the voters had seen the Democratic party in customary disarray. This internecine warfare had already helped erode its numerical supremacy over Republicans; internal conflict during 1968 and 1972 had substantially reduced the effectiveness of the national organization. Now the first meeting after the election saw another melee. Afterward, Strauss reaffirmed his support of the McGovern reforms; party leaders from across the country phoned in their congratulations; most liberals said they would test the new chairman by the future not the past; Senators McGovern, Kennedy, Humphrey, Muskie and future presidential hopefuls gave the usual blessings. Yet the divots down the Democratic fairway left little green visible. The DNC may have elected a new chairman but it had elevated no one.

The job of rebuilding would certainly be formidable. Nearly every segment of the party agreed that the proportionality section of the McGovern guidelines had to be redefined if not removed. But the task contained its own dangers. Women would not simply return to their old junior partnership; the blacks had demonstrated heroic loyalty over a difficult decade and would not stand for any reneging on their new stature in the party; and to penalize young people would only accelerate the attrition in Democratic enrollment in the party's most rapidly enlarging element. Yet the exit from the party of more traditional voters somehow had to be stemmed. And, above all, a tolerable concord within the ranks had to be established if the oldest political organization in the nation was not to become its most recent casualty.

Despite those difficulties, the Democratic party had a residual strength that could provide a base for renewal. It still controlled both houses of Congress, occupied the governor's chair in thirty-one states and continued to dominate the urban scene. Even the suburbs were no longer invulnerable as more and more Democrats won local offices beyond the crabgrass curtain. Though the slippage in percentage of party enrollment was marked, Democrats still handily outnumbered Republicans. And around the country, a generation of new leaders had begun to move into the edges of national attention. To be sure, the public had expressed its mounting skepticism about politics, voting less and less each year. Yet there was no evidence that the alienation from institutions was permanent or irreversible. The 200th birthday of the Republic will no doubt witness a Democratic revival—with the permission, of course, of the party itself.

Appendix

CIVIL RIGHTS PLANK
DEMOCRATIC PLATFORM OF 1960
July 12, 1960

We shall also seek to create an affirmative new atmosphere in which to deal with racial divisions and inequalities which threaten both the integrity of our democratic faith and the proposition on which our nation was founded—that all men are created equal. It is our faith in human dignity that distinguishes our open free society from the closed totalitarian society of the Communists.

The Constitution of the United States rejects the notion that the Rights of Man means the rights of some men only. We reject it too.

The right to vote is the first principle of self-government. The Constitution also guarantees to all Americans the equal protection of the laws.

It is the duty of the Congress to enact the laws necessary and proper to protect and promote these constitutional rights. The Supreme Court has the power to interpret these rights and the laws thus enacted.

It is the duty of the President to see that these rights are respected and that the Constitution and laws as interpreted by the Supreme Court are faithfully executed.

What is now required is effective moral and political leadership by the whole Executive branch of our Government to make equal opportunity a living reality for all Americans.

As the party of Jefferson, we shall provide that leadership.

In every city and state in greater or lesser degree there is discrimination based on color, race, religion, or national origin.

If discrimination in voting, education, the administration of justice or segregated lunch counters are the issues in one area, discrimination in housing and employment may be pressing questions elsewhere.

The peaceful demonstrations for first-class citizenship which have recently taken place in many parts of this country are a signal to all of us to make good at long last the guarantees of our Constitution.

The time has come to assure equal access for all Americans to all areas of community life, including voting booths, schoolrooms, jobs, housing, and public facilities.

The Democratic Administration which takes office next January will therefore use the full powers provided in the Civil Rights Acts of 1957 and 1960 to secure for all Americans the right to vote.

If these powers, vigorously invoked by a new Attorney General and backed by a strong and imaginative Democratic President, prove inadequate, further powers will be sought.

We will support whatever action is necessary to eliminate literacy tests and the payment of poll taxes as requirements for voting.

A new Democratic Administration will also use its full powers—legal and moral—to ensure the beginning of good-faith compliance with the Constitutional requirement that racial discrimination be ended in public education.

We believe that every school district affected by the Supreme Court's school desegregation decision should submit a plan providing for at least first-step compliance by 1963, the 100th anniversary of the Emancipation Proclamation.

To facilitate compliance, technical and financial assistance should be given to school districts facing special problems of transition.

For this and for the protection of all other Constitutional rights of Americans, the Attorney General should be empowered and directed to file civil injunction suits in Federal courts to prevent the denial of any civil right on grounds of race, creed, or color.

The new Democratic Administration will support Federal legislation establishing a Fair Employment Practices Commission to secure effectively for everyone the right to equal opportunity for employment.

In 1949 the President's Committee on Civil Rights recommended a permanent Commission on Civil Rights. The new Democratic Administration will broaden the scope and strengthen the powers of the present commission and make it permanent.

Its functions will be to provide assistance to communities, industries, or individuals in the implementation of Constitutional rights in education, housing, employment, transportation, and the administration of justice.

In addition, the Democratic Administration will use its full executive powers to assure equal employment opportunities and to terminate racial segregation throughout Federal services and institutions, and on all Government contracts. The successful desegregation of the armed services took place through such decisive executive action under President Truman.

Similarly the new Democratic Administration will take action to end discrimination in Federal housing programs, including Federally assisted housing.

To accomplish these goals will require executive orders, legal actions brought by the Attorney General, legislation, and improved Congressional procedures to safeguard majority rule.

Above all, it will require the strong, active, persuasive, and inventive leadership of the President of the United States.

The Democratic President who takes office next January will face unprecedented challenges. His Administration will present a new face to the world.

It will be a bold, confident, affirmative face. We will draw new strength from the universal truths which the founder of our Party asserted in the Declaration of Independence to be "self-evident."

Emerson once spoke of an unending contest in human affairs, a contest between the Party of Hope and the Party of Memory.

For 7½ years America, governed by the Party of Memory, has taken a holiday from history.

As the Party of Hope it is our responsibility and opportunity to call forth the greatness of the American people.

In this spirit, we hereby rededicate ourselves to the continuing service of the Rights of Man—everywhere in America and everywhere else on God's earth.

JOHN F. KENNEDY, ACCEPTANCE SPEECH
Los Angeles, July 15, 1960

With a deep sense of duty and high resolve, I accept your nomination. I accept it with a full and grateful heart—without reservation—and with only one obligation—the obligation to devote every effort of body, mind, and spirit to lead our party back to victory and our nation back to greatness.

I am grateful, too, that you have provided me with such an eloquent statement of our party's platform. Pledges which are made so eloquently are made to be kept. "The rights of man"—the civil and economic rights essential to the human dignity of all men—are indeed our goal and our first principles. This is a platform on which I can run with enthusiasm and conviction.

And I am grateful, finally, that I can rely in the coming months on so many others—on a distinguished running mate who brings unity to our ticket and strength to our platform, Lyndon Johnson—on one of the most articulate statesmen of our time, Adlai Stevenson—on a great spokesman for our needs as a nation and a people, Stuart Symington—and on that fighting campaigner whose support I welcome, President Harry S. Truman.

I feel a lot safer now that they are on my side again. And I am proud of the contrast with our Republican competitors. For their ranks are apparently so thin that not one challenger has come forth with both the competence and the courage to make theirs an open convention.

I am fully aware of the fact that the Democratic party, by nominating someone of my faith, has taken on what many regard as a new and hazardous risk—new, at least, since 1928. But I look at it this way: The Democratic Party has once again placed its confidence in the American people, and in their ability to render a free, fair judgment.

And you have, at the same time, placed your confidence in me, and in my ability to render a free, fair judgment—to uphold the Constitution and my oath of office—and to reject any kind of religious pressure or obligation that might directly or indirectly interfere with my conduct of the Presidency in the national interest.

My record of fourteen years supporting public education—supporting complete separation of church and state—and resisting pressures from any source on any issue should be clear by now to everyone.

I hope that no American, considering the really critical issues facing this country, will waste his franchise by voting either for me or against me solely on account of my religious affiliation. It is not relevant, I want to stress, what some other political or religious leader may have said on this subject. It is not relevant what abuses may have existed in other countries or in other times. It is not relevant what pressures, if any, might conceivably be brought to bear on me.

I am telling you now what you are entitled to know: That my decisions on every public policy will be my own—as an American, a Democrat, and a free man.

Under any circumstances, however, the victory we seek in November will not be easy. We all know that in our hearts. We recognize the power of the forces that will be aligned against us. We know they will invoke the name of Abraham Lincoln on behalf of their candidate—despite the fact that his political career has often seemed to show charity toward none and malice for all.

We know that it will not be easy to campaign against a man who has spoken or voted on every known side of every known issue. Mr. Nixon may feel it is his turn now, after the New Deal and the Fair Deal—but before he deals, someone had better cut the cards.

That "someone" may be the millions of Americans who voted for President Eisenhower but balk at his would-be, self-appointed successor. For just as historians tell us that Richard I was not fit to fill the shoes of bold Henry II—and that Richard Cromwell was not fit to wear the mantle of his uncle—they might add in future years that Richard Nixon did not measure to the footsteps of Dwight D. Eisenhower.

Perhaps he could carry on the party policies—the policies of Nixon, Benson, Dirksen, and Goldwater. But this nation cannot afford such a luxury. Perhaps we could afford a Coolidge following Harding. And perhaps we could afford a Pierce following Fillmore.

But after Buchanan this nation needed a Lincoln—after Taft, we needed a Wilson—after Hoover we needed Franklin Roosevelt—and after eight years of drugged and fitful sleep, this nations needs strong, creative Democratic leadership in the White House.

But we are not merely running against Mr. Nixon. Our task is not merely one of itemizing Republican failures. Nor is that wholly necessary. For the families forced from the farm will know how to vote without our telling them. The unemployed miners and textile workers will know how to vote. The old people without medical care—the families without a decent home—the parents of children without adequate food or schools—they all know that it's time for a change.

But I think the American people expect more from us than cries of indignation and attack. The times are too grave, the challenge too urgent, and the stakes too high—to permit the customary passions of political debate. We are not here to curse the darkness, but to light the candle that can guide us through that darkness to a safe and sane future. As Winston Churchill said on taking office some twenty years ago: "If we open a quarrel between the present and the past, we shall be in danger of losing the future."

Today our concern must be with that future. For the world is changing. The old era is ending. The old ways will not do.

Abroad, the balance of power is shifting. There are new and more terrible weapons—new and uncertain nations—new pressures of population and deprivation. One-third of the world, it has been said, may be free—but one-third is the victim of cruel repression—and the other one-third is rocked by the pangs of poverty, hunger, and envy. More energy is released by the awakening of these new nations than by the fission of the atom itself.

Meanwhile, Communist influence has penetrated further into Asia, stood astride the Middle East, and now festers some ninety miles off the coast of Florida. Friends have slipped into neutrality—and neutrals into hostility. As our keynoter reminded us, the President who began his career by going to Korea ends it by staying away from Japan.

The world has been close to war before—but now man, who has survived all previous threats to his existence, has taken into his mortal hands the power to exterminate the entire species some seven times over.

Here at home, the changing fact of the future is equally revolutionary. The New Deal and the Fair Deal were bold measures for their generations—but this is a new generation.

A technological revolution on the farm has led to an output explosion—but we have not yet learned to harness that explosion usefully, while protecting our farmers' right to full parity income.

An urban population revolution has overcrowded our schools, cluttered up our surburbs, and increased the squalor of our slums.

A peaceful revolution for human rights—demanding an end to racial discrimination in all parts of our community life—has strained at the leashes imposed by timid Executive leadership.

A medical revolution has extended the life of our elder citizens without providing the dignity and security those later years deserve. And a revolution of automation finds machines replacing men in the mines and mills of America, without replacing their income or their training or their need to pay the family doctor, grocer, and landlord.

There have also been a change—a slippage—in our intellectual and moral strength. Seven lean years of drought and famine have withered the fields of ideas. Blight has descended on our regulatory agencies—and a dry rot, beginning in Washington, is seeping into every corner of America—in the payola mentality, the expense account way of life, the confusion between what is legal and what is right. Too many Americans have lost their way, their will, and their sense of historic purpose.

It is time, in short, for a new generation of leadership—new men to cope with new problems and new opportunities.

All over the world, particularly in the newer nations, young men are coming to power—men who are not bound by the traditions of the past—men who are not blinded by the old fears and hates and rivalries—young men who can cast off the old slogans and delusions and suspicions.

The Republican nominee-to-be, of course, is also a young man. But his approach is as old as McKinley. His party is the party of the past. His speeches are generalities from Poor Richard's Almanac. Their platform, made up of leftover Democratic planks, has the courage of our old convictions. Their pledge is a pledge to the status quo—and today there can be no status quo.

For I stand tonight facing west on what was once the last frontier. From the lands that stretch 3,000 miles behind me, the pioneers of old gave up their safety, their comfort, and sometimes their lives to build a new world here in the West.

They were not the captives of their own doubts, the prisoners of their own price tags. Their motto was not "every man for himself"—but, "all for the common cause." They were determined to make that new world strong and free, to overcome its hazards and its hardships, to conquer the enemies that threatened from without and within.

Today some would say that those struggles are all over—that all the horizons have been explored—that all the battles have been won—that there is no longer an American frontier.

But I trust that no one in this vast assemblage will agree with those sentiments. For the problems are not all solved and the battles are not all won—and we stand today on the edge of a new frontier—the frontier of the 1960's—a frontier of unknown opportunities and perils—a frontier of unfulfilled hopes and threats.

Woodrow Wilson's New Freedom promised our nation a new political and economic framework. Franklin Roosevelt's New Deal promised security and succor to those in need. But the New Frontier of which I speak is not a set of promises—it is a set of challenges. It sums up not what I intend to offer the American people, but what I intend to ask of them. It appeals to their pride, not their pocketbook—it holds out the promise of more sacrifice instead of more security.

But I tell you the New Frontier is here, whether we seek it or not. Beyond that frontier are uncharted areas of science and space, unsolved problems of peace and war, unconquered pockets of ignorance and prejudice, unanswered questions of poverty and surplus.

It would be easier to shrink back from that frontier, to look to the safe mediocrity of the past, to be lulled by good intentions and high rhetoric—and those who prefer that course should not cast their votes for me, regardless of party.

But I believe the times demand invention, innovation, imagination, decision. I am asking each of you to be new pioneers on that New Frontier. My call is to the young in heart, regardless of age—to the stout in spirit, regardless of party—to all who respond to the scriptural call: "Be strong and of good courage; be not afraid, neither be thou dismayed."

For courage—not complacency—is our need today—leadership—not salesmanship. And the only valid test of leadership is the ability to lead, and lead vigorously. A tired nation, said David Lloyd George, is a tory nation—and the United States today cannot afford to be either tired or tory.

There may be those who wish to hear more—more promises to this group or that—more harsh rhetoric about the men in the Kremlin—more assurances of a golden future, where taxes are always low and subsidies ever high. But my promises are in the platform you have adopted. Our ends will not be won by rhetoric and we can have faith in the future only if we have faith in ourselves.

For the harsh facts of the matter are that we stand on this frontier at a turning point in history. We must prove all over again whether this nation—or any nation so conceived—can long endure—whether our society—with its freedom of choice, its breadth of opportunity, its range of alternatives—can compete with the single-minded advance of the Communist system.

Can a nation organized and governed such as ours endure? That is the real question. Have we the nerve and the will? Can we carry through in an age where we will witness not only new breakthroughs in weapons of destruction—but also a race for mastery of the sky and the rain, the ocean and the tides, the far side of space, and the inside of men's minds?

Are we up to the task? Are we equal to the challenge? Are we willing to match the Russian sacrifice of the present for the future? Or must we sacrifice our future in order to enjoy the present?

That is the question of the New Frontier. That is the choice our nation must make—a choice that lies not merely between two men or two parties, but between the public interest and private comfort—between national greatness and national decline—between the fresh air of progress and the stale, dank atmosphere of "normalcy"—between determined dedication and creeping mediocrity.

All mankind waits upon our decision. A whole world looks to see what we will do. We cannot fail their trust; we cannot fail to try.

It has been a long road from that first snowy day in New Hampshire to this crowded convention city. Now begins another long journey, taking me into your cities and homes all over America. Give me your help, your hand, your voice, your vote. Recall with me the words of Isaiah: "They that wait upon the Lord shall renew their strength; they shall mount up with wings as eagles; they shall run, and not be weary."

As we face the coming challenge, we too shall wait upon the Lord and ask that He renew our strength. Then shall we be equal to the test. Then we shall not be weary. And then we shall prevail.

JOHN F. KENNEDY
SPEECH TO HOUSTON MINISTERIAL ASSOCIATION
September 12, 1960

I am grateful for your generous invitation to state my views.

While the so-called religious issue is necessarily and properly the chief topic here tonight, I want to emphasize from the outset that I believe that we have far more critical issues in the 1960 election: the spread of Communist influence, until it now festers only ninety miles off the coast of Florida—the humiliating treatment of our President and Vice-President by those who no longer respect our power—the hungry children I saw in West Virginia, the old people who cannot pay their doctor's bills, the families forced to give up their farms—an America with too many slums, with too few schools, and too late to the moon and outer space.

These are the real issues which should decide this campaign. And they are not religious issues—for war and hunger and ignorance and despair know no religious barrier.

But because I am a Catholic, and no Catholic has ever been elected President, the real issues in this campaign have been obscured—perhaps deliberately in some quarters less responsible than this. So it is apparently necessary for me to state once again—not what kind of church I believe in, for that should be important only to me, but what kind of America I believe in.

I believe in an America where the separation of church and state is absolute—where no Catholic prelate would tell the President (should he be a Catholic) how to act and no Protestant minister would tell his parishioners for whom to vote—where no church or church school is granted any public funds or political preference—and where no man is denied public office merely because his religion differs from the President who might appoint him or the people who might elect him.

I believe in an America that is officially neither Catholic, Protestant nor Jewish—where no public official either requests or accepts instructions on public policy from the Pope, the National Council of Churches or any other ecclesiastical source—where no religious body seeks to impose its will directly or indirectly upon the general populace or the public acts of its officials—and where religious liberty is so indivisible that an act against one church is treated as an act against all.

For while this year it may be a Catholic against whom the finger of suspicion is pointed, in other years it has been, and may someday be again, a Jew—or a Quaker—or a Unitarian—or a Baptist. It was Virginia's harassment of Baptist preachers, for example, that led to Jefferson's statute of religious freedom. Today, I may be the victim—but tomorrow it may be you—until the whole fabric of our harmonious society is ripped apart at a time of great national peril.

Finally, I believe in an America where religious intolerance will someday end—where all men and all churches are treated as equal—where every man has the same right to attend or not to attend the church of his choice—where there is no Catholic vote, no antiCatholic vote, no bloc voting of any kind—and where Catholics, Protestants and Jews, both the lay and the pastoral level, will refrain from those attitudes of disdain and division which have so often marred their works in the past, and promote instead the American ideal of brotherhood.

That is the kind of America in which I believe. And it represents the kind of Presidency in which I believe—a great office that must be neither humbled by making it the instrument of any religious group, nor tarnished by arbitrarily withholding it, its occupancy, from the members of any religious group. I believe in a President whose views on religion are his own private affair, neither imposed upon him by the nation or imposed by the nation upon him as a condition to holding that office.

I would not look with favor upon a President working to subvert the First Amendment's guarantees of religious liberty (nor would our system of checks and balances permit him to do so). And neither do I look with favor upon those who would work to subvert Article VI of the Constitution by requiring a religious test—even by indirection—for if they disagree with that safeguard, they should be openly working to repeal it.

I want a Chief Executive whose public acts are responsible to all and obligated to none—who can attend any ceremony, service or dinner his office may appropriately require him to fulfill—and whose fulfillment of his Presidential office is not limited or conditioned by any religious oath, ritual or obligation.

This is the kind of America I believe in—and this is the kind of America I fought for in the South Pacific and the kind my brother died for in Europe. No one suggested than that we might have a "divided loyalty," that we did "not believe in liberty" or that we belonged to a disloyal group that threatened "the freedoms for which our forefathers died."

And in fact this is the kind of America for which our forefathers did die when they fled here to escape religious test oaths, that denied office to members of less favored churches, when they fought for the Constitution, the Bill of Rights, the Virginia Statute of Religious Freedom—and when they fought at the shrine I visited today—the Alamo. For side by side with Bowie and Crockett died Fuentes and McCafferty and Bailey and Bedillio and Carey—but no one knows whether they were Catholics or not. For there was no religious test there.

I ask you tonight to follow in that tradition, to judge me on the basis of fourteen years in the congress—on my declared stands against an ambassador to the Vatican, against unconstitutional aid to parochial schools, and against any boycott of the public schools (which I attended myself)—instead of judging me on the basis of these pamphlets and publications we have all seen that carefully select quotations out of context from the statements of Catholic Church leaders, usually in other countries, frequently in other centuries, and rarely relevant to any situation here—and always omitting, of course, that statement of the American bishops in 1948 which strongly endorsed church-state separation.

I do not consider these other quotations binding upon my public acts—why should you? But let me say, with respect to other countries, that I am wholly opposed to the state being used by any religious group, Catholic or Protestant, to compel, prohibit or persecute the free exercise of any other religion. And that goes for any persecution at any time, by anyone, in any country.

And I hope that you and I condemn with equal fervor those nations which deny their Presidency to Protestants and those which deny it to Catholics. And rather than cite the misdeeds of those who differ, I would also cite the record of the Catholic Church in such nations as France and Ireland—and the independence of such statesman as de Gaulle and Adenauer.

But let me stress again that these are my views—for, contrary to common newspaper usage, I am not the Catholic candidate for President. I am the Democratic Party's candidate for President, who happens also to be a Catholic.

I do not speak for my church on public matters—and the church does not speak for me.

Whatever issues may come before me as President, if I should be elected—on birth control, divorce, censorship, gambling, or any other subject—I will make my decision in accordance with these views, in accordance with what my conscience tells me to be in the national interest, and without regard to outside religious pressure or dictate. And no power or threat of punishment could cause me to decide otherwise.

But if the time should ever come—and I do not concede any conflict to be remotely possible—when my office would require me to either violate my conscience, or violate the national interest, then I would resign the office, and I hope any other conscientious public servant would do likewise.

But I do not intend to apologize for these views to my critics of either Catholic or Protestant faith, nor do I intend to disavow either my views or my church in order to win this election. If I should lose on the real issues, I shall return to my seat in the Senate, satisfied that I tried my best and was fairly judged.

But if this election is decided on the basis that 40,000,000 Americans lost their chance of being President on the day they were baptized, then it is the whole nation that will be the loser in the eyes of Catholics and non-Catholics around the world, in the eyes of history, and in the eyes of our own people.

But if, on the other hand, I should win this election, I shall devote every effort of mind and spirit to fulfilling the oath of the Presidency—practically identical, I might add, with the oath I have taken for fourteen years in the Congress. For, without reservation, I can, and I quote, "solemnly swear that I will faithfully execute the office of President of the United States and will to the best of my ability preserve, protect and defend the Constitution, so help me God."

EXCERPTS FROM THE GREAT DEBATES
September and October 1960

First Debate

September 26, 1960

HOWARD K. SMITH, moderator: Good evening. The television and radio stations of the United States and their affiliated stations are proud to provide facilities for a discussion of issues in the current political campaign by the two major candidates for the presidency. The candidates need no introduction. The Republican candidate, Vice President Richard M. Nixon, and the Democratic candidate, Senator John F. Kennedy. According to rules set by the candidates themselves, each man shall make an opening statement of approximately eight minutes' duration and a closing statement of approximately three minutes' duration. In between the candidates will answer, or comment upon answers to questions put by a panel of correspondents. In this, the first discussion in a series of four joint appearances, the subject-matter has been agreed, will be restricted to internal or domestic American matters. And now for the first opening statement by Senator John F. Kennedy.

Senator KENNEDY: Mr. Smith, Mr. Nixon. In the election of 1860, Abraham Lincoln said the question was whether this nation could exist half-slave or half-free. In the election of 1960, and with the world around us, the question is whether the world will exist half-slave or half-free, whether it will move in the direction of freedom, in the direction of the road that we are taking, or whether it will move in the direction of slavery. I think it will depend in great measure upon what we do here in the United States, on the kind of society that we build, on the kind of strength that we maintain. We discuss tonight domestic issues, but I would not want that to be any implication to be given that this does not involve directly our struggle with Mr. Khrushchev for survival. Mr. Khrushchev is in New York, and he maintains the Communist offensive throughout the world because of the productive power of the Soviet Union itself. The Chinese Communists have always had a large population. But they are important and dangerous now because they are mounting a major effort within their own country. The kind of country we have here, the kind of society we have, the kind of strength we build in the United States will be the defense of freedom. If we do well here, if we meet our obligations, if we're moving ahead, then I think freedom will be secure around the world. If we fail, then freedom fails. Therefore, I think the question before the American people is: Are we doing as much as we can do? Are we as strong as we

Adapted from Sidney Kraus, ed., *The Great Debates* (Bloomington, Ind., 1962), 348-68, 369-72, 374-75, 391-93, 396-99, 414-16, 419-20.

should be? Are we as strong as we must be if we're going to maintain our independence, and if we're going to maintain and hold out the hand of friendship to those who look to us for assistance, to those who look to us for survival? I should make it very clear that I do not think we're doing enough, that I am not satisfied as an American with the progress that we're making. This is a great country, but I think it could be a greater country; and this is a powerful country, but I think it could be a more powerful country. I'm not satisfied to have fifty per cent of our steel-mill capacity unused. I'm not satisfied when the United States had last year the lowest rate of economic growth of any major industrialized society in the world. Because economic growth means strength and vitality; it means we're able to sustain our defenses; it means we're able to meet our commitments abroad. I'm not satisfied when we have over nine billion dollars worth of food—some of it rotting—even though there is a hungry world, and even though four million Americans wait every month for a food package from the government, which averages five cents a day per individual. I saw cases in West Virginia, here in the United States, where children took home part of their school lunch in order to feed their families because I don't think we're meeting our obligations toward these Americans. I'm not satisfied when the Soviet Union is turning out twice as many scientists and engineers as we are. I'm not satisfied when many of our teachers are inadequately paid, or when our children go to school part-time shifts. I think we should have an educational system second to none. I'm not satisfied when I see men like Jimmy Hoffa—in charge of the largest union in the United States—still free. I'm not satisfied when we are failing to develop the natural resources of the United States to the fullest. Here in the United States, which developed the Tennessee Valley and which built the Grand Coulee and the other dams in the Northwest United States at the present rate of hydropower production—and that is the hallmark of an industrialized society—the Soviet Union by 1975 will be producing more power than we are. These are all the things, I think, in this country that can make our society strong, or can mean that it stands still. I'm not satisfied until every American enjoys his full constitutional rights. If a Negro baby is born—and this is true also of Puerto Ricans and Mexicans in some of our cities—he has about one-half as much chance to get through high school as a white baby. He has one-third as much chance to get through college as a white student. He has about a third as much chance to be a professional man, about half as much chance to own a house. He has about four times as much chance that he'll be out of work in his life as the white baby. I think we can do better. I don't want the talents of any American to go to waste. I know that there are those who say that we want to turn everything over to the government. I don't at all. I want the individuals to meet their responsibilities. And I want the states to meet their responsibilities. But I think there is also a national responsibility. The argument has been used against every piece of social legislation in the last twenty-five years. The people of the United States individually could not have developed the Tennessee Valley; collectively they could have. A cotton farmer in Georgia or a peanut farmer or a dairy farmer in Wisconsin and Minnesota, he cannot protect himself against the forces of supply and demand in the market place; but working together in effective governmental programs he can do so. Seventeen million

Americans, who live over sixty-five on an average Social Security check of about seventy-eight dollars a month, they're not able to sustain themselves individually, but they can sustain themselves through the social security system. I don't believe in big government, but I believe in effective governmental action. And I think that's the only way that the United States is going to maintain its freedom. It's the only way that we're going to move ahead. I think we can do a better job. I think we're going to have to do a better job if we are going to meet the responsibilites which time and events have placed upon us. We cannot turn the job over to anyone else. If the United States fails, then the whole cause of freedom fails. And I think it depends in great measure on what we do here in this country. The reason Franklin Roosevelt was a good neighbor in Latin America was because he was a good neighbor in the United States. Because they felt that the American society was moving again. I want us to recapture that image. I want people in Latin America and Africa and Asia to start to look to America; to see how we're doing things; to wonder what the president of the United States is doing; and not to look at Khrushchev, or look at the Chinese Communists. That is the obligation upon our generation. In 1933, Franklin Roosevelt said in his inaugural that his generation of Americans has a rendezvous with destiny. I think our generation of Americans has the same rendezvous. The question now is: Can freedom be maintained under the most severe attack it has ever known? I think it can be. And I think in the final analysis it depends upon what we do here. I think it's time America started moving again.

Mr. SMITH: And now the opening statement by Vice President Richard M. Nixon.

Mr. NIXON: Mr. Smith, Senator Kennedy. The things that Senator Kennedy has said many of us can agree with. There is no question but that we cannot discuss our internal affairs in the United States without recognizing that they have a tremendous bearing on our international position. There is no question but that this nation cannot stand still; because we are in a deadly competition, a competition not only with the men in the Kremlin, but the men in Peking. We're ahead in this competiion, as Senator Kennedy, I think, has implied. But when you're in a race, the only way to stay ahead is to move ahead. And I subscribe completely to the spirit that Senator Kennedy has expressed tonight, the spirit that the United States should move ahead. Where, then, do we disagree? I think we disagree on the implication of his remarks tonight and on the statements that he has made on many occasions during his campaign to the effect that the United States has been standing still. We heard tonight, for example, the statement made that our growth in national product last year was the lowest of any industrial nation in the world. Now last year, of course, was 1958. That happened to be a recession year. But when we look at the growth of G.N.P. this year, a year of recovery, we find that it's six and nine-tenths per cent and one of the highest in the world today. More about that later. Looking then to this problem of how the United States should move ahead and where the United States is moving, I think it is well that we take the advice of a very famous campaigner: Let's look at the record. Is the United States standing still? Is it true that this Administration, as Senator Kennedy has charged, has been an Administration of retreat, of defeat, of stagnation? Is it true that, as far as this country is concerned, in the field of electric power, in all of the fields that he has mentioned, we have not been moving ahead? Well, we have a comparison that we can make. We have the record of the Truman Administration of seven and a half years and the seven and a half years of the Eisenhower Administration. When we compare these two records in the areas that Senator Kennedy has discussed tonight, I think we find that America has been moving ahead. Let's take schools. We have built more schools in these last seven and a half years than we built in the previous seven and a half, for that matter in the last twenty years. Let's take hydroelectric power. We have developed more hydroelectric power in these seven and a half years than was developed in any previous administration in history. Let us take hospitals. We find that more have been built in this Administration than in the previous Administration. The same is true of highways. Let's put it in terms that all of us can understand. We often hear gross national product discussed and in that respect may I say that when we compare the growth in this Administration with that of the previous Administration that then there was a total growth of eleven per cent over seven years; in this Administration there has been a total growth of nineteen per cent over seven years. That shows that there's been more growth in this Administration than in its predecessor. But let's not put it there; let's put it in terms of the average family. What has happened to you? We find that your wages have gone up five times as much in the Eisenhower Administration as they did in the Truman Administration. What about the prices you pay? We find that the prices you pay went up five times as much in the Truman Administration as they did in the Eisenhower Administration. What's the net result of this? This means that the average family income went up fifteen per cent in the Eisenhower years as against two per cent in the Truman years. Now, this is not standing still. But, good as this record is, may I emphasize it isn't enough. A record is never something to stand on. It's something to build on. And in building on this record, I believe that we have the secret for progress, we know the way to progress. And I think, first of all, our own record proves that we know the way. Senator Kennedy has suggested that he believes he knows the way. I respect the sincerity with which he makes that suggestion. But on the other hand, when we look at the various programs that he offers, they do not seem to be new. They seem to be simply retreads of the programs of the Truman Administration which preceded it. And I would suggest that during the course of the evening he might indicate those areas in which his programs are new, where they will mean more progress than we had then. What kind of programs are we for? We are for programs that will expand educational opportunites, that will give to all Americans their equal chance for education, for all of the things which are necessary and dear to the hearts of our people. We are for programs, in addition, which will see that our medical care for the aged is much better handled than it is at the present time. Here again, may I indicate that Senator Kennedy and I are not in disagreement as to the aims. We both want to help the old people. We want to see that they do have adequate medical care. The question is the means. I think that the means that I advocate will reach that goal better than the means that he advocates. I could give better examples, but for whatever it is, whether it's in the field of housing, or health, or medical care, or schools, or the development of electric power, we have programs which we believe will move America, move her forward and build on the wonderful record that we have made over these past seven and a half years. Now, when we look at these programs, might I suggest that in evaluating them we often have a tendency to say that the test of a program is how much you're spending. I will concede that in all the areas to which I have referred Senator Kennedy would have the federal government spend more than I would have it spend. I costed out the cost of the Democratic platform. It runs a minimum of thirteen and two-tenths billions dollars a year more than we are presently spending to a maximum of eighteen billion dollars a year more than we're presently spending. Now the Republican platform will cost more too. It will cost a minimum of four billion dollars a year more, a maximum of four and nine-tenths billion dollars a year more than we're presently spending. Now, does this mean that his program is better than ours? Not at all. Because it isn't a question of how much the federal government spends; it isn't a question of which government does the most. It's a question of which administration does the right thing. And in our case, I do believe that our programs will stimulate the creative energies of a hundred and eighty million free Americans. I believe the programs that Senator Kennedy advocates will have a tendency to stifle those creative energies. I believe, in other words, that his program would lead to the stagnation of the motive power that we need in this country to get progress. The final point that I would like to make is this: Senator Kennedy has suggested in his speeches that we lack compassion for the poor, for the old, and for others that are unfortunate. Let us understand throughout this campaign that his motives and mine are sincere. I know what it means to be poor. I know what it means to see people who are unemployed. I know Senator Kennedy feels as deeply about these problems as I do, but our disagreement is not about the goals for America but only about the means to reach those goals.

Mr. SMITH: Thank you, Mr. Nixon. That completes the opening statements, and now the candidates will answer questions or comment upon one another's answers to questions, put by correspondents of the networks. The correspondents: [*introducing themselves*: "I'm Sander Vanocur, NBC News;" "I'm Charles Warren, Mutual News;" "I'm Stuart Novins, CBS News;" "Bob Fleming, ABC News."] The first question to Senator Kennedy from Mr. Fleming.

Mr. FLEMING: Senator, the Vice President in his campaign has said that you were naive and at times immature. He has raised the question of leadership. On this issue, why do you think people should vote for you rather than the Vice President?

Mr. KENNEDY: Well, the Vice President and I came to the Congress together in 1946; we both served in the Labor Committee. I've been there now fourteen years, the same period of time that he has, so that our experience in government is comparable. Secondly, I think the question is what are the programs that we advocate, what is the party record that we lead? I come out of the Democratic party, which in this century has produced Woodrow Wilson and Franklin Roosevelt and Harry Truman, and which supported and sustained these programs which I've discussed tonight. Mr. Nixon comes out of the Republican party. He was nominated by it. And it is a fact that through most of these last twenty-five years the Republican leadership has opposed federal aid for education, medical care for the aged, development of the Tennessee Valley, development of our natural resources. I think Mr. Nixon is an effective leader of his party. I hope he would grant me the same. The question before us is: which point of view and which party do we want to lead the United States?

Mr. SMITH: Mr. Nixon, would you like to comment on that statement?

Mr. NIXON: I have no comment.

Mr. SMITH: The next question: Mr. Novins.

Mr. NOVINS: Mr. Vice President, your campaign stresses the value of your eight-year experience, and the question arises as to whether that experience was as an observer or as a participant or as an initiator of policy-making. Would you tell us please specifically what major proposals you have made in the last eight years that have been adopted by the Administration?

Mr. NIXON: It would be rather difficult to cover them in two and a half minutes. I would suggest that these proposals could be mentioned. First, after each of my foreign trips I have made recommendations that have been adopted. For example, after my first trip abroad, I strongly recommended that we increase our exchange programs particularly as they related to exchange of persons and of leaders in the labor field and in the information field. After my trip to South America, I made recommendations that a separate inter-American lending agency be set up which the South American nations would like much better than to participate in the lending agencies which treated all the countries of the world the same. I have made other recommendations after each of the other trips; for example, after my trip abroad to Hungary I made some recommendations with regard to the Hungarian refugee situation which were adopted, not only by the President but some of them were enacted into law by the Congress. Within the Administration, as a chairman of the President's Committee on Price Stability and Economic Growth, I have had the opportunity to make recommendations which have been adopted within the Administration and which I think have been reasonably effective. I know Senator Kennedy suggested in his speech at Cleveland yesterday that that committee had not been particularly effective. I would only suggest that while we do not take the credit for it—I would not presume to—that since that committee has been formed the price line has been held very well within the United States.

Mr. KENNEDY: That's what I found somewhat unsatisfactory about the figures, Mr. Nixon, that you used in your previous speech, when you talked about the Truman Administration. Mr. Truman came to office in nineteen forty-four and at the end of the war, and difficulties that were facing the United States during that period of transition—1946 when price controls were lifted—so it's rather difficult to use an over-all figure taking those seven and a half years and comparing them to the last eight years. I prefer to take the over-all percentage record of the last twenty years of the Democrats and the eight years of the Republicans to show an over-all period of growth. In regard to price stability I'm not aware that that committee did produce recommendations that ever were certainly before the Congress from the point of view of legislation in regard to controlling prices. In regard to the exchange of students and labor unions, I am chairman of the subcommittee on Africa and I think that one of the most unfortunate phases of our policy towards that country was the very minute number of exchanges that we had. I think it's true of Latin America also. We did come forward with a program of students for the Congo of over three hundred which was more than the federal government had for all of Africa the previous year, so that I don't think that we have moved, at least in those areas, with sufficient vigor.

Mr. SMITH: The next question to Senator Kennedy from Mr. Warren.

Mr. WARREN: Senator Kennedy, during your brief speech a few minutes ago you mentioned farm surpluses.

Mr. KENNEDY: That's correct.

Mr. WARREN: I'd like to ask this: It's a fact, I think, that presidential candidates traditionally make promises to farmers. Lots of people, I think, don't understand why the government pays farmers for not producing certain crops—or paying farmers if they overproduce for that matter. Now, let me ask, sir, why can't the farmer operate like the business man who operates a factory? If an auto company overproduces a certain model car Uncle Sam doesn't step in and buy up the surplus. Why this constant courting of the farmer?

Mr. KENNEDY: Well, because I think that if the federal government moved out of the program and withdrew its supports then I think you would have complete economic chaos. The farmer plants in the spring and harvests in the fall. There are hundreds of thousands of them. They really are not able to control their market very well. They bring their crops in or their livestock in, many of them about the same time. They have only a few purchasers that buy their milk or their hogs—a few large companies in many cases—and therefore the farmer is not in a position to bargain very effectively in the market place. I think the experience of the twenties has shown what a free market could do to agriculture. And if the agricultural economy collapses, then the economy of the rest of the United States sooner or later will collapse. The farmers are the number one market for the automobile industry of the United States. The automobile industry is the number one market for steel. So if the farmers' economy continues to decline as sharply as it has in recent years, then I think you would have a recession in the rest of the country. So I think the case for the government intervention is a good one. Secondly, my objection to present farm policy is that there are no effective controls to bring supply and demand into better balance. The dropping of the support price in order to limit production does not work, and we now have the highest surpluses—nine billion dollars worth. We've had a higher tax load from the Treasury for the farmer in the last few years with the lowest farm income in many years. I think that this farm policy has failed. In my judgment the only policy that will work will be for effective supply and demand to be in balance. And that can only be done through governmental action. I therefore suggest that in those basic commodities which are supported, that the federal government, after endorsement by the farmers in that commodity, attempt to bring supply and demand into balance—attempt effective production controls—so that we won't have that five or six per cent surplus which breaks the price fifteen or twenty per cent. I think Mr. Benson's program has failed. And I must say, after reading the Vice President's speech before the farmers, as he read mine, I don't believe that it's very different from Mr. Benson's. I don't think it provides effective governmental controls. I think the support prices are tied to the average market price of the last three years, which was Mr. Benson's theory. I therefore do not believe that this is a sharp enough breach with the past to give us any hope of success for the future.

Mr. SMITH: Mr. Nixon, comment?

Mr. NIXON: I of course disagree with Senator Kennedy insofar as his suggestions as to what should be done on the farm program. He has made the suggestion that what we need is to move in the direction of more government controls, a suggestion that would also mean raising prices that the consumers pay for products and imposing upon the farmers controls on acreage even far more than they have today. I think this is the wrong direction. I don't think this has worked in the past; I do not think it will work in the future. The program that I have advocated is one which departs from the present program that we have in this respect. It recognizes that the government has a responsibility to get the farmer out of the trouble he presently is in because the government got him into it. And that's the fundamental reason why he can't let the farmer go by himself at the present time. The farmer produced these surpluses because the government asked him to through legislation during the war. Now that we have these surpluses, it's our responsibility to indemnify the farmer during that period that we get rid of the farmer—the surpluses. Until we get the surpluses off the farmer's back, however, we should have a program such as I announced, which will see that farm income holds up. But I would propose holding that income up not through a type of program that Senator Kennedy has suggested that would raise prices, but one that would indemnify the farmer, pay the farmer in kind from the products which are in surplus.

Mr. SMITH: The next question to Vice President Nixon from Mr. Vanocur.

Mr. VANOCUR: Mr. Vice President, since the question of executive leadership is a very important campaign issue, I'd like to follow Mr. Novin's question. Now, Republican campaign slogans—you'll see them on signs around the country as you did last week—say it's experience that counts—that's over a picture of yourself, sir, implying that you've had more governmental executive decision-making experience than your opponent. Now, in his news conference on August twenty-fourth, President Eisenhower was asked to give one example of a major idea of yours that he adopted. His reply was, and I'm quoting: "If you give me a week I might think of one. I don't remember." Now that was a month ago, sir, and the President hasn't brought it up since, and I'm wondering, sir, if you can clarify which version is correct—the one put out by Republican campaign leaders or the one put out by President Eisenhower?

Mr. NIXON: Well, I would suggest, Mr. Vanocur, that if you know the President, that was probably a facetious remark. I would also suggest that insofar as his statement is concerned, that I think it would be improper for the President of the United States to disclose the instances in which members of his official family had made recommendations, as I have made them through the years to him, which he has accepted or rejected. The President has always maintained and very properly so that he is entitled to get what advice he wants from his cabinet and from his other advisers without disclosing that to anybody—including as a matter of fact the Congress. Now, I can only say this. Through the years I have sat in the National Security Council. I have been in the cabinet. I have met with the legislative leaders. I have met with the President when he made the great decisions with regard to Lebanon, Quemoy and Matsu, other matters. The President has asked for my advice. I have given it. Sometimes my advice has been taken. Sometimes it has not. I do not say that I have made the decisions. And I would say that no president should ever allow anybody else to make the major decisions. The president only makes the decisions. All that his advisers do is to give counsel when he asks for it. As far as what experience counts and whether that is experience that counts, that isn't for me to say. I can only say that my experience is there for the people to consider; Senator Kennedy's is there for the people to consider. As he pointed out, we came to the Congress in the same year. His experience has been different from mine. Mine has been in the executive branch. His has been in the legislative branch. I would say that the people now have the opportunity to evaluate his as against mine and I think both he and I are going to abide by whatever the people decide.

Mr. SMITH: Senator Kennedy.

Mr. KENNEDY: Well, I'll just say that the question is of experience— and the question also is what our judgment is of the future, and what our goals are for the United States, and what ability we have to implement those goals. Abraham Lincoln came to the presidency in 1860 after a rather little known session in the House of Representatives and after being defeated for the Senate in fifty-eight and was a distinguished president. There's no certain road to the presidency. There are no guarantees that if you take one road or another that you will be a successful president. I have been in the Congress for fourteen years. I have voted in the last eight years and the Vice President was presiding over the Senate and meeting his other responsibilities. I have made decisions over eight hundred times on matters which affect not only the domestic security of the United States, but as a member of the Senate Foreign Relations Committee. The question really is: which candidate and which party can meet the problems that the United States is going to face in the sixties?

Mr. SMITH: The next question to Senator Kennedy from Mr. Novins.

Mr. NOVINS: Senator Kennedy, in connection with these problems of the future that you speak of, and the program that you enunciated earlier in your direct talk, you call for expanding some of the welfare programs for schools, for teacher salaries, medical care, and so forth; but you also call for reducing the federal debt. And I'm wondering how you, if you're president in January, would go about paying the bill for all this. Does this mean that you—[1]

Mr. KENNEDY: I didn't indicate—[1] I did not advocate reducing the federal debt because I don't believe that you're going to be able to reduce the federal debt very much in nineteen sixty-one, two, or three. I think you have heavy obligations which affect our security, which we're going to have to meet. And therefore I've never suggested we should be able to retire the debt substantially, or even at all in nineteen sixty-one or two.

---

[1] The opening words of Mr. Kennedy's reply overlapped the last few words of this portion of Mr. Novins' question, partially obscuring both.

Mr. NOVINS: Senator, I believe in one of your speeches—
Mr. KENNEDY: No, never.
Mr. NOVINS: —you suggested that reducing the interest rate would help toward—
Mr. KENNEDY: No. No. Not reducing the interest—[2]
Mr. NOVINS:—a reduction of the Federal debt.[2]
Mr. KENNEDY:—reducing the interest rate. In my judgment, the hard money, tight money policy, fiscal policy of this Administration has contributed to the slow-down in our economy, which helped bring the recession of fifty-four; which made the recession of fifty-eight rather intense, and which has slowed, somewhat, our economic activity in 1960. What I have talked about, however, the kind of programs that I've talked about, in my judgment, are fiscally sound. Medical care for the aged, I would put under social security. The Vice President and I disagree on this. The program—the Javits-Nixon or the Nixon-Javits program—would have cost, if fully used six hundred million dollars by the government per year, and six hundred million dollars by the state. The program which I advocated, which failed by five votes in the United States Senate, would have put medical care for the aged in Social Security, and would have been paid for through the Social Security System and the Social Security tax. Secondly, I support federal aid to education and federal aid for teachers' salaries. I think that's a good investment. I think we're going to have to do it. And I think to heap the burden further on the property tax, which is already strained in many of our communities, will provide, will insure, in my opinion, that many of our children will not be adequately educated, and many of our teachers not adequately compensated. There is no greater return to an economy or to a society than an educational system second to none. On the question of the developemnt of natural resources, I would pay as you go in the sense that they would be balanced and the power revenues would bring back sufficient money to finance the projects, in the same way as the Tennessee Valley. I believe in the balanced budget. And the only conditions under which I would unbalance the budget would be if there was a grave national emergency or a serious recession. Otherwise, with a steady rate of economic growth—and Mr. Nixon and Mr. Rockefeller, in their meeting, said a five per cent economic growth would bring by 1962 ten billion dollars extra in tax revenues. Whatever is brought in, I think that we can finance essential programs within a balanced budget, if business remains orderly.
Mr. SMITH: Mr. Nixon, your comment?
Mr. NIXON: Yes. I think what Mr. Novins was referring to was not one of Senator Kennedy's speeches, but the Democratic platform, which did mention cutting the national debt. I think, too, that it should be pointed out that of course it is not possible, particularly under the proposals that Senator Kennedy has advocated, either to cut the national debt or to reduce taxes. As a matter of fact it will be necessary to raise taxes. As Senator Kennedy points out that as far as his one proposal is concerned—the one for medical care for the aged—that that would be financed out of Social Security. That, however, is raising taxes for those who pay Social Security. He

[2]These two remarks overlapped and partially obscured each other.

points out that we would make pay-as-you-go be the basis for our natural resources development. Where our natural resources development—which I also support, incidentally, however—whenever you appropriate money for one of these projects, you have to pay now and appropriate the money and while they eventually do pay out, it doesn't mean that the government doesn't have to put out the money this year. And so I would say that in all of these proposals Senator Kennedy has made, they will result in one of two things: either he has to raise taxes or he has to unbalance the budget. If he unbalances the budget, that means you have inflation, and that will be, of course, a very cruel blow to the very people—the older people—that we've been talking about. As far as aid for school construction is concerned, I favor that, as Senator Kennedy did, in January of this year, when he said he favored that rather than aid to teacher salaries. I favor that because I believe that's the best way to aid our schools without running any risk whatever of the federal government telling our teachers what to teach.

Mr. SMITH: The next question to Vice President Nixon from Mr. Warren.

Mr. WARREN: Mr. Vice President you mentioned schools and it was just yesterday I think you asked for a crash program to raise education standards, and this evening you talked about advances in education. Mr. Vice President, you said—it was back in 1957—that salaries paid to school teachers were nothing short of a national disgrace. Higher salaries for teachers, you added, were important and if the situation wasn't corrected it could lead to a national disaster. And yet, you refused to vote in the Senate in order to break a tie vote when that single vote, if it had been yes, would have granted salary increases to teachers. I wonder if you could explain that, sir.

Mr. NIXON: I'm awfully glad you got that question because as you know I got into it at the last of my other question and wasn't able to complete the argument. I think that the reason that I voted against having the federal government pay teachers' salaries was probably the very reason that concerned Senator Kennedy when in January of this year, in his kick-off press conference, he said that he favored aid for school construction, but at that time did not feel that there should be aid for teachers' salaries—at least that's the way I read his remarks. Now, why should there be any question about the federal government aiding teachers' salaries? Why did Senator Kennedy take that position then? Why do I take it now? We both took it then, and I take it now, for this reason: we want higher teachers' salaries. We need higher teachers' salaries. But we also want our education to be free of federal control. When the federal government gets the power to pay teachers, inevitably in my opinion, it will acquire the power to set standards and to tell the teachers what to teach. I think this would be bad for the country; I think it would be bad for the teaching profession. There is another point that should be made. I favor higher salaries for teachers. But, as Senator Kennedy said in January of this year in this same press conference, the way that you get higher salaries for teachers is to support school construction, which means that all of the local school districts in the various states then have money which is freed to raise the standards for teachers' salaries. I should also point out this: once you put the responsibility on the federal government for paying a portion of teachers' salaries, your local communities and your states are not going to meet the responsibility as much as they should. I believe, in other words, that we have seen the local communities and the state assuming more of that responsibility. Teachers' salaries very fortunately have gone up fifty per cent in the last eight years as against only a thirty-four per cent rise for other salaries. This is not enough; it should be more. But I do not believe that the way to get more salaries for teachers is to have the federal government get in with a massive program. My objection here is not the cost in dollars. My objection here is the potential cost in controls and eventual freedom for the American people by giving the federal government power over education, and that is the greatest power a government can have.

Mr. SMITH: Senator Kennedy's comment?

Mr. KENNEDY: When the Vice President quotes me in January, sixty, I do not believe the federal government should pay directly teachers' salaries, but that was not the issue before the Senate in February. The issue before the Senate was that the money would be given to the state. The state then could determine whether the money should be spent for school construction or teacher salaries. On that question the Vice President and I disagreed. I voted in favor of that proposal and supported it strongly, because I think that that provided assistance to our teachers for their salaries without any chance of federal control and it is on that vote that Mr. Nixon and I disagreed, and his tie vote defeated—his breaking the tie defeated—the proposal. I don't want the federal government paying teachers' salaries directly. But if the money will go to the states and the states can then determine whether it shall go for school construction or for teachers' salaries, in my opinion you protect the local authority over the school board and the school committee. And therefore I think that was a sound proposal and that is why I supported it and I regret that it did not pass. Secondly, there have been statements made that the Democratic platform would cost a good deal of money and that I am in favor of unbalancing the budget. That is wholly wrong, wholly in error, and it is a fact that in the last eight years the Democratic Congress has reduced the requests for the appropriations by over ten billion dollars. That is not my view and I think it ought to be stated very clearly on the record. My view is that you can do these programs—and they should be carefully drawn—within a balanced budget if our economy is moving ahead.

Mr. SMITH: The next question to Senator Kennedy from Mr. Vanocur.

Mr. VANOCUR: Senator, you've been promising the voters that if you are elected president you'll try and push through Congress bills on medical aid to the aged, a comprehensive minimum hourly wage bill, federal aid to education. Now, in the August post-convention session of the Congress, when you at least held up the possibility you could one day be president and when you had overwhelming majorities, especially in the Senate, you could not get action on these bills. Now how do you feel that you'll be able to get them in January—

Mr. KENNEDY: Well as you take the bills—[3]

Mr. VANOCUR:—if you weren't able to get them in August?[3]

---

[3]The opening words of Mr. Kennedy's reply overlapped the last few words of Mr. Vanocur's question, partially obscuring both.

Mr. KENNEDY: If I may take the bills, we did pass in the Senate a bill to provide a dollar twenty-five cent minimum wage. It failed because the House did not pass it and the House failed by eleven votes. And I might say that two-thirds of the Republicans in the House voted against a dollar twenty-five cent minimum wage and a majority of the Democrats sustained it—nearly two-thirds of them voted for the dollar twenty-five. We were threatened by a veto if we passed a dollar and a quarter—it's extremely difficult with the great power that the president has to pass any bill when the president is opposed to it. All the president needs to sustain his veto of any bill is one-third plus one in either the House or the Senate. Secondly, we passed a federal aid to education bill in the Senate. It failed to come to the floor of the House of Representatives. It was killed in the Rules Committee. And it is a fact in the August session that the four members of the Rules Committee who were Republicans joining with two Democrats voted against sending the aid to education bill to the floor of the House. Four Democrats voted for it. Every Republican on the Rules Committee voted against sending that bill to be considered by the members of the House of Representatives. Thirdly, on medical care for the aged, this is the same fight that's been going on for twenty-five years in Social Security. We wanted to tie it to Social Security. We offered an amendment to do so. Forty-four Democrats voted for it, one Republican voted for it. And we were informed at the time it came to a vote that if it was adopted the President of the United States would veto it. In my judgment, a vigorous Democratic president supported by a Democratic majority in the House and Senate can win the support for these programs. But if you send a Republican president and a Democratic majority and the threat of a veto hangs over the Congress, in my judgment you will continue what happened in the August session, which is a clash of parties and inaction.

Mr. SMITH: Mr. Nixon, comment?

Mr. NIXON: Well obviously my views are a little different. First of all, I don't see how it's possible for a one-third of a body, such as the Republicans have in the House and the Senate to stop two-thirds, if the two-thirds are adequately led. I would say, too, that when Senator Kennedy refers to the action of the House Rules Committee, there are eight Democrats on that committee and four Republicans. It would seem to me again that it is very difficult to blame the four Republicans for the eight Democrats' not getting a something through that particular committee. I would say further that to blame the President in his veto power for the inability of the Senator and his colleagues to get action in this special session misses the mark. When the president exercises his veto power, he has to have the people—behind him, not just a third of the Congress. Because let's consider it. If the majority of the members of the Congress felt that these particular proposals were good issues—the majority of those who were Democrats—why didn't they pass them and send to the President and get a veto and have an issue? The reason why these particular bills in these various fields that have been mentioned were not passed was not because the President was against them; it was because the people were against them. It was because they were too extreme. And I am convinced that the alternate proposals that I have, that the Republicans have in the field of health, in the field of education, in the field of welfare, because they are not extreme, because they will accomplish the end without too great cost in dollars or in freedom, that they could get through the next Congress.

Mr. SMITH: The next question to Vice President Nixon from Mr. Fleming.

Mr. FLEMING: Mr. Vice President, do I take it then you believe that you can work better with Democratic majorities in the House and Senate than Senator Kennedy could work with Democratic majorities in the House and Senate?

Mr. NIXON: I would say this: that we, of course, expect to pick up some seats in both in the House and the Senate. We would hope to control the House, to get a majority in the House in this election. We cannot, of course, control the Senate. I would say that a president will be able to lead—a president will be able to get his program through—to the effect that he has the support of the country, the support of the people. Sometimes we—we get the opinion that in getting programs through the House or the Senate it's purely a question of legislative finagling and all that sort of thing. It isn't really that. Whenever a majority of the people are for a program, the House and the Senate responds to it. And whether this House and Senate, in the next session is Democratic or Republican, if the country will have voted for the candidate for the presidency and for the proposals that he has made, I believe that you will find that the president, if it were a Republican, as it would be in my case, would be able to get his program through that Congress. Now, I also say that as far as Senator Kennedy's proposals are concerned, that, again, the question is not simply one of a presidential veto stopping programs. You must always remember that a president can't stop anything unless he has the people behind him. And the reason President Eisenhower's vetoes have been sustained—the reason the Congress does not send up bills to him which they think will be vetoed—is because the people and the Congress, the majority of them, know the country is behind the President.

Mr. SMITH: Senator Kennedy.

Mr. KENNEDY: Well, now let's look at these bills that the Vice President suggests were too extreme. One was a bill for a dollar twenty-five cents an hour for anyone who works in a store or company that has a million dollars a year business. I don't think that's extreme at all; and yet nearly two-thirds to three-fourths of the Republicans in the House of Representatives voted against that proposal. Secondly was the federal aid to education bill. It—it was a very—because of the defeat of teacher salaries, it was not a bill that met in my opinion the need. The fact of the matter is, it was a bill that was less than you recommended, Mr. Nixon, this morning in your proposal. It was not an extreme bill and yet we could not get one Republican to join, at least I think four of the eight Democrats voted to send it to the floor of the House—not one Republican—and they joined with those Democrats who were opposed to it. I don't say the Democrats are united in their support of the program. But I do say a majority are. And I say a majority of the Republicans are opposed to it. The third is medical care for the aged which is tied to Social Security, which is financed out of Social Security funds. It does not put a deficit on the Treasury. The proposal advanced by you and by Mr. Javits would have cost six hundred millions of dollars—Mr. Rockefeller rejected it in New York, said he didn't agree with the financing at all, said it ought to be on Social Security. So these are three programs which are quite moderate. I think it shows the difference between the two parties. One party is ready to move in these programs. The other party gives them lip service.

Mr. SMITH: Mr. Warren's question for Senator Kennedy.

Mr. WARREN: Senator Kennedy, on another subject, Communism is so often described as an ideology or a belief that exists somewhere other than in the United States. Let me ask you, sir: just how serious a threat to our national security are these Communist subversive activities in the United States today?

Mr. KENNEDY: Well, I think they're serious. I think it's a matter that we should continue to give great care and attention to. We should support the laws which the United States has passed in order to protect us from those who would destroy us from within. We should sustain the Department of Justice in its efforts and the F.B.I., and we should be continually alert. I think if the United States is maintaining a strong society here in the United States, I think that we can meet any internal threat. The major threat is external and will continue.

Mr. SMITH: Mr. Nixon, comment?

Mr. NIXON: I agree with Senator Kennedy's appraisal generally in this respect. The question of Communism within the United States has been one that has worried us in the past. It is one that will continue to be a problem for years to come. We have to remember that the cold war that Mr. Khrushchev is waging and his colleagues are waging, is waged all over the world and it's waged right here in the United States. That's why we have to continue to be alert. It is also essential in being alert that we be fair; fair because by being fair we uphold the very freedoms that the Communists would destroy. We uphold the standards of conduct which they would never follow. And, in this connection, I think that we must look to the future having in mind the fact that we fight Communism at home not only by our laws to deal with Communists the few who do become Communists and the few who do become fellow travelers, but we also fight Communism at home by moving against those various injustices which exist in our society which the Communists feed upon. And in that connection I again would say that while Senator Kennedy says we are for the status quo, I do believe that he would agree that I am just as sincere in believing that my proposals for federal aid to education, my proposals for health care are just as sincerely held as his. The question again is not one of goals—we're for those goals—it's one of means.

Mr. SMITH: Mr. Vanocur's question for Vice President Nixon.

Mr. VANOCUR: Mr. Vice President in one of your earlier statements you said we've moved ahead, we've built more schools, we've built more hospitals. Now, sir, isn't it true that the building of more schools is a local matter for financing? Were you claiming that the Eisenhower Administration was responsible for the building of these schools, or is it the local school districts that provide for it?

Mr. NIXON: Not at all. As a matter of fact your question brings out a point that I'm very glad to make. Too often in appraising whether we are moving ahead or not we think only of what the federal government is doing. Now that isn't the test of whether America moves. The test of whether America moves is whether the federal government, plus the state government, plus the local government, plus the biggest segment of all—individual enterprise—moves. We have for example a gross national product of approximately five hundred billion dollars. Roughly a hundred billion to a hundred and a quarter billion of that is the result of government activity. Four hundred billion, approximately, is a result of what individuals do. Now, the reason the Eisenhower Administration has moved, the reason that we've had the funds, for example, locally to build the schools, and the hospitals, and the highways, to make the progress that we have, is because this Administration has encouraged individual enterprise; and it has resulted in the greatest expansion of the private sector of the economy that has ever been witnessed in an eight-year period. And that is growth. That is the growth that we are looking for; it is the growth that this Administration has supported and that its policies have stimulated.

Mr. SMITH: Senator Kennedy.

Mr. KENNEDY: Well, I must say that the reason that the schools have been constructed is because the local school districts were willing to increase the property taxes to a tremendously high figure—in my opinion, almost to the point of diminishing returns in order to sustain these schools. Secondly, I think we have a rich country. And I think we have a powerful country. I think what we have to do, however, is have the president and the leadership set before our country exactly what we must do in the next decade, if we're going to maintain our security in education, in economic growth, in development of natural resources. The Soviet Union is making great gains. It isn't enough to compare what might have been done eight years ago, or ten years ago, or fifteen years ago, or twenty years ago. I want to compare what we're doing with what our adversaries are doing, so that by the year 1970 the United States is ahead in education, in health, in building, in homes, in economic strength. I think that's the big assignment, the big task, the big function of the federal government.

Mr. SMITH: Can I have the summation time please? We've completed our questions and our comments, and in just a moment, we'll have the summation time.

VOICE: This will allow three minutes and twenty seconds for the summation by each candidate.

Mr. SMITH: Three minutes and twenty seconds for each candidate. Vice President Nixon, will you make the first summation?

Mr. NIXON: Thank you, Mr. Smith. Senator Kennedy. First of all, I think it is well to put in perspective where we really do stand with regard to the Soviet Union in this whole matter of growth. The Soviet Union has been moving faster than we have. But the reason for that is obvious. They start from a much lower base. Although they have been moving faster in growth than we have, we find, for example, today that their total gross national product is only forty-four per cent of our total gross national product. That's the same percentage that it was twenty years ago. And as far as the absolute gap is concerned, we find that the United States is even further ahead than it was twenty years ago. Is this any reason for complacency? Not at all. Because these are determined men. They are fanatical men. And we have to get the very most out of our economy. I agree with Senator Kennedy completely on that score. Where we disagree is in the means that we would use to get the most out of our economy. I respectfully submit that Senator Kennedy too often would rely too much on the federal government, on what it would do to solve our problems, to stimulate growth. I believe that when we examine the Democratic platform, when we examine the proposals that he has discussed tonight, when we compare them with the proposals that I have made, that these proposals that he makes would not result in greater growth for this country than would be the case if we followed the programs that I have advocated. There are many of the points that he has made that I would like to comment upon. The one in the field of health is worth mentioning. Our health program—the one that Senator Javits and other Republican Senators, as well as I supported—is one that provides for all people over sixty-five who want health insurance, the opportunity to have it if they want it. It provides a choice of having either government insurance or private insurance. But it compels nobody to have insurance who does not want it. His program under Social Security, would require everybody who had Social Security to take government health insurance whether he wanted it or not. And it would not cover several million people who are not covered by Social Security at all. Here is one place where I think that our program does a better job than his. The other point that I would make is this: this downgrading of how much things cost I think many of our people will understand better when they look at what happened when—during the Truman Administration when the government was spending more than it took in—we found savings over a lifetime eaten up by inflation. We found the people who could least afford it—people on retired incomes—people on fixed incomes—we found them unable to meet their bills at the end of the month. It is essential that a man who's president of this country certainly stand for every program that will mean for growth. And I stand for programs that will mean growth and progress. But it is also essential that he not allow a dollar spent that could be better spent by the people themselves.

Mr. SMITH: Senator Kennedy, your conclusion.

Mr. KENNEDY: The point was made by Mr. Nixon that the Soviet production is only forty-four per cent of ours. I must say that forty-four per cent and that Soviet country is causing us a good deal of trouble tonight. I want to make sure that it stays in that relationship. I don't want to see the day when it's sixty per cent of ours, and seventy and seventy-five and eighty and ninety per cent of ours, with all the force and power that it could bring to bear in order to cause our destruction. Secondly, the Vice President mentioned medical care for the aged. Our program was an amendment to the Kerr bill. The Kerr bill provided assistance to all those who were not on Social Security. I think it's a very clear contrast. In 1935, when the Social Security Act was written, ninety-four out of ninety-five Republicans voted against it. Mr. Landon ran in 1936 to repeal it. In August of 1960, when we tried to get it again, but this time for medical care, we received the support of one Republican in the Senate on this occasion. Thirdly, I think the question before the American people is: as they look at this country and as they look at the world around them, the goals are the same for all Americans. The means are at question. The means are at issue. If you feel that everything that is being done now is satisfactory, that the relative power and prestige and strength of the United States is increasing in relation to that of the Communists; that we've been gaining more security, that we are achieving everything as a nation that we should achieve, that we are achieving a better life for our citizens and greater strength, then I agree, I think you should vote for Mr. Nixon. But if you feel that we have to move again in the sixties, that the function of the president is to set before the people the unfinished business of our society as Franklin Roosevelt did in the thirties, the agenda for our people—what we must do as a society to meet our needs in this country and protect our security and help the cause of freedom. As I said at the beginning, the question before us all, that faces all Republicans and all Democrats is: can freedom in the next generation conquer, or are the Communists going to be successful? That's the great issue. And if we meet our responsibilities I think freedom will conquer. If we fail, if we fail to move ahead, if we fail to develop sufficient military and economic and social strength here in this country, then I think that the tide could begin to run against us. And I don't want historians, ten years from now, to say, these were the years when the tide ran out for the United States. I want them to say these were the years when the tide came in; these were the years when the United States started to move again. That's the question before the American people, and only you can decide what you want, what you want this country to be, what you want to do with the future. I think we're ready to move. And it is to that great task, if we're successful, that we will address ourselves.

Mr. SMITH: Thank you very much, gentlemen. This hour has gone by all too quickly. Thank you very much for permitting us to present the next president of the United States on this unique program. I've been asked by the candidates to thank the American networks and the affiliated stations for providing time and facilities for this joint appearance. Other debates in this series will be announced later and will be on different subjects. This is Howard K. Smith. Good night from Chicago.

Second Debate

October 7, 1960

Mr. NIVEN: Mr. Vice President, Senator Kennedy said last night that the Administration must take responsibility for the loss of Cuba. Would you compare the validity of that statement with the validity of your own statements in previous campaigns that the Truman Administration was responsible for the loss of China to the Communists?

Mr. NIXON: Well first of all, I don't agree with Senator Kennedy that Cuba is lost and certainly China was lost when this Administration came into power in 1953. As I look at Cuba today, I believe that we are following the right course, a course which is difficult but a course which under the circumstance is the only proper one which will see that the Cuban people get a chance to realize their aspirations of progress through freedom and that they get with our cooperation with the states in the Organization of American States. Now Senator Kennedy has made some very strong criticisms of my part—or alleged part—in what has happened in Cuba. He points to the fact that I visited Cuba while Mr. Batista was in power there. I can only point out that if we are going to judge the Administrations in terms of our attitude toward dictators, we're glad to have a comparison with the previous administration. There were eleven dicatators in South America and in Central America when we came in, in 1953. Today there are only three left including the one in Cuba. We think that's pretty good progress. Senator Kennedy also indicated with regard to Cuba that he thought that I had made a mistake when I was in Cuba in not calling for free elections in that country. Now I'm very surprised that Senator Kennedy, who is on the Foreign Relations Committee, would have made such a statement as this kind. As a matter of fact in his book, *The Strategy for Peace*, he took the right position. And that position is that the United States has a treaty—a treaty with all of the Organization of American States—which prohibits us from interfering in the internal affairs of any other state and prohibits them as well. For me to have made such a statement would have been in direct opposition to that treaty. Now with regard to Cuba, let me make one thing clear. There isn't any question but that we will defend our rights there. There isn't any question but that we will defend Guantanamo if it's attacked. There also isn't any question but that the free people of Cuba—the people who want to be free—are going to be supported and they they will attain their freedom. No, Cuba is not lost, and I don't think this kind of defeatist talk by Senator Kennedy helps the situation one bit.

Mr. McGEE: Senator Kennedy, would you care to comment?

Mr. KENNEDY: In the first place I've never suggested that Cuba was lost except for the present. In my speech last night I indicated that I thought that Cuba one day again would be free. Where I've been critical of the Administration's policy, and where I criticized Mr. Nixon, was because in his press conference in Havana in 1955, he praised the competence and stability of the Batista dictatorship—that dictatorship had killed over twenty thousand Cubans in seven years. Secondly, I did not criticize him for not calling for free elections. What I criticized was the failure of the Administration to use its great influence to persuade the Cuban government to hold free elections, particularly in 1957 and 1958. Thirdly, Arthur Gardner, a Republican Ambassador, Earl Smith, a Republican Ambassador, in succession—both have indicated in the past six weeks that they reported to Washington that Castro was a Marxist, that Raul Castro was a Communist, and that they got no effective results. Instead our aid continued to Batista, which was ineffective; we never were on the side of freedom; we never used our influence when we could have used it most effectively—and today Cuba is lost for freedom. I hope some day it will rise; but I don't think it will rise if we continue the same policies toward Cuba that we did in recent years, and in fact towards all of Latin America—when we've almost ignored the needs of Latin America; we've beamed not a single Voice of America program in Spanish to all of Latin America in the last eight years, except for the three months of the Hungarian revolution.

Mr. McGEE: Mr. Morgan, with a question for Senator Kennedy.

Mr. MORGAN: Senator, last May, in Oregon, you discussed the possibilities of sending apologies or regrets to Khrushchev over the U-2 incident. Do you think now that that would have done any good? Did you think so then?

Mr. KENNEDY: Mr. Morgan, I suggested that if the United States felt that it could save the summit conference that it would have been proper for us to have expressed regrets. In my judgment that statement has been distorted by Mr. Nixon and others in their debates around the country and in their discussions. Mr. Lodge, on "Meet the Press" a month ago, said if there was ever a case when we did not have law on our side it was in the U-2 incident. The U-2 flights were proper from the point of view of protecting our security. But they were not in accordance with international law. And I said that I felt that rather than tell the lie which we told, rather than indicate that the flights would continue—in fact, I believe Mr. Nixon himself said on May fifteenth that the flights would continue even though Mr. Herter testified before the Senate Foreign Relations Committee that they had been canceled as of May twelfth—that it would have been far better that if we had expressed regrets, if that would have saved the summit, and if the summit is useful—and I believe it is. The point that is always left out is the fact that we expressed regrets to Castro this winter; that we expressed regrets—the Eisenhower Administration expressed regrets—for a flight over Southern Russia in 1958. We expressed regrets for a flight over Eastern Germany under this Administration. The Soviet Union in 1955 expressed regrets to us over the Bering Sea incident. The Chinese Communists expressed regrets to us over a plane incident in 1956. That is the accepted procedure between nations; and my judgment is that we should follow the advice of Theodore Roosevelt: Be strong; maintain a strong position; but also speak softly. I believe that in those cases where international custom calls for the expression of a regret, if that would have kept the summit going, in my judgment it was a proper action. It's not appeasement. It's not soft. I believe we should be stronger than we now are. I believe we should have a stronger military force. I believe we should increase our strength all over the world. But I don't confuse words with strength; and in my judgment if the summit was useful, if it would have brought us closer to peace, that rather than the lie that we told—which has been criticized by all responsible people afterwards—it would have been far better for us to follow the common diplomatic procedure of expressing regrets and then try to move on.

Mr. McGEE: Mr. Vice President.

Mr. NIXON: I think Senator Kennedy is wrong on three counts. First of all, he's wrong in thinking, even suggesting that Mr. Khrushchev might have continued the conference if we had expressed regrets. He knew these flights were going on long before and that wasn't the reason that he broke up the conference. Second, he's wrong in the analogies that he makes. The United States is a strong country. Whenever we do anything that's wrong, we can express regrets. But when the president of the United States is doing something that's right, something that is for the purpose of defending the security of this country against surprise attack, he can never express regrets or apologize to anybody, including Mr. Khrushchev. Now in that connection Senator Kennedy has criticized the President on the ground not only of not expressing regrets, but because he allowed this flight to take place while the summit conference—or immediately before the summit conference occurred. This seems to me is criticism that again is wrong on his part. We all remember Pearl Harbor. We lost three thousand American lives. We cannot afford an intelligence gap. And I just want to make my position absolutely clear with regard to getting intelligence information. I don't intend to see to it that the United States is ever in a positiion where, while we're negotiating with the Soviet Union, that we discontinue our intelligence effort. And I don't intend ever to express regrets to Mr. Khrushchev or anybody else if I'm doing something that has the support of the Congress and that is right for the purpose of protecting the security of the United States. . . .

Mr. LEVY: Senator, on the same subject,[4] in the past you have emphasized the president's responsibility as a moral leader as well as an executive on civil rights questions. What specifically might the next president do in the event of an occurrence such as Little Rock or the lunch-counter sit-ins? From the standpoint of—[5]

Mr. KENNEDY: Well let me say that I think that the president operates in a number of different areas. First, as a legislative leader. And as I just said that I believe that the passage of the so-called Title Three, which gives the Attorney General the power to protect Constitutional rights in those cases where it's not possible for the person involved to bring the suit. Secondly, as an executive leader. There have been only six cases brought by this Attorney General under the voting bill passed in 1957 and the voting bill passed in 1960. The right to vote is basic. I do not believe that this Administration has implemented those bills which represent the will of the majority of the Congress on two occasions with vigor. Thirdly, I don't belive that the government contracts division is operated with vigor. Everyone who does business with the government should have the opportunity to make sure that they do not practice discrimination in their hiring. And that's in all sections of the United States. And then fourthly, as a moral leader. There is a very strong moral basis for this concept of equality of opportunity. We are in a very difficult time. We need all the talent we can get. We sit on a conspicuous stage. We are a goldfish bowl before the world. We have to practice what we preach. We set a very high standard for ourselves. The Communists do not. They set a low standard of materialism. We preach in the Declaration of Independence and in the Constitution, in the statement of our greatest leaders, we preach very high standards; and if we're not going to be charged before the world with hypocrisy we have to meet those standards. I believe the president of the United States should indicate it. Now lastly, I believe in the case of Little Rock. I would have hoped that the president of the United States would have been possible for him to indicate it clearly that the Supreme Court decision was going to be carried out. I would have hoped that it would have been possible to use marshals to do so. But it evidently— under the handling of the case it was not. I would hope an incident like that would not happen. I think if the president is responsible, if he consults with those involved, if he makes it clear that the Supreme Court decision is going to be carried out in a way that the Supreme Court planned—with deliberate speed—then in my judgment, providing he's behind action, I believe we can make progress. Now the present Administration— the President—has said—never indicated what he thought of the 1954 decision. Unless the president speaks, then of course the country doesn't speak, and Franklin Roosevelt said: "The presidency of the United States is above all a place of moral leadership." And I believe on this great moral issue he should speak out and give his views clearly. . . .

[4] [Civil rights—Ed.]
[5] The last portion of Mr. Levy's question overlapped with the first few words of Mr. Kennedy's reply, partially obscuring both.

Third Debate

October 13, 1960

Mr. McGEE: Senator Kennedy, yesterday you used the words "trigger-happy" in referring to Vice President Richard Nixon's stand on defending the islands of Quemoy and Matsu. Last week on a program like this one, you said the next president would come face to face with a serious crisis in Berlin. So the question is: would you take military action to defend Berlin?

Mr. KENNEDY: Mr. McGee, we have a contractual right to be in Berlin coming out of the conversations at Potsdam and of World War II. That has been reinforced by direct commitments of the president of the United States; it's been reinforced by a number of other nations under NATO. I've stated on many occasions that the United States must meet its commitment on Berlin. It is a commitment that we have to meet if we're going to protect the security of Western Europe. And therefore on this question I don't think that there is any doubt in the mind of any American; I hope there is not any doubt in the mind of any member of the community of West Berlin; I'm sure there isn't any doubt in the mind of the Russians. We will meet our commitments to maintain the freedom and independence of West Berlin.

Mr. SHADEL: Mr. Vice President, do you wish to comment?

Mr. NIXON: Yes. As a matter of fact, the statement that Senator Kennedy made was that—to the effect that there were trigger-happy Republicans, that my stand on Quemoy and Matsu was an indication of trigger-happy Republicans. I resent that comment. I resent it because it's an implication that Republicans have been trigger-happy and, therefore, would lead this nation into war. I would remind Senator Kennedy of the past fifty years. I would ask him to name one Republican president who led this nation into war. There were three Democratic presidents who led us into war. I do not mean by that that one party is a war party and the other party is a peace party. But I do say that any statement to the effect that the Republican party is trigger-happy is belied by the record. We had a war when we came into power in 1953. We got rid of that; we've kept out of other wars; and certainly that doesn't indicate that we're trigger-happy. We've been strong, but we haven't been trigger-happy. As far as Berlin is concerned, there isn't any question about the necessity of defending Berlin; the rights of people there to be free; and there isn't any question about what the united American people—Republicans and Democrats alike—would do in the event there were an attempt by the Communists to take over Berlin.

Mr. SHADEL: The next question is by Mr. Von Fremd for Vice President Nixon.

Mr. VON FREMD: Mr. Vice President, a two-part question concerning the offshore islands in the Formosa Straits. If you were president and the Chinese Communists tomorrow began an invasion of Quemoy and Matsu, would you launch the United States into a war by sending the Seventh Fleet and other military forces to resist this aggression; and secondly, if the regular conventional forces failed to half such an invasion, would you authorize the use of nuclear weapons?

Mr. NIXON: Mr. Von Fremd, it would be completley irresponsible for a candidate for the presidency, or for a president himself, to indicate the course of action and the weapons he would use in the event of such an attack. I will say this: in the event that such an attack occurred and in the event the attack was a prelude to an attack on Formosa—which would be the indication today because the Chinese Communists say over and over again that their objective is not the offshore islands, that they consider them only steppingstones to taking Formosa—in the event that their attack then were a prelude to an attack on Formosa, there isn't any question but that the United States would then again, as in the case of Berlin, honor our treaty obligations and stand by our ally of Formosa. But to indicate in advance how we would respond, to indicate the nature of this response would be incorrect; it would certainly be inappropriate; it would not be in the best interests of the United States. I will only say this, however, in addition to do what Senator Kennedy has suggested—to suggest that we will surrender these islands or force our Chinese Nationalist allies to surrender them in advance—is not something that would lead to peace; it is something that would lead, in my opinion, to war. This is the history of dealing with dictators. This is something that Senator Kennedy and all Americans must know. We tried this with Hitler. It didn't work. He wanted first, we know, Austria, and then he went on to the Sudetenland and then Danzig, and each time it was thought this is all that he wanted. Now what do the Chinese Communists want? They don't want just Quemoy and Matsu; they don't want just Formosa; they want the world. And the question is if you surrender or indicate in advance that you're not going to defend any part of the free world, and you figure that's going to satisfy them, it doesn't satisfy them. It only whets their appetite; and then the question comes, when do you stop them? I've often heard President Eisenhower in discussing this question, make the statement that if we once start the process of indicating that this point or that point is not the place to stop those who threaten the peace and freedom of the world, where do we stop them? And I say that those of us who stand against surrender of territory—this or any others—in the face of blackmail, in the face of force by the Communists are standing for the course that will lead to peace.

Mr. SHADEL: Senator Kennedy, do you wish to comment?

Mr. KENNEDY: Yes. The United States now has a treaty—which I voted for in the United States Senate in 1955—to defend Formosa and the Pescadores Island. The islands which Mr. Nixon is discussing are five or four miles, respectively, off the coast of China. Now when Senator Green, the chairman of the Senate Foreign Relations Committee, wrote to the President, he received back on the second of October, 1958—"neither you nor any other American need feel the U.S. will be involved in military hostilities merely in the defense of Quemoy and Matsu." Now, that is the issue. I believe we must meet our commitment to Formosa. I support it and the Pescadores Island. That is the present American position. The treaty does not include these two islands. Mr. Nixon suggests that the United States should go to war if these two islands are attacked. I suggest that if Formosa is attacked or the Pescadores, or if there's any military action in any area which indicates an attack on Formosa and the

Pescadores, then of course the United States is at war to defend its treaty. Now, I must say what Mr. Nixon wants to do is commit us—as I understand him, so that we can be clear if there's a disagreement—he wants us to be committed to the defense of these islands merely as the defense of these islands as free territory, not as part of the defense of Formosa. Admiral Yarnell, the commander of the Asiatic fleet, has said that these islands are not worth the bones of a single American. The President of the United States has indicated they are not within the treaty area. They were not within the treaty area when the treaty was passed in fifty-five. We have attempted to persuade Chiang Kai-shek as late as January of 1959 to reduce the number of troops he has on them. This is a serious issue, and I think we ought to understand completely if we disagree, and if so, where. . . .

Mr. VON FREMD: Senator Kennedy, I'd like to shift the conversation, if I may, to a domestic political argument. The chairman of the Republican National Committee, Senator Thruston Morton, declared earlier this week that you owed Vice President Nixon and the Republican party a public apology for some strong charges made by former President Harry Truman, who bluntly suggested where the Vice President and the Republican party could go. Do you feel that you owe the Vice President an apology?

Mr. KENNEDY: Well, I must say that Mr. Truman has his methods of expressing things; he's been in politics for fifty years; he's been president of the United States. They are not my style. But I really don't think there's anything that I could say to President Truman that's going to cause him, at the age of seventy-six, to change his particular speaking manner. Perhaps Mrs. Truman can, but I don't think I can. I'll just have to tell Mr. Morton that. If you'd pass that message on to him.

Mr. SHADEL: Any comment, Mr. Vice President?

Mr. NIXON: Yes, I think so. Of course, both Senator Kennedy and I have felt Mr. Truman's ire; and consequently, I think he can speak with some feeling on this subject. I just do want to say one thing, however. We all have tempers; I have one; I'm sure Senator Kennedy has one. But when a man's president of the United States, or a former president, he has an obligation not to lose his temper in public. One thing I've noted as I've traveled around the country are the tremendous number of children who come out to see the presidential candidates. I see mothers holding their babies up, so that they can see a man who might be president of the United States. I know Senator Kennedy sees them, too. It makes you realize that whoever is president is going to be a man that all the children of America will either look up to, or will look down to. And I can only say that I'm very proud that President Eisenhower restored dignity and decency and, frankly, good language to the conduct of the presidency of the United States. And I only hope that, should I win this election, that I could approach President Eisenhower in maintaining the dignity of the office; in seeing to it that whenever any mother or father talks to his child, he can look at the man in the White House and, whatever he may think of his policies, he will say: "Well, there is a man who maintains the kind of standards personally that I would want my child to follow."

Mr. SHADEL: Mr. Cater's question is for Vice President Nixon.

Mr. CATER: Mr. Vice President, I'd like to return just once more, if I may, to this area of dealing with the Communists. Critics have claimed that on at least three occasions in recent years—on the sending of American troops to Indochina in 1954, on the matter of continuing the U-2 flights in May, and then on this definition of—of our commitment to the offshore island—that you have overstated the Administration position, that you have taken a more bellicose position than President Eisenhower. Just two days ago you said that you called on Senator Kennedy to serve notice to Communist aggressors around the world that we're not going to retreat one inch more any place, where as we did retreat from the Tachen Islands, or at least Chiang Kai-shek did. Would you say this was a valid criticism of your statement of foreign policy?

Mr. NIXON: Well, Mr. Cater, of course it's a criticism that is being made. I obviously don't think it's valid. I have supported the Administration's position and I think that that position has been corrected; I think my position has been correct. As far as Indochina was concerned, I stated over and over again that it was essential during that period that the United States make it clear that we would not tolerate Indochina falling under Communist domination. Now, as a result of our taking the strong stand that we did, the civil war there was ended; and today, at least in the south of Indochina, the Communists have moved out and we do have a strong, free bastion there. Now, looking to the U-2 flights, I would like to point out that I have been supporting the President's position throughout. I think the President was correct in ordering these flights. I think the President was correct, certainly, in his decision to continue the flights while the conference was going on. I noted, for example, in reading a particular discussion that Senator Kennedy had with Dave Garroway shortly after his statement about regrets, that he made the statement that he felt that these particular flights were ones that shouldn't have occurred right at that time, and the indication was how would Mr. Khrushchev had felt if we had had a flight over the—how would we have felt if Mr. Khrushchev had had a flight over the United States while he was visiting here. And the answer, of course, is that Communist espionage goes on all the time. The answer is that the United States can't afford to have an espionage lack or should I say an intelligence lag—any more than we can afford to have a missile lag. Now, referring to your question with regard to Quemoy and Matsu. What I object to here is the constant reference to surrendering these islands. Senator Kennedy quotes the record, which he read from a moment ago, but what he forgets to point out is that the key vote—a vote which I've referred to several times—where he was in the minority was one which rejected his position. Now, why did they reject it? For the very reason that those Senators knew, as the President of the United States knew, that you should not indicate to the Communists in advance that you're going to surrender an area that's free. Why? Because they know as Senator Kennedy will have to know that if you do that you encourage them to more aggression.

Mr. SHADEL: Senator Kennedy?

Mr. KENNEDY: Well number one on Indochina, Mr. Nixon talked before the newspaper editors in the spring of 1954 about putting, and I quote him, "American boys into Indochina." The reason Indochina was preserved was the result of the

Geneva Conference which [partitioned] Indochina. Number two, on the question of the U-2 flights. I thought the U-2 flight in May just before the conference was a mistake in timing because of the hazards involved, if the summit conference had any hope for success. I never criticized the U-2 flights in general, however. I never suggested espionage should stop. It still goes on, I would assume, on both sides. Number three, the Vice President—on May fifteenth after the U-2 flight—indicated that the flights were going on, even though the Administration and the President had canceled the flights on May twelfth. Number three, the Vice President suggests that we should keep the Communists in doubt about whether we would fight on Quemoy and Matsu. That's not the position he's taking. He's indicating that we should fight for these islands come what may because they are, in his words, in the area of freedom. He didn't take that position on Tibet. He didn't take that position on Budapest. He doesn't take that position that I've seen so far in Laos. Guinea and Ghana have both moved within the Soviet sphere of influence in foreign policy; so has Cuba. I merely say that the United States should meet its commitments to Formosa and the Pescadores. But as Admiral Yarnell has said, and he's been supported by most military authority, these islands that we're now talking about are not worth the bones of a single American soldier; and I know how difficult it is to sustain troops close to the shore under artillery bombardment. And therefore, I think we should make it very clear the disagreement between Mr. Nixon and myself. He's extending the Administration's commitment. . . .

Fourth Debate

October 21, 1960

Mr. HOWE: Now the opening statement of Senator Kennedy.

Mr. KENNEDY: Mr. Howe, Mr. Vice President. First let me again try to correct the record on the matter of Quemoy and Matsu. I voted for the Formosa resolution in 1955. I have sustained it since then. I've said that I agree with the Administration policy. Mr. Nixon earlier indicated that he would defend Quemoy and Matsu even if the attack on these islands, two miles off the coast of China, were not part of a general attack on Formosa and the Pescadores. I indicated that I would defend those islands if the attack were directed against Pescadores and Formosa, which is part of the Eisenhower policy. I've supported that policy. In the last week, as a member of the Senate Foreign Relations Committee, I have re-read the testimony of General Twining representing the Administration in 1959, and the Assistant Secretary of State before the Foreign Relations Committee in 1958, and I have accurately described the Administration policy, and I support it wholeheartedly. So that really isn't an issue in this campaign. It isn't an issue with Mr. Nixon, who now says that he also supports the Eisenhower policy. Nor is the question that all Americans want peace and security an issue in this campaign. The question is: are we moving in the direction of peace and security? Is our relative strength growing? Is, as Mr. Nixon says, our prestige at an all-time high, as he said a week ago, and that of the Communists at an all-time low? I don't believe it is. I don't believe that our relative strength is increasing. And I say that not as the Democratic standard-bearer, but as a citizen of the United States who is concerned about the United States. I look at Cuba, ninety miles off the coast of the United States. In 1957 I was in Havana. I talked to the American Ambassador there. He said that he was the second most powerful man in Cuba. And yet even though Ambassador Smith and Ambassador Gardner, both Republican Ambassadors, both warned of Castro, the Marxist influences around Castro, the Communist influences around Castro, both of them have testified in the last six weeks, that in spite of their warnings to the American government, nothing was done. Our security depends upon Latin America. Can any American looking at the situation in Latin America feel contented with what's happening today, when a candidate for the presidency of Brazil feels it necessary to call—not on Washington during the campaign—but on Castro in Havana; in order to pick up the support of the Castro supporters in Brazil? At the American Conference—Inter-American Conference this summer, when we wanted them to join together in the denunciation of Castro and the Cuban Communists, we couldn't even get the Inter-American group to join together in denouncing Castro. It was rather a vague statement that they finally made. Do you know today that the Russians broadcast ten times as many programs in Spanish to Latin America as we do? Do you know we don't have a single program sponsored by our government to Cuba—to tell them our story, to tell them that we are their friends, that we want them to be free again? Africa is now the emerging area of the world. It contains twenty-five per cent of all the members of the General Assembly. We didn't even have a Bureau of African Affairs until 1957. In the Africa south of the Sahara, which is the major new section, we have less students from all of Africa in that area studying under government auspices today than from the country of Thailand. If there's one thing Africa needs it's technical assistance. And yet last year we gave them less than five per cent of all the technical assistance funds that we distributed around the world. We relied in the Middle East on the Bagdad Pact, and yet when the Iraqi Government was changed, the Bagdad Pact broke down. We relied on the Eisenhower Doctrine for the Middle East, which passed the Senate. There isn't one country in the Middle East that now endorses the Eisenhower Doctrine. We look to Asia because the struggle is in the under-developed world. Which system, Communism or freedom, will triumph in the next five or ten years? That's what should concern us, not the history of ten, or fifteen, or twenty years ago. But are we doing enough in these areas? What are freedom's chances in those areas? By 1965 or 1970, will there be other Cubas in Latin America? Will Guinea and Ghana, which have now voted with the Communists frequently as newly independent countries of Africa—will there be others? Will the Congo go Communist? Will other countries? Are we doing enough in that area? And what about Asia? Is India going to win the economic struggle or is China going to win it? Who will dominate Asia in the next five or ten years? Communism? The Chinese? Or will freedom? The question which we have to decide as Americans—are we doing enough today? Is our strength and prestige rising? Do people want to be identified with us? Do they want to follow United States leadership? I don't think they do, enough. And that's what concerns me. In Africa—these countries that have newly joined the United Nations. On the question of admission of Red China, only two countries in all of Africa voted with us—Liberia and the Union of South Africa. The rest either abstained or voted against us. More countries in Asia voted against us on that question than voted with us. I believe that this struggle is going to go on, and it may be well decided in the next decade. I have seen Cuba go to the Communists. I have seen Communist influence and Castro influence rise in Latin America. I have seen us ignore Africa. There are six countries in Africa that are members of the United Nations. There isn't a single American diplomatic representative in any of those six. When Guinea became independent, the Soviet Ambassador showed up that very day. We didn't recognize them for two months; the American Ambassador didn't show up for nearly eight months. I believe that the world is changing fast. And I don't think this Administration has shown the foresight, has shown the knowledge, has been identified with the great fight which these people are waging to be free, to get a better standard of living, to live better. The average income in some of those countries is twenty-five dollars a year. The Communists say, "Come with us; look what we've done." And we've been, on the whole, uninterested. I think we're going to have to do better. Mr. Nixon talks about our being the strongest country in the world. I think we are today. But we were far stronger relative to the Communists five years ago, and what is of great concern is that the balance of power is in danger of moving with them. They made a breakthrough in missiles, and by nineteen sixty-one, two, and three, they will be outnumbering us in missiles. I'm not as confident as he is that we will be the strongest military power by 1963. He talks about economic growth as a great indicator of freedom. I agree with him. What we do in this country, the kind of society that we build, that will tell whether freedom will be sustained around the world. And yet, in the last nine months of this year, we've had a drop in our economic growth rather than a gain. We've had the lowest rate of increase of economic growth in the last nine months of any major industrialized society in the world. I look up and see the Soviet flag on the moon. The fact is that the State Department polls on our prestige and influence around the world have shown such a sharp drop that up till now the State Department has been unwilling to release them. And yet they were polled by the U.S.I.A. The point of all this is, this is a struggle in which we're engaged. We want peace. We want freedom. We want security. We want to be stronger. We want freedom to gain. But I don't believe in these changing and revolutionary times this Administration has known that the world is changing—has identified itself with that change. I think the Communists have been moving with vigor—Laos, Africa, Cuba—all around the world today they're on the move. I think we have to revitalize our society. I think we have to demonstrate to the people of the world that we're determined in this free country of ours to be first—not first if, and not first but, and not first when—but first. And when we are strong and when we are first, then freedom gains; then the prospects for peace increase; then the prospects for our society gain. . . .

Mr. CRONKITE: Thank you Quincy. Mr. Vice President, Senator Fulbright and now tonight, Senator Kennedy, maintain that the Administration is suppressing a report by the United States Information Agency that shows a decline in United States prestige overseas. Are you aware of such a report, and if you are aware of the existence of such a report, should not that report, because of the great importance this issue has been given in this campaign, be released to the public?

Mr. NIXON: Mr. Cronkite, I naturally am aware of it, because I, of course, pay attention to everything Senator Kennedy says, as well as Senator Fulbright. Now, in this connection I want to point out that the facts simply aren't as stated. First of all, the report to which Senator Kennedy refers is one that was made many, many months ago and related particularly to the period immediately after Sputnik. Second, as far as this report is concerned, I would have no objection to having it made public. Third, I would say this with regard to this report, with regard to Gallup Polls of prestige abroad and everything else that we've been hearing about "what about American presitge abroad": America's prestige abroad will be just as high as the spokesmen for America allow it to be. Now, when we have a presidential candidate, for example—Senator Kennedy—stating over and over again that the United States is second in space and the fact of the matter is that the space score today is twenty-eight to eight—we've had twenty-eight successful shots, they've had eight; when he states that we're second in education, and I have seen Soviet education and I've seen ours, and we're not; that we're second in science because they may be ahead in one area or another, when over-all we're way ahead of the Soviet Union and all other countries in science; when he says as he did in January of this year that we have the worst slums, that we have the most crowded schools; when he says that seventeen million people go to bed hungry every night; when he makes statements like this, what does this do to American prestige? Well, it can only have the effect certainly of reducing it. Well let me make one thing clear. Senator Kennedy has a responsibility to criticize those things that are wrong, but he has also a responsibility to be right in his criticism. Every one of these items that I have mentioned he's been wrong—dead wrong. And for that reason he has contributed to any lack of prestige. Finally, let me say this: as far as prestige is concerned, the first place it would show up would be in the United Nations. Now Senator Kennedy has referred to the vote on Communist China. Let's look at the vote on Hungary. There we got more votes for condemning Hungary and looking into that situation than we got the last year. Let's look at the reaction to Khrushchev and Eisenhower at the last U.N. session. Did Khrushchev gain because he took his shoe off and pounded the table and shouted and insulted? Not at all. The President gained. America gained by continuing the dignity, the decency that has characterized us and it's that that keeps the prestige of America up, not running down America the way Senator Kennedy has been running her down.

Mr. HOWE: Comment, Senator Kennedy?

Mr. KENNEDY: I really don't need Mr. Nixon to tell me about what my responsibilities are as a citizen. I've served this country for fourteen years in the Congress and before that in the service. I've just as high a devotion, just as high an opinion. What I downgrade, Mr. Nixon, is the leadership the country is getting, not the country. Now I didn't make most of the statements that you said I made. I believe the Soviet Union is first in outer space. We may have made more shots but the size of their rocket thrust and all the rest—you yourself said to Khrushchev, "You may be ahead of us in rocket thrust but we're ahead of you in color television" in your famous discussion in the kitchen. I think that color television is not as important as rocket thrust. Secondly, I didn't say we had the worst slums in the world. I said we had too many slums. And that they are bad, and we ought to do something about them, and we ought to support housing legislation which this Administration has opposed. I didn't say we had the worst education in the world. What I said was that ten years ago, we were producing twice as many scientists and engineers as the Soviet Union and today they're producing twice as many as we are, and that this affects our security around the world. And fourth, I believe that the polls and other studies and votes in the United Nations and anyone reading the paper and any citizen of the United States must come to the conclusion that the United States no longer carries the same image of a vital society on the move with its brightest days ahead as it carried a decade or two decades ago. Part of that is because we've stood still here at home, because we haven't met our problems in the United States, because we haven't had a moving economy. Part of that, as the Gallup Polls show, is because the Soviet Union made a breakthrough in outer space. Mr. George Allen, head of your Information Service, has said that that made the people of the world begin to wonder whether we were first in science. We're first in other areas of science but in space, which is the new science, we're not first. . . .

LYNDON B. JOHNSON
"LET US CONTINUE" ADDRESS
November 27, 1963

Five days after the assassination of President Kennedy, President Johnson delivered the following speech to a joint session of Congress.

Mr. Speaker, Mr. President, Members of the House, Members of the Senate, my fellow Americans:

All I have I would have given gladly not to be standing here today.

The greatest leader of our time has been struck down by the foulest deed of our time. Today John Fitzgerald Kennedy lives on in the immortal words and works that he left behind. He lives on in the mind and memories of mankind. He lives on in the hearts of his countrymen.

No words are sad enough to express our sense of loss. No words are strong enough to express our determination to continue the forward thrust of America that he began.

The dream of conquering the vastness of space—the dream of partnership across the Atlantic—and across the Pacific as well—the dream of a Peace Corps in less developed nations—the dream of education for all of our children—the dream of jobs for all who seek them and need them—the dream of care for our elderly—the dream of an all-out attack on mental illness—and above all, the dream of equal rights for all Americans, whatever their race or color—these and other American dreams have been vitalized by his drive and by his dedication.

And now the ideas and the ideals which he so nobly represented must and will be translated into effective action.

Under John Kennedy's leadership, this Nation has demonstrated that it has the courage to seek peace, and it has the fortitude to risk war. We have proved that we are a good and reliable friend to those who seek peace and freedom. We have shown that we can also be a formidable foe to those who reject the path of peace and those who seek to impose upon us or our allies the yoke of tyranny.

The Nation will keep its commitments from South Viet-Nam to West Berlin. We will be unceasing in the search for peace; resourceful in our pursuit of areas of agreement even with those with whom we differ; and generous and loyal to those who join with us in common cause.

In this age when there can be no losers in peace and no victors in war, we must recognize the obligation to match national strength with national restraint. We must be prepared at one and the same time for both the confrontation of power and the limitation of power. We must be ready to defend the national interest and to negotiate the common interest. This is the path that we shall continue to pursue. Those who test our courage will find it strong, and those who seek our friendship will find it honorable. We will demonstrate anew that the strong can be just in the use of strength; and the just can be strong in the defense of justice.

And let all know we will extend no special privilege and impose no persecution. We will carry on the fight against poverty and misery, and disease and ignorance, in other lands and in our own.

We will serve all the Nation, not one section or one sector, or one group, but all Americans. These are the United States—a united people with a united purpose.

Our American unity does not depend upon unanimity. We have differences; but now, as in the past, we can derive from those differences strength, not weakness, wisdom, not despair. Both as a people and a government, we can unite upon a program, a program which is wise and just, enlightened and constructive.

For 32 years Capitol Hill has been my home. I have shared many moments of pride with you, pride in the ability of the Congress of the United States to act, to meet any crisis, to distill from our differences strong programs of national action.

An assassin's bullet has thrust upon me the awesome burden of the Presidency. I am here today to say I need your help; I cannot bear this burden alone. I need the help of all Americans, and all America. This Nation has experienced a profound shock, and in this critical moment, it is our duty, yours and mine, as the Government of the United States, to do away with uncertainty and doubt and delay, and to show that we are capable of decisive action; that from the brutal loss of our leader we will derive not weakness, but strength; that we can and will act and act now.

From this chamber of representative government, let all the world know and none misunderstand that I rededicate this Government to the unswerving support of the United Nations, to the honorable and determined execution of our commitments to our allies, to the maintenance of military strength second to none, to the defense of the strength and the stability of the dollar, to the expansion of our foreign trade, to the reinforcement of our programs of mutual assistance and cooperation in Asia and Africa, and to our Alliance for Progress in this hemisphere.

On the 20th day of January, in 1961, John F. Kennedy told his countrymen that our national work would not be finished "in the first thousand days, nor in the life of this administration, nor even perhaps in our lifetime on this planet. But," he said, "let us begin."

Today, in this moment of new resolve, I would say to all my fellow Americans, let us continue.

This is our challenge—not to hesitate, not to pause, not to turn about and linger over this evil moment, but to continue on our course so that we may fulfill the destiny that history has set for us. Our most immediate tasks are here on this Hill.

First, no memorial oration or eulogy could more eloquently honor President Kennedy's memory than the earliest possible passage of the civil rights bill for which he fought so long. We have talked long enough in this country about equal rights. We have talked for one hundred years or more. It is time now to write the next chapter, and to write it in the books of law.

I urge you again, as I did in 1957 and again in 1960, to enact a civil rights law so that we can move forward to eliminate from this Nation every trace of discrimination and oppression that is based upon race or color. There could be no greater source of strength to this Nation both at home and abroad.

And second, no act of ours could more fittingly continue the work of President Kennedy than the early passage of the tax bill for which he fought all this long year. This is a bill designed to increase our national income and Federal revenues, and to provide insurance against recession. That bill, if passed without delay, means more security for those now working, more jobs for those now without them, and more incentive for our economy.

In short, this is no time for delay. It is a time for action—strong, forward-looking action on the pending education bills to help bring the light of learning to every home and hamlet in America—strong, forward-looking action on youth employment opportunities; strong, forward-looking action on the pending foreign aid bill, making clear that we are not forfeiting our responsibilities to this hemisphere or to the world, nor erasing Executive flexibility in the conduct of our foreign affairs—and strong, prompt, and forward-looking action on the remaining appropriation bills.

In this new spirit of action, the Congress can expect the full cooperation and support of the executive branch. And in particular, I pledge that the expenditures of your Government will be administered with the utmost thrift and frugality. I will insist that the Government get a dollar's value for a dollar spent. The Government will set an example of prudence and economy. This does not mean that we will not meet our unfilled needs or that we will not honor our commitments. We will do both.

As one who has long served in both Houses of the Congress, I firmly believe in the independence and the integrity of the legislative branch. And I promise you that I shall always respect this. It is deep in the marrow of my bones. With equal firmness, I believe in the capacity and I believe in the ability of the Congress, despite the divisions of opinions which characterize our Nation, to act—to act wisely, to act vigorously, to act speedily when the need arises.

The need is here. The need is now. I ask your help.

We meet in grief, but let us also meet in renewed dedication and renewed vigor. Let us meet in action, in tolerance, and in mutual understanding. John Kennedy's death commands what his life conveyed—that America must move forward. The time has come for Americans of all races and creeds and political beliefs to understand and to respect one another. So let us put an end to the teaching and the preaching of hate and evil and violence. Let us turn away from the fanatics of the far left and the far right, from the apostles of bitterness and bigotry, from those defiant of law, and those who pour venom into our Nation's bloodstream.

I profoundly hope that the tragedy and the torment of these terrible days will bind us together in new fellowship, making us one people in our hour of sorrow. So let us here highly resolve that John Fitzgerald Kennedy did not live—or die—in vain. And on this Thanksgiving eve, as we gather together to ask the

Lord's blessing, and give Him our thanks, let us unite in those familiar and cherished words:

> America, America,
> God shed His grace on thee,
> And crown thy good
> With brotherhood
> From sea to shining sea.

LYNDON B. JOHNSON, "GREAT SOCIETY" SPEECH
May 22, 1964

The President spoke at the graduation exercises at the University of Michigan, Ann Arbor, after receiving an honorary degree of Doctor of Civil Law.

President Hatcher, Governor Romney, Senators McNamara and Hart, Congressmen Meader and Staebler, and other members of the fine Michigan delegation, members of the graduating class, my fellow Americans:

It is a great pleasure to be here today. This university has been coeducational since 1870, but I do not believe it was on the basis of your accomplishments that a Detroit High school girl said, "In choosing a college, you first have to decide whether you want a coeducational school or an educational school."

Well, we can find both here at Michigan, although perhaps at different hours.

I came out here today very anxious to meet the Michigan student whose father told a friend of mine that his son's education had been a real value. It stopped his mother from bragging about him.

I have come today from the turmoil of your Capital to the tranquility of your campus to speak about the future of your country.

The purpose of protecting the life of our Nation and preserving the liberty of our citizens is to pursue the happiness of our people. Our success in that pursuit is the test of our success as a Nation.

For a century we labored to settle and to subdue a continent. For half a century we called upon unbounded invention and untiring industry to create an order of plenty for all of our people.

The challenge of the next half century is whether we have the wisdom to use that wealth to enrich and elevate our national life, and to advance the quality of our American civilization.

Your imagination, your initiative, and your indignation will determine whether we build a society where progress is the servant of our needs, or a society where old values and new visions are buried under unbridled growth. For in your time we have the opportunity to move not only toward the rich society and the powerful society, but upward to the Great Society.

The Great Society rests on abundance and liberty for all. It demands an end to poverty and racial injustice, to which we are totally committed in our time. But that is just the beginning.

President Lyndon B. Johnson, Remarks at the University of Michigan, May 22, 1964, Doc. 357, *Public Papers of the Presidents of the United States* (Washington, 1965), I, 704-07.

The Great Society is a place where every child can find knowledge to enrich his mind and to enlarge his talents. It is a place where leisure is a welcome chance to build and reflect, not a feared cause of boredom and restlessness. It is a place where the city of man serves not only the needs of the body and the demands of commerce but the desire for beauty and the hunger for community.

It is a place where man can renew contact with nature. It is a place which honors creation for its own sake and for what it adds to the understanding of the race. It is a place where men are more concerned with the quality of their goals than the quantity of their goods.

But most of all, the Great Society is not a safe harbor, a resting place, a final objective, a finished work. It is a challenge constantly renewed, beckoning us toward a destiny where the meaning of our lives matches the marvelous products of our labor.

So I want to talk to you today about three places where we begin to build the Great Society—in our cities, in our countryside, and in our classrooms.

Many of you will live to see the day, perhaps 50 years from now, when there will be 400 million Americans—four-fifths of them in urban areas. In the remainder of this century urban population will double, city land will double, and we will have to build homes, highways, and facilities equal to all those built since this country was first settled. So in the next 40 years we must rebuild the entire urban United States.

Aristotle said: "Men come together in cities in order to live, but they remain together in order to live the good life." It is harder and harder to live the good live in American cities today.

The catalog of ills is long: there is the decay of the centers and the despoiling of the suburbs. There is not enough housing for our people or transportation for our traffic. Open land is vanishing and old landmarks are violated.

Worst of all expansion is eroding the precious and time honored values of community with neighbors and communion with nature. The loss of these values breeds loneliness and boredom and indifference.

Our society will never be great until our cities are great. Today the frontier of imagination and innovation is inside those cities and not beyond their borders.

New experiments are already going on. It will be the task of your generation to make the American city a place where future generations will come, not only to live but to live the good life.

I understand that if I stayed here tonight I would see that Michigan students are really doing their best to live the good life.

This is the place where the Peace Corps was started. It is inspiring to see how all of you, while you are in this country, are trying so hard to live at the level of the people.

A second place where we begin to build the Great Society is in our countryside. We have always prided ourselves on being not only America the strong and America the free, but America the beautiful. Today that beauty is in danger. The water we drink, the food we eat, the very air that we breathe, are threatened with pollution. Our parks are overcrowded, our seashores overburdened. Green fields and dense forests are disappearing.

A few years ago we were greatly concerned about the "Ugly American." Today we must act to prevent an ugly America.

For once the battle is lost, once our natural splendor is destroyed, it can never be recaptured. And once man can no longer walk with beauty or wonder at nature his spirit will wither and his sustenance be wasted.

A third place to build the Great Society is in the classrooms of America. There your children's lives will be shaped. Our society will not be great until every young mind is set free to scan the farthest reaches of thought and imagination. We are still far from that goal.

Today, 8 million adult Americans, more than the entire population of Michigan, have not finished 5 years of school. Nearly 20 million have not finished 8 years of school. Nearly 54 million—more than one-quarter of all America—have not even finished high school.

Each year more than 100,000 high school graduates, with proved ability, do not enter college because they cannot afford it. And if we cannot educate today's youth, what will we do in 1970 when elementary school enrollment will be 5 million greater than 1960? And high school enrollment will rise by 5 million. College enrollment will increase by more than 3 million.

In many places, classrooms are overcrowded and curricula are outdated. Most of our qualified teachers are underpaid, and many of our paid teachers are unqualified. So we must give every child a place to sit and a teacher to learn from. Poverty must not be a bar to learning, and learning must offer an escape from poverty.

But more classrooms and more teachers are not enough. We must seek an educational system which grows in size. This means better training for our teachers. It means preparing youth to enjoy their hours of leisure as well as their hours of labor. It means exploring new techniques of teaching, to find new ways to stimulate the love of learning and the capacity for creation.

These are three of the central issues of the Great Society. While our Government has many programs directed at those issues, I do not pretend that we have the full answer to those problems.

But I do promise this: We are going to assemble the best thought and the broadest knowledge from all over the world to find those answers for America. I intend to establish working groups to prepare a series of White House conferences and meetings—on the cities, on natural beauty, on the quality of education, and on other emerging challenges. And from these meetings and from this inspiration and from these studies we will begin to set our course toward the Great Society.

The solution to these problems does not rest on a massive program in Washington, nor can it rely solely on the strained resources of local authority. They require us to create new concepts of cooperation, a creative federalism, between the National Capital and the leaders of local communities.

Woodrow Wilson once wrote: "Every man sent out from his university should be a man of his Nation as well as a man of his time."

Within your lifetime powerful forces, already loosed, will take us toward a way of life beyond the realm of our experience, almost beyond the bounds of our imagination.

For better or for worse, your generation has been appointed by history to deal with those problems and to lead America toward a new age. You have the chance never before afforded to any people in any age. You can help build a society where the demands of morality, and the needs of the spirit, can be realized in the life of the Nation.

So, will you join in the battle to give every citizen the full equality which God enjoins and the law requires, whatever his belief, or race, or the color of his skin?

Will you join in the battle to give every citizen an escape from the crushing weight of poverty?

Will you join in the battle to make it possible for all nations to live in enduring peace—as neighbors and not as mortal enemies?

Will you join in the battle to build the Great Society, to prove that our material progress is only the foundation on which we will build a richer life of mind and spirit?

There are those timid souls who say this battle cannot be won; that we are condemned to a soulless wealth. I do not agree. We have the power to shape the civilization that we want. But we need your will, your labor, your hearts, if we are to build that kind of society.

Those who came to this land sought to build more than just a new country. They sought a new world. So I have come here today to your campus to say that you can make their vision our reality. So let us from this moment begin our work so that in the future men will look back and say: It was then, after a long and weary way, that man turned the exploits of his genius to the full enrichment of his life.

Thank you. Goodby.

LYNDON B. JOHNSON, MESSAGE REQUESTING
GULF OF TONKIN RESOLUTION
August 5, 1964

See the following document for the text of the Joint Resolution.

To the Congress of the United States:

Last night I announced to the American people that the North Vietnamese regime had conducted further deliberate attacks against U.S. naval vessels operating in international waters, and that I had therefore directed air action against gunboats and supporting facilities used in these hostile operations. This air action has now been carried out with substantial damage to the boats and facilities. Two U.S. aircraft were lost in the action.

After consultation with the leaders of both parties in the Congress, I further announced a decision to ask the Congress for a resolution expressing the unity and determination of the United States in supporting freedom and in protecting peace in southeast Asia.

These latest actions of the North Vietnamese regime have given a new and grave turn to the already serious situation in the southeast Asia. Our commitments in that area are well known to the Congress. They were first made in 1954 by President Eisenhower. They were further defined in the Southeast Asia Collective Defense Treaty approved by the Senate in February 1955.

This treaty with its accompanying protocol obligates the United States and other members to act in accordance with their constitutional processes to meet Communist aggression against any of the parties or protocol states.

Our policy in southeast Asia has been consistent and unchanged since 1954. I summarized it on June 2 in four simple propositions:

1. America keeps her word. Here as elsewhere, we must and shall honor out commitments.

2. The issue is the future of southeast Asia as a whole. A threat to any nation in that region is a threat to all, and a threat to us.

3. Our purpose is peace. We have no military, political, or territorial ambitions in the area.

4. This is not just a jungle war, but a struggle for freedom on every front of human activity. Our military and economic assitance to South Vietnam and Laos in particular has the purpose of helping these countries to repel aggression and strengthen their independence.

Congressional Record, 88th Cong., 2d sess., August 5, 1964, vol. 111, p. 18132.

The threat to the free nations of southeast Asia has long been clear. The North Vietnamese regime has constantly sought to take over South Vietnam and Laos. This Communist regime has violated the Geneva accords for Vietnam. It has systematically conducted a campaign of subversion, which includes the direction, training, and supply of personnel and arms for the conduct of guerilla warfare in South Vietnamese territory. In Laos, the North Vietnamese regime has maintained military forces, used Laotian territory for infiltration into South Vietnam, and most recently carried out combat operations—all in direct violation of the Geneva agreements of 1962.

In recent months, the actions of the North Vietnamese regime has become steadily more threatening. In May, following new acts of Communist aggression in Laos, the United States undertook reconnaissance flights over Laotian territory, at the request of the Government of Laos. These flights had the essential mission of determining the situation in territory where Communist forces were preventing inspection by the International Control Commission. When the Communists attacked these aircraft, I responded by furnishing escort fighters with instructions to fire when fired upon. Thus, these latest North Vietnamese attacks on our naval vessels are not the first direct attack on Armed Forces of the United States.

As President of the United States I have concluded that I should now ask the Congress, on its part, to join in affirming the national determination that all such attacks will be met, and that the United States will continue in its basic policy of assisting the free nations of the area to defend their freedom.

As I have repeatedly made clear, the United States intends no rashness, and seeks no wider war. We must make it clear to all that the United States is united in its determination to bring about the end of Communist subversion and aggression in the area. We seek the full and effective restoration of the international agreements signed in Geneva in 1954, with respect to South Vietnam, and again at Geneva in 1962, with respect to Laos.

I recommend a resolution expressing the support of the Congress for all necessary action to protect our Armed Forces and to assist nations covered by the SEATO Treaty. At the same time, I assure the Congress that we shall continue readily to explore any avenues of political solution that will effectively guarantee the removal of Communist subversion and the preservation of the independence of the nations of the area.

The resolution could well be based upon similar resolutions enacted by the Congress in the past—to meet the threat to Formosa in 1955, to meet the threat to the Middle East in 1957, and to meet the threat to Cuba in 1962. It could state in the simplest terms the resolve and support of the Congress for action to deal appropriately with attacks against our Armed Forces and to defend freedom and preserve peace in southeast Asia in accordance with the obligations of the United States under the Southeast Asia Treaty. I urge the Congress to enact such a resolution promptly and thus to give convincing evidence to the aggressive Communist nations, and to the world as a whole, that our policy in southeast Asia will be carried forward—and that the peace and security of the area will be preserved.

The events of this week would in any event have made the passage of a congressional resolution essential. But there is an additional reason for doing so at a time when we are entering on 3 months of political campaigning. Hostile nations must understand that in such a period the United States will continue to protect its national interests and that in these matters there is no division among us.

Lyndon B. Johnson

The White House, August 5, 1964

GULF OF TONKIN RESOLUTION
August 10, 1964

See the preceding document for President Johnson's message to Congress requesting a resolution "expressing the unity and determination of the United States in supporting freedom and in protecting peace in southeast Asia."

Joint Resolution to promote the maintenance of international peace and security in Southeast Asia.

Whereas naval units of the Communist regime in Vietnam, in violation of the principles of the Charter of the United Nations and of international law, have deliberately and repeatedly attacked United States naval vessels lawfully present in international waters, and have thereby created a serious threat to international peace; and

Whereas these attacks are part of a deliberate and systematic campaign of aggression that the Communist regime in North Vietnam has been waging against its neighbors and the nations joined with them in the collective defense of their freedom; and

Whereas the United States is assisting the peoples of southeast Asia to protect their freedom and has no territorial, military or political ambitions in that area, but desires only that these peoples should be left in peace to work out their own destinies in their own way: Now, therefore, be it

Resolved by the Senate and House of Representatives of the United States of America in Congress assembled, That: The Congress approves and supports the determination of the President, as Commander in Chief, to take all necessary measures to repel any armed attack against the forces of the United States and to prevent further aggression.

Sec. 2. The United States regards as vital to its national interest and to world peace the maintenance of international peace and security in Southeast Asia. Consonant with the Constitution of the United States and the Charter of the United Nations and in accordance with its obligations under the Southeast Asia Collective Defense Treaty, the United States is, therefore, prepared, as the President determines, to take all necessary steps, including the use of armed force, to assist any

P.L. 88-408, 78 Stat. 384, August 10, 1964.

member or protocol state of the Southeast Asia Collective Defense Treaty requesting assistance in defense of its freedom.

Sec. 3. This resolution shall expire when the President shall determine that the peace and security of the area is reasonably assured by international conditions created by action of the United Nations or otherwise, except that it may be terminated earlier by concurrent resolution of the Congress.

EUGENE McCARTHY
STATEMENT ANNOUNCING HIS CANDIDACY
November 30, 1967

I intend to enter the Democratic primaries in four states, Wisconsin, Oregon, California and Nebraska. The decision with reference to Massachusetts and also New Hampshire will be made within the next two or three weeks.

As far as Massachusetts is concerned it will depend principally upon the outcome of a meeting which is being held there if they finish their work this weekend—a meeting of the Democratic State Committee.

Since I first said that I thought the issue of Vietnam and the issues related to it should be raised in the primaries of the country I have talked with Democratic leaders from about 25 to 26 states. I've talked particularly to candidates for re-election to the Senate—Democratic candidates—some House members and also to students on campus and to other people throughout the country.

My decision to challenge the President's position and the Administration position has been strengthened by recent announcements out of the Administration, the evident intention to escalate and to intensify the war in Vietnam and on the other hand the absence of any positive indication or suggestion for a compromise or for a negotiated political settlement.

I am concerned that the Administration seems to have set no limit to the price which it's willing to pay for a military victory. Let me summarize the cost of the war up to this point:

The physical destruction of much of a small and weak nation by military operations of the most powerful nation in the world.

One hundred thousand to 150,000 civilian casualties in South Vietnam alone, to say nothing of the destruction of life and property in North Vietnam.

The uprooting and the fracturing of the structure of the society of South Vietnam where one-fourth to one-third of the population are now reported to be refugees.

For the United States as of yesterday over 15,000 combat dead and nearly 95,000 wounded through November.

A monthly expenditure in pursuit of the war amounting somewhere between $2-billion and $3-billion.

I am also concerned about the bearing of the war on other areas of the United States responsibility, both at home and abroad.

The failure to appropriate adequate funds for the poverty program here, for housing, for education, and to meet other national needs and the prospect of additonal cuts as a condition to the possible passage of the surtax tax bill.

New York Times, December 1, 1967.

The drastic reduction of our foreign aid program in other parts of the world.

A dangerous rise in inflation and one of the indirect and serious consequences of our involvement in Vietnam, the devaluation of the British pound, which in many respects is more important east of Suez today than the British Navy.

In addition, there is growing evidence of a deepening moral crisis in America—discontent and frustration and a disposition to take extralegal if not illegal actions to manifest protest.

I am hopeful that this challenge which I am making, which I hope will be supported by other members of the Senate and other politicians, may alleviate at least in some degree this sense of political helplessness and restore to many people a belief in the processes of American politics and of American government.

That the college campuses especially—on those campuses—and also among adult thoughtful Americans, that it may counter the growing sense of alienation from politics which I think is currently reflected in a tendency to withdraw from political action, to talk of nonparticipation, to become cynical and to make threats of support for third parties or fourth parties or other irregular political movements.

I do not see in my move any great threat to the unity and strength of the Democratic party, whatever that unity may be today and whatever strength it may be.

The issue of the war in Vietnam is not really a separate issue but one that must be dealt with in the configuration of other problems to which it is related. It is within this broader context that I intend to make the case to the people of the United States.

To say that I'm—as I'm sure I shall be charged—I am not for peace at any price, but for an honorable, rational and political solution to this war, a solution which I believe will enhance our world position, encourage the respect of our allies and our potential adversaries, which will permit us to give the necessary attention to other commitments both at home and abroad, military and non-military and leave us with resources and moral energy to deal effectively with the pressing domestic problems of the United States itself.

In this—this total effort—I believe we can restore to this nation a clearer sense of purpose and of dedication to the achievement of our traditional purposes as a great nation in the 20th century.

Thank you very much.

ROBERT F. KENNEDY
STATEMENT ANNOUNCING HIS CANDIDACY
March 16, 1968

I am announcing today my candidacy for the Presidency of the United States.
I do not run for the Presidency merely to oppose any man but to propose new policies. I run because I am convinced that this country is on a perilous course and because I have such strong feelings about what must be done, and I feel that I'm obliged to do all that I can.

I run to seek new policies—policies to end the bloodshed in Vietnam and in our cities, policies to close the gap that now exists between black and white, between rich and poor, between young and old in this country and around the rest of the world.

I run for the Presidency because I want the Democratic party and the United States of America to stand for hope instead of despair, for reconciliation of men instead of the growing risk of world war.

I run because it is now unmistakably clear that we can change these disastrous divisive policies only by changing the men who are now making them. For the reality of recent events in Vietnam has been glossed over with illusions.

The report of the riot commission has been largely ignored.

The crisis in gold, the crisis in our cities, the crisis in our farms and in our ghettos have all been met with too little and too late.

No one who knows what I know about the extraordinary demands of the Presidency can be certain that any mortal can adequately fill that position.

But my service on the National Security Council during the Cuban missile crisis, the Berlin crisis of 1961 and 1962 and later, the negotiations on Laos and on the nuclear test ban treaty have taught me something about both the uses and the limitations of military power, about the value of negotiations with the opportunities and the dangers which await our nation in many corners of the globe in which I have traveled.

As a member of the Cabinet and a member of the Senate I have seen the inexcusable and ugly deprivations which cause children to starve in Mississippi, black citizens to riot in Watts, young Indians to commit suicide on their reservations because they've lacked all hope and they feel they have no future, and proud and able-bodied families to wait out their lives in empty idleness in eastern Kentucky.

I have traveled and I have listened to the young people of our nation and felt their anger about the war that they are sent to fight and about the world that they are about to inherit.

New York Times, March 17, 1968.

In private talks and in public I have tried in vain to alter our course in Vietnam before it further saps our spirit and our manpower, further raises the risk of wider war and further destroys the country and the people it was meant to save.

I cannot stand aside from the contest that will decide our nation's future and our children's future.

The remarkable New Hampshire campaign of Senator Eugene McCarthy has proven how deep are the present divisions within our party and within our country. Until that was publicly clear my presence in the race would have been seen as a clash of personalities rather than issues.

But now that that fight is won and over policies which I have long been challenging, I must enter that race. The fight is just beginning and I believe that I can win.

I have previously communicated this decision to President Johnson and late last night my brother, Senator Edward Kennedy, traveled to Wisconsin to communicate my decision to Senator McCarthy.

I made clear through my brother to Senator McCarthy that my candidacy would not be in opposition to his but in harmony. My aim is to both support and expand his valiant campaign in the spirit of his Nov. 30 statement, taking one month at a time.

It is important now that he achieve the largest possible majority next month in Wisconsin, in Pennsylvania and in the Massachusetts primaries.

I strongly support his effort in those states and I urge all my friends to give him their help and their votes.

Both of us will be encouraging like-minded delegates to the national convention, for both of us want above all else an open Democratic convention in Chicago, free to choose a new course for our party and for our country.

To make certain that this effort will still be effective in June, I am required now to permit the entry of my name into the California primaries to be held in that month. And I do so in the belief, which I will strive to implement, that Senator McCarthy's forces and mine will be able to work together in one form or another.

My desire is not to divide the strength of those forces seeking a change, but rather to increase it.

Under the laws of Oregon and Nebraska this decision requires the Secretary of State in each of these states to place my name on the ballot, but in no state will my efforts be directed against Senator McCarthy.

Both of us are campaigning to give our forces and our party an opportunity to select the strongest possible standard bearer for the November elections.

To insure that my candidacy must be tested beginning now, five months before the convention and not after the primaries are over, I think that is the least that I can do to meet my responsibilities to the Democratic party and to the people of the United States.

Finally, my decision reflects no personal animosity or disrespect toward President Johnson. He served President Kennedy with the utmost loyalty and was extremely kind to me and members of my family in the difficult months which followed the events of November of 1963.

I have often commended his efforts in health, in education, and in many areas, and I have the deepest sympathy for the burden that he carries today.

But the issue is not personal. It is our profound differences over where we are heading and what we want to accomplish.

I do not lightly dismiss the dangers and the difficulties of challenging an incumbent President. But these are not ordinary times and this is not an ordinary election.

At stake is not simply the leadership of our party and even our country. It is our right to the moral leadership of this planet.

I thank you. I appreciate the members of my family and my office showing up.

LYNDON B. JOHNSON, ADDRESS TO THE NATION
Washington, March 31, 1968

Tonight I want to speak to you of peace in Vietnam and Southeast Asia.

No other question so preoccupies our people. No other dream so absorbs the 250 million human beings who live in that part of the world. No other goal motivates American policy in Southeast Asia.

For years, representatives of our Government and others have traveled the world seeking to find a basis for peace talks.

Since last September they have carried the offer that I made public at San Antonio. And that offer was this:

That the United States would stop its bombardment of North Vietnam when that would lead promptly to productive discussions—and that we would assume that North Vietnam would not take military advantage of our restraint.

Hanoi denounced this offer, both privately and publicly. Even while the search for peace was going on, North Vietnam rushed their preparations for a savage assault on the people, the Government and the allies of South Vietnam.

Their attack—during the Tet holidays—failed to achieve its principal objectives.

It did not collapse the elected Government of South Vietnam or shatter its army—as the Communists had hoped. It did not produce a "general uprising" among the people of the cities, as they had predicted.

The Communists were unable to maintain control of any of the more than 30 cities that they attacked, and they took very heavy casualties.

But they did compel the South Vietnamese and their allies to move certain forces from the countryside into the cities.

They caused widespread disruption and suffering. Their attacks, and the battles that followed, made refugees of half a million human beings.

The Communists may renew their attack any day. They are, it appears, trying to make 1968 the year of decision in South Vietnam—the year that brings, if not final victory or defeat, at least a turning point in the struggle.

This much is clear: If they do mount another round of heavy attacks, they will not succeed in destroying the fighting power of South Vietnam and its allies.

But tragically, this is also clear. Many men—on both sides of the struggle—will be lost. A nation that has already suffered 20 years of warfare will suffer once again. Armies on both sides will take new casualties. And the war will go on.

There is no need for this to be so. There is no need to delay the talks that could bring an end to this long and this bloody war.

Tonight, I renew the offer I made last August: to stop the bombardment of North Vietnam. We ask that talks begin promptly, that they be serious talks on the substance of peace. We assume that during those talks Hanoi will not take advantage of our restraint.

We are prepared to move immediately toward peace through negotiations. So tonight, in the hope that this action will lead to early talks, I am taking the first step to de-escalate the conflict. We are reducing—substantially reducing—the present level of hostilities, and we are doing so unilaterally and at once.

Tonight I have ordered our aircraft and our naval vessels to make no attacks on North Vietnam except in the area north of the demilitarized zone where the continuing enemy build-up directly threatens allied forward positions and where the movement of their troops and supplies are clearly related to that threat.

The area in which we are stopping our attacks includes almost 90 per cent of North Vietnam's population, and most of its territory. Thus there will be no attacks around the principal populated areas, or in the food-producing areas of North Vietnam.

Even this very limited bombing of the North could come to an early end—if our restraint is matched by restraint in Hanoi. But I cannot in good conscience stop all bombing so long as to do so would immediately and directly endanger the lives of our men and our allies. Whether a complete bombing halt becomes possible in the future will be determined by events.

Our purpose in this action is to bring about a reduction in the level of violence that now exists. It is to save the lives of brave men—and to save the lives of innocent women and children. It is to permit the contending forces to move closer to a political settlement.

And tonight I call upon the United Kingdom and I call upon the Soviet Union—as co-chairmen of the Geneva conferences and as permanent members of the United Nations Security Council—to do all they can to move from the unilateral act of de-escalation that I have just announced toward genuine peace in Southeast Asia.

Now, as in the past, the United States is ready to send its representatives to any forum, at any time, to discuss the means of bringing this ugly war to an end.

I am designating one of our most distinguished Americans, Ambassador Averell Harriman, as my personal representative for such talks. In addition, I have asked Ambassador Llewellyn Thompson, who returned from Moscow for consultation, to be available to join Ambassador Harriman at Geneva or any other suitable place—just as soon as Hanoi agrees to a conference.

I call upon President Ho Chi Minh to respond positively, and favorably, to this new step toward peace.

But if peace does not come now through negotiations, it will come when Hanoi understands that our common resolve is unshakable, and our common strength is invincible.

Tonight, we and the other allied nations are contributing 600,000 fighting men to assist 700,000 South Vietnamese troops in defending their little country.

Our presence there has always rested on this basic belief: The main burden of preserving their freedom must be carried out by them—by the South Vietnamese themselves.

We and our allies can only help to provide a shield behind which the people of South Vietnam can survive and can grow and develop. On their efforts—on their determinations and resourcefulness—the outcome will ultimately depend.

That small, beleaguered nation has suffered terrible punishment for more than 20 years.

I pay tribute once again tonight to the great courage and the endurance of its people. South Vietnam supports armed forces tonight of almost 700,000 men, and I call your attention to the fact that that is the equivalent of more than 10 million in our own population. Its people maintain their firm determination to be free of domination by the North.

There has been substantial progress, I think, in building a durable government during these last three years. The South Vietnam of 1965 could not have survived the enemy's Tet offensive of 1968. The elected Government of South Vietnam survived that attack—and is rapidly repairing the devastation that it wrought.

The South Vietnamese know that further efforts are going to be required to expand their own armed forces; to move back into the countryside as quickly as possible; to increase their taxes; to select the very best men they have for civil and military responsibility; to achieve a new unity within their constitutional government, and to include in the national effort all those groups who wish to preserve South Vietnam's control over its own destiny.

Last week President Thieu ordered the mobilization of 135,000 additional South Vietnamese. He plans to reach as soon as possible a total military strength of more than 800,000 men.

To achieve this, the Government of South Vietnam started the drafting of 19-year-olds on March 1. On May 1, the Government will begin the drafting of 18-year-olds.

Last month, 10,000 men volunteered for military service. That was two and a half times the number of volunteers during the same month last year. Since the middle of January, more than 48,000 South Vietnamese have joined the armed forces, and nearly half of them volunteered to do so.

All men in the South Vietnamese armed forces have had their tours of duty extended for the duration of the war, and reserves are now being called up for immediate active duty.

President Thieu told his people last week, and I quote:

"We must make greater efforts, we must accept more sacrifices, because as I have said many times, this is our country. The existence of our nation is at stake, and this is mainly a Vietnamese responsibility."

He warned his people that a major national effort is required to root out corruption and incompetence at all levels of government.

We applaud this evidence of determination on the part of South Vietnam. Our first priority will be to support their effort.

We shall accelerate the re-equipment of South Vietnam's armed forces in order to meet the enemy's increased firepower. And this will enable them progressively to undertake a large share of combat operations against the Communist invaders.

On many occasions I have told the American people that we would send to Vietnam those forces that are required to accomplish our mission there. So with that as our guide we have previously authorized a force level of approximately 525,000.

Some weeks ago to help meet the enemy's new offensive we sent to Vietnam about 11,000 additional Marine and airborne troops. They were deployed by air in 48 hours on an emergency basis. But the artillery and the tank and the aircraft and medical and other units that were needed to work with and support these infantry troops in combat could not then accompany them by air on that short notice.

In order that these forces may reach maximum combat effectiveness, the Joint Chiefs of Staff have recommended to me that we should prepare to send during the next five months the support troops totaling approximately 13,500 men.

A portion of these men will be made available from our active forces. The balance will come from reserve component units, which will be called up for service.

The actions that we have taken since the beginning of the year to re-equip the South Vietnamese forces; to meet our responsibilities in Korea, as well as our responsibilities in Vietnam; to meet price increases and the cost of activating and deploying these reserve forces; to replace helicopters and provide the other military supplies we need, all of these actions are going to require additional expenditures. this fiscal year and $2.6-billion in the next fiscal year. . . .

So these times call for prudence in this land of plenty. And I believe that we have the character to provide it, and tonight I plead with the Congress and with the people to act promptly to serve the national interest and thereby serve all of our people.

Now let me give you my estimate of the chances for peace—the peace that will one day stop the bloodshed in South Vietnam. That will—all the Vietnamese people will be permitted to rebuild and develop their land. That will permit us to turn more fully to our own tasks here at home.

I cannot promise that the initiative that I have announced tonight will be completely successful in achieveing peace any more than the 30 others that we have undertaken and agreed to in recent years.

But it is our fervent hope that North Vietnam, after years of fighting that has left the issue unresolved, will now cease its efforts to achieve a military victory and will join with us in moving toward the peace table.

And there may come a time when South Vietnamese—on both sides—are able to work out a way to settle their own differences by free political choice rather than by war.

As Hanoi considers its course, it should be in no doubt of our intentions. It must not miscalculate the pressures within our democracy in this election year. We have no intention of widening this war. But the United States will never accept a fake solution to this long and arduous struggle and call it peace.

No one can foretell the precise terms of an eventual settlement.

Our objective in South Vietnam has never been the annihilation of the enemy. It has been to bring about a recognition in Hanoi that its objective—taking over the South by force—could not be achieved.

We think that peace can be based on the Geneva accords of 1954, under political conditions that permit the South Vietnamese—all the South Vietnamese—to chart their course free of any outside domination or interferences, from us or from anyone else.

So tonight I reaffirm the pledge that we made at Manila: that we are prepared to withdraw our forces from South Vietnam as the other side withdraws its forces to the North, stops the infiltration, and the level of violence thus subsides.

Our goal of peace and self-determination in Vietnam is directly related to the future of all of Southeast Asia, where much has happened to inspire confidence during the past 10 years. And we have done all that we knew how to do to contribute and to help build that confidence.

A number of nations have shown what can be accomplished under conditions of security. Since 1966, Indonesia, the fifth largest nation in all the world, with a population of more than 100 million people, has had a government that's dedicated to peace with its neighbors and improved conditions for its own people.

Political and economic cooperation between nations has grown rapidly.

And I think every American can take a great deal of pride in the role that we have played in bringing this about in Southeast Asia. We can rightly judge—as responsible Southeast Asians themselves do—that the progress of the past three years would have been far less likely, if not completely impossible, if America's sons and others had not made their stand in Vietnam.

At Johns Hopkins University about three years ago, I announced that the United States would take part in the great work of developing Southeast Asia, including the Mekong valley, for all the people of that region. Our determination to help build a better land—a better land for men on both sides of the present conflict—has not diminished in the least. Indeed, the ravages of war, I think, have made it more urgent than ever.

So I repeat on behalf of the United States again tonight what I said at Johns Hopkins—that North Vietnam could take its place in this common effort just as soon as peace comes.

Over time, a wider framework of peace and security in Southeast Asia may become possible. The new cooperation of the nations of the area could be a foundation stone. Certainly friendship with the nations of such a Southeast Asia is what the United States seeks—and that is all that the United States seeks.

One day, my fellow citizens, there will be peace in Southeast Asia. It will come because the people of Southeast Asia want it—those whose armies are at war tonight; those who, though threatened, have thus far been spared.

Peace will come because Asians were willing to work for it and to sacrifice for it—and to die by the thousands for it.

But let it never be forgotten: peace will come also because America sent her sons to help secure it.

It has not been easy—far from it. During the past four and a half years, it has been my fate and my responsibility to be Commander in Chief. I have lived daily and nightly with the cost of this war. I know the pain that it has inflicted. I know perhaps better than anyone the misgivings it has aroused.

And throughout this entire long period I have been sustained by a single principle: that what we are doing now in Vietnam is vital not only to the security of Southeast Asia but it is vital to the security of every American.

Surely, we have treaties which we must respect. Surely, we have commitments that we are going to keep. Resolutions of the Congress testify to the need to resist aggression in the world and in Southeast Asia.

But the heart of our involvement in South Vietnam under three different Presidents, three separate Administrations, has always been America's own security.

And the larger purpose of our involvement has always been to help the nations of Southeast Asia become independent, and stand alone self-sustaining as members of a great world community, at peace with themselves, at peace with all others. And with such a nation our country—and the world—will be far more secure than it is tonight.

I believe that a peaceful Asia is far nearer to reality because of what America has done in Vietnam. I believe that the men who endure the dangers of battle there, fighting there for us tonight, are helping the entire world avoid far greater conflicts, far wider wars, far more destruction, than this one.

The peace that will bring them home someday will come. Tonight, I have offered the first in what I hope will be a series of mutual moves toward peace.

I pray that it will not be rejected by the leaders of North Vietnam. I pray that they will accept it as a means by which the sacrifices of their own people may be ended. And I ask your help and your support, my fellow citizens, for this effort to reach across the battlefield toward an early peace.

Yet, I believe that we must always be mindful of this one thing—whatever the trials and the tests ahead, the ultimate strength of our country and our cause will lie, not in powerful weapons or infinite resources or boundless wealth, but will lie in the unity of our people.

Finally, my fellow Americans, let me say this: Of those to whom much is given much is asked, I cannot say—and no man could say—that no more will be asked of us. Yet I believe that now, no less than when the decade began, this generation of Americans is willing to pay the price, bear any burden, meet any hardship, support any friend, oppose any foe, to assure the survival, and the success of liberty.

Since those words were spoken by John F. Kennedy, the people of America have kept that compact with mankind's noblest cause. And we shall continue to keep it.

This I believe very deeply. Throughout my entire public career I have followed the personal philosophy that I am a free man, an American, a public servant and a member of my party—in that order—always and only.

For 37 years in the service of our nation, first as a Congressman, as a Senator and as Vice President, and now as your President, I have put the unity of the poeple first. I have put it ahead of my divisive partisanship. And in these times, as in times before, it is true that a house divided against itself by the spirit of faction, of party, of region, of religion, of race, is a house that cannot stand.

There is division in the American house now. There is divisiveness among us all tonight. And holding the trust that is mine, as President of all the people, I cannot disregard the peril of the progress of the American people and the hope and the prospect of peace for all peoples, so I would ask all Americans whatever their personal interest or concern to guard against divisiveness and all of its ugly consequences.

Fifty-two months and ten days ago in a moment of tragedy and trauma, the duties of this office fell upon me.

I asked then for your help, and God's, that we might continue America on its course binding up our wounds, healing our history, moving forward in new unity to clear the American agenda and to keep the American commitment for all of our people.

United we have kept that commitment. And united we have enlarged that commitment. And through all time to come I think America will be a stronger nation, a more just society, a land of greater opportunity and fulfillment because of what we have all done together in these years of unparalleled achievement.

Our reward will come in the life of freedom and peace and hope that our children will enjoy through ages ahead.

What we won when all of our people united just must not now be lost in suspicion and distruct and selfishness and politics among any of our people. And believing this as I do I have concluded that I should not permit the Presidency to become involved in the partisan divisions that are developing in this political year.

With American sons in the fields far away, with America's future under challenge right here at home, with our hopes and the world's hopes for peace in the balance every day, I do not believe that I should devote an hour or a day of my time to any personal partisan causes or to any duties other than the awesome duties of this office—the Presidency of your country.

Accordingly, I shall not seek, and I will not accept, the nomination of my party for another term as your President. But let men everywhere know, however, that a strong and a confident and a vigilant America stands ready tonight to seek an honorable peace; and stands ready tonight to defend an honored cause, whatever the price, whatever the burden, whatever the sacrifice that duty may require.

Thank you for listening. Good night and God bless all of you.

ROBERT F. KENNEDY, STATEMENT ON THE ASSASSINATION OF MARTIN LUTHER KING, JR.
April 4, 1968

Indianapolis

Ladies and gentlemen, I am going to talk to you for only a few moments. I have sad news for all of you, and sad news for all our citizens.

Martin Luther King was shot and killed tonight.

Martin Luther King dedicated his life to love and to justice between his fellow human beings. He died in the cause of that effort.

For those of you who are black—considering the evidence that white people are responsible for the shooting—you can be filled with bitterness and hatred and a desire for revenge.

We can move in the direction of . . . greater polarization, black among black, white among white, filled with hatred toward one another. Or we can make an effort—as Martin Luther King did—to understand, to comprehend and replace the violence and the stain of bloodshed with compassion and love.

For those of you who are black and tempted to be filled with hatred at the injustice of such an act, I can also feel in my heart the same kind of feeling.

I had a member of my family killed . . . killed by a white man.

So I ask you tonight to return home and say a prayer for the family of Martin Luther King. That's true. But more importantly, to say a prayer for our country which all of us love.

HUBERT H. HUMPHREY
SPEECH ON AMERICAN CITIES
July 2, 1968

In this address before the City Club in Cleveland, Ohio, the Vice President proposed a Marshall Plan for American cities.

What happens in America's cities happens to America.

It is by the quality of life in our cities that the character of our civilization will be judged.

It is in our cities that American democracy will either succeed or fail.

It is there that the American dream—the dream of a free and equal people, living together in harmony—will or will not be achieved.

The urgent problems of our cities today are evident to anyone who tries to walk in them . . . or drive . . . or breathe . . . or find a quiet park, or a home, or a hospital, or a school a child could be proud of.

The harsh tragic facts of the slum and ghetto have become so familiar that detailing them is a filibuster . . . to put off action.

The truth, at least here in Cleveland—yes, and in Washington—is that a great deal is being done. There have been substantial gains.

But we are far short of the mark. As a nation, we haven't given this job the priority it must have.

We haven't yet made up our minds to pay what it costs—both in resources and in commitment.

We are still on the defensive. We know—or think we know—what we are against. We are less clear about what we are for.

We have declared a war on poverty. But we still need a crusade for opportunity.

We are against slums. But should we wipe them out or rebuild them or both?

We realize increasingly that the city itself is not the problem. The city is only the place where a score of different problems converge. And we have not yet developed that central, unifying idea which will be a rallying point for action.

That is why I have called for a Marshall Plan for America's cities.

The Marshall Plan was effective in Western Europe, above all, because of its concentration on a clear and feasible purpose.

It depended on a moral commitment . . . on planning . . . and on money to back both up.

Congressional Record, 90th Cong., 2d sess., 1968, vol. 114, pt. 17, pp. 22307-09.

It also depended on the use of American funds only as a catalyst to activate Western Europe's own human and material resources.

The American people put nearly 14 billion dollars into Western Europe over a five-year period. This sum was less by far than the cost to us—or to Europe—of economic chaos . . . or utter despair . . . or violence or another war.

Our money did not buy a new Europe. Nor could ten times as much have done so.

It helped Western Europeans build their own new Europe.

It generated a far greater amount of European capital.

It put jobless people on the job of rebuilding.

And it was used with enormous efficiency because of carefully coordinated planning by the European nations themselves.

Local initiative, careful planning, coordinated policy, strict priorities, and massive commitment—these techniques brought a new Europe from the ashes of World War II.

These are also the requirements for perfecting the American city.

The Marshall Plan produced a quick and visible impact—not only in bricks and mortar but in people's lives.

The initial investment was large enough, and the vision grand enough, to inspire hope . . . to show that the job could be done . . . to generate the will for self-help which brought Europe to self-sufficiency and prosperity.

This is the necessary element in a nationwide attack on the urban problem in America today.

There has in recent years been an unprecedented direction of federal funds and efforts to the problems of the cities.

A new Department of Housing and Urban Development has been set up—and a Department of Transporation, with responsibilities that bear directly on the urban problem.

A Model Cities Program is now funding comprehensive planning efforts in slum neighborhoods of 75 cities—150 next year.

Planning under Model Cities is done where it should be done—in the community. The plans must be total plans—to take account of housing, jobs, education, transportation, health, recreation and open spaces, and their interrelationship.

The Housing and Urban Development Act of 1968, now before the Congress, will initiate an unprecedented ten-year housing compaign to produce 26 million homes, 6 million of them federally assisted.

I hope that the events of the next year, especially in Vietnam, will let us advance that schedule.

The Economic Opportunity Act . . . the Manpower Development and Training Act . . . the Education Acts . . . the Health Acts . . . improvements in the Social Security Act and many more, have had a substantial impact on the problems of the cities.

But these all still appear as scattered efforts.

Now we must concentrate and coordinate our efforts.

How many houses? How many schools? How many health care centers? When? What is the timetable?

How much will it cost?

It will cost money—a great deal of it.

To help solve the central problems of financing, I propose the creation of a National Urban Development Bank, financed through subscription of private funds.

I propose federal underwriting of the unusual "risk" elements which are inevitably going to be involved in meeting the hardest and most critical urban problems.

Such a bank would have enough borrowing and lending authority to do the job. And we are talking here about billions of dollars each year.

An appropriation of federal funds would get the bank started. The balance of the funds would come from federally-guaranteed bonds, to be sold by the bank to private investors.

It would provide for private equity participation in the bank's operations.

Affiliated regional banks would be chartered by the National Bank for specific metropolitan areas.

Regional bank funds would be available to both public and private borrowers for programs which cannot be financed through any other means, but which are found essential to urban development.

They would be available, at varying interest rates depending on the circumstances of the need, to finance or help finance publicly-sponsored projects—especially, but not exclusively, in the inner cities.

These regional banks would aid in the financing of public facilities of all types and would include:

Funding of nonprofit neighborhood development corporations;

Guaranteed loans, made through conventional private lenders, for inner city and metropolitan-wide development;

Loans to inner city small businessmen whose contribution to the economy of their communities is now limited by lack of financing;

Funding of quasi-public housing development corporations.

Regional banks would provide technical management assistance in urban planning and development.

The establishment of a National Urban Development Bank with an assured source of funds would facilitate and encourage longrange planning for metropolitan area development—planning now inhibited by the uncertainties of the annual appropriation process.

Congressional surveillance would be maintained in appropriations, covering the differential between market and subsidized rates, technical assistance and other special grants for community and metropolitan developments.

Regional Bank Boards would include representation of local governments, as well as the broad spectrum of the population—white and black, rich and poor. Further community participation would be encouraged through direct equity investment in the Regional Bank by the people themselves.

This is essentially a program for federal underwriting of loans.

This is even more essentially a proposal to commit ourselves, as a country, to paying whatever is the cost not just saving, but of perfecting, our cities.

I shall ask Congress and the people of America to make this commitment.

I will urge that meeting the needs of America's cities be made in effect a prior lien on the additional several billions which we will realize each year in increased revenues from present taxes on our vastly-expanded national income.

I will urge, too, that we use, on these problems, a fair share of the "peace dividend" which can be ours—if we are steadfast in our determination to achieve an honorable settlement in Paris—and if we can achieve mutual deescalation in the costly and futile arms race between our nation and the Soviet Union.

Now let me make this equally clear: Any single proposal must not diminish to any degree whatsoever the other efforts which are essential to meet the urban crisis.

Social progress in our free enterprise economy has never been—nor should it be—primarily a responsibility of the public sector.

Private business, labor, banks, industry, and our universities must assume their full share of the urban development burden.

And we must create new mechanisms to stimulate private invesment to meet our social priorities.

If we are to perfect our cities within the traditions of American free enterprise, much of the money—and much of the initiative—must come from the private sector.

Six out of seven jobs in our economy are in the private sector.

Housing is almost entirely a private industry in America.

Most of the new buildings are designed by private architects, built by private contractors, and paid for by private concerns.

I am for keeping it that way. I think we can.

The life insurance companies of America have made an important start, not only with their billion-dollar commitment to build inner-city housing and create jobs, but also with the television documentary we saw last week on the dimensions of our urban challenge.

The National Alliance of Businessmen is ahead of schedule with pledges to hire and train the hard-core unemployed.

Business leaders in many of our cities have joined together in urban coalitions to begin improving their total communities.

This is only a beginning.

We can never build the cities we need without the full commitment of private enterprise.

We must, therefore, be prepared to offer financial and tax incentives to engage the enormous power of the private sector.

We must also offer these incentives, in addition to schools and first-class public services, as magnets to draw new industry and populations to the smaller city and new town—which can become the well-planned metropolis of tomorrow.

We are dependent on the vigorous exercise of private ingenuity, modern business methods, free enterprise to do most of the job in our cities.

There must clearly be a reordering and simplification of the local, state, and federal structures for administering the programs that are needed for urban and human redevelopment.

To begin to control the forces of urbanization, we must develop planning on an area-wide scale. We must avoid the irrational patchworks that have marked our urban growth patterns.

No matter what the federal govenment does, however, the consequences of urban disorganization cannot be avoided until localities recognize and accept their common destiny.

Constitutional reform and modernization of county and municipal government are no longer subjects for academic debate and editorial discussion. They are imperatives if our democracy is to survive.

Councils of governments—regional associations whose members are the governmental units of the metropolitan area—can provide an effective forum for attacking those problems whose solutions demand inter-governmental cooperation and coordination—law enforcement, transportation, air pollution, sanitation and garbage disposal, and employment.

As difficult as it will be, the next president must undertake a fundamental reorganization of all federal urban activities.

We must provide a structure which rewards innovation and a desire to act—not one which slowly drains and destroys the enthusiasm, effectiveness, and vision of urban leaders.

Then there is the problem of construction standards and technology—one of many places where we need uniform codes and state laws.

We shall never meet our national housing goals so long as 5,000 local jurisdictions apply different building-code standards.

Federal housing assistance, whether in the form of direct grants, loans, or mortgage insurance, should be contingent on the modernization of local land-use laws and building codes.

I urge, too, the adoption of the plain principle of public administrative responsibility: that the worst problems get the first attention.

In most cities today, public services are poorest where needs are greatest.

Schools are weakest where learning is hardest. This is wrong.

Garbage collection is slowest where the rats are.

Building codes are not enforced where the conditions they were designed to prevent are most prevalent.

Where health problems are most severe, medical facilities and personnel are least adequate—and often the most expensive.

Mr. Mayor, City Councilmen, Taxpayers: It is time to change that pattern. I don't suggest we impair city services in the better neighborhoods. I only say: We must make these services available to all our citizens.

But these courses of action—essential to progress—only make feasible the truly critical element: The motivation and capacity for effective action in the community itself.

The last several years have demonstrated the striking ability of citizens to assume major responsibility for shaping their own destinies—on their block, in their neighborhood, and throughout their city.

Persons supposedly lacking sophisticated training and preparation for community leadership have mounted some of our most successful and broadly-supported urban programs.

Cleveland: Now! Is a foremost example of the creative role which people can assume in saving a city. Under Mayor Carl Stokes' leadership, this is a community team in action—and achieving results.

But in many places this popular initiative has been thwarted—by lack of operating funds—by an unresponsive or even hostile bureaucracy in city hall, the state capitol or Washington—by unrealistic sets of rules, guidelines, regulations and procedures.

Whether the vehicle is a community corporation, neighborhood council, or city-wide planning body, we must prove our faith in democracy by getting people into the act.

New forms of neighborhood government must be considered by state legislatures and city councils.

I call particularly on those who are young to bring their capacities for invention, for faith, for commitment, and for human compassion, to the task of recreating cities that have gotten old before their time.

Let today's young people prove themselves as the generation of city builders.

I propose no miracles.

I make no promises that cannot be kept.

I have no promises that cannot be kept.

I have been the mayor of a great city. I know the weakness as well as the virtue of civic pride . . . how easy it is to start something—and how hard to finish it.

I know that stopping what is goinng on in our cities today is like stopping cancer.

But I know, too, that the American city is not going to die.

I know every mistake we have made in building our cities is a human mistake—which means it is within human capacity to correct.

We have everything it takes to recreate our cities . . . not in "Gleaming Alabaster" but surely "Undimmed by Human Tears."

There is no need—and it will compound our previous error—to settle for minimum housing, minimum health, minimum wages and employment, minimum schools, minimum neighborhoods.

We don't believe in a minimum American—and we won't fight hard enough if that is all we are after.

We believe—and we will fight for that belief—in creating an urban environment that calls forth the best quality in every person . . . that liberates the human spirit.

What is at stake today is not the urban—but the human condition.

We propose not to improve—but to perfect—that condition.

I say we can.

I say we will.

I say we can build an America that may be seen throughout the world, and by us, as Carl Sandburg saw her:

> I see America, not in the setting sun of a black night of despair ahead of us. I see America in the crimson light of a rising sun fresh from the burning, creative hand of god. I see great days ahead, great days possible to men and women of will and vision.

MAJORITY AND MINORITY WAR PLANKS
DEMOCRATIC PLATFORM OF 1968

MAJORITY PLANK

Our most urgent task in Southeast Asia is to end the war in Vietnam by an honorable and lasting settlement which respects the right of all the people of Vietnam. In our pursuit of peace and stability in the vital area of Southeast Asia we have borne a heavy burden in helping South Vietnam to counter aggression and subversion from the North.

We reject as unacceptable a unilateral withdrawal of our forces which would allow that aggression and subversion to succeed. We have never demanded, and do not now demand, unconditional surrender by the Communists.

We strongly support the Paris talks and applaud the initiative of President Johnson which brought North Vietnam to the peace table. We hope that Hanoi will respond positively to this act of statesmanship.

In the quest for peace no solutions are free of risk. But calculated risks are consistent with the responsibility of a great nation to seek a peace of reconciliation.

Recognizing that events in Vietnam and the negotiations in Paris may affect the timing and the actions we recommend we would support our Government in the following steps:

Bombing—Stop all bombing of North Vietnam when this action would not endanger the lives of our troops in the field; this action should take into account the response from Hanoi.

Troop Withdrawal—Negotiate with Hanoi an immediate end or limitation of hostilities and the withdrawal from South Vietnam of all foreign forces—both United States and allied forces, and forces infiltrated from North Vietnam.

Election of Postwar Government—Encourage all parties and interests to agree that the choice of the postwar government of South Vietnam should be determined by fair and safeguarded elections, open to all major political factions and parties prepared to accept peaceful political processes. We would favor an effective international presence to facilitate the transition from war to peace and to assure the protection of minorities against reprisal.

Interim Defense and Development Measures—Until the fighting stops, accelerate our efforts to train and equip the South Vietnamese army so that it can defend its own country and carry out cutbacks of U.S. military involvement as the South Vietnamese forces are able to take over their larger responsibilities. We should simultaneously do all in our power to support and encourage further economic, political and social development and reform in South Vietnam, including an extensive land reform program. We support President Johnson's repeated offer to provide a substantial U.S. contribution to the post-war reconstruction of South Vietnam as well as to the economic development of the entire region, including North Vietnam. Japan and the European industrial states should be urged to join in this post-war effort.

For the future, we will make it clear that U.S. military and economic assistance in Asia will be selective. In addition to considerations of our vital interests and our resources, we will take into account the determination of the nations that request our help to help themselves and their willingness to help each other through regional and multilateral cooperation.

We want no bases in South Vietnam; no continued military presence and no political role in Vietnamese affairs. If and when the Communists understand our basic commitment and limited goals and are willing to take their chances, as we are, on letting the choice of the post-war government of South Vietnam be determined freely and peacefully by all of the South Vietnamese people, then the bloodshed and the tragedy can stop.

MINORITY PLANK

Nearly 200,000 American men have been casualties in Vietnam, and 25,000 have died. The United States has spent more than $100-billion. This war has cost us heavily in human life and in all the resources we so badly need to rebuild our cities, improve the quality of life for all Americans and to meet our other obligations around the world.

Discarding judgment about the wisdom of the past, we must now act to secure and enrich our future by bringing the war in Vietnam to a swift conclusion. It is to this cause of early peace that the Democratic party now commits itself.

Nor can we be content with the vague and ambiguous statements which mark the platform of the Republican party. For a meaningful pledge of peace also demands the courage to make commitments to those concrete and specific acts most likely to hasten the end of the conflict and destruction. We have taken so many risks for war, we must now take some for peace.

That war must be ended now. It will not be ended by a military victory, surrender or unilateral withdrawal by either side: It cannot be ended by further United States escalation, either increasing our troops, introducing nuclear weapons, or extending the conflict geographically: it must therefore be ended by a fair and realistic compromise settlement.

Although the war in Vietnam is complex, the steps towards peace can be simply stated.

First, an unconditional end to all bombing of North Vietnam, while continuing to provide, in the South, all necessary air and other support for American troops.

Second, we will then negotiate a mutual withdrawal of all United States forces and all North Vietnamese troops from South Vietnam. This should be a phased withdrawal over a relatively short period of time.

Third, we will encourage our South Vietnamese allies to negotiate a political reconciliation with the National Liberation Front looking toward a Government which is broadly representative of these and all elements in South Vietnamese society. The specific shape of this reconciliation will be a matter for decision by the South Vietnamese, spurred to action by the certain knowledge that the prop of American military support will soon be gone.

In addition, the South Vietnamese will assume increasing responsibility for the resolution of the conflict, and full responsibility for the determining their own political destiny. We will, of course, extend economic and other assistance to help rebuild in peace the society which has been ravaged by war.

Fourth, to reduce American casualties and the suffering of Vietnamese civilians we will lower the level of violence by reducing offensive operations in the Vietnamese countryside, thus enabling an early withdrawal of a significant number of our troops. We will, of course, at all times continue to provide all necessary military support in the South for American troops confronted by hostile forces.

In this way we can eliminate all foreign forces from South Vietnam. Our troops will leave and those of North Vietnam will also depart. It will be up to the South Vietnamese to achieve a political and social reconciliation among their warring peoples. We will also seek to enlist the participation of international authority to guarantee troop withdrawals and the granting of asylum to political refugees.

Thus we can reasonably anticipate that as we leave, the Vietnamese will be well on the way to a solution of their own problems, and a Government in which all can have a share of power and responsibility.

We are also resolved to have no more Vietnams. We accept as basic each nation's right to choose its political, economic and social system. Our deep concern for the welfare of human beings everywhere will be expressed through economic and technical assistance, predominantly under international auspicies.

We shall neither assume the role of the world's policeman, nor lend our support to corrupt oppressive regimes unwilling to work for essential reforms and lacking the consent of the governed.

Above all, we shall avoid the unilateral use of military means where the issues are political in nature and our national security is not involved.

HUBERT H. HUMPHREY
CAMPAIGN SPEECH ON VIETNAM
September 30, 1968

Televised Address from Salt Lake City

Tonight I want to share with you my thoughts as a citizen and a candidate for President of the United States.

I want to tell you what I think about great issues which I believe face this nation.

I want to talk with you about Vietnam, and about another great issue in the search for peace in the world—the issue of stopping the threat of nuclear war.

After I have told you what I think, I want you to think.

And if you agree with me, I want you to help me.

For the past several weeks, I have tried to tell you what was in my heart and on my mind.

But sometimes that message has been drowned out by the voices of protesters and demonstrators.

I shall not let the violence and disorder of a nosiy few deny me the right to speak or to destroy the orderly democratic process.

I have paid for this television time this evening to tell you my story uninterrupted by noise—by protest—or by second-hand interpretation.

When I accepted the Democratic party's nomination and platform, I said that the first reality that confronted this nation was the need for peace in Vietnam.

I have pledged that my first priority as President shall be to end the war and obtain an honorable peace.

For the past four years I have spoken my mind about Vietnam, frankly and without reservation, in the Cabinet and in the National Security Council—and directly to the President.

When the President has made his decisions, I have supported them.

He has been the Commander in Chief. It has been his job to decide. And the choices have not been simple or easy.

President Johnson will continue—until Jan. 20, 1969—to make the decisions in Vietnam. The voice at the negotiating table must be his. I shall not compete with that voice. I shall cooperate and help.

We all pray that his efforts to find peace will succeed.

But, 112 days from now, there will be a President—a new Administration—and new advisers.

If there is no peace by then, it must be their responsibility to make a complete reassessment of the situation in Vietnam—to see where we stand and to judge what we must do.

As I said in my acceptance speech: The policies of tomorrow need not be limited by the policies of yesterday.

We must look to the future. For neither vindication nor repudiation of our role in Vietnam will bring peace or be worthy of our country.

The American people have a right to know what I would do—if I am President—after Jan. 20, 1969, to keep my pledge to honorably end the war in Vietnam.

What are the chances for peace?

The end of the war is not yet in sight. But our chances for peace are far better today than they were a year or even a month ago.

On March 31, the war took on an entirely new dimension.

On that date President Johnson by one courageous act removed the threat of bombing from 90 per cent of the people, and 78 per cent of the land area, of North Vietnam.

On that date President Johnson sacrificed his own political career in order to bring negotiations that could lead to peace.

Until that time, the struggle was only on the battlefield.

Now our negotiators are face to face across the table with negotiators from North Vietnam.

A process has been set in course. And lest that process be set back, our perseverance at the conference table must be great as our courage has been in the war.

There have been other changes during these past few months.

The original Vietnam decision—made by President Eisenhower—was made for one basic reason.

President Eisenhower believed it was in our national interest that Communist subversion and aggression should not succeed in Vietnam.

It was his judgment—and the judgment of President Kennedy and President Johnson since then—that if aggression did succeed in Vietnam, there was a danger that we would become involved on a more dangerous scale in a wider area of Southeast Asia.

While we have stood with our allies in Vietnam, several things have happened.

Other nations of Southeast Asia—given the time we have bought for them—have strengthened themselves—have begun to work together—and are far more able to protect themselves against any future subversion or aggression.

In South Vietnam itself, a constitution has been written—elections have been stepped up—and the South Vietnamese Army has increased its size and capacity, and improved its equipment, training and performance—just as the Korean Army did during the latter stages of the Korean war.

So—in sharp contrast to a few months ago—we see peace negotiations going on.

We see a stronger Southeast Asia.

We see a stronger South Vietnam.

Those are the new circumstances which a new President will face in January.

In light of those circumstances—and assuming no marked change in the present situation—how would I proceed as President?

Let me first make clear what I would not do.

I would not undertake a unilateral withdrawal.

To withdraw would not only jeopardize the independence of South Vietnam and the safety of other Southeast Asian nations. It would make meaningless the sacrifices we have already made.

It would be an open invitation to more violence—more aggression—More instability.

It would, at this time of tension in Europe, cast doubt on the integrity of our word under treaty and alliance.

Peace would not be served by weakness or withdrawal.

Nor would I escalate the level of violence in either North or South Vietnam. We must seek to de-escalate.

The platform of my party says that the President should take reasonable risks to find peace in Vietnam. I shall do so.

North Vietnam, according to its own statements and those of others, has said it will proceed to prompt and good faith negotiations, if we stop the present limited bombing of the North.

We must always think of the protection of our troops.

As President, I would stop the bombing of the North as an acceptable risk for peace because I believe it could lead to success in the negotiations and thereby shorten the war. This would be the best protection for our troops. In weighing that risk—and before taking action—I would place key importance on evidence—direct or indirect—by deed or word—of Communist willingness to restore the demilitarized zone between North and South Vietnam.

Now if the Government of North Vietnam were to show bad faith, I would reserve the right to resume the bombing.

Now secondly, I would take the risk that South Vietnamese would meet the responsibilities they say they are now ready to assume in their own self-defense.

I would move, in other words, toward de-Americanization of the war.

I would sit down with the leaders of South Vietnam to set a specific timetable by which American forces could be systematically reduced while South Vietnamese forces took over more and more of the burden.

The schedule must be a realistic one—one that would not weaken the overall Allied defense posture. I am convinced such action would be as much in South Vietnam's interest as in ours.

What I am proposing is that it should be basic to our policy in Vietnam that the South Vietnamese take over more and more of the defense of their own country.

That would be an immediate objective of the Humphrey-Muskie Administration as I sought to end the war.

If the South Vietnamese Army maintains its present rate of improvement, I believe this will be possible next year—without endangering either our remaining troops or the safety of South Vietnam.

I do not say this lightly. I have studied this matter carefully.

Third, I would propose once more an immediate cease-fire—with United Nations or other international supervision and supervised withdrawal of all foreign forces from South Vietnam.

American troops are fighting in numbers in South Vietnam today only because North Vietnamese forces were sent to impose Hanoi's will on the South Vietnamese people by aggression.

We can agree to bring home our forces from South Vietnam, if the North Vietnamese agree to bring theirs home at the same time.

External forces assisting both sides could and should leave at the same time, and should not be replaced.

The ultimate key to an honorable solution must be free elections in South Vietnam—with all people, including members of the National Liberation Front and other dissident groups, able to participate in those elections if they were willing to abide by peaceful processes.

That, too, would mean some risk.

But I have never feared the risk of one man, one vote. I say: let the people speak. And accept their judgment, whatever it is.

The Government of South Vietnam should not be imposed by force from Hanoi or by pressure from Washington. It should be freely chosen by all the South Vietnamese people.

A stopping of the bombing of the North—taking account of Hanoi's actions and assurances of prompt good faith negotiations and keeping the option of resuming that bombing if the Communists show bad faith.

Careful, systematic reduction of American troops in South Vietnam—a de-Americanization of the war—turning over to the South Vietnamese Army a greater share of the defense of its own country.

An internationally supervised cease-fire—and supervised withdrawal of all foreign forces from South Vietnam.

Free elections, including all people in South Vietnam willing to follow the peaceful process.

Those are risks I would take for peace.

I do not believe any of these risks would jeopardize our security or be contrary to our national interest.

There is, of course, no guarantee that all these things could be successfully done.

Certainly, none of them could be done if North Vietnam were to show bad faith.

But I believe there is a good chance these steps could be undertaken with safety for our men in Vietnam.

As President, I would be dedicated to carrying them out—as I would be dedicated to urging the Government of South Vietnam to expedite all political, economic and social reforms essential to broadening popular participation including high priority to land reform—more attention to the suffering of refugees—and constant Government pressure against inflation and corruption.

I believe all of these steps could lead to an honorable and lasting settlement, serving both our own national interest and the interests of the independent nations of Southeast Asia.

We have learned a lesson from Vietnam.

The lesson is not that we should turn our backs on Southeast Asia, or on other nations or peoples in less familiar parts of the world neighborhood.

The lesson is, rather, that we should carefully define our goals and priorities. And within those goals and priorities, that we should formulate policies which will fit new American guidelines.

Applying the lesson of Vietnam, I would insist as President that we review other commitments made in other times, that we carefully decide what is and is not in our national interest.

I do not condemn any past commitment.

I do not judge the decisions of past Presidents when, in good conscience, they made those decisions in what they thought were the interests of the American people.

But I do say, if I am President, I owe it to this nation to bring our men and resources in Vietnam back to America where we need them so badly, and to be sure we put first things first in the future.

Let me be clear: I do not counsel withdrawal from the world.

I do not swerve from international responsibility.

I only say that, as President, I would undertake a new strategy for peace in this world, based not on American omnipotence, but on American leadership, not only military and economic but moral.

That new strategy for peace would emphasize working through the United Nations—strengthening and maintaining our key alliances for mutual security, particularly including NATO—supporting international peacekeeping machinery—and working with other nations to build new institutions and instruments for cooperation.

In a troubled and dangerous world we should seek not to march alone, but to lead in such a way that others will wish to join us.

Even as we seek peace in Vietnam, we must for our own security and well-being seek to halt and turn back the costly and even more dangerous arms race.

Five nations now have nuclear bombs.

The United States and the Soviet Union already possess enough weapons to burn and destroy every human being on this earth.

Unless we stop the arms race—unless we stop 15 to 20 more nations from getting nuclear bombs and nuclear bomb technology within the next few years, this generation may be the last.

For 20 years we have lived under the constant threat that some irresponsible action or even some great miscalculation could blow us all up in the wink of an eye.

There is danger that we have become so used to the idea that we no longer think it abnormal—forgetting that our whole world structure depends for its stability on the precarious architecture of what Winston Churchill called the "balance of terror." This is no longer an adequate safeguard for peace.

There is a treaty now before the Senate which would stop the spread of nuclear weapons. That treaty must be ratified now.

If this nation cannot muster the courage to ratify this treaty—a treaty which in no way endangers our national security, but adds to it by keeping these weapons out of the hands of a Nasser, a Castro—and many others—then there can be little hope for our future in this world. We must ratify this treaty.

I also believe that we must have the courage—while keeping our guard up and fulfilling our commitments to NATO—to talk with the Soviet Union as soon as possible about a freeze and a reduction of offensive and defensive nuclear missiles systems.

To escalate the nuclear missile arms race is to raise the level of danger and total destruction. It is costly, menacing, fearsome and offers no genuine defense.

Beyond that, if I am President, I shall take the initiative to find the way—under carefully safeguarded, mutually acceptable international inspection—to reduce arms budgets and military expenditures systematically among all countries of the world.

Our country's military budget this year is $80-billion.

It is an investment we have to make under existing circumstances. It protects our freedom.

But if we can work with other nations so that we can all reduce our military expenditures together, with proper safeguards and inspection, then it will be a great day for humanity.

All of us will have moved further away from self-destruction. And all of us will have billions of dollars with which to help people live better lives.

The American people must choose the one man they believe can best face these great issues.

I would hope that Mr. Nixon, Mr. Wallace and I could express our views on Vietnam not only individually, but on the same public platform.

I call for this because—on the basis of our past records and past careers—there are great differences between our policies and programs.

Those views of Governor Wallace which I have seen reported indicate that he would sharply escalate the war.

Mr. Nixon's past record reveals his probable future policies.

In 1954—at the time of the French defeat at Dienbienphu—he advocated American armed intervention in Vietnam in aid of French colonialism. It was necessary for President Eisenhower to repudiate his proposal.

Since then, he has taken a line on Vietnam policy which I believe could lead to greater escalation of the war.

In January of this year, Mr. Nixon described as "bunk" the idea that free elections in South Vietnam were of importance.

In February of this year, when questioned about the use of nuclear weapons in Vietnam, Mr. Nixon said that a general "has to take the position that he cannot rule out the use of nuclear weapons in extreme situations that might develop."

Since then, he has indicated he has a plan to end the war in Vietnam but will not disclose it until be becomes President.

If he has such a plan, he has an obligation to so inform President Johnson and the American people.

A few days ago the Republican Vice-Presidential nominee said there is not now and never has been a Nixon-Agnew plan for peace in Vietnam. It was, he said, a ploy "to maintain suspense."

And then he said: "Isn't that the way campaigns are run?"

I think we need some answers about this from Mr. Nixon.

Mr. Nixon's public record shows, also, consistent opposition to measures for nuclear arms controls.

He attacked Adlai Stevenson and myself for advocating a nuclear test ban treaty—a treaty to stop radioactive fallout from poisoning and crippling people the world over. He called our plan "a cruel hoax." We can be thankful that President Kennedy and the Congress did not follow his advice.

Today, he is asking for delay of ratification of a treaty carefully negotiated over several years and signed by 80 nations—the nuclear nonproliferation treaty designed to stop the spread of nuclear weapons.

I speak plainly: I do not believe the American Presidency can afford a return to leadership which would increase tension in the world; which would, on the basis of past statements, escalate the Vietnam war; and which would turn the clock back on progress that has been made at a great sacrifice to bring the great powers of the world into a saner relationship in this nuclear age.

On the great issues of Vietnam, of the arms race and of human rights in America, I have clear differences with Mr. Nixon and Mr. Wallace.

I call on both the these men to join me in open debate before the American people.

Let us put our ideas before the people. Let us offer ourselves for their judgment —as men and as leaders.

Let us appear together—in front of the same audiences or on the same television screens, and at the same time—to give the people a choice.

We must not let a President be elected by the size of his advertising budget.

We cannot let a President be elected without having met the issues before the people.

I am willing to put myself, my programs, my capacity for leadership, before the American people for their judgment.

I ask the Republican nominee and the third-party candidate to do the same.

I ask, before Election Day, that we be heard together as you have heard me alone tonight.

I appeal to the people—as citizens of a nation whose compassion and sense of decency and fair play have made it what Lincoln called "the last best hope on earth."

I appeal to you as a person who wants his children to grow up in that kind of country.

I appeal to you to express and vote your hopes and not your hates.

I intend, in these five weeks, to wage a vigorous, tireless and forthright campaign for the Presidency. I shall not spare myself, or those who will stand with me.

I have prepared myself. I know the problems facing this nation. I do not shrink from these problems. I challenge them. They were made by men. I believe they can be solved by men.

If you will give me your confidence and support, together we shall build a better America.

"MANDATE FOR REFORM," McGOVERN COMMISSION REPORT ON DELEGATE SELECTION
September 1971

THE OFFICIAL GUIDELINES OF THE COMMISSION

On November 19 and 20, 1969, the Commission, meeting in open session in Washington, D.C., adopted the following Guidelines for delegate selection.

Part I—Introduction

The following Guidelines for delegate selection represent the Commission's interpretation of the "full, meaningful, and timely" language of its mandate. These Guidelines have been divided into three general categories.

A. Rules or practices which inhibit access to the delegate selection process—items which compromise full and meaningful participation by inhibiting or preventing a Democrat from exercising his influence in the delegate selection process.

B. Rules or practices which dilute the influence of a Democrat in the delegate selection process, after he has exercised all available resources to effect such influence.

C. Rules and practices which have some attributes of both A and B.

A. Rules or practices inhibiting access

1. Discrimination on the basis of race, color, creed, or national origin.
2. Discrimination on the basis of age or sex.
3. Voter registration.
4. Costs and fees.
5. Existence of Party rules.

B. Rules or practices diluting influence

1. Proxy voting.
2. Clarity of purpose.
3. Quorum provisions.
4. Selection of alternates; filling of delegate and alternate vacancies.
5. Unit rule.
6. Adequate representation of political minority views.
7. Apportionment.

Congressional Record, 92d Cong., 1st sess., vol. 117, no. 138, pp. 13-18.

C. Rules and practices combining attributes of A and B

1. Adequate public notice.
2. Automatic (ex-officio) delegates.
3. Open and closed processes.
4. Premature delegate selection (timeliness).
5. Committee selection processes.
6. Slate-making.

Part II—The Guidelines

A–1 Discrimination on the basis of race, color, creed, or national origin

The 1964 Democratic National Convention adopted a resolution which conditioned the seating of delegations at future conventions on the assurance that discrimination in any State Party affairs on the grounds of race, color, creed or national origin did not occur. The 1968 Convention adopted the 1964 Convention resolution for inclusion in the Call to the 1972 Convention. In 1966, the Special Equal Rights Committee, which had been created in 1964, adopted six and anti-discrimination standards—designated as the "six basic elements"[1] —for the State Parties to meet. These standards were adopted by the Democratic National Committee in January 1968 as its official policy statement.

These actions demonstrate the intention of the Democratic Party to ensure a full opportunity for all minority group members to participate in the delegate

---

[1] *Six basic elements, adopted by the Democratic National Committee as official policy statement, January 1968:*

1. All public meetings at all levels of the Democratic Party in each State should be open to all members of the Democratic Party regardless of race, color, creed, or national origin.

2. No test for membership in, nor any oaths of loyalty to, the Democratic Party in any State should be required or used which has the effect of requiring prospective or current members of the Democratic Party to acquiesce in, condone or support discrimination on the grounds of race, color, creed, or national origin.

3. The time and place for all public meetings of the Democratic Party on all levels should be publicized fully and in such a manner as to assure timely notice to all interested persons. Such meetings must be held in places accessible to all Party members and large enough to accommodate all interested persons.

4. The Democratic Party, on all levels, should support the broadest possible registration without discrimination on grounds of race, color, creed or national origin.

5. The Democratic Party in each State should publicize fully and in such manner as to assure notice to all interested parties a full description of the legal and practical procedures for selection of Democratic Party Officers and representatives on all levels. Publication of these procedures should be done in such fashion that all prospective and current members of each State Democratic Party will be fully and adequately informed of the pertinent procedures in time to participate in each selection procedure at all levels of the Democratic Party organization.

6. The Democratic Party in each State should publicize fully and in such manner as to assure notice to all interested parties a complete description of the legal and practical qualifications for all officers and representatives of the State Democratic Party. Such publication should be done in timely fashion so that all prospective candidates or applicants for any selected or appointed position within each State Democratic Party will have full and adequate opportunity to compete for office.

selection process. To supplement the requirements of the 1964 and 1968 Conventions, the Commission requires that:

1. State Parties add the six basic elements of the Special Equal Rights Committee to their Party rules and take appropriate steps to secure their implementation;

2. State Parties overcome the effects of past discrimination by affirmative steps to encourage minority group participation, including representation of minority groups on the national convention delegation in reasonable relationship to the group's presence in the population of the State."[2]

A-2 Discrimination on the basis of age or sex

The Commission believes that discrimination on the grounds of age or sex is inconsistent with full and meaningful opportunity to participate in the delegate selection process. Therefore, the Commission requires State Parties to eliminate all vestiges of discrimination on these grounds. Furthermore, the Commission requires State Parties to overcome the effects of past discrimination by affirmative steps to encourage representation on the national convention delegation of young people— defined as people of not more than thirty nor less than eighteen years of age—and women in reasonable relationship to their presence in the population of the State.[2] Moreover, the Commission requires State Parties to amend their Party rules to allow and encourage any Democrat of eighteen years or more to participate in all party affairs.

When State law controls, the Commission requires State Parties to make all feasible efforts to repeal, amend, or otherwise modify such laws to accomplish the stated purpose.

A-3 Voter registration

The purpose of registration is to add to the legitimacy of the electoral process, not to discourage participation. Democrats do not enjoy an opportunity to participate fully in the delegate selection process in States where restrictive voter registration laws and practices are in force, preventing their effective participation in primaries, caucuses, conventions and other Party affairs. These restrictive laws and practices include annual registration requirements, lengthy residence requirements, literacy tests, short and untimely registration periods, and infrequent enrollment sessions.

The Commission urges each State Party to assess the burdens imposed on a prospective participant in the Party's delegate selection processes by State registration laws, customs and practices, as outlined in the report of the Grass Roots Subcommittee of the Commission on Party Structure and Delegate Selection, and use its good offices to remove or alleviate such barriers to participation.

---

[2]It is the understanding of the Commission that this is not to be accomplished by the mandatory imposition of quotas.

A–4 Costs and fees; petition requirements

The Commission believes that costs, fees, or assessments and excessive petition requirements made by State law and Party rule or resolutions impose a financial burden on (1) national convention delegates and alternates; (2) candidates for convention delegates and alternates; and (3) in some cases, participants. Such costs, fees, assessments or excessive petition requirements discouraged full and meaningful opportunity to participate in the delegate selection process.

The Commission urges the State Parties to remove all costs and fees involved in the delegate selection process. The Commission requires State Parties to remove all excessive costs and fees, and to waive all nominal costs and fees when they would impose a financial strain on any Democrat. A cost or fee of more than $10 for all stages of the delegate selection process is deemed excessive. The Commission requires State Parties to remove all mandatory assessments of delegates and alternates.

The Commission requires State Parties to remove excessive petition requirements for convention delegate candidates of presidential candidates. Any petition requirement, which calls for a number of signatures in excess of 1% of the standard used for measuring Democratic strength, whether such standard be based on the number of Democratic votes cast for a specific office in a previous election or Party enrollment figures, is deemed excessive.

When State law controls any of these matters, the Commission requires State Parties to make all feasible efforts to repeal, amend or otherwise modify such laws to accomplish the stated purpose.

This provision, however, does not change the burden of expenses borne by individuals who campaign for and/or serve as delegates and alternates. Therefore, the Commission urges State Parties to explore ways of easing the financial burden on delegates and alternates and candidates for delegate and alternate.

A–5 Existence of party rules

In order for rank-and-file Democrats to have a full and meaningful opportunity to participate in the delegate selection process, they must have access to the substantive and procedural rules which govern the process. In some States the process is not regulated by law or rule, but by resolution of the State Committee and by tradition. In other States, the rules exist, but generally are inaccessible. In still others, rules and laws regulate only the formal aspects of the selection process (e.g., date and place of the State convention) and leave to Party resolution or tradition the more substantive matters (e.g., intrastate apportionment of votes; rotation of alternates; nomination of delegates).

The Commission believes that any of these arrangements is inconsistent with the spirit of the Call in that they permit excessive discretion on the part of Party officials, which may be used to deny or limit full and meaningful opportunity to participate. Therefore, the Commission requires State Parties to adopt and make available readily accessible statewide Party rules and statutes which prescribe the State's delegate selection process with sufficient details and clarity. When relevant to the State's delegate selection process, explicit written Party rules and procedural rules should include clear provisions for: (1) the apportionment of delegates and votes within the State; (2) the allocation of fractional votes, if any; (3) the selection and responsibilities of convention committees; (4) the nomination of delegates and alternates; (5) the succession of alternates to delegate status and the filling of vacancies; (6) credentials challenges; (7) minority reports.

Furthermore, the Commission requires State Parties to adopt rules which will facilitate maximum participation among interested Democrats in the processes by which National Convention delegates are selected. Among other things, these rules should provide for dates, times, and public places which would be most likely to encourage interested Democrats to attend all meetings involved in the delegate selection process.

The Commission requires State Parties to adopt explicit written Party rules which provide for uniform times and dates of all meetings involved in the delegate selection process. These meetings and events include caucuses, conventions, committee meetings, primaries, filing deadlines, and Party enrollment periods. Rules regarding time and date should be uniform in two senses. First, each stage of the delegate selection process should occur at a uniform time and date throughout the State. Second, the time and date should be uniform from year to year. The Commission recognizes that in many parts of rural America it may be an undue burden to maintain complete uniformity, and therefore exempts rural areas from this provision so long as the time and date are publicized in advance of the meeting and are uniform within the geographic area.

B–1 Proxy voting

When a Democrat cannot, or chooses not to, attend a meeting related to the delegate selection process, many States allow that person to authorize another to act in his name. This practice—called proxy voting—has been a significant source of real or felt abuse of fair procedure in the delegate selection process.

The Commission believes that any situation in which one person is given the authority to act in the name of the absent Democrat, on any issue before the meeting, gives such person an unjustified advantage in affecting the outcome of the meeting. Such a situation is inconsistent with the spirit of equal participation. Therefore, the Commission requires State Parties to add to their explicit written rules provisions which forbid the use of proxy voting in all procedures involved in the delegate selection process.

B–2 Clarity of purpose

An opportunity for full participation in the delegate selection process is not meaningful unless each Party member can clearly express his preference for candidates for delegates to the National Convention, or for those who will select such delegates. In many States, a Party member who wishes to affect the selection of the delegation must do so by voting for delegates or Party officials who will engage in many activities unrelated to the delegate selection process.

Whenever other Party business is mixed, without differentiation, with the delegate selection process, the Commission requires State Parties to make it clear to voters how they are participating in a process that will nominate their Party's candidate for President. Furthermore, in States which employ a convention or committee system, the Commission requires State Parties to clearly designate the delegate selection procedures as distinct from other Party business.

B–3 Quorum provisions

Most constituted bodies have rules or practices which set percentage or number minimums before they can commence their business. Similarly, Party committees which participate in the selection process may commence business only after it is determined that this quorum exists. In some States, however, the quorum requirement is satisfied when less than 40% of committee members are in attendance.

The Commission believes a full opportunity to participate is satisfied only when a rank-and-file Democrat's representative attends such committee meetings. Recognizing, however, that the setting of high quorum requirements may impede the selection process, the Commission requires State Parties to adopt rules setting quorums at not less than 40% for all party committees involved in the delegate selection process.

B–4 Selection of alternates; filling of delegate and alternate vacancies

The Call to the 1972 Convention requires that alternates be chosen by one of the three methods sanctioned for the selection of delegates—i.e., by primary, convention or committee. In some States, Party rules authorize the delegate himself or the State Chairman to choose his alternate. The Commission requires State Parties to prohibit these practices—and other practices not specifically authorized by the Call—for selecting alternates.

In the matter of vacancies, some States have Party rules which authorize State Chairmen to fill all delegate and alternate vacancies. This practice again involves the selection of delegates or alternates by a process other than primary, convention or committee. The Commission requires States Parties to prohibit such practices and to fill all vacancies by (1) a timely and representative Party committee; or (2) a reconvening of the body which selected the delegate or alternate whose seat is vacant; or (3) the delegation itself, acting as a committee.

When State law controls, the Commission requires State Parties to make all feasible efforts to repeal, amend or otherwise modify such laws to accomplish the stated purposes.

B–5 Unit rule

In 1968, many States used the unit rule at various stages in the processes by which delegates were selected to the National Convention. The 1968 Convention defined unit rule,[3] did not enforce the unit rule on any delegate in 1968, and added language to the 1972 Call requiring that "the unit rule not be used in any stage of the delegate selection process." In light of the Convention action, the Commission requires State Parties to add to their explicit written rules provisions which forbid the use of the unit rule or the practice of instructing delegates to vote against their stated preferences at any stage of the delegate selection process. [4]

B–6 Adequate representation of minority views on presidential candidates at each stage in the delegate selection process

The Commission believes that a full and meaningful opportunity to particiate in the delegate selection process is precluded unless the presidential preference of each Democrat is fairly represented at all levels of the process. Therefore, the Commission urges each State Party to adopt procedures which will provide fair representation of minority views on presidential candidates and recommends that the 1972 Convention adopt a rule requiring State Parties to provide for the representation of minority views to the highest level of the nominating process.

The Commission believes that there are at least two different methods by which a State Party can provide for such representation. First, in at-large elections it can divide delegate votes among presidential candidates in proportion to their demonstrated strength. Second, it can choose delegates from fairly apportioned districts no larger than congressional districts.

The Commission recognizes that there may be other methods to provide for fair representation of minority views. Therefore, the Commission will make every effort to stimulate public discussion of the issue of representation of minority views on presidential candidates between now and the 1972 Democratic National Convention.

B–7 Apportionment

The Commission believes that the manner in which votes and delegates are apportioned within each State has a direct bearing on the nature of participation. If the

---

[3] *Unit Rule.* "This Convention will not enforce upon any delegate with respect to voting on any question or issue before the Convention any duty or obligation which said delegate would consider to violate his individual conscience. As to any legal, moral or ethical obligation arising from a unit vote or rule imposed either by State law by a State convention or State committee or primary election of any nature, or by a vote of a State delegation, the Convention will look to each individual delegate to determine for himself the extent of such obligation if any."

[4] It is the understanding of the Commission that the prohibition on instructed delegates applies to favorite-son candidates as well.

apportionment formula is not based on Democratic strength and/or population the opportunity for some voters to participate in the delegate selection process will not be equal to the opportunity of others. Such a situation is inconsistent with a full and meaningful opportunity to participate.

Therefore, the Commission requires State Parties which apportion their delegation to the National Convention to apportion on a basis of representation which fairly reflects the population and Democratic strength within the State. The apportionment is to be based on a formula giving equal weight to total population and to the Democratic vote in the previous presidential election.

The Commission requires State Parties with convention systems to select at least 75% of their delegations to the National Convention at congressional district or smaller unit levels.

In convention or committee systems, the Commission requires State Parties to adopt an apportionment formula for each body actually selecting delegates to State, district and county conventions which is based upon population and/or some measure of Democratic strength. Democratic strength may be measured by the Democratic vote in the preceding presidential, senatorial, congressional or gubernatorial election, and/or by party enrollment figures.

When State law controls, the Commission requires State Parties to make all feasible efforts to repeal, amend or otherwise modify such laws to accomplish the stated purpose.

C–1 Adequate public notice

The Call to the 1968 convention required State Parties to assure voters an opportunity to "participate fully" in party affairs. The Special Equal Rights Committee interpreted this opportunity to include adequate public notice. The Committee listed several elements—including publicizing of the time, places and rules for the conduct of all public meetings of the Democratic Party and holding such meetings in easily accessible places—which comprise adequate public notice. These elements were adopted by the Democratic National Committee in January 1968 as its official policy statement and are binding on the State Parties.

Furthermore, the Commission requires State Parties to circulate a concise and public statement in advance of the election itself of the relationship between the party business being voted upon and the delegate selection process.

In addition to supplying the information indicated above, the Commission believes that adequate public notice includes information on the ballot as to the presidential preference of (1) candidates of slates for delegate or (2) in the States which select or nominate a portion of the delegates by committees, candidates or slates for such committees.

Accordingly, the Commission requires State Parties to give every candidate for delegate (and candidate for committee, where appropriate) the opportunity to state his presidential preferences on the ballot at each stage of the delegate selection process. The Commission requires the State Parties to add the word "uncommitted" or like term on the ballot next to the name of every candidate for delegate who does not wish to express a presidential preference.

When State law controls, the Commission requires the State Parties to make all feasible efforts to repeal, amend or otherwise modify such laws to accomplish the stated purposes.

C–2 Automatic (ex-officio) delegates (see also C–4)

In some States, certain public or Party officeholders are delegates to county, State and National Conventions by virtue of their official position. The Commission believes that State laws, Party rules and Party resolutions which so provide are inconsistent with the Call to the 1972 Convention for three reasons:

1. The Call requires all delegates to be chosen by primary, convention or committee procedures. Achieving delegate status by virtue of public or Party office is not one of the methods sanctioned by the 1968 Convention.

2. The Call requires all delegates to be chosen by a process which begins within the calendar year of the Convention. Ex-officio delegates usually were elected (or appointed) to their positions before the calendar year of the Convention.

3. The Call requires all delegates to be chosen by a process in which all Democrats have a full and meaningful opportunity to participate. Delegate selection by a process in which certain places on the delegation are not open to competition among Democrats is inconsistent with a full and meaningful opportunity to participate.

Accordingly, the Commission requires State Parties to repeal Party rules or resolutions which provide for ex-offico delegates. When State law controls, the Commission requires State Parties to make all feasible efforts to repeal, amend or otherwise modify such laws to accomplish the stated purpose.

C–3 Open and closed processes

The Commission believes that Party membership, and hence opportunity to participate in the delegate selection process, must be open to all persons who wish to be Democrats and who are not already members of another political party; conversely, a full opportunity for all Democrats to participate is diluted if members of other political parties are allowed to participate in the selection of delegates to the Democratic National Convention.

The Commission urges State Parties to provide for party enrollment that (1) allows non-Democrats to become Party members, and (2) provides easy access and frequent opportunity for unaffiliated voters to become Democrats.

C–4 Premature delegate selection (timeliness)

The 1968 Convention adopted language adding to the Call to the 1972 Convention the requirement that the delegate selection process must begin within the calendar year of the Convention. In many States, Governors, State Chairmen, State, district and county committees who are chosen before the calendar year of the Convention, select—or choose agents to select—the delegates. These practices are inconsistent with the Call.

The Commission believes that the 1968 Convention intended to prohibit any untimely procedures which have any direct bearing on the processes by which National Convention delegates are selected. The process by which delegates are nominated is such a procedure. Therefore, the Commission requires State Parties to prohibit any practices by which officials elected or appointed before the calendar year choose nominating committees or propose or endorse a slate of delegates—even when the possibility for a challenge to such slate or committee is provided.

When State law controls, the Commission requires State Parties to make all feasible efforts to repeal, amend, or modify such laws to accomplish the stated purposes.

C–5 Committee selection processes

The 1968 Convention indicated no preference between primary, convention, and committee systems for choosing delegates. The Commission believes, however, that committee systems by virtue of their indirect relationship to the delegate selection process, offer fewer guarantees for a full and meaningful opportunity to participate than other systems.

The Commission is aware that it has no authority to eliminate committee systems in their entirety. However, the Commission can and does require State Parties which elect delegates in this manner to make it clear to voters at the time the Party committee is elected or appointed that one of its functions will be the selection of National Convention delegates.

Believing, however, that such selection system is undesirable even when adequate public notice is given, the Commission requires State Parties to limit the National Convention delegation chosen by committee procedures to not more than 10 percent of the total number of delegates and alternates.

Since even this obligation will not ensure an opportunity for full and meaningful participation, the Commission recommends that State Parties repeal rules or resolutions which require or permit Party committees to select any part of the State's delegation to the National Convention. When State law controls, the Commission recommends that State Parties make all feasible efforts to repeal, amend, or otherwise modify such laws to accomplish the stated purpose.

C–6 Slate-making

In mandating a full and meaningful opportunity to participate in the delegate selection process, the 1968 Convention meant to prohibit any practice in the process of selection which made it difficult for Democrats to participate. Since the process by which individuals are nominated for delegate positions and slates of potential delegates are formed is an integral and crucial part of the process by which delegates are actually selected, the Commission requires State Parties to extend to the nominating process all guarantees of full and meaningful opportunity to participate in the delegate selection process. When State law controls, the Commission requires State Parties to make all feasible efforts to repeal, amend or otherwise modify such laws to accomplish the stated purpose.

Furthermore, whenever slates are presented to caucuses, meetings, conventions, committees, or to voters in a primary, the Commission requires State Parties to adopt procedures which assure that:

1. the bodies making up the slates have been elected, assembled, or appointed for the slate-making task with adequate public notice that they would perform such task;

2. those persons making up each slate have adopted procedures that will facilitate widespread participation in the slate-making process, with the proviso that any slate presented in the name of a presidential candidate in a primary State be assembled with due consultation with the presidential candidate or his representative,

3. adequate procedural safeguards are provided to assure that the right to challenge the presented slate is more than perfunctory and places no undue burden on the challengers.

When State law controls, the Commission requires State Parties to make all feasible efforts to repeal, amend or otherwise modify such laws to accomplish the stated purpose.

CONCLUSION

The Guidelines that we have adopted are designed to open the door to all Democrats who seek a voice in their Party's most important decision: the choice of its presidential nominee. We are concerned with the opportunity to participate, rather than the actual level of participation, although the number of Democrats who vote in their caucuses, meetings and primaries is an important index of the opportunities available to them. As members of the Commission, we are less concerned with the product of the meetings than the process, although we believe that the product will be improved in the give and take of open and fairly conducted meetings.

We believe that popular participation is more than a proud heritage of our party, more even than a first principle. We believe that popular control of the Democratic Party is necessary for its survival.

We do not believe this is an idle threat. When we view our past history and present policies alongside that of the Republican Party, we are struck by one unavoidable fact: our Party is the only major vehicle for peaceful, progressive change in the United States.

If we are not an open party; if we do not represent the demands of change, then the danger is not that people will go to the Republican Party; it is that there will no longer be a way for people committed to orderly change to fulfill their needs and desires within our traditional political system. It is that they will turn to third and fourth party politics or the anti-politics of the street.

We believe that our Guidelines offer an alternative for these people. We believe that the Democratic Party can meet the demands for participation with their adoption. We trust that all Democrats will give the Guidelines their careful consideration.

We are encouraged by the response of state Parties to date. In 40 states and territories the Democratic Party has appointed reform commissions (or subcommittees of the state committee) to investigate ways of modernizing party procedures. Of these, 17 have already issued reports and recommendations. In a number of states, party rules and state laws have already been revised, newly written or amended to insure the opportunity for participation in Party matters by all Democratics.

Rhode Island and Maryland, for example, were states that in 1968 chose their delegates by a State Committee selected in an untimely manner—that is, by a process that began before the calendar year of the convention. In 1969, the legislative bodies of those States passed presidential primary bills at the urging of Democratic members of those legislatures and Democratic Party officials. This year, the Maryland legislature has improved on the bill enacted in 1969.

Legislatures in the states of Illinois and New Mexico have also passed presidential primary laws, the latter being the first state to adopt a primary providing for proportional representation. In Nevada, a bill supported by the Democrats and calling for a presidential preference primary with proportional representation was approved by the legislature, but was vetoed by Republican Governor Paul Laxalt. A presidential primary bill has passed one house of the Delaware legislature.

In March, the Idaho legislature, at the prodding of its Democratic members, passed a law that will allow for complete modernization of the delegate selection process.

In several states there has been substantial reform of party rules governing delegate selection and party structure. In Minnesota, a new party constitution has been adopted that provides for proportional representation and modified "one Democrat—one vote." In Michigan, a meeting of 2,000 Democrats convened in January and adopted the broad recommendations of the Haber Reform Commission. In North Carolina, the State Party has adopted comprehensive reforms of its party structure, including one provision for 18-year-old participation in all party affairs and another for reasonable representation on all party committees and delegations of women, minority racial groups and young people. In Colorado, the State Committee has adopted a proposal that will ensure proportional representation for all presidential candidates at the next convention. In Oklahoma, rules have been proposed which will assure that not more than 60 percent of the membership of any committee or convention will be of the same sex, and will eliminate the role of untimely committees in the delegate selection process. In Missouri, statewide public hearings have been held to discuss proposals for party rules.

In other states, the Democratic Party has adopted significant changes in the structure and selection of their state and constituent committees. In January, Alabama reapportioned its State Committee on a one-man, one-vote basis with members now elected from districts rather than at large. The Florida Democratic Advisory Committee has provided for ex-officio representation of minority groups and youth on the State Committee.

In Washington and Virginia, the State Committee has adopted party rules that require 18-year-old participation in all party affairs. In an additional 30 states, at the urging of Democratic leaders, the 18-year-old vote is before the legislature or will be on the ballot in November.

In Mississippi, South Dakota and the Canal Zone the first set of comprehensive party rules has been adopted. The Missouri State Central Committee, upon completing its extensive statewide hearings, will adopt its first party constitution.

All of these efforts lead us to the conclusion that the Democratic Party is bent on meaningful change. A great European stateman once said, "All things are possible, even the fact that an action in accord with honor and honesty ultimately appears to be a prudent political investment." We share this sentiment. We are confident that party reform, dictated by our Party's heritage and principles, will insure a strong, winning and united Party.

O'HARA COMMISSION REPORT ON RULES
October 1971

Final Recommendations, Standing Committees of the Convention

I. Election of Convention Committees and Chairmen

Platform, Credentials, Rules Committee

1. The members of the Platform, Credentials, and Rules Committees shall be elected by the state's national convention delegates present at a meeting of which adequate notice of time and place shall be given and at which a majority of the state's delegates shall be present.

2. If, at the time any convention committee meets, any state's delegates to the Democratic National Convention have not yet been elected, such state's temporary representatives on such committee shall be elected by a procedure which takes place during the calendar year of the Convention at an open, well-publicized meeting of a democratically-elected party committee. It is also provided that members selected in this manner are temporary, and permanent members of the committees be elected as soon as possible after the regular delegate selection process has been completed.

3. The Chairman of the Platform Committee shall be elected by the Platform Committee at its first meeting. The Chairman of the Rules Committee shall be elected by the Rules Committee at its first meeting. The Chairman of the Credentials Committee shall be elected by the Credentials Committee at its first meeting. These meetings will be called by the Chairman of the Democratic National Committee who will request nominations for Chairman from the membership of these Committees. An Acting Chairman of the Credentials Committee shall be elected whenever the Chairman of the Democratic National Committee shall deem such election advisable, on the majority vote of those members of the Democratic National Committee present and voting at a meeting of the Democratic National Committee.

4. States that elect a single committee member to each of the standing committees should divide their representatives to the committees as equally as possible between men and women. States that elect two or more representatives to the committees should elect an equal or nearly equal number of men and women to each committee, giving due regard to the race and age of the men and women elected.

Congressional Record, 92d Cong., 1st sess. (daily ed. October 20, 1971), vol. 117, E11182-87.

Arrangements Committee

1. The members of the Arrangements Committee shall be elected by the majority vote of those members present and voting at a meeting of the Democratic National Commiteee held at such time as the Chairman of the Democratic National Committee deems advisable but only after notice to the members of the Democratic National Committee that such election will be conducted at such meeting. The election of the members of the Arrangements Committee shall be held no later than the first meeting of the Democratic National Committee in the year in which an election is held for the office of President of the United States. The Chairman of the Democratic National Committee, after appropriate consultation shall make nominations for the membership of the Arrangements Committee and shall report his reasons therefor. Nominations may be also made by any other Democratic National Committeeman. Each Presidential Candidate shall, upon qualifying as a Presidential Candidate, be entitled to appoint one non-voting member to the Arrangements Committee.

2. The members of the Arrangements Committee and its Chairman need not be delegates to the Democratic National Convention.

3. The Chairman of the Arrangements Committee shall be elected from its elected membership at the Arrangements Committee's first meeting.

II. Arrangements Committee

Authority

The Arrangements Committee shall be responsible for and have authority over all of the Convention's business and operations, including pre-Convention activities, except as specifically otherwise delegated in these rules, including, but not limited to—

1. housing.
2. communications, radio, television, and press.
3. seating of delegates in the Convention.
4. security.
5. transportation.
6. finances.

Number of Members

The Arrangements Committee shall consist of between five and fifteen members.

III. Platform Committee

Authority

The Platform Committee shall be responsible for drafting and presenting to the Democratic National Convention the Platform of the Democratic Party.

Number of Members

The Platform Committee shall be composed of 150 members allocated to the states in accordance with the state's delegation size, with the provision that each state shall have at least one member.

Regional Hearings

The Chairman of the Platform Committee shall determine the number (which shall in no case be less than eight), place and time for conducting Regional Hearings and shall name the presiding panel for each Regional Hearing. The Chairman of the Platform Committee shall, to the maximum extent possible, arrange, in consultation with members of the Platform Committee, for these hearings and for a representative group of witnesses to testify at the Regional Hearings.

Written Submissions

Any person may submit a written statement concerning the Platform to the Platform Committee at any time and may request permission to testify at any hearing.

Drafting

Prior to the first meeting of the Platform Committee, the Chairman of the Democratic National Committee shall arrange to distribute to the members of said Committee a document outlining the issues and alternative positions to be considered by the Platform Committee. The Platform Committee shall, at its first meeting, elect 15 persons to serve on a Drafting sub-Committee and shall also elect the Chairman of the Drafting sub-Committee. The Chairman of the Platform Committee shall, after appropriate consultation, make nominations for membership on the Drafting sub-Committee and shall nominate one of such persons as the Chairman thereof. In addition, one non-voting representative of each Presidential Candidate, appointed by each Presidential Candidate, may serve on the Drafting sub-Committee. The Drafting sub-Committee shall be responsible for the Drafting of the Platform's provisions under the direction and with the approval of the full Platform Committee.

Participation of Presidential Candidates

Each Presidential Candidate shall be invited to submit to the Platform Committee a written statement of recommendations at any time.

Committee Report

The Report of the Platform Committee and any Minority Report shall be prepared for public distribution and shall be mailed to all of the delegates no later than ten days prior to the commencement of the National Convention.

Minority Report

Upon the request of 10 per cent of the members of the Platform Committee present and voting at a meeting, a Minority Report shall be prepared for distribution to the Convention delegates as part of the Committee's report. The Committee staff shall assist in the preparation of such report.

Open Meetings

All meetings of the Platform Committee shall be open to the public.

IV. Credentials Committee

Authority

The Credentials Committee shall determine and resolve all questions concerning the seating of delegates at the Democratic National Convention, subject to the full Convention.

Number of Members

The Credentials Committee shall be composed of 150 members allocated to the states in accordance with the state's delegation size, with the provision that each state shall have at least one member.

Notice of Intent to Challenge

1. Written Notice of Intent to Challenge shall be filed with the Chairman of the Credentials Committee, the State's Democratic Chairman, and the challenged delegate or delegates within 10 calendar days after the completion of the delegate selection process in the state.
2. The Notice of Intent to Challenge may be filed only by a resident of the state in which the challenged delegate resides.
3. As soon thereafter as possible, but in no event more than 5 calendar days after the filing of the Notice provided in C(1), the challenger shall file with the Credentials Committee the following:
   (a) A description of the delegates or portion of the delegates challenged, including their names and addresses if known to him.
   (b) A short and concise statement of the alleged violations by the challenged delegates of provisions included in but not limited to the Call of the Convention, National Party standards and guidelines or state laws or party rules.
   (c) If the challenger proposes that he be seated in the state's delegation, a short and concise statement of the relief requested.

(d) A Request for Findings of Fact in the form of distinct numbered propositions of the facts; each separate proposition shall be separately numbered.

(e) A list of witnesses and each witness' address and telephone number if any are known at the time of filing.

(f) A list of documents which the challenger proposes to have considered by the Committee if any are available at the time of filing.

(g) A statement indicating whether a hearing is desired and the place which the challenger believes would be most convenient to the parties and witnesses to have the hearing held.

(h) The name, address, and telephone number of the challenger's attorney of record or other representative, if any.

4. The challenger shall have reserved to him the right to amend any of the matters required in this paragraph 3 prior to the hearing with due notice to the Committee.

Answer

1. Within 10 calendar days of receipt of written Notice of Intent to Challenge, each challenged delegate shall file with the Committee the name, address, and telephone number of his attorney of record or other representative, if any.

2. Within 10 calendar days of receipt by the State Democratic Chairman of Notice of Intent to Challenge, the State Chairman shall file with the Committee 5 complete sets of his state's relevant laws, regulations, and rules and his state's party rules relating to selection of delegates to the Democratic National Convention.

3. Not later than 10 days after receipt of the challenger's Request for Findings of Fact, the challenged delegate or group of delegates shall file with the Committee:

(a) A specific answer, by paragraph, to the facts alleged by the challenger. A separate response must be made to each fact alleged. Such answer shall state agreement with or denial of each fact alleged. Where a fact is denied, the challenged delegate must submit in his answer the facts the challenged delegate believes to be true which should substantiate the denial. Failure to so respond in good faith shall automatically deem the challenger's alleged facts to be admitted as true.

(b) The challenged delegate may submit additional facts or a counterstatement of facts provided it conforms with the form set forth in 3(d) above.

(c) A list of witnesses and each witness' address and telephone number if any are known at the time of filing.

(d) A list of documents the challenged delegate proposes to have considered by the Committee if any are available at the time of filing.

(e) A statement indicating whether the challenged delegate desires a hearing and a designation of the place which the challenged delegate believes would be most convenient to the parties and witnesses to have the hearing held.

(f) A short and concise statement of why the challenge should be dismissed and of why the challenged delegate should be seated.

(g) The name, address, and telephone number of the attorney of record or other representative if any.

4. The challenged delegate or delegates shall have reserved to him the right to amend any of the matters required in this paragraph 3 prior to the hearing with due notice to the Committee.

Hearing Officer

1. After the challenged delegate has filed his Answer to the challenger's Request for Findings of Fact, the Chairman of the Credentials Committee shall appoint a Hearing Officer, who shall be responsible for finding the facts.

2. The Hearing Officer shall be a person who is known by reputation to be fair and impartial in the context of the challenge and is experienced in the law, particularly in fact finding and procedural due process.

3. The Chairman of the Credentials Committee shall make a reasonable effort to secure the agreement of the parties to the Hearing Officer appointed by him for the challenge.

Hearings

1. If any party so requests, an open and public hearing shall be held within the state at such times and places as shall be determined by the Hearing Officer. The Hearing Officer may select one or more assistant Hearing Officers to assist in conducting the hearing.

2. The Hearing Officer shall inform the parties or their attorneys of record, if any, of the time and place where the hearing will be held.

3. The Hearing Officer shall hear the evidence, conduct the hearing, dispose of procedural requests and similar matters, and, to the extent possible, obtain stipulations of the parties as to the facts of the challenge.

4. Evidence

(a) If a hearing is held, each challenger and challenged delegate shall have the right to present his case or defense by oral and documentary evidence, to submit rebuttal evidence, and to conduct such cross-examination as, in the discretion of the Hearing Officer, may be required.

(b) The Hearing Officer may require one or more challenges or challenged delegates to consolidate or separate their challenge or defense for purpose of the hearing.

Findings of Fact

1. The Hearing Officer shall make written Findings of Fact which shall be submitted to the parties or to their attorneys of record or other representative and to the Credentials Committee in sufficient time so that respective cases may be prepared for argument before the Credentials Committee.

2. Any challenger or challenged delegate or group of delegates may submit to the Credentials Committee written Exceptions to the Findings of Fact and to the rulings on procedural matters which are alleged to have prejudicial effect.

3. The Findings of Fact shall not include recommendations concerning the seating of delegates. This determination shall be made only by the full Committee.

4. All hearings and meetings shall be open to the public.

Record

The official papers and pleadings shall be maintained in the offices of the Democratic National Committee in Washington, D.C., and shall be open and available for public inspection at reasonable times and for duplicating at actual cost to the Democratic National Committee.

Consideration by the Full Committee

1. The Credentials Committee shall begin meeting not later than two weeks before the commencement of the Democratic National Convention to consider the challenges to the seating of the delegates.

2. All meetings of the Credentials Committee shall be open to the public.

3. Request for Consideration.

Within 5 days after receipt of the Hearing Officer's Findings of Fact, the challenger or challenged delegate may file written Notice of Request for Consideration by the Full Committee with the Chairman. Each Notice must contain a short and concise statement of the grounds upon which the Request for Consideration is based.

4. Briefs.

(a) Any party may file a brief to the Credentials Committee prior to 20 calendar days before the commencement of the Democratic National Convention.

(b) Any party filing a brief shall file as many copies as there are members of the Committee plus 10 copies for the Chairman and his staff.

5. Argument.

(a) Each party shall be entitled to oral argument before the full Committee, but not exceeding 30 minutes.

(b) The Chairman of the Credentials Committee shall notify the parties of the time for oral argument.

(c) The Chairman of the Credentials Committee may require one or more challenger or challenged delegates to consolidate or separate their challenge or defense for purpose of oral argument.

6. Decisions.

(a) The Chairman shall convene the whole Committee at convenient times to decide challenges.

(b) Committee members and a representative of the challengers from the state in which a challenge is made may participate but may not vote on their state's challenge.

Committee Report

The Report of the Credentials Committee shall be prepared for public distribution and made conveniently available to all of the delegates no later than 48 hours prior to the commencement of the National Convention.

Minority Report

Upon the request of 10 per cent of the members of the Credentials Committee present and voting at a meeting, a Minority Report shall be prepared for distribution to the Convention delegates as part of the Committee's Report. The Committee staff shall assist in the preparation of such report.

General

1. All papers filed by a party with the Committee shall contain a certificate of service of such papers upon all other parties to the challenge.

2. These Rules shall be interpreted so as to provide justice and fairness to the parties. The Chairman or the Committee may waive any provision of the Rules when such waiver is required so as to provide justice and fairness or to prevent undue economic hardship to any party.

3. In the event that any of the state's delegates are selected less than 70 days prior to the convening of the Democratic National Convention, the Chairman of the Credentials Committee may provide such special procedural rules, for such state, in respect of written submissions by the parties, hearings, and consideration by the full Credentials Committee, so as to achieve the resolution of any Credentials challenge for such state at the meeting of the full Credentials Committee held during the second week preceding the commencement of the Democratic National Convention.

4. Section IV of these Rules pertaining to Credentials challenges shall be distributed and made available to the people of the states.

V. Rules Committee

Authority

The Rules Committee shall have the authority for recommending the Rules of the Convention, the Convention's agenda, and resolutions providing for the consideration of any other matter not provided for in the Rules of the Convention and not contained in the report of other Committees.

Number of Members

The Rules Committee shall be composed of 150 members allocated to the states in accordance with the state's delegation size, with the provision that each state shall have at least one member.

Committee Meetings

Meetings shall be convened in advance of the Convention at such time and places as the Chairman shall determine.

Committee Report

The Report of the Rules Committee and any Minority Report shall be prepared for public distribution and shall be mailed to all of the delegates no later than ten days prior to the commencement of the National Convention.

Minority Report

Upon the request of 10 per cent of the members of the Rules Committee present and voting at a meeting, a Minority Report shall be prepared for distribution to the Convention delegates as part of the Committee's report. The Committee staff shall assist in the preparation of such report.

Open Meetings

All meetings of the Rules Committee shall be open to the public.

Presentation by Rules Commission

The Chairman of the Committee on Rules shall arrange for the presentation of the recommendations of this Commission by its Chairman or his designees to the Rules Committee at the first meeting thereof or as soon thereafter as shall be appropriate.

VI. Certification of Delegates and Committee Members

Each state's Democratic Chairman shall certify in writing to the Chairman of the Democratic National Committee the election of his state's delegates to the National Convention within 3 days after the completion of the delegate selection process in the state and shall certify the election of Committee members within 3 days after their election, giving the full name and address of each of such persons. . . .

PART II: LOGISTICAL ARRANGEMENTS. . .

PART III: DELEGATE ALLOCATION FORMULA. . .

PART IV: PROCEDURAL RULES

Final Recommendations, Procedural Rules of the Convention

I. Temporary Chairman

The Chairman of the Democratic National Committee shall call the Convention to order and shall preside until a Chairman of the Convention shall be chosen in accord with these rules.

He shall appoint a temporary secretary and such other temporary officers as may be required to assist him in the conduct of the business of the Convention. These temporary officers shall be composed equally of men and women.

II. Temporary Roll

The Democratic National Committee shall determine a temporary roll of delegates to the Convention which shall consist of those persons whose names have been certified as delegates unless a credentials contest shall have arisen with respect to any such person, in which case the Democratic National Committee shall include on the temporary roll the name of the credentials contestant recommended for inclusion by the Committee on Credentials in its report.

Persons whose names are included on the temporary roll shall be permitted to vote on all matters before the Convention until after adoption of the report of the Committee on Credentials provided that no person shall be permitted to vote on his own credentials contest.

III. Order of Business

The order of business for the Democratic National Convention shall be as provided in these Rules and in any special order of business adopted under Article IV. The Chairman of the Convention may, at appropriate times, interrupt the order of business provided for in these Rules for introductions, announcements, addresses, presentations, resolutions of tribute and appreciation or remarks appropriate to the business of the Convention.

Report of Committee on Credentials

The report of the Committee on Credentials shall be acted upon before the consideration of other business.

1. The Chair shall recognize the Chairman of the Committee on Credentials for thirty minutes to present the Committee's Report unless a longer period of time shall

be provided in a special order of business agreed to by the Convention. The Chairman of the Committee may present committee amendments, may yield part of his time to others and may yield for the presentation and disposition of minority reports without losing his right to the floor.

2. The Chair shall arrange for the orderly presentation of amendments offered at the direction of the committee and of minority reports. Twenty minutes shall be allowed for the presentation of each committee amendment or minority report unless a longer period for any committee amendment or minority report is provided in special orders of business agreed to by the Convention. Time shall be equally allotted to proponents and opponents of each committee amendment or minority report. The question shall be put on each committee amendment or minority report immediately following its presentation without intervening motion.

3. Upon conclusion of the consideration and disposition of committee amendments and minority reports, the Chair shall put the question on the adoption of the report of the Committee on Credentials with amendments previously adopted, if any, presentation without intervening motion.

4. In the event that the Committee's Report shall not be agreed to when voted upon, the Committee shall immediately reconvene to reconsider its Report and shall present a new Report to the Convention as soon as possible. The Convention shall be in temporary recess until the Committee shall have adopted a new Report.

Convention Chairman

The Convention shall then proceed to elect the Convention Chairman in the following manner:

1. The Chairman of the Committee on Rules shall be recognized to offer a nomination for Convention Chairman as recommended by the Committee on Rules. Nominations from the floor shall then be received.

2. When there are no further nominations or upon adoption of a motion to close nominations, the Chair shall, after giving any nominee the opportunity to decline nomination, conduct a vote for Convention Chairman.

3. A majority vote of the delegates present and voting shall be required to elect the Convention Chairman. Balloting shall continue until a Chairman is elected.

Convention Vice Chairman

The Convention shall then proceed to elect the Convention Vice Chairman in the same manner in which it elected the Chairman except that nominations shall not be accepted for persons of the same sex as the Chairman. The Vice Chairman shall perform all of the duties of the Chairman in the Chairman's absence.

Report of Committee on Rules and Order of Business

The Chair shall then recognize the Chairman of the Committee on Rules and Order of Business to present the Committee's Report for the Rules of the Convention and minority reports, if any, in the same manner as that provided for the presentation of the Report of the Committee on Credentials.

Committee on Resolutions and Platform

The Chairman shall then recognize the Chairman of the Committee on Resolutions and Platform to present the Committee's Report and minority reports, if any, in the same manner as that provided for the presentations of the reports of the Committees on Credentials and Rules.

Nomination of the Democratic Candidate for President

The Chair shall then receive nominations from the floor for the office of President of the United States in the following manner:

1. Requests to nominate a Presidential Candidate shall be in writing and shall have affixed thereto the written approval of the nominee and the name of the delegate who shall be recognized to nominate the Presidential Candidate and shall be delivered to the Convention Chairman not later than 6:00 P.M. of the day preceding the day designated in the official Convention Program for the commencement of Presidential nominations.

2. Each such request must be accompanied by a petition indicating support for the proposed nominee signed by delegates representing not less than 50 nor more than 200 delegate votes, not more than 20 of which may come from one delegation. No delegate may sign more than one nominating petition.

3. The order for nominating Presidential Candidates shall be determined by the Committee on Rules by lot at a drawing, that shall be open to the public, on the morning of the day designated in the official Convention Program for the commencement of Presidential nominations.

4. Each Presidential Candidate shall be allowed a total of 15 minutes time for the presentation of his name in nomination by a nominating speech and not more than two seconding speeches; the time to run without interruption from the recognition of the nominator.

5. Delegates and alternates shall maintain order during and following nominations for the office of President, and demonstrations on behalf of Candidates shall not be permitted.

Roll Call Ballot for Presidential Candidate

After nominations for Presidential Candidates have closed, the Convention shall immediately proceed to a roll call vote by States on the selection of the Presidential Candidate. A majority vote of the Convention's certified delegates shall be required to nominate the Presidential Candidate. Delegates may vote for the candidate of their choice whether or not the name of such candidate was placed in nomination. Balloting will continue until a nominee is selected.

Acceptance Speech by Presidential Candidate

Immediately after the selection of the Democratic nominee for President, the Chairman shall appoint a committee to advise the nominee of his selection, to determine if he will accept the nomination and to invite the nominee to deliver an acceptance speech to the Convention.

Nomination for the Democratic Candidate for Vice President

The selection of a nominee for Vice President of the United States shall be conducted in the same manner as that heretofore provided for the selection of the nominee for President of the United States except that:

1. There shall be at least a 12 hour interval between the nomination of the President and the opening of the nominations for the Vice President.

2. A request to nominate must be filed not later than 3 hours before the scheduled opening of the nominations for the Vice President.

Roll Call Ballot for Vice Presidential Candidate

After nominations for Vice Presidential candidates have closed, the Convention shall immediately proceed to a roll call vote by states on the selection of the Vice Presidential Candidate. A majority vote of the Convention's certified delegates shall be required to select the Vice Presidential Candidate. Delegates may vote for the candidate of their choice whether or not the name of such candidate was placed in nomination.

Acceptance Speech by Vice Presidential Candidate

Immediately after the selection of the Democratic nominee for Vice President, the Chairman shall appoint a committee to advise the nominee of his selection, to determine if he will accept the nomination and to invite the nominee to deliver an acceptance speech to the Convention.

IV. Special Orders of Business

It shall be in order at any time for the Committee on Rules and Order of Business to report to the Convention a resolution providing a special order of business for debate of any resolution, motion, committee report or minority report or amendment to a committee report or for the consideration of any matter for which provision is not made under these rules.

V. Powers and Duties of Chairman

It shall be the responsibility of the Chairman to conduct and expedite the business of the Convention and to preserve order and decorum in its proceedings.

The Chairman is authorized to:

1. Appoint a secretary and such other officers as may be required to assist him in the conduct of the business of the Convention, to be composed equally of men and women.

2. Appoint any delegate temporarily to perform the duties of the Chair in the absence of the Vice Chairman.

3. Take such lawful action as may be necessary and appropriate to preserve order throughout the Convention hall.

VI. Voting

Secret Ballot

No secret ballots shall be permitted at any stage of the Convention or its committee proceedings.

Proxy Voting

Neither delegate nor alternate delegate votes may be cast by proxy.

Roll Call Votes

1. Voting shall be by voice vote or, when prescribed by these rules, by roll call vote. A roll call vote may also be had if the Chair is in doubt or upon the demand of any delegate supported by 20 percent of the delegate body as evidenced by (a) a petition submitted to the Chair indicating support of the demand by delegations which comprise not less than 20 percent of the authorized delegate body or, (b) by the rising in support of the demand of not less than 20 percent of the delegates present. In the case of a petition in support of a demand for a roll call vote, a delegation shall be taken to support the demand if a majority of its delegates vote to do so.

2. When a roll call vote is ordered the roll shall be called by states in the sequence determined by the results of the drawing for seating preference and the Chairman of each delegation or his designee shall report the vote of his delegation and shall send to the rostrum a tally showing the vote of each member of his delegation indicating whether such vote was cast in person or by an alternate. It shall be the duty of the Chair to arrange to have copies of roll call tally sheets received by him promptly made available to the news media.

3. On a roll call by States, the vote of a delegation as announced, may be challenged by any member of the delegation before the next State is called and the votes of that delegation shall then be recorded as polled without regard to any state law, Party rule, resolution or instruction binding the delegation or any member thereof to vote as a unit with others or to cast his vote for or against any candidate or proposition. The Convention Chairman may send a representative to the delegation to

conduct the poll. At the discretion of the Convention Chairman, the roll call may continue instead of awaiting the result of the polling.

4. A demand to poll a delegation may be withdrawn at any time before the actual polling has begun.

Interruption of Vote

When the question has been put, the vote thereon may not be interrupted for any purpose other than a demand for a roll call vote or a point of order directed to the conduct of the vote.

Determination of Question

Except as otherwise provided in these rules, all questions, including the question of nominations of candidates for President and Vice President of the United States, shall be determined by a majority vote of the delegates to the Convention.

VII. Death, Resignation or Disability of a Democratic Nominee

In the event of the death, resignation or disability of a nominee of the Party for President or Vice President, the Democratic National Committee is authorized to fill the vacancy or vacancies by a majority of the total number of votes provided at the Convention. The full vote of each delegation is to be cast by its duly qualified member or members of the Committee with each member casting a proportionate share of his delegations votes.

VIII. Interpretation of Rules

In interpreting these rules the Chair may have recourse to the rulings of Chairmen of previous Democratic National Conventions, to the precedents of the United States House of Representatives and to general parliamentary law.

IX. Appeals

The Chair shall decide all questions of order subject to an appeal by any delegate which may be debated for not more than ten minutes, the time to be equally divided between the delegate appealing the ruling and a delegate in favor of sustaining the ruling of the Chair; provided that an appeal shall not be in order while another appeal is pending or from decisions on recognition, or from decisions on dilatoriness of motions, or during a roll call vote or on a question on which an appeal has just been decided or when in the opinion of the Chair, such appeal is clearly dilatory.

Before the question is put on any appeal, the Chair shall be entitled to briefly state the reasons for the ruling being appealed.

X. Motion To Suspend The Rules

The Chair shall entertain a motion to suspend the rules which shall be decided without debate and which shall require a vote of 2/3 of the delegates voting, a quorum being present.

XI. Motions

No question of privilege nor any motion other than those provided under these rules shall be entertained except the motion to recess (to a time certain or at the call of the Chair) which shall be privileged, and the motion to adjourn which shall be of the highest privilege.

Motions to adjourn or to recess shall be in order at any time except when the question has been put or a vote is in progress and shall be decided without debate. The Chair shall not entertain motions to adjourn or recess when such motion closely follows another such motion if in the opinion of the Chairman such motion is dilatory.

XII. Amendments

No amendments to resolutions or motions before the Convention shall be permitted except amendments to Committee Reports offered at the direction of the Committee or in a minority report of the Committee and amendments to resolutions reported from a Committee offered at the direction of the Committee or with the written support of 10 percent of the membership of the Committee, provided, that no motion or proposition on a subject different from that under consideration shall be admitted under color of amendment.

XIII. Minority Reports

Minority reports of committees shall not be considered as such unless adopted by at least 10 percent of the members of a committee present and voting at a committee meeting.

XIV. Responsibility

By participation in the Democratic National Convention each delegate assumes the responsibility for doing all within his power to assure that voters of his state will have the opportunity to cast their election ballots for the Presidential and Vice Presidential nominees selected by the Convention and expressly agrees that he will not publicly support or campaign for any candidate for President or Vice President other than the nominees of the Convention.

XV. Debate

Unless otherwise provided in these Rules or in a resolution providing for a special order of business, debate on any question shall be limited to a total of 20 minutes and shall be equally divided between proponents and opponents unless they and the Chairman agree on an additional or lesser amount of time.

XVI. Division of A Question

When a question contains two or more separate propositions so distinct in substance that one being taken away a substantive proposition shall remain, it shall, on the demand of any delegate, before the question is put, be divided for voting.

XVII. Quorum

A majority of the delegates to the Convention shall constitute a quorum thereof for the purpose of transacting business. Upon a point of order of no quorum being made, the Chairman shall ascertain the presence or absence of a quorum by visual estimation and shall not proceed until a quorum is present provided that a motion to adjourn may be offered and voted upon without a quorum present.

XVIII. Journal of Proceedings

A record of all actions taken each day by the Convention shall be printed and made available to all delegates and alternates the morning of the following day.

In addition, a journal of the full proceedings of the Convention shall be printed within the year following the Convention.

Bibliographical Note

There is no general history of the Democratic party in the last decade, but the topic has drawn the attention of many journalists, scholars and participants in the events. Theodore White's three volumes, *The Making of the President, 1960, The Making of the President, 1964* and *The Making of the President, 1968* (New York, 1961, 1965, 1969) cover the campaigns of those years and each book includes a good deal on internal party matters. Theodore Sorensen's *Kennedy* (New York, 1965) and Arthur M. Schlesinger's *A Thousand Days* (Boston, 1965) deal with the administration of John F. Kennedy. Hugh Sidey's *Very Personal Presidency: Lyndon Johnson in the White House* (New York, 1968) covers 1963-1968. Since the Democratic party has been the majority party, a great many political analysts have commented on its composition and prospects. Among the most useful are Samuel Lubell's *The Hidden Crisis in American Politics* (New York, 1970) and Richard M. Scammon and Ben J. Wattenburg, *The Real Majority: An Extraordinary Examination of the American Electorate* (New York, 1971). *The Emerging Republican Majority* (New York, 1969) by Kevin Phillips necessarily analyzes the Democratic party, as does Mark R. Levy and Michael S. Kramer in *The Ethnic Factor* (New York, 1972). Indispensable to an understanding of the theme of this essay are the proceedings of the O'Hara and McGovern Commissions whose recommendations can be found in *Mandate for Reform* and *Call to Order* (both available from the Democratic National Committee).

The Republican Party
1952-1972

LEE W. HUEBNER serves as a Special Assistant to President Nixon and is associate director of the White House writing staff. He is a founding member and former president of the Ripon Society, a Republican research and policy organization.

The Republican Party 1952-1972

by *Lee W. Huebner*

The Republican party faced two great and interrelated challenges as it returned to power in 1953 for the first time in twenty years. The first concerned its relationship
to the American electorate: how effectively could the mandate of a single November be
transformed into a stable new pattern of public support? The second concerned the
party's internal relations: how effectively could the divisions which plagued the party
during its years of impotence and exile be reduced and relieved amid the new responsibilities of governing?

Both these challenges—the quest for majority and the quest for unity—were met
uncertainly in the 1950's, an uncertainty which was symbolized in the still unknown results of the 1960 election. The apparent opportunities of the 1950's were squandered in
part because of President Eisenhower's seeming indifference to party politics; in part perhaps because the party was not ready to follow his highly distinctive lead.

Once out of power, the Republicans were unable to hold even the limited gains of
the Eisenhower era. Both public support and party harmony went into deep decline. The
old GOP split between East and West reopened sharply, though the issues and the battle
lines were changed.

The years of Kennedy and Johnson rang for the Republicans with echoes of the
Roosevelt-Truman period. To be sure, the exile of the 1960's began much less
decisively than that of the 1930's and 1940's, and it ended much sooner. But even its
ending recapitulated the circumstances of 1952, as an incumbent Democratic president

was hounded out of office, largely by members of his own party, amid fearful domestic upheaval and an unpopular Asian war.

As the Republicans came back to Washington in 1969, they found waiting for them the same two political questions which they had left unresolved during the 1950's. Appropriately, the leader who would have the greatest opportunity to shape their answers was the same man, Richard Nixon, to whom these questions had often been delegated during the previous decade.

The first professional Republican to be elected to the presidency in over four decades, Nixon's institutional concern for the GOP had been a hallmark of his career. But while his personal influence over Republican affairs was now much greater than it had been as a relatively junior member of the Eisenhower administration, the party's room for maneuver was considerably reduced. Nixon's margin of victory in 1968 was nearly as slim as his margin of defeat eight years before. He was the first new president since Zachary Taylor to face both Houses of Congress under opposition control. The increasing complexity of domestic and foreign challenges—particularly with respect to the economy and Vietnam—also limited the new president's political opportunities. And so, of course, did the continuing appeal of George Wallace.

Eager as most Republicans—including the president—were to build a unified majority party, 1968 did not present them with the same advantages they gained in 1952. Whether inclination and opportunity would finally converge for the Republicans during a second Nixon administration was still a highly uncertain matter as the party looked beyond the 1972 elections.

Perhaps the greatest obstacle to a new Republican hegemony in the 1970's was a development which emerged in the Eisenhower years—the growing reluctance of American voters to make lasting commitments to any party. The indifferent Republican performance of the 1950's may well have resulted from President Eisenhower's de-emphasis on politics. That de-emphasis, on the other hand, may in fact have been the best of political strategies in a new age of declining partisanship. Similarly, the recovery of Republican prospects in the late 1960's and early 1970's may have represented a much deserved reward for the party's new sense of discipline and determination. But it also seemed to reflect the highly momentary reactions to particular Republicans and Democrats of an increasingly agnostic electorate.

Would the breakdown of party allegiance be a relatively permanent condition in the 1970's, or did it represent instead only a prolonged transition on the road to party realignment? The answer to that question would not be entirely clear until long after the 1972 campaign. Only when that answer became more evident would history prove whether Dwight D. Eisenhower was merely an early and uncertain prophet of an emerging Republican majority or rather the confident messiah of a new era of non-partisan politics.

II

The search for a new Republican majority to displace the New Deal Democratic coalition was guided in large measure during the 1950's and 1960's by the nature of

Eisenhower's victory in 1952. Essentially that victory and the strategies which grew out of it were centered on the traditional base of Republican voters, augmented by three new sources of electoral strength:

1) A rapidly expanding vote in normally Republican suburbs, a gain which was forecast by Thomas Dewey's suburban successes in 1948. If Eisenhower was the white collar Roosevelt, then Dewey was Eisenhower's Al Smith. Dewey won fifty-six percent of the vote in suburbs surrounding the country's twelve largest non-southern cities in 1948; Eisenhower raised this to sixty-one percent in 1952 and sixty-three percent in 1956, a larger slice of a pie which itself was growing larger. Adlai Stevenson's old pro from Illinois, Colonel Jacob Arvey, looked at the returns and summed up the election in four words: "the suburbs are murder."

2) Growing Republican appeal among blue-collar workers in the industrialized cities of the North. Eisenhower won forty-five percent of manual workers in 1952 and fifty percent four years later. His inroads were especially significant—as the seasoned Democratic observer Jim Farley was quick to note—among Roman Catholics, the heart of New Deal strength. Dewey won about one-third of the Catholic vote in 1948; Eisenhower received better than two-fifths in the 1952 election. Anti-Communism—dramatized by an Irish-Catholic senator from Wisconsin—may have played some role in this development, though Eisenhower's share of the Catholic vote rose to nearly fifty percent in 1956, when the Communist issue was no longer prominent. Stevenson's divorce may also have been a factor.

3) Significant GOP inroads into the "solid" Democratic South. To the small pockets of traditional GOP southern strength, Eisenhower added new Republican votes among the younger city dwellers of the "new South"—many of them transplanted from northern states. He also picked up some support among Dixiecrats who voted for Strom Thurmond in 1948. Though Dewey polled well under one-third of the southern vote both in 1944 and 1948, Eisenhower won more than forty-eight percent and fifty-seven southern electoral votes, the best GOP showing since 1928. In 1956, Eisenhower added a fifth southern state, Louisiana, to the four he carried in 1952. His vote fell off a bit in the Deep South following the Supreme Court's school desegregation decision of 1954, but he more than compensated with gains in outer, peripheral southern states.

In all three of these constituencies, the unique Eisenhower personality was a significant component in the Republican breakthrough. Eisenhower placed first in a poll to determine the most admired American in March, 1952, and forty-one percent of the Democrats indicated that June that they wanted him to run on their ticket if the GOP turned him down. In addition, there undoubtedly were many Democrats who voted for Eisenhower in 1952 as an expression of their special frustration with

Communism, corruption and Korea, but who intended to return to their old voting habits when those issues were removed.

Yet there was reason to believe after the 1952 elections that many Democratic Eisenhower voters would become regular Republican voters in time. Most important was the apparent blunting of the economic issue on which the New Deal coalition had been forged. For one thing, Eisenhower was unsullied by the taint of Hooverism which had damaged both Dewey and Taft. Even more significant was the nation's growing prosperity, a phenomenon most evident in the postwar spreading of suburbia, but a force which was also felt in the urban centers of the nation—both North and South.

Shortly after the 1952 election, a Truman aide poked his head in the door of the president's White House office and exclaimed: "You did it. It's all your fault." As Truman looked up in amazement his assistant went on: "You just made it too good for the people. They could afford to vote Republican."

The point was an appropriate one. For twenty years, Democrats had told the voters that if they wanted to live like Republicans they should vote like Democrats. Wartime and postwar prosperity apparently had vindicated that claim. The only problem for the Democrats was that once voters could afford to live like Republicans they could also afford to vote like Republicans—and with increasing frequency they did.

Or at least they did at the presidential level. Farther down the ballot, however, the drift to the GOP was far less impressive. While Eisenhower gained 55.1 percent of the vote in 1952, Republican congressional candidates polled only 49.8 percent. A net gain of twenty-two House seats and one Senate seat allowed the Republicans to take control of the Congress—but only by the narrowest of margins.

In 1953, the loss of a Republican governor and senator in New Jersey, along with GOP defeats in municipal and special congressional elections, led National Chairman Leonard Hall to conclude that his party was "in trouble." His assessment was confirmed in 1954 when the Democrats won back nineteen House seats, one Senate seat and nine governorships, and cut the Republican percentage of state legislative seats from 50.3 after 1952 to 43.5. Vice President Richard Nixon, after 20,000 miles of slam-bang campaigning, concluded that the 1954 election had been "a dead heat," and indeed the GOP congressional losses were less than normal for the party in power in mid-term ballotting. On the other hand, the weakness of Eisenhower's coattails in 1952 had automatically reduced the potential for a Democratic rebound. Economic problems in farm areas were a special GOP burden in 1954; on the whole, where the economy was doing well so did the Republicans.

The most important fact about the 1954 elections, however, was that the Republicans narrowly lost control of both Houses of Congress—and with it the argument that only a Republican Congress could work effectively with the president.

As the 1956 election approached, Eisenhower could point to a number of substantial successes. He had ended the war in Korea and avoided a war in Indochina. "Open skies," "atoms for peace," and "the spirit of Geneva" all gave promise of further thaws in the Cold War. Social security and the minimum wage had been liberalized; the St. Lawrence Seaway and the Department of Health, Education and Welfare had been established; significant tax reform, highway construction, and soil bank programs had been passed.

The Republican National Committee could accurately claim in 1955 that "everything is booming but the guns." But while the electorate was ready to credit Eisenhower for this condition, they were increasingly unready to credit his party: After the president's heart attack in September, 1955, polls concerning possible successors showed that no other Republican could win the presidency in 1956. An Iowa survey indicated that the Democrats would carry even that bastion of Republican sentiment if Ike did not run again. As Nixon put it in 1956: "The Republican party is not strong enough to elect a president. We have to have a presidential candidate strong enough to get the Republican party elected."

But in 1956, even Eisenhower was not strong enough to accomplish that feat. Determined to achieve a victory margin large enough to provide leverage during the lame duck term which lay ahead of him, fired by a Democratic campaign attack on his brother Milton, and boosted at the polls by pre-election crises in Hungary and the Suez, Eisenhower raised his victory percentage to 57.4. Yet even in the face of this landslide, the Democrats gained two House seats, one Senate seat and one governorship. Republican congressional candidates trailed the top of the ticket by 6.5 million votes, as four of every ten voters split their presidential and congressional ballots. Although Republican strength in the Congress was no weaker as a result than it had been in 1951 and 1952, the GOP lost its best opportunity in decades to make smashing advances. While Eisenhower made strong gains over 1952 among northeastern Catholics, his performance slumped a bit in the West.

Nineteen hundred and fifty-seven and 1958 were not happy years for the president or his party. When Eisenhower looked back on them in his memoirs he quoted from Hamlet: "When sorrows come, they come not single spies, but in battalions." Early in 1957, Treasury Secretary George Humphrey's attack on the Eisenhower budget opened the floodgates of conservative criticism. In the Fall, the president was forced to send troops to Little Rock to enforce school desegregation, and shortly afterward the Russians launched their Sputnik. In November, Eisenhower suffered a slight stroke. Meanwhile, the economy was spinning into the most serious recession of the postwar period. Republican prospects were also damaged by conflict of interest charges concerning the White House Chief of Staff, Sherman Adams, a revolt against administration farm policies, a continuing crisis in the Formosa Straits, and the insistence by conservatives that referenda on right-to-work laws be placed on the 1958 ballot in several states.

Though there had been no general Republican landslide in 1956, the Democratic rebound in 1958 was much greater than normal. The Democrats picked up six new governorships, forty-eight House seats and fifteen Senate seats, the greatest switching of Senate seats in history, save only for the loss of Democratic seats after the southern secession in 1860 and the gain of Republican seats from the reconstructed South in 1868. Republican strength in the state legislatures fell from 43.8 percent to 34.1 percent.

Most alarming for Republicans were the setbacks the party sustained in traditionally Republican areas. Twenty-three House seats were lost in the Midwest alone. All six of Connecticut's congressional seats swung from Republican to Democratic. The right-to-work issue was particularly damaging in Republican Ohio and in

California, which elected a Democratic governor and senator and gave the Democrats control of the legislature for the first time since 1888.

Six years earlier the Republicans had been plotting further inroads into solid Democratic bastions. Now—suddenly—they found themselves losing votes in their own suburban, small town, and rural backyards. Some described the 1958 election as a restoration of the New Deal coalition, and indeed the Democrats had solidified their strength in the cities and in the South—which reacted sharply against Eisenhower's intervention in Little Rock and the passage in 1957 of the first civil rights act since Reconstruction. But the 1958 election was also an indication that realignment could work both ways. If the Republicans would not fulfill the promise of 1952, then Democratic candidates would try to move into the moderate vacuum. Their reward was the support of millions of Eisenhower voters, from Maine to California.

Late in 1958, Leonard Hall—who had already begun to plan Richard Nixon's presidential campaign—estimated the odds against Republican success in 1960 at five to one—and many Republicans thought he was being optimistic. The fact, of course, was that Hall was far too pessimistic. Though Eisenhower Democrats might often return to their New Deal habits, and though Dewey Republicans might stray on occasion to the Democratic camp, the Eisenhower breakthroughs had not been entirely for naught. Under the right circumstances, the coalitions of 1952 and 1956 could still be reassembled.

This was the task which Richard Nixon undertook in 1960, and, considering the distance he had to travel after the 1958 catastrophe, he achieved remarkable success. It is significant to note that only a Democratic ticket which contained both a Catholic *and* a southerner was able to displace the Republican party in 1960—and only by the narrowest of margins.

III

Samuel Lubell has described American politics in the 1950's as "a revolt of the moderates"—and the concept is helpful in understanding both the successes and the failures of the Eisenhower Republicans.

Tired of sterile debates between Republican appeals which rang of 1896 and Democratic rhetoric which still echoed the themes of 1936, the voters called for a truce in the 1950's and, to a remarkable extent, they got one. The presidential elections of 1952, 1956, and 1960 were all marked by a minimum of ideological debate. The issues which emerged in these campaigns were largely peripheral and procedural, differences not of kind but of degree.

In his person and in his outlook, Dwight Eisenhower was the decade's preeminent symbol of conciliation and consolidation. The nation's search for consensus found its perfect fulfillment in Eisenhower's "middle way." The important thing, the president was fond of saying, was to move straight down the center of history's broad road, steering clear of the gutters on both the left and right. In practice this meant a general acceptance and even a mild expansion of many New Deal programs (Senator Goldwater would later refer to Eisenhower's "dime store New Deal") and a continuation of the internationalist foreign policies in which he had long been so deeply involved.

The labels which Eisenhower placed on his philosophy are instructive: sometimes he was "basically conservative," at other times he was "forward looking." On various occasions he described his outlook as "non-ideological," "positive," "sensible" and "practical." In 1954 he said he was "liberal in human relations, conservative in economic affairs." In 1955, he told the Finance Committee of the Republican National Committee: "I have said we were 'progressive moderates.' Right at the moment I rather favor the term 'dynamic conservatism.'" (An aide had earlier suggested "conservative dynamism" but Eisenhower turned it around.) In 1956, the president declared that the only issue was his own "progressive and dynamic" program, his "great middle-of-the-road philosophy."

One of the president's favorite expositions of political philosophy was Arthur Larson's 1956 treatise, *A Republican Looks at His Party*, which was intended to distill out of the approaches of Eisenhower's first term a credo for the "New Republicans" who occupied "The Authentic American Center." "In politics—as in chess—the man who holds the center holds a position of almost unbeatable strength," concluded Larson, who was quickly brought on as Eisenhower's personal speechwriter.

On election night in 1956, the president devoted his victory statement to the concept of "modern Republicanism": "I think that modern Republicanism has now proved itself. And America has approved of modern Republicanism." But when conservative critics began to attack the phrase in 1957, he told the party's new chairman, Meade Alcorn, that he was ready to abandon it. All he meant to imply, he said, was that his views were in the "mainstream" and were characterized by "hard commonsense." In the end, many Republicans decided that the term "Eisenhower Republicanism" was the most useful label of all.

Eight years after he left office, in an article released during the week of his death, Eisenhower was still urging the nation to avoid extremes and follow the middle way. He praised the new president, Richard Nixon, as "a man of the center," whose administration would renew the Eisenhower legacy of "government by commonsense." (Nixon aides, meanwhile, had coined the phrase "dynamic stability" to describe their own approach.)

Eisenhower's determination to avoid restrictive labels was far more the result of cunning than of confusion, for labels define and definitions limit, and Eisenhower was not a man to limit either his options or his constituency. Through his long military career he had come to think of himself as the servant of a whole people; during its latter, glorious stages he had become their surrogate and unifying symbol as well. It was a unique position, with unique responsibilities. To clarify and specify and distinguish, to embrace a particular movement or ideology or cause, to make an irrevocable commitment to some one part of his country—all these temptations could compromise his identification with the entire nation. When others chose up sides, it was his duty to stand apart.

Eisenhower never voted during his military service, but not because of inconvenience or disdain. It was instead a matter of principle; even the ballot could be compromising. Wooed by both parties after the war, he was reluctant to be identified with either. Even after he entered the White House he reminded friends that he could just as well have become "a conservative Democrat." As Lubell put it, he was "a clean sheet of paper, free of all the bitter repetitive particular scrawlings of the past," and he did what he could to preserve that unique advantage.

Eisenhower's reluctance to be a strong partisan leader was reenforced after his inauguration by his firm whiggish belief in a limited presidency, by his philosophy of leadership—which relied on quiet persuasion and distrusted arbitrary orders—and by his sense of personal humility. He frequently described himself as "a rank amateur" in politics and was more than ready to leave political matters to those supposedly more expert than he.

Eisenhower's "strong aversion to engaging in partisan politics," as Sherman Adams put it, was constantly in evidence. At the Republican National Convention in 1952, he instructed Adams, his floor manager, to make no "private deals"—even if it cost him the nomination. Nor would he be directly involved in the selection of a vice presidential nominee. When a new Republican National Chairman was chosen early in his first administration, Eisenhower refused to take a position on the matter, lest the new chairman be marked as "my man." He instructed his cabinet to join him in staying completely aloof from the Senate leadership contest which followed the death of Robert Taft. And later, though he was personally sympathetic to the effort, he also turned down Congressman Charles Halleck's request for help in unseating House Minority Leader Joseph Martin.

When Vice President Nixon urged cabinet members to use their patronage powers to advance the Eisenhower program, the president said he hoped such tactics would not prove necessary. He warned his very first cabinet meeting, in fact, against "any revival of the spoils system." He became increasingly impatient when the party chairman, Leonard Hall, raised the subject of patronage at early cabinet meetings and finally declared in October, 1953, that he was sick and tired of the entire subject. When Sherman Adams exploded to one petitioner: "Nuts, we're doing quite enough for the goddamn Republican party," he was clearly reflecting his boss's attitude.

Though he was finally persuaded to do some electioneering in 1954 and after, Eisenhower basically felt it was "improper" for a president to campaign. In March, 1958, he told Arthur Larson that "frankly, I don't care too much about the congressional election." He even claimed at one point that if he had known two months earlier "that a guy as decent as Stevenson was going to be the nominee, they might never have gotten me to take a nomination." As it did not really matter which party he joined, so it did not really matter which party governed. Party distinctions were superficial, after all; what really counted was character.

The Democratic platform in 1956 opened with a sharp attack on "political amateurs." But for Eisenhower that term was not one of opprobrium at all. To the contrary, he shared the typical American notion that politicians were the cause of more problems than they solved and that only the political amateurs could save the republic. Throughout his political career, Eisenhower felt a special fondness for the "Citizens for Eisenhower" organizations that were created to promote his candidacy outside the party channels. "We have been through a lot together," he told the "Citizens" as they gathered to plan for the 1956 campaign. "I came home [in 1952] in response . . . to a call from you people." He went on to say that he never faced "any grave question" as president without thinking: "The citizens would have expected this; this is the way they would have done it. Or this we believe is more in keeping with what the citizens meant when they elected us to office." Citizen politics—by which he meant non-partisan politics—was the only politics for him.

Despite the general's success in attracting millions of new voters to the Republican banner in 1952 and 1956, despite his continuing and genuine concern for bringing young people into the party, and despite his warning that it would be a tragic mistake for Republicans to "rely on any one man" or on "old timers like me," the Eisenhower administration was notably unsuccessful in recruiting or developing effective younger candidates for high office. Eisenhower would frequently try to create presidential candidacies out of thin air merely by listing his personal favorites. But the party's list of plausible successors rarely carried more than a single name. "Why can't we be like the British Conservative party?" Eisenhower once complained. "They always seem to have two or three men all ready to go." And as he looked at the state of his party during his last year in office, he wistfully asked Sherman Adams: "What happened to all those fine young people with stars in their eyes who sailed balloons and rang doorbells for us in 1952?"

Perhaps part of the problem was simply the age of the Eisenhower administration. Most of the president's advisers and cabinet officers had been recommended to him by the Dewey machine; like Eisenhower himself they were leaders who had emerged in the 1940's. In this sense, the Eisenhower administration was the last act of a political drama which had begun two decades before. There was no strong affirmative effort to develop fresh talent and when the star himself retired, so did most of his supporting cast.

The Eisenhower years also failed to revive the party's dwindling intellectual resources. Conservative intellectuals, many of whom gathered around a new magazine founded in 1955 (*National Review*) were generally antipathetic to both Eisenhower and Nixon. Liberal intellectuals were disturbed by the party's compromises with Joseph McCarthy and the apparent harsh and simple moralism of foreign policy under John Foster Dulles, Eisenhower's Secretary of State. Both groups were put off by what they saw as the muddled moderation of the president and the business club atmosphere of his administration.

It was sometimes difficult to remember in the 1950's and 1960's that the Republican party, from the time of its founding down through the early years of the twentieth century, had been the party of the nation's intellectuals. This condition had begun to change in 1912 when Theodore Roosevelt led many of them into the Bull Moose Movement and thus out of the Republican mainstream. The attractions of Wilson and the second Roosevelt reinforced this trend and the yawning gap which opened between the Republicans and the intellectual community became unbridgeable during the McCarthy period. Walter Lippmann—who supported Eisenhower in 1952 and Nixon in 1968—warned the party after the 1954 election of the need to "end its alienation from the best brains of the nation." But the warning was largely ignored.

IV

As Eisenhower would not be an aggressive Republican leader in battles against the Democrats, so he would not be an aggressive moderate leader in battles against the conservatives. Though the party's moderates had produced his nomination, he refused to regard himself as their captive. They had come to him, after all. He had been *their* vehicle to power and not vice versa.

Within the party as within the country, Eisenhower hated to be identified with conflict. When the nomination was clinched in 1952, and after he had spoken alone for a moment with his wife, his first move was to phone Bob Taft and say: "I'd very much like to come over and see you. . . ." The first call he made after his election was to Herbert Hoover.

Eisenhower's concern for party rapprochement was most dramatically symbolized by the joint statement he issued with Taft in September, 1952. The press, the Democrats and some of Eisenhower's more liberal supporters described it as "the surrender of Morningside Heights," but in truth there was no surrender. Placed well to the left of Taft strategically, Eisenhower was not far from him ideologically. On some domestic questions, he once told Taft, "You're twice as liberal as I am." Taft, for example, supported an expanded federal role in fields such as housing, education, welfare, agriculture and health care. He accepted unbalanced budgets and supported an increased minimum wage. Eisenhower, on the other hand, was opposed to the TVA—and often worried aloud about "creeping socialism." Their biggest differences were in foreign policy, but even here there seemed to be some room for accommodation.

Robert Taft died of leukemia in July, 1953. Eisenhower felt the loss deeply. After receiving the news, he went to visit Martha Taft, an invalid, and took her hand in both of his and said: "I don't know what I'll do without him—I don't know what I'll do without him." "If fate had permitted him to continue in his post," Eisenhower wrote in his memoirs, "the Republican party would have developed into a much stronger and better-unified political organization." Taft's death, he said, was "a loss that possibly could never be made good." He could have left out the word "possibly."

For Taft, less conservative than many of his followers, and Eisenhower, less liberal than some of his, both held positions of unassailable influence with their respective wings of the party. Their willingness to work with one another and learn from one another just might have fashioned the unified majority party of which so many Republicans dreamed. It would not have been an easy task in any event, but without Taft it was nearly impossible.

When Eisenhower refused to become involved in the fight over Taft's successor, as Senate majority leader, William Knowland of California won the post. As Sherman Adams would later write: "It would have been difficult to find anybody more disposed to do battle with much of the president's program in Congress." With Knowland's permission and often with his encouragement, conservative stalwarts such as Senators Eugene Milliken of Colorado, Styles Bridges of New Hampshire, Congressmen John Taber and Daniel Reed of New York and Clare Hoffman of Michigan worked effectively to cripple much of the Eisenhower program.

As the resulting sense of impasse grew, so did Eisenhower's impatience. "Don't the damn fools realize that the public thinks the dollar sign is the only respected symbol in the Republican party?" he exclaimed during a dispute on domestic policy. Concerning foreign affairs, he exploded one day to Knowland: "My God, you can't stand back and assume a nation is safe from all harm because the Republicans won the last election." Privately he complained that Knowland has "the most cockeyed notions about world affairs." He grew tired, he said, of being "kicked in the shins," especially on mutual security questions, by members of his own team. But just as he had done nothing to prevent that development, so he did very little to achieve conservative support. One reason there was "often little semblance of party unity," said Sherman Adams, was that there were "no penalties for deserting the party line."

Perhaps even more upsetting to Eisenhower than the programmatic opposition of conservatives in the Congress, however, was the growing standing of Senator Joseph McCarthy. As McCarthyism swept the land in 1953 and 1954, the Republican party was again divided against itself. Adlai Stevenson declared in 1954 that the "GOP is one-half McCarthy and one-half Eisenhower," and while his fractions may have been inaccurate, his speech hit a very raw nerve. Eisenhower's personal attitude toward McCarthy, according to Adams, was one of "disdain." To General Wilton B. Persons, his Assistant for Congressional Relations, the president remarked one day: "Jerry, I don't understand how you can come in this office altogether clean after shaking hands with that fellow." Yet, to the immense disappointment of his more liberal supporters, Eisenhower's attitude toward McCarthyism, like his attitude toward congressional obstructionism, was one of public restraint. He had avoided confrontation with McCarthy in the 1952 campaign. From time to time thereafter he made comments which distinguished his views from McCarthy's—as when he denounced "book burning" in a speech at Dartmouth College. But as far as public confrontation was concerned, Eisenhower simply would not, as he put it, "get into the gutter with that guy."

In his memoirs, Eisenhower explained his position this way: "Convinced that the only person who could destroy McCarthy as a political figure was he, himself, and finding evidence piling up that he was gradually doing exactly that, I continued in my determination to ignore him." In a sense, his gamble paid off. McCarthy did destroy himself, chiefly during the Army-McCarthy hearings in the Spring of 1954, and by the time he issued his famous apology for having supported Eisenhower in December, 1954, his influence was substantially reduced.

Eisenhower's reluctance to confront McCarthy was very much in character. Just as the party could not be coerced into unity, just as whites could not be forced to accept blacks as equals, just as the Indo-Chinese peoples could not be forced to fight Communism, so the public could not be forced to condemn McCarthy until they came to realize his excesses for themselves.

The decline of McCarthy did much to free Eisenhower from the frustrations of Republican factionalism, but the Democratic takeover of the Congress in 1955 may have done even more. Now the president was free to cope with Republican divisions by ignoring them. Whatever pressures there may earlier have been for negotiating with right-wing leaders, for disciplining errant Republicans, and for building the political strength of his own moderate adherents, all were considerably reduced when Sam Rayburn and Lyndon Johnson took over the congressional reins.

The new Democratic leaders hastened to assure the president that he had been wrong in his pre-election prediction that Democratic victories would usher in "a cold war of partisan politics." The Rayburn-Johnson strategy accorded perfectly with the Eisenhower temperament. He began to talk more about the Republican's minority status and the need to deal with Democrats. If partisanship becomes an issue, "we are foredoomed to defeat," he concluded. The only way to build the Republican party up was by working to play it down.

Eisenhower's personal distaste for intraparty maneuver had been evident in 1953 when he gave serious consideration to the possibility of starting a new party as a way of escaping the plague of factionalism. After 1954, it was possible for him to make that same escape through the magic of bipartisanship. With the cooperation of moderate Democrats and moderate Republicans, Eisenhower became, in effect, the leader of a centrist coalition government. Even that most partisan of Republicans, Richard Nixon, would later recall the period with some nostalgia—comparing the Eisenhower-Johnson relationship to that of a king and his prime minister and acknowledging that the arrangement had much to recommend it. Once established, the bipartisan approach quickly gained momentum. For one thing, the arrangement made conservative Republicans even angrier and more intractable, which in turn made it even more difficult for Eisenhower to do business with them. At the same time, the concept of party responsibility was further damaged among the electorate. Eisenhower's popularity continued to climb, but the party's popularity did not. As bipartisanship further weakened the Republicans, it made further bipartisanship inevitable.

The conservative Republicans did not however, disappear. Free now of the burden of McCarthy's excesses, they prepared themselves to take the party back. At first they did not attack Eisenhower frontally. Yet at this stage the typical conservative attitude toward Eisenhower was still that of Senator Jenner: "We'll run him if we have to run him stuffed" though Knowland was quick to announce his potential candidacy for president during the period of uncertainty following Eisenhower's heart attack.

The relatively liberal 1956 Republican platform, the highly personal nature of Eisenhower's victory that year, the president's election night heralding of "modern Republicanism," and—above all—the substantial spending increases in the budget which Eisenhower presented in early 1957 brought conservative patience to an end. On the very day the budget was presented, Treasury Secretary George Humphrey opened fire: if it was not cut, he said, "you will have a depression that will curl your hair." As if by signal, other conservative guns began to boom. The fresh and appealing voice of Barry Goldwater led the way, declaring, in April, 1957, that "the American mind is a conservative mind." Senator Karl Mundt of South Dakota put together a five-point strategy for building a formal bipartisan coalition of Republican conservatives and southern Democrats. The Young Republicans voted to reject certain

Eisenhower policies. *Time* magazine reported that moderates and conservatives "came close to hair pulling" at the biennial meeting of the League of Republican Women.

For the first time since he took office, Eisenhower was sharply criticized by the National Association of Manufacturers. A conclave of conservative Republicans gathered in Chicago to talk about "Real Republicanism versus 'Modern Republicanism.' " Congressman Clare Hoffman of Michigan, describing himself as one of the president's "loyal supporters, who keeps him from going too far," charged that "the president and his left wing, free spending international one-world advisers proposed to disinfect, fumigate, unify and remake the Republican party," and then suggested that the president run in 1960 as a Democrat. As the 1958 elections approached, emboldened conservatives across the country decided to mount a great offensive against the power of labor unions. In cooperation with liberal Democrats, they went after the scalp of Sherman Adams—and got it.

The stunning Democratic sweep in the 1958 election shocked many Republicans into a more cooperative posture. Moreover, many of the conservative leaders had departed by now from both the Congress and the cabinet. Less than half the Republicans in the Senate in 1959 had been there in 1953. Vice President Nixon—always closer than Eisenhower to the conservatives and to the Republican professionals—became increasingly prominent as the 1960 election approached and this fact also fostered a sense of party concord, as did the efforts of a new Committee on Program and Progress to reexamine and rearticulate the Republican philosophy. On Nixon's recommendation, an Illinois businessman, Charles H. Percy, was chosen to head the group—and to head the 1960 platform committee which built on its findings.

In the House, Congressman Halleck successfully challenged Joseph Martin for the Republican leadership (he won seventy-four to seventy). In the Senate, Everett Dirksen succeeded William Knowland, who had been solidly defeated in his attempt to change jobs with California's liberal Republican Governor Goodwin Knight. The Halleck-Dirksen team, though it would be widely ridiculed as "the Ev and Charlie Show" in the heady Camelot days of the early 1960's, was regarded by President Eisenhower as a breath of fresh air in 1959. For the first time, he told associates, he enjoyed going to congressional leadership meetings.

But perhaps the most important factor in the new cohesiveness of the GOP was the fact that the Democrats had suddenly grown too strong for bipartisanship. As the Eighty-sixth Congress gathered in January, 1959, its leaders realized that they had the votes, the issues, and, above all, the incentive—the presidential election of 1960—to play a much tougher partisan game. As a result, for the first time in his presidency, it was consistently easier for Eisenhower to deal with his own party than with the opposition. On the domestic front he continued to retreat from modern Republicanism to a more conventional conservatism. He took a sharper partisan line, handing down, for example, a stinging series of vetoes of Democratic "big spending" bills and fighting to ensure that his vetoes were upheld. He also called for an all-out effort to strengthen party machinery.

At the same time, the issue which had caused the greatest differences between Eisenhower and the right in his first years in office, old-fashioned isolationism with its emphasis on reduced military spending, was transformed by the end of the decade. The newer conservatism took its foreign policy cues less from Taft than from the militant anti-Communist leaders of the early 1950's; the eventual result was conservative support for larger defense budgets, while many aspects of Taft's neo-isolationist policy eventually found their way into the thinking of the left.

Republican divisions were largely compromised or obscured at the end of the 1950's. But they had not been eliminated. While the party was a somewhat more cohesive institution in 1960 than in 1952, the problems that plagued it then still lurked in the shadows.

V

"We have rotted since 1952. It wasn't 1964 that caused the debacle. Don't blame it on '64. There was a steady rotting process since 1952."

The words were those of Ray Bliss, the Republican National Chairman in the mid-1960's. His sentiments were widely shared in the party at that time. Eisenhower himself, writing in 1965, recalled that "one of the goals I set for myself when I agreed to run again for the presidency was to unify and strengthen the Republican party." Then he allowed: "My success was slight."

His success was slight because the party failed in the 1950's to expand the traditional resources for political success. It failed to use patronage effectively and to build organization; it failed to recruit workers and candidates; it failed to develop intellectual resources; it failed to enforce party discipline. These failures had an important impact on all elements of the Eisenhower coalition. Democrats and Independents who worked for Eisenhower found little reason to change their party registration. Arch-conservative Republicans were encouraged to travel down highly independent paths. Professional politicians were generally demoralized. "Modern" Republicans—who came to Washington with high hopes of building and renewing the party along dynamic new lines—became increasingly cautious about risking the wrath of congressional regulars without the shield of a strong White House blessing.

And yet after all the arguments have been made about Eisenhower's apparent failings as a political leader, it must also be acknowledged that the most significant obstacles to party growth and reunion in the 1950's may well have been beyond his control.

In the first place, Eisenhower took over a party which had been out of power for twenty years. The attrition of the 1930's and 1940's was not easy to reverse. Consider the question of organization, for example. In two areas most ripe for conversion—the cities and the South—local Democratic organizations were overwhelmingly dominant. A vote for Eisenhower or Nixon was one thing in such places; a vote against one's own community was quite another. In many American neighborhoods in the 1950's, especially in the urban North and the rural South, Democratic allegiance was woven deeply into the fabric of community life. Habits formed during decades of one-party rule could not be undone in one or two elections—particularly when there was no great issue to discredit Democrats and help Republicans, no great new appeal to offset the impact of Reconstruction and the Great Depression on basic party strength. As Samuel Lubell put it, only "finger by finger" could the grip of the past be unlocked.

The same thing was true concerning the recruitment of new candidates. The young Democrats who won so many congressional and senatorial and gubernatorial races in the 1950's were largely products of the Roosevelt era. Many of those who succeeded in traditionally Republican districts came from Republican families; their conversion from the party of Hoover to the party of Roosevelt during the 1930's and 1940's was an old debt which the GOP of the 1950's inherited and was forced to pay. By the same token, the rise of a new generation of popular Republican leaders in the 1960's—including such varied types as Rockefeller, Goldwater, Romney, Scranton, Reagan, Percy, Brooke, Hatfield, Baker, and Tower—can be seen as the delayed harvest of the 1950's, the period when most of these men began their Republican careers.

Finally, and perhaps most important, Eisenhower may well have read the new political realities of the 1950's much more perceptively than most Republicans. For the apparent breakup of the New Deal coalition in 1952 may not in fact have heralded a new era of Republican hegemony but rather a new age of personal politics and party decline. The leverage of patronage, after all, had been considerably reduced during the New Deal; lasting party affiliations were increasingly alien to highly mobile, highly educated Americans after the Second World War. Above all, there was television. Theodore H. White has reported that between 1950 and 1960 the percentage of American families with television sets in their homes increased from eleven percent to eighty percent.

The ability of the average voter to cast an intelligent ballot for the man and not the party increased enormously in the 1950's and so did the public disposition for ticket splitting. As Walter DeVries and V. Lance Tarrance have reported, some eighty percent of all presidential voters cast straight ballots before the Second World War, a figure which declined to sixty-six percent in 1952, sixty-one percent in 1956 and which has since continued to fall. The number of congressional districts carried by one party in the presidential race and another for the House of Representatives, about fourteen percent throughout the Roosevelt era, had more than doubled by 1956.

It can always be said, of course, that the decline of partisan politics was the *result* of Eisenhower's behavior rather than its cause. David Broder has charged, for example, that Eisenhower made it respectable for voters to take "a holiday from party responsibility," a habit they were later unable to shake. Still, a number of other forces were also working to undercut party allegiance in the 1950's. It is hard to see how even a partisan president could have reversed the trend.

If one begins with the premise that the opportunity of 1952 was a partisan one, then Eisenhower's political performance must be judged a failure. On the other hand, if one sees the 1952 election as signaling a departure from conventional politics, then Eisenhower's response to that new reality can be viewed as a political masterpiece. Asking not what he could do for his party but what his party could do for him, Eisenhower managed to delay the non-partisan trend among Republicans while accelerating it among Democrats. He gained the maximum personal advantage from his Republican affiliation, but usually leapt clear of its liabilities. Gary Wills summarized well the case for Eisenhower made by a number of revisionist writers in the late 1960's and early 1970's when he wrote that "Eisenhower was as superior to [the conventional rules of politics] as Renoir to a Paint-by-Number set. Eisenhower was not a political sophisticate; he was a political genius."

The Eisenhower administration was something less than a breakthrough into a period of new Republican dominance. But it was probably something more than what V. O. Key once described as a "brief Republican interlude" in a basically Democratic era. While it cannot be denied that Eisenhower failed to give his fellow Republicans effective partisan leadership, he did provide them with an extremely instructive example.

VI

The growing Republican unity of the late 1950's resulted, in part at least, from the growing inevitability of Richard Nixon's 1960 nomination. More than any other figure in the party, Nixon was the heir to Robert Taft's title, "Mr. Republican." Like his hero, Woodrow Wilson, Nixon was a firm believer in responsible party government. In an administration which often neglected party affairs, he made it his business to be the party man *par excellence*. In an administration which often drifted into bipartisanship, he was the thoroughgoing partisan.

Most importantly, Nixon provided an essential communications link between the party's warring wings. It was his acceptability to all factions of the party which put him on the Republican ticket in 1952. His strong anti-Communist credentials pleased the right; yet at the same time he was an ardent internationalist. Just as the Democratic party for years had relied heavily on brokers from the outer South—on Garner and Truman and Barkley and Rayburn and Johnson—to negotiate between its sharply divided southern and northern wings, so the Republicans had desperate need in the 1950's for figures who could bridge the foreign policy gulf in their party. Nixon was one of the few who emerged. After Taft's death, Nixon became the administration's emissary to the right wing of the party, and especially to Senator McCarthy. Nixon negotiated with McCarthy until, as he put it, he was "blue in the face," but the senator proved recalcitrant. Yet even while Nixon built a political base with the congressional conservatives and with the non-ideological professionals, he also retained the confidence of his mentors in the moderate wing. His sensitive performance during Eisenhower's convalescence in 1955 reassured many who had been taken aback by his touch campaigning. When Harold Stassen tried to bump him from the 1956 ticket, liberal and conservative Republicans alike came to his support.

Nixon's decision to constitute himself as a central meeting ground for highly diversified Republicans was not without its price. Inevitably, his reputation for aggressive campaigning was augmented by a reputation for imprecision and ambiguity. When Senator Hugh Scott commented later on "Richard Nixon's portable center," he did so with professional appreciation for the indispensability of such a figure. But while this function may have enhanced Nixon's standing with party leaders, it tarnished his image with the general public.

With Eisenhower himself, Nixon's relationship was cordial though not particularly close. The gap in their ages and Eisenhower's distrust of excessive partisanship precluded intimacy. For his part, Nixon could not help wondering why Eisenhower had not been quicker to reassure him about his place on the ticket after the fund controversy of 1952; he was quick to note that Taft had been among the first to defend him. Eisenhower's apparent uncertainty about Nixon's place on the ticket in 1956—resolved in part by the vice president's strong showing in the New Hampshire primary—further strained their relationship, as did the president's habit of including Nixon's name as only one of many on his list of possible successors.

Yet despite their different ages and attitudes toward politics, the bond of confidence between the two men grew steadily stronger during Eisenhower's presidency—and stronger still in the 1960's. Eisenhower endorsed Nixon from his hospital room before the GOP convention in 1968—and said afterward that his great remaining ambition was to live to greet two events: the marriage of his grandson, David, to Julie Nixon in December of that year and the inauguration of Richard Nixon the following January. Both wishes were fulfilled.

Better than most of the Republican moderates, Nixon knew how to survive in a party largely dominated by conservatives. Better than most conservatives in the party he also understood the more liberal general electorate. As he prepared to face that electorate in 1960, therefore, it was only natural that he would begin to emphasize a number of progressive themes. Younger moderates in the Eisenhower cabinet—men like Arthur Flemming, James Mitchell, William Rogers and Thomas Gates—came to look upon him as their strongest ally and secret weapon. This progressive emphasis seemed particularly important with the emergence of Governor Nelson Rockefeller of New York as Nixon's main GOP rival.

Rockefeller seriously considered confronting Nixon in the primaries. Some polls demonstrated he could win. Despite serious problems with the New York State legislature, the governor assembled a sizable campaign organization and began to scout the political terrain. What he found, however, was that Nixon had already been there—six years of labor in the Republican vineyards had produced their reward. The party machinery—left, right and center, contributors and office holders, Taft people and Eisenhower people were already behind the vice president. On Christmas Eve, 1959, Rockefeller announced that he would not be a candidate for president, adding: "This decision is definite and final." But Rockefeller's finality was provisional. Even Eisenhower's warning that he might appear to be "off again, on again, gone again, Finnegan," did not deter Rockefeller from announcing his availability for a draft. When an American U-2 plane was shot down over the Soviet Union, he plunged even further into the fray. On June 8, 1960, he issued a detailed nine-point critique of the Eisenhower record, along with a vigorous plea that the party not "march to meet the future with a banner aloft whose only emblem is a question mark."

The Rockefeller declaration—written with the help of Emmet John Hughes who, like Rockefeller, was a disillusioned former member of Eisenhower's staff—marked the first breach in the Eisenhower-Nixon-Percy concord. After eight years of battle on its right flank, the administration was suddenly under intraparty attack from the left. After endless complaints from conservative congressmen about excessive defensive spending, a cry for greater defensive spending had emerged, not only from Senator John F. Kennedy and other Democrats, but from within the governing party. Eisenhower considered this highly fashionable, post-Sputnik alarm about the nation's military and scientific posture exaggerated and ill-informed. His concern led him to insert in his farewell speech the next January a passage on the dangers of "the military-industrial complex."

Although Rockefeller had little leverage in the party, Nixon needed Rockefeller's help to win the election. Above all, he wanted to avoid a floor fight in Chicago which would give further ammunition to Kennedy. On the eve of the convention, he visited Rockefeller in New York at his Fifth Avenue apartment building (where Nixon himself would later reside), talked with him from 10:00 p.m. to 4:30 a.m., and achieved an historic meeting of minds.

The famous Fourteen-Point Compact of Fifth Avenue appeared at first glance to move significantly in Rockefeller's direction on foreign policy, national defense, government reorganization, economic growth, medical care for the elderly, and civil rights. In many cases, however, the movement involved little more than the use of a stronger adjective or adverb. What was not immediately evident was that Rockefeller had also done some compromising; originally, for example, he had demanded the use of specific target figures for new defense spending and economic growth but they did not appear in the joint statement.

Like the Eisenhower-Taft Morningside Heights agreement eight years earlier (to which it was immediately compared), the Fifth Avenue Compact was a conciliatory gesture by the party leader to a dissident group. The symbol was far more important than the substance. But again, as eight years earlier, the man who made the gesture was widely attacked for his "surrender." The fact that it was Nixon who went to see Rockefeller reenforced this impression. Senator Goldwater described the event as the "Munich of the Republican party" and the Platform Committee went into headlong revolt. With the help of Congressman Melvin Laird of Wisconsin (to whom Percy yielded the chair), Nixon was able to put down the rebellion and to painstakingly negotiate adjustments in the platform which were acceptable both to Rockefeller and the White House.

The Rockefeller episode may have worked to Nixon's immediate advantage in 1960. As one of Nixon's aides put it later, Rockefeller had taken "high ground" for Nixon that the candidate could not have taken on his own. He had given him an excuse to move his "portable center" another notch to the left. But the battle of the 1960 convention had other implications for the party which may not have been immediately evident. It hurt Nelson Rockefeller's standing not only with the White House but with party conservatives who came to see him as a dangerous liberal and with party professionals who came to see him as a spoiler. Meade Alcorn had concluded earlier that Rockefeller was a sure bet for the 1964 nomination if Nixon lost in 1960, but after the platform challenge he changed his mind "Now he will never be the nominee. Never," he said.

At the same time, Nixon had unavoidably clouded his relationship with the Republican right, especially with younger conservatives, many of them from the South, who looked to Barry Goldwater as their champion. Triggered by the Fifth Avenue Compact, conservative displeasure was compounded by Nixon's decision to wage an all out fight for Rockefeller's position on civil rights. The ensuing debate marked the emergence of civil rights as the critical dividing issue between the party's moderate and conservative wings. Also, the ruffled feathers of the right wing were not smoothed by Nixon's selection of the archetypical eastern establishmentarian, Henry Cabot Lodge, as his running mate, rather than Senator Thruston Morton of Kentucky or Congressman Walter Judd of Minnesota whom the conservatives preferred. Barry Goldwater finally stilled the conservative protest by asking that his own presidential nomination be withdrawn. Even as he did so, he hinted at the long shadow which the event would cast on the party's future. "Let's grow up, conservatives," he told a cheering convention. "If we want to take this party back, and I think we can someday, let's get to work."

The convention of 1960 evidenced that a new Republican left and a new Republican right were already jockeying for position. At the peak of convention warfare, a close Nixon aide who had once worked for Taft and would later work for Goldwater, was heard to ask in a weary moment: "I wonder what those Eisenhower people are up to." He meant, of course, to say "those Rockefeller people," but amid tension and fatigue, the ghosts of 1952 walked again. It may well be that someone else in that same hotel that night who had been with Eisenhower eight years earlier was momentarily confusing in his mind the forces of Senator Goldwater with the forces of Senator Taft.

Goldwater and Rockefeller represented new forces in the party, and their differences from the Taft and Eisenhower factions were as important as their similarities. Moreover, throughout 1960, Nixon commanded the full allegiance of virtually all who fought for Eisenhower or Taft eight years before. Yet there was a tendency in Chicago to hear in the Rockefeller-Goldwater maneuvering the echoes of a half century of fratricidal Republican warfare. That fact would have great significance for the party's future.

VII

The presidential campaign of 1960 was later remembered—by participants and observers alike—as a "classic" political confrontation, an exceptionally compelling drama. In part this resulted from the closeness of the race. From start to finish every moment counted, every decision was critical, and virtually every campaign development could later be blamed or credited for the result.

The closeness of the race was matched by the closeness of the candidates' strategies. Both worked to assemble broad national coalitions; virtually every region and every constituency became a battleground. Both Kennedy and Nixon tried to win southern votes without losing Negro votes. Kennedy campaigned in Republican suburbs and Nixon in Democratic cities. Neither party wrote off any significant bloc of votes.

Nixon's insistence on visiting all fifty states in 1960 was not a strategic quirk; Kennedy, after all, campaigned in forty-six states. Rather, it symbolized the central objective of each candidate: to establish himself as the legitimate heir of the Eisenhower consensus by identifying himself with the whole of the nation. Nixon's strong identification with the president was of substantial advantage to him in this effort, though his identification with his party was not. He promised essentially to become a "new" Eisenhower, continuing to travel down the middle of the road, but moving in what he described as a "more forceful and coherent" manner. For his part, Kennedy did all he could to portray himself as a natural successor to the general—another hero of the Second World War who could also articulate the Great American Consensus. Like Eisenhower, he shunned dogma and embraced pragmatism, emphasizing his ability to make the proper "judgments" as situations arose. While Eisenhower's judgments were rooted in the common sense of the Kansas soil, Kennedy's would draw on the intellectual resources of a newer frontier. Yet his was still the non-ideological middle way and the chief distinction he drew between himself and Eisenhower concerned his energy and age.

Perhaps more than any other election in the nation's history, the battle of 1960 turned on tactics rather than strategy, on nuances of personality, and on accidents of history. Trailing Kennedy in the polls forty-one percent to fifty-nine percent in November, 1958, and by an even more decisive thirty-nine percent to sixty-one percent just before his Russian trip in 1959, Nixon found that his television exposure in Moscow closed the gap forty-eight to fifty-two. By November, 1959, he moved into a fifty-three to forty-seven percent advantage and, with the help of his involvement in ending the steel strike, held that margin until the 1960 primary season. Kennedy's exposure in the primaries and at the Democratic convention, along with the collapse of Eisenhower's good will diplomacy after the U-2 incident, cut into Nixon's margin; the vice president trailed again forty-eight to fifty-two percent just before the Democratic convention and by a forty-five to fifty-five percent margin just after. But he made up the lost ground during the Republican convention and entered the Fall campaign with the same lead he had held the previous November; fifty-three to forty-seven percent.

When Nixon lost in November by 303 to 219 electoral votes, every critic had his own explanation. Given the close outcome, almost every theory was plausible. In his own post mortems, Nixon emphasized the slumping economy almost as much as Kennedy had emphasized it in his campaign speeches; both men clearly recognized its central role. Most of the Monday morning quarterbacking, however, focused on the four television debates, especially the first, which did so much to undercut Nixon's experience issue. In later years Nixon would joke that he had "flunked debating in the Electoral College"—but in fact it was not his debating so much as his physical appearance which was decisive. Polls revealed that among those who listened to the first debate on the radio, Nixon gained the advantage. On television, however, he projected an unfavorable image—the result in large part of a ten pound weight loss during his recent hospitalization for a knee infection. Forty-three percent of respondents in a Gallup Poll believed that Kennedy had won the first debate to twenty-three percent for Nixon; twenty-nine percent called it a tossup and five percent were undecided. While Nixon did much better in the last three confrontations, he never fully recovered from the impact of the first meeting. Dr. Elmo Roper concluded that the four television debates switched some two million votes to Kennedy.

Much criticism was also directed at Nixon's apparent indecision over how best to pursue both Negro and southern votes. General Eisenhower later felt that Nixon would have won the election had Kennedy not stolen a march on him with Negro voters by placing a celebrated phone call to Mrs. Martin Luther King, Jr., after her husband was jailed in Atlanta. The Nixon forces had considered such a move, but hesitated because of their growing belief—spurred by Nixon's warm reception in Atlanta early in the campaign—that the southern white vote held unusual Republican potential. Yet even this impulse was compromised by Lodge's statement that the new Republican administration would have a Negro in the cabinet. In the end, the vice president seemed to lose both ways, among white and black voters alike.

Nixon's reluctance to change his fifty state campaign plan after his hospitalization, his failure to conserve his energies, his desire to make too many decisions, his alleged tendency to isolate himself from both the press and politicians—all these factors were also blamed for his defeat. Yet if just 32,500 votes had been cast for Nixon rather than Kennedy in Illinois and Texas—or for that matter if only 11,124 had changed columns in Illinois, Missouri, Hawaii and Nevada—every small Kennedy error would have been magnified into an historic blunder and the many strengths of Nixon's campaign, including his very effective use of television in its closing stages, would have been widely remembered and loudly cheered.

Of course, some observers concluded that Nixon did win the election. An investigation by Earl Mazo revealed that at least 100,000 Democratic voters in Texas (which the Kennedy-Johnson ticket won by 46,257 votes) were "non-existent" and that "mountains of affidavits" in Chicago testified to electoral fraud in a state which Kennedy carried by less than 9,000 votes. For example, in one precinct where 86 ballots had been cast, the results were reported as 148 Democratic and 24 Republican. However, when Mazo began to detail his findings in the *New York Herald Tribune* he was quickly called off. The argument was made to him that his challenge could only produce a prolonged period of uncertainty which would badly damage the national interest. The man who made the argument was Richard Nixon.

Even by one official count, Nixon won the 1960 popular vote. Alabama voters in 1960 did not elect a Kennedy slate of electors but rather eleven individuals, only five of whom finally voted for Kennedy. If Kennedy is credited with the votes received in Alabama by the highest single Kennedy elector (318,303) he wins the national popular election. If, on the other hand, he is credited with only 5/11 of the highest Democratic elector vote (147,295, the figure the Democratic party used in apportioning seats to its 1964 convention) then he loses the national popular count to Nixon by 58,205 votes.

Where did Nixon fall short in his bid to reassemble the Eisenhower coalition? His most significant failure came with Catholics, who split nearly evenly between Eisenhower and Stevenson in 1956 but gave their co-religionist seventy-eight percent of their 1960 vote. Catholic voters who accounted for most of the new Republican votes from 1948 to 1956 also accounted for most of the losses from 1956 to 1960.

How crucial was this vote? The University of Michigan Survey Research Center has estimated that when those who voted *for* Kennedy because he was a Catholic are subtracted from those who voted *against* him for that reason, the net result is a nationwide *loss* for Kennedy of 2.2 percent of the total vote. On the other hand, this same study concludes that those who left Kennedy because of his religion were overwhelmingly southerners and that in the northern states—including most of the crucial battleground states—Kennedy's religion was a plus. He gained 5.2 percent and lost only 3.6 percent of the northern vote because of his Catholicism—a net increment of 1.6 percent.

What did the return of the Catholics to the Democratic fold portend for the future? Did it mean that Republicans were foolish to think they could repeat the urban successes of Eisenhower? Or was Kennedy's triumph among Catholics a one-time affair, a vote not for the Democratic party nor even for a Catholic, but only for the *first* Catholic president?

In the months immediately following the election, moderate and liberal Republicans would argue for the latter interpretation, claiming that Republicans must win future elections where they lost the 1960 election—in the cities. Party Chairman Thruston Morton established a special task force under Ohio State Chairman Ray Bliss to develop specific plans for winning the urban vote. Conservatives, on the other hand, argued that the big city vote was a will-o-the-wisp, one which could tempt the party into foolish economic liberalism. As the power of the right grew within the party, the Bliss Report was shelved and the party's resources were focused on the South.

In time, however, the conservative position changed as the reaction of Catholic and other urban whites to the social revolutions of the 1960's presented Republicans with new opportunities to win their support. From this new perspective, conservative strategists like Kevin Phillips, looking back at 1960, argued that the Catholic vote for Kennedy was a part of a Catholic quest for status, a quest which had led many Catholics into the Republican fold in the 1950's and would continue to do so in the 1960's. By this reasoning, Kennedy did not reverse the Republican-Catholic trend; he scarcely even interrupted it. In a sense, he even added to its momentum.

In the South, the second New Deal bastion turned GOP target, the results in 1960 were more encouraging for Republicans. Nixon actually out-ran Eisenhower in six of the old Confederate states, though his total southern vote, 47.7 percent, was closer to Eisenhower's performance of 1952 than of 1956. Lyndon Johnson's presence on the Democratic ticket, along with the growing identification of the Eisenhower administration with school integration and Nixon's own reputation as a civil rights advocate, worked to diminish the Republican southern vote. On the other hand, the Catholic issue did much to inflate Nixon's southern showing. The University of Michigan Survey Research Center showed a net gain of 16.5 percentage points for Nixon in the South as a direct result of the Catholic issue.

The returns of 1960 also pointed to the new significance in both southern and northern politics of the rising Negro vote. Prospects for Republican gains among Negroes were encouraging at the start of the 1960 campaign. At the time of the Democratic convention, Kennedy's popularity with black voters was the lowest of any Democratic candidate, including Lyndon Johnson. The GOP platform took a strong civil rights position and the original Republican campaign plan called for continuing this emphasis. But the plan changed after the resounding reception in Atlanta (Nixon called it the warmest he had ever encountered) and Kennedy's phone call to Mrs. King helped to spotlight the transformation. On election day, Kennedy polled almost as well among Negro voters as Stevenson in 1952 and better than Stevenson in 1956. Negro leaders claimed after the election that the black vote had been critical in delivering eleven states to Kennedy—including three in the South. Theodore White concluded that if Nixon had even held Eisenhower's 1956 percentage of the Negro vote he would have carried Illinois, New Jersey, Michigan, South Carolina and Delaware.

Whether Eisenhower's early success in adding blacks to his coalition could have been matched by Republicans in the 1960's is a difficult question. Economic issues would undoubtedly have given Democrats an automatic advantage with many black voters, though it must also be remembered that Negro voters, like Catholics and southerners, were becoming increasingly middle class. Had race not become a polarizing issue in the 1960's, Republicans may well have been able to hold at least that one-third of the non-white electorate which Nixon won in 1960. Yet when Nixon's showing is compared with what preceded and what followed, it is evident that the glass of black 'Republicanism in 1960 was two-thirds empty and not one-third full.

Finally, the 1960 election revealed an ominous trend for Republicans in the habits of suburban voters. Kennedy decided in October to devote a major portion of his remaining time and resources to the traditionally Republican suburbs, focusing especially on their younger residents. The strategy worked. In the same northern suburbs where Eisenhower had polled sixty-three percent of the vote in 1956, Nixon was held to fifty-two percent, a return to the GOP levels of 1940 and 1944. The percentage of college graduates, professional and business people, and white-collar workers voting Republican also fell about ten percent from 1956 to 1960. Though Nixon's strength still came largely from the traditional Republican bases, the drift away from the Republican banner which was apparent in those areas in 1958 showed up again two years later. While the Republicans picked up twenty House seats, two Senate seats, and a handful of state legislative seats in the 1960 election, the presidential candidate, as usual, ran well ahead of his party.

Nor did the Republicans make major inroads nationally in the next midterm election as they had in 1950, the last time they were out of office. In 1962, the Republicans picked up only two House seats, lost four senators, held their own in governorships and made only slight state legislative advances. On both left and right, the demands would grow in the early 1960's for the party to try *something* different.

VIII

The most important fact about the Republican party in the early 1960's was the enormous leadership vacuum created when General Eisenhower returned to his farm at Gettysburg and Richard Nixon returned to suburban Los Angeles. Two men tried to fill that vacuum in the middle 1960's: Nelson Rockefeller in 1961 and 1962, and Barry Goldwater in 1963 and 1964. Neither was able to win the confidence of the broad center of the party—much less of his ideological opponents. As a result, the Republican party flew through the 1964 election with only one wing. And when a new generation of Republicans still failed to produce plausible, unifying leadership in 1968, the party returned to the one man who had united them earlier.

The Book of Genesis tells the story of Jacob's love for Rachel, a love so deep that he was willing to serve her father seven years in order to marry her. "And they seemed unto him but a few days, for the love he had to her." And yet at the end of that time it was not Rachel but her sister Leah whom he received. The price of Rachel's hand was another seven years of service. It may well be that Richard Nixon's seven years of service to the Republican party from 1953 to 1960 "seemd unto him but a few days," because of the prize he thought awaited him. When that prize was denied him, however, he did not abandon his goal but returned to the vineyards of party service for another seven years.

The party which Nixon served in the 1950's was a divided, minority party—but at least it was the party in power. In the 1960's it was still weaker, even more divided and once again out of power. The Dirksen-Halleck team in the Congress was now the party's strongest policy voice; yet "the Ev and Charlie Show" presented on television a caricature of negative, Old Guard leadership which Republicans of all ideologies regarded as a public relations disaster. In one survey of thirty Republican congressmen, only two gave favorable marks to the team, and those two were Ev and Charlie. In the mid-1960's, the situation improved somewhat as Dirksen made a dramatic series of policy reversals, supporting Democratic presidents in the old bipartisan manner on issues such as the nuclear test ban treaty and civil rights. In the House both liberal and conservative congressmen tried to burnish the GOP image in the early 1960's by improving the level of minority staffing on House committees. But Halleck, jealous of his prerogatives, blocked all such plans. Nor was there a ready alternative to congressional image-making. The GOP had only sixteen governors now—and with the decline of patronage and the rise of the media, few of them had access to the critical levers of influence.

The party's titular leader, Richard Nixon, was also much weaker than he had been in the 1950's. No longer the precocious young vice president who had never lost an election, he was suddenly transformed into a national symbol for "the loser"—and after 1962, the poor loser at that. Jokes about the unfortunate man who drove an Edsel with a Nixon bumper sticker brought laughter across the country.

Even his party base had been undermined. Liberals complained that Nixon had over-emphasized the pursuit of southern votes in 1960; conservatives griped that he had been another me-too candidate. Party professionals complained about their exclusion from the campaign and pointed to abundant technical errors. Nevertheless, when Nixon returned to California in 1961 to practice law and write his memoirs, many thought he would inevitably run for president again three years later.

But Nixon thought otherwise. Convinced that it would be impossible to beat Kennedy in 1964, he decided to run instead for the governorship of California in 1962—pledging to serve a full, four-year term. Nixon sought the governorship not as a stepping stone to the presidency, but as a shelter from a second, fatal defeat. It was highly ironic that the argument which hurt him the most in the race against Governor Brown in 1962 was the fear of California voters that he was merely gaining a foothold for another assault on Kennedy. Nixon was also hurt when the right, whose candidate he had beaten two to one in the primary, failed to support him—in part because they saw him as a rival to Goldwater in 1964. Though he had led Governor Brown by sixteen percentage points in preliminary polls a year earlier, Nixon received only 47.4 percent of the two party vote. Then his famous explosion at his "last press conference" the day after the election seemed to end any remaining hope that he could fill the party's national leadership vacuum.

But if not Nixon, then who? One by one the possibilities were brought forward, and one by one they were eliminated.

First was Nelson Rockefeller. Despite the enemies he had made in 1960, his divorce in 1961, the reduced margin of his 1962 victory, a liquor control scandal involving a close associate, and growing tax problems in the New York State legislature, Rockefeller was still the odds on choice of both the public and the party for the Republican nomination. James Reston wrote in 1963 that the governor had "as much chance of losing the Republican nomination as he has of going broke." Said Walter Lippmann: "He could not prevent it if he wanted to." Rockefeller's recovery testified to the power of the leadership vacuum. But it also rested on the advice and assistance of his close associate, George Hinman, who worked carefully and traveled widely in 1961 and 1962 to reestablish the governor's regular Republican credentials.

As Hinman worked to reassure party leaders, Rockefeller concentrated on reassuring Goldwater. The two men discussed their views at a series of breakfast meetings and found they had much in common, particularly on national defense matters. A personal friendship ripened; Goldwater was one of the few Republican leaders whom Rockefeller phoned to tell about his remarriage. As Goldwater reported to his associates that the New York governor was "not so bad," many of them began to acquiesce in what looked to be an inevitable Rockefeller nomination. The two men found, moreover, that they shared a common conviction that the party must move beyond what they both regarded as the bland compromises of Eisenhower and Nixon. Both leaders distrusted the All-Republican Conference called by General Eisenhower at his Gettysburg farm in the Summer of 1962 and the Republican Citizens Committee which grew out of it. To Rockefeller and Goldwater, it seemed a likely front for Richard Nixon or even for William Scranton of Pennsylvania or George Romney of Michigan who won major governorship races in 1962.

Meanwhile, Rockefeller's popularity continued to impress the professionals, especially at a time when the Kennedy administration seemed to have monopolized the nation's attention. The appeal of the young president also helped to persuade both Goldwater and Nixon that the 1964 nomination was not worth much to any Republican and this too worked in Rockefeller's favor. Rockefeller's position was nevertheless extremely fragile. While a survey of delegates to the 1960 Republican convention showed that two-thirds *expected* Rockefeller to win the 1964 nomination, it also reported that only one-third thought he *should* be chosen. The New Yorker's strength rested on a series of uncertain supports: Goldwater's personal good will, Rockefeller's strong public standing, Kennedy's apparent invulnerability, and the muffling of those issues on which Rockefeller's positions were least acceptable to conservative Republicans.

One by one, all these props gave way in 1963. The first domino to fall was Rockefeller's public popularity. After his marriage on May 4 to Margaretta Fitler Murphy, Rockefeller's Gallup Poll rating plummeted immediately from a seventeen point lead over Goldwater to a five point deficit. Rockefeller's support had begun to slip in some polls even before the remarriage. But that event provided an excuse for many of the governor's less enthusiastic adherents to reconsider their support. Once his poll ratings began to fall, the governor was in deep trouble. For unlike Nixon, who typically moved out from his party base to a wider public, Rockefeller's public support was the base of his party strength.

Almost simultaneously with the remarriage, the dramatic flaring of the civil rights revolution brought into the national spotlight a highly emotional issue on which Rockefeller's views departed most dramatically from those of the party's conservatives. All these developments led to a Rockefeller decision in the Summer of 1963 which finally swept away the last major prop on which his inevitable nomination had rested, Senator Goldwater's friendship.

Desperate to recover his standing in the opinion polls, Rockefeller moved to dramatize two major issues which he hoped would strike a responsive public chord and reverse his declining fortunes: civil rights and extremism. Both were issues which President Kennedy had been developing with some success. But both also risked a sharp break with Republican conservatives. The bomb shell was dropped on Bastille Day, July 14. "The time for temporizing is over," declared the governor as he declared all-out war on the "unprincipled extremism of the radical right." At the same time, however, he also criticized those who were opposed to new civil rights legislation—and blended the two discussions in such a way as to imply that Senator Goldwater himself was an "unprincipled extremist." Goldwater's reaction to the statement was immediate and decisive. "There will be no more breakfasts," he said, "none at all."

IX

From Bastille Day on, the relationship between the Rockefeller and Goldwater factions was one of increasing animosity. The resulting polarization not only compromised Rockefeller's bid for party leadership, but also badly damaged the prospects of the second suitor to bid for the party's allegiance, Barry Goldwater.

Just as Rockefeller was not the direct heir of the Dewey-Eisenhower group in the Republican party—most of whom at this stage were looking to Nixon or Romney or Scranton or Lodge or some other moderate—so Goldwater was not the direct descendant of Taft. Many Taft conservatives—Everett Dirksen and Ray Bliss were good examples—did not feel particularly at home with the new ideologues who provided the backbone of Goldwater's support. Worried about the Arizonan's electability, many such leaders hung loose during 1963 and 1964, hoping some alternative candidacy would appear. F. Clifton White, a Dewey-Eisenhower supporter who played the critical role in Goldwater's nomination, emphasized the non-Taftian nature of the Goldwater movement in his invaluable memoir and manual, *Suite 3505* (named after the office from which the Draft Goldwater effort was managed in its early days). White points out that the great burst of Goldwater enthusiasm at the 1960 Republican convention did not originate among heartland conservative delegates, who were solid for Nixon, but among the more intense and more youthful delegations from South Carolina and other southern states. Those who began to organize for Goldwater in 1961 viewed Nixon and the party's professional politicians, many of them older Taft conservatives, as the foremost enemies of their effort to remake the party.

The same point has been emphasized by White's close associate, William Rusher, the publisher of *National Review*. It was Rusher who first came to White in 1961 with the important realization that the old Taft wing was virtually dead, that the old pros were "dreadfully out of condition" ("sitting ducks" White called them), and that the closeknit Young Republican group of "old friends"—in which Rusher, White, and Representative John Ashbrook of Ohio were the principal movers and shakers—was now "about the third or fourth largest faction" in the party.

Intellectually, the Goldwater movement also looked to forces which had very little to do with the placid conservatism of the small-town Middle West. In fact, it was two young and florid eastern Roman Catholics, steeped in European conservatism, who provided a major intellectual focus for the new conservative movement with the founding of *National Review* in 1955. William F. Buckley, Jr., the author of *God and Man and Yale*, and L. Brent Bozell, a writer for McCarthy and later for Goldwater, came to their new project fresh from a book called *McCarthy and His Enemies*, which described McCarthyism the movement (though not McCarthy the man) as something around which "men of good will and stern morality may close ranks."

Despite the protests of sometime associates like Whittaker Chambers, the group that gathered around *National Review* deeply distrusted Nixon in particular and the Republican party in general. The magazine argued effectively for a third force strategy which would marshal a conservative constituency for or against Republican candidates as circumstances dictated. (Unlike the conservatives of the 1940's, this group did not covet the title "Mr. Republican" as an honor for its heroes.) The message of *National Review* was that it was no longer enough "to hold by the accustomed" and that what the country needed was an entirely new "conscious conservatism"—a much more radical and aggressive "counter-revolutionary" doctrine. The role of *National Review,* in the words of its publisher, was not only that of a magazine but also "of a church, a school and a political party."

Many of the young conservatives who cheered Goldwater from the floor and the galleries of the Chicago convention in 1960 were activists not so much in party affairs as in crusading right-wing citizens organizations. Goldwater's stern warning that conservatives should grow up and get active in the party was primarily addressed to this audience of extra-party enthusiasts, not to older conservatives who had bled for the party for decades. A number of those who heard the speech nevertheless marched off from Chicago to Sharon, Connecticut, where they founded the nonpartisan Young Americans for Freedom. While the young intellectuals who supported Goldwater often complicated his relationship with the Republican party, it was their inspiring creed and sense of purpose which gave the Goldwater movement much of its power in the 1960's. They provided a resource which moderates and liberals in the party sorely lacked. Senator Goldwater—a proudly non-intellectual man—became an effective political mouthpiece for these thinkers, giving his name to two books, a regular newspaper column and many speeches which they drafted for him in the early 1960's. "Oh hell, I have ghosts all over the place," he laughingly acknowledged.

When White, Rusher, Ashbrook and nineteen other highly trusted old friends gathered at 2:00 p.m. on Sunday, October 8, 1961, in the Avenue Motel in Chicago, their aim was not to restore a displaced faction but to capture and revolutionize a political party. Few of that original group were active politicians; their average age was forty. They were not particularly close to Goldwater—White even had some difficulty getting through to tell the senator about their meeting—and initially they organized on behalf of a cause rather than a candidate. They operated at first on a shoe string, spending only about $43,000 in the first year. Despite budgetary problems, Goldwater's ambivalent attitude, and even the Arizonan's decision to forgo the presidential race in January, 1963, they laid the groundwork so well that the bottom did not drop out of the Goldwater campaign after plummeting polls and primary defeats in early 1964.

What the Clif White operation demonstrated above all else was the growing ability of disciplined minorities to quietly work their will in a mass society by carefully seeking its points of maximum vulnerability. One such vulnerable point in an age of declining political discipline was the delegate selection process for national political conventions, especially in non-primary states. In the Republican party, with no incumbent president and only sixteen incumbent governors, the prospects for revolution were particularly ripe. White understood, as did the Kennedy forces in 1960 and the McGovern forces in 1972, what he called the "whole new dimension to preconvention politics," one which required candidates to develop "national organizations, not mere coalitions of local Tammany type machines."

The Goldwater movement was supported by a vast grassroots army of dedicated volunteers who regarded the effort as a crusade to save the country. Many were women, convinced that the best thing they could do for their children was to put Barry in the White House. If that meant missing a meal while addressing envelopes or distributing another round of conservative literature in their neighborhoods, that was all right because it was for their children that they were writing and walking. Their contribution of time was matched by their contribution of money. It was later estimated that some 650,000 individuals contributed to the 1964 Goldwater campaign, of whom 560,000 made contributions of $100 or less. "Never," reporter Walter Pincus would later write, "have so many given so much for a candidate who garnered so few votes."

To all these resources, the Goldwaterites added a persuasive electoral strategy. Impatient with the slow pace of southern and Catholic conversions to the party, ambitious Republican strategists were ready to consider a new southern strategy which would supposedly produce a profound and immediate Republican breakthrough. The strategy argued that an aggressive conservative defense of states' rights and limited government could revolutionize political alignments in a South that was growing ever more hostile to federal involvement in racial matters. To be sure, a Republican chief justice, president, and attorney general had been closely identified with such involvement in the 1950's, but this fact was now obscured by the slowly growing identification of the Kennedy administration with the more turbulent civil rights revolutions of the 1960's. The new southern strategy would build a new majority coalition by adding what was once the solid Democratic South to traditional Republican strength in the North and West. One of the best summations of the strategy was William Rusher's article, "Crossroads for the GOP" which appeared in the *National Review* for February 12, 1963, and was widely circulated by the Draft Goldwater movement.

The strategy was spurred by the fact that nine of the fourteen new congressional seats the Republicans gained in the midterm elections of 1962 came in the South. John Tower's election in May, 1961, as the first Republican senator from Texas since Reconstruction and James Martin's narrow loss in the Senate race against Lister Hill in Alabama in 1962 also raised hopes for continuing Republican inroads in Dixie. Under Chairman William Miller, the Republican National Committee's Operation Dixie started by Meade Alcorn in 1957, became increasingly important, increasingly conservative and increasingly ready, in Senator Goldwater's 1961 phrase, to "go hunting where the ducks are" by writing off the southern Negro vote. Meanwhile, the cities report had been shelved and the minorities division diminished.

Finally, the new conservatives also had the advantage of a clearly defined enemy, and in this respect more than any other they looked back to former lines of party cleavage. The enemy they identified was the so-called eastern establishment, the power brokers of the financial and communication industries in New York City who presumably had prevented conservatives from gaining Republican presidential nominations for more than twenty years. This conservative theory fed on the same frustration Robert Taft had felt in 1952 when he complained that GOP presidential candidates were perennially selected "by the Chase National Bank." It was given its most ambitious expression—complete with smoke filled rooms and secret kingmakers and insidious propaganda machines—in a small book written by Mrs. Phyllis Schlafly of Alton, Illinois and published under the title *A Choice Not an Echo*—a phrase from Goldwater's speech declaring his presidential candidacy. Some 600,000 copies of the work were printed in May, 1964, and another million copies in June. While only seventy-two percent of all the Goldwater delegates to the San Francisco convention had ever heard Goldwater speak and while only eighty-two percent had read his *Conscience of a Conservative*, fully 92.8 percent of Goldwater delegates said afterward that they had read Mrs. Schlafly's book. In the event that conservative Republicans could not agree on just what they were for, they all knew very clearly whom they were against.

Senator Goldwater's best opportunity to take the leadership of a relatively united Republican party came in the Summer and Fall of 1963. Though he would later win the party's nomination, he would never again have as good a chance to win its heart.

Despite Rockefeller's Bastille Day broadside, the senator's image with most Republicans remained relatively free of extremist overtones in 1963. During twelve years of national travel, much of it as Chairman of the Republican Senatorial Campaign Committee, his candor and charm had helped him to achieve general acceptance as a legitimate party leader. In a poll taken on November 2, 1963, 85.1 percent of local Republican officials declared their preference for Goldwater as the 1964 nominee (some 1194 persons) compared to only 3.9 percent for Rockefeller and 3.1 percent for Nixon. At the same time, of rank and file Republicans, forty-five percent preferred Goldwater; twenty-three percent, Rockefeller; sixteen percent, Romney; and five percent, Scranton. October polls showed Goldwater leading Rockefeller by fifty-eight to twenty percent among Republicans in New Hampshire, the scene of the first presidential primary.

Meanwhile, Goldwater was also moving up on Kennedy. One poll even showed him leading fifty-two to forty-eight percent in Texas, a fact which helped persuade the president to schedule a late-November visit to Dallas. It was Kennedy's assassination which marked the end of the Goldwater ascendancy. Clif White later guessed that, had Kennedy lived, other centrist rivals to Goldwater would never have emerged as candidates, the Arizonan would have defeated Rockefeller for the nomination and, with William Scranton as his running mate, led a reasonably united party the following Autumn.

But when Lyndon Johnson became the Republican's opponent for 1964, the party's strategic assumptions and interests changed abruptly. For now the area of peculiar vulnerability for the Democrats was no longer the conservative South but the liberal North and East; now liberal Republican practitioners of Kennedy-style politics suddenly became a more valuable party asset. When a new group of Young Republican moderates, the Ripon Society, issued its first public statement in January, 1964, its central argument was that "the center is once again contestable," and that the Republicans should fight for that center through appeals to the "new Americans who are not at home in the politics of another generation." Goldwater himself, deeply shaken by Kennedy's assassination and hobbled by a painful bone spur in his heel, seemed to lose his zeal for politics and again came very close to quitting the race. Though he finally decided to announce his candidacy early in January, 1964, he did not recover his original buoyancy.

Much as Rockefeller's Bastille Day statement had underscored the fade which began with his remarriage, so Goldwater's New Hampshire campaign underscored the decline in his fortunes which had begun in November. Plagued by a series of verbal and tactical blunders, Goldwater saw his New Hampshire support drop steadily and he polled only twenty-two percent in the primary election.

What happened in New Hampshire, moreover, was also happening in the country. Goldwater's standing against other Republicans fell to twenty-seven percent in December and was down to fourteen percent by the following April.

X

The leadership vacuum persisted. The party's non-ideological professionals and Eisenhower centrists searched harder now for someone to fill it, another Eisenhower if they could find one, and if they could not, then another Nixon—or even Nixon himself. Despite his retirement from politics and his move to New York, the former vice president led other Republican candidates in the polls at the beginning of 1964 and was clearly "standing in the wings," as Nelson Rockefeller put it.

But Nixon felt he was still too weak—and the subsurface Draft Goldwater movement too strong—to allow him aggressively to seek renomination. His best chance lay in inheriting at least some of Goldwater's support as the Goldwater candidacy faded. But if he were the agent who helped cause that defeat, he would forfeit support on the right—with little hope of compensating gains among the moderates. Having been sidelined early in the fray, he would now have to wait for the nomination to come to him. Always the apostle of party unity, Nixon could not afford to be the spoiler.

Who else was there? To begin with there was Henry Cabot Lodge, like Rockefeller, the grandson of one of the party's staunchest turn-of-the-century conservatives. It was Lodge who had gone to Europe to bring home Eisenhower in 1952. Now he himself became the object of ardent requests that he come home from his post as ambassador to South Vietnam. Like Eisenhower, Lodge scored a spectacular victory in absentia in the New Hampshire primary—thanks to a joyous, almost madcap drive for write-in votes conducted by four young volunteers from Boston. Rockefeller's managers took to speaking in New Hampshire of "Henry Sabotage," but it is unclear that Lodge's protest vote could ever have been won by either of the two announced candidates—who gained less than half the vote between them.

Lodge had a great deal going for him in the early Spring of 1964. Rank and file Republicans remembered him not as an eastern liberal senator but as the man who stood up to the Russians in the United Nations. By April, forty-two percent of Republican poll respondents listed him as their first choice for president, while Rockefeller and Goldwater together had only twenty percent. Yet, unlike Eisenhower, Lodge was no blank sheet of paper. To old Taft supporters he was still the villain of 1952, and to many party professionals, his lackadaisical vice presidential campaign was disqualifying. Unlike Eisenhower, he did not come back to the country to rally his scattered supporters.

Favorite son candidacies had sharply limited the opportunities for primary election victories in 1964, and the Lodge forces missed the deadline for filing in the California primary, the most significant of the remaining contests. As a result, there was no ready method for translating Lodge's amorphous public support into concrete convention strength. When the voters came to realize this fact, Lodge's poll ratings began to tumble. Shortly after Rockefeller defeated him in the Oregon primary with the argument "he cared enough to come," Lodge announced his own support for Rockefeller, the only candidate other than Goldwater actually in the field.

On December 23, 1963, the *New York Herald Tribune*, described by many as the voice of the eastern Republican establishment, published a full page editorial entitled "Calling Governor Scranton." An Eisenhower protégé with a Kennedyesque background, Scranton seemed to many to be the perfect candidate against Lyndon Johnson. Throughout the Winter and Spring, inquiries concerning his potential candidacy began to mount, from the West as well as from the East, and from conservatives as well as moderates. Most of all, they came from the party's non-ideological professionals.

But those who supported Scranton ran into three unusual problems. In the first place, Scranton was not particularly interested in being president. Secondly, he was even less interested in intraparty combat. And thirdly, he shared Nixon's strategic assumption concerning the ability of the Goldwater forces to veto the nomination of anyone who earned their enmity. For all these reasons, Scranton determined that until Goldwater was stopped, he, too, would hold to a course of strict neutrality.

The other governor to emerge in the 1962 elections with a certain national following was George Romney. Len Hall and Cliff Folger, key Nixon men in 1960, began to launch trial balloons for Romney in 1963, but they found that he generated even less public support than Scranton and, hampered by legislative problems in Michigan, was equally disinclined to make an open race.

And so nothing happened. The vacuum persisted. Both the party professionals with Nixon and the Eisenhower centrists with Scranton adopted wait-until-Summer strategies, hopeful that they could then fill the vacuum on their own terms. It was the Goldwater forces who widely distributed Phyllis Schlafly's book, but it was the party's moderates and professionals who were victimized by the myth of the kingmakers. If the conspiracy theory made conservatives work harder, it only reenforced the moderates' tendency to temporize. "If only we were half the conspiracy they say we are," one moderate leader sighed as she looked back on the 1964 maneuvering. Like Mrs. Schlafly, the moderates too often forgot that Willkie from Indiana, Dewey from Michigan, and Eisenhower from Kansas—whatever their eastern associations—were candidates with national followings and nationwide organizational support.

Those who depended in 1964 on the wait-until-Summer strategy made a number of misjudgments. They overestimated both Eisenhower's remaining influence and his interest in a stop Goldwater movement. They neglected the fact that communications and financial power, once monopolized in Manhattan, had been substantially diluted in recent years. They overrated the influence of key political leaders with whom they were accustomed to dealing. As one of them later noted concerning last-minute stop

Goldwater efforts: "It was just incredible. We called all the old names; but they weren't there any longer, or they weren't in politics any longer. It was as if the Goldwater people had rewired the switchboard of the party and the numbers were all dead."

Finally, the moderates underestimated Goldwater's power. The fact that the senator was still slipping in general public opinion polls obscured the fact that Clif White was picking up Goldwater convention delegates by the dozens in the non-primary states. As Republican professionals surveyed the barren GOP landscape in the Spring of 1964, White's busy figure was the only impressive sight on the landscape. While they were not particularly happy with Goldwater, some of the professionals began to drift back in his direction once again. "You can't beat somebody with nobody," they said as they gave up the stop-Goldwater fight.

Still, the bulk of the party leaders waited on the results of the California primary before making their final move. Everett Dirksen was one. The man whose denunciation of Governor Dewey had expressed the depth of conservative despair in 1952, the man whose nominating speech for Goldwater, "the peddler's grandson," would express the heights of conservative euphoria in 1964, did not board the Goldwater express until well after the California primary, when he had nowhere else to go.

In California, Goldwater's managers wisely cut his speaking schedule by seventy-five percent. Then they turned loose their legions of doorbell pushers and book distributors and, as Richard Kleindienst, a top Goldwater assistant put it: "Those little old ladies in tennis shoes turned out to be the best political organization you ever saw." The senator's forces also exploited effectively the weaknesses of their only opponent, Nelson Rockefeller. They were helped by the continued unwillingness of Rockefeller's tacit allies, Nixon, Scranton and Romney, to give them any offense. All three took pains to deny Rockefeller's perfectly accurate implication that their prospects now depended on his success. Even Eisenhower rushed to say that the statement he had given to the *New York Herald Tribune* describing the ideal mainstream Republican, a description which appeared to exclude Goldwater, was meant to do no such thing. Said Nelson Rockefeller after Eisenhower's clarification: "We've got a meandering mainstream."

Fresh from his Oregon victory, Rockefeller campaigned hard and well in California, converting a nine percent deficit into a nine percent poll advantage in just three weeks. But when he returned to New York to greet the birth of his son on the weekend before the election, the issue which had damaged him so badly a year earlier was brought to the forefront again. His lead evaporated overnight; with 51.4 percent of the vote Goldwater narrowly won the election.

The tipping of California, once a liberal Republican stronghold, was the culmination of a rightward drift in that state which had been underway at least since 1958. It was the most important single shift in the balance of party power in a generation. Yet the tenacity of the conservative movement was so great that it may well have prevailed even if Goldwater had lost in California. To be sure, both the Scranton and Nixon camps had scheduled meetings after the primary to discuss the Rockefeller victory and how they best could capitalize on it. Yet Clif White contends that, even without California, he had more than 550 strong commitments to Goldwater by the time of the primary with another 100 yet to be selected but clearly in sight. (655 convention votes were required for nomination.) He had, in his own words, built a "fire escape" for Goldwater in non-primary states which could save him even if "all his bridges went up in flame in California." His greatest worry, said White, was that Nixon would be able to talk Goldwater into getting out of the race.

Robert Novak, on the other hand, has argued that impact of the California defeat would have loosened a number of these commitments, and that the hard Goldwater delegate count at the time of the primary was closer to 400. Firmness of commitment is a difficult thing to measure; suffice it to say that while a Rockefeller victory in California would have left the door partly open for Nixon and Scranton, it was still likely that Goldwater and White could soon have closed it again, or at the very least have dictated the terms on which another candidate walked through it.

XI

Goldwater's win in California removed the last real obstacle to his nomination. But many Republican moderates were unwilling—or unable—to accept that fact. The Cleveland governor's conference which convened a few days later thus became a showcase for their futility—and one of the most humiliating moments in the history of the Republican left. First Scranton prepared to launch a last-ditch candidacy, retreating suddenly, however, when General Eisenhower withdrew the support which Scranton thought he had pledged. Romney went through a similar dance, claiming that Nixon had tried to lure him into the race. ("George, you're six months late," said Oregon's Mark Hatfield.) Nixon, still hoping to be the compromise candidate, went so far as to suggest that "it would be a tragedy if Senator Goldwater's views as previously stated were not challenged and repudiated." The statement brought from Goldwater the observation that Richard Nixon sounds "more and more like Harold Stassen every day."

In sharp contrast to the way in which moderate governors in Houston in 1952 had rallied behind the Fair Play Rule which opened the doors to Eisenhower's nomination, the Republican governors at Cleveland, in Robert Donovan's words, were "reduced to a gaggle of Micawbers waiting for something to turn up." The rules of the political game had changed between 1952 and 1964. The fact that most of the Republican governors opposed the Goldwater candidacy no longer made any difference. Nor, for that matter, did the opposition of the party rank and file—who went two to one for Scranton in pre-convention polls. While the attention of the nation had been focused on leaders, polls and primaries, the work of picking the next Republican presidential candidate had been going on in the living rooms, church basements and school houses of the non-primary states. It was only at Cleveland that the party fully came to realize that fact. In Theodore White's words: "Like the Kerensky government, they were unaware of revolution until the Red Guards were already ringing the Winter Palace."

It was partly to redeem the humiliation of Cleveland that William Scranton decided in mid-June to make a last-ditch campaign for the presidential nomination.

Motivated, too, by Goldwater's vote against the civil rights bill—which also jolted Richard Nixon and almost reawakened his candidacy—Scranton launched out on what was essentially a moral crusade, bearing witness to what he called "the traditional principles of the party," and giving Republicans "a choice." But the choice had already been made.

So it was that Barry Goldwater, having failed to grasp firmly the brass ring of Republican leadership when he first touched it in 1963, seized it the second time around. In the meantime, however, much had changed with Goldwater and Goldwaterism. No longer the popular favorite of rank and file Republicans, he now owed his nomination to the power of an ideological crusade. Embittered by the coolness of the party professionals and especially by the recalcitrance of his moderate friends even after California, Goldwater drew more and more into his own coterie of highly dogmatic and politically inexperienced associates. He came to rely almost exclusively on an "Arizona Mafia," led by Denison Kitchel, and on a small group of intellectuals headed by William Baroody of the American Enterprise Institute.

Goldwater's isolation was accelerated by the continuing polarization which occurred at the San Francisco convention. A public letter, one which bore Governor Scranton's name but not his approval, helped to trigger the process with its charge that "Goldwaterism has come to stand for a whole crazy-quilt collection of absurd and dangerous positions that would be soundly repudiated by the American people in November." The booing of Governor Rockefeller as he rose to speak on the subject of extremism, though much of it came from the galleries, further widened the gap. The implacable resistance of the Goldwaterites to any compromise in the platform (though Goldwater later said he would have accepted Governor Romney's suggestions concerning extremism had he read them at the time) seemed to confirm the worst suspicions of the moderates. Many moderates felt that when Goldwater selected party chairman and New York Congressman William E. Miller as his running mate (with the explanation that "he gives Lyndon fits") and when he named his Arizona friend, Dean Burch, as the new National Chairman, he was deliberately rubbing salt in their gaping wounds.

But the last straw for Republicans like Governor Rockefeller, who had still intended to support the ticket, came with Goldwater's acceptance speech. Rather than inviting the vanquished moderates back into the party he seemed to read them out:

> Anyone who joins in all sincerity we welcome. Those who do not care for our cause we do not expect to enter our ranks in any case. And let our Republicanism, so focused and dedicated, not be made fuzzy and futile by unthinking and stupid labels. I would remind you that extremism in the defense of liberty is no vice. Moderation in the pursuit of justice is no virtue.

Properly interpreted and in their proper context, these words may well have been unexceptional. But Professor Harry Jaffa, who originally included the lines in a private memorandum, had never intended their use in this particular speech. White and his Draft Goldwater crew were stunned when they heard the words; they regarded the speech as a "betrayal" of all they had been working for.

If Goldwater had any chance to be accepted as the legitimate leader of a unified party before San Francisco, that chance effectively ended at the convention. In the following weeks—despite a "unity" meeting at Hershey, Pennsylvania—intraparty bitterness did not substantially decline. Having fought so long and so passionately against "me-too" Republicans, it was difficult for the conservatives now to suddenly embrace them as allies.

Many moderates returned the feeling. As the Fall wore on, many GOP candidates avoided Goldwater as a matter of self preservation. The *New York Herald Tribune* opposed a Republican presidential candidate for the first time since 1872. On election day, millions of Republicans cast their first Democratic presidential ballots ever; the 1964 election dealt yet another sharp blow to the party discipline at the ballot box.

Just as the chance for Republican reconciliation was missed in San Francisco, so Goldwater failed to rehabilitate his image with the national electorate during the Fall campaign. Forty-nine percent of the respondents in one post-convention poll said they knew "very little" about the senator from Arizona—but the chance to educate and convert them was missed. "My God," said one Goldwater lieutenant at the end of the San Francisco convention, "he's going to run as Barry Goldwater." And so he did. But it was not the candid, personable, sensible-sounding Goldwater of the late 1950's and early 1960's who emerged in the Fall campaign. Rather, it was Goldwater of the New Hampshire primary—irritable, defensive, and highly erratic—who came before the electorate during the Fall. He suggested the sale of TVA in Tennessee, attacked the poverty bill in Appalachia, and condemned Medicare in St. Petersburg. Rightly or wrongly, he was perceived as a man who would end social security, oppose the United Nations, defoliate the jungles of Vietnam, and stop progress toward civil rights. He was also portrayed as one who would be careless in the use of nuclear weapons. Some sixty percent of the voters in a pre-election survey said they feared that Goldwater would "shoot from the hip."

The radical caricature which haunted Goldwater throughout the Fall was built on the most careless of his past statements and embellished by the most strident criticisms of Rockefeller, Scranton and Nixon from the previous Summer and Spring. The Democrats fully exploited the caricature; by mid-campaign, fully forty-six percent of poll respondents said they considered Goldwater "an extremist—a radical." Constructive proposals such as his five year program of tax cuts, his revenue sharing suggestions and his draft reform recommendations were scarcely even heard. There were ample grounds for conservative complaints after the election that their true philosophy never had a real test.

Many in the Goldwater high command seemed to care more about the purity of the campaign than about its effectiveness. The Arizona Mafia, which had been working to limit Clif White's influence since the previous Winter, banished him and most of his people to second line campaign posts. Professionals like Ray Bliss were virtually frozen out. At the National Committee, long time loyalists were fired. Even Richard Nixon, who campaigned in thirty-six states for Goldwater, was treated with immense suspicion by many on the candidate's staff. The most effective single moment of the campaign, Ronald Reagan's half hour television speech called "A Time for Choosing," was aired only when Goldwater personally overruled his top assistants. Goldwater did not give a single campaign press conference and reporters were barred from the National Committee headquarters. As Theodore White concluded: "No man ever began a presidential effort . . . suffering more unsurmountable handicaps. And . . . he made the worst of them."

XII

The election results of 1964 seemed to demonstrate Thomas Dewey's prediction about what would happen if the parties were realigned on an ideological basis: "The Democrats would win every election and the Republicans would lose every election." Among virtually every voting bloc in every section of the country and at all levels of government, the Republicans were badly hurt. It almost seemed as though voters singled out for defeat candidates at lower levels whom they could associate with Goldwaterism.

Goldwater's decision to seek the presidency had been based on the assumption that he could win at least forty-five percent of the vote, and thus leave the conservative movement with a reasonable base for future building. His final percentage, however, was only 38.5 percent. The "hidden" conservative vote did not emerge. Goldwater carried only five deep southern states plus Arizona; in thirty-six of the forty-four states he lost he did not gain even forty-five percent of the vote. In addition to the sixty congressional districts he carried in the South, he won only sixteen others—six in southern California, five in the suburban Chicago area, and one each in Arizona, Kentucky, Idaho, Nebraska and Oklahoma. (Nixon had carried 228 congressional districts to Kennedy's 206). Despite the number of Democrats who had won in traditionally Republican states six years earlier, the party suffered a net loss of two Senate seats, reducing their total to thirty-two, the lowest level since the early 1940's. With the loss of thirty-eight House seats, GOP strength fell to 140, the lowest level since the defeat of 1936. Of the fifty-four Republican congressmen who declared in June, 1964, that Goldwater's candidacy would increase Republican strength in the House and Senate, seventeen were defeated, three who retired saw their districts go Democratic, and only seven—four of them southerners—ran stronger than in 1962. Of the twenty-one Republicans who joined Goldwater in opposing the 1964 Civil Rights Act, eleven were defeated.

The party showed a net increase of one governorship, but gains in state legislatures which had been mounting since 1958 were wiped out. Republicans lost ninety seats in the upper chambers of state legislatures and some 450 lower house seats, reducing their share of state legislative seats from the 39.9 percent level after the 1962 election to 33.2 percent. They lost control of both houses of the legislature in six states, losing fourteen lower houses and seven upper houses overall. In New York, Democrats controlled both houses of the legislature for the first time since 1935. In staunchly Republican Maine, a twenty-nine to five edge for the Republicans in the state Senate was turned into a twenty-nine to five edge for the Democrats. One Maine Republican explained that she and her friends wanted to "wipe out the entire slate so we can start fresh the next time." What about the three crucial constituencies which Republicans had identified in the 1950's?

The promise of gains in the South had been the heart of the Goldwater electoral strategy. But Goldwater merely traded Eisenhower-Nixon strength in peripheral southern states for the electoral votes of the deep South. His overall vote in the South was actually down one percent from Nixon's showing, as gains among rural southerners were offset by the losses in the cities and among blacks. Goldwater also lost Republican mountain areas in the South that had not gone Democratic since the Civil War.

The loss of southern Negro votes was especially damaging. Nationally, Republican support among non-whites dropped from Nixon's thirty-two percent to only six percent; in the South, where nearly twice as many Negroes were qualified to vote in 1964 as in 1960, the black vote tipped several states to Johnson. In Pine Bluff, Arkansas, 97.8 percent of the black vote went to President Johnson while 88.5 percent went to the Republican candidate for governor, Winthrop Rockefeller—a reminder of the support Republicans had once enjoyed among southern blacks. Analysts also pointed to the fact that most of Goldwater's gains over Nixon's showing came in areas where Negroes comprised a majority of the population but were not eligible to vote.

In big cities, the Republican vote fell from thirty-eight to twenty-six percent in the North and from forty-eight to thirty-nine percent in the West. Goldwater made a slight gain among Catholic voters, winning twenty-four percent as compared to Nixon's twenty-two percent in 1960. But this showing was still only half of what Eisenhower had achieved in 1956 and was largely explained by the fact that the Democratic ticket was once again headed by a Protestant.

As for suburbia, the Democratic beachheads of 1960 were enormously expanded in 1964. In suburban areas around the twelve largest cities, where the GOP had polled sixty-one, sixty-three, and fifty-two percent in the last three presidential races, the Goldwater showing was only forty percent—a lower level even than that of 1936. Many middle class suburban areas went Democratic for the first time in the century. The Republican share of the college-educated, professional and business, and white collar vote—which had fallen about ten percent between 1956 and 1960 fell another ten percent in 1964.

At the same time, the Republicans lost the farm belt for the first time since World War II. Many of Goldwater's sharpest losses came in the small town middlewestern areas which had once been solid for Taft. In Iowa, the Democrats won 101 of 124 lower house seats and 35 of 50 Senate seats to take control of both bodies. They also swept all of Iowa's state offices and displaced incumbent Republicans in five of the state's six congressional districts. Johnson carried ninety-three of Iowa's ninety-nine counties, the same number Nixon carried in 1960. He carried Vermont, a state which had never gone Democratic, by almost two to one. In William Miller's home congressional district, the Goldwater-Miller ticket received less than one-third of the vote.

The Democratic bid to become the party of national consensus—a design well symbolized by their 1964 convention slogan: "One nation, one party"—was significantly advanced in November. Yet amid prophecies of doom for the GOP, there were some slight reasons for encouragement. Voters again split their ballots in unprecedented numbers. The fact that voter participation was down in thirty-six states compared to 1960 was a hint of President Johnson's potential vulnerability. A Minnesota housewife spoke for many voters when she sighed just before the election: "Can't I vote no?"

In the wake of the 1964 defeat, many conservative Republicans would rally around the slogan "Twenty-seven million Americans can't be wrong." The Goldwater vote, they contended, was a substantial conservative base. But just how conservative was it? Louis Harris concluded that only six million of the twenty-seven million could be considered hard core Goldwater supporters, that some eighteen million were simply party loyalists and that some three million had been motivated mainly by the issue of race. A majority of Goldwater voters told Harris they were moderates or liberals and that they opposed a right-wing takeover of the party. A *New York Times* survey showed that some three-fifths of Goldwater voters felt the candidate should be replaced as the party leader. Louis Bean and Roscoe Drummond reported in *Look* Magazine that the "pure" Goldwater vote was no more than three million. In answer to Gallup's question as to who was the most representative Republican, fifteen percent of those who voted Republican in 1964 mentioned Goldwater and eighty-five percent mentioned Nixon and even more liberal figures.

XIII

The Goldwater people regarded 1964 not as the end of the road but as the beginning. Their fundraising successes, coupled with the decision to cut spending in the campaign's final hopeless days, had even produced a surplus in the treasury of the party—whose machinery they still controlled. As for conservative citizen groups, just three weeks after the election, a front page headline in the *New York Times* announced that the "Rightists" had been "buoyed by the elections" and were opening "new drives." Twenty-seven million Americans could not be wrong.

Some conservatives even thought about another Goldwater race, and their spirits were lifted when the Arizonan's presidential poll ratings went from eleven percent to nineteen percent during the Spring of 1965. Goldwater himself was more realistic—and increasingly preoccupied with winning back his Senate seat. Moreover, as Goldwater found himself and conservative Senate colleagues like Milton Young, Karl Mundt, and John Tower as well, fighting off pockets of John Birch Society resistance in their own bailiwicks, his taste for crusaders faded and his regular Republican instincts came to the fore. He slowly began to detach himself from the movement which had created his candidacy and turned instead toward the center of the party, grasping hands as he did so with Richard Nixon, who was simultaneously looking for support on the right. Meanwhile, many of those who had helped to launch Goldwater's candidacy four years before now began to talk of a new conservative hero for 1968, Ronald Reagan.

The first setback to the ambitions of the Goldwater-Reagan wing came in January, 1964, with the removal of Dean Burch as Republican National Chairman. His successor was the Ohio State party chairman, Ray C. Bliss, a Taft protégé under whose stewardship Ohio Republicans had won fifty-one of seventy-one statewide races, including three out of four presidential contests, since 1949. Bliss had experienced his most serious setbacks in 1958 and 1964 when right-wing diversions had undercut Republican strength and the experiences had deepened his natural distrust of dogma. After the 1964 convention, Bliss had been seen still sitting in the emptying Cow Palace, his head in his hands, bewildered that he had lost control of his delegation and worrying aloud that the Goldwater ticket would pull Robert Taft, Jr. to defeat in his Senate race.

For Bliss, the key to successful politics—as he would say almost hourly for the next four years—was "nuts and bolts"—and the money to pay for them. He organized seminars in electronic data processing, in public relations techniques, and in the methods of campaign management. The fact that the candidates had to take positions on the issues was a necessary evil that Bliss was willing to live with—but he steadfastly refused to take any such positions himself. "I'll work as hard for Jack Javits as for Strom Thurmond," he said, and he meant it.

The Bliss approach matched the mood of many rank and file Republicans. It suited quite exactly the requirements of the shaken party regulars, including the congressional leaders, whose passionate desire was for tranquillity and peace. In their view, the party desperately needed a respite from factional pressures of any variety—a suspension of all intraparty debate. The best expression of their mood was the 11th Commandment of California State Chairman Gaylord Parkinson: "Thou shalt not speak ill of any other Republican." (The National Committee actually adopted the 11th Commandment as an informal resolution just before the convention in 1968.)

The call of the party leaders, then, was *not* for compromise and negotiation but for the healing powers of silence. What they sought was essentially a ceasefire in place.

One other important shift in party leadership occurred in early 1965, but it had even less significance than the Bliss takeover in terms of factional influence. Congressman Gerald Ford of Michigan, who had helped to lead Charles Halleck's ouster of Joseph Martin in 1959 and who had himself replaced Iowa's Congressman Hoeven as Chairman of the House Republican Conference in 1963, brought down Halleck as House Minority Leader in 1965 with support from a broad coalition of conservative and moderate young turks. The Ford-Halleck fight, however, was one of generations and styles, not one of philosophy. To be sure, Ford was much more ready than Halleck to talk about replacing southern Democrats with Republicans rather than viewing them as indispensable legislative allies. He was also anxious to reverse Halleck's essentially negative image by developing "constructive Republican alternative proposals"—a phrase which Democratic acronymists seized upon with glee. To further this end he set up a new Planning and Research Group under the leadership of New York Congressman Charles Goodell.

On the other hand, Ford lost his bid to replace the veteran Les Arends with the more liberal Peter Frelinghuysen as party whip. Throughout the next four years he shared large portions of his power with Melvin Laird, who replaced him as chairman of the House Republican Conference. One of the party's most skillful politicians, Laird had chaired the 1964 platform committee, though Nixon had vetoed him for that job in 1960 because he was too conservative. Ford readily confessed that if the Republicans should ever take control of the House, Laird would certainly challenge him for the speakership.

It was partly because of Laird's fear that the Republican governors would provide a powerful voice for progressive Republicanism after 1964 that Ray Bliss allowed a single exception to his issues moratorium. The National Committee set up a new Republican Coordinating Committee—in which representatives of the governors, along with the party's past presidential candidates and other high officials, would join with the congressional leaders in developing party positions. Potentially, the group was the counterpart of the Democratic Advisory Council established by Paul Butler when his party was out of power in the late 1950's; more important for the moment, however, it provided a mechanism for ensuring that the reliable congressional leadership would call the party's ideological tune.

While party orthodoxy in 1965 and after called for a moratorium on ideology, the conservative movement retreated no further than a series of strategically placed base camps and waited for an opportunity to scale the mountain peak again. Most of the Goldwater true believers continued to believe deeply after 1964—and they regarded their baptism of fire that year as a training exercise for the future. The conservative network after 1964 included a number of public membership organizations such as Americans for Constitutional Action, which had been founded in 1959, Young Americans for Freedom, which dated from 1960, and the American Conservative Union and Free Society Association, which were established in 1965. The United Republicans of America beat the drums for conservative congressional candidates. On the intellectual front, *National Review* and the American Enterprise Institute continued to play their important roles. Publications such as *Human Events*, *Battle Line* and the *New Guard* also provided the communications links indispensable in building a strong sense of community across the land. With their own publishing houses, radio programs, book clubs and pooled mailing lists, the movement could sustain a sense of nationwide conservative purpose to which every lonely deed and donation could contribute.

In states like New York and later in Michigan and Massachusetts, where the GOP was controlled by progressives, conservatives organized third party movements. William Buckley's candidacy may have helped elect John Lindsay as the Republican mayor of New York in 1965 but it also helped to lay the groundwork for his brother's election to the Senate on the Conservative ticket five years later.

Within the party, Goldwater Republicans continued to hold critical places in the congressional leadership. By 1967, both the House and Senate Campaign Committees and the party's women's auxiliary were led by California conservatives.

The right also continued to rule the Young Republicans through the so-called "Syndicate" of "old friends" which had spearheaded the Draft Goldwater effort. Clif White's executive assistant in that effort soon became the president of the National Young Republicans, virtually a party within a party. Young Republican autonomy was so strong that Ray Bliss and a unanimous Republican National Committee were rebuffed when they attempted in 1967 to make the group more accountable to the senior party, which provided most of its funds.

Meanwhile, most moderates in the party were still heavily influenced by an instinctive aversion to political combat. They simply had little taste for the day in, day out, year in, year out fight to control at the grassroots. Many of their leaders, despite the lesson of 1964, still found it easier to trust in the "kingmaker" myth. There was virtually no attempt to duplicate the careful efforts of Thomas E. Dewey and Herbert Brownell to build an effective political network all across the country. An important symbol of what changed in progressive Republicanism between the 1940's and the 1960's was the fact that Dewey's roots—like those of the Republican party—were firmly planted in the small town Middle West. There he had been born and raised and educated, and there his family had remained. Though he avidly pursued the considerable power that resided in Manhattan, he never overestimated its unilateral impact in a highly diversified nation.

Dewey's successor as a builder of effective Republican coalitions in the 1960's was not the able patrician son of America's wealthiest family who succeeded him as the Republican governor of New York. Despite George Hinman's efforts in 1961 and 1962, Rockefeller's organizational talents were rarely exercised beyond the borders of New York State. When non-New Yorkers came to him with projects designed to advance his interests, they seldom got to first base. Dewey's role was played instead by two other small town boys—both of whom were Dewey protégés, Richard Nixon and F. Clifton White.

The problem with most moderates in the 1960's was essentially their moderation; they were balanced and sensible, in style as well as substance, and reluctant to enlist in great crusades. Like Eisenhower, they were proud of their "amateur" status. They continued to talk of citizen politics—which meant part-time politics for most of them. Few committed their whole lives to politics, as did Richard Nixon, for example. Most continued to underrate the power of the right, rationalizing away their 1964 experience by attributing it to "accidents," like Rockefeller's remarriage. Cool and technocratic, most moderates distrusted dogma and built their politics instead around highly attractive personalities. With little sense of common purpose or strategy or tactics, the moderate wing was a very loose and sometimes jealous coalition of highly independent elements.

In terms of rank and file strength, the moderates had a great deal to draw upon. Mid 1960 polls showed that a majority of Republicans supported moderate, Eisenhower-style positions on issues such as support for the United Nations, social security, foreign aid, reciprocal trade, aid to education, co-existence with the Russians, and arms reduction. In fact, the Republican rank and file took more progressive positions than did most Democrats on controversial issues such as Vietnam and civil rights. But while moderates could win elections and dominate the media, conservatives now controlled the presidential nominating machinery.

The conservative "base camp" organizations did have their counterparts on the GOP left in the wake of 1964. A Council of Republican Organizations was even organized as an umbrella group for a number of them, including Republicans for Progress, the Republican Citizens Committee, the Ripon Society, the National Council of Republican Workshops, the National Negro Republican Assembly, and other, more locally-oriented groups. But their size and influence were limited. By one estimate, conservative citizen organizations were spending about $1 million a year in 1967 compared to only $150,000 a year for all the moderate groups. By 1968, many of these moderate organizations had faded from the scene, and by 1970, for the first time in more than a decade, there was not even a common fund-raising effort for moderate GOP candidates. Except for the *Ripon Forum*, a monthly publication with very limited circulation, there was no effective communications link on the Republican left. A magazine called *Advance* attempted the role in the early 1960's but could not raise sufficient finances. The *New York Herald Tribune* stopped publishing in 1966.

Among officeholders, there was even less interest in organizing an effective counterforce to Goldwaterism. In 1963, a small group of progressive congressmen organized the Wednesday Group, which worked effectively to influence civil rights legislation in 1964. But the Wednesday Group was generally too small and its members too junior to have a continuing impact. On the one occasion where a close division among House Republicans might have given the Wednesdays the balance of power, Gerald Ford's challenge to Minority Leader Charles Halleck in 1965, the group was immobilized by internal divisions.

The Republican officeholders with the greatest potential for progressive influence after 1964 were the governors, who had been so important in 1952 and had remained a strong bastion of Eisenhower support throughout the 1950's. In the early 1960's, the governors discovered that their cohesion on civil rights matters gave them a perfect opportunity to embarrass the highly divided Democrats at national Governors Conferences, and in 1963 they formally organized the Republican Governors Association as a means for translating their cohesion into a position of greater influence within the party. Their chairman, Idaho's Governor Robert Smylie, described the new group as "a third major force" along with the National Committee and the congressional leadership in directing the party's affairs.

The "third force" prospect, however, was not warmly welcomed by either of the first two major forces—and many conservatives looked upon it with absolute horror. National Chairman William Miller issued a strong request that the group's congressional relations and financial activities be handled through his office. The governors acquiesced. Geographically scattered, preoccupied with state affairs, and with virtually no collective staff, the governors accomplished little in 1964 beyond securing the keynote speaker slot at the San Francisco convention for one of their colleagues, Mark Hatfield of Oregon. The governors led the effective assault on Dean Burch in the weeks following the 1964 election, and their association began to speak more frequently on issues in 1965 and 1966. But the potential of the Association was never realized. Goldwater attacked it as a divisive "splinter group" and there was evidence that Chairman Bliss agreed.

Ray Bliss consistently opposed the array of "splinter" organizations on the right and the left of the party. Not only did they threaten the return of ideological debate, but they also competed for funds with his hard-pressed treasury. A former chairman, Hugh Scott, responded by distinguishing the explicitly non-partisan organizations (mostly on the right) which hinted now and then of developing into conservative third parties from those groups (mostly on the left) which worked to convert independents and Democrats to the Republican cause. With only twenty-five percent of the electorate identifying themselves as Republicans, Scott argued, unity and harmony were not sufficient Republican virtues. A unified minority was still a minority. But Bliss remained convinced that the first priority for the party's shattered nerves was a prolonged rest cure.

For Bliss, the ultimate test of his leadership would come at the polls—and the test was passed with flying colors. In 1965, urban victories by John Lindsay in New York and Arlen Spector in Philadelphia along with the strong gubernatorial showing of the moderate Virginian, Linwood Holton, began to lift at least some Republican spirits, though the party suffered a shattering setback in New Jersey. And one year later, the Republicans staged a comeback impressive both in its depth and in its diversity. Election day, 1966, was the brightest for the GOP since 1952. "It's a very lively elephant" declared Ray Bliss. "Once again," said the Ripon Society, "it's fun to be a Republican."

GOP victories in 1966 came at all levels of government, in all parts of the country, and—most notably—with candidates of all ideological varieties. While the conservative Republicans cheered Ronald Reagan's election as governor of California, moderates pointed out that Nixon's progressive protégé, Robert Finch, ran 100,000 votes ahead of Reagan in winning the lieutenant governorship. While moderates cheered the Senate victories of Mark Hatfield, Charles Percy and Ed Brooke—the first Negro senator since Reconstruction, conservatives pointed to the strong southern showings of John Tower and Strom Thurmond and Howard Baker. In all, the number of Republican senators jumped from thirty-three to thirty-six, while Republican strength in the House of Representatives increased by forty-seven. Of the 180 Republicans in the new House of Representatives, only 89 had been there before the 1962 election.

At the same time, the number of Republican governors jumped from seventeen to twenty-five and the GOP share of state legislative seats increased from 33.2 to 41.1 percent. Gubernatorial victories included Maryland's Spiro T. Agnew, who carried ninety-four percent of the Negro vote. Governors Rockefeller, Romney, Chafee and John Volpe of Massachusetts all were elected to their *third* terms, despite the fact that rising taxes had created an extraordinarily high rate of gubernatorial mortality in the 1960's.

The era of live and let live allowed a thousand flowers to bloom in 1965 and 1966 and on election day the party was able to offer "something for everyone." Some commentators, looking for a common theme in the various Republican successes, spoke of the youth and physical attractiveness of the winners. Others emphasized their pragmatic, problem-solving approach, contrasting it with the dogmatism of Goldwater. (That dogmatism was still strong enough in some quarters, however, to make words like "pragmatic" and "problem-solving" synonyms for left-wing Republicanism.) When Stephen Hess and David S. Broder wrote their thoroughgoing study of *The Republican Establishment* in 1967, they began and ended the book with a quotation from a man they considered the quintessential Republican victor of 1966, Washington's Governor Daniel Evans, a young attractive, pragmatic engineer. "What 1966 has given us," said Evans, "is the luxury of choice." Indeed it had. Hess and Broder were able to list more than fifteen plausible dark horse candidates for president and vice president. But the luxury of choice did not obviate the necessity to choose.

In his own discussion of the victory, a jubilant Ray Bliss spoke of the "teamwork and dedicated effort" of the "candidates and party leaders of every level, the precinct workers, financial contributors, and the many thousands of volunteers. . . ." It was, in short, a victory for nuts and bolts—a victory for professionalism. It was also—it must be emphasized—a victory over a Democratic party badly damaged by the growing unpopularity of President Johnson and the Vietnam War. In 1967, even the successful Republican candidate for governor of Kentucky used the slogan, "Tired of War? Vote Nunn." As 1968 approached, the question was whether the same electorate which had used the Republican party so enthusiastically to check Johnson in 1966 would also use it to replace him.

XIV

In the wake of the 1966 election, the heavy favorite for the next presidential nomination was George Romney. Polls taken just after the election showed him leading President Johnson fifty-four percent to forty-six percent—while Nixon, Rockefeller and Percy all trailed Johnson by the same margin and Reagan received only thirty-three percent to Johnson's sixty-seven percent. Romney continued to hold his lead into the following year. At this stage Richard Nixon calculated that Romney was an even money bet to win the nomination, while Percy and Nixon himself were two to one shots and the odds on Reagan were four to one. Rockefeller, Nixon said, had no chance of being nominated—a prospect he had helped to reinforce just after the 1964 elections with a blistering attack on the governor for failing to support Goldwater. Romney, despite Barry Goldwater's comment that "I cannot forgive him" for his 1964 apostasy, had a far more moderate image.

The nascent Romney campaign did all it could to portray Romney as the heir not of Rockefeller and Dewey but of Nixon and Eisenhower. A devout Mormon, Romney had originally come into the Michigan political scene as a citizen advocate of constitutional reform. He had been so pleased by his experiences with Citizens for Michigan that he contemplated the formation of a Citizens for America organization which would develop new political programs and sell them to the regular parties. Like Eisenhower, Romney's appeal grew out of his ability to rise above partisanship; he largely shunned the Republican label in his first campaign in 1962. "One Eisenhower in a generation is enough," Barry Goldwater once said of Romney—and in this case he spoke not only for conservative Republicans but for many of the party's professionals. Melvin Laird seemed to cut to the heart of the weakness Romney shared with Eisenhower when he insisted that the governor demonstrate his ability to carry an entire slate of GOP candidates to victory in 1966 before he could legitimately aspire to national party leadership. To Laird's surprise (and perhaps to Romney's as well) the governor passed the test, pulling in Senator Robert Griffin and five new GOP congressmen and leading the party to control of the State legislature.

Rockefeller, sensitive to the charge that his personal vulnerability had torpedoed the moderate cause in 1964, now removed himself entirely from the presidential competition and gave his complete support to Romney. "I am not, will not, and under no circumstances will be a candidate again," he declared after the 1966 election. But he could not entirely eliminate the suspicion that Romney was his stalking horse, and the suspicion inevitably damaged Romney's candidacy.

As he looked back on 1964, Rockefeller recalled most vividly the failure of other moderates to support him in New Hampshire and California and concluded that the party's anti-Goldwater majority had simply failed to focus its energies. Determined to avoid the same mistake in 1968, he took it upon himself to rally Republican progressives around the Romney candidacy—actively discouraging other potential candidates such as Charles Percy, whom Nixon regarded as potentially his toughest rival. Trial balloons for General James Gavin, Mark Hatfield, Thruston Morton and others also failed to rise. "If Romney fails," all were told, "then you can make your case. But we don't want to find your fingerprints on the body."

Nelson Rockefeller's "non-proliferation treaty" was highly effective; moderate aspirants learned to wait in line rather than compete for public favor. But in his anxiety to avoid the mistakes of 1964, Rockefeller may well have repeated the greatest error. For what plagued the moderates in the fight against Goldwater was not so much the proliferation of candidates late in the campaign as the failure of candidates to proliferate early. When the leading candidate was wounded in 1963, there was no one else to take his place—and the same thing happened in 1967. As in 1964, the moderate Republicans put all their eggs in one basket and as in the previous quadrennium they had no contingency plan when the bottom fell out of the basket.

While Nixon was taking a highly strategic vacation from politics through much of 1967, Romney was forced to prepare himself for the presidential race in the bright spotlight which inevitably follows the front runner. He was subjected to an intense and sometimes cruel grilling by a national press corps which fundamentally distrusted his fervent evangelical style. He was unable to quiet widespread doubts about his depth and experience—especially in foreign policy. Early in 1967, Romney remarked before a press conference in Pocatello, Idaho on the "political expedience" of President Johnson's policies in Vietnam and elsewhere. But he refused to elaborate on the comments, holding adamantly to his position that he would not go into the Vietnam issue in any detail until he had given the matter further study. The incident, repeatedly revived by the press, marked the beginning of the end for Romney. The governor himself joked at a fund raising dinner that Spring that success in politics meant "blood, sweat, and avoiding press conferences." Nixon could avoid press conferences in 1967, but Romney, the front runner, could not.

Every day of Romney silence on the nation's number one issue further corroded his foundation of public trust. When he finally delivered a long-awaited and highly sophisticated speech on Vietnam in Hartford in April, the White House cleverly thanked him for his support and effectively blunted its impact. The beneficial effects of the speech were also limited by its sheer complexity and its clearly collective origins. (Rockefeller had even sent his foreign policy consultant, Henry Kissinger, to consult with Romney on Vietnam.) When the press and the public learned over the Labor Day weekend in 1967 of Romney's comment that he had been "brainwashed" by the government on Vietnam, they were already highly suspicious of the governor's competence in foreign policy. The innocent brainwashing remark, which would probably have gone unnoticed had most other candidates uttered it, was seized upon as final proof of their suspicions. It was circulated over the following weeks not so much as direct evidence of Romney's shortcomings but as the shorthand symbol for months of accumulated misgivings.

Romney's brainwashing interview was the 1967 equivalent of Rockefeller's remarriage in 1963. Both candidates were vulnerable before the event—and virtually hopeless afterward. In the days immediately following the comment, Romney dropped sixteen points in the Harris Poll. In October, 1967, the party rank and file—who preferred the Michigan governor early in the year—now came down forty-two percent for Nixon, eighteen percent for Rockefeller, fourteen percent for Reagan and thirteen percent for Romney. Though Romney drove doggedly on, many of his supporters began to look elsewhere.

Some went to Nixon, joining progressive leaders like the Kansas congressman and Wednesday Group member, Robert Ellsworth, who had been with Nixon from the start. Respectful of Nixon's proven abilities, many moderates were still confident that he was essentially a centrist. Other Romney supporters looked now to Rockefeller, whose intention to remain in the background was becoming far more difficult. Romney, meanwhile, plunged headlong into New Hampshire, hoping that his warm, whirlwind campaign style might still reverse his fortunes.

By late February, however, polls in New Hampshire showed Nixon with seventy-five percent and Romney with ten percent, while Rockefeller—whose name was not on the ballot—was at eight percent and rising. Even Romney's own polls showed him at nineteen percent to seventy-three percent for Nixon. With characteristic directness, the governor pulled out of the race. And so, for the third time in the decade, liberal Republican hopes seemed to ride with Nelson Rockefeller.

Or did they? On March 21, the day he was expected to announce his candidacy, Rockefeller surprised the nation by declaring that he was not an "active" candidate. But what did Rockefeller mean by his statement and why did he make it? Many observers suggested that the governor, having twice braved hostile fire in the service of progressive Republicans, was simply not ready to move out again without the assurance of considerable support. When that support did not emerge rapidly enough after Romney's pullout, they said, Rockefeller decided that he should make his followers come to him.

Other considerations may also have been important. For one thing, the Rockefeller forces, not foreseeing Nixon's spectacular southern successes, anticipated a deadlocked convention. There seemed no reason to hurry. The announcement also allowed Rockefeller to avoid a primary showdown with Nixon in Nebraska, where he was almost certain to lose, though it precluded a race in Oregon. But even in Oregon, his chances were only estimated at fifty-fifty and, with most of the other remaining primaries preempted by favorite sons, it was easy to conclude that in 1968, as in 1964, the primaries would be relatively unimportant.

Nevertheless, in ways he may not have anticipated, the March 21 declaration was costly to Rockefeller. Its very abruptness turned off many of his supporters—including Governor Agnew who had assembled reporters to watch the sprouting of seeds he planted as head of the Draft Rockefeller effort. No one told Agnew that the seeds would not sprout on March 21. "The most important telephone call never made" thus started the irritated governor down a new road which led eventually to the vice presidency. Many moderates mistakenly read into Rockefeller's announcement a final rejection of any candidacy. Determined to stop Reagan at all costs and anxious to be with the eventual winner as early as possible, they scampered now to board the Nixon bandwagon.

The March 21 decision helped Nixon in another way as well, for it ended any chance of a setback at the polls, the place where he felt himself most vulnerable. Strong with party leaders, but weaker with the public, Nixon managed to win renomination in 1968 without facing even a single open test in any primary state by any major candidate. The most telling strength of the progressive Republicans, their ability to win elections, was never used at all during the 1968 primary season. Nixon had said he would pull out of the race if he lost in New Hampshire and Wisconsin. But as one observer noted, "He didn't even work up a sweat," as he won every primary he entered.

In many ways, Rockefeller in 1968 was in the same position Nixon held in 1964; his best chance depended on finding someone else to stop the front runner. But there was one major difference. In 1964 Nixon could hope that a candidate on the left would block the front runner on the right so that he could emerge as a middle ground compromise. In 1968, however, the front runner was in the middle. The sacrificial blocking move would therefore have to come from one flank or the other—and it seemed likely that Nixon's supporters would then swing to whichever alternate candidate had *not* been the spoiler. This meant, of course, that it was in Rockefeller's interest to have the conservative leader, Governor Reagan, lead a stop-Nixon movement and vice versa. The result was a period of watchful waiting to see who, as William Rusher put it, would be the first to "chicken in."

It was Rockefeller who moved first. Just six weeks after quitting the race he joined it again on April 30, and was rewarded that very day with an upset write-in victory over the favorite son, John Volpe, in the Massachusetts primary.

The period between March 21 and April 30 had been an extraordinary time in the nation's history. First Lyndon Johnson, under growing pressure from Eugene McCarthy and Robert Kennedy, announced he would not stand for re-election. Then the assassination of Dr. Martin Luther King threw the nation into turmoil.

The sense of crisis which followed King's assassination, rising pressure from a new Draft Rockefeller movement, and a growing realization that the convention would not be deadlocked unless somebody moved to deadlock it, all helped produce

Rockefeller's April 30 turnaround. But the Rockefeller candidacy did not begin to stir an emotional response until June, after Robert Kennedy's assassination. For nearly ten years, one of Rockefeller's great political strengths was that he seemed to be a Republican answer to the Kennedys. Now, with the second Kennedy tragically gunned down, millions of shaken Americans in both parties looked to Rockefeller as the one leader who could lift the fallen torch and calm the nation's fevers.

Rockefeller's strategy now sought to maximize this asset. This meant directing his campaign to a liberal national constituency rather than to the more conservative party regulars. Hopefully, the awakening of this national constituency would have a dramatic impact on his standing in public opinion polls and these polls, in turn, would have a powerful impact on the party. The strategy paralleled that which Romney had pursued in 1967 when his slogan had been: "Winning is the name of the game." But as it had for Romney, the public opinion poll strategy eventually failed for Rockefeller.

Rockefeller supporters—including five recent GOP national chairmen (Scott, Hall, Alcorn, Morton and Miller)—knew the risks of the polling strategy. For one thing, it required the governor to launch an attack on Nixon, even while he was wooing Nixon delegates in an impressive series of private sessions. Some argued afterward that more attention to those delegates and less attention to the polls would have brought greater returns at the national convention. Only six percent of Rockefeller's budget was spent on delegate hunting, while the overwhelming share of campaign funds went for television advertising to boost the governor's public standing.

But even in the polls, Rockefeller began to have problems. His apparent springtime indecision hurt him; many shared Gary Wills' feeling that Rockefeller "was not only a late starter; he had developed a fascination with the starting gate, and kept circling through it as if it were a revolving door." At the same time, Nixon's image benefitted from his dignified walk through the uncontested primaries. Moreover, his familiarity and experience became an even greater asset as a deeply troubled nation recalled the relative tranquillity of the Eisenhower era. Like Romney, Rockefeller offered the party chiefly his popularity and like Romney, he was finally beaten by Nixon at his own game.

The former vice president, of course, had always been favored over Rockefeller by the party's rank and file. By July, 1968, he led Rockefeller by sixty to twenty-three percent among Republicans. His problem, like that of Hubert Humphrey, who was also the favorite of his party, was his standing with the general electorate. Then, just before the Republican National convention opened in Miami Beach, a Gallup poll showed Nixon doing better than Rockefeller among all voters against both Humphrey and McCarthy. Suddenly Rockefeller's strongest argument became an argument for Nixon. Even the subsequent release of a Harris poll which showed Rockefeller doing somewhat better could not put Humpty Dumpty together again. It was all the pollsters could do to rescue their own image as Gallup and Harris issued an unusual joint statement arguing that voter shifts between the times the polls were taken could account for their discrepancies. But the damage had been done. Now Rockefeller's only hope was Ronald Reagan.

XV

Reagan, an actor who had never run for public office, was the phoenix who rose from the ashes of the Goldwater defeat—and in the end he did not fall too far short of the 1968 nomination. That he was able to move so far so fast, while moderates were generally so defensive about their 1968 prospects, told a great deal about the strength and outlook of the party's factions.

To begin with, most moderates did not take Reagan seriously. Senator Thomas Kuchel, the only man who could have defeated Reagan in a primary election in 1965, decided to forego the race for the governorship of California. San Francisco Mayor George Christopher was no match for Reagan—especially after the Brown forces persuaded columnist Drew Pearson to revive a twenty-five year old smear involving Christopher's dairy company. (Christopher had been "arrested" when he lowered milk prices to test the constitutionality of a depression era price-pegging law.) Pearson later apologized for the story, but Christopher's poll ratings, which had been climbing until that point, fell eleven percent in one month and Reagan scored a two to one primary victory. Then, in a significant departure from Goldwater's 1964 pattern, he took pains to invite the Christopher people into a united and generally moderate campaign which won a smashing victory in November.

Like many of the conservative leaders, Reagan was a convert from liberalism. His reputation in the 1940's had been so left-wing, in fact, that Helen Gahagan Douglas refused to allow his name to appear on her literature when she ran for the Senate against Richard Nixon in 1950. By the 1960's, Reagan had become a firm conservative, whose political style, like that of Dwight Eisenhower, emphasized common sense approaches and his amateur "citizen" status.

The first Reagan for President banners had been unfurled at his victory party in Sacramento on election night in 1966. By December of that year, a Reagan aide, Tom Reed, had developed a careful week by week timetable for the governor which culminated in his nomination for the presidency in August, 1968. Early in 1967, the *Washington Post* carried the front page headline: "After a Spectacular Seven Weeks—Reagan Credited With Rising Presidential Hopes." That Summer he was the overwhelming presidential favorite at the Young Republican National convention—a significant fact since the favorite at such conventions had almost invariably gone on one year later to become the presidential nominee of the senior party. Barry Goldwater even said he would reconsider his support for Nixon if the California governor continued to climb and John Tower was forced to reject the possibility of becoming Nixon's campaign manager because of Reagan pressures in Texas. By 1968, when Clif White joined the Reagan team, the governor's timetable seemed to be very much in order. "It's like a prairie waiting for a match," said one observer in describing Reagan's national potential.

Reagan finally declared his candidacy as the national convention opened in 1968. But White did not hold all the cards he had once expected to hold as he climbed into his Miami Beach command post—a trailer marked "Suite 3505A." Nineteen hundred and sixty-eight would not be another 1964. For one thing, many conservatives were gunshy about another Goldwater-style debacle. For another, Reagan had created a great deal of controversy as governor, and, most important, Richard Nixon was back in the field.

XVI

Nixon's pursuit of the 1968 nomination began before the 1964 convention, when he finally accepted the inevitability of Goldwater. He used the San Francisco convention to build bridges to Goldwater Republicans—most importantly through his plea for party unity as he introduced Goldwater—and he used the Fall campaign that year to further advance the process. Traveling some 50,000 miles in thirty-six states, he was also able to reestablish his ties with the party's traditional leaders. He found that many who had griped most loudly about his mistakes in 1960 now looked back almost nostalgically on that campaign.

In 1965, Nixon campaigned in New Jersey and Virginia and in 1966 he traveled to thirty-five states and undertook a series of critical fund raising missions for Republican candidates. The net effect of all these efforts was that he once again became the party's titular leader. In a sense, he took this role back by default; there was no one else to claim it. Goldwater had never been accepted as the legitimate leader of the entire party, and Nixon simply reassumed a role in 1966 which had been his until his defeat in California.

The restoration was completed when President Johnson lashed out bitterly against Nixon's criticisms of the recent Manila Conference on Vietnam at the end of the 1966 campaign. The Republican Congressional Campaign Committee purchased time for Nixon, speaking now on behalf of all GOP congressional candidates, to answer the attack. Until Ray Bliss objected that Nixon possessed no unique standing to speak for the entire party, plans were also underway to have the National Committee sponsor an election-eve telecast which would combine films of Johnson's emotional outburst with Nixon's cool response. (The identical plan was used by the Democrats four years later when Senator Edmund Muskie's quiet response to President Nixon established him for a moment as the chief spokesman for his party.)

As he began campaigning for himself again after the moratorium of 1967, Nixon capitalized on the fact that he was virtually the only figure in the party acceptable to all its factions—the only person still in a position to reestablish an Eisenhower-style compromise. "The center must lead," he declared in one discussion of the party's future and when asked where he would place himself within the party spectrum, he answered: "I am perhaps at dead center." His frequent journeys abroad also burnished his image with the centrists. To pragmatic politicians who admired expertise, Nixon appeared to be the quintessential expert, especially when compared to the proud and defiant amateurs, Romney and Reagan.

Nixon's conservative credentials were also strong, however. The same Nixon who wrote a sophisticated treatise on "Asia after Vietnam" for *Foreign Affairs* magazine later in 1967 was simultaneously represented by a hardline law and order article in the *Reader's Digest*. "They don't like me, but they tolerate me," he once said of the Goldwater Republicans. Appreciating the indispensability of their support, he worked to encourage their toleration. He spoke of the need to make "responsible conservatism respectable again" and he joked during a 1966 visit in Birmingham, Alabama, that he had shaken more hands on the right side of the aisle than on the left. "It is hard for me to turn left," he said.

Nixon's attention to the conservatives paid sizable dividends, especially among those whose dogmatism had been tempered by the bitter experiences of 1964. Early in 1965, Goldwater himself described Nixon to the faithful as the man "who worked harder than any one person for the ticket. Dick," he said, "I'll never forget it. I know that you did it in the interest of the Republican party and not for any selfish reasons. But if there ever comes a time I can turn those into selfish reasons, I am going to do all I can to see that it comes about." Many Goldwaterites across the country followed their leader's example over the next three years. Among them were a group of leaders whom Nixon met in Atlanta on May 31 and June 1, 1968, fresh from his impressive seventy-three percent showing in the Oregon primary. The Oregon results, and especially Reagan's poor showing in a neighboring state, gave Nixon important leverage in Atlanta, and he pinned down critical support from Senators Tower, Thurmond and Baker and from the State Chairmen of Florida, Georgia, Virginia and Mississippi. The southern potential which had first beguiled Nixon on his visit to Atlanta in August, 1960, now came to fruition in that same city, though he would still have to work hard to keep his southern support in Miami Beach under Reagan's intense assault.

Despite covert efforts at coordination, the Rockefeller and Reagan wings of the party were too far apart to mount an effective set of stop-Nixon maneuvers at Miami Beach. Instead, Nixon was able to play them off against one another—using the threat of Rockefeller to scare conservative Nixonites back into line and using the threat of a Reagan nomination to hold his own moderate strength. The two governors countered by arguing to potential converts that Nixon would pick someone from the opposite wing as his running mate, but most wavering delegates found it easier to stay with Nixon and risk some lesser ideological opponent for vice president rather than to bolt him and have that ideological opponent as presidential nominee. In the end, Rockefeller and Reagan failed to prevent Nixon's nomination primarily because Reagan was unable to win the southern support both camps had attributed to him. When the heat was on during the final hours in Miami Beach, it was one of the party's newest converts, Strom Thurmond, who played the critical role in holding the South for Nixon.

When the balloting finally took place, and before the switching began, Nixon had 692 votes, 25 more than a majority; Rockefeller, 277; Reagan, 182. Clif White contended that less then ten votes in key southern states operating under the unit rule would have turned the entire South around on that first ballot. Delegates who bolted to Nixon in the generally liberal Pennsylvania and New Jersey delegations also might have held if Nixon had fallen short elsewhere. Theodore White later estimated that 100 of Nixon's votes would have been vulnerable on another ballot. Still, Nixon had reserve strengths in Ohio, Michigan and California which he did not need to tap. Moreover, even if he had been stopped on the first ballot, it seems likely that either Reagan or Rockefeller delegates would have moved to Nixon later in order to prevent a less acceptable outcome. But it was also generally agreed that the candidate with the next best shot at the nomination was Ronald Reagan. If the balloting had been secret, some Nixon men acknowledged, Reagan might even have come close to winning.

With Nixon's nomination, the party's mainstream reemerged from its long underground journey. Virtually all segments of the party prepared to give their support to the candidate–though virtually all were stunned the day following the nomination when Nixon named Governor Agnew as his vice presidential choice. "You're kidding," said Chairman Bliss when he received the news.

The objections to Agnew were not primarily philosophical. Progressives generally viewed him as one of their own during his term as governor, while most conservatives regarded him as less liberal than Nixon's apparent second choice, Governor Volpe, or most of the other likely designees. Nixon's polls had shown that no potential running mate added to his strength. As he reminded his counselors all through the long night of consultations on the matter, he would have to win this one "on my own." The important thing was to choose a man who–like himself–would be acceptable to all segments and give no great offense to any. A border state governor with urban experience, a progressive record and a strong law and order image (earned primarily when he chastised black leaders after an outbreak of violence in the Spring of 1968), Agnew seemed to fit Nixon's requirements perfectly. In addition, he had impressed Nixon with his "calm strength" and "coolness under fire," a point which Nixon repeated when he chose him again four years later.

The objections to Agnew were based in part on his relative obscurity, and in part on the irritation of some Rockefeller backers over Agnew's betrayal of their leader. Most important, however, was the disappointment of many party professionals and congressional leaders–who had hoped for a running mate with potent appeal in the North and East where the ticket had the best chance to pull in congressional candidates. A number of delegates, including both conservatives and liberals, joined in a brief revolt on behalf of New York's Mayor John Lindsay. That effort ended, however, when Lindsay realistically agreed to second Agnew's nomination–in part because trusted advisers like Herbert Brownell persuaded him that this display of regularity would advance the chances for his own presidential nomination at some future date. Some of the rebels turned next to George Romney, who received 186 votes in the vice presidential balloting. But once the ticket had officially been nominated and Nixon had delivered a rousing acceptance speech, the entire party began to prepare for the Fall campaign.

XVII

The party's sense of unity and purpose after the Miami Beach convention was further buoyed when Nixon's lead over Humphrey in the Gallup Poll jumped to sixteen percentage points. The man who had united an impossibly divided party seemed to have struck a responsive chord in a badly divided nation. And, while the Republican convention had displayed a party coming together, the traumatic Democratic convention in Chicago at the end of August seemed to reveal a party falling apart. Humphrey (contrary to most later recollections) did pick up some ground on Nixon during the convention, but not very much. The margin at the beginning of September was down to twelve percent but it widened again to fifteen percent at the end of that month.

The very size of the lead became a handicap for Nixon. Earlier, the emphasis had been on the impossible comeback, the refreshing challenge, and the failures of the incumbent administration. But as the public came to accept the likelihood of a Nixon presidency, Johnson's record faded and Nixon became the issue. Now it was Humphrey who was making the comeback and on the attack, while Nixon, fighting opponents on both the left and the right, found himself increasingly on the defensive. Meanwhile, like Harry Truman, Humphrey was able to exchange the image of the bungling incumbent for that of the battling underdog. When he finally managed to get off the defensive on the Vietnam issue with his televised speech from Salt Lake City on September 30, Humphrey slowly began to gain.

The Nixon dilemma in 1968 grew out of his need to maximize his strength with two constituencies, the swing voters deciding between Wallace and Nixon and the swing voters deciding between Nixon and Humphrey. The two constituencies were so different, however, that the appeals which were effective with one risked driving off the other. In these circumstances, Nixon could only try to make some appeals in both directions, avoid controversy whenever possible, and hope that the Autumn days would dwindle faster than his plurality.

It was evident in the late Summer of 1968 that a substantial majority of the American people wanted a change. But there were two anti-incumbent candidates in 1968, and it was very possible for them to divide the vote between them in a way which would return the incumbent party to power. As Alabama Governor George Wallace's position in the polls climbed over twenty percent in late September, this danger became compelling for many Nixon strategists. Persuaded, too, that it was easier to win converts among those who had already taken an anti-incumbent posture than for those who were inclined to vote Democratic, the Nixon campaign set out to cut back Wallace.

Determined to avoid racist appeals, Nixon emphasized many of the same positions that had helped him hold southern Republican votes at the convention: his resistance to forced integration, his concern for law and order, his determination to appoint a more conservative Supreme Court, and especially his deep commitment to a strong national defense—an issue which had been crucial in winning Strom Thurmond's support. Meanwhile, Thurmond and other Nixon supporters hammered at the theme that Wallace could never win and that a Wallace vote was a wasted ballot.

At the same time, however, the Nixon command also recognized that the anti-incumbent vote was not necessarily a constant; even as they battled with Wallace for a larger share of the protest vote, they were also competing with Humphrey. The "new Nixon" of the primary season thus continued his fight for the center. His experience in foreign affairs received special emphasis; he campaigned as the man best equipped to cope with the Vietnam nightmare. In other fields too, his seasoned judgment and expertise had genuine appeal for moderates. To make the most of these virtues, the campaign was built around a series of regional question and answer programs in which Nixon, "the man in the arena," faced panels of citizen interrogators.

While his stump speeches took up the harder line, a series of radio addresses and position papers were beamed at the wavering center. Nixon's September 19 radio speech on "The Nature of the Presidency" was described by some usually critical commentators as one of the most impressive presidential campaign speeches since the days of Adlai Stevenson. A series of nightly radio speeches on specific issues was hastily scheduled in October. The campaign also drew on the capital achieved among many moderates by earlier, highly substantive campaign documents, including the discussions of black capitalism which had helped to rehabilitate Nixon's image in the Spring. Above all, the candidate emphasized the theme of bringing the nation together. He pledged to replace the trend toward confrontation with a commitment to negotiation, both in domestic affairs and in foreign policy, to reinforce the rule of reason and reject the rule of force. Later he would focus his victory statement on this same theme and make it the centerpiece as well of his First Inaugural Address.

Nixon took pains in 1968 to avoid the procedural mistakes of 1960, keeping well rested, delegating technical decisions, and avoiding television debates. The fact that he could unite the party and run a sound campaign was perhaps in itself some reason to argue that he could also unite the country and run an effective government.

The critical moment came on October 31 when President Johnson announced that he was suspending the bombing of North Vietnam in the expectation that this would produce significant progress at the negotiating table. Many in the Nixon camp—which had expected some such action for some time—thought the development would cost them the election. But at least part of its impact was offset a day later when the South Vietnamese government balked at the purported agreement. The tide was stemmed and Nixon narrowly won with 43.4 percent of the vote.

XVIII

Just four years after suffering one of the worst defeats in its history, the Republican party recaptured the presidency. Nixon received 301 electoral votes to 191 for Humphrey and 46 for Wallace. The Alabama governor appeared to have hurt each candidate about equally in the electoral college, costing Nixon the electoral votes of Maryland and the deep southern states according to some analysts, while taking enough votes from Humphrey to cost him New Jersey, Illinois, Missouri, Alaska and Delaware.

The lessons of the 1968 election were hotly debated. ithin the administration and without, before the 1969 inauguration and long afterward. For the Republican party was still a party in flux in the late 1960's, a party still struggling to determine its identity. Diversity had served it well in 1966, and ambiguity had been a useful tool in 1968, but the responsibilities of governing would require harder choices and a clearer profile. What Republicans took to be the meaning of 1968 would do much to shape the party's behavior in the 1970's.

The 1968 election, however, was an especially difficult election to analyze. The close result, the sharp shifts of opinion in the last days of the campaign, and the role of Wallace all vastly complicated the picture. Many observers read into the low voter turnout a sense of public reservation about all the candidates; only sixty percent of voting age Americans cast ballots in 1968 compared to sixty-four percent in 1964 and sixty-nine percent in 1960. Gallup's report that fifty-four percent of the voters had split their ticket in 1968 made many analysts even more reluctant to draw far-reaching conclusions about the future of voter allegiances. (One symbol of the trend toward ticket-splitting was the fact that the winning candidates in Arkansas included a Republican governor, a Democratic senator and the American Independent party's candidate for president.)

Both Houses of Congress went Democratic in 1968, a particular disappointment to Republicans given their long early lead. The GOP gained only five seats in the House, including one which was added earlier in the year. In the Senate, the Republicans showed a gain of five—the largest since 1950—taking away seats from Democrats in Oregon, Maryland, Pennsylvania, Florida, Oklahoma, and Ohio but losing California, where Thomas Kuchel had been defeated by the ultra-conservative Max Rafferty in the Republican primary. The GOP also realized a net increase of five governorships and increased their share of state legislative seats from 41.1 to 42.3 percent. After the election—and before Governor Agnew became vice president, Republicans controlled thirty of the fifty state houses and could claim that eighty-five percent of the population outside the South now lived in states governed by Republicans.

Many analysts suggested that, except for the South, Humphrey essentially reassembled the New Deal Coalition in 1968. Others, like Kevin Phillips, contended that the disintegration process had also continued in most of the cities. Phillips made a great deal of the fact that Nixon's share of the Catholic vote rose substantially to thirty-three percent, compared to Goldwater's twenty-four percent and Nixon's own twenty-two percent in 1960. Yet, by repeatedly emphasizing the comparison with 1960, when a Roman Catholic led the Democratic ticket, Phillips grossly misled his readers. For the party's Catholic showing in 1968 was far less impressive when compared with other less extraordinary elections. Even Nixon and Wallace together did not equal the forty-nine percent Republican Catholic vote of 1956, for example; Humphrey did better among Catholics than Stevenson, even against two opponents.

Humphrey's comeback in 1968 was spearheaded by organized labor. On election day, the Democrat received fifty-six percent of the union vote, about the same showing as Stevenson's in 1956 but down nine percentage points from Kennedy's showing and considerably lower than Lyndon Johnson's. Nixon's twenty-nine percent of the labor vote was only two percent better than Goldwater's performance. Yet it was clear that if Wallace labor voters could be kept from returning to the Democratic party, then the 1968 election could mark yet another milestone in the conversion of America's working class to Republicans.

The availability of the labor vote to the GOP was also demonstrated by the fact that millions of working-class Democrats who finally returned to the fold had been prepared to break with Humphrey only a few months before the election. As Democratic National Chairman O'Brien put it: "The old Cadillac Square syndrome" was dead.

Meanwhile, the growing bloc of black voters continued to move toward the Democrats, despite the fact that large numbers of black families were moving into the middle-class. Nixon polled only twelve percent of the overall non-white vote, double Goldwater's six percent but less than two-fifths of his own thirty-two percent showing in 1960.

Whatever ambiguities there may have been in the cities, it was clear that GOP strength in the South was continuing to grow—despite the influence of George Wallace. Perhaps one ironic reason was that Wallace had precluded the deep South strategy followed by Barry Goldwater and had forced the Republicans to return to that emphasis on the peripheral South which had characterized the old Eisenhower-Nixon strategy. For the sixth consecutive presidential election, the deep South and the peripheral South did *not* vote together in the 1968 election.

In the South, even more than in the cities, the lessons of 1968 depended very much on the future of George Wallace. The southern Wallace vote, for the most part, seemed naturally more available to the Republicans, since loyalty to the National Democratic party had been crumbling there for a good long time. As Thurmond had been a way station for some southern Democrats who went on to vote for Eisenhower in 1952, so Wallace could be seen as a way station for millions of southern voters on their way to a new Republican party. How long they decided to remain at the Wallace way station, however, would be a very critical question. As long as Wallace was available, the Republicans would have to compete with him for conservative support, with attendant risks in the center.

These risks were very evident in 1968. One of the most striking facts of the campaign was that Nixon's showing in the polls had scarcely changed throughout it. From the time of the Republican convention to the day of the election, it remained virtually paralyzed at forty-three percent. Humphrey, on the other hand, climbed steadily from twenty-nine percent to 42.7 percent, while Wallace, beginning with his designation of General Curtis Le May as his running mate in early October, fell from a high of twenty-one percent to the 13.5 percent level. The undecided vote, which stood at eight percent as late as mid-September, seemed to go largely for Humphrey in November. But what happened to the millions of voters who left Wallace during the last month of the campaign? It appeared that perhaps half the Wallace vote went to Nixon, a critical factor in border and southern areas, while the other half helped Humphrey, chiefly in working-class areas of the North.

Yet despite the new votes he won from Wallace, Nixon did not gain ground. There was only one explanation. Even while he was gaining about five percent of the vote on the right from Wallace, Nixon was losing about the same number of votes on the left to Humphrey. But though the exchange kept Nixon at forty-three percent, he did not really break even. Every vote lost to Humphrey narrowed the Humphrey-Nixon margin by two—adding one to Humphrey's column even while it subtracted one from Nixon's. The vote gained from Wallace, however, affected the Humphrey-Nixon margin only once. The election thus became a much closer affair than anyone had expected.

A great deal of attention was paid, before the election *and* after, to the traditional Democrats in the South and the cities who bolted to Wallace or Nixon. But far less attention was given, before the election *or* after, to the traditional Republicans and Independents in small towns and suburbs who were leaning to Nixon when the campaign began, but who later moved to the Democratic standard. Referred to by some as the "frontlash vote," this block was generally the same, well-educated, middle-class constituency which had gone so strongly for Eisenhower in 1952 and 1956, but which had begun to move away from the GOP in 1958 and 1960.

After leaving the party in large numbers in 1964, these voters returned in 1966 to buttress the Republican comeback. Now in 1968 they turned in a distinctly mixed performance. One survey showed Nixon gaining only fifty-one percent of the suburban vote. Among college educated, professional and business, and white-collar voters the Republican percentages were up from 1964 but down from 1960. Even the combined "conservative" Nixon-Wallace vote in these categories did not equal the Eisenhower showings. All the polls showed that it was among these "frontlash" voters that Humphrey had made his greatest gains during the campaign's closing stages.

Some Republicans argued after the election that this drift of votes to Humphrey had been inevitable. The frontlash, they suggested was composed of liberals whose antipathy to the Johnson administration had led them to declare for Nixon in August but who never realistically could be relied upon. Kevin Phillips went on to emphasize that even with the frontlash defections, there was still a solid conservative vote of fifty-six percent, including Nixon's forty-three percent and Wallace's thirteen percent, which could be assembled into a new Republican majority. Yet in his much-heralded *The Emerging Republican Majority* in 1969, Phillips acknowledged that the pursuit of that conservative majority would probably cost the party "several million liberal Republican voters from Maine and Oregon to Fifth Avenue."

The casual attitude of many conservatives to the frontlash potential grew out of an emotion which had infused much Republican thinking for many decades, a deep antipathy to an over-refined eastern elite, resting on geographic resentments in the West and the South and on social resentments among more recent immigrant groups in the cities. Phillips' writings, for example, abounded with bitter descriptions of the over-educated Yankee elitists, the supercilious adherents of radical chic. This was the effete enemy establishment which seemed constantly to sneer down on Irish Catholics and other working-class populations as they tried to make their way up the ladder of success. In 1972, Phillips would refer to them as the Pucci and Porsche set, symbolized by New York Mayor John Lindsay and Congressman Ogden Reid, both of whom had recently defected to the Democratic party. Phillips' impulse may have paralleled that of Richard Nixon who tended to dismiss many of the "young, attractive" heroes of the party's left in a single phrase: "the glamour boys." Or, as another GOP strategist put it when queried about liberal Republican defections: "Why get so worried about a few preppies?"

But whatever the explanations for these resentments and whatever their merits, they misrepresented the full nature of independent Republicanism. Potential frontlash voters were not all urbane northeastern Yankees. Though concentrated in the middle and upper middle classes, economically and educationally, frontlash voters came from all parts of the country and from all ethnic and religious backgrounds. Polls in 1972, for example, showed middle class Roman Catholics to be exceptionally concerned about achieving racial justice.

Many of these frontlash voters thought of themselves as moderate conservatives. The candidates with whom they most closely identified were not so much the Lindsays and Reids nor even always the Rockefellers, but rather the Griffins and Tafts and Millikens and Lugars of the upper Middle West, the Coopers and Cooks and Mortons of Kentucky, northeastern Catholics like Volpe and Cahill, devoted fundamentalists like Romney and Hatfield, pragmatic westerners like Finch and Evans, maverick originals like Hickel and Saxbe, and new southerners like Holton and Bush and Baker. A leader like Charles Percy won their favor far more because of his square Horatio Alger image and his Christian Science piety than because of his eastern social connections or the aura of jet set glamour.

Though many frontlash voters had spurned Goldwater's candidacy, most had supported Nixon. Fully one-fourth of Nixon's 1968 votes came from people who had voted for Johnson in 1964. But even as they returned to the GOP on the presidential line, they cast critical ballots which sent liberals like McGovern, Hughes, Bayh, Nelson, Church and Cranston to the Senate, each of them from states which Nixon simultaneously carried. In 1970, other Senate candidates—Stevenson, Tunney, Moss, Burdick, Hartke, Montoya—would also win because thousands of Nixon voters gave them their support.

In short, many of Nixon's votes in 1968 came from the growing ranks of the ticket-splitters. Clearly, the Nixon-Wallace fifty-six percent majority was not made up exclusively of conservative doctrinaires. The danger for Republicans was that the revolving door, bringing in Wallace voters on the one side, would usher out frontlash supporters on the other. The danger was manifested when a poll to determine party preferences in 1971 showed that for the first time ever, business and professional persons preferred the Democrats.

Could the loss of "several million liberal Republicans and Independents from Maine and Oregon to Fifth Avenue" possibly be made up? Only if Wallace were out of the picture and if three quarters of his supporters joined the Republicans. Even this result would leave the parties evenly divided. "From Maine and Oregon to Fifth Avenue"—well perhaps the party, with Phillips, could say good riddance to the Fifth Avenue portion of that constituency. But from Maine to Oregon, all across the Midwest and in the urban South, "several million" lost Republicans would surely turn the party's emerging majority into a distinct minority once again.

A number of other objections were raised against the Phillips thesis. Many critics jumped on him for suggesting that racial polarization in the South would be a good thing for the party, since an increasingly black Democratic party would drive even more whites to the Republicans. Others claimed that his theories were fine as far as presidential politics were concerned but that they ignored the continuing weakness of grassroots Republicans in the South and the continuing strength of state and local liberal Republicans in the North. Some wondered how a book which purported to explain the 1968 election could avoid any mention of Vietnam. Still others suggested that the 1968 election patterns which Phillips used to establish the inevitability of the conservative tide, had in fact resulted from his own influence in the campaign. As the author himself put it in 1972: his work as a special assistant to the campaign director, John Mitchell, had "helped keep the Nixon drive aimed at southerners, Wallaceites and Catholics." Little wonder, some said, that the results of the campaign confirmed the premises of the strategy.

When Phillips argued that the most conservative areas of the country were also those which were growing fastest, some critics asked how he could be so sure that the influx of new voters would necessarily adopt the voting habits of the old. It was also pointed out that Phillips' contention that the Northeast *always* lagged behind great historic movements was based on an extremely selective and highly inaccurate reading of the nation's critical elections.

Despite the fact that Phillips dedicated his book to Richard Nixon and John Mitchell, "the architects of the emerging Republican majority," and despite conservative efforts to label the Phillips book as the "Bible of the Nixon Administration," its views were never fully adopted by the new administration's most powerful strategists. The strategy of writing off any sizable group of Republicans was risky and unnecessary, they said. The new Republican majority must be built by inclusion and not by exclusion. The party would therefore attempt to join the South and the cities, the suburbs and small towns, in a grand new coalition of the center.

XVIX

The great discovery of conservative Republicans in the 1960's was that the pursuit of the South and the pursuit of the cities were complementary endeavors. This rightward trend in both constituencies was far more than a reaction against racial disturbance. It involved a general cultural rebellion against the elite establishment, a frustration among little people who felt they had lost control over their own lives. The feeling focused on various issues as time went by: on the race question, yes, but particularly on the busing of school children, on the breakdown in an older morality and the tendency toward "permissiveness," on rising crime and ghetto riots and the belief that the Supreme Court had been soft on criminals, on rising taxes which seemed to accompany declining services, on a welfare system which seemed to defy the work ethic, on drug abuse and campus unrest and no school prayer and on all the trappings of "limousine liberalism."

It was to all of these frustrations that political analysts referred in the late 1960's when they spoke of the "middle Americans," the "silent majority," the "status rebellion," the "morality issue," the "law and order issue," the "cultural issue," and the "social issue." The latter phrase was used in 1970 by Richard Scammon and Ben J. Wattenberg in an influential book called *The Real Majority* which argued, essentially, that "the man who chooses the president of this country is the man who bowls on Thursday nights." *The Real Majority* also popularized the mythical machinist's wife in Dayton as the symbol of the middle aged, middle class, middle minded voter who presumably decided most elections.

In many ways, the Scammon-Wattenberg discussion confirmed the judgments of Kevin Phillips—and even strengthened them by pointing to conservative potential among northern Democrats who were non-Catholic as well as Catholic and who lived outside the great cities as well as within. Phillips thanked Scammon at one symposium for helping to rehabilitate his much maligned conclusions. But the thesis of *The Real Majority* also differed from that of the *Emerging Republican Majority* in significant ways. Scammon and Wattenberg did not subscribe to Phillips' almost metaphysical notion about the inevitable cycles of history. They denied that the social issue must unavoidably lead to Democratic decline. They described the outlook of the typical Middle American as a highly complex mixture of conservative and liberal tenets. A decade after Eisenhower's retirement, the nation still clung to the "attitudinal center," they contended, still scorning the gutters on the left and the right.

Essentially, *The Real Majority* was a book written *by* Democrats *for* Democrats, telling them how to neutralize pressures from the right. By wearing a flag in one's lapel, for example, and by emphasizing the economic liberalism which had continuing appeal in middle America, Democrats could still retain their old supporters—and many of them did in 1970 and 1972. Meanwhile, Phillips himself talked more and more of blending conservative social appeals with more progressive economic positions.

The alienated, frustrated, resentful but still loyal Americans described by both of these post-election analyses had been a major focus of Nixon's 1968 campaign. His acceptance speech described them as the Forgotten Americans: "The non-shouters; the non-demonstrators . . . They are not racist or sick; they are not guilty of the crime that plagues the land. They are good people, they are decent people; they work, they save, they pay their taxes, and they care."

This theme had been growing in the Republican consciousness for at least a decade. Senator Goldwater said almost exactly the same thing in 1961 when he charged that "minority groups now speak much more loudly than do majority groups which I classify as the forgotten American, the man who pays his taxes, prays, behaves himself, stays out of trouble, and works for his government. . . ." Raymond Moley emphasized the same point in his 1962 primer on GOP strategy, *The Republican Opportunity*, in which he quoted from William Graham Sumner's nineteenth century description of the Forgotten Man, "delving away in patient industry, supporting his family, paying his taxes, casting his vote, supporting the church and the school, reading the newspaper, and cheering for the politician of his admiration, but he is the only one for whom there is no provision in the great scramble and the big divide. . . ."

When Goldwater introduced the Forgotten American theme in 1961, in what was then known as the Goldwater Manifesto, it was part of an ambitious blueprint for a new Republican party which had been largely developed by Michael J. Bernstein, an innovative and pragmatic Goldwater adviser. Bernstein was convinced that conservatism and Republicanism had to expand their appeal through constructive Federal programs. As things worked out, however, the senator from Arizona could not square the moderate new programs which his staff began to outline with his rugged individualism and rock-ribbed suspicion of federal power. The Bernstein approach, which could conceivably have provided a broad ideological tent for Republicans in the 1960's, died aborning—though similar impulses were to run through the Nixon administration eight years later.

Just as the Republican party was still too much the party of Lincoln to "out-Wallace" the Wallaceites in the South, so it was still too much the party of Taft to out-promise the Democrats in the North. It would approach both constituencies energetically and openly, but it would try to approach them without denying its essential historic character.

XX

The difficulty of trying to broaden the center with converts from the right and left was also evident in the 1970 election. The president returned from Europe early in October of that year intending to refrain from general campaigning and to appear instead as a world statesman who needed a more compatible Congress to strengthen his diplomatic hand. But the poll data which greeted him upon his return was not encouraging. For two years the party had looked to the 1970 elections as its golden opportunity, especially in the Senate where so many now-vulnerable Democrats had been elected in the landslides of 1958 and 1964. But despite the president's determined efforts to recruit strong candidates, most of his horses were now running well behind. By October 12, the president had decided to step up his direct involvement in the campaign and by election day he had managed to visit twenty-two states. Meanwhile, the Scammon-Wattenberg thesis—though intended for Democrats—had gained wide attention in the Republican party. Ignoring the passages which told Democrats how to neutralize the social issue, ignoring warnings that the issue would backfire if it was pushed too far and ignoring the suggestion that Republicans should complement their natural advantage on the social issue by finding ways to neutralize the Democrats' economic advantages, many Republicans decided to make the social issue the center of the Fall campaign.

Just as Vice President Nixon had provided the heavy artillery for the GOP attack in 1954 and 1958, so Vice President Agnew now led the assault on the radical-liberal Democrats. The president's own campaign speeches also hit hard on the social issue—as dramatized by his constant hecklers—though the president still gave the bulk of his attention to foreign policy and economic affairs. The impression that he was "running for sheriff" as John Mitchell later put it, came partly from fragmentary reports on his speeches and also from the decision to broadcast on election eve a technically marred television tape of the president's address in Phoenix. The speech had been triggered by a controversial rock throwing incident involving the presidential motorcade a few days earlier in San Jose and was especially tough. The president later said that he would not have broadcast the tape had he been making that decision. Moreover, even when the decision was made, it could be known that the tape would be followed immediately by Senator Muskie's calm fireside chat from Maine.

The results of the 1970 election were mixed. The Silent Majority did not speak clearly, as one observer put it, but seemed rather to be clearing its throat. There were many reasons for Republicans to be encouraged. Compared with earlier off-year election results, the party did well merely to hold its own (though it must be remembered that in 1968, as in 1952, the limited power of Nixon's coattails had decreased the potential for a Democratic rebound). The GOP had recovered ground during the campaign that seemed lost in early October, and the president's campaigning had helped to win new Republican senate seats in Maryland, Ohio, Connecticut, and Tennessee. Though Republican senators lost in Illinois and California, the party still showed a net gain of two Senate seats. And while Republican Senator Charles Goodell was defeated in New York, the winner, with tacit support from the president and not quite so tacit support from the vice president, was James Buckley, who added the Republican designation to his Conservative label after entering the Senate. In addition, a liberal Democrat was replaced by a conservative Democrat in Texas. The overall result, said the White House, was a new "ideological majority" for the president in the upper chamber.

In the House, the Republicans lost only nine seats compared with the October projection of thirty losses, despite the dampening impact on many GOP candidates of high unemployment rates. Still, compared to the glowing expectations of the Spring, Republicans could not help feeling disappointed. Twenty-five Democratic senators had been up for election in 1970, compared to only ten Republicans. Many of the Democrats were from conservative western states. Yet in ten races for Democratically held senate seats west of the Mississippi, the GOP failed to win a single one.

The most unhappy aspect for Republicans of the 1970 results came at the state level, though losses there may have been a natural correction after the strong GOP showings of 1966 and 1968. Eleven governorships and over 200 state legislative seats were lost to the Democrats. Republicans lost control of the legislatures of California, Pennsylvania and Illinois.

And what of southern Republicanism in the Nixon era? It was increasingly apparent in 1969 and 1970 that George Wallace was not a one-time phenomenon. His poll ratings did not fade. After being elected governor again in 1970, his position became even more powerful.

The Phillips strategy, premised on a solid Republican South, grew less tenable as a repeat Wallace candidacy in 1972 grew more likely. Southern Republican pleas for administration policies that would provide leverage against Wallace grew stronger. And in areas such as trade and tariff policy, defense programs, Supreme Court appointments, and opposition to busing to achieve racial balance, the administration worked to solidify responsible southern support.

One factor which encouraged Republicans to fight for the South—Wallace candidacy or no Wallace candidacy—was the continuing emergence of a new southern constituency, basically conservative and not particularly responsive to Wallace's populist appeals. This was the New South in which Eisenhower had been so successful, the constituency to which Samuel Lubell referred when he wrote that "the Wallaceites and the Nixon Republicans represent two clashing streams of southern life, culturally, economically, and historically." It was this New South—including traditional Republicans, younger voters, urban dwellers and blacks—which elected Howard Baker as senator from Tennessee in 1966 and Linwood Holton as governor of Virginia in 1969. The election in 1970 of the first Republican governor in Tennessee in fifty years, after a non-ideological campaign, helped to illustrate the same point. Senator John Tower of Texas built two election victories on his ability to win liberal and minority group support against arch-conservative opponents. After Albert Watson was defeated by a racial moderate in the race for governor of South Carolina in 1970, Senator Strom Thurmond did an about-face and began to cultivate the Negro vote in an effort to preserve his senate seat in 1972.

In short, the standard conservative approach to the South, as articulated by Rusher and embellished by Phillips, had to be adjusted in light of the continuing difficulty of attracting low income southern voters to the Republican banner, the growing importance of blacks in the southern electorate, and the continuing tendency toward moderation among middle and upper class whites.

The success of moderate Democrats throughout the South in 1970, including the fact that the Republicans picked up only one congressional seat in Dixie, demonstrated the dangers of depending too exclusively on social issues to pull in poor white voters whose economic outlook favored the Democrats. Wallace could combine social conservatism with economic populism but most Republicans could not. The future of southern Republicanism seemed after 1970 to require either a sharp reversal of the party's economic image or a somewhat more mellow appeal which would allow the party to pick up at least some small percentage of black votes and renew its claim on urban moderates.

Whatever the disappointments of 1970 when measured against the ideal, it was true, nevertheless, that the party's 22 governorships, 177 House seats and 45 Senate seats put it in a much stronger position as it approached the 1972 election than it had been in 1960, the last time it held the White House during a presidential race. More than that, observers after 1970 were increasingly inclined to interpret shifts in party strength as fluctuations of the moment rather than as reliable predictors of emerging party lines. More and more it seemed as though the voters had given up their search for permanent party homes. More and more it seemed as if they were consciously using the two parties to check and balance one another, treating them, in Samuel Lubell's phrase, the way a cowboy carries a pistol on both his hips, distributing votes between and among the parties in whatever fashion seemed best designed to send their messages to the government.

There were, of course, continuing predictions of party realignment in the early 1970's, particularly when Mayor Lindsay and later Congressman Reid transferred to the Democratic party, and when John Connally, a close associate of President Johnson and leader of Texas Democrats, became a highly valued member of the Nixon administration and a powerful influence in winning Democratic support for the president's reelection campaign. But the evidence of declining party allegiance also continued to be persuasive. Between 1952 and 1968, for example, only one-fifth of the nation's counties voted for the same party in all five presidential elections. Of the fifteen states with simultaneous gubernatorial and senatorial elections in 1968, nine divided the victories between the two parties and in 1970, eleven out of twenty-four states did so.

It was perhaps with this highly independent voter in mind that President Nixon, speaking just two months after the 1970 election at the dedication of the Republican National Committee's new headquarters on Capitol Hill, declared that the Republican party should become "the party of the open door, open to people of all races, all religions, and all ideologies." On another occasion he told reporters that he would be wearing his presidential, non-political hat in 1971 and he continued to pursue this non-partisan, non-factional theme well into his 1972 campaign.

Within the party, factional lines seemed to be shifting some as 1972 approached. For one thing, the Senate—with the infusion of fresh Republican blood in 1966, 1968 and 1970—became the center of gravity for the party's moderate wing, while the Governors Association grew more conservative and less visible. Fully twenty of the Senate's forty-five Republicans—many of them from well beyond the traditionally liberal East Coast—became members of the Senate's new Wednesday Group. When Everett Dirksen died in 1969, a moderate team, Hugh Scott of Pennsylvania and Robert Griffin of Michigan, took over the Senate Republican leadership. In the House, Congressman John Anderson of Illinois became Chairman of the Republican Conference when Melvin Laird became Secretary of Defense. Anderson, whose record had slowly moderated over the years, was symbolic of the gradual shift of heartland Republicans from the party's right wing to its center. Another such symbol, perhaps a more dramatic one simply because of his name, was Robert Taft, Jr., a leader in the civil rights struggles of the mid 1960's as a member of the House of Representatives and a strong centrist figure in the Senate after 1970.

From its very beginnings, as Christopher Beal has demonstrated the story of the Republican party can be seen as an ongoing battle between New York and Ohio, a battle Ohio usually won. From Grant in the 1860's to Harding in the 1920's, seven of the nation's nine Republican presidents were native Ohioans and the two exceptions were New Yorkers (Arthur and Roosevelt) who succeeded to the presidency after Ohioans had died.

William Howard Taft's defeat of Theodore Roosevelt at the 1912 convention and Roosevelt's embittered reaction was the most dramatic moment in the long New York-Ohio struggle. That struggle broke out again in the 1940's as Taft's son battled another New Yorker, Thomas Dewey, and in the 1950's as eastern internationalists fought the efforts of Ohio Senator John Bricker to limit presidential power. In 1964, though Governor Rhodes and Chairman Ray Bliss tried to prevent it, the Ohio delegation went for Goldwater and opposed yet another New Yorker, Nelson Rockefeller. With the one exception of a very late ballot at the convention of 1876, as Howard Reiter has shown, the New York and Ohio delegations were on opposite sides of every disputed presidential nomination in the history of the party.

But in 1968, even this century-old rule changed as Rhodes led his delegation away from Nixon and behind his favorite son candidacy. By the 1970's moreover, both of Ohio's Republican senators were members of the moderate Wednesday Group while New York had produced the Senate's only Conservative party spokesman. When Ohio voted with the moderates—and with New York—during the symbolic rules fight at the 1972 convention, many argued that an important wheel had come full cycle. They also noted that the moderates were led in that fight by a decidedly regular Republican from Wisconsin, Congressman William Steiger.

As the 1960's turned into the 1970's, it seemed that the line of demarcation between areas of moderate and conservative Republican strength was slowly shifting to the West.

XXI

Despite the splinter protest candidacies of two Congressmen, Ohio's John Ashbrook and California's Paul N. ("Pete") McCloskey, the party entered the 1972 campaign with a higher degree of unity than many party regulars had ever known before. To be sure, neither wing of the party was entirely happy with every detail of the president's record. But on the issues that mattered most to their constituencies, each wing was generally pleased.

The salient issue of the bitter fight between Eisenhower and Taft had been the question of isolationism versus internationalism; ever since that time, foreign policy had continued to be of central concern to liberal Republicans. With the assistance of Nelson Rockefeller's former aide, Henry Kissinger, the president went well beyond most of their expectations with his trips to Peking and Moscow and his progress toward arms control. Progressive Republicans also praised a number of the president's domestic programs, especially the new economic policy he introduced in August, 1971, and his program for reforming the welfare system. The Ripon Society acknowledged that virtually all of the policy positions it had endorsed or developed before the 1968 election had become a part of the Nixon program.

For most of the conservatives in the party, the subjects that aroused the deepest feelings in the 1960's centered around the social issue and the need for law and order. They were encouraged, therefore, by the president's efforts to change the direction of the Supreme Court, his crackdown on crime and drugs, and the spirited defense of traditional values in which both the president and the vice president enthusiastically engaged.

Both wings of the party joined in supporting a number of positions which the party had developed during the 1960's which could not be easily classified by traditional ideological criteria. They ranged from revenue sharing to the volunteer army, from reorganizing and decentralizing the federal bureaucracy to the "reprivatization" of government functions (a vogue word the administration borrowed from Peter Drucker). With the early help of Daniel Patrick Moynihan, a liberal Democrat grown tired of conventional liberalism, and other thinkers, many of whom shared Moynihan's affiliation with *The Public Interest*, the Nixon administration began to put together a series of humanistic but anti-bureaucratic domestic programs which gave renewed promise that the party's disparate factions would yet find that their agreements were more important than their differences. The president's course in Vietnam also drew broad party support.

To be sure, conservatives who cared most deeply about foreign policy and liberals who cared most deeply about domestic policy—particularly civil rights and civil liberties—voiced continuing complaints. But even the most serious intraparty rebellions did not begin to match those of the Eisenhower years. Protests among party liberals over what they described as "the purging" of Senator Goodell in 1970 was quelled by strong reassurances that his case was a distinct exception. Conservative rebellion in late 1971 and early 1972 concerning wage and price controls, budget deficits, and inadequate military spending generally died when Senator Goldwater, Governor Reagan and other prominent conservatives continued to stand with the president and when Vice President Agnew was retained on the 1972 ticket.

The Republican National Committee—under the chairmanship of Maryland Congressman Rogers C. B. Morton, who succeeded Ray Bliss, and Kansas Senator Robert Dole, who succeeded Morton when the latter became Secretary of the Interior—took on a generally noncontroversial posture as the bulk of political decision-making moved to the White House. When a Texan, George Bush, became party chairman in 1973, he was generally welcomed by all factions.

Despite the fight over rules, the 1972 convention, like the campaign which followed, was largely a celebration of party unity. With a new sense of cohesion and with added running room among the general electorate both to the left and to the right, the Republican party entered the 1972 campaign with its best chance since 1952 to become the nation's majority party. In seeking however, to establish the grand coalition of the center, in trying to win both ways—the Republicans necessarily risked losing both ways, becoming just conservative enough to offend upper middle class suburbanites and just liberal enough to turn off the Archie Bunkers of Queens and the clay farmers of Georgia. Still, most Republican leaders were confident in the early 1970's that a responsible and effective and balanced administration could assemble a broad and balanced coalition of support. This would be far easier, they realized, if either of two conditions were met: 1) if George Wallace were not a candidate in 1972 and 2) if the Democrats heeded the advice of their more militant liberals rather than battling with Nixon for the center. And, as the twists and turns of fate would have it, the Republicans suddenly found, as the 1972 convention season ended and the Fall campaign began, that both of these conditions existed.

XXII

On November 7, 1972, the Republican party won its fourth presidential victory in the last six tries. With nearly sixty-one percent of the vote, Richard Nixon achieved a winning margin which easily topped that of the two Eisenhower wins and which was rivaled in the long history of the party only by the 1920 success of Warren Harding.

The slow erosion of Democratic strength in the South and the cities became a landslide in 1972. The Nixon vote in the South reached seventy-two percent, greater than the combined Wallace-Nixon vote of 1968. Early estimates showed the Catholic vote going fifty-three percent to Nixon. Members of labor union families went fifty-four percent for the GOP. Just as millions of Republicans had cast their first Democratic ballots in 1964, so the controversial candidacy of George McGovern seemed to speed the disintegration of solid Democratic voting blocs in 1972. Overall, about one-third of registered Democrats voted for Nixon.

Like 1964, however, the 1972 election seemed an unreliable indicator of general voting trends. In both cases, a strong majority of voters seemed to decide very early in the campaign against the challenging candidate—some because of his apparent ideology, some because they simply doubted his competence. In both cases an incumbent president was returned to office with strong support all across the country.

President Nixon carried forty-nine states in 1972. He had strong backing in both rural and urban areas, and in all economic groups. Even the unemployed gave him fifty percent of their support. He roughly doubled his 1968 showing among such minority groups as Jews, blacks and Spanish-speaking Americans. New voters between eighteen and twenty-four seemed to divide their votes about evenly, defying the early assumptions of most Democratic strategists. And as Lou Harris pointed out just after the election, Nixon also carried well-educated, affluent independents—what some called the frontlash vote and what Harris now termed the "constituency for change." Foreign policy seemed to be the critical issue which brought many of these voters back to the GOP banner—a banner from which they had gradually been drifting for nearly two decades.

And yet, in the aftermath of this massive presidential triumph, almost none claimed that the long-sought Republican majority had at last emerged. At the state and local level, in fact, the results could be described as a slight Republican setback. The GOP picked up only a dozen House seats and actually lost two seats in the Senate. They won four previously Democratic seats in the South and Southwest (Virginia, North Carolina, Oklahoma, New Mexico), but lost six northern seats (Maine, Delaware, Iowa, Kentucky, South Dakota, and Colorado) which had once seemed safely Republican. The party suffered a net loss of one additional governorship and lost strength in several state legislatures. Richard Nixon's triumph in 1972 was indeed a lonely landslide.

As had been the case with Eisenhower, party officials were inclined to blame the weakness of the coattails on the man who wore the coat. Nixon's cool and cautious non-campaign had ruined the chances for a party sweep, they said, though many of these same leaders had also complained that Nixon had done too much campaigning two years earlier. Other observers pointed to a so-called "penance vote"—suggesting that undecided Democratic voters resolved their doubt in favor of Democratic candidates at lower levels in order to assuage guilty consciences for having broken party ranks at the presidential level.

One explanation of voting behavior which was emphatically confirmed by the 1972 results was that which pointed to the growing role of the ticket-splitter in a new age of centrist, non-partisan politics. If party label and party allegiance seemed a minor factor in the campaigns of the candidates, it was because party allegiance seemed an increasingly irrelevant factor in the minds of the voters. One poll even showed that the same electorate which gave Nixon his landslide victory would have voted Democratic if the presidential choice had been between Senator Edward Kennedy and Vice President Spiro Agnew.

As the polls closed on November 7, 1972, an era ended for the Republican party. For the first time in twenty years, Richard Nixon was not a candidate for national office, a fact which had important implications for both his presidency and his party. As that party began to think about future elections and future leaders, it was not a notably stronger institution than it had been in 1952. But potentially, at least, it was a more competitive party, capable of winning majorities in places where the GOP label had once scarcely been respectable.

Whether the Republicans would capitalize on this potential in the 1970's seemed to depend largely on whether they waited passively for outside forces—be they the successes of their president or the cycles of history—to sweep them to inevitable majority status, or whether instead they worked to develop at every level of government and in every part of the country an array of candidates and programs which could win the confidence of an ever more demanding and less predictable public.

Appendix

DWIGHT D. EISENHOWER, FIRST INAUGURAL ADDRESS
January 20, 1953

My friends, before I begin the expression of those thoughts which I deem appropriate to this moment, would you permit me the privilege of uttering a little private prayer of my own, and I ask that you bow your heads.

Almighty God, as we stand here, at this moment, my future associates in the executive branch of Government join me in beseeching that Thou wilt make full and complete our dedication to the service of the people in this throng and their fellow citizens everywhere. Give us, we pray, the power to discern clearly right from wrong and allow all our words and actions to be governed thereby and by the laws of this land.

Especially we pray that our concern shall be for all the people—regardless of station, race, or calling. May cooperation be permitted and be the mutual aim of those who, under the concepts of our Constitution, hold to differing political beliefs, so that all may work for the good of our beloved country and for Thy glory. Amen.

My fellow citizens, the world and we have passed the midway point of a century of continuing challenge. We sense with all our faculties that forces of good and evil are massed and armed and opposed as rarely before in history.

This fact defines the meaning of this day. We are summoned, by this honored and historic ceremony, to witness more than the act of one citizen swearing his oath of service, in the presence of his God. We are called, as a people, to give testimony, in the sight of the world, to our faith that the future shall belong to the free.

Since this century's beginning, a time of tempest has seemed to come upon the continents of the earth. Masses of Asia have wakened to strike off shackles of the past. Great nations of Europe have waged their bloodiest wars. Thrones have toppled and their vast empires have disappeared. New nations have been born.

For our own country, it has been a time of recurring trial. We have grown in power and in responsibility. We have passed through the anxieties of depression and of war to a summit unmatched in man's history. Seeking to secure peace in the world, we have had to fight through the forests of the Argonne, to the shores of Iwo Jima, and to the mountain peaks of Korea.

In the swift rush of great events, we find ourselves groping to know the full sense and meaning of the times in which we live. In our quest of understanding, we beseech God's guidance. We summon all our knowledge of the past and we scan all signs of the future. We bring all our wit and will to meet the question: How far have we come in man's long pilgrimage from darkness toward light? Are we nearing the light—a day of freedom and of peace for all mankind? Or are the shadows of another night closing in upon us?

Congressional Record, 83d Cong., 1st sess., 1953, 99, pt. 1, 451-52.

Great as are the preoccupation absorbing us at home, concerned as we are with matters that deeply affect our livelihood today and our vision of the future, each of these domestic problems is dwarfed by, and often even created by, this question that involves all human kind.

This trial comes at a moment when man's power to achieve good or to inflict evil surpasses the brightest hopes and the sharpest fears of all ages. We can turn rivers in their courses, level mountains to the plains. Ocean and land and sky are avenues for our colossal commerce. Disease diminishes and life lengthens.

Yet, the promise of this life is imperilled by the very genius that has made it possible. Nations amass wealth. Labor sweats to create—and turns out devices to level not only mountains but also cities. Science seems ready to confer upon us, as its final gift, the power to erase human life from the earth.

At such a time in history, we who are free must proclaim anew our faith.

This faith is the abiding creed of our fathers. It is our faith in the deathless dignity of man, governed by eternal moral and natural laws.

This faith defines our full view of life. It establishes, beyond debate, those gifts of the Creator that are man's inalienable rights, and that make all men equal in His sight.

In the light of this equality, we know that the virtues most cherished by free people—love of truth, pride of work, devotion to country—all are treasures equally precious in the lives of the most humbled and of the most exalted. The men who mine coal and fire furnaces and balance ledgers and turn lathes and pick cotton and heal the sick and plant corn, all serve as proudly, and as profitably, for America as the statesmen who draft treaties or the legislators who enact laws.

This faith rules our whole way of life. It decrees that we, the people, elect leaders not to rule but to serve. It asserts that we have the right to choice of our own work and to the reward of our own toil. It inspires the initiative that makes our productivity the wonder of the world. And it warns that any man who seeks to deny equality in all his brothers betrays the spirit of the free and invites the mockery of the tyrant.

It is because we, all of us, hold to these principles that the political changes accomplished this day do not imply turbulence, upheaval, or disorder. Rather this change expresses a purpose of strengthening our dedication and devotion to the precepts of our founding documents, a conscious renewal of faith in our country and in the watchfulness of a divine providence.

The enemies of this faith know no god but force, no devotion but its use. They tutor men in treason. They feed upon the hunger of others. Whatever defies them, they torture, especially the truth.

Here, then, is joined no pallied argument between slightly differing philosophies. This conflict strikes directly at the faith of our fathers and the lives of our sons. No principle or treasure that we hold, from the spiritual knowledge of our free schools and churches to the creative magic of free labor and capital, nothing lies safely beyond the reach of the struggle.

Freedom is pitted against slavery; light against dark.

The faith we hold belongs not to us alone but to the free of all the world. This common bond binds the grower of rice in Burma and the planter of wheat in Iowa, the shepherd in southern Italy, and the mountaineer in the Andes. It confers a common dignity upon the French soldier who dies in Indochina, the British soldier killed in Malaya, the American life given in Korea.

We know, beyond this, that we are linked to all free peoples not merely by a noble idea but by a simple need. No free people can for long cling to any privilege or enjoy any safety in economic solitude. For all our own material might, even we need markets in the world for the surpluses of our farms and of our factories. Equally, we need for these same farms and factories vital materials and products of distant lands. This basic law of interdependence, so manifest in the commerce of peace, applies with thousandfold intensity in the event of war.

So are we persuaded by necessity and by belief that the strength of all free peoples lies in unity, their danger in discord.

To produce this unity, to meet the challenge of our time, destiny has laid upon our country the responsibility of the free world's leadership. So it is proper that we assure our friends once again that, in the discharge of this responsibility, we Americans know and observe the difference between world leadership and imperialism; between firmness and truculence; between a thoughtfully calculated goal and spasmodic reaction to the stimulus of emergencies.

We wish our friends the world over to know this above all: We face the threat—not with dread and confusion—but with confidence and conviction.

We feel this moral strength because we know that we are not helpless prisoners of history. We are free men. We shall remain free, never to be proven guilty of the one capital offense against freedom—a lack of stanch faith.

In pleading our just cause before the bar of history and in pressing our labor for world peace, we shall be guided by certain fixed principles.

These principles are:

(1) Abhorring war as a chosen way to balk the purposes of those who threaten us, we hold it to be the first task of statesmanship to develop the strength that will deter the forces of aggression and promote the conditions of peace. For, as it must be the supreme purpose of all free men, so it must be the dedication of their leaders, to save humanity from preying upon itself.

In the light of this principle, we stand ready to engage with any and all others in joint effort to remove the causes of mutual fear and distrust among nations, and so to make possible drastic reduction of armaments. The sole requisites for undertaking such effort are that, in their purpose, they be aimed logically and honestly toward securing peace for all; and that, in their result, they provide methods by which every participating nation will prove good faith in carrying out of its pledge.

(2) Realizing that common sense and common decency alike dictate the futility of appeasement, we shall never try to placate an aggressor by the false and wicked bargain of trading honor for security. For in the final choice a soldier's pack is not so heavy a burden as a prisoner's chains.

(3) Knowing that only a United States that is strong and immensely productive can help defend freedom in our world, we view our Nation's strength and security as a trust upon which rests the hope of free men everywhere. It is the firm duty of each of our free citizens and of every free citizen everywhere to place the cause of his country before the comfort of himself.

(4) Honoring the identity and heritage of each nation of the world, we shall never use our strength to try to impress upon another people our own cherished political and economic institutions.

(5) Assessing realistically the needs and capacities of proven friends of freedom, we shall strive to help them to achieve their own security and well-being. Likewise, we shall count upon them to assume, within the limits of their resources, their full and just burdens in the common defense of freedom.

(6) Recognizing economic health as an indispensable basis of military strength and the free world's peace, we shall strive to foster everywhere, and to practice ourselves, policies that encourage productivity and profitable trade. For the impoverishment of any single people in the world means danger to the well-being of all other peoples.

(7) Appreciating that economic need, military security, and political wisdom combine to suggest regional groupings of free peoples, we hope, within the framework of the United Nations, to help strengthen such special bonds the world over. The nature of these ties must vary with the different problems of different areas.

In the Western Hemisphere, we join with all our neighbors in the work of perfecting a community of fraternal trust and common purpose.

In Europe, we ask that enlightened and inspired leaders of the western nations strive with renewed vigor to make the unity of their peoples a reality. Only as free Europe unitedly marshals its strength can it effectively safeguard, even with our help, its spiritual and cultural treasures.

(8) Conceiving the defense of freedom, like freedom itself, to be one and indivisible, we hold all continents and peoples in equal regard and honor. We reject any insinuation that one race or another, one people or another is in any sense inferior or expendable.

(9) Respecting the United Nations as the living sign of all peoples' hope for peace, we shall strive to make it not merely an eloquent symbol but an effective force. And in our quest of honorable peace, we shall neither compromise, nor tire, nor ever cease.

By these rules of conduct, we hope to be known to all peoples.

By their observance, an earth of peace may become not a vision but a fact.

This hope—this supreme aspiration—must rule the way we live.

We must be ready to dare all for our country. For history does not long entrust the care of freedom to the weak or the timid. We must acquire proficiency in defense and display stamina in purpose.

We must be willing, individually, and as a nation, to accept whatever sacrifices may be required of us. A people that values its privileges above its principles soon loses both.

These basic precepts are not lofty abstractions, far removed from matters of daily living. They are laws of spiritual strength that generate and define our material strength. Patriotism means equipped forces and a prepared citizenry. Moral stamina means more energy and more productivity, on the farm and in the factory. Love of liberty means the guarding of every resource that makes freedom possible—from the sanctity of our families and the wealth of our soil to the genius of our scientists.

So each citizen plays an indispensable role. The productivity of our heads, our hands, and our hearts is the source of all the strength we can command, for both the enrichment of our lives and the winning of peace.

No person, no home, no community can be beyond the reach of this call. We are summoned to act in wisdom and in conscience; to work with industry, to teach with persuasion, to preach with conviction, to weigh our every deed with care and with compassion. For this truth must be clear before us: Whatever America hopes to bring to pass in the world must first come to pass in the heart of America.

The peace we seek, then, is nothing less than the practice and the fulfillment of our whole faith, among ourselves and in our dealings with others. It signifies more than stilling the guns, easing the sorrow, of war.

More than an escape from death, it is a way of life.

More than a haven for the weary, it is a hope for the brave.

This is the hope that beckons us onward in this century of trial. This is the work that awaits us all, to be done with bravery, with charity, and with prayer to Almighty God.

RICHARD M. NIXON
TELEVISION ADDRESS ON "McCARTHYISM"
March 13, 1954

Before I get into my talk tonight I want to thank the radio and television stations for providing time for me to reply to the attack which was made by Mr. Stevenson over these same stations on President Eisenhower and his administration last week, to give both sides a chance to be heard is in the fair, best American tradition.

At the outset I must confess this hasn't been an easy talk to prepare, not that I haven't had plenty of advice. All week long the wires and the letters, the telephone calls have been pouring into my office in Washington. The trouble is, of course, they haven't agreed.

For example, I brought a few down here.

Here is a batch that says to attack McCarthy.

And then here's a batch that says to attack Stevenson.

And over here is a group of people who say to attack both of them.

And then over here is a group that says, "Don't take on either one."

But after talking to the President we decided this issue is too important to answer in kind with a rip-roaring political tirade, before a cheering partisan audience.

The President believes, and I agree, that the best answer to an attack any time is the facts, and that is why I am sitting in this studio alone tonight. I want to talk to you just as if you were sitting across this desk from me. That is why I don't have a prepared written text. I find that when I feel very strongly on a subject I speak a little more effectively when I just refer to notes I have made myself.

Well, to begin, what did Mr. Stevenson say? Cutting away the quips and the fancy adjectives and the cheer lines you usually find in political speeches, he has criticised the Eisenhower administration on three counts.

First, he raised the question about military foreign policy, which has been referred to as the New Look. Secondly, he criticised the administration's handling of the problem of communism in the Government. Third, he claims that President Eisenhower is not providing the leadership he should to his party and to the country.

I want to take each one of these charges up in order of their importance. First one in order of importance, of course, is his criticism of our foreign and military policy—because nothing is more important than developing the policy which will allow Americans to live at peace with their neighbors. What is this new policy and why was it adopted? How does it differ from the old? I think I can tell you something about that because I was there when it was made.

Congressional Record, 83d Cong., 2d sess., 1954, 100, pt. 3, 3210-12.

Every Thursday morning since Eisenhower's administration has been in Washington there has been a meeting of the National Security Council. For two and a half to three hours, the President, Secretary of State, Secretary of Defense, and other top advisers in these fields have discussed our foreign and our military policies. They had only one objective in mind in those discussions: What is the best policy for America?

We began by asking ourselves the question—Was the policy we inherited from the previous administration good enough? And our answer was no, because of its results. What were those results?

We found that in 7 years of Truman-Acheson policies 600 million people had been lost to the Communists, and not a single Russian soldier had been lost in combat. We found when we went to Washington that we were still involved in a war in Korea that had cost us 125,000 American boys as casualties. Again not a single Russian soldier was lost in that war. We found that we inherited a budget, a policy which if continued as recommended by the Truman administration would have added $40 billion to the national debt. This would have meant had we approved that policy, more controls and higher prices for all Americans. We found that despite record spending for military purposes, that, in our efforts to be strong everywhere, we weren't strong enough anywhere. So, since our former policy had failed, we then asked ourselves the question: What kind of a new policy should we adopt?

In determining what that policy should be, we decided to find out what the men in the Kremlin were up to. We found that militarily their plan, apparently, was to destroy us by drawing us into little wars all over the world with their satellites, and where, due to our inability to bring to bear our great, superiority on the sea and in the air, we would be unable to win those wars. We found that economically their plan, apparently, was to force the United States to stay armed to the teeth, to be prepared to fight anywhere, in the world that they, the men in the Kremlin, chose.

Why? Because they knew that this would force us into bankruptcy, that we would destroy our freedom in attempting to defend it.

We decided we would not fall into these traps. So we adopted a new plan, which summed up, is this: rather than let the Communist nibble us to death all over the world in little wars, we would rely, in the future, primarily on our massive, mobile retaliatory power. This we could use at our discretion against the major source of aggression, at times and places that we chose.

We adjusted our armed strength to meet the requirements of this new concept. What was just as important, we let the world and we let the Communists know what we intended to do. Right now the question is how has that policy worked?

Well, what has happened in the first year of the Eisenhower administration? First the Korean war has been brought to an end.

Second, two American divisions have been brought home because under our new policy we have decided that we will not fight the Communists on their terms if they engage in aggression again in Korea.

Third, our budget is approaching a balance and this means that controls have ended, that taxes can be reduced, and that inflation has been stopped.

Fourth, and this is vitally important, we have finally seized the ideological offensive from Communists all over the world.

The President in his magnificent speech of April 16th before the U. N. Assembly, Secretary Dulles in his superb performance at Berlin, have finally placed the responsibility where it belongs—on the Communists—for blockading the road to peace.

Incidentally, in mentioning Secretary Dulles, isn't it wonderful, finally, to have a Secretary of State who isn't taken in by the Communists, who stands up to them?

We can be sure now that the victories our men win on the battlefields will not be lost in the future by our diplomats at the council table.

Finally, during the one year of the Eisenhower administration, in not one area of the world have the Communists made a significant gain, and in several areas we have.

Well, that's the New Look—and those are some of the results.

Now, since Mr. Stevenson objects to this policy, and since he hasn't said what he's for, I would like to ask him some questions:

First, does he think the Korean war should not have been stopped?

Second, does he think the two divisions that were brought home to America because of the New Look policy should be sent back to Korea?

Third, does he think that the Soviet Union and Communist China should not be held responsible when they commit aggression against a free nation by using one of their satellites?

Fourth, does he favor having more Korean-type wars all over the world?

Fifth, does he favor a return to the Truman-Acheson foreign policy?

And finally, in discussing this subject, may I add just two things: The best way to avoid war is to let the great aggressive powers who threaten war know that if they begin one they will be held responsible for their acts.

That's what we've done. I think the great majority of the American people will agree with the decision of this administration in doing just that.

Then I would like to say this: I am not a military strategist, and, for that matter, neither is Mr. Stevenson. I don't imagine many of you listening to this program are military experts either. But, fortunately, the man who is President of the United States is one of the greatest military leaders in the world today. He is an expert. He is the one who made the final decision on this policy. I believe that we can and should have confidence in his decision, and in that policy, particularly when the nonexpert who criticizes it offers nothing but return to a policy which failed, and was rejected overwhelmingly by the American people in the elections of November 1952.

So much for that criticism.

Now, to the second criticism Mr. Stevenson makes—the administration's handling of the problem of Communists in Government.

Here again let's see what the administration's policy is, and also let's see how it differs from that of the previous administration.

The first great difference is that this administration recognizes the danger of Communist infiltration in the United States.

We don't agree with Mr. Truman in kissing off that danger by calling it a red herring, nor do we agree with Mr. Stevenson, referring as he did to the investigations of that danger as chasing "phantoms among ourselves."

We know from studying history of the past 10 years that men like Alger Hiss and Harry White turned over secret papers to the Communists, and we know also that they were in a position to exert influence—for the Communists—on policies of the United States.

We know that our atomic experts say the Russians got the secret of the atomic bomb 3 to 5 years before they would have gotten it otherwise, because of the help they received from Communist spies right here in the United States. Consequently—because we recognize this danger—under the President's direction the executive branch of this Government has developed a program to deal with this problem.

Now, this program does two things. First, we make just as sure as we can that we don't put Communists on the payroll. Second, under a new security-risk program, we recognize that it is a privilege, not a right, to work for the Government, and that we should remove from the payroll those who are undoubted risks, and those who might be easy prey to espionage agents because of their personal habits or their backgrounds.

How does this policy work? Now, since May, when the policy was adopted, fairly and effectively, under this program we have been weeding out individuals of this type. To give you an idea, I have here a breakdown of the files of over 2,400 people who have left the Federal payroll either by resignation or discharge under this program since May. A great majority of these, incidentally, were inherited from the previous administration.

This is what their files showed: 422 of the files showed that they contained information indicating subversive activities or associations; 198 of them showed information indicating sexual perversion; 611 showed information indicating conviction for felonies or misdemeanors; 1,424 of these files showed information indicating untrustworthiness, drunkenness, mental instability, or possible exposure to blackmail.

I think all of you will agree that people with information like this in their files shouldn't be working for the Federal Government. That is what we think, and that is why they aren't working for the Federal Government today. Now, that is what the administration in the executive branch has done.

In addition, the President and this administration recognize the right and the responsibility of congressional committees to investigate in this field. Here I want to make a statement that some of you are going to agree with, and some of you are not, but which should be made.

The President and this administration, the responsible leadership in the Republican Party, insist that, whether in the executive branch or in the legislative branch of the Government, the procedures for dealing with the threat of communism in the United States must be fair and they must be proper.

Now, I can imagine some of you who are listening will say, "Why all this hullabaloo about being fair when you are dealing with a gang of traitors?" As a matter of fact, I have heard people say, "After all, we are dealing with a bunch of rats. What we ought to do is go out and shoot them."

I agree they are a bunch of rats. But just remember this, when you go out to shoot rats, you have to shoot straight, because when you shoot wildly, it not only means that the rats may get away more easily but you make it easier on the rats. Also, you might hit someone else who is trying to shoot rats, too. And so we have got to be fair for two very good reasons:

1. Because it is right; and
2. Because it is the most effective way of doing the job.

Why is it right? Well, why do we fight communism in the first place? Because communism threatens freedom, and when we use unfair methods to fight Communists, we help to destroy freedom ourselves.

Now, why is the most effective way to fight Communists to do it fairly?

I have had some experience in this field. I think I know what I am talking about. I know that even when you do it fairly, you will get criticism from some of those who object not to how you are investigating, but to what you are investigating. When you do it unfairly, and with irresponsibility, all that you do is give ammunition to those who oppose any action against the Communist. When, through carelessness, you lump the innocent and the guilty together, what you do is give the guilty a chance to pull the cloak of innocence around themselves.

In recent weeks we have see a striking example of the truth of these principles I have enunciated. Men who have in the past done effective work exposing communism in this country have, by reckless talk and questionable methods, made themselves the issue, rather than the cause they believe in so deeply. When they have done this, you see, they not only have diverted attention from the danger of communism, but have diverted that attention to themselves. Also, they have allowed those whose primary objective is to defeat the Eisenhower administration to divert attention from its great program to these individuals who follow those methods.

Now may I make a personal reference on this subject? I have fought Communists all my political life and I am proud to say that they have fought me all my political life, too.

I believe in congressional investigations because I know that if it had not been for the investigations conducted by the Committee on Un-American Activities, Alger Hiss would be free today. And it is because I believe in congressional investigations, that I know the President is right in insisting on fair procedures in those investigations. I would also like to say something else on this subject. I can assure you this administration, under President Eisenhower, will never tolerate disloyalty in any place we find it, and that when mistakes are made, we will admit them rather than to try to cover them up.

Don't you agree that is the best answer to this problem? I believe it is. Because, you see, we must remember that the extremes of those who ignored the Communist danger or who covered it up when it was exposed, have led to the extremes of those who exaggerate it today.

Well, I think that is enough on that subject.

Now let us go to the final criticism Mr. Stevenson made. In a way, it is related to the issues I just discussed. He says that President Eisenhower is not giving proper leadership to the Republican administration and to the country.

My answer to that one is pretty short, and it is very simple. President Eisenhower is not only the unquestioned leader of the Republican Party, but he has the confidence and the support of the great majority of Americans, Democrats and Republicans alike. And both his leadership and their support, believe me, are undivided.

Why would anyone raise such a question? Well, I think possibly because they mistake abuse and rhetoric for leadership. It is true that President Eisenhower does not engage in personal vituperations and vulgar name-calling, or promiscuous letterwriting, in asserting his leadership, and I say thank God he doesn't. I think the American people have had enough of that kind of leadership in the White House. Let us never forget that no really great American President ever resorted to such tactics.

How does a great man lead? How does President Eisenhower lead? He leads by example, by what he is for—and President Eisenhower is for the greatest, positive program presented to Americans in a whole generation. Its very simple objective is that all Americans can have peace and prosperity, and have peace and prosperity at the same time. That is something we haven't had in this country for 20 years.

And so I say that it is time to get behind the President's program. Let's quit being diverted from the business of putting that program into effect by fighting, and by controversy over an issue we ought to be together on.

Incidentally, you know Mr. Stevenson was good enough to give some advice to President Eisenhower and the Republican Party last week.

I am sure that he won't mind if I give a little advice to him. It is this: As the recognized leader of the Truman wing of the Democratic Party I advise Mr. Stevenson that if he has a better program to offer to the American people, either in the foreign field or in the domestic field than President Eisenhower has, to offer it and let's debate it. But if he hasn't, then I say come along with the rest of the American people and support the President's program.

And now I am going to say a final word. I believe in America's destiny, as I know all of you do. I studied America's history and I recall in our periods of great crisis America has always been blessed by having great Presidents. This may surprise some of you for me to say this, but some of those great Presidents have been Republicans and some of them have been Democrats.

Today we need the very best leadership that America can provide. I believe that we have that leadership in President Eisenhower.

I say that because I've had the opportunity of working with him.

I say it because I know not only is he respected in the United States, not only is he respected in Europe, where he has worked, but he's also known and respected and loved in countries on this earth which he's never visited.

May I tell you a little story? When Mrs. Nixon and I were on our trip around the world, we went to Bangalore, India. It was the first stop we made in India, and I remember, as we were driving through the streets the crowds were very, very heavy. So I had the car stopped at an intersection and we got out of the car to shake hands with some of the people. But the press of the crowd was so great I asked Mrs. Nixon to get back in the car, and I jumped up on the hood to make a little talk to this group of people.

Now, get the picture. Only 25 to 30 percent of these people, I imagine, even understood English.

I said two things. I said: "I want to thank you for welcoming Mrs. Nixon and me as graciously as you have on our visit to your country."

And: "I bring you the greetings not only of the people of the United States, but I bring you the greetings of the President of the United States, Dwight Eisenhower."

And then a wonderful thing happened. At the mention of the word "Eisenhower," that whole tremendous crowd broke into applause. And so we have a leader who is not only an American leader; he is a world leader, and he is a man who is mobilizing world opinion for the free nations and for us.

I have seen him make some great decisions during this past year. I see him make them day after day. But no matter how tiring the conferences have been, no matter how long, I can tell you that when he has made those decisions, I have never seen him mean; I have never seen him rash; I have never seen him impulsive; I have never seen him mad; and I have never seen him make a decision which was motivated by political purposes. His only test was the one that he said he was going to use all through the campaign—what is good for America.

I think we are lucky to have this man as President of the United States.

You know this is a great and good country.

Let's quit fighting among ourselves about an issue that all Americans should be united on. Let's join together and get behind our President in making the American dream come true.

Well, I see my time is up, and to all of you who have listened and agreed with me, my appreciation To all of you who have listened and disagreed with me, my respect—and to everybody who on a busy Saturday night took the time to hear this program, thank you, and good night.

ARTHUR LARSON
A REPUBLICAN LOOKS AT HIS PARTY
1956

PRINCIPLES OF THE NEW REPUBLICANISM

The principles of New Republicanism, which give expression and direction to our National Consensus on fundamentals, are these:

1. *We begin by acknowledging reverently the existence of a God of order, justice and love.*

Because this is a universe of order, we may frame our plans around a faith that the innate motivations given us by the Creator will drive us toward progress, prosperity and happiness.

Since this is a universe of justice, then our insistence on the highest standards in government, on a framework of fair play for the settlement of disputes brought on by the free forces of our society, and on the firm and even-handed enforcement of the laws is justified on a higher level than that of good administration; it is justified on the necessity of attuning government to the deepest moral and ethical principles.

And since there is a God of love, our efforts to allay the suffering of the unfortunate, to temper the exercise of raw economic force at the expense of the less strong, and to provide opportunity for each individual person to realize the best that is in himself, are not sentimentalism; they are the governmental counterpart of a rule of life accepted by devout Americans as an expression of their religious convictions.

2. *The individual person is the pre-eminent object of all our political arrangements.*

Governments as such—whether federal, state or municipal—unions as such, business or nonbusiness organizations as such, are only means toward a better life for the person.

This means that in all we do, we must respect his pride, his independence, his right to be himself, his right to come and go as he chooses, and his age-old franchise to work out or fight out his own destiny and keep the rewards of his exertions and ingenuity, so long as he respects the similar rights of others.

It also means that our legislation must deal in separate people as far as possible; we do not deal in classes or masses, and we are not satisfied with statistically average

Arthur Larson, "Principles of the New Republicanism," ch. 8, *A Republican Looks at His Party* (New York, 1956), 198-204.

welfare. The well-being of a member of a minority—even a very small minority—is as important as that of the dominant majority, because each member of that small minority is just as much created in God's image as if he happened to be associated with a larger group. God's image is not to be arrived at by drawing a composite portrait using the average features of the majority.

Finally, it means that the person must remain sovereign in his dealings with government. He must not be maneuvered into the position of cringing before it for largesse; he must not be pushed around unnecessarily in his everyday affairs; and he is entitled to have as large a share in government as is administratively feasible.

3.   Government should be as local as possible.

If the individual is to have as large a share as possible in government, the principle of localism as against centralization follows, since it is axiomatic that a person has a larger say in the running of his school board than in the decisions of the United States Senate.

The convergence of all lines of power in Washington is dangerous, not only because it separates people more widely from their government, but also because it has the potentiality of gradually drawing us into the kind of totalitarianism that almost brought a new Dark Age on the world.

State governments must be built up in prestige, strength, fiscal sturdiness and sense of responsibility; and the great municipalities, where most of our people now live, must similarly shoulder an unprecedented share of the over-all job of government.

We believe that the tradition of localization of authority in matters not clearly demanding central concern is fundamental to our federal form of government and to its original wise purpose of keeping a swollen Executive, whether arrogant or beneficent or both, from becoming the master of the people.

4.   Whatever can be done privately should be done privately.

Even under this principle, and under the principle that government should be as local as possible, there will always be more than enough for the federal government to do, confining itself to matters that neither private entities nor local governments can handle.

But if there is added to the unavoidable federal responsibilities a layer of further jobs that could be managed by states and a still further layer of activities that should be in the hands of private enterprise, the combination is almost certain to inflate the central government to perilous proportions.

Therefore, the government should stay out of business, and when it is necessary to regulate business, it should not cut into the main channel of activity, but simply police the boundaries of the channel to protect the public interest.

5.   The government has a responsibility for prosperity which it discharges best by aiding and releasing, not by over-ruling, the forces of private enterprise.

The principle of private enterprise, comprising the ideas of free competition, rewards for incentive, penalties for sloth and opportunity for everyone, is intrinsically right. The government's principal responsibilities are: to adopt wise tax policies that will stimulate both investment and purchasing power; to battle inflation by striking at its sources rather than by trying to trim off its effects; to attune its own gigantic fiscal movements to the times, so as to aid orderly growth and stability; to use its facilities and resources to help build up areas not sharing in the general prosperity; and to act upon unhealthy turns in the business cycle by guiding the inherent forces of private enterprise, such as credit, rather than by usurping and invading the domain of private enterprise and by affronting and violating its rules.

Dr. Gabriel Hauge, Assistant to President Eisenhower on economic matters, cites a phrase for it: the government should attempt to influence the economic weather and not try to ration raindrops.

6.   *The government has a responsibility for enabling working people to improve their lot through fair collective bargaining, which it discharges best by encouraging free trade unionism, guaranteeing the right of genuine representative collective bargaining, and then avoiding interference with these free negotiations.*

Just as the attitude toward private enterprise stems from a deep faith in the inner soundness of that system, so the attitude toward unionism and collective bargaining is an expression of the fullest faith in those institutions.

Note also the consistency between this policy and the policy of governmental withdrawal from interference with private affairs. Where good unions exist, the government does not have to intervene in the interest of raising labor standards. Where unions are lacking, it sometimes becomes necessary to have minimum wage laws, maximum hours laws and other compulsory laws to eradicate substandard working conditions. The government, therefore, in carrying out its objective of withholding its hand from private matters, is glad to have the job of protecting labor standards more and more taken over by free nongovernmental agencies.

7.   *The government has a responsibility for the general welfare of people, which it discharges best by initiating systems of income insurance, disaster relief, aid for education, health, safety and the like, with a maximum of private and local content and a minimum of centralized control.*

It is the objective of New Republicanism to combine a dignified provision against the more serious personal risks inherent in a fast-changing competitive economy with actual strengthening of both individual values and business vigor. It is its objective also to combine the generous marshaling of federal resources in aid of traditionally local activities such as education, roads, health, safety and relief with the building-up rather than the chopping-away of state responsibility and stature.

These combinations are not impossible, but can be achieved only if the determination to achieve them is never for a moment slackened, and if we are willing to apply to the task all the ingenuity, diligence and patience at our disposal. The "easy way" to go at the job of welfare is by abdicating the entire responsibility to a governmental welfare state created by a few strokes of federal legislation. To get comparable benefits—while preserving our American division of function—is "the hard way," but it is our way and it can succeed.

8.   *America has its own political philosophy, stemming not from the European left-wing, right-wing concept, but from the ideals of our Revolution and Constitution, and drawing its flexibility and vitality from the American tradition of willingly employing novel mechanisms in changing times to preserve our oldest ideals.*

Our history is one of inventing and applying original and daring devices to spread across a new continent the enduring virtues of personal liberty, equality of opportunity and self-realization of individual persons.

The struggle which formed the basis of our traditions is not that of class against class in a land which has had centuries in which to sort people into aristocrat, gentleman and villein, or in more modern times, into Right and Left; it is rather that of millions of people from every conceivable background fighting side by side against the wilderness, the prairie, the forest, the sea and the forces of nature. The difference is crucial: the former struggle is in essence a contest to divide what is already in hand—mainly a struggle of the have-nots to take away from the haves; the latter struggle is a struggle to create something where nothing was before, and to produce ever more and more. It is the difference between the storming of the Bastille, and the California gold rush; it is the difference between inventing the guillotine and inventing the reaper; it is the difference between the Corn Laws and the Homestead Act.

As a result of our people's essentially classless tradition and sense of similarity of background, it is natural and fitting that our political scene should display, not a division into left-wingers and right-wingers, but a large and powerful Center. A good image of the story of European class conflicts and left-right struggles is contained in a remark of Martin Luther: "Mankind is a drunken peasant on a donkey. You heave him up on one side and he only slides down on the other." But that is not the pattern for America in the mid-century and in the critical years ahead. This is no time to harry the American public from crisis to crisis, nor to drive breaches between groups for transient political advantage. The nation which must shoulder the gravest world responsibilities of the Thermonuclear Age cannot heave from one side to another like a drunken peasant on a donkey. Fortunate indeed it is that the period which assigned us these responsibilities was also the period in which there appeared the strong, confident, center-of-the-road American Consensus.

NELSON A. ROCKEFELLER, STATEMENT ON PROBLEMS FACING THE REPUBLICAN PARTY AND HIS WITHDRAWAL FROM THE PRESIDENTIAL RACE
June 8, 1960

We have come to a time that calls for plain talk.

It is a difficult and testing time.

It is so for the world—with the forces of freedom challenged as never before.

It is so for the nation—with the hope and strength of freedom everywhere reliant upon us.

It is so therefore for the Republican party—with the vigor of our own democracy at stake.

The vitality and integrity of the Republican party, at so critical a time as the present, become matters of national concern. Without a two-party system that works with candor and courage, the American Republic—the very processes of democratic government—cannot work responsibly. Without the Republican party displaying such candor and courage, the two-party system cannot work creatively.

A responsible patriotism thus does not deny—but does demand—a responsible partisanship. For the way a party speaks and acts can—and should—inspire the way a nation speaks and acts.

I am deeply convinced, and deeply concerned, that those now assuming control of the Republican party have failed to make clear where this party is heading and where it proposes to lead the nation.

Now is the time to face and weigh these facts.

We, as Republicans, have much to give us pride in our history. This history reaches from the principles of a Lincoln to the principles of an Eisenhower. No attack or abuse from any quarter can diminish—it can only dramatize—the dignity and the integrity of the leadership that President Eisenhower has given to both nation and party.

This man who led us to victory over the Nazi menace has steadfastly faced the Communist tyranny in tireless pursuit of a just peace. He thus has won a place unique in our age and in the hearts of free men everywhere.

As he lays down his burdens, this historic term of service comes to its end.

A new period now begins. It summons new men. New problems demand new ideas, new actions.

Where do they begin?

They begin, I believe, with this awareness: we cannot and we must not confuse taking pride in the past with taking measure of the future.

What—and who—is this future? It is a host of men and nations, problems and forces, to be ignored or evaded only at deadly peril to our own national life and freedom. It is: nuclear power, either serving to better lives and to defend peoples—or serving to shatter nations and shake the planet. It is: the rise of new nations across the earth, either to learn and to enjoy the ways of freedom—or to suffer and to serve the ways of tyranny. It is: a great technological revolution changing the lives of all men, for better or for worse, as it is disciplined and directed. It is: an immensely complex problem of national defense for an exposed America—a problem either to be resolved by strong action or to be evaded by strong slogans. It is: the need for the American economy to grow faster—to prove that freedom will not become static or sterile, but forever be fertile and creative. It is: the proving by political action (or the disproving by partisan evasion) that we do love and respect the dignity of man—as we assure civil rights for all our people, education for our young, health for our aged.

The people, confronting these great and basic challenges, look to their political parties.

They need an assurance—and a strategy—of national purpose for the future.

I deeply believe they are asking for this.

They cannot be answered—by either political party—with mere petty designs of partisan maneuver.

The challenge this poses to the Republican party is made more urgent by the state of leadership of the Democratic party. This leadership can inspire no citizen with great hope. It has been confused and uncertain. It has seemed to answer—almost mechanically—great questions of the future with worn answers from the past. In all the area of foreign policy, it has contributed little of force or relevance to even the discussion of foreign affairs—through eight years of vocal opposition. In all the area of domestic policy, no matter is more critical than civil rights—and no matter so deeply divides the Democratic party.

These facts do not make the task and the duty of the Republican party more easy.

They make this duty more stern and demanding—for the nation's sake.

I cannot pretend to believe that the Republican party has fully met this duty.

I know it is unconventional—on the political scene—to mention lacks or lapses in one's own party.

But the times we live in are not conventional.

And the scene we must view is not simply one of partisan politics, but the politics—perhaps the destiny—of all the world.

This is not extreme. It is merely realistic.

In this spirit, I am compelled to say two things bluntly.

1. I find it unreasonable—in these times—that the leading Republican candidate for the Presidential nomination has firmly insisted upon making known his program and his policies not before, but only after, nomination by his party.

2. I find it reasonable—and urgently necessary—that the new spokesmen of the Republican party declare now, and not at some later date, precisely what they believe and what they propose, to meet the great matters before the nation.

I had hoped—in months past—that anyone aspiring to lead the party would do precisely this. I have been waiting for this.

It has not been done.

I can no longer be silent on the fact.

We cannot, as a nation or as a party, proceed—nor should anyone presume to ask us to proceed—to march to meet the future with a banner aloft whose only emblem is a question mark.

The duty of this time is no less binding on myself than upon others—this duty to talk plainly.

In this spirit, I wish to state a number of problems, concrete and crucial, on which the Republican party—and any of its leaders—must state their stands.

1. I believe that the future development of our foreign policy must begin with the fact that our position in the world is dramatically weaker today than fifteen years ago, at the end of World War II. The blame for this can be placed on no one party, on no one administration. The fact is that world upheaval, exploited by communism, now challenges America and the West more gravely than at any time in our history.

These facts must be honestly faced. To speak of them is to confess neither weakness nor fear.

Strength begins with truth.

Future pretenses could damage us far more than past reverses.

We can begin clearly to succeed in the future only as we begin to know clearly where we failed in the past.

We, as a people, must act with firmer knowledge of the dynamic nature and aggressive purpose of Communist imperialism.

We must quickly strengthen the forces of freedom and the unity and common effort of free peoples.

2. I believe our national defense needs great strengthening to meet the physical danger in which America lives. This danger has to be made completely clear to the people whose freedom—and lives—are at stake. And this danger is measured by such plain facts as these:

a. Our long-range missiles are not only inferior in number to those at Soviet disposal, but also are dangerously vulnerable to Soviet attack.

b. Our strategic bombers, though reasonably large in number, are concentrated on less than fifty bases, all clearly identified by the Soviets, every one defenseless against a direct missile-hit.

c. For all our reliance upon Polaris submarines, not one is operational now, and only two will be operational by the start of 1961.

d. For all the dangers of local aggression, our forces for limited war are inadequate in strength and mobility.

Every one of these facts is fully known to the Soviet Union.

3. I believe these facts require immediate actions to increase both the strength and the efficiency of our defenses—including:

a. An additional $3,000,000,000 for immediate defense needs, including additional and improved bombers, air-borne alert, more missiles, more Polaris submarines, modernized equipment for our ground forces.

b. A $500,000,000 program for civil defense.

c. A more flexible and balanced military establishment and doctrine to meet all contingencies including local aggression.

d. A more tightly organized Department of Defense.

4. I believe the needs of our defense structure reflect the still wider need of our whole government structure for an organization adapted to meet modern problems and threats in all their complexity and swiftness. This is essential for effective conduct of both our international relations and our national affairs. This need found instant and sobering proof in the conduct of government departments during the U-2 incident.

5. I believe in the urgent need for adequate and formal international inspection and control of arms. Never before in history have nations been armed and able to devastate one another—in mere minutes. Yet we, as a nation, have seemed, on occasion, no better prepared to meet this critical and continuing challenge than to confront sudden accident or crisis. Thus one month before the start of the Ten Nations Disarmament Conference in Geneva there simply did not exist a prepared American position.

The machinery of free government can and must be geared to do better than this.

6. I believe that, as our economic strength must match and sustain our military power, we must quicken the growth of the American economy to meet all challenges and needs, domestic and foreign. This demands raising of sights—and of effort by both labor and management—throughout the private economy that is the mainspring of our growth. It further requires that we gear our economic policies and practices to work toward an annual rate of growth of 5 to 6 per cent. And these policies will have to include:

a. Revision of tax policies to encourage investment;

b. Elimination of all featherbedding or restrictive practices by labor or management; and

c. Redefinition of our farm program to make low-income farmers more productive members of the economy.

7. I believe this economic strength further requires firm discipline upon forces threatening to unleash inflation, weaken defense production, and disrupt our economy. The Administration of President Eisenhower has written a notable record in the field of fiscal integrity. Yet our economy must not be tormented by periodic crises or clashes that invite solution by political pressure or political expediency. I believe firmly in the democratic process of collective bargaining, and I am firmly opposed to automatic or general use of compulsory arbitration. Yet I believe the President should be given discretionary authority to use compulsory arbitration if an economic conflict reaches the point of clearly endangering the national welfare and if all honest attempts of collective bargaining, mediation and arbitration have been exhausted. Such a procedure would help to avoid the kind of surrender to forces of inflation that marked the long-delayed settlement of the steel strike last year. This settlement carefully postponed until after next election day the cost of its consequences—a rise in steel costs of more than $1,000,000,000 annually. For this the public must pay the price.

8. I believe we must practice at home such a respect for law and equality as we wish to reach—and serve—in the world at large. The record of the Republican party on civil rights is a very creditable one—certainly on any comparative basis. But no record

can claim to be good enough so long as discrimination, segregation, and disenfranchisement persist on almost massive scale. The Supreme Court has called for respect of the basic laws and principles of our nation "with all deliberate speed." The deliberateness must not be sabotage. The time has come for progress. And this can come with the summoning of cooperative efforts by leaders in communities throughout the nation.

9. I believe that, for a nation traditionally passionate about the need for good and general education, we have seemed singularly slow to assure—through Federal aid to needy areas—equality of educational opportunity for all. This can be done—without interfering with local control of education—by Federal aid for school construction and increased Federal scholarships. If the Democratic party has done little or nothing in this area, the fact is no less true that a number of Republican leaders have managed, one way or another, to join with Democrats to block effective action. A whole generation should not be asked to wait much longer. Even a hugely prosperous country cannot afford such investment in purely partisan maneuvering—with the price paid in citizenship.

10. I believe that we must meet the growing problem of medical help for the aged. The formula recently proposed by the Administration, while admirable in purpose, is basically unsound from a fiscal viewpoint. It is based largely on a concept of subsidy. It would be both costly and cumbersome to administer. We have a long-established contributory system of social insurance. Its soundness is proven. We should build on it.

These are the serious matters before us.

As we meet and weigh them, we need realize that the very life of our democratic system requires the Republican party to speak and to argue its views with vigor—but also with responsibility and reason. I accordingly deplore any voices suggesting, by inference or innuendo, that our national unity requires any stifling of debate.

We should remember, too, that one vital sign of our national political health is given not only by full debate between our two parties, but also by open debate within each of our political parties. Each party itself serves as a forum—preceding the greater forum that is the national electorate. Real party unity and strength can be based only on honest debate. And in the watching eyes of the people, such debate will be understood as a sign not of disunity but of vitality.

All these specific things I firmly believe.

This is not just another election year.

The stakes are historically high.

The occasional, or frequent, trappings of a political campaign cannot suffice for either party—the resounding platitudes, the hollow clichés, the eloquent evasions, the slick slogans.

The time—I do repeat—calls for plain talk.

The talk must be of specific problems, specific actions, specific purposes.

A century ago, in the shadow of civil war, the Republican party proved itself master of the challenge it met.

It must prove itself again—in no less historic a way.

There remain less than two months before the Republican party assembles in convention to set its course and to choose its leaders.

This time must be spent in one way: in placing the facts before the people and in summoning the people to the great endeavors that these facts demand.

This is the way—the only way—a living democracy works.

The people—I am convinced—are ready.

The question remains: is the party ready?

The path of great leadership does not lie along the top of a fence.

It climbs heights.

It speaks truths.

The people want and need one thing above all others: a leadership of clear purpose, candidly proclaimed.

"THE TREATY OF FIFTH AVENUE"
ROCKEFELLER-NIXON PACT ON GOP PLATFORM
July 23, 1960

STATEMENT BY GOVERNOR ROCKEFELLER

The Vice-President and I met today at my home in New York City.

The meeting took place at the Vice President's request.

The purpose of the meeting was to discuss the platform of the Republican party. During the course of the meeting we discussed our views with Chairman Percy and other members of the platform committee by telephone.

The Vice Preisdent and I reached agreement on the following specific and basic positions on foreign policy and national defense:

1. The growing vigor and aggressiveness of communism demands new and profound effort and action in all areas of American Life.

2. The vital need of our foreign policy is new political creativity—leading and inspiring the formation, in all great regions of the free world, of confederations, large enough and strong enough to meet modern problems and challenges. We should promptly lead toward the formation of such confederations in the North Atlantic community and in the Western Hemisphere.

3. In the field of disarmament we shall
   a. Intensify the quest for better detection methods;
   b. Discontinue nuclear weapon tests in the atmosphere;
   c. Discontinue other tests as detection methods make possible, and,
   d. Resume immediately underground nuclear testing for purposes of improving methods of detection.

4. In national defense, the swiftness of the technological revolution—and the warning signs of Soviet aggressiveness—makes clear that new efforts are necessary, for the facts of our survival in the Nineteen Fifties give no assurance of such survival, in the same military posture, in the Nineteen Sixties.

5. The two imperatives of national security in the Nineteen Sixties are:

New York Times, July 24, 1960.

    a.   A powerful second-strike capacity—a nuclear retaliatory power capable of surviving surprise attack to inflict devastating punishment on any aggressor, and,

    b.   A modern, flexible and balanced military establishment with forces capable of deterring or meeting any local aggression.

6.   These imperatives require: More and improved bombers, airborne alert, speeded production of missiles and Polaris submarines, accelerated dispersal and hardening of bases, full modernization of the equipment of our ground forces, and an intensified program for civil defense.

7.   The United States can afford and must provide the increased expenditures to implement fully this necessary program for strengthening our defense posture. There must be no price ceiling on America's security.

The Vice President and I also reached agreement on the following specific positions on domestic affairs:

1.   Our government must be reorganized—especially in supporting the President in the crucial decision-making process—to cope effectively with modern problems and challenges. Specifically, this calls for:

    a.   Creation of a post to assist the President in the whole area of national security and international affairs;

    b.   Creation of a post to assist in planning and management of domestic affairs, and,

    c.   Reorganization of defense planning and command to achieve under the President, unified doctrine and unified direction of forces.

2.   The rate of our economic growth must, as promptly as possible, be accelerated by policies and programs stimulating our free enterprise system—to allow us to meet the demands of national defense and the growing social needs and a higher standard of living for our growing population. As the Vice President pointed out in a speech in 1958, the achievement of a 5 per cent rate of growth would produce an additional $10,000,000,000 of tax reserve in 1962.

3.   Our farm programs must be realistically reoriented by:

    a.   Finding and encouraging ways for our low income farmers to become more productive members of our growing economy;

    b.   At least doubling of the Conservation Reserve;

    c.   Use of price supports at level best-fitted to specific commodity in order to widen markets, ease production controls, and help achieve equitable farm income;

d. Faster disposal of surpluses through an expanded "Food for Peace" program and allocation of some surplus to a stock pile for civil defense.

4. Our program for civil rights must assure aggressive action to remove the remaining vestiges of segregation or discrimination in all areas of national life—voting and housing, schools and jobs. It will express support for the objectives of the sit-in demonstrators and will commend the action of those business men who have abandoned the practice of refusing to serve food at their lunch counters to their Negro customers and will urge all others to follow their example.

5. Our program for health insurance for the aged shall provide insurance on a sound fiscal basis through a contributory system under which beneficiaries have the option of purchasing private health insurance.

6. Our program for labor, while reaffirming our efforts to support and strengthen the processes of free collective bargaining, shall provide for improved procedures for the resolution of disputes endangering the national welfare.

7. Our program for educational needs [sic] by calling for prompt and substantial grant aid for school construction primarily on the basis of financial needs, under an equalization formula, and with matching funds by the states—including these further measures for higher education: grants-in-aid for such buildings as classrooms and laboratories, an expanded loan program for dormitories, expanded student loan and graduate fellowship programs and inauguration of a program of federal scholarships for the most able undergraduates.

These constitute the basic positions for which I have been fighting.

If they are embodied in the Republican Party platform, as adopted by the convention, they will constitute a platform that I can support with pride and vigor.

STATEMENT BY VICE PRESIDENT NIXON

Governor Rockefeller and I have been in consultation with the Platform Committee since its sessions began. By yesterday, it was apparent that there was a general agreement among members of the committee and between the Governor and myself regarding the basic philosophy to be followed as we go into the 1960 campaign.

Whatever differences that existed between Governor Rockefeller and myself were matters more of specifics than of principle. I felt it in the best interests of both our country and the Republican party at this critical time in history that it be made clear that we stood firmly together on these important issues.

Therefore, I called Governor Rockefeller and arranged a private meeting last night. The text of the statement released by the Governor defines our area of agreement and provides a guide to our thinking for the consideration of the Platform Committee.

BARRY GOLDWATER, "GROW UP, CONSERVATIVES" ADDRESS TO GOP CONVENTION WITHDRAWING HIS NOMINATION, 1960

Mr. Chairman, delegates to the convention and fellow Republicans:

I respectfully ask the chairman to withdraw my name from nomination. Please, I release my delegation from their pledge to me and, while I'm not a delegate, I would suggest that they give these votes to Richard Nixon.

Now, Mr. Chairman, with your kind permission and indulgence, as a conservative Republican I would like to make a few statements that will not take more than a few moments, and I think might help in this coming election.

We are conservatives. This great Republican party is our historic house. This is our home. Now some of us don't agree with every statement in the official platform of our party, but I might remind you that this is always true in every platform of an American political party.

Both of the great historic parties represent a broad spectrum of views spread over a variety of individual and group convictions. Never are all of these views expressed totally and exclusively in the platform of either party.

We can be absolutely certain of one thing. In spite of the individual points of difference the Republican platform deserves the support of every American over the blueprint for socialism presented by the Democrats.

Over the years, however, it is clear what the historic position of both the great parties has been. There has been a real difference over-all in the two great parties.

I might suggest to you that during the past thirty years it is true beyond any doubt that those with more radical views have felt more at home in the Democratic party, while those with strong historic beliefs have felt more at home in the Republican party.

The same condition prevails today. Yet if each segment, each section of our great party, were to insist on the complete and unqualified acceptance of its views, if each viewpoint were to be enforced by a Russian-type veto, the Republican party would not long survive.

There are tides of sentiment, tides of belief, that rise and fall inside the party. And under these changes in emphasis the basic core convictions of the party endure from generation to generation.

Now radical Democrats who rightfully fear that the American people will reject their extreme program in November are watching this convention with eager hopes that some split may occur in our party.

I am telling them now that no such split will take place.

New York Times, July 28, 1960.

This very morning the press carried a story that the nominee for the Vice-Presidency on the Democratic ticket was speaking hopefully of a split in the Republican party. Let him know that the conservatives of the Republican party do not intend by any act of theirs to turn this country over by default to a party which has lost its belief in the dignity of man, a party which has come to believe that the United States is a second-rate power.

I am proud to call myself a Republican as well as conservative. And let me tell you something and let me remind the members of the press who might think otherwise:

I've been campaigning across this country for six years for Richard Nixon. And I see no reason to change my mind tonight.

Now you conservatives and all Republicans, I'd like you to listen to this. While Dick and I may disagree on some points, they're not many. I would not want any negative action of mine to enhance the possibility of a victory going to those who by their very words have lost faith in America.

I know that conservatives here and in November will show the strong sense of responsibility which is a central characteristic of the conservative temper.

We must remember that Republicans have not been losing elections because of more Democrat votes—now get this—we have been losing elections because conservatives too often fail to vote.

Why is this? And you conservatives think this over—we don't gain anything when you get mad at a candidate because you don't agree with his every philosophy. We don't gain anything when you disagree with the platform and then do not go out and work and vote for your party.

I know what you say. You say, "I'll get even with that fellow. I'll show this party something!" But what are you doing when you stay at home? You are helping the opposition party elect candidates dedicated to the destruction of this country!

We have lost election after election in this country in the last several years because conservative Republicans get mad and stay home. Now I implore you. Forget it! We've had our chance, and I think the conservatives have made a splendid showing at this convention!

We've had our chance: we've fought our battle. Now let's put our shoulders to the wheels of Dick Nixon and push him across the line. Let's not stand back. This country is too important for anyone's feelings: this country in its majesty is too great for any man, be he conservative or liberal, to stay home and not work just because he doesn't agree. Let's grow up, conservatives.

Let's, if we want to take this party back—and I think we can someday—let's get to work.

I'm a conservative and I'm going to devote all my time from now until November to electing Republicans from the top of the ticket to the bottom of the ticket, and I call upon my fellow conservatives to do the same. Just let us remember that we are facing Democrat candidates and a Democrat platform that signify a new type of New Deal, far more menacing than anything we have seen in the past.

Just remember this: The Democratic party is no longer the party of Jefferson, Jackson and Woodrow Wilson; it is now the party of Bowles, Galbraith, and Walter Reuther.

RICHARD M. NIXON, ACCOUNT OF FIRST TELEVISION DEBATE WITH SENATOR KENNEDY, 1960

[For excerpts from the Great Debates, see pp. 2879-2908.]

. . . All the previous week I had used every spare minute preparing my opening statement and studying the issues that might be raised by the panel of newsmen. I got up early Sunday morning and worked through the day, without interruption, until it was time to go to the airport for a ten o'clock night flight to Chicago. As I pored over my material I wished that I had arranged to have Saturday free as well as Sunday for this preparation. But it was too late to do anything about the situation now, except to ask Jim Bassett to lighten the schedule somewhat before each of the next three debates so that I could have more time for studying the issues and also for some needed rest after a hard week of campaigning.

Our flight was scheduled for a 10:30 arrival in Chicago, Central Time, which would make it possible for me to get to bed by midnight for a good night's sleep. But our plans did not work out exactly as we had expected. Despite the late hour, we were met at the airport by a crowd of some 5000. And the Chicago Republican leaders had planned street rallies in each of the five wards we would be passing through on our way from the airport to the Pick-Congress Hotel. Only a brief 15-minute stop was required in each case, but it was past one o'clock Monday morning before we finally arrived downtown.

The next morning I made an eleven o'clock appearance before the annual convention of the Carpenters Union, my second campaign speech to a labor organization. While the Carpenters, like the Machinists, were expected to end up in the Kennedy camp, I thought it important to accept their invitation, particularly in view of the fact that Republican strength among the rank-and-file is probably greater in the Carpenters' membership than in any other union.

For five solid hours that afternoon I read through and digested material which my staff had prepared, on every issue that might conceivably be raised during the course of the debate. By the time I had completed my boning and was ready to take off for the television station, I felt that I was as thoroughly prepared for this appearance as I had ever been in my political life up to that time. I had crammed my head with facts and figures in answer to more than a hundred questions which my staff suggested might be raised in the field of domestic affairs.

The tension continued to rise all afternoon. My entire staff obviously felt it just as I did. As we rode to the television studio, conversation was a a minimum as I continued to study my notes up to the last minute.

Richard M. Nixon, *Six Crises* (New York, 1962), 336-42.

The presidents of the four major networks greeted me as I walked into the studio and I was immediately ushered onto the set so that the lighting and sound technicians could make their final tests. About ten minutes later, Kennedy arrived. This was the first time we had met each other since the Senate had adjourned. I had never seen him look more fit. I remarked on his deep tan and he jokingly replied that he had gotten it from riding in open cars while touring sunny California. We posed for pictures for four or five minutes and then each of us went to the rooms assigned us to wait for broadcast time.

I had vetoed Ted Rogers' recommendation that I wear makeup and agreed only that Ev Hart of our TV staff might apply some "beard stick" powder to help cover my perpetual "five o'clock shadow"—which the television cameras always pick up, even five minutes after I have shaved. I continued to pore over my notes until Rogers came in the room and told me, with five minutes until broadcast time, that we should move on-stage.

Howard K. Smith of CBS News, Moderator for the evening, stuck to the classic script, said "the candidates need no introduction"—and then proceeded to introduce us anyway—and history's first television debate between presidential candidates, and what may have been the most important and most decisive appearance either Kennedy or I was to make during the entire campaign, was on.

Kennedy had the opening argument. He took roughly the line I had expected and he spoke as effectively as I have ever heard him. He did exactly what I would have done under similar circumstances: he attacked. Depressed and distressed areas, the unemployed, Puerto Rican and Negro victims of discrimination, the downtrodden farmers, the old people who couldn't afford adequate medical care, the underpaid teachers—all these were the fault of the Eisenhower Administration. We wanted to stand still—he wanted to move ahead. We didn't care about these problems—he did. For eight lagging years America had been stuck on dead-center—it is time to get her moving again. The Russians are catching up with us and will soon leave us in the dust—unless we get going.

When he finished, eight minutes later, I realized that I had heard a very shrewd, carefully calculated appeal, with subtle emotional overtones, that would have great impact on a television audience. And particularly it would impress unsophisticated voters who—far from questioning the facts in the matter—would not even ask themselves: How does he propose to do all these things? How much is it going to cost? How is he going to keep all these promises? Whose money is he going to spend anyway—his or ours?

Against this appeal, and in the mood thus established, it was now my turn. Looking back, I suppose the politically expedient course would have been for me to grant without argument that we had been standing still for the past eight years and then to promise, if I were elected, to do everything he had promised, and more besides. But I rejected this demagogic approach and proceeded to answer him, point-by-point. I said that, far from standing still, the nation had experienced eight years of its greatest progress in history under Eisenhower, largely because of his sound policies. I pointed out that there was no difference between us in "caring" about the problems of less fortunate people. We had the same ultimate goals—sustained growth and prosperity widely shared. Our differences—and all-important ones—arose over how best to solve all these problems. Kennedy would do it by primary emphasis on huge and costly Federal Government programs—which would have to be paid for right out of the pockets of the people he was trying to help, and in cheapened dollars to boot. I proposed to solve them with a necessary minimum of government action but with primary emphasis on and encouragement of individual initiative and private enterprise. The great gulf of difference between us, I strongly implied, was that of a bureaucratic society vs. a free society.

The issue had been joined. Now came the questions. One of them—of no real substantive importance actually—was to plague me the rest of the campaign. It was put by Sander Vanocur of NBC. He referred to a statement President Eisenhower had made in a press conference on August 24. Someone had asked him, "What major decisions of your Administration has the Vice President participated in?" Eisenhower had replied: "If you give me a week, I might think of one." Later that same day, Eisenhower had called me on the phone and expressed chagrin at the way this exchange had been handled by the press. He pointed out that he was simply being facetious and yet they played it straight and wrote it seriously. I could only reply to Vanocur's question in the same vein, but I am sure that to millions of unsophisticated televiewers, this question had been most effective in raising a doubt in their minds with regard to one of my strongest campaign themes and assets—my experience as Vice President.

With that teaser out of the way, the panel turned to more important issues—Kennedy's and my farm programs, the probable cost of the "New Frontier," school aid, the seriousness of the internal threat of Communist subversion, Kennedy's prediction as to his probable success in getting Congress to pass all the new legislation he was proposing, especially in view of his failure to get any major legislation passed during the post-Convention congressional session. But because of the format of the program, there was no time for answers in depth. And because the members of the panel jumped from subject to subject with no apparent attempt to provide any continuity, the question period took on a decidedly scatter-shot tone. In our closing statements, both Kennedy and I returned to the basic positions we had taken at the outset, I to the need for sound and stable progress with an emphasis on free choice and private initiative, and Kennedy to a demand that we simply "get moving."

Finally, the hour came to an end. Kennedy and I shook hands. The press asked us who had won. I replied that we would learn the answer to that question on Election Day. We then left the studio and I returned to the hotel.

As we rode back, I tried to analyze the debate objectively. I felt that Kennedy had done extremely well. He had been on the offensive throughout, just as I had expected him to be. I thought that as far as the arguments were concerned, point-by-point, I might have had a little the better of it. But also, from a great deal of experience with television, I knew that appearance may at times count more than substance, and I was anxious to make a check as soon as possible on the key question: how did each of us come through on the TV screen?

When I got to my hotel suite, I asked Don Hughes to get Len Hall, Fred Seaton, Bob Finch, Jack Drown, Jim Shepley, and any others who were available to come by and give me an appraisal. Before they arrived, however, Rose Mary Woods, my personal secretary and also one of my most honest critics, came in with some disturbing information. Her parents had called—from their home in Sebring, Ohio—and asked if I were feeling up to par. They said that on their TV set I had looked pale and tired. I asked Rose what she thought. She said she tended to agree with their reaction, despite the fact that she thought I had had the better of the argument on substance.

This proved to be the unanimous reaction of my campaign advisers. At the conclusion of our post-mortem, I recognized the basic mistake I had made. I had concentrated too much on substance and not enough on appearance. I should have remembered that "a picture is worth a thousand words." I would be the first to recognize that I have many weaknesses as a politician candidate, but one of my strengths is that I try to be my own severest critic. In this instance, I realized that the lesson was plain: next three times out we must not make the same mistake. If the picture was bad, it could not be blamed on the technicians. If we felt the technicians were not competent, then it was our responsibility to find better ones.

My growing conviction about how bad I must have looked was further confirmed when my mother called from California, after the program was carried there, to ask Rose if I were "feeling all right."

It would be a most convenient excuse for me to blame my poor physical appearance on the fact that I really wasn't feeling up to par. But this simply is not the truth. I had never felt better mentally before any important appearance than I did before the first debate. My knee still bothered me a bit, but when I am keyed up, as I was on this occasion, I do not notice physical pain at all. What then was the trouble? Some of it was technical, over which I had no control. But in all honesty, I must admit in retrospect that some of it was avoidable. The TV camera is like a microscope: it shows not how one feels but what his physical condition actually is.

Dr. Malcolm Todd, who had joined us by this time, talked to me like a Dutch uncle after the program. He asked me how much I weighed because he had noticed that my shirt—collar-size 16, standard with me since college days—fit loosely. I had to admit that I had not been on the scales since leaving the hospital over two weeks before. I stepped on the scales in the bathroom at the Pick-Congress and realized for the first time how much had been taken out of me, physically, by two weeks in a hospital bed followed immediately by two weeks of intensive campaigning. I weighed 160—ten pounds below normal and five pounds less than I could remember having weighed at any time in the last thirty years. Dr. Todd said, "You looked weak and pale and tired tonight on TV because, in fact, you *are* weak and pale and tired—even though you don't feel that way at all, in your own mind. We have to lighten up the schedule, get more food into you, and get you up to par before the next debate." His prescription incidentally, was a pleasant one. There happens to be nothing I like better than a rich milkshake but because of trying to keep my weight in check, I had not had one for years. The doctor ordered me to have one with each meal—plus another in mid-afternoon—for the next two weeks. The prescription worked. For the second debate, I had put on five pounds.

During the next few days, as we resumed the campaign, I tried to put the probable effect of the first debate into reasonable perspective. I concluded that it had been a setback—but not a disaster. As far as the television audience was concerned, Claude Robinson and the other pollsters recorded a clear edge for Kennedy. But at the same time, they noted that the debate had in itself had but slight effect on the way people said they were going to vote: rather than changing voters' intentions, in other words, it intensified previous decisions and preferences.

The press, almost without exception, called it a "draw." Typical reactions were: the Philadelphia *Inquirer*—"inconclusive, won by neither." William S. White: "It is impossible to say who won. It is not even easy to say who came out ahead on points." Robert Albright of the Washington *Post*: "A dead heat." The St. Louis *Post-Dispatch*: "We should not say that anybody won." Richard Starnes in the New York *World-Telegram and Sun*: "Neither made a mistake or scored a point." The Denver *Post*: "A draw." But while the press was calling it a draw, I knew that they were basing their conclusions primarily on what had been said, not on how the candidates had looked. I knew, too, that how the candidates looked, to many viewers, was going to be a great deal more important than what they said.

Radio reaction was just the opposite from that on television. All the polls gave me a clear advantage. Ralph McGill of the Atlanta *Constitution,* a Kennedy supporter, had run an actual test. This is what he concluded: "Kennedy looked better . . . But I had a number of persons listen on the radio . . . They unanimously thought Mr. Nixon had the better of it." This information was of very little comfort to me, however. The TV audience ran five-to-six times bigger than the radio audience and it was concentrated in the big industrial states which would be decisive in determining the election outcome. It was, then, essential that we make a comeback, and the time and place to start was October 7 in Washington when we were to have the second debate. . . .

DWIGHT D. EISENHOWER, FAREWELL ADDRESS
January 17, 1961

My fellow Americans:

Three days from now, after half a century in the service of our country, I shall lay down the responsibilities of office as, in traditional and solemn ceremony, the authority of the Presidency is vested in my successor.

This evening I come to you with a message of leave-taking and farewell, and to share a few final thoughts with you, my countrymen.

Like every other citizen, I wish the new President, and all who will labor with him, Godspeed. I pray that the coming years will be blessed with peace and prosperity for all.

Our people expect their President and the Congress to find essential agreement on issues of great moment, the wise resolution of which will better shape the future of the Nation.

My own relations with the Congress, which began on a remote and tenuous basis when, long ago, a member of the Senate appointed me to West Point, have since ranged to the intimate during the war and immediate post-war period, and, finally, to the mutually interdependent during these past eight years.

In this final relationship, the Congress and the Administration have, on most vital issues, cooperated well, to serve the national good rather than mere partisanship, and so have assured that the business of the Nation should go forward. So, my official relationship with the Congress ends in a feeling, on my part, of gratitude that we have been able to do so much together.

II.

We now stand ten years past the midpoint of a century that has witnessed four major wars among great nations. Three of these involved our own country. Despite these holocausts America is today the strongest, the most influential and most productive nation in the world. Understandably proud of this pre-eminence, we yet realize that America's leadership and prestige depend, not merely upon our unmatched material progress, riches and military strength, but on how we use our power in the interests of world peace and human betterment.

Public Papers of the Presidents of the United States, Dwight D. Eisenhower, (Jan. 1) 1960—(Jan. 20) 1961, Item 421, pp. 1035-40.

III.

Throughout America's adventure in free government, our basic purposes have been to keep the peace; to foster progress in human achievement, and to enhance liberty, dignity and integrity among people and among nations. To strive for less would be unworthy of a free and religious people. Any failure traceable to arrogance, or our lack of comprehension or readiness to sacrifice would inflict upon us grievous hurt both at home and abroad.

Progress toward these noble goals is persistently threatened by the conflict now engulfing the world. It commands our whole attention, absorbs our very beings. We face a hostile ideology—global in scope, atheistic in character, ruthless in purpose, and insidious in method. Unhappily the danger it poses promises to be of indefinite duration. To meet it successfully, there is called for, not so much the emotional and transitory sacrifices of crisis, but rather those which enable us to carry forward steadily, surely, and without complaint the burdens of a prolonged and complex struggle—with liberty the stake. Only thus shall we remain, despite every provocation, on our charted course toward permanent peace and human betterment.

Crises there will continue to be. In meeting them, whether foreign or domestic, great or small, there is a recurring temptation to feel that some spectacular and costly action could become the miraculous solution to all current difficulties. A huge increase in newer elements of our defense; development of unrealistic programs to cure every ill in agriculture; a dramatic expansion in basic and applied research—these and many other possibilities, each possibly promising in itself, may be suggested as the only way to the road we wish to travel.

But each proposal must be weighed in the light of a broader consideration: the need to maintain balance in and among national programs—balance between the private and the public economy, balance between cost and hoped for advantage— balance between the clearly necessary and the comfortably desirable; balance between our essential requirements as a nation and the duties imposed by the nation upon the individual; balance between actions of the moment and the national welfare of the future. Good judgment seeks balance and progress; lack of it eventually finds imbalance and frustration.

The record of many decades stands as proof that our people and their government have, in the main, understood these truths and have responded to them well, in the face of stress and threat. But threats, new in kind or degree, constantly arise. I mention two only.

IV.

A vital element in keeping the peace is our military establishment. Our arms must be mighty, ready for instant action, so that no potential aggressor may be tempted to risk his own destruction.

Our military organization today bears little relation to that known by any of my predecessors in peacetime, or indeed by the fighting men of World War II or Korea. Until the latest of our world conflicts, the United States had no armaments industry. American makers of plowshares could, with time and as required, make swords as well. But now we can no longer risk emergency improvisation of national defense; we have been compelled to create a permanent armaments industry of vast proportions. Added to this, three and a half million men and women are directly engaged in the defense establishment. We annually spend on military security more than the net income of all United States corporations.

This conjunction of an immense military establishment and a large arms industry is new in the American experience. The total influence—economic, political, even spiritual—is felt in every city, every State house, every office of the Federal government. We recognize the imperative need for this development. Yet we must not fail to comprehend its grave implications. Our toil, resources and livelihood are all involved; so is the very structure of our society.

In the councils of government, we must guard against the acquisition of unwarranted influence, whether sought or unsought, by the military-industrial complex. The potential for the disastrous rise of misplaced power exists and will persist.

We must never let the weight of this combination endanger our liberties or democratic processes. We should take nothing for granted. Only an alert and knowledgeable citizenry can compel the proper meshing of the huge industrial and military machinery of defense with our peaceful methods and goals, so that security and liberty may prosper together.

Akin to, and largely responsible for the sweeping changes in our industrial-military posture, has been the technological revolution during recent decades.

In this revolution, research has become central; it also becomes more formalized, complex, and costly. A steadily increasing share is conducted for, by, or at the direction of, the Federal government.

Today, the solitary inventor, tinkering in his shop, has been overshadowed by task forces of scientists in laboratories and testing fields. In the same fashion, the free university, historically the fountainhead of free ideas and scientific discovery, has experienced a revolution in the conduct of research. Partly because of the huge costs involved, a government contract becomes virtually a substitute for intellectual curiosity. For every old blackboard there are now hundreds of new electronic computers.

The prospect of domination of the nation's scholars by Federal employment, project allocations, and the power of money is ever present—and is gravely to be regarded.

Yet, in holding scientific research and discovery in respect, as we should, we must also be alert to the equal and opposite danger that public policy could itself become the captive of a scientific-technological elite.

It is the task of statesmanship to mold, to balance, and to integrate these and other forces, new and old, within the principles of our democratic system—ever aiming toward the supreme goals of our free society.

V.

Another factor in maintaining balance involves the element of time. As we peer into society's future, we—you and I, and our government—must avoid the impulse to live only for today, plundering, for our own ease and convenience, the precious resources of tomorrow. We cannot mortgage the material assets of our grandchildren without risking the loss also of their political and spiritual heritage. We want democracy to survive for all generations to come, not to become the insolvent phantom of tomorrow.

VI.

Down the long lane of the history yet to be written America knows that this world of ours, ever growing smaller, must avoid becoming a community of dreadful fear and hate, and be, instead, a proud confederation of mutual trust and respect.

Such a confederation must be one of equals. The weakest must come to the conference table with the same confidence as do we, protected as we are by our moral, economic, and military strength. That table, though scarred by many past frustrations, cannot be abandoned for the certain agony of the battlefield.

Disarmament, with mutual honor and confidence, is a continuing imperative. Together we must learn how to compose differences, not with arms, but with intellect and decent purpose. Because this need is so sharp and apparent I confess that I lay down my official responsibilities in this field with a definite sense of disappointment. As one who has witnessed the horror and the lingering sadness of war—as one who knows that another war could utterly destroy this civilization which has been so slowly and painfully built over thousands of years—I wish I could say tonight that a lasting peace is in sight.

Happily, I can say that war has been avoided. Steady progress toward our ultimate goal has been made. But, so much remains to be done. As a private citizen, I shall never cease to do what little I can to help the world advance along that road.

VII.

So—in this my last good night to you as your President—I thank you for the many opportunities you have given me for public service in war and peace. I trust that in that service you find some things worthy; as for the rest of it, I know you will find ways to improve performance in the future.

You and I—my fellow citizens—need to be strong in our faith that all nations, under God, will reach the goal of peace with justice. May we be ever unswerving in devotion to principle, confident but humble with power, diligent in pursuit of the Nation's great goals.

To all the peoples of the world, I once more give expression to America's prayerful and continuing aspiration:

We pray that peoples of all faiths, all races, all nations, may have their great human needs satisfied; that those now denied opportunity shall come to enjoy it to the full; that all who yearn for freedom may experience its spiritual blessings; that those who have freedom will understand, also, its heavy responsibilities; that all who are insensitive to the needs of others will learn charity; that the scourges of poverty, disease and ignorance will be made to disappear from the earth, and that, in the goodness of time, all peoples will come to live together in a peace guaranteed by the binding force of mutual respect and love.

NELSON A. ROCKEFELLER
CALL FOR A UNITED REPUBLICAN PARTY IN 1964 ELECTION
July 14, 1963

Over the past months, many leaders of the Republican Party, myself included, have been working to put the Party in a position to face the challenge of the 1964 election as a strong and united fighting force.

A minority party must be united for principle to provide the effective opposition and constructive alternatives that our country sorely needs. It must be united for principle and reach beyond its own boundaries to win. It must be united for principle to command broad support.

The paralysis of government that we are witnessing today in Washington stems from the fact that the Democratic Party is not united for principle, but in effect is two parties of opportunism proceeding in opposite directions.

In making this effort toward unity for principle, it was my conviction that the activities of the radical right, while deeply disturbing in many ways, would represent an inconsequential influence on the Republican Party.

It was my conviction that despite differences in emphasis among the Party's responsible elements, there was an overwhelming consensus within the Party on the fundamental articles of Republican faith.

In broadest terms, these articles of faith are:

1. Unswerving dedication to the preservation of our own freedom and the extension of freedom throughout the world through a firm, resolute and positive foreign policy.

2. Equality of opportunity for a better life for all Americans regardless of economic status, geographic location, race, creed, color or national origin.

3. Faith in our federal system of government as the best assurance of freedom and equal opportunity and as the only hope of keeping democratic government close to the people and responsive to their will.

4. Faith in the private enterprise system as the dynamic, creative base for social progress in a free society and of freedom of individual initiative without which men cannot be really free or equal.

5. Faith in the fundamental importance of fiscal integrity in government as the indispensable political base for economic growth and the vitally needed expansion of job opportunities.

6. Faith in our heritage of freedom of speech and of information and in the right and need of the people to know all the facts on the issues confronting them as essential to the preservation of a free society.

While as a party and as a people, we have been keenly aware of the grave threat to these principles posed by international communism, I have now come to the conclusion that many of us have been taking too lightly the growing danger to these very same principles through subversion from the radical right.

I am now convinced that, unless the vast majority of Republicans who subscribe to these principles, are aroused from present inaction—whether this inaction stems from complacency, from fear or from a fantastically short-sighted opportunism—the Republican Party is in real danger of subversion by a radical, well-financed and highly-disciplined minority.

For it has now become crystal clear that the vociferous and well-drilled extremist elements boring within the Party utterly reject these fundamental principles of our heritage. They are, in fact, embarked on a determined and ruthless effort to take over the Party, its platform and its candidates on their own terms—terms that are wholly alien to the sound and honest conservatism that has firmly based the Republican Party in the best of a century's traditions, wholly alien to the sound and honest Republican liberalism that has kept the Party abreast of human needs in a changing world, wholly alien to the broad middle course that accommodates the mainstream of Republican principle.

This cannot be allowed to happen. The continuing commitment of the Republican Party to its historic principles, including its fundamental dedication to equality of opportunity for all men, cannot and must not be betrayed. No temptation of political gain through cynical expediency can be permitted to becloud our commitment to principle and purpose.

` No one could fail to be deeply disturbed by the proceedings at the recent Young Republican National Convention in San Francisco. I am completely confident that the overwhelming majority of Young Republicans of this country respond today, as they always have, to the idealism of the Party's tradition. I am confident that they want it to continue to be a positive and responsible party serving the best interest of all the people.

But every objective observer at San Francisco has reported that the proceedings there were dominated by extremist groups, carefully organized, well-financed and operating through the tactics of ruthless, rough-shod intimidation. These are the tactics of totalitarianism.

Unfortunately, this cannot be brushed off as irresponsibility. For youth *is* responsible. The leaders of the Birchers and others of the radical right lunatic fringe—every bit as dangerous to American principles and American institutions as the radical left—who successfully engineered this disgraceful subversion of a great and responsible auxiliary of the Republican Party are the same people who are now moving to subvert the Republican Party itself. They claim initial success and predict ultimate victory for their efforts.

These people have no program for the Republican Party or the American people except distrust, disunity and the ultimate destruction of the confidence of the people in themselves. They are purveyors of hate and distrust in a time when, as never before, the need of the world is for love and understanding.

They have no concern with and offer no solution for the problems of chronic unemployment, of education and training, of housing, of racial injustice and strife, of all the other problems which must have answers if our democratic ideals are to be translated into living reality.

And in the political sphere, they offer something equally sinister:

Completely incredible as it is to me, it is now being seriously proposed to the Republican Party that as a strategy for victory in 1964, that it write off the Negro and other minority groups, it deliberately write off the great industrial states of the North (representing nearly 50% of the country's population), that it write off the big cities, and that it direct its appeal primarily to the electoral votes of the South, plus the West and a scattering of other states.

The transparent purpose behind this plan is to erect political power on the outlawed and immoral base of segregation and to transform the Republican Party from a national party of all the people to a sectional party for some of the people.

No such plan ever has, or ever will succeed. It cannot stand the light of day. It will be rejected out of hand by the Republican Party. It will be rejected by the nation. It will be rejected by the South.

The South has long pointed out that the racial problem is not a sectional problem, but a national problem. I know that there is southern leadership that wants to participate in a national solution.

A program based on racism or sectionalism would in and of itself not only defeat the Republican Party in 1964, but would destroy it altogether.

The Republican Party is the Party of Lincoln. It was founded to make men free and equal in opportunity. It is the party of all men, the only truly national party in America. For that Party to turn its back on its heritage and its birthright would be an act of political immorality rarely equalled in human history.

No cloak of so-called "states' rights" can conceal the real purpose behind this strategy. The political rights of states are clear within the Federal system and their realization depends importantly upon the exercise of states' responsibilities within that system. But a century ago, a great war decided for all time that in the area of human dignity, states' rights must forever yield to the rights of the individual. And so in this area, the invocation of states' rights can only be regarded as a pretext.

For the Republican Party, political success cannot be divorced from political morality and the fact is that the Party's dedication to the equality of all men is still, and must more than ever before, be its guide to leadership and to victory.

Far from abandoning this dedication, the whole burden of the distinguished 1961 report by Chairman Bliss of Ohio was that both the Party's greatest challenge and its brightest opportunity lay in its willingness to deal with the great urban problems confronting our Nation, and the people of the cities, especially the minority groups.

The path to victory is not in running away from the people of this country. The path to victory is in seeking out the people in the areas where they live, in accepting the responsibilities of leadership in the solution of their problems and demonstrating to them, as the Republican Party has in many areas, that in it is to be found the will, the sincerity, the competence, and the drive to make this a better land for all its people.

The issue that confronts the Republican Party today is the gravest in its history.

I have no doubt whatever that responsibility, modernization and sound progress continue to be the spiritual allegiance of the overwhelming majority of the Republicans of this country.

But a complacent majority, or a fearful one, or a majority misled to betrayal of its principles in pursuit of political fantasies will be as surely subverted by militant extremism as such majorities always have been throughout all history.

No Republicans can stand by idly in the face of this threat. No Republican can stand aloof from the issue that it presents. One must be either for or against these forces. The time for temporizing is over.

Some in the Party have already spoken out against this threat. This is a responsibility for all of us. I for one will do everything in my power, working with others to counter the influence of these forces and to defeat their purposes.

For the future of this great Nation lies not in the unprincipled extremism of the radical right any more than it lies in the unprincipled opportunism that has captured the Democratic Party.

It lies in the fiscally-responsible, humanely-principled mainstream of American thought and leadership that the party of Abraham Lincoln, of Theodore Roosevelt, of Robert Taft has always represented and will continue to represent.

It is said that in the next presidential election, the voters should be given a choice.

I agree.

There must be an alternative to a faltering administration that has suffered a Communist military base to be established 90 miles off our shores—the most visible symbol, but by no means the only one of a general deterioration in our national security and our posture of leadership before the world.

There must be an alternative to an administration that is floundering in its fiscal management, that has been unable to settle on a program, let alone effect a solution, for our stagnant economy and our millions of unemployed.

There must be an alternative for an administration that by inaction has plunged our country into the most soul-searing racial strife of our history.

There must be an alternative. But, in the sound instincts of the American people, that alternative will never be found in a party of extremism, a party of sectionalism, a party of racism, a party that disclaims responsibility for most of the population before it even starts its campaign for their support.

Such an alternative is not a choice but a mockery.

The choice that must be provided to the American people is to be found only in a party of responsible Republicanism, truly faithful to its Lincolnian heritage, truly national in scope, concerned with the opportunity and well-being of every individual citizen and thus commanding the confidence of the country as a whole. Last but not least, it must be responsibly and constructively concerned with the strengthening of this country's leadership of the free world.

The choice as to whether such a party shall be presented to the electorate is a choice of all Republicans. In the days between now and the Republican Convention, where the final decision will be made, that choice and these issues must be submitted to them. I have no doubt as to the outcome. And I have no doubt that out of this process will come the kind of moral strength, the strength of principle, that is needed to win and that is needed to govern.

The Republican Party stands today at the crossroads of its destiny. Its destiny is to save the nation by first saving itself.

WILLIAM W. SCRANTON
LETTER ATTACKING SENATOR GOLDWATER
July 13, 1964

As we move rapidly toward the climax of this convention, the Republican party faces continuing struggle on two counts.

The first involves, of course, selection of a candidate.

Here the issue is extremely clear. It simply is this: Will the convention choose the candidate overwhelmingly favored by the Republican voters, or will it choose you?

Your organization does not even argue the merits of the question. They admit that you are a minority candidate, but they feel they have bought, beaten and compromised enough delegate support to make the result a foregone conclusion.

With open contempt for the dignity, integrity and common sense of the convention, your managers say in effect that the delegates are little more than a flock of chickens whose necks will be wrung at will.

I have doublechecked the arithmetic of my staff, and I am convinced that a true count at this minute puts your first ballot strength at only some 620 votes.

Our count differs from that of your managers because we have calculated an important element which they are incapable of comprehending. That is the element of respect for the men and women who make up the delegations to this convention.

We are not taking them for granted. We are not insulting their intelligence or their integrity.

We're not counting noses, we're counting hearts.

We're not issuing orders, we're providing a rallying point for responsibility in the Republican party.

You will be stopped on the first ballot because a sufficient number of your nominal supporters have already indicated to us that they will not vote for you.

They are not breaking commitments to you; you have broken commitments to them.

You have too often casually described nuclear war as a solution to a troubled world.

You have too often allowed the radical extremists to use you.

You have too often stood for irresponsibility in the serious question of racial holocaust.

You have too often read Taft and Eisenhower and Lincoln out of the Republican party.

And that brings me to the second count on which the Republican party is fighting for its soul.

New York Times, July 14, 1964.

In the last few days the ill-advised efforts to make us stand for Goldwaterism instead of Republicanism has set off ripples of public opinion across the nation.

All of us in San Francisco are so close to the hour-by-hour story unfolding here that there is a danger we may overlook the over-all impression being created in the minds of the American people.

Goldwaterism has come to stand for nuclear irresponsibility.

Goldwaterism has come to stand for keeping the name of Eisenhower out of our platform.

Goldwaterism has come to stand for being afraid to forthrightly condemn right-wing extremists.

Goldwaterism has come to stand for law and order in maintaining racial peace.

In short, Goldwaterism has come to stand for a whole crazy-quilt collection of absurd and dangerous positions that would be soundly repudiated by the American people in November.

Meanwhile, we have tried as best we can in the rigged situation engineered by your organization to articulate another point of view.

These are not surface differences between you and the vast majority of Republicans. These are soul-deep differences over what the Republican party stands for.

We cannot lightly ignore the deep convictions of 60 per cent of the Republican party that Goldwaterism is wrong. Circumstances have given me the responsibility of speaking up for their position. Inclination has given you the task of defending far different opinions.

Neither of us can ignore our responsibilities.

I feel that I have nothing to fear from the convention or from the millions of Americans watching it because my position is a right one.

Certainly you should not fear a convention you claim to control, and I would hope that we have not reached the point where you fear to face the nation.

Therefore I am asking that you join me in a request to allow both of us to appear before the convention on Wednesday prior to the nominating speeches.

Each of us should be permitted to speak on the issues.

Then we ought to have the opportunity to question each other.

Frankly, few people expect that you will accept my invitation.

If that is true, the implication will be quite clear. You have taken comfort in the inflated claims of your managers and you no longer have any regard for the opinions of uncommitted delegates or of the American public.

So it is up to you. You must decide whether the Goldwater philosophy can stand public examination—before the convention and before the nation.

BARRY GOLDWATER, ACCEPTANCE SPEECH
San Francisco, July 17, 1964

My good friend and great Republican, Dick Nixon and your charming wife, Pat; my running mate—that wonderful Republican who has served us so well for so long—Bill Miller and his wife, Stephanie; to Thurston Morton, who's done such a commendable job in chairmaning this convention; to Mr. Herbert Hoover who I hope is watching, and to that great American and his wife, General and Mrs. Eisenhower. To my own wife, fellow Republicans here assembled, and Americans across this great nation:

From this moment, united and determined, we will go forward together dedicated to the ultimate and undeniable greatness of the whole man.

Together we will win.

I accept your nomination with a deep sense of humility. I accept, too, the responsibility that goes with it, and I seek your continued help and your continued guidance. My fellow Republicans, our cause is too great for any man to feel worthy of it. Our task would be too great for any man did he not have with him the heart and the hands of this great Republican party.

And I promise you tonight that every fibre of my being is consecrated to our cause, that nothing shall be lacking from the struggle that can be brought to it by enthusiasm by devotion and plain hard work.

In this world no person, no party can guarantee anything, but what we can do and what we shall do is to deserve victory and victory will be ours. The Good Lord raised this mighty Republican—Republic to be a home for the Brave and to flourish as the land of the free—not to stagnate in the swampland of collectivism, not to cringe before the bully of Communism.

Now my fellow Americans, the tide has been running against freedom. Our people have followed false prophets. We must, and we shall, return to proven ways—not because they are old, but because they are true.

We must, and we shall, set the tide running again in the cause of freedom. And this party, with its every action, every word, every breath and every heart beat, has but a single resolve, and that is freedom.

Freedom made orderly for this nation by our constitutional government. Freedom under a government limited by laws of nature and of nature's God. Freedom balanced so that order lacking liberty will not become the slavery of the prison cell; balanced so that liberty lacking order will not become the license of the mob and of the jungle.

Congressional Record, 88th Cong., 2d sess., 1964, 110, pt. 12, pp. 16387-88.

Now, we Americans understand freedom, we have earned it; we have lived for it, and we have died for it. This nation and its people are freedom's models in a searching world. We can be freedom's missionaries in a doubting world.

But, ladies and gentlemen, first we must renew freedom's mission in our own hearts and in our own homes.

During four futile years the Administration which we shall replace has distorted and lost that faith. It has talked and talked and talked and talked the words of freedom but it has failed and failed and failed in the works of freedom.

Now failure cements the wall of shame in Berlin; failures blot the sands of shame at the Bay of Pigs; failures marked the slow death of freedom in Laos; failures infest the jungles of Vietnam, and failures haunt the houses of our once great alliances and undermine the greatest bulwark ever erected by free nations, the NATO community.

Failures proclaim lost leadership, obscure purpose, weakening wills and the risk of inciting our sworn enemies to new aggressions and to new excesses.

And because of this Administration we are tonight a world divided. We are a nation becalmed. We have lost the brisk pace of diversity and the genuis of individual creativity. We are plodding along at a pace set by centralized planning, red tape, rules without responsibility and regimentation without recourse.

Rather than useful jobs in our country, people have been offered bureaucratic makework; rather than moral leadership, they have been given bread and circuses; they have been given spectacles, and, yes, they've even been given scandals.

Tonight there is violence in our streets, corruption in our highest offices, aimlessness among our youth, anxiety among our elderly, and there's a virtual despair among the many who look beyond material success toward the inner meaning of their lives. And where examples of morality should be set, the opposite is seen. Small men seeking great wealth or power have too often and too long turned even the highest levels of public service into mere personal opportunity.

Now, certainly simple honesty is not too much to demand of men in government. We find it in most. Republicans demand it from everyone.

They demand it from everyone no matter how exalted or protected his position might be.

The growing menace in our country tonight, to personal safety, to life, to limb and property, in homes, in churches, on the playgrounds and places of business, particularly in our great cities, is the mounting concern or should be of every thoughtful citizen in the United States. Security from domestic violence, no less than from foreign aggression, is the most elementary and fundamental purpose of any government, and a government that cannot fulfill this purpose is one that cannot long command the loyalty of its citizens.

History shows us, demonstrates that nothing, nothing prepares the way for tyranny more than the failure of public officials to keep the streets safe from bullies and marauders.

Now we Republicans see all this as more—much more—than the result of mere political differences, or mere political mistakes. We see this as the result of a fundamentally and absolutely wrong view of man, his nature and his destiny.

Those who seek to live your lives for you, to take your liberty in return for relieving you of yours; those who elevate the state and downgrade the citizen, must see ultimately a world in which earthly power can be substituted for Divine Will. And this nation was founded upon the rejection of that notion and upon the acceptance of God as the author of freedom.

Now those who seek absolute power, even though they seek it to do what they regard as good, are simply demanding the right to enforce their own version of heaven on earth, and let me remind you they are the very ones who always create the most hellish tyranny.

Absolute power does corrupt, and those who seek it must be suspect and must be opposed. Their mistaken course stems from false notions, ladies and gentlemen, of equality. Equality, rightly understood as our founding fathers understood it, leads to liberty and to the emancipation of creative differences; wrongly understood, as it has been so tragically in our time, it leads first to conformity and then to despotism.

Fellow Republicans, it is the cause of Republicanism to resist concentrations of power, private or public, which enforce such conformity and inflict such despotism.

It is the cause of Republicanism to insure that power remains in the hands of the people—and, so help us God, that is exactly what a Republican President will do with the help of a Republican Congress.

It is further the cause of Republicanism to restore a clear understanding of the tyranny of man over man in the world at large. It is our cause to dispel the foggy thinking which avoids hard decisions in the delusion that a world of conflict will somehow resolve itself into a world of harmony, if we just don't rock the boat or irritate the forces of aggression—and this is hogwash.

It is, further, the cause of Republicanism to remind ourselves, and the world, that only the strong can remain free; that only the strong can keep the peace.

Now I needn't remind you, or my fellow Americans regardless of party, that Republicans have shouldered this hard responsibility and marched in this cause before. It was Republican leadership under Dwight Eisenhower that kept the peace, and passed along to this Administration the mightiest arsenal for defense the world has ever known.

And I needn't remind you that it was the strength and the believable will of the Eisenhower years that kept the peace by using our strength, by using it in the Formosa Strait, and in Lebanon, and by showing it courageously at all times.

It was during those Republican years that the thrust of Communist imperialism was blunted. It was during those years of Republican leadership that this world moved closer not to war but closer to peace than at any other time in the last three decades.

And I needn't remind you, but I will, that it's been during Democratic years that our strength to deter war has been stilled and even gone into a planned decline. It has been during Democratic years that we have weakly stumbled into conflicts, timidly refusing to draw our own lines against aggression, deceitfully refusing to tell even our own people of our full participation and tragically letting our finest men die on battlefields unmarked by purpose, unmarked by pride or the prospect of victory.

Yesterday it was Korea: tonight it is Vietnam. Make no bones of this. Don't try to sweep this under the rug. We are at war in Vietnam. And yet the President, who is the Commander in Chief of our forces, refuses to say, refuses to say mind you, whether or not the objective over there is victory, and his Secretary of Defense continues to mislead and misinform the American people, and enough of it has gone by.

And I needn't remind you, but I will, it has been during Democratic years that a billion persons were cast into Communist captivity and their fate cynically sealed.

Today—today in our beloved country we have an Administration which seems eager to deal with Communism in every coin known—from gold to wheat; from consulates to confidence, and even human freedom itself.

Now the Republican cause demands that we brand communism as the principal disturber of peace in the world today. Indeed, we should brand it as the only significant disturber of the peace. And we must make clear that until its goals of conquest are absolutely renounced, and its relations with all nations tempered, Communism and the governments it now controls are enemies, of every man on earth who is or wants to be free.

Now, we here in America can keep the peace only if we remain vigiliant, and only if we remain strong. Only if we keep our eyes open and keep our guard up can we prevent war.

And I want to make this abundantly clear—I don't intend to let peace or freedom be torn from our grasp because of lack of strength, or lack of will—and that I promise you Americans.

I believe that we must look beyond the defense of freedom today to its extension tomorrow. I believe that the Communism which boasts it will bury us will instead give way to the forces of freedom. And I can see in the distant and yet recognizable future the outlines of a world worthy of our dedication, our every risk, our every effort, our every sacrifice along the way. Yes, a world that will redeem the suffering of those who will be liberated from tyranny.

I can see, and I suggest that all thoughtful men must contemplate, the flowering of an Atlantic civilization, the whole world of Europe reunified and free, trading openly across its borders, communicating openly across the world.

This is a goal far, far more meaningful than a moon shot.

It's a truly inspiring goal for all free men to set for themselves during the latter half of the twentieth century. I can see and all free men must thrill to the events of this Atlantic civilization joined by a straight ocean highway to the United States. What a destiny! What a destiny can be ours to stand as a great central pillar linking Europe, the Americans and the venerable and vital peoples and cultures of the Pacific.

I can see a day when all the Americas—North and South—will be linked in a mighty system—a system in which the errors and misunderstandings of the past will be submerged one by one in a rising tide of prosperity and interdependence.

We know that the misunderstandings of centuries are not to be wiped away in a day or wiped away in an hour. But we pledge, we pledge, that human sympathy—what our neighbors to the South call an attitude of sympatico—no less than enlightened self-interest will be our guide.

And I can see this Atlantic civilization galvanizing and guiding emergent nations everywhere. Now I know this freedom is not the fruit of every soil. I know that our own freedom was achieved through centuries of unremitting efforts by brave and wise men. And I know that the road to freedom is a long and a challenging road, and I know also that some men may walk away from it, that some men resist challenge, accepting the false security of governmental paternalism.

And I pledge that the America I envision in the years ahead will extend its hand in help in teaching and in cultivation so that all new nations will be at least encouraged to go our way; so that they will not wander down the dark alleys of tyranny or to the dead-end streets of collectivism.

My fellow Republicans, we do no man a service by hiding freedom's light under a bushel of mistaken humility.

I seek an America proud of its past, proud of its ways, proud of its dreams and determined actively to proclaim them. But our examples to the world must, like charity, begin at home.

In our vision of a good and decent future, free and peaceful, there must be room, room for the liberation of the energy and the talent of the individual, otherwise our vision is blind at the outset.

We must assure a society here which while never abandoning the needy, or forsaking the helpless, nurtures incentives and opportunity for the creative and the productive.

We must know the whole good is the product of many single contributions. And I cherish the day when our children once again will restore as heroes the sort of men and women who, unafraid and undaunted, pursue the truth, strive to cure disease, subdue and make fruitful our natural environment, and produce the inventive engines of production, science and technology.

This nation, whose creative people have enhanced this entire span of history, should again thrive upon the greatness of all those things which we—we as individual citizens—can and should do.

During Republican years, this again will be a nation of men and women, of families proud of their role, jealous of their responsibilities, unlimited in their aspirations—a nation where all who can will be self-reliant.

We Republicans see in our constitutional form of government the great framework which assures the orderly but dynamic fulfillment of the whole man, and we see the whole man as the great reason for instituting orderly government in the first place.

We see in private property and in economy based upon and fostering private property the one way to make government a durable ally of the whole man rather than his determined enemy.

We see in the sanctity of private property the only durable foundation for constitutional government in a free society.

And beyond that we see and cherish diversity of ways, diversity of thoughts, of motives, and accomplishments. We don't seek to live anyone's life for him. We only seek to secure his rights, guarantee him opportunity, guarantee him opportunity to strive with government performing only those needed and constitutionally sanctioned tasks which cannot otherwise be performed.

We, Republicans, seek a government that attends to its inherent responsibilities of maintaining a stable monetary and fiscal climate, encouraging a free and competitive economy and enforcing law and order.

Thus do we seek inventiveness, diversity and creative difference within a stable order, for we Republicans define government's role where needed at many, many levels, preferably through the one closest to the people involved: our towns and our cities, then our counties, then our states, then our regional contacts and only then the national government.

That, let me remind you, is the land of liberty built by decentralized power. On it also we must have balance between the branches of government at every level.

Balance, diversity, creative difference—these are the elements of Republican equation. Republicans agree, Republicans agree heartily, to disagree on many, many of their applications. But we have never disagreed on the basic fundamental issues of why you and I are Republicans.

This is a party—this Republican party is a party for free men. Not for blind followers and not for conformists.

Back in 1858 Abraham Lincoln said this of the Republican party, and I quote him because he probably could have said it during the last week or so: It was composed of strained, discordant, and even hostile elements. End of the quote, in 1958 [sic].

Yet all of these elements agreed on one paramount objective: to arrest the progress of slavery, and place it in the course of ultimate extinction.

Today, as then, but more urgently and more broadly than then, the task of preserving and enlarging freedom at home and of safeguarding it from the forces of tyranny abroad is great enough to challenge all our resources and to require all our strength.

Anyone who joins us in all sincerity we welcome. Those, those who do not care for our cause, we don't expect to enter our ranks in any case. And let our Republicanism so focused and so dedicated not be made fuzzy and futile by unthinking and stupid labels.

I would remind you that extremism in the defense of liberty is no vice!

And let me remind you also that moderation in the pursuit of justice is no virtue!

By the—the beauty of the very system we Republicans are pledged to restore and revitalize, the beauty of this Federal system of ours is in its reconciliation of diversity with unity. We must not see malice in honest differences of opinion, and no matter how great, so long as they are not inconsistent with the pledges we have given to each other in and through our Constitution.

Our Republican cause is not to level out the world or make its people conform in computer-regimented sameness. Our Republican cause is to free our people and light the way for liberty throughout the world. Ours is a very human cause for very humane goals. This party, its good people, and its unquestionable devotion to freedom will not fulfill the purposes of this campaign which we launch here now until our cause has won the day, inspired the world, and shown the way to a tomorrow worthy of all our yesteryears.

I repeat, I accept your nomination with humbleness, with pride and you and I are going to fight for the goodness of our land. Thank you.

RICHARD M. NIXON, ACCEPTANCE SPEECH
Miami Beach, August 8, 1968

Mr. Chairman, delegates to this convention, my fellow Americans.

Sixteen years ago I stood before this convention to accept your nomination as the running mate of one of the greatest Americans of our time or of any time—Dwight D. Eisenhower.

Eight years ago I had the highest honor of accepting your nomination for President of the United States.

Tonight I again proudly accept that nomination for President of the United States.

But I have news for you. This time there's a difference—this time we're going to win.

We're going to win for a number of reasons. First a personal one.

General Eisenhower, as you know, lies critically ill in the Walter Reed Hospital tonight. I have talked, however, with Mrs. Eisenhower on the telephone.

She tells me that his heart is with us. She says that there is nothing that he lives more for, and there is nothing that would lift him more than for us to win in November.

And I say let's win this one for Ike.

We're going to win because this great convention has demonstrated to the nation that Republican party has the leadership, the platform and the purpose that America needs.

We're going to win because you have nominated as my running mate a statesman of the first rank who will be a great campaigner, and one who is fully qualified to undertake the new responsibilities that I shall give to the next Vice President of the United States.

And he is a man who fully shares my conviction and yours that after a period of 40 years when power has gone from the cities and the states to the Government in Washington, D.C., it's time to have power go back from Washington to the states and to the cities of this country all over America.

We're going to win because at a time that America cries out for the unity that this Administration has destroyed, the Republican party, after a spirited contest for its nomination for President and Vice President, stands united before the nation tonight.

And I congratulate Governor Reagan, I congratulate Governor Rockefeller, I congratulate Governor Romney, I congratulate all those who have made the hard fight that they have for this nomination, and I know that you will all fight even harder for

Congressional Record, 90th Cong., 2d sess., 1968, 114, pt. 20, pp. 26880-81.

the great victory our party is going to win in November because we're going to be together in that election campaign.

And a party that can unite itself will unite America.

My fellow Americans, most important we're going to win because our cause is right. We make history tonight, not for ourselves but for the ages. The choice we make in 1968 will determine not only the future of America but the future of peace and freedom in the world for the last third of the 20th century, and the question that we answer tonight: can America meet this great challenge?

Let us listen to America to find the answer to that question.

As we look at America, we see cities enveloped in smoke and flame. We hear sirens in the night. We see Americans dying on distant battlefields abroad. We see Americans hating each other; fighting each other; killing each other at home.

And as we see and hear these things, millions of Americans cry out in anguish: Did we come all this way for this? Did American boys die in Normandy and Korea and in Valley Forge for this?

Listen to the answers to these questions.

It is another voice, it is a quiet voice in the tumult of the shouting. It is the voice of the great majority of Americans, the forgotten Americans, the non-shouters, the non-demonstrators. They're not racists or sick; they're not guilty of the crime that plagues the land; they are black, they are white, they're native born and foreign born; they're young and they're old.

They work in American factories, they run American businesses. They serve in government; they provide most of the soldiers who die to keep it free. They give drive to the spirit of America. They give lift to the American dream. They give steel to the backbone of America.

They're good people. They're decent people; they work and they save and they pay their taxes and they care.

Like Theodore Roosevelt, they know that this country will not be a good place for any of us to live in unless it's a good place for all of us to live in.

And this I say, this I say to you tonight, is the real voice of America. In this year 1968, this is the message it will broadcast to America and to the world.

Let's never forget that despite her faults, America is a great nation. And America is great because her people are great.

With Winston Churchill we say, we have not journeyed all this way, across the centuries, across the oceans, across the mountains, across the prairies because we are made of sugar candy.

America's in trouble today not because her people have failed, but because her leaders have failed. And what America needs are leaders to match the greatness of her people.

And this great group of Americans—the forgotten Americans and others—know that the great question Americans must answer by their votes in November is this: Whether we shall continue for four more years the policies of the last five years.

And this is their answer, and this is my answer to that question: When the strongest nation in the world can be tied down for four years in a war in Vietnam with no end in sight, when the richest nation in the world can't manage its own economy, when the nation with the greatest tradition of the rule of law is plagued by unprecedented lawlessness, when a nation has been known for a century for equality of opportunity is torn by unprecedented racial violence, and when the President of the United States cannot travel abroad or to any major city at home without fear of a hostile demonstration—then it's time for new leadership for the United States of America.

Thank you. My fellow Americans, tonight I accept the challenge and the commitment to provide that new leadership for America and I ask you to accept it with me.

And let us accept this challenge not as a grim duty but as an exciting adventure in which we are privileged to help a great nation realize its destiny and let us begin by committing ourselves to the truth, to see it like it is and tell it like it is, to find the truth, to speak the truth and to live the truth. That's what we will do.

We've had enough of big promises and little action. The time has come for an honest government in the United States of America.

And so tonight I do not promise the millenium in the morning. I don't promise that we can eradicate poverty and end discrimination and eliminate all danger of wars in the space of four, or even eight years. But I do promise action. A new policy for peace abroad, a new policy for peace and progress and justice at home.

Look at our problems abroad. Do you realize that we face the stark truth that we are worse off in every area of the world tonight than we were when President Eisenhower left office eight years ago? That's the record.

And there is only one answer to such a record of failure, and that is the complete house cleaning of those responsibile for the failures and that record.

The answer is the complete reappraisal of America's policies in every section of the world. We shall begin with Vietnam.

We all hope in this room that there's a chance that current negotiations may bring an honorable end to that war. And we will say nothing during this campaign that might destroy that chance.

But if the war is not ended when the people choose in November, the choice will be clear. Here it is: For four years this Administration has had at its disposal the greatest military and economic advantage that one nation has ever had over another in a war in history. For four years America's fighting men have set a record for courage and sacrifice unsurpassed in our history. For four years this Administration has had the support of the loyal opposition for the objective of seeking an honorable end to the struggle.

Never has so much military and economic and diplomatic power been used so ineffectively. And if after all of this time, and all of this sacrifice, and all of this support, there is still no end in sight, then I say the time has come for the American people to turn to new leadership not tied to the mistakes and policies of the past. That is what we offer to America.

And I pledge to you tonight that the first priority foreign policy objective of our next Administration will be to bring an honorable end to the war in Vietnam.

We shall not stop there. We need a policy to prevent more Vietnams. All of America's peace-keeping institutions and all of America's foreign commitments must be reappraised.

Over the past 25 years, America has provided more than $150-billion in foreign aid to nations abroad. In Korea, and now again in Vietnam, the United States furnished most of the money, most of the arms, most of the men to help the people of those countries defend themselves against aggression. Now we're a rich country, we're a strong nation, we're a populous nation but there are 200 million Americans and there are two billion people that live in the free world, and I say the time has come for other nations in the free world to bear their fair share of the burden of defending peace and freedom around this world.

What I call for is not a new isolationism. It is a new internationalism in which America enlists its allies and its friends around the world in those struggles in which their interest is as great as ours.

And now to the leaders of the Communist world we say, after an era of confrontations, the time has come for an era of negotiations.

Where the world superpowers are concerned there is no acceptable alternative to peaceful negotiation. Because this will be a period of negotiations we shall restore the strength of America so that we shall always negotiate from strength and never from weakness.

And as we seek through negotiations let our goals be made clear. We do not seek domination over any other country. We believe deeply in our ideas but we believe they should travel on their own power and not on the power of our arms. We shall never be belligerent. But we shall be as firm in defending our system as they are in expanding theirs.

We believe this should be an era of peaceful competition not only in the productivity of our factories but in the quality of our ideas. We extend the hand of friendship to all people. To the Russian people. To the Chinese people. To all people in the world. And we shall work toward the goal of an open world, open sky, open cities, open hearts, open minds. The next eight years my friends. . . .

This period in which we're entering—I think we will have the greatest opportunity for world peace, but also face the greatest danger of world war of anytime in our history.

I believe we must have peace. I believe that we can have peace. But I do not underestimate the difficulty of this task.

Because, you see, the art of preserving peace is greater than that of waging war, and much more demanding.

But I am proud to have served in an Administration which ended one war and kept the nation out of other wars for eight years afterward.

And it is that kind of experience, and it is that kind of leadership, that America needs today and that we will give to America, with your help.

And as we commit the new policies for America tonight, let me make one further pledge—For five years hardly a day has gone by when we haven't read or heard a report of the American flag being spit on, and our embassy being stoned, a library being burned, or an ambassador being insulted some place in the world, and each incident reduced respect for the United States until the ultimate insult inevitably occurred.

And I say to you tonight that when respect for the United States of America falls so low that a fourth-rate military power like Korea will seize an American naval vessel in the high seas, it's time for new leadership to restore respect for the United States of America.

Thank you very much. My friends, America is a great nation. It is time we started to act like a great nation around the world.

It's ironic to note, when we were a small nation, weak militarily and poor economically, America was respected. And the reason was that America stood for something more powerful than military strength or economic wealth.

The American Revolution was a shining example of freedom in action which caught the imagination of the world, and today, too often, America is an example to be avoided and not followed.

A nation that can't keep the peace at home won't be trusted to keep the peace abroad. A president who isn't treated with respect at home will not be treated with respect abroad. A nation which can't manage its own economy can't tell others how to manage theirs.

If we are to restore prestige and respect for America abroad, the place to begin is at home—in the United States of America.

My friends, we live in an age of revolution in America and in the world. And to find the answers to our problems, let us turn to a revolution—a revolution that will never grow old, the world's greatest continuing revolution, the American Revolution.

The American Revolution was and is dedicated to progress. But our founders recognized that the first requisite of progress is order.

Now there is no quarrel between progress and order because neither can exist without the other.

So let us have order in America, not the order that suppresses dissent and discourages change but the order which guarantees the right to dissent and provides the basis for peaceful change.

And tonight it's time for some honest talk about the problem of order in the United States. Let us always respect, as I do, our courts and those who serve on them, but let us also recognize that some of our courts in their decisions have gone too far in weakening the peace forces as against the criminal forces in this country.

Let those who have the responsibility to enforce our laws, and our judges who have the responsibility to interpret them, be dedicated to the great principles of civil rights. But let them also recognize that the first civil right of every American is to be free from domestic violence. And that right must be guaranteed in this country.

And if we are to restore order and respect for law in this country, there's one place we're going to begin: We're going to have a new Attorney General of the United States of America.

I pledge to you that our new Attorney General will be directed by the President of the United States to launch a war against organized crime in this country.

I pledge to you that the new Attorney General of the United States will be an active belligerent against the loan sharks and the numbers racketeers that rob the urban poor in our cities.

I pledge to you that the new Attorney General will open a new front against the pill peddlers and the narcotics peddlers who are corrupting the lives of the children of this country.

Because, my friends, let this message come through clear from what I say tonight. Time is running out for the merchants of crime and corruption in American society. The wave of crime is not going to be the wave of the future in the United States of America.

We shall re-establish freedom from fear in America so that America can take the lead of re-establishing freedom from fear in the world.

And to those who say that law and order is the code word for racism, here is a reply: Our goal is justice—justice for every American. If we are to have respect for law in America, we must have laws that deserve respect. Just as we cannot have progress without order, we cannot have order without progress.

And so as we commit to order tonight, let us commit to progress.

And this brings me to the clearest choice among the great issues of this campaign.

For the past five years we have been deluged by Government programs for the unemployed, programs for the cities, programs for the poor, and we have reaped from these programs an ugly harvest of frustrations, violence and failure across the land. And now our opponents will be offering more of the same—more billions for Government jobs, Government housing, Government welfare. I say it's time to quit pouring billions of dollars into programs that have failed in the United States of America.

To put it bluntly, we're on the wrong road and it's time to take a new road to progress.

Again we turn to the American Revolution for our answers. The war on poverty didn't begin five years ago in this country; it began when this country began. It's been the most successful war on poverty in the history of nations. There's more wealth in America today, more broadly shared than in any nation in the world.

We are a great nation. And we must never forget how we became great. America is a great nation today, not because of what government did for people, but because of what people did for themselves over 190 years in this country.

And so it is time to apply the lessons of the American Revolution to our present problems.

Let us increase the wealth of America so we can provide more generously for the aged and for the needy and for all those who cannot help themselves.

But for those who are able to help themselves, what we need are not more millions on welfare rolls but more millions on payrolls in the United States of America.

Instead of Government jobs and Government housing let Government use its tax and credit policies to enlist in this battle the greatest engine of progress ever developed in the history of man—American private enterprise.

Let us enlist in this great cause the millions of Americans in volunteer organizations who will bring a dedication to this task that no amount of money can ever buy.

And let us build bridges, my friends, build bridges to human dignity across the gulf that separates black America from white America.

Black Americans—no more than white Americans—do not want more Government programs which perpetuate dependency. They don't want to be a colony in a nation. They want the pride and the self-respect and the dignity that can only come if they have an equal chance to own their own homes, to own their own businesses, to be managers and executives as well as workers, to have a piece of the action in the exciting ventures of private enterprise.

I pledge to you tonight that we shall have new programs which will provide that equal chance. We make great history tonight. We do not fire a shot heard round the world, but we shall light the lamp of hope in millions of homes across this land in which there is no hope today.

And that great light shining out from America will again become a beacon of hope for all those in the world who seek freedom and opportunity.

My fellow Americans, I believe that historians will recall that 1968 marked the beginning of the American generation in world history. Just to be alive in America, just to be alive at this time is an experience unparalleled in history. Here's where the action is.

Think: Thirty-two years from now most of Americans living today will celebrate a New Year that comes once in a thousand years.

Eight years from now, in the second term of the next President, we will celebrate the 200th anniversary of the American Revolution.

And by our decision in this we—all of us here, all of you listening on television and radio—we will determine what kind of nation America will be on its 200th birthday. We will determine what kind of a world America will live in in the year 2000.

This is the kind of a day I see for America on that glorious Fourth eight years from now: I see a day when Americans are once again proud of their flag; when once again at home and abroad it is honored as the world's greatest symbol of liberty and justice.

I see a day when the President of the United States is respected and his office is honored because it is worthy of respect and worthy of honor. I see a day when every child in this land, regardless of his background, has a chance for the best education that our wisdom and schools can provide, and an equal chance to go just as high as his talents will take him.

I see a day when life in rural America attracts people to the country rather than driving them away.

I see a day when we can look back on massive breakthroughs in solving the problems of slums and pollution and traffic which are choking our cities to death.

I see a day when our senior citizens and millions of others can plan for the future with the assurance that their government is not going to rob them of their savings by destroying the value of their dollar.

I see a day when we will again have freedom from fear in America and freedom from fear in the world. I see a day when our nation is at peace and the world is at peace and everyone on earth—those who hope, those who aspire, those who crave liberty will look to America as the shining example of hopes realized and dreams achieved.

My fellow Americans, this is the cause I ask you to vote for. This is the cause I ask you to work for. This is the cause I ask you to commit to not just for victory in November but beyond that to a new Administration because the time when one man or a few leaders could save America is gone. We need tonight nothing less than the total commitment and the total mobilization of the American people if we are to succeed.

Government can pass laws but respect for law can come only from people who take the law into their hearts and their minds and not into their hands.

Government can provide opportunity, but opportunity means nothing unless people are prepared to seize it.

A president can ask for reconciliation in the racial conflict that divides Americans, but reconciliation comes only from the hearts of people.

And tonight, therefore, as we make this commitment, let us look into our hearts, and let us look down into the faces of our children.

Is there anything in the world that should stand in their way? None of the old hatreds mean anything when you look down into the faces of our children. In their faces is our hope, our love and our courage.

Tonight, I see the face of a child. He lives in a great city, he's black or he's white, he's Mexican, Italian, Polish, none of that matters. What matters he's an American child.

That child in that great city is more important than any politician's promise. He is America, he is a poet, he is a scientist, he's a great teacher, he's a proud craftsman, he's everything we've ever hoped to be in everything we dare to dream about.

He sleeps the sleep of a child, and he dreams the dreams of a child. And yet when he awakens, he awakens to a living nightmare of poverty, neglect and despair.

He fails in school, he ends up on welfare. For him the American system is one that feeds his stomach and starves his soul. It breaks his heart. And in the end it may take his life on some distant battlefield.

To millions of children in this rich land this is their prospect, but this is only part of what I see in America.

I see another child tonight. He hears a train go by. At night he dreams of faraway places where he'd like to go. It seems like an impossible dream. But he is helped on his journey through life. A father who had to go to work before he finished the sixth grade sacrificed everything he had so that his sons could go to college.

A gentle Quaker mother with a passionate concern for peace, quietly wept when he went to war but she understood why he had to go.

A great teacher, a remarkable football coach, an inspirational minister encouraged him on his way. A courageous wife and loyal children stood by him in victory and also in defeat.

And in his chosen profession of politics, first there was scores, then hundreds, then thousands, and finally millions who worked for his success.

And tonight he stands before you, nominated for President of the United States of America.

You can see why I believe so deeply in the American dream.

For most of us the American revolution has been won, the American dream has come true. What I ask of you tonight is to help me make that dream come true for millions to whom it's an impossible dream today.

One hundred and eight years ago the newly elected President of the United States, Abraham Lincoln, left Springfield, Ill., never to return again.

He spoke to his friends gathered at the railroad station. Listen to his words:

"Today I leave you. I go to assume a greater task than devolved on General Washington. The Great God which helped him must help me. Without that great assistance I will surely fail. With it, I cannot fail."

Abraham Lincoln lost his life but he did not fail.

The next President of the United States will face challenges which in some ways will be greater than those of Washington or Lincoln, because for the first time in our nation's history an American President will face not only the problem of restoring peace abroad, but of restoring peace at home.

Without God's help, and your help, we will surely fail.

But with God's help and your help, we shall surely succeed.

My fellow Americans, the dark long night for America is about to end.

The time has come for us to leave the valley of despair and climb the mountain so that we may see the glory of the dawn, a new day for America, a new dawn for peace and freedom to the world.

RICHARD M. NIXON, INAUGURAL ADDRESS
January 20, 1969

Senator Dirksen, Mr. Chief Justice, Mr. Vice President, President Johnson, Vice President Humphrey, my fellow Americans—and my fellow citizens of the world community:

I ask you to share with me today the majesty of this moment. In the orderly transfer of power, we celebrate the unity that keeps us free.

Each moment in history is a fleeting time, precious and unique. But some stand out as moments of beginning, in which courses are set that shape decades or centuries.

This can be such a moment.

Forces now are converging that make possible for the first time, the hope that many of man's deepest aspirations can at last be realized.

The spiraling pace of change allows us to contemplate, within our own lifetime, advances that once would have taken centuries.

In throwing wide the horizons of space, we have discovered new horizons on earth.

For the first time, because the people of the world want peace and the leaders of the world are afraid of war, the times are on the side of peace.

Eight years from now America will celebrate its 200th anniversary as a nation. Within the lifetime of most people now living, mankind will celebrate that great new year which comes only once in a thousand years—the beginning of the Third Millennium.

What kind of nation we will be, what kind of world we will live in, whether we shape the future in the image of our hopes, is ours to determine by our actions and our choices.

The greatest honor history can bestow is the title of peacemaker. This honor now beckons America—the chance to help lead the world at last out of the valley of turmoil, and onto that high ground of peace that man has dreamed of since the dawn of civilization.

If we succeed, generations to come will say of us now living that we mastered our moment, that we helped make the world safe for mankind.

This is our summons to greatness.

I believe the American people are ready to answer this call.

The second third of this century has been a time of proud achievement. We have made enormous strides in science and industry and agriculture. We have shared our wealth more broadly than ever. We have learned at last to manage a modern economy to assure its continued growth.

Congressional Record, 91st Cong., 1st sess., 1969, 115, pt. 1, 1290-92.

We have given freedom new reach, and we have begun to make its promise real for black as well as for white.

We see the hope of tomorrow in the youth of today. I know America's youth, I believe in them. We can be proud that they are better educated more committed, more passionately driven by conscience than any generation in our history.

No people has ever been so close to the achievement of a just and abundant society, or so possessed of the will to achieve it.

Because our strengths are so great, we can afford to appraise our weaknesses with candor and to approach them with hope.

Standing in this same place a third of a century ago, Franklin Delano Roosevelt addressed a nation ravaged by depression and gripped in fear. He could say in surveying the nation's troubles: "They concern, thank God, only material things."

Our crisis today is the reverse.

We have found ourselves rich in goods, but ragged in spirit; reaching with magnificent precision for the moon, but falling into raucous discord on earth.

We are caught in war, wanting peace. We are torn by division, wanting unity. We see around us empty lives, wanting fulfillment. We see tasks that need doing, waiting for hands to do them.

To a crisis of the spirit, we need an answer of the spirit.

To find that answer, we need only look within ourselves.

When we listen to "the better angels of our nature," we find that they celebrate the simple things, the basic things—such as goodness, decency, love, kindness.

Greatness comes in simple trappings.

The simple things are the ones most needed today if we are to surmount what divides us, and cement what unites us.

To lower our voices would be a simple thing.

In these difficult years, America has suffered from a fever of words: from inflated rhetoric that promises more than it can deliver; from angry rhetoric that fans discontents into hatreds; from bombastic rhetoric that postures instead of persuading.

We cannot learn from one another until we stop shouting at one another—until we speak quietly enough so that our words can be heard as well as our voices.

For its part, government will listen. We will strive to listen in new ways—to the voices of quiet anguish, the voices that speak without words, the voices of the heart—to the injured voices, the anxious voices, the voices that have despaired of being heard.

Those who have been left out, we will try to bring in.

Those left behind, we will help to catch up.

For all of our people, we will set as our goal the decent order that makes progress possible and our lives secure.

As we reach toward our hopes, our task is to build on what has gone before—not turning away from the old, but turning toward the new.

In this past third of a century, government has passed more laws, spent more money, initiated more programs, than in all our previous history.

In pursuing our goals of full employment, better housing, excellence in education; in rebuilding our cities and improving our rural areas; in protecting our environment and enhancing the quality of life—in all these and more, we will and must press urgently forward.

We shall plan now for the day when our wealth can be transferred from the destruction of war abroad to the urgent needs of our people at home.

The American dream does not come to those who fall asleep.

But we are approaching the limits of what government alone can do.

Our greatest need now is to reach beyond government, to enlist the legions of the concerned and the committed.

What has to be done, has to be done by government and people together or it will not be done at all. The lesson of past agony is that without the people we can do nothing; with the people we can do everything.

To match the magnitude of our tasks, we need the energies of our people—enlisted not only in grand enterprises, but more importantly in those small, splendid efforts that make headlines in the neighborhood newspaper instead of the national journal.

With these, we can build a great cathedral of the spirit—each of us raising it one stone at a time, as he reaches out to his neighbor, helping, caring, doing.

I do not offer a life of uninspiring ease. I do not call for a life of grim sacrifice. I ask you to join in a high adventure—one as rich as humanity itself, and exciting as the times we live in.

The essence of freedom is that each of us shares in the shaping of his own destiny.

Until he has been part of a cause larger than himself, no man is truly whole.

The way to fulfillment is in the use of our talents; we achieve nobility in the spirit that inspires that use.

As we measure what can be done, we shall promise only what we know we can produce, but as we chart our goals we shall be lifted by our dreams.

No man can be fully free while his neighbor is not. To go forward at all is to go forward together.

This means black and white together, as one Nation, not two. The laws have caught up with our conscience. What remains is to give life to what is in the law; to ensure at last that as all are born equal in dignity before God, all are born equal in dignity before man.

As we learn to go forward together at home, let us also seek to go forward together with all mankind.

Let us take as our goal: where peace is unknown, make it welcome; where peace is fragile, make it strong; where peace is temporary, make it permanent.

After a period of confrontation, we are entering an era of negotiation.

Let all nations know that during this Administration our lines of communication will be open.

We seek an open world—open to ideas, open to the exchange of goods and people, a world in which no people, great or small, will live in angry isolation.

We cannot expect to make everyone our friend, but we can try to make no one our enemy.

Those who would be our adversaries, we invite to a peaceful competition—not in conquering territory or extending dominion, but in enriching the life of man.

As we explore the reaches of space, let us go to the new worlds together—not as new worlds to be conquered, but as a new adventure to be shared.

With those who are willing to join, let us cooperate to reduce the burden of arms, to strengthen the structure of peace, to lift up the poor and the hungry.

But to all those who would be tempted by weakness, let us leave no doubt that we will be as strong as we need to be for as long as we need to be.

Over the past twenty years, since I first came to this Capitol as a freshman Congressman, I have visited most of the nations of the world.

I have come to know the leaders of the world, and the great forces, the great hatreds, the fears that divide the world.

I know that peace does not come through wishing for it—that there is no substitute for days and even years of patient and prolonged diplomacy.

I also know the people of the world.

I have seen the hunger of a homeless child, the pain of a man wounded in battle, the grief of a mother who has lost her son. I know these have no ideology, no race.

I know America. I know the heart of America is good.

I speak from my own heart, and the heart of my country, the deep concern we have for those who suffer, and those who sorrow.

I have taken an oath today in the presence of God and my countrymen to uphold and defend the Constitution of the United States and to that oath I now add this sacred commitment: I shall consecrate my office, my energies, and all the wisdom I can summon, to the cause of peace among nations.

Let this message be heard by strong and weak alike.

The peace we seek to win is not victory over any other people, but the peace that comes "with healing in its wings;" with compassion for those who have suffered; with understanding for those who have opposed us; with the opportunity for all the peoples of this Earth to choose their own destiny.

Only a few short weeks ago, we shared the glory of man's first sight of the world as God sees it, as a single sphere reflecting light in the darkness.

As the Apollo astronauts flew over the moon's gray surface on Christmas Eve, they spoke to us of the beauty of Earth—and in that voice so clear across the lunar distance, we heard them invoke God's blessing on its goodness.

In that moment, their view from the moon moved poet Archibald MacLeish to write:

To see the Earth as it truly is, small and blue and beautiful in that eternal silence where it floats, is to see ourselves as riders on the Earth together, brothers on that bright loveliness in the eternal cold—brothers who know now they are truly brothers.

In that moment of surpassing technological triumph, men turned their thoughts toward home and humanity—seeing in that far perspective that man's destiny on earth is not divisible: telling us that however far we reach into the cosmos, our destiny lies not in the stars but on Earth itself, in our own hands, in our own hearts.

We have endured a long night of the American spirit. But as our eyes catch the dimness of the first rays of dawn, let us not curse the remaining dark. Let us gather the light.

Our destiny offers, not the cup of despair, but the chalice of opportunity. So let us seize it, not in fear, but in gladness—and, "riders on the earth together," let us go forward, firm in our faith, steadfast in our purpose, cautious of the dangers; but sustained by our confidence in the will of God and the promise of man.

SELECTED SPEECHES OF SPIRO T. AGNEW
October and November 1969

CITIZENS' TESTIMONIAL DINNER

October 19, 1969
New Orleans, Louisiana

Sometimes it appears that we are reaching a period when our senses and our minds will no longer respond to moderate stimulation. We seem to be approaching an age of the gross. Persuasion through speeches and books is too often discarded for disruptive demonstrations aimed at bludgeoning the unconvinced into action.

The young, and by this I don't mean by any stretch of the imagination all the young, but I'm talking about those who claim to speak for the young, at the zenith of physical power and sensitivity, overwhelm themselves with drugs and artificial stimulants. Subtlety is lost, and fine distinctions based on acute reasoning are carelessly ignored in a headlong jump to a predetermined conclusion. Life is visceral rather than intellectual, and the most visceral practitioners of life are those who characterize themselves as intellectuals.

Truth to them is "revealed" rather than logically proved, and the principal infatuations of today revolve around the social sciences, those subjects which can accommodate any opinion and about which the most reckless conjecture cannot be discredited.

Education is being redefined at the demand of the uneducated to suit the ideas of the uneducated. The student now goes to college to proclaim rather than to learn. The lessons of the past are ignored and obliterated in a contemporary antagonism known as the generation gap. A spirit of national masochism prevails, encouraged by an effete corps of impudent snobs who characterize themselves as intellectuals.

It is in this setting of dangerous oversimplification that the war in Vietnam achieves its greatest distortion.

The recent Vietnam Moratorium is a reflection of the confusion that exists in America today. Thousands of well-motivated young people, conditioned since childhood to respond to great emotional appeals, saw fit to demonstrate for peace. Most did not stop to consider that the leaders of the Moratorium had billed it as a massive public outpouring of sentiment against the foreign policy of the President of the United States. Most did not care to be reminded that the leaders of the Moratorium refused to disassociate themselves from the objective enunciated by the enemy in Hanoi.

John R. Coyne, Jr., ed., *The Impudent Snobs: Agnew vs. the Intellectual Establishment* (New Rochelle, 1972), 248-53, 257-61, 265-70, 270-74.

If the Moratorium had any use whatever, it served as an emotional purgative for those who felt the need to clease themselves of their lack of ability to offer a constructive solution to the problem.

Unfortunately, we have not seen the end. The hard-core dissidents and the professional anarchists within the so-called "peace movement" will continue to exacerbate the situation. November 15 is already planned—wilder, more violent, and equally barren of constructive result.

Is all this justified? Are we imperialist warmongers? Let's look for a moment at the President's policy in Vietnam in the light of political and military conditions as they were and as they are today.

The situation as of January 20, 1969

MILITARY CONDITIONS

—The number of U.S. troops to Vietnam was still increasing.

(When the men on their way there on January 20 finally arrived, it reached an all-time high level in February.)

—We appeared still to be seeking a military solution.

—Military operations were characterized by maximum military pressure on the enemy, through emphasis on offensive operations.

—Progress in strengthening the South Vietnamese army was slow; not enough resources were being devoted to that effort.

POLITICAL CONDITIONS

—We found only a general and vague set of proposals for political settlement of the war. While they called for "self-determination," they provided no specific program for achieving it.

—Mutual withdrawal of forces was provided for under the Manila Declaration which envisioned that the Allied withdrawal would be completed within six months of the withdrawal of North Vietnamese forces. But everyone knew at that time that the North Vietnamese were not about to pull out while we were still there.

The situation today

MILITARY CONDITIONS

—We have instituted a Vietnamization program which envisages South Vietnamese responsibility for all aspects of the war—coping with both Viet Cong insurgency and regular North Vietnamese forces—even if we cannot make progress in the political negotiations in Paris.

—We have offered the withdrawal of U.S. and Allied forces over a 12-month period, if North Vietnamese forces also withdraw.

—We have declared that we would retain no military bases.

—We have begun to reduce our presence in South Vietnam by setting in motion the replacement of over 60,000 U.S. troops (twelve percent of total troops, or twenty percent of combat troops). This is a meaningful act of deescalation.

—We have emphasized to our military commanders the requirement that losses be held to an absolute minimum, consistent with their mission to protect Allied forces and the civilian population.

(Casualties in the first nine months of this administration are one-third less than during the comparable period last year.)

POLITICAL CONDITIONS

For the first time, concrete and comprehensive political proposals for the settlement of the war have been made:

—We have proposed free elections organized by joint commissions under international supervision.

—We and the government of South Vietnam have announced that we are prepared to accept any political outcome which is arrived at through free elections.

—We have offered to negotiate supervised cease fires under international supervision to facilitate the process of withdrawal.

—We have expressed willingness to discuss the ten-point program of the other side, together with plans to be put forward by the other parties.

In short, the only item which has been declared non-negotiable is the right of the people of South Vietnam to determine their future, free of outside interference.

Progress made to date in Vietnam:

—The enemy was unable to launch the summer offensive which everyone predicted for this year.

—The infiltration rate is down by two-thirds (which means that the possibility of an offensive this fall has receded).

—Casualties for the first nine months of this year are down one-third, as I indicated.

—The South Vietnamese army is larger, stronger, and more well-equipped.

—The influence of the government of South Vietnam has expanded substantially throughout the countryside. That government has made significant progress in coping with its domestic problems.

That is what is happening in Vietnam. There's a constructive program. What do the marchers in the Moratorium offer in place of that? Nothing. Absolutely nothing except an emotional bath for the people of the United States and this country can't afford to be torn to pieces by that kind of demonstrating in the streets.

Let us turn for a moment to a legitimate complaint of our young people—the draft.

The draft, at best, is a necessary evil—one that President Nixon wants to do away with as soon as possible. But while the draft is still necessary, our government has a moral obligation to make it as fair and as reasonable as possible. Our failure to do so mocks the ideals we profess so often.

What is it that makes our draft system so *unfair* and so *unreasonable?*

Essentially, there are two problems: first—the present system creates for our young men a long period of draft vulnerability, one which begins at age nineteen and stretches for seven long years—unless the young man is drafted sooner. During this time, his educational plans, his career, even his decisions concerning marriage and family are distorted by his inability to predict the impact of the draft. All of this constitutes a terrible pressure, a dark shadow which falls across the lives of young Americans at the very time when they should be greeting the opportunities of adulthood with the greatest sense of excitement and adventure.

Prolonged uncertainty is one problem with the draft. Unfair selection is the second. Though all are technically vulnerable to the draft, those who are able to go on to college and then into certain graduate programs or occupations are often able to escape induction. In short, the current draft system creates frustration and mocks justice; it is both unfair and unreasonable.

This is not my opinion alone. It is widely shared—by members of all age groups in all parts of the country. Two panels composed of distinguished citizens—one headed by General Mark Clark and one headed by Mr. Burke Marshall—have reached the same conclusion in recent years. So have the many leaders of both parties in the House and Senate.

Months ago President Nixon took the lead in the battle to reform the draft. On May 13, 1969, he sent a message to the Congress in which he asked that body to reduce the period of prime vulnerability from seven years to one year and to institute a fair, random-selection system. Under this arrangement, everyone would be eligible for the draft at age nineteen and would be randomly assigned a place in the order of call at that time. He would remain in a condition of prime eligibility for twelve months. If he were not drafted in twelve months, he would move into less vulnerable categories. Those who chose to take a deferment at age nineteen, to go on to college, for example, would do so knowing where they fell in that order of call and could plan their lives accordingly. They would then spend their year in the prime vulnerability group at the time they left school.

Few of the President's statements have brought more favorable reaction than his suggestions for reforming the draft. Despite the widespread dissatisfaction with the draft and despite the widespread praise which greeted the President's message—the Congress waited until this week to act. The House Armed Services Committee this week unanimously reported the bill favorably, and early House action is expected. Senate action will depend on prompt attention by Senator Stennis' Committee.

As Secretary Laird recently explained, all that is necessary is that one sentence be changed in the current draft law, a sentence introduced as a last-minute after-thought back in 1967. This single sentence now prevents the President from switching to the random-selection process. Now if they just take care of this one problem, if

Congress takes care of that, the President can avoid doing it by administrative order which would eliminate the systematic inequity by scrambling the 365 days of the year and rearranging them so that birthdays fell randomly and the oldest in that year would not have to be taken. This is clearly the fairest system.

Certainly this is the time for the people to join the President in making their desires felt in this matter of draft reform. For if reform is frustrated, it will be a defeat not only for the President, but for the Democratic process. Above all it will be a retreat from the principles of reason and justice which we value so highly in this country, principles which we preach with great ardor to our young people, but which we have not yet achieved in our selective service legislation.

Among the inaccurate tirades against the present foreign policy of the United States is an oft-repeated allegation that we are mostly at fault for the strategic arms race with Russia.

If we examine the record of the past few years, it is quite clear that the United States has exercised considerable restraint in its strategic weapons programs, probably more than was prudent. Now, just listen carefully to these facts. You have heard it said on many occasions by Senators and Congressmen, for both parties, that the United States is responsible for this arms race. These are the facts:

—We built up to a force of about 1,000 ICBMs by mid-1967 and held it there;

—We began building the last of our forty-one ballistic missile submarines in 1965 and we have built none since;

—Even though President Kennedy was being pressed to deploy an ABM system as early as 1961, the U.S. refrained from a decision to deploy an ABM until 1967. And that was the time President Johnson suggested the Sentinel system. However, because of pressure, it was decided to modify the previous administration's ABM system to emphasize further that the U.S. deployment was not intended to be provocative to the Soviet Union, so we got the Safeguard system.

—We have stretched out a decision to deploy a new manned bomber for nearly a decade.

The Soviet Union's record should be judged against this background of U.S. restraint.

—The Soviets have already deployed sixty-four ABMs, and they are pursuing an active ABM development program today; they have more ABMs today than we will have by 1974, if the Safeguard program goes forward as planned;

—Their recent SS-9 tests with multiple warheads suggest that they are also pursuing a MIRV system; a development which is of grave concern to us;

—They have several ICBMs in development and production and have overcome our lead in deployed ICBMs; already this year they have started construction on upwards of 100 new ICBMs, and they show no signs of slacking off;

—They are continuing to build and deploy ballistic missile submarines and test new missiles for them;

—They are continuing to build up their air defense systems;

—They are developing mobile missile systems which move these ICBMs around the countryside.

In summary, they are active across the board in developing and deploying strategic systems.

Interest in arms control cannot be one-sided. It takes two sides to have a competition. I believe our record is clearly one of restraint. Moreover, since this administration took office, we have studied in detail every aspect of limiting strategic weapons.

—For example, for many weeks we have had a panel of experts examining in depth the possibilities and pitfalls in limiting the development and deployment of MIRVs.

—We have had another panel doing a detailed study of U.S. intelligence capabilities and our ability to verify compliance with an arms control agreement.

These studies have shown that clear cutoff points are very difficult to establish. For example, it would not be enough simply to ban MIRV testing in order to stop MIRV deployment. We would have to have collateral restrictions on the testing of most space and weapons systems involving multiple or maneuvering objects in order to have confidence that MIRV deployment was in fact banned. This makes a unilateral moratorium very risky.

Complex questions such as these cannot be resolved overnight. We look forward to discussing strategic arms limitation issues with the Soviet Union. We have asked them in April to set up a date for the talks. We asked them again in July to set a date for the talks. We are still waiting to begin those talks on strategic arms limitations.

We gain nothing, and the prospects for successful negotiations are not advanced one iota by restraints which are not reciprocated. Why should the Soviet Union bargain seriously with us if they can have what they want without paying any price whatever? We would be playing Russian roulette with U.S. security if we failed to take the minimum essential steps to maintain our security.

Finally, we are beset with the accusation that this administration is insensitive to domestic needs; that we are not spending enough on the problems of the poor; and that we, in fact, do not have a domestic program.

The decisions and actions of this administration, since it came to office on January 20th, have been conditioned by the economic environment that we inherited. By Inauguration Day, 1969, the federal government had run for eight years an unbroken string of budget deficits that added more than $78 billion to the federal debt. The impact of these deficits on the national economy was far reaching.

By this past January, price inflation had been generated and propelled to the point where the cost of living was surging upward at a rate of five per cent a year. These price increases, coupled with tax increases, meant that the average American working-man had made no gain at all in real income in more than three years. For those below the national average—the Americans who live on pensions or fixed income—these three years had been even more difficult. These Americans were worse off economically in terms of real income in January of 1969 than they had been in December of 1965—despite the growth in the economy.

The imperatives of this economic situation dictated to a great extent our legislative and administrative priorities.

We made initial cuts of some $4 billion in the proposed 1970 fiscal year budget. Later we made additional cuts of more than $4 billion to hold to our spending ceiling of $192.9 billion for this fiscal year. A short, tight leash on federal spending is the most effective means of controlling inflation—we are going to continue to use that leash.

We recommended an orderly phase-out of the surtax at the full ten percent for the second half of 1969 and at five percent for the first six months of calendar year 1970. Congress has so far only granted the first and most vital part of this request. We ordered a cutback of seventy-five percent in all federal construction; we have asked the states to cut back construction as much as they can; we have followed the restrained and restrictive monetary policy which our precarious economic situation requires.

While controversial and unpopular, I will agree, in the short-run to many Americans, these measures are essential to the long-run stability and security of the economy on which the well-being of the public sector and the private sector ultimately depend.

Even with a tight budget leaving little room for fiscal maneuver, we have come forward with legislative initiatives that break new ground in half a dozen areas that entail historic reform in others, and that will enable us to test a philosophy of government that rejects the old centralism that guided federal policy for most of the past four decades.

Among our recommendations to this first session of the Ninety-First Congress are:

1. The most extensive overhaul of the welfare system since the beginning of the New Deal. What a failure that welfare system has been. Just this week, we read that in the City of New York alone, there has been a $66 million waste of welfare money by giving it to people who are not even eligible to receive it under the AFDC program.

2. The beginning of a historic redistribution of power from the national capital to the state capitals and city halls through a sharing of federal income tax revenues with the states. Now I will agree that everyone talked about that for a long time, but this is the first time a President of the United States and administration have ever submitted legislation which will permit this revenue sharing to take place to reach within five years the level of $5 billion.

3. The first major reform of the Federal Tax Code in fifty years.

4. The first major reform of the Selective Service System since conscription became a permanent part of American life in 1948.
5. A major attack on organized crime and the narcotics traffic.
6. A concerted national effort to eliminate the vestiges of hunger and malnutrition from our national life.
7. Replacement of the 189-year-old United States Post Office Department with a government-owned corporation operating on business principles rather than political patronage.
8. The most extensive federal commitment to mass transit and aviation in history, a level of $10 billion in new spending for mass transit within the next twelve years.

Taken together, these recommendations represent our best judgment as to the priority of the competing and legitimate claims on the federal government. This is our assessment of where existing federal resources can best be distributed for the good of the country. If our diplomatic policies can produce an honorable peace in Asia, and our economic policies can halt inflation in the economy, we shall be able to take up at once other urgent needs of our people.

Great patriots of past generations would find it difficult to believe that Americans would ever doubt the validity of America's resolve to protect free men from totalitarian attack. Yet today we see those among us who prefer to side with an enemy aggressor rather than stand by this free nation. We see others who are shortsighted enough to believe that we need not protect ourselves from attack by governments that depend upon force to control their people—governments which came into being through force alone and continue to exist by force alone.

I do not want to see this nation spend one dollar more on defense than is absolutely necessary, but I would hate to see this nation spend one dollar less on defense than is absolutely necessary. Until the principle of open representative government exists among all nations, the United States must not abandon its moral obligation to protect by any means necessary the freedoms so hard won by past generations. The freedoms so hard won by the 400,000 Americans who made the ultimate sacrifice in dedicated belief that some things are more precious than life itself.

PENNSYLVANIA REPUBLICAN DINNER

October 30, 1969
Harrisburg, Pennsylvania

A little over a week ago, I took a rather unusual step for a Vice President . . . I said something. Particularly, I said something that was predictably unpopular with the people who would like to run this country without the inconvenience of seeking public office. I said I did not like some of the things I saw happening in this country. I criticized those who encouraged government by street carnival and suggested it was time to stop the carousel.

It appears that by slaughtering a sacred cow I triggered a holy war. I have no regrets. I do not intend to repudiate my beliefs, recant my words, or run and hide.

What I said before, I will say again. It is time for the preponderant majority, the responsible citizens of this country, to assert *their* rights. It is time to stop dignifying the immature actions of an arrogant, reckless, inexperienced element within our society. The reason is compelling. It is simply that their tantrums are insidiously destroying the fabric of American democracy.

By accepting unbridled protest as a way of life, we have tacitly suggested that the great issues of our times are best decided by posturing and shouting matches in the streets. America today is drifting toward Plato's classic definition of a degenerating democracy . . . a democracy that permits the voice of the mob to dominate the affairs of government.

Last week I was lambasted for my lack of "mental and moral sensitivity." I say that any leader who does not perceive where persistent street struggles are going to lead this nation lacks mental acuity. And any leader who does not caution this nation on the danger of this direction lacks moral strength.

Now let me make it clear, I believe in Constitutional dissent. I believe in the people registering their views with their elected representatives, and I commend those people who care enough about their country to involve themselves in its great issues. I believe in legal dissent within the Constitutional limits of free speech, including peaceful assembly and the right of petition. But I do not believe that demonstrations, lawful or unlawful, merit my approval or even my silence where the purpose is fundamentally unsound. In the case of the Vietnam Moratorium, the objective announced by the leaders—immediate unilateral withdrawal of all our forces from Vietnam—was not only unsound but idiotic. The tragedy was that thousands who participated wanted only to show a fervent desire for peace, but were used—yes, used—by the political hustlers who ran the event.

It is worth remembering that our country's founding fathers wisely shaped a constitutional republic, not a pure democracy. The representative government they contemplated and skillfully constructed never intended that elected officials should decide crucial issues by counting the number of bodies cavorting in the streets. They recognized that freedom cannot endure dependent upon referendum every time part of the electorate desires it.

So great is the latitude of our liberty that only a subtle line divides use from abuse. I am convinced that our preoccupation with emotional demonstration, frequently crossing the line to civil disruption and even violence could inexorably lead us across that line forever.

Ironically, it is neither the greedy nor the malicious, but the self-righteous who are guilty of history's worst atrocities. Society understands greed and malice and erects barriers of law to defend itself from these vices. But evil cloaked in emotional causes is well disguised and often undiscovered before it is too late.

We have just such a group of self-proclaimed saviours of the American soul at work today. Relentless in their criticism of intolerance in America, they themselves are intolerant of those who differ with their views. In the name of academic freedom, they destroy academic freedom. Denouncing violence, they seize and vandalize buildings of great universities. Fiercely expressing their respect for truth, they disavow the logic and discipline necessary to pursue truth.

They would have us believe that they alone know what is good for America; what is true and right and beautiful. They would have us believe that their reflective action is superior to our reflective action; that their revealed righteousness is more effective than our reason and experience.

Think about it. Small bands of students are allowed to shut down great universities. Small groups of dissidents are allowed to shout down political candidates. Small cadres of professional protesters are allowed to jeopardize the peace efforts of the President of the United States.

It is time to question the credentials of their leaders. And, if in questioning we disturb a few people, I say it is time for them to be disturbed. If, in challenging, we polarize the American people, I say it is time for a positive polarization.

It is time for a healthy in-depth examination of policies and a constructive realignment in this country. It is time to rip away the rhetoric and to divide on authentic lines. It is time to discard the fiction that in a country of 200 million people, everyone is qualified to quarterback the government.

For too long we have accepted superficial categorization—young versus old; white versus black; rich versus poor. Now it is time for an alignment based on principles and values shared by all citizens regardless of age, race, creed, or income. This, after all, is what America is all about.

America's pluralistic society was forged on the premise that what unites us in ideals is greater than what divides us as individuals. Our political and economic institutions were developed to enable men and ideas to compete in the marketplace on the assumption that the best would prevail. Everybody was deemed equal, and by the rules of the game they could become superior. The rules were clear and fair: in politics, win an election; in economics, build a better mousetrap. And as time progressed, we added more referees to assure equal opportunities and provided special advantages for those whom we felt had entered life's arena at a disadvantage.

The majority of Americans respect these rules . . . and with good reason. Historically, they have served as a bulwark to prevent totalitarianism, tyranny, and privilege . . . the old world spectres which drove generations of immigrants to American sanctuary. Pragmatically, the rules of America work. This nation and its citizens—collectively and individually—have made more social, political and economic progress than any civilization in world history.

The principles of the American system did not spring up overnight. They represent centuries of bitter struggle. Our laws and institutions are not even purely American—only our federal system bears our unique imprimatur.

We owe our values to the Judeo-Christian ethic which stresses individualism, human dignity, and a higher purpose than hedonism. We owe our laws to the political evolution of government by consent of the governed. Our nation's philosophical heritage is as diverse as its cultural background. We are a melting pot nation that has for over two centuries distilled something new and, I believe, sacred.

Now, we have among us a glib, activist element who would tell us our values are lies, and I call them impudent. Because anyone who impugns a legacy of liberty and dignity that reaches back to Moses, is impudent.

I call them snobs for most of them disdain to mingle with the masses who work for a living. They mock the common man's pride in his work, his family and his country. It has also been said that I called them intellectuals. I did not. I said that they characterized themselves as intellectuals. No true intellectual, no truly knowledgeable person, would so despise democratic institutions.

America cannot afford to write off a whole generation for the decadent thinking of a few. America cannot afford to divide over their demagoguery . . . or to be deceived by their duplicity . . . or to let their license destroy liberty. We can, however, afford to separate them from our society—with no more regret than we should feel over discarding rotten apples from a barrel.

The leaders of this country have a moral as well as a political obligation to point out the dangers of unquestioned allegiance to any cause. We must be better than a charlatan leader of the French Revolution, remembered only for his words: "There go the people; I am their leader; I must follow them."

And the American people have an obligation, too . . . an obligation to exercise their citizenship with a precision that precludes excesses.

I recognize that many of the people who participated in the past Moratorium Day were unaware that its sponsors sought immediate unilateral withdrawal. Perhaps many more had not considered the terrible consequences of immediate unilateral withdrawal.

I hope that all citizens who truly want peace will take the time to read and reflect on the problem. I hope that they will take into consideration the impact of abrupt termination; that they will remember the more than 3,000 innocent men, women, and children slaughtered after the Viet Cong captured Hue last year and the more than 15,000 doctors, nurses, teachers and village leaders murdered by the Viet Cong during the war's early years. The only sin of these people was their desire to build their budding nation of South Vietnam.

Chanting "Peace Now" is no solution, if "Peace Now" is to permit a wholesale bloodbath. And saying that the President should understand the people's view is no solution. It is time for the people to understand the views of the President they elected to lead them.

First, foreign policy cannot be made in the streets.

Second, turning out a good crowd is not synonymous with turning out a good foreign policy.

Third, the test of a President cannot be reduced to a question of public relations. As the eighteenth-century jurist, Edmund Burke, wrote, "Your representative owes you not his industry only but his judgment; and he betrays instead of serving you, if he sacrifices it to your opinion."

Fourth, the impatience—the understandable frustration over this war—should be focused on the government that is stalling peace while continuing to threaten and invade South Vietnam—and that government's capital is not in Washington. It is in Hanoi.

This was not Richard Nixon's war . . . but it will be Richard Nixon's peace if we only let him make it.

Finally—and most important—regardless of the issue, it is time to stop demonstrating in the streets and start doing something constructive about our institutions. America must recognize the danger of constant carnival. Americans must reckon with irresponsible leadership and reckless words. The mature and sensitive people of this country must realize that their freedom of protest is being exploited by avowed anarchists and communists—yes, I say communist because a member of one of those committees is a member of the communist party and proud of it—who detest everything about this country and want to destroy it.

This is a fact. These are the few . . . these are not necessarily all the leaders. But they prey upon the good intentions of gullible men everywhere. They pervert honest concern to something sick and rancid. They are vultures who sit in trees and watch lions battle, knowing that win, lose or draw, they will be fed.

Abetting the merchants of hate are the parasites of passion. There are the men who value a cause purely for its political mileage. There are the politicians who temporize with the truth by playing both sides to their own advantage. They ooze sympathy for "the cause" but balance each sentence with equally reasoned reservations. Their interest is personal, not moral. They are ideological eunuchs whose most comfortable position is straddling the philosophical fence, soliciting votes from both sides.

Aiding the few who seek to destroy and the many who seek to exploit is a terrifying spirit, the new face of self-righteousness. Former HEW Secretary John Gardner described it: "Sad to say, it's fun to hate . . . that is today's fashion. Rage and hate in a good cause! Be vicious for virtue, self-indulgent for higher purposes, dishonest in the service of a higher honesty."

This is what is happening in this nation . . . we are an effete society if we let it happen here.

I do not overstate the case. If I am aware of the danger, the convicted rapist Eldridge Cleaver is aware of the potential. From his Moscow hotel room he predicted, "Many complacent regimes thought that they would be in power eternally—and awoke one morning to find themselves up against the wall. I expect that to happen in the United States in our lifetimes."

People cannot live in a state of perpetual electric shock. Tired of a convulsive society, they settle for an authoritarian society. As Thomas Hobbes discerned three centuries ago, men will seek the security of a Leviathan state as a comfortable alternative to a life that is "nasty, brutish, and short."

Right now we must decide whether we will take the trouble to stave off a totalitarian state. Will we stop the wildness now before it is too late, before the witch-hunting and repression that are all to inevitable begin?

Will Congress settle down to the issues of the nation and reform the institutions of America as our President asks? Can the press ignore the pipers who lead the parades? Will the head of great universities protect the rights of all their students? Will parents have the courage to say no to their children? Will people have the intelligence to boycott pornography and violence? Will citizens refuse to be led by a series of Judas goats down tortuous paths of delusions and self-destruction?

Will we defend fifty centuries of accumulated wisdom? For that is our heritage. Will we make the effort to preserve America's bold, successful experiment in truly representative government? Or do we care so little that we will casually toss it all aside?

Because on the eve of our nation's 200th birthday, we have reached the crossroads. Because at this moment totalitarianism's threat does not necessarily have a foreign accent. Because we have a home-grown menace, made and manufactured in the U.S.A. Because if we are lazy or foolish, this nation could forfeit its integrity, never to be free again.

I do not want this to happen to America. And I do not think that you do either. We have something magnificent here . . . something worth fighting for . . . and now is the time for all good men to fight for the soul of their country. Let us stop apologizing for our past. Let us conserve and create for the future.

MIDWEST REGIONAL REPUBLICAN COMMITTEE MEETING

November 13, 1969
Des Moines, Iowa

Tonight I want to discuss the importance of the television news medium to the American people. No nation depends more on the intelligent judgment of its citizens. No medium has a more profound influence over public opinion. Nowhere in our system are there fewer checks on vast power. So, nowhere should there be more conscientious responsibility exercised than by the news media. The question is . . . are we demanding enough of our television news presentations? . . . And, are the men of this medium demanding enough of themselves?

Monday night, a week ago, President Nixon delivered the most important address of his administration, one of the most important of our decade.[1] His subject was Vietnam. His hope was to rally the American people to see the conflict through to a lasting and just peace in the Pacific. For thirty-two minutes, he reasoned with a nation that has suffered almost a third of a million casualties in the longest war in its history.

When the President completed his address—an address that he spent weeks in preparing—his words and policies were subjected to instant analysis and querulous criticism. The audience of seventy million Americans—gathered to hear the President of the United States—was inherited by a small band of network

[1] See the following document—*Ed.*

commentators and self-appointed analysts, the *majority* of whom expressed, in one way or another, their hostility to what he had to say.

It was obvious that their minds were made up in advance. Those who recall the fumbling and groping that followed President Johnson's dramatic disclosure of his intention not to seek reelection have seen these men in a genuine state on non-preparedness. This was not it.

One commentator twice contradicted the President's statement about the exchange of correspondence with Ho Chi Minh. Another challenged the President's abilities as a politician. A third asserted the President was "following the Pentagon line." Others, by the expressions on their faces, the tone of their questions, and the sarcasm of their responses, made clear their sharp disapproval.

To guarantee in advance that the President's plea for national unity would be challenged, one network trotted out Averell Harriman for the occasion. Throughout the President's address he waited in the wings. When the President concluded, Mr. Harriman recited perfectly. He attacked the Thieu government as unrepresentative; he criticized the President's speech for various deficiencies; he twice issued a call to the Senate Foreign Relations Committee to debate Vietnam once again; he stated his belief that the Viet Cong or North Vietnamese did not really want a military takeover of South Vietnam; he told a little anecdote about a "very, very responsible" fellow he had met in the North Vietnamese delegation.

All in all, Mr. Harriman offered a broad range of gratuitous advice—challenging and contradicting the policies outlined by the President of the United States. Where the President had issued a call for unity, Mr. Harriman was encouraging the country not to listen to him.

A word about Mr. Harriman. For ten months he was America's chief negotiator at the Paris Peace Talks—a period in which the United States swapped some of the greatest military concessions in the history of the warfare for an enemy agreement on the shape of a bargaining table. Like Coleridge's Ancient Mariner, Mr. Harriman seems to be under some heavy compulsion to justify his failures to anyone who will listen. The networks have shown themselves willing to give him all the airtime he desires.

Every American has a right to disagree with the President of the United States, and to express publicly that disagreement.

But the President of the United States has a right to communicate directly with the people who elected him, and the people of this country have the right to make up their own minds and form their own opinions about a presidential address without having the President's words and thoughts characterized through the prejudices of hostile critics before they can even be digested.

When Winston Churchill rallied public opinion to stay the course against Hitler's Germany, he did not have to contend with a gaggle of commentators raising doubts about whether he was reading public opinion right, or whether Britain had the stamina to see the war through. When President Kennedy rallied the nation in the Cuban Missile Crisis, his address to the people was not chewed over by a roundtable of critics who disparaged the course of action he had asked America to follow.

The purpose of my remarks tonight is to focus your attention on this little group of men who not only enjoy a right of instant rebuttal to every presidential address, but more importantly, wield a free hand in selecting, presenting, and interpreting the great issues of our nation.

First, let us define that power. At least forty million Americans each night, it is estimated, watch the network news. Seven million of them view ABC; the remainder being divided between NBC and CBS. According to Harris polls and other studies, for millions of Americans the networks are the sole source of national and world news.

In Will Rogers' observation, what you knew was what you read in the newspaper. Today, for growing millions of Americans, it is what they see and hear on their television sets.

How is this network news determined? A small group of men, numbering perhaps no more than a dozen "anchormen," commentators, and executive producers, settle upon the twenty minutes or so of film and commentary that is to reach the public. This selection is made from the 90 to 180 minutes that may be available. Their powers of choice are broad. They decide what forty to fifty million Americans will learn of the day's events in the nation and in the world.

We cannot measure this power and influence by traditional democratic standards for these men can create national issues overnight. They can make or break—by their coverage and commentary—a Moratorium on the war. They can elevate men from local obscurity to national prominence within a week. They can reward some politicians with national exposure and ignore others. For millions of Americans, the network reporter who covers a continuing issue, like ABM or Civil Rights, becomes in effect, the presiding judge in a national trial by jury.

It must be recognized that the networks have made important contributions to the national knowledge. Through news, documentaries, and specials, they have often used their power constructively and creatively to awaken the public conscience to critical problems.

The networks made "hunger" and "black lung" disease national issues overnight. The TV networks have done what no other medium could have done in terms of dramatizing the horrors of war. The networks have tackled our most difficult social problems with a directness and immediacy that is the gift of their medium. They have focused the nation's attention on its environmental abuses . . . on pollution in the Great Lakes and the threatened ecology of the Everglades.

But it was also the networks that elevated Stokely Carmichael and George Lincoln Rockwell from obscurity to national prominence . . . nor is their power confined to the substantive.

A raised eyebrow, an inflection of the voice, a caustic remark dropped in the middle of a broadcast can raise doubts in a million minds about the veracity of a public official or the wisdom of a government policy.

One Federal Communications Commissioner considers the power of the networks to equal that of local, state, and federal governments combined. Certainly it represents a concentration of power over American public opinion unknown in history.

What do Americans know of the men who wield this power? Of the men who produce and direct the network news—the nation knows practically nothing. Of the commentators, most Americans know little, other than that they reflect an urbane and assured presence, seemingly well informed on every important matter.

We do know that, to a man, these commentators and producers live and work in the geographical and intellectual confines of Washington, D.C. or New York City—the latter of which James Reston terms the "most unrepresentative community in the entire United States." Both communities bask in their own provincialism, their own parochialism. We can deduce that these men thus read the same newspapers, and draw their political and social views from the same sources. Worse, they talk constantly to one another, thereby providing artificial reinforcement to their shared viewpoints.

Do they allow their biases to influence the selection and presentation of the news? David Brinkley states, "objectivity is impossible to normal human behavior." Rather, he says, we should strive for "fairness."

Another anchorman on a network news show contends: "You can't expunge all your private convictions just because you sit in a seat like this and a camera starts to stare at you ... I think your program has to reflect what your basic feelings are. I'll plead guilty to that."

Less than a week before the 1968 election, this same commentator charged that President Nixon's campaign commitments were no more durable than campaign balloons. He claimed that, were it not for fear of a hostile reaction, Richard Nixon would be giving into, and I quote the commentator, "his natural instinct to smash the enemy with a club or go after him with a meat-ax."

Had this slander been made by one political candidate about another, it would have been dismissed by most commentators as a partisan assault. But this attack emanated from the privileged sanctuary of a network studio and therefore had the apparent dignity of an objective statement.

The American people would rightly not tolerate this kind of concentration of power in government. Is it not fair and relevant to question its concentration in the hands of a tiny and closed fraternity of privileged men, elected by no one, and enjoying a monopoly sanctioned and licensed by government?

The views of this fraternity do *not* represent the views of America. That is why such a great gulf existed between how the nation received the President's address—and how the networks reviewed it.

As with other American institutions, perhaps it is time that the networks were made more responsive to the views of the nation and more responsible to the people they serve.

I am not asking for government censorship or any other kind of censorship. I am asking whether a form of censorship already exists when the news that forty million Americans receive each night is determined by a handful of men responsible only to their corporate employers and filtered through a handful of commentators who admit to their own set of biases.

The questions I am raising here tonight should have been raised by others long ago. They should have been raised by those Americans who have traditionally considered the preservation of freedom of speech and freedom of the press their special provinces of responsibility. They should have been raised by those Americans who share the view of the late Justice Learned Hand that "right conclusions are more likely to be gathered out of a multitude of tongues than through any kind of authoritative selection."

Advocates for the networks have claimed a first amendment right to the same unlimited freedoms held by the great newspapers of America.

The situations are not identical. Where the *New York Times* reaches 800,000 people, NBC reaches twenty times that number with its evening news. Nor can the tremendous impact of seeing television film and hearing commentary be compared with reading the printed page.

A decade ago, before the network news acquired such dominance over public opinion, Walter Lippmann spoke to the issue:

> There is an essential and radical difference between television and printing . . . the three of four [*sic*] competing television stations control virtually all that can be received over the air by ordinary television sets. But, besides the mass circulation dailies, there are the weeklies, the monthlies, the out-of-town newspapers, and books. If a man does not like his newspaper, he can read another from out of town, or wait for a weekly news magazine. It is not ideal. But it is infinitely better than the situation in television. There, if a man does not like what the networks are showing, all he can do is turn them off, and listen to a phonograph.

"Networks," he stated, "which are few in number, have a virtual monopoly of a whole medium of communication." The newspapers of mass circulation have no monopoly of the medium of print.

"A virtual monopoly of a whole medium of communication" is not something a democratic people should blithely ignore.

And we are not going to cut off our television sets and listen to the phonograph because the airwaves do not belong to the networks; they belong to the people.

As Justice Byron White wrote in his landmark opinion six months ago, "It is the right of the viewers and listeners, not the right of the broadcasters, which is paramount."

It is argued that this power presents no danger in the hands of those who have used it responsibly.

But as to whether or not the networks have abused the power they enjoy, let us call as our first witnesses, former Vice President Humphrey and the City of Chicago.

According to Theodore H. White, television's intercutting of the film from the streets of Chicago with the "current proceedings on the floor of the convention created the most striking and *false* political picture of 1968—the nomination of a man for the American presidency by the brutality and violence of merciless police."

If we are to believe a recent report of the House Commerce Committee, then television's presentation of the violence in the streets worked an injustice on the reputation of the Chicago police.

According to the Committee findings, one network in particular presented "a one-sided picture which in large measure exonerates the demonstrators and protesters." Film of provocation of police that was available never saw the light of day, while the film of the police response which the protestors provoked was shown to millions.

Another network showed virtually the same scene of violence—from three separate angles—without making clear it was the same scene.

While the full report is reticent in drawing conclusions, it is not a document to inspire confidence in the fairness of the network news.

Our knowledge of the impact of network news on the national mind is far from complete. But some early returns are available. Again, we have enough information to raise serious questions about its effect on a democratic society.

Several years ago, Fred Friendly, one of the pioneers of network news, wrote that its missing ingredients were "conviction, controversy, and a point of view." The networks have compensated with a vengeance.

And in the networks' endless pursuit of controversy, we should ask what is the end value ... to enlighten or to profit? What is the end result ... to inform or to confuse? How does the ongoing exploration for more action, more excitement, more drama, serve our national search for internal peace and stability?

Gresham's law seems to be operating in the network news.

Bad news drives out good news. The irrational is more controversial than the rational. Concurrence can no longer compete with dissent. One minute of Eldridge Cleaver is worth ten minutes of Roy Wilkins. The labor crises settled at the negotiating table is nothing compared to the confrontation that results in a strike—or, better yet, violence along the picket line. Normality has become the nemesis of the network news.

The upshot of all this controversy is that a narrow and distorted picture of America often emerges from the televised news. A single dramatic piece of the mosaic becomes, in the minds of millions, the entire picture. The American who relies upon television for his news might conclude that the majority of American students are embittered radicals, that the majority of black Americans feel no regard for their country; that violence and lawlessness are the rule, rather than the exception, on the American campus. None of these conclusions is true.

We know that television may have destroyed the old stereotypes—but has it not created new ones in their place?

What has this passionate pursuit of "controversy" done to the politics of progress through logical compromise, essential to the functioning of a democratic society?

The members of Congress or the Senate who follow their principles and philosophy quietly in a spirit of compromise are unknown to many Americans—while the loudest and most extreme dissenters on every issue are known to every man in the street.

How many marches and demonstrations would we have if the marchers did not know that the ever-faithful TV cameras would be there to record their antics for the next news show?

We have heard demands that Senators and Congressmen and Judges make known all their financial connections—so that the public will know who and what influences their decisions or votes. Strong arguments can be made for that view. But when a single commentator or producer, night after night, determines for millions of people how much of each side of a great issue they are going to see and hear; should he not first disclose his personal views on the issue as well?

In this search for excitement and controversy, has more than equal time gone to the minority of Americans who specialize in attacking the United States, its institutions, and its citizens?

Tonight, I have raised questions. I have made no attempt to suggest answers. These answers must come from the media men. They are challenged to turn their critical powers on themselves. They are challenged to direct their energy, talent and conviction toward improving the quality and objectivity of news presentation. They are challenged to structure their own civic ethics to relate their great selling with the great responsibility they hold.

And the people of America are challenged too . . . challenged to press for responsible news presentations. The people can let the networks know that they want their news straight and objective. The people can register their complaints on bias through mail to the networks and phone calls to local stations. This is one case where the people must defend themselves . . . where the citizen—not the government—must be the reformer . . . where the consumer can be the most effective crusader.

By way of conclusion, let me say that every elected leader in the United States depends on these men of the media. Whether what I have said to you tonight will be heard and seen at all by the nation is not *my* decision; it is not *your* decision; it is *their* decision.

In tomorrow's edition of the *Des Moines Register* you will be able to read a news story detailing what I said tonight; editorial comment will be reserved for the editorial page, where it belongs. Should not the same wall of separation exist between news and comment on the nation's networks?

Now, my friends, we would never trust such powers, I've described, over public opinion in the hands of an elected government—it is time we questioned it in the hands of a small and unelected elite. The great networks have dominated America's airwaves for decades; the people are entitled to a full accounting of their stewardship.

ALABAMA CHAMBER OF COMMERCE

November 20, 1969
Montgomery, Alabama

One week ago tonight I flew out to Des Moines, Iowa, and exercised my right to dissent. This is a great country. In this country every man is allowed freedom of speech—even the Vice President.

Of course, there has been some criticism of what I had to say out there in Des Moines.

Let me give you a sampling.

One Congressman charged me with, and I quote, "A creeping socialistic scheme against the free enterprise broadcast industry." Now this is the first time in my memory anybody ever accused Ted Agnew of having socialist ideas.

On Monday, largely because of this address, Mr. Humphrey charged the Nixon Administration with a "calculated attack" on the right of dissent and on the media today. Yet, it is widely known that Mr. Humphrey himself believes deeply that the unfair coverage of the Democratic Convention in Chicago, by the same media, contributed to his defeat in November. Now, his wounds are apparently healed, and he is casting his lot with those who were questioning his own political courage a year ago. But let us leave Mr. Humphrey to his own conscience. America already has too many politicans who would rather switch than fight.

There were others who charged that my purpose was to stifle dissent in this country. Nonsense. The expression of my views has produced enough rugged dissent in the last week to wear out a whole covey of commentators and columnists.

One critic charged that the speech was "disgraceful, ignorant and base," that it "leads us as a nation into an ugly era of the most fearsome suppression and intimidation." One national commentator, whose name is known to everyone in this room, said "I hesitate to get into the gutter with this guy." Another commentator charges that it was "one of the most sinister speeches that I have ever heard made by a public official." The president of one network said that it was an "unprecedented attempt to intimidate a news medium which depends for its existence upon government licenses." The president of another charged me with "an appeal to prejudice," and said that it was evident that I would prefer the kind of television "that would be subservient to whatever political group happened to be in authority at the time."

And they say *I* have thin skin.

Here indeed are classic examples of overreaction. These attacks do not address themselves to the questions I raised. In fairness, others—the majority of critics and commentators—did take up the main thrust of my address. And if the debate they have engaged in continues, our goal will surely be reached—our goal which is, of course, a thorough self-examination by the networks of their own policies—and perhaps prejudices. That was my objective then; and that's my objective now.

Now, let me repeat to you the thrust of my remarks the other night, and perhaps make some new points and raise some new issues.

I am opposed to censorship of television or the press in any form. I don't care whether censorship is imposed by government or whether it results from management in the choice and presentation of the news by a little fraternity having similar social and political views. I am against—I repeat, I am against censorship in all forms.

But a broader spectrum of national opinion *should* be represented among the commentators of the network news. Men who can articulate other points of view *should* be brought forward.

And a high wall of separation *should* be raised between what is news and what is commentary.

And the American people *should* be made aware of the trend toward the monopolization of the great public information vehicles and the concentration of more and more power in fewer and fewer hands.

Should a conglomerate be formed that tied together a shoe company with a shirt company, some voice will rise up righteously to say that this is a great danger to the economy; and that the conglomerate ought to be broken up.

But a single company in the nation's capital holds control of the largest newspaper in Washington, D.C., *and* one of the four major television stations, *and* an all-news radio station, *and* one of the three major national news magazines—all grinding out the same editorial line—and this is not a subject that you have seen debated on the editorial pages of the *Washington Post* or the *New York Times.*

For the purpose of clarity—before my thoughts are obliterated in the smoking typewriters of my friends in Washington and New York—let me emphasize I am not recommending the dismemberment of the Washington Post Company. I am merely pointing out that the public should be aware that these four powerful voices hearken to the same master.

I am raising these questions so that the American people will become aware of—and think of the implications of—the growing monopolization of the voices of public opinion on which we all depend—for our knowledge and for the basis of our views.

When the *Washington Times-Herald* died in the nation's capital, that was a political tragedy; and when the *New York Journal-American,* the *New York World-Telegram and Sun,* the *New York Mirror* and the *New York Herald-Tribune* all collapsed within this decade, that was a great, great political tragedy for the people of New York. The *New York Times* was a better newspaper when they were all alive than it is now that they are gone.

And what has happened in the city of New York has happened in other great cities in America.

Many, many strong independent voices have been stilled in this country in recent years. And lacking the vigor of competition, some of those who have survived have, let us face it, grown fat and irresponsible.

I offer an example. When 300 Congressmen and 59 Senators signed a letter endorsing the President's policy in Vietnam it was news—it was big news. Even the *Washington Post* and the *Baltimore Sun*—scarcely house organs of the Nixon Administration—placed it prominently on their front pages.

Yet the next morning the *New York Times,* which considers itself America's paper of record, did not carry a word. Why?

If a theology student in Iowa should get up at a PTA luncheon in Sioux City and attack the President's Vietnam policy, my guess is that you would probably find it reported somewhere in the next morning's issue of the *New York Times.* But when 300 Congressmen endorse the President's Vietnam policy, the next morning it is apparently not considered news fit to print.

Just this Tuesday, when the Pope, the spiritual leader of half a billion Roman Catholics, applauded the President's efforts to end the war in Vietnam, and endorsed the way he was proceeding—that news was on page 11 of the *New York Times*. But the same day, a report about some burglars who broke into a souvenir shop at St. Peters and stole $9,000 worth of stamps and currency—that story made page 3. How's that for news judgment?

A few weeks ago here in the South, I expressed my views about street and campus demonstrations. Here is how the *New York Times* responded:

> He [that's me] lambasted the nation's youth in sweeping and igno-
> rant generalizations, when it is clear to all perceptive observers that
> American youth today is far more imbued with idealism, a sense of service,
> and a deep humanitarianism than any generation in recent history, includ-
> ing particularly Mr. Agnew's [generation].

That seems a peculiar slur on a generation that brought America out of the Great Depression without resorting to the extremes of either fascism or communism. That seems a strange thing to say about an entire generation that helped to provide greater material blessings and more personal freedom—out of that Depression—for more people than any other nation in history. We have not finished the task by any means—but we are still on the job.

Just as millions of young Americans in this generation have shown valor and courage and heroism fighting the longest and least popular war in our history—so it was the young men of my generation who went ashore at Normandy under Eisenhower and with MacArthur into the Philippines.

Yes, my generation, like the current generation, made its own share of great mistakes and great blunders. Among other things, we put too much confidence in Stalin and not enough in Winston Churchill.

But whatever freedom exists today in Western Europe and Japan exists because hundreds of thousands of young men of my generation are lying in graves in North Africa and France and Korea and a score of islands in the Western Pacific.

This might not be considered enough of a "sense of service" or a "deep humanitarianism" for the *"perceptive critics"* who write editorials for the *New York Times,* but it's good enough for me; and I am content to let history be the judge.

Now, let me talk briefly about this younger generation. I have not and do not condemn this generation of young Americans. Like Edmund Burke, I would not know how to "draw up an indictment against a whole people." After all, they are our sons and daughters. They contain in their numbers many gifted, idealistic, and courageous young men and women.

But they also list in their numbers an arrogant few who march under the flags and portraits of dictators, who intimidate and harass university professors, who use gutter obscenities to shout down speakers with whom they disagree, who openly profess their belief in the efficacy of violence in a democratic society.

Oh yes, the preceding generation had its own breed of losers—and our generation dealt with them through our courts, our laws, and our system. The challenge now is for the new generation to put their own house in order.

Today, Dr. Sidney Hook writes of "Storm Troopers" on the campus; that "fanaticism seems to be in the saddle." Arnold Beichman writes of "young Jacobins" in our schools who "have cut down university administrators, forced curriculum changes, halted classes, closed campuses, and set a nationwide chill of fear all through the university establishment." Walter Laqueur writes in commentary that "the cultural and political idiocies perpetrated with impunity in this permissive age have gone clearly beyond the borders of what is acceptable for any society, however liberally it may be constructed."

George Kennan has devoted a brief, cogent, and alarming book to the inherent dangers of what is taking place in our society and in our universities. Irving Kristol writes that our "radical students . . . find it possible to be genuinely heartsick at the injustice and brutalities of American society, while blandly approving of injustice and brutality committed in the name of 'the revolution.' " Or as they like to call it—the movement.

Now those are not names drawn at random from the letterhead of an Agnew-for-Vice-President Committee.

Those are men more eloquent and erudite than I. And they raise questions that I have tried to raise.

For we must remember that among this generation of Americans there are hundreds who have burned their draft cards and scores who have deserted to Canada and Sweden to sit out the war. To some Americans—a small minority—these are the true young men of conscience in the coming generation. Voices are and will continue to be raised in the Congress and beyond asking that amnesty—a favorite word—should be provided for "these young and misguided American boys." And they will be coming home one day from Sweden and from Canada, and from a small minority of our citizens they will get a hero's welcome.

They are not our heroes. Many of our heroes will not be coming home; some are coming back in hospital ships; without limbs or eyes; with scars they shall carry the rest of their lives.

Having witnessed firsthand the quiet courage of wives and parents receiving posthumously for their heroes Congressional Medals of Honor, how am I to react when people say, "Stop speaking out, Mr. Agnew, stop raising your voice."

Should I remain silent while what these heroes have done is vilified by some as "a dirty and immoral war" and criticized by others as no more than a war brought on by the chauvinistic, anticommunism of Presidents Kennedy, Johnson, and Nixon?

No. These young men made heavy sacrifices so that a developing people on the rim of Asia might have a chance for freedom that they obviously will not have if the ruthless men who rule in Hanoi should ever rule over Saigon. What is dirty or immoral about that?

One magazine this week said that I will go down as the "great polarizer" in American politics. Yet, when that large group of young Americans marched up

Pennsylvania and Constitution Avenues last week—they sought to polarize the American people against the President's policy in Vietnam. And that was their right.

And so it is my right, and my duty, to stand up and speak out for the values in which I believe. How can you ask the man in the street in this country to stand up for what he believes if his own elected leaders weasel and cringe?

It is not an easy thing to wake up each morning to learn that some prominent man or some prominent institution has implied that you are a bigot, a racist, or a fool.

I am not asking any immunity from criticism. That is the lot of the man in politics; we would not have it any other way in this democratic society.

But my political and journalistic adversaries sometimes seem to be asking something more—that I circumscribe my rhetorical freedom, while they place no restrictions on theirs.

As President Kennedy once observed in a far more serious situation, this is like offering an apple for an orchard.

We do not accept those terms for continuing the national dialogue. The day when the network commentators and even the gentlemen of the *New York Times* enjoyed a form of diplomatic immunity from comment and criticism of what they said is over. Yes, gentlemen, that day is past.

Just as a politician's words—wise and foolish—are dutifully recorded by the press and television to be thrown up at him at the appropriate time, so their words should likewise be recorded and likewise recalled.

When they go beyond fair comment and criticism they will be called upon to defend their statements and their positions just as we must defend ours. And when their criticism becomes excessive or unjust, we shall invite them down from their ivory towers to enjoy the rough-and-tumble of public debate.

I do not seek to intimidate the press, the networks, or anyone else from speaking out. But the time for blind acceptance of their opinions is past. And the time for naïve belief in their neutrality is gone.

But, as to the future, each of us could do worse than take as our own the motto of William Lloyd Garrison who said: "I am in earnest. I will not equivocate. I will not excuse. I will not retreat a single inch. And I will be heard."

RICHARD M. NIXON, VIETNAM ADDRESS
November 3, 1969

Good evening, my fellow Americans: Tonight I want to talk to you on a subject of deep concern to all Americans and to many people in all parts of the world—the war in Viet-Nam.

I believe that one of the reasons for the deep division about Viet-Nam is that many Americans have lost confidence in what their Government has told them about our policy. The American people cannot and should not be asked to support a policy which involves the overriding issues of war and peace unless they know the truth about that policy.

Tonight, therefore, I would like to answer some of the questions that I know are on the minds of many of you listening to me.

How and why did America get involved in Viet-Nam in the first place?

How has this administration changed the policy of the previous administration?

What has really happened in the negotiations in Paris and on the battlefront in Viet-Nam?

What choices do we have if we are to end the war?

What are the prospects for peace?

Let me begin by describing the situation I found when I was inaugurated on January 20.

—The war had been going on for 4 years.

—31,000 Americans had been killed in action.

—The training program for the South Vietnamese was behind schedule.

—540,000 Americans were in Viet-Nam, with no plans to reduce the number.

—No progress had been made at the negotiations in Paris and the United States had not put forth a comprehensive peace proposal.

—The war was causing deep division at home and criticism from many of our friends, as well as our enemies, abroad.

In view of these circumstances there were some who urged that I end the war at once by ordering the immediate withdrawal of all American forces.

From a political standpoint this would have been a popular and easy course to follow. After all, we became involved in the war while my predecessor was in office. I could blame the defeat which would be the result of my action on him and come out as the peacemaker. Some put it to me quite bluntly: This was the only way to avoid allowing Johnson's war to become Nixon's war.

But I had a greater obligation than to think only of the years of my administration and the next election. I had to think of the effect of my decision

Department of State Bulletin, November 24, 1969, 437-46.

on the next generation and on the future of peace and freedom in America and in the world.

Let us all understand that the question before us is not whether some Americans are for peace and some Americans are against peace. The question at issue is not whether Johnson's war becomes Nixon's war.

The great question is: How can we win America's peace?

History of U.S. Involvement in Vietnam

Let us turn now to the fundamental issue. Why and how did the United States become involved in Viet-Nam in the first place?

Fifteen years ago North Viet-Nam, with the logistical support of Communist China and the Soviet Union, launched a campaign to impose a Communist government on South Viet-Nam by instigating and supporting a revolution.

In response to the request of the Government of South Viet-Nam, President Eisenhower sent economic aid and military equipment to assist the people of South Viet-Nam in their efforts to prevent a Communist takeover. Seven years ago President Kennedy sent 16,000 military personnel to Viet-Nam as combat advisers. Four years ago President Johnson sent American combat forces to South Viet-Nam.

Now, many believe that President Johnson's decision to send American combat forces to South Viet-Nam was wrong. And many others, I among them, have been strongly critical of the way the war has been conducted.

But the question facing us today is: Now that we are in the war, what is the best way to end it?

Consequences of Precipitate Withdrawal

In January I could only conclude that the precipitate withdrawal of American forces from Viet-Nam would be a disaster not only for South Viet-Nam but for the United States and for the cause of peace.

For the South Vietnamese, our precipitate withdrawal would inevitably allow the Communists to repeat the massacres which followed their takeover in the North 15 years before.

—They then murdered more than 50,000 people, and hundreds of thousands more died in slave labor camps.

—We saw a prelude of what would happen in South Viet-Nam when the Communists entered the city of Hue last year. During their brief rule there, there was a bloody reign of terror in which 3,000 civilians were clubbed, shot to death, and buried in mass graves.

—With the sudden collapse of our support, these atrocities of Hue would become the nightmare of the entire nation—and particularly for the million and a half Catholic refugees who fled to South Viet-Nam when the Communists took over in the North.

For the United States, this first defeat in our nation's history would result in a collapse of confidence in American leadership not only in Asia but throughout the world.

Three American Presidents have recognized the great stakes involved in Viet-Nam and understood what had to be done.

In 1963 President Kennedy, with his characteristic eloquence and clarity, said: "...we want to see a stable government there, carrying on a struggle to maintain its national independence. We believe strongly in that. We are not going to withdraw from that effort. In my opinion, for us to withdraw from that effort would mean a collapse not only of South Viet-Nam, but Southeast Asia. So we are going to stay there."

President Eisenhower and President Johnson expressed the same conclusion during their terms of office.

For the future of peace, precipitate withdrawal would thus be a disaster of immense magnitude.

—A nation cannot remain great if it betrays its allies and lets down its friends.

—Our defeat and humiliation in South Viet-Nam without question would promote recklessness in the councils of those great powers who have not yet abandoned their goals of world conquest.

—This would spark violence wherever our commitments help maintain the peace—in the Middle East, in Berlin, eventually even in the Western Hemisphere.

Ultimately, this would cost more lives. It would not bring peace; it would bring more war.

For these reasons I rejected the recommendation that I should end the war by immediately withdrawing all our forces. I chose instead to change American policy on both the negotiating front and the battlefront.

U.S. Peace Proposals

In order to end a war fought on many fronts, I initiated a pursuit for peace on many fronts.

In a television speech on May 14, in a speech before the United Nations, and on a number of other occasions, I set forth our peace proposals in great detail.

—We have offered the complete withdrawal of all outside forces within 1 year.

—We have proposed a cease-fire under international supervision.

—We have offered free elections under international supervision, with the Communists participating in the organization and conduct of the elections as an organized political force. The Saigon Government has pledged to accept the result of the elections.

We have not put forth our proposals on a take-it-or-leave-it basis. We have indicated that we are willing to discuss the proposals that have been put forth by the other side. We have declared that anything is negotiable, except the right of the people of South Viet-Nam to determine their own future. At the Paris peace conference, Ambassador Lodge has demonstrated our flexibility and good faith in 40 public meetings.

Hanoi has refused even to discuss our proposals. They demand our unconditional acceptance of their terms, which are that we withdraw all American forces immediately and unconditionally and that we overthrow the Government of South Viet-Nam as we leave.

Private Initiatives Undertaken

We have not limited our peace initiatives to public forums and public statements. I recognized in January that a long and bitter war like this usually cannot be settled in a public forum. That is why, in addition to the public statements and negotiations, I have explored every possible private avenue that might lead to a settlement. . . .

But the effect of all the public, private, and secret negotiations which have been undertaken since the bombing halt a year ago and since this administration came into office on January 20 can be summed up in one sentence: No progress whatever has been made except agreement on the shape of the bargaining table.

Now, who is at fault?

It has become clear that the obstacle in negotiating an end to the war is not the President of the United States. It is not the South Vietnamese Government.

The obstacle is the other side's absolute refusal to show the least willingness to join us in seeking a just peace. It will not do so while it is convinced that all it has to do is to wait for our next concession, and our next concession after that one, until it gets everything it wants.

There can now be no longer any question that progress in negotiation depends only on Hanoi's deciding to negotiate, to negotiate seriously.

I realize that this report on our efforts on the diplomatic front is discouraging to the American people, but the American people are entitled to know the truth—the bad news as well as the good news—where the lives of our young men are involved.

New Direction in U.S. Foreign Policy

Now let me turn, however, to a more encouraging report on another front.

At the time we launched our search for peace, I recognized we might not succeed in bringing an end to the war through negotiation.

I therefore put into effect another plan to bring peace—a plan which will bring the war to an end regardless of what happens on the negotiating front. It is in line with a major shift in U.S. foreign policy which I described in my press conference at Guam on July 25.

Let me briefly explain what has been described as the Nixon doctrine—a policy which not only will help end the war in Viet-Nam but which is an essential element of our program to prevent future Viet-Nams.

We Americans are a do-it-yourself people. We are an impatient people. Instead of teaching someone else to do a job, we like to do it ourselves. And this trait has been carried over into our foreign policy.

In Korea and again in Viet-Nam, the United States furnished most of the money, most of the arms, and most of the men to help the people of those countries defend their freedom against Communist aggression.

Before any American troops were committed to Viet-Nam, a leader of another Asian country expressed this opinion to me when I was traveling in Asia as a private citizen. He said: "When you are trying to assist another nation defend its freedom, U.S. policy should be to help them fight the war, but not to fight the war for them."

Well, in accordance with this wise counsel, I laid down in Guam three principles as guidelines for future American policy toward Asia:

—First, the United States will keep all of its treaty commitments.

—Second, we shall provide a shield if a nuclear power threatens the freedom of a nation allied with us or of a nation whose survival we consider vital to our security.

—Third, in cases involving other types of aggression, we shall furnish military and economic assistance when requested in accordance with our treaty commitments. But we shall look to the nation directly threatened to assume the primary responsibility of providing the manpower for its defense.

After I announced this policy, I found that the leaders of the Philippines, Thailand, Viet-Nam, South Korea, and other nations which might be threatened by Communist aggression welcomed this new direction in American foreign policy.

The Vietnamization Plan

The defense of freedom is everybody's business—not just America's business. And it is particularly the responsibility of the people whose freedom is threatened. In the previous administration we Americanized the war in Viet-Nam. In this administration we are Vietnamizing the search for peace.

The policy of the previous administration not only resulted in our assuming the primary responsibility for fighting the war but, even more significantly, did not adequately stress the goal of strengthening the South Vietnamese so that they could defend themselves when we left.

The Vietnamization plan was launched following Secretary [of Defense Melvin R.] Laird's visit to Viet-Nam in March. Under the plan, I ordered first a substantial increase in the training and equipment of South Vietnamese forces.

In July, on my visit to Viet-Nam, I changed General Abrams' orders so that they were consistent with the objectives of our new policies. Under the new orders, the primary mission of our troops is to enable the South Vietnamese forces to assume the full responsibility for the security of South Viet-Nam.

Our air operations have been reduced by over 20 percent.

And now we have begun to see the results of this long-overdue change in American policy in Viet-Nam:

—After 5 years of Americans going into Viet-Nam, we are finally bringing American men home. By December 15, over 60,000 men will have been withdrawn from South Viet-Nam, including 20 percent of all of our combat forces.

—The South Vietnamese have continued to gain in strength. As a result, they have been able to take over combat responsibilities from our American troops.

Two other significant developments have occurred since this administration took office:

—Enemy infiltration, infiltration which is essential if they are to launch a major attack, over the last 3 months is less than 20 percent of what it was over the same period last year.

—Most important, United States casualties have declined during the last 2 months to the lowest point in 3 years.

Our Program for the Future

Let me now turn to our program for the future.

We have adopted a plan which we have worked out in cooperation with the South Vietnamese for the complete withdrawal of all U.S. combat ground forces and their replacement by South Vietnamese forces on an orderly scheduled timetable. This withdrawal will be made from strength and not from weakness. As South Vietnamese forces become stronger, the rate of American withdrawal can become greater.

I have not and do not intend to announce the timetable for our program. There are obvious reasons for this decision, which I am sure you will understand. As I have indicated on several occasions, the rate of withdrawal will depend on developments on three fronts.

One of these is the progress which can be, or might be, made in the Paris talks. An announcement of a fixed timetable for our withdrawal would completely remove any incentive for the enemy to negotiate an agreement. They would simply wait until our forces had withdrawn and then move in.

The other two factors on which we will base our withdrawal decisions are the level of enemy activity and the progress of the training program of the South Vietnamese forces. I am glad to be able to report tonight progress on both of these fronts has been greater than we anticipated when we started the program in June for withdrawal. As a result, our timetable for withdrawal is more optimistic now than when we made our first estimates in June.

This clearly demonstrates why it is not wise to be frozen in on a fixed timetable. We must retain the flexibility to base each withdrawal decision on the situation as it is at that time rather than on estimates that are no longer valid.

Along with this optimistic estimate, I must in all candor leave one note of caution: If the level of enemy activity significantly increases, we might have to adjust our timetable accordingly.

However, I want the record to be completely clear on one point.

At the time of the bombing halt just a year ago, there was some confusion as to whether there was an understanding on the part of the enemy that if we stopped the bombing of North Viet-Nam, they would stop the shelling of cities in South Viet-Nam. I want to be sure that there is no misunderstanding on the part of the enemy with regard to our withdrawal program.

We have noted the reduced level of infiltration, the reduction of our casualties, and are basing our withdrawal decisions partially on those factors.

If the level of infiltration or our casualties increase while we are trying to scale down the fighting, it will be the result of a conscious decision by the enemy.

Hanoi could make no greater mistake than to assume that an increase in violence will be to its advantage. If I conclude that increased enemy action jeopardizes our remaining forces in Viet-Nam, I shall not hesitate to take strong and effective measures to deal with that situation.

This is not a threat. This is a statement of policy which as Commander in Chief of our Armed Forces, I am making in meeting my responsibility for the protection of American fighting men wherever they may be.

My fellow Americans, I am sure you can recognize from what I have said that we really only have two choices open to us if we want to end this war:
- —I can order an immediate, precipitate withdrawal of all Americans from Viet-Nam without regard to the effects of that action.
- —Or we can persist in our search for a just peace, through a negotiated settlement if possible or through continued implementation of our plan for Vietnamization if necessary—a plan in which we will withdraw all of our forces from Viet-Nam on a schedule in accordance with our program, as the South Vietnamese become strong enough to defend their own freedom.

I have chosen this second course. It is not the easy way. It is the right way. It is a plan which will end the war and serve the cause of peace, not just in Viet-Nam but in the Pacific and in the world.

In speaking of the consequences of a precipitate withdrawal, I mentioned that our allies would lose confidence in America.

Far more dangerous, we would lose confidence in ourselves. Oh, the immediate reaction would be a sense of relief that our men were coming home. But as we saw the consequences of what we had done, inevitable remorse and divisive recrimination would scar our spirit as a people.

We have faced other crises in our history and have become stronger by rejecting the easy way out and taking the right way in meeting our challenges. Our greatness as a nation has been our capacity to do what had to be done when we knew our course was right.

I recognize that some of my fellow citizens disagree with the plan for peace I have chosen. Honest and patriotic Americans have reached different conclusions as to how peace should be achieved.

In San Francisco a few weeks ago I saw demonstrators carrying signs reading: "Lose in Viet-Nam, bring the boys home."

Well, one of the strengths of our free society is that any American has a right to reach that conclusion and to advocate that point of view. But as President of the United States, I would be untrue to my oath of office if I allowed the policy of this nation to be dictated by the minority who hold that point of view and who try to impose it on the Nation by mounting demonstrations in the street.

For almost 200 years, the policy of this nation has been made under our Constitution by those leaders in the Congress and in the White House elected by all of the people. If a vocal minority, however fervent its cause, prevails over reason and the will of the majority, this nation has no future as a free society.

And now I would like to address a word, if I may, to the young people of this nation who are particularly concerned—and I understand why they are concerned— about this war.

I respect your idealism.

I share your concern for peace.

I want peace as much as you do.

There are powerful personal reasons I want to end this war. This week I will have to sign 83 letters to mothers, fathers, wives, and loved ones of men who have given their lives for America in Viet-Nam. It is very little satisfaction to me that this is only one-third as many letters as I signed the first week in office. There is nothing I want more than to see the day come when I do not have to write any of those letters.

—I want to end the war to save the lives of those brave young men in Viet-Nam.

—But I want to end it in a way which will increase the chance that their younger brothers and their sons will not have to fight in some future Viet-Nam someplace in the world.

—And I want to end the war for another reason.

I want to end it so that the energy and dedication of you, our young people, now too often directed into bitter hatred against those responsible for the war, can be turned to the great challenges of peace: a better life for all Americans, a better life for all people on this earth.

I have chosen a plan for peace. I believe it will succeed.

If it does succeed, what the critics say now won't matter. If it does not succeed, anything I say then won't matter.

I know it may not be fashionable to speak of patriotism or national destiny these days. But I feel it is appropriate to do so on this occasion.

Two hundred years ago this nation was weak and poor. But even then, America was the hope of millions in the world. Today we have become the strongest and richest nation in the world. The wheel of destiny has turned so that any hope the world has for the survival of peace and freedom will be determined by whether the American people have the moral stamina and the courage to meet the challenge of free-world leadership.

Let historians not record that when America was the most powerful nation in the world we passed on the other side of the road and allowed the last hopes for peace and freedom of millions of people to be suffocated by the forces of totalitarianism.

And so tonight—to you, the great silent majority of my fellow Americans—I ask for your support.

I pledged in my campaign for the Presidency to end the war in a way that we could win the peace. I have initiated a plan of action which will enable me to keep that pledge.

The more support I can have from the American people, the sooner that pledge can be redeemed; for the more divided we are at home, the less likely the enemy is to negotiate at Paris.

Let us be united for peace. Let us also be united against defeat. Because let us understand: North Viet-Nam cannot defeat or humiliate the United States. Only Americans can do that.

Fifty years ago, in this room and at this very desk, President Woodrow Wilson spoke words which caught the imagination of a war-weary world. He said: "This is the war to end wars."

His dream for peace after World War I was shattered on the hard realities of great-power politics, and Woodrow Wilson died a broken man.

Tonight I do not tell you that the war in Viet-Nam is the war to end wars. But I do say this: I have initiated a plan which will end this war in a way that will bring us closer to that great goal to which Woodrow Wilson and every American President in our history has been dedicated—the goal of a just and lasting peace.

As President I hold the responsibility for choosing the best path to that goal and then leading the Nation along it.

I pledge to you tonight that I shall meet this responsibility with all of the strength and wisdom I can command in accordance with your hopes, mindful of your concerns, sustained by your prayers.

RICHARD M. NIXON, ACCEPTANCE SPEECH
Miami Beach, August 23, 1972

Mr. Chairman, delegates to this convention, my fellow Americans:

Four years ago, standing in this very place, I proudly accepted your nomination for President of the United States.

And with your help, and with the votes of millions of Americans, we won a great victory in 1968.

Tonight, I again proudly accept your nomination for President of the United States.

And let us pledge ourselves to win an even greater victory this November in 1972.

I congratulate Chairman Ford, I congratulate Chairmen Dole and Armstrong, the hundreds of others who have laid the foundation for that victory by their work at this great convention.

Our platform is a dynamic program for progress for America and for peace in the world.

And speaking in a very personal sense, I express my deep gratitude to this convention for the tribute that you have paid to the best campaigner in the Nixon family, my wife, Pat. In honoring her, you have honored millions of women in America who contributed in the past and will contribute in the future so very much to better government in this country.

And again, as I did last night when I was not at the convention, I express the appreciation of all of the delegates and of all America for letting us see young America at its best at our convention.

As I express my appreciation to you, I want to say that you have inspired us with your enthusiasm, with your intelligence, with your dedication at this convention. You have made us realize that this is a year when we can prove the experts' predictions wrong because we can set as our goal winning a majority of the new voters for our ticket this November.

And I pledge to you, I pledge to you, all of the new voters in America who are listening on television and listening here in this convention hall, that I will do everything that I can over these next four years to make your support be one that you can be proud of, because as I said to you last night—and I feel it very deeply in my heart—years from now I want you to look back and be able to say that your first vote was one of the best votes you ever cast in your life.

New York Times, August 24, 1972.

Mr. Chairman, I congratulate the delegates to this convention for renominating as my running mate the man who has so eloquently and graciously introduced me, Vice President Ted Agnew.

I thought he was the best man for the job four years ago. I think he is the best man for the job today, and I'm not going to change my mind tomorrow.

And finally, as the Vice President has indicated, you have demonstrated to the nation that we can have an open convention without dividing Americans into quotas. Let us commit ourselves to root out every vestige of discrimination in this country of ours.

But, my fellow Americans, the way to end discrimination against some is not to begin discrimination against others.

Dividing Americans into quotas is totally alien to the American tradition. Americans don't want to be part of a quota—they want to be part of America.

And this nation proudly calls itself the United States of America. Let's reject any philosophy that would make us the divided people of America.

In that spirit I address you tonight, my fellow Americans, not as a partisan of party which would divide us but as a partisan of principles which can unite us. Six weeks ago our opponents at their convention rejected many of the great principles of the Democratic party. To those millions who have been driven out of their home in the Democratic party, we say, come home. We say come home not to another party, but we say come home to the great principles we Americans believe in together.

And I ask you, my fellow Americans, tonight to join us, not in a coalition held together only by a desire to gain power. I ask you to join us as members of a new American majority bound together by our common ideals.

I ask everyone listening to me tonight—Democrats, Republicans, independents—to join our new majority, not on the basis of the party label you wear in your lapel, but on the basis of what you believe in your hearts.

And in asking for your support, I shall not dwell on the record of our Administration, which has been praised, perhaps too generously, by others at this convention.

We have made great progress in these past four years.

It can be truly said that we have changed America and that America has changed the world. As a result of what we have done, America today is a better place and the world is a safer place to live in than was the case four years ago.

We can be proud of that record but we shall never be satisfied. A record is not something to stand on, it's something to build on.

And tonight I do not ask you to join our new majority because of what we have done in the past. I ask your support of the principles I believe should determine America's future.

The choice, the choice in this election is not between radical change and no change, the choice in this election is between change that works and change that won't work."

I begin with an article of faith. It has become fashionable in recent years to point up what is wrong with what is called the American system. The critics contend it is so unfair, so corrupt, so unjust that we should tear it down and substitute something else in its place.

I totally disagree. I believe in the American system.

I have traveled to 80 countries in the past 25 years, and I have seen Communist systems, I've seen Socialist systems, I have seen systems that are half-Socialist and half-free.

Every time I come home to America I realize how fortunate we are to live in this great and good country.

Every time I am reminded that we have more freedom, more opportunity, more prosperity than any people in the world, that we have the highest rate of growth of any industrial nation, that Americans have more jobs at higher wages than in any country in the world, that our rate of inflation is less than that of any industrial nation, that the incomparable productivity of America's farmers has made it possible for us to launch a winning war against hunger in the United States, and that the productivity of our farmers also makes us the best-fed people in the world with the lowest percentage of the family budget going to food of any country in the world.

We can be very grateful in this country that the people on welfare in America would be rich in most of the nations of the world today.

Now my fellow Americans, in pointing up those things we do not overlook the fact that our system has its problems. Our Administration, as you know, has provided the biggest tax cut in history, but taxes are still too high. That is why one of the goals of our next Administration is to reduce the property tax, which is such an unfair and heavy burden on the poor, the elderly, the wage earner, the farmer and those on fixed incomes.

As all of you know, we have cut inflation in half in this Administration, but we've got to cut it further. We must cut it further so that we can continue to expand on the greatest accomplishment of our new economic policies—for the first time in five years wage increases in America are not being eaten up by price increases.

And as a result of the millions of new jobs created by our new economic policies, unemployment today in America is less than the peacetime average of the sixties, but we must continue the unparalleled increase in new jobs so that we can achieve the great goal of our new prosperity—a job for every American who wants to work, without war and without inflation.

The way to reach this goal is to stay on the new road we have charted to move America forward and not to take a sharp detour to the left which would lead to a dead end for the hopes of the American people.

And this points up one of the clearest choices in this campaign. Our opponents believe in a different philosophy. Theirs is the politics of paternalism, where master planners in Washington make decisions for people.

Ours is the politics of people—where people make decisions for themselves.

The proposal that they have made to pay $1,000 to every person in America insults the intelligence of the American voters. Because you know that every politician's promise has a price—the taxpayer pays the bill.

The American people are not going to be taken in by any scheme where Government gives money with one hand and then takes it away with the other.

And their platform promises everything to everybody but at a net increase in the budget of $144-billion, but listen to what it means to you, the taxpayers of the country.

That would mean an increase of 50 per cent in what the taxpayers of America pay. I oppose any new spending programs, which will increase the tax burden on the already overburdened American taxpayers.

And they have proposed legislation which would add 93 million people to the welfare rolls. I say that instead of providing incentives for millions of more Americans to go on welfare, we need a program which will provide incentives for people to get off welfare and to get to work.

We believe that it is wrong for anyone to receive more on welfare than for someone who works. Let us be generous to those who can't work, without increasing the tax burden of those who do not work.

And while we're talking about welfare, let us quit treating our senior citizens in this country like welfare recipients. They have worked hard all their lives to build America, and as the builders of America they haven't asked for a handout. What they ask for is what they have earned, and that is retirement in dignity and self-respect. Let's give that to our senior citizens.

And now when you add up the cost of all of the programs our opponents have proposed, you reach only one conclusion: they would destroy the system which has made America No. 1 in the world economically.

Listen to these facts: Americans today pay one-third of all of their income in taxes. If their programs were adopted, Americans would pay over one-half of what they earn in taxes. This means that if their programs are adopted, American wage-earners would be working more for the Government than they would for themselves, and once we cross this line, we cannot turn back, because the incentive which makes the American economic system the most productive in the world would be destroyed.

Their is not a new approach. It has been tried before in countries abroad and I can tell you that those who have tried it have lived to regret it.

We cannot and will not let them do this to America.

Let us always be true to the principle that has made America the world's most prosperous nation—that here in America a person should get what he works for and work for what he gets.

Let me illustrate the difference in our philosophies. Because of our free economic system, what we have done is to build a great building of economic wealth and might in America. It is by far the tallest building in the world, and we are still adding to it. Now, because the windows are broken, they say tear it down and start again. We say, replace the windows and keep building. That's the difference.

Let me turn now to a second area where my beliefs are totally different from those of our opponents. Four years ago crime was rising all over America at an unprecedented rate. Even our nation's capital was called the crime capital of the world. I pledged to stop the rise in crime.

In order to keep that pledge I promised in the election campaign that I would appoint judges to the Federal courts and particularly to the Supreme Court who would recognize that the first civil right of every American is to be free from domestic violence.

I have kept that promise. I am proud of the appointments I have made to the courts and particularly proud of those I have made to the Supreme Court of the United States.

And I pledge again tonight as I did four years ago that, whenever I have the opportunity to make more appointments to the courts, I shall continue to appoint judges who share my philosophy that we must strengthen the peace forces in the United States.

We have launched an all-out offensive against crime, against narcotics, against permissiveness in our country.

And I want the peace officers across America to know that they have the total backing of their President in their fight against crime.

My fellow Americans, as we move toward peace abroad, I ask you to support our programs which will keep the peace at home.

And now, I turn to an issue of overriding importance, not only to this election but for generations to come—the progress we have made in building a new structure of peace in the world.

Peace is too important for partisanship.

There have been five Presidents in my politicial lifetime—Franklin D. Roosevelt, Harry Truman, Dwight Eisenhower, John F. Kennedy and Lyndon Johnson.

They had differences on some issues, but they were united in their beliefs that where the security of America or the peace of the world is involved, we are not Republicans, we are not Democrats, we are Americans first, last and always.

These five Presidents were united in their total opposition to isolation for America and in their belief that the interest of the United States and the interest of world peace required that America be strong enough and intelligent enough to assume the responsibilities of leadership in the world.

They were united in the conviction that the United States should have a defense second to none in the world. They were all men who hated war and were dedicated to peace.

But not one of these five men and no President in our history believed that America should ask an enemy for peace on terms that would betray our allies and destroy respect for the United States all over the world.

And as your President, I pledge that I shall always uphold that proud bipartisan tradition.

Standing in this convention hall four years ago, I pledged to seek an honorable end to the war in Vietnam. We have made great progress toward that end.

We have brought over half a million men home and more will be coming home. We have ended America's ground combat role. No draftees are being sent to Vietnam. We have reduced our casualties by 98 per cent.

We've gone the extra mile—in fact, we've gone tens of thousands of miles trying to seek a negotiated settlement of the war. We have offered a cease-fire, a total withdrawal of all American forces, an exchange of all prisoners of war, internationally supervised free elections with the Communists participating in the elections and in the supervisions.

There are three things, however, that we have not and that we will not offer:

We will never abandon our prisoners of war.

And, second, we will not join our enemies in imposing a Communist government on our allies—the 17 million people of South Vietnam.

And we will never stain the honor of the United States of America.

Now, I realize that many—particularly in this political year—wonder why we insist on an honorable peace in Vietnam. From a political standpoint they suggest that, since I was not in office when over a half a million American men were sent there, that I should end the war by agreeing to impose a Communist government on the people of South Vietnam and just blame the whole catastrophe on my predecessors.

This might be good politics. But it would be disastrous to the cause of peace in the world. If at this time we betray our allies, it will discourage our friends abroad and it will encourage our enemies to engage in aggression.

In areas like the Mideast, which are danger areas, small nations who rely on the friendship and support of the United States would be in jeopardy.

To our friends and allies in Europe, Asia, the Mideast and Latin America, I say the United States will continue its great bipartisan tradition—to stand by our friends and never to desert them.

Now in discussing Vietnam, I have noticed that in this election year there's been a great deal of talk about providing amnesty for those few hundred Americans who chose to desert their country rather than to serve it in Vietnam.

I think it's time that we put the emphasis where it belongs. The real heroes are two and a half million young Americans who chose to serve their country rather than desert it.

And I say to you tonight in these times when there is so much of a tendency to run down those who have served America in the past and who serve it today, let's give those who serve in our armed forces and those who have served in Vietnam the honor and the respect that they deserve and that they've earned.

Finally, in this connection, let one thing be clearly understood in this election campaign. The American people will not tolerate any attempt by our enemies to interfere in the cherished right of the American voter to make his own decision with regard to what is best for America without outside intervention.

Now, it is understandable that Vietnam has been a major concern in foreign policy, but we have not allowed the war in Vietnam to paralyze our capacity to initiate historic new policies to construct a lasting and just peace in the world.

And when the history of this period is written, I believe it will be recorded that our most significant contributions to peace resulted from our trips to Peking and to Moscow. The dialogue that we have begun with the People's Republic of China has reduced the danger of war and has increased the chance for peaceful cooperation between two great peoples.

And, within the space of four years in our relations with the Soviet Union, we have moved from confrontation to negotiation and then to cooperation in the interest of peace.

We have taken the first step in limiting the nuclear arms race.

We have laid the foundation for further limitations on nuclear weapons, and, eventually, of reducing the armaments in the nuclear area.

We can thereby not only reduce the enormous cost of arms for both our countries, but we can increase the chances for peace.

More than on any other single issue, I ask you, my fellow Americans, to give us the chance to continue these great initiatives that can contribute so much to the future of peace in the world.

And it can truly be said that as a result of our initiatives the danger of war is less today than it was, the chances for peace are greater.

But a note of warning needs to be sounded. We cannot be complacent. Our opponents have proposed massive cuts in our defense budget which would have the inevitable effect of making the United States the second strongest nation in the world. For the United States unilaterally to reduce its strength with the naive hope that other nations would do likewise would increase the danger of war in the world. It would completely remove any incentive of other nations to agree to a mutual limitation to reduction of arms, the promising initiatives we have undertaken to limit arms would be destroyed, the security of the United States and all the nations in the world who depend upon our friendship and support would be threatened.

Let's look at the record on defense expenditures. We have cut spending in our Administration. It now takes the lowest percentage of our national product in 20 years. We should not spend more on defense than we need, but we must never spend less than we need.

What we must understand is spending what we need on defense will cost us money. Spending less than we need could cost us our lives or our freedom.

And so tonight, my fellow Americans, I say, let us take risks for peace, but let us never risk the security of the United States of America.

And it is for that reason that I pledge that we will continue to seek peace and the mutual reduction of arms. The United States during this period, however, will always have a defense second to none.

There are those who believe that we can entrust the security of America to the goodwill of our adversaries. And those who hold this view do not know the real world. We can negotiate limitation of arms, and we have done so. We can make agreements to reduce the danger of war, and we have done so. But one unchangeable rule of international diplomacy that I've learned over many, many years is that, in negotiations between great powers, you can only get something if you have something to give in return.

And that is why I say tonight, let us always be sure that when the President of the United States goes to the conference table he never has to negotiate from weakness.

There is no such thing as a retreat to peace.

My fellow Americans, we stand today on the threshold of one of the most exciting and challenging eras in the history of relations between nations. We have the opportunity in our time to be the peacemakers of the world.

Because the world trusts and respects us, and because the world knows that we shall only use our power to defend freedom, never to destroy it; to keep the peace, never to break it.

A strong America is not the enemy of peace, it is the guardian of peace.

The initiatives that we have begun can result in reducing the danger of arms as well as the danger of war which hangs over the world today.

Even more important, it means that the enormous creative energies of the Russian people and the Chinese people and the American people and all the great peoples of the world can be turned away from production of war and turned toward production for peace.

And in America it means that we can undertake programs for progress at home that will be just as exciting as the great initiative we have undertaken in building a new structure of peace abroad.

My fellow Americans, the peace dividend that we hear so much about has too often been described solely in monetary terms—how much money we could take out of the arms budget and apply to our domestic needs. By far the biggest dividend, however, is that achieving our goal of a lasting peace in the world would reflect the deepest hopes and ideals of all of the American people.

Speaking on behalf of the American people, I was proud to be able to say in my television address to the Russian people in May, we covet no one else's territory, we seek no dominion over any other nation, we seek peace, not only for ourselves, but for all the people of the world.

This dedication to idealism runs through America's history. During the tragic war between the states, Abraham Lincoln was asked whether God was on his side. He replied, "My concern is not whether God is on our side but whether we are on God's side."

May that always be our prayer for America.

We hold the future of peace in the world and our own future in our hands.

Let us reject, therefore, the policies of those who whine and whimper about our frustrations and call on us to turn inward. Let us not turn away from greatness.

The chance America now has to lead the way to a lasting peace in the world may never come again.

With faith in God and faith in ourselves and faith in our country, let us have the vision and the courage to seize the moment and meet the challenge before it slips away.

On your television screens last night, you saw the cemetery in Leningrad I visited on my trip to the Soviet Union where 300,000 people died in the siege of that city during World War II. At the cemetery, I saw the picture of a 12-year-old girl. She was a beautiful child. Her name was Tanya. I read her diary. It tells the terrible story of war. In the simple words of a child, she wrote of the deaths of the members of her family—Zhenya in December, Grannie in January, then Leka, then Uncle Vasta, then Uncle Lyosha, then Mama in May.

And finally these were the last words in her diary: "All are dead, only Tanya is left."

Let us think of Tanya and of the other Tanyas and their brothers and sisters everywhere in Russia and in China and in America as we proudly meet our responsibilities for leadership in the world in a way worthy of a great people.

I ask you, my fellow Americans, to join our new majority not just in the cause of winning an election but in achieving a hope that mankind has had since the beginning of civilization.

Let us build a peace that our children and all the children of the world can enjoy for generations to come.

Bibliographical Note

In addition to standard reference works such as *The Congressional Quarterly*, various compilations of documents and voting statistics, and an abundant periodical literature, the following are among the most useful books concerning the Republican party from 1952 to 1972: Sherman Adams, *Firsthand Report* (New York, 1961); Stewart Alsop, *The Reporter's Trade: Rockefeller and Nixon* (Garden City, N.Y., 1960); David S. Broder, *The Party's Over: The Failure of Politics in America* (New York, 1972); Angus Campbell, Philip E. Converse, Warren E. Miller, Donald E. Stokes, *The American Voter* (Abridged version, New York, 1964); and *Elections and the Political Order* (New York, 1966); Lewis Chester, Godfrey Hodgson, and Bruce Page, *An American Melodrama* (New York, 1969); John R. Coyne, Jr., *The Impudent Snobs: Agnew vs. the Intellectual Establishment* (New Rochelle, N.Y., 1972); Walter DeVries and V. Lance Tarrance, *The Ticket Splitter: A New Force in American Politics* (Grand Rapids, Mich., 1972); Robert Donovan, *Eisenhower: The Inside Story* (New York, 1956); and *The Future of the Republican Party* (New York, 1964); Dwight D. Eisenhower, *The White House Years, Mandate for Change: 1953-1956* (Garden City, N.Y., 1963); and *The White House Years, Waging Peace: 1956-1961* (Garden City, N.Y., 1965); Roland Evans, Jr. and Robert D. Novak, *Nixon in the White House* (New York, 1971); George F. Gilder and Bruce K. Chapman, *The Party That Lost Its Head* (New York, 1966); Barry Goldwater, *Conscience of a Conservative* (Shepherdsville, Ky., 1960); and *Why Not Victory?* (New York, 1963); Louis Harris, *Is There a Republican Majority?* (New York, 1954); Karl Hess, *In a Cause That Will Someday Triumph* (Garden City, N.Y., 1967); Stephen Hess and David S. Broder, *The Republican Establishment* (New York, 1967); Emmet John Hughes, *The Ordeal of Power: A Political Memoir of the Eisenhower Years* (New York, 1963); Charles O. Jones, *Party and Policy-Making: The House Republican Policy Committee* (New

Brunswick, N.J., 1964); Arthur Larson, *A Republican Looks at His Party* (New York, 1956); and *Eisenhower: The President Nobody Knew* (New York, 1968); Samuel Lubell, *The Future of American Politics*, 3d ed. (New York, 1968); *The Revolt of the Moderates* (New York, 1956); and *The Hidden Crisis in American Politics* (New York, 1970); Leonard Lurie, *The King Makers* (New York, 1971); Joseph Martin, *My First Fifty Years in Politics* (New York, 1960); Earl Mayo and Stephen Hess, *Nixon, A Political Portrait* (New York, 1968); Joe McGinniss, *The Selling of the President* (New York, 1961); Raymond Moley, *The Republican Opportunity* (New York, 1962); Richard E. Neustadt, *Presidential Power* (New York, 1960); Richard Nixon, *Six Crises* (New York, 1962); Robert D. Novak, *The Agony of the GOP, 1964* (New York, 1965); Kevin Phillips, *The Emerging Republican Majority* (New Rochelle, 1969); The Ripon Society, *From Disaster to Distinction* (New York, 1965); and *The Lessons of Victory* (New York, 1969); Richard M. Scammon and Ben J. Wattenberg, *The Real Majority* (New York, 1970; 2d ed., 1971); Phyllis Schlafly, *A Choice Not An Echo* (Alton, Ill., 1964); Steven Shadegg, *What Happened to Goldwater?* (New York, 1965); Nick Thimmesch, *The Condition of Republicanism* (New York, 1968); F. Clifton White, *Suite 3505: The Story of the Draft Goldwater Movement* (New Rochelle, 1967); Theodore H. White, *The Making of the President, 1960* (New York, 1961); *The Making of the President, 1964* (New York, 1965); and *The Making of the President, 1968* (New York, 1969); Gary Wills, *Nixon Agonistes* (Boston, 1970); Jules Witcover, *White Knight: The Rise of Spiro Agnew* (New York, 1972); and *The Resurrection of Richard Nixon* (New York, 1970).

Other important books published recently include: Richard J. Whalen, *Catch the Falling Flag* (Boston, 1972); Herbert S. Parmet, *Eisenhower and the American Crusades* (New York, 1972); John Osborne, *The Nixon Watch* (New York, 1970); *The Second Year of the Nixon Watch* (New York, 1971); and *The Third Year of the Nixon Watch* (New York, 1972); James Keogh, *President Nixon and the Press* (New York, 1972); John S. Saloma and Frederick H. Sontag, *Parties* (New York, 1972).

The American Communist Party

JOSEPH R. STAROBIN is Associate Professor of Political Science, Glendon College, York University, Toronto. He is author of *American Communism in Crisis: 1943-1957; Paris to Peking* and *Eyewitness in Indo-China.*

The American Communist Party

by *Joseph R. Starobin*

The American Communist party has long been one of the most widely-publicized of the minor parties in national life, the focus of attack, the subject of derision not unmixed with a certain awe, and increasingly the object of detached examination by historians. The charge of "Communism" against one's political opponents is less of a staple in political combat than it was a quarter of a century ago. Fear of "infiltration" in a bewildering variety of organizations has receded. Nevertheless, the evocation of such ghosts and skeletons gives the impression that American Communism was a far more influential force than any detailed examination of its history and the net result of its activity would support. It was always a minor movement, even in the heyday of its impact but minor in a way that differentiated it from other minor parties. The C.P.U.S.A., as Daniel Bell has suggested, was a "dye suffusing the American scene," and penetrating the body politic with greater power than its numbers warranted. It "provided an unmatched political sophistication to a generation that went through its ranks and gave an easy-going, tolerant, sprawling America a lesson in organizational manipulation, and hard-bitten ideological devotion which this country, because of its tradition and temperament, found hard to understand . . ."[1]

What distinguished the American Communists from their minor counterparts was the attempt to grapple with major questions. In the aftermath of the First World War and certainly after the economic crisis of 1929-1931, the values of a society devoted so exclusively to individual mobilization, and the injustices associated with such a society came under sharp scrutiny; whether the democratic process could survive under America's commitment to the massing of goods and wealth, unfairly distributed, both when this commitment worked wonders and when it ignominiously broke down, came into question.[2] The Communists not only joined in the scrutiny and questioning but proposed an answer, supporting it with a capacity for organizing men and women in everyday battles that was perhaps peculiarly American in its stubbornness and scope. In addition, the Communist answer was backed by the promise and the alleged performance of the "Soviet experiment." The claim to have a franchise on Marxism—an "ism" which still had great analytic power and predicted nothing less than the regeneration of mankind—combined with American Communism's frank adherence to an international movement which seemed to be the "wave of the future," enhanced its position at home as much as it drew attack. Americans of many derivations, with a characteristic universalism and often an inferiority complex toward the outside world, were receptive to the claim that a century of wars, the catastrophe of repeated economic crisis, and flagrant injustice to labor and minorities could be ended by a transition to a Promised Land. The aura of certainty which the Communists gave to this hope made them different from other sects. For a generation, they ceased being a sect at all. Moreover, the Communists advanced specific programs to overcome generic evils and not only related these to an organic process of historical evolution, but gave their faith a sharp cutting-edge of "works," of organizational expertise.

In at least three realms, the Communists could claim a distinct contribution. The first related to the helplessness of the American worker, largely unorganized in the mass production industries which were the new feature of the corporate economy. Throughout the dismal 1920's, and even though constantly zigzagging because of the changing emphases of the Communist International, American Communists grappled with the practical problem of organizing the unorganized on industrial rather than craft lines. The party's foremost recruit of the early 1920's, William Z. Foster, was unique among the hacks and the quasi-intellectuals who occupied the uneasy seats of C.P. eminence because he had been identified with the enormous effort, in 1919, to build industrial unions among the packinghouse and steel workers of the Chicago area. The great strikes which Foster and close associates led were supported by the Chicago Federation of Labor; its leader, John Fitzpatrick, was among the many who realized that a purely craft basis could not serve the changing needs of labor.

Having failed, Foster and his colleagues, among them Earl Browder, his junior by ten years, projected the idea of "amalgamation," which achieved considerable resonance through the Trade Union Educational League. The Communists were at that time connected with thousands of authentic radicals of different ideological persuasions, from Socialist to "Wobbly," who placed modern unionism in the forefront of their objectives. In bitter battles with John L. Lewis in the coal fields of southern

Illinois, and in wide-ranging, sometimes bizarre, sometimes tragic actions among the textile workers of Passaic, N.J. and Gastonia, N.C., the Communists wrestled with the problem.[3]

By 1929, they had changed the T.U.E.L. to the Trade Union Unity League, (the T.U.U.L.), a frankly "dual union" effort which corresponded to the Comintern's new emphasis after its Sixth Congress in 1928 and Stalin's victory in Moscow. The American Communists concentrated their efforts in the T.U.U.L., and also educated a corps of tough, practical, experienced unionists. Once ten leading unions of American labor broke out of their A.F.L. framework in 1935 to champion industrial unionism, and were favored in doing so by the New Deal's Wagner Act, these men and women rapidly came into the leadership of the organizational upsurge. The Communists were, among a variety of other radicals, brought into the top ranks of powerful new unions. Many were employed by their old enemy and new mentor, John L. Lewis. In Nathan Glazer's phrase,[4] they were carried to leadership "like corks on a flood." By the mid-1930's, they were leading at least a third of the C.I.O. unions,[5] a leverage never before, and never since, achieved by any wing of American radicalism.

A second preoccupation was the "Negro question." The American Communists gave this issue much practical and strategic attention, even after they had themselves lost influence and several times contradicted their original analysis. The United States was unique in having within its white majority a population ten percent black, racially distinct, originally slave and even after the formal freedom brought by the bitter Civil War, unable to be integrated into American life because the economic basis for such freedom was reversed after Reconstruction. Neither slave, nor serf, not a freeholder on the land, nor yet an industrial worker, what was the Negro? Where did his struggles fit into the larger battle in which the Socialists and then the Communists were engaged?

As Theodore Draper's research has shown,[6] the Communists tried during the 1920's—in emergent cultural nationalism and in Marcus Garvey's "back-to-Africa" movement—to make contact with a force which required definition and without whose freedom no progress could be made either in the South or in changing the resistance by the Bourbon South to the forward movement of the North and the West. Here, too, the Communist record shows changes of tactics, and frustration. Originally, the C.P. shared the attitude of the Socialists and syndicalists that the "race question" would be resolved by the emancipation of the working class as a whole and hence required no separate preoccupation. By the end of the 1920's, however, as an offshoot of Comintern discussions about South Africa, the American Communists opted for what was really a version of "black power." They called it "self-determination for the Black Belt." They envisaged a Negro republic in the South, carved out across state lines, which blacks would govern, and in which they would develop their own economy, speed their liberation from quasi-feudal circumstances and decide themselves how to order their relations with the country as a whole and the whites within that autonomous "black republic."

The concept leaned heavily on Stalin's theoretical solution for the Tsarist and eastern European conditions. As a practical matter, it got nowhere. But it did pose the central question of whether Negro liberation could be accomplished within the system, or would, as it unfolded, help burst the confines of the system. This theoretical emphasis helped to energize Communist championship of practical matters—the anti-lynching and anti-poll tax campaigns, the defense of the Scottsboro boys,[8] and a new national sensitivity to the harsh realities. At the same time, it helped the Communists build an integrated organization in their own party and movements influenced by them. During the Second World War, ten percent of their membership was black and a similar proportion were among the thousands of new recruits who came and went.[9] By the late 1940's, the party's integration broke down in the cross-current of new movements among blacks and bitter failures of the Communists themselves. Yet they could claim to have projected the issue, despite all their own inadequacies.[10]

A third change in America, of which the Communists were a part and which they helped to stimulate even as they failed to consolidate their gains, was in the realm of culture, taken in its largest sense. The 1920's witnessed a widespread revolt against Puritan mores, against the confines of Sinclair Lewis' *Main Street*; intellectuals were exhilarated by H. L. Mencken's contempt for the "booboisie." It was a time of sexual experimentation, a migration to the urban environment, a quest for contact with the older or wider world of the Orient, of Latin America and of Europe out of which the "rediscovery of America" which Waldo Frank sought could be found. The earlier edition of the "greening of America" had in fact begun just before the First World War, when Woodrow Wilson's New Freedom vied with Teddy Roosevelt's "Bull Moose" movement and the popularity of Eugene Victor Debs; the *Masses*[11] had embodied in its cartoons and its poetry and journalism that irreverence for capitalism which was to be heightened by the disillusion over the war's outcome. Not the least of the new tendencies of the time was accentuated feminism, following the victory of the suffragettes, but seeking something much beyond the vote.

Radicalism in politics went hand in hand with radicalism in culture. What in the 1920's had been a certain iconoclasm and bohemianism became in the 1930's a distinctive trend. In the 1932 presidential campaign, fifty-two intellectuals demonstratively supported the Communist candidates, Foster and Ford, among them some of the most prestigious and promising figures in the arts, letters and sciences.[12] Later, in what Eugene Lyons lamented as the "red decade," disillusion with the party took hold under the impact of the Moscow Trials and the Soviet-German Non-Aggression Pact. Yet if important writers (distinguished artists hung on) left the "locomotive of history" as it took a sharp turn, new segments of white-collar workers and professionals—part of the shift within the economy as such—showed an extraordinary penchant for left-wing causes. Communism became fashionable on Broadway, which was for many but a stepping-stone to Hollywood. Among editors, magazine and newspaper craftsmen, librarians, technicians, doctors, dentists, and teachers, the Communists found an unusual array of supporters,[13] not to mention the college students among whom a series of anti-war strikes had radicalized part of a generation; many had gone from the colleges into the alphabetical jungle of New Deal agencies and into the labor movement.[14] But more fundamental than the organizational and political fact was the growth of a basic conception—that the gulf between culture and mass-politics had to be overcome, that culture had to be politicized, and the political process made more sensitive to cultural change. The average man, the common denominator of the "masses," had himself to take part in creative achievement, not leaving it to the ivory tower of poets and philosophers. The Communists had by no means the monopoly of this emphasis, but they gave it more substance than any other movement. Was it accidental that under their aegis Waldo Frank and Theodore Dreiser had traveled at the pit of the depression to bear witness to the agony of the Harlan, Kentucky coal miners; or that Vernon L. Parrington and Thorstein Veblen had affirmed in their last years the hope which Communism represented in a world of apparent decay?

Not the least important feature of American Communism which further separates it from other minor parties was its international tie, its commitment both to the Soviet Union as the "bulwark of world Socialism," and to the parties which made up the Communist International, conceived as the "general staff" of a world revolutionary vanguard. Nothing gave the Communists such zeal, such hope—and so much difficulty and grief—as their participation in the world movement. Nothing about them was so criticized, and the sources of this fixation are easily misunderstood. It is true that foreign-born workers played an inordinate part in the founding of the Communist party. In the breakaway from the Socialists, the language federations, especially those of eastern European and Russian origin, were certainly dominant. It could be argued, even in the late 1940's,[15] that a very large group in the party's leadership and essential cadres were first and second generation Americans out of European stock, out of Russia itself and the countries later to become part of the Soviet bloc. Wonder and pride at the great doings in the "old country" surely stimulated the party's beginnings. Yet this does not itself explain why millions of Americans of first and second generation stock out of this same area did not sympathize with Communism; more important, it does not explain the attraction to the party's cause of radicals of Anglo-Saxon and Scandinavian stock, many of them tracing their forebears to colonial times.

Only if one realizes the dilemma of the Socialists of the Debsian vintage and the syndicalists of "Big Bill" Haywood's time can one grasp the impact of the Russian Revolution upon them. Neither the Socialists nor the syndicalists had any conception, for all their devotion and not-insignificant impact, of how the revolution was to come about. The First World War saw the collapse of the formal international solidarity solemnly pledged by the Second International. Almost alone, the American Socialist party opposed the war. When Lenin, an unknown in America, succeeded overnight, and a Socialist experiment suddenly loomed over one-sixth of the earth and helped bring the war to an end, the prestige of Russia soared. It became an easy, magnetic *non-sequitur* to assume that the kind of party Lenin had built was a model for revolutionaries everywhere. Both in the immediate period when revolution appeared to have a chance in Germany and Hungary, and later when those prospects waned, the idea of a "general staff," a tightly-knit organism for which Russia was not a nation in itself but a base in the further unfolding of the revolutionary process, took a tenacious hold. All this corresponded with a peculiarly Whitmanesque assumption that the ideal of the brotherhood of all men could be transfigured into a world movement. Such assumptions and complexes were by no means un-American.

To be sure, the American comrades out-Lenined Lenin. Whereas the Russian leader by 1922 was musing that the Comintern's program was too Russian, and could be translated abroad but not emulated, the emulation of the Soviet experience prevailed.[16] All manner of changes, conflicts, and crimes within the Soviet party did not weaken the Soviet Union's image as the base of revolution in the minds of American Communists. The party's experience in the 1920's, as Theodore Draper's two painstaking studies have shown,[17] is the chronicle of desperate, sometimes pathetic efforts to keep in step with the Soviet party's Byzantine inner strife, always reflected within the International itself whose task was brusquely changed, under Stalin, from leading a complex world movement into serving as an arm of Soviet state policy. Under the grip of such assumptions, under the illusion of a "world party," the American Communists were ready for anything demanded of them, and did things which they only *imagined* were demanded—whether it was the gathering of information, not too far from espionage,[18] or the submission of their leadership to whatever changes Moscow proposed, or abrupt gyrations of policy no matter at what cost to themselves. "Why is the American Party like the Brooklyn Bridge," asked Jay Lovestone (deposed by Stalin in 1929 despite his majority at home) and then he answered in bitter jest: "Because it is suspended at both ends by cables."[19] Indeed, cables, Comintern "letters," emissaries of Finnish, German, Japanese, Hungarian and Russian extraction went back and forth throughout the 1920's, and well into the 1930's. Only toward the end of that decade did the *Daily Worker*, which had been founded in 1924 with a Comintern subsidy, remove from its masthead its identification as the organ of a Communist party, U.S.A. (Section of the Communist International).

Ironically, one major reason why American Communists found this tie normal lay in the fact that the pressure for "Americanization" came from the Comintern itself. The foreigners who made up the commissions that scrutinized C.P.U.S.A. activities were altogether conscious that the American comrades were unrepresentative.[20] The pressure to subordinate the language federations and to find roots within the native-born population came from Moscow; so did the Open Letter of 1933 which sparked the revival of the C.P.U.S.A. Moreover, when the Soviet Union turned in 1935 to a policy of "collective security" and sought to build its defenses by treaties with France, Britain, and China against the threat of the fascist Axis, the Communist International, in its Seventh Congress of 1935, made a strategic reorientation: it encouraged each party to find roots in native soil and native democratic traditions, and to unite with a large cross-section of the nation in a Popular Front against fascism.

Under this impact, the American Communists blossomed, and became a pervasive factor in the burgeoning second New Deal. Whatever doubts persisted as to the wisdom of placing so much reliance upon, and giving such obedience to, Soviet policy was offset by the developing coincidence of interest developed between the United States and the Soviet Union. In singing the Star Spangled Banner at their Madison Square Garden meetings amid billowing streamers that "Communism is 20th Century

Americanism," the Communists made their underlying reliance on Moscow more palatable.[21] If they paid a heavy price for abandoning this policy in 1939-1941 during the Soviet-German Non-Aggression Pact (a flipflop which hung as a pall over the next twenty years), they nimbly recovered during wartime national unity. And when their general secretary of that time, Earl Browder, attempted a departure from the Leninist structure, and tried to adapt his movement's policy to what he believed would be the postwar imperatives of American-Soviet cooperation, he expressed in a tentative, hesitating way the nascent polycentrism which was gripping the Communist movement. Browder was encouraged by the dissolution of the Communist International in May-June, 1943 and by the rationale that "fundamental differences of the historical development of the separate countries of the world" justified this move. The Comintern's last declaration also averred that Communists "were never advocates of the preservation of outmoded historical forms."[22] One of the C.I.'s last acts was to ratify the decision of the American C.P. in 1940 to disaffiliate from the International, an action which spared it prosecution under the Voorhis Act.

Yet for all the accusation of "revisionism" which cost Browder his leadership and career, the American Communists were unable to make an independent analysis of that which was new in American society as the war fostered changes in the direction of a welfare state. Browder never reexamined, except at fleeting moments, the distinctively new aspects of neo-capitalism. Nor could the Communists shake free of their commitment to the Soviet Union as the postwar polarization developed and became ominous. The opportunity presented by the Soviet Union's rupture with Tito's Yugoslavia was passed up, indeed hardly considered. Throughout the 1940's, as will be shown later, American Communists had such difficulty keeping in step with a world movement guided by strategic considerations to which they were not privy, which in any case never force their interests into account, that when the inevitable *denouement* came in 1956, American Communism found itself in trauma. Eugene Dennis, the party's secretary in the 1956 reexamination, lamented that the C.P. had suffered from the "decades-old weakness" of transposing foreign conditions to the American scene.[23]

Thousands of members, who streamed out of the ranks from 1956-1958, were humiliated by the realization that having dumped Browder and engaged in a self-defeating attempt to keep up with Stalin's contortion of the world movement, they had also defeated themselves. They were being told by Nikita Khrushchev in 1956 that many of Browder's propositions—once denounced as revisionism—had now become the new orthodoxy. The attempt of the 16th National Convention, in February, 1957, to declare its autonomy of the world movement and to seek an independent course within it was by then altogether doomed. Neither the political nor organizational vitality to pursue such a course was any longer available.[24]

Were the American Communists "agents of a foreign power"? Not in the sense of deliberately enrolling in a conspiracy, and readily accepting the consequences. Were they creative members of a world movement which might be justified in its own terms? This they tried to be, never quite succeeding, and never being taken into the confidence of the "general staff" itself. Stalin had, in 1929, flattered the American

Communists by declaring that "history had entrusted them with tasks of world-decisive importance." Yet there is no evidence that Moscow ever trusted the American Communists, accepted their initiatives nor invited them to help map the world battle plan. Most of the evidence of the tortuous half century shows that the C.P. was expected to follow the waving of the Soviet baton blindly, asking few questions, rarely getting answers.

And when that situation began to change, what loomed up was the necessity of so fundamental a revision of doctrine and structure that the Communists could only have become a radical force of a social-democratic character, or diminish into a caricature of the Leninist model. Faced with this dilemma, they could only follow the international movement by zodiac signs, by a sort of Couéism, or Pavlovian reflex. Even direct consultations with Moscow and with other parties hardly helped them.[25] Thus, one of the most important characteristics which differentiate the C.P.U.S.A. from other minor parties, namely its internationalism, an internationalist impulse which was generous and distinctively American and yet which also stamped it so indelibly as un-American, was the seedbed of its undoing. The Communists were more like a self-proclaimed guerrilla band, operating without any real contact with the "main force" which took their existence for granted. Accepting this role of expendability, they were in fact expended.

Unlike other minor parties, including those of the radical tradition, the American Communists set themselves the task of becoming a Leninist party, a "party of a special type." Their problem was to forge an organism capable of taking power in the very citadel of a highly-developed capitalism, power not in the electoral sense but on the model of the Bolsheviks in Tsarist Russia, a power intended to transform—against expected opposition—the whole of bourgeois society.

Although they stressed the importance of propaganda and education, it was not in mere education or even by exemplary action which would have an educational effect that the American Communists saw as their distinctive role. Nor was it by running candidates within the American party system. They did this on many occasions without viewing the matter as the true measure of their purpose; their record in balloting for local or national office was not, in their eyes, the real index of success or failure.[26] A "party of a special type" implied building a quasi-military, highly-disciplined movement. While they were constantly engaged in recruitment of rank and file members, they were at bottom concerned with what Philip Selznick[27] has called their "deployable cadres," those who could aspire to become the prime movers, the spark-plugs of activity in their chosen field. The highest rung, the greatest honor of the most proven and tested cadres was to be accepted in the category of "professional revolutionary," the "full-timers." On the other hand, such "professional revolutionaries" adaptable to any and every "task," were not born to this calling. They had to aspire to it, be trained and tested.

Thus, as Nathan Glazer[28] has pointed out, the Communists were constantly engaged in a "human alchemy"—turning intellectuals into proletarians, working men into "proletarian intellectuals." The movement became a vehicle for social mobility with the highest objective the transformation of ordinary men into "Bolsheviks," that is, counterparts of those who had scaled the pinnacle of achievement and had "made the Revolution." Such an ideal called for men and women capable of self-sacrifice, able to maintain their cool under fire, animated by a capacity for the scientific analysis of society, objective in their judgments, yet deeply committed and therefore permeated by a love of humanity, and especially of that segment of it, the oppressed and humble folk, which were, in the Marxian definition, the bearers of a new social order and alone capable of rescuing humanity from the slough of capitalism.

Nor should the chronicler of Communism be derisive of the nobility of this purpose and the very important contribution which it made in the lives of individual Communists. The party was, in striving to be a liberating army, also a family, a community. Many an individual worker, student, doctor, lawyer found in it an avenue for self-improvement, in some cases, an educational stimulus and a vehicle whereby hidden talents and organizational skills were brought to flower.[29]

It was also true, given a missionary type of community hierarchically organized on the basis of "democratic centralism," and given the mentality of "class war" which permeated its fiber, that the Communists exhibited intense factionalism, a capacity for dogmatism, a cruelty not only to foes but to friends, an ability to break the hearts of many who were both rank and file members as well as leaders. Communism had a record of profligate waste of human beings, absence of solidarity, honesty and love among themselves not so different from the bourgeois society that they were trying to replace. If what Daniel Bell has called the "schwärmerei and grubbiness" pervading the party's inner life was not so different from the same state of affairs in other radical movements, indeed in all organizational life, nevertheless the Communists were constantly confronted with the question of why they were unable to do any better than others?

At the apex of repeated crises, in which the floodgates of suppressed self-criticism were broken, as in 1945 and again in 1956, the self-portrait of the Communists was not at all flattering.[30] How to define the thin line between devotion to principle and dogmatism, between detached, scientific weighing of hard and even unpleasant facts and the determination to cling to one's premises, between firmness under heavy fire and a suicidal fanaticism? The Communists tried to walk this difficult, narrow path. For all their own experience, and the presumed lessons of an international movement tested in this moral and ideological tight-rope walking, they did not succeed. What was the ultimate reason for this much-lamented failure? Arthur Koestler, himself a former Communist, attributed the result to the "mentality of a person who lives in a closed system of thought, Communist or other." Such a person's problem, he continued, "can be summed up in a single formula: he can prove anything he believes and he believes everything he can prove. The closed system sharpens the faculties of the mind, like an overefficient grindstone, to a brittle edge; it produces a scholastic, Talmudic, hair-splitting brand of cleverness which affords no protection against committing the crudest imbecilities."[31]

The "closed system" needs, of course, to be extended from the intellectual and ideological plane to the level of political and organizational structure. There was something uniquely closed and unchanging about the American Communist party's leadership over several decades. It was largely unable to advance new forces out of the hundreds of thousands, perhaps close to a million Americans who came and went through the revolving doors of the party.[32] What must also be explored in some detail were the inner contradictions of a movement that was trying to fashion an instrument of revolutionary change in a time and a country in which nothing like the Leninist revolution was possible. In this respect, too, the Communists were prisoners of their closed system.

Surveying membership and leadership, one is struck by the pre-eminence of a relative handful of men and women over about four decades, almost all of whom cut their eyeteeth in the split of the Socialist party, the collapse of the I.W.W. (providing many recruits) and the first three or four years during which two parties existed, each with its own underground. It was not until 1923-1924 that the American Communists, guided in detail by Comintern "reps," succeeded in forming an open, legal, and united structure. In the next five years they went through intense factional battles. Only by 1930 did they arrive at the semblance of a collective leadership in which Earl Browder was to become the rising star.

Some of the men and women of this first decade passed away early, notably Charles Ruthenberg. Louis Fraina disappeared for a decade and did not return to the C.P.[33] James P. Cannon, unionist become Trotskyist, was expelled by the group around Jay Lovestone and Bertram Wolfe, who were themselves later expelled as "Bukharinists." The C.P. leaders who remained were to dominate the party throughout the 1930's and 1940's and even through the 1950's. In a sense, a gerontocracy governed American Communism. Important leaders, among them Clarence Hathaway, William F. Dunne and Samuel Darcy disappeared in Browder's time, and their fate was sealed by William Z. Foster's accession to power after the war. Yet in the top and middle leadership, the older generation persisted. The stamp of its experience—the experience prior to the emergence of the party as a formidable movement in the 1930's—was indelibly engraved on the organism. Although the 1930's formed a new chapter, and although the party's membership rose from 7,000 in 1930 to almost 90,000 during the war—and this was the decade during which more members came and went than in any other—the main leaders remain those of the 1920's.[34] Younger men, such as Eugene Dennis, Gilbert Green and Gus Hall, John Steuben and Steve Nelson, came out of the youth movement of that same decade: their common characteristic is their attendance at the Lenin School and post-graduate work in the Comintern's apparatus.

Men and women of some prestige who were persuaded to join in the mid-1930's, such as Elizabeth Gurley Flynn, Louis F. Budenz, Arnold Johnson, Vern Smith and Harrison George—remained figureheads; they did not hold the key levers of party control. As for the cadres who came out of the youth movement of the 1930's—one of American Communism's most successful achievements—one finds them in the Abraham Lincoln Brigade in Spain and then among the 15,000 American Communists who went into the military service during the war. But they do not come into the party leadership until after the war. John Gates, Henry Winston, Robert Thompson— to name only the most prominent—achieved positions of power only after the great upheaval of 1945.

This means that the American Communist movement remained in the tight control of the men whose formative period, deepest experience and most fundamental lessons were of the 1920's. It means also that while the party's work was done by newcomers, by fresh recruits, the decision-making always remained in the hands of the older generation. Whereas in other parties, notably in Western Europe, the great refreshment of cadres, and to some extent new ideas, came during the Resistance, the American Communists experienced their Resistance prior to the Second World War. In fact, the war was a rupture for the party. Tens of thousands of its most experienced activists were forced during the war to see the vastness of the American problem and the relative impotence of the party to solve it. Many did not return to the fold. Even in the fruitful 1930's, there was a "generation gap" within the party, which meant that at moments of great crisis, the reflexes of the decision-making strata impelled them to return to what they knew was solid, firm, traditional and proven in their own minds.[35] If the younger cadres and the newer membership did not agree, they quietly left. Or, they went into other fields of left-wing activity in which they did not have to take direct party responsibility.

This brings up a central characteristic of American Communism, part of its inner sociology and the dilemma of its strategy, which was rarely visible to either its members or dispassionate observers. Early in its career, the American C.P. realized that mere advocacy of a new social order, the inscription of Socialism on its banners or even the most imaginative outline of what a new social order might look like in the future would not be enough to enlist the American working class. *Advocacy* of Socialism was not enough. Nor could the masses be impelled by exemplary action on to the Socialist path. The activism of the syndicalists was impressive but altogether too sporadic; some link between advocacy and confrontation was required. The Communists found this link in the theory of fighting for "immediate, partial demands." This formula was sanctioned by the Comintern's emphasis after 1922 that the Communists of the western world get into the existing labor movement and abandon what Lenin had called the "infantile disorder" of demonstratively separating themselves from the main body of the working people. As William Z. Foster, who came to Communism after his reputation as a trade union leader had been built, put it: the American militant "must participate in the unions, and through day-to-day detailed work through close association with the masses, convince the masses that he is a good union man, interested in their welfare. The idea was to use their control to put across their radical philosophy, not to use their radical philosophy to get control."[36] The same thought had been expressed succinctly by Max Bedacht: "The working class must travel the road of these immediate struggles to reach the battlefields of power."

The next fifteen years of the Communist party's "line" was a refinement and amplification of this tactic. The Communists were to become indefatigable organizers, champions of practical issues, the builders of a complex network of *ad hoc* organizations. America was, especially in the face of the new needs of the Great Crisis after 1929, an organizational *tabula rasa*. It needed only the enterprise of dedicated people to build new expressions of popular demands. It was not difficult, by this activity, to rise to leadership.

Yet this conception of the road to revolution contained within itself a fundamental ambiguity and dilemma, which caused a crucial organizational feedback into the Communist apparatus. For what if "the masses" were to show their gratitude to the Communist organizers by elevating them to high posts without necessarily accepting their radical philosophy? What if the masses were, in fact, to find immediate satisfaction of their needs without, for all that, proceeding to draw radical conclusions?

The Communist assumption was that capitalism would prove incapable of satisfying the needs of the people, would prove recalcitrant to their demands, and thus by a constant escalation of these demands the masses would come to accept the necessity of revolutionary transformation. Yet what if the system was more elastic than the Communists supposed? In that case, the masses would have achieved what they wanted. They might or might not continue the Communists in positions of control. They might accept them *despite* their views, or ultimately consent to the ouster of the Communists from strategic positions without so much as a "thank you" for the hard work they had done. The masses might feel that—at moments when the party's needs collided with the needs of its operatives who had achieved strategic control—to dump the Communist organizers on the ground that their private political faith was being used to further the party's interest rather than the interests of the organizations which the party faithful had built.[37]

On the other hand, the strategy of achieving control of popular organizations, not only the trade unions but *ad hoc* movements of every type, was bound to have the grave consequences for the inner life of the party. If the revolutionary *denouement* were delayed, if the masses were not to move consistently from reliance on party-led reforms toward acceptance of the party's revolutionary solutions, there would inevitably take place a certain stabilization and institutionalization of the organizational life. Men who were Communists might find themselves in control of organizations in which the dedicated Communist rank and filers were few in number. Such "influentials," as I have called them elsewhere,[38] might find themselves obliged to carry on with budgets, programs, staffs, and all the paraphernalia of bureaucratic life under a very specific tension: if they voiced their political views, their control might be jeopardized; if they did not voice their views and concealed them, they might be vulnerable to loss of control on grounds of duplicity.

This state of affairs constituted a very intense strain. To accept responsibility for the party and openly participate in formulating its political policy might become very difficult and hazardous. On the other hand, for the best of the party's cadres, to stand aside from the party's political tasks, and to refrain from using their power in the party's interests would lead to a gulf between them and the movement which had been the original stimulus of their success. The influentials could become alienated from the party itself. The party's leadership would become nothing more than a system of brokerage between a "center," which had little standing among the masses, and a network of operatives. Such operatives had the autonomous power within their organizations to separate themselves from the party. They could abandon it abruptly and still be factors in American life. Or they could remain private revolutionaries in their own self-image, without any respect for, or obedience to, the party.

The American Communist party had to face the divergence between what Max Weber has called the "ethics of responsibility," that is, the realm of action which sought pragmatic, concrete and specific reforms, and the "ethics of ultimate ends," the realm which set itself absolute, revolutionary goals. As the discussion of the 1944-1945 crisis will show, the C.P.'s transformation to a political association and then the abrupt return to the party form did not make an explicit choice of either of the Weberian ethics. The Communists straddled both, and tried to combine both. They attempted the revolutionary solution, but largely by verbalism. The United States was not confronted by revolutionary change in the classic sense of that word. Their revolutionary striving was largely abstract, and expressed itself in following the international movement where the contradiction between revolutionary objectives and non-revolutionary realities was less apparent.

In practice, the American Communists were by the logic *of their own successes rather than their failures* propelled in the direction of becoming a movement of a social-democratic character, a movement of radical reform. Yet they recoiled from this alternative. To avow it meant to acknowledge that their Leninist commitment was outmoded. It could not be realized and had to give way to something else. But this commitment was too deep. The Communists could not face up to the reality that the only possible political future which could capitalize on their achievements and con-tinue them as a genuine factor in American life would be the abandonment of the Leninist illusion, the reupholstering of their structure and purpose with ideological garments more appropriate than those which had been inherited under the impact of the great split of 1919 and the great hallucination of a world revolution. Earl Browder attempted this change in 1944. It was essentially a straddle, an experiment with a new name and form, which he justified by the construct of a new American-Soviet relationship in world affairs, by a judgment about the radically altered relationship of world forces following the war. Browder had prophetic insights about this new relationship, but it was at that time only a potential, not yet a reality.

Thus, the American Communists became a casualty of the Cold War. They had an intimation that the Second World War had transformed the nature and the terrain of the struggle between opposing systems, and as a result would oblige Communism to alter itself and in so doing contribute to a basic re-orientation of capitalism as well, but they could not pursue the logic of this intimation nor give it political substance.

II

History, fickle and contradictory, did not work out for the American Com-munists as they had supposed it would. Two circumstances contributed to the party's growth but also undermined its ideological assumptions. If the Great Crisis of 1929 appeared to have confirmed that capitalism was on the verge of collapse, it was also true that a vast movement of social, cultural and political change was generated in response to the crisis. The New Deal was led by Franklin D. Roosevelt, a conservative of the Burkean tradition, who believed in the elasticity of the society and for the sake of conserving it was prepared for reform. The Communists flourished in the whirlpool of the era of reform. They could claim to have contributed to it in substantial measure. Their contribution, as has been shown, dovetailed with their conception that the revolutionary road was paved with the struggle for immediate, partial demands. Whereas in much of the world and notably in Germany, the response to the crisis was repression, the destruction of democratic liberties, the rise of fascism and the eclipse of Communism, American life in the 1930's showed that a different outcome was possible. This in itself distinguished the American Communist experience from that of fraternal movements in much of the world.

The second circumstance, equally fundamental but even more perplexing, was the confluence of interest between the United States and the Soviet Union—the conjunction of their self-defence against the Axis. The war brought vast changes in the direction of the welfare state within the United States and the entire capitalist world while it also brought about an upheaval among the colonial peoples whose most striking feature was the prospect of a Communist China. The war enabled the American Communists to defend the Soviet Union while participating in the defense of their own country. At the same time, the question was posed whether the postwar period would necessarily witness a polarization or mortal conflict between the Communist-led revolutionary states and the democratic capitalist world.

The prospect of "peace for many generations" was pledged by Stalin, Roosevelt and Churchill at their first wartime meeting in Teheran, December, 1943. But peace for many generations was a new concept. It challenged the basic Leninist contention that imperialism as a system could only be overthrown by a transition to Socialism throughout a half century of wars. The alterations within capitalist society which the war had wrought also raised the question of whether the Communist analysis was not subject to revision. Whereas the advance of Socialism had, in the 1920's and early 1930's, been envisaged as an extension of Soviet power from its base within the Soviet Union, there now loomed up a polycentric, differentiated advance, relatively peaceful in some countries, violent in others, *but possible at a distance from Soviet arms*. The prospect of social transformation within the framework of democracy and by methods quite different from those which had until then been Leninist orthodoxy now emerged within the framework of a coexistence and interpenetration of systems such as Lenin had not anticipated. The dissolution of the Communist International in 1943 appeared to give sanction to this very polycentrism and the abandonment of forms which, as the C.I.'s last document suggested, had become "historically outmoded."

The American Communist party, minor as it was and minor within the world movement in which it had been born and bred, found itself in the vortex of the great issues impiled by the exciting possibilities, as Earl Browder put it in 1944, that "capitalism and socialism have begun to find the way to peaceful coexistence and collaboration in the same world."[39] The American Communist experiment with the implications of this affirmation lasted only eighteen months. It was reversed in the Spring of 1945, long before it was reversed in 1947 throughout the international Communist movement. But the experiment dealt with such fundamental issues that it formed a decisive chapter not only in the annals of this movement but in the origins of the Cold War, examined as such origins must be in terms of the crisis of Communism which the war had brought about.[40] In the succeeding twelve years, the C.P.U.S.A. wrestled with the implications of overturning the experiment of 1944, a wrestling identified with the preeminence of Browder's long-time mentor and rival, William Z. Foster. Nor will the crisis of 1955-1957, and the party's collapse, be comprehended without returning to the wartime reorientation which Browder proposed and virtually the entire leadership at that time accepted—and then a year later rejected—also rejecting Browder himself.

The party's general secretary proposed to adapt his movement to what he believed was a vast world turning-point, a long-term peace between the United States and the Soviet Union. Browder was aware that labor's domestic gains and the generally progressive environment of the wartime period could be reversed by a defeat of the Roosevelt policies. No doubt, Browder wished to assist the Soviet Union itself; he reckoned that it required a period of recuperation which could best be hastened by avoiding revolutionary confrontation. The American C.P. leader was impressed by the extreme caution with which Stalin proceeded in Eastern Europe as the Soviet armies arrived. The local Communists and those who returned from Moscow were under plain orders not to project Sovietization. True to his deal with Churchill, Stalin did not support the Greek uprising. By recognizing Charles de Gaulle as head of a tripartite regime to which the French Communists turned in their arms and undertook responsibility for economic reconstruction, (not measures of socialization) the tone was set for avoiding any clash of ideologies and/or ideological armies. At that same time, the Chinese Communists, it may be remembered, were still involved in a united front with Chaing Kai-shek; while keeping their own armies intact, they were seeking to extend joint action against Japan, but were also envisaging a postwar united government. No one knew how long the war would continue in its Pacific theatre. Support for inclusion of the Chinese Communists in a postwar government was growing in Washington—a sentiment which the American Communists encouraged, and which also encouraged them.

Early in 1944, it was not certain that FDR would run for an unprecedented fourth term. The left wing in the labor movement sparked the campaign to assure Roosevelt's candidacy. Whereas the main leaders of labor had fought to continue Henry Wallace as FDR's vice president, the Communists did not think the dropping of Wallace was a disaster; their conception of postwar national unity certainly included senators like Harry S. Truman. The overall situation, in Browder's words, required of the Communists "the reaffirmation of our wartime policy that we will not raise the issue of socialism in such a form or manner as to endanger or weaken that national unity."[41] The Communists proposed to cooperate with the "decisive sections" of American capitalism, against those reactionary sections who had been hostile to the joint war effort, and opposed postwar friendship with Russia. Since the American economy had vastly expanded its productive forces during the war, it seemed to Browder that overseas markets as well as a doubling of domestic purchasing power were essential to avoid economic crisis. Only participation of Communists abroad in stable, liberation governments as well as their own commitment not to extend Socialist power by arms or *coups*, would give the United States a world order in which its new economic capacity could find outlets. While the Communists never went quite as far as the left-wing labor leader, Harry Bridges, in suggesting a postwar no-strike pledge, it was widely assumed that he spoke for them. Bridges, a syndicalist in his origins, was on the closest terms with the C.P., although denying membership in it.[42]

To dramatize the party's commitment to such postwar conceptions, Browder proposed his movement's transformation into the Communist Political Association. It was to be a Marxist vanguard, but would act as a lobby and pervade the whole of organizational life. It would work as a non-partisan force and ally itself with that substantial minority which was independent, and from the vantage point of this independence voted for one or another ticket as the issue or the personality of a candidate warranted. Browder sought political mileage for his movement within the two-party system. At bottom, he was seeking to legitimatize his movement to give the party's influentials a way of functioning openly as left wingers, assuming responsibilities for a Marxist organization.[43] He abandoned the premises of a Leninist party because the Leninist task of leading revolutionary change was not, in fact, on the order of the day.

At first, Browder was quite tentative and avoided any "theoretical generalizations" to characterize the new period. Nor did he make any re-analysis of the changes within the structure of American capitalism. The new prospects were only possibilities, not yet realities. They were worth fighting for, if only to throw responsibility for their failure on the opponents of Teheran. But Browder also exuded a sense of pioneering. "For the first time we are meeting and solving problems," he told his National Board at its meeting of January 7-9, 1944, "for which there are no precedents in history and no formulas from the classics which give us the answers." Exhibiting a certain independence but implicitly admitting the dependence which had always been denied, Browder added: "Perhaps we could say that our Party is standing on its own feet for the first time." Marxism, he continued, "was never a series of dogmas and formulas; it was never a catalogue of prohibitions listing the things we must not do irrespective of new developments and new situations; it does not tell us that things cannot be done; it tells us how to do the things that have to be done . . . Marxism is a theory of deeds, not of dont's. . . ."[44]

Two leaders opposed Browder's projections. One was Samuel Adams Darcy, the Philadelphia organizer, the other William Z. Foster, by then an emeritus figure having been shunted aside over the previous decade, and yet a major personality. He presented a critical letter to a national committee meeting ten days after Browder's report to the national board. Foster took no strong exception to the conversion of the party to a political association. It did not seem to him then a "dissolution" of the Communist movement as was to be charged a year later. But he believed that Browder was underestimating "the deepening crisis of world capitalism caused by the war," and falling prey to illusions that capitalism "had somehow been rejuvenated and was entering a new period of expansion and growth."

In attempting to apply the Teheran decisions to the United States, Browder was mistakenly evoking a perspective of a "smoothly-working national unity, including the decisive sections of American finance capital not only during the war but in the post-war." In this outlook, Foster argued "American imperialism virtually disappears, there remains hardly a trace of the class struggle, and socialism plays practically no role whatsoever." The task of Communists was not to persuade any section of capitalism to follow a progressive course, much less to rely on it to do so. Instead, the task was to "rally the great popular masses . . . and resist the forces of big capital now, during the war, and also to curb their power drastically in the post-war period." Browder, he continued "goes too far when he says that world capitalism and world Socialism have learned to live peacefully together." Foster envisaged refusal of the capitalists to "tolerate a repetition of the New Deal," and with a "growing fascist spirit in their ranks," they "would adopt, if necessary the most drastic means to clip the strength of labor and prevent the return of any popular, progressive government."[45]

Foster's projections stemmed from the classic, traditional view that capitalism as a system was in ever-deeper crisis; no "temporary stabilization" nor growth was probable. To "curb the power of monopoly capital," without specifying by what means short of basic revolutionary change this might come about, had a Populist ring, strongly infused by the syndicalist certainty. It was defiant and comforting even if it lacked strategic scope and would be tactically hard to implement. In Foster's eyes, there had been nothing more than a coincidence of American and Soviet interest. The inevitable polarization between the two systems would produce new revolutionary advances and with them the implicit danger of world war. This theme was to become a preoccupation, even an obsession in later years. With it went the companion theme of a fascist solution for the American crisis, unless a revolutionary *denouement* were somehow to arrive in the nick of time.

Hopelessly isolated in the January, 1944 meetings, Foster made no public fight for his position. The party's membership knew nothing of the controversy between its most prestigious leaders. Samuel Darcy, who argued essentially that Browder was premature in raising postwar problems, was expelled in April; Foster himself presided over the commission which expelled his only ally. The real reason for Foster's reluctance to press his views, and the real reason why Browder did not move to expel his longtime rival and also the real story of how this conflict came to the attention of Moscow and resulted within a year in the famous article by Jacques Duclos remained hidden.[46]

Scarcely one year later, Browder's ambitious experiment received an earthquake blow in the form of a denunciation by the French Communist leader Jacques Duclos.[47] By then, much that the American Communists had worked for did in fact materialize. Roosevelt accepted and won a fourth term. The Allied invasion of Normandy sealed the fate of the Nazi armies, and the partition of Germany. A new international labor body, the World Federation of Trade Unions, brought the C.I.O. into contact with the British, Soviet and the unified left-led unions of France and Italy. A few American labor leaders (there were eleven left-wingers in the C.I.O.'s executive of thirty-three members) did announce themselves by joining the C.P.A.[48] All the evidence—the rapid membership growth and enhanced prestige—indicated a promising future.[49] As for the world outlook, Marshal Stalin made the judgment in his November, 1944 address, that while differences existed among the Big Three "the surprising thing is not that differences exist, but that there are so few of them and that as a rule, in practically every case, they are resolved in a spirit of unity and coordination of among the three great powers." The alliance, said Stalin, is founded "not on casual, short-lived considerations but on vital, lasting interests," and having withstood the strain of the war "will all the more certainly stand the strain of the concluding phase of the war."[50] The American Communists were attuned to exactly this wave-length.

Yet by the late Spring of 1945, such optimism had given way to serious forebodings. The president's death in mid-April preceded a sharp confrontation between Molotov, the Soviet foreign minister, *en route* to the founding conference of the United Nations with FDR's successor, Harry S. Truman. The Yalta accords, as regards Poland, were being interpreted very differently. The beginnings of a deliberate anti-Soviet campaign were evident at San Francisco itself from quarters such as Ambassador Averell Harriman, whom the American Communists had regarded as an "intelligent capitalist" and a champion of the Teheran concept.[51]

When the Duclos article arrived it was by no means immediately accepted among the top Communist leaders. A detailed study of their reactions,[52] in their National Board early in May, and then in national committee meetings late in May, and again in June, reveals astonishment and even anger against Duclos. Many of his facts, alleging a fall-off in C.P.A. membership were wrong. Equally unbelievable was his assertion that the movement which had so vigorously expanded had in reality undergone "dissolution." His rebuke to the Communists for their failure to appreciate the antimonopolist emphasis of former Vice President Henry Wallace was also puzzling.

The most vital passage accused Browder of not only a "notorious revisionism," but of transforming the Teheran declaration of December, 1943, "which is a document of a diplomatic character," into "a political platform of class peace in the United States." The Duclos article quoted Browder as having declared, "that at Teheran capitalism and socialism had begun to find the means of peaceful coexistence and collaboration in the framework of one and the same world." This was now held to have been his basic error. "The Teheran agreements mean to Earl Browder that the great part of Europe, west of the Soviet Union, will probably be reconstituted on a bourgeois-democratic basis, and not on a fascist or Soviet basis."[53]

Many weighty difficulties arose. Was Duclos speaking simply for himself? In that case, as Browder tried to suggest to his colleagues, this was but a viewpoint in an increasingly polycentric Communist world. It could be argued on its merits. Yet the internal evidence made it plain that Duclos could only have been assisted by someone in Moscow; the article contained allusions to events which took place before the August, 1944 liberation of Paris, that is, while Duclos himself was in hiding, and thus could only have been assembled by one news-gathering agency, TASS. If the Soviet party were involved, this was a much graver matter.

Was Browder's leadership itself at stake, and was his removal being demanded?[54] That, too, was equally grave. For several weeks, the Communist leaders, including Foster, begged Browder to make an appropriate self-criticism and continue as party leader. Only when Browder refused was this plea abandoned. There was still another difficulty. By suggesting that Europe, even Western Europe, might *not* be reconstituted on a basis acceptable to the West, and might be the scene of an acute struggle for power, the Duclos article was not in keeping with any other expressions of policy in the Communist world at that time. In fact, as Browder was to argue, it contradicted French Communist policy. Against the charge of "revisionism," Browder replied that his whole political projection was but an adaptation, to American conditions, of a general line. Accused of having stepped out of line, Browder insisted that he had merely implemented world Communist policy with appropriate American terminology.

Once again, as in 1929 in the case of Lovestone, the foremost U.S. Communist leader was being accused of "American exceptionalism." The top leader was to be disgraced again and the enormous investment in the build-up of his authority squandered. At a moment when the prestige of both the Soviet Union and the world movement was at its highest, the American public was treated to the spectacle of a self-flagellating criticism, an abrupt reversal of course, a declaration by the Communists to all those whom they wanted and needed as allies that they were going to be harder to live with. Browder's own expulsion did not come until February, 1946. By then, perhaps 50,000 members (not all of them wartime recruits) had departed.[55] Many important trade unionists were confirmed in their suspicion of the party's ineptitude, and their private distance from it increased. The emergency convention of July, 1945, reconstituted the party with the peculiarity—which also undermined confidence—that William Z. Foster, avenger of the party's orthodoxy, was now obliged to draw on the very same cadres who had been formed in the Browder decade. Men and women, compromised by a previous policy, tried to implement a new one. Uncertain as to what weapons of their political armory of the 1930's were now appropriate to an increasingly defensive and complex battle, they went into the 1940's and 1950's refurbishing the weapons of the 1920's.

III

American Communism's postwar decade, from its rededication to Marxism-Leninism in 1945-1946 until the moral crisis of 1956-1957, appears in retrospect as the period of decline. This was not simply the judgment of historians.[56] The *post-mortem* was made by the party's general secretary, Eugene Dennis; he spoke in April, 1956, to the first national Committee meeting after five years during which his movement's top leaders were in jail under the Smith Act and its most important cadres attempted to maintain "an underground" in the expectation of American-Soviet war and the onset of fascism. The Dennis report[57] found that his party had done practically nothing right. On every key issue, it was unable to judge the real processes in American life despite the guidance Marxism-Leninism was supposed to provide. Although its burden was a collective self-criticism, the Dennis review became an indictment of William Z. Foster. The latter cast the sole negative vote at the April, 1956 meeting, and until that Autumn of disasters—the repercussion of de-Stalinization in Hungary and Poland—Foster stood alone and discredited. Thus, within ten years, American Communism downgraded its two most eminent leaders. Foster, like Browder before him, was held culpable in turn.

By 1957, the party's membership was reduced to perhaps 17,000—not far from the level[58] at which it began its rise and in the aftermath of the crisis, it probably went lower. The dissolution which Duclos had charged to Browder in 1944 was accomplished under Foster. By 1958, the daily newspaper ceased to appear.[59] Connections between the party and the political life had virtually been severed. For example, in 1956 the American Labor party, once such an ambitious progressive coalition, disbanded having failed four years earlier to garner the necessary 50,000 votes in New York State. In 1948, this movement had given Wallace (as four years earlier in the case of Roosevelt) half a million votes.

Influence in the labor movement had also declined drastically. Those left-wing leaders who had made their way into the now unified A.F.L.-C.I.O. no longer looked to the party for advice. Nor could their positions assist the party in its travail. Those leaders of the few left-led unions which had remained viable after expulsion from the C.I.O., rejected the party's advice to join the "mainstream," a term of contempt in their circles. Few of them participated in the agonizing reappraisal of 1956 or the discussions[60] preceding the Sixteenth National Convention in February, 1957. Nor did the one-time "influentials" take part. Most of them were by then to be found as supporters of the *National Guardian* and *Monthly Review*, and in many cases their private revolutionary pretensions increased in proportion as they separated from the party and often from any sort of political life.

The most striking evidence of the party's inability to recover from the 1956-1958 crisis was the experience of the Sixteenth National Convention which demonstratively proclaimed its readiness for a creative and independent Marxism, rejected the interference of the perennial Jacques Duclos and passed declarations such as few parties—until the great surge of polycentrism a decade later—were capable of doing. Nevertheless, the supporters of a new course also left the movement by the thousands, including most of the cadres formed in the 1930's and most of those who had piloted the movement from the "unavailable" category in 1951-1956. The reexaminationists won the convention. But they did not believe their movement was worth maintaining. They admitted this by their own exodus.[61] The center of gravity shifted back to the Old Guard simply because its adherents stayed to hold the franchise.

With a few years, many of the key leaders of the party's heyday had passed away, most of them within a short time span: Foster himself,[62] Elizabeth Gurley Flynn, Pettis Perry, Benjamin J. Davis, jr., Jack Stachel, Robert Thompson, and Eugene Dennis. The party's *eminence grise* on all phases of policy, Alexander Bitlelman, was expelled, after forty years, by those with whom he had been most close, because he persisted in seeking some way out of the ideological *cul de sac*.[63] Gus Hall now achieved a life-long ambition of becoming general secretary only to find that all his own energy plus intimate contact with the international movement did not make for American Communism's revival. The New Left which arose in the 1960's with such elemental force derived little inspiration from Communism. The discontinuity of the New Left from the orthodoxies of the earlier tradition has, paradoxically, been at once its most promising feature and perhaps also a contributing factor to its own volatility and decline.[64]

Yet if one returns to 1945 and examines the American Communists in the first postwar years, it is not immediately apparent why they suffered such a debacle. All the outward indications, if one eliminates the knowledge of hindsight, show a movement which not only restored itself after a severe crisis, but prospered despite difficulties. The immediate postwar years witnessed a malestrom of class struggle. In 1946, more than two million American workers, and in the most decisive industries such as coal, automobile, packinghouse, and the railways were on strike at almost the same time; one Communist labor expert noted that by contrast with the 1920-1921 experience, "not a single strike was lost."[65] Left-led unions actively took part and benefitted from the settlements even when they did not decide them. Within the C.I.O., President Philip Murray rejected the urgings of Social-Democratic and Catholic influences to divide the organization by a witch-hunt[66] against the Left Wing. The expulsion of the eleven left-led unions did not come until 1949-1950, and then only after Murray had been exasperated by the Wallace movement and the Left's opposition to the Marshall Plan. Although repressive measures were foreshadowed as early as March, 1947, by the government's executive order 9385, which forbade Communists to work in the public service (and this ban was soon extended to defense firms) it is also true that direct measures against the C.P. leadership do not come until mid-1948. The trial of the party's national board under the Smith Act occupied the whole of 1949, but the final verdict did not go into force until mid-1951. Proceedings against about 100 local Communist leaders did not come until much later. The McCarran Act, for example, which required registration of the party or Communist-influenced organizations as "foreign agents" was not passed until the Autumn of 1950 and was never really applied.

Until the outbreak of the Korean War in mid-1950, Communists did not face the ostracism, the pillorying and goring of individual members, sympathizers or alleged sympathizers that characterized the McCarthy era in the early 1950's. When Secretary of Labor Lewis Schwellenbach, proposed in March, 1947, to outlaw the party, many of Communism's opponents protested the idea as unconstitutional and unwise. The party raised $250,000 in twenty-five days for its self-defense. This feat was repeated a year later under the threat of the Mundt-Nixon Bill. Such resources suggest a vitality and a considerable sympathy from the non-Communist public, which was in fact characteristic of the first three postwar years.[67]

In terms of membership, the party had not only been reconstituted in the South, where it had been converted during the war into Peoples Educational Associations, but was reported higher than ever in its history.[68] At the Fourteenth National Convention, in August, 1948, Organizational Secretary Henry Winston disclosed that the reconversion of the loose, wartime structure now resulted in a party with 1,700 community clubs and 3,425 industrial clubs; of the latter 300 were factory cells. Some 200 professional and an equal number of student clubs existed. With a membership of "over 60,000," the report[69] continued, half were industrial workers. The Communist apparatus had roots in 600 cities, towns and rural communities, even if in large areas of the country it did not have even a toehold. The fact that half the members were not industrial workers did not militate, at the time, against the party's relative effectiveness; for it set itself in those years the building of an anti-monopoly coalition, and believed it was achieving this goal in Henry Wallace's Progressive party. The non-industrial membership certainly facilitated this ambitious effort.

Nor can it be said that with the expulsion of Browder the Communist leadership faced an "opposition" of the kind with which it had to contend in the case of Jay Lovestone or James P. Cannon; Browder did not form a competing movement. His trajectory was, in fact, very peculiar. In May, 1946, Browder demonstratively travelled to Moscow, was received by very high Soviet officials, and then took a post as distributor of Soviet literature; his activity was independent of the party, directed toward advocacy of American-Soviet friendship. In August, 1948, Browder tried to rejoin the party and was refused. As late as 1949 he negotiated with the party's lawyers as a possible witness in the Smith Act trial. Although a series of pamphlets from 1948 to 1950 disclose his increasing contempt for his erstwhile colleagues, it was not until well into the 1950's that Browder gave up the hope of some ultimate return, and began a critique of Communism on a basis which foreclosed such return. Thus, it was not because of serious competition from this direction that the post-Browder leadership had such difficulties; the major fire appears in 1946 to have been directed against "leftist" figures, several of whom were expelled that year. For all the cleansing of the movement of its "leftists," it was ironical that ten years later Dennis lamented the party had suffered primarily from "left-sectarian" errors.

Where then, did these fatal errors come from? Why was a movement which had found the *juste milieu* in its political line, and presumably recharged its political batteries having such an immensely difficult time, to be ultimately smashed up more by what it did to itself than by increasing governmental repression and public repudiation?

Detailed answers to these questions require much more documentation than is possible here. Even a cursory study suggests that these were the years in which the peculiar duality of structure—the existence of a formally-legal party combined with a wide body of influentials who were not avowed Communists—began to take its toll. The cohesion of the Communist movement came apart because it was essentially unable to legitimatize its most important cadres, and these cadres in turn were faced with problems to which the party leadership had no answer. The Communist hold in the labor movement began to weaken because the needs of the left-wing unionists ran in the direction of autonomy from the party's political objectives. Except in one or two unions, there was no solid corps of workers of Communist persuasion. The top leaders could only cling to their positions if they were not obliged to implement the party's dictates, especially on foreign policy issues. These left-wing unionists now found themselves subject not only to the inevitable bureaucratic problems of institutional life, but also subject to competition often from union leaders whom they had helped into strategic posts.

The National Maritime Union and the Automobile Workers Union offered examples. In the former, President Joseph Curran no longer needed the Left and was able to base himself on new strata of seamen to whom the Communist party's contribution in the formative years of the union was meaningless. In the latter case, an able ideological opponent, Walter Reuther, had won the U.A.W. presidency in 1946 but was surrounded for another year by an executive board hostile to him in which the Communists had influence not by any position of deep principle but by factional combinations. When these factional ties came apart, the party's operatives were quickly isolated.

Yet it must not be supposed that in its relations with its own influentials, the party was always in the position of counselling the more immoderate or headlong course. In 1946 and again in 1947, Dennis complained to his National Committee that the pressure for rupturing alliances with the Murray-Hillman leadership was coming from the left-wing unionists. At the July, 1946 meeting Dennis urged a continued united front relationship with the Center in the C.I.O., affirming that "our relations with the Murray-Hillman forces are not temporary, are not based on transitory considerations but are based on the long-range perspective of friendly collaboration for progressive aims. . . ." Dennis complained that

> . . .unfortunately not everyone in the Left-Wing grasps this. Unfortunately, there are even some Communists who have a cavalier attitude with respect to relations between the Center . . . and the Left Wing. . . . Unfortunately, even some Communists in the C.I.O. misjudge and distort the middle-of-the-road though generally progressive position of the Murray-Hillman forces. Instead of seeking to resolve tactical and similar dif ferences in a friendly fashion as between allies, some Leftwingers are frequently inclined to blow up each point of disagreement and every divergency of view into a major conflict, into a head-on collision. . . .[70]

One cannot grasp why the Wallace movement was such a crucial watershed for the Communist Left without crediting this inner tension between the party's operatives and the formal leadership. The precipitate decision to run Wallace as the head of a separate party rather than as a candidate within the Democratic party was, as will be shown, the result of a last-minute change by the Communists who during 1947 had been very reluctant to jeopardize their positions in the C.I.O. and doubted that a third party could be viable without the participation of center-led unions. Announcement of the Cominform and its call for world-wide militancy caused the change. Within this precipitate decision there was another determining element: many party influentials believed themselves to be better Communists than the leadership, and desired to overcome their own anomalous position; they saw in the Progressive party a possible refuge if they were ousted from positions in the labor movement, a possible vehicle for political self-expression more normal than what they had experienced as concealed C.P.'ers. Thus, while many unionists such as Michael Quill, of the Transport Workers Union, turned against the party because its demand that he support a third party jeopardized fifteen years of hard work and eminence within the C.I.O., other unionists welcomed the pending split within the C.I.O. They saw in it the chance to "go it alone," perhaps to make their control of unions a surrogate for the party in the anarcho-syndicalist tradition, or find for themselves a political expression which they could espouse without political penalty. Wallace's movement appeared to give that channel.

In essence, what undid the Communist party in the labor movement was the fatal, inner defect of the strategy of the "manipulated revolution" which had been adopted in 1922, the Leninist compulsion to gain strategic control. Unable to win adherents as an educational sect, and anxious to take part in real politics, the Communists had in fact gained important posts of control. But unable to legitimatize their supporters by changing the form and nature of their party as they started to do during the war, they found themselves forced in the Social-Democratic direction of giving their unionists autonomy at a moment when their Marxist-Leninist commitment was most vehemently affirmed. Refusing this course, the party imposed on its influentials tasks they could fulfill only at the price of their self-destruction. At the same time, the influentials imposed on the party tactics which the party leadership itself knew to be ruinous.[71] All factors in this unstable equation oscillated, veered in one direction and then another. By 1948, this tension became intolerable. By 1949, it was too late. With the failure of Wallace's third party, the Communist unionists were now either forced to accept the new relationship of forces within the C.I.O. and become minor factors within it, or in "going it alone" to increase their distance from the party proper and spurn its authority.

A second distinguishing feature of the immediate postwar years was the immense difficulty which the revitalized Communist leadership experienced in judging the dynamics of capitalism within their own country, as well as the process of maneuver and conflict within the international Communist movement.

Despite improved contacts with the world movements, the American Communists found themselves out of step with it, and tried fitfully to get into step. World Communism was in fact in ideological and strategic disarray between 1943 and 1947, and Stalin's moves in 1947-1948 which exacerbated the Cold War were efforts to overcome this disorder since it hindered Soviet objectives and made a synchronized prosecution of the Cold War more difficult. The American party's gyrations offer a mirror of this disarray.

The problem of judgment arose largely in three respects: the nature of the postwar confrontation between the United States and the Soviet Union and whether this could lead to early war, or a prolonged political tug-of-war, or some truce that involved partial settlements and a *de facto* coexistence; secondly, whether an early economic crisis was to be expected, and if so what measures the Communists would propose to avoid it; and third, whether the attack on the Left presaged a period of fascism, coinciding perhaps with war or with economic crisis, and by what means the Communists could make credible their readiness to defend democratic forms while preparing their own organization for the worst. On all three matters, the party was to admit, in the 1956 reappraisal, that its estimates had been wrong. But no particular probe was ever made as to why this had been so.

What impeded a detached, objective consideration of factual data and the weighing of alternatives which would have been the essence of a scientific approach was the dogmatic Communist commitment to the proposition that capitalism had entered a phase of rapid decay, that its ruling circles were united, that little short of a radical transformation within the United States could block the apocalyptic ending. Trapped in what was its ultimate and approaching dead-end—American monopoly—capitalism would go down fighting. Anything less than such a view involved the American Communists in what seemed some variety of the Browderism which they had just abandoned.

To suggest that the United States might in fact enjoy a very considerable postwar boom and that government intervention, including limited rearmament, could postpone or deflect the tendencies toward crisis ran counter to that fundamentalist creed about a doomed society that pervaded Communist thinking after 1945. In the next several years, Foster was to offer as his chief theoretical contribution a series of philippics against the theories of John Maynard Keynes; yet the program of the labor movement and of all the allies the Communists needed postulated a Keynsian governmental policy to countervail the innate tendencies of the system. The party inhibited itself from projecting policies short of putting "the axe to the root of the evil" for fear that in so doing the distinction between itself and others would be blurred. The Communists were, therefore, seeking an alliance, in fact nothing less than an anti-monopoly coalition which they believed the Wallace movement to be, while simultaneously proclaiming their disbelief in any of the ideas of "progressive capitalism" which Wallace projected and which were the concepts then prevailing throughout the labor movement. Rejecting any point of contact, in terms of ideas, with those whom they wanted as allies, it is not surprising that their own integrity as allies was discounted. To defend the right of Americans to be protected in their Communist beliefs also required a commitment to constitutional procedures. The record of the American Communists, not to mention Communists abroad, whom the C.P. defended so blindly, militated against the credibility of their professions in this regard.

As early as the Autumn of 1945, American Communist leaders began to speculate on a "war danger," the prospect of an early clash with the Soviet Union. The now reunited American capitalist class was presumably driven by its contradictions and its compulsion to dominate the world, and by its monopoly of the atomic bomb, to destroy the Socialist bloc. But the Communists found it difficult to advance any terms for a settlement or even a truce promised on the continuation of capitalism as a system. This appeared to undermine their own thesis that the war danger was in fact generated by capitalism itself. They came close to the proposition that only the overthrow of capitalism could insure world peace, which was not, of course, a tenable platform for an era of coexistence. Neither could they allow for existing or future differences within the ruling class. Any such suggestion rattled too many ideological skeletons in the closets of the very recent past.

Nor could any serious distinction be tolerated between the Democrats and the Republicans, since both were said to be embarked on a bipartisan foreign policy that precluded any settlement. The Communists, therefore, found it hard to deploy their own cadres within the two-party system although their positions in the labor movement allowed them precisely such a deployment. The party found itself precluded from offering any credible economic program, comparable to the Marshall Plan for example, as an alternative to an ever-growing war danger. The very concept of a compromise or even a truce in the Cold War, giving capitalism some economic viability in the process of peace, involved it in too many contradictions.

In the Autumn of 1946, the *Daily Worker* bitterly criticized Henry Wallace's Madison Square Garden Address in which the Secretary of Commerce proposed a sphere-of-influence settlement with Stalin. A few days later, upon Wallace's ouster from the cabinet, the Communists found themselves obliged to support him. Almost simultaneously, the party ideologists were thrown into turmoil[72] when Stalin himself, in the interview with Alexander Werth, decried the talk of war and denied that the ruling circles of the United States were planning war. The C.P.U.S.A. had been saying exactly the opposite for a year. Foster visited Europe in the Winter of 1946-1947 to discover that few Communist leaders agreed with his spectral vision of a rampant American imperialism, imposing its will at the risk of war, not even Jacques Duclos.[73]

Beginning with the Summer of 1947, Stalin was confronted both with a deadlock over Germany at the foreign minister's conference and a disarray in his own world movement. To conduct the Cold War with any efficacy required mobilizing the world movement and overcoming its disarray, bringing to a close the cautious policies in Eastern Europe and the themes of peaceful development among the western parties. Stalin vetoed the Czech and Polish readiness to join the Marshall Plan; the Communist Information Bureau was brought into being that Autumn; the Prague *coup* followed in February, 1948, and shortly after, the test of strength over Berlin began. By the middle of 1948, the Yugoslav Communists, hitherto pursuing a most "leftist" line almost alone, were expelled from the Socialist bloc and the allegations of a Titoist conspiracy was used to cleanse the Eastern European leadership of all but sycophants.

This entire trend militated against the success of Wallace's third party, which as a matter of fact the Communists had been reluctant to crystallize as an independent party. During 1947, they repeatedly said it could not succeed without more than left-wing labor support.[74] Yet they did help to precipitate it in November-December, 1947, in response to their interpretation of the Cominform's declarations. Having gambled their entire, hard-won position on a high Wallace vote, conceiving it as their contribution to the international confrontation, the U.S. Communists now celebrated the worsening of the Cold War as a proof that the international Communist movement had now caught up with them. Foster told his party's Fourteenth National Convention of his disappointment, when visiting London sixteen months earlier, that very few of the delegates from thirty-four countries to a conference of the British Empire Communist parties "indicated any sense of the real danger of war and fascism from American imperialism." Continuing in this vein, Foster said: "By indicating the world drive of American imperialism, with its implications of fascism and war, as we did very definitely and very clearly in our 1945 resolution, it appears to me that we did some international pioneering. In fact, our Party was among the first, if not the very first Party, to speak out clearly on the world drive of American imperialism and its accompanying dangers."[75]

This sense of having been justified by the sharpening of world tensions was reinforced by the doomsday mood resulting from the Foley Square trial as well as the collapse of the Left's positions after the defeat of the Progressive party. The main leaders of the C.I.O. now turned vindictively against their opponents, sensing their weakness just as the Truman administration gave short shrift to those who had done their best to make his 1948 victory as narrow as possible. Unable to reorient their movement either by major strategic changes and facing all the difficulties of tactical retreats, it was perhaps inevitable that their plight should be rationalized by a further development of apocalyptic themes.

It also became necessary to rationalize the partial settlement at Berlin and the new initiatives which the Communist movements were making in Western Europe, as well as the approaching victory of the Chinese Revolution. Even accepting the premise of an American drive to war over the previous years, how explain that this drive was *not* winning, that all the circumstances were favorable to the victory of peace? Foster now asserted that the obstacles confronting American imperialism were bound to make it more desperate. The war danger therefore increased if U.S. imperialism were unchecked, and also increased if it were checked.

Such a perspective was, of course, politically immobilizing. While the foremost American Communist leader thundered that the American people would "have to accept the logic of the situation," very few would be found that could make a political platform or a mode of political activism out of this Calvinistic sense of doom and perdition. The American Communists found it difficult to take part in the world-wide movement for peace with the new emphasis that peace *could be won*, and the increasing emphasis, even in foreign Communist circles, that no matter who started the Cold War, the time had come to stop it.

The American Communists had, as a matter of principle, refused any suggestion that some responsibility might have rested within their own camp. At the Progressive party's convention in July, 1948, the famous "Vermont Resolution" had been voted down with little thought either from Wallace supporters or Communist supporters as to what was being done. This resolution had asserted rather moderately that "although we are critical of the present foreign policy of the United States, it is not our intention to give blanket endorsement to the foreign policy of any nation." Nobody at the convention would vote for this pathetic disclaimer except three delegates from Vermont!

By 1949, the world Communist movement was accentuating the struggle for peace, indeed making it the major task;[76] the American Communists found themselves in the acute difficulty that their own propaganda had undermined their faith in the possibility of peace.[77] They were, in fact, preparing their movement for the "logic of the situation." They had painted themselves into an ideological corner, with the premise that peace could only be imposed on American imperialism, that the only distinction to be made about its ruling circles were between those who wanted war immediately and those who were willing to wait a while longer.[78]

Even the concept that the "peace camp" would impose coexistence on the United States did not remove, in their minds, the ideological stumbling block they had themselves created, namely, that American capitalism could accept peaceful solutions without fundamental changes within itself. Hobbled by such premises, a good part of their movement nonetheless tried desperately and valiantly (and not without some success) to collect signatures for the Stockholm Pledge and to build broader organizations than the diminished audience of the far Left itself. Unlike other countries, however, where the peace movement helped to revive or keep weaker political movements going, the same could not be said of the United States. Peace would have to be won despite the American Communists and without much help from them.

If the researcher into the party's history can come up with any other clue to the excruciating posture in which it found itself by 1950, apart from the grip of an hallucinatory view of politics, and the impossibility of maintaining the balance between its unavowed supporters (themselves at bay) and a legal party (under heavy attack) one would have to explore the inner tensions of the leadership itself. By contrast with other movements, Communism invariably proclaimed that it had the secret of cohesion and unity, even when its leaders had profound differences of opinion. The American Communists had gone through the withering experience of factionalism in the 1920's. Democratic centralism was supposed to oblige men and women who had opposing views to debate them but to accept the party's decision in the higher interest of maintaining a functioning organism.

It had been observed, however, that for all the expulsion of individuals (some of them eminent), no outward factions appear to have troubled the American Communists in the decade of their decline. This was perhaps exactly its dilemma and the secret of the decline itself. The factions existed but were repressed and hence had a more devastating effect. Having apparently united his movement after 1945, using all the men whom he had known as the staunchest supporters of Browder, Foster now had a certain leverage. His associates, many of whom had the gravest doubts about the party's course, were afraid to speak up for fear of being accused of residual Browderist tendencies. The extraordinary duality in the writings and behavior of the Communist leadership finds its explanation in this fact: the fear of being labelled as Browderist proved more paralyzing and more devastating to a great many men and women who knew their movement was being carried to its destruction than Browderism in its heyday. Democratic centralism, the unique cohesive force that presumably distinguished a Leninist party from all others, proved to be the straitjacket that kept the differences within the Communist ranks and leadership from being expressed in a way that might have been helpful. In reality, factions had been formed. The most powerful was led by Robert Thompson, secretary of the New York State organization and his closest associate, Benjamin J. Davis, jr., the most eminent black leader, and Foster himself. More dynamic, more determined and conscious of the self-imposed disadvantage in which the fear of Browderism placed their associates, they imposed their political line, even against the resistance, hesitation and better judgment of their colleagues. Herein lies the hidden story of the party's "underground," how it was decided and why it did not work.[79]

Once the movement entered the narrowing corridor of the 1950's, other factors coincided. A great many of the talented Negro leaders who had joined Communism because they saw in it the avenue of Negro liberation, were in despair as the Left Wing on which they counted seemed to fail them. Many departed. Others turned against their white comrades demanding purification of innate "white chauvinism" as though by some purging of their own personal faults they could somehow compensate for the party's let-down of Negro hopes. The "white chauvinism" campaign of the early 1950's, which paralyzed the dwindling party at a moment of all its other tribulations, ran its destructive course until Foster himself was obliged to stop it. This, too, was given its theoretical figleaf. The impotence of the American Left coincided with the advance of the colonial peoples, mostly peoples of color. It soon became fashionable in Communist ranks to suggest that the leading role in revolutionary change was now being taken over by American blacks. The classic position, namely that the working-class, both black and white, was the backbone and ramrod of change gave way to the primacy of the "black power." All of this, so familiar in the late 1960's in the New Left, had happened before. The fear of Browderism coupled with the fear of being accused of minimizing the importance of the Negro question was a potent combination. It inhibited all rational examination and resulted shortly in the destruction of that aspect of the American C.P. which had been its proudest claim, namely, that it was an integrated organization.

Not until 1956 did Eugene Dennis, in his review of the decade of crisis, disclose what all participants in the drama knew, namely, that the unity of the leadership had been fictitious. "As the attacks on the Party mounted," Dennis declared, "the unity of the Party itself was at stake," and "sharp political differences which arose in the leadership were often temporized and left unresolved for long periods. . . ."

IV

Taken as a whole, the American Communist party made a major effort to overcome its minor status. Its devotion to Marxism-Leninism did not spare it all the vicissitudes that confronted parties which made no claim to an effective ideology as the matrix of its organizational and political ambitions. Despite a wealth of practical experience, the American Communists thrashed about at the outer limits of what had become a dogma and were not able to escape its effects. Within a single decade they went through all the themes which were later to be recognized in the great schism within Communism represented by its Russian and Chinese variants. The C.P.U.S.A. had in fact a precocious and premature experience with these variants under Browder, and then under Foster. They were never able to stake out a single path and follow it to any logical conclusion. They did not choose any single course which the diverse experience of American and world revolutionary movements offered. Their story lies in having tried them all, and for many years pursued them at one and the same time.

NOTES

[1] Daniel Bell, *Marxian Socialism in the United States*, rev. ed., (Princeton, 1968).
[2] See Edmund Wilson, *The American Earthquake* (Garden City, 1968).
[3] J. B. S. Hardman and Maurice F. Neufeld, *The House of Labor* (New York, 1930). See also, Len DeCaux, *Labor Radical: from the Wobblies to the C.I.O.* (Boston, 1970); Theodore Draper, "Gastonia Revisited," *Social Research*, 38, No. 1, Spring, 1971.
[4] Nathan Glazer, *The Social Basis of American Communism* (New York, 1961).
[5] Arthur Goldberg, *A.F.L.-C.I.O. United* (New York, 1956); Arnold Beichman, *Christian Science Monitor*, Oct. 16, 1956.
[6] Theodore Draper, *The Rediscovery of Black Nationalism* (New York, 1970).
[7] Harry Haywood, *Negro Liberation* (New York, 1938).
[8] Wilson Record, "Race and Radicalism" (Ithaca, 1964).
[9] Wilson Record, *The Negro and the Communist Party* (Chapel Hill, 1951). Cf. John Williamson, *The Communist*, Oct. 1943.
[10] Harold Cruse, *The Crisis of the Negro Intellectual* (New York, 1967).
[11] William L. O'Neill, *Echoes of Revolt: The Masses* (Chicago, 1966). Also Joyce Kornbluth, *Voices of Revolt* (Chicago, 1966).
[12] Daniel Aaron, *Writers on the Left* (New York, 1961). Granville Hicks, *Where We Came Out* (New York, 1954) says that five of the original fifty-two signers of the "Culture and the Crisis" statement were anti-Communist by 1939, and only nine of the original group were to be found among the supporters of the Waldorf-Astoria peace conference in 1949.
[13] Arthur M. Schlesinger, jr. remarks, rather contemptuously, in his *The Age of Roosevelt: The Politics of Upheaval* (Boston, 1960): "For the discontented magazine writer, the guilty Hollywood scenarist, the aggrieved university instructor, the underpaid high school teacher, the politically inexperienced scientist, the intelligent clerk, the culturally aspiring dentist—as well as for a diminishing number of genuinely creative people—Marxism as a system of explanation and consolation carried great appeal."
[14] For a portrait of the student movement at that time, see Joseph P. Lash and James A. Wechsler, *War Our Heritage* (New York, 1936). Cf. also Harold L. Wilensky, *Intellectuals in Labor Unions* (Glencoe, Ill., 1956).
[15] Report of Attorney General Tom Clark, 1952. U.S. Senate Committee on the Judiciary, Hearings on S. 1832, 81 Cong. 1st sess., pt. 1.
[16] V. I. Lenin, "Report of the Fourth Congress of the Communist International," Nov. 13, 1922. Selected Works, Vol. X (New York, 1938): "At the Third Congress in 1921, we adopted a resolution on the organizational structure of the Communist Parties and on the methods and content of their work. The resolution is an excellent one, but it is almost thoroughly Russian, that is to say, everything is taken from Russian conditions. I have the impression that we made a big mistake with this resolution, namely that we have blocked our own road to further success. . . . The resolution is too Russian; it reflects Russian experience. That is why it is unintelligible to foreigners. But they cannot be content with hanging it in a corner like an icon and praying to it."
[17] Theodore Draper, *The Roots of American Communism* (New York, 1957) and *American Communism and Soviet Russia* (New York, 1960).
[18] Earl Latham, *The Communist Controversy in Washington* (Cambridge, 1966).
[19] This anecdote was told me by the former Canadian Communist leader, J. B. Salsberg.
[20] J. B. S. Hardman, an ex-Communist himself and later an authoritative writer on labor, quotes a one-time C.I. "rep," H. Walecki, a Polish mathematician, as saying: "Granted that the American Party is plainly crazy, still we must work with the material at hand." *New Republic*, a series of articles, Aug.-Sept., 1930.
[21] This attractive slogan was abandoned by 1939, evidently under Comintern pressure. Cf. *The Communist*, Dec. 1938.
[22] Kermit E. McKenzie, *Comintern and World Revolution* (New York, 1964).
[23] Eugene Dennis, *The Communists Take a New Look* (New York, 1956).
[24] John Gates, *The Story of an American Communist* (New York, 1958).
[25] For details on the contacts between the C.P.U.S.A., Moscow and foreign Communists after the Second World War, as well as in the experiment of 1944, see my book, *American Communism in Crisis* (Cambridge, 1972).

[26] The Workers' party nationwide vote in 1924 was 33,316; it was 48,228 in 1928, and reached a peak, as the Communist party, of 102,991 in 1932. In the 1936 campaign, it was 80,181 and 46,251 four years later.

[27] Philip Selznick, *The Organizational Weapon* (New York, 1952). Cf. also Frank S. Meyer, *The Moulding of Communists* (New York, 1961).

[28] Nathan Glazer, *The Social Basis of American Communism* (New York, 1961).

[29] One example would be the career of Henry Winston, a bootblack in a Tennessee town who became a Young Communist leader in the 1930's, was charged with the C.P.'s organizational secretaryship in the 1940's, and is now the C.P. chairman. See also Richard O. Boyer, *Pettis Perry: the Story of a Workingclass Leader* (New York, 1952).

[30] In the self-examination after the criticism by Jacques Duclos in the June-July, 1945 *Daily Worker* and particularly after this same paper opened its columns for discussion in the Spring of 1956, following Nikita Khrushchev's revelations about Stalin, there will be found the most revealing, searing details of inner party life. Gus Tyler in the *A.D.A. World*, Mar. 1957, called it "the soul-sickness of Communism." See also, Irving Howe and Lewis Coser, *The American Communist Party* (New York, 1962).

[31] Arthur Koestler, *Arrow in the Blue* (New York, 1961).

[32] Morris Ernst and David Loth, *Report on the American Communist* (New York, 1952) give this figure, although Howe and Coser consider it high and speak of "several hundred thousands."

[33] Theodore Draper, in his *Roots of American Communism*, uncovers the hitherto hidden story of Louis Fraina and his subsequent reincarnation as Lewis Corey.

[34] Nathan Glazer, *The Social Basis*, says the party doubled its membership in the first three years of the Depression, then doubled again in the first two years of the New Deal, and again in the next two years. By October, 1936, the majority of members were native born, "an important watershed" reached in New York by September, 1938.

[35] The C.P. converted itself into the Communist Political Association and experienced a large rise in a relatively new membership during the war, for example, two-thirds of the party in Michigan was newly recruited in 1944. John Williamson, organizational secretary, observed: "We cannot expect to be the same well-knit organization that we were when we were smaller and composed of a group of conscious and tested Communists." He also complained that "a small handful of loyal comrades" tend to "jell into an ever tighter group" and "without rest (keep) going themselves, trying to carry the entire load." *Political Affairs*, Apr., 1945. This was the group that reacted most bitterly and decisively, reversing the C.P.'s course after the criticism from abroad in mid-1945.

[36] This was Foster's view in Apr., 1922, after his first contact with Moscow and the Profintern (the Red International of Trade Unions) to whose congress he has gone on the urging of his colleague, Earl Browder. See Theodore Draper's "The Manipulated Revolution" in *The Roots of American Communism.*

[37] Kenneth Boulding, in *The Organizational Revolution* (New York, 1953) says: "The unforgivable sin of the Communists is that they regard the union as a means to gain their own ends and not as an organization with its own life and purposes." This observation points up the dilemma although it was not entirely fair to many Communist unionists. They did regard the trade union as "an organization with its own life and purposes" but were confronted with the problem of how to square this devotion with another loyalty–to the party which had urged them to go into the unions. This proved particularly acute in the 1948 Wallace campaign and in the battle against the Marshall Plan. Many Communists resolved the dilemma by separating from the party.

[38] See my *American Communism in Crisis* (Cambridge, 1972).

[39] Earl Browder, *Teheran and America* (New York, 1944). This was Browder's report to the Jan., 1944 meeting of the C.P.'s national committee where the change to the Communist Political Association was first proposed.

[40] See my article in *Foreign Affairs*, July, 1969, "Origins of the Cold War: the Communist Dimension."

[41] Earl Browder, *Teheran and America.*

[42] After four trials in which Bridges was charged with perjury for denying C.P. membership, the government gave up. Bridges never denied his accessibility to the party and close connection with it; his orientation always remained, however, syndicalist rather than Marxist. C.f. Compare Charles P. Larrowe, *Harry Bridges: The Rise and Fall of Radical Labor in the United States* (New York, 1972).

[43] Roy Hudson, responsible for trade union work, wrote in the discussion pamphlet, *Shall the Communist Party Change its Name?* "It has not always been possible for Communists in some industries to fully make their influence felt as Communists. . . . However, if the change of name . . . helps us to achieve those changes in our relationship with broader Labor forces it will also soon—and very soon—create those conditions where every Communist trade unionist will be able to contribute a maximum in helping to determine our policies . . . and if this comes about . . . it will be very important indeed."

[44] Earl Browder, *Teheran and America.*

[45] Foster's letter of Jan. 20, 1944, was reprinted in *Political Affairs*, July, 1945.

[46] In the Columbia University Oral History Project, there will be found an extended interview by myself with Earl Browder, as of 1965. Browder reveals (for the first time to my knowledge) that he himself sent to Georgi Dimitrov, the outgoing general secretary of the Communist International, all the documentation on his differences with Foster, including Foster's letter and Darcy's remarks. Browder received a message from Dimitrov urging Foster not to press his differences. Browder shrugged his shoulders when I asked why he felt obliged to communicate with Dimitrov, ten months after the dissolution of the International! This was consistent with the long-time practice. Thus, Foster did not press the point because Dimitrov urged him not to. Browder did not press for disciplinary measures against Foster for the same reason. Browder felt fortified by Dimitrov's support, although he also received a congratulatory letter from another power in the C.I., Andre Marty. The documentation got to Moscow not by Foster's guile or persistance but because Browder sent it there, which means that Duclos could not have known of all this, except via Moscow.

[47] The Duclos article was published in the Apr., 1945 issue of the French theoretical magazine, *Cahiers du Communisme.* Internal evidence suggests it was written before Roosevelt's death in mid-April but after the Yalta conference in February. It did not reach the American Communist leaders until early in May, and was published in the *Daily Worker* on May 24, 1945, several days after it appeared in the New York *World Telegram.*

[48] For example, the N.Y. Teachers Union leader, Bella Dodd.

[49] In *The Communist*, Apr., 1944, the Ohio secretary, Arnold Johnson, gave an enthusiastic appraisal of the C.P.A.'s prospects. In a twelve week recruiting drive, 1,233 new members had joined and the movement was at its membership peak. Browder shared the platform at a Cleveland meeting with Democratic and Republican councilmen, and some Negro political figures joined the C.P.A. "We have brought into our ranks a far larger number of trade union leaders, especially local officers, shop stewards and others," Johnson wrote, adding that "of the several thousand who were visited only a handful of 'professional sympathizers' shook their heads in skepticism" at the new Communist line.

Entirely unpublicized, however, were Browder's discussions with Wendell Willkie, the maverick industrialist who had been the Republican nominee for president in 1940, and who during the war actively discussed a realignment of both parties along liberal-conservative lines with Roosevelt himself. Browder denies ever having met the president. But he did latch on to the Willkie-Roosevelt negotiations. By this time, Willkie had helped win the important Schneiderman decision in the Supreme Court which upheld the advocacy of Socialism as within the terms of the First Amendment. In March, 1945, the C.P.A. contributed $5,000 to the Freedom House memorial to Willkie who had passed away the previous year.

[50] Joseph Stalin, *For Victory and Enduring Peace* (New York, 1944).

[51] Newspapermen *en route* to San Francisco on a specially arranged train which the State Department provided—I was among them—were aware that Ambassador Harriman was briefing selected correspondents, stressing the theme that American and Soviet interests were "irreconcilable." Roy Howard, publisher of the Scripps-Howard papers, exclaimed at one such off-the-record briefing that if this were true "the United States should be helping Japan, instead of urging Russia to enter the war against Japan."

[52] Stenograms of the May and June, 1945 meetings of the C.P.A.'s top bodies are in the private collection of Philip J. Jaffe.

[53] For the English translation of the Duclos article, see the *Daily Worker*, May 24, 1945.

[54] Browder, Foster and Eugene Dennis met secretly in Washington with two important French Communist leaders, Francois Billoux, then minister of health and a member of France's delegation to the U.N., and Benoit Frachon, a secretary of the French Confederation of Labor, also *en route* to San Francisco for a W.F.T.U. meeting. Both were silent when Browder complained that the tone

of the Duclos article implied that his removal from leadership was being demanded. The fact of this meeting was mentioned in Browder's remarks during the argument with his colleagues. But when these remarks were published in mid-July, it was said that Browder, Foster and Dennis had met with "two trade unionists." The party did not know that its top leaders had conferred with the closest co-workers of Duclos.

[55] This figure is given by Eugene Dennis, in his report to the February, 1946 National Committee meeting. See *What America Faces* (New York, 1946). By then, recruiting drives had brought the membership up to over 60,000. Robert Thompson complained in *Political Affairs*, Jan., 1946, that many veterans of the war "including a few former leading party *actives*" were not returning to activity, and he cited reasons for this "underlying . . . doubts about the correctness of the Party's role, underestimation of the urgency of the problems confronting our Party and the labor movement."

[56] One of the few books on this decade, by David A. Shannon, is entitled *Decline of American Communism* (New York, 1959). See also Irving Howe and Lewis Coser, *The American Communist Party* rev. ed. (New York, 1963).

[57] Eugene Dennis, *The Communists Take a New Look* (New York, 1956).

[58] This estimate is given by the last *Daily Worker* editor, and leader of the re-examinationist group, John Gates, *The Story of an American Communist* (New York, 1958).

[59] How this came about, see Gates, *ibid.* In the 1960's, the party resumed a daily paper, *The Daily World*. On the West coast, the *People's World*, a daily until the mid-1950's, is now a weekly. Both papers circulate in less than ten thousand copies.

[60] On the West coast, prominent left-wing leaders talked of founding a new party in those years, without ever doing anything of the kind. Essentially dinner-table conversation, such talk was also a measure of their refusal to take responsibility for the party which had nurtured them at the point when it needed them.

[61] For a poignant portrait, see George Charney, *A Long Journey* (Chicago, 1968).

[62] Foster, who was partly paralyzed, insisted on travelling to Moscow, preferring to die there rather than in his own land. Edmund Wilson, watching Foster's impressive bearing at a Fish Committee hearing, mused on "why I should have been so stirred by Foster's appearance" and then noted (*New Republic*, Dec. 24, 1930) that "an element appears in his language which is quite alien to anything which has hitherto been characteristic of the militant American workingman—it is the idiom of Russian Communism." Foster was carried to his grave by Soviet leaders, already then in deep conflict with the Chinese Communists. They could not have realized the ironic fact that only a few years earlier, Foster had written to Mao Tse-tung, hailing him as the foremost Marxist since Stalin and expressing a desire to visit Peking. After the Sino-Soviet split became public, *People's Daily*, in Peking, Mar. 8, 1963, criticized the American C.P.'s pro-Moscow line, and said its leaders "can show that they really understand their international obligations and are fulfilling them, if they carry on and enrich the revolutionary tradition of Comrade Foster." Cf. my article in Leo Labedz, ed. *International Communism after Khrushchev* (Cambridge, 1965). Miss Flynn and Pettis Perry also died while visiting Moscow.

[63] For Bittelman's effort to relate Socialism to the welfare state and peaceful coexistence, see the book which he printed privately in 1960 when the party refused it publication, *A Communist Views America's Future*.

[64] Gilbert Green, *The New Radicalism: Anarchist or Marxist?* (New York, 1971) reveals the current dilemmas of the Communist party in grappling with the radical youth.

[65] Harold Simon, *Political Affairs*, June, 1946.

[66] For Murray's refusal in 1946, see Curtis MacDougall, *Gideon's Army* (New York, 1965), I. The irritation of the anti-Communists with Murray is well expressed in Max Kampelman, *The Communist Party and the C.I.O.* (New York, 1957).

[67] Communist candidates for local offices received comparatively high votes: A. R. Krchmarek, running for the school board in Cleveland, got 64,264 votes in 1947; William Harrison, in a race for the Massachusetts legislature in 1946, got 3,124 votes, or one-sixth of the total; Archie Brown, in a write-in vote for the California governorship in 1946 got 22,206 votes.

[68] N. Ross, *Political Affairs*, Oct., 1947.

[69] Henry Winston, *Political Affairs*, Sept., 1948.

[70] Eugene Dennis, *Political Affairs*, Sept., 1946.

[71] At the C.I.O. convention in October, 1946, left-wing unionists supported a resolution brought in by a committee under Michael Quill, the famous "resent and reject" declaration affirming that no

interference from outside organizations such as the Communist party would be tolerated. This was a milestone in the increasing tension of the party's influentials, and increased the "credibility gap" for them among rank and file workers as well as political opponents.
[72]Max Weiss, in *Political Affairs*, Nov., 1946, grappled with the meaning of Stalin's declaration and had the utmost difficulty squaring the C.P.'s emphasis with Stalin's realistic judgment.
[73]Foster made no mention of his encounter with Duclos in *The New Europe* (New York, 1947) but the Canadian Communist leader, Tim Buck, who accompanied Foster, showed no such reticence. His own account, *Europe's Rebirth* (Toronto, 1947) describes the Duclos rebuke to Foster plainly.
[74]At the June, 1947 National Committee meeting, John Gates, among others, warned against any attempt to crystallize a third party unless there were a substantial breakaway in the Democratic party and support for a third party by unions such as the Amalgamated Clothing Workers or the United Automobile Workers. Many supporters of Wallace, for example, former attorney general of California, Robert Kenny, wanted Wallace to enter Democratic primaries and come to the Democratic convention as a candidate. At a meeting between Kenny and Foster in the Autumn of 1947, the Communist leader seemed impressed with this strategy. There appears to be no realistic explanation of the party's switch in the late Fall of 1947 other than the impact on it of the formation of the Information Bureau and a feeling that a decisive stage in the Cold War was being reached which required a dramatic contribution on their part. Cf. Curtis MacDougall, *Gideon's Army*. For detailed analysis of this switch, see my own book, *American Communism in Crisis*.
[75]William Z. Foster, *Political Affairs*, Sept., 1948.
[76]The new phase of the peace campaign was ushered in with a declaration by the Italian Communist leader, Palmiro Togliatti, and his French counterpart, Maurice Thorez, to the effect that if the Soviet armies, in the course of pursuing an aggressor, had to enter France or Italy, the peoples of those countries would not fight against the Russians. In effect, the western Communists lent themselves to the threat of civil war at the moment when the North Atlantic Treaty Organization was taking shape. The Togliatti-Thorez initiative was rapidly taken up by Communist parties everywhere, including those to whom it could not conceivably apply, in Latin America and even Australia! The American Communist leaders, Foster and Dennis, felt constrained to support this declaration with variations appropriate to the American scene. This came during the Foley Square trial and evoked the retort from President Truman that the C.P. leaders were "traitors."
[77]Only in 1949 did articles begin to appear in the American Communist press, seriously arguing the case for coexistence. The foreign editor of *L'Humanité*, Pierre Courtade, visiting the U.N. in 1949, was charged with bringing the American C.P.'s draft theses for its Fifteenth National Convention for the approval of Jacques Duclos. Courtade returned with the word that the French C.P. was struck by the absence of any real emphasis on coexistence.
[78]As late as Apr. 8, 1955—after Stalin's death, and after the Indo-China and Bandung peace conferences and the general thaw of that time—William Z. Foster was still arguing in the *Daily Worker* about the "war now-war later" division in the American ruling class.
[79]Cf. "How the Die Was Cast, and Other Skeletons," in my book, *American Communism*.

Appendix

DECLARATION OF THE AMERICAN DELEGATION TO THE SECOND CONGRESS OF THE COMINTERN
Moscow, July 24, 1920

The Bureau has received the following declaration from the American delegation, addressed to the Second Congress of the Communist International:

"In accordance with the decision of the Executive Committee of the Communist International, and the requirements of the American Communist movement itself, it is necessary to unite the two Communist Parties.

Accordingly we greet the formation of a united Communist Party, composed of the Communist Labour Party and a substantial portion of the Communist Party. But this unity is not complete.

The complete unification of the American Communist movement being imperative, we, delegates of the Communist Party and the Communist Labour Party agree:

(1)   To work as one group in the Congress.

(2)   To call upon the Executive Committee of the International to intervene again, in mandatory fashion, to compel any elements who may resist complete unity, to unite on the basis of the International.

(3)   To abide by the decisions of the Executive Committee of the International on the question of unity."

Communist Party of America:

Louis C. Fraina.
Alexander Stokiltsky.

Communist Labour Party of America:

John Reed.
John Jurgis.
Alexander Bilan.

JOHN REED AND LOUIS C. FRAINA ON
"THE NATIONAL AND COLONIAL QUESTIONS"
Moscow, July 26, 1920

The following "Supplementary Theses on the National and Colonial Questions" were made at the Second Congress of the Communist International by two American delegates.

REED—There are ten million negroes in America, mostly concentrated in the Southern States; but of late years many thousands have gone North. The negroes in the North are in industry, while the greater part of the Southern negroes are agricultural workers or small tenant farmers. The position of the negroes especially in the Southern States is a terrible one. They are barred from all political rights. The sixteenth amendment of the Constitution of the United States grants the negroes full citizenship. Most Southern States, however, disenfranchise the negroes. In others in which the negroes may legally vote they do not dare to do so.

Negroes cannot travel in the same cars with white men, enter the same hotels and restaurants, or live in the same parts of the towns. There are separate and inferior schools for negroes and separate churches. This segregation of the negroes is called the "Jim Crow" system, and the ministers of Southern churches preach a "Jim Crow" heaven. In industry the negroes are unskilled workers. Until recently they were excluded from most unions of the American Federation of Labour. The I.W.W., of course, organised the negroes. The old Socialist Party did not seriously attempt to organise the negroes. In some states negroes were not admitted to the Party at all, in others they were organised in separate branches; and in the Southern States generally the Party constitutions forbade the use of Party funds for the propaganda among negroes.

The negro in the South generally has no right in the Law, and no protection from it. Negroes can be killed by white men with impunity. The great institution of the Southern white men is the lynching of negroes. This consists in mobbed murder, which commonly takes the form of drenching the negro with oil, hanging him to a telegraph pole, and setting him on fire. The entire population of the town, men, women, and children, come out to see the show, and carry home pieces of the negro's clothing and flesh as souvenirs.

I have too short a time to give the historical background of the negro problem in the United States. Descendents of a slave population, the negroes were emancipated while still politically and economically undeveloped—as a military measure in the Civil War. They were then given full political rights, in order to create a vicious class war in the South, which would prevent the development of Southern capitalism until the Northern capitalists had seized the resources of the country.

The negro displayed no aggressive consciousness of race until recently. The first awakening of the negroes came after the Spanish American War, in which the black regiments fought with extreme bravery, and returned home with the sense of equality as men with the white soldiers. Up to this time the only movement among the negroes had been a sort of semi-philanthropic educational movement, headed by Booker T. Washington, supported by the white capitalists, consisting in the establishment of schools to train the negroes to be good servants in industry, and mentally to train them to reconcile to the position of a subject people. Following the Spanish War there is an aggressive reform movement among the negroes, demanding social and political equality with the whites.

The outbreak of the European War sent half a million negroes, drafted into the American Army, to France, where, brigaded with the French troops, they found themselves suddenly considered as equals of white soldiers, socially and in every other way. American General Headquarters sent an order to the French Command asking that the negroes be excluded from all places frequented by white men and be treated as inferiors.

Returning from the war, after this experience, many of the negroes being decorated for gallantry by the French and Belgian Governments, the negroes went back to their Southern villages and were lynched because they had dared to wear their uniforms and decorations in the streets.

At the same time a tremendous movement was taking place among the negroes who remained. Thousands of them went North into the war industries, and there came in contact with the broad stream of the Labour movement. The high wages paid were more than offset by the immensely high prices of the necessities of life, and, moreover, the negroes revolted against speeding up, against the merciless driving to work, much quicker than the white workers, who had been used to the terrible exploitation for years.

The negroes went on strike with the white workers, and rapidly became identified with the industrial proletariat. They proved extremely susceptible to revolutionary propaganda. At this time was founded a magazine called the "Messenger," edited by a young negro Socialist named Randolph, which combined Socialist propaganda with appeals to the race consciousness of the negroes to defend themselves against the brutal attacks of the whites. This magazine, however, urged the closest possible union with the white workers, even though the white workers sometimes took part in pogroms against the negroes, pointing out that it was the capitalists who maintained race antagonism of both blacks and whites for capitalist interests.

The return of the army from the war threw immediately four million white workers on the labour market. Unemployment immediately followed, and the impatience of the demobilised soldiers grew so formidable that the employers were forced to turn this discontent away from themselves by telling the soldiers that their places had been taken by the negroes—thus provoking massacres of the negroes by the white workers.

The first of these outbreaks occurred in the national capital, Washington, where the petty Government office holders came back from the war to find their places occupied by negroes. Most of these office holders were Southerners anyway. They organised night attacks upon the negro quarters in order to terrorise the negroes into surrendering their positions. To the astonishment of everyone, the negroes poured into the streets fully armed, and a battle raged during which the negroes boasted that they killed three white men to every negro murdered. Several months later another riot broke out in Chicago, which lasted for several days, many negroes and white men being killed. Still a third massacre took place in Omaha later. In all those fights, for the first time in history, the negroes showed that they were armed, well organised, and absolutely unafraid of the whites. The effect of the negro resistance was in the first place belated Government interference, and in the second place the opening of the labour unions of the American Federation of Labour to negro workers.

Among the negroes themselves a great racial consciousness arose. There was and is among the negroes now a section which advocates armed insurrection against the whites. Defence societies were organised everywhere by the returned negro soldiers for resistance to white lynchers. But while the Communists should energetically support the negro defence movement, they should discourage all ideas of a separate armed insurrection of the negroes. Many people think that a negro rising would be the signal for the general Revolution in America. We know that without the co-operation of the white proletariat it would be the signal for the counter-revolution.

The "Messenger" rapidly increased in circulation, with its tone of outright defiance, until at present more than 150,000 copies a month are distributed. At the same time Socialist ideas rapidly spread and are spreading among the negroes in industry.

Considered as an oppressed and subject people, the negroes present a twofold problem: that of a strong racial and social movement, and of a proletarian labour movement advancing very fast in class-consciousness. The negroes have no demands for national independence. All movements aiming at a separate national existence for negroes fail, as did the "Back to Africa Movement" of a few years ago. They consider themselves first of all Americans at home in the United States. This makes it very much simpler for the Communists.

The policy of the American Communists towards the negroes should be primarily to consider the negroes as workers. The agrarian workers and tenant farmers of the South present problems identical to those of the white agrarian proletariat, although the negroes are extremely backward. Among the negro industrial workers of the North Communist propaganda can be spread. In both sections of the country, among all negroes, every effort must be made to organise them in the labour unions with the white workers, as the best and quickest means of breaking down race prejudice and developing class solidarity. But the Communists must not stand aloof from the negro movement for social and political equality, which in the present growth of racial consciousness enlists the negro masses. The Communists must use this movement to point out the futility of bourgeois equality, and the necessity of the Social Revolution, not only to free all workers from servitude, but also as the only means of freeing the negroes as a subject people.

FRAINA–The previous speaker spoke of the negroes as a subject people in the United States, but we have two other kind of subject peoples–the foreign workers and the peoples in the colonies.

The terrible suppression of strikes and revolutionary movements in the United States is not a consequence of the war, but an intensified political expression of the previously existing attitude towards the unorganised unskilled workers. The strikes of these workers were brutally crushed. Why? Because these unorganised unskilled workers are mostly foreigners (constituting about 60 per cent. of the industrial proletariat), and the foreign workers in the United States are practically in the status of colonial peoples. After the Civil War (1861-1865) capitalism developed rapidly; the great undeveloped West was opened by the trans-continental railway system. The investment capital for this development came from the Eastern states and Europe; while immigrants became the human raw material precisely as the peoples in a backward colonial country are being "developed" by an imperialistic force.

Concentration of industry and monopoly arose–all the typical conditions of an internal imperialism, before the United States developed its external imperialism.

The horrors practised upon colonial peoples are not worse than those practised upon foreign workers in the United States. For example, in 1912 there was a miners' strike in Ludlow; soldiers were used and the miners thrown out of their homes, being compelled to live in tents. One day, while the men were some miles away fighting with the mine-guards, a contingent of soldiers surrounded the tents, set them afire, hundreds of women and children being burned to death. Under these conditions the class struggle in the United States partly assumes a racial form. Precisely as in the case of a negro revolt being the signal not for the proletarian revolution but for the bourgeois counter-revolution, so in the case of a revolt of the foreign workers. The great task is to unite these with the American workers in one revolutionary movement.

The whole of Latin America must be considered as a colony of the United States, and not simply the actual colonies, such as the Philippines, etc., in Central America; the United States is in complete control by means of an army of occupation. But this control also exists in Mexico and North America, exercised in two ways: (1) By means of economic and financial penetration, all the more powerful since the expropriation of German interests in these countries; (2) by means of the Monroe Doctrine, which from its original form of protecting the Americans from monarchical schemes, has been transformed into an instrument to assure the supremacy of United States Imperialism in Latin America. One year before the war President Wilson interpreted the Monroe Doctrine as giving the American Government power to prevent British capitalists acquiring new oil wells in Mexico. In other words, Latin America is the colonial basis of the imperialism of the United States. The economic conditions in the rest of the world become more and more disturbed; the imperialism of the United States recoups itself by increasing the exploitation and development of Latin America. It is necessary to strike at this imperialism by developing revolutionary movements in Latin America precisely as it is necessary to strike at British Imperialism by developing revolutionary movements in its colonies. The movement in the United States has up till now paid no attention to the Latin American movement, with the consequence that this movement ideologically depends upon Spain instead of the United States. The Latin American movement must be liberated from this dependence, as well as from its Syndicalist prejudices. The American Federation of Labour and reactionary Socialist Party are trying to arrange pan-American organisations, but these are not for revolutionary purposes. The Communist movement in the United States in particular, and the Communist International in general, must actively intervene in the Latin American movement. The movement in the United States and in Latin America must be considered as one movement, war strategy and tactics must be envisaged in terms of the American Revolution, comprising the whole of the Americas, a fundamental task of the Communist International, the accomplishment of which alone will assure the World Revolution, is the destruction of United States Imperialism; and this destruction is possible only by means of a gigantic revolutionary movement embracing the whole of the Americas, each national unit of which subordinates itself to the unified problems of the American Revolution.

THE COMINTERN ON THE NEGRO QUESTION
1928

The following is from "The Revolutionary Movement in the Colonies and Semi-Colonies," a thesis adopted by the Sixth World Congress of the Communist International held in Moscow, July-August 1928.

THE NEGRO QUESTION

39. In connection with the colonial question, the Sixth Congress draws the close attention of the Communist Parties to the negro question. The position of the negroes varies in different countries and accordingly requires concrete investigation and analysis. The territories, in which compact negro masses are to be found, can be divided according to their general features into the following groups:

(i) The United States and some South American countries, in which the compact negro masses constitute a minority in relation to the white population.

(ii) The Union of South Africa, where the negroes are the majority in relation to the white colonists.

(iii) The negro States which are actually colonies or semi-colonies of imperialism (Liberia, Haiti, San-Domingo).

(iv) The whole of Central Africa divided into the colonies and mandated territories of various imperialist Powers (Great Britain, France, Portugal, etc.). The tasks of the Communist Parties have to be defined in their dependence on the concrete situation.

In the United States are to be found 12 million negroes. The majority of them are tenants, paying rent in kind and living under semi-feudal and semi-slave conditions. The position of these negro tenant farmers is exactly the same as that of agricultural labourers, being only formally distinguishable from the slavery that the constitution is supposed to have abolished. The white landowner, uniting in one person, landlord, merchant and usurer, employs the lynching of negroes, segregation and other methods of American bourgeois democracy, reproducing the worst forms of exploitation of the slavery period. Owing to the industrialisation of the South a negro proletariat is coming into existence. At the same time, the emigration of the negroes to the North continues at an ever-increasing rate, where the huge majority of negroes become unskilled labourers. The growth of the negro proletariat is the most important phenomenon of recent years. At the same time there arises in the negro quarters—the negro ghetto—a petty bourgeoisie, from which is derived a stratum of intellectuals and a thin stratum of bourgeoisie, the latter acting as the agent of imperialism.

One of the most important tasks of the Communist Party consists in the struggle for a complete and real equality of the negroes, for the abolition of all kinds of racial, social and political inequalities. It is the duty of the Communist Party to carry on the most energetic struggle against any exhibition of white chauvinism, to organise active resistance against lynching, to strengthen its work among negro proletarians, to draw into its ranks the most conscious elements of the negro workers, to fight for the acceptance of negro workers in all organisations of white workers, and especially in the trade unions (which does not exclude, if necessary, their organisation into separate trade unions), to organise the masses of peasants and agricultural workers in the South, to carry on work among the negro petty bourgeois tendencies such as "Garveyism" and to carry on a struggle against the influence of such tendencies in the working class and peasantry. In those regions of the South in which compact negro masses are living, it is essential to put forward the slogan of the "Right of Self-determination for Negroes." A radical transformation of the agrarian structure of the Southern States is one of the basic tasks of the revolution. Negro Communists must explain to non-negro workers and peasants that only their close union with the white proletariat and joint struggle with them against the American bourgeoisie can lead to their liberation from barbarous exploitation and that only the victorious proletarian revolution will completely and permanently solve the agrarian and national questions of the Southern United States in the interests of the overwhelming majority of the negro population of the country.

JOSEPH STALIN
SPEECH ON THE AMERICAN COMMUNIST PARTY
May 6, 1929

The speech which follows was delivered in the American Commission of the Presidium of the Executive Committee of the Communist International.

Comrades, since quite a few speeches have been delivered here and the political position of both groups in the Communist Party of the United States of America has been sufficiently clarified, I do not intend to speak at great length. I shall not deal with the political position of the leaders of the majority and the minority. I shall not do so since it has become evident during the course of the discussion that both groups are guilty of the fundamental error of exaggerating the specific features of American capitalism. You know that this exaggeration lies at the root of every opportunist error committed both by the majority and the minority group. It would be wrong to ignore the specific peculiarities of American capitalism. The Communist Party in its work must take them into account. But it would be still more wrong to base the activities of the Communist Party on these specific features, since the foundation of the activities of every Communist Party, including the American Communist Party, on which it must base itself, must be the general features of capitalism, which are the same for all countries, and not its specific features in any given country. It is on this that the internationalism of the Communist Party is founded. Specific features are only supplementary to the general features. The error of both groups is that they exaggerate the significance of the specific features of American capitalism and thereby overlook the basic features of American capitalism which are characteristic of world capitalism as a whole. Therefore, when the leaders of the majority and the minority accuse each other of elements of a Right deviation, it is obviously not without some measure of truth. It cannot be denied that American conditions form a medium in which it is easy for the American Communist Party to be led astray and to exaggerate the strength and stability of American capitalism. These conditions lead our comrades from America, both the majority and the minority, into errors of the type of the Right deviation. Owing to these conditions, at times one section, at others, the other section, fails to realize the full extent of reformism in America, underestimates the left-ward swing of the working class and, in general, is inclined to regard American capitalism as something apart from and above world capitalism. That is the basis for the unsteadiness of both sections of the American Communist Party in matters of principle.

Having made these general observations, let us now pass to practical political questions.

What are the main defects in the practice of the leaders of the majority and the minority?

Firstly, that in their day-to-day work they, and particularly the leaders of the majority, are guided by motives of unprincipled factionalism and place the interests of their faction higher than the interests of the Party.

Secondly, that both groups, and particularly the majority, are so infected with the disease of factionalism that they base their relations with the Comintern, not on the principle of confidence, but on a policy of rotten diplomacy, a policy of diplomatic intrigue.

Let us take a few examples. I will mention such a simple fact as the speculations made by the leaders both of the majority and the minority regarding the differences within the Communist Party of the Soviet Union. You know that both groups of the American Communist Party, competing with each other and chasing after each other like horses in a race, are feverishly speculating on existing and non-existing differences within the C.P.S.U. Why do they do that? Do the interests of the Communist Party of America demand it? No, of course not. They do it in order to gain some advantage for their own particular faction and to cause injury to the other faction. Foster and Bittelman see nothing reprehensible in declaring themselves "Stalinites" and thereby demonstrating their loyalty to the C.P.S.U. But, my dear comrades, that is disgraceful. Do you not know that there are no "Stalinites," that there must be no "Stalinites"? Why does the minority act in this unseemly fashion? In order to entrap the majority group, the group of Comrade Lovestone, and to prove that the Lovestone group is opposed to the C.P.S.U. and, hence, to the basic nucleus in the Comintern. That is, of course, incorrect. It is irresponsible. But the minority cares nothing about that; their chief aim is to ensnare and discredit the majority in the interests of the faction of the minority.

And how does the Lovestone group act in this connection? Does it behave more correctly than the minority group? Unfortunately, not. Unfortunately, its behavior is even more disgraceful than that of the minority group. Judge for yourselves. The Foster group demonstrate their closeness to the C.P.S.U. by declaring themselves "Stalinites." Lovestone perceives that his own faction thereby may lose something by this. Therefore, in order not to be outdone, the Lovestone group suddenly performs a "hair raising" feat and, at the American Party Congress,[1] carries through a decision calling for the removal of Comrade Bukharin from the Comintern. And so you get a game of rivalry on the principle of who will outdo whom. Instead of a fight on principles you get the most unprincipled speculation on the differences within the C.P.S.U.

Such are the results of a policy which places the interests of faction higher than the interests of the Party.

Another example. I refer to the case of Comrade Pepper. You are all more or less acquainted with that case. Twice the Comintern demanded Comrade Pepper's return to Moscow. The Central Committee of the American Communist Party resisted and, in fact, ignored a number of decisions of the Executive Committee of the Communist International regarding Pepper. Thereby the majority of the American Communist

---

[1] Comrade Stalin speaks here of the Sixth Convention held in 1929.

Party demonstrated its fellowship with Pepper, whose opportunist vacillations everybody knows. Finally, a delegation from the Executive Committee of the Communist International sent to the 6th Congress of the American Communist Party, advances again, in the name of the Executive Committee of the Communist International, the immediate recall of Comrade Pepper. The majority under the leadership of Lovestone and Gitlow again resists this demand and does not find it necessary to carry out the decision of the E.C.C.I. Foster's group utilizes this situation against the Lovestone group, stating that the majority group within the American Communist Party is against the Comintern. The Lovestone group finally senses that its interests might suffer should it find itself in a position of opposition to the Comintern. Accordingly, the Lovestone group performs another "hair-raising" feat and expels Comrade Pepper from the Party! The same Pepper whom only the day before they had defended against the C.I. Another game of rivalry—who can spit furthest. How can we explain the resistance to the decisions of the Comintern regarding Pepper on the part of the majority group? Not, of course, in the interests of the Party. It was exclusively in the interests of the majority faction. Why is it that the majority made a sudden right-about-face and unexpectedly expelled Pepper from the Party? Was it in the interests of the Party? Of course not. It was purely in the interests of the Lovestone faction, who were anxious not to surrender a trump card to their enemy, namely, the Foster-Bittelman factional group. Faction interests above all!

The Foster group want to demonstrate their devotion to the C.P.S.U. by declaring themselves "Stalinites." Very good. We, the Lovestoneites, will go still further than the Foster group and demand the removal of Comrade Bukharin from the Comintern. Let the Fosterites try to beat that! Let them know over there in Moscow that we Americans know how to play the stock market.

The Foster group want to demonstrate their solidarity with the Comintern by demanding the carrying out of the decision of the Comintern regarding Pepper's recall. Very good. We, the Lovestoneites, will go still further and will expel Comrade Pepper from the Party. Let the Fosterites try to beat that! Let them know over there in Moscow that we Americans know how to play the stock market.

There you have the fruits of the factionalism of the majority and the minority.

But, Comrades, the Comintern is not a stock market. The Comintern is the holy of holies of the working class. The Comintern, therefore, must not be confused with a stock market. *Either* we are Leninists, and our relations one with another, as well as the relations of the sections with the Comintern, and vice versa, must be built on mutual confidence, must be as clean and pure as crystal—in which case there should be no room in our ranks for rotten diplomatic intrigue; *or* we are not Leninists—in which case rotten diplomacy and unprincipled factional struggle will have full scope in our relations. One or the other. We must chose, comrades.

In order to show how pure Communist morals are depraved and defiled in the course of a factional struggle, I could cite yet another fact as, for instance, my conversation with Comrades Foster and Lovestone. I refer to the conversation that took place at the time of the Sixth Congress. It is characteristic that in correspondence with his friends Comrade Foster makes this conversation out to be something secret, something which must not be talked about aloud. It is characteristic that Comrade Lovestone, in bringing his charges against Comrade Foster, in connection with this conversation, refers to his talk with me and boasts here that he, Comrade Lovestone, unlike Foster, is able to keep a secret and that under no conditions would he consent to divulge the substance of his conversation with me. Why this mysticism, dear comrades; what purpose does it serve? What could there be mysterious in my talk with Comrades Foster and Lovestone? Listening to these comrades, one might think I spoke to them of things which one would be ashamed to relate here. But that is stupid, comrades. What is the purpose of this mystical game? Is it difficult to understand that I have nothing to conceal from comrades? Is it difficult to understand that I am ready at any moment to tell comrades the substance of my conversation with Foster and Lovestone from beginning to end? What will then become of the famous mysticism so zealously spread here by Foster and Lovestone?

What did Comrade Foster talk to me about? He complained of the factionalism and unprincipledness of Comrade Lovestone's group. What did I answer him? I admitted these sins on the part of the Lovestone group, but at the same time added that the same sins were characteristic of the Foster group. On the basis of this Comrade Foster arrives at the singular conclusion that I sympathize with the minority group. Where is the foundation, one asks? On what grounds is Foster pleased to think that I fail to see the defects of the minority group and even sympathize with that group? Is it not obvious that with Comrade Foster *the wish is father to the thought*?

What did Comrade Lovestone talk about? Of the worthlessness of the Foster-Bittelman group. What did I answer? I answered that both groups were suffering from serious defects and advised him to take measures to liquidate factionalism. That was all.

What is there mysterious here that cannot be spoken about aloud?

Is it not strange that out of these simple and clear facts the comrades of the majority and the minority make a secret worthy of arousing the laughter of serious-minded people? Is it not obvious that there would be no mystification if there were no factional atmosphere poisoning the life of the American Communist Party and defiling simple and pure Communist morals?

Or let us take, for instance, another fact. I refer to the talk with Comrade Lovestone that took place *the other day*. It is characteristic that Comrade Lovestone has also been spreading absurd rumors about this conversation of mine and making a secret of it. Why this incomprehensible passion for the "mysterious"? . . . What did he speak about to me the other day? He asked that the Presidium of the E.C.C.I. should rescind the decision to withdraw him from America. He said that he, Lovestone, would undertake to carry out the proposed decision of the Presidium of the E.C.C.I., provided it would not be directed sharply against the leaders of the majority of the Communist Party of America. He promised to be a loyal soldier of the Comintern and to prove it in practice, if the Comintern would give him the necessary instructions. He said he was not looking for high positions in the American Communist Party, but only begged that he should be tested and given the opportunity to prove his loyalty to the Comintern. What did I reply to this? I told him that experiments in testing the loyalty of Comrade Lovestone to the Comintern have already been going on for three years, but no good has come of them. I said it would be better both for the Communist Party of America and for the Comintern, if Comrades Lovestone and Bittelman were kept in Moscow for a time. I said that this method of action on the part of the Comintern was one of the surest means of curing the American Communist Party of factionalism and saving it from disintegration. I said that although this was my opinion, I agreed to submit the proposal of Comrade Lovestone to the consideration of the Russian comrades, and undertook to inform him of the opinion of the Russian comrades.

That seems perfectly clear. Yet Comrade Lovestone again tries to make a secret of these obvious facts and is spreading all kinds of rumors regarding this conversation.

It is obvious that there would be no such mystification and simple things would not be turned into mysterious legends, if it were not for a policy which places the interests of a faction higher than the interests of the Party, the interests of diplomatic intrigue higher than the interests of the Comintern.

In order to put an end to these foul methods and place the American Communist Party on the lines of Leninist policy, it is necessary first of all to put an end to factionalism in that Party.

That is the conclusion to which the above-mentioned facts bring us. What is the solution?

Comrade Foster mentioned one. According to his proposal, the leadership should be handed over to the minority. Can that solution be adopted? No, it can not. The delegation of the Executive Committee of the Communist International committed an error when it sharply dissociated itself from the majority, without at the same time dissociating itself *equally sharply* from the minority. It would be very unfortunate if the Commission of the Presidium repeated the error of the delegation of the E.C.C.I. I think the Commission of the Presidium of the E.C.C.I. should in its draft dissociate itself both from the errors of the majority and from the errors of the minority. And for the very reason that it must dissociate itself from both, it must not propose to turn over the leadership to the minority. Hence the proposal of Comrade Foster with all its implications, automatically falls to the ground.

The American delegation proposed a different solution, directly contrary to the proposal of Comrade Foster. As you know, the proposal of the American delegation consists of ten points. The substance of this proposal is to the effect that the leadership of the majority should be fully rehabilitated, the factional work of the majority should be considered correct, that the decision of the Presidium of the E.C.C.I. to withdraw Comrade Lovestone should be annulled, and that thus the practice of suffocating the minority should be endorsed. Can this solution be adopted? No, it can not, for it would mean, not eradicating factionalism, but elevating it to a principle.

What then is the solution?

The solution consists in the following:

1. The actions and the proposals of the delegation of the E.C.C.I. must, in the main, be approved, with the exclusion from the proposals of those points which approximate to the proposals of Comrade Foster.

2. An open letter must be sent in the name of the E.C.C.I. to the members of the American Communist Party setting forth the errors of both sections of the Party and sharply emphasizing the question of eradicating all factionalism.

3. The action of the leaders of the majority at the Convention of the Communist Party of America, particularly on the question of Pepper, must be condemned.

4. An end must be put to the present situation in the Communist Party of America, in which the questions of positive work, the questions of the struggle of the working class against the capitalists, questions of wages, working hours, work in the trade unions, the fight against reformism, the fight against the Right deviation—when all these questions are kept in the shade, and are replaced by petty questions of the factional struggle between the Lovestone group and the Foster group.

5. The Secretariat of the Executive Committee of the American Communist Party must be reorganized with the inclusion of such workers therein as are capable of seeing something more than the factional struggle, the struggle of the working class against the capitalists, who are capable of placing the interests and the unity of the Party above the interests of individual groups and their leaders.

6. Comrades Lovestone and Bittelman must be summoned and placed at the disposal of the Comintern, in order that the members of the American Communist Party should at last understand that the Comintern intends to fight factionalism in all seriousness.

Such is the solution, in my opinion.

A word or two regarding the tasks and the mission of the American Communist Party. I think, comrades, that the American Communist Party is one of those few Communist Parties in the world upon which history has laid tasks of a decisive character from the point of view of the world revolutionary movement. You all know very well the strength and power of American capitalism. Many now think that the general crisis of world capitalism will not affect America. That, of course, is not true. It is entirely untrue, comrades. The crisis of world capitalism is developing with increasing rapidity and cannot but affect American capitalism. The three million now unemployed in America are the first swallows indicating the ripening of the economic crisis in America. The sharpening antagonism between America and England, the struggle for markets and raw materials and, finally, the colossal growth of armaments—that is the second portent of the approaching crisis. I think that the moment is not far off when a revolutionary crisis develops in America, that will be the beginning of the end of world capitalism as a whole. It is essential that the American Communist Party should be capable of meeting the leadership of the impending class struggle in America. Every effort and every means must be employed in preparing for that, comrades. For that end the American Communist Party must be improved and bolshevized. For that end we must work for the complete liquidation of factionalism and deviations in the Party. For that end we must work for the reestablishment of unity in the Communist Party of America. For that end we must work in order to forge real revolutionary cadres and a real revolutionary leadership of the proletariat, capable of leading the many millions of the American working class toward the revolutionary class struggles. For that end all personal factors and factional considerations must be laid aside and the revolutionary education of the working class of America must be placed above all.

That is why I think, comrades, that the most serious attention must be paid to the proposals of the Commission of the Presidium of the E.C.C.I. for your consideration here, for the aim of these proposals is to render the Communist Party of America a healthy Party, to eradicate factionalism, to create unity, to strengthen the Party and to bolshevize it.

COMINTERN ADDRESS TO THE AMERICAN
COMMUNIST PARTY, 1929

See the following document for the American Communist party's response to this address.

AN ADDRESS BY THE EXECUTIVE COMMITTEE OF
THE COMMUNIST INTERNATIONAL

To All Members of the Communist Party of the United States

Dear Comrades: The Executive Committee of the Communist International together with the delegation of the Sixth Convention of the Communist Party of the United States has very carefully discussed the situation in the American Communist Party. Having given to all delegates the fullest opportunity for expressing their views and for making proposals, having carefully examined all material presented and having considered the question from all aspects, the Executive Committee of the Communist International deems it necessary to place in all seriousness the situation within the Party before all members of the Communist Party of the United States.

The Open Letter of the Executive Committee of the Communist International to the Sixth Convention of the American Communist Party, which placed before it the fundamental tasks arising in connection with the accentuation of the inner and outer contradictions of American imperialism in the present period, pointed out the necessity of the Party's converting itself as soon as possible from a numerically small propagandistic organization into a mass political party of the working class, which particularly at the present juncture is indissoluably connected with the intensification of the struggle against the right danger. This Open Letter declared categorically that the fundamental prerequisite for the successful carrying out of these tasks is the cessation of the unprincipled struggle of many years standing.

The Executive Committee of the Communist International is compelled to record that at the Convention itself and after it not only was there no appreciable result achieved in the matter of doing away with factionalism, but on the contrary the factional struggle has become still more accentuated. Due to the unprincipled factional struggle the Sixth Convention of the American Communist Party failed to produce the results which it should have produced in regard to bolshevization and the establishment of a healthier condition within the American Communist Party. Many of the most important political questions and tasks confronting the Party were not discussed by the Convention. The errors of the Majority and of the Minority of the Party were

Daily Worker, May 20, 1929.

not explained at the Convention as they should have been as a matter of Bolshevik self-criticism. The Party was not mobilized for the struggle against the right danger. No consolidation of all forces of the Party for struggle against factionalism was secured at the Convention. On the contrary this Convention, which was composed of the best proletarian elements of the American Communist Party who uphold the line of the Comintern, became an arena for unprincipled maneuvers on the part of the top leaders of the Majority as well as on the part of the leaders of the Minority. The Convention was forced off of the line proposed by the Comintern and was mobilized for purposes of further factional struggle by both groups.

A gross distortion of the line of the Comintern was the theory inoculated into the Convention alleging that organization proposals of the Executive Committee of the Communist International were in contradiction to its political letter instead of being a necessary guarantee for carrying out the line of the Open Letter to the American Communist Party. A clearly factional distortion of the meaning of the organizational proposals of the Executive Committee of the Communist International were also the efforts to interpret them as handing over the leadership of the Party to the Minority, which was not and is not intended by the Comintern since the fundamental task of the Open Letter and organizational proposals of the Executive Committee of the Communist International to the Sixth Convention was the consolidation of the Party on the basis of the line of the Comintern in the direction of the struggle against the factionalism of both groups. The Minority of the Central Committee of the Communist Party of the United States endeavored to make the Open Letter and organizational proposals of the Executive Committee of the Communist International an instrument for getting the leadership of the Party into its own hands. The Executive Committee of the Communist International condemns these attempts of the Minority which show that it factionally distorted the meaning of the Open Letter of the Executive Committee of the Communist International and its organizational proposals and that certain leaders of the Minority have shown themselves unfit to play a role of a uniting factor in the struggle of the Party against factionalism in conformity with the directions of the Executive Committee of the Communist International. It is the factional leaders of the Majority with Comrade Lovestone at the head that are mainly responsible for making use of the Convention for factional purposes, for misleading honest proletarian Party members who uphold the line of the Comintern, for playing an unprincipled game with the question of the struggle against the Right danger in the Comintern and in the Communist Party of the Soviet Union, for inadmissable personal hounding of the delegation of the Comintern at the Convention, for the organization of caucus meetings of the delegates of the Majority in direct contradiction with the Open Letter of the Executive Committee of the Communist International and in spite of verbal acceptance of that letter, for hounding those comrades who departed from the Majority faction and unconditionally accepted the line of the Executive Committee of the Communist International, for a campaign against certain responsible comrades of the Minority who were carrying out the line of the Executive Committee of the Communist International—for all these methods and intrigues which cannot be tolerated in any section of the Comintern and which clearly bear the imprint of petty bourgeois politiciandom.

Both factions of the American Communist Party have been guilty of right errors. Both factions show serious deviations to the right from the general line of the Comintern, which creates the danger of an openly opportunist right deviation crystallizing within the Party.

Since the Sixth World Congress of the Communist International the Majority of the Central Committee of the American Communist Party has been committing a series of gross right errors pointed out in the Open Letter of the Executive Committee of the Communist International. These errors found their expression in overestimating American imperialism and putting the question of inner and outer contradictions in a wrong way, which led to the obscuring of the inner contradictions of American capitalism, in underestimating the swing to the left of the American working class, in underestimating American reformism which led to weakening the struggle against it, in underestimating the right danger in the American Communist Party, in substituting in place of the question of the right opportunist danger only the question of Trotskyism, in dealing with the question in a manner which led to the obscuring of the right danger.

The Minority of the Central Committee of the American Communist Party was committing, in regard to questions dealing with the crisis of American capitalism and the swing of the masses to the left, "left", but in reality right opportunist errors; it dissociated the development of the inner contradictions of American capitalism from its external contradictions and from the general crisis of world capitalism, and in regard to the question of the struggle against the war danger it was sliding down to petty bourgeois pacifist slogans ("no new cruisers"—Comrade Bittelman). The Minority of the Central Committee was unable to dissociate itself at the right time from Trotskyism and did not properly struggle against it. An ideological level of right errors in the American Communist Party was the so-called theory of "exceptionalism" which found its clearest exponents in the persons of Comrades Pepper and Lovestone whose conception was as follows: There is a crisis of capitalism but not of American capitalism, there is a swing of the masses leftwards but not in America, there is the necessity of accentuating the struggle against reformism but not in the United States, there is a necessity for struggling against the right danger but not in the American Communist Party. And yet the present period, when the process shaking the foundation of capitalist stabilization is going on, signifies for the United States that it is being ever more closely involved in the general crisis of capitalism. In America too the fundamental contradiction of capitalism—the contradiction between the growth of productive forces and the lagging behind of markets—is becoming more accentuated. The bourgeoisie is increasing its efforts to find a way out of the growing crisis by means of rationalization, i.e., by increased exploitation of the working class. The internal class contradictions are growing; the struggle for markets and spheres for investment of capital against other imperialist states is becoming more accentuated; there is a feverish growth of armaments and the war danger is getting nearer and nearer. With a distinctness unprecedented in history, American capitalism is exhibiting now the effects of the inexorable laws of capitalist development, the laws of the decline and downfall of capitalist society. The general crisis of capitalism is growing more rapidly than it may seem at first glance. This crisis will shake also the foundation of the power of American imperialism.

Under these conditions the theory of "exceptionalism" is a reflection of the pressure of American capitalism and reformism which is endeavoring to create among the mass of workers the impression of absolute firmness and "exceptional" imperialist might of American capital in spite of its growing crisis and to strengthen the tactic of class collaboration in spite of the accentuation of class contradictions. The Executive Committee of the Communist International points out that not only the mistakes of the Majority but also the most important mistakes of the Minority were based on the conception of American "exceptionalism." While it records the political mistakes of both groups as well as the growth of the right danger in the American Communist Party, the Executive Committee of the Communist International regards as a factional exaggeration the claim alleging that the group of the Majority as a whole is a bearer of the right tendency as well as the claim alleging that the Minority group represents the Trotskyist deviation. There are in the ranks of both groups elements with strong right tendencies which either show themselves openly or are masked by "left" phraseology. Neither of the two groups has carried on a proper struggle against these right tendencies in the ranks of its own faction and the factionalism of both groups has been the great impediment to the development within the Party of the necessary self-criticism and to the political education of the Party members in the spirit of Bolshevik steadfastness based upon principle. A factional lack of principle which is also an expression of opportunism finds its expression in the fact that both groups were putting the interests of their faction above the interests of the Party. On the strength of this the American Communist Party is confronted now in all sharpness with the question of the danger of the political disintegration of the present leading cadres which threatens to undermine the whole work of the Party. A characteristic manifestation of rotten factional diplomacy in regard to the Communist International is the attitude of the Majority of the Central Committee of the American Communist Party on the question of Comrade Pepper's conduct. In spite of repeated decisions of the Comintern on the removal from work in the American Communist Party of Comrade Pepper who repeatedly exhibited opportunistic tendencies, the Majority of the Central Committee violated these decisions of the Comintern, shielding the political errors and gross breaches of discipline which were being committed by Comrade Pepper. The inconsistency and lack of principle in the attitude of the leaders of the Majority of the Central Committee in regard to Comrade Pepper found vivid expression in the fact that the Central Committee of the American Communist Party expelled him from the Party, pointing out that "the political platform of Comrade Pepper is no doubt the real cause of his cowardly disinclination to do his duty and to go and place himself at the disposal of the Comintern" (decision of the Secretariat of the Central Committee of the American Communist Party approved by the Political Bureau of the Central Committee), whereas a few days later in spite of the political characteristic given to Comrade Pepper the Central Committee reinstated him to the ranks of the Party. The Majority as well as the Minority in 1929 was engaged in inadmissable, unprincipled speculation with questions of the situation in the

Communist Party of the Soviet Union and in the Comintern. If the Minority speculated in the version as if it were the only group in the American Communist Party sharing the attitude of the Communist Party of the Soviet Union in its struggle against right deviations, the Majority, making use of methods of rotten diplomacy, went to the length of unprincipled maneuvering in regard to this question. This has found expression in the adoption by the Convention at the initiative of Comrades Lovestone and Gitlow and without the least attempt at informing the delegates of the Convention about the situation in the Communist Party of the Soviet Union, of a resolution which proposed organizational measures in the struggle against the right deviation. And subsequently to the arrival in Moscow the delegation of the Majority in the person of Comrade Gitlow made a declaration which practically disavows this resolution and upholds the slanderous attacks of the right elements on the leadership of the Communist Party of the Soviet Union and of the Comintern.

The Executive Committee of the Comintern draws special attention to attacks entirely unworthy of a Communist, which during the Convention, Comrade Lovestone permitted himself to make on the leadership of the Comintern (Comrade Lovestone's reference to "a running sore" in the apparatus of the Executive Committee of the Communist International). The Executive Committee of the Communist International emphasizes that these attacks of Comrade Lovestone represent a repetition of slanderous attacks upon the Comintern made by right opportunists.

The Executive Committee of the Communist International draws special attention to the declaration of May 9th in which Comrades Bedacht, Lovestone and others tried to discredit beforehand the decision of the Comintern by stating that "the Executive Committee of the Communist International wants to destroy the Central Committee and is therefore following a policy of legalizing forever the factionalism of the opposition block and is recommending that it carry it on also in future."

The Executive Committee of the Communist International holds that this most factional and entirely impermissible anti-Party declaration of Comrades Bedacht, Lovestone and others represents a direct attempt at preparing a condition necessary for paralyzing the decisions of the Comintern and for a split in the Communist Party of America. The same manifest determination to oppose their faction to the Comintern found expression also in a second statement of May 14th submitted by the delegation from the Convention only in more diplomatic form. The assertion of the leaders of the Majority faction concerning their "loyalty" to the Comintern contained in that statement was clearly exposed at the very session of the Presidium of the Executive Committee of the Communist International at which the statement was reported, by the refusal of the majority of the signers unconditionally to carry into effect the decisions contained in this letter. The Executive Committee of the Communist International declares that in case the authors of the declaration refuse unconditionally to submit to the decisions of the Comintern and to actively put them into practice, the Executive Committee of the Communist International will be forced to adopt all measures necessary to put a stop to all attempts at splitting the Party, to secure unity in the ranks of the Communist Party of America and to realize the decisions adopted by the Comintern.

In the course of years the Executive Committee of the Communist International had repeatedly demanded the liquidation of factionalism in the Communist Party of America. Thus for example in the resolution of the 5th enlarged Plenum of the Executive Committee of the Communist International in 1925 it is stated: "The Executive Committee holds firmly to the opinion that the factional struggle between the two groups must absolutely cease."

In a resolution of the 6th Enlarged Plenum of the Executive Committee of the Communist International in 1926 on the American question, among other things it is stated: "To enable the American Communist Party to fulfil its historic mission the first prerequisite is complete and unconditional termination of the factional fight within the Communist Party not in words but in deeds."

In its resolution of July 1st 1927 the Executive Committee of the Communist International again reminded the Party that "this demand was not being carried out seriously enough" and that there is still in the Party "an impermissible situation of faction formation" which may lead to "a crisis in the Party."

The Sixth World Congress of the Comintern in 1928, while mentioning in its political theses that in the Party there is to be "observed a slackening of the long standing factional struggle," nevertheless found sufficient ground for deciding that "the most important task confronting the Party is to put an end to factional strife—which is not based on any serious controversies on points of principle."

Finally the Executive Committee of the Communist International, with the object of carrying out the decisions of the World Congress and in view of the fact that the inner-Party situation in the United States became anew accentuated, had addressed an open letter to the American Party in December 1928 and demanded from the Convention then pending that it begin at last really to carry out the decisions of the Comintern concerning the liquidation of factionalism. All of this was absolutely of no avail so far. The leaders of the Majority as well as the leaders of the Minority of the Central Committee, who repeatedly gave their verbal pledges to the Executive Committee of the Communist International that they will carry out the decisions of the Comintern, have systematically violated the decisions of the Executive Committee of the Communist International and their own pledges. Therefore the Executive Committee of the Comintern, approving in the main the work of the delegation of the E.C.C.I. to the Sixth Convention of the American Communist Party, resolves to adopt the following measures:

1. To place the Majority as well as the Minority of the Central Committee under the obligation of dissolving immediately all factions and ceasing all factional work. To call upon all organizations of the American Communist Party to secure the putting into practice of this instruction, not shrinking from the application in regard to factionalism of the most severe disciplinary measures clear up to expulsion from the Party.

2. Comrades Lovestone and Bittelman as the extreme factionalists of the Majority and Minority, to be removed for a time from work in the American Communist Party.

3. To reject the demand of the Minority of the Central Committee in regard to the calling of a special Convention.

4. To recognize as necessary the reorganization and extension of the Secretariat of the Central Committee on a basis of securing real collective, non-factional activity, and to render to the Central Committee every possible help in the matter of putting an end to all factionalism in the Party.

5. To turn over Comrade Pepper's case to the International Control Commission for consideration.

The Executive Committee of the Communist International calls upon all members of the Party to get together for the struggle against unprincipled factionalism in the Party, to be able to carry on the struggle against the right danger, for the healing and bolshevization of the American Communist Party, for the genuine carrying out of inner-Party democracy and proletarian self-criticism. With these objects in view the Party must initiate on a large scale a discussion of the questions concerning the situation within the Party and the political tasks confronting the Party. It is necessary to carry on in all Party and young Communist organizations a thorough enlightenment campaign concerning the decisions of the Sixth Congress of the Comintern, the Open Letter of the E.C.C.I. to the Sixth Convention of the Communist Party of America, and concerning the present address of the Executive Committee of the Communist International. In the course of this enlightenment campaign, while waging a struggle against all opportunists who want to fight the Comintern, while uniting in that struggle all honest and disciplined comrades who are loyal to the Communist movement, the Communist Party must concentrate its attention on the most important questions of revolutionary struggle of the proletariat of America—on questions of unemployment, struggle for social insurance, wages, working hours, work in existing trade unions, work for the organization of new unions, struggle against reformism and struggle against the war danger. The Communist Party of the United States must strengthen its work in regard to recruiting and retaining in its ranks new cadres of workers that are joining the Party, especially of the working youth. It must widen its agitational and organizational work in the big plants in the main branches of industry and among the Negroes and must secure for the Party an independent leading role in the industrial struggles of the working class that are developing, organizing in the process of the struggle the unorganized workers.

It is only by relentless struggle against unprincipled factionalism, which is eating into the vitals of the Party, only by consolidating the whole Party for carrying out its fundamental practical tasks on the basis of the line of the Comintern and by more energetic struggle against the right danger that the American Communist Party will become the genuine Bolshevik vanguard of the American proletariat and will be converted into a mass political Party of the American workers in the ranks of which inner-Party democracy is being actually unfolded while at the same time an iron proletarian discipline is strengthened, to which all organizations and each individual member unconditionally submits; in the ranks of which is practised the submission of the Minority to the Majority on the basis of the Party's persual of the line and practical directions of the Comintern. Such a Party will be capable to lead the American proletariat to victorious struggle against capitalism.

With Communist Greetings,

Executive Committee Communist International

AMERICAN COMMUNIST PARTY'S RESPONSE
TO COMINTERN ADDRESS
May 18, 1929

See the preceding document for the text of the Address by the Executive Committee of the Communist International to the American Communist Party.

DECISIONS OF CENTRAL COMMITTEE OF COMMUNIST
PARTY OF THE U.S.A. ON THE ADDRESS OF
THE COMMUNIST INTERNATIONAL

(Decisions made Saturday, May 18, 1929.)

1. The Central Committee accepts and endorses the Address to the American Party membership by the Executive Committee of the Communist International and undertakes to win the entire Party membership for the support of the Comintern Address.

2. The Central Committee pledges itself unconditionally to carry into effect the decisions contained in this Address.

3. The Central Committee pledges itself and its members to defend the Address of the Comintern before the membership against any ideological or other opposition to the Address.

4. The Central Committee calls upon the members of the delegation in Moscow to withdraw all opposition to the Address and to the decisions contained therein and to do all in their power to assist the Comintern and the Central Committee of the American Party to unify the Party in support of these decisions.

5. The Central Committee instructs the Secretariat to proceed immediately, in agreement with the Executive Committee of the Communist International, to take all measures necessary to put into application the decisions and to realize the objectives of the Comintern as expressed in the Address.

6. The Central Committee approves all decisions of the Secretariat of the same date, accepting and ordering immediate publication in the entire Party press of the Address of the E.C.C.I. to the American Party membership, and instructs the Secretariat to put these decisions into effect immediately.

Daily Worker, May 20, 1929.

CULTURE AND THE CRISIS, 1932

PREFACE

We of this generation stand midway between two eras. When we look backward, we see our American past like a great tidal wave that is now receding, but that was magnificent indeed in the sweep of its socially purposeless power. When we look ahead, we see something new and strange, undreamed of in the American philosophy. What we see ahead is the threat of cultural dissolution. The great wave piled up too much wreckage—of nature, of obsolete social patterns and institutions, of human blood and nerve.

We who write this, listed among the so-called "intellectuals" of our generation, people trained, at least, to think for ourselves and hence, to a degree for our time and our people—we have no faintest desire to exaggerate either our talents or our influence. Yet on the other hand, we are not humble, especially with respect to the power that measures itself in dollar signs and ciphers, the thought that is not thought, but merely the stereotype of habit, the action that is not will, not choice, but the reflex of fear. Why should we as a class be humble? Practically everything that is orderly and sane and useful in America was made by two classes of Americans; our class, the class of brain workers, and the "lower classes", the muscle workers. Very well, we strike hands with our true comrades. We claim our own and we reject the disorder, the lunacy spawned by grabbers, advertisers, traders, speculators, salesmen, the much-adulated, immensely stupid and irresponsible "business men". We claim the right to live and to function. It is our business to think and we shall not permit business men to teach us our business. It is also, in the end, our business to act.

We have acted. As responsible intellectual workers we have aligned ourselves with the frankly revolutionary Communist Party, the party of the workers. In this letter, we speak to you of our own class—to the writers, artists, scientists, teachers, engineers, to all honest professional workers—telling you as best we can why we have made this decision and why we think that you too should support the Communist Party in the political campaign now under way.

AN OPEN LETTER TO THE INTELLECTUAL
WORKERS OF AMERICA

There is only one issue in the present election. Call it hard times, unemployment, the farm problem, the world crisis, or call it simply hunger—whatever name we

League of Professional Groups for Foster and Ford, *Culture and the Crisis: An Open Letter to the Writers, Artists, Teachers, Physicians, Engineers, Scientists and Other Professional Workers of America* (New York, 1932), 1-11, 17-19, 23-30.

use, the issue is the same. What do the major political parties propose to do about it?

The Republicans propose, in effect, to do nothing whatever. Twelve to fifteen million men and women have lost their jobs; twenty-five to thirty-five million people will go hungry this winter; nobody knows the exact figures. The Republican Party, three years after the crash, does not even promise to take a census of our misery. The best its candidate can offer is a pledge to continue the policies which are depriving these millions of work, food and shelter.

Somebody must pay the cost of the depression: will it be the rich or the poor, the capitalists or the workers and farmers? In the battle now raging between them, the Republican administration has taken the side of the rich. To banks, railroads and industrial corporations, it has offered government loans, millions, billions, anything to keep them from going bankrupt. To the Rockefellers and Mellons it has offered a pledge to keep their taxes down—by discharging government employees and refusing government help to the unemployed. It offers nothing to the poor except higher taxes, lower wages and the chance to share their misery. If they ask for more, it gives them bayonets and tear-gas.

The Democrats, in the present election, have tried to appeal to both sides. Their candidate has promised as much as he safely could to as many people as he thought were influential. He has promised progressivism to progressives and conservatism to conservatives. He has promised to lower the price of electric power without lowering the inflated value of power company stock. He has promised more and less regulation of the railroads. He has promised to lower the protective tariff and at the same time make it more protective. He has promised higher prices to the farmers by means of a measure which cannot be put into effect until hundreds of thousands of farms have been sold for taxes and mortgages. He has promised beer to industrial workers, if they have the money to buy it. On the one real issue he promises nothing.

If Roosevelt is elected—and Wall Street expects him to win—there will be changes here and there in the machine of government. The leaks in the boiler will be stuffed with cotton waste, the broken bolts mended with hay wire. A different gang of engineers will run the machine for the profit of the same owners.

The causes of the crisis will be untouched. The results of the crisis—hunger, low wages, unemployment—will still be with us. If there is a temporary return to a limited degree of prosperity, it can only be succeeded by another crisis. The United States under capitalism is like a house that is rotting away; the roof leaks, the sills and rafters are crumbling. The Democrats want to paint it pink. The Republicans don't want to paint it; instead they want to raise the rent.

*   *   *

The Logic of Capitalism

The value of the debacle of 1929, to all thinking persons, must have been that it revealed, as in a lightning-flash, the fatal character of the post-war society. The equilibrium of this society was false; its rotten foundations had been changed in no way. Outside of Soviet Russia, nearly all human services were still administered through the profit-seeking of capitalists. From this condition arose the contradictions, the frauds and imbecilities which became so apparent after the coming of depression.

Our industrialists and bankers, for all their patriotic promises to continue the New Era, to maintain "high wages" (which had been practically stationary from 1923 to 1929), began at once a work of ruthless deflation. They discharged labor, lowered wages, speeded up operations. It was a vast work of *hoarding* which they had begun, a hoarding of which they accused the masses of people. With one hand they opened charity "drives" or conducted "block-aid" campaigns, but with the other they hoarded. And the left hand could not withstand the destructive labors of the right hand. The workers and professionals have been forced to pay for relief of the unemployed.

The prosperity spree of bankers had over-capitalized our industries, added productive power beyond people's buying capacity to already over-extended enterprises. To save the banks, the government revenues were to be raised by means of taxation, further reducing the national buying power. Thus, capital, after years of profiteering and speculation, exacted prodigal doles for itself while opposing the "dole" (unemployment insurance) for the workers and other forms of adequate relief for professionals, workers and farmers.

To a dispassionate scrutiny the statesmanship of the depression, in government and big business, seems like the random movements of lunacy; yet such a course as we have watched, such reasoning as we have been able to distinguish, represents the "logic" of capitalism.

Serfs and Vagabonds

After three years the flag is still at half mast, the economic activities of the country are at a rate of approximately 50 per cent of capacity. Our heavy industries are almost motionless; the giant steel plants, the magnificent motor factories, such as those of Ford, are shut down in great part. Our means of production, efficient enough to sustain all of us in comfort, function at half-pressure or rust away. Whole regions seem devastated as if by a plague or a war; whole industries on which millions depend seem permanently blighted. Thus the farming population, the largest and most conservative section of the country, has been driven to violence, after deepening poverty of many years standing. They have too much food to sell in a country whose masses are hungry. Though their produce is fearfully needed, it may not be sold save at terms which drive them from the land. In addition to 12,000,000 or 15,000,000 unemployed workers, other millions are employed only part time. One of the most tragic aspects of the capitalist-made depression are the 300,000 children who, according to government reports, are completely homeless, wandering to and fro.

At a given day in 1931 the heads of several great industrial corporations, such as the United States Steel, the General Motors, the Standard Oil, in concert announced universal wage-cuts for all their workers, of 10 to 20 per cent. (Soon afterward the railroads and many other industries followed their example.) By this command most of the 40,000,000 workers in this country had their earnings and their standard of living deeply altered. And we saw at once what oppressive power a few men exercised; and how the mass of workers, largely unorganized—the conservative labor unions dare not strike back at any rate—were literally returned to serfdom. Unable to control their own destiny they became simply the army of slave-labor which capital requires.

But a great part of the army of workers were totally deprived, by the same command, of the means of living. Some of them grouped as army veterans or starving miners participated in mass uprisings or hunger riots. Many of them began to wander about hopelessly, on freight-cars or cast-off automobiles.

"Hooverville", the new No Man's Land of tin and paper covered shanties, located along the fringes of civilization, by the freight yards or ports of cities, now became the transitory gathering place of the unemployed. "Hooverville", monument to the depression, is incredible; yet, in the long run, given our present conditions and philosophy, "Hooverville" must grow larger. The future, more and more, is bound up with "Hooverville" as new classes of the population steadily fall under the system of depression.

The Professionals Suffer Too

The brain workers who give technical or educational services are not spared from misfortune. As an illuminating instance of the experience of this middle class, we need only look at the political-financial chaos which has come to such an urban center as Chicago. Here, the school teachers had, up to recently, received only five months pay out of the previous thirteen months. Two thousand of them had lost their savings in bank failures. Yet at one moment the city government undertook to sell for tax defaults the houses of its employees, unable to pay their taxes, because of the city's own default in wages!

In New York City alone there are about 8,000 unemployed teachers. The American Association of University Professors has revealed that a nation-wide drive of wage-cuts and lay-offs is on. By closing classes for adults, cutting the school year and doubling the size of classes, the rulers of the educational system throw increasing numbers of teachers out of work. In one New Jersey town, more than 100 white collar workers have turned to ditch-digging, competing with underpaid workers for their jobs. Dean Williamson of the Columbia University School of Library Service has declared that students must be barred since there are already "too many" librarians. Last June, the New York City school system had to eliminate 85 per cent of its architects, engineers and draftsmen. The New York City Chemists Club reports large numbers of trained chemists out of work. The head of the Medical Society of New York State, reports that doctors have taken to taxi driving and similar jobs to keep alive. The Dental Association reports that its members average 25 per cent of their incomes of three years ago. An Engineering School opened free graduate courses for unemployed Alumni. The Journalism College Dean reports that there are as many students as jobs, and the jobs are already filled to overflowing. Theatres close while actors and playwrights starve. Musicians suffer not only from the crisis but permanently from technological unemployment through the development of radio, talking-movies and the like. Artists find no market for their wares. Writers find no publishers, or must accept miserable terms, and then can count upon only a most limited sale of books. Even those business posts which require some technical training have become scarce. The personnel managers of the great trusts no longer comb the colleges for bright seniors whom they will set on a royal road to riches. Department stores have their pick of Ph. D.'s at $12.00 a week. Anxious employers seek to stem the flood of trained applicants for jobs. Professors F. W. Taussig and C. S. Joslyn of Harvard have shown that business leadership is in the hands of a caste, selected by birth and connections, and Professors A. B. Crawford and S. N. Clement of Yale have armed employers with a plan to further bar the way to jobs by instituting an "interneship" for business. And down at the bottom, scores of thousands of students struggle through college barely able to keep alive, since adults have taken away their part-time jobs, and wonder what they will do when they graduate. All this unemployment and misery, all this training and talent thrown away, not because there are too many doctors, teachers, artists, writers and the like, but despite the fact that this country has never yet been able to provide its population with a sufficiently large body of trained intellectuals and professionals to satisfy its cultural needs. This cultural crisis of course grows directly out of the economic crisis.

* * *

Toward a New Society

The spectacle of catastrophic economic collapse—the magnificent and recurrent capitalist spectacle of starvation in the midst of plenty—presents the issue of social reorganization as the major issue in this campaign. The history of capitalism shows that crises and depressions are inevitable under the system of production for profit, of money making, and that the development of capitalism aggravates their violence. This depression, moreover, is no mere dip in the business cycle; it is a manifestation of the general crisis and collapse of capitalism. Even capitalist economists admit that capitalism cannot survive "as is".

Fundamental social reorganization must eliminate the basic causes of cyclical fluctuations and depressions—production for profit, speculation, the anarchy of production, the unequal distribution of income which creates a disparity between production and consumption, the exploitation of the working class. Only Socialism can eliminate the exploitation and misery which prevail under capitalism.

Social ownership and management of the means of production and distribution become the starting point of social reorganization, economic and cultural. Industry ceases being a means of exploitation, of the accumulation of profits and fortunes; it ceases being the master of life and becomes the server of life. Socialist industry is planned, deliberately, purposively, unhampered by predatory capitalist interest—there can be neither the poverty which prevails under capitalism even in the most prosperous times nor the catastrophe and aggravated mass misery of depression. Industry becomes the creative technical problem of calculating social needs and mobilizing and reorganizing the necessary labor, machinery and raw materials.

The Professional Classes Will Be Liberated

Under Socialism science and technology are freed from their dependence upon private profit; their scope and social application are enormously increased. The professional workers, whom capitalism either exploits or forces to become exploiters, are liberated to perform freely and creatively their particular craft function—the engineer need consider only the efficiency of his work, the economist and statistician can purposively plan the organization, management and social objectives of industry, the architect is released from profit and speculative motives and may express his finest aspirations in buildings of social utility and beauty, the physician becomes the unfettered organizer of social preventive medicine, the teacher, writer, and artist fashion the creative ideology of a new world and a new culture.

It is an ideal worth fighting for, and it is a practical and realizable ideal, as is being proved in the Soviet Union. It would, moreover, be much easier to build Socialism in the United States than in Russia because of the infinitely higher development of our technology and our means of production and distribution.

*   *   *

The Communist Party

The Communist Party stands for a Socialism of deeds, not of words. It appeals for the support of the American working classes, not like the Socialist Party on the basis of broken and unfulfilled promises, but with concrete evidence of revolutionary achievement both at home and abroad.

Already in Soviet Russia, under the leadership of the Communists, unemployment has been wiped out, a gigantic reconstruction of industry to extend a Socialist planned economy has been undertaken, and a cultural revolution of tremendous dimensions has been won on many fronts. The Soviet Union has freed women from age-old social disabilities and discrimination, provided national and racial minorities with an opportunity to develop their own cultural life, broken down the barriers between city and country and adopted the most advanced system of social insurance in the world. For the first time in recorded history a civilization has emerged unified by a living faith in man's ability to create a classless society in which "the free development of each is the condition of the free development of all", in which every human being is privileged to participate in the collective effort of the whole.

Whatever burdens must be shouldered fall upon all alike. These will be conquered in the future just as famine, blockade, invasion, have been conquered. Until then no one lives in luxury and no one suffers from need. Contrast this with capitalist America in which the luxury of a few is flaunted in the face of hungry and homeless millions.

The Communist Party of America proposes as the real solution of the present crisis the overthrow of the system which is responsible for all crises. This can only be accomplished by the conquest of political power and the establishment of a workers' and farmers' government which will usher in the Socialist commonwealth. The Communist Party does not stop short merely with a proclamation of its revolutionary goal. It links that goal up with the daily battles of the working class for jobs, bread and peace. Its actions and achievements are impressive evidence of its revolutionary sincerity.

The Communist Party is the only party which has stood in the forefront of the major struggle of the workers against capital and the capitalist state. It has unflinchingly met every weapon of terror which frenzied capitalist dictatorship has let loose upon it—clubbings, imprisonment, deportation and murder. It has rallied thousands of workers to resist the onslaught upon their already low standard of living. It has fought the Jim Crow system used by the capitalist class to divide and weaken the working class. It has fought the evictions of the unemployed. It has fought and is prepared to fight in the struggles of every group of exploited workers in the country—the miner, the steel worker, the farmer, the ex-serviceman. It has unmasked the class character of justice dispensed in American courts and led mass demonstrations in behalf of victims of legal frame-ups—notably Tom Mooney and the Scottsboro boys and against the deportations of militant workers. In the present crisis the Communist Party has been the only party which has thrown down a militant challenge to the ruling class and unfolded a program of mass activity.

The Communist Party Platform

Let us judge it by its election program of immediate demands:

1. The Communist Party demands *unemployment and social insurance at the expense of the state and employers*. This demand is radically distinguished from all other programs for unemployment insurance in that it does not seek to saddle the worker with the costs of his own insurance. All other schemes involve a form of insurance in which payments made to workers are in part, at least, nothing but deferred wages. Since the total profit of capitalist enterprise is derived from the unpaid labor of the worker, the Communist Party as an immediate measure demands that the cost of insurance be paid by those who appropriate the profits.

2. The Communist Party demands a *militant struggle against Hoover's wage-cutting policy*. The attempts made to conceal the extent of unemployment by spreading work through the stagger system, the Share-the-Work movement, is the most transparent device for reducing the wages and standards of living of the working class. An acceptance of a wage-cut by any group of workers not only tends to induce wage cuts among other groups; it undermines the fighting morale of their organizations and leaves them helpless for further action.

3. The Communist Party demands *emergency relief for the impoverished farmers without restrictions by the government and the banks; exemption of impoverished farmers from taxes and no forced collection of rents or debts.* No other measures can save the poorer farmers from losing their heavily mortgaged farms and being thrust into peonage or pauperism. While in the cities the demagogues cry "back to the land," the working farmers are actually being put off the land.

4. The Communist Party demands *equal rights for the Negroes and self-determination for the Black Belt.* It calls for an end to the policy of supine acceptance of legal and extra-legal lynchings, of social discrimination and political disfranchisement. It holds that the necessary condition for all equality is social equality and that social equality can only be won by the joint struggle of white and Negro workers against their common oppressors. It breaks with the policy of empty promises, deceit and betrayal which has characterized the attitudes of the Republican, Democratic and Socialist Parties towards the Negro masses. It has sealed its sincerity in the struggle for the liberation of the Negroes with the blood of its organizers—heroic white and colored workers who have fallen victims of the lynch terrorism of the Southern landlords and the Northern capitalists.

5. The Communist Party appeals for a united front *against capitalist terror; against all forms of suppression of the political rights of the workers.* The more the crisis eats its way into the vitals of capitalist society, the more ruthlessly does the capitalist class set itself to destroy all militant workers' organizations. It does not hesitate to sweep aside its own "sacred" constitutional guarantees of freedom of speech and assembly and at the same time accuses Communists of attempting to undermine constitutional rights. It has met peaceful demonstrations for bread with bullets. It has resorted to the crudest frame-ups in order to railroad working-class leaders to jail. As the crisis sharpens, the campaign of injunctions, deportations and violence threatens to develop into an organized war against radical trade unions, unemployed councils and workers' defense organizations. The Communist Party alone calls upon the working class for action to meet capitalist class terror.

6. The Communist Party appeals for a united front *against imperialist war; for the defense of the Chinese people and of the Soviet Union.* Capitalism breeds war as inevitably as it breeds crisis. The quest for profits leads to the search for foreign markets—the search for foreign markets, to struggle with suppressed nationalities and rival capitalist groups. War is welcomed by the capitalist class as a method of disposing of surplus commodities and surplus wage workers. War under modern conditions of technology and science recognizes no distinction between the front and the rear, between and combatant and non-combatant. It means pitting the workers of one country against the workers of another in order to call them off from the war of class against class. At the present moment imperialist war is raging in China; tomorrow world capitalism is prepared to launch its holy crusade against the Soviet Union. The Communist Party demands an open war against capitalist war. It rallies the workers in munition factories and on the sea-front to strike against shipping war materials. It calls upon the working class to be prepared to transform the coming imperialist war against mythical enemies without into a revolutionary war against the real class enemy within.

The Communist Road to a New Society

What is the relationship between these immediate demands and the revolutionary goal of Communism? It does not require much reflection to see that they are integrally connected. The immediate demands of the Communist Party differ from those of the reformist parties in that they are not proposed as sops to be thrown to discontented workers and farmers in order to prevent revolution. They are the first steps, under existing conditions, toward the overthrow of capitalism. Each demand furnishes the basis for a broad mass organization and mass activity.

The so-called reform plans in the election platforms of other parties call for the perpetuation of the capitalist system under the guise of patching up either the currency system or the tariff or the farm policy. Their voice of protest against the abuses of capitalism is merely the swan song of the middle classes which the processes of centralization of industry and concentration of wealth have put on the auction-block. Those parties of reform first confuse the minds of the workers with radical words and then betray them by their official acts. They no more can prevent wage cuts, unemployment and war than their soup kitchens can wipe out want.

The Communist Party does not sit back in sectarian blindness waiting for Communism to come by gentle inevitability in the distant future. It organizes the workers in the factories and mines, in offices and schools, in the city and country, in the army and navy, to fight for their rights, and to resist the attempt of the capitalists to make the masses shoulder the burdens of the world crisis.

Why Vote Communist

* * *

The history of the class struggle in America since 1929 proves that it has been the revolutionary demands of the Communist Party which have forced the national and local governments to recognize unemployment and at least make gestures at relief. It was only after March 6, 1930, when Communist demonstrations against unemployment had been broken up throughout the country, and Wm. Z. Foster served six months in prison after his arrest for leading the demonstration, that the country awoke to the effects of the collapse of the previous fall. In New York it was only after a deputation of unemployed under Communist leadership had been clubbed by the police, that the Board of Estimate was compelled to make grants for relief. In St. Louis it required a march on city hall by thousands of workers under Communist leadership before the municipal government restored hungry families to the relief rolls. Even where the Communist Party fails to attain its immediate objective, its failure, by bringing into action great masses with potential revolutionary capacities, accomplishes more for the workers than the successes of the capitalist parties.

A vote for any party but the Communist Party is worse than a wasted vote. It is a vote for the class enemies of the workers. A vote for hunger, war, unemployment; for the thousand-fold material and spiritual oppressions which flow from capitalism. A vote for the Communist Party is not a wasted vote. It is an effective protest against a system which permits the necessities of life to be destroyed rather than let them be consumed by those who cannot pay for them.

Why should intellectual workers be loyal to the ruling class which frustrates them, stultifies them, patronizes them, makes their work ridiculous, and now starves them? There are teachers on the bread lines, engineers patching the sheet-iron shacks in the "Hooversvilles," musicians fiddling in the "jungles." The professionals are not yet starving as the proletariat is starving. But since 1929 there reigns a permanent superfluity in the ranks of the professional groups. We "intellectuals," like the workers, find ourselves superfluous. Is that because there is too much civilization, too much "culture"? No, it is because there is not enough.

We, too, the intellectual workers, are of the oppressed, and until we shake off the servile habit of that oppression we shall build blindly and badly, to the lunatic specifications of ignorance and greed. If we are capable of building a civilization, surely it is time for us to begin; time for us to assert our function, our responsibility; time for us to renew the pact of comradeship with the struggling masses, trapped by the failure of leadership in the blind miseries of a crumbling madhouse. In a few years dwindling opportunities for employment brought on by progressive rationalization of industry, capitalist economies in the social services of government and the whole anarchistic system of education which prevails under capitalism—will mean the pauperization of the most highly creative groups in society.

What is worse, the spiritual degradation which every independent intellectual or professional worker suffers when false money-standards are applied to his creative craft, will grow deeper. Today it is difficult for the professional conscientiously to perform his work in the face of demands made by his employers—that he use his art, his science, his skill for ends that are foreign to his professional activity. Tomorrow it will be impossible for the intellectual to function as a free personality under the pressure of vocational unemployment and the necessity of serving those upon whom he is dependent.

It is important that the professional workers realize that they do not constitute an independent economic class in society. They can neither remain neutral in the struggle between capitalism and Communism nor can they by their own independent action effect any social change. Their choice is between serving either as the cultural lieutenants of the capitalist class or as allies and fellow travelers of the working class. That for them is the historic issue which cannot be straddled by the multiform varieties of personal escape or settled by flying to the vantage points of above-the-battle moralities.

The struggle for the emancipation of society from the blight of capitalism is not only an economic question, it is a cultural question as well. Both in theory and in practice, capitalism is hostile to the genuine culture of the past and present and bitterly opposed to the new cultural tendencies which have grown out of the epic of working class struggle for a new society. "The bourgeoisie has robbed of their haloes various occupations hitherto regarded with awe and veneration. Doctor, lawyer, priest, poet and scientist have become its wage-laborers . . . it has left no other bond between man and man . . . but crude self-interest and unfeeling 'cash payment.' " No genuine culture can thrive in a society in which malnutrition is a natural cause of death, the exploitation of man by man the natural cause of wealth, and foreign war and domestic terror the natural means of retaining political power. It is capitalism which is destructive of all culture and Communism which desires to save civilization and its cultural heritage from the abyss to which the world crisis is driving it.

The intellectual worker is confronted on all sides by the massed unity of capitalism—chaotic and benighted in itself, yet organized enough when it works with its pawns—enforcing its own needs, confining them to its own limited and sterilizing program. How long will he suffocate within this narrow house? When will he attempt to break through this closed circle by alliance with the only militant force which seeks renovation?

In the interests of a truly human society in which all forms of exploitation have been abolished; in behalf of a new cultural renaissance which will produce intergrated, creative personalities, we call upon all men and women—especially workers in the professions and the arts—to join in the revolutionary struggle against capitalism under the leadership of the Communist Party.

Vote Communist—for Foster and Ford—on November 8.

GEORGI DIMITROFF, "THE UNITED FRONT"
August 2, 1935

Written by the Comintern's General Secretary, Georgi Dimitroff, "The United Front: The Struggle Against Fascism and War" was the main report delivered to the Seventh World Congress of the Communist International. An excerpt follows.

2. UNITED FRONT OF THE WORKING CLASS AGAINST FASCISM

Comrades, millions of workers and toilers of the capitalist countries ask the question: How can fascism be prevented from coming to power and how can fascism be overthrown after it has been victorious? To this the Communist International replies: *The first thing that must be done, the thing with which to begin, is to form a united front, to establish unity of action of the workers in every factory, in every district, in every region, in every country, all over the world. Unity of action of the proletariat on a national and international scale is the mighty weapon which renders the working class capable not only of successful defense but also of successful counter-attack against fascism, against the class enemy.*

Importance of the United Front

Is it not clear that joint action by the supporters of the parties and organizations of the two Internationals, the Communist and the Second International, would make it easier for the masses to repulse the fascist onslaught, and would heighten the political importance of the working class?

Joint action by the parties of both Internationals against fascism, however, would not be confined in its efforts to influencing their present adherents, the Communists and Social-Democrats; it would also exert a powerful influence on the ranks of the *Catholic, Anarchist and unorganized workers, even upon those who had temporarily become the victims of fascist demagogy.*

Moreover, a powerful united front of the proletariat would exert tremendous influence on *all other strata of the working people*, on the peasantry, on the urban petty bourgeoisie, on the intelligentsia. A united front would inspire the wavering groups with faith in the strength of the working class.

But even this is not all. The proletariat of the imperialist countries has possible allies not only in the toilers of its own countries but also in the *oppressed nations of*

Georgi Dimitroff, *The United Front: The Struggle Against Fascism and War* (New York, 1938), 30-43.

the colonies and semi-colonies. Inasmuch as the proletariat is split both nationally and internationally, inasmuch as one of its parts supports the policy of collaboration with the bourgeoisie, in particular its system of oppression in the colonies and semi-colonies, a barrier is put between the working class and the oppressed peoples of the colonies and semi-colonies, and the world anti-imperialist front is weakened. Every step on the road to unity of action in the direction of supporting the struggle for the liberation of the colonial peoples by the proletariat of the imperialist countries means transforming the colonies and semi-colonies into one of the most important reserves of the world proletariat.

If, finally, we bear in mind that international unity of action by the proletariat relies on the *steadily growing strength of the proletarian state, the land of socialism, the Soviet Union,* we see what broad perspectives are revealed by the realization of proletarian unity of action on a national and international scale.

The establishment of unity of action by all sections of the working class, irrespective of the party or organization to which they belong, is necessary *even before the majority of the working class is united in the struggle for the overthrow of capitalism and the victory of the proletarian revolution.*

Is it possible to realize this unity of action of the proletariat in the individual countries and throughout the whole world? Yes, it is. And it is possible at this very moment. The Communist International *puts no conditions for unity of action except one, and that an elementary condition acceptable for all workers, viz., that the unity of action be directed against fascism, against the offensive of capital, against the threat of war, against the class enemy.* This is our condition.

The Chief Arguments of the Opponents of the United Front

What objections can the opponents of the united front have and how do they voice their objections?

Some say: "To the Communists the slogan of the united front is merely a maneuver." But if it is a maneuver, we reply, why don't you expose the "Communist maneuver" by your honest participation in the united front? We declare frankly: We want unity of action by the working class, so that the proletariat may grow strong in its struggle against the bourgeoisie, in order that while defending today its current interests against attacking capital, against fascism, the proletariat may reach a position tomorrow to create the preliminary conditions for its final emancipation.

"The Communists attack us," say others. But listen, we have repeatedly declared: We shall not attack anyone, whether persons, organizations or parties, standing for the united front of the working class against the class enemy. But at the same time it is our duty, in the interests of the proletariat and its cause, to criticize those persons, organizations and parties that hinder unity of action by the workers.

"We cannot form a united front with the Communists, since they have a different program," says a third group. But you yourselves say that your program differs from the program of the bourgeois parties, and yet this did not and does not prevent you from entering into coalitions with these parties.

"The bourgeois-democratic parties are better allies against fascism than the Communists," say the opponents of the united front and the advocates of coalition with the bourgeoisie. But what does Germany's experience teach? Did not the Social-Democrats form a bloc with those "better" allies? And what were the results?

"If we establish a united front with the Communists, the petty bourgeoisie will take fright at the 'Red danger' and will desert to the fascists," we hear it said quite frequently. But does the united front represent a threat to the peasants, small traders, artisans, working intellectuals? No, the united front is a threat to the big bourgeoisie, the financial magnates, the *Junkers* and other exploiters, whose regime brings complete ruin to all these strata.

"Social-Democracy is for democracy, the Communists are for dictatorship; therefore we cannot form a united front with the Communists," say some of the Social-Democratic leaders. But are we offering you now a united front for the purpose of proclaiming the dictatorship of the proletariat? We make no such proposal now.

"Let the Communists recognize democracy, let them come out in its defense, then we shall be ready for a united front." To this we reply: We are adherents of Soviet democracy, the democracy of the toilers, the most consistent democracy in the world. But in the capitalist countries we defend and shall continue to defend every inch of bourgeois-democratic liberties, which are being attacked by fascism and bourgeois reaction, because the interests of the class struggle of the proletariat so dictate.

"But the tiny Communist Parties do not add anything by participating in the united front brought about by the Labor Party," say, for instance, the Labor leaders of Great Britain. Recall how the Austrian Social-Democratic leaders said the same things with reference to the small Austrian Communist Party. And what have events shown? It was not the Austrian Social-Democratic Party headed by Otto Bauer and Karl Renner that proved right, but the tiny Austrian Communist Party which at the right moment signaled the fascist danger in Austria and called upon the workers to struggle. The whole experience of the labor movement has shown that the Communists, with all their relative insignificance in number, are the motive power of the militant activity of the proletariat. Besides this, it must not be forgotten that the Communist Parties of Austria or Great Britain are not only the tens of thousands of workers who are adherents of the Party, but are *parts* of the world Communist movement, are *Sections of the Communist International,* the *leading* Party of which is the Party of a proletariat which has already achieved victory and rules over one-sixth of the globe.

"But the united front did not prevent fascism from being victorious in the Saar," is another objection advanced by the opponents of the united front. Strange is the logic of these gentlemen! First they leave no stone unturned to ensure the victory of fascism and then they rejoice with malicious glee because the united front which they entered into only at the last moment did not lead to the victory of the workers.

"If we were to form a united front with the Communists, we should have to withdraw from the coalition, and reactionary and fascist parties would enter the government," say the Social-Democratic leaders holding cabinet posts in various countries. Very well. Was not the German Social-Democratic Party in a coalition government? It was. Was not the Austrain Social-Democratic Party in office? It was. Were not the Spanish Socialists in the same government as the bourgeoisie? They were, too. Did the participation of the Social-Democratic Parties in the bourgeois coalition governments in these countries prevent fascism from attacking the proletariat? It did not. Consequently it is as clear as daylight that participation of Social-Democratic ministers in bourgeois governments *is not* a barrier to fascism.

"The Communists act like dictators, they want to prescribe and dictate everything to us." No. We prescribe nothing and dictate nothing. We only put forward our proposals, being convinced that if realized they will meet the interests of the working people. This is not only the right but the duty of all those acting in the name of the workers. You are afraid of the "dictatorship" of the Communists? Let us jointly submit all proposals to the workers, both yours and ours, jointly discuss them together with all the workers, and choose those proposals which are most useful to the cause of the working class.

Thus all these arguments against the united front *will not stand the slightest criticism.* They are rather the flimsy excuses of the reactionary leaders of Social-Democracy, who prefer their united front with the bourgeoisie to the united front of the proletariat.

No. These excuses will not hold water. The international proletariat has experienced the suffering caused by the split in the working class, and becomes more and more convinced that *the united front, the unity of action* of the proletariat *on a national and international scale, is at once necessary and perfectly possible.*

Content and Forms of the United Front

What is and ought to be the basic content of the united front at the present stage? The defense of the immediate economic and political interests of the working class, the defense of the working class against fascism, must form the *starting point* and *main content* of the united front in all capitalist countries.

We must not confine ourselves to bare appeals to struggle for the proletarian dictatorship. We must also find and advance those slogans and forms of struggle which arise from the vital needs of the masses, from the level of their fighting capacity at the present stage of development.

We must point out to the masses what they must do *today* to defend themselves against capitalist spoliation and fascist barbarity.

We must strive to establish the widest united front with the aid of joint action by workers' organizations of different trends for the defense of the vital interests of the toiling masses. This means:

First, joint struggle really to shift the burden of the consequences of the crisis onto the shoulders of the ruling classes, the shoulders of the capitalists, landlords—in a word, to the shoulders of the rich.

Second, joint struggle against all forms of the fascist offensive, in defense of the gains and the rights of the toilers, against the destruction of bourgeois-democratic liberties.

Third, joint struggle against the approaching danger of imperialist war, a struggle that will make the preparation of such a war more difficult.

We must tirelessly prepare the working class for a *rapid change in forms and methods of struggle* when there is a change in the situation. As the movement grows and the unity of the working class strengthens, we must go further, and prepare the transition *from the defensive to the offensive against capital,* steering toward the *organization of a mass political strike.* It must be an absolute condition of such a strike to draw into it the main trade unions of the countries concerned.

Communists, of course, cannot and must not for a moment abandon their own *independent work* of Communist education, organization and mobilization of the masses. However, to ensure that the workers find the road of unity of action, it is necessary to strive at the same time both for short-term and for long-term agreements that provide for *joint action with Social-Democratic Parties, reformist trade unions and other organizations of the toilers* against the class enemies of the proletariat. The chief stress in all this must be laid on developing *mass action* locally, *to be carried out by the local organizations* through local agreements.

While loyally carrying out the conditions of all agreements made with them, we shall mercilessly expose all sabotage of joint action on the part of persons and organizations participating in the united front. To any attempt to wreck the agreements—and such attempts may possible be made—we shall reply by appealing to the masses while continuing untiringly to struggle for restoration of the broken unity of action.

It goes without saying that the practical realization of the united front will take *various* forms in various countries, depending upon the condition and character of the workers' organizations and their political level, upon the situation in the particular country, upon the changes in progress in the international labor movement, etc.

These forms may include, for instance: coordinated joint action of the workers to be agreed upon *from case to case* on definite occasions, on individual demands or on the basis of a common platform; coordinated actions in *individual enterprises* or by *whole industries;* coordinated actions on a *local, regional, national* or *international scale;* coordinated actions for the organization of the *economic* struggle of the workers, carrying out of mass *political* actions, for the organization of joint *self-defense* against fascist attacks; coordinated action in rendering *aid to political prisoners and their families,* in the field of struggle against *social reaction;* joint actions in the defense of the *interests of the youth* and *women,* in the field of the *cooperative movement, cultural activity, sport, etc.*

It would be insufficient to rest content with the conclusion of a pact providing for joint action and the formation of contact committees from the parties and organizations participating in the united front, like those we have in France, for instance. That is only the first step. The pact is an auxiliary means for obtaining joint action, but by itself it does not constitute a united front. A contact commission between the leaders of the Communist and Socialist Parties is necessary to facilitate the carrying out of joint action, but by itself it is far from adequate for a real development of the united front, for drawing the widest masses into the struggle against fascism.

The Communists and all revolutionary workers must strive for the formation of elected (and in the countries of fascist dictatorship—selected from the most authoritative participants in the united front movement) *class bodies of the united front chosen irrespective of party*, at the *factories*, among the *unemployed*, in the *working class districts*, among the *small townsfolk* and in the *villages*. Only such bodies will be able to include also in the united front movement the vast masses of unorganized toilers, and will be able to assist in developing mass initiative in the struggle against the capitalist offensive of fascism and reaction, and on this basis create the necessary *broad active rank and file of the united front* and train hundreds and thousands of non-Party Bolsheviks in the capitalist countries.

Joint action of the *organized* workers is the beginning, the foundation. But we must not lose sight of the fact that the unorganized masses constitute the vast majority of workers. Thus, in *France* the number of organized workers—Communists, Socialists, trade union members of various trends—is altogether *about one million*, while the total number of workers is *eleven million*. In *Great Britain* there are approximately *five million* members of trade unions and parties of various trades. At the same time the total number of workers is *fourteen million*. In the *United States of America* about *five million workers* are organized, while altogether there are *thirty-eight million* workers in that country. About the same ratio holds good for a number of other countries. In "normal" times this mass in the main does not partitipate in political life. But now this gigantic mass is getting into motion more and more, is being brought into political life, comes out in the political arena.

The creation of non-partisan class bodies is the *best form* for carrying out, extending and strengthening the united front among the rank and file of the masses. These bodies will likewise be the best bulwark against any attempt of the opponents of the united front to disrupt the established unity of action of the working class.

The Anti-Fascist People's Front

In mobilizing the mass of working people for the struggle against fascism, the formation of a *wide, popular anti-fascist front on the basis of the proletarian united front* is a particularly important task. The success of the whole struggle of the proletariat is closely bound up with establishing a fighting alliance between the proletariat on the one hand, and the toiling peasantry and basic mass of the urban petty bourgeoisie, who together form the majority of the population even in industrially developed countries, on the other.

In its agitation, fascism, desirous of winning these masses to its own side, tries to set the mass of working people in town and countryside against the revolutionary proletariat, frightening the petty bourgeoisie with the bogey of the "Red peril." We must *turn this weapon against those who wield it* and show the working peasants, artisans and intellectuals whence the real danger threatens. We must *show concretely* who it is that piles the burden of taxes and imposts on to the peasant and squeezes usurious interest out of him; who it is that, while owning the best land and every form of wealth, drives the peasant and his family from his plot of land and dooms him to unemployment and poverty. We must explain concretely, patiently and persistently who it is that ruins the artisans and handicraftsmen with taxes, imposts, high rents and competition impossible for them to withstand; who it is that throws into the street and deprives of employment the wide masses of the working intelligentsia.

But this is *not enough*.

The fundamental, the most decisive thing in establishing the anti-fascist People's Front is *resolute action of the revolutionary proletariat* in defense of the demands of these sections of the people, particularly the working peasantry—demands in line with the basic interests of the proletariat—and in the process of struggle combining the demands of the working class with these demands.

In forming the anti-fascist People's Front, a correct approach to those organizations and parties which have in them a considerable number of the working peasantry and the mass of the urban petty bourgeoisie is of great importance.

In the capitalist countries the majority of these parties and organizations, political as well as economic, are still under the influence of the bourgeoisie and follow it. The social composition of these parties and organizations is heterogeneous. They include big kulaks (rich peasants) side by side with landless peasants, big business men alongside of petty shopkeepers; but control is in the hands of the former, the agents of big capital. This obliges us to *approach the different organizations in different ways*, taking into consideration that not infrequently the bulk of the membership does not know anything about the real political character of its leadership. Under certain conditions, we can and must try to draw these parties and organizations or certain sections of them to the side of the anti-fascist People's Front, despite their bourgeois leadership. Such, for instance, is today the situation in France with the Radical Party, in the United States with various farmers' organizations, in Poland with the "Stronnictwo Ludowe," in Yugoslavia with the Croatian Peasants' Party, in Bulgaria with the Agrarian League, in Greece with the Agrarians, etc. But regardless of whether or not there is any chance of attracting these parties and organizations as a whole to the People's Front, our tactics must *under all circumstances* be directed toward drawing the small peasants, artisans, handicraftsmen, etc., among their members into the anti-fascist People's Front.

Hence, you see that in this field we must all along the line put an end to what frequently occurs in our practical work—neglect or contempt of the various organizations and parties of the peasants, artisans and the mass of petty bourgeoisie in the towns.

Key Questions of the United Front in Individual Countries

There are in every country certain *key questions* which at the present stage are agitating vast masses of the population and around which the struggle for the establishment of the united front must be developed. If these key points, or key questions, are properly grasped, it will ensure and accelerate the establishment of the united front.

A. The United States of America

Let us take, for example, so important a country in the capitalist world as the United States of America. There millions of people have been set into motion by the crisis. The program for the recovery of capitalism has collapsed. Vast masses are beginning to abandon the bourgeois parties and are at present at the crossroads.

Embryo American fascism is trying to direct the disillusionment and discontent of these masses into reactionary fascist channels. It is a peculiarity of the development of American fascism that at the present stage this fascism comes forward principally in the guise of an opposition to fascism, which it accuses of being an "un-American" tendency imported from abroad. In contradistinction to German fascism, which acts under anti-constitutional slogans, American fascism tries to portray itself as the custodian of the Constitution and "American democracy." It does not yet represent a directly menacing force. But if it succeeds in penetrating to the wide masses who have become disillusioned with the old bourgeois parties it may become a serious menace in the very near future.

And what would the success of fascism in the United States involve? For the mass of working people it would, of course, involve the unrestrained strengthening of the regime of exploitation and the destruction of the working-class movement. And what would be the international significance of this success of fascism? As we know, the United States is not Hungary, or Finland, or Bulgaria, or Latvia. The success of fascism in the United States would vitally change the whole international situation.

Under these circumstances, can the American proletariat content itself with organizing only its class-conscious vanguard, which is prepared to follow the revolutionary path? No.

It is perfectly obvious that the interests of the American proletariat demand that all its forces dissociate themselves from the capitalist parties without delay. It must find in good time ways and suitable forms to prevent fascism from winning over the wide mass of discontented working people. And here it must be said that under American conditions the creation of a mass party of working people, a *"Workers' and Farmers' Party,"* might serve as such a suitable form. *Such a party would be a specific form of the mass People's Front in America* and should be put in opposition to the parties of the trusts and the banks, and likewise to growing fascism. Such a party, of course, will be *neither* Socialist *nor* Communist. But it *must be* an anti-fascist party and *must not be* an anti-Communist Party. The program of this party must be directed against the banks, trusts and monopolies, against the principal enemies of the people, who are gambling on the woes of the latter. Such a party will correspond to its name only if it defends the urgent demands of the working class, only if it fights for genuine social legislation, for unemployment insurance; only if it fights for land for the white and black sharecroppers and for their liberation from debt burdens; only if it tries to secure the cancellation of the farmers' indebtedness; only if it fights for equal status for Negroes; only if it defends the demands of the war veterans and the interests of members of the liberal professions, small businessmen and artisans. And so on.

It goes without saying that such a party will fight for the election of its own candidates to local government, to the state legislatures, to the House of Representatives and the Senate.

Our comrades in the United States acted rightly in taking the initiative for the creation of such a party. But they still have to take effective measures in order to make the creation of such a party the cause of the masses themselves. The question of forming a "Workers' and Farmers' Party," and its program, should be discussed at mass meetings of the people. We should develop the most widespread movement for the creation of such a party, and take the lead in it. In no case must the initiative of organizing the party be allowed to pass to elements desirous of utilizing the discontent of the millions who have become disillusioned in both the bourgeois parties, Democratic and Republican, in order to create a "third party" in the United States, as an anti-Communist party, a party directed against the revolutionary movement. . . .

DOCUMENTS ON THE DISSOLUTION OF
THE COMINTERN, 1943

Proposal of the Presidium of the Executive Committee of the Communist International for the Dissolution of the Communist International

May 15, 1943

The historical role of the Communist International, organized in 1919 as the result of the political collapse of the overwhelming majority of the old pre-war workers' parties, consisted in that it preserved the teachings of Marxism from vulgarization and distortion by opportunist elements of the labor movement. In a number of countries it helped to unite the vanguard of the advanced workers into genuine workers' parties, and it helped them to mobilize the mass of toilers in defense of their economic and political interests for struggle against fascism and war, which fascism had been preparing, and for the support of the Soviet Union as the main bulwark against fascism.

The Communist International revealed in good time the true significance of the "Anti-Comintern Pact" as a weapon in the war preparations of the Hitlerites. Long prior to the war the Communist International tirelessly exposed the base, undermining activities of the Hitlerites in foreign states, who masked these with outcries about alleged interference of the Communist International in the internal affairs of these states.

But long before the war it had already become increasingly clear that to the extent that the internal as well as the international situation of individual countries became more complicated, the solution of the problems of the labor movement of each individual country through the medium of some international center would meet with insuperable obstacles.

The deep difference in the historical roads of development of each country of the world; the diverse character and even the contradiction in their social orders; the difference in level and rate of their social and political development, and finally, the difference in the degree of consciousness and organization of the workers, conditioned also the various problems which face the working class of each individual country.

The entire course of events for the past quarter of a century, as well as the accumulated experiences of the Communist International, have convincingly proven that the organizational form for uniting the workers as chosen by the First Congress of the Communist International, and which corresponded to the needs of the initial period of the rebirth of the labor movement, more and more outlived itself in proportion to the growth of this movement and to the increasing complexity of

The Communist, XXII (July 1943), 668-72.

problems in each country; and that this form even became a hindrance to the further strengthening of the national workers' parties.

The world war unleashed by the Hitlerites still further sharpened the differences in the conditions in various countries, showing the deep line of demarcation between the countries which became the bearers of Hitlerite tyranny and the freedom-loving peoples united in the mighty anti-Hitler coalition.

Whereas in the countries of the Hitlerite bloc the basic task of the workers, toilers and all honest people is to contribute in every conceivable way toward the defeat of this bloc by undermining the Hitlerite war machine from within and by helping to overthrow the governments responsible for the war, in countries of the anti-Hitler coalition the sacred duty of the broadest masses of the people and first and foremost of the progressive workers is to support in every way the war efforts of the governments in these countries for the sake of the speediest destruction of the Hitlerite bloc and to secure friendly collaboration between nations on the basis of their equal rights.

At the same time it must not be overlooked that the individual countries which adhere to the anti-Hitler coalition also have their specific tasks. Thus, for instance, in countries occupied by Hitlerites and which have lost their state independence, the basic task of progressive workers and broad masses of people is to develop the armed struggle which is growing into a national war of liberation against Hitlerite Germany.

At the same time, the war of liberation of the freedom-loving peoples against Hitlerite tyranny, which set into motion the broadest masses of people who are uniting in the ranks of the mighty anti-Hitler coalition irrespective of party or religion, made it still more evident that the national upsurge and mobilization of the masses for speediest victory over the enemy can best and most fruitfully be supplied by the vanguard of the labor movement of each country within the framework of its state.

The Seventh Congress of the Communist International, held in 1935, taking into consideration the changes which had come to pass in the international situation as well as in the labor movement—changes which demanded greater flexibility and independence of its sections in solving the problems facing them—already then emphasized the need for the Executive Committee of the Communist International, when deciding upon all the problems of the labor movement, "to proceed in deciding any question from the concrete situation and specific conditions obtaining in each particular country and as a rule to avoid direct intervention in internal organizational matters of the Communist Party."

The Executive Committee of the Communist International was guided by these same considerations when it took note of and approved the decision of the Communist Party of the United States of America in November, 1940, to leave the ranks of the Communist International.

Communists, guided by the teachings of the founders of Marxism-Leninism, have never advocated the preservation of those organizational forms which have become obsolete. They have always subordinated the organizational forms of the labor movement and its methods of work to the basic political interests of the labor movement as a whole, to the peculiarities of given concrete historical conditions, and to those problems which arise directly from these conditions.

They remember the example of the great Marx who united the progressive workers into the ranks of the International Workingmen's Association. And after the First International had fulfilled its historical task, having laid the basis for the development of workers' parties in the countries of Europe and America, Marx, as a result of the growing need to create national workers' mass parties, brought about the dissolution of the First International, inasmuch as this form of organization no longer corresponded to this need.

Proceeding from the above-stated considerations, and taking into account the growth and political maturity of the Communist Parties and their leading cadres in the individual countries, and also in view of the fact that during the present war a number of sections have raised the question of the dissolution of the Communist International as the guiding center of the international labor movement, the Presidium of the Executive Committee of the Communist International, unable owing to the conditions of world war to convene a congress of the Communist International, permits itself to submit for approval by the sections of the Communist International the following proposal:

To dissolve the Communist International as the guiding center of the international labor movement, releasing the sections of the Communist International from obligations ensuing from the constitution and decisions of the congresses of the Communist International.

The Presidium of the Executive Committee of the Communist International calls upon all adherents of the Communist International to concentrate their forces on all-round support and active participation in the liberation war of the peoples and states of the anti-Hitler Coalition in order to hasten the destruction of the mortal enemy of the working people—German fascism and its allies and vassals.

Signed by the members of the Presidium of the Executive Committee of the Communist International: Gottwald, Dimitroff, Zhdanov, Kolarov, Koplenig, Kuusinen, Manuilsky, Marty, Pieck, Thorez, Florin, Ercoli.

This resolution was endorsed by representatives of the following parties: Bianco (Italy), Dolores Ibarruri (Spain), Lehtinen (Finland), Pauker (Rumania), Rakosi (Hungary).

The Letter of Joseph Stalin to Harold King, Reuter Correspondent, in Reply to a Question with Reference to the Dissolution of the Communist International

May 28, 1943

Dear Mr. King: I have received your request to answer a question referring to the dissolution of the Communist International. I am sending you my answer.

Question: "The British comment on the decision to wind up the Comintern has been very favorable. What is the Soviet view of this matter and of its bearing on future international relations?"

Answer: This dissolution of the Communist International is proper and timely because it facilitates the organization of the common onslaught of all freedom-loving nations against the common enemy—Hitlerism.

The dissolution of the Communist International is proper because:

A. It exposes the lie of the Hitlerites to the effect that "Moscow" allegedly intends to intervene in the life of other nations and to "Bolshevize" them. An end is now being put to this lie.

B. It exposes the calumny of the adversaries of Communism within the labor movement to the effect that the Communist Parties in the various countries are allegedly acting not in the interest of their people but on orders from the outside. An end is now being put to this calumny too.

C. It facilitates the work of the patriots in the freedom-loving countries for uniting the progressive forces of their respective countries, regardless of party or religious faith, into a single camp of national liberation—for unfolding the struggle against fascism.

D. It facilitates the work of the patriots of all countries for uniting all the freedom-loving peoples into a single international camp for the fight against the menace of world domination by Hitlerism, thus clearing the way to the future organization of the companionship of nations based upon their equality.

I think that all these circumstances taken together will result in the further strengthening of the united front of the allies and other United Nations in their fight for victory over Hitlerite tyranny.

I feel that the dissolution of the Communist International is perfectly timely because it is exactly now, when the fascist beast is exerting its last strength, that it is necessary to organize the common onslaught of the freedom-loving countries to finish off this beast and to deliver the peoples from fascist oppression.

With respect,

J. Stalin

The Statement of Georgi Dimitroff, in Behalf of the Presidium of the Executive Committee of the Communist International, on the Approval by the Comintern Sections of the Proposal to Dissolve the Communist International

June 10, 1943

At its last meeting on June 8, 1943, the Presidium of the Executive Committee of the Communist International considered the resolutions received from its affiliated sections with regard to the decision of May 15, 1943, proposing the dissolution of the Communist International, and established:

1. That the proposal to dissolve the Communist International has been approved by the Communist Party of Argentina, the Communist Party of Australia, the Communist Party of Austria, the Communist Party of Belgium, the Communist Party of Bulgaria, the Communist Party of Canada, the United Socialist Party of Catalonia, the Communist Party of Chile, the Communist Party of China, the Communist Party of Colombia, the Revolutionary Communist Union of Cuba, the Communist Party of Czechoslovakia, the Communist Party of Finland, the Communist Party of France, the Communist Party of Germany, the Communist Party of Great Britain, the Communist Party of Hungary, the Communist Party of Ireland, the Communist Party of Italy, the Communist Party of Mexico, the Workers' Party of Poland, the Communist Party of Rumania, the Communist Party of the Soviet Union (Bolsheviks), the Communist Party of Spain, the Communist Party of Sweden, the Communist Party of Switzerland, the Communist Party of Syria, the Communist Party of the Union of South Africa, the Communist Party of Uruguay, the Communist Party of Yugoslavia, and the Young Communist International (affiliated to the Communist International as one of its sections).

2. That not one of the existing sections of the Communist International raised any objections to the proposal of the Presidium of the Executive Committee.

In view of the above-mentioned, the Presidium of the Executive Committee of the Communist International hereby declares:

1. That the proposal to dissolve the Communist International has been unanimously approved by all of its existing sections (including the most important ones) which were in a position to make their decisions known.

2. That it considers the Executive Committee of the Communist International, the Presidium and Secretariat of the Executive Committee, as well as the International Control Commission dissolved as of June 10, 1943.

3. It instructs the committee composed of Dimitroff (chairman), M. Ercoli, Dmitri Manuilsky and Wilhelm Pieck to wind up the affairs, dissolve the organs and dispose of the staff and property of the Communist International.

G. Dimitroff

On behalf of the Presidium of the Executive Committee of the Communist International.

EARL BROWDER
"THE CHANGES IN COMMUNIST ORGANIZATION"
1944

The organized Communists, or Marxists, of our country consider that the perspective and tasks which have been opened up by the Teheran concord are so basic and new that as a consequence some important changes are called for in our form of organization and methods of work. Final decisions are still to be made at a National Convention in the month of May. But already the nationwide discussions have revealed such unanimity of opinion that the main outline of the decisions to be taken can be given accurately in advance.

American Communists are relinquishing for an extended period the struggle for partisan advancement for themselves as a separate group, which is the main characteristic of a political party. The Communists foresee that the practical political aims they hold will for a long time be in agreement on all essential points with the aims of a much larger body of non-Communists, and that therefore our political actions will be merged in such larger movements. The existence of a separate political party of Communists, therefore, no longer serves a practical purpose but can be, on the contrary, an obstacle to the larger unity.

The Communists will, therefore, dissolve their separate political party, and find a new and different organizational form and name, corresponding more accurately to the tasks of the day and the political structure through which these tasks must be performed.

There will no longer be a Communist Party in the United States.

People who had been loudly demanding that the Communist Party should dissolve have been strangely disappointed now that their demand is being realized; they now say that it doesn't make a bit of difference, since there will still be Communists and they will freely associate for common work in another form. Evidently what they wanted, and still want, is that Communists should be required to commit suicide! A certain Dr. Counts, who but a few months ago published a whole book to prove that the Communist Party should dissolve, has suddenly changed his mind without any explanation and is equally vociferous in his demand that the Communists must be required to have their own separate party whether they wish it or not! Perhaps if history did not thus provide its own comic relief, it would be too oppressively serious for human nature.

Of course the Marxists, the Communists, will have an organization. But it will be *non-partisan* in character.

Earl Browder, *Teheran: Our Path in War and Peace* (New York, n.d.), ch. XVI, 117-21.

The political aims which we hold with the majority of Americans we will attempt to advance through the existing party structure of our country, which in the main is that of the peculiarly American "two-party system."

In my book *Victory—and After*, published in 1942, I gave an extended analysis of the two-party system and its workings. I showed how the Democratic and Republican parties had become semi-official institutions, buttressed in laws and customs which rendered difficult if not impossible the rise of new major parties. The complex and ever-changing currents of American political life have been channelized into these traditional forms which took shape in previous periods and in response to issues and political relations now long obsolete. The result is that today's political issues are fought out, not *between* the two parties, but *within* both of them. The adherents of a party are bound together by tradition rather than a common current agreement, and a growing portion of the population, now more than a third, identify themselves as *independent* of both parties, choosing between them not *en bloc* but anew on each office and issue presented for decision.

No one can predict any more which party has the majority in the country, because neither has a stable majority at any time. The independent voters who "split their vote," and who agree with neither party as a whole, hold a growing balance of power. Their role is enhanced by the system of "direct primaries" whereby in many states the government itself conducts the election of party leadership and candidates for public office, and in which any citizen can participate (sometimes by registering in a particular party, in other cases simply by choosing which ballot he will use when he enters the polling place).

We need not debate the question as to whether this is the best possible electoral system. It is the one we have, and there is no early perspective of any fundamental change. Our task is to do everything possible to make it work for the benefit of the nation.

Several ambitious attempts have been made in modern times to break out of this political strait jacket of the two-party system, when it was too obviously and drastically falsifying the political relations within the country. Such attempts were the Teddy Roosevelt "Bull Moose" movement of 1912, and the LaFollette movement of 1924. These revolts were of the most tremendous political significance, and hastened many modifications of the two-party practice, but they were not organizationally successful and brought no permanent major changes in the system.

The Farmer-Labor Party of Minnesota broke away from the Democratic Party in that state, and had a successful but brief career; but in 1944 it has almost unanimously decided to fuse once more with the traditional Democratic Party, finding the complications of a three-party system in their state an obstacle to unity. The Progressive Party in Wisconsin experienced some short-lived successes, but soon disintegrated under the Nazi-imitating leadership of Phil LaFollette.

In New York the American Labor Party has been able to rise to an important role because the state election laws, unlike most states, permit of fusion between parties by the expedient of naming a common candidate for the particular office, with the vote of both tickets being combined for the final count. The A.L.P. has been able, therefore, to maintain a coalition with the Democratic Party in national elections, with the Republican Party on some particular state offices, and run its own candidates for other posts, thus furnishing a very valuable organizational weapon for the independent voters. How precarious is its position, however, was shown when a bill was introduced in Albany to change the state election laws to prohibit a candidate from appearing on more than one ticket—that of the party with which he is registered. The bill was not adopted, but if the Republican majority in the legislature had considered it sufficiently in their interest, nothing could have prevented them making it law and thereby destroying the efficacy of the American Labor Party as it now operates. Thus the A.L.P. is always at the mercy of whichever other party controls the state legislature.

The Communists are not joining any existing political party as a group or organization. They are joining the body of independent voters who choose the best candidates from among those put forward by all parties. Individual Communists are at liberty to register under any party designation they see fit, in a way the independent progressives with whom they habitually associate may judge best.

The new organization which the Communists establish for their common non-partisan activities will take over and continue all those educational-political activities formerly carried on by the Communist Party, dropping the party-electoral features which embody the struggle for partisan advancement.

A name for the new Communist organization has not been agreed upon at the time this book goes to press. There is general agreement that the name will be something like *American Communist Political Association*. Another suggestion that will be considered is *Non-partisan Political Association*. The issue as between two such names is that of whether the term "Communist" should be continued. This is a question as to what is most expedient: to emphasize the long-term political character of the organization in its name or to emphasize its method of work with the broad democratic-progressive majority of the American people. In any case, the American public will be in no doubt whatever as to who are the Communists in our country, what they think, where they are and what they are doing. Communists have never been known as persons who habitually and by choice dissolve into the general landscape.

There has been in some quarters a misconception that the change in Communist organization and practice would mean that no Communist would henceforth run for office. That is no more true for Communists than it would be for other independents with whom we are joining our efforts. It does mean, however, that Communists will not run for office as the nominees only of their own group, and on a purely Communist platform. If a Communist is nominated for office it will be an act of broad circles of independent voters, similar to the naming of Benjamin J. Davis, Jr., and Peter Cacchione, to the New York City Council, in which case the candidates represented a circle of unity much larger than all but one or two of the entire list of candidates. Whenever a Communist will properly represent and help weld the larger unity by accepting a nomination, there will be no hesitation to run for office.

We may sum up the whole question of the changes in Communist organization and procedure by saying they are guided by the single thought—to make the

Communists more active and efficient participants in the unification of the American working class and the nation as a whole, to fight for progress and enlightenment, for victory in the war and for a durable peace of prosperity and freedom.

We know from our own experience, and from the experience of most countries of the world, that the Communists have a great and growing contribution to make to our own country, the United States.

JACQUES DUCLOS, CRITIQUE OF EARL BROWDER
April 1945

Duclos was Secretary of the Communist Party of France. "On the Dissolution of the Communist Party of the United States" originally appeared in the April 1945 issue of Cahiers du Communisme, *the theoretical organ of the Communist Party of France.*

Many readers of *Cahiers du Communisme* have asked us for clarification on the dissolution of the Communist Party of the U.S.A. and the creation of the Communist Political Association.

We have received some information on this very important political event, and thus we can in full freedom give our opinion on the political considerations which were advanced to justify the dissolution of the Communist Party.

The reasons for dissolution of the Communist Party in the U.S.A. and for the "new course" in the activity of American Communists are set forth in official documents of the Party and in a certain number of speeches of its former secretary, Earl Browder.

In his speech devoted to the results of the Teheran Conference and the political situation in the United States, delivered December 12, 1943, in Bridgeport and published in the Communist magazine in January, 1944, Earl Browder for the first time discussed the necessity of changing the course of the C.P.U.S.A.

The Teheran Conference served as Browder's point of departure from which to develop his conceptions favorable to a change of course of the American C.P. However, while justly stressing the importance of the Teheran Conference for victory in the war against fascist Germany, Earl Browder drew from the Conference decisions erroneous conclusions in no wise flowing from a Marxist analysis of the situation. Earl Browder made himself the protagonist of a false concept of the ways of social evolution in general, and in the first place, the social evolution of the United States.

Earl Browder declared, in effect, that at Teheran capitalism and socialism had begun to find the means of peaceful co-existence and collaboration in the framework of one and the same world; he added that the Teheran accords regarding common policy similarly presupposed common efforts with a view to reducing to a minimum or completely suppressing methods of struggle and opposition of force to force in the solution of internal problems of each country.

> That (the Teheran Declaration) is the only hope of a continuance of civilization in our time. That is why I can accept and support and believe in the Declaration at Teheran and make it the starting point for all my

Jacques Duclos, "On the Dissolution of the Communist Party of the United States," *Political Affairs*, XXIV (July 1945), 656-63.

thinking about the problems of our country and the world. (Address at Bridgeport, Conn., December 12, 1943.)

Starting from the decisions of the Teheran Conference, Earl Browder drew political conclusions regarding the problems of the world, and above all the internal situation in the United States. Some of these conclusions claim that the principal problems of internal political problems of the United States must in the future be solved exclusively by means of reforms for the "expectation of unlimited inner conflict threatens also the perspective of international unity held forth at Teheran." (*Teheran and America*, pp. 16-17.)

The Teheran agreements mean to Earl Browder that the greatest part of Europe, west of the Soviet Union, will probably be reconstituted on a bourgeois-democratic basis and not on a fascist-capitalist or Soviet basis.

But it will be a capitalist basis which is conditioned by the principle of complete democratic self-determination for each nation, allowing full expression within each nation of all progressive and constructive forces and setting up no obstacles to the development of democracy and social progress in accordance with the varying desires of the peoples. It means a perspective for Europe minimizing, and to a great extent eliminating altogether, the threat of civil war after the international war. (Bridgeport speech, *The Communist*, January, 1944, p. 7.)

And Earl Browder adds:

Whatever may be the situation in other lands, in the United States this means a perspective in the immediate postwar period of expanded production and employment and the strengthening of democracy within the framework of the present system—and not a perspective of the transition to socialism.

We can set our goal as the realization of the Teheran policy, or we can set ourselves the task of pushing the United States immediately into socialism. Clearly, however, we cannot choose both.

The first policy, with all its difficulties, is definitely within the realm of possible achievement. The second would be dubious, indeed, especially when we remember that even the most progressive section of the labor movement is committed to capitalism, is not even as vaguely socialistic as the British Labor Party.

Therefore, the policy for Marxists in the United States is to face with all its consequences the perspective of a capitalist postwar reconstruction in the United States, to evaluate all plans on that basis, and to collaborate actively with the most democratic and progressive *majority* in the country, in a *national unity* sufficiently broad and effective to realize the policies of Teheran. (*Teheran and America*, p. 20.)

To put the Teheran policy into practice, Earl Browder considers that it is necessary to reconstruct the entire political and social life of the United States.

> Every class, every group, every individual, every political party in America will have to readjust itself to this great issue embodied in the policy given to us by Roosevelt, Stalin and Churchill. The country is only beginning to face it so far. Everyone must begin to draw the conclusion from it and adjust himself to the new world that is created by it. Old formulas and old prejudices are going to be of no use whatever to us as guides to find our way in this new world. We are going to have to draw together all men and all groups with the intelligence enough to see the overwhelming importance of this issue, to understand that upon its correct solution depends the fate of our country and the fate of civilization throughout the world.
> We shall have to be prepared to break with anyone that refuses to support and fight for the realization of the Teheran Agreement and the Anglo-Soviet-American Coalition. We must be prepared to give the hand of cooperation and fellowship to everyone who fights for the realization of this coalition. If J. P. Morgan supports this coalition and goes down the line for it, I as a Communist am prepared to clasp his hand on that and join with him to realize it. Class divisions or political groupings have no significance now except as they reflect one side or the other of this issue. (Bridgeport speech, January, 1944, *The Communist*, p. 8.)

Browder's remark regarding Morgan provoked quite violent objections from members of the American C.P. Explaining this idea to the plenary session of the central committee, Browder said that:

> . . . I was not making a verbal abolition of class differences, but that I was rejecting the political slogan of "class against class" as our guide to political alignments in the next period. I spoke of Mr. Morgan symbolically as the representative of a class, and not as an individual—in which capacity I know him not at all. (*Teheran and America,* p. 24.)

As Browder indicates, creation of a vast national unity in the U.S. presupposes that the Communists would be a part of this. Thus, the Communist organization must conclude a long-term alliance with far more important forces. From these considerations, Browder drew the conclusion that the Communist organization in the U.S. should change its name, reject the word "party" and take another name more exactly reflecting its role, a name more in conformity, according to him, with the political traditions of America.

Earl Browder proposed to name the new organization "Communist Political Association," which, in the traditional American two-party system, will not intervene as a "party," that is, it will not propose candidates in the elections, will neither enter the Democratic or Republican Party, but will work to assemble a broad progressive and democratic movement within all parties.

In his report to the plenary session of the central committee of the C.P.U.S.A., Browder spoke in detail of the economic problems of U.S. postwar national economy, and their solution on the basis of collaboration and unity of different classes. Browder indicated that American business men, industrialists, financiers and even reactionary organizations do not admit the possibility of a new economic crisis in the U.S. after the war. On the contrary, all think that U.S. national economy after the war can preserve and maintain the same level of production as during the war.

However, the problem is in the difficulties of transition from wartime economic activity to peacetime production, and in the absorption by home and foreign markets of $90 billions in supplementary merchandise which the American government is now buying for war needs. In this regard, Earl Browder claims that the Teheran Conference decisions make possible the overcoming of Anglo-American rivalry in the struggle for foreign outlets, and that the government of the United States, in agreement with its great Allies, and with the participation of governments of interested states, can create a series of giant economic associations for development of backward regions and war-devastated regions in Europe, Africa, Asia and Latin America.

As to extension of the home market, to permit absorption of a part of the $90,000,000,000 worth of merchandise, Browder suggests doubling the purchasing power of the average consumer, notably by wage increases.

> Marxists will not help the reactionaries, by opposing the slogan of "Free Enterprise" with any form of counter-slogan. If anyone wishes to describe the existing system of capitalism in the United States as "free enterprise," that is all right with us, and we frankly declare that we are ready to cooperate in making this capitalism work effectively in the postwar period with the least possible burdens upon the people. (*Teheran and America*, p. 21.)

Further, Browder claims that national unity could no more be obtained by following a policy based on slogans aimed at the monopolies and big capital.

> Today, to speak seriously of drastic curbs on monopoly capital, leading toward the breaking of its power, and imposed upon monopoly capital against its will, is merely another form of proposing the immediate transition to socialism. . . . (*Teheran and America*, p. 23.)

In his closing speech to the plenary session of the C.P. Central Committee in January, 1944, Browder tried to base himself on "theoretical" arguments to justify the change of course of the American C.P. Also he expressed his concept of Marxism and its application under present conditions.

Browder thinks that by pronouncing the dissolution of the C.P. and creating the C.P.A., the American Communists are following a correct path, resolving problems which have no parallel in history and demonstrating how Marxist theory should be applied in practice.

Marxism never was a series of dogmas and formulas; it never was a catalogue of prohibitions listing the things we must not do irrespective of new developments and new situations; it does not tell us that things cannot be done; it tells us how *to do* the things that have to be done, the things that history has posed as necessary and indispensable tasks. Marxism is a theory of deeds, not of don'ts. Marxism is therefore a positive, dynamic, creative force, and it is such a great social power precisely because, as a scientific outlook and method, it takes living realities as its starting point. It has always regarded the scientific knowledge of the past as a basis for meeting the new and unprecedented problems of the present and the future. And the largest problems today are new in a very basic sense.

We have more than ever the task to refresh ourselves in the great tradition of Marxism, completely freeing ourselves from the last remnants of the dogmatic and schematic approach. . . .

True, according to all of the textbooks of the past, we are departing from orthodoxy, because none of our textbooks foresaw or predicted a long period of peaceful relations in the world before the general advent of socialism. (*Teheran and America*, pp. 43-45.)

The new political course outlined by Browder found but few adversaries among the leading militants of the C.P.U.S.A. At the enlarged session of the political bureau of the Party, those who spoke up violently against Browder were William Foster, president of the C.P.U.S.A., and Darcy, member of the central committee and secretary of the Eastern Pennsylvania district.

Foster expounded his differences with Browder in two documents—in a letter to the national committee of the C.P.U.S.A. and in his introductory speech to the extraordinary session of the national committee on Feb. 8, 1944.

In these two documents, Foster criticizes Browder's theoretical theses regarding the change in the character of monopoly capital in the U.S.A., the perspectives of postwar economic development as well as Browder's position on the question of the Presidential elections.

In his Feb. 8 speech Foster also attacks those who, on the basis of Browder's theses, suggested that strikes be renounced in the postwar period.

But in neither one of these documents did Foster openly take a stand against the dissolution of the Communist Party.

In his report Comrade Browder, in attempting to apply the Teheran decisions to the United States, drew a perspective of a smoothly working national unity, including the decisive sections of American finance capital, not only during the war but also in the postwar; a unity which (with him quoting approvingly from Victory and After), would lead to "a rapid healing of the terrible wounds of the war" and would extend on indefinitely, in an all-class peaceful collaboration, for a "long term of years." In this picture, American imperialism virtually disappears, there remains hardly a trace of the class struggle, and Socialism plays practically no role whatever. (*Foster Letter to Members of N.C.*)

Foster violently criticized Browder because the latter while outlining a new course in the activity of the American C.P., had lost sight of several of the most fundamental principles of Marxism-Leninism.

It seems to me that Comrade Browder's rather rosy outlook for capitalism is based upon two errors. The first of these is an underestimation of the deepening of the crisis of world capitalism caused by the war. When questioned directly in Political Bureau discussion, Comrade Browder agreed that capitalism has been seriously weakened by the war, but his report would tend to give the opposite implication. The impression is left that capitalism has somehow been rejuvenated and is now entering into a new period of expansion and growth. (*Ibid.*)

According to Foster, world capitalism can surely count on a certain postwar boom, but it would be wrong to think that capitalism, even American capitalism, could maintain itself at the production level attained in wartime, and resolve, in a measure more or less satisfactory to the working class, the complex problems which will arise after the war.

Without diminishing the importance of the Teheran conference, Foster considered, nevertheless, that it would be an extremely dangerous illusion to think that Teheran had in any way changed the class nature of capitalism, that the Teheran conference had liquidated the class struggle, as it appears from Browder's speech. The fact that capitalism has learned to live in peace and in alliance with socialism is far from meaning that American monopoly capitalism has become progressive and that it can henceforth be unreservedly included in national unity in the struggle for the realization of the Teheran conference decisions.

The class nature of imperialistic capitalism, Foster asserted, is reactionary. This is why national unity with it is impossible. The furious attack of these circles against the democratic Roosevelt government—does this not supply a convincing proof? Can one doubt, after that, that the monopolist sections in the U.S. are enemies and not friends of the Teheran decisions as Earl Browder thinks?

The danger in this whole point of view is that, in our eagerness to secure support for Teheran, we may walk into the trap of trying to cooperate with the enemies of Teheran, or even of falling under their influence. Trailing after the big bourgeoisie is the historic error of social-democracy, and we must be vigilantly on guard against it. (*Foster Letter to Members of N.C.*)

Foster also criticized Browder for his attitude toward the National Association of Manufacturers, which is, in his opinion, one of the most reactionary organizations of monopoly capital in the U.S. However, Browder thought he had to approve a certain number of the economic measures of this association. He accepts its central slogan, that of "free private enterprise," which is in reality basically reactionary and contrary to the Roosevelt policy. What is more, Browder, counting on seeing workers' wages increased 100 per cent after the war, invites U.S. monopolists to share his good intentions and says to them: "[You] must find the solution in order to keep their plants in operation."

Citing these words of Browder's Foster declared:

In my opinion, it would be a catastrophe for the labor movement if it accepted such a plan or such an idea, even if only provisionally. Starting from a notoriously erroneous conception, that U.S. monopoly capitalism can play a progressive role Comrade Browder looks askance at all suggestions tending to subdue the monopolies, whereas the C.P. can accept only one policy, that of tending to master these big capitalists now and after the war. In calling for the collaboration of classes, Browder sows wrong illusions of tailism in the minds of trade union members. Whereas the job of the trade unions is to elaborate their policy and dictate it to the big employers.

As to the problems of postwar organization, Foster repudiated all illusions regarding the self-styled progressive role of monopoly capital. America, Foster declared, will emerge from the war as a powerful state in the world, the industrial magnates will be rather inclined to dictatorial acts than to compromises, and it is hardly likely, he added, that we can expect a progressive program from them.

So far as the bulk of finance capital is concerned, starting out with a prewar record of appeasement, it has, all through the war, followed a course of rank profiteering and often outright sabotage of both the domestic and foreign phases of the nation's war program, especially the former. While these elements obviously do not want the United States to lose the war, they are certainly very poor defenders of the policy of unconditional surrender. In the main, their idea of a satisfactory outcome of the war would be some sort of a negotiated peace with German reactionary forces, and generally to achieve a situation that would put a wet blanket on all democratic governments in Europe. (*Foster Letter to Members of N.C.*)

Foster thinks that Browder is right when he says that the question of socialism is not the issue of the present war and that to pose this question would only result in restricting the framework of national unity. But considering the fact that the successes of the U.S.S.R., will increase the interest of the masses in socialism, the Communists must explain to the workers the importance of the socialist development of our epoch and the way in which it concerns the U.S., for otherwise the Social Democrats could represent themselves as a part of socialism.

> The enforcement of the Teheran decisions, both in their national and international aspects, demands the broadest possible national unity, and in this national unity there must be workers, farmers, professionals, small businessmen and all of the capitalist elements who will loyally support the program. (*Foster Letter to Members of N.C.*)

Foster's letter to the National Committee and his speech at the extraordinary session of the National Committee on Feb. 8, 1944, against Browder's line, provoked violent criticism from those in attendance. Most speakers rejected Foster's arguments and supported the "new course" of the C.P.U.S.A. outlined by Browder.

Speaking during the meeting against Browder, Darcy said that in his opinion Foster's speech was not aimed at diminishing Browder's authority. Like Foster, Darcy violently criticized the interpretation given by Browder of the Teheran decisions and asserted that the political agreement of the big three powers who constitute the Teheran conference should not be considered as an agreement on the principal postwar economic problems.

Afterwards Darcy was expelled from the Party by the Congress on the proposal of a commission named by the Central Committee and headed by Foster, because, as the decision says, by sending to Party members a letter containing slanderous declarations on Party leaders, he attempted to create a fraction within the Party, and because he submitted the letter in question to the bourgeois press.

After the extraordinary session of the National Committee, a discussion on Browder's report to the plenary assembly of the Central Committee was opened in the basic organizations of the Party, in regional congresses and the Party press.

According to information published in the *Daily Worker*, after the discussion the organizations and regional congresses of the Party unanimously accepted Browder's proposals. As to Foster, he declared at the extraordinary session of the National Committee that he did not intend to make known his differences with Browder outside the Party Central Committee.

The Congress of the C.P.U.S.A. (held May 20, 1944) heard Browder's report in which he expressed his opinions regarding the political situation in the U.S. and he proposed adoption of a new course in the policy of Communists of the U.S.

Proposing a resolution on the dissolution of the C.P.U.S.A., Browder declared:

> On Jan. 11 the National Committee of the Communist Party in the interest of national unity and to enable the Communists to function most effectively in the changed political conditions and to make still greater contributions toward winning the war and securing a durable peace, recommended that the American Communists should renounce the aim of partisan advantage and the party form of organization. . . .

With that purpose, I propose in the name of the National Committee and in consultation with the most important delegations in this Convention, the adoption of the following motion:

I hereby move that the Communist Party of America be and hereby is dissolved. . . . (*Proceedings*, p. 11.)

After having accepted the resolution on dissolution of the C.P., the Congress of the C.P.U.S.A. proclaimed itself the Constituent Congress of the Communist Political Association of the United States and adopted a programmatic introduction to the Association's statutes. In this introduction it is said:

The Communist Political Association is a non-party organization of Americans which, basing itself upon the working class, carries forward the traditions of Washington, Jefferson, Paine, Jackson and Lincoln, under the changed conditions of modern industrial society.

It seeks effective application of democratic principles to the solution of the problems of today, as an advanced sector of the democratic majority of the American people.

It upholds the Declaration of Independence, the United States Constitution and its Bill of Rights, and the achievements of American democracy against all the enemies of popular liberties.

It is shaped by the needs of the nation at war, being formed in the midst of the greatest struggle of all history; it recognizes that victory for the free peoples over fascism will open up new and more favorable conditions for progress; it looks to the family of free nations, led by the great coalition of democratic capitalist and socialist states, to inaugurate an era of world peace, expanding production and economic well-being, and the liberation and equality of all peoples regardless of race, creed or color.

It adheres to the principles of scientific socialism, Marxism, the heritage of the best thought of humanity and of a hundred years' experience of the labor movement, principles which have proved to be indispensable to the national existence and independence of every nation: it looks forward to a future in which, by democratic choice of the American people, our own country will solve the problems arising out of the contradiction between the social character of production and its private ownership, incorporating the lessons of the most fruitful achievements of all mankind in a form and manner consistent with American traditions and character. . . . (Preamble, *Proceedings*, pp. 47-48.)

The Constituent Congress of the C.P.A. adopted a main political resolution, "National Unity for Victory, Security and a Durable Peace."

The resolution points out the exceptional importance of the Teheran conference decisions for victory over the aggressor and establishment of a lasting peace. It calls for reinforcement of national unity as the necessary conditions for the application of those historic decisions.

By national unity is meant union of all patriotic forces from Communists, Laborites to adherents of the Democratic and Republican parties. All ideological, religious and political differences must be subordinated to this unity. The resolution stresses the exceptional importance of the 1944 elections on whose results depend the country's unity and destiny. It recognizes the increasingly important role of the working class in national unity, its growing activity and its political influence.

The resolution flays the reactionary policy of groups led by Du Pont, Hearst, McCormick, characterizing this policy as pro-facist and treason, and calling on the American people to struggle against these groups.

The resolution then says that the majority of the American people is not yet convinced of the need for a more radical solution to social and economic problems with the aid of nationalization of big industry or by means of establishing socialism.

That is why, the immediate task consists in obtaining a higher level of production in the framework of the existing capitalist regime. With this, private employers must receive all possibilities to solve the problem of production and employment of labor. Solution of these problems is likewise, in the first place, linked to the maximum increase in the American people's purchasing power and extension of foreign commerce. If private industry cannot solve these tasks, the government must assume responsibility for their realization.

The resolution expresses itself against anti-Semitism, anti-Negro discrimination, calls for the outlawing of the "fifth column" and for the banning of calls by the latter for a negotiated peace with the aggressor.

The resolution concludes in these terms:

> For the camp of national unity, which is composed of the patriotic forces of all classes, from the working people to the capitalists, rests and depends upon the working class, the backbone and driving force of the nation and its win-the-war coalition. . . . It requires the extension of labor's united action of the A. F. of L., the C.I.O. and Railroad Brotherhoods. It requires the most resolute development of labor's political initiative and influence, with labor's full and adequate participation in the government. . . .
>
> . . . we Communists, as patriotic Americans, renew our sacred pledge to the nation to subordinate everything to win the war and to destroy fascism. . . . (*Resolutions*, p. 7.)

In addition to the resolution on "National Unity," the C.P.A. Congress passed a series of other decisions: on transition from war to peacetime production; on international trade union unity; on the C.P.A.'s wage policy; on political life as it regards demobilized veterans; on war among women; on farmers; on the situation in the southern states; on suppressing the poll tax; on the fight against anti-Semitism; on unity among countries of the western hemisphere and on the 25th anniversary of the Communist movement in the U.S.

The congress unanimously elected Browder president of the C.P.A.

The C.P.A. Congress addressed a message to Comrade Stalin and the Red Army saying especially:

In every American city and village, every factory and farm of our great land, men and women and children of all classes speak with wonder and deep gratitude of the heroic achievements of the Soviet Union and its valiant Red Army. Every day since the brutal and treacherous common Fascist enemy violated your borders on June 22, 1941, more of the American people have come to know and love your leaders and your people.

The political and military leadership of the U.S.S.R and its mighty Red Army is applauded not only by our great political and military leaders, but by our workers, farmers, businessmen, professional people, artists, scientists and youth. The appeasers of the Hitlerites and the enemies of our common victory, who have been trying to frighten us with Hitler's "Soviet bogey," have not succeeded in blinding our people to the realities. Your deeds daily speak with an authority that drowns their poisonous words.

As the relentless offensives of your mighty forces drive the Nazis from your soil, bringing nearer the day of your common and final victory over the Fascist enemy, we grow ever more conscious of our enormous debt to you, the leaders and fighters and peoples of the great Soviet land. The names of your liberated towns and villages are daily on our lips, the name of Stalin and the names of your countless heroes enshrined in our hearts.

Daily more and more of our people understand why it is that yours, the world's first Socialist state, has given the world such an unparalleled example of unity, heroism, individual initiative and a new discipline in the art and science of warfare.

All patriotic Americans are determined to strengthen still further the concerted action of the United Nations, and its leading coalition of our country, the Soviet Union and England on which our assurance of victory rests. They are determined to continue and deepen this coalition in the peace to come and to extend the friendship among our peoples which will cement the alliance of our two powerful nations as the mainstay of victory, national freedom and an enduring peace." (Message to Stalin, *Proceedings*, pp. 13-14.)

After the Constituent Congress, the leadership of the C.P.A. waged a campaign of explanation on the aims and tasks of the Association.

In one of his speeches Browder said:

. . . That is why we dissolved the Communist Party, renounced all aims of partisan advancement, and regrouped ourselves into the non-partisan

Communist Political Association. This is why we are ready and willing to work with any and all Americans who place victory in the war as the first law, and who move toward such a minimum program as we have outlined for the solution of our postwar problems. This is why we do not associate ourselves with any other political party, but rather with the most forward-looking men in all parties. ("The War and the Elections," *Daily Worker*, June 18, 1944.)

Explaining the functions of the C.P.A., its organizational secretary, Williamson, declared:

As regards the functioning of the Association, we emphasize that this means manifold increase and improvement in every aspect of political-educational activity, on a national, state and local club basis. We must become known as an organization whose grasp of Marxism provides us with correct answers to the complex political problems confronting the people. While the members belong to, and are active in, every type of mass organization—political, economic, cultural, fraternal, etc.—the Association in its own name will speak out boldly and with initiative on all issues and policies." (Williamson, *Proceedings*, pp. 55-56.)

The practical activity of the C.P.A. since the Congress was subordinated to the principal task of the hour: active participation of the C.P.A. in the 1944 election campaign.

The national C.P.A. Congress unanimously backed Mr. Roosevelt's Presidential candidacy. In their speeches, Browder, and the other leaders of the C.P.A. in the name of the C.P.A. supported Mr. Roosevelt's election to a fourth term. The regional-state organizations of the C.P.A. and local clubs carried on an active propaganda campaign in favor of Mr. Roosevelt and congressional candidates favorable to Mr. Roosevelt.

On Sept. 25, 1944, during a meeting called by the New York C.P.A. on the 25th anniversary of the Communist movement in the U.S., Browder gave a speech in which he declared:

... every group, however small, just as every individual has the same supreme duty to make its complete and unconditional contribution to victory. We must give not only our lives, but we must be ready also to sacrifice our prejudices, our ideologies, and our special interests. We American Communists have applied this rule first of all to ourselves.

We know that Hitler and the Mikado calculated to split the United Nations on the issue of Communism and anti-Communism; we know that the enemy calculated to split America on this issue in the current elections, and thus prepare our country for withdrawal from the war and a compromise peace. We therefore set ourselves, as our special supreme task, to remove the Communists and Communism from this election campaign as in any way an issue, directly or indirectly.

To this end we unhesitatingly sacrificed our electoral rights in this campaign, by refraining from putting forward our own candidates; we went to the length of dissolving the Communist Party itself for an indefinite period in the future; we declared our readiness to loyally support the existing system of private enterprise which is accepted by the overwhelming majority of Americans, and to raise no proposals for any fundamental changes which could in any way endanger the national unity; we went out into the trade unions and the masses of the people, straightforwardly and frankly using all our influence to firmly establish this policy of national unity; we helped with all our strength to restrain all impulses toward strike movements among the workers, and to prepare the workers for a continuation of national unity after the war. . . .

As spokesman for American Communists I can say for our small group that we completely identify ourselves with our nation, its interests and the majority of its people, in this support for Roosevelt and Truman for President and Vice-President.

We know quite well that the America that Roosevelt leads is a capitalist America, and that it is the mission of Roosevelt, among other things, to keep it so. We know that only great disaster for our country could change this perspective of our country from that of capitalism to that of socialism, in the forseeable future. Only failure to carry through the war to victory, or a botching of the peace and failure to organize it, or the plunging of our country into another economic catastrophe like that of the Hoover era, could turn the American people to socialism.

We do not want disaster for America, even though it results in socialism. If we did, we would support Dewey and Hoover and Bricker and their company. We want victory in the war, with the Axis powers and all their friends eliminated from the world. We want a world organized for generations of peace.

We want our country's economy fully at work, supplying a greatly multiplied world market to heal the wounds of the world, a greatly expanded home market reflecting rising standards of living here, and an orderly, cooperative and democratic working out of our domestic and class relationships, within a continuing national unity that will reduce and eventually eliminate large domestic struggles. . . .

That is why American Communists, even as our great Communist forebears in 1860 and 1864 supported Abraham Lincoln, will in 1944 support Franklin Delano Roosevelt for President of the United States. . . .

As to Browder's attitude toward the Soviet Union, he highly appreciates the U.S.S.R.'s role in the United Nations system and in the work of finally crushing Hitlerite Germany and establishing a lasting peace after the war. Browder stressed more than once that the Soviet state built by Lenin and Stalin constitutes the irreplaceable force which saved the world from fascist slavery and he called for it to be made known to all Americans all the wisdom of Leninist-Stalinist theory that made the Soviet Union great and powerful.

From an organizational point of view, the C.P.A. structure is as follows: the basic organizational cell is the territorial club whose general meeting is called once a month. Between general membership meetings all the work planned by the club is carried out by its committee, made up of the most active members. The clubs are subordinated to regional C.P.A. councils. The leading organization of the C.P.A. is the National Committee elected for two years at the Association Congress. The Association's president and 11 vice-presidents elected by the Congress comprise the permanent leading organization of the Association.

The C.P.A. Congress set forth maintenance of the principle of democratic centralism as the structural basis of the Association. Williamson, C.P.A. organizational secretary, explained to the Congress in these terms the application of the democratic centralism principle of the C.P.A.:

> ... While maintaining a structure and minimum organizational requirements compatible with the character of a Marxist political educational association, we must grant greater autonomy to the lower organizations, emphasize that democracy is a two-way street from top to bottom and bottom to top, and eliminate all rigidity of organization. (Williamson, *Proceedings*, p. 58.)

The national Congress of the Political Association adopted the C.P.A. constitution in which it said that everyone who wishes to belong to the C.P.A. accepts its program and its line.

Explaining who can belong to the Association, the *Daily Worker* wrote:

> We can ask of new applicants to membership in the Party only loyalty to the principles that are already comprehensive to all workers, devotion to the most basic duties of action today; plus a willingness and eagerness to study the program and history and the theory which will make them thorough Communists. And above all a willingness to fight, to sacrifice in the war of mankind against Nazi enslavement is the first requirement for entering the Communist Party. (Minor, *Daily Worker*, February, 1944.)

At the time of its dissolution the Communist Party of the United States, according to Browder's declaration, had 80,000 members without counting the 10,000 Party members in the army. According to the Congress decisions all members of the C.P.U.S.A. are members of the C.P.A. and must register before July 4, 1944. As the *Daily Worker* announced up to July 16, 1944, hardly 45,000 persons had gotten themselves registered.

Without analyzing in detail Browder's full position on the dissolution of the C.P.U.S.A. and creation of the Communist Political Association, and without making a developed critique of this position, one can nevertheless deduce from it the following conclusions.

1. The course applied under Browder's leadership ended in practice in liquidation of the independent political party of the working class in the U.S.

2. Despite declarations regarding recognition of the principles of Marxism, one is witnessing a notorious revision of Marxism on the part of Browder and his supporters, a revision which is expressed in the concept of a long-term class peace in the United States, of the possibility of the suppression of the class struggle in the postwar period and of establishment of harmony between labor and capital.

3. By transforming the Teheran declaration of the Allied governments, which is a document of a diplomatic character, into a political platform of class peace in the United States in the postwar period, the American Communists are deforming in a radical way the meaning of the Teheran declaration and are sowing dangerous opportunist illusions which will exercise a negative influence on the American labor movement if they are not met with the necessary reply.

4. According to what is known up to now, the Communist Parties of most countries have not approved Browder's position and several Communist Parties (for example that of the Union of South Africa and that of Australia) have come out openly against this position, while the Communist Parties of several South American countries (Cuba, Colombia) regarded the position of the American Communists as correct and in general followed the same path.

Such are the facts. Such are the elements of understanding which permit passing judgment on the dissolution of the American Communist Party. French Communists will not fail to examine in the light of Marxist-Leninist critique the arguments developed to justify the dissolution of the American Communist Party. Once can be sure that, like the Communists of the Union of South Africa and of Australia, the French Communists will not approve the policy followed by Browder for it has swerved dangerously from the victorious Marxist-Leninist doctrine whose rigorously scientific application could lead to but one conclusion, not to dissolve the American Communist Party but to work to strengthen it under the banner of stubborn struggle to defeat Hitler Germany and destroy everywhere the extensions of fascism.

The fact that all the members of the Communist Party of the United States did not sign up automatically in the Communist Political Association shows that the dissolution of the Party provoked anxieties, perfectly legitimate besides.

In the United States the omnipotent trusts have been the object of violent criticism. It is known, for instance, that the former Vice-President of the United States, Henry Wallace, has denounced their evil doings and their anti-national policy.

We too, in France, are resolute partisans of national unity, and we show that in our daily activity, but our anxiety for unity does not make us lose sight for a single moment of the necessity of arraying ourselves against the men of the trusts.

Furthermore one can observe a certain confusion in Browder's declarations regarding the problem of nationalization of monopolies and what he calls the transition from capitalism to socialism.

Nationalization of monopolies actually in no sense constitutes a socialist achievement, contrary to what certain people would be inclined to believe. No, in nationalization it is simply a matter of reforms of a democratic character, achievement of socialism being impossible to imagine without preliminary conquest of power.

Everyone understands that the Communists of the United States want to work to achieve unity in their country. But it is less understandable that they envisage the solution of the problem of national unity with the good will of the men of the trusts, and under quasi-idyllic conditions, as if the capitalist regime had been able to change its nature by some unknown miracle.

In truth, nothing justifies the dissolution of the American Communist Party, in our opinion. Browder's analysis of capitalism in the United States is not distinguished by a judicious application of Marxism-Leninism. The predictions regarding a sort of disappearance of class contradictions in the United States correspond in no wise to a Marxist-Leninist understanding of the situation.

As to the argument consisting of a justification of the Party's dissolution by the necessity of not taking direct part in the presidential elections, this does not withstand a serious examination. Nothing prevents a Communist Party from adapting its electoral tactics to the requirements of a given political situation. It is clear that American Communists were right in supporting the candidacy of President Roosevelt in the last elections, but it was not at all necessary for this to dissolve the Communist Party.

It is beyond doubt that if, instead of dissolving the Communist Party of the United States all had been done to intensify its activity in the sense of developing an ardent national and anti-fascist policy, it could very greatly have consolidated its position and considerably extended its political influence. On the contrary, formation of the Communist Political Association could not but trouble the minds and obscure the perspectives in the eyes of the working masses.

In France, under cover of Resistance unity, certain suggestions for the liquidation of the parties have been circulated, with more or less discretion, during the last months, but none among us has ever thought of taking such suggestions seriously. It is not by liquidating the Party that we would have served national unity. On the contrary we are serving it by strengthening our Party. And as far as the American Communists are concerned, it is clear that their desire to serve the unity of their country and the cause of human progress places before them tasks which pre-suppose the existence of a powerful Communist Party.

After the Teheran decisions came the Yalta decisions which expressed the will of the Big Three to liquidate fascism in Germany and to help the liberated peoples to liquidate the remnants of fascism in the different countries.

It is scarcely necessary to recall that the material bases for fascism reside in the trusts, and the great objective of this war, the annihilation of fascism, can only be obtained to the extent in which the forces of democracy and progress do not shut their eyes to the economic and political circumstances which engendered fascism.

The American Communists have an especially important role to play in the struggle taking place between the progressive forces of the earth and fascist barbarism.

Without any doubt they would have been in a better position to play this role in the interests of their country and human progress if, instead of proceeding to dissolve their Party, they had done everything to strengthen it and make of it one of the elements of the assembling of the broad democratic masses of the United States for the final crushing of fascism, that shame of the 20th Century. It would be useless to hide the fact that fascism has more or less concealed sympathizers in the United States, as it has in France and other countries.

The former Vice-President of the U.S., Henry Wallace, present Secretary of Commerce, said rightly that one cannot fight fascism abroad and tolerate at home the activity of powerful groups which intend to make peace "with a simple breathing spell between the death of an old tyranny and the birth of a new."

The Yalta decisions thwart these plans, but the enemies of liberty will not disarm of their free will. They will only retreat before the acting coalition of all the forces of democracy and progress.

And it is clear that if Comrade Earl Browder had seen, as a Marxist-Leninist, this important aspect of the problems facing liberty-loving peoples in this moment in their history, he would have arrived at a conclusion quite other than the dissolution of the Communist Party of the United States.

AMERICAN COMMUNIST PARTY DRAFT RESOLUTION
September 13, 1956

The party's National Committee prepared this lengthy statement for their 16th National Convention. It re-examines their past and adopts a more independent, post-Stalinist course. Excerpts follow.

A LETTER ON THE RESOLUTION

To all Members of the Communist Party

Dear Comrades: On Lincoln's Birthday 1957 our Party will hold its National Convention. The National Committee in accordance with its responsibilities to the party presents this Draft Resolution to serve as a basis for the pre-convention discussion.

In presenting this resolution, we feel that it indicates a sound approach for our Party towards overcoming its present isolation and strengthening its ties with the American working class and people; towards advancing the struggle for civil rights and security, and the cause of democracy and peace.

It should be borne in mind that this resolution is a draft. Everything in it is subject to discussion by the Party membership. Undoubtedly numerous amendments will result from the discussion. Final action on the resolution can be taken only by the convention.

The Resolution is the result of several weeks of work by the Resolution Committee. The Committee had before it the numerous rich contributions made by comrades in the preceding discussion in the Central and District Discussion Bulletins, in the letters to the Daily Worker, in resolutions from Party clubs and sections and in Party meetings from club to district levels.

The successive drafts were discussed in general and in detail at two lengthy meetings of the National Committee, and the Draft Resolution represents the collective thinking of the National Committee.

All members of the N.C. present voted for the resolution. Comrades Foster and Ben Davis voted "Yes" with qualifications. Each comrade will make known the nature of his qualifications shortly in the form of articles.

This does not mean that there were no other differences in the Resolution Committee and in the National Committee. Minor differences were resolved in the give and take of discussion. Major differences on the Resolution as a whole, or on important sections of the resolution will be brought before the Party as follows:

1. The National Committee has requested members of the N.C. to give their views in forthcoming issues of Political Affairs or in the Party Discussion Bulletin which will be published every two weeks beginning Nov. 1.

2. The N.C. will request certain of its members to write articles explaining how the position in the Resolution on various key questions was arrived at.

The Worker, September 23, 1956.

3. The National Committee is making its members available to speak at membership meetings and meetings of Party committees at all levels throughout the country.

The National Committee acknowledges the widespread criticism in the ranks of the Party, of our failure to participate adequately in the discussion in the past few months. There have been three meetings of the National Committee since the April session. The last two meetings revolved around the preliminary drafts of this Resolution. The N.C. decided that the most fruitful way to bring the thinking of its members to the Party was through the publication of the Draft resolution and subsequent individual articles and discussions at Party meetings. In doing this, the N.C. now recognizes that it had made inadequate preparations for participation in the general discussion in the interim.

We are conscious of the fact that the Resolution has certain weaknesses. It is over-long. It does not deal with the specific problems in the field of work among the youth, the farmers, in the women's movements or in the field of cultural work, with the question of Social-Democracy, nor in sufficient detail with the situation and developments in the labor movement. Additional material on these questions, and particularly on the Negro question and the right of self-determination, will be issued in the course of the discussion. It does not deal adequately with the new questions in the field of economics arising from the new situation that we confront today. These questions require extended study of the facts and the National Committee is appointing a special commission to develop such studies.

The discussion of the Resolution in the districts and lower organizations of the Party should be combined with a discussion of the concrete developments and trends among the masses in the states and counties, as well as an examination of the work of the respective Party organizations.

While the Resolution is reaching the Party as promised in the middle of September, the formal pre-convention discussion will not open until Nov. 1 so as to enable all Party organizations to participate fully during the month of October in the national election campaign.

This Resolution proposes far-reaching changes in our program, practices and outlook. We believe these changes are necessary if we are to meet the new situation that confronts us. We feel it will provide a focus for the discussion through which the membership will be able to make their views effective. We hope that this Resolution, shaped and amended as it will be by the membership, by the clubs, counties, state and national organizations in the course of the discussion, will provide a basis for our Party to consolidate its ranks, strengthen its mass work and open a new chapter in its record of service to the American working class and people.

Our pre-convention discussion will be unfolding against the background of important struggles of the American people. It will be truly fruitful only if it strengthens our participation in these current struggles and draws renewed inspiration from them. The National Committee calls for an intensification of all mass activities of the Party as the discussion proceeds.

Comradely yours,

National Committee,
Eugene Dennis,
General Secretary.

Foreword

We open our pre-convention discussion against the background of profound change on the world scene and many favorable developments at home.

The pulse of our people is quickened with high hope that the world is entering an era that can bring lasting peace, freedom and equality and an end to poverty and oppression.

This hope is rooted in reality. Out of World War II and the people's strivings of the postwar period have come great transformations, and more are in the making.

The defeat of fascism, to which our own country contributed, opened the way to the liberation of hundreds of millions. The people of China, whose land had for so long been the prey of foreign exploiters, and the countries of Eastern Europe took the path of socialism, along which the Soviet Union had blazed the trail. Socialism emerged as a world system embracing a third of mankind—a system which based its relations with the capitalist states on the perspective of peaceful economic competition and coexistence.

Nearly another third of mankind, in former colonial lands such as India and Indonesia, won their freedom from imperialism. Increasingly they pursued a course of neutrality and non-alignment in the cold war. They joined with other Asian and African nations at the historic Bandung Conference and endorsed the principles of peaceful coexistence and national independence for all peoples and states.

A new world situation and a new relationship of forces have come into being. America is part of this vast process of change. A gigantic united labor movement has been born, a tower of growing strength in the whole democratic struggle. The Negro people are on the march as they have not been since Reconstruction days. Together with many white citizens they are writing new imperishable pages in the history of the fight for American freedom. Atomic energy and new technological developments are revealing unprecedented possibilities of peace, progress and a life of abundance for all.

The American people stand on the threshold of great democratic advance. In crossing this threshold—and it can be crossed only by the most determined and united struggle—there is lost ground to be recovered as well as ground to be won. There are new vistas of peace; of a successful struggle against poverty and economic insecurity; of progress in housing, health and education; of securing full citizenship for the Negro people, undoing the evils of McCarthyism and Eastlandism, and achieving new gains for democracy.

As we look back to December 1950, when the last convention of the Communist Party was held, we can see how far our country and the world have moved.

At that time the war in Korea was at its height. The McCarran Act had just taken its place alongside the anti-labor Taft-Hartley Act. A divided labor movement had suffered a new political defeat in the November Congressional elections. The Supreme Court was soon to uphold the Smith Act convictions of Comrades Dennis, Winston and the other National Board members. Reaction was pressing its assault upon the Constitution and the Bill of Rights. Throughout the world, the men of Wall Street were prosecuting the cold war with mounting vigor.

Our party at its 15th Convention nevertheless saw that there were forces at work in our country and abroad that could save America and the world from disaster. Asserting its confidence in those forces, it proclaimed, "Peace Can Be Won."

Today, international tension has eased and the danger, though still present, has been reduced. The Geneva summit conference registered the possibility of ending the cold war, sharply cutting armaments and achieving peaceful coexistence.

Rampant McCarthyism has been checked and the deep democratic sentiments of the American people are reasserting themselves. Though Smith Act prosecutions continue and the McCarran Act still threatens American liberties, the wave of repression, fed by war hysteria, is becoming increasingly unpopular.

Any great new advance today, however, inevitably encounters the real enemy of peace, progress and democracy—the giant monopolies which have become ever more powerful during these same years.

These are the same corporations that in the thirties plunged our country into the worst economic disaster in our history. They aided and abetted the rise of Hitler and the Axis and engaged in a profit orgy during World War II. They are the same corporations that during the past decade were responsible for the reactionary foreign policy whose symbol was the cold war. They are the corporations that today breed poverty and insecurity for millions of Americans, gouge the farmers and drive small and medium size business to the wall. They are the economic beneficiaries from the many sided discrimination against and economic robbery of the Negro tenth of our population.

These monopolies are the real enemy of America. Only through united action against them can our people move forward toward realizing their aspirations.

We Communists in the future as in the past will seek to contribute our utmost to the realization of these aspirations. As advocates of socialism, we shall—in the course of the struggle against the trusts—help the American working class and people in their great majority come to see that these aspirations can be completely and permanently fulfilled only by a basic change in the economic system. This will require the replacement of the system of profits for the few with a system of production owned by the people and operated for the use of all.

For a number of months we Communists have been re-examining our policies and our methods of work and organization. This reappraisal is necessary because we, like other forward-looking political forces in America, have begun to see that there is a new situation in our country and in the world today. We need to study this new situation, summoning the full measure of our collective understanding as Marxists. We need to determine what it means as regards certain theoretical propositions and past policies and forms of organization.

There is, however, a further compelling reason that adds urgency to this reappraisal. It lies in the fact that although we have made many important contributions to the struggles of the American working class and people and have stood up honorably under intense political persecution, we have made a number of errors over the years. These errors need to be rectified and the necessary conclusions drawn therefrom if we are to measure up to the great responsibilities which confront our party and the working class in the period ahead, a period which will be marked by big political and economic struggles on the home front.

THE SITUATION TODAY

I

For a Prosperous America; for an end to poverty; for a new program of social advance

Production, total employment and profits in 1956 are at boom levels. For the past decade, this country has enjoyed a postwar period of relative prosperity. Since 1947, despite temporary declines, industrial production has risen by 42 percent.

Corporate profits before taxes jumped from $23.5 billion in 1946 to an annual rate of $43.6 billion in the first half of 1956. And by mid-1956, employment reached a record level of 66½ million.

Underlying this high level of the economy is a high rate of investment in fixed capital throughout the postwar period, motivated by the need to replace obsolete and worn equipment, by the requirements of large-scale arms production, and by technological advances. Added to this is, in recent years, a large investment in inventory accumulation.

No small part has been played by arms expenditures, which during the Korean war hit a peak rate of $55 billion a year, and are today running at an annual rate of some $41 billion.

Another factor is the boom in housing construction. Since 1949, non-farm housing starts have averaged well over a million a year. Still another is the steady growth in consumer credit, which now stands at a peak of over $36 billion.

For much of the postwar period, production was sparked chiefly by expanding arms budgets. Since 1954, however, a new upsurge has taken place, this time with no increase in military spending, but stimulated instead by tax rebates and giveaways, and by a huge credit inflation. The American economy today has taken on much of the aspect of a speculative peacetime boom, reminiscent in some respects of that of the 20s.

But the boom has by no means brought prosperity for all. The past several years have seen farm incomes falling by one-third between 1947 and the middle of 1956. The Department of Agriculture reports that in terms of purchasing power the net income of farmers in 1955 was lower than in any year since 1940.

The number of small and family-sized farms has declined while the biggest operators and corporation farms have grown. This agricultural depression is persistent and represents a heavy economic burden on the shoulders of the small marginal and family-size operators. The outbreak of a general economic crisis would have a catastrophic effect on the small farmers, for never in the nation's history was the agricultural economy so closely bound up with the industrial and financial life, and never was it under such sharp pressure from monopoly.

One-fifth of a nation suffers poverty in the midst of plenty; one family in five earns less than $2,000 a year—that is, less than $40 a week. Among Negro families, the proportion is more than two in five. Ten million American children live in slums. The country has a number of depressed areas suffering high unemployment.

During 1956 the cost of living, which appeared to have reached a plateau, resumed its upward movement and is now at its highest point in history.

Despite record levels of employment, the rise in production since 1954 has brought no corresponding rise in employment. And the past months have witnessed a growth of unemployment in the auto and farm equipment industries. With the further extension of automation, unemployment is likely to increase.

Nor has small business flourished in the recent period. In fact, bankruptcies of small business ventures have been on the rise.

The chief beneficiaries of the boom have been the giant trusts and monopolies. The year 1956, says Fortune, was "very definitely the best year ever for big business."

The monopolies have continued to grow and to become ever more powerful. Today, the 500 largest industrial corporations account for about half of all production and employment. These giants rake in the lion's share of the profits. In the first quarter of 1956, profits per dollar of sales for the biggest companies (those with assets of $100,000,000 or more) were nearly five times those of the smaller companies (with assets under $250,000). And under the Cadillac Cabinet, with its giveaways and its policies favoring big business, mergers are taking place at a higher rate than ever before.

The enormous profits of the trusts are obtained at the expense of the workers, the small farmers and small business. Their growing stranglehold on the economy increases further the imbalance between production and the market.

Such is the present-day prosperity.

How long will it last? The Eisenhower Administration and big business spokesmen maintain that prosperity has become a permanent feature of the American scene. "Adjustments" may occur, but crises, they say, are a thing of the past. They assert that, the government, through its capacity to intervene and to "manage" the economy, can prevent any major disaster.

But this theory rests on a most shaky foundation. Thus, for the past six months, although industrial production has failed to rise, inventories have mounted. Nevertheless, in the face of this situation, capital investment continues to expand.

This does not mean that a crisis is around the corner. In fact, there may well be an upturn in production prior to the onset of the next recession. But it does indicate that the expansion of capital investment—the very factor on which the high level of the economy principally rests, is aggravating the imbalance between productive capacity and the market. The underlying instability of the economy is increased, and the factors making for a cyclical economic crisis continue to operate. The boom, with its growing credit inflation, only conceals the sharpening contradiction between the forces of production and the capitalist relations of production—a contradiction which can only be finally resolved in the people's interest through the establishment of a socialist society.

The economy may be given new shots in the arm. There may be new rises in production, especially if foreign trade is expanded by such measures as the removal of trade barriers between our country and the Socialist world.

There are also many new features in the economy which have an important bearing on the frequency and depth of the cyclical crisis which we need to examine.

The National Committee proposes that a special commission shall make a study of the total economic outlook in light of such new features.

But there is no foundation for Wall Street inspired illusions of permanent prosperity.

In this day of automation and rapid technological change, labor faces new and more acute problems. Though production today is at a higher point than a few years ago, factory employment has fallen off. Among industrial workers, there is a growing sense of job insecurity and mounting pressure for the 30-hour week without reduction in take home pay. There are intensified problems of speedup and deterioration of working conditions. In many industries the runaway shop evil is reaching more and more serious proportions.

To meet these problems there is a new, strengthened labor movement, growing out of the merger of the AFL and CIO. This historic merger, proceeding in the first place from the growing unity demands among the members, was the outstanding positive labor development of the past decade. In ending 20 years of division, the AFL-CIO entered a new and higher stage in the process of unifying the American workers. The merger has strengthened labor's ability to defend its economic and political interests and thereby has increased its contribution to the life of the nation.

Within the labor movement the first fruits of unity are already becoming apparent in the lessening of jurisdictional disputes, the decline in raiding, a greater degree of solidarity and mutual aid in economic struggles, and the first tentative plans for undertaking the organization of the unorganized in the South.

There are, however, a number of important unresolved issues within the leadership of the AFL-CIO. These include such questions as new demands of the craft union leadership that would weaken the industrial unions; differences on political action, involving attitude toward the two major parties, as well as the degree of participation of the union membership in political and legislative struggles. The issues still to be fought out also encompass the question of a democratic foreign policy and peaceful coexistence as well as the whole field of the rights of Negro workers.

In the struggle around these issues alignments are still in process of developing and will undoubtedly continue to do so for a considerable time.

However, the merger has already strengthened the hand and multiplied the voice of the labor movement in the halls of Congress, within the political parties and among the people generally.

Organized labor has developed a comprehensive program to combat poverty, to improve social welfare, to aid the farmers and small business. In formulating this program it is recognizing its responsibility to the nation in this age of atomic energy and automation.

We Communists endorse and support the forward looking domestic and legislative proposals of the labor movement and other democratic organizations for economic betterment and social welfare. It is through struggle for such a program and the forging of unity around it that the workers and the people generally can advance their own interests against the opposition of the monopolies and the administration which they dominate.

The age of automation and the atom stands in glaring contradiction to widespread poverty, to inadequate educational and health facilities, and to growing job insecurity and fear of the future. But to fulfill the promise of plenty which automation and atomic engergy hold forth will require concerted struggle by labor and its allies against the trusts. In the course of such struggles, if Communists and other socialist-minded Americans work effectively, the working people of this country can achieve a fuller understanding of the need of a socialist economy as the only basic answer to their problems.

A NEW STAGE FOR MANKIND

For Peaceful Co-Existence and an End to the Cold War

Having lived for a decade under the threat of atomic war, the American people, like peoples everywhere, deeply desire to enjoy in peace the great benefits which they rightfully demand of the coming atomic age.

Today, they are becoming ever more confident that this desire can be realized. The prospect has opened up of bringing the cold war to an end and ushering in a new era of peaceful co-existence and competition of different social systems.

Soon after World War II, the giant corporations which dominate American political and economic life set about trying to extend their domination to the rest of the world. They caused our government to scrap FDR's policy of American-Soviet friendship and Big Three unity for peace. They also brought about the scuttling of FDR's "good neighbor" policy in Latin America, which despite serious limitations, had curbed aggressive intervention and developed better relations with the peoples of that area. Acting through the Truman and Eisenhower Administrations, the economic royalists replaced these policies with one of atom-bomb diplomacy, military alliances, war bases, and active intervention in the internal affairs of other countries. Under the pretext of "defense" against a mythical "Soviet menace" they built up a very profitable arms economy at home.

This policy had its domestic counterpart in the smog of intimidation and conformity that polluted American life, in the persecutions, repressions and witchhunts that steadily eroded the Bill of Rights. The pall of McCarthyism grew until it threatened to blot out American liberties.

Over the years Wall Street's war-like, anti-American policy suffered one setback after another. Our country became isolated, its good name dishonored. Aggressive acts and threats of "massive retaliation" precipitated differences with our "allies." The newly independent nations of Asia refused to tow the State Department and Pentagon line. A great people's peace movement embracing hundreds of millions all over the world, insisted on an end to the cold war and the settlement of differences through negotiations. The Soviet Union refused to behave in accordance with the myth of "Soviet aggression," and instead, the socialist countries directed all their efforts toward preventing war and achieving peaceful co-existence.

The growing crisis in American foreign policy finally reached the point where in July, 1955, the Eisenhower Administration was compelled to drop its opposition to great power negotiations, meet with the Soviet Union at Geneva, and formally renounce the use of force to resolve differences.

The changed world situation symbolized by Geneva, came about because the American people, no less firmly than other peoples, refused to accept the prospect of atomic annihilation. In 1952 they elected Eisenhower on the strength of his pledge to stop the war in Korea; in 1954 they vetoed Nixon's plan to use American troops in Indochina; in 1955 they quashed the Dulles-Radford provocations around Quemoy and Matsu.

And Geneva was also made possible because the American people refused to bow to McCarthyism, but instead, through their struggles in 1953 and 1954, administered serious defeats to the McCarthyites and began the still incomplete process of restoring the Bill of Rights.

Now there has come into being a vast "zone of peace," embracing socialist and non-socialist peace seeking states populated by well over half the human race. And this "zone of peace" may also be said to include the peoples of all other countries irrespective of the policies of their governments.

The pressures that brought Eisenhower to the Summit meeting are today stronger than ever. They are producing an "agonizing reappraisal" on the part of big business and of various political circles.

It is widely recognized that the bankrupt and dangerous Dulles diplomacy of "massive retaliation" and "brink of war" has brought American prestige to a new low. Influential spokesmen are casting about for the means of restoring this prestige and counteracting the recurring Soviet and Chinese proposals for disarmament, trade, and cultural relations. The foreign policy debate continues amidst much confusion, shifting and partisan maneuvering. Among the trends reflected are in broad outline the following:

A. Certain of the most reactionary financial and political circles openly oppose Geneva and flatly reject peaceful negotiations, trade, and co-existence, especially with China. They want to heat up the cold war and compel the "allies," the neutrals, and the UN to tow the line. Their ultimate aim is a fascist Fortress America, equipped with overwhelming superiority in air-atomic terms. In its crudest form this is the view of the McCarthy-Jenner-Eastland forces and in a more released form, of Knowland and of Nixon. It influences some of the Dulles bluff-and-bluster policies. The virulent anti-Sovietism finds an echo in the utterances of a number of leading Democrats.

B. The predominant Wall Street forces, whose policies are reflected in the Eisenhower wing of the GOP and most of the Democratic leadership, still favors a continuation in somewhat altered form of the main features of the cold war— especially the arms budgets, NATO and the like. But with varying emphasis they call for greater flexibility in relations with "allies" and neutrals as the international struggle shifts more and more to the economic and ideological plane. Nor do they close the door altogether to negotiating, some partial steps to disarmament.

C. Some spokesmen for Big Business (Lippmann, Eaton, Flanders, Bowles) appear to go farther. They put their main stress on the shift to economic competition and Point 4, while advocating the retention of the arms budget. They favor increased trade and exchange, and continued efforts to achieve some progress towards disarmament.

Meanwhile, the American people at the grass-roots are making their own reappraisal. The result is a rising peace demand which insistently calls upon the United States to take further steps to reduce tensions, promote East-West trade and exchange, halt the arms race, suspend A and H-bomb tests, and support the colonial peoples in their demand for liberation.

War is not inevitable, though the danger still exists. Imperialism breeds this danger, as shown again in the Suez crisis. Nor have the big trusts and corporations given up their aim of world domination. But the danger of war has considerably subsided. This is the main feature of the present situation.

This feature can be a powerful stimulant to the people's struggle to unfold the new era of peaceful co-existence and end the cold war altogether. This struggle will also be accelerated, and the myth of the "Soviet menace" further dissipated, as our people come to understand the profound changes and corrections of serious errors now taking place in the Socialist countries. It will also be helped by the new initiative displayed in Soviet foreign policy correcting past weaknesses and improving relations with other countries. This already is beginning to exert a favorable influence on the attitude toward peaceful negotiations and co-existence in labor and liberal ranks.

The immediate outlook is for the further growth of broad popular movements on specific peace issues. Influential groups in women's church, Negro, farm, youth and other organizations are calling for concrete steps toward universal disarmament, especially for an immediate ban on A and H-bomb tests. These and other United Nations supporters are asking that that body be strengthened by the admission of China.

The unprecedented rise of the Negro people is closely linked with rising sympathy and support for the liberation struggles of the colonial peoples in Africa and elsewhere.

In the labor movement there has been growing differentiation on foreign policy and peace within the past few years. On the one hand certain national leaders have adopted an aggressive and rigid anti-co-existence, anti-Geneva position. On the other hand, the sentiment of the majority of the rank and file has found expression in varying degree in the position of other leaders of important international unions, and in a number of trade union publications. The leaders and publications criticize the more aggressive aspects of Washington's foreign policy and urge negotiations, curbing the A and H-bombs, support of anti-colonial struggles, expanded foreign economic aid and various forms of peaceful competition with the lands of socialism.

There is growing concern in the labor movement on the question of economic aid to underdeveloped countries. In contrast to Meany's anti-co-existence position, Reuther's 10 point program for aid envisages joint action through the UN by the USA and USSR. Such proposals, along with a program for expansion of East-West trade and exchange of delegations, can win broad support in labor and liberal political circles.

Such movements as these will bring to bear the influence of labor and the other main sectors of the American people upon the foreign and domestic policies of the new Administration and Congress. They will help realize the new perspectives of peaceful co-existence.

For Full Economic, Political and Social Equality for the Negro People

The new level achieved by the Negro people's freedom movement during the past few years has made civil rights one of the most dynamic issues in American political life today. This freedom movement has stimulated a new political awakening among a majority of the American people, who are recognizing the inescapable, urgent, democratic and moral responsibility to remove from American national life the last remaining barriers to first-class citizenship for the 16,000,000 American Negroes.

The Negro freedom movement is today marked by such features of historic significance as: a) the increasingly active leadership role being exercised by the Negro urban population in general and the organized workers in particular; b) the focal point of the freedom struggle is shifting to the urban centers of the Deep South, the region whose agrarian relations and institutions have historically been the incubator of the whole odious system of oppression suffered by the Negro people, and c) the mounting anti-imperialist struggles of the colored colonial peoples all over the world have had a profound ideological impact on the Negro freedom movement, its program and tactics, which in turn more and more identifies itself with and contributes to the colonial liberation movements.

Note must be taken, not only of the shift of the center of Negro freedom struggle to the South, but of the important changes that have taken place in the South during the past 20 years.

Under the stimulus of industrialization and urbanization, the size of the working class in the South has more than doubled; and the number of white and Negro Southern trade unionists now approaches two million. Southern workers have learned important lessons in Negro-white unity in the course of struggle for common economic advancement. The relations between the Negro people and the white intellectuals and professionals in the South have been strengthened, as well as between the South and the rest of the United States. The impact of the moral weight of the Negro question on the largely churchgoing population among white Southerners has been positive. The struggle for the democratic right to vote spearheaded by the Negro people has stimulated an advance in political activity among all the working people in the South.

The situation in every Southern state is today marked, politically, by a growing cleavage between the Dixiecrat rulers, on the one hand, and the Southern democratic majority who are compelled to struggle against Dixiecratism, on the other. The forms vary from state to state but the content is everywhere the same.

The democratic gains won by the Negro people during the past two decades (including gains in literacy, union organizations, limited exercise of political rights, and certain material improvements in living standards) provide the organizational, material and cultural basis for the enhanced political role being played in the life of our country by the Negro freedom movement and the principal organization, the NAACP.

Negro-white solidarity movements are achieving great breadth in various parts of the country. A number of big unions and leading church bodies are helping to organize concrete economic and moral support for the Montgomery boycotters. The AFL-CIO has a special committee to aid the South. Labor in general, and the Textile Workers of America in particular, are taking a firmer stand against the activities of the White Citizens Council.

Nevertheless, there has not been any radical change in the fundamental status of special oppression of the Negro people as an oppressed people. At this late date the average American Negro family is forced to live on 44 percent less income than the average white family; the rate of unemployment among Negroes is double that of whites. This economic robbery produces the social consequences of higher death rate, generally poorer health, less opportunity for securing wholesome food, decent housing, higher education and cultural fulfillment.

The absence or sharp restriction of political rights for Negroes in the South, including the elementary democratic right to vote and the right to representation on all levels of government; the overwhelming inequality in educational opportunity which continues more than two years after the Supreme Court decision; the disproportionate landlessness of the Negro rural population; and the humiliation and indignities which are the daily experiences of the Negro people, limiting participation in the normal streams of human activity (admission in restaurants, hotels etc.)—these are the bitter facts of life that cannot be ignored.

Outside the South, although the oppression of the Negro does not constitute a system of punitively enforced Jim Crow law, there are no legislative safeguards to secure their rights as equal citizens. These conditions are marked by discrimination in employment, wages and working conditions, Jim Crow housing in slums, inequalities in educational and social facilities and opportunities, denial of political representation, police brutality and other indignities which all emphasize that the struggle for Negro freedom is nationwide.

The economic robbery, political subjugation, social ostracism and frustrated cultural development of the Negro people constitute a special system of oppression maintained by monopoly capitalism. This system continues to be more lucrative source of profit for Big Business than the latter's multibillion investments in Latin America. The limited but important democratic gains scored in the struggle for Negro freedom open up new possibilities for further developing a fruitful alliance between the Negro people and the democratic majority of the American people, led by organized labor. It opens up the possibilities for realizing the full citizenship of the Negro people, for the preservation of the Bill of Rights, for curbing the abuses and power of the monopolies and for improvements in the material well-being of the entire population.

The growing alliance between the Negro people and the labor movement is one of the positive features of American life, with great potentialities for the future. Labor needs to increase its participation in the struggle for Negro rights as part of the defense of its own interests. More attention is also required to the upgrading of Negroes in industry and the election and appointment of Negroes to leading positions in trade unions. We believe too that labor has the main responsibility for taking the initiative in overcoming the strains and further strengthening the bonds in the alliance with the Negro people.

A political crisis in Dixiecrat rule of historic significance is shaping up in the South. The Eastland-led Dixiecrat rebellion against the Constitution and the Supreme Court desegregation decision aims to maintain the poisonous political and ideological influence of racism and white supremacy in the national life of our country. The national positions of influence held by the Dixiecrats—who are the servitors of the most reactionary sector of monopoly capital—can only be maintained on the traditional basis of violating the Constitutional and human rights of the Negro people in particular and of the majority of the Southern population in general.

From this historically developed set of circumstances flows the No. 1 unfinished democratic task confronting the whole American people, namely to win the battle for equal rights for the Negro people and thereby open the way for a broad, new advance for American democracy.

The healthy, democratic response which millions are giving to the Negro people's demand for full freedom has generated a mood of desperation among the Dixiecrats. They are actively at work stirring up the most backward prejudices, inspiring acts of terrorism and murder, promoting racist ideas through the White Citizens Councils, attempting to split the labor movement in the South along racist lines, etc. The Dixiecrats aim to push back the frontiers of progress and wipe out the democratic gains won by the people in order to perpetuate their monopoly of political power in the South. In this un-American effort they have found common cause with the pro-fascist McCarthyites outside the South.

Our Party must play its indispensable role in implementing a program of struggle for equal rights and democracy which includes:

a) Mobilizing national material, moral and financial support to the embattled Negro freedom forces in the South;

b) Helping to win universal suffrage for all in the South, without restrictions;

c) Advancing the struggle for Negro representation on all levels of government;

d) Helping to facilitate organized labor's drive to organize the unorganized in the South and to end the North-South wage differential;

e) Organizing the rural poor.

f) Winning governmental measures to secure land and land tenure for Negro sharecroppers, tenants and small owners.

On this basis, an effective national action program for Negro equality could be worked out in the spirit of the slogan "Free by '63." It would seek Federal and state executive and legislative action to guarantee the right to vote, equal job opportunities, security of person and property, an end to segregated schools, housing and all other forms of discrimination and oppression of the Negro people. It would prepare now to curb the Dixiecrat filibusters through a successful fight to amend Senate Rule 22 on the opening day of the new 85th Congress. It would organize to guarantee a general breakthrough in Negro representation in local, state and national elections in 1957 and 1958. Our Party pledges its dedicated support to such a program.

For the Defense of the Constitution and the Bill of Rights

Looking back over the past ten years, the American people can well take pride in the fact that their profound attachment to democratic traditions remained basically intact throughout the storm and stress of the post-war period. However, this needs to be tempered with the realization that the vast damage done by reaction to the Constitution and the Bill of Rights is still to be repaired and that powerful enemies of freedom—the Brownells and Nixons, the Eastlands and McCarthys—are still at their subversive work.

The year 1954 marked a certain turning point. McCarthyism, the most virulent expression of pro-fascist reaction, was checked. A new political climate began to be reflected in the election defeat of the McCarthyites and their Administration friends and in the Senate censure of McCarthy. This in turn facilitated the easing of world tensions at the Geneva Conference. It helped make possible a number of significant Supreme Court decisions favorable to democratic liberties. It led to curbing some of the worst excesses of Congressional Administrations and local witch hunting. It created a favorable atmosphere for the American people to take the counter-offensive for civil liberties that the CIO called for late in 1954.

The basic responsibility for the rise of McCarthyism and other reactionary movements lay with the big trusts and their cold war policies. To the myth of a "Soviet menace" abroad they joined the myth of a "Communist conspiracy" at home. It was the Truman Administration, as Dean Acheson recently acknowledged in a frank admission of error, that first opened the flood-gates with its "loyalty" program. Eisenhower and the Cadillac Cabinet took up where Truman left off, continuing the Smith Act and McCarran Act prosecutions initiated by their predecessors. Chiefly through Nixon and Brownell, they exploited for political purposes McCarthy's main weapon, the "Communist conspiracy" hoax, directing it at Truman himself.

That the menace of pro-fascist reaction has receded is due primarily—in additon to the pressure of world democratic opinion—to the great resurgence of democratic expressions by the American people. A many-sided anti-McCarthy sentiment took shape in 1953 and 1954. A high point was the Joe-Must-Go movement in Wisconsin. McCarthy soon became a political liability to the Eisenhower Administration.

Since 1954, this resurgence has taken on a multitude of forms. Outstanding have been the energetic campaign of the AFL-CIO unions against the state "right-to-work" laws and the Taft-Hartley Act; the broad movements for the repeal or revision of the McCarran-Walter Immigration Act; the rising opposition to "loyalty" and "security" programs in industry and government; the American Association of University Professors defense of the right of Communists to teach; the resolutions of many influential labor, liberal and progressive organizations condemning the Smith Act and the McCarran Act; the petition to cease Smith Act prosecutions and grant amnesty to Smith Act prisoners, sponsored by Mrs. Roosevelt, Norman Thomas and A. J. Muste. But within this, a considerable gap still exists between the extent and level of the movement for defense of civil liberties in the broad sense, and the much more limited scope of the fight against the attacks on the Communist Party itself—attacks which are far from ended.

Moreover, the democratic resurgence confronts new challenges today, as the drive of reaction continues. The Dixiecrats have organized the White Citizens Councils to advocate and practice force and violence against the Negro people and the Constitution. They then proceeded to outlaw the NAACP in a number of Southern states. Dixiecratism allies itself with McCarthyism in the Eastland-McCarthy-Jenner conspiracy. Their immediate aim is to intimidate the Supreme Court (now preparing to review the Smith Act), block enforcement of the desegregation decision and demand of the next Congress legislation to nullify that historic finding as well as the vital verdict against state sedition laws. Meanwhile, the big anti-labor corporations are seeking to spread the "right-to-work" laws from the South to such labor centers as the state of Washington.

Thus the defense of the Communists, whose Smith Act convictions are now on appeal in the Supreme Court or in lower courts, is an integral part of the defense of trade union rights. It is an integral part of the struggle to enforce the desegregation decision and break down the other barriers to full Negro equality. The defense of the Constitutional liberties of Communists is inseparable from the whole movement to rout McCarthyism and Dixiecratism and restore the Bill of Rights for all Americans. All the more necessary is it for trade unions to put an end to the red-baiting, witch-hunts and political discrimination that still continue in some sections of the labor movement.

In this connection it should be noted that the extension of Smith Act prosecutions to Puerto Rico has introduced new anti-democratic evils; crass violation of the national rights of an oppressed people that mocks the so-called commonwealth status granted to Puerto Rico.

Thus events point up to the need and possibility for a new extension of the struggle to defend the Constitution and the Bill of Rights against their reactionary enemies of all types. A closer relationship is emerging among the movements for equal rights for the Negro people, for labor's political and economic rights and for freedom of political expression and association.

A major feature of a civil liberties program would be a series of legislative proposals for the next session of Congress. In additon to repeal of the Taft-Hartley and McCarran-Walter Acts and the enactment of effective civil rights legislation, these proposals would include a number of vital points advanced by labor and liberal spokesmen in recent months; curbing or abolishing the Congressional witch-hunt committees, revision or repeal of such "anti-subversive" laws as the Smith and McCarran Acts and the like. Such a civil liberties program would likewise undertake to defend the Supreme Court against Dixiecrat-McCarthyite attacks, to combat state and local infringements of the Bill of Rights, and to press for an end to the Smith Act prosecutions, for a new trial or freedom for Morton Sobell, freedom for all political prisoners, and amnesty for all political prisoners who are now in jail. . . .

AMERICAN ROAD TO SOCIALISM

III

The people's anti-monopoly coalition would have as its central aim the improvement of the conditions of the American people and the defense and extension of their democratic rights. Its success in electing a people's anti-monopoly government would open the way to a vast and unprecedented expansion of democracy. Such a government could curb the repressive economic and political powers of the monopolies and deprive them of the ability to promote violence to frustrate the will of thc people. Under such conditions, whenever the majority of the American people become convinced of the necessity of a socialist reorganization of society, they would be able to advance to their goal along peaceful and constitutional lines.

Ever since the rise of the struggle against fascism and the fascist danger in the 30s, our Party has been elaborating such a program for a peaceful and constitutional transition to socialism. In 1938 the 10th Party convention adopted the first written constitution of the Communist Party. It expressly stated that any advocate of force and violence would be excluded from the Party.

In the succeeding years many additional steps were taken. The leading spokesmen of the Party, Chairman Foster and General Secretary Dennis, expressed this position of the Party in 1947-48 in articles, statements and interviews with such leading newspapers as the New York Times and Herald Tribune. A high point in the presentation of this question was Comrade Foster's deposition "In Defense of the Communist Party and Its Indicted Leaders," at the first Smith Act trial in 1949. This statement of policy was endorsed by the National Committee of the Party. It was expressed in the Party Program, "The American Way," adopted in 1954. Comrades Dennis and Gates at the first meeting they addressed after their release from jail, at Carnegie Hall, Jan. 20, 1956, reiterated our Party's advocacy of a peaceful and constitutional road to socialism in our country.

Some have challenged this view on the ground that the capitalist class of the U.S. is strong and the forces of repression at its disposal are powerful. They point to the character and sharpness of the class and people's struggle in the past and today. These points are unquestioned. The trusts will continue to try to promote demagogy, division and force and violence to halt social progress and democratic advance.

Titanic economic and political struggles will intervene in our country before the majority of the people take the path to socialism. In the course of and as a consequence of such struggles of the working class, the Negro people and others, the power of the monopolies could be drastically curbed through the election of an anti-monopoly government. There would be a new strength, a new class-consciousness and political maturity within the labor and people's movements which would also be reflected in the strength of the party or parties of socialism.

That is why we state that the possibility exists for the peaceful and constitutional transition to socialism. This transition to socialism will become possible when the majority of the American people so decide in the course of their struggles against the monopolies. Only the American people will make that decision.

The history of our country, the struggles of our people to fulfill the Bill of Rights, their attachment to the Constitution all point to the conclusion that socialism in the U.S. will provide full civil liberties to all, including the right to dissent, and, as long as the people so desire, a multi-party system. This is not an academic question for our Party. This stand by our Party on civil liberties under socialism is of value in clarifying our perspective of socialism and also assists in strengthening the unity of the democratic forces of our land for common action today.

Socialism in America will be the realization of the dream of economic independence and political freedom, of "life, liberty, and the pursuit of happiness" under the conditions of today, in the age of atomic energy and automation. It will carry forward the best traditions of Jefferson, Lincoln and Frederick Douglass, and of the great American pioneer labor and socialist leaders, William Sylvis and Gene Debs.

Socialism is no more un-American than is capitalism particularly American. Capitalism and socialism are social systems growing out of the evolution of society and its struggle towards greater progress. Capitalism in the U.S., because of the peculiar features and historical conditions of its development, has brought a relatively high standard of living to a large number of people. But it also has brought economic crisis, wars, colonial exploitation and oppression, unemployment, insecurity, crime, social degradation and discrimination.

The people had to fight for their standard of living and for their democratic liberties against the forces of privilege and reaction at every stage in the history of our country. They fought for independence, for the Bill of Rights, for the right to vote, for the right to education, for the abolition of slavery, for the rights of women, for the abolition of child labor, for the right to build unions, for social insurance. And to this day the Negro people are denied equal rights, are discriminated against, and are doubly exploited.

Today socialism, embracing a third of the world's people, has grown to a world system. In the coming period the superiority of socialism over capitalism will become ever more apparent to all peoples.

Socialism in the U.S. from the beginning will be able to provide all our people with the highest standard of living, the fullest economic security. For ours is the most technically advanced country in the world. Our resources, our skills, our technology, our organizing capacity and experience, our workers, scientists, will assure a rapidly increasing standard of living for all. Socialism in our country will bring not only the fullest satisfaction of our material needs but also the fullest democratic liberty and cultural satisfaction.

The Communist Party from its inception has been the party of socialism. Because of this it has brought strength and understanding much greater than its numbers to the struggles in which it fought as part of the American working people. But our Party never fully mastered the task of how to successfully combine the immediate struggle and socialist education. In the early period policies and slogans were put forward as if socialism were around the corner. Later on, when the Party, making a more sober and realistic analysis of the situation, came to the conclusion that socialism was not on the immediate order of the day in the U.S. educational work for socialism was neglected. This resulted from our narrow and sectarian conception of socialism, of what it would be like in the U.S. and of how it would be achieved. We failed to see in the many struggles for greater economic security, in the strong anti-monopoly tendencies, the basis for reaching the people with fundamental discussions of issues and for promoting socialist education among them.

But the enemies of socialism have never ceased their attacks and are today carrying on widespread propaganda not only against the socialist lands and against the Communist Party of the United States but also against the ideas of socialism.

This should make clear that the Communist Party cannot limit itself to a mere declaration that socialism is not on the immediate order of the day in our land. This is undoubtedly true. But socialism is nonetheless an issue: socialism in the Soviet Union and other socialist countries, and most of all, what socialism would be like in the U.S., and how the Communist Party hopes the American people will achieve socialism.

The historic conditions deriving from the First World War, the Russian Revolution, and the split in the socialist movement have now given way to new conditions. . . .

These conditions make possible a great new trend towards unity among socialist minded people which has already begun to be felt not only abroad but in our own country. The new features of independence and mutual criticism in the relationships among Communist Parties also tend to remove barriers between Communists and other supporters of socialism.

For some months our Party has had under consideration the question presented in Gene Dennis' report to the National Committee last April, of our attitude towards the perspective of a united party of socialism in this country.

The new developments point to a certain revitalization and growth of socialist-oriented and pro-Marxist currents and groupings. In the past we tended to assume that all that was worth while in other socialist currents and groupings would inevitably flow into our own organization. This assumption was always incorrect and should be replaced by serious and painstaking efforts to assist in the eventual development of the broadest possible unity of all socialist-minded elements.

Such a development can by no means be expected as a quick and easy solution to the common problems of all socialist groupings, or to the specific problems of our own Party. Least of all could this objective be advanced by any tendency to weaken or dissolve the Communist Party. On the contrary, it is essential that the Communist Party strengthen in every way its organization, mass work and general influence.

The prospect we hold forth for our Party requires a reinvigoration of the Marxist press. A prerequisite for an effective hearing for Marxist ideas and for making their influence felt in respect to the course of our country's development is that we spare no effort in helping to finance and solve the distribution problems of The Worker and the Daily Worker. Stabilizing the financial base of the Marxist press and building its circulation will establish the practical foundation for a steady improvement in its political and journalistic quality.

The attainment of unity among socialist-minded forces lies along the path of common struggle on the broadest issues facing the American people, in the course of which ideological and tactical questions will become clarified and common bonds be forged.

It would be wrong to identify the extent of socialist traditions and thinking with the low level of socialist organization today. Among the trade unions, in the building of which Socialists and Communists played a major role, among the Negro people, the working farmers, the professionals and the youth who are pondering the significance of the growth of the socialist world system, as well as among the many thousands who at one time were members of our Party or who participated in mass struggles under our leadership, are to be found many who would welcome the perspective of a united party of socialism. The National Committee should be charged with fostering this perspective.

The historic objective of achieving unity of all honest socialist-minded forces to develop the American people's anti-monopoly coalition, as well as the ultimate achievement of socialism, throws an added light on our reappraisal for our Party's past and present functioning, its mass activities, and its vital role in the period ahead.

Our Party

The Communist Party made a vital contribution to the welfare of our country since the end of World War II by its unflinching fight for peace, against the danger of fascism, for the civil rights of the Negro people, and for the economic needs of the working people. It continues to do so.

Communists fought consistently through the years of the cold war to help bring about the present improved political situation. In so doing, they served the best national interests of our country with patriotic selflessness.

At its Emergency Convention in 1945 the Communist Party warned the American people about the dangers inherent in the developing plans of Wall Street to dominate the world. As this aggressive drive for world domination unfolded, the

Communist Party alerted the American people to the emergence of a serious danger of a new world war. It exposed and combatted every policy and action which jeopardized or broke the peace; the notorious "get tough with Russia" policy; the war-inciting Fulton, Missouri, speech of Winston Churchill; the Truman doctrine of "containment," atom-bomb diplomacy and military intervention in China and Greece; the Marshall Plan; the "position of strength" policy embodied in the Atlantic Pact, NATO, SEATO and other military alliances, as well as building of military bases all over the world. The Communist Party fought consistently under difficult conditions for a negotiated peace to end the Korean War. It vigorously combatted the Big Lie of an alleged threat of Soviet aggression. It called for the negotiation of differences between the Big Powers, the ending of the cold war and its replacement by a policy of peaceful coexistence between our country and the Soviet Union.

During this period the Communist Party took the lead in combatting a whole host of repressive measures and policies designed to silence those fighting for peace and to intimidate the American people into acceptance of unpopular military adventures. It exposed and fought against the Schwellenbach proposal for outlawing the Communist Party, the Mundt-Nixon Bill, the McCarran Act, the Taft-Hartley Act, the Attorney General's "subversive list," the thought-control "loyalty" order and civil service witchhunts, the persecution by Congressional committees, the Smith Act prosecutions, the McCarthyite inquisition and the "atom-spy" hoax which resulted in the frame-up and execution of Julius and Ethel Rosenberg, as well as the imprisonment of Morton Sobell. The Party exposed and fought against repressive measures and policies adopted in many states.

Throughout this period the Communist Party actively supported labor's struggles for improved economic and working conditions, particularly during the big strikes of the miners, the railway, packinghouse, steel, auto, electrical and farm equipment workers. Communists championed labor's united action in defense of its hard won gains. They contributed to labor's growing appreciation of its unique and decisive role in the life of the nation. They helped labor gain a better understanding of its relations to the struggle for Negro rights. They urged closer working relationships between labor and the farm population. They fought for democratic, militant trade unionism and against expulsions, raiding, secessions and the fragmentation of the labor movement. They popularized independent political action as the key to the future not only of the labor movement but of the entire nation.

The Communist Party energetically championed the struggles of the Negro people for full economic, social and political equality. It made notable contributions in defending Willie McGee, the Martinsville Seven, the Trenton Six, Mrs. Rosa Lee Ingram and Wesley Wells; in combatting segregated housing in Stuyvesant Town, Levittown and Parkchester in New York, in Park Manor, Peoria Street and Trumbull Park in Illinois, and in many other communities throughout the nation, in popularizing the battle for Negro representation in all elective and appointive government bodies; in promoting the struggle for inclusion of model FEPC clauses in union contracts; in fighting for election and appointment of Negro leaders to top positions in the lily-white leadership of many nations. These and similar activities of the Communist Party contributed substantially to the emergence of the current broad movement for civil rights.

The struggles waged by the Communist Party in the past decade constitute a notable chapter in the history of the American working class. As the tide continues to turn against McCarthyism and the cold war, sweeping away the frenzied insanity of a decade of red-baiting, lies and distortions, the justice and courage of the Communist Party's struggle will be increasingly vindicated in the eyes of all Americans who have the real welfare of our country at heart. Every member and friend of the Communist Party has reason to be proud of the contribution made to the great task of helping save America from catastrophe of war and fascism.

The Communist Party and its supporters have reason to be proud of the staunchness with which they met the wave of persecution against them. Nonetheless this persecution was not without effect. It took the form of an expanding pattern of repression including: Taft-Hartley Act affidavits and perjury prosecutions; Smith Act arrests, trials, convictions and jail sentences; Congressional committee inquisitions and contempt citations; the screening of whole industries and the entire civil service; firings from jobs, hounding from professions, establishment of industry-wide blacklists; McCarran Act persecutions; widespread deportations of foreign-born; deprivation of legal rights to halls, radio time, advertising space, etc. All this put the Communist Party in a position of de facto illegality.

This attack was designed to destroy the Communist Party. In this it did not succeed. It did succeed in weakening and isolating it. It is necessary for all members of the Communist Party to face up soberly to the fact that in this period the Party suffered heavy organizational losses, decline in political influence in many areas of work and fields of activity, became dangerously isolated from important sectors of the labor and people's movements; that the Marxist press is in jeopardy, and that generally the Party is confronted with a critical situation.

Was it inevitable, in view of these attacks and adverse objective conditions, that the Party should suffer such heavy organizational losses and become so severely isolated as it did? The answer must be NO.

The attacks on the Party occurred at a time when the overall economic situation, with the exception of the chronic postwar agricultural crisis was characterized by high levels of general employment and increased total earnings by workers' families. This situation gave rise to two trends in the ranks of the working class. On the one hand, the absence of an army of unemployed who might be used as a club against them encouraged workers to fight militantly throughout this period for wage increases and important fringe benefits. On the other hand, the growth of class consciousness among the workers was inhibited by continued high levels of employment and rising earnings for almost 15 years, combined with the propaganda of views in the labor movement reflecting the influence of Keynesian theories about the ability of capitalism to solve permanently the problem of "boom and bust" through a "managed economy" of built-in stabilizers.

What is more, this factor has helped erode the class consciousness of many labor leaders who in past years considered themselves adherents of socialism but who today have abandoned their socialist convictions, or even oppose socialist ideas in favor of an illusory "permanently expanding capitalism" as the ultimate solution for the problem of American workers.

Past Errors

Against the background of this economic situation and its consequences, the errors and long standing weaknesses of our Party had a particularly damaging effect.

The most important of these errors include:

A) In the Fight for Peace:

The Party's estimate that Wall Street's drive for world domination created a serious danger of a new world war was correct. With this analysis our Party made a significant contribution to the mobilization of American and world peace forces. At the same time some serious sectarian mistakes were made in analyzing important phases of the struggle between the forces of peace and war. While we repeatedly asserted that World War III was not inevitable, we tended to weaken this correct estimate by declaring that each new defeat for American imperialism increased its desperation and hence, increased the danger of war. This was coupled with an analysis that the only major difference in the ranks of monopoly capital was between those who want war now and those who want war later.

This overlooked the fact that Wall Street's ability to achieve its predatory aims was diminishing and that the setbacks to the imperialist drive sharpened all differences within the ranks of monopoly capital as well as between the imperialists of various countries. It overlooked the fact that the overall situation of American imperialism still gave it room to maneuver short of world war rather than reducing it to desperate alternatives.

In effect, such estimates excluded the possibility of the peaceful settlement of differences except through a major change in the relation of class forces in the United States. They made it difficult to convince the Party membership and the masses of the possibility of achieving under existing conditions a protracted period of peaceful coexistence.

Certainly, when Dulles three times took our country "to the brink of war," this represented on each occasion a acute sharpening of the danger of wars which might have had global repercussions. But Dulles' inability to take our country over the brink revealed the strength of the obstacles to war. It was precisely this strength that our Party underestimated.

That is why, despite our statements regarding the profound significance of the armistice in Korea and the negotiated peace in Indo-China, our Party did not draw conclusions from the favorable changes in international relations which these events signalized.

Because of a narrow concept of the division of the world into two camps we did not properly assess the growth of a neutralist bloc in the world, especially the newly liberated colonial countries, as well as like forces in our country.

In fact, up to the very eve of the Geneva Summit meeting there were strong tendencies to underestimate the ability of the peace forces, within our country and internationally, to compel the Eisenhower Administration to enter into peaceful negotiations with the socialist world.

B) In the Fight Against Fascist Danger:

The Party correctly assessed the connection between American imperialism's aggressive foreign policy and the host of reactionary and pro-fascist measures which began to be promulgated, adopted or enforced in the late 1940s. These measures were designed to intimidate and suppress all opposition to the aggressive foreign policies of Big Business. Contrary to opinions prevalent in some circles that this development was a temporary post-war aberration which would automatically subside in time, the Party emphasized the potential fascist danger if it was not checked by the active struggle of the American people.

However, the errors made by the Party in estimating various phases of the struggle against the war danger also influenced its judgment of the fascist menace, particularly in relation to attempts to outlaw the Party. This took the form of overestimating the scope, level and tempo of the process of fascization under way generally. Our evaluation also tended to equate the attempted outlawing of the Party with fascism.

This led to wrong organizational decisions of 1950, including conscious efforts to reduce the size of the Party membership. While this particular error was quickly recognized by the Districts and the National Committee and corrective steps were taken, it nevertheless resulted in serious damage to the Party organization.

Subsequently, in 1951, the National Committee statement on the Vinson decision upholding the first Smith Act conviction of Communist leaders estimated that we had entered a wholly "new situation"; in other words, that a qualitative change had taken place in the process of the fascization of our country. This led to the introduction of a system of leadership which virtually gave up the fight for legality, tended to accept a status of illegality and abandoned many possibilities for the public functioning of the Party.

While it was essential to safeguard the Party and enable it to function under the difficult conditions it faced, and while numerous Communists displayed great steadfastness in this task, nevertheless, as a result of a sectarian approach to this effort, the Party needlessly lost thousands of members. This facilitated the efforts of reaction to isolate us from the masses who, naturally, could not understand the Party's course in the given situation.

Contributing to these left-sectarian errors were:

a) the failure to recognize that the ruling class was not so hard pressed as to be unable to continue its established method of governmental rule even as it sharply curtailed the Bill of Rights by launching unprecedented attacks against the labor and people's movements, and in the first place, against the Communist Party;

b) underestimation of the strength of American democratic traditions among the people, their readiness to defend the Constitution and the Bill of Rights, the latent power of the trade unions as a bulwark against fascism, the peculiarities of American governmental structure, as well as the struggles between and within the two major parties which act as impediments to the repressive drive of the most reactionary circles;

c) On imminence of Economic Crisis.

Repeatedly since 1945, the Party has erred in assessing economic developments in the United States. In 1945, in 1949 and 1954 it predicted that the current decisions would develop into crises of major proportions.

At certain moments the Party's analysis wrongly appraised effects of the continuing arms program. Even more important, it overlooked the extent of continuing investments in fixed capital to replace, expand and modernize equipment which had worn out or become obsolete since the last major cycle of fixed capital renewal in the thirties. Together with this it failed to size up adequately the level of commercial and residential construction as well as the scope of unsatisfied consumer demand and the possibilities of credit expansion. Also, it overlooked the temporary stimulating effect of the government's tax program which provided for rebates, attractive amortization terms, lower excess profits taxes.

The Party's judgment in each case was faulty because it never made an adequate analysis of the specific features of American capitalism. Instead, it based itself on a one-sided and incomplete study of economic data, applying the Marxian theory of economic crisis in a routine, formal and doctrinaire manner.

These repeated estimates of impending economic crisis had many harmful effects: projection of unrealistic economic programs, overestimation of the tempo of radicalization of the masses with resultant mistakes in tactical approaches to united front relations especially in the trade unions; and, finally, encouragement of all tendencies to overestimate the imminence of war and fascism.

Sectarian Policies

The foregoing mistaken estimates contributed to a series of sectarian errors in the Party's policies in the main areas of work.

Our policies and tactics in regard to the most important aspect of our work, our relations with the labor movement, did not escape the influence of sectarianism. This took the form of a sectarian attitude to the labor movement itself and to the relations that should exist between the Communist Party and the trade unions. We did not view the labor movement realistically in the light of its actual level of development. Rather, our point of departure was our own concept of what the labor movement should be. We therefore projected standards of achievement for Communists and progressives in the labor movement, as well as for the labor movement as a whole, based on our estimate of what was urgently needed rather than on what was possible under existing conditions.

This led to cumulative strains in the relations between the Party and the most friendly sections of the labor movement. It was in great part responsible for isolating us from the membership and the leadership of the unions, towards whom we often adopted not only a sectarian but even a factional attitude. This was demonstrated not only in the failure to wage a skillful and consistent fight to prevent an irreconcilable rupture with the progressive and center forces in several CIO unions, but also in the development of a policy of waging the sharpest struggle against those we characterized as the "center forces" in the CIO and as "Social Democrats."

Within the conservative-led unions this sectarian approach also proved to be very costly. Communists and progressives were often faced with the alternative of either pursuing policies which led to their isolation, to loss of positions of leadership and often loss of jobs in the shop as well; or taking a more flexible position and being branded as opportunists by the Party. The history of the past period is replete with examples of both consequences. In the vast majority of cases it led to the isolation of the most militant trade unionists from the masses of the workers. In many cases it caused militant and progressive workers and union leaders to break relations of long standing with our Party. These mistakes are in large part responsible for our failure to build the strength of the Left in the AFL and the conservative-led unions of the CIO.

A flagrant example of this leftism is to be found in the series of events that led up to the expulsion of the progressive-led unions from the CIO. These expulsions and the all-out effort to destroy the unions led by progressives were part of a well organized campaign to split the labor movement in every major country. This plan was not only the brainchild of certain labor leaders but was supported, if not initiated, by the State Department and the other anti-labor forces. Nevertheless, we must recognize that their efforts were facilitated by our own errors in policy and tactics.

Our Party urged all progressives to fight for unity of the CIO. We were sharply critical of tendencies to withdraw from the CIO at the 1949 Cleveland convention. In the main the progressive unions made great efforts to maintain a united CIO and were prepared to accept any formula for the settlement of the issues involved as long as their autonomous rights were respected. The expulsions were completely unjustified and those who pressed for them did irreparable harm to the CIO and to the whole labor movement.

But the numerous head-on collisions which took place at the Boston, Portland and Cleveland conventions and in between those conventions on questions of policy relating to political action, foreign affairs, economic outlook and trade union democracy, were not seen by our Party from the beginning as laying the groundwork for expulsion. Our sectarian policy and tactics prevented us from throwing our weight behind a policy calculated to ease these collisions, to avoid them where possible and generally to keep the two trends in the labor movement from becoming so sharply polarized as to lead to an organizational split. Our errors also contributed to making it more difficult for the Communists in the unions to advocate the adoption of steps after the expulsion for re-entry of the progressive-led unions into the mainstream of the American labor movement, either through a fight for re-affiliation or through merger with other unions.

Sectarianism also led our Party at times into a position opposite to our traditional and true policy of fighting for over-all unity of the labor movement. We have played a leading and positive role in advocating the reunification of the labor movement ever since the organization of the CIO. We have always been champions of the organic unity of the labor movement. But the growing sentiment for the merger of the AFL and CIO after the Republican victory of 1952 did not evoke from us the enthusiastic support that it deserved. Instead there was the tendency to a negative approach, counterposing united labor action to organic unity and at times even a tendency to be influenced by opinions which some expressed that the merger was being consummated on the initiative of the State Department for ulterior purposes.

In fighting to rid the Party of sectarianism in policy and tactics, we must also clearly define what we consider to be the correct relations between the Party and the trade union movement, as well as between Communists and their fellow unionists, as follows:

The Communist Party recognizes and respects the complete political and organizational independence of the trade unions and other organizations of the working class and people. It rejects any policy of interference in their internal affairs. It repudiates any allegation that it seeks to capture or control these organizations or to "bore from within." Its attitude to them is the same as to the working class and the people generally whom it tries to influence publicly by political discussion, persuasion and example. Communists belonging to these organizations adhere to and abide by the discipline and democratic decisions of the organizations. They are guided only by their devotion to the best interests of the working class and people.

Communists will be found among those who work for democratic procedures in the unions, for the full involvement of the membership in the policy-making as well as the activities of the unions. They will endeavor to be among the foremost in carrying out the main task of the unions, the defense and improvement of the wage and working conditions of the membership, and in promoting the united action of all labor to achieve these objectives. As workers imbued with class consciousness, Communists have much to contribute in helping their fellow workers attain a greater understanding on such questions as:

The need for a firm alliance and brotherly relationship between Negro and white; the role that labor's independent political action can play in the workers' daily life and in advancing the cause of labor's future, as well as the importance of gaining allies among other sections of the population; the perspective of a great people's anti-monopoly coalition, headed by labor, leading the nation towards greater democracy, economic betterment and peace. In the tradition of Sylvis, Debs and Foster, Communists will bring the great ideas of socialism to the labor movement, seeking to help the trade unions achieve their full stature as representative organizations of the American working class.

FOR CREATIVE MARXISM

The April 1956 meeting of the National Committee inaugurated a new phase in the struggle against sectarianism. The report of Comrade Dennis advanced the struggle against left-sectarianism by examining the basic estimates in which the sectarian tactical line of the Party has been rooted. The report established that the main task of the Party in the present period was to eliminate every vestige of left-sectarianism in policies and activities.

The roots of these errors are not to be found in the events of the past ten years alone.

The Marxist movement in our country has suffered historically from dogmatic application of Marxist theory to the American scene. The Communist Party inherited these weaknesses. Insufficient development of the independent theoretical work of our Party over the past decades has contributed towards our doctrinaire acceptance and mechanical application of many theoretical propositions.

Our Party has also suffered from an oversimplified approach to and an uncritical acceptance of many views of Marxists and Marxist parties in other countries.

Doctrinaire forms of party organization, bureaucratic methods of leadership, failure to develop inner party democracy and a frequent intolerant attitude to the people we worked with have been in large measure responsible for our inability to correct mistakes in time as well as for much of our sectarianism. All these factors are interrelated; each helped to reinforce the other.

To advance the struggle in the United States for peace, democracy, civil rights and socialism, the Communist Party must further develop its independent theoretical work. It must free itself from deeply ingrained habits of dogmatism and doctrinairism which breed sectarianism, and which in turn lend encouragement to right opportunism.

In order to succeed in this, the Party must study thoroughly the realities of American life today, the history and traditions of our working class and people, the special features of capitalist economy and bourgeois democracy in our country, the distinctive features of the American road to socialism.

The principles of scientific socialism were first put forward by Marx and Engels. They were further developed in the imperialist era by Lenin. They were later enriched by contemporary Marxists in many countries. Basing ourselves on these Marxist-Leninist principles as interpreted by the Communist Party of our country, we must learn much better how to extract from the rich body of this theory that which is universally valid, combining it with the specific experiences of the American working class in the struggle for socialism in the United States. The Party must distinguish better between the additions to Marxist theory made by Lenin which are valid for all countries and those specific aspects of Lenin's writings which reflect exclusively certain unique features of the Russian revolution or of Soviet society.

Likewise, the Communist Party will have to be bolder in re-examining certain Marxist-Leninist theories which, while valid in a past period, may have become outdated and rendered obsolete by new historical developments. For entirely new and unprecedented problems are emerging today which were never treated by Marx, Engels or Lenin. They arise from the new world situation and its impact on all countries.

Already, in response to these new developments, profoundly important and qualitatively new elements have been introduced into the body of Marxist theory by

Marxists of many countries. For example, we as well as other Marxist parties have already discarded as obsolete Lenin's thesis that war is inevitable under imperialism. We have long since rejected as incorrect Stalin's thesis about the alleged law of inevitable violent proletarian revolution. Likewise, we are making important modifications in the theory of the state, as evidenced in our advocacy of the peaceful, constitutional path to socialism.

We must undertake to make our own independent contributions to the further development and enrichment of the theory of scientific socialism. Creative Marxism is impossible without the ceaseless re-examination and reappraisal of theory in the light of ever-changing reality.

The National Committee feels that it is incorrect to continue to function without a comprehensive and basic written program. The program adopted in 1954 is inadequate for that purpose. Such a program is necessary in order to define clearly and unequivocally the viewpoint of American Communists on all fundamental problems of the struggle for socialism in the United States.

The National Committee recommends that the coming Party convention elect a program committee to begin drafting such a document, which will be submitted to the membership for general discussion.

The Communist Party is an independent party of American workers dedicated to socialism. Its primary concern is for the present and future welfare of the American people. Its only allegiance is to the working class and people of our country. Its consistent objective is to promote the national welfare and advance our country's true national interests.

The Communist Party formulates its policies independently. It is not subject to any external allegiance or discipline either of an organizational or political character.

The Communist Party works for friendship between all peoples so that our country may prosper in a world at peace. In this spirit it advocates friendship and cooperation between our country and the socialist countries. This has been one of its major contributions to the national welfare.

The Soviet Union, People's China and Peoples' Democracies of Eastern Europe are socialist countries. The system of capitalist exploitation has been abolished in these countries and, together with it, the cause of poverty, fascism, war, national oppression and race discrimination. From the beginning the Communist Party has greeted and supported the efforts of the working people of these countries to build a new life for themselves on socialist foundations.

Big Business tries to vilify these countries, to slander and defame them, to incite hostility against them. In the interest of the American people the Communist Party is concerned with nailing these lies and exposing these slanders.

The attitude of the Communist Party to these countries reflects devotion to the great principle of working class internationalism which has deep roots in our country's history. This tradition of international solidarity is a proud one. The Communist Party continues it and considers it a badge of honor.

At the same time the Communist Party recognizes that over the years it held certain wrong and over-simplified concepts of what its relations should be to other Marxist parties.

The Party tended to accept uncritically many views of Marxists of other countries. Not all these views were correct; some did not correspond to American conditions.

The Party also viewed uncritically developments in the Soviet Union and other socialist countries. It mistakenly thought that any public criticism of the views or policies of the Marxist parties of these countries would weaken the bonds of international working class solidarity or bring comfort to the enemies of peace and socialism.

The incorrectness of this view was highlighted by the revelations in Khrushchev's special report to the 20th Congress of the CPSU. Because it held this view, the Communist Party of our country was entirely unprepared for and deeply shocked by the admissions of crimes, violations of socialist justice, mistreatment of certain national minorities, and the basis for the rupture of relations with Yugoslavia—all at variance with the truly liberating character of socialism. The courage shown in making these disclosures and the profound process of self-correction, begun some years ago and sharply accelerated since the 20th Congress, are irrefutable evidence of the historic role and vitality of the socialist system.

Socialism is strengthened, not weakened, by the fraternal and constructive criticism of Marxists of many lands. Such criticism has nothing in common with those who deprecate the epic achievements of the USSR, People's China and the other socialist countries or those who seek to engender hostility to socialism at home and abroad.

Our attitude was used to refurbish the slanderous calumny which has been used historically against all radical movements in our country—the lie that the Communist Party is "the agent of a foreign power."

This despicable charge is a lie cut from the whole cloth. We are American Communists, patriots. Our allegiance is to our own country, the United States. In representing and advancing the fundamental welfare of the working class we aim always to serve our country's true national interests.

The Communist Party must continue to correct the oversimplified relations which have existed between itself and other Marxist parties. These relations must be based on the principles of scientific socialism, on proletarian internationalism they must be based on each Communist Party serving the best national interests of its people and thereby the common interests of all progressive humanity. This requires the equality and independence of Marxist parties in the mutual discussion and resolution of common problems; the right and duty of the Communists of all countries to engage in comradely criticism of the policies and practices of the Communists of any country whenever they feel this necessary. This will strengthen, not weaken, international solidarity. It will advance the cause of socialism in all countries.

Bureaucratic concepts of Party organization, systems of leadership and relations between the Party and the masses have been a prime factor in contributing to our errors. They hindered the early and timely correction of these errors. Wrong concepts of leadership discouraged full and free participation of the membership in the discussion of policy and tactics. They stood as insurmountable obstacles to the efforts of comrades in mass organizations to challenge sectarian policies and tactics. They contributed to the weakening of inner party democracy. In many cases they resulted in departure from the very procedures established by our own constitution. They resulted in disciplinary actions which further inhibited expressions of disagreement. They made the life of the party largely routine, devoted, at least between pre-convention discussion periods, to the organization of a multitude of campaigns without adequate examination and testing of our policies and tactics in actual life by our members in the shops and mass organizations.

These bureaucratic methods of work, system of leadership and organization have been accentuated in part by the mechanical application of certain principles of organization adopted by other Communist parties that functioned under different historical conditions.

The history of factional struggle which almost destroyed our Party in its early years gave rise to a correct desire to defend party unity against the danger of factional splits. But this was distorted by efforts to achieve formal unity instead of uniting the party on the basis of principle, full democratic inner life and free, open discussion of differences.

This convention must completely abolish these bureaucratic methods of work, organization and leadership. It must clearly define the character of our Party and its proper method of organization and functioning.

The Communist Party is an American working class political party. It is a Party of white and Negro unity. It is devoted to the struggle for the constant advancement of the welfare of the working class, the Negro people, the farming population, small businessmen and professional people. Its ultimate aim is the socialist reorganization of society in a peaceful, constitutional manner by the majority choice of the American people.

The Communist Party is a democratic organization based on majority rule. It is a cohesive organization for the purpose of acting unitedly to carry out the policies and program decided by its members. The inner life of the Party shall be regulated by the provisions and rules of its constitution which will emerge from this convention, following prior discussion by the whole membership. The unfolding of a correct mass policy by the Party, as well as its ability to attract and hold masses of socialist-minded Americans, requires extensive changes in its structure and methods of work. Among these are the following:

Guarantees of real inner-party democracy through provision of channels for freedom of discussion, dissent and criticism within the framework of carrying out the majority will.

The National Committee should issue a special publication on a regular monthly basis devoted exclusively to articles or letters discussing, debating or differing with party policies, whether current or long-range. Such a publication is necessary to encourage the greatest possible participation by the membership in the formulation, correction or abandonment of policies or tactics.

FOR PARTY DEMOCRACY

The decisions of all Party bodies shall continue to be made by majority rule. Minorities or individuals opposed to such decisions shall be required to abide by them. But the right of such individuals or minorities to express their views shall be guaranteed in all cases. However, this does not mean that factions—groupings with their own platform, discipline, organization and publications set up in opposition to the regular program, discipline, organization and publications of the Party—can be tolerated. The whole history of the Communist Party shows that factionalism actually destroys inner-Party democracy and shatters Party unity.

Between pre-convention discussion periods the National Committee must take special steps to involve the membership in making basic changes in policy. Such methods may involve setting aside limited periods for Party-wide discussion on draft policy resolutions; or convening special delegated conferences with power to act on specific questions presented beforehand to the membership; or the organization of referendum votes on questions.

Establishment of closest ties between membership and leadership and creation of political and organizational guarantees against bureaucratic separation of leadership from membership by the following:

a) Proceedings of the National Committee shall be publicized, including digests of speeches or reports as well as votes of National Committee members on important questions. Where possible State Committees shall do likewise.

b) Minutes of National Board meetings shall be circulated among all members of the National Committee. Periodic summaries should be sent to State Committees.

c) The National Committee should be considerably enlarged.

d) The National Committee shall meet a minimum of three times per year, with agendas and draft documents to be discussed sent in advance to all members.

IN FELLOWSHIP WITH THE AMERICAN PEOPLE

The National Committee feels that the important and deep-going changes on questions of program, policy and organization that it proposes for discussion will expand the opportunities of our members to work with ever larger sections of progressive Americans and their organizations.

It will provide the basis for building our Party into an effective Marxist organization capable of coping with the challenging problems before the American working class and people. There are no valid grounds for any destructive attitude toward the Party's past contribution and the vital role the Party has to play in the future. Neither is there any justification for proposals to liquidate our Party so as to "clear the way" for a broader party of socialism at some future time.

Another view with which the National Committee disagrees is that the Communist Party should change its character by transforming itself into an educational league which would simply conduct propaganda for socialism and the eventual formation of a united socialist Party. This would be a harmful retrograde step. It flows from an abstract understanding of socialist education that separates it from political struggles and class organization.

The foregoing two proposals are liquidationist in character. However, others of an entirely different character have also been offered. One such proposal is that the Communist Party become a political action association. In the opinion of the National Committee, circumstances today do not justify such a change.

In the immediate period ahead these struggles will largely focus around the November elections and their consequences. It should be our concern to help the labor and people's movements bring the decisive issues to the forefront and win significant gains.

High among these issues is the people's standard of living: job security, farm income, the high cost of living, the crisis in schools, housing, and health, the chronic poverty of one-fifth of the nation, segregation and discrimination.

The new outburst of struggles in the South at the opening of the school term again highlights the central importance of the civil rights struggle of the Negro people and their allies. Therefore we demand full equality in jobs, housing, education and political representation, and the abolition of all forms of segregation.

Vital questions affecting the civil liberties of all Americans will be at issue before the Supreme Court and the new Congress and Administration: the Taft-Hartley Act, the "loyalty" program, the Smith Act, the McCarran Act, the McCarran-Walter Act and the demand for amnesty for Smith Act prisoners. These require the rallying of the American people to regain their lost liberties and defend the Constitution and the Bill of Rights.

Above all, the people's profound desire for peace and an end to the cold war calls for concrete steps toward disarmament and a policy of peaceful co-existence: for an end to H-bomb tests, for drastic cuts in the arms budget and the like.

In the struggles around these issues in the shops and communities our concern at all times must be to help strengthen and unite the organizations of labor and the people. It must be to help build under labor's leadership an ever more effective people's coalition directed against the great monopolies and striving to elect a people's anti-monopoly government.

Our Party stretches out its hand to all workers and the whole American people in the fellowship of common struggle for the goal of peace, democracy and social progress.

Bibliographical Note

For further information on the American Communist party the following books should be consulted: Daniel Aaron, *Writers on the Left* (New York, 1961); Gabriel Almond, et al., *The Appeals of Communism* (Princeton, 1954); Daniel Bell, *Marxian Socialism in the United States*, rev. ed. (Princeton, 1968); Earl R. Browder, *Memoirs and Interviews*, Oral History Project, Columbia University, New York; *Teheran and America* (New York, 1944); *Teheran* (New York, 1944); and *Writings and Speeches, May-July, 1945* (privately printed, n.d.); George Charney, *A Long Journey* (Chicago, 1968); Eugene Dennis, *What America Faces* (New York, 1946); and *The Communists Take a New Look* (New York, 1956); Theodore Draper, *The Roots of American Communism* (New York, 1957); *American Communism and Soviet Russia* (New York, 1960); and *The Rediscovery of Black Nationalism* (New York, 1970); Len DeCaux, *Labor Radical: From the Wobblies to the C.I.O.* (Boston, 1970); William Z. Foster, *World Capitalism and World Socialism* (New York, 1941); *The Twilight of World Capitalism* (New York, 1949); and *History of the Communist Party of the United States* (New York, 1952); John Gates, *The Story of an American Communist* (New York, 1958); Nathan Glazer, *The Social Basis of American Communism* (New York, 1961); Irving Howe and Lewis Coser, *The American Communist Party*, rev. ed. (New York, 1962); Max Kampelman, *The Communist Party and the C.I.O.* (New York, 1957); Curtis R. MacDougall, *Gideon's Army*, 3 vols. (New York, 1965); Frank S. Meyer, *The Moulding of Communists* (New York, 1961); Earl Latham, *The Communist Controversy in Washington* (Cambridge, 1966); Wilson Record, *The Negro and the Communist Party* (Chapel Hill, 1951); and *Race and Radicalism: The N.A.A.C.P. and the Communist Party in Conflict* (Ithaca, 1964); Philip Selznick, *The Organizational Weapon* (New York, 1952); David A. Shannon, *Decline of American Communism* (New York, 1959); Joseph R. Starobin, chapter on North America in Leo Labedz. ed., *International Communism after Khrushchev* (Cambridge, 1965); "Origins of the Cold War: the Communist Dimension," *Foreign Affairs, July 1969*; and *American Communism in Crisis* (Cambridge, 1972); Edmund Wilson, *The American Earthquake* (Garden City, N.Y., 1968).

The Progressive and States'
Rights Parties of 1948

LEONARD DINNERSTEIN is Professor of History at the University of Arizona. He is the author of *The Leo Frank Case,* editor of *Antisemitism in the United States,* and coeditor of *Jews in the South; American Vistas*; and *The Aliens.*

The Progressive and States' Rights Parties of 1948

by *Leonard Dinnerstein*

The Progressive and States' Rights (commonly known as the Dixiecrats[1]) parties of 1948 were products of dissension within the Democratic ranks. Both parties began with hopes of displacing the dominant core in the Democratic party and both failed miserably. The Progressives had envisioned uniting all liberals in a forward-looking, socialistic, movement. The Dixiecrats believed that the time had come for southern segregationists and economic conservatives to oust the northern liberals from their policy making roles. In the end, both Progressives and Dixiecrats lasted only one presidential election.

The Progressive party of 1948 wanted, more than anything else, to reverse the direction of Truman's foreign policy. Many of the early Progressives believed that the president's determination to contain the expansion of Communism constituted a reversal of Franklin D. Roosevelt's attempts at coexistence with Russia and other nations whose cultural attributes and political needs differed from our own. They regarded Truman's policies as a betrayal of the spirit of the United Nations. The Progressives fervently desired to educate the country about the ultimate consequences of what they considered a blatantly aggressive American posture in international affairs. They foresaw, about a generation earlier than most other Americans, that

American troops could not act as policemen of the world, and that the United States could not remake divergent national groups in its own image. They tried to persuade the American government to work within the United Nations in international affairs and to recognize that coexistence with Communism provided the world's best chance for peace.

The Dixiecrats, on the other hand, had no quarrel with the president's foreign policy but vigorously opposed his attempt to curb racism in the United States. Truman's proposed civil rights program in 1948 struck many southerners as the most serious national threat to their way of life since Reconstruction. A good deal of financial support for southern dissidents came from the oil industry, which was alarmed by Truman's determination to have federal control of off-shore oil deposits in the Gulf of Mexico. The combination of a civil rights bill and programs of federal intervention in the economy united two groups who together provided the backbone for the States' Rights party: bigots and businessmen.

During the campaign of 1948 both the minor parties aimed their major attacks at the Democrats. Neither paid much attention to the other. After the election both passed from the scene while the Democratic party emerged not only unscathed, but stronger than it had been during Truman's early years in the White House.

As early as 1946, astute political observers predicted the emergence of a third party in 1948. A number of pacifists, religious leaders, scientists, old-time midwestern isolationists, professional friends of Russia, devotees of peaceful coexistence and American Communists viewed President Truman's cold war anti-Communism with misgivings. Labor concerns about the president's threat to draft striking railroad workers and the administration's generally lackluster efforts to promote social and economic welfare legislation alienated many members of the New Deal coalition. Finally, Truman's replacement of liberal appointees with representatives of big business and the military upset a goodly number of other Democrats.

Henry Wallace, former vice president and Secretary of Agriculture and Commerce under Franklin D. Roosevelt, emerged as the spokesman for these disgruntled groups. Born in Iowa on October 7, 1888, Wallace had a long and varied career. A graduate of Iowa State College, he worked on, and then edited, the family's successful journal, *Wallace's Farmer*. He won renown as a plant geneticist, conducting original experiments which led to higher yields and finer strains of corn. His father served as Secretary of Agriculture during Warren Harding's presidency but Wallace broke family tradition by supporting Democrats Al Smith in 1928 and Franklin D. Roosevelt in 1932. Many of Roosevelt's associates credited him with putting Iowa in the Democratic column in the election of 1932. With his background he seemed an ideal selection for his father's old job as Secretary of Agriculture.

In Washington, Wallace emerged as one of the major spokesmen for New Deal policies. He believed that the government should help the "common man" achieve a decent standard of living, and advocated government intervention where necessary, to provide jobs for the unemployed. A deeply religious man who frequently quoted from the Bible, he struck some observers as a mystic.

In 1940, President Roosevelt insisted on having Wallace as his running mate. Ideologically Wallace was to the left of Roosevelt and most other Democrats; but, since the president made the Iowan's nomination a condition for accepting a third term, convention delegates could do nothing about it. As Vice President Wallace's demands for "a better world right now" won approval from the liberals and the downtrodden, his outspoken position about racial equality offended southerners and his refusal to ingratiate himself with party bosses hurt him with key officials. In 1944, the St. Louis *Post-Dispatch* succinctly and candidly summarized the Iowan's liabilities as the politicos interpreted them: he is "impractical, theoretical, enigmatical and 'too damned independent.' He is too pro-labor, too outspoken for racial equality. And besides, he speaks Russian." In view of the opposition, Roosevelt did not insist on having Wallace on the ticket again. He therefore agreed to have Senator Harry S. Truman of Missouri, who had many boosters and few enemies in political circles, as the vice presidential nominee.

Feeling somewhat guilty, and perhaps ashamed that he had not backed Wallace as staunchly as he might have, President Roosevelt offered the Iowan any cabinet secretaryship except the State Department when his tenure as vice president ended in January, 1945. Wallace chose Commerce. He remained there, a liberal symbol of the New Deal era, until Truman requested his resignation in September, 1946. The circumstances under which this occurred left some of the more outspoken liberals throughout the country bitter and reinforced their impression that Henry Wallace, rather than Harry Truman, was the rightful political heir to Franklin D. Roosevelt.

On September 12, 1946, Wallace delivered an address in New York City's Madison Square Garden calling for peaceful coexistence with Russia. He warned against allowing Great Britain to dominate American thinking in foreign policy, predicted that "the tougher we get with Russia, the tougher they will get with us," and pleaded for the United States to recognize Russia's legitimate interests in Eastern Europe. President Truman had at first approved the speech but under pressure from Secretary of State James F. Byrnes reversed himself and then, shortly afterwards, requested Wallace's resignation from the cabinet. This dismissal, more than any other single factor, united dissident liberals behind Henry Wallace.

During the next year and a half, Wallace toured the country speaking out against the policies of the Truman administration. He opposed aid to Greece and Turkey claiming that military aid was not the answer to social crisis: "The world is hungry and insecure, and the people of all lands demand change. American loans for military purposes won't stop them. . . . America will become the most hated nation in the world." He also opposed the Marshall Plan, arguing that the European Recovery Program should be administered through the United Nations rather than through the United States. As such it would be of great humanitarian value. As constituted, though, it looked to Wallace like a political tool and a boon to the American businessman.

Although Wallace emphasized foreign policy differences with the Truman administration, he did not ignore domestic concerns. In this area, however, Wallace differed with the president more in degree than in kind. He spoke about the high cost of living and urged greater governmental action to provide adequate medical care, decent housing and comprehensive social security. Moreover, he condemned Jim Crowism and the lack of adequate protection for free speech. "Neither party defends the First Amendment," he lamented. "Both stand mute while freedom of speech and thought are under attack. Both cry, 'Red! Communist!' at all opponents and use the Red Scare to cover up their plunder of the people." Wallace vigorously opposed the Taft-Hartley Act[2] but since Truman had already vetoed the bill the president could not be held to account for it.

With each succeeding speech Wallace sounded more like a presidential candidate. California's state attorney general, Robert Kenny, started a Wallace-for-President movement on the Democratic ticket on July 28, 1947, and a number of other groups soon sprung up throughout the country. Some wanted to start a new party. Wallace, in a speech at Los Angeles, hinted that he would not be averse to a new organization: "If the Democratic Party departs from the ideals of Franklin D. Roosevelt I shall desert altogether from that party." Then he predicted that the day was coming when labor would agree to join a real labor party with forward-looking farmers, businessmen, professionals, and scientists.

Wallace hesitated about stating his political plans during his speech tours. He never quite said that he would leave the Democratic party and head a new one; but his vigorous criticisms of existing governmental policies suggested that he might be receptive to such a scheme if approached properly. Progressives of varying political persuasions, including leaders of New York City's American Labor party, the Independent party of California, the Progressive party of Illinois, and especially the Progressive Citizens of America, began pressuring him to lead a new party. Finally, on the night of December 2, 1947, in the New York City home of sculptor Jo Davidson, Wallace agreed. Conferring with the Iowan that evening were C. B. "Beany" Baldwin, executive vice president of the Progressive Citizens of America; Lewis Frank, Jr., of *The New Republic*; and Hannah Dorner, former executive director of the Independent Citizens Committee of the Arts, Sciences and Professions.

Of all those encouraging Wallace to run for the presidency, the Progressive Citizens of America had the largest following. The PCA had resulted from a merger in 1946 of the National Citizens Political Action Committee and the Independent Citizens Committee of the Arts, Sciences and Professions. In 1947 it also included dissatisfied Democrats who deplored many of Truman's domestic and foreign policies. This group spearheaded the movement for the formation of a third party, and Henry Wallace's similarity of viewpoint, his New Deal associations, and his reputation as the most outspoken liberal Democrat in the country made him the likely choice to head a new coalition party.

Not all PCA leaders wanted a third party or Wallace. The organization's president, Frank Kingdom, who according to Wallace had been pressuring him to run independently for the presidency, resigned as soon as the Iowan's nomination seemed set. This surprised Wallace who had counted him one of his most enthusiastic supporters. Bartley Crum, the PCA national vice-chairman, also resigned because of

Wallace's nomination. In addition, many liberal Progressives did not want to sabotage the Democratic party or associate themselves with a man, such as Wallace, whose policies sounded more extreme than they preferred. Some, like Kingdom, believed that the American Communist party was playing too large a role in the third party movement.

Starting a new political party in December, 1947, may have been unwise. There was no broad base of popular discontent throughout the country. Despite the existence of concern, uncertainty and even forthright opposition to some aspects of President Truman's programs, most of the population believed that the American government sincerely wanted peace in the world and that Russia and the other Communist nations thwarted this goal. The idea of a monolithic Communist doctrine—with its stated intent of overthrowing the capitalistic world—seemed convincing to most Americans in the 1947 political climate. The expressions of American government officials condemning Russian policies and alleged Communist subversion reinforced this viewpoint. As a result, political candidates who appeared sympathetic to Russian needs or views, or who spouted ideals similar to those enunciated by Communists, struck most Americans as traitors, fools, dupes, or fellow-travelers. Neither Henry Wallace nor the majority of Progressives realized this when they launched their new party on the night of December 29, 1947.

In a radio address to the nation that evening Henry Wallace offered himself to the people. He pledged to fight against evil and to obtain "peace, progress and prosperity" for all Americans. He concluded his speech with a biblical allusion:

> We have assembled a Gideon's Army, small in number, powerful in conviction, ready for action. We have said with Gideon, "Let those who are fearful and trembling depart." For every fearful one who leaves, there will be a thousand to take his place. A just cause is worth a hundred armies. We face the future unfettered, unfettered by any principle but the general welfare. We owe no allegiance to any group which does not serve that welfare. By God's grace, the people's peace will usher in the century of the common man.

Announcing a new party is one thing. Forming and organizing the constituent units of a viable political machine is something else again. Wallace's new party could count on three already established organizations: the American Labor party in New York, the Independent Progressives of California and the Progressive party in Illinois as a nucleus. Furthermore, the Progressive Citizens of America, the strongest group that had agitated for the third party, would merge with the others. But state and local units had to be developed and nominating petitions had to be filed in states to qualify Wallace and his party for a place on the November ballot. The task appeared monumental.

Wallace's failure to impose his views or direct party affairs closely, disagreement among Progressives on organizational strategy, and an insufficient number of qualified individuals to staff fledgling political clubs hampered development. Wallace wanted local units open to "all people who wish for a peaceful understanding between the United States and Soviet Russia," but others fought for narrower, tightly disciplined, cell-like units, primed for future thrusts on the national level. Some labor leaders favored deemphasizing international relations and playing up the "slave labor" aspects of the Taft-Hartley Bill. One pressing problem—that of communications—the party never solved. There simply were too few individuals available as field organizers and national party leaders to meet regularly and exchange ideas.

The general pattern of development in each state—although variations abounded —consisted of the establishment of local groups which then merged into state committees which held conventions, nominated candidates for different offices and started drumming up support for the candidates. Outside of New York, California and Illinois, most of the constituent units of the party had to be formed from scratch. Organizers from New York went out to help where needed. No central committee exerted control over the local units, and, not surprisingly, the chaos and variations in the end led to a smaller vote than would have come out had there been a well oiled machine. In Connecticut, for example, the party attracted mostly white-collar workers; in Colorado a split between those who wanted a narrow party and those who favored a broader based group culminated in a victory for the former and the latter left the organization.

Progressives also had problems in getting a place on the ballot. Ohio's Secretary of State refused to allow Progressive nominees to run in the Buckeye State because they had not been duly chosen by delegates elected in the primary. He also questioned whether they could qualify on security grounds. The state's Supreme Court reversed his decision, and the Progressives ran in Ohio. In Illinois, on the other hand, the state's high court ruled in the party's favor; but state election officials, by claiming that the decision came too late to print new ballots in time for the election, in effect nullified the legal decision. Nevertheless, the party did appear on the ballot in forty-five states—all but Illinois, Nebraska and Oklahoma—and fielded 9 candidates for the United States Senate and 114 congressional nominees in 23 states.

In addition, a number of Progressives withdrew from their contests before the election to allow Democrats with fairly similar views an opportunity to win. This was often done to avoid splitting the liberal vote and letting the conservative candidate be elected. Yale Law School Professor Thomas Irwin Emerson, dropped out of Connecticut's gubernatorial race; this, no doubt, helped elect Democrat Chester Bowles whose margin of victory barely exceeded 2,000. The Progressive party also endorsed, in the words of its national chairman, "Beany" Baldwin, twenty-four "outstanding Democrats with liberal records" for reelection to the House of Representatives. It also, however, ran candidates against other liberal Democrats, such as Paul H. Douglas in the senatorial contest in Illinois.

The immediate cause of the southern bolt appeared to be President Truman's Civil Rights message of February 2, 1948. The president asked Congress to abolish segregation in interstate travel, grant residents of the District of Columbia the right to vote, end the poll tax, make lynching a federal crime, and establish a Fair Employment Practices Commission. The program riled southerners and provided a sharp focus for a revolt in the South. Alabama's *Hale County News* wrote in September, 1948, however, that Dixiecrat protests

> against civil rights and for states rights are merely a camouflage to cover their real purposes. The bolt has been led by a coalition of entrenched reactionaries who are primarily interested in maintaining their privileged stations. Their stranglehold upon the politics of their respective states has been challenged and seriously endangered by the sweep of a liberal movement across the South that is interested in progress and the development of our resources. The reactionaries have seized upon the strategy of stirring up prejudice and fomenting racial strife as a blind to their real purposes.

Ever since the New Deal southern conservatives had felt their influence waning in the Democratic party. They resented elimination of the two-thirds rule at the 1936 convention. They scorned policies which elevated the economic circumstances of blacks. They deplored President Roosevelt's order barring segregation in defense plants during the Second World War. Moreover, the liberal trend in the Democratic party in the North lessened southern influence in policy formulation and also in political appointments. Claims were also made about centralization of power in the hands of the federal government, but such fears were voiced primarily by those who objected to how that power was being used. Many prominent business corporations, for example those companies controlling the tidelands oil, felt that state governments would be more sympathetic to their needs than the federal government. Ralph McGill, former publisher of the *Atlanta Constitution*, pithily analyzed the goals of the southern dissenters with the comment, "Hell, this ain't a fight to preserve State rights, this is a fight to preserve State wrongs."

Displays of southern wrath had occurred earlier. The conservative coalition—a combination of Republicans and southern Democrats—surfaced in Congress in the mid-1930's, frustrating the extension of New Deal programs after 1938. Governors Sam Jones of Louisiana and Frank Dixon of Alabama had invited the conference of southern governors to join them in forming a new southern Democratic party in 1943 but met with a chilly reception. The following year a number of southern delegations helped thwart the renomination of Henry Wallace for vice president because they found his brand of liberalism much too distasteful. Only Franklin D. Roosevelt's strength and position prevented many southern delegations from attacking him publicly in 1944.

In 1948, however, Harry S. Truman had little prestige. Almost no astute political observer expected him to win the election in November. Those leading the movement for a new party foresaw the possibility that the eleven states of the Confederacy would give the new southern party all of their electoral votes and that neither the Republican nor Democratic nominees would achieve a majority in the electoral college. That would force the presidential election into the House of Representatives where the southerners believed they would hold the balance of power. Senator James Eastland of

Mississippi predicted that, in the event the House had to make a decision, the southern nominee would probably win because the northern Democrats would prefer any Democrat to a Republican, while the Republicans would feel more comfortable with a southern Democrat in the White House than with a northern Democrat. Even less optimistic southerners saw themselves exerting greater influence in the federal government with the formation of their own party and the defeat of Truman. They hoped that the Republicans might win such a landslide vote as to wipe most liberal Democrats from office, thereby giving southern Democrats all the positions of congressional control in the minority party. Even if these two events did not come to pass, the least the southern Democrats expected by starting a new party was to contribute to Truman's defeat and gain additional influence in the national Democratic party.

Those southerners who wanted to bolt the party were still few in number by February, 1948, despite the president's civil rights speech. But they attracted attention because their leaders occupied the governor's mansions of several states. Governor Fielding Wright of Mississippi had called for a break with the national party in his January, 1948 inaugural address, and was instrumental in bringing about the Walkulla Springs, Florida, conference of southern governors on February 7, 1948, only five days after Truman's address. At Walkulla Springs, the governors served notice that the national Democratic party had forty days to reverse its stand on civil rights. A five-man committee, consisting of the governors of Arkansas, North Carolina, Texas, South Carolina and Virginia then met with the Democratic National Chairman, J. Howard McGrath, to express opposition to the civil rights report and ask that it be withdrawn from Congress. McGrath refused to intercede with the president on their behalf. The governors (without the chief executives of Florida, Louisiana, North Carolina and Tennessee) met again in Washington on March 13, 1948, to hear the conferees' report. Since the Democratic national chairman refused to yield, the governors urged each other to send anti-civil rights statements to the national convention which would meet in July.

The major pre-convention conclave of southerners opposed to the civil rights program took place in Jackson, Mississippi, on May 10, 1948. The Mississippi state executive committee had called a conference of "all true white Jeffersonian Democrats" to assemble at the state capitol. Two thousand, five hundred people responded to the invitation. Governor Wright presided. Whoever opposed civil rights and supported states rights, which in effect meant anyone who felt like coming, received a warm welcome. South Carolina Governor J. Strom Thurmond gave the keynote address. He implored his listeners to work diligently "to restore the prestige of the South in political affairs of the nation." Speaking in a similar vein earlier in the meeting Governor Wright had said, "We must teach the party leaders and the nation once and for all that we mean what we say and that from henceforward we will no longer tolerate slanderous, unwarranted attacks upon us and our customs."

Before the conference broke up, it authorized the establishment of an executive committee headed by Governor Ben Laney of Arkansas, and composed of two members from each of the eleven states representing the "Solid South." Resolutions were passed authorizing a bolt from the national party if the civil rights plan won majority approval in July at the party convention.

The southerners spoke with determined voice, but at the Democratic National Convention in Philadelphia two months later, the majority of the delegates completely ignored their wishes. The national party refused to restore the two-thirds rule in selecting candidates and approving platform positions, and pointedly ignored southern sensitivities by adopting the strongest civil rights plank in the history of the party. The adoption of the civil rights program resulted in the withdrawal of the Mississippi delegation and half of the Alabamans. But other southerners remained and most gave their votes for presidential nominee to Georgia's United States Senator Richard Russell. (Thirteen of North Carolina's thirty-two votes, though, went to President Truman.)

The northern control of the national Democrats—as evidenced by the adoption of the civil rights plank and the refusal to restore the two-thirds rule—infuriated Governor Wright, who invited those delegates who opposed Truman to meet in Birmingham, Alabama, on Saturday, July 17, to select a better candidate. A number of disaffected Democrats heeded his plea. For many it was a continuation of the states rights convention which had met in Jackson on May 10.

Birmingham's Municipal Auditorium, which seated 6,000, served as the meeting place. The organizers could not decide what to call the gathering and therefore labeled it a "conference." Delegates, reporters, and others, however, referred to it as a "convention." Whatever the sobriquet, it opened at 10:45 a. m. on July 17, 1948, with Ruby Mercer of the Metropolitan Opera singing the "Star Spangled Banner" and "Dixie" in that order.

Most prominent southern Democratic leaders on both state and national levels shunned the Birmingham affair despite their opposition to Truman and the party's national platform. They did not want to jeopardize seniority rights in Congress or possible patronage plums that might fall to them in the future. Moreover, they saw nothing to be gained by joining an obviously futile cause like a fourth party. Even Governor Ben Laney of Arkansas, who sympathized with the opponents of civil rights legislation, came to Birmingham but refused to appear on the convention floor. He wanted no part of a formal break with the national party.

As a consequence of the key politicos' refusal to participate at Birmingham, virtually anyone who claimed allegiance to the cause could get a delegate's badge. Most southern states did not bother to send official representatives even though placards supposedly identified thirteen state groups. Four University of Virginia students and an Alexandrian woman on her way home from New Orleans represented the Old Dominion. Reporters tried, but could not find anyone who would identify himself as coming from North Carolina or Kentucky. Louisiana, Florida and Texas supported delegations of between fifteen and twenty-five each. Arkansas had twelve; Oklahoma three. Four students from the University of Tennessee, six from Cumberland College and five "sympathizers" not otherwise identified, met under the Tennessee banner. Governor Thurmond brought a large retinue from South Carolina. Alabama and Mississippi had full delegations. Georgia remained unrepresented.

Besides the "delegates," the "conference" attracted, in the words of one observer, "political hacks and has-beens, reactionaries . . . Ku Kluxers, Negro baiters-and-haters, Confederate-flag-waving-Dixie-singing sentimentalists, wifebeaters, dog poisoners, eaters of popcorn in movies, and many who wear wool hats in the summertime. . . ." Gerald L. K. Smith, the notorious Arkansas anti-semite, appeared under the pseudonym S. Goodyear, while "Alfalfa Bill" Murray, the former Oklahoma governor who credited America's progress to "Christian principles and white men's brains" also made the scene.

Gessner McCovey, chairman of the Alabama Democratic Executive Committee, served as the "conference's" temporary chairman, and Walter Sillers, speaker of the Mississippi House of Representatives, held the permanent chairmanship. Houston attorney Ralph Lee was the permanent secretary. Former Governor Frank M. Dixon gave the keynote address. As thousands cheered, he warned that Truman's civil rights program would "reduce us to the status of a mongrel, inferior race, mixed in blood, our Anglo-Saxon heritage a mockery." He vowed that "the South will fight the attempt to mongrelize our people."

Many of those present danced and sang, shouted epithets—one group of Mississippi students chanted "To hell with Truman"—and waved Confederate flags. Life size pictures of Robert E. Lee abounded. The delegates relished the opportunity of openly expressing contempt for the national Democratic party and reverence for their southern heritage.

The "conference" issued a "Declaration of Principles," one of which condemned the Democratic party's "infamous and iniquitous program of equal access to all places of public accommodation for persons of all races, colors, creeds, and national origin." The Declaration of Principles also noted the southern commitment to the United States Constitution, reiterated the words of the Tenth Amendment that powers not delegated to the federal government are reserved to the states, accused the president of creating a totalitarian state by allowing the federal government to interfere in state affairs, charged the Philadelphia convention with deliberately attempting to demoralize the South, and reasserted southern loyalty to the Democratic party and the ideals of Thomas Jefferson and Andrew Jackson.

In addition to an excoriation of the president and his enunciated policies, the conference also "recommended" Governors J. Strom Thurmond of South Carolina and Fielding Wright of Mississippi as its candidates for president and vice president respectively. Thurmond received the nomination, in all probability, because the favorite, Governor Ben Laney of Arkansas, who eventually decided to remain in the Democratic fold, did not want it. (Ralph McGill believed that Thurmond and Wright took the nominations to gain strength for their projected races in the United States Senate primaries in 1950.)

Governor Strom Thurmond, born on December 5, 1902, had attended Clemson College in his home state and received a B. S. in 1923. He taught high school for the next six years while studying for a law degree. In the 1930's he won admittance to the bar. During the New Deal years he favored improvement of education, aid to conservation and betterment of working conditions for farmers and laborers alike. In 1938 he became the youngest circuit judge in South Carolina and during World War II served in the Army's 82nd Airborne Division. After the war he ran successfully for governor. Under his administration the legislature increased appropriations for education, libraries, hospitals and other social services. A devout Baptist, he neither smoked nor drank.

Governor Wright, a native Mississippian, born on May 16, 1895, was also a lawyer with a long record of service in the Mississippi legislature. He won a seat in the state Senate in 1928, and in the House of Representatives four years later. In 1936 he became Speaker of the House. During his legislative years Wright worked to improve the state's social services, including increased aid for Negro education. Elected lieutenant governor in 1943 he succeeded to the governorship in 1946 upon the death of the incumbent. A Methodist, he smoked cigars but was never seen drinking in his legally dry state.

In accepting their nominations, Governors Wright and Thurmond said just what the audience wanted to hear. "We cannot, we will not turn back. This is the opportunity of the South to prove we are the Democratic Party," the Mississippi governor proclaimed. Thurmond, speaking after him, announced, "We must prove that the South means business this year." "If the South should vote for Truman this year," the South Carolina governor continued, "we might just as well petition the Government to give us colonial status."

Most of the Dixiecrats considered themselves the nation's "true Democrats." They believed that the northern wing had corrupted the party's purpose and had to be defeated. That Thurmond still considered himself a Democrat after his nomination is evidenced by the fact that when Democratic National Chairman J. Howard McGrath requested his resignation as national party committeeman, the South Carolina governor refused.

The objectives of the Dixiecrats were threefold: (1) to defeat Truman and his civil rights planks; (2) to show Democrats that they could not win an election without southern support, thereby gaining greater southern influence in future party conclaves; and (3) "to restore the Democratic Party to the American way and to guarantee that the principle of state sovereignty" be forever continuous.

In contrast to the Dixiecrats, the Wallaceites—originally known as members of the "New party" before their convention officially changed the name to the "Progressive party"—were, in the words of *New York Times* correspondent Anne O'Hare McCormick, "fresh as daisies and politically innocent . . . political 'displaced persons,' seeking a leader to help them overcome their half-articulate fears, frustrations and resentments." Among the 3,200 at their convention in Philadelphia, one found "scores of boys with bristly crew haircuts, wearing sports jackets and open-collar shirts, and girls in oxfords, bobby socks and dirndls." Decidedly thinner, younger and more sincere than their Republican and Democratic counterparts, many in attendance had joined the party because of idealistic commitments to brotherhood and good will towards men. The poverty, insecurity, poor health, inequities, and cold war atmosphere that they saw in this country disheartened them and they viewed the Progressive party as the vehicle through which society could be regenerated.

On the convention floor, Negroes talked about racism, and Jews about anti-semitism, midwestern Scandinavians worried about farmers' cooperatives and Townsendites expressed fears of poverty in old age. A *New Republic* analysis showed the delegates most concerned with discrimination, labor's rights and the cost of living, in that order. Joseph and Stewart Alsop reported, though, that "sooner or later they all talk of peace."

Most of the assembled were Socialists either emotionally or intellectually. The gathering included authors, musicians, scientists, union members, a few well known politicians like Rexford G. Tugwell and New York City's American Labor party leader Vito Marcantonio, and a host of ordinary folk who simply wanted to make the world a better place to live in. One woman delegate, when asked why she was there, responded, "Wallace is the only one interested in seeing that my sons aren't turned into cannon fodder for the Wall Street imperialists."

The Progressives possessed a penchant for song unrivaled in American political history. The *New York Post* dubbed their rallies as the "singingest political convention in American history." Delegates sang on busses and streetcars on their way to the convention hall and each morning and afternoon session opened with chanting voices. Paul Robeson performed "The House I Live In" and "Old Man River." To the tune of the "Battle Hymn of the Republic," Pete Seeger blared out:

> From the bay of Massachusetts
> Out into the Golden Gate
> Henry Wallace leads his army
> 'Gainst destruction, fear and hate.
> We Americans will save the
> Precious land that we create
> For the people's march is on.

In between choruses delegates pinpointed their goals in rousing chants like:

> 1-2-3-4
> We Don't Want Another War
> 5-6-7-8
> We Don't Want a Fascist State

and slogans such as:

> Truman is tired of talking over international
>   differences.
> We're tired of dying over them.
> People before Profits.
> Wallace or War.

The idealists may have been in a majority at the convention but the platform committee reflected the views of hardheaded individuals. Rexford G. Tugwell, former Under-Secretary of Agriculture in the 1930's, chaired the seventy-four man group. Newspaper reporters carelessly dubbed many of these people Communists and fellow-travellers. John Cotton Brown, a political scientist who attended the platform committee meetings, has written that the policymaking group did not divide along "left-wing" or "right-wing" splits. According to Brown, only fifty-five members of the committee attended any sessions, of these only thirty-nine expressed identifiable views; perhaps eight were "left-wingers," and "these eight were seldom if ever unanimous on any matter at issue."

After sharp debate, the platform committee deleted a statement from the platform endorsing a "unified homeland" for the Macedonian people; this had been one of the heresies for which Stalin had recently excommunicated Tito. The committee also turned down a resolution sponsored by delegates from Vermont proclaiming that "it is not our intention to give blanket endorsement to the foreign policy of any nation." The Vermont resolution was considered to be "red-baiting." Such actions raised the question of Communist associations that plagued the Progressive party throughout its brief history. Many Progressives believed that Communists and non-Communists could work together and therefore made no effort to purge the pink element. Henry Wallace endorsed this position. So too did most, but not all, of the party leaders, who included New York City Congressman Vito Marcantonio, Albert Fitzgerald, president of the United Electrical Workers, "Beany" Baldwin, T.I. Emerson, and Elmer Benson, national chairman of the Wallace-for-President group and former governor of Minnesota. At the party's state convention in Nevada, though, the chairman had resigned because the delegates refused to take a stand against Communism; in New Mexico six Progressive leaders left the party because of "undue Communist influence." Young George S. McGovern who attended the Philadelphia convention, soon dropped out of the party because of the prominence of the Communists. Tugwell also declined to take an active part in the campaign.

The association of Communists with the Progressive party led to savage accusations in the press. Dorothy Thompson, in a radio address, proclaimed, "The Communist party—let's tell the truth—initiated the movement for Wallace." Columnists Joseph and Stewart Alsop wrote that the Progressive convention had been "quite obviously stage managed by the American Communist Party in the interests of the foreign policy of the Soviet Union." *Time* reported that the national convention had "assembled under careful Communist supervision." It claimed that "the Communists, their fellow-travelers and their stooges—many of whom deny that they are Communists but all of whom walk the Communist chalk line" were behind Wallace. These tactics conditioned the public's reaction to Progressive candidates and issues and also lessened the party's total votes at the polls in November.

To make matters worse, Henry Wallace reinforced the connection of Communism and Progressivism in people's minds with politically maladroit comments. When reporters asked him why the Progressive platform "in almost every major particular" paralleled the Communist party's published statements of goals, Wallace responded, "I'd say they have a good platform." In another context he indicated his belief "that the Communists are the closest things to the early Christian martyrs." The political consequences of such a statement were profound. Most Americans, including those with socialistic tendencies, had no affinity for Communism either in theory or as it was practiced in Russia. To win votes Wallace could have emphasized the world's desire for peace and this country's need for domestic reform without tying his platform to views associated with other nations.

On the last night of the convention 32,000 fans paid anywhere from $.65 to $2.60 to hear Henry Wallace deliver his acceptance speech at Philadelphia's Shibe Park. "I am committed to the policy of placing human rights above property rights," he told the members of his audience, and they howled their approval. He also enunciated support for old line Socialist and New Deal programs, such as subjecting corporate monopolies to greater public control and increasing federal assistance to build schools, houses, dams, power plants and highways. In sum, he favored "progressive capitalism." He closed his speech that night with a renunciation:

> . . .of those who practice hate and preach prejudice; of those who would limit the civil rights of others; of those who would restrict the use of the ballot; of those who would advocate force and violence; and I am committed to accept and do accept the support of all those who truly believe in democracy.

As Wallace's running mate, the convention chose Glen Taylor, Idaho's junior Democratic United States senator. Taylor, the twelfth of thirteen children, was born on April 12, 1904. Economic necessity forced him to leave school and go to work after the eighth grade. At seventeen, he joined a dramatic stock company and later on formed part of the "Glendora Ranch Gang," a folk-singing group. He ran unsuccessfully for a seat in the United States House of Representatives in 1937, and for the Senate in 1938 and 1940. When he finally won the coveted Senate seat in 1944, he campaigned on two issues: the need for an international organization to preserve peace, and federal aid to establish a Columbia Valley Authority similar to the Tennessee Valley Authority.

Sometimes known as "The Singing Cowboy," Taylor came to Washington in 1945 and immediately amused reporters by sitting down on the Capitol steps, taking out his guitar, and twanging out, "Give Me a Home 'Neath the Capitol Dome." Anxious to avoid another war, the Idahoan spoke out against the militarists in the government. He ridiculed the two major cabinet posts as the "State of War Department." When Truman proposed to help Turkey and Greece, Senator Taylor labeled the program "not a relief plan but an oil grab." To dramatize his opposition to the Marshall Plan, he attempted to ride horseback from Hollywood to Washington. This feat won him national attention as well as a reputation for being a "genial oddball." At the Progressive convention he and his family gave a rendition of "When You Were Sweet Sixteen." Taylor's crooning may have pleased the ear but he lacked the dignity necessary to impress voters with the seriousness and purposefulness of the Progressive program. Still, he was a New Dealer, had publicly taken the same positions as Wallace, and as a United States senator had the requisite prestige for a vice presidential nomination.

Henry Wallace did not need any press buildup. He had had a distinguished career in Washington and no one questioned his dedication to the cause of peace or the welfare of the common man. Many people had reservations, though, about his methods and programs. For a politician he was curiously aloof and distant, unable to deal with people in a friendly, casual way. A poor speaker and careless organizer, he had an enigmatic quality which gave him the reputation of a mystic. Collectively, these characteristics mitigated his impact as party leader.

Wallace focused Progressive goals on peace, freedom and abundance. He wanted a secure world in which the major powers—Russia and the United States—showed respect and understanding for each other's needs; the rights of all persons to express their views—no matter how bizarre or obnoxious—without fear of being branded a traitor; the establishment of a civil rights program which would abolish segregation and second-class citizenship for Negroes; and a prosperous economy where everyone shared the fruits of industrial progress. He predicted the inevitability of the welfare state and promised that after the Progressives became the nation's dominant party they would place banks, railroads, gas, power, and atomic energy under public ownership.

Wallace did not have the ability to sell his programs to a suspicious public. More specifically, he had difficulty even finding audiences who would listen to him. The Wallace entourage usually entered an area unheralded and without fanfare. Few leading citizens greeted the former vice president. The parade and hullabaloo which every Republican and Democratic standard bearer could expect as a matter of course eluded the Progressive candidate. Once into a city Wallace sometimes encountered difficulties in conducting his campaign. In Topeka, Kansas, Progressives could not rent the municipal auditorium, which sat 4,000, so the candidate had to make his presentation in a city park seating 400. The University of Missouri refused to allow a Wallace rally on the campus, while the Mayor of Asheville, North Carolina, wired the candidate, "Your presence is not desired here."

In Birmingham, Alabama, the Public Safety Commissioner, Eugene "Bull" Connor, refused Wallace permission to speak before an integrated audience. "I ain't gonna let no darkies and white folk mix together in this town," Connor indignantly proclaimed. Wallace also endured ruffians' thumping fists on his fenders and shouts like "nigger lover" and "Why don't you go back to Russia?" In other cities the populace expressed its displeasure differently. During the campaign Wallace served as target for eighty-four eggs, forty tomatoes, four peaches, two lemons, one orange, one bun and an unspecified number of green peppers. *Time* magazine concluded that the attacks came because his "wild parroting of the Communist line had given most voters a feeling of disgust."

When Wallace's advance men successfully found a suitable area for him to speak, the meetings generally followed a regular pattern. There would be an invocation, often by a Negro minister, opening remarks by local politicos, a nod to the Progressive candidate running in the area and finally the presentation of Henry Wallace who would proceed with his "dry, earnest discourse." One remarkable aspect that astounded observers was that the Progressives charged admission to most of their rallies.

The Progressive party also differed from most other parties (but not the Dixiecrats) in that it did not lack financial resources. At the end of the campaign the party coffers contained a surplus of $20,000. At no time did any plans or programs have to be cancelled for lack of funds. The party spent over $3 million. About half of these contributions came from people giving less than $100 and living on either the East or West coasts. In general, middle America contributed little. Four states—New York, Pennsylvania, Illinois, and California—contributed the bulk of all the monies collected. Chicago's Anita McCormick Blaine, daughter of Cyrus McCormick and daughter-in-law of James G. Blaine, gave lavishly. One chronicler of the Progressive party's history estimated her donations at about $800,000.

Because they were so well financed, the Progressives publicized their candidates and programs in comic books, on billboards and films, and on the radio. The national party distributed 25 million copies of more than 140 different leaflets, pamphlets, posters, buttons, films, and phonograph records. When Henry Wallace's crowds diminished so that further public appearances were practically worthless, the presence of adequate funds allowed him, after October 17, to cancel whistle-stop speeches and purchase radio time for his statements.

The Progressives, more than any other party before or since, vigorously supported efforts to give all Americans opportunities equal to their abilities. Women served as the party directors in Georgia, Louisiana, North Carolina and Missouri, and performed two-thirds of the work done in California. They also ran for Congress on the Progressive slate. Others quite visible among the Progressives included Negro and Spanish-speaking candidates wherever these groups constituted a significant proportion of the population.

In direct contrast to the many full state slates of the Progressives, the Dixiecrats ran only two nominees—Thurmond and Wright, had no room for minorities in their ranks, and allowed women to serve in the traditional roles that society had assigned to them: as hostesses, secretaries, and button-sellers. The Dixiecrats established no party organizations but utilized the existing Democratic apparatus wherever possible. Outside the South the Dixiecrats won a place on the ballot only in the state of North Dakota.[3] But the sharpest contrast between Progressives and Dixiecrats lay in the realm of programs. Whereas the former spelled out numerous steps it would take to make the federal government more responsive to human needs, the latter sputtered out platitudes and argued strenuously for a do-nothing federal government.

Governor Thurmond travelled 25,975 miles and made 107 speeches, mostly against Truman's "Civil Wrongs Proposals." He capitalized on his audiences' fear of Communism, charged that Russia supported Truman and his Fair Employment Practices Commission and claimed that Truman "patterned" the F.E.P.C. "after a Russian law written by Joseph Stalin in 1920." Even if the Dixiecrat campaign failed, Thurmond proclaimed, "we shall have accomplished our most important objective—to rebuild the Democratic party, to prevent passage of the un-American force bills and to restore the Southern states to a position of respect from every political party."

One concern of the Dixiecrats, which Thurmond did not publicize, centered around the needs of the major southern industrialists who financed the party lavishly. Hugh Roy Cullen, the Texas millionaire who sparked the oil industry's support of the States' Righters, furnished a private plane for Governor Thurmond and his entourage to use when he went to Houston, Texas, to accept the Dixiecrat nomination, and also placed a special train at the disposal of Governor Wright and his associates for the same purpose. One experience of Georgia's Governor Ellis Arnall, suggests that others may have been equally solicitous. Governor Arnall had attended a football game in New Orleans with friends and associates, and had occupied expensive suites in a local hotel. When he left and attempted to pay the bill the desk clerk told him, "That's all right, Governor, your bill has been taken care of." She then explained that the Mississippi Power and Light Company had paid for the expenses. Arnall must have looked quite surprised because the clerk countered, "You are the Governor of Mississippi, aren't you?"

It is impossible to know exactly who supported the Dixiecrats, or the extent of their financial contributions to the party, but the roster of names known to favor the movement includes those associated with some of the most prominent business interests in the region at that time. In Mississippi, fifty-four year old Wallace Wright (no relation to the governor), president of the largest wholesale grocery firm in the state in 1948, served as financial backer and guiding spirit. In Alabama, the party's state chairman, lawyer Marion Rushton, counted New York's Chase Manhattan Bank, Buckeye Cotton Oil and Capitol Fertilizer among his clients. In South Carolina, Alabama, Louisiana and Texas, lawyers for Esso, Humble Oil, Gulf Oil, Magnolia Petroleum, Tennessee Coal and Iron, and the National Association of Manufacturers, and officials of the National Cotton Council (the NAM of the plantation South) stood out prominently in the ranks of the Dixiecrats.

The oil people supported the Dixiecrats primarily because they wanted Truman defeated. They believed that with a Republican in the White House control of the offshore oil discoveries would be given to the states whose legislatures would be more sympathetic to their needs. The oil men worked well with the southern politicians who, in economic matters, did not differ from the Republicans.

On the political level, the Dixiecrats won the support of state and local politicians whose careers did not depend on federal patronage. In local campaigns Dixiecrat orators aroused partisans who turned out in large numbers, gave rebel yells, and sang "Dixie" interminably. Audiences encouraged speakers who insisted that Negroes be kept in their place, that home rule be preserved, and that constitutional rights be restored. Twenty-five dollar a plate dinners and $5 admission picnics to finance party activities sold out quickly. Dixiecrats proudly sported "Thurmond-and-Wright" buttons and in Birmingham the daughters of a local steel executive and the president of Coca-Cola sold these emblems in public at $1 each.

Ardor and dedication to principles, though, could not turn minority positions into winning combinations. Although the results of the election of 1948 surprised the nation, Harry Truman and the Democrats, not the Progressives or Dixiecrats, won impressive numbers of votes. Instead of hurting Truman, the two new parties may actually have helped him—the Dixiecrats by bringing out the black vote for the Democrats; and the Progressives by making it impossible for the Republicans to apply the Communist label to the Democrats as they would attempt to do in later years, thereby holding the Catholic vote for Truman.

Polls taken in February, 1948, indicated that the Progressives might capture 11.5 percent of the votes. This figure dwindled as the year progressed, but just before the election different pollsters estimated that Wallace would get between 3.3 percent and 4.4 percent of the final tally. When the Progressives received 2.38 percent of the ballots cast, party leaders and followers wondered what had caused such a dismal showing. The party elected no senators and only one congressman, Vito Marcantonio of New York's American Labor party. Wallace and Taylor received only 1,157,063 votes. They had needed about 5 or 10 million to demonstrate strong opposition to the administration and to lay the foundations for a viable new party. Wallace carried only thirty precincts in the nation and those contained the most downtrodden minorities: seven in Tampa, Florida, inhabited mainly by Cuban cigar workers; a number in New York and Los Angeles with poor Jewish and Negro neighborhoods; and eight in Marcantonio's East Harlem district in New York City which housed mostly Negroes, Puerto Ricans and Italians. In short, the Progressives received their greatest support from those elements of the population most directly concerned with civil rights and equal opportunities.

The Progressives received their largest votes in New York (509,559; 8.12 percent of the total vote), California (190,381; 4.73 percent), and Pennsylvania (55,111; 1.47 percent). Wallace also took enough votes away from Truman in New York, Connecticut, Michigan and Maryland to allow New York's Governor Thomas E. Dewey, the Republican presidential nominee, to carry those states.

The Progressive failure dashed the hopes of the party stalwarts who had envisioned an election outcome which would provide a base for a strong run in 1952 and 1956. Wallace, a poor political leader, had not discouraged anyone, regardless of his degree of leftist leanings, from joining the party. As a result the public believed that the Communists pulled the strings and dictated party positions. Wallace may have been misguided, and perhaps even elusive, but his desire for peace and for the end of racial prejudice and economic inequities did not stem from any commitment to a foreign ideology. He sincerely believed in the goals for which he fought. Unfortunately, he failed to make it abundantly clear that his beliefs resulted from his own convictions and education and not from the wishes of any other political groups. His inability to establish an image of the Progressives independent of foreign ideologies proved catastrophic for the party.

The formation of the Americans for Democratic Action—an organization devoted to quite similar economic and social programs at home as the Progressives but one that opposed Stalinism and backed the containment policy—also hurt Wallace's party by providing dissident liberals with a home outside of the Democratic party. Moreover, Truman had undercut the impact of the Progressive domestic issues by his own domestic program. Why then should the poor and the downtrodden throw away their votes on a third party that could not possibly win when the Democrats promised a good civil rights program, increased federal assistance for housing, a rise in the minimum wage, additional social security benefits, and support for national health insurance?

Truman also had good luck on his side in foreign affairs. While Wallace toured the country denouncing American imperialism, labeling the Marshall Plan a pork barrel for American business interests, and pleading for an understanding of Soviet needs and policies, the Russians became more belligerent. They engineered a Communist coup in Czechoslovakia in February and a few weeks later were apparently responsible for the death of Jan Masaryk, the country's national hero. The Russian blockade of allied ground transportation into Berlin in June and increasing Societ bellicosity in the United Nations made it difficult for Wallace to get sympathy or agreement from American audiences when he said "the tougher we get with Russia, the tougher they will get with us." Henry Wallace did not realize that his pleas for Americans to understand Russian views and Soviet needs smacked of appeasement and weakness to a nation that clearly remembered Western Europe's sellout of Czechoslovakia to Hitler in Munich ten years earlier.

Many American Jews, deeply concerned about Israel, rallied behind Truman after he recognized the infant nation shortly after its independence in May, 1948. He chose James G. McDonald as this country's first ambassador to the new nation. McDonald, League of Nations Refugee Commissioner in the 1930's, had almost singlehandedly lobbied among the world's nations to find a place for German-Jewish outcasts, and his appointment in 1948 won Truman even more friends and good will among liberals in the United States.

The Progressives could not have won the election under any circumstances, but numerous factors weakened the prospect of even a respectable showing. The party lacked central direction, right organizational units, and enough people to perform the unspectacular tasks at ward and precinct levels. No major bloc gave Progressives whole-hearted support. Henry Wallace had no charisma and failed to attract voters whom a more popular or sympathetic leader could have won over. The media proved extremely unfriendly by slanting stories against the Progressives and emphasizing Communist associations whenever possible. People were also reluctant to vote out an administration in times of economic prosperity and this, too, aided Truman and hurt Wallace. Finally, in the voting booths, many of those who favored Wallace wound up casting their ballots for Truman because they were appalled at the prospect of Thomas E. Dewey as president; they believed that a vote for the Progressives would aid the Republican party.

The Dixiecrats' expectations also misfired. They did not force the presidential race into the House of Representatives, and won only 2.4 percent of the total vote. The party did carry, though, the thirty-eight electoral votes of the four states where it had expropriated the Democratic machinery and party banners: Louisiana, Mississippi, South Carolina and Alabama.[4] The electoral votes of these states gave the Dixiecrats the highest total of any third party since the 1912 Bull Moosers captured eighty-eight. Thurmond and Wright polled nineteen percent of the total southern vote. They scored their greatest victories in southern counties with high proportions of disenfranchised Negroes but did poorly where whites were not living in fear of black domination or where the economy did not revolve around plantations with their attendant racial and social attitudes. Of the country's 3,072 counties, the Dixiecrats captured two in the border states and 252 in the South. The Dixiecrat supporters had, in the past, been the staunchest backers of southern solidarity. The same counties that opted for secession in 1861 and that voted for Al Smith in 1928, also embraced Thurmond and Wright.

"They were, in short," Alexander Heard has written, "the Democrats with the firmest traditional attachment to the Democratic party."

After the 1948 election, Dixiecrats hastened to return to the Democratic fold. Governor Thurmond urged all Americans to "close ranks" behind President Truman. He claimed that the Dixiecrat bolt was merely "a fight within our own family," and insisted that he had "voted the ticket of the Democratic party of South Carolina." Other Dixiecrats engaged in similar gyrations. Some, including Thurmond, eventually joined the Republican party, but none announced his switch immediately.

The Progressives faded rapidly after the 1948 election. The defeat destroyed the political careers of both Wallace and Taylor. The latter returned to the Democratic fold but failed to hold on to his seat in the 1950 Idaho primary. The Progressives held a national convention in February, 1950, but one observer wrote that they looked "more like a sect than a major political party." The outbreak of the Korean War that summer brought a showdown. Wallace publicly supported the American position and formally resigned from the Progressive party along with numerous others who would not condemn Truman and support the Communists on this issue. A crippled organization did run two unknowns—Vincent Hallinan and Mrs. Charlotta Bass—for president and vice president in 1952, but that Fall *Fortune Magazine* informed its readers that "the Progressives today consist almost entirely of Communists, fellow travelers, and the most determined innocents." By 1954 the Progressive party had disintegrated so much that it just dissolved.

It took almost twenty years before a segment of the national Democrats recognized that the policies of the Cold War may have been misguided, that military assistance was not the answer to deep-seated social problems, and that the capitalist nations had to make efforts to understand, and get along with, the Communist nations in the world. Wallace is now dead, and his memory has not been hallowed, but a recent commentator did acknowledge that despite its errors and distortions, the Progressive party was nevertheless "a desperate attempt to reverse the tide which less than twenty years later has brought [the United States] to the brink of disaster."

In the final analysis, both the Dixiecrats and Progressives failed to establish viable parties because they misjudged the popular temper. Both groups opted for programs which a basically middle-of-the-road population found too extreme. The premises of these dissident wings of the Democratic party simply frightened too many Americans who were unwilling to base all of their hopes on either a racist determined to neutralize New Deal economic and social gains or on a mystic intent on changing the course of an established bipartisan foreign policy.

NOTES

[1] The term "Dixiecrat" seems to have originated when a telegraph editor for the *Charlotte News* (North Carolina) could not squeeze the party name—States' Rights Democrats—into a headline. So he coined the sobriquet, Dixiecrat, and it stuck.

[2] Congress passed the Taft-Hartley Labor Relations Act in 1947 over Truman's veto. Many ardent unionists labeled it a "slave labor" law. It forbade coercion of employees, excessive union dues, jurisdictional strikes, strikes by government employees, and secondary boycotts. It made unions responsible for acts of violence committed by members and prohibited unions from contributing to political campaigns. It also required some union officials to take oaths that they were not Communists. In addition, it banned the closed shop and allowed states to outlaw union shops. Finally, it set up machinery which the president could use to deal with strikes that might adversely affect the national welfare.

[3] The Dixiecrats appeared on the North Dakota ballot because an enterprising young army officer who lived in North Carolina solicited several of his friends to get 300 signatures for the party in that state. The friends thought of it as a lark but set out to get the requisite figure. They were never very serious about it and after they achieved their goal they disappeared as a group. No Dixiecrat headquarters appeared in the state, no one made a speech for Thurmond and Wright, and no one distributed literature for the party.

[4] One Tennessee elector cast his ballot for the Dixiecrats in the electoral college.

Appendix

HENRY A. WALLACE, SPEECH ON FOREIGN POLICY
September 12, 1946

The Secretary of Commerce delivered this speech before a joint meeting held in New York of the National Citizens Political Action Committee and the Independent Citizens Committee of the Arts, Sciences, and Professions. The prepared text follows.

First off, I want to give my own personal endorsement to the candidates chosen by the Democratic Party and the American Labor Party in New York. James Mead long has been one of the ablest public servants in Washington—a constant, faithful and intelligent proponent of the New Deal of Franklin Roosevelt. The Senate will miss him—but Albany needs him. He will make a great governor—worthy of the tradition of Smith and Roosevelt and Lehman.

Herbert Lehman knows full well the problems and the opportunities facing the State of New York, the United States, and the United Nations. His great heart and great mind will be increasingly useful when he is a member of the United States Senate.

Victory for Mead and Lehman in November will mean a long stride in the people's progress.

Tonight I want to talk about peace—and how to get peace. Never have the common people of all lands so longed for peace. Yet, never in a time of comparative peace have they feared war so much.

Up till now peace has been negative and unexciting. War has been positive and exciting. Far too often, hatred and fear, intolerance and deceit have had the upper hand over love and confidence, trust and joy. Far too often, the law of nations has been the law of the jungle; and the constructive spiritual forces of the Lord have bowed to the destructive forces of Satan.

During the past year or so, the significance of peace has been increased immeasurably by the atom bomb, guided missiles and airplanes which soon will travel as fast as sound. Make no mistake about it—another war would hurt the United States many times as much as the last war. We cannot rest in the assurance that we invented the atom bomb—and therefore that this agent of destruction will work best for us. He who trusts in the atom bomb will sooner or later perish by the atom bomb—or something worse.

I say this as one who steadfastly backed preparedness throughout the Thirties. We have no use for mamby-pamby pacificism. But we must realize that modern inventions have now made peace the most exciting thing in the world—and we should be willing to pay a just price for peace. If modern war can cost us $400 billion, we should be willing and happy to pay much more for peace. But certainly, the cost of peace is to be measured not in dollars but in the hearts and minds of men.

The price of peace—for us and for every nation in the world—is the price of giving up prejudice, hatred, fear, and ignorance.

Let's get down to cases here at home.

First we have prejudice, hatred, fear and ignorance of certain races. The recent mass lynching in Georgia was not merely the most unwarranted, brutal act of mob violence in the United States in recent years; it was also an illustration of the kind of prejudice that makes war inevitable.

Hatred breeds hatred. The doctrine of racial superiority produces a desire to get even on the part of its victims. If we are to work for peace in the rest of the world, we here in the United States must eliminate racism from our unions, our business organizations, our educational institutions, and our employment practices. Merit alone must be the measure of man.

Second, in payment for peace, we must give up prejudice, hatred, fear and ignorance in the economic world. This means working earnestly, day after day, for a larger volume of world trade. It means helping undeveloped areas of the world to industrialize themselves with the help of American technical assistance and loans.

We should welcome the opportunity to help along the most rapid possible industrialization in Latin America, China, India, and the Near East. For as the productivity of these people increases, our exports will increase.

We all remember the time, not so long ago, when the high tariff protectionists blindly opposed any aid to the industrialization of Canada. But look at our exports to Canada today. On a per capita basis our Canadian exports are seven times greater than our exports to Mexico.

I supported the British loan of almost four billion dollars because I knew that without this aid in the rehabilitation of its economy, the British government would have been forced to adopt totalitarian trade methods and economic warfare of a sort which would have closed the markets of much of the world to American exports.

For the welfare of the American people and the world it is even more important to invest $4 billion in the industrialization of undeveloped areas in the so-called backward nations, thereby promoting the long-term stability that comes from an ever-increasing standard of living. This would not only be good politics and good morals, it would be good business.

The United States is the world's great creditor nation. And low tariffs by creditor nations are a part of the price of peace. For when a great creditor demands payment, and at the same time, adopts policies which make it impossible for the debtors to pay in goods—the first result is the intensification of depression over large areas of the world; and the final result is the triumph of demagogues who speak only the language of violence and hate.

Individual Republicans may hold enlightened views—but the Republican party as a whole is irrevocably committed to tariff and trade policies which can only mean world-wide depression, ruthless economic warfare and eventual war. And if the Republicans were in power in the United States today, intelligent people all over the world would fear that once more we would be headed straight for boom, bust and world-wide chaos.

I noticed in the papers recently that Governor Dewey doesn't like my prophecies. I said weeks before the last election—and said it repeatedly—that Franklin Roosevelt would carry 36 states and have a popular majority of three million. Of course, Mr. Dewey didn't like that one. I say now—as I have said repeatedly—that Republican foreign economic policies carried into action would mean disaster for the nation and the world. Mr. Dewey won't like that one either.

The Republican Party is the party of economic nationalism and political isolation—and as such is as anachronistic as the dodo and as certain to disappear. The danger is that before it disappears it may enjoy a brief period of power during which it can do irreparable damage to the United States and the cause of world peace.

Governor Dewey has expressed himself as favoring an alliance of mutual defense with Great Britain as the key to our foreign policy. This may sound attractive because we both speak the same language and many of our customs and traditions have the same historical background. Moreover, to the military men, the British Isles are our advanced air base against Europe.

Certainly we like the British people as individuals. But to make Britain the key to our foreign policy would be, in my opinion, the height of folly. We must not let the reactionary leadership of the Republican party force us into that position. We must not let British balance-of-power manipulations determine whether and when the United States gets into war.

Make no mistake about it—the British imperialistic policy in the Near East alone, combined with Russian retaliation, would lead the United States straight to war unless we have a clearly-defined and realistic policy of our own.

Neither of these two great powers wants war now, but the danger is that whatever their intentions may be, their current policies may eventually lead to war. To prevent war and insure our survival in a stable world, it is essential that we look abroad through our own American eyes and not through the eyes of either the British Foreign Office or a pro-British or anti-Russian press.

In this connection, I want one thing clearly understood. I am neither anti-British nor pro-British—neither anti-Russian nor pro-Russian. And just two days ago, when President Truman read these words, he said that they represented the policy of his administration.

I plead for an America vigorously dedicated to peace—just as I plead for opportunities for the next generation throughout the world to enjoy the abundance which now, more than ever before, is the birthright of man.

To achieve lasting peace, we must study in detail just how the Russian character was formed—by invasions of Tartars, Mongols, Germans, Poles, Swedes, and French; by the czarist rule based on ignorance, fear and force; by the intervention of the British, French and Americans in Russian affairs from 1919 to 1921; by the geography of the huge Russian land mass situated strategically between Europe and Asia; and by the vitality derived from the rich Russian soil and the strenuous Russian climate. Add to all this the tremendous emotional power which Marxism and Leninism gives to the Russian leaders—and then we can realize that we are reckoning with a force which cannot be handled successfully by a "Get tough with Russia" policy. "Getting tough" never bought anything real and lasting—whether for schoolyard bullies or businessmen or world powers. The tougher we get, the tougher the Russians will get.

Throughout the world there are numerous reactionary elements which had hoped for Axis victory—and now profess great friendship for the United States. Yet, these enemies of yesterday and false friends of today continually try to provoke war between the United States and Russia. They have no real love of the United States. They only long for the day when the United States and Russia will destroy each other.

We must not let our Russian policy be guided or influenced by those inside or outside the United States who want war with Russia. This does not mean appeasement.

We most earnestly want peace with Russia—but we want to be met half way. We want cooperation. And I believe that we can get cooperation once Russia understands that our primary objective is neither saving the British Empire nor purchasing oil in the Near East with the lives of American soldiers. We cannot allow national oil rivalries to force us into war. All of the nations producing oil, whether inside or outside of their own boundaries, must fulfill the provisions of the United Nations Charter and encourage the development of world petroleum reserves so as to make the maximum amount of oil available to all nations of the world on an equitable peaceful basis—and not on the basis of fighting the next war.

For her part, Russia can retain our respect by cooperating with the United Nations in a spirit of openminded and flexible give-and-take.

The real peace treaty we now need is between the United States and Russia. On our part, we should recognize that we have no more business in the *political* affairs of Eastern Europe than Russia has in the *political* affairs of Latin America, Western Europe and the United States. We may not like what Russia does in Eastern Europe. Her type of land reform, industrial expropriation, and suppression of basic liberties offends the great majority of the people of the United States. But whether we like it or not the Russians will try to socialize their sphere of influence just as we try to democratize our sphere of influence. This applies also to Germany and Japan. We are striving to democratize Japan and our area of control in Germany, while Russia strives to socialize eastern Germany.

As for Germany, we all must recognize than an equitable settlement, based on a unified German nation, is absolutely essential to any lasting European settlement. This means that Russia must be assured that never again can German industry be converted into military might to be used against her—and Britain, Western Europe and the United States must be certain that Russia's Germany policy will not become a tool of Russian design against Western Europe.

The Russians have no more business in stirring up native communists to political activity in Western Europe, Latin America and the United States than we have in interfering in the politics of Eastern Europe and Russia. We know what Russia is up to in Eastern Europe, for example, and Russia knows what we are up to. We cannot permit the door to be closed against our trade in Eastern Europe any more than we can in China. But at the same time we have to recognize that the Balkans are closer to Russia than to us—and that Russia cannot permit either England or the United States to dominate the politics of that area.

China is a speical case and although she holds the longest frontier in the world with Russia, the interests of world peace demand that China remain free from any sphere of influence, either politically or economically. We insist that the door to trade and economic development opportunities be left wide open in China as in all the world. However, the open door to trade and opportunities for economic development in China are meaningless unless there is a unified and peaceful China—built on the cooperation of the various groups in that country and based on a hands-off policy of the outside powers.

We are still arming to the hilt. Our excessive expenses for military purposes are the chief cause for our unbalanced budget. If taxes are to be lightened we must have the basis of a real peace with Russia—a peace that cannot be broken by extremist propagandists. We do not want our course determined for us by master minds operating out of London, Moscow or Nanking.

Russian ideas of social-economic justice are going to govern nearly a third of the world. Our ideas of free enterprise democracy will govern much of the rest. The two ideas will endeavor to prove which can deliver the most satisfaction to the common man in their respective areas of political dominance. But by mutual agreement, this competition should be put on a friendly basis and the Russians should stop conniving against us in certain areas of the world just as we should stop scheming against them in other parts of the world. Let the results of the two systems speak for themselves.

Meanwhile, the Russians should stop teaching that their form of communism must, by force if necessary, ultimately triumph over democratic capitalism—while we should close our ears to those among us who would have us believe that Russian communism and our free enterprise system cannot live, one with another, in a profitable and productive peace.

Under friendly peaceful competition the Russian world and the American world will gradually become more alike. The Russians will be forced to grant more and more of the personal freedoms; and we shall become more and more absorbed with the problems of social-economic justice.

Russia must be convinced that we are not planning for war against her and we must be certain that Russia is not carrying on territorial expansion or world domination through native communists faithfully following every twist and turn in the Moscow party line. But in this competition, we must insist on an open door for trade throughout the world. There will always be an ideological conflict—but that is no reason why diplomats cannot work out a basis for both systems to live safely in the world side by side.

Once the fears of Russia and the United States Senate have been allayed by practical regional political reservations, I am sure that concern over the veto power would be greatly diminished. Then the United Nations would have a really great power in those areas which are truly international and not regional. In the world-wide, as distinguished from the regional field, the armed might of the United Nations should be so great as to make opposition useless. Only the United Nations should have atomic bombs and its military establishment should give special emphasis to air power. It should have control of the strategically located air bases with which the United States and Britain have encircled the world. And not only should individual nations be prohibited from manufacturing atomic bombs, guided missles and military aircraft for bombing purposes, but no nation should be allowed to spend on its military establishment more than perhaps 15 per cent of its budget.

Practically and immediately, we must recognize that we are not yet ready for World Federation. Realistically, the most we can hope for now is a safe reduction in military expense and a long period of peace based on mutual trust between the Big Three.

During this period, every effort should be made to develop as rapidly as possible a body of international law based on moral principles and not on the Machiavellian principles of deceit, force and distrust—which, if continued, will lead the modern world to rapid disintegration.

In brief, as I see it today, the World Order is bankrupt—and the United States, Russia and England are the receivers. These are the hard facts of power politics on which we have to build a functioning, powerful United Nations and a body of international law. And as we build, we must develop fully the doctrine of the rights of small peoples as contained in the United Nations Charter. This law should ideally apply as much to Indonesians and Greeks as to Bulgarians and Poles—but practically, the application may be delayed until both British and Russians discover the futility of their methods.

In the full development of the rights of small nations, the British and Russians can learn a lesson from the Good Neighbor policy of Franklin Roosevelt. For under Roosevelt, we in the Western Hemisphere built a workable system of regional internationalism that fully protected the sovereign rights of every nation—a system of multilateral action that immeasurably strengthened the whole of world order.

In the United States an informed public opinion will be all-powerful. Our people are peace-minded. But they often express themselves too late—for events today move much faster than public opinion. The people here, as everywhere in the world, must be convinced that another war is not inevitable. And through mass meetings such as this, and through persistent pamphleteering, the people can be organized for peace—even though a large segment of our press is propagandizing our people for war in the hope of scaring Russia. And we who look on this war-with-Russia talk as criminal foolishness must carry our message direct to the people—even though we may be called communists because we dare to speak out.

I believe that peace—the kind of peace I have outlined tonight—is the basic issue, both in the Congressional campaign this fall and right on through the Presidential election in 1948. How we meet this issue will determine whether we live not in "one world" or "two worlds"—but whether we live at all.

HENRY A. WALLACE
BROADCAST ANNOUNCING HIS CANDIDACY
December 29, 1947

The following was delivered over the Mutual Broadcasting System, Chicago, Illinois.

For the past fifteen months I have traveled up and down, and back and forth across this country. I have talked with half a million people in public meetings and with thousands in private gatherings. I have been working for, and I shall continue to work for, peace and security in America, grounded on a foundation of world peace and security.

Everywhere in the United States today, among farmers, workers, small business-men and professional men and women, I find confusion, uncertainty and fear. The people do not ask, "will there be another war"—but "when will the war come?"

Everywhere I find that people are spending so much for food and rent that they can't afford their customary services from the doctor and dentist. They do not ask, "will there be another depression"—but "when will the depression start?"

Peace and abundance mean so much to me that I have said at a dozen press conferences and in many speeches when asked about a third party, "if the Democratic party continues to be a party of war and depression, I will see to it that the people have a chance to vote for peace and prosperity." To those who have come to me asking the conditions of my adherence to the present Democratic administration, I have said, "let the administration repudiate universal military training and rid itself of the Wall Street-military team that is leading us toward war."

I have insisted that the Democratic administration curb the ever-growing power and profits and monopoly and take concrete steps to preserve the living standards of the American people. I have demanded that the Democratic administration cease its attacks on the civil liberties of Americans. In speeches in the North and in the South at non-segregated meetings I have stated the simple truth that segregation and discrimination of any kind or character have no place in America.

My terms to the Democratic high command have been well known. By their actions and finally by their words, they have said—"Henry Wallace, we welcome your support but we will not change our policies."

In answering me, the Democratic leadership also gave its answer to millions of Americans who demand the right to vote for peace and prosperity. Thus, the leader-ship of the Democratic party would deprive the American people of their rightful opportunity to choose between progress and reaction in 1948. As far as the Repub-lican party is concerned, there is no hope—as George Norris, Fiorello LaGuardia, and Wendell Willkie long ago found out.

When the old parties rot, the people have a right to be heard through a New Party. They asserted that right when the Democratic party was founded under

Jefferson in the struggle against the Federalist party of war and privilege of his day. They won it again when the Republican party was organized in Lincoln's time. The people must again have an opportunity to speak out with their votes in 1948.

The lukewarm liberals sitting on two chairs say, "why throw away your vote?" I say a vote for a new party in 1948 will be the most valuable vote you ever have cast or ever will cast. The bigger the peace vote in 1948, the more definitely the world will know that the United States is not behind the bi-partisan reactionary war policy which is dividing the world into two armed camps and making inevitable the day when American soldiers will be lying in their Arctic suits in the Russian snow.

There is no real fight between a Truman and a Republican. Both stand for a policy which opens the door to war in our lifetime and makes war certain for our children.

Let us stop saying, "I don't like it but I am going to vote for the lesser of two evils."

Rather than accept either evil, come out boldly, stand upright like men, and say so loudly all the world can hear—"We are voting peace and security for ourselves and our children's children. We are fighting for old-fashioned Americanism at the polls in 1948. We are fighting for freedom of speech and freedom of assembly. We are fighting to end racial discrimination. We are fighting for lower prices. We are fighting for free labor unions, for jobs, and for homes in which we can decently live."

We have just passed through the holiday season when every radio and every church proclaimed the joyous tidings of peace. Every year at this time the hearts of the American people swell with genuine good will toward all mankind. We are a kindly, well-meaning people. But the holiday season soon passes and one of the first items on the agenda of the new Congress is Universal Military Training. I say the first political objective of progressives is the defeat of this bill, which would deliver our eighteen-year-olds over to the Army and cost the nation $2,000,000,000 a year.

The American people read of the fantastic appropriations that are being made for military adventures in Greece, Turkey, China—and billions for armaments here at home. Slowly it dawns on us that these newspaper headlines have stepped into our everyday lives at the grocery store when we pay $1 for butter, 95 cents for eggs, and 90 cents for meat. We suddenly realize that we can't have all the people of the world getting ready for the next war without paying for it in our daily lives with less food, clothing and housing. War preparations create record profits for big business, but only false prosperity for the people—their purchasing power shrinks as prices rise, their needs go unfilled, and they are burdened with new debts. Yes, corporate profits are over three times what they were in 1939, but every family is paying for our war policy at the grocery store.

Two years ago I denounced those who were talking up World War III as criminals. Of course, the bulk of our people are not criminals, but it is possible for a little handful of warmongers to stampede them. As Mark Twain long ago pointed out: "—The nation will rub its sleepy eyes and try to make out why there should be a war and will say, earnestly and indignantly, 'for it is unjust and dishonorable and there is no necessity for it.' The handful will shout louder—and now the whole nation will take up the war cry and shout itself hoarse, and mob any honest man who ventures to open his mouth and presently such mouths will cease to open. Next the statesmen will invent cheap lies, putting the blame on the nation that is attacked, and every man will be glad of those conscience-soothing falsities."

This pattern, as Mark Twain saw it fifty years ago, is repeating itself on a scale so vast as to threaten the destruction of humanity. The rich monopolists have always been more ready to sacrifice their sons than their money, but now they have reached a point where they are willing to sacrifice both for the sake of world control.

It just doesn't make sense. The time has come for a new party to fight these war makers. We say that peace is mandatory and that it can be had if we only want it.

Universal Military Training is the first decisive step on the road toward Fascism. We shall fight it to the limit and all Congressmen who vote for it.

A New Party must stand for a positive youth program of abundance and security, not scarcity and war. We can prevent depression and war if we only organize for peace in the same comprehensive way we organize for war.

I personally was for the humanitarian aspects of the Marshall Plan long before it was announced. Because I saw the post-war need of helping human beings I was accused of wanting a quart of milk for every Hottentot. I pushed for help for Greece against the opposition of the Administration eight months before the Truman Doctrine was announced.

But I have fought and shall continue to fight programs which give guns to people when they want plows. I fight the Truman Doctrine and the Marshall Plan as applied because they divide Europe into two warring camps. Those whom we buy politically with our food will soon desert us. They will pay us in the basic coin of temporary gratitude and then turn to hate us because our policies are destroying their freedom.

We are restoring western Europe and Germany through United States agencies rather than United Nations agencies because we want to hem Russia in. We are acting in the same way as France and England after the last war and the end result will be the same—confusion, digression and war.

It just doesn't need to happen. The cost of organizing for peace, prosperity and progress is infinitely less than the organizing for war.

We who believe this will be called "Russian tools" and "Communists," but let the fearmongers not distort and becloud the issue by name calling. We are not for Russia and we are not for Communism, but we recognize Hitlerite methods when we see them in our own land and we denounce the men who engage in such name-calling as enemies of the human race who would rather have World War III than put forth a genuine effort to bring about a peaceful settlement of differences.

One thing I want to make clear to both Russia and the United States—peace requires real understanding between our peoples. Russia has as much to gain from peace as the United States, and just as we here fight against the spreaders of hate and falsehood against Russia, the Russian leaders can make a great contribution by restraining those extremists who try to widen the gap between our two great countries.

I insist that the United States will not be fully secure until there is real peace between this country and Russia and until there is an international police force stronger than the military establishment of any nation, including Russia and the United States. I am utterly against any kind of imperialism or expansionism whether sponsored by Britain, Russia or the United States, and I call on Russia, as well as the United States to look at all our differences objectively and free from that prejudice which the hatemongers have engendered on both sides. What the world needs is a U.N. disarmament conference to rid humanity for all time of the threat, not only of atomic bombs, but also of all other methods of mass destruction.

It happens that all of my mother's and three-fourths of my father's ancestors came to this country before the American Revolution. I love the Americanism I was taught to respect in the public schools of Iowa half a century ago. That Americanism was betrayed after World War I by forces which found their origin in monopoly capitalism, yellow journalism and racial bigotry. Today there is a greater menace than ever before—a menace more serious than has ever confronted the human race.

That menace can be met and overcome only by a new political alignment in America which requires the organization of a new political party.

To that end I announce tonight that I shall run as an independent candidate for President of the United States in 1948.

Thousands of people all over the United States have asked me to engage in this great fight. The people are on the march. I hope that you who are listening to me tonight will lead the forces in peace, progress and prosperity throughout your communities and throughout our country. Will you let me know that you have come out fighting against the powers of evil?

We have assembled a Gideon's Army, small in number, powerful in conviction, ready for action. We have said with Gideon, "Let those who are fearful and trembling depart." For every fearful one who leaves, there will be a thousand to take his place. A just cause is worth a hundred armies. We face the future unfettered—unfettered by any principle but the general welfare. We owe no allegiance to any group which does not serve that welfare. By God's grace, the people's peace will usher in the century of the common man.

HENRY A. WALLACE, "STAND UP AND BE COUNTED"
January 5, 1948

Wallace had been editor of the New Republic *for about a year when the following editorial appeared, accompanied by his brief announcement that " . . . since I cannot be both the candidate of a political movement and the editor of an independent progressive magazine, I am relinquishing with this issue my editorship. . . ."*

I am convinced the time has come for an independent presidential candidacy. I believe in the hope of world democracy. I believe that this hope can be realized, for Americans and for all peoples, in our time. But I see this hope endangered by present trends.

I have been saddened by the sight of the richest, most powerful and, to me, most beautiful nation in the world being haunted by fear. Today, we alone of the peoples of the world speak as though Doomsday were just around the corner. We fear war. We expect depression. We await the destruction of the United Nations and the break-up of One World into two worlds. To those who admit the truth of all this and add: This is a time for waiting, I reply: We cannot wait; the welfare of Americans demands that we act now.

Our workers fear the instability of present employment. As their real wages fall with rising prices, they suffer a steadily declining standard of living, and they also feel the burden of new debts.

Our mothers and their sons in school fear the onrushing program of compulsory military training which will take a year out of the lives of millions of American boys for no useful purpose.

Our businessmen fear the instability of their markets. Thousands upon thousands of small independent producers are feeling, as never before, the squeeze of giant monopolies.

Our farmers fear their prosperity will soon end.

Millions upon millions of Americans fear to speak out against policies they know are dangerous and potentially ruinous. If they speak frankly, they know they may suffer loss of jobs and social standing. They have been intimidated by the current campaign which brands every progressive idea "communistic."

In the lifetime of my generation we have seen two world wars and half a dozen depressions and recessions of varying length. But there is no sound historic reason for assuming that a major catastrophe must be inevitable. I know that man has the resources and the knowledge with which to prevent both depression and war. To accept the inevitability of war and depression is to deny democracy. The companion notion that personal insecurity is a necessary part of our life is outrageous.

[Editorial] , *New Republic*, CXVIII (January 5, 1948), 5-10.

I believe in the old-fashioned American doctrine of standing up, speaking your mind, and letting the chips fall where they may. I am determined that the American people shall have a chance to speak their minds, free of intimidation.

The Bipartisan Bloc

Today we live under a one-party rule. No scrapping over spoils, no disagreements over strategy and timing, no amount of fine-sounding speeches and gestures for liberal support can obscure this fundamental fact. Our democracy lives by expressing the free choice of its citizens. Yet, on the basic foreign and domestic issues that affect the lives of all Americans, we are today denied any opportunity to choose. Even in wartime, party politics continued under Roosevelt. Now, in the third year since victory, a bipartisan bloc governs us in the name of an undeclared emergency. In peacetime one-party rule is a real threat to our democracy.

Of course there is an emergency. All over the world devastated nations depend on American aid. It was not to meet this emergency that the bipartisan bloc was formed. It was formed to perpetuate a foreign policy based on hatred and fear. It is made up of men who opposed resistance to fascism, who killed UNRRA, who attacked the heart of the United Nations in creating the Truman Doctrine, and who again bypassed the United Nations with the Marshall Plan. A coalition government might be desirable, if it represented all the people. But the bipartisan bloc is no broad coalition. It represents only a small minority of powerful interests. Rejecting our nation's history and traditions, it allies the American people with reactionaries and dictators who have no respect whatever for American ideals.

Only when Americans reject the bipartisan bloc and all the hysteria it stirs up can we move on to real progress at home and abroad. Millions of Americans know this today. Many more will come to understand it, as the facts are made clear. My reason in striking out for independent action is to give these Americans their democratic right to choose.

Our World Policy

When I was Vice President, and again after I returned from Europe in May of 1947, I came out for a comprehensive program for aid to the outside world. I am not and never have been an isolationist. I stood for a Marshall Plan before there was a Marshall Plan, but it was a plan to unite the world, not divide it.

I have insisted that aid should be given under international auspices for productive purposes. I have always advocated trucks, not tanks; plows, not guns. I have advocated international planning through scientific technicians to increase the productivity of the world.

Some of the same reactionaries who called this "globaloney" now support the Administration's dangerous program for aid. They want political strings and unilateral administration. They are interested in political meddling abroad. They use the same language to sell their program that I used in presenting what they used to call "globaloney," but their purposes are far different.

It is curious to see men who have never displayed real interest in health, education and social security at home pull out all the stops when they talk about the needy peoples of Europe. They are not genuinely concerned with the welfare of those peoples any more than they have been concerned with the welfare of the American people. Their program of aid will not really and fully serve those peoples. In the long run their program will make us the most hated nation in the world. I would resent it if a banker to whom I owed money insisted that I vote for his man for President, against my own conviction. The United States is the world banker, and the present European-aid plan, under congressional action, proposes to tell the borrowers how they shall vote.

We stand for an America that can unite the world for peace. The Charter of the United Nations is our guide. In seeking world recovery we do not hold the Russians blameless. Neither is there any justification for trying to put all the blame on the Russians. If we should accept every criticism made of the Soviet Union, there would still be no excuse for an American policy which does not conform to American principles and American hopes.

There is no question that the American people want to help peoples abroad. But the proposed foreign-aid program does not reflect their democratic sentiments. Indeed, it may create an antipathy for future aid, *unless it is coupled with sound planning and controls here at home.* Rising prices resulting from foreign aid and the heavy armaments program needed to support a badly conceived policy, may cause housewives and wage-earners to turn from their devotion to the principles of One World.

The policy of propping up Greek reaction with American dollars, led by Truman, controlled by Wall Street, backed by the military and paid for by peace-loving citizens, has failed. Our first loan, sold to the American people as aid for rehabilitation, has been spent mostly on arms to destroy a few thousand guerrillas. Today the guerrillas are stronger than ever. For every guerrilla killed by American bullets, ten others are made by the terrorism and corruption of the State Department-sponsored Greek government. The love of America in other peoples is strong, but not limitless. And I say that our one-party coalition is squandering the love and moral leadership that America has earned over centuries and, under Roosevelt, continued to command.

A European Recovery Program based on the idea of fighting Russia and communism will be an endless drain on American resources. The Communists in France and Italy, who polled substantial votes in all postwar elections and have been forced out of their democratically won posts in government by the pressure of American dollars, will take foolish, though understandably human, action to defeat the American aid program.

Eventually, as more and more strings are attached to our aid by those who dominate American foreign policy, the Social Democrats and others will turn on us. Finally, the cold war will turn to a war with bombs and with soldiers lying in their Arctic suits in the Russian snow.

Independent Action

I repeat, our foreign-aid program must be free of political meddling, and this requires international administration through the United Nations. With its record of circumventing the UN, we cannot expect the present bipartisan leadership to fight for this principle.

I repeat, our foreign-aid program must be coupled with sound planning and controls here at home. A failure to control inflation here at home will result in a resurgence of isolationist sentiment that may be ruinous to all hopes of One World.

Yet these are present trends, and, because present trends lead to disaster, we cannot wait. For two years, with all the facts at our command, we have tried to awaken the established parties to the urgent necessity of taking action to prevent inflation. For a year we have looked in vain to these parties for some sign of willingness to work in a new spirit for world peace and understanding. The leaders of the bipartisan bloc have held fast to their basic policy of world division. Once we based our appeal on the self-interest of all Americans to take obvious and necessary measures to avoid inflation and international breakdown. Now we realize that this appeal, directed to the great selfish interests that dominate the present parties, is useless. All they can understand is the pressure of the people's will. And that pressure today must be organized, directed pressure; organized in progressive political machinery, directed to the achievement of an over-all program for progress.

Monopoly

The conquering of the carefully nurtured and self-perpetuating fears, which daily breed new dangers to our country, will require full exposure of the grip which the monopolists have on our national life.

The fundamental fact is that the directing of this country of ours does not at present belong to the people, but to a relative handful of wealthy men. The foundation of the government, as presently constituted, is not the general welfare, but the special privilege of industrial and financial giants. These giants control both parties. I had to sit in the chair of Herbert Hoover and Jesse Jones, as Secretary of Commerce, really to understand the machinations of these key giants.

Neither the Republican nor the Democratic Party can act for the welfare of the American people, for the primary concern of both parties is for the profits of monopoly. That is why the average weekly wage of American workers—$49—has shrunk until it buys no more than $29.50 bought in 1939. That is why corporation profits have pyramided to $17.5 billion, as contrasted with $5 billion in 1939. That is why both parties have shrunk away from genuine price control as if it were the plague. High prices mean high profits, and high profits are the major goal of those who control the two political parties.

The present exorbitant prices and profits were planned that way. They were planned by men who oppose democratic planning for peace and abundance. Shrill denials and scornful denunciations can mount to the stratosphere, but this will continue to be a fact until the American people regain control of their own destiny.

Monopoly control, long fought by Americans of every persuasion and every time, is not new, but it has grown until today it threatens every man, woman and child in the entire world with catastrophe.

In opposing it we are returning to the faith of our fathers. We are speaking once again in the American tongue, fighting monopoly as our fathers have fought it from the time of Jefferson to that of Franklin Roosevelt. Jefferson won such a fight in the very earliest days of our republic, even though monopoly capital as we know it did not begin to develop until after the Civil War. Abraham Lincoln, with his remarkable prescience, sensed its beginnings. In grave warning to the American people he said he feared this concentration of financial power might grow and swell and pyramid until it, and not the people, owned the American earth and the American government.

As early as 1888 Grover Cleveland declared in a message to Congress: "Corporations, which should be carefully restrained creatures of the law and the servants of the people, are fast becoming the people's masters."

In 1913 President Wilson declared: "The masters of the government of the United States are the combined capitalists and manufacturers of the United States." In Wilson's day the 200 largest non-financial corporations owned more than one-third of the assets of all non-financial corporations. By the middle thirties they owned more than 55 percent.

In 1938, President Roosevelt declared in a message to Congress: "The liberty of a democracy is not safe if the people tolerate the growth of private power to a point where it becomes stronger than their democratic state itself. That, in its essence, is fascism." And he added the warning that "among us today a concentration of private power without equal in history is growing."

During the war and after it, this concentration of private power has continued to swell at such an unprecedented rate that today it can be said: *Never before in the history of the world have so few owned so much at the expense of so many.*

Both major parties serve faithfully the few who own so much at the expense of the many. Both killed price control, both support the bipartisan foreign policy, passed the Taft-Hartley bill, favor the rebuilding of Germany. Weak, lip-service opposition is provided to some of these acts by the present Administration, but there is neither the will nor the power to fight the great financial interests.

The Third Party

Franklin Roosevelt, by the most masterful political maneuvering ever seen in the United States, brought the Democratic Party back to the principles of Jefferson, Jackson and Wilson. He humored Southern reactionaries, cajoled the big-city machines, and reconciled the most diverse regional, religious and racial interests, as he went to the people for support for progressive programs. But when Roosevelt passed on, the jackals were ready to pounce. In a very short time they destroyed practically everything he stood for, while still paying lip-service to his principles and program.

The Democrats, like the Republicans, stand silent when they do not aid and abet the nullification of the Constitution and the Bill of Rights. Both parties are apparently unmindful of the fact that the liberty of no American can be secure when the rights of any American are wrongfully invaded.

Neither party puts up any effective fight against racial and religious discrimination, for the rights of the Negro people, for the elimination of restrictive covenants and anti-Semitism, for the creation of a genuine FEPC, for the defeat of the poll tax and passage of a federal anti-lynch law. Neither party defends the First Amendment. Both stand mute while freedom of speech and thought are under attack. Both cry, "Red! Communist!" at all opponents and use the Red scare to cover up their plunder of the people. We pay $1.05 a pound for butter today, and commensurate prices for other necessities, partly because the American people have been distracted from the real issues by the demagogic cry of "Red."

These generated fears must be quelled. *I believe the American people must have an opportunity to express their hopes as well as their fears.*

My decision to help provide a means of expression is the result of months of careful consideration following years of political activity. I have tried for long to be patient and optimistic concerning this administration. I had hoped that a brightening international scene might make agreement possible. I hoped that the feelings of the people shown at all our great meetings this year might have led the Administration to progress. I still think I was right in waiting for as long as possible. My final decision was made solely on the basis of giving the American people a chance to vote for peace and security. Election laws in key states make delay impossible if there is to be an effective independent candidacy.

Election-Year Lip-Service

I am satisfied that progressives must control political machinery, or the principles they hold dear will win nothing more than election-year lip-service from the major parties. The Democratic Party leadership will pay more effusive lip-service than will that of the Republicans. Its actions will not be materially different.

Two years ago President Truman's State of the Union message contained a magnificent New Deal program. The Democratic Party controlled Congress, yet no significant part of that program was enacted into law. I am sure that the program Truman announces in this election year will meet the same fate. If any part of it is enacted by Congress, it will be because of the work of organized, independent progressives prepared to deliver votes, speaking the language politicians understand.

There is a great difference between an FDR announcing a program and rallying the people to support it, and the mere proclamation of a program by a politician who does not believe in it and is not prepared to fight for it. FDR is gone. The only substitute is practical political machinery manned by genuine, dyed-in-the-wool progressives.

Back in 1944 I made a fight against the corrupt machines and the Southern reactionaries in the Democratic Party. I lost that fight. Many progressives urged me to bolt the party and form a third party. Roosevelt, they said, had sold out to reaction. He hadn't, of course. He was making a compromise in order to win the peace following the war—to bring conservatives and even some reactionaries along, under his leadership, on a program for coöperation with Russia to win the war and preserve the peace. He was not going to insist that I receive the nomination if it would antagonize those who disliked my stand on domestic economics, the poll tax and other issues.

It is curious that some of those who argued for that course in 1944, who were willing to risk a split of the Roosevelt supporters at the height of the war, are now opposed to an independent ticket. I said "no" most emphatically in 1944, because Roosevelt was at the helm and there was a large group of progressive congressmen to be saved. I thought then that we could eventually win the fight against the corrupt and reactionary forces in the Democratic Party.

I retained some lingering hopes when I went out to campaign for progressive Democrats right after I left the cabinet in the fall of 1946. These men and women are of great importance today. There are many excellent progressives within the Democratic Party—a few members of Congress and hundreds of local and state officials. I believe that the surest way of getting them reëlected is to supplement their efforts with a hard-hitting campaign based on principle, not on political expediency. Such a campaign will bring out millions of voters who will stay at home if they have only a choice between evils in the major contest for the presidency.

The bankruptcy of a policy of voting for the lesser of two evils was demonstrated conclusively in the 1946 campaign. The CIO Political Action Committee then felt it necessary to follow that policy. They gave money and working support to "lesser evils." A substantial number of the lesser evils, who were elected, voted for the Taft-Hartley bill.

It seems to be generally agreed, among those who speak of the lesser evil, that the Republicans are the greater evil, the Democrats the lesser. It is thus admitted that our choice is between two degrees of evil. Personally, I have yet to be convinced that the welfare of the American people can be served by voting for any degree of evil.

The Communist Issue

Many of the friends who have supported my decision argued in advance that it was dangerous because the Communists want it. But I have never believed in turning from a principled position because it happened to win the support of others with whom you have important disagreements. I have been told in times past that I shouldn't fight the poll tax because the Communists wanted its abolition. I continued to fight it. The argument is no good.

During the past year I have been urging a foreign policy based on understanding with Russia. I was told that this was dangerous because the Communists wanted it. The alternatives were support of the present militaristic bipartisan policy or a retreat to isolationsim. This would be a particularly dangerous time to leave the advocacy of peace and understanding with Russia solely to a handful of Communists. If we are to build a significant progressive movement, we shall only succeed by taking leadership and fighting for the things we seek.

I welcome the support of all people who sincerely believe you get peace by preparing for peace rather than for war. I want to mobilize all the sentiment there is for planning peace. I want the peoples of the world to know that there is another America than that which attempts to dominate their politics and dictate their economics. I want them to know that American workers, farmers, small businessmen and professional people are their brothers, not would-be masters. I want to kill off the Universal Military Training program, which is the entering wedge of military fascism in the United States.

Those who call us "Russian tools" and "Communists" as we fight for the peace, security and welfare of our country and the world are using the weapons of Adolf Hitler. They are demonstrating that they prefer war with Russia to settlement of differences in a peaceful way. We are fighting for peace with Russia—yes. But we are fighting with confidence that we can make our system work. We are not for Russia and we are not for communism, but we are for peace and for bringing real Americanism back again to the United States.

Our Future

There is talk that an independent candidacy is doomed to failure because of financing. It is said that many millions of dollars will be required for such a campaign. As sure as I am that the two major parties are controlled by big-money interests, and as realistic as I am about the opposition of the big-money press, I still have confidence in democracy. I have confidence that a people's campaign can be waged in 1948.

If money for political campaigns is to come only from the "big boys," then America has become what Russia says it is. I repudiate this idea. I think the people can still make the democratic system work. I am not worried about money because I know that we shall get millions of dollars donated by housewives, stenographers, professional people, workers and shop stewards, and others who will work with a devotion big money can't buy.

We shall need money and I think we shall have it. We shall not need the Wall Street-military backing because we shall build on fundamental principles rather than expediency. We expect abuse and we shall weather it, with a remembrance of the abuse accorded Jefferson, Jackson, Lincoln and their followers. We shall not let the House Un-American Activities Committee and other smear-artists distract us. We shall keep our eyes on the future and remain confident that in November the American people will stand up and be counted. Then the whole world will know how strong is the sentiment in the United States for peace and security.

ALFRED FRIENDLY, *WASHINGTON POST* ARTICLE
May 2, 1948

Widely distributed by the Americans for Democratic Action, this article sought to document charges concerning Communist control of the Wallace movement.

The Communist Party, as a means of blocking the Marshall Plan, decided last October to back a third party headed by Henry A. Wallace, long before the former Vice President himself announced his candidacy.

The strategy, adopted in October, 1947, by the Party's Central Committee, was to force the CIO to reverse its position, taken the week before, indorsing the European Recovery Program.

In this way, it was hoped there would be created a large and powerful labor pressure group against the pending foreign aid program.

Considerations of Russian foreign policy were the almost exclusive reasons moving the Communists to found the third party and pick Wallace as its candidate.

The two primary goals were defeating the Marshall Plan and winning a Communist victory in the Italian elections.

The Central Committee of the American Communist Party ordered labor's indorsement of Wallace to be secured even if that resulted in "splitting the CIO right down the middle."

The points presented above are the highlights of the carefully planned scheme which culminated in Wallace's formal acceptance of the role of candidate last December 29.

But there is nothing to suggest that Wallace was a party to, or had direct knowledge of the Communists' inception and creation of the third party.

There is now an indication—not firm, but nevertheless of possible significance—that the Communist Party, having used Wallace and having failed in its objectives—is now thinking of new strategy, involving the dumping of Wallace. This indication will be discussed later.

The Communists' support of the Wallace campaign and their key roles in it have been, of course, obvious for many months. But it was not until last week that a competent authority stated flatly that the Communists were "directly responsible" for founding the third party movement.

The speaker was Phillip Murray, CIO president, addressing the Textile Workers Union at Atlantic City, N.J., on Wednesday. He said the decision was made at a Communist Party meeting in New York City last October. He gave no further details.

The Washington Post is now able to supply a number of those details, with some exactness.

Its information is mainly from persons who participated directly in the series of meetings where the plans and decisions were made in addition, there is confirming information from individuals close to the actual participants, who have been told by them what happened.

The chronology:

The CIO national convention was held in Boston last year, beginning on October 13. Two days later it heard a speech by Secretary of State Marshall. The convention concluded its sessions with a vigorous indorsement of the Marshall Plan.

It refrained from indorsing President Truman for reelection, but it did not lay any foundations, nor even provide an opening for support of a third party movement.

The ERP resolution and the cold shoulder to a third party were distressing in the extreme to the Communist Party.

Such mass support as it has, it should be remembered at this point, is in the 10 or a dozen left-led CIO unions. Its main hope for further mass support, by the same token, lies in organized labor, mainly in the CIO. For a decade the party's principal prospect for growing strong has been to gain ultimate control of the whole CIO.

Accordingly, the CIO convention action was a body blow. Party leaders immediately summoned a meeting of the top Communist members and sympathizers among CIO union officers. The meeting was held within a few days of the convention's close, when the union leaders were still in the area.

The meeting, in New York, lasted all day and well into the night. The theme was how to recover the loss just suffered in the convention.

There was a long discussion of how to put pressure on the unions, and on Congress to defeat passage of the ERP.

At this meeting, the organization of a third party was not discussed in concrete terms. But delegates from Illinois and California noted that they would move to organize third-party campaigns in their States.

Wallace was mentioned as a possible candidate by Michael A. Quill, president of the Transport Workers Union, who—only in the last month—has now broken with the Communists.

In general terms there was a discussion of how to get the CIO to reserve its convention stand and to accept the idea of dumping Mr. Truman and helping a third party get under way.

Very soon after this meeting—still in October—there was a meeting in New York of the Central Committee of the Communist Party. This is the party organ which frames all high policy decisions.

It consists of William Z. Foster, national chairman of the party; Eugene Dennis, the executive secretary; John Williamson, chief labor official of the party, and several CIO union officials.

The Central Committee decided to create a third party and to obtain Wallace as its candidate.

The best evidence of what transpired at that meeting are descriptives given to the Washington Post of a subsequent gathering at which the official orders were handed out.

APPENDIX 3353

It took place about December 15. Those in attendance were the Communist-minded leaders of unions in the New York area.

Some 26 persons were present. There were from one to three representatives of every CIO union in New York except the Amalgamated Clothing Workers.

Party Chairman Foster was not present, but Dennis, generally considered the best brains of the organization, was there.

The most active figure, however, was Robert Thompson, Communist Party chairman for New York State.

He opened the meeting with a long speech, saying that it had been decided to create a third party, with Wallace as its head.

Therefore, he continued, the Communist Party wanted all union leaders to get busy preparing petitions for the candidacy, and literature to be distributed immediately after Wallace's formal announcement of acceptance was made. This event was anticipated—correctly, as it turned out—sometime during the next couple of weeks.

CIO unions, Thompson said, should be ready to follow the announcement with an immediate indorsement of Wallace.

Quill thereupon spoke out in what now seems to have been the beginning of his breakaway from the party.

[Quill has denied that he has ever been a card-carrying member of the party, but he has never denied that he was high in its councils.

His ultimate break came recently over the issue of a raise in New York City subway and transit fares. The raise was opposed by the Communist Party, but it was essential if Quill's union members were to get a pay increase. Quill would have lost his union at once had he supported the Communist position—Editor's note.]

"Red Mike"—or, more properly, "Ex-Red Mike"—demanded to know who had made such a decision.

The Central Committee, said Thompson.

Quill attacked it bitterly. He said the Central Committee could not tell him or his union that they had to go for Wallace, and that it had no right to do so. He said he would not go along and that the proposed action might split the CIO.

The Communists in the CIO and those unions which they could influence must pressure for an indorsement of Wallace, Thompson replied, "even if it splits the CIO right down the middle."

"The hell with you and our Central Committee," Quill said. He told Thompson to relay his remarks to "that crackpot" Foster.

Despite his opposition, the meeting continued on the original line.

The strategy was made clear. The pressure to be created, it was explained, would be such that Phillip Murray could not hold out against it. He would be forced to get a reversal of the convention stand. To save the CIO and his position in it, he would have to indorse Wallace and denounce the ERP.

Start the division from the convention policy as soon as possible, delegates were ordered, and stop the Marshall Plan from going into effect.

Thompson said the Communists and the unions and locals they led should not be wishy-washy about supporting Wallace. The CIO, he went on, was rapidly moving toward the right and that trend must be stopped. The Communist-led unions should now "stand up and be counted."

Already, Thompson continued, the Communist Parties in France and Italy were making their decision and there would be revolutions in both countries within two weeks.

Whether anyone else at the meeting took Thompson seriously about the imminent revolutions is not known. But Thompson took himself seriously. The support of Wallace and the campaign to that end in the CIO was to "help the revolution."

The meeting, it may be noted, took place at about the end of the serious Communist strikes in France and Italy.

At a New York meeting, the talk went on into an hour's discussion on the question of whether Wallace was "reliable."

His meteoric shifts were recalled as well as an occasion a year or so ago when, at a Madison Square Garden rally, he had made disparaging remarks about the Communists. The question was would he turn against the Communists again, or would he stay in line?

The Washington Post has two accounts, not necessarily inconsistent, on how this question was resolved.

According to one, it was admitted that Wallace was not so adhesively consistent as might be desired, but that he could be held as long as the Communists surrounded him and worked on him. The answer was to the effect that, "To the extent that we encircle him, to that extent he'll stick."

According to the second account, it was decided that it did not make much difference if Wallace finally turned against them. The argument was that Wallace was to be used as a tool or lever for the Communist foreign policy. The immediate goals were defeat of the Marshall Plan and a Communist victory in the Italian elections. Wallace could be used as the rallying and magnetic point for a great pressure bloc for these goals. He was not going to be elected President, so it didn't matter what position he might take later.

The Communist plans fell far short of expectations.

The CIO reaction was not as hoped. The pressure was less—not enough to bother Murray seriously. The dissent from the CIO convention policy was much less than was anticipated. Only fractions of a few unions fell into the Communist Party line.

When the matter came to a head in the CIO, at a meeting of its executive board late in January, the board voted a strong denunciation of Wallace and the third party and a vigorous reaffirmation of the ERP support.

The vote was 33 for the resolution and only 11 against, far fewer than the Communists had hoped. It was not enough seriously to disturb the unity of the organization, and not enough to create an effective labor pressure group against American foreign policy.

There are signs abroad that Russia is vamping a new policy to adjust itself to its defeats in Italy and on the ERP. Left Socialist groups are already making friendly overtures to work cooperatively with the Marshall Plan.

Some students of Communist policy think that that policy is indeed in a state of flux, and that reflections of the shift will soon be seen here.

There are some straws in the wind. Recently, locals of the United Office Workers and the United Public Workers, both far to the left in their leadership, found the pressure from their officers swiftly relaxed when the rank-and-file balked at indorsing Wallace. Leaders grew surprisingly "soft." They said that "for the sake of CIO unity" they would drop the suggestion.

The same theme has turned up in a remarkable letter recently sent to Phillip Murray. It is signed by a subordinate official of the Fur Workers, the ne-plus-ultra of Communist unions.

The letter says that its contents have been reviewed and approved by the top international officials of the union. For practical purposes, then, the letter has the sanction of union president Ben Gold, member of the Central Committee, and of New York's joint furrier council manager Irving Potash, an important figure in the Communist Party.

The letter purports to come from victor to vanquished and to offer a "deal" out of generosity. Actually, it is plain that the reverse is to be understood. The letter suggests that "in the interest of CIO unity" it might be possible for both sides to get together if Murray could find a suitable presidential candidate from within the Democratic Party ranks.

Conceivably, the letter could be a feeler or trial balloon. It might mean that the Communists recognize defeat on their recent objectives, plan to change tactics and are willing to forget Wallace now that their use of him was without results.

PROGRESSIVE PLATFORM OF 1948

PREAMBLE

Three years after the end of the second world war, the drums are beating for a third. Civil liberties are being destroyed. Millions cry out for relief from unbearably high prices. The American way of life is in danger.

The root cause of this crisis is Big Business control of our economy and government.

With toil and enterprise the American people have created from their rich resources the world's greatest productive machine. This machine no longer belongs to the people. Its ownership is concentrated in the hands of a few and its product used for their enrichment.

Never before have so few owned so much at the expense of so many.

Ten years ago Franklin Delano Roosevelt warned: "The liberty of a democracy is not safe if the people tolerate the growth of private power to a point where it becomes stronger than their democratic state. That, in its essence, is fascism."

Today that private power has constituted itself an invisible government which pulls the strings of its puppet Republican and Democratic parties. Two sets of candidates compete for votes under the outworn emblems of the old parties. But both represent a single program—a program of monopoly profits through war preparations, lower living standards, and suppression of dissent.

For generations the common man of America has resisted this concentration of economic and political power in the hands of a few. The greatest of America's political leaders have led the people into battle against the money power, the railroads, the trusts, the economic royalists.

We of the Progressive Party are the present-day descendants of these people's movements and fighting leaders. We are the political heirs of Jefferson, Jackson and Lincoln—of Frederick Douglass, Altgeld and Debs—of "Fighting Bob" LaFollette, George Norris, and Franklin Roosevelt.

Throughout our history new parties have arisen when the old parties have betrayed the people. As Jefferson headed a new party to defeat the reactionaries of his day, and as Lincoln led a new party to victory over the slave-owners, so today the people, inspired and led by Henry Wallace, have created a new party to secure peace, freedom, and abundance.

With the firm conviction that the principles of the Declaration of Independence and of the Constitution of the United States set forth all fundamental freedoms for all people and secure the safety and well being of our country, the Progressive Party pledges itself to safeguard these principles to the American people.

BETRAYAL BY THE OLD PARTIES

The American people want peace. But the old parties, obedient to the dictates of monopoly and the military, prepare for war in the name of peace.

They refuse to negotiate a settlement of differences with the Soviet Union.

They reject the United Nations as an instrument for promoting world peace and reconstruction.

They use the Marshall Plan to rebuild Nazi Germany as a war base and to subjugate the economies of other European countries to American Big Business.

They finance and arm corrupt, fascist governments in China, Greece, Turkey, and elsewhere, through the Truman Doctrine, wasting billions in American resources and squandering America's heritage as the enemy of despotism.

They encircle the globe with military bases which other peoples cannot but view as threats to their freedom and security.

They protect the war-making industrial and financial barons of Nazi Germany and imperial Japan, and restore them to power.

They stockpile atomic bombs.

They pass legislation to admit displaced persons, discriminating against Catholics, Jews, and other victims of Hitler.

They impose a peacetime draft and move toward Universal Military Training.

They fill policy-making positions in government with generals and Wall Street bankers.

Peace cannot be won—but profits can—by spending ever-increasing billions of the people's money in war preparations.

Yet these are the policies of the two old parties—policies profaning the name of peace.

The American people cherish freedom.

But the old parties, acting for the forces of special privilege, conspire to destroy traditional American freedoms.

They deny the Negro people the rights of citizenship. They impose a universal policy of Jim Crow and enforce it with every weapon of terror. They refuse to outlaw its most bestial expression—the crime of lynching.

They refuse to abolish the poll tax, and year after year they deny the right to vote to Negroes and millions of white people in the South.

They aim to reduce nationality groups to a position of social, economic, and political inferiority.

They connive to bar the Progressive Party from the ballot.

They move to outlaw the Communist Party as a decisive step in their assault on the democratic rights of labor, of national, racial, and political minorities, and of all those who oppose their drive to war. In this they repeat the history of Nazi Germany, Fascist Italy, and Franco Spain.

They support the House Committee on Un-American Activities in its vilification and persecution of citizens in total disregard of the Bill of Rights.

They build the Federal Bureau of Investigation into a political police with secret dossiers on millions of Americans.

They seek to regiment the thinking of the American people and to suppress political dissent.

They strive to enact such measures as the Mundt-Nixon Bill which are as destructive of democracy as were the Alien and Sedition Laws against which Jefferson fought.

They concoct a spurious "loyalty" program to create an atmosphere of fear and hysteria in government and industry.

They shackle American labor with the Taft-Hartley Act at the express command of Big Business, while encouraging exorbitant profits through uncontrolled inflation.

They restore the labor injunction as a weapon for breaking strikes and smashing unions.

This is the record of the two old parties—a record profaning the American ideal of freedom.

The American people want abundance.

But the old parties refuse to enact effective price and rent controls, making the people victims of a disastrous inflation which dissipates the savings of millions of families and depresses their standards.

They ignore the housing problem, although more than half the nation's families, including millions of veterans, are homeless or living in rural and urban slums.

They refuse social security protection to millions and allow only meagre benefits to the rest.

They block national health legislation even though millions of men, women, and children are without adequate medical care.

They foster the concentration of private economic power.

They replace progressive government officials, the supporters of Franklin Roosevelt, with spokesmen of Big Business.

They pass tax legislation for the greedy, giving only insignificant reductions to the needy.

These are the acts of the old parties—acts profaning the American dream of abundance.

No glittering party platforms or election promises of the Democratic and Republican parties can hide their betrayal of the needs of the American people.

Nor can they act otherwise. For both parties as the record of the 80th Congress makes clear, are the champions of Big Business.

The Republican platform admits it.

The Democratic platform attempts to conceal it.

But the very composition of the Democratic leadership exposes the demogogy of its platform. It is a party of machine politicians and Southern Bourbons who veto in Congress the liberal planks "won" in convention.

Such platforms, conceived in hypocrisy and lack of principle, deserve nothing but contempt.

PRINCIPLES OF THE PROGRESSIVE PARTY

The Progressive Party is born in the deep conviction that the national wealth and natural resources of our country belong to the people who inhabit it and must be employed in their behalf; that freedom and opportunity must be secured equally to all; that the brotherhood of man can be achieved and scourge of war ended.

The Progressive Party holds that basic to the organization of world peace is a return to the purpose of Franklin Roosevelt to seek areas of international agreement rather than disagreement. It was his conviction that within the framework of the United Nations different social and economic systems can and must live together. If peace is to be achieved capitalist United States and communist Russia must establish good relations and work together.

The Progressive Party holds that it is the first duty of a just government to secure for all the people, regardless of race, creed, color, sex, national background, political belief, or station in life, the inalienable rights proclaimed in the Declaration of Independence and guaranteed by the Bill of Rights. The government must actively protect these rights against the encroachments of public and private agencies.

The Progressive Party holds that a just government must use its powers to promote an abundant life for its people. This is the basic idea of Franklin Roosevelt's Economic Bill of Rights. Heretofore every attempt to give effect to this principle has failed because Big Business dominates the key sectors of the economy. Anti-trust laws and government regulation cannot break this domination. Therefore the people, through their democratically elected representatives, must take control of the main levers of the economic system. Public ownership of these levers will enable the people to plan the use of their productive resources so as to develop the limitless potential of modern technology and to create a true American-Commonwealth free from poverty and insecurity.

The Progressive Party believes that only through peaceful understanding can the world make progress toward reconstruction and higher standards of living; that peace is the essential condition for safe-guarding and extending our traditional freedoms; that only by preserving liberty and by planning an abundant life for all can we eliminate the sources of world conflict. Peace, freedom, and abundance—the goals of the Progressive Party—are indivisible.

Only the Progressive Party can destroy the power of private monopoly and restore the government to the American people. For ours is a party uncorrupted by privilege, committed to no special interests, free from machine control, and open to all Americans of all races, colors, and creeds.

The Progressive Party is a party of action. We seek through the democratic process and through day-by-day activity to lead the American people toward the fulfillment of these principles.

We ask support for the following program:

PEACE

American-Soviet Agreement

Henry Wallace in his open letter suggested, and Premier Stalin in his reply accepted, a basis for sincere peace discussions. The exchange showed that specific areas of agreement can be found if the principles of non-interference in the internal affairs of other nations and acceptance of the right of peoples to choose their own form of government and economic system are mutually respected.

The Progressive Party therefore demands negotiation and discussion with the Soviet Union to find areas of agreement to win the peace.

The Progressive Party believes that enduring peace among the peoples of the world community is possible only through world law. Continued anarchy among nations in the atomic age threatens our civilization and humanity itself with annihilation. The only ultimate alternative to war is the abandonment of the principle of the coercion of sovereignties by sovereignties and the adoption of the principle of the just enforcement upon individuals of world federal law, enacted by a world federal law, enacted by a world federal legislature with limited but adequate powers to safeguard the common defense and the general welfare of all mankind.

Such a structure of peace through government can be evolved by making of the United Nations an effective agency of cooperation among nations. This can be done by restoring the unity of the Great Powers as they work together for common purposes. Since the death of Franklin Roosevelt, this principle has been betrayed to a degree which not only paralyzes the United Nations but threatens the world with another way in which there can be no victors and few survivors.

Beyond an effective United Nations lies the further possibility of genuine world government. Responsibility for ending the tragic prospect of war is a joint responsibility of the Soviet Union and the United States. We hope for more political liberty and economic democrary throughout the world. We believe that war between East and West will mean fascism and death for all. We insist that peace is the prerequisite of survival.

We believe with Henry Wallace that "there is no misunderstanding or difficulty between the USA and USSR which can be settled by force or fear and there is no difference which cannot be settled by peaceful, hopeful negotiation. There is no American principle of public interest, and there is no Russian principle of public interest, which would have to be sacrificed to end the cold war and open up the Century of Peace which the Century of the Common Man demands."

We denounce anti-Soviet hysteria as a mask for monopoly, militarism, and reaction. We demand that a new leadership of the peace-seeking people of our nation—which has vastly greater responsibility for peace than Russia because it has vastly greater power for war—undertake in good faith and carry to an honorable conclusion, without appeasement of sabre-rattling on either side, a determined effort to settle current controversies and enable men and women everywhere to look forward with confidence to the common task of building a creative and lasting peace for all the world.

End the Drive to War

The Progressive Party calls for the repeal of the peacetime draft and the rejection of Universal Military training.

We call for the immediate cessation of the piling up of armament expenditures beyond reasonable peacetime requirements for national defense.

We demand the repudiation of the Truman Doctrine and an end to military and economic intervention in support of reactionary and fascist regimes in China, Greece, Turkey, the Middle East, and Latin America. We demand that the United States completely sever diplomatic and economic relations with Franco Spain.

We call for the abandonment of military bases designed to encircle and intimidate other nations.

We demand the repeal of the provisions of the National Security Act which are mobilizing the nation for war, preparing a labor draft, and organizing a monopoly-militarist dictatorship.

These measures will express the American people's determination to avoid provocation and aggression. They will be our contribution to the reduction of mistrust and the creation of a general atmosphere in which peace can be established.

United Nations

The Progressive Party will work to realize Franklin Roosevelt's ideal of the United Nations as a world family of nations, by defending its Charter and seeking to prevent its transformation into the diplomatic or military instrument of any one power or group of powers.

We call for the establishment of a United Nations Reconstruction and Development Fund to promote international recovery by providing assistance to the needy nations of Europe, Africa and Asia, without political conditions and with priorities to those peoples that suffered most from Axis aggression.

We call for the repudiation of the Marshall Plan.

We urge the full use of the Economic and Social Council and other agencies of the United Nations to wipe out disease and starvation, to promote the development of culture and science, and to develop the peaceful application of atomic energy.

We demand that the United States delegation to the Untied Nations stop protecting fascist Spain and press for effective economic and diplomatic sanctions against Franco's dictatorship.

Disarmament

The Progressive Party will work through the United Nations for a world disarmament agreement to outlaw the atomic bomb, bacteriological warfare, and all other instruments of mass destruction; to destroy existing stockpiles of atomic bombs and to establish United Nations controls, including inspection, over the production of atomic energy; and to reduce conventional armaments drastically in accordance with resolutions already passed by the United Nations General Assembly.

Germany and Japan

The Progressive Party calls for cooperation with our wartime allies to conclude peace treaties promptly with a unified Germany and with Japan. The essentials for a German settlement are denazification and democratization, punishment of war criminals, land reform, decartelization, nationalization of heavy industry, Big-Four control of the Ruhr, reparations to the victims of Nazi aggression, and definitive recognition of the Oder-Neisse line as the Western boundary of Poland. On this basis, we advocate the speedy conclusion of a peace treaty and a simultaneous withdrawal of all occupation troops.

Similar principles should govern a settlement with Japan.

State of Israel

The Progressive Party demands the immediate de jure recognition of the State of Israel.

We call for admission of Israel to the United Nations.

We call for a Presidential proclamation lifting the arms embargo in favor of the State of Israel.

We pledge our support for and call upon the Government of the United States to safeguard the sovereignty, autonomy, political independence, and territorial integrity of the State of Israel in accordance with the boundaries laid down by the Resolution of the General Assembly of the United Nations of November 29, 1947.

We support the prompt extension of Israel of generous financial assistance without political conditions.

We oppose any attempt to interfere with Israel in its sovereign right to control its own immigration policy.

We call upon the United States Government to provide immediate shipping and other facilities for the transportation of Jewish displaced persons in Europe who desire to emigrate to Israel.

We support, within the framework of the United Nations, the internationalization of Jerusalem and the protection of the Holy Places.

We appeal to the Arab workers, farmers and small merchants to accept the United Nations decision for a Jewish and Arab state as being in their best interest. We urge them not to permit themselves to be used as tools in a war against Israel on behalf of British and American monopolies, for the latter are the enemies of both Arabs and Jews.

The Far East

The Progressive Party supports the struggle of the peoples of Asia to achieve independence and to move from feudalism into the modern era. We condemn the bipartisan policy of military and economic intervention to crush these people's movements. World peace and prosperity cannot be attained unless the people of China, Indonesia, Indo-China, Malaya and Asian lands win their struggle for independence and take their place as equals in the family of nations.

We call for the immediate withdrawal of American troops and abandonment of bases in China.

We demand cessation of financial and military aid to the Chiang Kai-shek dictatorship.

We follow the policy of Franklin Roosevelt in encouraging the creation of a democratic coalition government in China. We urge support for the granting of large scale economic assistance to such a government.

We support the efforts of the people of Korea to establish national unity and the kind of government they desire. We demand an early joint withdrawal of occupation troops.

Colonial and Dependent Peoples

We believe that people everywhere in the world have the right to self-determination. The people of Puerto Rico have the right to independence. The people of the United States have an obligation toward the people of Puerto Rico to see that they are started on the road toward economic security and prosperity.

We demand the repeal of the Bell Trade Act relating to the Philippines and the abrogation of other unequal trade treaties with economically weaker peoples.

We urge action by the people of the United States and cooperation with other countries in the United Nations to abolish the colonial system in all its forms and to realize the principle of self-determination for the peoples of Africa, Asia, the West Indies, and other colonial areas.

We support the aspirations for unified homelands, of traditionally oppressed and dispersed people such as the Irish and Armenians.

Latin America

The Progressive Party urges a return to, and the strengthening of, Franklin Roosevelt's good-neighbor policy in our relations with republics to the South.

We demand the abandonment of the inter-American military program.

We call for economic assistance without political conditions to further the independent economic development of the Latin American and Caribbean countries.

Displaced Persons

The Progressive Party calls for the repeal of the anti-Catholic, anti-semitic Displaced Persons Act of 1948 which permits the entry into the United States of fascists and collaborators. We call for the enactment of legislation to open our doors in the true American tradition to the victims of fascist persecution.

FREEDOM

End Discrimination

The Progressive Party condemns segregation and discrimination in all its forms and in all places.

We demand full equality for the Negro people, the Jewish people, Spanish-speaking Americans, Italian Americans, Japanese Americans, and all other nationality groups.

We call for a Presidential proclamation ending segregation and all forms of discrimination in the armed services and Federal employment.

We demand Federal anti-lynch, anti-discrimination, and fair-employment-practices legislation, and legislation abolishing segregation in interstate travel.

We call for immediate passage of anti-poll tax legislation, enactment of a universal suffrage law to permit all citizens to vote in Federal elections, and the full use of Federal enforcement powers to assure free exercise of the right to franchise.

We call for a Civil Rights Act for the District of Columbia to eliminate racial segregation and discrimination in the nation's capital.

We demand the ending of segregation and discrimination in the Panama Canal Zone and all territories, possessions and trusteeships.

We demand that Indians, the earliest Americans, be given full citizenship rights without loss of reservation rights and be permitted to administer their own affairs.

We will develop special programs to raise the low standard of health, housing, and educational facilities for Negroes, Indians and nationality groups, and will deny Federal funds to any state or local authority which withholds opportunities or benefits for reasons of race, creed, color, sex or national origin.

We will initiate a Federal program of education, in cooperation with state, local, and private agencies to combat racial and religious prejudice.

We support the enactment of legislation making it a Federal crime to disseminate anti-Semitic, anti-Negro, and all racist propaganda by mail, radio, motion picture or other means of communication.

We call for a Constitutional amendment which will effectively prohibit every form of discrimination against women—economic, educational, legal, and political.

We pledge to respect the freedom of conscience of sincere conscientious objectors to war. We demand amnesty for conscientious objectors imprisoned in World War II.

The Right of Political Association and Expression

The Progressive Party will fight for the constitutional rights of Communists and all other political groups to express their views as the first line in the defense of the liberties of a democratic people.

We oppose the use of violence or intimidation, under cover of law or otherwise, by any individual or group, including the violence and intimidation now being committed by those who are attempting to suppress political dissent.

We pledge an all-out fight against the Mundt-Nixon Bill and all similar legislation designed to impose thought control, restrict freedom of opinion, and establish a police state in America.

We demand the abolition of the House Un-American Activities Committee and similar State Committees, and we mean to right the wrongs which these committees have perpetrated upon thousands of loyal Americans working for the realization of democratic ideals.

We pledge to eliminate the current "Loyalty" purge program and to reestablish standards for government service that respect the rights of Federal employees to freedom of association and opinion and to engage in political activity.

We demand the full right of teachers and students to participate freely and fully in the social, civic and political life of the nation and of the local community.

We demand that the Federal Bureau of Investigation and other Government agencies desist from investigating, or interfering with, the political beliefs and lawful activities of Americans.

We demand an end to the present practices of Congressional committees—such as the House Labor Committee—in persecuting trade unionists and political leaders at the behest of Big Business.

We demand an end to the present campaign of deportation against foreign-born trade unionists and political leaders, and will actively protect the civil rights of naturalized citizens and the foreign born.

Nationality Groups

The Progressive Party recognizes the varied contributions of all nationality groups to American cultural, economic, and social life, and considers them a source of strength for the democratic development of our country.

We advocate the right of the foreign born to obtain citizenship without discrimination.

We advocate the repeal of discriminatory immigration laws based upon race, national origin, religion, or political belief.

We recognize the just claims of the Japanese Americans for indemnity for the losses suffered during their wartime internment, which was an outrageous violation of our fundamental concepts of justice.

We support legislation facilitating naturalization of Filipinos, Koreans, Japanese, Chinese, and other national groups now discriminated against by law.

We support legislation facilitating naturalization of merchant seamen with a record of war service.

Democracy in the Armed Forces

The Progressive Party demands abolition of Jim Crow in the armed forces.

We demand abolition of social inequalities between officers and enlisted personnel.

We call for basic revision in the procedure of military justice, including the more adequate participation of enlisted men in courts-martial.

We urge that admission to West Point and Annapolis be based on the candidates' qualifications, determined by open competitive examinations, and that an increasing percentage of young men admitted to be drawn from the ranks.

Representative Government

The Progressive Party proposes a constitutional amendment providing for the direct election of the President and Vice President by popular vote.

We call for Home Rule and the granting of full suffrage to the disfranchised citizens of the District of Columbia.

We favor the immediate admission of Hawaii and Alaska as the 49th and 50th states of the Union.

We urge that all general and primary election days be declared holidays to enable all citizens to vote.

Separation of Church and State

The Progressive Party intends to maintain the traditional American separation of church and state and protect the freedom of secular education.

ABUNDANCE

High Cost of Living

The living standards of the American people are under bipartisan attack through uncontrolled inflation. The only effective method of combating inflation is to take the profits out of inflation.

The Progressive Party calls for legislation which will impose controls that will reduce and keep down the prices of food, shelter, clothing, other essentials of life, and basic materials. Such controls should squeeze out excessive profits, provide for the payment of subsidies to farmers wherever necessary to maintain fair agricultural prices, and allocate materials and goods in short supply.

We call for removal by the President of the Housing Expediter who is administering rent control in the interests of the real estate lobby.

We call for strengthening rent control, providing protection against evictions, and eliminating the present "hardship" regulations which are a bonanza for the large realty interests.

Economic Planning

The Progressive Party believes in the principle of democratic economic planning and rejects the boom-and-bust philosophy of the old parties.

We mean to establish a Council of Economic Planning to develop plans for assuring high production, full employment, and a rising standard of living.

We mean to develop, on the TVA pattern, regional planning authorities in the major river valleys the country over to achieve cheap power, rural electrification, soil conservation, flood control and reforestation, and to accelerate the growth of undeveloped areas, particularly in the South and West.

We mean to promote, through public ownership and long-range planning, the peaceful use of atomic energy to realize its great potential as a source of power and as a tool in science, medicine, and technology.

Only through the planned development of all our resources will the full benefit of the nation's wealth and productivity be secured for the people.

Breaking the Grip of Monopoly

Monopoly's grip on the economy must be broken if democracy is to survive and economic planning become possible. Experience has shown that antri-trust laws and government regulation are not by themselves sufficient to halt the growth of monopoly. The only solution is public ownership of key areas of the economy.

The Progressive Party will initiate such measures of public ownership as may be necessary to put into the hands of the people's representatives the levers of control essential to the operation of an economy of abundance. As a first step, the largest banks, the railroads, the merchant marine, the electric power and gas industry, and industries primarily dependent on government funds or government purchases such as the aircraft, the synthetic rubber and synthetic oil industries must be placed under public ownership.

We mean to strengthen and vigorously enforce the anti-trust laws to curb monopoly in the rest of the economy.

We call for the immediate abolition of discriminatory freight rates, which help to keep the South and West in bondage to Wall Street.

Tideland oil resources belong to the people, and we fight the efforts of the oil companies to steal them. We support Federal control of such resources.

We demand the repeal of the Bulwinkle law which exempts railraods from anti-trust prosecution.

We call for the repeal of the Miller-Tydings legislation which eliminated retail competition in branded goods, excluding these from the coverage of the Anti-trust laws.

Labor

The Progressive Party recognizes that from the earliest period of its history the organized labor movement has taken leadership in the struggle for democratic and humanitarian objectives. Organized labor remains the mainspring of America's democratic striving, and the just needs of labor are of special concern to the Progressive Party.

We hold that every American who works for a living has an inalienable right to an income sufficient to provide him and his family with a high standard of living. Unless the rights of labor to organize, to bargain collectively, and to strike are secure, a rising standard of living cannot be realized.

We demand the immediate repeal of the Taft-Hartley Act and the reinstatement of the principles of the Wagner and Norris-LaGuardia acts. These last measures are essential to restore labors equality in collective bargaining and to prevent business from using government to establish a dictatorship over labor by injunction.

We will demand the right for employees in publicly owned industries to organize, to bargain collectively, and to strike.

We call for the establishment of collective bargaining machinery for Federal employees.

We support the legitimate demands of all wage and salary earners, including Federal employees, for wage and salary increases and improved working conditions. We demand the enactment of a minimum wage of $1 an hour, extension of the Fair Labor Standards Act to cover all workers, enforcement of equal pay for equal work regardless of age or sex, and the elimination of any regional wage differential.

We oppose governmental strike-breaking through seizure of struck industries under the pretext of Federal operation, while profits continue to go to private employers.

We urge the enactment and stringent enforcement of Federal and State laws establishing adequate safety and health standards for miners, longshoremen, railroad workers, merchant seamen, and all other workers in hazardous industries.

We pledge drastic amendment of the Railway Labor Act to make certain that the railroad workers enjoy genuine collective bargaining and the right to strike. We call for amendment of the Railroad Retirement Act to grant railroad workers pensions of $100 minimum after 30 years' service or when they become 60 years old.

We call for Federal legislation to improve railroad working conditions by establishing a 40-hour, 5-day week for non-operating and terminal employees, and a six-hour day for roadmen, and train limit and full crew provisions.

We actively support measures to repair and improve the living standards of the 12 million white collar and professional employees, who have suffered particularly under the inflation.

We call for an end to the second-class citizenship of our nation's two and a half million agricultural wage workers, and the thousands of food processing workers who are excluded from the protection of social and labor legislation. We stand for legislation to protect the right of agricultural workers to bargain collectively. We call for extension of social security and fair labor standards coverage to all agricultural and food processing workers.

We demand an immediate end to the arbitrary security orders issued by the Department of National Defense which blacklist employees in private industries under government contracts.

Agriculture

The Progressive Party recognizes that the welfare of farmers is closely tied to the living standards of consumers. We reject the "eat-less" policy of the old parties and proclaim our intention to develop within the framework of an economy of planned abundance, a long-range program of full agricultural production, combined with necessary safe-guards for the security of farmers and for the conservation of our natural resources.

We stand for the family-type farm as the basic unit of American agriculture. The Farmer's Home Administration, (formerly, Farm Security Administration) must be expanded to provide ample low-cost credit to assist tenants, sharecroppers, and returned veterans to become farm-owners. Marginal farmers must be assisted to become efficient producers. Where farming is incapable of yielding an adequate family income, supplementary employment on needed conservation and public works projects must be provided.

We propose as a major goal of Federal farm programs that all farm families be enabled to earn an income of not less than $3,000 a year. We repudiate the program of Big Business which would eliminate as many as two-thirds of the nation's farmers.

We call for a 5-year program of price-supports for all major crops at not less than 90 percent of parity—parity to be calculated according to an up-to-date formula. Dairy products and certain specialties should be supported at higher rates than 90 percent.

We demand that all essential crops be insured against hazards which are beyond the control of the individual farmer.

We support the principle of direct payments to farmers for soil conservation practices, crop adjustment, and rodent control.

We favor the principle of compensating payments and production subsidies when needed to encourage a high level of consumption without jeopardizing farm income. We also call for assistance to low-income consumers through such programs as the food stamp plan and the school hot-lunch program.

We favor international commodity agreements and a World Food Board under the United Nations Food and Agriculture Organization to stabilize world markets and to move farm surpluses to deficient areas.

We call for a long-range national land policy designed to discourage the growth of corporation farms and absentee ownership. This policy is especially important in the South to promote the proper development of its resources and to provide land for the landless. Priority in the purchase of land made available by river-valley projects must be given to tenants, sharecroppers, and small farmers.

We regard it as of utmost importance that programs of conservation, production, marketing, and price-support be administered by democratically elected farmer committeemen, as in the Triple-A program.

We stand for the principle of a graduated land tax and for the 160-acre limitation in the use of public irrigation.

We support farmer and consumer cooperatives as a highly important answer to the problem of monopoly control over markets and supplies. We oppose the tax drive being staged by Big Business against cooperatives.

We favor immediate flood control projects and universal electrification of all farms. REA lines and generating facilities should be rapidly expanded, and river-valley projects for power and irrigation should be undertaken as promptly as possible.

Independent Business

The Progressive Party believes that independent businessmen can survive only in an economy free from monopoly domination, where workers and farmers receive incomes sufficient to permit them to purchase the goods they need.

We propose to encourage and safeguard independent business by providing adequate working capital and development loans at low interest rates, granting tax relief, and giving independent and small business a fair share of government contracts. We propose to make available to independent business, through an expanded government research program, the know-how essential to efficient operation.

Housing

The Progressive Party charges that private enterprise, under monopoly control, has failed to house the American people. It is the responsibility of democratic government to guarantee the right of every family to a decent home at a price it can afford to pay.

We demand a Federal emergency housing program to build within the next two years four million low-rent and low-cost dwellings for homeless and doubled-up families, with priority to veterans.

We recognize that to accomplish this objective it will be necessary to curb non-essential construction, to allocate scarce materials, and to reduce the cost of land, money, and building materials.

We pledge an attack on the chronic housing shortage and the slums through a long-range program to build 25 million new homes during the next ten years. This program will include public subsidized housing for low-income families.

We pledge that as a part of our general program of economic planning the building industry will be reorganized and rationalized, capacity to produce presently scarce materials will be expanded, and year-round employment will be guaranteed to workers in the building trades.

Government—Federal, state and local—has the responsibility to insure that communities are well-planned, with homes conveniently located near places of employment and with adequate provision for health, education, recreation, and culture.

We pledge the abolition of discrimination and segregation in housing.

Security and Health

The Progressive Party demands the extension of social security protection to every man, woman and child in the United States.

We recognize the service which the Townsend Plan has performed in bringing to national attention the tragic plight of the senior citizens of America, and we condemn the bipartisan conspiracy in Congress over the past ten years against providing adequate old-age pensions.

We pledge our active support for a national old-age pension of $100 a month to all persons at 60 years of age, based on right and not on a pauperizing need basis.

We call for a Federal program of adequate disability and sickness benefits. protecting all workers and their standards of living.

We call for maternity benefits for working mothers for thirteen weeks, including the period before and after childbirth, and the granting of children's allowances to families with children under 18.

We favor adequate public assistance for all persons in need, with Federal grants-in-aid proportionate to the needs and financial ability of the states, pending the enactment of a comprehensive Federal Social Security program.

We support the right of every American to good health through a national system of health insurance, giving freedom of choice to patient and practitioner, and providing adequate medical and dental care for all.

We favor the expenditure of Federal funds in support of an effective program for public health and preventive medicine and a program of dental care.

We favor the expenditure of Federal funds for the promotion of medical and dental education and research.

We look forward to the eventual transfer of the entire cost of the security and health program to the government as an essential public service.

Women

The Progressive Party proposes to secure the rights of women and children and to guarantee the security of the American family as a happy and democratic unit and as the mainstay of our nation.

We propose to raise women to first-class citizens by removing all restrictions— social, economic, and political—without jeopardizing the existing protective legislation vital to women as mothers or future mothers.

We propose to extend fair labor standards for women, to guarantee them healthful working conditions, equal job security with men, and their jobs back after the birth of children.

We propose to guarantee medical care for mother and child prior to, during and after birth, through a national system of health insurance.

We propose a program of Federal assistance for the establishment of day care centers for all children.

Young People

The Progressive Party believes young people are the nation's most valuable asset: their full potentialities can be realized only by implementing our complete program for peace, freedom and abundance. We challenge the failure of the old parties to meet the special problems of youth.

We call for the right to vote at eighteen.

We call for the enforcement and extension of child labor laws.

We call for Federal and state expenditures for recreational facilities, particularly in needy rural communities.

Veterans

The Progressive Party recognizes the veterans' special sacrifices and contributions in the nation's most critical period.

We demand priority for veterans in obtaining homes.

We call for a Federal bonus to veterans based on length of service.

We demand the expansion of the Veterans Administration program and increased G.I. benefits and allowances and the elimination of discrimination.

We demand that the coverage of the GI Bill of Rights and other servicemen's benefits be extended to war widows and the merchant seamen with war service.

We call for the prompt refund of the overcharges collected from veterans by National Service Life Insurance.

We demand that the government enforce the right of Negro veterans in the South to file terminal leave applications and to collect their benefits.

We call for increased benefits for disabled veterans and a program to guarantee them jobs at decent wages.

Taxation

The Progressive Party demands the overhaul of the tax structure according to the democratic principle of ability to pay. We propose to employ taxation as a flexible instrument to promote full employment and economic stability.

We propose to exempt from personal income taxes all families and individuals whose income falls below the minimum required for a decent standard of living. We propose that income from capital gains be taxed at the same graduated rate as ordinary income.

We propose to enact effective excess profits and undistributed profits taxation.

We propose to curb tax dodging by closing existing loopholes.

We propose to work towards the progressive elimination of Federal excise taxes on the basic necessities of life.

We oppose all state and local sales taxes.

We propose to close existing loopholes in estate and gift taxes and establish an integrated system of estate and gift taxation.

Education

The Progressive Party proposes to guarantee, free from segregation and discrimination, the inalienable right to a good education to every man, woman, and child in America. Essential to good education are the recognized principles of academic freedom—in particular, the principle of free inquiry into and discussion of controversial issues by teachers and students.

We call for the establishment of an integrated Federal grant-in-aid program to build new schools, libraries, raise teachers' and librarians' salaries, improve primary and secondary schools, and assist municipalities and states to establish free colleges.

We call for a system of Federal scholarships, fellowships, and cost-of-living grants, free from limitations or quotas based on race, creed, color, sex or national origin, in order to enable all those with necessary qualifications but without adequate means of support to obtain higher education in institutions of their own choice.

We call for a national program of adult education in cooperation with state and local authorities.

We oppose segregation in education and support legal action on behalf of Negro students and other minorities aimed at securing their admission to state-supported graduate and professional schools which now exclude them by law.

We call for a Department of Education with a Secretary of Cabinet rank.

Culture

The Progressive Party recognizes culture as a potentially powerful force in the moral and spiritual life of a people and through the people, in the growth of democracy and the preservation of peace, and realizes that the culture of a democracy must, like its government, be of, by, and for the people.

We pledge ourselves to establish a department of government that shall be known as the Department of Culture, whose function shall be the promotion of all the arts as an expression of the spirit of the American people, and toward the enrichment of the people's lives, to make the arts available to all.

Promotion of Science

The Progressive Party calls for the enactment of legislation to promote science, including human and social sciences, so that scientific knowledge may be enlarged and used for the benefit of all people.

We condemn the militarization of science and the imposition of military control over scientific expression and communication.

We support measures for public control of patents and licensing provisions to insure that new inventions will be used for the benefit of the people.

The Progressive Party has taken root as the party of the common man. It has arisen in response to, and draws growing strength from, the demand of millions of men and women for the simple democratic right to vote for candidates and a program which satisfy their needs. It gives voters a real choice.

Purposeful and deeply meant, the program of the Progressive Party carries forward the policies of Franklin Roosevelt and the aspirations of Wendell Willkie and holds forth the promise of a reborn democracy ready to play its part in one world. The American people want such a program. They will support it.

Under the leadership of Henry A. Wallace and Glen H. Taylor, a great new people's movement is on the march. Under the guidance of Divine Providence, the Progressive Party, with strong and active faith, moves forward to peace, freedom and abundance.

HENRY A. WALLACE, ACCEPTANCE SPEECH
Philadelphia, July 24, 1948

Four years and four days ago, as Vice President of the United States and head of the Iowa delegation to the Democratic convention, I rose to second the nomination of Franklin Roosevelt, and said:

> The future belongs to those who go down the line unswervingly for the liberal principles of both political democracy and economic democracy regardless of race, color or religion. . . . Roosevelt can and will lead the United States, in cooperation with the rest of the world, toward that type of peace which will prevent World War III.

That was four years ago. Do you remember that summer of casualty lists, and the wreckage still smoldering on the beaches of Normandy? A time of dying and destruction . . . and, yet, something more.

For in that time, you remember, every one of us held a dream. At the lathe, in the fields in early morning, at the kitchen window, sweating out a barrage in the line, everyone of us dreamed of a time when the sound of peace would come back to the land, and there would be no more fear, and men would begin to build again.

And in that dark time, you remember, Franklin Roosevelt looked beyond the horizon and gave us a vision of peace, an economic bill of rights; the right to work, for every man willing. The right of every family to a decent home. The right to protection from the fears of old age and sickness. The right to a good education. All the rights which spell security for every man, woman and child, from the cradle to the grave.

It was the dream that all of us had, and Roosevelt put it into words, and we loved him for it.

Two years later the war was over, and Franklin Roosevelt was dead.

And what followed was the great betrayal.

Instead of the dream, we have inherited disillusion.

Instead of the promised years of harvest, the years of the locust are upon us.

In Hyde Park they buried our President and in Washington they buried our dreams.

One day after Roosevelt died Harry Truman entered the White House.

And forty-six days later Herbert Hoover was there.

It was a time of comings and goings.

Into the Government came the ghosts of the great depression, the banking house boys and the oil-well diplomats.

In marched the generals—and out went the men who had built the TVA and the Grand Coulee, the men who had planned social security and built Federal housing, the men who had dug the farmer out of the dust bowl and the workman out of the sweatshop.

A time of comings and goings ... the shadows of the past coming in fast—and the lights going out slowly—the exodus of the torchbearers of the New Deal.

I was still in the Cabinet—hoping that we might yet return, somehow, to the course Franklin Roosevelt had charted for the nation in peace. And in that great hope, two years ago this month I wrote to the President.

I warned him that we had fallen upon cynical counsel, that the bankers and the brokers and the big brass had launched us upon a dangerous policy—the "get tough policy."

I said then that "our post-war actions have not yet been adjusted to the lessons gained from experience of allied cooperation during the war and the facts of the atomic age."

I said that it would be fruitless to seek solutions for specific problems without establishing an atmosphere of mutual trust and confidence—and I warned that our "get tough" policy would only produce a "get tougher" policy. That warning was before the crises in Greece, in Italy, in Palestine, in Czechoslovakia. That warning was two years ago—two years before Berlin.

You have read your papers. In the two years since the people who planned for living were eased out of Washington, and the ghosts who plan for destruction were invited in—in those two short years during which the Department of State has been subtly annexed to the Pentagon, and the hand of military has come to guide the pen of the diplomat—we have ricocheted from crisis to crisis.

The "get tough policy" has spawned its inevitable bread—the "get tougher policy."

And what harvest do we have of all our hoping, what fruits of the hard-won victory? Not peace—but the sword; not an economic bill of rights—but a mounting bill of wrongs.

Not life—but tens of thousands of deaths, on unnecessary battlefields in Greece—in Palestine—in China.

One world, yes—frozen in one fear.

The world's eyes today focus upon the burning spot of the cold war—Berlin.

Berlin need not have happened. Berlin did not happen. Berlin was caused.

When we were set on the road of "get tough" policy, I warned that its end was inevitable. Berlin is becoming that end.

There is no reason why the peace of a world should hang on the actions of a handful of military men stationed in Germany!

In all earnestness, I assure you that if I were president, there would be no crisis in Berlin today. I assure you that without sacrificing a single American principle or public interest, we would have found agreement long before now with the Soviet Government, and with our other wartime allies.

Long before now we could have embarked upon a policy for Germany upon which a sound foundation could be built for peace throughout Europe.

It is not by accicident that Germany has become, once again, the heart of a crisis.

Germany will be the core of every world crisis until we have come to an agreement with the Soviet Union. We have been manoeuvred into a policy whose specific purpose has been this, and only this: to revive the power of the industrialists and cartelists who heiled Hitler and financed his fascism, and who were the wellspring of his war chest.

In the western zone of Germany today, we are told, there is enjoyed "peace and justice."

This so-called just peace is not just. It is a peace which rebuilds the warmaking potential of German industry in the western zone.

This justice is being dispensed by local judges, of whom 10 per cent are former Nazi officials. German war industry is on the rise again—and its managers are the same Krupp and I.G. Farben men who made Germany into Hitlerland.

There is no peace, no justice—for either allies or former enemies in our German policy. It is a child born of lust for power and profit.

With a Germany groomed and muscled as the eastern-most outpost of another war, we cannot make a peace. Nor can the world which watches helplessly.

I repeat. If I were President, there would be no crisis in Berlin. Do you remember when—only two months ago—our Ambassador to Moscow sent a note to the Kremlin? It was a note which seemed to be an invitation to sit around the table of reason—an invitation to talk over the problems which have created this continued state of crisis? Do you remember how the Russians responded with what seemed like real eagerness? You remember that day.

It was as if somebody had suddenly declared peace. Sit down and talk it over, we said—that's the way. But what happened?

Within twenty-four hours, our Administration, having consulted its carbon-copy opposite party, slammed the door it had itself swung open.

On that day, I addressed an open letter to Premier Stalin. I detailed a program which would have safeguarded the interests of both nations and preserved the peace. Ten days later, when Stalin responded to that open letter, the "get tough" boys slammed the door again. Since that time there have been no more approaches—except toward conflict. There are two sides to every curtain.

And so, Germany still festers at the heart of all peacemaking—yet, by closing the door to peace talks with Russian leaders, nothing remains but the fruitless discussions of minor officials in Berlin.

I say the peace of the world is far too fragile to be shuttled back and forth through a narrow air corridor in freighter planes.

I say the lives of our children, and our children's parents, are far too precious to be left to the tempers of second lieutenants at road barriers where zone meets zone—or to the generals who are quoted calmly as favoring a "show of strength."

I say that if reasonable men, men without special interests, peace-loving men—if Franklin Roosevelt were in Washington today—there would be no crisis in Berlin. Long before this the leaders of both nations would have rooted out the causes for conflict.

We hear it said that we should have a showdown at Berlin. But what is the showdown about? What is the American public interest which will be served by a showdown? There may be some private interests . . . some interests of Dillon, Read and international bankers. But there is no public interest. Dillon, Read's distinguished alumni, Secretary Forrestal and General Draper and Dewey's Wall Street lawyer, John F. Dulles, are major advisers on this issue, but I have yet to meet the American in shop or field or college or independent business who wants to give up his life to defend Dillon, Read.

I think we should look coldly at some of the facts which confront us if the cold war developed into a hot war:

There is not a single nation on the European Continent prepared to put an army into the field to defend Anglo-Saxon, that is, British and American policies.

We can buy generals with dollars, but we can't buy wartime armies. These generals won't die in battle. Soldiers would. We can support—and we are supporting—armies during this time of cold war, but we can't purchase suicide. We can buy governments, but we can't buy people.

It is said that we must have a showdown or lose prestige. Truman may lose prestige. Dulles may lose prestige. But the American people won't lose prestige by demanding fundamental discussions looking to peace. Our prestige in Germany went sinking when we divided Germany and established the western sector as an American and British Puerto Rico—as a colony. When we did that we gave up Berlin politically and we can't lose anything by giving it up militarily in a search for peace.

We who are met here tonight—who are met here at a time of crisis—are talking to the people of the United States and the world on behalf of the everlasting principles of the founding fathers of our country.

We who are gathered here tonight recall the crisis of 150 years ago, when Thomas Jefferson was attacked here in the city of Philadelphia—attacked because he spoke courageously for the peaceful settlement of alleged differences between the United States and France.

It was a time of terror unsurpassed till now.

Thomas Jefferson was slandered as the tool of French revolutionaries bought with French gold.

One hundred and fifty years ago Thomas Jefferson took leadership in forming a new party—a successful new party, which overcame the odds of a hostile press, of wealth and vested interests arrayed against it, and of a Government which sought to undermine the new movement by jailing its leaders.

The party Jefferson founded 150 years ago was buried here in Philadelphia last week. It could not survive the Pauleys, the Hagues, the Crumps, the racists and bigots, the generals, the admirals, the Wall Street alumni. A party founded by a Jefferson died in the arms of a Truman.

But the spirit which animated that party in the days of Jefferson has been captured anew. It has been captured by those who have met here this weekend with a firm resolve to keep our tradition of freedom that we may fulfill the promises of an abundant, peaceful life for all men.

Four score and seven years ago, the successful candidate of another new party took office in Washington.

Lincoln, with the Emancipation Proclamation fulfilled the promise of the new party which he led to victory. He headed a government of the people, by the people, and for the people. In the generations which followed his party became a party of the corporations, by the corporations, and for the corporations. The party of a Lincoln has been reduced to the party of a Dewey.

But we here tonight—we of the Progressive party—we here dedicate ourselves to the complete fulfillment of Lincoln's promise; we consecrate ourselves to a second emancipation; an emancipation that will achieve for the Negro and all Americans of every race, creed, and national origin a full, free, and complete citizenship everywhere in these United States.

We ally ourselves against those who turn to nightmares the peoples' dreams of peace and equality.

We ally ourselves to stand against the kings of privilege who own the old parties—the corrupted parties, the parties whose founders rebelled in times past, even as we do today, against those whose private greed jeopardizes the general welfare.

We stand against their cold war and their red smear, under cover of which they steal our resources, strike terror into our hearts, and attempt to control our thoughts and dominate the life of man everywhere in the world.

We stand together to stop the disasters—economic, political, and military, which their policies must breed.

Only those who take the spirit of Jefferson and Lincoln and apply it to the present world situation can bring the peace and security which will end fear and unleash creative force beyond the power of man to imagine.

It was in the spirit of Jefferson and Lincoln that Roosevelt challenged the money changers in his first inaugural address fifteen years ago. It was in the spirit of Jefferson and Lincoln that he told the Wall Street crowd in 1940 that they had met their master. In the spirit of Jefferson and Lincoln he outlined the Four Freedoms and the economic bill of rights.

It was in the spirit of Jefferson and Lincoln that he addressed that great Senator, George Norris, and said: "I go along with you because it is my honest belief that you follow in their footsteps—radical like Jefferson, idealist like Lincoln, wild like Theodore Roosevelt, theorist like Wilson—dare to be all of these as you have in bygone years."

Franklin Roosevelt did not fear; he reveled in the names hurled by those who feared the shape of his vision. We of the new party—the Progressive party—shall cherish the adjectives and mound of hate thrown at us. They are a measure of the fear in the temples of the money changers and the clubs of the military. The base metal of vituperation cannot withstand the attack of truth.

We of the Progressive party must—and will—carry on where Roosevelt and Norris and LaGuardia left off. They preserve for us all that was most precious, the old-fashioned Americanism that was built for us by Jefferson, Jackson, Lincoln, Theodore Roosevelt and Woodrow Wilson.

There are some who say they agree with our objectives, but we are ahead of our times. But we are the land of pioneers and trail blazers. Though we have reached the end of the old trails to the West, a new wilderness rises before us. The wilderness of poverty and sickness and fear.

Once again America has need of frontiersmen. A new frontier awaits us—no longer west of the Pacific—but forward across the wilderness of poverty and sickness, and fear. We move, as the Pilgrim ships moved, as the Conestoga wagons moved, not ahead of our time, but in the very tide. And always before us, the bright star, the dream of the promised land, of what this nation might be.

But the American dream is no Utopian vision. We do not plan rocket ships for weekend trips to Mars. The dream is the hard and simple truth of what can be done. In one fleet of heavy bombers lies wealth and skill that could have saved Vanport from the flood waters, that could have taken a million veterans out of trailer camps and chicken coops.

We can build new schools to rescue our children from the fire-traps where they now crowd two at a desk. We can end the murderous tyranny of sickness and disease. The dream is nothing but the facts. The facts are that we spend $20,000,000,000 a year for cold war. The facts are that world health authorities, given one-tenth of this sum, could, in one year, with $2,000,000,000, wipe from the face of the earth tuberculosis, typhoid, malaria and cholera!

The cold war has already brought death to millions of Americans.

Look at your friends. Read the papers. Here are casualty lists. Millions—sick of cancer, tuberculosis, of pellagra, of heart disease and polio. We can prevent and cure not only these diseases but a vast host of others by devoting our science as enthusiastically to peace as to war.

A nation that is shaped for life, not death, can save these lives—your lives, the lives of your families. Together we must rise up and write an end to the casualty lists of the cold war. This is the American way—to conquer the forces of nature, not our fellow men.

Within the past month other men, candidates of the graveyard parties, have stood in this city, have flexed their muscles, and have declared their intention to continue the cold war whose heaviest tolls have been taken here at home. Both have said that "partisan politics must stop at the water's edge." They have declared their agreement. It is an agreement which would doom the nation and the world.

It is the policies which operate beyond the water's edge; the policies which demand heavy arms, and draft acts, and the waste of resources and skills in producing for disaster— it is those policies which determine the real wages for American workers, prices for American consumers, and the life-span of all the people of the world.

Yes, other candidates have stood before the American people to declare that they have made no commitments to obtain their nominations. But they have committed themselves; they have committed themselves to the policies of the big brass and big gold; to the policies of militarization and imperialism; to the policies which cast a shroud over the life-giving, life-saving course Franklin Roosevelt had charted for this post-war world.

I tell you frankly that in obtaining the nomination of the Progressive party—a nomination I accept with pride—I have made commitments. I have made them in every section of this land. I have made them in great halls and sports arenas, in huge open air meetings and in small gatherings. I have made commitments in the basement of a Negro church and in union halls and on picket lines. I have made commitments. I have made them freely. I shall abide by them. I repeat them with pride:

I am committed to the policy of placing human rights above property rights.

I am committed to using the power of our democracy to control rigorously and, wherever necessary, to remove from private to public hands, the power of huge corporate monopolies and international big business.

I am committed to peaceful negotiations with the Soviet Government. I am committed to do everything I can through the new party to save the lives of those who are now to be drafted through the establishment of peace without sacrificing any American principle or public interest.

I am committed to appointing to positions in the Cabinet and Administration men whose training and private interests cannot conflict with their public responsibilities.

I am committed to building and strengthening the United Nations as an instrument which can peacefully resolve differences between nations.

I am committed to using the power and prestige of the United States to help the peoples of the world, not their exploiters and rulers; to help the suffering, frustrated people in the colonial areas of the world even as we help other civilizations which have felt the full destructive force of war.

I am committed to planning as carefully and thoroughly for production for peace as the militarists and bankers plan and plot for war. For many of today's 60 million jobs are cold war jobs, unstable jobs, suicide jobs. I am committed to making 60 million—and more—jobs of producing for peace—house building jobs, school building jobs, the jobs of building dams and power plants and highways and clinics.

I am committed to a program of progressive capitalism—a program which will protect from the tentacles of monopolists the initiative and creative and productive powers of truly independent enterprise.

I am committed to fighting, with everything I have, the ugly practice of stifling with Taft-Hartley injunctions and the power of Government the free trade union organizations of our workers.

I am committed to rooting out the causes of industrial conflict and anti-labor practices; to returning us to the basic principles of the National Labor Relations Act and to strengthening the democratic organizations which give our workers safeguards against economic and political injustice.

I am pledged to fight the murderers who block, impede and stifle legislation and appropriations which would eliminate segregation and provide health and education facilities to bridge the gap of ten years life expectancy between a Negro child and a white child born this day.

I am pledged to licking inflation by stopping the cold war, the ruthless profiteering of monopolies, and the waste of resources which could give us an abundance of the goods of peace.

I am committed to helping lift the heavy hand of fear from our elder citizens, whose minds and bodies have served to build this America and whose reward must be the economic security which will enable them to spend their days with the peace of mind that comes from work well done and appreciated. And I am committed to those programs—principally the program for peace, which will lift from our young people the dread of war and drafts and unemployment and which will replace these fears with hope born of security and the equal opportunity to develop fully their individual talents and careers.

I am committed—as I have been my whole life through— to advancing those programs for agriculture which will increase the productivity of our land and better the lives of our farmers and their families.

I am committed to stopping the creation of fear; to using all my powers to prevent the fear-makers from clogging the minds of the people with the "red issue." The American people want and deserve fewer red issues and more red meat. Millions know and millions more must see that it is not the Kremlin, not the Communists who have sent milk to 24 cents a quart and meat to $1.30 a pound; that is the red issue not the reds who did this to us.

Yes. I am committed and I am confident the new party will commit itself to the principle of using our democratic process to the end that all men may enjoy the benefits made possible by modern science.

And I am committed and do renounce the support of those who practice hate and preach prejudice; of those who would limit the civil rights of others; of those who would restrict the use of the ballot; of those who advocate force and violence; and I am committed to accept and do accept the support of those who favor the program of peace I have outlined here; the support of all those who truly believe in democracy.

HENRY A. WALLACE, CAMPAIGN SPEECH
New York, September 10, 1948

The following was delivered at a Progressive party rally by the party's presidential candidate.

Just two years ago I spoke to many thousands of you who are here tonight. I said then as I say tonight that peace is the basic issue of the 1948 election campaign. I say now that the first job of national defense: the most important job in maintaining the peace is the job of conquering hate here at home, the job of protecting the civil rights of all Americans.

This is a great American meeting.

It is a meeting in the best American tradition—a meeting of men and women of all races, of all creeds.

Last week—in smaller gatherings—we proved that such meetings can be held in the much-maligned Southern states. We proved that such meetings—meetings of all the people—can be held wherever men respect the Constitution of the United States; and wherever they respect the Christian principles of brotherhood on which so much of our modern civilization has been built.

The news reported from the South last week was news of eggs and tomatoes. It was news of violence and threats of violence.

And there were eggs. And there were tomatoes. And there was violence and there were threats of violence.

Yes, and there were the ugly spewings of hate and prejudice; and the sad sight of men and women and children whose faces were contorted with hate.

But the significance of our trip south was not the dramatic proof that there are seeds of violence and fascism and deep prejudice in the Southern states. The significance was not in proving what is known.

No. The significance of our Southern trip lies in the two dozen completely unsegregated, peaceful meetings which we were able to hold.

The significance lies in those meetings in Virginia, North Carolina, Alabama, Mississippi, Arkansas and Tennessee which were held—even as this meeting tonight—in the best American tradition.

We held such meetings by insisting on our American rights to freely assemble and freely speak.

And if there is one message above all other messages which I bring you as a result of that Southern trip, it is this: Fear is a product of inactivity and the greatest remedy for fear is to stand up and fight for your rights.

In the course of private and public life I have traveled many places. I have experienced many fields. I have had a wide variety of emotional experiences. But I have never had such deeply moving experiences as those of the first week of September, 1948, when I traveled South to campaign for peace.

I had seen the victims of mass prejudice in a DP camp.

I had seen and felt—as any decent human being must feel—for the Jewish orphans interned in Italy.

I had visited foreign lands—Latin America, China and many parts of Europe, and had my heart go out to victims of oppression.

I have deplored and felt that I truly understood the plight of workers who have faced picket line violence.

I had been South before—many times—and I thought I understood the plight of our Negro citizens.

But I discovered last week that my understanding was only the limited understanding; the sympathetic feeling of a friend for a man who is afflicted.

To me fascism is no longer a second-hand experience—a motion picture, a photograph on the deeply moving words of a great writer.

It is no longer a mere definition of an economic and political system in which freedom is stifled by private power; in which prejudices are bred and nourished; in which man is set against man for the profit of powerful and greedy forces.

No, fascism has become an ugly reality—a reality which I have tasted.

I have tasted it neither so fully nor so bitterly as millions of others. But I have tasted it.

And in tasting it I have reinforced my solemn resolution to fight it wherever and whenever it appears so long as I live.

Last week—when I had a chance to live—to live very briefly and relatively mildly—the kind of life which millions of Americans live every waking hour, last week I learned what prejudice and hatred can mean. I learned to know the face of violence, although I was spared the full force of violence. I saw the ugly reality of how hate and prejudice can warp good men and women; turn Christian gentlemen into raving beasts; turn good mothers and wives into jezebels.

I didn't like that part of what I saw. I didn't like to see men and women fall victims to the catchwords of prejudice and the slogans of hate, even as the poor people of Germany were victimized by the catchwords and slogans of Hitler and Streicher.

I saw how a few hate mongers carefully placed in a crowd of decent folks can set off a dangerous spark.

I saw a young college student—a Progressive party worker—who was severely cut across his chest and arms by the agents of hate.

I was a passenger in the car of a prominent businessman in a Southern city as he raced down dark streets and alleys to elude all who might be following us, so that he could take me, unknown to anyone else, to his home for dinner.

He was a courageous man. The precautions he took were necessary. His business in that Southern town would have been ruined, if it were known that a candidate for the Presidency, a former Vice President, was having dinner at his home.

I saw an irate landlord rouse a quiet neighborhood where I had gone quietly to rest and work on a radio speech at the apartment of a young couple.

I saw how fear is bred and perpetuated and capitalized—and I didn't like it.

But I also saw the kind of courage; the kind of real, deep human fighting spirit which promises a new day for the South and for the world.

I saw men and women, white and Negro, who have been leading the fight against hate and prejudice and intolerance in the South.

I saw them standing up and fighting for the very foundations of our American way of life—standing up to all kinds of intimidation. And from them radiates a contagious spirit; the same kind of spirit of resistance which stopped the armies of Adolf Hitler in half a dozen European countries.

I heard Clark Foreman say so truthfully that "Down here, to believe in the Constitution means you are automatically called a Communist"; and I heard a young college student, a veteran, add: "It's like General Carlson said, 'To be called a Red here is a badge of honor.'"

I am confident that their spirit—the spirit of the progressive Southerners—will triumph in the South. I am hopeful that our trip helped to build their forces; helped rally new strength; helped along the movement which will free the South. Rich in resources—proud and courageous, the South must be—and will be—freed from the shackles in which it has been held by huge corporations with headquarters only four miles south of here—not in Virginia, not in Tennessee, but in Wall Street.

The free South and the feudal South live side by side in the State of Alabama. In one day we received courteous receptions and held free meetings in the best American tradition in Decatur and Huntsville and Gunthersville in the great TVA area; and on the same day we could not hold meetings in Gadsden and Birmingham and Bessemer, cities which are dominated by Northern-owned steel corporations. We did not hold meetings because the police insisted on dividing Americans by the color of their skins. We did not hold meetings because the constitutional right to freely assemble and speak was denied by the police authorities of those company towns.

Here—in Alabama—in a single day, we saw the economic basis of hate and segregation.

In the steel towns it is profitable to keep labor divided.

North against South, race against race, farmer against worker—the profits of the men who own the South are multiplied by keeping the people divided.

But their days are numbered.

The good people of the South have learned their scriptures. They know the fundamental Christian doctrine of the Fatherhood of God and the Brotherhood of Man. They know that "God hath made of one blood all the nations to dwell upon the face of the earth." They know that we are all members, one of another. Just as surely as men everywhere, they want the Kingdom of Heaven here on earth; and they are not going to be stopped any longer by those who spew hate.

It is the owners of the mines and mills, the great plantations, and newspapers who incite violence.

They don't personally engage in lynching either free speech or human beings, just as they don't personally engage in fighting the wars from which they profit.

But they inflame the passions of others. They have had others do their dirty work. But the ranks of new recruits for their dirty work are narrowing as more and more men and women of the South see how they have been victimized by prejudice— as they see how it has profited the few, and brought misery for themselves and their neighbors.

And the workers and farmers and independent businessmen of the South are turning from the false leadership of those who have been styled "Southern liberals"— they are turning from those who have preached the tolerance of intolerance, tolerance of segregation; tolerance of murderous Jim Crow. They are learning that such men are only slightly to the left of Hitler and Rankin.

They are learning that no man can believe in both segregation and democracy.

In a radio interview the editor of an Arkansas paper asked me about FEPC. He wanted to know if I would interfere with the right of men to choose their own associates. And I replied that I considered that a most important right. I replied that it was precisely my devotion to that right that leads me to fight segregation—segregation which deprives both white and Negro from freely choosing their own associates.

I told this same man; this same champion of segregation that while I knew we couldn't legislate love, we most certainly could and will legislate against the acts of hate.

Throughout the South we spoke for the full protection of all citizens under the Constitution of the United States. Tonight, I want to call upon the candidates of the Republican and Democratic parties to pledge with me that whosoever shall be elected, he will enforce the second section of the Fourteenth Amendment no less than the other provisions of the Constitution. That section of our Constitution calls for the reduction of the number of Congressmen for each state where the right to vote is abridged.

In 1946 the votes cast to elect fourteen Congressmen from Louisiana and Mississippi were less than the votes cast in the Twenty-fifth Congressional District here in New York.

John Rankin and thirteen others, all together, received less votes than are cast here in the Twenty-fifth District.

That is not only unfair to the people of New York's Twenty-fifth District; it is grossly unfair to the people of the Southern states whose freedom has been limited by the failure of the Congress to enforce the Fourteenth Amendment.

If every Congressional candidate, if each of the Presidential candidates will take a pledge to secure constitutional reapportionment on the basis of the next census, I predict that we shall see an end to the many hindrances to free suffrage in the South.

We pledge ourselves to enforce this constitutional right.

In pledging to live by the Constitution, we have earned enemies. And we are proud of our enemies.

The men who stand for Jim Crow.

The men who stand for Taft-Hartley.

The men who support fascists in Greece and China.

The men who prefer an atmosphere of war, because they profit by it.

The men who hated Franklin Roosevelt and the New Deal and who now find their unity in hatred for the Progressive party.

These men, Republicans and Democrats bound together by hate, are using every mechanism which bipartisan fear can suggest to defeat congressional candidates who stand for peace.

The Democrats, the Republicans, and the self-styled Liberals have joined hands to support single candidates against the candidates of the Progressive party; against candidates of the American Labor party.

They have joined hands in their bipartisan wrath against two men with the best liberal and labor voting records in the Congress of the United States.

They have honored—these corrupt and dangerous men—they have honored two real servants of the people. Vito Marcantonio and Leo Isacson. They have honored Leo Isacson with a single opponent. They have honored Vito Marcantonio with a joint campaign of vituperation and hate.

They are afraid of our strength. They saw what the people could do last February when they sent Leo Isacson to the Congress.

They have seen, time and again, the devotion of Vito Marcantonio's constituents to that dynamic champion of progressive principles. They have reason for their fear—and though they have combined their resources and efforts, we shall lick them on election day and return Vito Marcantonio and Leo Isacson to the Congress.

It is with great sadness that I note that the bipartisans have some new allies; fearful men who call themselves liberals and leaders of labor; men who cry out against Wall Street running the country and then ask workers to give dollar bills to keep President Truman and his Wall Street gang in Washington.

I say such action, such double talk, such duplicity is shameful, immoral, and corrupt.

These illiberal liberals; these labor leaders who fight monopoly with words, but whose actions support the candidates of monopoly, these men make possible the Truman double talk. They make it possible for Truman to condemn Taft-Hartley while using it to destroy unions and the Wagner Act; to call for civil rights, while maintaining segregation in the Armed Forces and conducting loyalty purges; to call for price controls after killing them; to call for peace, while preparing for war.

The surest proof that we of the Progressive party are not impractical in our politics is in the alliances of hate which have been formed against us.

Some of the liberals, some of the Pied Pipers of labor will tell us that they have compromised because Roosevelt compromised; but they slander a great man when they draw that comparison.

Roosevelt, by the deftest political maneuvering in all history, made many a political deal, but always advancing the cause of the common man.

The men who are bargaining with corruption today hope for no gains, no advancements. They are bargaining to minimize losses. They are fearful men. They are men who might well heed the lesson that the only cure for fear is to stand up and fight for right.

The bipartisans have learned that the Progressives are not for sale. They have found out—through their leading agent in New York City, Mayor O'Dwyer, that the party in which Fiorello LaGuardia was proud to enroll himself is not for sale.

Bill O'Dwyer found it out when he tried with his fanciest offers to get John Rogge to quit the race for the surrogate's bench. Bill O'Dwyer heard Vito Marcantonio say "no." He heard John Rogge say "no." And he knows that John Rogge will conduct the kind of dynamic, fighting campaign against corruption which he himself should have fought against Tammany.

O'Dwyer, who has Trumanized his local administration by serving the same interests as the Republicans, by pitting police against strikers, by fighting inflation with increased subway fares, by invoking local loyalty orders; Bill O'Dwyer has found that Progressives know double-talk when they hear it.

As President Truman has demonstrated that he could not fill the shoes of Roosevelt; so Mayor O'Dwyer has shown that he cannot fill the shoes of LaGuardia.

Yes, our "no sale" sign has earned us many names. But it does not matter if they call us red or black, if they lie about us or egg us or stone us. We will not join the Republican-Democratic poker match which governs out of the backroom—from the bottom of the deck.

The shop-worn, the discredited, the cheap political tricksters have joined with those who all their lives have practiced black reaction. They have set up one camp, though there are many banners.

And what are they joined against? What are we that they should forget old feuds to fight against us?

We are those who stand against the course which leads to war.

We are those who would take from the hands of monopoly the power to say who shall starve and who shall feast. We are those who protest a policy toward minority groups that is administered by a policeman's nightstick. We are those who feel attacked whenever the color of man's skin or the color of his political beliefs is the official excuse for brutality, whether in Mississippi or in Harlem, whether at home or abroad.

We must go now into every building of this city, into every suburban home, onto every street corner. We must tell the people who we are. We will stand up and take the jeers of hirelings.

We must work—we will work, so that on Nov. 2, Americans can clearly choose.

TABLE 1

1948 STATE REQUIREMENTS FOR QUALIFYING PRESIDENTIAL ELECTORAL CANDIDATES FOR PLACES ON BALLOTS*

I. PETITIONS

A. Required Number of Registered Voters' Signatures Determined by Percentage of Vote in Prior Election for Specified Office

Arizona	2	of vote in last gubernatorial election (from each of at least 5 counties)
California	10	of vote in last gubernatorial election.†
Connecticut	1	of vote in last presidential election.
Georgia	5	of registered voters.†
Indiana	½ of 1	of vote for Secretary of State in last election.
Michigan	1 to 4	of vote for Secretary of State in last election.
Nevada	5	of vote in last congressional election.
Ohio	1	of vote in last gubernatorial election (to qualify independent electors).
(or)	15	of vote in last general election (to qualify as third party).
Oregon	5	of vote in last congressional election.†
Pennsylvania	½ of 1	of highest vote for any state office in last election (State Judge—1947).
South Dakota	2	of vote for Governor in last election (qualify as independent).
or	20	of vote for Governor in last election (qualify as third party).
Vermont	1	of vote for Governor in last election.
West Virginia	1	of vote in last presidential election.

B. Required Number of Registered Voters' Signatures Determined by Statute

Arkansas	no specified number	
Colorado	500	
Delaware	750	250 in each of 3 counties.
Illinois	25,000	at least 200 from each of 50 counties (of 102).
Kansas	2,500	separate petitions for each of 8 electors.
Kentucky	100	
Louisiana	1,000	not affiliated with any major party.
Maine	1,000	
Maryland	2,000	

TABLE 1 (Continued)

Massachusetts	50,000	
Minnesota	2,000	separate petitions for each elector.
Mississippi	50	
New Hampshire	1,000	
New Jersey	800	
New York	12,000	at least 50 in each county.
North Carolina	10,000	nonaffiliated.
North Dakota	300	
Oklahoma	5,000	
Rhode Island	500	
Tennessee	1,425	15 from each of 95 counties.†
Utah	300	
Virginia	250	
Wisconsin	1,000	separate petitions for each of 12 electors, plus 1 each for presidential and vice-presidential candidates.
Wyoming	100	separate petition for each of 3 electors.

II. CONVENTIONS

Delegates Required

Alabama	no designated number of delegates.
Idaho	200
Iowa	2 (1 to sign as chairman, 1 as secretary.)
Montana	no designated number.
Nebraska	750
Oregon	250†
Tennessee	no designated number.†
Washington	25

III. OTHER METHODS

A. Change of Registration

California	1% of voters in last gubernatorial election.†
Florida	5% of registered voters.‡

B. Miscellaneous

Mississippi	any group may name slate.
New Mexico	formal organization and filing.
South Carolina	print and distribute ballots at polling places.
Texas	formal organization.

*This table was assembled primarily from newspaper sources. The *New York Times*, January 2, 1948, published a summary as compiled by the Associated Press. This was corrected in the light of later reports and information. The most recent scholarly works in the field at the time were an article by Joseph R. Starr, "The Legal Status of American Political Parties," *American Political Science Review*, June and August, 1940, and a compilation, "Legal Obstacles to Minority Party Success," published in the *Yale Law Journal*, July, 1948.

†Alternate methods provided.

‡Law amended in course of 1948 campaign to allow presidential electoral nominees to file without meeting formal requirements.

TABLE 2

COMBINED TOTALS OF CONTRIBUTIONS AND EXPENDITURES FOR THE PROGRESSIVE PARTY AND THE NATIONAL WALLACE-FOR-PRESIDENT COMMITTEE

	Total Contributions *	*Adjusted Total, or "Actual" Contributions* †
Progressive Party	$ 382,825.12	$ 491,090.84
National Wallace-for-President Committee	578,370.47	789,188.65
	$ 961,195.59	$1,280,279.49

	Total Expenditures *	*Adjusted Total, or "Actual" Expenditures*
Progressive Party	$ 535,050.13	$ 490,385.61
National Wallace-for-President Committee	813,532.67	769,717.30
	$1,348,582.80	$1,260,102.91

	Refund of Expenditures *	
Progressive Party	$ 152,920.24	
National Wallace-for-President Committee	254,633.55	
	$ 407,553.79	

Net Expenditures	941,029.01	
Surplus †	$ 20,166.58 ‡	$ 20,176.58 ‡

* Figures as filed with the Clerk of the House.

† These figures were arrived at by breaking down the party's "Refund of Expenditures" item as follows: "Admissions less than $100" and "Sale of Campaign Material at Cost" were added to contributions; "Advances," "Redeposits," "Exchanges," and "Reimbursed Expenditures" were deducted from expenditures.

‡ The $10 discrepancy arises from what appears to be an incorrect addition in the report of "Refund of Expenditures" for the Progressive Party during the period Oct. 29–Dec. 31, 1948. The reported total is $51,523.43, but the figures submitted actually total $51,533.43.

TABLE 3

REPORTED CONTRIBUTIONS BY ASSOCIATED GROUPS TO THE PROGRESSIVE PARTY AND TO THE NATIONAL WALLACE-FOR-PRESIDENT COMMITTEE

Labor
Fur and Leather Workers Committee for Wallace, Taylor, and Progressive Candidates	$5,000.00

Labor
Independent Political Committee of the Greater New York Council	1,425.00
Committee for Wallace, AFL Food, Hotel and Restaurant Workers	1,000.00
PAC (Local 1139, Minneapolis and Chicago Joint Board, IFLW)	500.00
Labor Committee for Wallace, New York City	500.00
FTA-CIO Wallace Committee, Philadelphia	500.00
Labor Committee for Wallace and Taylor, Local 430	100.00
	$9,025.00

Nationalities
Armenians for Wallace	$1,648.00
Greeks for Wallace	443.20
Irish-American Committee for Wallace	100.00
Italian-American Committee for Wallace	300.00
Lithuanian Wallace Committee	200.00
Romanians for Wallace	120.00
Russian Club for Wallace	100.00
Serbian-American Committee for Wallace	309.00
Slovenian-American National Council	1,887.00
Ukrainians for Wallace	100.00
Yugoslav-Americans for Wallace	200.00
	$5,407.20

Progressive Citizens of America (PCA)
California Chapters	$1,350.00
New York Chapters	1,298.90
Other Chapters	1,456.00
	$4,104.90

Women-for-Wallace
Greater New York Branches	$ 782.85

TABLE 4

DISTRIBUTION OF REPORTED STATE AND LOCAL ORGANIZATIONAL CONTRIBUTIONS TO THE PROGRESSIVE PARTY AND TO THE NATIONAL WALLACE-FOR-PRESIDENT COMMITTEE IN COMPARISON WITH DISTRIBUTION OF VOTE

State	Amount Contributed	1948 Votes for Electors	Rank in Total Organizational Contributions	Rank in Total Vote
New York	$76,466.85	509,559	1	1
Pennsylvania	56,734.00	55,161	2	3
Illinois	46,450.63	*	3	
California	38,864.00	190,381	4	2
Missouri	14,500.00	3,998	5	22
Texas	14,375.32	3,764	6	24
Indiana	13,173.00	9,649	7	16
New Jersey	12,650.00	42,683	8	5
Minnesota	12,543.10	27,866	9	9
Ohio	12,250.62	37,596	10	7
Colorado	12,000.00	6,115	11	19
Maryland	8,980.00	9,983	12	15
Connecticut	8,450.00	13,713	13	12
District of Columbia	7,650.00	†	14	
Michigan	6,475.00	46,515	15	4
Wisconsin	5,400.00	25,282	16	10
Iowa	4,996.43	12,125	17	13
Idaho	4,200.00	4,972	18	20
Florida	4,000.00	11,620	19 ‡	14
Oregon	4,000.00	14,978	19 ‡	11
Washington	3,683.30	31,692	21	8
Georgia	3,000.00	1,636	22 ‡	35
Massachusetts	3,000.00	38,157	22 ‡	6
Kansas	2,416.30	4,603	24	21
Nevada	1,900.00	1,469	25	38
New Mexico	500.00	1,037	26	41
Utah	385.00	2,679	27	29
Virginia	200.00	2,047	28 ‡	31
Puerto Rico	200.00	†	28 ‡	
Montana	111.02	7,313	30	18

Note: These totals represent only contributions from the various state parties and committees. Other group contributions will be found in Table 3.

   * Wallace electoral slate did not appear on ballot.

   † No vote in presidential elections.

   ‡ Tie.

TABLE 5

CONTRIBUTIONS AND ADMISSIONS REPORTED
IN THE PRESS FOR RALLIES AND DINNERS

Rallies

Date (1948)	Place	Attendance	Admissions	Contributions
Jan. 18	Chicago			$ 3,300.00 *
Feb.	Minnesota	16,000	$ 15,000.00	20,000.00
Apr. 10	Chicago (2 rallies)			70,000.00
Apr.	Midwest, East (10 rallies)			10,000.00
May 12	New York (Madison Square Garden)		50,000.00	
May 17	Los Angeles	31,000	30,000.00	20,000.00
May 21	San Francisco			40,000.00 *
May 30	Denver	3,200		5,000.00 *
June 25	Philadelphia (Shibe Park)	25,000		60,000.00
June 26	Washington, D.C.			22,000.00 *
Sept. 20	New York (Yankee Stadium)	60,000	78,000.00	52,000.00
Oct. 27	New York (Madison Square Garden)	19,000	23,000.00	24,000.00
			$196,000.00	$326,300.00

Dinners

Date (1948)	Place	Attendance	Admissions	Contributions
Jan. 17	Chicago			$ 32,200.00
Apr. 20	New York ($100.00 a plate)	1,400		100,000.00
June 22	New York (Businessmen's Lunch)	600		25,000.00
Sept. 22	New York ($100.00 a plate)	400		35,000.00
Oct. 2	Hollywood ($12.50 a plate)	several hundred		2,000.00
Oct. 20	Philadelphia ($25.00 a plate)	425		8,500.00
				$202,700.00

Women-for-Wallace Dinners

Date (1948)	Place	Attendance	Admissions	Contributions
Feb. 26	Brooklyn			$ 5,000.00
Apr. 21	Bronx			2,000.00
Oct. 27	New York ($100.00 a plate)	250		20,000.00
				$ 27,000.00
			Grand Total	$752,000.00

* Identification of separate figures impossible for Admissions and Contributions.

TABLE 6

COMPARISON OF EXPENDITURES BY NATIONAL GROUPS AND A LOCAL GROUP

National Wallace-for-President Committee and National Progressive Party * (Jan. 1–Oct. 31, 1948)			Progressive Party District of Columbia † (Apr. 1–Dec. 31, 1948)		
Item	*Expenditures*	*Percentage*	*Item*	*Expenditures*	*Percentage*
Advertising, Mail Solicitations	$ 18,311.60	1.6			
Tours (Wallace, Robeson, Taylor)	61,700.27	5.5	Travel	$ 693.94	2.0
Fundraising Events	207,624.50	18.2	Meetings, Rallies, and Special Events	4,682.42	13.2
Cost of Campaign Material	171,589.46	15.0	Publicity	3,525.14	9.9
Non-Fundraising Events	55,622.70	4.9			
Direct Contributions to State Campaigns and Candidates	43,312.67	3.8	Contributions (of which $14,000.00– 39.4 per cent– was to national groups)	14,612.00	41.1
Budgetary Expenses	583,484.25	51.0	Salaries	5,082.65	14.3
			Office Supplies	2,519.54	7.1
			Telephone and Telegraph	1,144.51	3.2
			General	351.61	1.0
			Taxes	919.34	2.6
			Non-Itemized (expenditures of less than $10,000 each)	2,003.93	5.6
Total Expenditures	$1,141,645.45	100.0	*Total Expenditures*	$35,535.08	100.0

* Figures for the expenditures of the Propressive Party (national) and National Wallace-for-President Committee from Consolidated Surplus Statement prepared for national headquarters.

† Figures for the expenditures of the Progressive Party of the District of Columbia taken from report filed with the Clerk of the House, Rept. 1987.

TABLE 7

PERCENTAGES OF STATES' VOTES RECEIVED BY 1948
WALLACE PROGRESSIVE PARTY

State	Percentage	State	Percentage
New York	8.12	Maryland	1.67
California	4.73	Connecticut	1.55
North Dakota	3.81	Pennsylvania	1.47
Washington	3.51	Ohio	1.28
Montana	3.27	Colorado	1.19
Oregon	2.86	Iowa	1.17
Nevada	2.37	South Dakota	1.12
Idaho	2.32	Vermont	1.04
Minnesota	2.30	Utah	0.97
Michigan	2.20	Wyoming	0.92
New Jersey	2.19	New Hampshire	0.85
Florida	2.01	Rhode Island	0.79
Wisconsin	1.98	Delaware	0.76
Arizona	1.87	Louisiana	0.73
Massachusetts	1.77	Maine	0.71
Alabama	0.71	Texas	0.33
Kansas	0.58	Arkansas	0.31
Indiana	0.58	Missouri	0.25
New Mexico	0.56	Kentucky	0.19
North Carolina	0.49	Mississippi	0.12
Virginia	0.49	South Carolina	0.11
West Virginia	0.44	Illinois	*
Georgia	0.39	Nebraska	*
Tennessee	0.34	Oklahoma	*

*Progressive Party did not appear on ballot.

TABLE 8

COMPARISON OF PERCENTAGES OF STATES' VOTES
RECEIVED BY SOME MINOR PARTIES

State	Wallace Progressive Party, 1948	All Minor Parties, 1864–1936	La Follette Progressive Party, 1924	Roosevelt Progressive Party, 1912	Populist (People's) Party, 1892
Alabama	0.71%	4.8%	4.9%	19.8%	36.60%
Arizona	1.87	6.5	23.2	34.3	*
Arkansas	0.31	3.8	9.5	18.8	8.07
California	4.73	9.3	33.2	49.7	9.38
Colorado	1.19	8.0	20.4	29.4	57.07
Connecticut	1.55	3.3	10.6	19.3	
Delaware	0.76	2.5	5.4	18.7	
Florida	2.01	4.3	7.9	10.1	16.06
Georgia	0.39	4.1	7.6	17.2	19.17
Idaho	2.32	10.6	36.5	27.6	54.66
Illinois		6.2	17.5	37.0	2.54
Indiana	0.58	4.0	5.6	27.2	4.00
Iowa	1.17	6.9	28.1	34.6	4.65
Kansas	0.58	8.6	14.9	35.5	48.44
Kentucky	0.19	2.7	5.0	23.3	6.92
Louisiana	0.73	1.3	3.3	12.6	5.30
Maine	0.71	3.7	5.9	38.4	2.04
Maryland	1.67	3.6	13.2	25.6	
Massachusetts	1.77	5.4	12.5	30.1	0.82
Michigan	2.20	6.2	10.5	41.4	4.32
Minnesota	2.30	11.0	41.3	42.4	11.35
Mississippi	0.12	2.2	3.1	5.7	19.42
Missouri	0.25	3.5	6.4	18.8	7.59
Montana	3.27	10.0	37.8	32.6	16.55
Nebraska		8.2	22.9	30.8	41.00
Nevada	2.37	8.7	36.2	33.4	66.76
New Hampshire	0.85	2.6	5.4	20.9	
New Jersey	2.19	4.2	10.0	35.3	0.28
New Mexico	0.56	3.4	8.5	18.0	*
New York	8.12	5.4	14.4	26.0	1.20
North Carolina	0.49	2.1	1.4	28.5	15.94
North Dakota	3.81	11.2	45.3	32.9	48.96
Ohio	1.28	5.2	17.6	23.6	1.74
Oklahoma		4.3	7.8	0.1	*
Oregon	2.86	9.5	24.5	31.5	16.24
Pennsylvania	1.47	5.7	14.3	39.9	
Rhode Island	0.79	3.9	3.2	22.5	0.43
South Carolina	0.11	0.6	1.0	2.5	3.42
South Dakota	1.12	12.4	37.0	54.6	37.58
Tennessee	0.34	2.8	3.5	22.1	8.92
Texas	0.33	4.5	6.5	9.7	23.64
Utah	0.97	6.5	20.8	23.5	*
Vermont	1.04	3.2	5.9	36.4	4.17
Virginia	0.49	1.7	4.6	16.1	
Washington	3.51	14.7	35.8	42.0	21.79
West Virginia	0.44	3.6	6.2	31.8	2.49
Wisconsin	1.98	9.9	54.0	17.5	2.66
Wyoming	0.92	9.0	31.5	23.6	46.14
National Percentage	2.3	5.7	16.85	29.6	8.63

* Not yet admitted to Union.

TABLE 9

VOTES RECEIVED BY PROGRESSIVE PARTY CANDIDATES,
NOVEMBER 2, 1948

State	Votes for Wallace-Taylor Electors	Votes for Progressive Senatorial Candidates	Votes for Progressive House Candidates	Number of House Candidates
Alabama	1,522			
Arizona	3,310	*	1,478	1
Arkansas	751			
California	190,381	*	228,180	14
Colorado	6,115	2,981		
Connecticut	13,713	*	9,186	5
Delaware	1,050	681		
Florida	11,620	*		
Georgia	1,636			
Idaho	4,972	3,154	3,130	2
Illinois			19,155	4
Indiana	9,649	*	1,076	1
Iowa	12,125	3,387	2,167	4
Kansas	4,603			
Kentucky	1,567	924	686	1
Louisiana	3,035			
Maine	1,884			
Maryland	9,983	*	12,172	3
Massachusetts	38,157			
Michigan	46,515		1,608	4
Minnesota	27,866			
Mississippi	225			
Missouri	3,998	*	3,039	4
Montana	7,313			
Nebraska				
Nevada	1,469	*		
New Hampshire	1,970	1,538	1,512	2
New Jersey	42,683	22,658	16,035	7
New Mexico	1,037	705	805	1
New York	509,559	*	512,148	44
North Carolina	3,915	3,490	3,345	6
North Dakota	8,391	*	1,758	1
Ohio	37,596	*		
Oklahoma				
Oregon	14,978		18,741	2
Pennsylvania	55,161	*	6,969	2
Rhode Island	2,587			
South Carolina	154			
South Dakota	2,801			
Tennessee	1,864		3,670	1
Texas	3,764		1,449	4
Utah	2,679	*		
Vermont	1,279	*		
Virginia	2,047	5,347	3,037	2
Washington	31,692	*	13,739	3
West Virginia	3,311			
Wisconsin	25,282	*	10,382	5
Wyoming	931			
Total	1,157,140	44,865	875,467	123

* No senatorial seat was at stake.

GOV. FIELDING WRIGHT OF MISSISSIPPI, STATEMENT TO DEMOCRATIC PARTY LEADERS
January 1948

Facing the future, as your chief executive, I would be remiss in my responsibilities if your attention were not directed to the fact that we are living in unsettled, uncertain, and even perilous times. One need not be a diplomat nor a student of international affairs to see the many danger flags flying throughout the world in the field of international relations as democracy clashes with communism in a struggle which will determine whether or not these two ideologies can live together in cooperation or if we must once again maintain our heritage and our freedom in the cold and cruel crucible of war. Nor need one be an economic prophet to realize that the inflation running rampant in this country today—if allowed to continue its mad flight unchecked—will eventually, and in the not-too-distant future, lead us into the depths of another great depression.

But, serious as these problems may be, they can be met and solved if approached in the spirit of common sense, honesty, and unselfishness which has characterized our efforts in so many difficult and trying times in the past.

And as we search for the answers to these problems, there is yet another most serious conflict being thrust upon the people of Mississippi and our beloved Southland; thrust upon us in the Congress of the United States and through press and radio services throughout the country. That is the campaign of abuse and misrepresentation being levelled against our section by those who seek to tear down and disrupt our institutions and our way of life. They are using as their tools such infamous proposals as FEPC, anti-lynching legislation, anti-poll-tax bills, and now the antisegregation proposals.

The charge of dereliction of duty could be hurled at me by the citizens of this State were I to fail to direct your thoughts to the vicious effect of the proposals of the committee appointed by the President of the United States to study and make recommendations under the guise of preservation of civil liberties. Those of you who read and studied the report recognize in it a further, and I might say, the most dangerous step, toward the destruction of those traditions and customs so vital to our way of life, particularly in our Southland.

These measures and the proposals of this committee are deliberately aimed to wreck the South and our institutions. But they are far more sinister than being mere pieces of antisouthern legislation and recommendations, for hidden under their misleading titles and guarded phraseology are elements so completely foreign to our American way of living and thinking that they will, if enacted,

Congressional Record, 80th Cong., 2d sess., 1948, 94, pt. 1, 466-67.

eventually destroy this Nation and all of the freedoms which we have long cherished and maintained.

The advocates of today's antisouthern legislation disregard the great instrument creating this Government which makes of us a union of sovereign States. This Nation, of which we are so justly proud, has grown great amid our very many differences of ideas. Each of our 48 States has made singular and specific contributions to the national whole because while they are different the people had the individual leeway to decide their own best methods for solving their local problems. Individuals in this Nation have achieved the heights because they had the right to use their own personal talents, and no man was standardized or limited to any given level of attainment or service to or among his fellows.

With this record of achievement which has made our country the greatest in the world—with our structure of republican government which has enabled our sovereign States to live together in relative harmony and progress and which has brought to all our people a standard of living never before achieved in human history—I cannot understand why there are those in this land today and in the Congress of the United States who would begin its disintegration by such types of nefarious legislation as I have previously mentioned. The legislation to which I have referred flagrantly invades the sovereign rights of the individual States. It undertakes to destroy our proper privilege of solving our own individual problems in the light of all our circumstances.

Aside from this fundamental right, such legislation violates the very experience of man, namely, that the problems of human relationships are so varied and diverse that we can never begin to solve all of them by laws. They can only be answered by education and continuing progress in the light of truth as God may give us wisdom to see and embrace the truth. And they can only be solved by the people who understand and know and are familiar with the problem.

Here in Mississippi and the South may be found the greatest example in human history of harmonious relationships ever recorded as existing between two so different and distinct races as the white and the Negro, living so closely together and in such nearly equal numbers. The uninterrupted progress which has been made will be continued in an orderly, effective manner if both races are left alone by those unfamiliar with the true situation. This problem is being solved by Mississippians and by southerners in a wholesome and constructive manner. We know that human relationship cannot be equalized and balanced by legislation, unless through such legislation the power of the State is exercised to force all men into a pattern—a rigid pattern which would operate to destroy the freedoms of all and cut off our march of progress.

We believe that the people of each of the 48 States—north, south, east, and west—are the most capable of judging their own respective local needs and meeting them. We know that this was the program set up by our founding fathers and guaranteed in our Constitution.

In Mississippi, and I think in the other States known as the South, we feel that our rights are being threatened by enemies of the South who are in fact also enemies of the Nation. We are convinced that in upholding our position in this current struggle, we are in fact maintaining the interests of all the American people and each of the 48 States. Yes, we are confident that we are by our position upholding the rights of the members of all races and sections.

As a lifelong Democrat, as a descendant of Democrats, as the Governor of this Nation's most Democratic State, I would regret to see the day come when Mississippi or the South should break with the Democratic Party in a national election. But vital principles and eternal truths transcend party lines, and the day is now at hand when determined action must be taken.

We have repeatedly seen the proposal of various measures in the Congress which were not for the best interests of the Nation but definitely designed to appeal to certain voting groups holding the balance of power in other States. We of the South will no longer tolerate being the target for this type of legislation which would not only destroy our way of life, but which, if enacted, would eventually destroy the United States. The time has come for the militant people of the South and the Nation, who have never shirked any patriotic responsibility, to band together for the preservation of true Americanism. United in our cause, we serve not only ourselves and our neighbors, but all of our fellow citizens throughout the Nation.

As we face this particular task I invite the patience, calm deliberation, counsel, and cooperation of all men of good will and true Americanism, wherever they may be. We are Democrats; we have been loyal to the Democratic Party at all times, in its periods of success as well as in the dark days of despair. We voted the Democratic ticket when no other section stayed with the banner. We have never shirked, nor have we ever faltered in our loyalty to our party. There are some who subscribe to the belief that due to this record of faithful service we are taken for granted and are not deemed worthy of consideration in formulating party policy and platforms. A continuation of the harassing and unfair legislation to which I have referred will compel all of us to such a conclusion.

This is a new day in State and national politics and circumstances may make necessary a new, and, we hope, a temporary approach to national politics by our State and Southland. We have always remained true to the traditions of our party and will continue to do so, but when the national leaders attempt to change those principles for which the party stands, we intend to fight for its preservation with all means at our hands. We must make our national leaders fully realize we mean precisely what we say, and we must, if necessary, implement our words with positive action. We warn them now, to take heed. Drastic though our methods may be, and as far reaching as the results may prove, we are certain that the ultimate consequence will fully justify any temporary set-back that may follow our action.

HARRY S. TRUMAN, CIVIL RIGHTS MESSAGE
February 2, 1948

To the Congress of the United States:

In the state of the Union message on Jan. 7, 1948, I spoke of five great goals toward which we should strive in our constant effort to strengthen our democracy and improve the welfare of our people. The first of these is to secure fully our essential human rights. I am now presenting to the Congress my recommendations for legislation to carry us forward toward that goal.

This nation was founded by men and women who sought these shores that they might enjoy greater freedom and greater opportunity than they had known before. The founders of the United States proclaimed to the world the American belief that all men are created equal, and that Governments are instituted to secure the inalienable rights with which all men are endowed. In the Declaration of Independence and the Constitution of the United States, they eloquently expressed the aspirations of all mankind for equality and freedom.

These ideals inspired the peoples of other lands and their practical fulfillment made the United States the hope of the oppressed everywhere. Throughout our history men and women of all colors and creeds, of all races and religions, have come to this country to escape tyranny and discrimination. Millions strong, they have helped build this democratic nation and have constantly reinforced our devotion to the great ideals of liberty and equality.

With those who preceded them, they have helped to fashion and strengthen our American faith—a faith that can be simply stated:

We believe that all men are created equal and that they have the right to equal justice under law.

We believe that all men have the right to freedom of thought and of expression and the right to worship as they please.

We believe that all men are entitled to equal opportunities for jobs, for homes, for good health and for education.

We believe that all men should have a voice in their government and that government should protect, not usurp, the rights of the people.

These are the basic civil rights which are the source and the support of our democracy.

Today, the American people enjoy more freedom and opportunity than ever before. Never in our history has there been better reason to hope for the complete realization of the ideals of liberty and equality.

New York Times, February 3, 1948.

We shall not, however, finally achieve the ideals for which this nation was founded so long as any American suffers discrimination as a result of his race, or religion, or color, or the land of origin of his forefathers.

Unfortunately, there still are examples—flagrant examples—of discrimination which are utterly contrary to our ideals. Not all groups of our population are free from the fear of violence. Not all groups are free to live and work where they please or to improve their conditions of life by their own efforts. Not all groups enjoy the full privileges of citizenship and participation in the government under which they live.

We cannot be satisfied until all our people have equal opportunities for jobs, for homes, for education, for health and for political expression, and until all our people have equal protection under the law.

One year ago, I appointed a committee of fifteen distinguished Americans and asked them to appraise the condition of our civil rights and to recommend appropriate action by Federal, State and local governments.

The committee's appraisal has resulted in a frank and revealing report. This report emphasizes that our basic human freedoms are better cared for and more vigilantly defended than ever before. But it also makes clear that there is a serious gap between our ideals and some of our practices. This gap must be closed.

This will take the strong efforts of each of us individually, and all of us acting together through voluntary organizations and our governments.

The protection of civil rights begins with the mutual respect for the rights of others which all of us should practice in our daily lives. Through organizations in every community in all parts of the country—we must continue to develop practical, workable arrangements for achieving greater tolerance and brotherhood.

The protection of civil rights is the duty of every government which derives its powers from the consent of the people. This is equally true of local, state and national governments. There is much that the states can and should do at this time to extend their protection of civil rights. Wherever the law enforcement measures of State and local governments are inadequate to discharge this primary function of government, these measures should be strengthened and improved.

The Federal Government has a clear duty to see that constitutional guarantees of individual liberties and of equal protection under the laws are not denied or abridged anywhere in our Union. That duty is shared by all three branches of the Government, but it can be fulfilled only if the Congress enacts modern, comprehensive civil rights laws, adequate to the needs of the day, and demonstrating our continuing faith in the free way of life.

I recommend, therefore, that the Congress enact legislation at this session directed toward the following specific objectives:

1. Establishing a permanent Commission on Civil Rights, a Joint Congressional Committee on Civil Rights, and a Civil Rights Division in the Department of Justice.

2. Strengthening existing civil rights statutes.

3. Providing Federal protection against lynching.

4. Protecting more adequately the right to vote.

5. Establishing a Fair Employment Practice Commission to prevent unfair discrimination in employment.

6. Prohibiting discrimination in interstate transportation facilities.

7. Providing home rule and suffrage in Presidential elections for the residents of the District of Columbia.

8. Providing statehood for Hawaii and Alaska and a greater measure of self-government for our island possessions.

9. Equalizing the opportunities for residents of the United States to become naturalized citizens.

10. Settling the evacuation claims of Japanese-Americans.

As a first step, we must strengthen the organization of the Federal Government in order to enforce civil rights legislation more adequately and to watch over the state of our traditional liberties.

I recommend that the Congress establish a permanent Commission on Civil Rights, reporting to the President. The Commission should continuously review our civil rights policies and practices, study specific problems and make recommendations to the President at frequent intervals. It should work with other agencies of the Federal Government, with state and local governments and with private organizations.

I also suggest that the Congress establish a Joint Congressional Committee on Civil Rights. This committee should make a continuing study of legislative matters relating to civil rights and should consider means of improving respect for and enforcement of those rights.

These two bodies together should keep all of us continuously aware of the condition of civil rights in the United States and keep us alert to opportunities to improve their protection.

To provide for better enforcement of Federal civil rights laws, there will be established a Division of Civil Rights in the Department of Justice. I recommend that the Congress provide for an additional assistant Attorney General to supervise this division.

I recommend that the Congress amend and strengthen the existing provisions of Federal law which safeguard the right to vote and the right to safety and security of person and property. These provisions are the basis for our present civil rights enforcement program.

Section 51 of Title 18 of the United States Code, which now gives protection to citizens in the enjoyment of rights secured by the Constitution or Federal laws, needs to be strengthened in two respects. In its present form, this section protects persons only if they are citizens, and it affords protection only against conspiracies by two or more persons.

This protection should be extended to all inhabitants of the United States. Whether or not they are citizens and should be afforded against infringement by persons acting individually, as well as in conspiracy.

Section 52 of Title 18 of the United States Code, which now gives general protection to individuals against the deprivation of Federally secured rights by public officers, has proved to be inadequate in some cases because of the generality of its language. An enumeration of the principal rights protected under this section is needed to make more definite and certain the protection which the section affords.

A specific Federal measure is needed to deal with the crime of lynching—against which I cannot speak too strongly.

It is a principle of our democracy, written into our Constitution, that every person accused of an offense against the law shall have a fair, orderly trial in an impartial court. We have made great progress towards this end, but I regret to say that lynching has not yet finally disappeared from our land. So long as one person walks in fear of lynching, we shall not have achieved equal justice under law.

I call upon the Congress to take decisive action against this crime.

Under the Constitution, the right of all properly qualified citizens to vote is beyond question.

Yet the exercise of this right is still subject to interference. Some individuals are prevented from voting by isolated acts of intimidation. Some whole groups are prevented by outmoded policies prevailing in certain states or communities.

We need stronger statutory protection of the right to vote. I urge the Congress to enact legislation forbidding interference by public officers or private persons with the right of qualified citizens to participate in primary, special and general elections in which Federal officers are to be chosen. This legislation should extend to elections for state as well as Federal officers in so far as interference with the right to vote results from discriminatory action by public officers based on race, color, or other unreasonable classification.

Requirements for the payment of poll taxes also interfere with the right to vote. There are still seven states which, by their Constitutions have this barrier between their citizens and the ballot box. The American people would welcome voluntary action on the part of these states to remove this barrier.

Nevertheless, I believe the Congress should enact measures insuring that the right to vote in elections for Federal officers shall not be contingent upon the payment of taxes.

I wish to make it clear that the enactment of the measures I have recommended will in no sense result in Federal conduct of elections. They are designed to give qualified citizens Federal protection of their right to vote. The actual conduct of elections, as always, will remain the responsibility of state governments.

We in the United States believe that all men are entitled to equality of opportunity. Racial, religious and other invidious forms of discrimination deprive the individual of an equal chance to develop and utilize his talents and to enjoy the rewards of his efforts.

Once more I repeat my request that Congress enact fair employment practice legislation prohibiting discrimination in employment based on race, color, religion or national origin. The legislation should create a Fair Employment Practice Commission with authority to prevent discrimination by employers and labor unions, trade and professional associations and Government agencies and employment bureaus.

The degree of effectiveness which the wartime Fair Employment Practice Committee attained shows that it is possible to equalize job opportunity by Government action, and thus to eliminate the influence of prejudice in employment.

The channels of interstate commerce should be open to all Americans on a basis of complete equality. The Supreme Court has recently declared unconstitutional state laws requiring segregation on public carriers in interstate travel. Company regulations must not be allowed to replace institutional state laws. I urge the Congress to prohibit discrimination and segregation, in the use of interstate transportation facilities, by both public officers and the employes of private companies.

I am in full accord with the principle of local self-government for residents of the District of Columbia. In addition, I believe that the Constitution should be amended to extend suffrage in Presidential elections to the residents of the district.

The District of Columbia should be a true symbol of American freedom and democracy for our own people and for the people of the world. It is my earnest hope that the Congress will promptly give the citizens of the District of Columbia their own local, elective government.

They themselves can then deal with the inequalities arising from segregation in the schools and other public facilities and from racial barriers to places of public accommodation which now exist for one-third of the district's population.

The present inequalities in essential services are primarily a problem for the District itself, but they are also of great concern to the whole nation. Failing local corrective action in the near future, the Congress should enact a model civil rights law for the nation's capital.

The present political status of our territories and possessions impairs the enjoyment of civil rights by their residents.

I have in the past recommended legislation granting statehood to Alaska and Hawaii, and organic acts for Guam and American Samoa, including a grant of citizenship to the people of these Pacific islands. I repeat these recommendations.

Furthermore, the residents of the Virgin Islands should be granted an increasing measure of self-government and the people of Puerto Rico should be allowed to choose their form of government and their ultimate status with respect to the United States.

All properly qualified legal residents of the United States should be allowed to become citizens without regard to race, color, religion or national origin.

The Congress has recently removed the bars which formerly prevented persons from China, India and the Philippines from becoming naturalized citizens. I urge the Congress to remove the remaining racial or nationality barriers which stand in the way of citizenship for some residents of our country.

During the last war more than 100,000 Japanese-Americans were evacuated from their homes in the Pacific States solely because of their racial origin. Many of these people suffered property and business losses as a result of this forced evacuation and through no fault of their own.

The Congress has before it legislation establishing a procedure by which claims based upon these losses can be promptly considered and settled. I trust that favorable action on this legislation will soon be taken.

The legislation I have recommended for enactment by the Congress at the present session is a minimum program if the Federal Government is to fulfill its obligation of insuring the Constitutional guarantees of individual liberties and of equal protection under the law.

Under the authority of existing law, the Executive Branch is taking every possible action to improve the enforcement of the Civil Rights Statutes and to eliminate discrimination in Federal employment, in providing Federal services and facilities, and in the Armed Forces.

I have already referred to the establishment of the Civil Rights Division of the Department of Justice. The Federal Bureau of Investigation will work closely with this new division in the investigation of Federal Civil Rights Cases. Specialized training is being given to the Bureau's agents so that they may render more effective service in this difficult field of law enforcement.

It is the settled policy of the United States Government that there shall be no discrimination in Federal employment or in providing Federal services and facilities. Steady progress has been made toward this objective in recent years. I shall shortly issue an Executive Order containing a comprehensive restatement of the Federal non-discrimination policy, together with appropriate measures to ensure compliance.

During the recent war and in the years since its close we have made much progress toward equality of opportunity in our Armed Services without regard to race, color, religion or national origin. I have instructed the Secretary of Defense to take steps to have the remaining instances of discrimination in the Armed Services eliminated as rapidly as possible. The personnel policies and practices of all the Services in this regard will be made consistent.

I have instructed the Secretary of the Army to investigate the status of civil rights in the Panama Canal Zone with a view to eliminating such discrimination as may exist there. If legislation is necessary, I shall make appropriate recommendations to the Congress.

The position of the United States in the world today makes it especially urgent that we adopt these measures to secure for all our people their essential rights.

The peoples of the world are faced with the choice of freedom or enslavement, a choice between a form of government which harnesses the State in the service of the individual and a form of government which chains the individual to the needs of the State.

We in the United States are working in company with other nations who share our desire for enduring world peace and who believe with us that, above all else, men must be free. We are striving to build a world family of nations—a world where men may live under governments of their own choosing and under laws of their own making.

As part of that endeavor, the Commission on Human Rights of the United Nations is now engaging in preparing an international bill of human rights by which the nations of the world may bind themselves by international covenant to give effect to basic human rights and fundamental freedoms. We have played a leading role in this undertaking designed to create a world order of law and justice fully protective of the rights and the dignity of the individual.

To be effective in these efforts, we must protect our civil rights so that by providing all our people with the maximum enjoyment of personal freedom and personal opportunity we shall be a stronger nation—stronger in our leadership, stronger in our moral position, stronger in the deeper satisfactions of a united citizenry.

We know that our democracy is not perfect. But we do not know that it offers a fuller, freer, happier life to our people than any totalitarian nation has ever offered.

If we wish to inspire the peoples of the world whose freedom is in jeopardy, if we wish to restore hope to those who have already lost their civil liberties, if we wish to fulfill the promise that is ours, we must correct the remaining imperfections in our practice of democracy.

We know the way. We need only the will.

Harry S. Truman

J. STROM THURMOND
MOTION AT SOUTHERN GOVERNORS' CONFERENCE
Wakulla Springs, Florida
February 7, 1948

The people of the States represented by the members of this conference here have been shocked by the spectacle of the political parties of this country engaging in competitive bidding for the votes of small pressure groups by attacking the traditions, customs, and institutions of the section in which we live.

Our people have been engaged for many years in a tremendous effort to restore our section to the place in the economy of the Nation which it should rightfully occupy. On the solution of our economic problems depend the education, welfare, and progress of all of our people and we have spared no effort to solve those problems. Economic underprivilege in the South has known no color line; it has fallen heavily on all races alike. The people of the Nation are well aware of the headway which we have already made toward solving the economic problems of our people, and it will be as a result of the solution of our economic problems that our racial problems will disappear.

Despite our sound, constructive, and sure progress, the political leaders of the country have been unwilling to respect our accomplishments and to let us continue with the task. Their political attacks are calculated only to hamper our efforts and actually militate against the welfare of the very people whom they assert they are trying to help. Under the compulsion of petty political considerations, they have seen fit to outrage and insult our people because they think we have no place to which we can turn.

Without sincerity and in utter disregard of the facts, they again propose a so-called antilynching bill. They ignore the fact that the crime of lynching has been virtually stamped out in the South without outside interference. It is a matter of common knowledge that this legislation would be an unconstitutional invasion of the field of government of the several States.

They have again sponsored a so-called anti-poll-tax bill. It is a matter of common knowledge that this type of legislation is an unconstitutional infringement upon the right of the several States to prescribe voting qualifications.

They talk about breaking down the laws which knowledge and experience of many years have proven to be essential to the protection of the racial integrity and purity of the white and the Negro races alike. The superficial objections to these laws arise from economic rather than political causes, and their sudden removal would jeopardize the peace and good order which prevails where the two races live side by

Congressional Record, 80th Cong., 2d sess., 1948, 94, pt. 1, 1198-99.

side in large numbers. As a nation we have favored the protection of racial autonomy and integrity in other lands, such as Palestine and India, but a different doctrine is sought to be applied here at home.

They advocate a so-called fair employment practice law, which every thinking American citizen, upon reflection, will recognize to be an anti-American invasion of the fundamental conception of free enterprise upon which our economic structure is erected and which made America great. The right of a man to own and operate his own business, in which he has his savings and to which he devotes his labor and his energy, is to be impaired or destroyed by governmental interference under the guise of protecting the right to work. In effect, such a law would render every private business in this Nation a quasi-public one. Employer and employee alike are adversely affected by this type of legislation, and the concepts upon which it is based are appropriate, not to the American way of life but only to the economic and political philosophy of the Communist Party.

We are expected to stand idle and let all of this happen, for the sole purpose of enticing an infinitesimal minority of organized pressure blocs to vote for one or another candidate for the Presidency. It is thought that we have no redress. This assumption ignores the electoral college set up in the Constitution of the United States.

We should approach the situation thus presented with dignity, self-respect and restraint. We should refuse to be stampeded or to indulge in idle oratory. We must consider the matter calmly and deliberately to the end that by joint and common action and decision we may demand and obtain for our people the consideration and respect to which they are entitled. We must no longer permit pressure groups by their adroit activities to establish by propaganda and political maneuvering a nuisance value for themselves in election years which threatens to defeat the political rights of others and endanger the progress which we in the South have made to better the lot and circumstance of all our people.

Therefore, I move, Mr. Chairman, that this conference go on record as deploring all ill-considered proposals which have the effect of dividing our people at a time when national unity is vital to the establishment of peace in this troubled world; and that this conference set a meeting not later than 40 days from this date, at a time and place to be designated by the chairman, for the careful consideration of the problems of the Southern States arising from such proposals; and that the chair do appoint a committee from the membership of this conference to make careful inquiry and investigation into such problems, and their solution by joint and common action, and to report to the conference at that meeting, with their recommendations as to further action which may be taken in the premises.

SOUTHERN GOVERNORS' COMMITTEE
STATEMENT OF DEMOCRATIC CIVIL RIGHTS PROGRAM
Washington, February 23, 1948

The following statement was made after the Committee had conferred with Democratic National Chairman J. Howard McGrath on Truman's civil rights program.

Following the Southern Governors' conference at Tallahassee setting up our committee, we began an inquiry to determine the most effective ways and means of securing concerted action on the part of the South in opposing the so-called civil-rights program. We have communicated with party leaders in the various Southern states. We have secured the viewpoints of the Democratic members of Congress from the South. We have surveyed the opinion of rank-and-file Democrats in every walk of life—the people who have furnished the votes which have made the South solid for the Democratic party.

As a part of our study and inquiry, we asked for a conference with the operating head of the party, Chairman J. Howard McGrath of the Democratic National Committee. We propounded certain questions to Chairman McGrath which have been made public.

Governor Lane of Maryland, Chairman of the Southern Governors Conference, who sat with us in our meetings in Washington, will announce shortly the time and place of the meeting of the full conference to receive and consider the committee's report. In the interest of concerted and unified action, we shall not make public our report and recommendations until they have been passed on by the Southern Governors Conference.

The committee, however, feels that the following statement should be made at this time:

> A vast majority of the Democrats of the South are determined to restore the Democratic party to the principles of Jefferson and Jackson and will resort to whatever means are necessary to accomplish this end. The Democrats of the South are united in their opposition to the so-called civil-rights program proposed by the President and effective action in the Southern states will be taken to prevent adoption of this program.
>
> We feel we are expressing the firm conviction of our people when we say that the present leadership of the Democratic party has deserted the

New York Times, February 24, 1948.

principles of government upon which the Democratic party was founded. As never before, the time has come for strong and effective action by the Southern states not only to save the Democratic party but to preserve the rights of the states to govern themselves and preserve American democracy.

In this fight we are not only expecting support from the Democrats of the South but support from Democrats everywhere who are opposed to a centralized government invading the rights of the people and the rights of the respective states.

The Southern states are aroused and the present leadership of the Democratic party will soon realize that the South is no longer "in the bag." Each Southern state, under the framework of an over-all program, will work out the most effective means of resisting the proposals of the present leadership of the party, but resist them we will.

SOUTHERN GOVERNORS' CIVIL RIGHTS RESOLUTION
March 13, 1948

Resolved by the Conference of Southern Governors in meeting assembled in Washington this 13th day of March 1948:

1. That we go on record as repudiating the present national leadership of the Democratic Party in sponsoring the so-called civil-rights program;

2. That we recommend to the people of the Southern States that they fight to the last ditch to prevent the nomination of any candidate for President or Vice President who advocates such invasions of State sovereignty as those proposed in the said program; and we pledge our influence in our respective States to the objectives that the delegates to the national convention will support and fight for a positive declaration for States' rights in the party platform and will support only candidates for President and Vice President who entertain similar views;

3. That we recommend to the people of the Southern States that if the National Democratic Party should nominate any candidate who advocates such invasions of State sovereignty as those proposed in the said program, they shall see to it that the Electoral College votes of their States are not cast for such nominees; and we pledge our influence in our respective States to this end.

Resolved further, That in order to carry out the foregoing recommendations, we urge that the people of the respective Southern States, with due regard to the time available and the local circumstances, take all effective political action possible, which may include some or all of the following:

(a) The adoption and transmission to the chairman of the Democratic National Committee of a resolution by the State conventions or the authorized body of the State Democratic Party expressing the opposition of the party in the State to the usurpation and infringement of the sovereignty of the States of the Union required by the enactment of any portion of the so-called civil-rights program; an outright declaration that the party within the State will not support the candidacy of any candidate for the Democratic nomination for President or Vice President who is in sympathy with the same; a clear statement of their belief that the principles involved are above and beyond personalities and parties and cannot be surrendered under any circumstances; and their determination to do everything possible to see that the electoral vote of the State shall not be cast for candidates who do not have the same belief.

(b) The instruction by the respective State conventions of their delegates to the national convention to propose and work for the adoption of a plank in the national

Congressional Record, 80th Cong., 2d sess., 1948, 94, pt. 10, *Appendix,* pp. A1594-95.

party platform upholding the sovereignty of the several States of the Union, and opposing the enactment of such invasions of that sovereignty as the proposed FECP law, the proposed antilynching law, the proposed antipoll tax law, and Federal laws interfering with State and local laws relating to the separation of the races, and any other laws violating State sovereignty.

(c) The instruction by the respective State conventions of their delegates to the national convention to propose and work for the restoration of the two-thirds rule.

(d) That the Democratic State organizations which send delegates to the National Democratic Convention do so with advance notice in writing to the national convention, given before the delegates take any part therein, containing the terms and reservations prescribed by the State convention upon which the said delegates shall participate in the national convention.

(e) The deferring by State conventions of the nomination of their electors for President and Vice-President until after the holding of the national convention.

(f) The adoption of a resolution by the respective State conventions pledging their electors to vote only for candidates in the electoral college not in sympathy with such violations of in the sovereignty of the States of the Union as those required by the so-called civil-rights program.

(g) The adoption by the respective State conventions of a resolution providing that the electors for President and Vice President shall be pledged to cast their electoral ballots in the electoral college as requested to do by the party's State convention of State executive committee.

(h) A caucus of the Presidential and Vice Presidential electors of the Southern States so that they can take concerted action in the electoral college if necessary.

(i) The holding of the party leaders in the Southern States of conferences for the purpose of developing and carrying out direct, positive, effective, and aggressive joint action, in order that the political strength of the South will be exerted to the fullest in national party councils and in the national convention.

Resolved further, That the State conventions take action to provide that the Democratic Party in the respective States shall continue to function as such on all other levels, including the election of local, county, and State officials, and United States Senators and Congressmen, without regard to the action which may be taken in the State in reference to the election of Presidential and Vice Presidential electors.

Resolved further, That we recognize and commend the efforts of our Senators and Representatives in the National Congress who have fought, and are engaged in fighting, the so-called civil-rights program, and we urge them to carry on their fight to the end, with the assurance that our people are standing firmly and irrevocably behind them.

GOV. FRANK M. DIXON OF ALABAMA,
KEYNOTE ADDRESS AT SOUTHERN DEMOCRATIC CONVENTION
Birmingham, July 17, 1948

It is an honor to be called upon to make this keynote speech to this great gathering today—an honor I deeply feel. For this is a gathering of militant followers of those democratic principles near and dear to us all.

The meeting is a continuation of the Jackson convention which was held on May 10, and in which nearly all of the Southern States were represented. In the resolutions of that convention, it was provided that if Truman was the nominee of the Democratic Party, or if a platform was adopted at Philadelphia hostile to the South, then the Birmingham meeting should be held.

You are familiar with what happened in Philadelphia. You know that the definite decision was made there by the National Democratic Party to approve Truman's actions in trying to enforce a social revolution in the South. You heard the jeers of the followers of the city machines of the North when the fine southerners of Alabama and Mississippi walked out of that convention. You heard the demands for the destruction of the social structure of the South coming from Democrats in sections where not one single elective public officer is a Democrat—not even a justice of the peace. I cite the case of Minnesota. You heard the deliberate adoption of a program meant to destroy us.

Everyone in America is familiar with the history of democratic action so far as this civil-rights program is concerned. Not all are familiar with the personnel of the Truman Committee on Civil Rights. Suffice to say, without attempting to go into the various personalities, that it was a committee stacked for the purpose of rendering the report which it did, a committee biased and prejudiced in advance. Its appointment, with that personnel as if it were a committee to make an impartial investigation, was a sham and a fraud on the American people. The report which it rendered required no deliberation—it required simply the stenographic services necessary to write down the prejudices and animosities of its members.

What is this so-called civil-rights program which Truman, our Democratic President, has recommended to Congress? I do not want any misunderstanding about it among the Southern white people. Here is part of what it means:

First. The elimination of segregation in the public schools from grade schools through colleges. Your children are to be required to work and play in the company, with the forced association, of Negroes. Negroes are to teach them, guide them. What will that mean to your children, to your hopes for them? What

---

Congressional Record, 80th Cong., 2d sess., 1948, 94, pt. 12, *Appendix,* pp. A 4672-73.

will it mean in immorality, in vice, in crime? Just what it means in those slum areas of the Northern cities where like conditions prevail, with results fatal to decency.

Second. The elimination of segregation in private and ultimately in denominational schools, such as Judson, Huntington, Howard, and Birmingham-Southern, as to students and teachers as well. I am using local, Alabama institutions as examples, but the application is not solely to them. The effect is to be the same in all schools, boys' and girls' as well, from Maine to California. Suppose that you are determined not to subject your children to biracial schools, and are willing to make any sacrifice to that end. You are helpless, since even private schools are to be forced to permit Negroes to attend.

Third. The elimination of segregation in trains, busses, restaurants, theaters, beauty shops, hotels, swimming pools, ball games, churches, and everywhere else people congregate. Picture life with us, men and women, when every time we leave our homes these conditions are forced upon us. Picture the stores, the streetcars, the busses, restaurants, the churches. Picture the bitterness, the racial hostility, the violence which will follow.

Fourth. The elimination of segregation in places of residence and homes. This means that Negroes can build in any neighborhood, live in any apartment house.

Fifth. The employment of Negroes in every business establishment, office, factory and store, in the same numerical proportion that the Negro race bears to the white. While the ratio is not written into the report, we well know from the operation of the wartime FEPC of infamous memory that this is the aim and that the tools of oppression will be devoted to that end. In my own county of Jefferson there are 43 percent Negroes, in Alabama generally 35 percent, in some counties 6 to 1. A department store in Jefferson County that has 100 clerks must have 43 Negroes among them; a restaurant or beauty shop employing 10 must have 4 to 5; a plant employing 1,000 must have 430. If this ratio does not now prevail, then enough white employees must be fired to make it possible. How else can it be obtained? Any law office, any physician's office, comes under the law just as much and no more than any other place of business.

Sixth. There is to be an upgrading in jobs, and promotions on an equal basis, and the ratio must apply to all levels. There must be as many Negro foremen, as many department heads, as many bosses, as the ratio calls for. They are to be over whites and Negroes alike, mixed together without regard to the wishes of anyone.

Seventh. There is to be no segregation in hospitals, either as to physicians, patients or nurses. White men and women who must necessarily use the hospitals, public and private, are to be attended by Negro physicians and nurses, as well as by white.

Eighth. All segregation in labor unions and professional associations such as the Bar Association and the Medical Association is to be done away with.

Ninth. The poll tax is to be eliminated, all Negroes to be registered to vote without regard to intelligence or capacity, and all segregation is to be done away with in the armed services.

Is all this a real threat, or is it just politics? Are these so-called Democrats actually determined to destroy our way of life? I assure you that the danger is deadly in its seriousness.

The Civil Rights Section of the Department of Justice is to be reorganized to enforce it. Constant police inspection and supervision, through a Federal Gestapo, is recommended, without waiting for complaints. The law is to be changed to make conviction easy. Enforcement is to be taken away from the local officials. Civil-court orders, punished as contempt of court, are to supplement the criminal proceedings enforceable by the FBI. Criminal penalties are to be by fine up to $5,000, and imprisonment up to 10 years. Every local police officer and deputy sheriff is to be subject to Federal criminal and civil laws, and under constant scrutiny.

Tax-exemption privileges are to be taken away from the private and ultimately denominational schools which resist, and from the churches.

Federal grants-in-aid are to be taken from States or cities which resist.

Fines and jail terms are to be part of local officials or private citizens who resist.

This vicious program means to eliminate all difference, all separation between black and white. It so declares itself, in words. It means to create a great melting pot of the South, with white and Negroes intermingled socially, politically, economically. It means to reduce us to the status of a mongrel, inferior race, mixed in blood, our Anglo-Saxon heritage a mockery; to crush with imprisonment our leadership, and thereby kill our hopes, our aspirations, our future and the future of our children.

It seems to me to be useless to repeat the arguments as to the unconstitutionality of the proposed enactment by Congress of an antilynching act. Such an act was declared unconstitutional by the Supreme Court of the United States in the seventies when it bore the nomenclature of the force bill. Such an act has been fought by some of the best and most distinguished Americans of other sections of the country—men of the character of President McKinley, and Senators Norris and Borah. The proposed antilynching act, as recommended by the committee and as supported by Truman, goes far beyond the old iniquitous force bills. It was written patently and obviously to buy the Negro vote in the doubtful States—we of the South know that there is no lynching in the South. They of the North know it. And they also know that the race riots and the killings which have made some northern cities famous in these last few years have no duplicate in any State or city in the South.

They know, also, these who seek to create a police state, that the surest way to do it is to take over the enforcement of criminal law. Lynching is murder. There is a law in every State against it, and these laws are enforced. Bring the Federal Government into the field of local law enforcement and you have broken down one of the great safeguards of personal freedom. Break this first one, and the precedent has been laid for persecution against which no citizen is safe.

With this the program of the National Democratic Party, do we belong to it? If this is the meaning of the plank adopted at Philadelphia, are our people to remain in it? Are they to say to the Nation: "All right, we don't like it, but we choose, and our people choose, to wear the shackles of this kind of slavery rather than to break with the national democracy, rotten though it may be, and the avowed enemy of our people."

Is this civil rights program constitutional? Not under any decisions of the courts in the past, not with any court save possibly our Supreme Court as at present constituted. The tenth amendment to the Constitution reads as follows: "The powers not delegated to the United States by the Constitution, nor prohibited by it to the States, are reserved to the States respectively, or to the people." The powers of local self-government are not given to Congress, but are reserved to the States, and these include every feature of the so-called civil rights program. We are fundamentally sound in this fight, whatever the present-day politics of the doubtful States, for whose benefit we are being sold down the river.

The term "States' rights" means much more than simple theory—it means the preservation of democracy and freedom itself. The oldest form of government in the world is the highly centralized one, with all power concentrated, as in Washington. There were tyrannies in the dim mists of history. It is only with the founding of this country that democracy developed, and it came, and this country grew great, because the Federal government was locked and tied down by the Constitution to the point that it could not impose its will on the people in their daily lives.

Schools are local affairs, as is the police force, the fire department, the city and county governments, the habits of the people, the building of roads, the conduct of local business, all the myriad affairs of daily life. The right to work or to loaf, to choose your vocation, and change your job, to guide the education of your children, to attend the church of your choice, to work with whom you please, to go where you choose, these are not inherent and divine rights. They are ours solely because the Federal Government was denied the power to interfere with them.

In this so-called civil-rights program, Truman advocates granting the power to the Federal Government to invade these and all other freedoms. The program is aimed at us, of course, since it is to secure Negro votes in the doubtful States. But those leaders hostile to us will find their people, as well as we, come under such a program. They will find that their freedom, as well as ours, is gone. Properly understood in all its viciousness and danger, this program will receive the condemnation of right-thinking people everywhere. We will not stand alone in this fight.

How is it possible for a man who calls himself a Democrat, for a man who is a follower of the principles which have made the Democratic Party great, to lend himself to any scheme meant to aggrandize the power of the Federal Government in Washington and to permit the formation of a gestapo charged with the mission of revolutionizing the social life of the Nation. The Democratic Party has been a tower of strength throughout the years in the maintenance of the personal freedoms of the individual. The Democratic Party has believed forever in the limited powers of the Federal Government under the Constitution. The great men through the pages of history who have been placed in high positions by the Democratic Party have been men who were firm in their refusal to permit the seizure of power in Washington.

Government essentially is a dangerous thing. There is no truth more fundamental than that power seeks always to increase. Human nature is a compound of many things. Its sole, continuously recurring characteristic is the desire deep in the hearts of all for power. Government is a dangerous thing, and the great leaders of the past, except the military men who have been despots, the great leaders since there came into existence the theory of the rights of men, have with universal tongue cautioned the people against the danger of power in the hands of the Government. This was understood and completely understood by the great founders of this Republic. It was understood, and completely understood, by the founders of the party of Democrats. And yet in this day and generation, the national Democratic Party has sunk so low as to be willing to barter, for the votes of racial minorities in doubtful States, the liberties of all of us.

The term "States rights" is an unfortunate term. It does not express the meaning of the thought which is in our minds. In the beginning of this Republic, the States were supreme. They surrendered a portion of their power to the Federal Government in order that the Union might exist. But there were three great bodies of rights. There were the rights which the State had over its citizens; there were the rights which the States surrendered to the Federal Government; there were the great body of rights which neither State nor Federal Governments ever had over its citizens, those rights which contain personal liberty and the freedoms which make life worth while. When the Federal Government moves against rights which the States had, then the term "States' rights" is applicable. When it moves against that great body outside any government to control, as it is doing now, then it becomes the enemy of every free American. That will not stop government, that thought, since government lives and thrives on power. But it behooves those of us over our citizens in a Republic still free to be on guard always against the invasion of our freedoms and to remain determined to resist to the end.

As most of Alabama knows, I have never been one of those who fomented hatred between the two races. There is room for both, separate and apart. Segregation is our way of life, essential to peace and good will. There are many Negroes among us completely worthy of full citizenship, honest, decent, self-respecting, and God-fearing people. They are being given the vote; they live their own lives, leaders among their own. They wish no forced association with white people; they know its consequences in bitterness and terror. They, as we, are victims of the political situation in the doubtful States, where Republican and Democrat alike offer us as the mess of pottage with which elections are to be purchased—cynically betraying their own blood and heritage for political spoils.

We are faced by facts, not theories. We have worked out a way of life, in difficult circumstances, between the two races. The Negro race has progressed further in threescore years than any race in history. It has progressed because it has had the sympathetic help of the southern white people of good will. It can continue to progress only with a continuance of that sympathetic help. That assistance is based on segregation, on keeping the races apart, a system necessary for white as well as blacks. Destroy it and chaos will result.

The question is continually asked, "What can we do? Where are we going?" This is what the convention is here to decide. We have several possible courses of action. I will mention only two. We can name a candidate for President and Vice President and recommend to the people of the several States that they elect electors pledged to those nominees. It is thought by some that this is the proper method of procedure. Another route which can be followed is to suggest to the various Southern States the selection of free electors. This is the system that we have followed in Alabama, and in the beginning of this movement, we planned that the electors from Alabama should, after the general elections in November, meet with the electors from the other Southern States and agree upon a candidate for whom their votes should be cast. This was the system which was planned by the founding fathers of this Republic, and this is the system which we in Alabama have wanted to follow. We are not, however, determined to follow any course that will not fit the needs and necessities of the other Southern States. We are willing to go to any length to secure unanimity of action.

Should this be a Republican year, then of course we will have accomplished nothing, save to enforce our demands for recognition in the Democratic Party. Should the party of Truman succeed between now and the general election in gaining enough strength to be a real contender, then this movement could easily become the deciding factor in the American political scene, since we would have approximately 129 electors and might easily be able to throw the election into Congress. There is not much satisfaction with Dewey among the Republican States. There is not much satisfaction with Truman among the Democratic States. Congress might easily turn to an outstanding American selected by us for the next President of the United States.

A word of caution also to those who are of the opinion that this is not a grass roots movement. I have been in receipt of hundreds of telephone calls, most of them from so-called little people, not office holders, not people of particular prominence. There is a firm conviction in their minds that they are not being properly represented by those who are in positions of authority over them. There is a feeling in their minds that the office holder is more afraid of the loss of his job and of his perquisites than he is enthusiastic for the call of the people. I have been amazed at the intensity of this action. There may be those among the occupiers of high public positions in the South who think that they can weasel their way through and weather the storm. But if I am any political prophet, our people are more aroused than they have been in many, many years, and they will repay by retirement to private life the efforts of any so-called southern leaders who hope to carry them into the camp of Harry S. Truman in the coming election.

We people of the South have had our divisions. The Nation was treated to a sample of those divisions at the Philadelphia Convention, when a portion of the Alabama delegation and the Mississippi delegation in a body walked out, while other States with people just as truly southern and as truly loyal as ours remained in their seats after the adoption of the plank approving this iniquitous so-called civil rights legislation. We have our divisions in Alabama politics, every southern State has divisions within itself in its political life. These are part of the workings of democracy itself. These divisions, however, cease in the face of a common danger to us and to our wives and children. These divisions cease in the face of the threat to our very existence. We who are active in this movement want the help of every man, woman, and child—we want all divisions forgotten. We want the strength that comes with unity. We want and must have, if we are to have any hope of success, the men and women of the South united, determined, self-sacrificing, devoted to this common cause.

The people of the South are still a proud people, and they are determined not to submit to those who have repudiated the doctrines which have been those of democracy throughout all the years. They are determined not to submit to those who would wreck and destroy their civilization and mongrelize our people. They are determined, thank God, to preserve the basic principles of democracy and to prevent the establishment in this land of ours of a police state, vicious as all police states are vicious, and to prevent the end of human and personal freedom throughout this land.

STATES' RIGHTS PLATFORM OF 1948

The following was adopted by the Southern Democratic Convention held at Birmingham, Alabama, July 17, 1948.

We affirm that a political party is an instrumentality for effectuating the principles upon which the party is founded; that a platform of principles is a solemn covenant with the people and with the members of the party; that no leader of the party, in temporary power, has the right or privilege to proceed contrary to the fundamental principles of the party, or the letter or spirit of the Constitution of the United States; that to act contrary to these principles is a breach of faith, a usurpation of power, and a forfeiture of the party name and party leadership.

We believe that racial and religious minorities should be protected in their rights guaranteed by the Constitution, but the bold defiance of the Constitution in selfish appeals to such groups for the sake of political power forges the chains of slavery of such minorities by destroying the only bulwark of protection against tyrannical majorities. The protection of the constitutional rights of a minority does not justify or require the destruction of constitutional rights of the majority. The destruction of constitutional limitations on the power of the central government threatens to create a totalitarian state and to destroy individual liberty in America.

We believe that the protection of the American people against the onward march of totalitarian government requires a faithful observance of article X of the American Bill of Rights which provides that: "The powers not delegated to the United States by the Constitution, nor prohibited by it to the States, are reserved to the States respectively, or to the people.

THE PRINCIPLE OF STATES' RIGHTS

We direct attention to the fact that the first platform of the Democratic Party, adopted in 1840, resolved that: "Congress has no power under the Constitution to interfere with or control the domestic institutions of the several States, and that such States are the sole and proper judges of everything appertaining to their own affairs not prohibited by the Constitution." Such pronouncement is the cornerstone of the Democratic Party.

A long train of abuses and usurpations of power by unfaithful leaders who are alien to the Democratic Parties of the States here represented has become intolerable to those who believe in the preservation of constitutional government and individual liberty in America."

The executive department of the Government is promoting the gradual but certain growth of a totalitarian state by domination and control of a politically minded Supreme Court. As examples of the threat to our form of government, the executive department, with the aid of the Supreme Court, has asserted national dominion and control of submerged oil-bearing lands in California, schools in Oklahoma and Missouri, primary elections in Texas, South Carolina, and Louisiana, restrictive covenants in New York and the District of Columbia, and other jurisdictions, as well as religious instruction in Illinois.

PERIL TO BASIC RIGHTS

By asserting paramount Federal rights in these instances, a totalitarian concept has been promulgated which threatens the integrity of the States and the basic rights of their citizens.

We have repeatedly remonstrated with the leaders of the national organization of our party but our petitions, entreaties, and warnings have been treated with contempt. The latest response to our entreaties was a Democratic convention in Philadelphia rigged to embarrass and humiliate the South. This alleged Democratic assembly called for a civil-rights law that would eliminate segregation of every kind from all American life, prohibit all forms of discrimination in private employment, in public and private instruction and administration and treatment of students; in the operation of public and private health facilities; in all transportation, and require equal access to all places of public accommodation for persons of all races, colors, creeds, and national origin.

PROPOSED FBI POWERS

This infamous and iniquitous program calls for the reorganization of the Civil Rights Section of the Department of Justice with a substantial increase in a bureaucratic staff to be devoted exclusively to the enforcement of the civil-rights program; the establishment within the FBI of a special unit of investigators and a police state in a totalitarian, centralized, bureaucratic government.

This convention hypocritically denounced totalitarianism abroad but unblushingly proposed and approved it at home. This convention would strengthen the grip of a police state upon a liberty-loving people by the imposition of penalties upon local public officers who failed or refused to act in accordance with its ideas in suppressing mob violence.

We point out that if a foreign power undertook to force upon the people of the United States the measures advocated by the Democratic convention in Philadelphia, with respect to civil rights, it would mean war and the entire Nation would resist such effort.

The convention that insulted the South in the party platform advocated giving the Virgin Islands and other dependencies of the United States the maximum degree of local self-government. When an effort was made to amend this part of the platform so as to make it read that the party favored giving the Virgin Islands and the several States the maximum degree of local self-government, the amendment adding the words 'these several States' was stricken out and the sovereign States were denied the rights that the party favors giving the Virgin Islands.

PAST LOYALTY

We point out that the South, with clocklike regularity, has furnished the Democratic Party approximately 50 percent of the votes necessary to nominate a President every 4 years for nearly a century. In 1920 the only States in the Union that went Democratic were the 11 Southern States. Notwithstanding this rugged loyalty to the party, the masters of political intrigue now allow Republican States in which there is scarcely a Democratic officeholder to dominate and control the party and fashion its policies.

NEW POLICY

As Democrats who are irrevocably committed to democracy as defined and expounded by Thomas Jefferson, Andrew Jackson, and Woodrow Wilson, and who believe that all necessary steps must be taken for its preservation, we declare to the people of the United States as follows:

1. We believe that the Constitution of the United States is the greatest charter of human liberty ever conceived by the mind of man.

2. We oppose all efforts to invade or destroy the rights vouchsafed by it to every citizen of this Republic.

3. We stand for social and economic justice, which, we believe, can be vouchsafed to all citizens only by a strict adherence to our Constitution and the avoidance of any invasion or destruction of the constitutional rights of the States and individuals. We oppose the totalitarian, centralized, bureaucratic government and the police state called for by the platforms adopted by the Democratic and Republican conventions.

4. We stand for the segregation of the races and the racial integrity of each race; the constitutional right to choose one's associates; to accept private employment without governmental interference, and to earn one's living in any lawful way. We oppose the elimination of segregation, employment by Federal bureaucrats called for by the misnamed civil-rights program. We favor home rule, local self-government, and a minimum interference with individual rights.

5. We oppose and condemn the action of the Democratic Convention in sponsoring a civil-rights program calling for the elimination of segregation, social equality by Federal fiat, regulation of private employment practices, voting, and local law enforcement.

6. We affirm that the effective enforcement of such a program would be utterly destructive of the social, economic, and political life of the southern people, and of other localities in which there may be differences in race, creed, or national origin in appreciable numbers.

7. We stand for the checks and balances provided by the three departments of our Government. We oppose the usurpation of legislative functions by the executive and judicial departments. We unreservedly condemn the effort to establish Nation-wide a police state in this Republic that would destroy the last vestige of liberty enjoyed by a citizen.

8. We demand that there be returned to the people, to whom of right they belong, those powers needed for the preservation of human rights and the discharge of our responsibility as Democrats for human welfare. We oppose a denial of those rights by political parties, a barter or sale of those rights by a political convention, as well as any invasion or violation of those rights by the Federal Government.

We call upon all Democrats and upon all other loyal Americans who are opposed to totalitarianism at home and abroad to unite with us in ignominiously defeating Harry S. Truman and Thomas E. Dewey, and every other candidate for public office who would establish a police state in the United States of America.

Bibliographical Note

Aside from the vast number of contemporary accounts in journals such as *The Nation, The New Republic, The Progressive, Time* and *Newsweek,* there is only a small bit of worthwhile literature on the Progressives and the Dixiecrats.

A good start on the Progressives would be Karl M. Schmidt, *Henry A. Wallace: Quixotic Crusade* (Syracuse, 1960). A more detailed account is Curtis D. MacDougal, *Gideon's Army*, 3 vols. (New York, 1965). MacDougal ran in Illinois as the 1948 Progressive candidate for the U.S. Senate. Some unpublished material which gives additional sidelights and insights are John Cotton Brown, "The 1948 Progressive Campaign: A Scientific Approach" (Ph.D. thesis, University of Chicago, 1949); Cynthia Letts Adcock, "Popular Front Politics in America, 1948-1954: A Study of the Left Progressives" (M.A. thesis, Columbia University, 1963); and Verna W. Spinrad, "Henry Wallace and the Progressive Party of 1948" (M.A. thesis, Columbia University, 1956).

For biographical material on Henry Wallace one might start with Russell Lord, *The Wallaces of Iowa* (Boston, 1947); and Edward L. and Frederick H. Schapsmeier, *Henry A. Wallace of Iowa*, 2 vols. (Ames, Iowa, 1968; 1970). On Glenn Taylor it might be helpful to read the following: Richard L. Neuberger, "Glenn Taylor: Leftwing Minstrel," *The Progressive,* April 1948; and two essays in the *Pacific Northwest Quarterly:* William C. Pratt, "Glenn H. Taylor: Public Image and Reality," 60 (January 1969), 10-16, and F. Ross Peterson, "Fighting the Drive Toward War:

Glenn H. Taylor, the 1948 Progressives, and the Draft," 61 (January 1970), 41-45.

There are three particularly insightful essays on the Dixiecrats: Sarah McCulloh Lemmon, "The Ideology of the 'Dixiecrat' Movement," *Social Forces,* 30 (December 1952), 162-71; William G. Carleton, "The Fate of Our Fourth Party," *The Yale Review,* 38 (March 1949), 449-59; and Emile B. Ader, "Why the Dixiecrats Failed," *Journal of Politics,* 15 (August 1953), 356-69. Ader expanded his essay into *The Dixiecrat Movement: Its Role in Third Party Politics* (Washington, D.C., 1955), but the article should provide sufficient information for most interested persons. Extensive discussions of the Dixiecrats also appear in two excellent books: V.O. Key, Jr., *Southern Politics in State and Nation* (New York, 1950), and Alexander Heard, *"A Two-Party South?"* (Chapel Hill, 1952). Unpublished material worth examining includes Frank W. Ashley, "Selected Southern Liberal Editors and the States' Rights Movement of 1948" (Ph.D. thesis, University of South Carolina, 1959), and Barbara E. Berg, "The Dixiecrat Party in the 1948 Election" (M.A. thesis, Columbia University, 1967). Biographical material on Thurmond and Wright is limited but Alberta Lachicotte, *Rebel Senator* (New York, 1967) provides some basic facts about the former. Contemporary journalistic accounts and brief sections in *Current Biography* can be consulted also.

The American Independent Party

MARSHALL FRADY is a southern journalist who covered George Wallace's approaches to his first presidential campaign in 1968. He is the author of *Wallace: Across a Darkling Plain*, and is currently working on another large volume on Wallace.

The American Independent Party

by *Marshall Frady*

It was the peculiar nature of the American Independent party (AIP) that it was really not so much a party, or even a particular ideology, as it was simply a personality. In terms of its inception, its operative vitality, its whole reason for being, it consisted finally of a single figure—the stumpy, audacious, indefatigable person of George Corley Wallace, governor of Alabama, who managed almost single-handedly to translate a parochial segregationist evangelism into an authentic national political insurgency.

Around Wallace there collected, in time, a haphazard assortment of small, fractious, strident groups from the more obscure reaches of the American right, along with a motley company of ideological outriders, radio gospel patriots and such antedeluvian southern politicians as Louisiana's Leander Perez and Georgia's Roy Harris and Lester Maddox. These interests, by their very nature, did not lend themselves particularly to any general cohesion. But Wallace, himself a kind of congenitally sullen political orphan, gave these various citizens of the fringe a momentary unity and coherence and, for once in their long unavailing careers, a certain tangible and heady potential for actually impinging on the course of the country.

These parties, along with local vigilante cells of citizens here and there, and the administrative apparatus of the state capitol in Alabama, made up what formal structure the American Independent party could be said to have had. For the most part, as a national political operation, it was rather an interim and ephemeral Rube Goldberg contraption, a homemade affair willed and contrived into being and sustained exclusively by Wallace's own swashbuckling ambition, dauntless optimism, and uncanny guttural political savvy. It was strictly a personal phenomenon, a personal exigency with no life of its own, and evidence enough would be the fact that, in 1972, when Wallace occupied himself in what seemed then the more promising instrumentalities of the regular Democratic party, the American Independent party seemed by all indications to have dematerialized.

To be sure, Wallace and the American Independent party did not occur accidentally in a vacuum. The times, back during the early and middle 1960's, were singularly propitious for such a political insurrection. When Wallace made his first excursions beyond the South in the 1964 Democratic primaries in Wisconsin and Indiana, he was generally dismissed as merely an antic and slightly odious southern curiosity bent on a mission of ill-tempered mischief. But the stunning response to him in these primary votes indicated he was in touch with large subterranean popular frequencies. Gradually, it was recognized that Wallace was articulating, in the enormous complications and tensions of the mid-1960's in America, a nostalgia for the old simplicity of the village ethos and village values of the nation's past. These first tentative ventures beyond Alabama became something like a camp-meeting revival for the old harsh elemental assumptions about the nature of human beings, a retrenchment against sociologists and intellectuals and the whole national intelligentsia, the national elite. With a certain weariness, enervation and even nausea beginning to suffuse the national life after all the immense social exertions of the previous thirty years, it seemed the American commonfolk were asserting themselves at last against a vaguely-defined national establishment which had sought to involve them in a conscience, in sacrifices, and in an experience which they had difficulty comprehending. In a sense, Wallace coincided with a gathering confrontation between the village ethic and the Manhattan sophistication—a revolt of Main Street America against alien sensibilities which were no longer confined to literary periodicals and academic salons, but which had begun to impose effectively on their lives, and their vision of themselves and their society.

This unease, in fact, lingered on well beyond the 1968 campaign, if anything had actually gained magnitude by 1972, when it was enunciated more precisely by a new figure in the American Independent party, California Congressman John Schmitz:

> An elitist power structure has been established, dominating both the Republican and Democratic parties and manipulating public opinion through clever propaganda. The favored few escape the burden of high taxes, continuing inflation, tightening government controls, invasion of privacy, endless no-win wars, compulsory busing of school children, and virtually all the other ugly products of the system they run, while the 'forgotten Americans' who bear the burdens are given no hearing and find no voice.... The very foundations of [this 'forgotten American's'] life and livelihood and the land he loves and the education of his children are undermined and shifted without his prior knowlege or consent....

As much as anything else, what had happened was that, through the happenstance of television, with its counterfeit immediacy and intimacy, these people began to feel menaced and besieged by confrontations and figures—not only black militants but psychedelic prophets, student revolutionists, counter-culture apostles—that were actually quite remote from the perimeters of their own existences, and which in another time would have remained quite abstract and incidental to their lives. It had truly become one continental community when steel workers in Gary, Indiana, or sheep-farmers in New Mexico could become exercised about, and feel accosted by, civil turmoils in Oakland or Harvard Square.

But it was a community perversely composed of a passionate sense of divisions and embattlement—a malaise of alienation, not only between white and black, but between youth and age, between the common man and the intellectual estate, between the general citizenery and the system presiding over it. Indeed, not the least of the dynamics at work in the Wallace phenomenon was a kind of surly class assortment against the affluent, privileged and powerful. America's economically-harried white commoners could identify, as a class, with Wallace in a way they couldn't identify with other figures of similar persuasions but more urbane upper-class auras, like Goldwater: Wallace talked like they did, angered like them, even dressed like them. He was one of their own. In an almost mystical way, he answered their vague sense of dread and inadequacy and uncertainty and dull unremitting pettiness: he brought to them a special glee and exhilaration that refreshed, however fleetingly, the general staleness of their lives.

The truth is, massive divisions among people tended to enthrall and excite Wallace much more than commonalities; he always seemed more intrigued and invigorated by prospects for confrontations than by hopes for reconciliations. In this respect, he was only a natural occurrence in a time of deep popular schisms. More than that, though, his national campaigns all along proceeded tacitly and basically on what might be the most ominous of all separations—that increasing dissolution in American society between language and meaning in the conduct of the nation's business. Before his 1968 campaign was fully mounted, a magazine article appeared which quoted him as observing soberly that most federal judges needed more than anything else a simple brisk crack on the back of the skull to straighten out their thinking: this quote scandalized a number of Wallace's advisers, but he himself, in the privacy of the governor's office one afternoon, proposed to a newsman, "Well, hell, of course we can't be going around saying that officially as part of our platform, but just between you and me now—what's so bad about that? Whole heaps of folks in this country feel exactly the same way." Another time, during a television interview at the governor's mansion in Montgomery, he leaned back in a maroon-velvet settee when the camera lights were turned off to change film, and began chatting with the network correspondent about the disparities between black and white neighborhoods. "It don't have anything to do with the buildings or the environment or anything like that," he confided. "You and I both know why Nigra schools and communities are inferior, but it's not something we're going to talk about. You know what I mean, but neither one of us going to say it out loud." An hour later, when the television crew had departed, he squatted for awhile on a step midway up the sweeping red-carpeted stairway of the mansion, remarking to an aide, "Course, they were asking me all that stuff about the U.N. and what my policies would be there. If you want to know the truth, the U.N.'s just a cannibal club, but I couldn't be going and saying that on TV, you know."

Finally and fundamentally, Wallace and the American Independent party, for all the accompanying baggage of legitimate anxieties and discontents, amounted to a kind of massive unspoken collaboration of racism in all its varieties, from blatant to furtive, deliberate to unwitting, malevolent to amicable. To journalists close to Wallace, there was a hallucinatory quality about the inconclusive speculation they heard elsewhere on this point through the campaign. That Wallace and his retainers managed with their strenuous coyness on the issue even to accomplish any debate about it was one of their most surprising triumphs. Wallace has always thrived on being misfocused by the national press, in his early years, as a caricature of southern red-neck boobery, and then, in 1968, by investing both himself and the American Independent party with a certain careful stilted deacon-like circumspection and gravity, which eventually made any thought of broaching the subject of racism seem like a breach of taste. One AIP official in Davenport, Iowa, suggested that the matter of whether or not Wallace was a racist was really as irrelevant as "Jack Kennedy's religion. If Kennedy happened to be a Catholic, that was his own private business." But there's no question that the American Independent party was conceived in the racial travail of the South during the 1960's: as the Second Reconstruction, unlike the First a century earlier, eventually began to ramify over the rest of the nation, Wallace discerned—as he had expected—a national magnification of the white need in Alabama, and his own ambitions amplified accordingly. As governor during these lightening-struck years in the South from 1962 to 1966, he had always insisted, "When they start catching this mess up North and everywhere else, then you gonna see this whole country southernized, from Boston to Los Angeles." Then, during one of his northern junkets in 1967, he quietly remarked to a newsman in the lobby of a Cleveland hotel after one appearance, "Let 'em call me a racist in the press. It don't make any difference. If you want to know the truth, race is what's gonna win this thing for us."

His private professions of this conviction, even during the campaign, would make up an interminable catalogue: "Nigguhs hate whites and whites hate nigguhs. Everybody knows that deep down. Hell, that's just the way folks are." But as his campaign gained momentum, he sedulously maintained a gap between the reality of this private persuasion, and his public appearance of ambivalence on the matter. Nevertheless, the white backfire that ensued as the black awakening extended into the rest of the country constituted the essential political energy of Wallace and the AIP. The fact that their outrider campaign wound up figuring as seriously as it did in the political speculations and determinations that year confirmed the suspicion of many that the country, in its heart of hearts, was irredeemably, however elusively, racist.

Before long, in the appalled liberal commentaries that Wallace's prosperity began to increasingly provoke, there were suggestions that his count on election day would represent a rough approximation of the potential for an American totalitarianism—a strictly indigenous and unique variety, ferociously decent, conventionally patriotic and righteous, mostly innocent and unrecognizable to a great number of citizens. The specific spectre of Naziism was sometimes invoked, it being cited that the American Independent party like national Socialism in Germany, was dependent on a single and somewhat disreputable wildcat political figure of a special uncontainable angry genius, which was made up of a mixture of popular politics and authoritarianism that seemed to flourish on violent street encounters. All this was taking place in the classic conditions of a pre-facist society: a massive unease among average non-political citizens in the face of disruptions and events they didn't understand and a sudden dread and uncertainty about the future, a growingly virulent anti-intellectualism and anti-culturalism prompted perhaps by a rebellion against the sense of guilt imposed on many citizens by years of moral crisis, along with a passing of faith in the traditional processes of the governmental system. The speculation was heard during 1968 that Hitler was merely the first lurid and violent eruption of what was soon to become a new theme in the history of man-race—which, as the world contracted into an ever-more intimate neighborhood, would dominate world affairs for at least the next century. Wallace and the AIP, supposedly signalled the arrival of that overt racial preoccupation into American politics.

If so, Wallace himself was supremely impervious to such implications of his candidacy. One Alabama politician declared at the time, "He doesn't ever talk about purposes, causes, destinies, significancies, anything like that. He differs from every other politician I've ever known in that respect." Wallace himself cheerfully allowed once, "Naw, we don't stop and figger and think about history or theories or none of that. We just go ahead. History can take care of itself." Abstractions did not seem to exist for him, and for that reason it was beyond him to retreat to the top floor of a hotel like Huey Long and come back down six weeks later with *Every Man a King*—or, for that matter, to compose in solitude anything like a *Mein Kampf* prospectus. This peculiar innocence was, at once, part of his personal political genius and the ultimate reason there appeared no hope of the American Independent party ever sustaining itself on its own as a lasting systematized political infrastructure or program.

Wallace first caught national notice with his inauguration as governor of Alabama in 1963, when he proclaimed, "In the name of the greatest people that have ever tred the earth, I draw the line in the dust and toss the gauntlet before the feet of tyranny, and I say, segregation now! segregation tomorrow! segregation forever!" Not surprisingly, for some time after that, he was regarded as just another of the hopelessly provincial segregationist curios of the day, perhaps a bit grimmer than most, but certain to wane back into oblivion after his phosphorescent local glare.

But his deepest political hankerings had always been on a larger, national scale. Throughout the third-party Dixiecrat gambit that followed the 1948 Democratic convention, he remained fast in the national party fold, and even before the convention in Philadelphia, when he was running for alternate-delegate, "he was a hot loyalist," remembers a former national partyman in Alabama. Elected an alternate-delegate, when Wallace arrived in Philadelphia, it turned out he might be elevated to a full-fledged delegate—a stroke of luck owing to the fact that the regular delegate from Wallace's district was confined to a hospital bed back in Alabama. But the official Alabama delegation knowing Wallace was a committed loyalist, ignored him as long as possible and excluded him from their pre-convention caucus in which they decided by a vote of thirteen to twelve to stalk out of the convention if an offensive civil rights platform was adopted. But when the convention opened, the delegate from Wallace's district was still prostrate in his bed back in Alabama, so there was no choice but to swear in Wallace and seat him with the rest of the Alabama party. Shortly thereafter, recalls a delegate who was there, "Our Dixiecrat faction stood up and charged out of the hall, and it was none other than George Wallace who ran up the aisle after them, literally grabbed the state banner out of Bull Connor's hands, and ran back onto the convention floor with it." Then, barely a blink later, he was making a seconding speech for the presidential nomination of Richard Russell.

From then on, as he steadily enlarged his political horizons at home, he continued showing up at national Democratic conclaves for as long as it remained politically seemly back in Alabama. One of his old colleagues remembers, "George was always borrowing money off me to go to another goddam national party soiree somewhere. The further away it was, Colorado or Idaho, the hotter he was to get there. If he hadn't finally decided to turn renegade, I'd of probably gone broke."

At some point during the segregationist delirium of the late 1950's in Alabama, while Wallace was a circuit judge, he made the calculation that continuing to pursue any political career that would be compatible with the national party disposition would mean public extinction in Alabama, whereas what would be required to cultivate any political fortune in Alabama would render him thoroughly indigestible to the national party. With that determination, the American Independent party had its inception. Then, as governor in 1963, he struck his pose in the schoolhouse door at the University of Alabama, standing on a soft-drink crate behind a lectern to deny entrance to two black students, the "forever" of his inauguration speech turning out to last in this case about four hours. But however ephemeral and ineffectual his gesture, it was magnified by the formidable registers of television over the entire nation, and with that—though no one suspected it at the moment—he ceased for all time to be merely a provincial parochial figure. Though he had decided to repudiate his possibilities in the national Democratic context and opt for a folk popularity in Alabama, he found that the brief performance which had derived from that decision had also touched off the most congenial continental resonances. But to exploit these underground intimations of support, he realized, very likely meant that he would still have to operate for awhile outside the conventional structure of the national Democratic party. It was shortly after the University of Alabama episode that acquaintances recall hearing him first muse audibly about the possibilities for a national "movement."

His stance in the schoolhouse door had, among other things, brought into his office a flurry of invitations from all over the country for speaking appearances, especially from college campuses whom he primarily interested as the most garish of the southern gargoyles of that day. These latter invitations he accepted with a particular alacrity. Most of his campus appearances wound up in the most indecorous and disheveled melees of kibbitzing and tomato-tossing, but Wallace, out of his own mute private instinct about the larger effect of student unruliness, alchemized his receptions by these unwitting audiences into occasions which further endeared him to a much vaster audience beyond the lecture halls. In the same way, in his appearances before panels of interviewers on television, he used the conspicuous superciliousness and impatience of some newsmen to futher nourish his growing national political vitality. He was playing a much wider game than any of his antagonists.

Nevertheless, it was still in the most haphazard and improvisational manner that, in the course of all this circuit-riding, he found himself in three of the 1964 Democratic primaries. Late one afternoon, for instance, after a speech at the University of Wisconsin, someone called Wallace's suite at a Madison hotel with the announcement that he had a plan for Wallace's entry into the upcoming presidential primary in that state. "I thought he was a crackpot," remembers one former Wallace aide.

> Wisconsin seemed like the last state to run in anyway—they had no Negro problem, they had their own civil rights law. The whole idea seemed like a joke, and we'd been on this speaking tour for two weeks, everybody was wanting to get on back home. But this nut wouldn't quit calling, so we finally told him to meet us at this radio station downtown where Wallace had to appear on a call-in program before we flew back to Alabama. He was from Oshkosh, seventy miles away, and it was snowing, but he drove all the way over, with us sitting in that radio station for an hour and a half waiting on him.

Wallace's conversation with the man was hurried, and he emerged from the radio station with an outline of the primary qualifications tucked into his briefcase. Once aboard his plane, he withdrew the papers from his briefcase and studied them all the way back to Alabama.

In this inauspicious manner, Wallace sidled not only into the Wisconsin primary, but those in Indiana and Maryland. The general sophistication regarded his enterprise as an absurdity, ranging from slapstick to malignant. But in these makeshift improbable free-lance expeditions, Wallace accomplished an astonishing measure of political mayhem. In Wisconsin, he made off with about thirty-five percent of the Democratic vote, and in Indiana, he drew almost thirty percent. Then in Maryland, the last of the three, he officially captured forty-five percent of the vote—and since then, from the private acknowledgements of some Maryland party officials, there has materialized reason to suppose that he might have actually won that primary, a wonder reportedly averted by a late-night "recapitulation" of the count at precinct level.

If Wallace had perpetuated his presidential venture that year as he contemplated doing for awhile—clapping together campaigns in Alabama and perhaps other southern states where he could run as an extra-curricular candidate—it's quite probable he would have pilfered from Republican candidate Barry Goldwater enough votes in the general election to leave Goldwater in the mortifying position of carrying only his own home state of Arizona. But under the urgings of his advisors and chief supporters, Wallace somewhat grudgingly withdrew in deference to Goldwater; despite his startling showings in the three primaries he had entered, Wallace still headed no more than a guerilla operation nowhere brawny and concerted enough to accomplish more than a vandalism at Goldwater's campaign. The resentment this would have incurred among a number of conservatives could have been an imposing liability later on. His demurral in 1964, then, was a studied investment of a kind in 1968.

But through most of these four intervening years, the American Independent party remained a tentative and rudimentary affair, consisting of little more than an address in Montgomery for contributions. In fact, almost up to the last possible statuatory minute, it even remained nameless, with Wallace and his aides, during their forays about the country, endlessly inventing titles for it at odd moments in elevators or car rides from airports. "Dammit, we got to decide what we gonna call this thing now," Wallace would fume abstractedly while munching a cigar, and someone would offer, "What about 'The Free American party'?" Wallace would retort, "Well, what would the initials say—FAP? Hell, that don't sound too hot—FAP."

In rather the same off-hand manner, he plotted the financing for the enterprise, scribbling on the back of a manila envelope with a ball-point pen: "Let's see, we got better than $380,000 when we went into three states back in 1964; three goes into fifty about seventeen times, yes, and seventeen times $380,000, that oughtta be—that $6,460,000. That oughtta be enough." The truth was, Wallace seemed to regard all formal political organization, including arrangements for financing, with a vague contempt as a sign of political effeteness, an absence of vitality. Power to him simply did not lie in the traditional equations of press celebration and business support and the interests of political establishments. He bypassed all the classic brokers of political power with a personal formula that was almost childishly naive and ingenuous: power lies with the folks, and nothing else. His assumption was that he was already naturally blessed with what political organization exists to create.

At the same time, he seemed to suspect that any kind of elaborate organization would actually subvert the integrity of his campaign as a singularly personal phenomenon. For that reason, he simply did not trust holding a national convention: there was too great a risk that it might romp off on its own beyond his particular personal designs. He explained once, "You get a big bunch of folks together like that, there'll always be a few who'll try to take the thing over."

So Wallace deliberately kept the AIP in the embryonic form of isolated hot enclaves of volunteers dappled over the map of the country, a few minor government officials like city councilmen and state legislators, along with a handful of professional political operatives who collected in the AIP's Montgomery headquarters from far-flung points like Nevada. Most of them were of obscure background and, almost necessarily, tended to be congenital outsiders and dissidents. Actually, without Wallace, there was no likelihood such an assembly could have achieved any more sturdy and explicit form anyway. Finally, the nearest approximation of a viable campaign machinery was afforded by all the accoutrements of the Alabama governor's office itself. "What you're going to see throughout 1968," said one Alabama politician, "is this whole state used as the aircraft carrier for Wallace's invasion of the rest of the country." It worked out more or less that way. Both logistically and in personnel, in airplanes, telephones and bodyguards, not to mention the financial constraints available to the office, the resources of Alabama's governorship served as the true engine-system of the campaign—a tidy bit of thrifty adaptation on Wallace's part to compensate for his poverty in the customary assets of a national presidential campaign.

Even so, the outlook for this improvised political collage remained eminently bleary. With Wallace providing the party with its sole image and articulation, there loomed now a new and not inconsiderable question, as the moment of truth drew nearer, of whether or not he might not actually be confounded by a simple subtle matter of style. He still carried with him a surpassingly southern presence, had an incorrigibly regional character about him, and it began to seem increasingly possible that all his cultural dissonances might render him finally and implausibly foreign to assembly-line workers in Detroit and retirees in Orange County, whatever their angers and desperations. Could a governor of Alabama, in the gravity of an actual presidential election, really take nationally?

But most formidably, there was the staggering problem of getting on the ballot in each of the fifty states. Any third-party movement with authentic national aspirations faces fifty different fronts of bureaucratic and statuatory difficulties, some of them almost impossibly stubborn. The complications in California, for instance, were so Byzantine that the state was generally counted out, even by the American Independent party, as beyond the resources of its campaign.

In the end, however, the AIP pulled off the monumental feat of official listing on the general election ballots of all the states in the Union. It was a coup that seemed to surprise even Wallace, and not incidentally it retired forever any doubts about the national popular response to his essential southern style. Whatever was to befall the AIP from then on, with this triumph it was cast into a magnitude of consequence, for all its organizational amorphousness, enjoyed by no other third party in the country within recent memory.

While the AIP materialized more or less empirically as a movement without any real ideological coherence, only a leader, it was the advent of a general sentiment reminiscent of other popular surges in the American past. There were suggestions of the Know-Nothing party's xenophobic suspicion of all alien impingements on what was assumed to be the American character, along with that sullen antipathy toward all elitism and a somewhat brutish bullying elemental egalitarianism which has recurred not infrequently throughout the American experience. But most notably, the Wallace phenomenon was a kind of twentieth century reassertion of that old Populist political sensibility which lingered on in the South after those days of its lustiness between the Civil War and turn of the century, when it enfevered not only the South but much of the Midwest. A peculiar fusion of the rural pentecostal Calvanist ethic and a breeding economic discontent, Populism posed a truly revolutionary potential in its day. It allied an impoverished white yeomanry and, initially, blacks with a few sympathetic landowners—a coalition which pitted itself against the proprietorial interests of Wall Street, the merchants, bankers, railroad barons, textile magnates and petty capitalists of the Gilded Age, all of whom tended to regard the movement, not without some legitimacy, as an ominous insurgency.

In the South, the Bourbons of the new industrial order finally baffled and dispersed the Populist offensive by cultivating, through their proxy press and politicians, the illusionary menace of Marxism and black pillage. But the Populist movement was probably doomed from the beginning because it finally answered, in the fact of a rampant industrialization of American society, to agrarian nostalgias and sensibilities, in particular the old dream of a democracy of small farmers. In a sense, it was like the last struggle of the country against the city.

Then, in the 1960's, Wallace appeared like the incarnate annunciation of Populism's translation into a somehow more meager and rancorous urban mutation. As governor, he proved to be of compulsive Populist inclinations; he built a gallery of new junior colleges and trade schools, initiated a free-textbook program, scattered new nursing homes and medical clinics over the state. The proportion of Alabama citizens participating in public welfare programs at the end of his first term was exceeded by only one other state in the Union—Louisiana. Whenever it was noted, somewhat wryly, that he exhibited notably liberal impulses for someone so widely regarded as a ferocious conservative, Wallace would reply, "Well, I'm not one of these ultra-conservatives. They against everything. The only thing they want to conserve is the dollar. If they talking about me borrowing money to build roads and bridges over the state, well, we gonna build these roads and bridges whatever it takes to do it. And spending money for the blind and crippled and elderly, that's no giveway, that's just helping folks, that's what we *supposed* to do."

But Wallace was something of an abberation on the traditional Populist mentality. Though he had entertained the old Populist notion that "cities do something to people, makes them meaner and smaller in some way," he vigorously set about industrializing the Alabama countryside as soon as he became governor. Also, the larger share of his taxing programs—on cigarettes, sports events, and gas—fell on the "common folks" to the benefit of big business in the state. In 1968, when the American Independent party at last performed the formality of producing a party platform, that document, like all party platforms, having about as much relation to the actual realities of the political merchandise as a Madison Avenue incantation about breakfast cereal, nevertheless held in it hints of the mutations the Populist psychology had undergone in its transition from the earth to the city. Its preoccupations, essentially those of the new white urban Jacquerie in America, were generally involved with "riots, minority group rebellions, domestic disorders, spiralling living costs, searing interest rates, a frightening increase in the crime rate. . .minority appeasement as the country burns and decays." To contend with these urban distresses, the platform invoked many of the old egalitarian sentiments—"freedom from interference and harassment from and by the government at all levels," and, perhaps its most radical proposition, "the adoption of an amendment whereby members of the federal judiciary at district level be required to face the electorate at periodic intervals, "with the same amendment requiring 're-confirmation' of Courts of Appeals and Supreme Court judges 'at reasonable intervals'."

Its fundamental deviation from aboriginal Populism, though was the unusual solicitude it exhibited for big business. Its most intriguing proposal was the diffusion of industry out over the scantily-inhabited spaces of the country, which presumably would begin to alleviate the congestion in metropolitan areas and restore a measure of the population back to the graces of life in small communities. But this project was to be effected through making it "economically attractive to industry through tax incentives and other means of economic benefit, believing fully that the answer to the problem lies in the vigor and capability of our tremendous free enterprise system—curious sanctitudes to issue from Populist instincts.

The truth is, though, the Populist temperament has always been especially susceptible to eventual beguilement by these pieties and orthodoxies by which, historically, its constituency's voice and interests have always been confounded. The American custodial estate, in fact, has managed to befuddle and finally dispel every gathering movement of Populist politics—not only in the South but throughout the country, and known by many other names besides Populism, such as the IWW—through not only brandishing the spectre of racial and Bolshevist peril, but through nuturing a kind of conventional decency made up of the Horace Greeley romance and *Saturday Evening Post* respectabilities. Noted political scientist James Clotfelter observes: "One problem with Populism has always been that the people who speak for it tend to be very unsophisticated and naive to begin with. Their perspectives are those of people who have grown up on the periphery of power, which leaves them somehow especially vulnerable to corruption and blandishment once they approach all the bemusements of power themselves."

Accordingly, it soon became Wallace's aspiration to realize in the AIP, a "fusion" of the working man with the large industrialists and tycoons, not of Wall Street, but of mid-America. "We got part of it already," he declared early in 1967, "we got the working man, and now we're gonna get the other part of it—the high hoi-polloi. They'll come around in time, you wait." One of the great mysteries of 1968 is to what extent he succeeded in striking this consortium of basically antagonistic interests. There were various mutterings that the American Independent party enjoyed substantial patronage from Texas oil potentate H.L. Hunt—though one of Wallace's aides protested, "Sure, he's sent us about two million pamphlets, but we ain't seen a dollar bill from him yet."

In the course of the party's exertions to place itself on the general election ballots of the various states, it became necessary, to satisfy the technicalities in a number of these states, to rummage up someone to posture for awhile as Wallace's vice presidential candidate until the decision on the actual candidate was reached. This was a detail which afforded Wallace a special discomfort. Having never been one for associating himself politically whatsoever with anyone else, he now had to accept an alter-ego, a second, which constituted an inevitable complication of identity, a more closely defining qualification which could not help but be constricting, a compromise and violation of the totally personal nature of his campaign. That a party's presidential candidate had to be attended by a vice presidential candidate was a stipulation, in fact, which Wallace would have given anything in the world to avoid if it had been possible.

After some extensive groping about, Wallace finally came up with, as an interim stand-in, Georgia's old winsome redoubtable segregationist governor, Marvin

Griffin—who hardly lent the American Independent party any more cosmopolitan dimensions. As it happened, even Griffin seemed more aware than Wallace himself that his temporary presence on the AIP's bridge was something of a dowdy embarrassment, and with noticeably enormous relief, he receded into south Georgia anonymity when Wallace finally produced his actual running mate: retired Air Force General Curtis LeMay.

LeMay, perhaps, was the consummate incongruity of the AIP's short career. Almost a parody of the uniformed American militarist, whose sole bluff suggestion for resolving international frustrations tended to be obliteration by bomb, he could not have seemed more remote from Wallace's own political origins. In fact, early in Wallace's own career when he ran for circuit judge in his native Barbour County, his opponent was a local patrician who had been a lieutenant colonel in World War II; the man remembered later that Wallace had advertised himself almost exclusively during the campaign as a veteran of low rank who still nurtured an implacable animosity toward all officers: "He went all over the county saying, 'Now, all you officers can vote for Clayton, but all you privates and corporals now, you vote for me.' "

But more significantly, it has also been one of the characteristics of the Populist disposition—while fiercely isolationist and anti-militaristic in the innocence of irrelevancy—to begin evidencing, once at the threshold of any consequence of import, an exuberance for the glamors of the military. Accordingly, in the AIP platform, there were robust assurances that the Wallace administration would "restore to their proper duties, functions and authority the leaders of our military services so that the nation may once again profit from their wisdom and experience," and it would, furthermore, "seek the advice and good judgement of the Joint Chiefs of Staff as to ways and means of reaching a military conclusion to [the Vietnam] conflict with the least loss of life to our American servicemen and our South Vietnamese allies . . . through the use of conventional weapons." On the whole, the platform's defense section bristled with rather bizarre military belligerencies, promising among other things to accelerate the construction of an anti-ballistic missile system, to cultivate a new concern for "the captive satellite nations of Eastern Europe," and to "deny foreign aid and assistance to those nations who oppose us militarily in Vietnam and elsewhere, as well as those who seek our economic and military destruction by giving aid and comfort to our avowed enemies." While the platform's general need of inhospitality toward foreign aid programs corresponded to Populism's primal disinclination toward any overseas entailments whatsoever, it was more a matter with the AIP of designing an overall foreign policy addressed toward "gaining the respect, if not always the admiration" of the community of nations.

Actually, Wallace himself had always shown that poignant vulnerability of the Populist sensibility to those figures of any heft and consequence in society, and no doubt it was his simple assumption that LeMay, as much as anything else, would lend the AIP's still somewhat irregular enterprise a certain measure of dignity and legitimacy. But many of those well-versed in Wallace's unique kind of political vitality recognized that the selection of LeMay was an uncanny lapse of judgment. He made the mistake of associating the AIP campaign with a Goldwater-like figure who had all of Goldwater's liabilities but few of his charms. Sure enough, as the campaign proceeded, General LeMay turned out to be about as politically graceful as an irate buffalo on a waxed waltz floor. Before long, it was obvious that Wallace himself recognized all this, if nothing else from his hasty and assiduous defensiveness on the subject of LeMay's appropriateness to his campaign. Whatever, it was about coincident with LeMay's appearance as an accessory to Wallace that his showings in the polls began to falter dramatically.

However awesome the AIP's feat of obtaining official status on the ballot of all fifty states, that had been transacted in the general decisiveness and imprecisions of the nation's pre-convention political theatre. But now, though the AIP had advanced further than any other third-party effort in over a generation, it began to fray and give like all third-party movements before it in the ultimate compressions and tensions of American politics grand climactic last act—the actual presidential selection itself. Wallace had hoped that the Republican nominee would be either George Romney or Nelson Rockefeller, liberal Republicans who would have left him with the conservative field to himself. But with the convention, the campaign and candidates came into final definition, and the Republican nominee, Richard Nixon, began immediately to assimilate that portion of Wallace's sympathizers who preferred a more conventionally respectable air in their spokesman.

At the same time, the heckling that began to accompany Wallace's rallies—which were really all that the AIP campaign consisted of now, like merely a continental rendition of Wallace's own stump-hopping style in Alabama—became progressively more cunning and sedulous, noticeably disconcerting him on several occasions. More importantly, it provided spectacular rhubarbs which had always worked to his enhancement in the lower stages of his political progression, but which now, in the deeper seriousness of the presidential campaign itself, invoked unsettling visions of what the temper of his actual presidency might be.

But most significant, perhaps, was the success of labor leadership and the Democratic establishment in persuading the great common ranks of working men outside the South to regard Wallace with suspicion. This was not totally without authenticity, since Wallace, given to the usual Populist aberrations once he acquired the Alabama governorship, had granted a handsome array of tax concessions to corporate interests in the state to encourage "industrialization" while remaining largely indifferent to the economic beleaguerment of the common citizenry. Even so, in about every other respect, Wallace had always identified himself first and fundamentally with the spiritual weather of the blue-collar white. Of anyone, the working man is the constituency whose tribune he has always labored to make himself. On the whole, then, the disaffection with Wallace which labor leadership finally managed to induce among the ranks of their unions was rather a triumph of propaganda over reality. But it dislodged Wallace, most disastrously, from his true popular ground.

Finally, there was Nixon's baroque ploy of enlisting that archaic irascible Dixie-crat-turned-Republican, Senator Strom Thurmond of South Carolina, in an odyssey through the South to convince Wallace folk there, in exchange for what turned out later to be some Supreme Court appointments and other gestures from the White House, that a vote for the AIP would be idle and profitless folly. In a sense, Thurmond owed the one moment he ever approached any possible national relevancy to Wallace, but he did succeed—most significantly in South Carolina—in sabotaging Wallace in some southern states.

Despite all this, Wallace did draw 9,906,473 popular votes—as well as 46 electoral votes. In both electoral and popular votes, though not in the proportion of the popular vote, the AIP surpassed the LaFollette Progressive party of 1924. Actually, Wallace's own expectations at the very outset of his campaign were modest, and though the polls later exalted his speculations somewhat, he wound up finishing about as he had originally and privately calculated he would.

But the import of Wallace and the American Independent party ranged beyond their numerical showing in the election. The prospect that the AIP might manage to pitch the presidential selection into the House of Representatives for the first time in 144 years did not materialize in the end. The disarray in the nation's electoral procedures which was intimated by Wallace's candidacy did occasion profound misgivings about these procedures which may, even yet, result in the elimination of the electoral college system. Perhaps even more important, Wallace alerted those who preside and mediate over the affairs of this country to a massive unsuspected, unanswered constituency of despair and estrangement submerged like a lost continent in the national population. One result of this, as early as the 1968 campaign, was that he became a kind of ghost-writer for many of the issues—though his effect was that of casting a precautionary chill over the expansiveness and adventurousness of these issues. Still, however illusionary the debate of presidential campaigns may be, it's hard to imagine, if there had not been a Wallace, the kind of rhetoric that has become commonplace since 1968—as well as Spiro Agnew having been conjured forth as the Republican vice presidential candidate. Wallace, in fact, flared out of nowhere as the oracle for what would become the central obsession of the campaign in 1972—the New Populism.

What began to emerge, after the AIP's prosperity in 1968, was a recognition of the profound chasm that had existed all along between what the general sophistication thought this nation was and wanted, and what it actually represented. The only way the nation has been able to finally describe itself has been by the choices it has had in presidential elections, and those descriptions up to 1968 were limited to the necessarily crude choice of only two candidates. But what any democracy has to fear is not so much fear itself, as unreality and illusion in its image and the issues and men with which its destiny is involved. At the least, Wallace and the AIP provided, for a time, a somewhat more detailed clarification on that score for the United States.

After its exertions in 1968, however, the AIP itself lapsed back almost completely into that unrecognizable state of noisy inchoate suspended distraction out of which it had been summoned, and made a party, by the single galvanic figure of Wallace. There were a few desultory efforts to assert itself as a party in random local elections, but Wallace, out of that aversion to attaching his political fortune to that of anyone else, maintained for the most part a scrupulous detachment. It seemed obvious that the AIP would be chronicled, at the most, as a party similar to the life pattern of locusts, which would exist only once every four years, solely on a national scale, and that in the person of Wallace and exclusively at his whim—if, indeed, it was ever to emerge again.

It remained in this state of nebulous abeyance while Wallace, with all apparent seriousness, began campaigning in the 1972 Democratic presidential primaries, having assumed this time a certain subdued and modulated manner—a new and strangely formal composure—which many attributed to the diligent cultivations of his politically canny and elegant second wife, but which nevertheless imparted the sense somehow that he aspired now to range beyond the faintly dowdy eccentricity of his old third-party equipage. Once again Wallace outstripped the conventional expectations. Beginning with Florida, he did boomingly in the primaries he entered, and actually was taken with increasing soberness as the Democratic convention approached, all the while, maintaining a studied evasiveness about what direction he might take after that event in Miami. Accordingly, suggestions began to amplify that Wallace—always mightily tempted by any prospect for actually counting in the traditional legitimate theatre of American politics—was becoming beguiled by a vision of winding up as the Democratic party's vice presidential nominee, despite the fact this would perfect the extinction of the AIP. But the most likely conjecture is that, expecting to be dismissed finally by the convention no matter how imposing his popular totals in the primaries (as it turned out, they out-bulked those of any other contender, including nominee George McGovern), Wallace was actually embarked throughout the primaries in a ploy to lend, after the convention's rebuff, a high melodrama to his subsequent plunge off into a second American Independent party campaign.

But all these intricately constructed surmises, of course, vanished with Wallace lying half-curled like a dropped dying squirrel on the concrete of a Maryland shopping-center parking lot. He was shot with a small pistol after a campaign rally there, on the very day when, with his victories that evening in the Maryland and Michigan primaries, he arrived at the highest crest of his long, rapt, furious political life. As so often happens, abrupt blurting intrusions of violence have disordered the traditional processes of government in the United States, until violence itself has become the dark abiding phantom extra-arbitrator of American history. In a way, it was only another instance of that peculiar uncanny luck that has attended Wallace throughout his political career that, in a season of assassinations, after the strikes at John Kennedy and Martin Luther King and then Robert Kennedy, he would be the only one of them who managed to survive. But after that act of highest vandalism in Maryland, Wallace seemed, when next glimpsed a few days later to have aged twenty years, to have become suddenly an old man—with the drab and empty gaze in his once crackling hot eyes of having been excarnated of his vitals, scooped out inside, like a sepulchral and incidental semblance of who he once was. He went through the motions, wanly and falteringly, of finishing out his gambit for the convention, though his superfluousness there now was confirmed. Elegies have always been notoriously treacherous propositions with Wallace's particular political fortunes, but after the spectacular ten-year flare as an irrepressible and ingenious poltergeist in national affairs, his day seemed now suddenly done. He seemed already to be passing into the dimming vague twilights of a yesterday. Whatever had been his own plot for the AIP after the Democratic convention was now lost.

Despite that, the American Independent party proceeded to hold its scheduled 1972 convention in Louisville, Kentucky, and the dogged disposition of its some 2,000 delegates from forty states was to nominate Wallace anyway, until Wallace himself addressed them by phone from a hospital bed in Birmingham, requesting that they select someone else. With that, the convention somewhat perfunctorily nominated, for vice president, Thomas Anderson, a farm magazine publisher long vigorous in the more lurid outer ranges of far-right billingsgate, and for president, John G. Schmitz—a John Birch Society member and briefly congressman from California's Orange Country. Schmitz, for his part, proposed, "The government of the United States of America today has ceased to speak for or represent, in any way, the hard-working, productive, taxpaying citizens who are the heart and backbone of our nation. . . . We do not have to stand for this any longer—and, God willing, we shall not. That is why the American party is in the presidential election contest this year, and why I agreed to be its candidate. . . ." For the most part, Schmitz maintained that both Republicans and Democrats were engaged in a conspiratorial Socialist collaboration, and asserted that President Nixon, in his intercourse with North Vietnam's allies during the Vietnamese conflict, had committed treason. He made such accusations, however, more with a certain stand-up humor than with Wallace's sullen ferocity.

With Wallace now having disengaged himself from a party conceived and sustained only as a personal expedient, the nomination of these two figures seemed to portend the American Independent party's inevitable contraction and atrophy into little more than an ossified remnant of Wallace's own expansive enterprise—another of those side-curious lingering from the long continuous evolution of America's central system of two opposition parties.

Appendix

AMERICAN INDEPENDENT PLATFORM OF 1968

PREAMBLE

A sense of destiny pervades the creation and adoption of this first Platform of the American Independent Party, a Platform personifying the ideals, hopes, aspirations and proposals for action of the Party and its candidates for the Presidency and Vice Presidency of the United States, George C. Wallace and Curtis E. LeMay.

As this great nation searched vainly for leadership while beset by riots, minority group rebellions, domestic disorders, student protests, spiraling living costs, soaring interest rates, a frightening increase in the crime rate, war abroad and loss of personal liberty at home; while our national political parties and their leaders paid homage to the legions of dissent and disorder and worshipped at the shrine of political expediency, only this Party, the American Independent Party, and its candidates, George C. Wallace and Curtis E. LeMay, possessed the courage and fortitude to openly propose and advocate to the nation those actions which are necessary to return this country to its accustomed and deserved position of leadership among the community of nations and to offer hope to our people of some relief from the continued turmoil, frustration and confusion brought about through the fearful and inept leadership of our national political parties.

It is to this end and for this purpose that this Platform is designed. Herein will be set forth the policies, attitude, proposals and position of this Party and its candidates, treating with those matters of deepest concern to the average American, his home, his family, his property, his employment, his right to freedom from interference and harassment from and by the government at all levels and, lastly, his pride in himself and his nation and all that it has stood for.

We feel that this American has an intense devotion to his country, glorifies in its accomplishments and is saddened by its failures and shortcomings; that he is tolerant of the mistakes of political leaders if he senses their actions to be in good faith and directed to the best interest of the country, but he is confused and dismayed when these leaders desert the principle of government for the people and dedicate themselves to minority appeasement as the country burns and decays.

This document treats of both foreign and domestic policy and is basically designed to present the proposals and action programs of this Party and its candidates in the area of:

1. Peace abroad and domestic tranquility at home.

2. An enlightened and advancing educational program, assisted but not controlled by the federal government.

3. Job training and opportunity for all Americans willing and able to seek and hold gainful employment.

4. An alliance and partnership with the private sector of our economy seeking an end to poverty among our people.

5. Efficiency and prudence in governmental spending leading to a helpful and stable economy free from the need for ever continuing taxation.

6. Inclusion of the farmer in our program of prosperity through his own efforts rather than total reliance of government subsidy.

7. Reestablishment of the authority and responsibility of local government by returning to the states, counties and cities those matters properly falling within their jurisdiction and responsibility.

8. Ending the inflationary spiral of the past decade through fiscal responsibility and efficiency to all echelons of government.

9. The orderly and economical utilization of the natural resources of this nation coupled with a sensible program of conservation of these resources.

10. An insistence that the laboring man and woman be given his fair share of responsibility and reward for the development of the mighty potential of this nation.

11. A re-dedication of this country to the love of God and country and the creation of a judiciary mindful of the attitudes of the people in this regard.

With these cardinal principles in mind, we herein set forth the precepts of our Party and Candidates in the following areas of concern:

DOMESTIC POLICY

Clearly, our citizens are deeply concerned over the domestic plight of this nation. Its cities are in decay and turmoil; its local schools and other institutions stand stripped of their rightful authority; law enforcement agencies and officers are hampered by arbitrary and unreasonable restrictions imposed by a beguiled judiciary; crime runs rampant through the nation; our farmers exist only through unrealistic government subsidies; welfare rolls and costs soar to astronomical heights; our great American institutions of learning are in chaos; living costs rise ever higher as do taxes; interest rates are reaching new heights; disciples of dissent and disorder are rewarded for their disruptive actions at the expense of our law-abiding, God fearing, hard working citizenry. America is alarmed that these conditions have come to exist and that our national leadership takes no corrective action. We feel that the programs and policies of our Party offers this leadership and provides constructive proposals of action for the elimination of the conditions now existing. This we would do in the following manner.

LOCAL GOVERNMENT

The Founding Fathers of our country, when they had won their freedom from King George III in the American Revolution, and were engaged in setting up our Federal Government, in their infinite wisdom, visualized the tyranny and despotism which would inevitably result from an omnipotent central government; and, they sought to avoid that peril by delegating to that central or federal government only those powers which could best be adminstered by a central or federal government, such as the laying and collecting of taxes to pay the national debt, providing for the common defense, regulating commerce between the states, declaring and waging war, coining money and establishing and maintaining a postal system. And then they provided, in Article X of the Bill of Rights, the Tenth Amendment to the Constitution of the United States, that:

> The powers, not delegated to the United States by the Constitution, nor prohibited by it to the states, are reserved to the states respectively, or to the people.

The Federal Government, in derogation and flagrant violation of this Article of the Bill of Rights, has in the past three decades seized and usurped many powers not delegated to it, such as, among others: the operation and control of the public school system of the several states; the power to prescribe the eligibility and qualifications of those who would vote in our state and local elections; the power to intrude upon and control the farmer in the operation of his farm; the power to tell the property owner to whom he can and cannot sell or rent his property; and, many other rights and privileges of the individual citizen, which are properly subject to state or local control, as distinguished from federal control. The Federal Government has forced the states to reapportion their legislatures, a prerogative of the states alone. The Federal Government has attempted to take over and control the seniority and apprenticeship lists of the labor unions; the Federal Government has adopted so-called "Civil Rights Acts," particularly the one adopted in 1964, which have set race against race and class against class, all of which we condemn.

It shall be our purpose to take such steps and to pursue such courses as may be necessary and required to restore to the states the powers and authority which rightfully belong to the state and local governments, so that each state shall govern and control its internal affairs without interference or domination of the Federal Government. We feel that the people of a given state are in better position to operate its internal affairs, such as its public schools, than is the Federal Government in Washington; and, we pledge our best efforts to restore to state governments those powers which rightfully belong to the respective states, and which have been illegally and unlawfully seized by the Federal Government, in direct violation of Article X of the Bill of Rights.

THE FEDERAL JUDICIARY

Our forebears, in building our government, wisely provided and established, in the Constitution of the United States, that the Federal Government should consist of three branches, the Legislative, represented by the Congress, whose duty and responsibility it is to enact the laws; the Executive, represented by the President, whose duty it is to enforce the laws enacted by the Congress; and, the Judicial, whose duty and responsibility it is to interpret and construe those laws, not to enact them.

The Constitution of the United States provides that the judicial power of the United States shall be vested in a Supreme Court and in such inferior courts as the Congress shall from time to time ordain and establish; and, further, that the judges of the Federal courts shall hold their offices for life, during good behavior.

In the period of the past three decades, we have seen the Federal judiciary, primarily the Supreme Court, transgress repeatedly upon the prerogatives of the Congress and exceed its authority by enacting judicial legislation, in the form of decisions based upon political and sociological considerations, which would never have been enacted by the Congress. We have seen them, in their solicitude for the criminal and lawless element of our society, shackle the police and other law enforcement agencies; and, as a result, they have made it increasingly difficult to protect the law-abiding citizen from crime and criminals. This is one of the principal reasons for the turmoil and the near revolutionary conditions which prevail in our country today, and particularly in our national capital. The Federal judiciary, feeling secure in their knowledge that their appointment is for life, have far exceeded their constitutional authority, which is limited to interpreting or construing the law.

It shall be our policy and our purpose, at the earliest possible time, to propose and advocate and urge the adoption of an amendment to the United States Constitution whereby members of the Federal judiciary at District level be required to face the electorate on his record at periodical intervals; and, in the event he receives a negative vote upon such election, his office shall thereupon become vacant, and a successor shall be appointed to succeed him.

With respect to the Supreme Court and the Courts of Appeals I would propose that this amendment require re-confirmation of the office holder by the United States Senate at reasonable intervals.

PRIVATE PROPERTY

We hold that the ownership of private property is the right and privilege of every American citizen and is one of the foundation stones upon which this nation and its free-enterprise system has been built and has prospered. We feel that private property rights and human rights are inseparable and indivisible. Only in those nations that guarantee the right of ownership of private property as basic and sacred under their law is there any recognition of human rights.

We feel that the American system of private property ownership, coupled with its system of free enterprise, upon the basis of which our country has grown and prospered for more than two hundred years, is sacred; and, we repudiate and condemn those who propose to transform our nation into a socialist state; and, we propose to furnish and provide a national leadership that is dedicated to the preservation and perpetuation of the great American system of private enterprise and private ownership of property.

We repudiate and condemn any federal action regulating or controlling the sale or rental of private property as a socialistic assault upon not only the system of private ownership of property, but upon the right of each American citizen to manage his private affairs without regulation from an all-powerful central government.

There is no provision in the Federal Constitution which gives Congress the power to regulate the sale or rental of private property. Such legislation strikes at the very heart of the American system and if followed to its logical conclusion will inevitably lead to a system alien to our concept of free government, where citizens are no longer able to make decisions for themselves or manage their personal affairs. We pledge to take the Federal Government out of the business of controlling private property and return to the people the right to manage their lives and property in a democratic manner.

CRIME AND DISORDER

Lawlessness has become commonplace in our present society. The permissive attitude of the executive and judiciary at the national level sets the tone for this moral decay. The criminal and anarchist who preys on the decent law abiding citizen is rewarded for his misconduct through never ending justification and platitudes from those in high places who seem to have lost their concern for that vast segment of America that so strongly believes in law and order.

We hear much of the "root causes" for the depredations committed in our streets and in our towns and cities. We hold that these are to be found in the apparent absence of respect for the law on the part of the perpetrators of these offenses, and the unexplainable compassion for the criminal evidenced by our executive and judicial officers and officials. We advocate and seek a society and a government in which there is an attitude of respect for the law and for those who seek its enforcement and an insistence on the part of our citizens that the judiciary be ever mindful of their primary duty and function of punishing the guilty and protecting the innocent.

We urge full support for law enforcement agencies and officers at every level of government and a situation in which their actions will not be unreasonably fettered by aribtrary judicial decrees.

We will insist on fair and equal treatment for all persons before the bar of justice.

We will provide every assistance to the continued training and improvement of our law enforcement facilities at federal and local level, providing and encouraging mutual cooperation between each in his own sphere of responsibility.

We will support needed legislation and action to seek out and bring to justice the criminal organizations of national scope operating in our country.

We will appoint as Attorney General a person interested in the enforcement rather than the disruption of legal processes and restore that office to the dignity and stature it deserves and requires.

We will provide leadership and action in a national effort against the usage of drugs and drug addiction, attacking this problem at every level and every source in a full scale campaign to drive this evil from our society.

We will provide increased emphasis in the area of juvenile delinquency and juvenile offenses in order to deter and rehabilitate young offenders.

We will not accept violence as the answer to any problem be it social, economic, or self-developed. Anarchists and law violators will be treated as such and subjected to prompt arrest and prosecution.

We will oppose federal legislation to enforce the registration of guns by our citizens, feeling that this measure would do little or nothing to deter criminal activity, but, rather, would prove restrictive to our decent, law abiding citizens, and could well encourage further activity by the criminal. We will preserve to the states their rights to take such reasonable measures as they deem appropriate in this area.

CITIES AND SUBURBS

The urban areas of our nation are in a state of social and economic unrest, largely brought about through unfilled promises hastily and carelessly made and the failure of ill-conceived programs enacted under duress and compulsion. For this, we must hold responsible the national leadership of the other two parties, for they were joint partners in this disastrous course of action resulting in the situation now existing in our cities.

We object to a federal policy which has poured billions of dollars into our cities over the past decades but which has not been able to prevent stagnation and decay and has resulted in the flight of millions to the suburbs. We reject the notion that the solution is untold additional billions to be poured into the cities in the same manner, whether such huge sums are to be raised from taxes on the middle class in general, or by unwelcome taxes on those who live in the suburbs of the individual cities. We submit that no government can buy contentment for those living in the cities, suburbs, or rural areas. We advocate the formulation of a mutually arrived at, joint federal, state and local policy which will make it economically and socially attractive and physically safe for people to live again in all sections of all of our cities. We submit that the science and technology, which made possible the development and growth of these cities, is the instrument whereby this can be brought about.

Specifically, there must be a restoration and maintenance of law and order before any program, no matter how well conceived, will succeed. We pledge ourselves to this accomplishment and will exert forceful leadership at local level to such effort.

Those totally unfitted by training, background and environment for urban living who have been lured to the metropolitan areas by the wholly false promises and commitments of self-seeking political leaders must be afforded an opportunity for training or, in the alternative, an opportunity to return to gainful employment in the less urbanized area from whence they came. This we propose to accomplish in conjunction with private industry through a program of diversification and de--centralization of expanding industry into areas away from metropolitan centers, thereby providing relief for many of the problems of the area while providing productive life for those afforded the opportunity to depart these overcrowded areas.

We advocate assistance, but not control, to local governmental units from the federal level to enable them to cope with their multiplicity of problems, feeling they are better prepared to offer solution than those more removed therefrom.

We advocate and will sponsor a partnership with the private sector of our economy in the restoration of job opportunity and a healthy living environment to our cities through program made economically attractive to industry.

We will support programs designed to provide means by which home-ownership can become a reality to our city dwellers, thereby instilling a greater feeling of dignity, stability and responsibility in those benefiting from such a program.

Above all, there must be a restoration of order in our cities as a prelude to any program of assitance, for without order neither government nor private industry will meet with success. Herein lies the cause of much failure in the past.

JOB OPPORTUNITY AND THE POOR

We feel that the matter of our citizens in need and the existence of job opportunities are so closely related as to warrant concurrent consideration.

We are convinced that the average American believes in the inherent dignity of gainful employment, preferring this method of attaining a livelihood to any welfare grant or benefit not earned through his own efforts. For this reason we consider the solution to the problem of our needy citizens, capable of gainful employment to be the provision of job opportunity. This will be the goal of our Party and our administration.

Our first consideration will be the inclusion of private industry in this program and effort. We believe that the private sector of our economy has the will and capability of providing a solution to the problem of poverty much more promptly and efficiently than any or all governmental programs of indiscriminate welfare contributions. Based on this premise, we will work in partnership with private industry in a program mutually beneficial to each to provide these job opportunities. We propose to make this program economically attractive to industry through tax incentives and other means of economic benefit, believing fully that the answer to this problem lies in the vigor and capability of our tremendous free enterprise system.

We would propose that the federal government aid and assist in a well designed program of job training or re-training for those in need thereof. This will be at the vocational school and lower level, depending on the needs of the trainees. We will encourage and assist the states in programs of job training or re-training through realistic productive efforts in this respect, including assistance to the establishment and maintenance of vocational trade schools and other like institutions designed to provide skilled and semi-skilled personnel for industrial employment, as well as means whereby "in-training" programs can be carried out by private industry in cooperation with government.

In the event a public works program becomes necessary to provide employment for all employable Americans, we will provide such a program assuring, however, that these programs be needful and productive and that the participants engage in labor beneficial to the nation and its economy rather than becoming wards of the government and the recipients of gratuitous handouts.

For those unemployable by reason of age, infirmity, disability or otherwise, provision will be made for their adequate care through programs of social services based on the requirements and needs of these persons. We hold that all Americans are deserving of and will have the care, compassion and benefits of the fullness of life.

HEALTH AND WELFARE

Senior Citizens

Social Security is basically an old age, survivors and disability Insurance Plan. It provides for citizens to pay into the Trust Fund during their working years and is designed to replace part of the earning capacity of the participant, or his family, lost due to retirement, death or disability. During past administrations, the Social Security Trust Fund has been depleted and current payments are being made from current revenues. Social Security cannot be financed from current revenues or from the Federal Treasury without raising taxes or jeopardizing other essential programs of government. Such a policy is irresponsible.

We pledge to restore the Social Security Trust Fund to a sound financial basis and by responsible fiscal policies to insure following:

1. An immediate increase in social security payments with a goal of a 60% increase in benefits.

2. An increase in the minimum payment to $100, with annual cost of living increases.

3. Restoration of the 100% income tax deduction for drugs and medical expenses paid out by people 65 and over.

4. Removal of the earnings limitation on people 65 and over in order that they may earn any amount of additional income.

Our goal is to make every senior citizen a first class citizen; to restore their dignity, prestige, self-respect, independence and their security, without intrusion into their private lives by federal bureaucrats and guideline writers.

Health Care

It is the obligation of a responsible government to help people who are unable to help themselves. There should be adequate medical assistance available to the aged and those unable to afford treatment. This can best be achieved through a partnership between federal and state governments and private enterprise. Medicare should be improved. It should be strengthened in conjunction with medical care provided at state and local governmental levels and by private insurance. Through sound fiscal management we set as a goal the following improvements in Medicare:

1. Relief to persons unable to pay deductible charges under Medicare.

2. Relief to persons unable to have deducted from their Social Security checks the monthly fee for physician service coverage under Medicare.

3. Providing for uninterrupted nursing home care for those with chronic illness who require such care.

4. We will encourage low cost insurance programs for the elderly and will assist the states and local communities in building hospitals, nursing homes, clinics as well as medical and nursing schools.

In this land of plenty, no one should be denied adequate medical care because of his financial condition.

We are particularly disturbed about the doctor-patient, and the hospital-patient relationship. We stand solidly for freedom of choice in this relationship. It is our intent that medical care programs be carried out without subjecting our professional people and our hospital administrators and personnel to the harassment which has been their lot since the implementation of the Medicare program. We believe that those assisted by the Medicare program should have some degree of selection in the medical and hospital services furnished to them, and that simplification in the administration of this program would prove of benefit to government, patient and the professional practitioner alike.

American medical and dental practice is the admitted marvel of the world. Its traditional freedom is one of the chief reasons why this is so. The American Independent Party pledges continuous study and effort to maintain that freedom both for doctor and for patient.

Other Social Services

The people of this land are the fiber of our nation. Their well-being is essential to a strong America. Unfortunately, many of our citizens are unable to earn an adequate living, due to no fault of their own. Our aged, our blind, and our disabled who are unemployed are the concern of us all.

In every area of social welfare, rehabilitation should be of paramount concern. This includes physical restoration where possible, training to develop new skills, adult education in many instances, and broad cooperative endeavors between government and private industry to develop jobs that the less skilled can fill. We believe that every American prefers independence and a wage earned. For those infirmities, age, or other problems prevent such independence, welfare services should be adequate to provide a living with dignity and honor.

Dependent children become the responsibility of government when they lack the care and support of parents or guardians. Every effort should be made to provide support by responsible persons rather than the government, where possible. However, when children are separated permanently, by death or other cause from their families, a facilities of government should safeguard, protect, serve and care for them.

In every area possible, federal grants should be administered through existing state and local governmental agencies, thus eliminating additional federal offices and agencies which merely duplicate efforts of existing state and local agencies.

We will review and examine the administration of these programs with a view to the elimination of waste and duplication and thereby better serve the purposes and people designed to be assisted. We subscribe to the principle of block grants, administered by state agencies as a possible solution to these problems.

NATIONAL ECONOMY

The national economy must be restored to and maintained in a healthy, viable posture under conditions assuring to each individual American the opportunity to participate in and enjoy the benefits arising from a real prosperity, as distinguished from the false, inflationary conditions presently existing. As a first step the nation's business, industry and other agencies and organizations of production must be freed from the ever increasing intrusions of government into the affairs of these institutions and organizations. This nation achieved its economic greatness under a system of free enterprise, coupled with human effort and ingenuity, and thus it must remain. This will be the attitude and objective of this Party.

There must be an end to inflation and the ever increasing cost of living. This is of vital concern to the laborer, the housewife, the farmer and the small business man, as well as the millions of Americans dependent upon their weekly or monthly income for sustenance. It wrecks the planned lives and retirement of our elderly who must survive on pensions or savings gauged by the standards of another day.

We will take immediate, affirmative steps to bring these conditions to an end through selective decreases in the lavish expenditures of our federal government and through the institution of efficiency into the operation of the machinery of government, so badly plagued with duplication, overlapping and excesses in employment and programs. Bureaucracy will cease to exist solely for bureaucracy's own sake, and the institutions and functions of government will be judged by their efficiency of operation and their contribution to the lives and welfare of our citizens.

We will support and assist business and industry in those areas needful and desirable, such as in the area of small business.

We will enforce those laws designed to protect the consumer and wage earner, but will eliminate those programs and agencies serving only to harass and intimidate our business community.

We will review and propose revisions to our present tax structure so as to ease the load of the small income citizen and to place upon all their rightful share of the tax burden.

We will work toward a reduction in the tax burden for all our citizens, using as our tools efficiency and economy in the operation of government, the elimination of unnecessary and wasteful programs and reduction in government expenditures at home and abroad.

We will eliminate the favorable treatment now accorded the giant, non-tax paying foundations and institutions and require these organizations to assume their rightful responsibility as to the operation of our government.

To achieve these goals and objectives, we would use government for the strengthening of the free enterprise system rather than the replacement of the free enterprise system by government. We believe that strength and confidence in the American political and economic system will tend to encourage domestic private investment and prosperity in our economy.

We would propose that effective use be made during our administration of economic advisors dedicated to the preservation and strengthening of our economic freedoms in the area of enterprise, labor and marketing that have contributed so much to the strength of the American system.

Our administration will be dedicated to the maintenance of prosperity and price stability in our economy. We will institute a strong anti-inflationary fiscal, monetary and debt management policy in our nation as the first requirement to solving international problems.

We propose to rely heavily upon a competitive market structure rather than upon prices administered or fixed by bureaucratic procedures.

We do not propose to use periodic, intermittent tax adjustments or surcharges as a tool of economic policy under the guise of stabilizing the inflationary spiral we are experiencing.

We feel little is done to curb inflationary trends in the nation's economy merely by taking from the taxpayer in order to enrich the spending programs of big government. We propose, rather, a stabilized and equitable tax base affording fair treatment to those of small income and designed to cause all persons, organizations and foundations to assume their rightful financial responsibility for government coupled with selective and prudent reductions in the wasteful expenditures of government.

AGRICULTURE

America's agriculture, and especially the small farmer, is on the brink of disaster. Under both Democratic and Republican administrations, the income of our farmers has steadily declined. Farm prices have been ranging at a parity level the lowest since the dark days of the great depression. Individual producers are unable to regulate the output or price of their products and stringent government controls have been forced upon farmers. Revolutionary methods of production have resulted in increased yield from less acreage and requiring less manpower. The farmer is hampered by a faulty system of distribution, and his costs have continued to increase at an astronomical rate. Yet, all America's farmers have received from either of the other two parties has been broken promises.

The following is the pledge of the American Independent Party to our nation's farmers:

1. We pledge ourselves to the protection and preservation of the family farm, which is the backbone of American Agriculture.

2. We pledge that the new Secretary of Agriculture will immediately begin to support prices at 90% of parity which is the highest level provided under present law.

3. Congress will be urged to increase the maximum support to 100% of parity.

4. Legislation will be sought to permit farmers to exercise their freedom of choice to vote whether or not to come under self-imposed controls.

5. We propose the creation of a National Feed Grain Authority, authorized to make long-term loans for development of farmer-owned and controlled warehouses, to be strategically located, permitting farmers to store large quantities of grain and to sell direct to the trade through their own local organizations.

6. We propose that no portion of the nation's emergency reserves of food, feed or fiber be sold for less that 115% of the prevailing farm price support of that commodity.

7. A limit to subsidy payments should be set in order to prevent an unfair advantage being built up by giant corporate farm structures over our small farmer or family farms.

8. We propose to impose reasonable limitations on the import of foreign farm and meat products into this country.

9. It is our belief that continued support of the REA and other cooperative programs designed to improve marketing methods conditions throughout the nation is vital to our farming interests.

10. It is our belief that federal support for farm research is important, and that Agriculture Colleges and Extension Services should be more effectively utilized.

11. Governmental agencies similar to the Farm Home Administration have been beneficial to farmers and should be improved and continued.

12. We propose that the State Department and the Agriculture Department work together in a joint effort to develop new foreign markets for our farm products and develop a vigorous export program.

13. We support a good soil conservation program and pledge the continuation and improvement of such program.

14. It is our policy to assist in improving farm production reporting in order that farmers obtain more accurate production forecasts for planning purposes.

15. It is our intention to simplify the administration of all farm programs, and to eliminate wasteful duplication and red tape within the Department of Agriculture.

16. We will work toward gradual relaxation and elimination of farm regulation and control with a concurrent reduction in required subsidization as farm income increases, the eventual goal being the elimination of both controls and the need for subsidy, such program being contingent upon the increase in farm income to a level making subsidy unnecessary.

17. We will require that programs for disease and insect control be continued and expanded where needed if it is indicated that state and local bodies need and desire assistance from the federal level. Such program would, among other things, provide for necessary steps to eradicate the imported fire ants. This pest is now

prevalent throughout a major portion of the southern region but will eventually affect three-fourths of the land area of the United States if eradication is not accomplished promptly.

The farmers of this nation are entitled to a fair, just and equitable profit on their investment, just as citizens in other fields of endeavor. It is our belief that a major step toward solving our problems in agriculture would be to insure a substantial increase in farm income. It is time for a new Secretary of Agriculture who represents the views and interest of the farmer and the rancher, and who will work ceaselessly and tirelessly to improve the income and the lives of America's farm families. We pledge to you such Secretary and such a program.

LABOR

America achieved its greatness through the combined energy and efforts of the working men and women of this country. Retention of its greatness rests in their hands.

Through the means of their great trade organizations, these men and women have exerted tremendous influence on the economic and social life of the nation and have attained a standard of living known to no other nation. In the meantime, American labor has become a bulwark against the intrusion of foreign ideology into our free society. America must be eternally grateful to it working men and women.

The concern of this Party is that the gains which labor struggled so long to obtain not be lost to them either through inaction or subservience to illogical domestic policies of our other national parties.

We propose and pledge

To guarantee to and protect labor in its right of collective bargaining;

To assert leadership at the federal level toward assuring labor its rightful reward for its contribution to the productivity of America;

To propose and support programs designed to improve living and employment conditions for our working men and women;

To prohibit intrusion by the federal government into the internal affairs of labor organizations, seeking to direct and control actions as to seniority and apprentice lists and other prerogatives;

To provide for and protect the working men and women in the exercise of democratic processes and principles in the conduct of the affairs of their organizations, free from threats, coercion, or reprisals from within or without such organization;

To support programs and legislation designed to afford an equitable minimum wage, desirable working hours and conditions of employment, and protection in the event of adversity or unemployment;

To add efficiency and dispatch to the actions and activities of the National Labor Relations Board, resulting in more prompt decisions by this agency;

To pledge and assure that labor will be adequately represented in all deliberations of this Party and its administration of the affairs of government;

To cause all agents of government to refrain from any coercive action in strike settlements, serving in the role of counselor and advisor only, believing that good faith bargaining between the parties concerned is the best solution to any settlement.

EDUCATION

Without question education offers the answer to many of the nation's social and economic problems. It is tragic that during the past decades, while governed alternately by the Republican and Democratic parties, we have witnessed the deterioration of our public school systems into a state of disruption wherein the maintenance of order is the major problem and quality education is a forgotten objective. Our educational leaders and administrators are discouraged and dismayed by the continuing attacks upon, and erosion of, their duties and authority by agents of the federal bureaucracy and members of the federal judiciary.

Local educational officials have been stripped of their authority to administer the affairs of their school systems. Harassing directives and requirements of an unreasonable and unrealistic nature are constantly being imposed upon them. Parents, students and educators alike are dismayed, confused and at a loss as to where to turn for relief. Many of our institutions of higher learning have been completely disrupted by a small band of revolutionaries, encouraged by the permissive attitude of executive and judicial officials of government and the activities of other anarchists throughout the nation.

Many of our primary and secondary school systems have become centers for social experimentation rather than centers of learning, serving merely as pawns for the whims and caprices of some member of the federal judiciary or some agent of the federal bureaucracy.

These conditions must come to an end. Our educational systems and institutions must once again be given the opportunity to resume their rightful duty of preparing the youth of America for entry into our highly competitive society.

As a first and immediate step we must absolutely prohibit the agencies and agents of the federal government from intruding into and seeking to control the affairs of the local school systems of the states, counties and cities of the nation. Control of these schools must be returned to the local officials, representatives of the people, who have the rightful duty and authority to administer such school.

Once returned to proper control, order must be restored and education of our children again become the primary matter of concern in these schools. Sociological experiments must cease. The people of the several states, counties, cities and communities must be given the right to administer the affairs of their schools as they see fit without fear or threat of reprisal, economic or punitive, from the federal government.

We must cooperate with the administrators of our institutions of higher learning now in the hands of revolutionaries. We must support these officials in the restoration of order on their campuses and we must assure that no assistance, financial or otherwise, from the federal level be given to those seeking to disrupt and destroy these great institutions.

America is a nation "Under God" and we must see that it remains such a nation. We will support with all the power of the Executive action to restore to our educational institutions and the children they serve the right and freedom of prayer and devotions to God.

We must assure that the federal government assist in all phases of the educational processes of the nation without attempting to control these processes.

With these thoughts in mind

We advocate a greater role of the states in administering federal aid and in determining national policy.

We advocate the return of our school systems to the states and to local, county and city officials.

We advocate support for administrators of our educational institutions in their efforts to restore order to these institutions.

We advocate fewer federal guidelines, regulations, and administrative procedures and greater simplification and consolidation of programs and procedures.

We advocate less categorical aid and more general aid to states with funding provided for well in advance.

We advocate educational opportunity for all people regardless of race, creed, color, economic or social status.

The complexities of education are many. State and local officials are faced with tremendous pressures to provide early childhood education, increased teacher salaries, provide vocational technical education, improved elementary and secondary education, provide adult education, continuing education, and urban and rural education, provide for higher education, graduate and professional education.

The goals of the American Independent Party are to improve the educational opportunity for all our citizens from early childhood through the graduate level. We believe that the improvement of educational opportunity can best be accomplished at the state and local level with adequate support from the federal level.

SCIENCE AND TECHNOLOGY

The scientific and technological skills and accomplishments of America are the marvel of modern civilization. Our potential in this area is unlimited. Our development of this potential must be commensurate with our capability. We live in a fiercely competitive world in the area of science and technology. For social, economic and security reasons we must not lag behind.

We would propose, encourage and provide from the federal level assistance to those of our youth showing demonstrated capacity in these areas of endeavor. Federal grants based on ability and aptitude will be provided to assure development of skills in this field.

Federal assistance will be made available for research in various fields of science for in research lies the key to tomorrow. Such assistance will be directed both to individuals and to institutions.

We propose that this research, development and scientific knowledge so acquired be directed to human problems as well as national security. In the fields of housing, transportation, education, industry and related activities, these skills and the knowledge so acquired can make for a better life for all Americans.

Emphasis on the further exploration and utilization of space must be renewed. This, again, is a highly competitive area between nations, but not for this reason alone, but for the welfare and security of this nation, we must not be lacking in our effort in this field.

We fully support renewed and expanded efforts in our space program with the objective of acquiring knowledge and experience of benefit to the peaceful pursuits of mankind as well as that essential to the military security of this nation.

TRANSPORTATION

The expansion of America's industry, commerce and its economy depends upon its transportation system. America cannot maintain its position as world leader in industry and commerce unless all modes of transportation are able to meet the demanding challenges of the future. To solve America's transportation problems requires ingenuity and planning.

Airport congestion around most major cities is not only a growing problem, but an ever increasing danger. We face a major railroad crisis and citizens in many urban areas are unable to travel short distances without delays due to congested highway traffic. Our merchant marine fleet has dwindled and our ship building industry suffers today. This not only affects our economy, but is a serious handicap to America's military might.

We therefore favor

1. The development of a modern, low cost domestic mass transportation system within our congested urban areas;

2. Development of high-speed passenger trains between urban areas;

3. An emergency program carried out cooperatively by the federal government and the airline industry to develop adequate methods of controlling air congestion, and for financing and improving airport facilities;

4. Developing a program of assistance to modernize and stimulate our merchant marine fleet and our ship building industry.

The Interstate Highway System is one of America's wisest investments. Every effort must be made to speed up construction on existing plans, and farsighted planning of additional facilities must be accomplished. The Interstate Highway System must be expanded, adding new routes between population centers, and extra attention should be given to constructing additional freeways in and around congested urban areas. Not only is this necessary for the expansion of commerce and the economy, but highway safety demands it.

Thousands of Americans lose their lives each year on the nation's highways. Most of these deaths are unnecessary. With proper highway planning, stricter enforcement of highway laws, and intensified driver education, along with proper safety devices provided on automobiles, we will be able to cut these needless and tragic fatalities to a small fraction.

Public safety and convenience demand that we engage in a vast program to improve and four-lane many of the local road and highway networks. Highway construction is financed by those persons using the highways and is one of the few federal programs that is self-financed which amounts to a capital investment of public funds, and this we greatly favor.

We will encourage the development within the transportation industry of organizations who are specialists in the movement of passenger and cargo from point to point, using all modes and means of transportation, and we will encourage healthy competition between such agencies and organizations.

NATURAL RESOURCES AND CONSERVATION

The preservation of our natural resources and the quality of our natural environment has greatly been ignored during the past decade. We are vitally concerned about the future well-being of our citizens and fully realize that positive action programs must be undertaken, in a cooperative effort between the federal government and the states, to assure adequate outdoor recreational facilities and to assure necessary health safeguards for generations to come.

To these ends we make the following pledge to the American people:

1. We will promote an agressive campaign at all levels of government to combat the serious air and water pollution problem.

2. Full support will be given to the establishment of adequate water quality standards to protect the present high quality waters, to abate pollution, and to improve the status of waters not now considered of high quality.

3. We will work in close cooperation with private industry and governmental agencies toward engineering designs to abate the mounting air pollution problems.

4. We will actively support research to control pests through biological means and chemical means which are more selective and less persistent than those now used.

5. Legislation and an active program are necessary to protect our endangered wildlife species. This problem is of serious concern and will receive our immediate attention and action.

6. We will work for protection of our waterfowl wetlands and nesting areas.

7. Our estuarine areas must be protected as vital to the production of fish, shellfish, furbearers, waterfowl and other aquatic creatures.

8. All federal assistance programs to the states in the areas of game and fish and for outdoor recreation will be streamlined to gain the maximum benefit from each dollar invested.

9. Our increasing population demands improved and additional outdoor recreational areas. To this end we will support active programs at all levels of government for the development of existing parks and proper outdoor recreational programs. Public lands must be utilized for multiple uses to benefit all of our people.

10. The preservation of our forest and timber resources is of utmost concern to the nation. We pledge federal cooperation with efforts of state and local governments and with private industry for a sound and economically regulated basis to avoid depletion of this vital natural resource. Government and industry will be encouraged to participate in planned reforestation programs, and programs for protection of our forests from the ravages of fire and other destructive causes.

America is blessed with an abundance of natural resources, with beautiful scenery and bountiful waters. This land of ours should not be marred and its resources wasted. We recognize that progress invites construction and industrial development and we recognize its necessity, but we must assure that the intangible values of our parks, forests and estuarine areas will be protected, promoted and developed and that America shall retain its scenic beauty for centuries to come.

We will place particular emphasis on the problems of air and water pollution and will initiate joint cooperative programs with industry to attack and solve these problems, as their correction is in the interest of all segments of our national life, the people, the government and the nation's industry.

VETERANS

America owes no other group of citizens so much as we do our veterans. To that group of self-sacrificing and patriotic individuals who have risked their lives for our nation and its principles in past wars and conflicts, and to our brave men and women returning from service in Vietnam, we pledge you the support of the American Independent Party. We pledge to you and your dependents our assurance of active and vigorous assistance in seeking out job opportunities; job training; further educational opportunities and business opportunities. We likewise support a program to provide educational benefits to children of deceased veterans in order that they may receive a quality education and participate in America's competitive society of the future.

We pledge to our veterans, their families and dependents the cooperation and active assistance of their government in providing adequate medical treatment and hospital care. Veterans' benefits and disability benefits will be updated and revised periodically in order to meet the increased cost of living. The Veterans Administration and its hospitals will remain as an independent agency of the government, and its one objective will be to serve our veterans and their families.

INDIAN AFFAIRS

For over 100 years the other two parties have been making promises to our fellow citizens, the American Indians and Eskimos. For over 100 years the promises of those parties have not been kept. Our Party offers to these independent and hard working people a new hope. We promise that all of the programs of the federal government which have so lavishly bestowed benefits upon minority groups of this country will be made equally applicable to the American Indians and Eskimos. There will be no discrimination with respect to these two ancient and noble races.

We also promise that the federal government will cooperate fully to insure that job opportunity, job training, full educational opportunity, and equal application of all health and housing programs are afforded to these, our native citizens, in order that they may enjoy the same benefits and privileges enjoyed by every American. We will foster and support measures through which the beauties and accomplishments of their native culture will be preserved and enhanced.

FOREIGN POLICY

One of the greatest needs of our country at this moment in history is a strong, realistic, well defined policy to guide our relationship with the other nations of the world. The policy developed to govern our actions in foreign affairs must be one well stated and well understood, first by our own people and, equally as important, by friends and foes alike throughout the world. The absence of any such well defined and consistent policy throughout the past two decades has contributed immeasurably to the chaotic world conditions now existing.

Our foreign policy will be one designed to secure a just and lasting peace. We feel that such a situation can best come to exist when nations deal with one another on a basis of mutual trust and understanding. If this be lacking, as is so often the case in today's world, the only alternative is complete frankness and determination to adhere to stated objectives and courses of action. If a nation, as is the case with an individual, will only say what it means and mean what it says, it will gain respect, if not always the admiration, of its sister nations. It is in this regard that we have failed, so often equivocating in such a manner as to cause friendly, as well as unfriendly, nations to have grave doubt as to our stability, determination and reliability of purpose.

We feel that the road to peace lies through international cooperation and understanding. We will pursue this goal to the limits consistent with our own national interest. We will become participants in international programs of aid and development from which all member nations, including our own, derive benefit.

We will not abandon the United Nations Organization unless it first abandons us. It should be given fair opportunity at resolving international disputes, however, we will not subordinate the interest of our nation to the interest of any international organization. We feel that in this organization, as in any other, participating members should bear proportionate shares of the cost of operation and we will insist on financial responsibility on the part of the member nations. We also feel that the officers and officials of such organization must conduct themselves with an abstract air of objectivity and impartiality, and we will so insist. We will give this organization every opportunity to succeed in its purpose but should it fail, we will reappraise our relationship with it.

FOREIGN AID

Foreign aid and assistance, both of an economic and military nature, will be granted on a basis of what is in the best interest of our own nation as well as the receiving nation.

We will deny aid and assistance to those nations who oppose us militarily in Vietnam and elsewhere, as well as those who seek our economic and military destruction by giving aid and comfort to our avowed enemies. This must be so in order to protect the economic welfare and national security of this country.

We will continue aid to those countries who need, deserve and have earned the right to our help. This will be done freely and willingly with every effort directed to elimination of waste and dishonesty from such programs.

Foreign aid must become an instrument of foreign policy and be used in such manner as to further the interest of this nation.

EXPORT-IMPORT

We believe strongly in the free enterprise system for America, internally as well as in its trade relations with other nations. However, should the increasing inflow of imports from low-wage nations endanger employment or marketing by American industry, we will approve reasonable quantitative limits on these imports. We feel that our home industry is entitled to a fair share of the present market and of future growth. Before seeking additional legislation in the import field all efforts will be exerted toward securing negotiated agreements that would fully protect American industry.

We will insist on equitable tax treatment for any industry adversely affected by foreign imports, in the area of depreciation allowances for plants and equipment and in like measure.

We will cause the Department of State and other interested agencies of government to work toward the lowering of trade barriers against American goods in a manner consistent with the policy of our administration on controlling imports into the American market.

In the event certain segments of our industrial economy are adversely affected by foreign imports to such an extent as to cause economic harm, we will sponsor and develop programs of re-training and re-employment for those so affected.

BALANCE OF PAYMENTS

A serious situation now exists in our balance of payments and this must be ended.

We feel that the adoption of the programs and proposals set out in this Platform will result in a more favorable balance of payments situation. Specifically, we feel that the relief we so badly need in this respect may be achieved through reductions in spending for foreign aid, more efficiency in the use of funds for international programs, and more reliance on our allies in meeting heavy military expenditures abroad.

We have earlier proposed that foreign aid be granted on a basis of need and in a manner consistent with the best interest of this country and that it be denied those who aggressively seek our destruction. We strongly advocate efficiency in operation and the elimination of waste and corruption from expenditures under international programs and we will insist that our allies assume their proportionate and rightful share of the burden of defenses in those areas in which we have mutual interest.

Our export-import situation remains in reasonable balance but our disastrous situation as to balance of payments is caused by excesses in our foreign aid program and other international gratuitous expenditures.

We will work to reduce our military expenditures overseas, not by lessening our military strength and preparedness, but by causing our allies to assume and bear their proportionate share of the burden.

MIDDLE EAST

The Middle East remains a source of high potential danger to world peace. In the interest of securing a stable peace in this part of the world, we will take the initiative in seeking mutual cooperation between the adversaries in this area in reaching agreement in their age-old dispute. We will encourage the initiation of multi-lateral discussions to arrive at the best possible terms of settlement. This will mean resolving and stabilizing boundaries and the free use of water and land routes throughout this area. Binding non-aggression agreements must be developed and we must seek the mutual respect of both Israel and the Arab nations.

First and foremost is the need for sincere negotiations between these two parties. Until this is accomplished we must assure that no imbalance of force comes to exist in this area. Nothing could more endanger the peace.

Should arms continue to be introduced into this area by foreign powers to such an extent as to endanger the peace in this part of the world, we must take steps to assure that a balance of force is brought to exist. We will join with other nations of the free world in providing the means whereby this balance of force will continue and the threat of aggression of one nation against another is made less likely. More importantly, this nation will strive in every way to merit and receive the friendship of all parties to this dispute and to earn the respect and good will of Israel and the Arab nations alike. The road to peace in the Middle East lies in this direction rather than in the continued use of military might.

EUROPE

We continue to regard Western Europe as an area of vital importance to America. In our concern with the interminable conflict in Southeast Asia we must not lose sight of the strategic importance of our relationship with our European allies. We must retain a posture of strength in this area and must work with and for our allies to assure that they remain economically and militarily strong.

We will continue to support the North Atlantic Treaty Organization and seek to strengthen it through the cooperative efforts of all member nations. We will retain the necessary troop strength in this vital area and will insist that our allies and member nations do likewise.

We will deal patiently but firmly with the present French government feeling that in due time its actions will, of necessity, be directed toward increased cooperation with its Western allies of long standing.

We will remain concerned for the captive satellite nations of Eastern Europe and share with them their hopes and aspirations for their eventual and inevitable return to the family of free nations.

LATIN AMERICA

The interests of the nations of Latin America are closely related to those of this country, economically, geographically, security-wise, socially and politically.

We must and will provide aid and assistance to these nations to enable them to achieve political and economic stability and to better prepare them to resist the threat of communist infiltration and subversion from the Red satellite, Cuba.

We will develope a program of assistance to these countries designed to relieve the conditions of economic and social poverty existing in some segments of these nations and to provide for their less fortunate citizens a better condition of life.

We will assist in the development of the agricultural and industrial potential of these nations and the development and proper utilization of their tremendous natural resources rather than the exploitation thereof, to the end that the nations of this hemisphere may live in peace, prosperity and harmony with one another and that the principles of the Monroe Doctrine may once again become a cornerstone of our national policy.

We will work with and support the Organization of American States.

CUBA

As for Cuba, we will continue and strengthen the economic pressures on the Castro tyranny. In order to do this, we must secure a greater degree of cooperation from nations of the free world than we have had in the past. Trade with Cuba by our allies must be effectively minimized, if not completely curtailed.

To frustrate Castro's attempt to export subversion, we must increase the quality and effectiveness of our military aid and assistance to Latin American allies with a primary objective of developing realistic indigenous counterinsurgency capabilities within those countries. Economic aid, more carefully planned and scrupulously administered, will be continued through the Alliance for Progress Program, or an improved version thereof.

AFRICA AND ASIA

The emerging nations of Africa and Asia desiring assistance and demonstrating a capability of reasonably assimilating such help and assistance will be aided. We will not aid in the replacing of one form of despotism with another, nor will be become concerned with the internal quarrelings of dissident groups and factions.

We disagree with present economic sanctions and pressures applied to Rhodesia and the Union of South Africa and will seek to have these removed and eliminated. We consider these to be nations friendly to this country and they will be respected and treated as such.

GENERAL

We will conduct the foreign affairs of this country on a basis of aiding, assisting and cooperating with our friends and recognizing and treating our enemies and adversaries as such. We feel that foreign affairs can be conducted effectively only when there is respect for our nation and this respect is best engendered by attaining a position of strength and adopting an attitude of firmness and fairness. This we will do.

We feel that when this nation again becomes a strong and determined nation, dedicated to a fixed national and international policy, many of our existing difficulties throughout the world will become resolved and new difficulties are less likely to arise.

We will oppose aggression and subversion. Communist or otherwise, whenever it infringes upon the national interest of this country or its friendly allies through means appropriate to the situation.

We do not propose, nor does this or any other nation have the capability, to police the entire world. We will avoid unilateral entanglement in situations not vital to our national interest and will seek the cooperation of our allies at every opportunity.

VIETNAM

The current situation in Southeast Asia, and particularly in Vietnam, is one of the most critical which has ever faced this nation. The American people are angry, frustrated and bewildered as they seek for leadership which apparently fails to exist. There is no parallel in American history of such a situation as now exists, not even our engagement in Korea, where there were at least vaguely defined objectives.

It is too late to engage in debate as to why we are so deeply involved and committed in Vietnam. The fact is that we are so involved. No one can retrace the steps of the last ten years and correct and adjust all that has gone wrong. We presently have more than one-half million Americans committed to this conflict and they must be supported with the full resources of this nation. The question now is what does America do to maintain its honor, its respect and its position in this most strategic part of the world, Southeast Asia.

The prime consideration at this time is the honorable conclusion of hostilities in Vietnam. This must be accomplished at the earliest possible moment.

We earnestly desire that the conflict be terminated through peaceful negotiations and we will lend all aid, support, effort, sincerity and prayer to the efforts of our negotiators. Negotiation will be given every reasonable and logical chance for success and we will be patient to an extreme in seeking an end to the war through this means. If it becomes evident that the enemy does not desire to negotiate in good faith, that our hopes of termination of hostilities are not being realized and that the lives and safety of our committed troops are being further endangered, we must seek a military conclusion.

Hopefully such a situation will never arise, but should it come to pass, I would then seek the advice and good judgment of my Joint Chiefs of Staff as to ways and means of reaching a military conclusion to this conflict with the least loss of life to our American servicemen and our South Vietnamese allies, stressing the fact that this is to be accomplished through the use of conventional weapons.

Military force has always been recognized as an instrument of national policy and its use to obtain objectives has always been accepted. However, once national policy is established by the civilian government and military force has been selected as one of the means of attaining national objectives, the tactical employment of this force should be left to the military so long as this employment is consistent with national policy, and the mission of the military should be to attain these national objectives—nothing less.

I would retain full control, as a civilian Commander-in-Chief, of final decision, but I would pay heed to and consider to the fullest extent the advice and judgment of my military advisors.

Unfortunately, there is not clearly defined national policy with respect to the conflict in Vietnam. If there were, much of the doubt, debate and despair of the American people would be eased. There is a total absence of clearly announced and understood national objectives with respect to Vietnam. We are told that it is not victory over the enemy we seek but something else—what we do not know. In battle, and certainly this is battle, there can be but one objective—that is victory. Anything worth dying for is worth winning.

As first step we must develop a clearly defined national policy as to Vietnam. This policy will be made known to the people of this country and will be based on our own national interest. The essence of this policy will be a timely and successful termination of the conflict, either through negotiation or by victory over the enemy. We will not allow this conflict to drag on indefinitely with its great drain on our national resources and manpower.

As President, we will designate a Secretary of Defense who holds the confidence and trust of the people, the Congress and the military establishments and one with the capability and desire of working in harmony with each. He will be required to reduce the excessive manpower of the Pentagon and rid the Department of Defense of those who have fostered the "no-win" policy.

We will then require the establishment of firm objectives in Vietnam. Should negotiations fail, and we pray that they will not fail, these objectives must provide for a military conclusion to the war. This would require the military defeat of the Vietcong in the South and the destruction of the will to fight or resist on the part of the government of North Vietnam, which is equipping and supporting the enemy troops in the South. We feel that the prompt and effective application of military force could achieve this objective with minimized loss of life, and the tactical employment of this force will be left in the hands of the military commanders, so long as they act pursuant to defined national policy.

We will require the military to plan and conduct military operations once policies and objectives are established and we will not, or will we permit civilian subordinates, to usurp these functions and assume the role of "commander" or "tactician." This must be a team effort with officials and leaders of civil government performing their required functions and the military establishment being allowed to perform in the manner and for the purpose for which it is trained.

Once hostilities have ceased, efforts must be undertaken to stabilize the government and economy of Vietnam. This must be through programs of self-help and not through completely meaningless "give away" programs. We are dealing with a proud people of ancient culture. They are not, and never will be, adapted to all the facets of western civilization, nor should they be. We must help them to become secure in their government, their lands, their economy and in their homes, as their friends and allies and not as sanctimonious intruders. In this manner, we will gain a lasting ally.

NATIONAL DEFENSE

Nothing is of greater importance to the American people at this time than the state of our National Defense, and sadly, there is no area of our national structure so fraught with misrepresentations and inconsistencies. As we near the end of the era of "computerized defense" and "cost effectiveness" rather than military reliability, it is difficult, if not impossible for the nation to ascertain the true state of its defenses.

We are aware of basic fallacies in the doctrines and logic of those who have been charged with the responsibility of our national security.

We have been told that strength is weakness and weakness in strength—This is not true.

We have been told that parity rather than superiority in weapons and munitions is sufficient to assure the keeping of the peace and the protection of this country—This is not true.

We have been told that a "deterrent" capability is preferable to an offensive capability in maintaining peace and assuring freedom from attack—This is not true.

We have been told that commitment of our military forces need not always be followed by a quest for victory—This is not true.

We have been led to believe in the proven invulnerability of our "second strike" capability—This is not true.

We have been told that the complete disruption of the structure of our Reserve Components resulted in a more readily responsive Reserve—This is not true.

We have been told that our research and development program, especially in the area of space research and development, is not lagging—This is not true.—And so on.

We propose an intensive and immediate review of the policies, practices and capabilities of the Department of Defense with a view to reestablishing sound principles of logic and reasoning to the decisions and directives of that agency and to eliminating from its ranks all of those who have been party to the dissemination and promulgation of the false doctrines of security and the coercion, intimidation and punishment of all who would oppose or disagree with them.

We are in accord with civilian control of our defense establishment but will insist that the civilian authorities work in partnership and harmony with the splendid military force with which this country is blessed. We propose to restore to their proper duties, functions and authority the leaders of our military services so that the nation may once again profit from their wisdom and experience.

We will require our civilian and military leaders of defense to establish a reasonable relationship between defense and offensive capabilities and provide our services with the proper arms, munitions and equipment to afford a proper mix of both type weapons and munitions.

We will place increased emphasis on research and development in the area of space, weaponry and mobility, as well as other areas vital to our national security.

We support the installation of an anti-ballistic missile defense for the protection of our nation and its citizens. We will expedite this program.

We will assure to our services the best attainable weapons, equipment, machines and munitions without resort to devious distinctions of cost effectiveness and the substitution of arbitrary, unsound judgment for that of the professional military.

We will guarantee to the services and to the nation that American troops will never be committed with less than full support of available resources.

We will seek efficiency in the collection and evaluation of vital intelligence throughout the services.

We will never permit a static situation to develop wherein America stands still while her potential enemies continue to advance in all areas of development.

We will hasten the reconstitution of an adequate and efficiently organized reserve force throughout the several states of the nation. We will accept these reserve component forces into full partnership with the regular military establishment and will assure stability to their organizational structure and operation.

We will take all steps necessary to return our Merchant Marine fleet to its rightful place among the maritime nations of the world. This is not only vital to our national security but to the economic progress and viability of the nation. Maritime shipping has been, and will once again become, a vital part of the nation's economy and trade activity.

We will take steps to make military service more attractive to the enlistee, the inductee and the career personnel at all levels. We will support programs for better pay; better housing and living conditions, both on and off post; more realistic programs of promotion potential so that merit and performance may be rewarded; equitable sharing of hardship assignment; and increase and more uniform retirement benefit to correct serious inequities now existing; a pay scale commensurate with that of private employment, with provisions for periodic increases measured by the cost of living index; improved and expanded medical and hospital benefits for dependents, and a restoration of the dignity and prestige rightfully due those engaged in the defense of our nation.

With military services becoming more attractive the requirement for involuntary inductions through the Selective Service System is reduced. However, we favor retention of such system for so long as there is a need for manpower being acquired by this means. We would approve any changes to such system designed to eliminate inequities in the selection of inductees, and quite likely some do exist.

We would feel that eventually manpower requirements may be met on a voluntary basis. In such event, a fair and equitable system of civilian induction will be kept in existence, on standby basis, for use in the event of national emergency.

CONCLUSION

This Platform represents the attitude, policy, position, judgment and determination of this Party with respect to the major problems confronting America.

We believe that our analysis of the nature of these problems is in keeping with the feelings of the great majority of our people. We further feel that our approach to solution of these matters is sound, logical, practical and attainable and in keeping with the basic, inherent good judgment of the American people.

Among other proposals,

We offer opportunity for early peace to a nation at war.

We offer order and domestic tranquility to a nation sorely beset by disorder.

We offer a program of job opportunity for the jobless.

We offer a return to respect for the law and an opportunity for every citizen to pursue his daily activities in safety and security.

We offer to relieve our citizens, their businesses and institutions, from harassment and intimidation by agents of the federal bureaucracy.

We offer to return to the officials of local government those matters rightly and properly falling within their scope of responsibility.

We offer the laboring man and woman an opportunity to provide for himself and his family a better and fuller life and a greater democratic freedom in the management of the affairs of his organizations, free from intrusion by the federal government.

We offer to the farmer an opportunity to regain a place of prominence in the economy of this nation, a fair price for the products of his labor and less dependence on federal subsidation.

We offer to restore the dignity, strength and prestige of this nation to a level commensurate with its position as acknowledged leader of the nations of the free world.

We offer a national defense designed to assure the security of this nation and its citizens.

And, above all, we offer to each individual citizen a system of government recognizing his inherent dignity and importance as an individual and affording him an opportunity to take a direct hand in the shaping of his own destiny and the destiny of this nation. Under such a system, we are convinced, America will reach new heights of greatness.

PRESS INTERVIEWS WITH GEORGE C. WALLACE
September and October 1968

BY NEW YORK TIMES EDITORS AND REPORTERS*
[Excerpts]

Dallas, September 17, 1968

Q. We have a Constitution that's served in this country over a great many years, and now we have got lots of new problems and things of that kind. Do you think the Constitution is as good today as it was when it was written or does it need some updating, an amendment or something?

A. The Constitution of the country is still just as good a document as it was when written, as far as I'm concerned. It has provisos for amendment process.

Q. Right.

A. And I can think of at least one amendment that ought to be submitted to the people of the country; submitted to the legislatures, rather. And that's the one involving the public school system.

Q. What would that be, Governor?

A. It would be an amendment declaring that absolute control of the public school systems should vest in the states, and all matters involving privileges and immunities and due process of law that arose thereunder, insofar as schools were concerned, would be decided by the state courts. That really was the law, in my judgement, prior to the take-over of the public school system by the Federal courts and the Federal Government. By usurpation of authority, the judges nullified the 10th Amendment.

Q. This would be, in essence, an amendment that would revoke the 1954 [school desegregation] decision of the Court?

A. Well, not necessarily—the 1954 decision was an anti-discrimination decision. I don't know that anybody argues with an anti-discrimination decision. In the long run, of course, what the argument was about was that they knew and we knew that this was not just anti-discrimination and we were correct. It was a matter of forceful take-over, and forced compliance with whatever guidelines are written by the Federal Government. They have jumped from non-discrimination to complete control.

For instance, we had freedom of choice in the public school system in Alabama and Texas and the other states of this region, but the Federal authorities filed a suit in which they said not enough people chose to go to the proper schools.

*New York Times, September 26, 1968.

That showed that they were not truthful when they said they believed in this decision; they really didn't believe in this decision unless it did what they wanted it to do.

And so the free choice proposition of being able to choose to go to any school you want to go to regardless of race didn't work, and bring about those changes that the pseudo-intellectuals, the smart folks, the people that want to handle my child's life and tell me what to do with my child, and what neighborhood for him to go to school wished,—It didn't work. That is, the people didn't choose like they thought they would choose.

And so now they say you must choose for them, and if you don't choose for them, then we are going to choose for them. And so, in Alabama, for instance, they just arbitrarily ordered the closing down of 100 schools, including some new multimillion-dollar high schools—just closed them down.

Q. We have a war in Vietnam today, and we never have declared war. I wonder why we don't do that?

A. I think the really important thing is that we are in Vietnam with a half million American servicemen whose lives are at stake and who are totally committed, whether we agree with the war or not. As long as they are there we must do whatever is necessary for their interest. That is what I am concerned about.

My main concern is the safety for those who are being shot at. Now, I was shot at during the war, and I know how it feels to be shot at. I think our main concern is their safety and health at the present time. And when you bring up the matter of aiding the Communists, why that's one reason this movement has strong support as all these pseudo-intellectual definitions of treason and academic freedom run counter to the common sense judgment of the average man.

While his sons are over there being shot at by the Communists, and his grandsons, you can let somebody go out and raise money and blood and fly the flag of the people trying to kill his son. And you let a professor make a speech that's reprinted in the Communist capitals saying, we wish defeat for our servicemen. And the theoreticians say [in Washington] we can't do anything about that because we really haven't declared war.

Q. Would you do something different?

A. Many people at the time questioned our moral position in World War II. But we got into it. I am glad we defeated the Nazis and Fascists. When we got into it we saw it to a conclusion. I think that we ought to have a reappraisal of our position with our allies, telling them that it is as much your interest as it is ours, that you have as much at stake as we do, and we expect you to help us.

Now, we can't make them help us. But we can think about our commitments, all the way from military to money, and we can think about what they owe us. I believe that since they need us and we need them, that they would respect us more and we would get more support for our position if we laid it on the line with them.

Q. I also think that you had something on your mind about Vietnam that you wanted to say, and we got off that subject.

A. Well, we talked about our involvement there and about our allies, and of course, like I say in my speeches, I hope and pray the peace talks in Paris are successful, and I believe if we could have an honorable peace through negotiations, that's best. Hopefully, diplomacy and political negotiations will settle the war honorably and peaceably and bring the servicemen home, but it looks like the Paris talks may fail.

Q. Do you have some pattern in your own mind about that settlement?

A. Well, of course, I don't think that settlement ought to be one in which we just completely surrender the South Vietnamese Government to the Vietcong and a coalition government really, in the long run, amounts to that.

If we fail in getting a guarantee of the integrity of South Vietnam, then I think that we are going to have to turn to the Joint Chiefs of Staff for advice and if they feel that a military conclusion through the use of conventional weapons can be brought up—that is, a military victory—then I would be for that.

Q. There's the question of the nuclear antiproliferation treaty that has come up in the campaign. Mr. Nixon says that he's for it, but he thinks we ought to delay making any moves for ratification of it. Mr. Humphrey is on the other side. Do you have any particular views about that?

A. Well, of course, I think it would be good to stop the proliferation of nuclear weapons. But, of course, the signing of a treaty doesn't necessarily mean the Communists will abide by the treaty, because they will proliferate, if they want to, and nonproliferate, if they don't want to proliferate.

So I think that any agreement we make with them in this field, or any other field, ought to be one providing for adequate inspection programs.

I just don't believe the Communists on their word, and I don't think you folks do either. But I think we should wait awhile on the ratification of the treaty, but with the understanding that we are still interested in nonproliferation of nuclear weapons.

In view of the recent actions of the Communists in Czechoslovakia I think perhaps it's good to delay it. But we should never say that we are going to forget about proliferation. I think we ought to stop the proliferation of atomic nuclear devices.

Q. Why not go ahead and sign it now?

A. Well, maybe in that way we can let the Russians know we are not pleased with their actions in Europe.

Q. What about the Supreme Court, Governor? You are talking about the Supreme Court and the decisions. Would you have any program dealing with the Supreme Court?

A. Yes, I'd sponsor a mountain climbing expedition for some of them to draw off some of their excess energy. However, attrition takes its toll under every Administration. And I would appoint people differently oriented in the first place.

In the second place, I would ask that Congress provide, through Constitutional amendment or otherwise, whichever is appropriate, that the term be limited to, say, eight years, and that they then have to be reconfirmed by the Senate of the United States. I'd also recommend an age limit, a retirement time.

Q. Governor, you have said a couple of times here, in discussing the strength of your movement and your chances for election, that one of the reasons you stand a good chance is because the people are angry and they are mad for a whole series of reasons. Is there a danger that that anger can fall over into actual violence?

A. No sir. Some of you folks—I don't mean you, personally, but I am talking about your paper and other papers—you sympathize with and help build up the forces who believe in violence because you have written editorials declaring what a great movement it was to lie down in the streets. Those are the people that have brought about the anarchy and violence in the country. Unless that is contained and controlled, you are going to have a movement that's not going to be on the left. It's going to be on the other side and it's going to stop all of this.

That's the fear, that's one reason I am running for President. I want to change some things in the country—within the constitutional context—at the ballot box and thus prevent violence.

We are not going out here and ask that a hundred thousand people march in Raleigh, N.C., that a hundred thousand march in Montgomery, Ala., or here in Dallas, or Houston. You have been with us and seen the crowds we had. We don't ask them to do that. We say, "You must obey the law and obey court orders, whether you like them or not."

You see, this is for the purpose of preventing what we are talking about and it is to stop this group of militants and anarchists from threatening the mass of people in the country. When you go to hear me speak and there are 200 in Milwaukee [anti-Wallace demonstrators] there with Father [James] Groppi and 7,000 inside and that many more on the outside supporting us, you understand how they are outnumbered in the nation as far as people are concerned. Those people that were applauding me outnumber this group.

We must control this group of militants and anarchists. Unless we stop their activities, I mean, their unlawful activities, they are going to be in danger themselves.

Q. But, is the only solution to this beating them on the head?

A. We have tried every other solution. The previous administrations have passed every civil rights bill known to man to placate the anarchists, including the open housing bill. Senator Robert Kennedy said when he was living, "Let's just pass these bills and get people out of the streets into the courts."

And the more bills they passed and laws and judgments they rendered, the more activity we had in the streets. So we have spent billions of dollars in the poverty program to give people money, and still have street mobs, so what else do you suggest?

Q. What do you suggest?

A. In France they were about to destroy the republic as a result of revolution in the street. What did de Gaulle say the last time? "This is the last of it," didn't he say? "We are going to suppress it next time with whatever suppression is necessary." Well, you haven't had any more of it, have you? Why not try that? The idea of people throwing bombs and looting and burning and laughing and carrying on while the police are ordered to stand around and watch them doesn't make sense.

Q. Do you think this represents the large percentage of the population?

A. No, I think it represents a small percentage of the population. I think the majority of black and white people are overwhelmingly against it, and want it stopped. It is a few folks who take advantage of the situation—a few militants.

Prior to this, if you had any mob action, the same newspapers who now say go soft on these rioters and looters said, "Shoot those folks." Now, it is turned around the other way, and then you want to handle looters and arsonists with kid gloves.

Maybe that is the way folks at The New York Times think it ought to be done, but the masses of people are tired of it. The man who goes out and works 25 years for a home, works every day and then his home is burned down, he is mad! He can't walk in his neighborhood in most cities of the United States at night without fear of something happening to him.

And the policeman who makes any effort to do anything about this crime often ends up being sued, demoted, fired or suspended.

People are tired of this, and there is a way to stop it. Proper use of the police power is the only thing left now to try to curtail anarchy in the country. Everything else has failed.

Q. May I ask you another question, a direct question? Are you a segregationist?
A. Well, what do you mean by a segregationist?

Q. Do you believe in segregation?
A. Well, segregation of the races? In what respect?

Q. Schools and hospitals?
A. In the first place, you are asking me a question about something that never has existed in the history of the country. We have never had what your definition of segregation is, to exist in the South. In fact, we have had more mixing and mingling and togetherness and association there than you have had in New York City, where The New York Times is located. We have worked together, we have sat together, we have ridden together, we have been completely together in the South.

We did have in the school system a separation because the schools in the rural South were the social center. And we did have social separation as you have in New York, and as you have in your family life. And so we just had a common sense social separation —the schools were the social center. But if you mean complete separation of the races, we have never had that and I hope we never will have it.

Q. But do you advocate a return to segregation of the schools?

A. No sir. I do not advocate that.

Q. In Alabama?

A. No, sir. I don't advocate that. I am running for the Presidency of the United States on the platform of turning the control of the public school systems back to the people of the states. And I would say that you would not have a completely segregated system in Alabama.

But, you would have a control of the system that would mean it would never deteriorate to such a status as the Washington school system, and some of the schools in New York City have deteriorated into. God help us if our schools ever get to be a jungle like you have some in New York City, and like you have in Washington, and like you have in Philadelphia—

Q. Well, the reason—

A. They can't even play high school football games before crowds. In Philadelphia they play football games behind locked gates with just the cheer-leaders—no spectators, because they had had a race riot at every football game. I think schools should be controlled locally.

Q. The reason I asked the question is that I wondered if you have changed your views?

A. No, sir, I haven't changed my views at all. I said I thought the segregated school system was the best school system in Alabama. It was a system that has peace and tranquility. And after all, there is something to say for peace and tranquility.

Although the theoreticians and the newspapers and others think it is not so important to have a peaceful and tranquil community and a peaceful and tranquil school system. It is a real good school system compared to some they have in some parts of the country. So a segregated system has been the best school system for Alabama, that is correct.

Q. Well, do you think—?

A. I am running for Presidency of the United States, and I want to leave it to the states. And so I would make no recommendation to Alabama.

Q. To the states or to local school boards?

A. Well, to the states, as every local school board is a creature of the state and the states created—all political subdivisions—so leave it to the states. The states have, by enactment of their legislatures, given authority to local school boards to administer school affairs in their particular localities.

The reason local school boards have control of schools in Alabama is because the State of Alabama, the sovereign, granted that power to the local school boards. The local school boards granted no authority to the states. So when you leave it to the states, you are leaving it, in effect, to the local school boards.

Q. Do you think whites and blacks, they just ordinarily want to stab one another?

A. Want to do what?

Q. Want to stab one another.

A. I didn't say that they want to stab one another. I just said in your school systems and parts of the country you have fights and friction and violence every week.

Q. Well, what does that have to do with segregation and integration, now?

A. Forced mixing in the big school systems at an abnormal rate has brought violence in the school systems, that's correct.

BY ASSOCIATED PRESS EDITORS*

Buffalo, October 4, 1968

Q. We would like to begin, Governor, by discussing the law and order issue. Law and order has been described by all three candidates in the presidential election as one of the main issues of the campaign. All are for law and order, but few specifics have been advanced to deal with the problem. What we would like to do is try to clarify this by suggesting that we take law and order and break it down to specific problems and ask you how you would deal with each of them.

First, how would you combat the growth of organized crime which has steadily increased despite the efforts of the FBI and other police forces?

A. Of course, at the federal level we have many federal statutes regarding organized crime. I think the Justice Department ought to be more vigilant and I think the President ought to speak out on the matter of organized crime. I think he ought to lend the moral support of the presidency to the local law enforcement officials in the combating of organized crime.

Q. As of now though you see no need for any additional federal laws to combat organized crime?

A. No, I don't think we need any additional laws. We need a common sense interpretation of existing laws. We need some common sense application of rules of jurisprudence involved in confessions, involving obtaining evidence so that each time you arrest and convict someone for crime they won't be turned loose because of the Supreme Court rule that the confession was taken, for instance, without a lawyer present. The different decisions of the court have handcuffed the police and law enforcement officials throughout the country in their fight against organized crime and also crime on the streets. It is almost impossible to convict anybody of any crime now from the highest to the lowest.

*Birmingham News, October 13, 1968.

Q. If you were President would you ask Congress to pass legislation that would overturn the so-called Miranda and Escobedo decisions?

A. Yes, I would. I said that many times. I think those two decisions have helped bring about the increase in the crime rate and they really, in effect, made second class citizens of the policeman in our country.

Q. How would you deal with the widespread growth in recent years of petty crime, mainly committed by young people, that infests every area of the country? Tied to this question is the growth of drug addiction, since much of the crime is committed to obtain money for narcotics?

A. Well, we see people in high places with their permissiveness on the matter of crime in the streets, the matter of looting and arson. No one has any respect for the law any more and I think this encourages and helps to bring about the commission of petty crime and also drug addiction and everything else, because it is the thing to do and you can do it and nothing happens to you, nobody is going to bother you, you can't convict anybody. I think that plays a part in that. I also think that the Justice Department and the states ought to really bear down on this matter of marijuana and LSD.

Q. Would you consider any federal legislation, perhaps to outlaw LSD and marijuana?

A. I don't know that you need any further federal legislation. I don't think we ought to move into any more areas of law enforcement. I think that the states ought to handle it. However transporting marijuana, LSD, across the state line is or should be a federal offense, but I think by and large we ought to leave the matter of law enforcement to the states.

Q. One other point on this, Governor, in the matter of heroin particularly, the hard narcotics, these are almost all imported. Would you have any ideas, perhaps for action by this country and other countries, in trying to cut off this traffic?

A. Of course I am not a law enforcement official and I cannot talk about items of strategy, logistics and mechanics of combating heroin or the importation of heroin, or anything else, but as President I would ask those federal agencies who are charged with law enforcement to stop the heroin traffic. Now how they are going to stop it would be left up to them.

Q. How would you deal with racial disorders, rioting and looting?

A. I don't know whether you should call them racial disorders. Usually racial disorder is between races, people of two races, you don't have much of this in the country at all. We do have a few militants who bring about the breakdown of law and order and then a few other people are caught up in the mob action, the hysteria of the moment, and loot and burn and commit arson. I think the police ought to be allowed to enforce the law. I think they have to be allowed to use whatever methods are necessary to prevent the breakdown of law and order and then if it does break down, they ought to be allowed to use whatever measures are necessary to stop it. We've used every other method of trying to stop disorder, we passed every piece of legislation advocated by the militants and otherwise. They passed the first bill called the civil rights bill. Senator Kennedy said we'd get folks out of the streets and into the courts and when you pass another bill you have more folks to get into the streets. I think we've tried every other method but that of the method of letting the police enforce the law.

Q. You talk about the militants being responsible, and "militant" seems to be something of a relative term. Would you identify the militants?

A. You might say militants are activists, revolutionaries, anarchists, and even Communists. Grand jury investigations in various parts of the country have shown the Communists involved. I'm talking about a person who stands up and says let us burn the town down is militant, he is a revolutionary.

Q. Would you characterize a person who advocates civil disobedience, non-violent protest, as a militant?

A. Civil disobedience is militancy, too. That is not the way to change laws or to air grievances. The people of our region of the country have been very upset about all the laws and court orders that destroyed their right to determine the policies involved in the education of their children. But they haven't advocated civil disobedience. They have advocated doing the best we could, and one reason my candidacy has the support of so many people in Buffalo and throughout the country is that we're going to change some of these procedures and laws and court orders within the constitutional context. So I think the matter of civil disobedience is just another method to disrupt and create chaos in the country and destroy our society.

Q. Since civil disobedience almost always involves a localized protest at the time, that is a march in Memphis or in Philadelphia or a march in New York, isn't it true that there is nothing a President can do to prevent them?

A. You have a right to march in Memphis peacefully saying we stand for so and so, but you don't have a right to march eight weeks and when I'm talking about civil disobedience I'm not talking about a march, people have a right to march for a candidate. I'm talking about lying in the streets, I'm talking about sitting down on thoroughfares and sitting down in buildings and assaulting the Pentagon, assaulting draft board stations, lying down on railroad tracks, in front of troop trains, that type of civil disobedience ought to be stopped. I'm certainly not talking about somebody who wants to make a march in protest, they have a right to do that.

Q. These acts of civil disobedience which you have just enumerated except for those that might have happened in the District of Columbia are outside federal jurisdiction. Do you have any plan of bringing them within the realm of federal authority?

A. No sir. I recognize what you are driving at. As President you don't have any right to go into the state of Alabama and stop this from happening but my election as

President is going to be a moral boost to the policemen and law enforcement officials in the country, and it is going to put some backbone in the back of the mayors and governors when we carry their states and is going to put backbone in the back of members of Congress whose districts we carry, because they really feel like we do . . . about stopping all this nonsense but they don't think it was politically expedient. I think my election is going to mean stronger law enforcement in this country, I think that's going to be a mandate to the people back in the states, that is the officials back in the states, to stand with their police and not handcuff them, not send them into a situation without even a gun and tell them don't do anything, don't hurt people's feelings. That is what happened many times.

Q. You said that you would urge the police to enforce the law by any means necessary. Precisely what do you mean by "any means necessary?"

A. I don't know that I said by any means necessary. I said enforce the laws with the means they know are necessary and that they know how to employ. The police have been trained how to stop looting and rioting and arson. They have been trained how to control people who infringe upon the rights of others by making it unsafe for folks on the street and maybe a situation involving a riot. Just let them employ the tactics that they've been taught to use in the past but are not allowed to use now because the politicians in charge of the police in many instances are afraid it's going to affect them politically.

Q. Would you agree that the police should employ the maximum force necessary to put down these disorders?

A. No, sir. They should use the minimum force necessary to put down the disorders. Don't use maximum force. You use whatever is necessary—the maximum could be the minimum sometimes. But you use the minimum force, not the maximum force. I don't want to see a situation exist where people just go out and want to knock people in the head. However sometimes when you knock a few in the head, it saves having to knock many in the head, and I think strong measures in the beginning save lives. We saved lives in our own state by saying in advance what we were going to do in case you break out windows or throw rocks at policemen or try to set something on fire. It will be the last place you set on fire, and as a consequence, nobody even got hit in the head because—there was no trouble.

Q. If it's necessary for the police to shoot to stop looting and burning do you think the police should be permitted to shoot?

A. To stop a riot and looting and destruction of property and the committing of arson yes. If that's the only way it can be done, yes. Now, I don't advocate we just go out and shoot to be shooting, but I think they ought to take whatever measures are necessary.

Q. What would you do about student demonstrations, some of which have been over opposition to the war in Vietnam?

A. Well, you have a right to demonstrate against the war, but when you make one march on a city street, you ought not to march for three straight weeks and tie up trade and commerce and business and imperil the safety of people as a result of continuous demonstration. You have a right to protest the war, although, I think common sense and judgment ought to be used by protesters who love our country, but who genuinely think that the war is not good for the United States. That's one thing, but now, those who go out and call for Communist victory and fly the Viet Cong flag and raise material for the Communists, I think that's violation of the law, to get up and make a speech that you think the war is not good or we ought to get out of the war, it's not good for our country, that's one thing. Just to make a speech saying I want the Communists to win and they print that speech in the Communist capitals, that's not legitimate dissent. That's an overt act of treason, because it aids and abets the enemies of our country and if you apply a little common sense you can tell a legitimate dissenter from one who's not a legitimate dissenter.

Q. What would you do, Governor, with the people—

A. I would—you see the courts have held that states cannot punish for sedition in the Steve Nelson case arising in Pennsylvania. So the Government of the United States, the Justice Department, ought to seek indictments against those who make speeches calling for Communist victory and those on college campuses, the few that do raise money and blood and clothes for the Communists. You ought to indict them and stick a few of them in jail and you'd stop it. I just don't understand sending grandsons and sons of American people to be killed by the Communists and allowing people in this country, some of them draft exempt, because they're going to college, raising material and supplies for the Communist and flying the Viet Cong flag. I don't understand it, but to me that's not academic freedom.

Q. Since all the three candidates have said they're for law and order, how would you describe your position as differing from those of your opponents?

A. Well, of course, a year ago when I was talking about law and order, these candidates were not talking about law and order. And a few years ago when I was talking about civil disobedience was going to culminate in anarchy, Mr. Nixon and Mr. Humphrey were endorsing this movement, saying it was a great movement. Now, since it engulfed the whole country in a siege of anarchy they both say law and order. Of course I knew they would start saying it when they sent their representative around to listen to me speak and hear the reception from the crowds that we've had all over the country, so there used to be no difference in what they said, or a dime's worth of difference I used to say. Now there's not a dime's worth of difference in what they say and what I'm saying about law and order, but this movement of ours brought it about, and I think they ought to have started saying it a long time ago.

Q. You're saying now that you and Mr. Nixon and Mr. Humphrey on this issue are saying essentially the same thing.

A. Saying essentially the same thing, but I don't think their hearts have been in it as long as mine because they have, on the other hand, actually endorsed this movement that brought about the breakdown of law and order.

Q. You have said that you hope an honorable settlement of the war in Vietnam can be negotiated. Specifically, what terms would you accept as constituting an honorable settlement?

A. The integrity of South Vietnam, remove the North Vietnamese armed forces, and the Viet Cong to lay down their arms and have free elections in Southeast Asia. I would consider coalition government being forced upon the South Vietnamese with the Communists represented, would not be an honorable settlement. I would say it would mean the end of South Vietnam. It would become Communist. Now if the people in South Vietnam vote Communist, that's another thing. I don't think they will, but that's what would constitute an honorable settlement as far as I'm concerned.

Q. Given the present situation in Vietnam, do you think the North Vietnamese are likely to settle for anything less than a coalition government with Communist participation in South Vietnam?

A. I don't have any idea what they would agree to. What they agree to would be based on how critical their situation happens to be and so I have no idea what the North Vietnamese would do. I frankly think they're using the peace talks for propaganda purposes and they're using it to rebuild that portion of North Vietnam that we're not bombing now.

Q. How would you go about increasing the pressure on North Vietnam to negotiate an acceptable settlement? Would you, for example, resume the bombing?

A. Well, of course, I don't want to talk about military strategy and tactics because I'm not a military man, but if I were the President and peace talks hadn't concluded and we don't have an honorable settlement by the time of the new administration, then I think we ought to set some time limit in the matter of negotiations, and then if they don't solve and settle the matter honorably, then we ought to win a military victory with conventional weapons and get out of Vietnam.

Q. In connection with winning a military victory with conventional weapons, we'd like to ask you what military actions are you prepared to take to win that victory?

A. I am not prepared to say what military action I would take because I would not be a military man, and I would ask the Joint Chiefs of Staff what military action we should take. But I will not abrogate my civilian responsibilities to the military. I would lean heavily upon them and probably accept their advice.

Q. Would you authorize an invasion of North Vietnam or the neutral states of Cambodia and Laos if the military should decide that such steps are necessary?

A. I would still lean on the Joint Chiefs of Staff and accept their recommendation about ending the war if we fail to end it in Paris.

Q. You would go along with what the Joint Chiefs of Staff recommended?

A. I don't say that I'd go along with everything they recommended. I would not give up my right as commander-in-chief to veto or to accept, but I would lean very heavily upon them.

Q. Invasion of North Vietnam and the bordering states has been suggested as a means of cutting off the lifeline of supplies from North Vietnam to its forces in South Vietnam and to the Communist guerrillas, the Viet Cong. Many people who oppose this, including some military men, contend that carrying the ground war into enemy territory would risk involving the United States in a war with Communist China. Do you agree? Is that a risk that you can—

A. Well, we took a calculated risk when we went to Vietnam. And we shouldn't have gone there by ourselves in the first place. I hear one of the other candidates say what I've said for a long time. It is just as much to Western Europe's and non-Communist Asia's interest to be there as it is for us to be there, but we took the calculated risk when we went in Vietnam. Now, if you're talking about Red China, in my judgment Red China would get involved in the war if she wanted to get involved in the war and won't get involved if she doesn't want to. And she doesn't have to have any excuse for getting in the war, she can concoct any excuse, because the leaders of Red China control all the news media and they could say tomorrow morning in their newpapers that we had invaded China whether we had invaded China or not and the Chinese people would not know any difference. So, we took the risk when we went over there, but if we lose diplomatically and politically, then we cannot stay in Vietnam forever. We cannot continue to have three or four hundred servicemen killed a week, in a war that we see no end to, and if we can't win it militarily—if we lose diplomatically and politically, what other recourse is there but to get out. So I would say we got out if we couldn't win militarily, but I think we should win militarily and I think that we have to take whatever risks we take, because we took those risks when we went there, I certainly don't want to get bogged down in any war with anybody else. I don't think we are going to.

Q. Do you believe that the United States should continue its policy of military intervention as exercised in Lebanon, the Dominican Republic and Vietnam?

A. I think that Western Europe, that has two hundred and fifty-five million people—more than we have in this country—ought to carry a larger share of the load of not only manpower, but munitions and money and also those in the Far East in Japan and Thailand and the Philippines and all other countries who have a stake in a free Asia. And when I said we shouldn't have gone there by ourselves, when we saw we were going, we should have talked to Western Europe and non-Communist Asia and they ought to have helped us. We ought to have talked to the SEATO signatories, some of them have a token force of a hundred people or five hundred and they have as much at stake as we do. They let us carry the load. And we should not have carried all the load by ourselves, with just token help. Now, we do have help from Australia and New Zealand, but they're small countries.

Q. What we asked, Governor, though, is that policy of being an international policeman?

A. No, sir, we cannot be a policeman for the entire world. In other parts of the free world they are going to have to shore up their defenses and their forces and they are going to have to take their share of the risks and take their share of the policing and we cannot be policeman for the entire world by ourselves. I don't want to say that we're going back to isolationism, because what happens in other parts of the world affects us.

Q. Would it be fair to say that you would reassess this policy?

A. Yes, sir.

Q. One possible trouble area is the Middle East where the United States has supported Israel in its continuing confrontation with the Arab states. Would you continue this policy?

A. Insofar as the Middle East is concerned, I would like to see stability and peace achieved at the conference table and that we wouldn't have a war every five years as we have had in the Mideast for the last fifteen years. And I would hope that by building our own defenses up in this country and having an attitude of superiority that we could then talk later with the great powers about trying to stop the arms race in the Mideast, which I think ought to be stopped if humanly possible. And the Arab nations and Israel both must give and take and see if they cannot solve their differences at the conference table, but there must be a military balance in the Mideast.

Q. Then given the Soviet Union's support of the Arab States, we have no alternative would you say?

A. I maintain that a military balance ought to exist, but that we ought to also try, if at all possible, through diplomacy, to gain respect of both sides, the Arab nations and the Israelis both, if that's possible, and help bring about a peaceful settlement with both sides giving and taking and that would stop the arms race. So I say there must be a military balance.

Q. In that connection, Governor, the other two presidential candidates have endorsed the sale of U.S. Phantom jets to Israel, which the Israelis say they need to maintain this military balance, but I don't believe you have.

A. Well, what I said was, Phantom jets are military hardware, and I said we must keep a balance. I don't know what is necessary to keep a balance, but whatever is necessary to keep a balance ought to be done. Not being a military man, I can't say submarines or M16 rifles or Phantom jets, but we ought to keep a balance, but at the same time trying to work with both sides for a peaceful settlement. And try to gain some respect from both sides. I would like to see this country friendly with all the peoples of the Mideast, which in my judgment would be a benefit to the Israelis and also to the Arabs.

Q. Governor, another source of potential trouble involves Korea, particularly the aggressiveness of the North Koreans as demonstrated in the seizure of the USS Pueblo and its crew. What would you have done about that seizure if you had been President?

A. Well, there is no need for me to say what I would have done, because I was not in possession of the intelligence that the State Department and the Defense Department had about the Pueblo. I'm sorry the matter happened and I think we should never forget the Pueblo and we should continue our efforts to get the crew back safely. I hope that we won't allow it to happen again and that we might have support in whatever area some ship of this sort happens to be. I can understand that with the delicate mission of this ship you couldn't have a flotilla around it, but I think that we ought to in the future see that it doesn't happen again. But since we've gone this far its been so long, the only recourse at the moment is diplomacy.

Q. Do you have any specific ideas for diplomatic maneuvers that might gain freedom of the crewman?

A. I don't have any specific ideas other than that I would ask the State Department with its trained diplomats and those in the career service to continue their efforts to get the crew back and we should never forget that either.

Q. You have said that you regard inflation as a major issue of the campaign. What steps do you feel must be taken to curb inflation?

A. Well, I think we ought to cut out some of the spending. We ought to take some of the welfare programs that really pay some able-bodied people not to work, and some of the so-called poverty programs and put on a public works program to employ able-bodied people in the building of highways and the building of streets, sewers, drainage systems, which enhances wealth and property values and helps to create trade and commerce. Some of the foreign aid programs ought to be cut out. The administration of domestic institutions which costs hundreds of millions of dollars of the taxpayers' money ought to be cut out. They should be administered in the districts and the political sub-divisions of the states that have elected officials. We ought to cut out on some spending.

Q. You have suggested at various times increasing personal income tax exemptions to $1,000, $1,200 and $1,500. Wouldn't any such increase be inflationary?

A. No sir, I don't consider it to be inflationary because I think it would stimulate production, stimulate employment and stimulate the need for additional production and there is nothing wrong with that. As long as production increases along with the spending capacity then you don't have inflation. You have inflation where you have an increase in spending and are status quo in production.

Q. Governor, there has been an increasing tendency in the government to use taxes or tax policy to attempt to control inflation or deflation. The recent

10 percent surtax is a case in point. Do you regard this sort of thing as an effective weapon?

A. Well, I think that naturally, that tax is an effective weapon against inflation, but we have so many tax exempt foundations that get by without paying their taxes. The government ought to remove some of the tax exemption status on the multibillion dollar tax exempt foundations and we should have gotten the money from them instead of from the average citizen on the street.

Q. Do you have any idea of how much money the Treasury could gain by removing those exemptions and do you think it would be enough to—

A. Yes sir. To raise a dependent's exemption from six hundred to a thousand dollars would cost nine billion dollars. I hope I'm correct on this but I've seen some reports estimate that from twenty-five to forty billion dollars is lost in taxes through tax loopholes as a result tax-exempt foundations and otherwise. So if you remove these tax loopholes, you could get as much as necessary to grant the dependent's exemption from six hundred to a thousand, maybe twelve hundred dollars, even in war time.

GEORGE C. WALLACE
SPEECH AT MADISON SQUARE GARDEN
October 24, 1968

Well, thank you very much ladies and gentlemen. Thank you very much for your gracious and kind reception here in Madison Square Garden. I'm sure that the *New York Times* took note of the reception that we've received here in the great city of New York. I'm very grateful to the people of this city and this state for the opportunity to be on the ballot on November 5, and as you know we're on the ballot in all 50 states in this union. This is not a sectional movement. It's a national movement, and I am sure that those who are in attendance here tonight, especially of the press, know that our movement is a national movement and that we have an excellent chance to carry the great Empire State of New York.

I have a few friends from Alabama with me and we have a number of others who were with us last week, but we have with us Willie Kirk, past president of Local 52, United Association of Plumbers and Pipefitters.

Well, I want to tell you something. After November 5, you anarchists are through in this country. I can tell you that. Yes, you'd better have your say now, because you are going to be through after November 5, I can assure you that.

I have also with me W. C. Williamson, business manager of Local 52, UAPP, Montgomery, Alabama, and R. H. Low, president of the Mobile Building and Construction Trades Council and business manager of Local 653 Operating Engineers.

And, you came for trouble, you sure got it.

And we have R. H. Bob Low, president of the MBC—We—why don't you come down after I get through and I'll autograph your sandals for you, you know?

And Charlie Ryan, recording secretary of the Steam Fitters Local 818, New York City. We have been endorsed in Alabama by nearly every local in our state: textiles workers, paper workers, steel workers, rubber workers, you name it. We've been endorsed by the working people of our state.

Regardless of what they might say, your national leaders, my wife carried every labor box in 1966, when she ran for governor of Alabama in the primary and the general election. And I also was endorsed by labor when I was elected governor in 1962.

Now, if you fellows will—I can drown—listen—if you'll sit down, ladies and gentlemen, I can drown that crowd out. If you'll just sit down, I'll drown 'em out—that—all he needs is a good haircut. If he'll go to the barbershop, I think they can cure him. So all you newsmen look up this way now. Here's the main event. I've been wanting to fight the main event a long time in Madison Square Garden, so here we are. Listen, that's just a preliminary match up there. This is the main bout right here. So let me say again as I said a moment ago, that we have had the support of the working people of our state. Alabama's a large industrial state, and you could not be elected governor without the support of people in organized labor.

Let me also say this about race, since I'm here in the state of New York, and I'm always asked the question. I am very grateful for the fact that in 1966 my wife received more black votes in Alabama than did either one of her opponents. We are proud to say that they support us now in this race for the presidency, and we would like to have the support of people of all races, colors, creeds, religions, and national origins in the state of New York.

Our system is under attack: the property system, the free enterprise system, and local government. Anarchy prevails today in the streets of the large cities of our country, making it unsafe for you to even go to a political rally here in Madison Square Garden, and that is a sad commentary. Both national parties in the last number of years have kowtowed to every anarchist that has roamed the streets. I want to say before I start on this any longer, that I'm not talking about race. The overwhelming majority of all races in this country are against this breakdown of law and order as much as those who are assembled here tonight. It's a few anarchists, a few activists, a few militants, a few revolutionaries, and a few Communists. But your day, of course, is going to be over soon. The American people are not going to stand by and see the security of our nation imperiled, and they're not going to stand by and see this nation destroyed, I can assure you that.

The liberals and the left-wingers in both national parties have brought us to the domestic mess we are in now. And also this foreign mess we are in.

You need to read the book "How to Behave in a Crowd." You really don't know how to behave in a crowd, do you?

Yes, the liberals and left-wingers in both parties have brought us to the domestic mess we are in also to the foreign policy mess we find our nation involved in at the present time, personified by the no-win war in Southeast Asia.

Now what are some of the things we are going to do when we become president? We are going to turn back to you, the people of the states, the right to control our domestic institutions. Today you cannot even go to the school systems of the large cities of our country without fear. This is a sad day when in the greatest city in the world, there is fear not only in Madison Square Garden, but in every school building in the state of New York, and especially in the City of New York. Why has the leadership of both national parties kowtowed to this group of anarchists that makes it unsafe for your child and for your family? I don't understand it. But I can assure you of this—that there's not ten cents worth of difference with what the national parties say other than our party. Recently they say most of the same things we say. I remember six years ago when this anarchy movement started, Mr. Nixon said: "It's a great movement," and Mr. Humphrey said: "It's a great movement." Now when they try to speak and are heckled down, they stand up and say: "We've got to have some law and order in this country." "We've got to have some law and order in this country." They ought to give you law and order back for nothing, because they have helped to take it away from you, along with the Supreme Court of our country that's made up of Republicans and Democrats.

It's costing the taxpayers of New York and the other states in the union almost a half billion dollars to supervise the schools, hospitals, seniority and apprenticeship lists of labor unions, and businesses. Every year on the federal level we have passed a law that would jail you without a trial by jury about the sale of your own property. Mr. Nixon and Mr. Humphrey, both three or four weeks ago, called for the passage of a bill on the federal level that would require you to sell or lease your own property to whomsoever they thought you ought to lease it to. I say that when Mr. Nixon and Mr. Humphrey succumb to the blackmail of a few anarchists in the streets who said we're going to destroy this country if you do not destroy that adage that a man's home is his castle, they are not fit to lead the American people during the next four years in our country. When I become your president, I am going to ask that Congress repeal this so-called open occupancy law and we're going to, within the law, turn back to the people of every state their public school system. Not one dime of your federal money is going to be used to bus anybody any place that you don't want them to be bussed in New York or any other state.

Yes, the theoreticians and the pseudo-intellectuals have just about destroyed not only local government but the school systems of our country. That's all right. Let the police handle it. So let us talk about law and order. We don't have to talk about it much up here. You understand what I'm talking about in, of course, the City of New York, but let's talk about it.

Yes, the pseudo-intellectuals and the theoreticians and some professors and some newspaper editors and some judges and some preachers have looked down their nose long enough at the average man on the street: the pipe-fitter, the communications worker, the fireman, the policeman, the barber, the white collar worker, and said we must write you a guideline about when you go to bed at night and when you get up in the morning. But there are more of us than there are of them because the average citizen of New York and of Alabama and of the other states of our union are tired of guidelines being written, telling them when to go to bed at night and when to get up in the morning.

I'm talking about law and order. The Supreme Court of our country has hand-cuffed the police, and tonight if you walk out of this building and are knocked in the head, the person who knocks you in the head is out of jail before you get in the hospital, and on Monday morning, they'll try a policeman about it. I can say I'm going to give the total support of the presidency to the policemen and the firemen in this country, and I'm going to say, you enforce the law and you make it safe on the streets, and the president of the United States will stand with you. My election as president is going to put some backbone in the backs of some mayors and governors I know through the length and breadth of this country.

You had better be thankful for the police and the firemen of this country. If it were not for them, you couldn't even ride in the streets, much less walk in the streets, of our large cities. Yes, the Kerner Commission Report, recently written by Republicans and Democrats, said that you are to blame for the breakdown of law and order, and that the police are to blame. Well, you know, of course, you aren't to blame. They said we have a sick society. Well, we don't have any sick society. We have a sick Supreme Court and some sick politicians in Washington,—that's who's sick in our country. The Supreme Court of our country has ruled that you cannot even say a simple prayer in a public school, but you can send obscene literature through the mail, and recently they ruled that a Communist can work in a defense plant. But when I become your president, we're going to take every Communist out of every defense plant in the United States, I can assure you.

The Kerner Commission report also recommended that the taxes of the American people be raised to pay folks not to destroy the country, and not to work. I never thought the day would come when a Republican and Democratic report would call for the taxes on the already over-taxed people of our country to pay people not to destroy. It is the most ludicrous and asinine report ever made to a president of our country. I want to tell you folks something. I was fighting the Nazis and Fascists before you were born. I was even shot at by them. I've been shot at by the Nazis—the Nazis and the Fascists. Now the Kerner Commission report—who is it writes these reports, ladies and gentlemen? It's usually some pointed head from one of those multi-billion dollar tax-exempt foundations. When they recommend that taxes be raised on you and me, they don't have to pay taxes because they're tax-exempt. When I become the president, I'm going to ask the Congress to remove the tax exemption feature on these multi-billion dollar tax-exempt foundations and let them pay taxes like the average citizen of New York pays also. It's estimated that 25 billion dollars goes through tax loopholes that ought to be paid by those able to pay and Senator Robert Kennedy himself said the same thing. So I say that what we ought to do is to remove that tax-exemption feature. And when we do, we can raise the workingman's dependent exemption from $600 to $1200 even in wartime.

Well now, all you television folks get a good picture over there now. Go ahead. You know—now its all over. Get this camera turned back this way. You know—everywhere we've spoken we've had this same kind of crowd, but the television puts all its footage on a few folks that don't know how to behave in a crowd and make it appear that there are no people supporting you here. And I frankly think the networks are doing that on purpose, myself. I don't think they want to show the support we have here in New York City and throughout the country. Yes sir, but I think they know tonight and have seen something they didn't expect in Madison Square Garden, and I reckon they'll try to explain it away tomorrow, the *New York Times*, and the other papers will. But you just remember that some of these newspapers can fool some of the people some of the time, but they can't fool all the people all the time. You remember that.

We have a comprehensive platform that I hope you get copies of before the election, in which we have dealt with every problem that faces the American people. But let me tell you briefly about foreign policy. The Democrats and the Republicans are always saying: "What do the folks at Madison Square Garden supporting the American Independent Party know about foreign policy?" I ask them: "What do you know about foreign policy? We've had four wars in the last 50 years. We've spent $122 billion of our money on foreign aid. We are bogged down in a no-win war in Southeast Asia, and anarchy in the streets. What do you know about foreign policy? You haven't been so successful in conducting American foreign policy in the last 50 years yourself." I can say this: we are in Vietnam. But General Lemay knows as I know and you know that the strongest deterrent to any further global conflict is superiority in offensive and defensive capabilities of our country. We can never be on a parity nor inferior because when you are superior, you can always go to the negotiating table; you can go to the peace table; you can go to the conference table. The way I would like to see every difference between any nation settled is around the conference table. But as long as there are tensions in the world, we cannot gamble upon the security of this city or this state or this nation by having anything but absolute superiority in the matter of defensive and offensive capabilities.

We are in Vietnam whether you like it or not. I sincerely hope and pray that the conflict is soon over, but we should have learned one thing about our involvement in Southeast Asia—the same thing that Mr. Humphrey now says in his speeches: we should not march alone. I said last year in California that we should never have gone to Vietnam—by ourselves. We should have looked our allies in the face in Western Europe and our non-Communist Asian allies and said to them: it is as much your interest as it is ours and you are going to go with manpower, munitions, and money, and if you don't go and help us in Southeast Asia, and if you don't stop trading with the North Vietnamese who are killing American servicemen, we are not only going to cut off every dime of foreign aid you're getting, but we're going to ask you to pay back all you owe us from World War I right on this very day.

Yes, the average taxpayer in New York doesn't understand his money going to those nations who not only won't support us, but on the other hand actively trade with the North Vietnamese. I'm not saying we must kick our allies out. We need them in Western Europe, and they need us. We need them in non-Communist Asia, and they need us. But NATO countries of Western Europe have 55 million people more than do the United States, and in the future they're going to have to carry their share of the defense burden because we cannot carry it alone. We will not carry it alone, even though we recognize that those things that happen in other parts of the world affect us in this country, they must carry their fair share of not only the manpower commitments, but also the commitments in munitions and money, and I know you agree with that.

I sincerely hope and pray that we have a successful negotiated peace. Well, I'll drown them out, come on. I sincerely hope and pray that we have an honorably negotiated peace to arise out of the Paris peace talks. I know that you pray that, and that the American servicemen can come home. But if we fail diplomatically and politically in Southeast Asia, we're not going to stay there forever, we're not going to see hundreds of American servicemen killed every week for years and months to come. If we do not win diplomatically and politically in Paris, that is, by honorable conclusion of the war, then in my judgment, we ought to end it militarily with conventional weapons and bring the American servicemen home. If we cannot settle it diplomatically and politically, and could not win it militarily with conventional weapons, then I wonder why we're there in the first place? We're going to conclude this war one way or the other either through honorable negotiations or conventional military power.

There's something else we ought to talk about and you see some of it here in the state of New York. We should stop the morale boost for the Communists in our own country. In every state in the union, this treasonable conduct on the part of a few, and their speeches, are printed in Hanoi, Peking, Moscow, and Havana. General Westmoreland said it is prolonging the war, and it is causing New Yorkers and Alabamans to be killed in Southeast Asia. When you ask the Attorney General of our nation: "Why don't you do something about this treasonable conduct" do you know what he says? "We are too busy bussing school children in New York and Los Angeles and we don't have time." We also have some college students who raise money, food, and clothes for the Communists and fly the Viet Cong flag in the name of academic freedom, and free speech. We didn't allow that in World War II; we did not allow for anybody to call for Nazi victory, or Fascist victory.

There is such a thing as legitimate dissent. Senator Robert Kennedy from this state said we should not be in Southeast Asia, and you have a right to say it yourself, if that's what you believe because you don't believe its in the interests of our country to be there. But if you arise and make a speech the next day and say I long for Communist victory, every average citizen in New York knows that one is dissent and the other is something else. I want to tell you that when I become your president, I'm going to have my Attorney General seek an indictment against any professor calling for Communist victory and stick him in a good jail somewhere. When you drag a few of these college students who are raising money for the Communists and put them in a good jail you'll stop that too, I can assure you. That'll stop them. We're going to destroy academic freedom in this country if we continue to abuse it as it has been abused at this time. Whether you agree with the war or not, we should agree that whatever we say or do should be in the national interests of getting the American servicemen home safely, and that sort of conduct is not conducive to the return of the American servicemen to New York and Alabama.

My friends, let me say this. We can win this election because it only takes a plurality to win when there are three or more running. If we get thirty-four percent of the vote in this state, and the other two get thirty-three percent apiece, then we win the entire electoral vote of the State of New York. That's all it takes. You know this, and that's one reason Mr. Nixon doesn't want to debate. Well, I want to tell Mr. Nixon it's a good thing he doesn't debate because if he ever does, we're going to point out that he's made so many inconsistent statements about so many matters, I would be happy to debate. But he cannot get a debate started.

That's alright. That's alright honey—that's right sweety-pie—oh, that's a he. I thought you were a she. I tell you what, I got. . . .

Well, don't worry what the newspapers say about us. Everything I've said tonight is logical and reasonable and constitutional. Not a single thing have I said tonight that anybody can argue logically with, and that's the reson they call us extremists and want to say we're Fascists. They cannot argue with the logic of the position we take here in Madison Square Garden tonight. They want to say, well, they're evil folks. I want to tell these newspapers something. These large newspapers that think they know more than the average citizen on the street of New York haven't always been right. I remember the time the *New York Times* said that Mao tse-Tung was a good man, and he turned out to be a Communist. I remember when they said that Ben Bella was a good man, and he turned out to be a Communist. When old Castro was in the hills of Cuba, the *New York Times* said he was the Robin Hood of the Caribbean, and they introduced him on national television as the George Washington of Cuba. They were mistaken about Castro.

They [newspapers] are mistaken about our movement, and they are mistaken about the good people of New York State who are here tonight supporting our candidacy because the two national parties (other than our party) has paid no attention to you. But they are paying attention to those who are making the most noise here at Madison Square Garden tonight and every other place in the country. You know that some of those people who make it unsafe for you and me are going to school on your tax money and they are exempt from the draft. Well, I tell you one thing. I'm tired of my tax money going to educate somebody who wants to raise money for the Communists in our country, and that's exactly what a lot of them do on some of the college campuses in this country. I'm certainly not talking about all the college students. You know the few that I'm talking about, and there are some in every state in the union.

Four years ago our movement received thirty-four percent of the vote in Wisconsin, thirty percent in Indiana, and forty-four percent in Maryland. We have won nearly every radio and television poll in every state in the union, so don't pay any attention to the pollsters. They said we were going to get fifteeen percent of the Midwest, well, Ohio's part of the Midwest, and we got eighteen percent of the voters in that one state to sign a petition to get us on the ballot, and I would say that for every one who signed a petition in the state of Ohio, there were four more who would have signed had they been given the opportunity. Yes, we got forty-four percent of the vote four years ago in the state of Maryland.

You know, I like to tell this because—if you'll listen to this, I'll tell you a good joke—you've heard it before, but it's very good. Down in the state of Maryland that night four years ago in the presidential primary, I was leading up until about 9:30 with several hundred thousand votes in, and they called the mayor of Baltimore to the television and asked him what he thought about this man from Alabama running first in the presidential primary in our free state. Well, do you know what he said, being a big-time politician? He said: "It's sad; it's sad. We'll never live this down. What has come over the people of the free state of Maryland?" Well, if he had gone out and asked a good cab driver in Baltimore, he could have told him. You vote for me and you are going to be through with all that. Let me tell you now you continue to support our movement until November 5, together we are going to change directions in this country, and we are going to return some sanity to the American government scene. I do appreciate you being here in Madison Square Garden tonight. Thank you very much, ladies and gentlemen.

Bibliographical Note

Unfortunately, a wealth of bibliographical information about the American Independent Party does not exist. However, additional material may be found in *Wallace* by Marshall Frady (New York, 1968) and *The Making of the President, 1968* by Theodore White (New York, 1968).

Acknowledgements

"Principles of the New Republicanism" in *A Republican Looks at His Party* by Arthur Larson. Copyright © 1956 by Arthur Larson. Reprinted by permission of Harper & Row, Publishers, Inc.

"Stand Up and be Counted" by Henry A. Wallace. Copyright © 1948, Harrison-Blaine of New Jersey, Inc. Reprinted by permission of *The New Republic*.

Article by Alfred Friendly. Copyright © 1948 by the *Washington Post*. Reprinted by permission.

"Wallace Says Law Stand Deters Reprisal by Right" by B. Franklin. Copyright © 1968 by *The New York Times* Company. Reprinted by permission.

Adlai Stevenson speeches, "The American Vision" and speech in Milwaukee, Sept. 29, 1956. Reprinted by permission of Adlai Stevenson III.

"The Changes in Communist Organization" in *Teheran: Our Path in War and Peace,* by Earl Browder, Copyright © 1944. Reprinted by permission of International Publishers Co., Inc.

"The Setting for John W. Davis" by Walter Lippmann. Copyright © 1927 by the *Atlantic Monthly* Company. Reprinted by permission of Walter Lippmann.

"An Open Letter to Alfred E. Smith" by Charles C. Marshall. Copyright © 1927 by the *Atlantic Monthly* Company. Reprinted by permission.

"Reply to Charles Marshall" by Alfred E. Smith. Copyright © 1927 by the *Atlantic Monthly* Company. Reprinted by permission of his daughter, Mrs. John Warner.

Index

A

Abern, Martin, 2428
abolition *see* anti-slavery movements;
     emancipation
abolitionists, 347, 740-51, 756, 760, 1141
Abraham Lincoln Brigade, 3178
Acheson, Dean, 2683, 2688, 2691, 2702, 2705
Adams, Charles Francis, 356, 361, 362, 755,
     1142
Adams, John, 12-15, 19, 22, 25, 240, 245-46,
     248-50, 255, 257
Adams, John Quincy, 22, 264, 502, 592, 1142,
     2402
     and elections, 24, 25, 258, 268, 271, 501,
          503, 504, 578, 579, 589
     National Republican party, 271, 333, 337
     as president, 259, 501, 502
     as Secretary of State, 268, 271
     slavery, 341, 500, 504
Adams, Samuel, 8-9, 154, 160
Adams, Sherman, 2703, 2989, 2992, 2993,
     2994, 2995, 2997
Adamson Act of *1916*, 1816
Addams, Jane, 2086, 2555
Advance, 3027
Advocate, 1710
Agnew, Spiro T., 2842, 2847, 3028, 3032,
     3037, 3046, 3053, 3123-46
agrarian interests *see* rural interests

Agrarian Reformers, 2404-05
Agricultural College Act *see* Morrill Act of
     1862
Agricultural Wheel, 1710
Aiken, William, 613
Akerman, Amos T., 1294
Albany Advertiser, 579
Albany Evening Journal, 586, 591
Albert, Carl, 2701
Alcorn, Meade, 2991, 3002, 3013, 3033
Aldrich, Chester H., 2552
Aldrich, Nelson W., 2079, 2088
Alexander, Thomas B., 349
Alien and Sedition Acts, 14, 15, 253, 254, 259
     Kentucky and Virginia Resolutions, 89-93,
          253, 525
Alinsky, Saul, 2858
Allen, Charles, 593
Allen, Henry J., 2564
Allen, Leo S., 2270, 2285
Allen, William V., 520, 1718, 1721, 1722
Allison, William B., 2079
Alsop, Joseph, 3320, 3321
Alsop, Stewart, 3320, 3321
Altgeld, John Peter, 999, 1000, 1003
Amalgamation party, 504
Ambler, John, 298
America First Committee, 2431
American, 1006
American and Foreign Anti-Slavery Society,
     746

American Anti-Slavery Society (AASS), 742-48
  passim, 751, 784-91
  see also The Emancipator; The Liberator
American Bimetallic League, 1721
American Confederation of the International
  Workingmen's Association, 2458-59
American Enterprise Institute, 3025
American Federation of Labor (AFL), 994,
  1728, 1943, 2076, 2111, 2114, 2264,
  2399, 2409-418 *passim*, 2420-23,
  2425, 2427, 2429-31 *passim*, 3171
AFL-CIO, 2399, 2438, 2439, 2440, 2854, 3188
*American Federation of Labor in the Time of
  Gompers, The,* 2412
American Historical Review, 1830
American Independent party (AIP), 3429-98
  constituent groups, 3429-31
  convention of *1972,* 3444
  decline, 3442-44
  platform of *1968,* 3439-40
  structure, 3436-37
American Labor party, 2430, 3188, 3313
American Liberty League, 1942
American Organ, 612
American party *see* Know Nothing party
American People's Money, The, 1721
American Philosophical Society, 142
American Railway Union (ARU), 999, 2070,
  2416
American Republican party, 514, 519
  see also Know Nothing party
American Revolution, 4, 6-7, 25
"American's Creed, The," 1823
Americans for Democratic Action, 2828, 3326
American Workers party, 2428
Ames, Fisher, 16, 17, 99-100
Ames, Nathaniel, 262
Anderson, John, 3049
Anderson, Robert, 1163
Annapolis convention, 8
anti-alcohol movements *see* prohibition and
  Prohibition party
Antifederalist party, 8, 9, 135-236
  Constitution, objections to, 153-63 *passim*,
    165, 166, 239
  and Federalist party, 8, 9, 135, 158, 159,
    160, 162, 164, 165, 166
Anti-Imperialist League, 2098
Antimasonic Enquirer, 579
Antimasonic party, 333, 334, 338, 504, 576-93
  passim, 595, 596, 597, 598, 603,
  604, 605, 607, 608, 618, 619, 620,
  623-79, 737
  and Democratic party (*1828-1860*), 334,
    578, 580, 582, 584-92 *passim*, 594,
    619
  and National Republican party, 580, 582,
    584, 585, 589, 590, 591
  and Whig party, 338, 341, 342, 346, 576,
    578, 579, 590, 591, 592, 623
Anti-Masonic Review, 580

Anti-Monopoly party, 1555, 1558, 1707, 1708
Anti-Saloon League, 1571, 1579-80
anti-slavery movement
  John Brown, 1150, 1156
  Dred Scott case, 1152
  and Kansas, 1153-54
  leadership, 1147-48, 1155, 1156
  see also emancipation, Liberty party
A. Philip Randolph Institute, 2438
Appeal of the Independent Democrats,
  1144-45
Appeal to Reason, 2418
Appleton, Nathan, 338, 355
Arena, 2075-76
Arends, Les, 3024
army, 7, 586
  Antifederalist party, 143, 151, 155, 157
  Federalist party, 14, 15, 154, 159
  Jeffersonian Republican party, 254, 259
Army of the Commonweal of Christ, 999
Arnall, Ellis, 3325
Aronson, Sidney, 18-19
Articles of Confederation, 7, 151, 152, 154,
  155, 157
Arthur, Chester A., 1427, 1429
Arvey, Jacob M., 2685, 2687, 2987
Ashbrook, John, 3011, 3012, 3049, 3050
Ashby, N. B., 1702
Askew, Reubin, 2847
Atchison, David R., 526, 1143
Atlanta Constitution, 1510-11, 1543-45
Avery, W. W., 566

B

Bailey, Gamaliel, 613, 749, 752, 824-27, 1146
Bailey, John M., 2700, 2706, 2832, 2834,
  2837
Bailey, Josiah W., 1949, 2122
Baker, Howard, 2999, 3028, 3036, 3043,
  3047-48
Baker, Newton D., 1816
Bakers' Union, 2410
Baldwin, "Beany," 3312, 3314, 3321
Baldwin, Roger, 2568
Baldwin, Simeon, 1017
Ball, Joseph H., 2283
Ballinger, Richard A., 2089, 2543
Baltimore-Ohio Railroad, 598
Banfield, Edward C., 2072
Bank of North America, 142, 147
Bank of the United States, First, 11, 25, 242
Bank of the United States, Second
  opposition to, 498, 504, 507, 509
    Andrew Jackson, 334, 335, 336, 337, 339,
      340, 505, 508-09, 541-43, 590, 591
  panic of *1819,* 498, 499

banking and monetary policy, 7, 499-500, 504,
    586, 590, 591, 748, 751, 1721,
    2071, 2074, 2107
    debt, national, 7, 11, 25, 141, 152, 156, 159,
        242, 254, 259
    debt, private, 141, 142, 148-52 *passim,*
        159, 165, 499, 504, 586
    inflations and panics, 1015, 1551, 1554,
        1941
    legislation
        Agricultural Credit Banks, 2124
        Bland-Allison Silver Purchase Act, 990,
            991, 993, 998, 1419, 1720
        Contraction Act, 1553
        Farm Loan Act of *1916,* 1730
        Federal Reserve Bill of *1913,* 1730,
            2093
        First Legal Tender Act, 888, 894, 1552
        Independent Treasury Act, 341, 350,
            511, 512, 748
        Intermediate Credit Act of *1923,* 1730
        Mint Act of *1792,* 1705
        National Banking System, 1167, 1552-
            53, 1705
        Pendleton or Ohio Plan, 894-95, 922-33
        Public Credit Act, 1553
        Reconstruction Finance Corporation
            (RFC), 2122-23, 2124, 2690
        Sherman Silver Purchase Act, 1720
        Specie Resumption Act, 895-96, 901,
            998-99, 1551, 1556, 1557, 1585-86,
            1705, 1708, 1720
        Warehouse Act of *1916,* 1730
    and political parties
        Antifederalist, 141-42, 148-52 *passim,*
            165
        Democratic, 334, 335, 336, 337, 339,
            340, 341, 498, 499, 505, 507-12
            passim, 514, 515, 516, 519, 527,
            530, 531, 541-49, 557, 590, 591,
            990-91, 1942, 1958
        Federalist, 9, 11, 12, 14, 17, 18, 25,
            142, 149, 151, 152, 156-57, 159,
            241-42
        Greenback, 894-96, 1553, 1554, 1708,
            1715
        Republican, 254, 259, 498, 500, 2079
        Whig, 347, 348, 350, 351, 352, 411-19,
            511, 516
    silver vs. gold standard, 898, 993, 995, 996-
        97, 1000-02, 1004, 1005, 1011,
        1012, 1417-20, 1552, 1705-06,
        1721-22, 2078
Bankhead, John, 1953
Bankhead, William, 1951
Banks, Nathaniel P., 613, 614-15, 617, 618,
    620, 1148, 1149, 1150, 1165
Banner, James M., Jr., 17, 20, 23
Baptists *see* religious interests
Barbour, P. P., 507, 508
Barker, James W., 593, 617

Barker, Wharton, 1725
Barkley, Alben, 1963, 2686, 3000
Barnburners *see* Democratic party, factions,
    Barnburners
Baroni, Gino C., 2858
Baroody, William, 3019
Barrett, Frank A., 2695
Bartlett, E. B., 612
Baruch, Bernard, 1814, 2122
Bass, Charlotta, 3328
Bates, Edward, 1159, 1160, 1165
Battle, John S., 2702
Battle Line, 3025
Bayard, James A., 16, 97-98, 534
Bayard, Thomas F., 989
Bayh, Birch, 2834, 2848, 2849, 3043
Bean, Louis, 3023
Beard, Charles and Mary, 2400, 2411
Beckley, John, 245, 247, 248-49, 250
Bedacht, Max, 3179
Bedini, Gaetano, 597
Belknap, Jeremy, 145
Bell, Daniel, 2415, 2417, 2418, 3169, 3177
Bell, John, 360, 362, 610, 619, 1161
Bellamy, Edward, 2080, 2413-14, 2416
Belmont, August H., 891, 895, 934-35, 1721
Belmont, Perry, 1010
Benedict, E. C., 994
Bennett, Wallace F., 2690
Benson, Elmer, 3321
Benson, Lee, 350
Bentley, Elizabeth Terrill, 2686
Benton, Thomas Hart, 520, 1150
Benton, William, 2696
Berger, Victor, 2104, 2415, 2424
Berle, Adolf, 1942, 1963
Bernstein, Michael J., 3045
Berrien, John, 334, 338, 506, 507, 508
Berry, George L., 2430
Bethune, Mary McLeod, 1947
Beveridge, Albert J., 2095, 2147-52, 2553,
    2554, 2556, 2557, 2564
Biden, J. R., 2856
Bigelow, Abijah, 24
Bigler, William, 597
Bimetallic Democratic National Committee,
    1002
Bingham, Kinsley S., 1146
Birney, James G., 353, 741, 743, 744-50, 752,
    755, 759, 794-801, 824-31, 835-40
Bitelman, Alexander, 3188
Black, James, 1571
blacks, 1729, 2083-84, 3027, 3171
    and civil rights, 892-93, 895, 898, 1961,
        2120, 2697, 2698
    and communism, 3171-72, 3196-97, 3211-
        12
    and Democratic party, 889, 1007, 1289,
        2838, 2840, 2857-59, 2862
    and elections, 1946, 2115, 2264, 2280,
        2689, 2694, 2697, 2701, 3007, 3022

blacks (*cont.*)
  and labor, 2406, 2438, 2676
  party loyalties, 1728, 2084, 2280, 2555,
    2829
  and Progressive party of *1948,* 3324, 3326
  racial unrest, 2838-39, 2840-41
  and Republican party, 1289, 2072, 2088,
    2115, 2262, 2285
  and F.D.R. administration, 1947, 1949,
    2269
  see also civil rights
Blaine, Anita McCormick, 3324
Blaine, James G., 886, 893, 902, 904, 988,
    1282, 1413-14, 1415, 1422, 1426,
    1429, 1460-80
Blair, Francis P.
  Washington Globe, 506, 517, 519, 527,
    895, 1145
Blair, Francis P., 1149, 1166, 1168
Blair, Henry W., 1423
Blair, Montgomery, 361, 1165, 1168, 1169,
    1172
Blair, William McCormick, Jr., 2693
Bland, Richard "Silver Dick," 995, 1001, 1002
Bland, Theodorick, 162
Bland-Allison Silver Purchase Act, 990, 991,
    993, 998, 1720
Blatchly, Cornelius C., 2401
Bliss, Ray, 2998, 3006, 3011, 3020, 3024-29
    passim, 3035, 3037, 3049, 3051
Blue, Frederick Judd, 755-56, 757, 758
Boies, Horace, 1001
Bolsheviks, 2425, 2432, 3176-77
Bonaparte, Charles Joseph, 2556
Borah, William E., 1946, 2103, 2104, 2107,
    2108, 2115, 2120, 2272, 2277,
    2547, 2549, 2556, 2562, 2569
Boston Atlas, 342
Botts, John Minor, 360
Bourdet, Edouard, 1827
Boutwell, George S., 895, 1553
Bovey, Alvan E., 1145
Bowles, Chester, 2681, 2685, 2690, 3314
Bowles, Samuel, 1148
Bowling, Kenneth, 9
Bozell, L. Brent, 3011
Bradley, Joseph H., 901
Bradley, Stephen R., 264
Branch, John, 334, 339, 506, 507, 508
Brandagee, Frank B., 2102
Branigan, Roger, 2840
Brandeis, Louis D., 1814, 1816, 2093
Breckinridge, John C., 535, 1151, 1161
Brennan, George, 1818
Bretz, Julian P., 751-52
Brewster, Owen, 2114
Bricker, John W., 2283, 2284, 3049
Bridges, Harry, 3184
Bridges, Styles, 2994
Bright, Jesse, 534

Brinkley, Wilfred E., 902
Brisbane, Albert, 2403
British Empire Communist parties, 3194
Broder, David, 2999, 3028, 3029
Brooke, Edward, 2999, 3028
Brooks, C. Wayland, 2687
Brooks, Preston, 1150
Brophy, John, 2430
Brotherhood of Locomotive Engineers, 1559-
    60
Brotherhood of Railroad Trainmen and Loco-
    motive Engineers, 2679
Brothers of Freedom, 1710
Brough, John, 1168
Browder, Earl, 1946, 2432-36 *passim,* 3170,
    3175, 3178, 3181-88 *passim,* 3190,
    3196, 3197, 3253-73 *passim*
Brown, Albert G., 563, 564-65
Brown, B. Gratz, 900
Brown, Edmund G., 2704, 2705, 3009
Brown, John, 1150, 1156
Brown, John Cotton, 3321
Brown, H. Rap, 2438
Brownell, Herbert, 3026, 3037
Browning, Orville, 1157
Brownlow, Parson, 601
Bryan, Charles W., 1823
Bryan, George, 158, 159
Bryan, Samuel, 154, 158
Bryan, William Jennings, 887, 987, 992, 994-
    97, 1000-19, 1578, 1717, 1811,
    1815, 1816, 1820, 1823, 1825,
    1856, 2078, 2080, 2098
  background, 1001-02
  and Cleveland, 1002, 1004, 1005, 1008,
    1009, 1012, 1013
  and election of *1896,* 1722, 1723, 1725,
    2076, 2077
  and election of *1912,* 1812, 1813, 2559
  speeches, 1013, 1102-07, 1061-79, 1086-
    1100, 1108-15, 1120-28
  "Cross of Gold," 1080-85
Bryant, William Cullen, 1145, 1148
Buchanan, James, 348, 513, 527, 604, 1151,
    1162, 1286
  and election of *1852,* 525
  and election of *1856,* 362, 530, 616, 617
  as president, 531, 532, 534, 1152-53, 1158,
    1163
  as Secretary of State, 519
Buchanan, John P., 1713
Buckley, Charles A., 2706, 2860
Buckley, James, 3025, 3047
Buckley, William F., Jr., 3011, 3025
Buckner, Simon Bolivar, 1002
Budenz, Louis F., 3178
Buell, Don Carlos, 1165
Bukharin, 2431
Bukarinism, 3178
Bull Moose party *see* Progressive party

Bumpers, Dale, 2847
Burch, Dean, 3019, 3024, 3027
Burchard, Samuel D., 904
Burke, Aedanus, 162
Burleson, Albert, 1815
Burlingame, Anson, 1156
Burner, David, 2117
Burnham, W. Dean, 2076
Burns, James M., 1943, 1962
Burr, Aaron, 16, 23, 242, 245
    and election of *1800,* 252, 256, 257, 258
    and election of *1804,* 263, 296
    and Alexander Hamilton, 16, 23, 97-98
    and Thomas Jefferson, 242, 252-53
business interests, 898, 988, 1704, 1954, 2094,
        2100, 2218-19, 2679, 2680, 3315,
        3441
    and Democratic party, 1002, 1816, 1825,
        1829, 1942, 1943, 1945
    entrepreneurial elites, 1554-56, 1558
    Muscle Shoals, 2240-46
    political strength, 2070, 2081, 2087
    and Republican party, 2073, 2077, 2083,
        2084, 2093, 2109, 2110, 2122,
        2123, 2271, 2997
    and Theodore Roosevelt, 2080, 2082,
        2546-47
    and States' Rights party, 3310, 3324-25
    tariff protection, 1415-17
    and trusts, 998, 1416, 1425
    see also Liberty League; National Civic
        Federation; banking and monetary
        policy
Butler, Andrew P., 526, 1150
Butler, Benjamin F., 510, 888, 976-82, 1145,
        1164, 1170, 1565, 1708
Butler, John M., 2690
Butler, Nicholas Murray, 2566
Butler, Marion, 1720, 1722, 1726, 1789-94
Butler, Paul, 2698, 2701, 3205
Butler, Pierce, 2112
Byrd, William, 1950, 1952, 2685, 2691
Byrnes, James, 1953, 2673, 2681-82, 2694,
        3311

C

Caesar's Column (I. Donnelly), 1726
Cain, Harry P., 2695
Calhoun, John C., 334, 336, 337, 340, 354,
        356, 505, 512, 514, 515, 535, 536,
        600, 602, 1152
    and Democratic party, 336, 341, 505, 506-07
        508, 511, 514, 517, 518, 519, 520,
        522
    and election of *1824,* 268, 501-02
    and election of *1828,* 502, 503, 506
    and election of *1832,* 507

and election of *1844,* 516, 517, 518
    R. M. T. Hunter, letter from, 517
    and A. Jackson, 505-06, 506-07
    R. Pakenham, letter to, 518, 550-52
    as Secretary of State, 353, 752
    as Secretary of War, 268, 505-06
    South Carolina Exposition and Protest, 502,
        503
    and Texas annexation, 517-18, 519, 550-52
    as vice president, 506
    and Whig party, 339, 353
Calhoun, Patrick, 162
Camden and Amboy Railroad, 334
Cameron, A. C., 2406
Cameron, Simon, 527, 605, 606, 620, 886,
        1156, 1159, 1160, 1165
Campbell, James, 528, 597
Campbell, John, 526
Canada and United States boundaries, 350
Canadian Rebellion of *1837,* 342
canals, 498, 499, 599
    Erie Canal, 500, 578, 585, 586, 599
    Pennsylvania Canal System, 586, 587
Cannon, James P., 2428, 3178, 3190
Cannon, Joseph G. "Uncle Joe," 1812, 2088,
        2089, 2090, 2543
Capper, Arthur, 2552
Carleton, William G., 896
Carlisle, John G., 996-97, 1008
Carmichael, Stokeley, 2438
Carpenter's Union, 2402
carpetbaggers *see* Reconstruction
Carrington, Edward, letter from A. Hamilton,
        275-83
Carroll, Charles, 150
Carroll, John A., 2701
Cary, Samuel F., 1708
Cass, Lewis, 356, 519, 520, 521
    and elections, 516, 518, 522-25 *passim,*
        755, 757
    A. O. P. Nicholson, letter to, 522, 553-55
Caudle, Theron Lamar, 2690
Center for Urban Ethnic Affairs, 2858
Challenge to Liberty, The (H. Hoover), 2267
Chambers, Whittaker, 2287-88, 2686, 3011
Chandler, "Happy," 1949
Chandler, William E., 1426
Chandler, Zechariah, 886, 1145, 1156, 1157
Channing, William Henry, 2403
Chapman, Oscar, 2705
Charles, Joseph, 11-12, 13
Chase, Katherine, 887
Chase, Salmon P., 607, 612, 752, 754-55, 895,
        1144, 1145, 1149, 1150, 1151, 1153,
        1159, 1160, 1165, 1167, 1170, 1175-
        80, 1152
    correspondence, 608, 754, 821-23
Chase, Samuel, 22, 150, 157, 161, 166
Chase, Solon, 1563
Chavez, Caesar, 2861

Chavez, Dennis, 2683, 2695
Chiang Kai-shek, 3183
Chicago Federation of Labor, 3170
Chicago platform *see* election of *1896,* Chicago
    platform
Chicago Tribune, 1223-28
    editorials, 1479-80, 1507-09, 1533-34,
        1538-40
Chicago *Union Signal,* editorial, 1647-50
Child, David Lee, 744
China, 2094, 2879-2908
Christian Advocate, 2153-56
Christian Index, 2095
Christopher, George, 3034
Church, Frank, 2701, 3043
civil rights
    "Black Codes," 1292
    and Democrats, 2685, 2869-70, 3317
    Dyer anti-lynching bill, 2115
    as election issue, 2115, 2286, 3007
    Fourteenth Amendment, 1282, 1292-93
    Fifteenth Amendment, 1290, 1293
    Little Rock, 2703, 2989, 2990
    and Republicans, 1289, 1290, 2115, 2120,
        2285, 2702-03
    and T. Roosevelt, 2083-84, 2089
    and socialists, 2436, 2437
    and South, 1282, 2697
    see also blacks
Civil Rights Act of *1957,* 2702-03, 2990
Civil Rights Act of *1964,* 2436
Civil Rights Bill of *1875,* 1293
Civil Rights Commission, 2702
Civil Service Commission, 990
Civil Service Law of *1883,* 989
civil service system, 886-87, 988, 1034
    reforms, 989, 1551
Civil War, 362, 593, 620, 888-92
    battles, 1165, 1168, 1171, 1172
    causes, 1162-63
    Congressional Committee on the Conduct
        of the War, 1165
    H. W. Davis letter on, 1275-77
    Emancipation Proclamation, 1252-56
    as issue, 885-86, 898, 909-13
    Wade-Davis Bill, 1268-72
    Wade-Davis Manifesto, 1273-74
Civilian Public Service, 2434
Claflin, Tennessee, 2406
Clark, Champ, 1017, 1812, 1813, 2553
Clark, Evans, 2421
Clark, Joseph, 2692, 2697, 2701
Clay, Henry, 344-45, 350-51, 353, 500-02,
        505, 1167, 1415, 2402
    and Compromise of *1850,* 358, 447-60
    correspondence, 426-31
    and election of *1824,* 24, 268, 271, 344,
        501
    and election of *1832,* 333-34, 335, 340,
        344-45, 589

and election of *1836,* 340
and election of *1840,* 342, 343, 352
and election of *1844,* 352-53, 517
and election of *1848,* 356
as Freemason, 576, 589
and National Republican party/Whig party,
    271, 333, 335, 337, 338, 339, 340,
    344, 345, 347, 348, 350-51, 352,
    358, 359, 360
Clayton, John M., 339, 346, 357
Clements, Earle C., 2685
Cleveland, Grover, 887, 904, 1034, 1040,
    2074, 2076
    annual messages, 1023-24, 1029-30, 1037,
        1041-44, 1051-55, 1059-60
    on Bryan, 1002, 1004, 1005, 1012, 1013
    Bryan comments on, 1006, 1008-09
    editorials on, 1479-80, 1531-32, 1535-37
    Inaugural Addresses, 996, 1021-22, 1031-33
    messages, 1025-28, 1035-36, 1038-39, 1045-
        50, 1056-58
    as president, 987-1004 *passim,* 1424, 1426-
        30
    as presidential candidate, 983, 1429, 1716
    and Sherman Silver Purchase Act, 1430,
        1720
Cleveland, John P., 1229-38
Clingman, Thomas L., 357
Clinton, DeWitt, 21, 266, 267, 310-20, 504,
    577, 578
Clinton, George, 18, 21, 138, 149, 150, 153,
    163, 245, 246, 256, 263, 265
Clotfelter, James, 3439
Cobb, Howell, 357, 358
Cockran, Bourke, 1005, 1011
Coin's Financial Fool (H. White), 1721
Coin's Financial School (W. H. Harvey), 1721
Cold War, 2834, 3192, 3194, 3195, 3327, 3328
Colfax, Schuyler, 602, 901, 1148
Collamer, Joseph, 1156
Colored Alliance, 1709
Colored Farmers' Alliance and Co-operative
    Union, 1710
Columbian Centinel, 12
Combs, Jerald, 13
Cominform, 3191, 3194
Comintern *see* Communist Internationals
commerce *see* trade
Commercial and Financial Chronicle, 2085
Committee for a Sane Nuclear Policy, 2436
Committee for Political Education (A.F.L-
    C.I.O.), 2423
Committee of Forty-eight, 2568
Committee on the Conduct of the War, 1165
Committee on Delegate Selection and Party
    Reforms (McGovern Commission),
    2952-64
Committee on Illinois Government (C.I.G.),
    2863
Committees of Correspondence, 6

Commoner, The, 1007, 1856
Commons, John R., 2086
Communism, 2432
    as election issue, 2291, 2687, 2987
    investigations, 2686, 2688, 2696
    and socialism, 2423-29
    and Truman administration, 2287-88
Communist Information Bureau, 3191, 3194
Communist International, 3173, 3175, 3178-79,
        3182, 3248-52
    and American Communist party, 3174,
        3178, 3220-26
    Second Congress (*1920*), 3205-10
    Sixth Congress (*1928*), 3171, 3211-12
    Seventh Congress, 2429, 2432, 3174, 3239-
        47
Communist International, Third, 2425, 3170,
        3174
Communist Labor party, 2424-25
Communist Manifesto (Karl Marx), 2405
Communist party, American
    appeal, 3170, 3172-73
    and blacks, 3171-72, 3196-97
    conventions
        emergency convention (*1945*), 3187
        Fourteenth national (*1948*), 3189, 3194
        Sixteenth national, 3175, 3188, 3274-
            305
    crises
        1944-45, 3181
        1956-57, 3175, 3177, 3183, 3187-88
    and culture, 3172-73, 3228-38
    factionalism, 2428-29, 2435, 3188, 3196
        Left-Wing, 3197, 3190, 3191
        revisionism, 3175, 3186, 3187
    government infiltration, 2288, 2432, 2688-
        89
    "influentials," 3180, 3184, 3188, 3190,
        3191, 3192
    international ties, 3173-76, 3227
    and labor, 2432, 2433, 3170-71, 3191,
        3192
    leadership, 3178-79, 3188
    National Board, 3184, 3185, 3186, 3187,
        3189
    and Progressive party, 2567, 3191-93, 3194,
        3195, 3313, 3320-22, 3326, 3351-
        55
    psychology of members, 3176-79
    and Second World War, 2433, 3182-87
    and socialism, 2424-25, 2429, 2436, 2439
    strength, 2433, 2435, 3171, 3178, 3185,
        3187, 3188-90
    structure, 3173, 3174, 3177, 3196
    tactics
        "immediate partial demands," 3179-81
        "manipulated revolution," 2439, 3192
    postwar decline, 3187-97
    and U.S.S.R., 2435, 3182-87, 3195-96,
        3213-19

    as arm of, 2431-35, 3174, 3182-83,
        3186-87, 3192
    see also "Red Scare"
Communist Political Association, 3184
Compromise of *1850,* 358, 359, 447-74, 524,
        525, 609, 758, 1142-43, 1144
Compromise of *1877,* 902, 989
Compromise Tariff of *1833,* 335, 340, 343,
        345, 508
Confederacy, 362, 1281, 1290
Confederate States of America, 1163
Confederation of Industrial Organizations,
        1763-65
Conference for Progressive Political Action
        (C.P.P.A.), 2421-23, 2567-68
Confiscation Acts, First and Second, 1166
congregationalists *see* religious interests
Congress, 1st (*1788-1790*), 9, 10, 239
Congress, 2nd (*1790-1792*), 241
Congress, 5th (*1796-1798*), 14
Congress, 7th (*1800-1802*), 240, 1144
Congress, 13th (*1812-1814*), 266
Congress, 15th (*1816-1818*), 1144
Congress, 18th (*1822-1824*), 2402, 2445-57
Congress, 23rd (*1832-1834*), 335, 337
Congress, 27th (*1840-1842*), 351
Congress, 28th (*1842-1844*), 351
Congress, 29th (*1844-1846*), 521
Congress, 30th (*1846-1848*), 355, 521
Congress, 31st (*1848-1850*), 357, 1142, 1143,
        1144, 1146
Congress, 33rd (*1852-1854*), 1143, 1144, 1175-
        84
Congress, 34th (*1854-1856*), 1149
Congress, 37th (*1860-1862*), 888, 1162, 1165,
        1166, 1169
Congress, 38th (*1862-1864*), 888-89, 1166-67,
        1169, 1268-74, 1284
Congress, 39th (*1864-1866*) 891-93, 902, 987,
        1167, 1284, 1292-93
Congress, 40th (*1866-1868*), 893, 1282, 1293
Congress, 41st (*1868-1870*), 892, 896
Congress, 43rd (*1872-1874*), 895, 900, 1556,
        1557
Congress, 44th (*1874-1876*), 895, 900-01,
        948-51, 1293, 1585-87
Congress, 45th (*1876-1878*), 902, 1419
Congress, 46th (*1878-1880*), 903, 904, 1412
Congress, 48th (*1882-1884*), 904, 970-75, 1422
Congress, 50th (*1886-1888*), 991, 1424
Congress, 51st (*1888-1890*), 992, 993, 1419,
        1425, 1429
Congress, 52nd (*1890-1892*), 993-95, 1429,
        1713
Congress, 53rd (*1892-1894*), 996, 997-98,
        1430-31
Congress, 54th (*1894-1896*), 999, 1000, 1720
        2070, 2075
Congress, 55th (*1896-1898*), 1724-25, 2076,
        2079, 2142-46

Congress, 56th (*1898-1900*), 2079-80
Congress, 57th (*1900-1902*), 1006
Congress, 58th (*1902-1904*), 1008
Congress, 59th (*1904-1906*), 1012, 2098
Congress, 60th (*1906-1908*), 2084-85, 2171-74
Congress, 61st (*1908-1910*), 1015
Congress, 62nd (*1910-1912*), 1017, 1812, 2089, 2090
Congress, 63rd (*1912-1914*), 1814, 2187-91, 2560
Congress, 64th (*1914-1916*), 1815, 1816
Congress, 65th (*1916-1918*), 2102-03, 2195-2201, 2202-08
Congress, 66th (*1918-1920*), 1817, 2103-04, 2209-11
Congress, 67th (*1920-1922*), 1822, 1948
Congress, 68th (*1922-1924*), 1820, 2218-19
Congress, 69th (*1924-1926*), 1824-26, 2220-21
Congress, 70th (*1926-1928*), 2222-28
Congress, 71st (*1928-1930*), 2119
Congress, 72nd (*1930-1932*)
    composition, 1831, 2120
    on Depression, 2247-54
    and H. Hoover, 2122-23
    Muscle Shoals, 2240-46
    voting record, 1830, 2123
Congress, 73rd (*1932-1934*), 1941, 1960, 2260, 2266
Congress, 74th (*1934-1936*), 1942-43, 2268, 2269
Congress, 75th (*1936-1938*), 1948, 1949
Congress, 76th (*1938-1940*), 1948, 1950, 2274
Congress, 77th (*1940-1942*), 1953, 2280
    W. Willkie testimony, 2352-60
Congress, 78th (*1942-1944*)
    composition, 1953, 2282
    Republican minority, 2282
    voting record, 1955, 1960
Congress, 79th (*1944-1946*), 1957, 2284
Congress, 80th (*1946-1948*), 2286, 2366-76, 2683, 2684-86
Congress, 81st (*1948-1950*), 2287, 2377-90, 2687-88
Congress, 82nd (*1950-1952*), 2690
Congress, 83rd (*1952-1954*), 2292, 2695-96, 2988, 2994-95
Congress, 84th (*1954-1956*), 2697-98, 2988, 2995-96
Congress, 85th (*1956-1958*), 2701, 2989
Congress, 86th (*1958-1960*), 2704-05, 2828 2989, 2997
Congress, 87th (*1960-1962*), 2833
Congress, 88th (*1962-1964*), 2834-35, 3013
Congress, 89th (*1964-1966*), 2837-38, 3021, 3024-25
Congress, 90th (*1966-1968*), 1966, 2838, 3028
Congress, 91st (*1968-1970*), 3040
Congress, 92nd (*1970-1972*), 2847, 3047
Congress, 93rd (*1972-1974*), 2856, 3052

Congress (*1870-1900*), composition analysis of, 1428, 2073
Congress (*1913-21*), voting record of, 2093
Congress (*1936-45*), Democratic losses in, 2676
Congress of Industrial Organizations (C.I.O.), 2431, 2433, 2689, 3171, 3185, 3189, 3191, 3192, 3195
    see also A.F.L-C.I.O.
C.I.O.-P.A.C. *see* Political Action Committee
Conkin, Paul, 1942
Conkling, Roscoe, 886, 1282, 1412, 1421, 1429
Connally, John, 2864, 3048
Connally, Tom, 1686-87, 2682, 2685, 2691
Connelly, Matthew J., 2689
Connor, Eugene "Bull," 3323
Conscience Whigs *see* Whig party
conservation, and F.D.R., 1830, 2080, 2084, 2089
    see also lands, public
Conservative party, 610
Constitution, United States
    amendments, 9, 154, 157, 160, 163, 164, 166
        Thirteenth, 892, 1166, 1281
        Fourteenth, 893, 988, 1281, 1282
        Fifteenth, 982, 988, 1281, 1290
        Eighteenth, 1579-81
        proposed by Maryland, 220-23
        proposed by Massachusetts, 218-20
        proposed by North Carolina, 229-33
        proposed by Rhode Island, 234-35
        proposed by Virginia, 224-28
    debates and ratification, 6, 7, 8-9, 45-63, 143, 146-53 *passim,* 158-66 *passim,* 239
Constitutional Convention, 6, 8, 9-10, 153, 158, 160, 162, 163
    Antifederalist party, 152-53, 157, 163, 164, 173-217
    Pennsylvania, minority dissent, 173-91
Constitutional Union party, 358-59, 362, 619
    see also Whig party
Continental Congress, 6, 7, 8
Contraction Act, 1553
Cook County Farmer's Alliance, 1709
Coolidge, Calvin, 1822, 1824, 1880-86, 2070, 2107
    and election of *1920,* 2105
    and election of *1924,* 2116, 2569
    on McNary-Haugen Bill, 2222-28
    as president, 2112-15
Cooper, Peter, 1558, 1708, 3043
Cooper, Thomas, *Political Arithmetic,* 253
Cooperative Commonwealth, The (L. Grunlund), 2413
Cooper Union speeches
    Bryan, 1006
    Tilden, 940-45

Copperheads *see* Democratic party, factions
Corcoran, Tommy, 1949, 2705
Corey, Lewis, 2405, 2424
Cornell, Alonzo, 903
Corwin, Thomas, 346
Coser, Lewis, 2433
Costello, Frank, 2691
Cotton Whigs *see* Whig party
Coughlin, Charles E., 1944, 1946, 2269
Covode, John, 1156
Cox, Eugene E., 2685
Cox, James M., 1818-20, 1824, 1830, 2105
Cox, Samuel S., 891
Coxey, Jacob, 999, 1719, 1722, 2069, 2074, 2568
Coyne, John R., Jr., 3123-46
Crane, Charles, 1814
Crawford, William Harris, 25, 267, 268, 269, 271, 501, 504
Credit Mobilier, revelations, 901
    see also scandals
Crittenden, John J., 362, 610, 1154
Crittenden Compromise, 1249-51
    see also Missouri Compromise
Crittenden-Johnson Resolutions of *1861,* 1169
Croker, Richard, 1005, 1006
Croly, Herbert, 2568
Cross, Wilbur, 2120
Crotty, Peter, 2706
Crum, Bartley, 3312-13
Crump, Edward, 2676, 2691
Cuba, 2094, 2097, 2107
Cullen, Hugh Roy, 3324
Cummins, Albert B., 2549, 2551, 2553, 2556, 2562, 2566
Cunliffe, Marcus, 10
Curley, James, 2676
Curran, Joseph, 3191
currency *see* banking and monetary policy
Currie, Lauchlin, 2686
Curtis, Benjamin, 1153
Curtis, George W., 904, 1283, 1421
Cushing, Caleb, 516, 524, 526, 597, 600
Cutting, Bronson, 2674

D

Daily Worker, 2435, 3174, 3188, 3194
Daley, Richard, 2707, 2844, 2851, 2854, 2862
Dana, Charles A., 995
Dangerfield, George, 6
Daniels, Josephus, 1831, 2077
Darcy, Samuel Adams, 3178, 3184, 3185
Daugherty, Harry, 1819, 2110, 2111
David, Paul T., 2077

Davidson, Jo, 3312
Davis, David, 1159, 1554
Davis, Henry Winter, 1169, 1170, 1275-77
Davis, Benjamin J., Jr., 3188, 3196
Davis, James J., 2111
Davis, Jefferson, 526, 533, 563, 886, 1144, 1159
Davis, John W., 1823, 1824, 1826, 1830, 1887-92, 2116, 2122
Davis, Matthew L., 256
Davis, O. K., 2557
Davis, Will, 2843, 2845
Dawes, Charles, 2107
Dawes Severalty Act, 990
Dawson, Donald S., 2690
Day, Horace, 1558
Dayton, William L., 615, 1151
Dearborn, Henry, 259
Debs, Eugene, 1724, 2084, 2417, 2421, 2426, 3173
    and American Railway Union, 999-1000, 2070
    described, 2416, 2483-85
    and election of *1904,* 2082, 2084, 2415
    and election of *1912,* 1814, 2091, 2399, 2418, 2427, 2559
    and election of *1920,* 1819, 2420
    "Revolutionary Unionism" speech, 2476-82
Debsian socialism *see* Socialist party
De Lancey family, 135, 137
Dell, Floyd, 2424
DeLeon, Daniel, 1728, 2409, 2412, 2414, 2415, 2417, 2435, 2439, 2467-75
Democracy, the *see* Democratic party
Democratic Advisory Council *see* Democratic party, structure
Democratic Digest, The, 2696
Democratic party
    and Antimasonic party, 334, 578, 580, 582, 584-92 *passim,* 594, 619
    "Independent Democrats," 1175-80
    Atlanta Constitution editorial on, 1510-11
    under Bryan, 887, 1001-17
    under Cleveland, 887, 904, 988-93, 995-1001
    coalitions and compromises with Republicans, 900, 902, 1168, 1283, 1284, 1811-12, 1819, 1825, 1962, 2090, 2122, 2704, 2996
    congressional voting record, 888, 893, 896, 900, 994-95, 1417, 1423, 2124, 2561, 2704-05
    constituent groups, 890, 892, 894, 896-98, 904, 988, 1014, 1288, 1427, 1816, 1819-21, 1940, 1946-48, 1953, 1958-59, 2071, 2125, 2269, 2561, 2675-76, 2843, 2851-52, 2864
    corruption charges, 1822, 2288-89, 2686, 2688-89, 2690-91

Democratic party (*cont.*)
  disaffection of South, 3314-17, 3399-3401,
    3441
    Governor's Conference of *1948,* 3316,
      3409-14
    1828-1860, 26, 271, 333-38 *passim,* 341,
      342, 343, 360, 361, 497-571, 588,
      591, 592, 595, 597, 598, 615, 616,
      617, 749-58 *passim*
  and elections *see* elections
  and ethnic minorities, 504, 514, 525, 530,
    606, 897, 1819, 1820-22, 1958,
    2071, 2076, 2082, 2830
  factions, 903, 999-1000, 1002, 1013, 1142-
    46, 1148, 1286, 1417, 1823-24,
    2099, 2675, 2677, 2680, 2682-84,
    2691, 2851
    Barnburners, 519, 521, 522, 523, 525-
      26, 753-58 *passim,* 851-70, 1142,
      1145, 1150
    Byrnes vs. Wallace, 2675-76, 2681-82
    conservatives, 1942-43, 1945, 1948,
      1949-51, 1952, 1956, 2561, 2864,
      3315
    conservatives, southern, 1960-61, 2678,
      2679, 2685, 2693, 2698, 2702-03
    Copperheads, 889-91
    fusionists, 1145-48
    Hunkers, 1142
    liberals, 1956, 2677-78, 2680-81, 2683,
      2689, 2693, 2697-98, 2701-02,
      2864, 3315
    progressivism, 1811-12, 1814-15, 1942-
      43, 1945, 1948, 1949-51
    rebels, 1815, 2275
    Reorganizers, 1005-06, 1008-11, 1015
    third party movements, 3309-10, 3312,
      3315-16
  failures analyzed, 887, 898, 903, 1003,
    1015, 1819-20, 1823, 2105, 2694,
    2855-56, 3029
  and Free Soil party, 523-24, 526, 757
  funding, 1813-14, 1958, 2071, 2077, 2698,
    2847-48, 3323-25
  ideologies
    New Deal *see* New Deal
    "New Departure," 898-99, 936-39, 988,
      1007, 1011
    "Fair Deal," 2688
    "Great Society," 2835, 2913-16
    "New Freedom," 1814, 1846-55, 2558
    "New Frontier," 2706, 2707, 2832,
      2871-75
  under L. B. Johnson, 2695-96, 2835, 2837-
    40
  under J. F. Kennedy, 2707, 2832-35
  and Know Nothing party, 530, 594, 600,
    610

  leaders
    1860-1900, 887, 888, 891, 989, 2017
    1900-1930, 1008-9, 1013, 1017, 1813,
      1825, 1893
    1930-1960, 1942, 1947, 1949, 1950-51,
      1953, 1963, 2695-96
    1960-1972, 2706, 2707, 2828, 2843, 2864
  and Liberty party, 750
  machines, 902, 1288, 1812-13, 1815, 1821,
    1958, 1960, 2071, 2559, 2676,
    2682, 2707, 2839, 2860, 2862-63
  and monetary policies, 894-96, 990-91, 995,
    997, 1000-02, 1004-05, 1430
  and N.F.A. and I.U., 1713
  and National Republican party, 335, 336,
    337, 338, 508
  patronage, 1811, 1814-15, 2269, 2830,
    2837
  and People's party, 1717, 1719, 1723
  purge of *1938,* 1949-50, 1956, 1960,
    2673
  and racial issue, 2697-98, 2703, 2829,
    2839, 2857-58
  and Republican party, 530, 535, 536, 617,
    759
  under F. D. Roosevelt, 1830-31, 1940-50
    passim, 1955, 1958, 1961-63
  under A. E. Smith, 1821, 1829-30
  and Southern Rights' parties, 522, 524,
    525, 526, 609
  states' rights and State Rights parties, 335,
    336, 502, 505, 508, 514, 525, 1427
  structure, 1145, 1824, 1830, 1953, 1959-
    61, 2829-30, 2832, 2834
    Democratic Advisory Council, 2701-2,
      2829, 3025
    Democratic National Committee
      (D.N.C.), 1813, 1815, 1824, 1825,
      1940, 1948, 2675, 2683, 2684,
      2696-97, 2834, 2837, 2847, 2863-
      64
    nationalities division (All-American
      Council), 2687, 2858-59
  structure reforms
    Committee on Delegate Selection and
      Party Reforms (McGovern Commis-
      sion), 2843-46, 2847, 2856, 2864,
      2952-64; guidelines, 2845-46, 2851,
      2864
    "Democrats" defined, 2845-47
    O'Hara Commission, 2843, 2846-47,
      2852, 2965-81
    unit rule, 2841, 2843-44
  success analyzed, 903-4, 1535-37, 1817,
    1946, 2273-74, 2707
  under H. S. Truman, 2674-91
  and Union parties, 524, 525, 609, 610, 615,
    616, 625

and Whig party, 336-44 *passim,* 348, 349-
    50, 352-53, 356, 357, 359-60, 363,
    508, 509, 510, 511, 513-14, 518,
    520, 521, 524, 525, 531, 595, 610,
    619, 620
  under W. Wilson, 1813-20
Dennis, Eugene, 3178, 3187, 3188, 3190,
    3191, 3197
DeSapio, Carmen, 2690, 2706, 2707, 2859-60
de Saussure, H. W., 96
Desert Lands Act, *1877,* 1702
DeVries, Walter, 2999
Dewey, Thomas E., 1957, 2095, 2686, 2690,
    2987, 2988, 3016, 3021, 3049
  background, 3026
  campaign speech, 2361-65
  and election of *1940,* 2279
  and election of *1944,* 2283
  and election of *1948,* 2286, 2434
  and election of *1952,* 2289-90
  as governor, 2282, 2283
De Witt, Alexander, 1175-80
Dickens, Samuel, 266-67
Dickinson, Daniel S., 526
Dickinson, Don M., 995
Dickinson, Lester J., 2270
Dilworth, Richardson, 2691, 2692, 2697
Dimitroff, Georgi, 3239-47
Dirksen, Everett M., 2689, 2997, 3008, 3011,
    3017, 3049
Dix, John Adams, 520, 526, 1286, 1287
Dix, John A., 1017
Dixiecrats *see* States' Rights parties
Dixon, Archibald, 361, 610
Dixon, Frank M., 3315, 3318, 3415-21
Dixon, Joseph M., 2551, 2553, 2554, 2557
Dodd, Thomas, 2836
Dodge, Cleveland, 1814
Doheny Edward L., 1822
Dole, Robert, 3051
Donelson, Andrew Jackson, 613-14
Donnelly, Ignatius, 993, 1708, 1714, 1716,
    1721, 1725, 1726
Donohoe, Bernard, 1953
Donovan, Robert, 3018
Doolittle, James R., 1156
Dorner, Hannah, 3312
Dos Passos, John, 2432
Douglas, Helen Gahagan, 2690, 3034
Douglas, Lewis, 1942
Douglas, Paul H., 2687, 2692, 2693, 2762,
    2862, 2863, 3314
Douglas, Stephen A., 358, 361, 522, 531, 533,
    888, 1143-44, 1153, 1159
  and election of *1852,* 525
  and election of *1856,* 526
  and election of *1860,* 531-36 *passim,* 562,
    1161

Freeport Doctrine, 533, 562, 563, 1155
  Lecompton Constitution, 532, 533, 562
  and A. Lincoln debates, 533, 562, 1155
  and slavery, 531, 532, 533, 562, 563, 566
Douglas, William O., 1951
Dow, Neal, 1573
Draper, Theodore, 2424, 2425, 3171, 3174
Dred Scott case, 531, 562, 1152
Dreiser, Theodore, 3173
Drucker, Peter, 3050
Drummond, Roscoe, 3023
Duane, James, 33-34, 149, 163
Duane, William, 260
Dubinsky, David, 2430
Du Bois, W. E. B., 2084, 2115
Duclos, Jacques, 3185, 3186, 3187, 3188,
    3194, 3257-73
Duff, James A., 2690
Dulles, John Foster, 2700, 2993
Dunn, Arthur J., 1013
Dunne, William F., 3178
DuPont, Samuel F., 1275
Durkee, Charles, 1148
Dwight, Theodore, 16, 99-100

E

Eagleton, Thomas, 2852-53
Earle, George, 1951
Earle, Thomas, 745
Early, Jubal A., 1171
Early, Steve, 1956
Eastland, James, 3315-16
Eastman, Max, 2424
Eaton, Dorman B., 1422
Eaton, John, 499-500, 506, 510
economy
  anti-depression legislation, 2120, 2122-24,
    2266, 2269, 2271, 2273, 2429,
    2678-80, 2702
  and Civil War, 1551-53
  depressions
    1812, 2412
    1857, 1153
    1870's, 1556
    1883-1885, 2408
    1890, 2411
    1895, 1719, 2075, 2080
    1921, 2110
    Great, 1830, 1939-40, 1942, 1943,
      1952, 2120, 2122, 2263, 2426-27,
      3181-82
    H. Hoover on, 2247-54, 2267-68
  as election issue, *1886-1896,* 1422-23,
    2070, 2072-73, 2075

economy (*cont.*)
  farm prices, 894, 993, 1001-03, 1555, 1941, 1953
  inflation, 1556, 1953, 2678-79
  national market, 1550-55, 1702-03
  panics
    1819, 498, 499
    1837, 341, 342, 510, 2403, 2406
    1857, 531
    1873, 895, 900, 1555, 2406, 2407
    1893, 2069
    1907, 1015, 2088, 2544
  recessions, 1949, 2702, 2989
Ector, Zales N., 2695
education, 141, 142, 347, 348, 2113-14, 2402-03, 2416
  Morrill Act of *1862,* 1167
  Roman Catholic schools, 514, 528, 597
Eighteenth Amendment *see* Constitution, U.S.
Eisenhower, Dwight D., 2685, 2702, 2830, 3009, 3016
  addresses, 3057-61, 3090-94
  background, 2291, 2987, 2990-93
  and civil rights, 2698, 2702-03
  and election of *1948,* 2290, 2685
  and election of *1952,* 2290-91, 2987-88
  and election of *1956,* 2988-89
  and election of *1958,* 2703
  and election of *1960,* 2833
  as party leader, 2991-3000
  as president, 2704, 2986, 2989-3000
  and Republican leaders, 1819, 2988, 2991, 2993-95, 3002, 3016-18
Eisenhower, Milton, 2989
elections, gubernatorial
  1861 (Ohio), 1168
  1862, 889
  1863 (Ohio), 890-91
  1867 (Ohio), 895
  1870 (Missouri), 899-900
  1875 (Ohio, Pennsylvania), 896
  1910, 1812
  1912, 1814, 2560
  1916 (New York), 2104
  1918-1926 (New York), 1821
  1924 (Maine), 2114
  1926, 1826
  1928 (New York), 1830
  1930 (Connecticut, New York), 2120, 1830
  1942 (New York), 1957, 2282
  1954, 2697
  1962, 1834, 3009
  1964, 2837
  1965 (Virginia), 3028
  1966, 3028-29
  1969 (Virginia), 3048
  1970, 2847, 3047
elections, local
  1863, 1168
  1872-1880, 1560, 1573

1872, 1621-24
1878, 1604-08
1879, 1707
1886 (New York mayoralty), 2400, 2405, 2408, 2409
1893-1931, 2077
1901, 1008
1903, 1009
1912, 2551-53, 2558-60
  Socialist party, 2418
1917 (New York mayoralty), 2419, 2424
1947, 2685
1950, 2690
1965, 3025-28
1972, 2863
elections, national
  1788, 166
  1792, 245
  1794, 13
  1796, 13, 15, 246-50 *passim,* 253, 255, 257, 291-92
  1800, 5, 15, 16, 17, 19, 22, 25, 94-96, 240, 250-59 *passim,* 263, 264
  1802, 21
  1804, 251, 263-64, 265, 296-300
  1808, 21, 251, 264, 265-66, 304-09
  1812, 21, 266, 267, 310-20
  1816, 267, 268
  1820, 267
  1824, 24, 25, 258-59, 263, 265, 268-71, 322-24, 344, 500, 501-02
  1828, 333, 344, 348, 497, 502-10 *passim,* 578, 579, 623
  1832, 333-34, 335, 340, 344-45, 507, 508, 509, 589-90, 662-79
  1836, 336, 337, 339-40, 342-43, 349, 384-89, 511, 515, 590, 591, 592
  1840, 342-44, 350, 352, 384-89, 400-10, 512, 513, 515, 591, 741, 744, 746, 747, 748
    Liberty party, 1141
  1844, 352-53, 384-89, 420-25, 516, 517, 518-19, 524, 550, 747, 748, 757, 1141
  1848, 356, 384-89, 433-46, 521-25 *passim,* 553, 750, 754, 755, 756, 757, 1142
  1852, 359-60, 384-89, 475-90, 525, 530, 557, 601, 609, 758, 1142
  1854, 527, 529, 530, 699-700
    results, 1147, 1149
  1856, 362, 525, 526, 527, 530, 557-61, 594, 595, 603, 608, 611-19 *passim,* 701-37
    American party, 1151
    Democrats, 1151
    Republicans, 1148-50, 1185-1222
    results, 1151
  1858, 532-33
    Republicans, 1154, 1159-60
    results, 1155

1860, 362, 525, 531-36 *passim,* 557, 562,
    563, 566-70, 618, 619, 620
    Constitutional Union party, 1161
    Democrats, 1159, 1161
    Republicans, 1160, 1161, 1239-47
    results, 1161
1862
    Democrats, 888-89
    results, 889, 1168
1864
    Democrats, 891, 895, 1171-72, 2836
    Republicans, 1166, 1170, 1171, 1259-
    67, 1282, 1283, 1297-1321
    results, 891-92, 1283, 1321
1866
    Republicans, 1293
    results, 893
1868
    Democrats, 895, 1290
    Republicans, 1283, 1287, 1290, 1322-43
1870, Prohibition party, 1571
1872
    Democrats, 900, 1290
    Prohibition party, 1571-72, 1619-20
    Republicans, 899, 1283, 1344-69, 1572
    results, 900, 1283, 1368-69, 1572
    Socialist party, 2458-59
1874-1910, results analyzed, 987-88
1874
    Republicans, 900-01
    results, 985, 900-01, 987
1876
    Democrats, 901, 1283, 1290
    Greenback party, 1587
    People's party, 1724
    Prohibition party, 1572, 1625-26
    Republicans, 1283-85, 1290-91, 1370-
    1407
    results, 888, 901-02, 987, 1283-84,
    1406-07, 1558-59
1878
    Greenback party, 1560-62, 1599-1601
    results, 903, 987, 1561-62
1880
    Democrats, 903
    Greenback party, 1609-11
    National Independent party, 1708
    Prohibition party, 1572, 1577
    Republicans, 1437-39
    results, 888, 903, 988, 1428-29, 1564,
    1576, 1708
1882, Democrats, 904
1884
    Democrats, 904, 976-83, 989, 1129
    Greenback party, 1612-14
    National party, 1708
    Prohibition party, 1575-76, 1577
    Republicans, 904, 1429, 1457-59
    results, 904, 988, 1130, 1429, 1708
1886, issues, 991

1888
    Democrats, 992
    issues, 991, 992, 1425
    Prohibition party, 1577, 1645-50
    Republicans, 1425, 1429, 1481-85
    results, 992, 1131, 1137, 1429, 1709
    Union labor party, 1709
1890
    Democrats, 1429
    Populist parties, 1712
    results, 993, 1712
1892
    Democrats, 995-96
    People's party, 1714, 1716, 1760, 1766-
    68
    Populist party, 994,
    Prohibition party, 1577
    Republicans, 994, 1512-15
    results, 996, 1003, 1132, 1137, 1429,
    1716-18
    Socialist Labor party, 2412
1894
    Democrats, 1431
    People's party, 1719-20
1896
    Democrats, 999-1005, 1012, 1722,
    2076
    issues, 2070
    National party, 1656-57
    People's party, 1795-98
    Populist party, 1002
    Prohibition party, 1578, 1658
    Republicans, 1002-03, 2077
    results, 1003-04, 1133, 1137, 1724,
    2076
1898
    results, 1004, 2079-80
    Socialist Labor party, 2412
1900
    Democrats, 1004-06, 1008, 1725
    Prohibition party, 1659-62
    results, 1006, 1134, 1137, 2080
    Socialist party, 2416
1902
    Democrats, 1008
    Republicans, 2082
    results, 1008
1904
    Democrats, 1009-12, 2097-98
    Republicans, 2097
    results, 1012, 1135, 1137, 2082-83
    Socialist party, 2415
1906, Democrats, 1013
1908
    Democrats, 1013-15
    results, 1015, 1136, 1137, 1811
    Socialist party, 2415
1910
    Democrats, 1016-17
    issues, 1812

elections, national (*cont.*)
   Republicans, 1016, 2543
   results, 1812, 2089, 2422, 2542
  1912, 594
   Democrats, 1016-17, 1812-15, 1835-45,
    2553, 2557-58
   issues, 1814
   Progressive party, 2090-91, 2551, 2553-
    58, 2562, 2567, 2584-95
   Republicans, 1813, 2090-91, 2541,
    2547, 2548-50, 2557
   results, 1814, 2091, 2559
   Socialist party, 2399, 2415, 2418, 2486-
    90
  1914
   Progressive party, 2564
   results, 1815, 2564
  1916, 1815
   Democrats, 1816, 2101
   issues, 1816
   Progressive party, 2566-67, 2635-36
   Republicans, 2100-01, 2566
   results, 1816-17, 2101
   Socialist party, 2418
  1918, results, 2103-04
  1920, 1824
   Debsian Socialist party, 2420
   Democrats, 1118-20, 1818-20, 1857-72
   issues, 2115
   Prohibition party, 1665-69
   Republicans, 1119, 1817, 1819, 2103,
    2105, 2108
   results, 1819, 2105
  1922, 2568
  1924
   Democrats, 1822-23, 1826, 2114-16
   Progressive party, 2422, 2423, 2568,
    2644-68
   Republicans, 2116
   results, 1824, 2116, 2569
  1926, 2116
  1928, 1824
   Democrats, 1822, 1826-29, 1914-27,
    2116, 2117
   Prohibition party, 1580, 1670-71
   Republicans, 2115, 2117-18, 2229-39
   results, 1829, 2118, 2262-63, 2426
   Socialist party, 2426, 2498-2503
  1930, 1831, 2120
  1932
   Communist party, 2432, 3172
   Democrats, 1831, 1933-36, 1941, 1967-
    89, 2263
   Republicans, 2259-60, 2295-2311
   results, 2125, 2263-64, 2427
   Socialist party, 2399, 2427, 2504-08
  1934
   Democrats, 1942-43
   Republicans, 2266-67
   results, 2268

  1936
   Communist party, 2432-33
   Democrats, 1197-1205, 1890-96, 1945-
    46, 1948, 1990-2005, 3315
   Republicans, 1945-46, 2270-74, 2338-
    43
   results, 1945, 1948, 2273, 2274, 2428
  1938
   Democrats, 1951, 1960, 1962
   Republicans, 2276
   results, 2276
  1940
   Democrats, 1951-52, 2031-41, 2042-47
   issues, 2277
   Prohibition party, 1672-73
   Republicans, 1952, 2279-80, 2344-51
   results, 1953, 2261, 2280, 2431
   Socialist party, 2431
  1942, 1953-55, 2282
  1944
   Democrats, 1956-57, 1961, 2056-59,
    2060-66, 2284, 2682-84
   Republicans, 1957, 2283-84, 2361-65
   results, 1957, 2284
   Socialist party, 2434
  1946, results, 2284, 2683
  1948
   ballot qualifications, 3314, 3389-90
   Democrats, 2286-87, 2685, 2686-87,
    2711, 2720, 3316-17, 3433-34
   Progressive party, 3195, 3314, 3320-21,
    3322-24, 3356-74, 3383-88
   Republicans, 2286
   results, 2287, 2687, 3325-27, 3396-98
   Socialist party, 2434
   States' Rights party, 3324-25
  1950, results, 2689-90
  1952
   Democrats, 2291, 2494, 2692-94, 2732
   issues, 2694, 2988
   Prohibition party, 1674-77
   Republicans, 2289-92, 2391-95
   results, 2291-92, 2694-95, 2987, 2988
   Socialist party, 2434
  1953, results, 2697
  1954
   Democrats, 2697
   results, 2988
  1956
   Democrats, 2699-2700, 2780, 2992
   issues, 2700, 2987-89
   Republicans, 2700, 2988-90, 2996
   results, 2701, 2987, 2989
  1958
   issues, 2990
   results, 2703-04, 2989-90, 2997
   Socialist party, 2435
  1960
   debates, 2879-2908, 3085-89
   Democrats, 2705, 2706, 2831-33, 2869-

78, 2997, 3003-07
issues, 2707, 2990, 3003-07
Prohibition party, 1678-85
Republicans, 2833, 2997, 3001-07,
    3010-12, 3079-84
results, 1829, 2706-07, 2833, 2997,
    3004, 3007
Socialist party, 2513-18
voting patterns, 3005
1962, results, 2834, 3007, 3013
1964
    Democrats, 2437-38, 2836, 3023, 3430,
        3435
    Republicans, 2837, 3008, 3012, 3014-
        21, 3102-08
    results, 2837, 3020, 3021
    Socialist party, 2437
1966, results, 2838, 3028-29
1968
    American Independent party, 2842
    Democrats, 934-35, 2439, 2839-42,
        2846, 2863, 2922-26, 2942-51, 3038
    Prohibition party, 1688-96
    Republicans, 2842, 2847, 3001, 3032,
        3037-39, 3109-17, 3441
    results, 2842, 2986, 3039, 3040
    Socialist party, 2519-37
1970
    Republicans, 3046
    results, 3046-48
1972
    Democrats, 2848, 2850-57, 3443
    "new media politics," 2854-55
    Republicans, 2854, 2856, 3050-51,
        3156-64
    results, 2855, 3051-52, 3444
1976, Democrats and
    "barometer states" (Cal., Ill., N.Y.),
        2859-63
conventions and platforms (Democratic)
    1856, 1151
    1860 (Baltimore), 1159, 1161
    1864 (Chicago), 891, 1171-72
    1868, 895, 934-35, 1290
    1872 (Baltimore), 900, 1290
    1876, 1290
    1880 (Cincinnati), 903
    1884 (Chicago), 976-82
    1892, 995-96
    1896 (Chicago), 999-1002, 1004, 1005,
        1012, 1722, 2076
    1900 (Kansas City), 1005, 1008, 1725
    1904 (St. Louis), 1010-11
    1908 (Denver), 1014
    1912 (Baltimore), 1813, 1815, 1835-45
    1916 (St. Louis), 1816
    1920 (Chicago), 1818-19, 1857-72
    1924 (New York City), 1822, 1823,
        2114, 2116
    1928, 1827, 1829, 1914-27, 2117

1932, 1831, 1933-36, 1967-70, 2263
1936, 1945, 1948, 1990-96, 3315
1940, 1952, 2031-41
1944, 1956, 2056-59
1948 (Philadelphia), 2685, 2711, 2720,
    3316-17, 3433-34
1952, 2692-93, 2732
1956, 2699-700, 2780, 2992
1960 (Los Angeles), 2706, 2831, 2832,
    2869-70
1964 (Atlantic City), 2437-38, 2836
1968 (Chicago), 895, 934-35, 2439,
    2941-42, 2846, 2863, 2942-44,
    3038
1972 (Miami), 2851-52, 2857
conventions and platforms (Greenback
    party)
    1876, 1587
    1878 (Toledo), 1560-62, 1599-1601
    1880, 1609-11
    1884, 1612-14
conventions and platforms (National party)
    1898, 1656-57
conventions and platforms (People's party)
    1892 (Omaha), 1714-15, 1760, 1766-68
    1896, 1795-98
conventions and platforms (Progressive
    party)
    1912 (Chicago), 2090-91, 2551, 2553-
        57, 2567, 2584-95
    1916, 2566-67, 2635-36
    1924 (Cleveland), 2568, 2644-48
    1948, 3195, 3320-21, 3356-74
conventions and platforms (Prohibition
    party)
    1869, 1617-18
    1872, 1571, 1619-20
    1876, 1625-26
    1880, 1577
    1884, 1577
    1888, 1577, 1645-50
    1892, 1577
    1896, 1658
    1900, 1659-62
    1920, 1665-69
    1928, 1670-71
    1940, 1672-73
    1952, 1674-77
    1960, 1678-85
    1968, 1688-96
conventions and platforms (Republican
    party)
    1856, 1149-50, 1185-1222
    1860, 1160-61, 1239-47
    1864, 1166, 1171, 1259-67, 1297-1321
    1868, 1287, 1290, 1322-43
    1872, 1344-69, 1572
    1876, 1285, 1290-91, 1370-1407
    1880, 1437-39
    1884, 1457-59

elections, national (*cont.*)
   1888, 1429, 1481-85
   1892 (Minneapolis), 994, 1512-15
   1912 (Chicago), 2090, 2541, 2547,
      2548-50
   1916, 2100, 2101, 2566
   1920, 2105
   1936, 2272-73
   1940, 2279
   1944, 2283-84
   1948, 2286
   1952, 2290-91, 2391-95, 2992
   1956, 2996
   1960, 2997, 3002-04, 3010-12, 3079-84
   1964, 3019-20, 3102-08
   1968, 3001, 3037, 3109-17
   1972, 3051, 3156-64
  conventions and platforms (United Labor
    party)
   1877, 1596-98
  primaries (Democratic)
   1924, 1822-23
   1956, 2699
   1960, 2705, 2831
   1964, 3430, 3435
   1968, 2839-40, 2922-26
   1972, 2850, 3443
  primaries (Republican)
   1960, 3001
   1964, 3012, 3017-18
   1968, 3032
  voter participation, 2070, 2075, 2082,
    2091-93, 2118, 2120, 2287
Electoral Commission, 901-02
Eliot, Thomas D., 1146
Ellis, Vesparian, 612, 613
Ellsworth, Robert, 3031
emancipation, 888, 1165-66, 1290
  First and Second Confiscation Acts of
    1861, 1166
Emancipation Proclamation, 1166, 1255-56
Emancipator, The, 818-20
Emerging Republican Majority, The, 3042
Emerson, Ralph Waldo, 349
Emerson, Thomas Irwin, 3314, 3321
Endicott, W.C., 989
Engels, Frederick, 203-06 *passim*, 2401, 2408,
    2409, 2412
Epstein, Jacob, 2086
Erie Canal, 500, 578, 585, 586, 599
Erie Railroad, 598
Esch-Cummins Act, 1818
ethnic groups, 2269, 2828, 2857-58
  and election of *1940*, 2280
  and election of *1948*, 3326-27
  and election of *1972*, 2852
  and political parties, 1549, 1570, 2424,
    2830, 2852, 3326-27

  see also immigration; religious interests
Evans, Daniel, 3029, 3043
Evans, George Henry, 2402-03, 2404, 2407
Evans, Hiram, 1822
Everett, Edward, 114, 362
Ewing, Thomas, 344

F

Fairchild, Charles S., 995
Fair Employment Practices Commission (F.E.
    P.C.), 2676, 2678, 3324
Fall, Albert B., 2102, 2104
Family party, 504
Farenthold, Cissy, 2852
Farley, James, 1831, 1948, 1951, 2006-11,
    2987
Farmer-Laborite party, 1948, 2263, 2421,
    2567, 2568
Farmer-Labor party of Minnesota, 1731
farmers and farming *see* rural interests
Farmer's Alliance, 1710
Farmer's Alliance, 1426, 1702, 1710
  see also People's party
Farmers' Clubs of North Carolina, 1710
Farmer's and Laborers Union, 1710
Farmer's League, 1709
Farmer's Mutual Benefit Association, 1709,
    1711
Farmer's party, 1707
Farmer's Union (Texas), 1731
Farm Loan Act of *1916*, 1730
Farragut, David G., 891, 1172
Fascism: A Challenge to Democracy (M. W.
    Howard), 1731
Faubus, Orval Lee, 2703
Fayssoux, John, 162
Federal Bureau of Investigation (F.B.I.), 2435
Federal Elections ("Force") Bill, 335, 508,
    993
Federal Farm Loan Act of *1916*, 1816
Federalist Papers, 9, 163, 240
Federalist party, 3-132, 139-43 *passim*, 146,
    147, 149, 152, 153, 157, 239, 247,
    265, 497, 498, 504
  and Antifederalist party, 8, 9, 135, 158,
    159, 160, 162, 164, 165, 166
  Hartford Convention, 20, 23-24, 116-31, 266
  and Jeffersonian Republican party, 4, 10,
    12, 13, 18, 19, 21, 22, 23, 166, 240,
    244, 246, 250, 253, 259, 260, 264,
    266, 267, 270, 271, 272, 504
  and Whig party, 348
Federal Reserve Act of *1913*, 1730, 1816

Federal Reserve Board, 1815
Federal Trade and Tariff Commissions, 1816
Federation of Organized Trades (A.F.L.), 2408
Fellowship Forum, 1828
feminism, 1651-52, 1827, 2090, 3172
    and Democratic convention of *1972,* 2852
    and Progressive party of *1948,* 3324
    and Prohibition party, 1577, 1647-50
    and Republican party, 1820, 1824, 2072
    under Roosevelt, 1947
Fenno, John, 242, 243
Fessenden, William P., 1146, 1157, 1166
Feuer, Lewis, 2404
Feverty, Clare Gerald, 2333-37
Field, James G., 994, 1716
Fillmore, Millard, 355, 356, 359, 360, 362,
    363, 591, 594, 595, 612-19 *passim,*
    1149, 1151, 1160
Finch, Robert, 3028, 3043
Finletter, Thomas K., 2860
Finney, Charles Grandison, 347
First Battle, The (W. J. Bryan), 1004
First World War, 2195-2201
    limitation of armament, 2212-17
    "Peace of Vengeance," 2202-08
    and Progressive party, 2561, 2565
    and Republican party, 2099
    and Socialist party, 2417, 2419-20
Fischer, David Hackett, 17, 19
Fisk, James, Jr., 898
Fitzgerald, Albert, 3321
Fitzgerald, "Honey Fitz," 1431
Fitzgerald, John F., 2114
Fitzpatrick, John, 3170
Flemming, Arthur, 3001
Fletcher, Henry P., 2267, 2312-16
Flinn, William, 2552, 2553, 2557
Flinn Plan, 2552
Flower, R. W., 2074
Floyd, John B., 335
Flynn, Ed, 1956
Flynn, Elizabeth Gurley, 3178, 3188
Folger, Cliff, 3016
Folk, Joseph W., 1013, 1017, 2086
Foner, Eric, 753, 755, 756, 1157
Force Bill, 335, 508, 993
Ford, Gerald, 3024, 3027
Ford, Henry, 2104, 2112
Ford, James, 2432, 3172
Ford, Thomas, 607, 611, 612, 613, 706
foreign policy, 1426, 2276-77, 2688, 3310,3311
    Asia, 2094-97, 2106, 2175-76, 2287
    and Democratic administrations, 1007,
        2287, 2684, 2834
    expansionism, 2093-2108
    Kellogg-Briand Pact, 2106
    Latin America, 2094, 2097-99, 2107-08
    Marshall Plan, 2684

NATO, 2377-90, 2688
Near East, 2366-76
    and Republican administrations, 2099-2103,
        2106-08, 2276-80, 2703, 2856,
        2989, 3147-55
    Root-Takahira Agreement, 2175-76
    Russia, 2096, 2681-82, 2703
    and Whig party, 350, 352, 353, 354
    W. Willkie on lend lease, 2352-60
Foreign Relations, 2175-76
Forney, John A., 531, 532
Foss, Eugene N., 1017
Foster, Lafayette, 1156
Foster, William Z., 2417, 2425, 2432, 3170-88
    passim, 3193-97 *passim*
Fourier, Francois Marie Charles, 2403
Fraina, Louis (Lewis Corey), 2424, 3206-10,
    3205
France
    and Great Britain, 244
    and the United States, 12, 14, 15, 244, 253
Francis, David R., 1008
Frank, Glenn, 2275
Frank, Lewis, Jr., 3312
Frank, Waldo, 3172, 3173
Franklin, Benjamin, 153, 576
Franklin, John Hope, 892
Frazier, Donald, 2843
Free Democratic party, 1141, 1142, 1145
Freedman's Bureau, 892
Freeman, Orville, 2697
Freemasons, 576-80 *passim*
    see also Antimasonic party
Free Soil party, 356, 357, 360, 361, 523, 525,
    529, 605, 741, 752, 754-61 *passim,*
    871-82, 1141, 1142, 1145
    and Democratic party, *1828-1860*, 523-24,
        526, 757
    formation, 1142
    and Liberty party, 750, 751, 757
    and Republican party, 617, 741, 1141
    and Whig party, 757, 758-59
free soil principle, 1141 ·
Frelinghuysen, Peter, 3024
Frelinghuysen, Theodore, 352
Fremont, Charles C. ("The Pathfinder"), 362,
    527, 594, 615, 616, 617, 619, 1150,
    1165, 1166, 1171, 1172, 1265-67
Freneau, Philip, 242-43
Fried, Albert, 2403, 2407
Fritchey, Clayton, 2696
From Marx to Lenin (M. Hillquit), 2425
Frye, William P., 1420
Fugitive Slave Act, 359, 524, 607, 614, 701,
    1143, 1146
Fulbright, J. William, 2683, 2690
Fuller, Henry M., 613
Fusion party, 615, 616

G

Gable, Hamilton, 1169
Galbraith, John Kenneth, 2426-27, 2702
Gallatin, Albert, 246, 247, 256, 258, 267
Gardner, August P., 2102
Gardner, Henry, 605, 607, 608, 616, 706
Gardner, John W., 2838
Garfield, James A., 601, 886, 903, 988, 1285, 1422, 1428
    acceptance letter, 1440-43
    campaign speeches, 1444-48
    editorials on, 1449-56
    as president, 1422, 1428, 1429
    and Republican party, 1414, 1429
Garfield, James R., 2556, 2564
Garfield, John, 1290
Garland, A. H., 989
Garner, John Nance, 1830, 1831, 1949, 1950, 1951, 2109, 2122, 2124, 3000
Garrison, William Lloyd, 741, 743, 744-45, 746, 760, 761, 792-93, 1141
    on third party issue, 794, 801-17
Garvey, Marcus, 3171
Gary, Elbert, 2111
Gates, Horatio, 256
Gates, John, 2435, 3178
Gates, Thomas, 3001
Gatlin, Alfred, 270
Gavin, James, 3030
Gayarre, Charles, 611
Gazette of the United States, 242, 243
Genet, Citizen (Edmond Charles Genet), 11, 246
George, Harrison, 3178
George, Henry, 2080, 2400, 2405, 2408, 2409, 2414, 2460-66
George, Milton, 1709
George, Walter, 1950, 1951, 1952, 2678
German Ideology, The (Karl Marx), 2403
German immigrants *see* immigrants; nativism
Gerry, Elbridge, 153, 154, 157, 166
Gettysburg, Battle of, 1168
Gibbons, James, 2408
Giddings, Joshua R., 355, 752, 757, 758, 1144, 1146, 1149, 1153, 1156, 1157, 1160, 1175-80
Gilder, Richard Watson, 994
Gillette, William, 1290
Gilligan, John, 2847
Gilmer, Thomas, 516
Glass, Carter, 1950, 1952, 2122
Glazer, Nathan, 3171, 3176
Godkin, E. L., 989, 1421
Goldfine, Bernard, 2703
Goldwater, Barry, 2991, 2999, 3002, 3008, 3012, 3023, 3034, 3040, 3045, 3049, 3051, 3435

"Arizona Mafia," 3019, 3020
    background, 2996, 3014
    and civil rights, 3013, 3019
    and election of *1960,* 3003, 3083-84
    and election of *1964,* 2835, 3013, 3014, 3015-23
    as party leader, 3010-15, 3018-21, 3023-29
    and Republican leaders, 3017, 3018, 3023, 3029, 3036, 3100-01
    speeches, 3083-84, 3102-08
Gompers, Samuel, 1014, 1425, 1724, 1728, 1818, 2076, 2414, 2417, 2418, 2420-22, 2460
Goodell, Charles, 3024, 3047, 3051
Goodell, William, 748, 750, 752, 758, 759, 840-47
    "Political Action Against Slavery," 777-83
Goodman, Paul, 16
Good Templars *see* Independent Order of Good Templars
Gore, Albert, 2696, 2704, 2847
Gorman, Arthur P., 1008, 1009, 2097
Government Executive Order *9385,* 3189
Grace, William R., 903
Graham, Frank P., 2689
Gramsci, Antonio, 2425
Grand Army of the Republic, 991, 1006, 1289, 1422, 2070-71
Grand State Farmer's Alliance, 1709, 1735-36
Grange, the *see* Patrons of Husbandry
Granger, Francis, 338, 355, 578-79, 585, 591
Granger laws, 1555
Grant, Ulysses S., 891, 892, 895, 898, 900, 901, 1171, 1284, 1413, 1556-57
    denial of third term nomination, 1283, 1428
    and election of *1864,* 1170
    and election of *1868,* 1290, 1322-43
    and election of *1872,* 1344-69
    and Reconstruction, 1293
Graves, Earl, 2843
Gray, George, 1009, 1011, 1013, 1014
Grayson, William, 162
Great Britain
    and American Revolution, 4, 6-7, 25
    and France, War of *1793,* 244
    and United States, 12
        Jay Treaty, 10, 12-13, 17, 18, 19, 246-47
        Oregon dispute, 351, 353, 354, 518, 520, 753
        Texas annexation, 516, 550
        trade, 12, 13, 17, 18
        War of *1812,* 20, 21, 23, 24, 106-15, 266
        Webster-Ashburton Treaty, 350
Greeley, Horace, 343, 361, 887, 900, 946-47, 1145, 1148, 1149, 1154, 1159, 1229-38, 1283, 1284, 1287, 1290, 1572, 2403, 3020

Log Cabin, 344
Green, Duff, 502, 506
Green, Edith, 2701
Green, Gilbert, 3178
Greenback Clubs, 1558
Greenback-Labor party *see* Greenback party
Greenback party, 896, 903, 1557, 1573, 1578,
  2070, 2406
  addresses on, 1593, 1602-03
  constituent groups, 1555, 1562
  conventions and platforms, national
    1875 (Cleveland), 1551, 1557
    1876 (Indianapolis), 1551, 1558, 1587,
      1708
    1878 (Toledo), 1560-62, 1599-601,
      1708
    1880, 1563, 1609-11
    1884, 1612-14
    1896, 1656-57
  conventions and platforms, state, 1558
    1877, 1590-95
    1878, 1604-05, 1606-08
  decline, 1419, 1559, 1565-66
  effect on major parties analyzed, 1418,
    1565-66
  factions, 1557-58, 1562, 1563
  as Independent party, 1555, 1557, 1707,
    1708, 1712
  social-economic background, 1549-51
  strength, *1876-1884,* 1558-65
  J. B. Weaver, 1769-78
Gresham, Walter Q., 1716
Grier, Robert C., 1152
Griffin, Marvin, 3440
Griffin, Robert, 3030, 3043, 3049
Grimes, James W., 1146
Griswold, Roger, 23
Grodzins, Morton, 15, 1963
Gronlund, Lawrence, 2413, 2416
Grow, Galusha, 1156
Grun, Karl, 2403
Grundy, Joseph P., 2119

H

Hadley, Herbert S., 2086, 2549-50, 2566
Hague, Frank, 2676, 2685, 2690
Hale, John P., 605, 606, 754, 755, 758, 1142,
  1145, 1156
Hale, William Bayard, 1846-55
Hall, Gus, 3178, 3188
Hall, Leonard, 2988, 2990, 2992, 3016, 3033
Halleck, Charles, 2704, 2992, 2997, 3008,
  3024, 3027
Hallinan, Vincent, 3328

Hamilton, Alexander, 13, 33-34, 139, 152,
  163, 239, 246, 348, 1415
  and John Adams, 14, 15
  and Aaron Burr, 16, 23, 97-98
  correspondence, 16, 33-34, 64-65, 94-95,
    97-98, 243, 275-83
  and election of *1796,* 247
  and election of *1800,* 16, 94-95, 258
  and Federalist party, 7, 9, 10, 12, 15, 16,
    25, 257, 258
  and John Fenno, 242, 243
  and Thomas Jefferson, 239, 241-42, 243-
    44, 246, 250, 284-88
  and James Madison, 239, 241, 243
  monetary policy, 9, 11, 12, 14, 17, 18,
    241-42, 1417
  on New York gubernatorial election of
    1792, 64-65
  on Republican party, 275-83
Hamilton, John, 1946
Hamlin, Hannibal, 527, 1145, 1160, 1171
Hancock, John, 9, 138, 160
Hancock, Winfield S., 888, 903, 967-69, 1415,
  1428
Handlin, Oscar, *The Uprooted,* 1827
Hanna, Don, 2557, 2562
Hanna, Marcus A., 1002, 1006, 1009, 1724,
  2077, 2078, 2082, 2095, 2421,
  2423, 2429, 2555
Hannegan, Edward, 520
Hannegan, Robert E., 1956, 2674, 2675,
  2678, 2682, 2683
"Hannegan's Torpedoes," 2678
Hanrahan, Edward V., 2862, 2863
Harding, Warren G., 1822, 2070, 2100, 2103,
  2110-11, 2115, 2426, 2550
  character, 1819
  and election of *1920,* 2105, 2108, 2115
  as president, 2110-12
Hare, Charles Willing, 21
Harlan, James, 1148
Harmon, Judson, 1017, 2553
Harper, Robert Goodloe, 18, 21
Harper's Weekly, 1283
Harriman, E. H., 2563
Harriman, William Averell, 2681, 2693, 2697,
  2699, 2701, 2704, 2859, 3186
Harris, Fred, 2843, 2847, 2849
Harris, Roy, 3429
Harrison, Benjamin, 162, 992, 993, 996, 1414,
  1425, 1427, 1716, 2074
  acceptance letters, 1486-90, 1516-30
  campaign speeches, 1492-502
  editorials on, 1503-09, 1531-32
  failure analyzed, 1533-37
  as president, 1429
Harrison, Carter, 1008
Harrison, William Henry
  and election of *1836,* 340, 342-43, 590,
    591, 592

Harrison, William Henry (*cont.*)
    and election of *1840,* 342-43, 343-44, 591,
        745, 746
    as president, 350
Hartford *Connecticut Courant,* 301-03
Hartke, Vance, 2849, 3043
Hartz, Louis, 363, 2404
Harvey, George, 1012
Harvey, William H., 1721
Haskell, Charles N., 1014
Haskill Affair, 1014
Hastings, Daniel O., 2270
Haswell, Anthony
    letter from T. Jefferson, 260
Hatfield, Mark, 2999, 3018, 3027, 3028,
        3030, 3043
Hathaway, Clarence, 3178
Hathaway, William, 2856
Hawkes, Albert W., 2282
Hay, John ("Banty Tim"), 1003, 1164, 1289,
        2095
Hayes, Max, 2417, 2421
Hayes, Rutherford B., 896, 901-02, 1416,
        1419, 1428
    and Congress, 1428
    and election of *1876,* 1283, 1284, 1294,
        1370-407
    as governor, 1284
    on Know Nothing party, 598, 601
    and patronage, 1412, 1421
    as president, 1411-12
Hays, Samuel P., 2092
Hays, Will, 1819, 1820
Haywood, "Big Bill," 2417, 3173
Heard, Alexander, 3328
Hearst, William Randolph, 1006, 1009, 1010,
        1011, 1013, 1812, 2098
Heatter, Gabriel, 2509-10
Heflin, Thomas, 1828
Hegel, G. W. F., 2413
Helper, Hinton Rowan, *The Impending Crisis
    of the South,* 1157
Henderson, Leon, 2685
Hendricks, Thomas A., 901
Henry, Aaron, 2843, 2845
Henry, Francis J., 2564
Henry, Patrick, 162, 166
Henshaw, David, 503, 510
Herrick, Myron T., 1009
Hess, Stephen, 3028, 3029
Hewitt, Abram S., 898, 901, 902, 958-66,
        2409
Hicks, Granville, 2432
Hicks, Thomas H., 1169
Higginson, Thomas W., 904
Hill, Benjamin, 893-94, 952-55
Hill, David B., 995, 1001, 1002, 1005, 1006,
        1008-11, 1013
Hill, Isaac, 503

Hill, Lister, 1949, 3013
Hillman, Sidney, 1961, 2282, 2430, 2676
Hillquit, Morris, 2415, 2416, 2419, 2423,
        2425, 2426
Hinman, George, 3009, 3026
Hiss, Alger, 2287-88, 2686, 2688
Hoar, George F., 1443, 2157-58
Hobart, H. C., 898
Hodges, Luther, 2702
Hoey, Clyde R., 2689
Hoff, Philip, 2834
Hoffman, Clare, 2270, 2994, 2997
Hofstadter, Richard, 14-15, 2071, 2405, 2413,
        2429
Hogan, Frank, 2860
Hogg, James S., 1713
Holley, Myron, 746, 747
Holton, Linwood, 3028, 3043, 3048
Home Protection party, 1574, 1575
homestead legislation, 1143, 1702
    Homestead Bill of *1860,* 1158
    Homestead Bill of *1862,* 1167
Hoopes, Darlington, 2434, 2435
Hoover, Herbert, 1830, 2070, 2108, 2111,
        2113, 2429
    background, 2116-17
    on blacks, 2115, 2262
    Challenge to Liberty, The, 2267
    and election of *1920,* 2105
    and election of *1928,* 2117-18, 2229-39
    and election of *1932,* 2124-25
    and election of *1934,* 2267-68
    and election of *1936,* 1946, 2272
    and Great Depression, 2121-22, 2247-54
    Muscle Shoals Veto Message, 2240-46
    as party leader, 2265-68, 2274-75, 2276
    personality, 2264-65
    as president, 2107, 2119-24
    and rural interests, 2119, 2262, 2271
    as Secretary of Commerce, 2106, 2110,
        2115
    speeches, 2229-39, 2295-2311
Hopkins, Harry, 1942, 1947, 1949, 1951-52
Hopkins, J. A. H., 2567
House, Edward, 1825
House Un-American Activities Committee,
        2287, 2686, 2696
Houston, David, 1818
Houston, Sam, 613
Howard, Milford W., 1718, 1731
Howe, Irving, 2433
Hughes, Charles Evans, 1817, 2087, 2102,
        2107, 2566, 2567
    and election of *1916,* 2100-01
    and election of *1920,* 2105
    and labor, 2103, 2111
    as Secretary of State, 2106-07
    speeches, 2192-93, 2212-17
Hughes, Emmet John, 3002

Hughes, Francis W., 1503-04
Hughes, Harold, 2843, 2847-48, 2849
Hughes, John, 597
Hughes, William, 1814
Hull, Cordell, 1824, 1951
Human Events, 3025
Humphrey, George, 2989, 2996
Humphrey, Hubert, 2439, 2685, 2693, 2696,
    2698, 2701, 2836, 2843, 3033,
    3037, 3040
  background, 2697, 2828
  candidate, national elections
    1960, 2831
    1968, 2841, 2842, 2935-41, 3038,
      3041
    1972, 2849, 2851
  candidate, primary elections
    1960, 2705
    1968, 2840
    1972, 2850-51
  speeches, 2935-41, 2945-51
Humphreys, David, 159
Hunkers, 1142
Hunt, H. L., 3439
Hunt, Worthington, 362
Hunter, David, 1166
Hunter, R. M. T., 517, 526
Hunter, Robert, 2420
Hutcheson, William L., 2429

I

Ickes, Harold, 1949, 2568, 2681
Illinois Farmers' Association, 1557
Illinois primary of *1912,* 1812
Illinois Staats Zietung, 1572
immigrants, 523, 528, 594, 596, 609, 751,
    1816, 2407-08
  and antimasonry, 586, 587, 590
  and Democratic party, 504, 513, 514, 515,
    519, 525, 528, 529, 530, 531, 597,
    598, 606, 897-98, 988, 1820-22,
    1958, 2102
  and election of *1894,* 2075
  and election of *1896,* 2078
  and election of *1916,* 2104
  and election of *1920,* 1819, 2105
  and election of *1928,* 2116
  and election of *1930,* 2120
  and First World War, 2099, 2105
  and Know Nothing party, 361, 529, 530,
    531, 576, 593-97 *passim,* 599, 600
    604, 605, 606, 609, 610, 618
  and labor force, 528, 598, 599, 890, 2408,
    2412, 2413

naturalization time and suffrage, 528, 593,
    596-97, 617
  and Republican party, 530, 616, 2072,
    2082, 2089, 2096, 2262
  restrictions, 2076, 2114
Impelliteri, Vincent, 2690
*Impudent Snobs: Agnew vs. the Intellectual
    Establishment, The,* 3123-46
Independent Citizens Committee of the Arts,
    Sciences and Professions, 3312
Independent Fusionists, 1712
Independent Order of Good Templars, 1567,
    1569
Independent party *see* Greenback party
Independent party of California, 3312
Independent Progressives of California, 3313
Independent Socialist League, 2435
Independent Voters of Illinois, 2863
Indiana Farmer, 1557
Indianapolis Working-Men's Resolutions of
    1877, 1588-89
Indians, 18, 136, 334, 347, 506
  and Democratic party of *1828-60,* 504, 505,
    584
Industrial Age, 1557
industrialization, 1415, 1550-51
Industrial party (Michigan), 1712
Industrial Union
  L. L. Polk address to, 1746-57
  St. Louis Demands, 1737-39
Industrial Workers of the World (I.W.W.), 2412,
    2415, 2417, 3178, 3439
Intermediate Credit Act of *1923,* 1730
Internal Revenue Act of *1862,* 1568
International Harvester Corporation, 2563
International Workingmen's Association
    (I.W.M.A.), 2406
Interstate Commerce Commission, 1424, 1815
Iowa Homestead, 1557
isolationism, 1816, 2229-39, 2997-98
Isthmus Holding Company, Ltd., 2169-70

J

Jackson, Andrew, 266, 505-07, 576, 578
  and election of *1824,* 24, 25, 268, 271,
    500, 501-02
  and election of *1828,* 333, 344, 348, 497,
    502-06 *passim,* 508, 509, 510, 578,
    579
  and election of *1832,* 333, 334, 340, 507,
    508, 509, 590
  as president, 333-39 *passim,* 348, 505-10
    passim, 514, 515, 516, 517, 584

Jackson, Andrew (*cont.*)
    Second Bank of the United States and
        monetary policy, 334-40 *passim*,
        505, 508-10, 511, 541-43, 590, 591,
        1417
    and slavery, 504, 508, 514, 515, 584
    and Martin Van Buren, 334, 337, 338, 340,
        348, 502-07 *passim*, 578
Jackson, Francis, 744
Jackson, Henry M., 2695, 2849
Jackson, Jesse, 2862
Jackson, John M., 427-28
Jackson, Jonathan, 3
Jackson, Robert, 1951
Jaffa, Harry, 3019
Jay, John, 7, 10, 12, 149, 163, 257
    Constitution supported by, 45-55
    and Alexander Hamilton correspondence,
        16, 94-95
Jay Treaty, 10, 12-13, 17, 18, 19, 246-47
Jefferson, Thomas, 154
    and John Adams, 15, 246, 250
    and Aaron Burr, 242, 252-53
    correspondence, 243, 246, 252-53, 260,
        284-88
    and election of *1796,* 246, 247-48, 249,
        253, 257, 291-92
    and election of *1800,* 15, 240, 251, 253-
        54, 255, 257, 258
    and election of *1804,* 263
    and Federalist party, 3, 5, 6, 9, 21
    First Inaugural Address, 259, 293-95
    and Alexander Hamilton, 239, 241-42, 243-
        44, 246, 250
        Washington's attempt at reconciliation,
            243, 284-88
    and James Madison, 239, 241, 242, 245,
        246, 253
    and James Monroe, 246, 253
    as president, 5, 15, 16, 17, 19, 21, 22, 23,
        240, 258, 259, 260, 263, 265-66,
        271, 272
    as Secretary of State, 11, 239, 241-42, 242-
        43, 245, 246
    as vice president, 246, 249-50, 252-53
Jeffersonian Republican party, 16, 18, 24, 25,
        146, 147, 153, 239-330, 341, 497,
        578
    and Antifederalist party, 166
    and Federalist party, 4, 10, 12, 13, 18, 19,
        21, 22, 23, 166, 240, 244, 246, 250,
        253, 259, 260, 264, 266, 267, 270,
        271, 272, 504
    Old Republicans, 498, 500-01, 504-08
        passim, 541
    see also National Republican party
Johnson, Andrew, 892, 893, 1284
    background, 1171
    and election of *1864,* 1171, 1297-1321
    and election of *1868,* 1287

as governor, 1169-70
near impeachment, 1282
as president, 1282, 1283, 1286, 1291,
    1292
Johnson, Arnold, 3178
Johnson, Arthur, 2084
Johnson, Hiram, 2103, 2277, 2278, 2553,
    2564
    and election of *1910,* 2542
    and election of *1912* (Bull Moose), 2549-
        51, 2560
    and election of *1916,* 2566
    and Republican party, 2086, 2108, 2120,
        2263, 2861
Johnson, James Weldon, 2115
Johnson, Lyndon B., 2703, 3014
    background, 2695
    and election of *1956,* 2699
    and election of *1960,* 2705, 2706, 2831,
        3006, 3007
    and election of *1968,* 2840, 2927-33, 3032
    and election of *1972,* 2854
    as party leader, 2695-96, 2835
    as president, 2835-40, 3029, 3035, 3039
    as senator, 2687, 2697-98, 2828, 2996
    and Socialist party, 2437, 2439
    speeches
        "Great Society," 2835, 2913-16
        "Let Us Continue," 2835, 2909-12
        requesting Gulf of Tonkin Resolution,
            2917-19
        to Senate Democrats, 2820
Johnson, Richard, 588
Johnson, Tom L., 1009
Johnston, Alvan Ley, 2679
Johnston, William F., 615
Jones, James K., 1002, 1723
Jones, Jesse, 1951
Jones, Samuel, 3315
Jones, Willie, 164
Jones Act, 1816
Judd, Norman, 1159
Judd, Walter, 3003
judiciary, 141, 143, 144, 152, 154, 155, 336,
    2269, 2546-47
    see also Supreme Court
Judiciary Act of *1801,* 21-23
Julian, George W., 758, 1142, 1145, 1146,
    1285

K

Kansas-Nebraska Act, 361, 526, 527, 529, 530,
    556, 595, 602, 607, 611, 612, 613,
    617, 701, 759, 1143-46, 1147,
    1181-84

Kefauver, Estes, 2679, 2687, 2690-91, 2702
  and election of *1952*, 2691-93
  and election of *1956*, 2699, 2700
Keitt, Lawrence, 1156
Kelley, Florence, 2086
Kelley, Oliver Hudson, 1555, 1706-07
Kelley, William D. ("Pig Iron"), 1415
Kellog, Edward, 2406
Kellogg, Frank B., 2106, 2107
Kellogg, William, 1162
Kelly, Edward J., 1956, 2676, 2685
Kelly, John, 903
Kendall, Amos, 509, 514
Kendall, George W., 351
Kenelly, Martin, 2685
Kennedy, Edward, 2706, 2847, 2864, 3053
  and election of *1968*, 2841
  and election of *1972*, 2851, 2852
Kennedy, John F., 2437, 2439
  background, 2699-2700, 2828-29
  debates of *1960*, 2879-908, 3085-89
  and Democratic party, 2701, 2832-35, 2860
  and election of *1952*, 2694
  and election of *1958*, 2704
  and election of *1960*, 2705-07, 2827,
    2831-32, 3003-07
  and election of *1964*, 2835
  and ethnic minority vote, 2857, 3007
  as president, 2833-35
  speeches, 2871-78
Kennedy, Robert F., 2834
  assassination, 2841, 2861, 3033
  and blacks, 2840-41
  and election of *1960*, 2705, 2832, 2860
  and election of *1964*, 2836
  and election of *1968*, 2839-40, 2924-26
  and L. B. Johnson, 2835-36, 3032
  and King assassination, 2840-41, 2934
  as senator, 2837, 2860
Kenny, John, 2690, 2707
Kenny, Robert, 3312
Kent, Frank R., 1015
Kentucky Resolutions, 89-93, 253, 525
Kenyon, William S., 2553
Keogh, Eugene, 2706
Kern, John W., 1014
Kern Act, 1816
Kern-McGillicuddy Workmen's Compensation
    Law, 1816
Kerr, Robert, 2686, 2691
Key, David M., 989
Key, V. O., 1960, 1961, 3000
Keynes, John Maynard, 3193
Khrushchev, Nikita, 2435, 3175
Kilgore, Harley M., 2683, 2695
King, John, 2834
King, Martin Luther, Jr., 2436, 2834, 2840-41,
    2862, 2934, 3032
King, Mrs. Martin Luther, Jr., 3005
King, Preston, 521, 527, 1148, 1156, 1157

King, Rufus, 21, 23, 24, 64-65
Kingdom, Frank, 3312-13
Kipnis, Ira, 2418
Kirwan, Mike, 2701
Kissinger, Henry, 2855, 3031, 3050
Kitchel, Denison, 3019
Kitchell, Aaron, 252
Kitchin, Claude, 1815
Kleindienst, Richard, 3017
Kleppner, Paul, 896-97, 1288
Knight, Goodwin, 2997
Knights of Labor, 994, 1564, 1711, 1728,
    1737-39, 2408-09
Knowland, William, 2704, 2994-97 *passim*
Know Nothing party (American party), 361-62,
    529, 530, 531, 576, 593-620,
    680-737, 1147, 1151, 1161, 3437
  and Democratic party, 530, 594, 600, 610
  factions
    Know Somethings, 607, 611, 706, 1148
    North Americans, 1148
    Order of the Star Spangled Banner, 593,
      1148
  and Republican party, 529, 530, 594, 595,
    606, 607, 611-19 *passim*, 736
  and Whig party, 576, 595, 600, 602, 605,
    608, 610, 614, 616
Knox, Frank, 2272, 2273, 2279, 2552
Knox, Philander C., 2096, 2097, 2566
Knutson, Harold, 2270, 2285
Koestler, Arthur, 3177
Kolb, Reuben F., 1717
Korean War, 2287, 2289, 2688, 2693, 2694
Kriege, Hermann, 2405
Krock, Arthur, 1823
Kuchel, Thomas, 3034, 3040
Ku Klux Klan, 1282, 1822, 1823, 1874-76,
    2114, 2116
Kurtz, Stephen, 15
Kyle, James H., 1712, 1716

L

labor, 1420, 1554, 2686, 3441
  and Communist party, 2682, 3170-71,
    3179, 3184, 3185, 3188, 3189,
    3190-92
  and Democrats, 334, 350, 514, 999, 1014,
    1817-18, 1826, 2679-80, 2682,
    2698, 2829
  and F.D.R., 1942, 1945, 1946-47, 1957,
    2060-66
  and economic crises, 1556, 2403, 2406
  and Bonus Expeditionary Force,
    Anacostia Flats, 2124

labor (*cont.*)
  and elections
    1896, 999, 1003, 2076
    1908, 1014, 1015
    1918, 2103
    1924, 1826
    1928, 1826, 2118
    1952, 2987
    1972, 2854
  expansion, 1551, 1941-45, 2676
  and Greenback party, 1561, 1563-65, 1606
  and immigrants, 528, 598, 599, 2076
  Indianapolis Working-Men's Resolutions,
    1588-89
  and Know Nothing party, 596, 598, 599-
    600
  legislation, 1425, 1560, 1830
    Case Bill, 2679
    Child Labor Bill of *1916*, 2093
    Clayton Act, 2422
    Taft-Hartley Act, 2688
  parties, 334, 350, 586, 1596-98, 2402-04,
    2409, 2414, 2421
  and People's party, 994, 1724
  and Republicans, 1007, 1416, 2073, 2074,
    2082, 2111, 2113, 2285, 2987
  on Second World War, 2100, 2676
  strikes, 999, 1560, 1943, 1953, 2074, 2111,
    2113, 3184
    railroad, 999, 1000, 1040, 1719, 1559-
      60, 2679
  unemployment, 1830, 1939, 1942, 1945,
    1952, 2069, 2110, 2120, 2121,
    2122, 2129-33, 2697
  unions, 1816, 2997, 3170-71
    politicization, 1554, 2092, 2399, 2405,
      2410-11, 2415, 2418, 2422-23,
      2428, 2430, 2439-40, 2676
    and socialism, 2399, 2438, 2476-82
    and voluntarism, 2429-30, 2440, 2679
  see also Independent party; Socialist party;
    individual unions
Labor for McGovern Committee, 2854
Labor party of Illinois, 2408
La Follette, Phillip, 1950
La Follette, Robert, 2086
  and election of *1912*, 2090, 2544, 2548,
    2551
  and election of *1924*, 1824, 1825, 2116,
    2422-23, 2649-61, 2662-68
  and isolationism, 2099, 2101, 2102, 2277
  and Progressive party, 1826, 2542, 2545,
    2547, 2551, 2556, 2567-68, 3442
  voting position, 2083-84, 2094, 2103, 2108
La Follette, Robert, Jr., 2120, 2123
La Follette Seamen's Act, 1816
La Guardia, Fiorello, 2568
Laird, Melvin, 3002, 3025, 3029, 3030, 3049
Lamar, L. Q. C., 989, 991

Landon, Alfred M., 2275-76, 2278
  and election of *1936*, 1946, 2272-73
  and election of *1940*, 2279, 2280
  speeches, 2327-32, 2338-43
land policy
  and Antifederalist party, 157, 165
  and Democratic party, 353, 507, 509, 515,
    518, 520, 526, 527, 531
  and Jeffersonian Republican party, 166,
    498
  and National Republican party, 335, 337,
    340
  reforms
    Desert Lands Act of *1877*, 1702
    Homestead Act, 1702
    Omaha platform of *1892*, 1715
    Pre-emption Act, 1702
    Timber Culture Act of *1873*, 1702
  and Whig party, 350-55 *passim*, 516
lands, public
  T. Roosevelt on, 2171-74
Lane, Henry S., 1195-97
Laney, Ben, 3316, 3317, 3318
La Palombara, Joseph, 25
Larson, Arthur, 2991, 2992, 3069-72
Lausche, Frank, 2695, 2701
Law, George, 612, 613
Lawrence, Abbott, 338, 355
Lawrence, David, 2697
Leader, George M., 2697
League for Industrial Democracy, 2438
League of Nations, 1819, 1820, 2104-05, 2194,
    2209-11
  and Republicans, 2102, 2104-6, 2281-82
League of Republican Women, 2997
Lease, Mary Ellen "Yellin," 993, 1712, 1716
Lecompton Constitution, 532, 533, 562, 563,
    1153-54
Lee, Arthur, 2544
Lee, Ralph, 3318
Lee, Richard Henry, 154, 162
Leedy, John W., 1725
Legal Tender Act, 894, 1552
Lehman, Herbert H., 2696
Le May, Curtis, 3041, 3440, 3441
Lemke, William, 1946
LeMoyne, Francis Julius, 746
Lend Lease, 2352-60
Lenin, V. I., 2404, 2425, 3173, 3174, 3179
Leninism, and American Communist party,
    3175, 3181, 3182, 3184
Lenin School, 3178
Lever Act of *1917*, 1817
Lewelling, Lorenzo Dow, 1702, 1718, 1787-88
Lewis, Dixon H., 508
Lewis, John L., 2111, 2118, 2429, 2430, 2433,
    3171
Lewis, Morgan, 296
Lewis, Samuel

J. G. Birney, letter from, 827-31
Lewis, Sinclair, *Main Street,* 3172
Lewis, William, 499-500
Lewis, William Draper, 2554, 2557
Liberal party, 2430
Liberal Tradition in America (L. Hartz), 2404
Liberator, The, 767-83, 792-817
Liberty League, 750-51, 754, 765, 758, 759,
    2317-26, 2333-37
Liberty party, 344, 353, 356, 523, 741, 744-61
    passim, 832-34 331, 1141-42
    and Free Soil party, 750, 751, 757
    see also blacks, Republican party
Lilienthal, David, 1961
Lincoln, Abraham, 347, 618-19, 891, 1146, 1287
    background, 1154, 1159-60
    and election of *1860,* 535, 618, 619, 620,
        1160-62
    and election of *1864,* 1172, 1282, 1283,
        1297-321
    Emancipation Proclamation, 1166, 1252-54,
        1255-56
    and Homestead Act of *1862,* 2404-05, 2407
    letter against territorial compromise, 1248
    and Lincoln-Douglas debates, 533, 562,
        1155
    as president, 5, 1162-72, 1282
    and Reconstruction, 1169-70, 1282, 1291,
        1293
    as a Republican, 1157, 1413
    speeches
        "House Divided," 1223-28
        Inaugural Address, 1163
    on Wade-Davis Bill, 1166, 1171-72
Lincoln Catechism, The, 891, 914-21
Lindsay, John, 2849, 2850, 3025, 3028, 3037
    3042, 3048
Lipow, Arthur, 2414
Lippmann, Walter, 1825, 1826, 1830, 1887-92,
    2100, 2123, 2993, 3009
Lipset, Seymour Martin, 2404
Lissner, Meyer, 2554
literacy tests, W. H. Taft on, 2187-91
    see also Henry Cabot Lodge
Literary Digest, 1822, 2274
Litwack, Leon, 756
Livermore, Shaw, Jr., 24
Livingston, Brockholst, 256
Livingston, Edward, 13
Livingston, Gilbert, 163
Livingston, Robert R., 149, 242
Livingston family, 135, 137
Lloyd, Henry Demarest, 999, 1722, 1728,
    1799-805
Locke, Matthew, 164
Locofocos, 510
Lodge, Henry C.
    and foreign policy, 2093-94, 2098, 2099,
        2277

    and League, 2102-04, 2209-11
    on literacy bill, 2076, 2078, 2134-38
    Peace of Vengeance speech, 2202-08
    and T. Roosevelt, 2099, 2543, 2566
    senatorial voting stance, 993, 1425-26,
        2093, 2115
Lodge, Mrs. Henry Cabot, 2077
Lodge, Henry Cabot, Jr., 3003, 3005, 3015-16
    and Eisenhower, 2290, 2694, 3011
Loeb, James, 2682
Logan, John A., 886, 888, 896, 1164, 1286,
    1287, 1289
London, Jack, 2415
Long, Huey, 1944, 1946, 1961, 2269, 2430
Long, John, Jr., 270
Longworth, Nicholas, 2119
Looking Backward (E. Bellamy), 2413-14
Look Magazine, 3023
Los Angeles Times, The, 2483-85
Loucks, H. L., 1718
Louisiana Farmer's Union, 1710
Louisiana Purchase, 1144
Louisville *Journal,* 351
Lovejoy, Owen, 1149, 1157, 1197-99
Lovestone, Jay, 2431, 3174, 3178, 3187, 3190
Lowden, Frank, 2108
Lowell, James Russell, 355
Lowenstein, Allard, 2839
Lowndes, Rawlins, 162
Lubell, Samuel, 1953, 2990, 2991, 2999, 3047,
    3048
Lucas, Scott W., 1953, 2689, 2695
Lyon, Cecil, 2557
Lyons, Eugene, 3172

M

MacArthur, Douglas, 2124, 2283, 2391-95,
    2693
McAdoo, William Gibbs, 1818, 1820-25, 2114,
    2568, 2569
McCarran Act, 3189
McCarthy, Eugene, 2704, 2836, 2863, 3032
    background, 2839
    and election of *1968,* 2839-41, 2844, 2922-
        23
    and election of *1972,* 2849, 2850
McCarthy, Joseph R., 1726, 2288-89, 2689,
    2690, 2696, 2703, 2830, 2993,
    2995, 3000
McCarthy and His Enemies, 3011
McCarthyism, 2425, 2433, 2696, 2993, 3062-
    68, 3189
    see also Red Scare

McClellan, George B., 888, 891, 1164, 1165, 1172
McClellan, George B., Jr., 1009
McClernand, John, 1164
McCloskey, Matthew, 2697
McCloskey, Paul N., 3050
McCombs, W. F. 1813
McCormack, John, 1963
McCormack, M., 2701
McCormick, Anne O'Hare, 3319
McCormick, Cyrus, 898, 1814
McCormick, Medill, 2552
McCormick, Richard, 20
McCovey, Gessner, 3318
McCulloch, Hugh, 1553
McDonald, James G., 3327
McDowell, Arthur, 2433
McFarland, Ernest, 2683, 2695, 2702
McGill, Ralph, 3315, 3318
McGovern, Francis E., 2548
McGovern, George, 2839, 2859, 2860, 2863, 2864, 3043, 3052
    background, 2841, 2848
    and election of 1972, 2841, 2848-55, 3443
    and "McGovern Commission," 2843-46
    and Progressive party of 1948, 3321
McGovern Commission see Democratic party, Committee on Delegate Selection and Party Reforms
McGrath, J. Howard, 2683, 2684, 3316, 3319
McHenry, James, 14
McIntyre, Thomas, 2834
McKean, Thomas, 23
McKinley, William, 1428, 2070
    background, 1431, 2078
    and election of 1894, 1431
    and election of 1896, 1002, 1003, 1722, 2076, 2078
    and election of 1900, 2080
    foreign policy, 1415, 2094-95, 2097
    as governor, 2073, 2078
    as president, 1004, 2078-79
    speeches, 2142-46, 2153-56
    tariff see McKinley tariff
McKinley tariff, 992, 993, 994, 998, 1415, 1416
McLean, John, 589, 601, 603-04, 1150, 1153
McLevy, Jasper, 2434
McMechen, David, 161
McNamara, Robert, 2833
McNary, Charles L., 2282
McNary-Haugen Bill, 1829, 2222-28
McNutt, Paul, 1951
McPherson, Edward, 1249-51
Macuve, Charles W., 1709, 1713, 1714, 1718
Macuve subtreasury plan, 994
Maddox, Lester, 3429
Madison, James, 7-10 passim, 153
    and election of 1792, 245
    and election of 1808, 264, 265, 304-09

and election of 1812, 266, 267, 310-20
and Philip Freneau, 242, 243
and Alexander Hamilton, 239, 241, 243
and Thomas Jefferson, 239, 241, 242, 245, 246, 253
Jeffersonian Republican party, 241, 245, 246, 247, 249, 256, 264, 265, 266
as president, 22, 258, 266
as Secretary of State, 240, 265
Mangum, Willie P., 337, 340, 360, 510
Manifest Destiny, doctrine of, 515
Mann, James R., 2100
Manning, Daniel, 989, 990
Mansfield, Mike, 2695, 2696, 2701, 2704, 2864
Marbury v. Madison, 22
Marcantonio, Vito, 3320, 3321, 3326
Marcus, Robert, 2073
Marcy, William Learned, 346, 519, 526, 608
Marshall, Charles C.
    open letter to Al Smith, 1894-1904
    answer by Smith, 1905-13
Marshall, Humphrey, 613
Marshall, John, 12, 14, 22
Marshall, Thomas R., 1813
Marshall Plan, 2684, 3189, 3194
Martin, James, 3013
Martin, John Bartlow, 2693
Martin, Joseph, 2282, 2992, 2997, 3024
Martin, Louis, 2843
Martin, Luther, 161, 166, 192-212
Marx, Karl, 2401, 2403-04, 2405, 2406, 2412
Marxian Socialism in the United States (D. Bell), 2417
Marxism, 2417, 2428, 2434, 3170, 3184, 3188
Maryland Unionist party, 1169
Mason, George, 153, 154, 162
Mason, James M., 526
Masons see Freemasons
Massachusetts Anti-Slavery Society, 743, 767-76
Massachusetts Greenback platform of 1877, 1594-95
Massachusetts Prohibition platform of 1877, 1628-29
Masses, 3172
Masters, Edgar Lee, 1016
Maurer, James Hudson, 2415
Maverick, Maury, 1950, 2693
Maysville Road bill, 505
Mazo, Earl, 3005
Meany, G., 2440
Mechanics Union of Trade Associations, 2402
Mellon, Andrew, 1825, 2112
Mencken, H. L., 1928-30, 3172
Mennonites, 587
Mercer, John Francis, 161
Mercer, Ruby, 3317
Meredith, Edwin T., 1818
Merrill, Horace and Marion, 2079, 2088

Metcalfe, Ralph, 2862
Methodist Board of Morals, 1579
Metropolitan, 2616-24, 2625-34
Mexican War (*1846-48*), 355, 520, 522, 752,
    753, 1142
Mexico, 521, 524, 527, 2098, 2101, 2107
Meyner, Robert B., 2703, 2705
Michelson, Charles, 1830, 2675
Michigan State Anti-Slavery Society, 835-39
Midwest, the, 896-97, 1285, 1417, 1707, 2081
    and election of *1894,* 2075
    and election of *1912,* 1813
    and election of *1918,* 2103
    and election of *1932,* 2263
    Republicans, 2147-52, 2261, 2278-80,
        2283
    see also rural interests
Military Reconstruction Act of *1867,* 1282,
    1293
Miller, Stephen F., 426
Miller, William, 3013, 3019, 3022, 3027, 3033
Millikin, Eugene D., 2282, 2994, 3043
Mills, Roger Q., 992
Mills, Wilbur, 2849
Mills Bill, 992
Minor, Robert, 2424
Minot, George Richards, 160
Minow, Newton, 2693
Mint Act of *1792,* 1705
Mississippi Freedom Democratic party, 2438,
    2836
Missouri Compromise of *1820,* 1144, 1146,
    1162
    repeal, 361, 526, 527, 556, 611, 1147,
        1149
    restoration, 612, 613, 614, 706, 709
Missouri party coalition, 900
Mitchell, Clarence, 2698
Mitchell, George, 2843, 2864
Mitchell, James, 3001
Mitchell, John, 3044, 3046
Mitchell, Stephen A., 2693
Mixner, David, 2843
Moley, Raymond, 1942, 1963, 3045
Molotov, V., 3186
monetary policy *see* banking and monetary
    policy
Monroe, James, 246, 253
    and election of *1792,* 245
    and election of *1808,* 264, 265
    and election of *1816,* 267, 268
    and election of *1820,* 267
    as president, 258, 266, 267, 272
Monroe Doctrine, 2097-98
Monthly Review, 3188
Moore, Edmond, 1823, 2117
Moore, Edward H., 2282
Morgan, Edwin D., 617
Morgan, John H., 891
Morgan, J. P., 1000, 1721, 2082, 2563

Morgan, Thomas J., 2410, 2411
Morgan, William, 577, 580, 584
Morgenthau, Henry, 1814, 1955
Morison, Elting E., 2157-58
Morison, William R., 1417
Morrill, Justin S., 1415, 1416
Morrill Tariff of *1861,* 894
Morris, Gouverneur, 7, 8, 106-15
Morris, Robert, 7, 147
Morrow, Dwight, 2107, 2120
Morton, J. Sterling, 995, 1001, 1008
Morton, Oliver P., 886, 896, 1289
Morton, Rogers C. B., 3051
Morton, Thruston, 3003, 3006, 3030, 3033,
    3043
Moskowitz, Belle, 1827
Mowry, George, 2085
Moynihan, Daniel Patrick, 3050
Mugwumps *see* Republican party, factions
Mundt, Karl, 2996, 3023
Mundt-Nixon Bill, 3189
Munroe, John A., 18
Munsey, Frank, 2545, 2546, 2549, 2556, 2557,
    2558, 2562
Murdock, Victor, 2560
Murphy, Charles, 1818, 1826
Murphy, Frank, 1950, 1951, 2430
Murray, "Alfalfa Bill," 3318
Murray, James E., 2684
Murray, Philip, 3189
Murray, William Vans, 13, 14
Murray-Hillman, 3191
Muscle Shoals, 2121, 2240-46
    see also Tennessee Valley Authority
Muskie, Edmund S., 2697, 2703, 2847, 2849,
    2863, 3035, 3046
    and election of *1972,* 2842, 2849, 2850-51
    and "McGovern Commission," 2843
Muste, A. J., 2428, 2435
Myers, Francis J., 2690
Myers, Gustavus, 2419

N

Nagel, Charles, 2187-91
Nation, The, 1877-79, 2169-70, 2509-10
National Anti-Imperialism League, 1005
National Association for the Advancement of
    Colored People (N.A.A.C.P.), 1947,
    2698
National Association of Manufacturers
    (N.A.M), 2074, 2997
National Banking Act, 1552-53, 1705
National Bimetallic Coinage Association, 1419
National Civic Federation (N.C.F.), 2421,
    2423, 2429

National Civil Service Reform League, 989
National Convention of the Conference for
    Progressive Political Action, 2568
National Cooperative Society, 2568
National Cotton Council, 3325
National Democratic party, 1002
National Economist, 1710
Naitonal Era (Washington, D.C.), 1144, 1145,
    1146
National Farmer's Alliance, 1709, 1710
National Farmer's Alliance and Industrial
    Union
  conventions and platforms
    1889 (St. Louis), 1711, 1712, 1737-39
    1890 (Ocala), 1713, 1746-59
    1891 (Cincinnati), 1713, 1761-63
    1892 (St. Louis), 1714, 1763-65
  Northern Alliance, 1737-39, 1760
  L. L. Polk address, Ocala, 1746-57
  Southern Alliance
    component groups, 1709-11
    Confederation of Industrial Organiza-
        tions 1713
    demise, 1718
    subtreasury play, 1711-12, 1740-45
  see also People's party
National Gazette, 242, 243
National Guardian, 3188
National Independent party *see* Greenback
    party
Nationalist Clubs, 2413-14
Nationalists, 7-8, 9, 17, 152
National Labor Congress, 1554
National Labor Convention, 1558
National Labor Reform party, 1554, 1708
National Labor Union (N.L.U.), 1554, 2405-
    06, 2414
National Maritime Union, 3191
National party *see* Greenback party
National Progressive Republican League, 2542,
    2544
National Protective Association, 1630-38
National Recovery Administration (N.R.A.),
    1942, 1943, 2429, 2430
National Reform party, 1555
National Reformers, 2404
National Republican party, 271, 335, 336, 337,
    338, 367-68, 583, 588, 589, 590,
    592
  and Antimasonic party, 580, 582, 584, 585,
      589, 590, 591
  and Democratic party (*1828-1860*), 335,
      336, 337, 338, 508
  see also Whig party
National Review, 2993, 3011, 3013, 3025
National Silver party, 1002, 1721, 1723
National Tariff Reform League, 991
National Temperance Society and Publication
    House, 1569
National Union Convention, 893

National Union party *see* Republican party,
    factions
nativism, 528-29, 593, 594, 596, 598, 599,
    600, 618
  and American Republican party, 514, 519
  and Antimasonic party, 587, 591, 597
  and Democratic party (*1828-1860*), 353,
      557
  and Know Nothing party, 361, 529, 530,
      576, 593, 594, 595, 599, 600, 604,
      605, 606, 609, 610, 680, 699
  see also Know Nothing party
  and Native American Democratic Associa-
      tion, 514
  and Republican party, 530, 616, 618
  and Whig party, 348, 353, 360, 513, 519,
      525, 594-95, 597, 601
Nativist party, 1146-48
Navy, and Federalist party, 15, 254, 259
Nearing, Scott, 2421
Negroes *see* blacks
Nelson, Gaylord, 2834
Nelson, Steve, 3178
Nevins, Allan, 362, 891, 1144
New America, 2436
Newark *Centinal of Freedom,* 252
Newberry, Truman, 2104
Newberry Bill, 1718
New Deal, the
  and Communist party, 2432, 3174, 3181-
      82, 3185
  criticism of, 1941-44, 1946, 1949-50, 2288-
      89, 2333-37, 2511-12
  and Democratic party, 1948, 1950-51
  and economy, 1941, 1942, 1943, 1945,
      1948-49, 1981-89
  ending of, 1950-51, 1954-56, 1962
  legislation, 1941, 1942, 1943, 1945, 1948-
      49, 1955
  reforms, 1941, 1943, 1945, 1947, 1948-49
  and Republican party, 1957, 2226-27,
      2260, 2272-74, 2285, 2286
  and Second World War, 1954-55
  and Socialism, 2481, 2422, 2429
  support for, 1945-46, 1949, 1953, 1960
Newell, Frederick H., 2080
New Freedom, The (Woodrow Wilson), 1846-55
New Guard, 3025
New Hampshire, Prohibition platform of *1872,*
    1621
New Left, the, 3188-89
New Nationalism, The, 2573-83
New Orleans *Picayune,* 351
New Orleans Riot of *1866,* 892-93
New Populism, 3442
New Republic, 1825, 1893, 2677
  on Democratic party, 1931-32
  on Ku Klux Klan, 1874-76
  on Alfred E. Smith, 1873
New York Central Labor Union, 2412

New York Central Railroad, 598
New York Herald, 2102, 2194
New York Herald Tribune, 3005, 3016, 3020, 3027
New York State Democratic-American Labor party, 2682
New York Sun, 1830, 2083
New York Times, The, 899, 1014, 1116-19, 1823, 1829, 2082, 2192-93, 2564, 3079-82, 3083-84, 3100-01, 3156-64
   survey, 3023
New York Tribune, 903, 1145, 1146, 2101-02
   editorials, 1453-56, 1477-78, 1503-04, 1535-37, 1541-42
New York World, 1009, 1014
   editorials, 946-47, 948-51, 970-75, 1101, 1449-52, 1475-76, 1505-06, 1531-32
Nicholson, Alfred Osborne Pope, 522, 553-55
Nicholson, James, 256
Niles, John M., letter to Welles Gideon, 519
Nixon, Richard M.
   background, 2842, 2986, 3000-03
   and election of *1950,* 2690
   and election of *1952,* 2291
   and election of *1956,* 2699, 2700
   and election of *1960,* 2706, 2827, 2990, 3003-07
   and election of *1962* (gubernatorial), 3009
   and election of *1964,* 3015, 3018, 3020-21
   and election of *1966,* 2838
   and election of *1968,* 2842, 3037-44
      bid for nomination, 3029-37
   and election of *1972,* 2850, 2854-55
   Kennedy debates of *1960,* 2879-2908, 3085 89
   as party leader, 3000-03, 3008-09, 3031-33, 3035-37, 3049, 3050-51
   policies, 2850, 2857, 3035, 3050
   as president, 2986, 3046, 3049-50
   and Republican leaders, 3000, 3001, 3018, 3020, 3025, 3035-36
   and Rockefeller, 3002-03, 3011, 3017, 3026, 3079-82
   speeches
      acceptance (*1960*), 3109-17
      acceptance (*1968*), 3156-64
      "Checkers," 2694
      First Inaugural Address, 3118-22
      on McCarthyism, 3062-68
      on Vietnam, 3147-55
   as vice president, 2287, 2686, 2988, 2989, 2992, 2997, 3000-3003
   voter support, 2859, 3040-43
Non-Partisan League, 1731, 2420, 2430, 2568
Norbeck, Peter, 2119
Norris, George W., 2084, 2674
   and congressional structure, 1017, 2089
   and elections, 1827, 1948, 2104, 2552, 2569
   and Progressive party, 2091, 2568, 2569

   speech against war, 2195-2201
   voting record, 2099, 2103, 2108, 2110, 2113, 2120
North American Federation of the International, 2407
North American Review, on Coolidge, 1880-86
NATO, R. A. Taft speech against, 2377-90
North Carolina Alliance, 1710
Northeast, the, 1145, 1820, 2070, 2081, 2118, 2543
Northern, W. J., 1713
Northern Alliance *see* National Farmer's Alliance and Industrial Union
Norton, Seymour F., 1721, 1723
nullifiers and nullification, 335, 337, 507-08, 511, 514
   Kentucky and Virginia Resolutions, 89-93, 253, 525

O

O'Brien, Lawrence, 2847, 2864, 3041
O'Connell, William, 2113, 2114
O'Connor, John, 1950
O'Conor, Charles, 1554
O'Conor, Herbert K., 2683
O'Dwyer, Paul, 2685
O'Dwyer, William, 2691
Office of Price Administration (O.P.A.), 2680
O'Hara, James, 2843, 2965-81
O'Hara Commission *see* Democratic party, conventions
Olcutt, Thomas, 510
Oldfield, William, 1824
Old Republicans *see* Jeffersonian Republican party, Old Republicans
Olds, Leland, 2695
Olleman, A. E., 1557
Olney, Richard, 999, 1008, 1009, 2094
Olson, Floyd, 1944
O'Mahoney, Joseph C., 2683, 2695
Oneal, James, 2421
O'Neill, Thomas, 2864
One World (W. Willkie), 2282
Order of the Star Spangled Banner, 593, 1148
Order of United Americans, 593, 601
Oregon Treaty, 753
Ostend Manifesto, 1151
Otis, Harrison Gray, 21, 23, 24
Otto, Louis-Guillaume, 156
Outlook, The, 2544, 2608-12
Overton, John, 499-500, 509-10
Owen, Robert, 2401-02, 2402-03
   speech to Congress, 2445-57

P

Paine, Ephraim, 146, 149
Paine, Thomas, *The Rights of Man,* Jefferson
  foreword, 242
Pakenham, Richard, letter from J. C. Calhoun,
  518, 550-52
Palfrey, John G., 752
Palmer, John M., 1002, 1003, 2078
Palmer, Mitchell A., 1817, 1818
Panama Canal, 2097, 2159-68, 2169-70
Parker, Alton B., 1008-12, 1015, 1813, 2082,
  2083, 2097, 2120
Parker, John M., 2555, 2566
Parker, Theodore, 341-42
Parkinson, Gaylord, 3024
Parrington, Vernon L., 3173
Parsons, Theophilus, 13
parties, political *see* political parties
party machines *see* Democratic party; Repub-
  lican party
"Pathfinder, The" *see* Fremont, John C.
Patrick, Luther, 2679
patronage
  Democratic and Republican compared,
    2269
  and Democratic party, 506, 525, 526, 531,
    989-90, 1145, 1421, 1811, 1814-15,
    2830, 2837
  and Jeffersonian Republican party, 259,
    260
  and Progressive party, 2560
  and Republican party, 886, 900, 1007,
    1144, 1166, 1421, 1425, 1960,
    1962, 2545-46, 2675, 2681, 2992,
    3441
  and States' Rights party, 3325
  and Whig party, 363, 610
Patrons of Husbandry (Grange), 1555, 1706-08
Patrons of Industry, 1709
Patterson, Basil, 2857
Patterson, R. C., 2263
Pauley, Edwin W., 1956, 2681
Payne, Henry P., 566
Peace Democrats *see* Democratic party, dissen-
  sion within
Pearson, Drew, 3034
Pecora, Ferdinand, 2690
Peffer, William A., 1712, 1713, 1715
Peña, Albert A., 2843
Pendergast, James, 2676
Pendergast, Tom, 2674
Pendleton, Edmund, 256
Pendleton, George H., 891, 894-95, 922-33
Pendleton, Nathaniel, 18
Penn family, 136-37
Pennington, William, 1157
Pennsylvania Canal System, 586, 587

Pennsylvania Railroad, 598
Pennsylvania State Constitution, debate over,
  8, 146
Pennsylvania United Labor Platform of *1877,*
  1596-98
Penrose, Boise, 2552
People's Educational Associations, 3189
People's Independents, 1712
People's party, 603, 615, 617, 618, 747, 1701-
  1806
  beginnings, 1713-14
  and Bryan, 994, 1002-03, 1005, 1010, 1013
  constituents, 1716-18
  conventions and platforms
    1891, 1761-62
    1892 (Omaha), 1714, 1763-68
    1896, 1721-24, 1789-98, 1799-1805
    1904 (Springfield), 1725
    1908, 1725
  and currency issue, 1555, 1704-06
  and election of *1816,* 999
  and election of *1854,* 1146
  and election of *1892,* 1429
  and election of *1894,* 1431, 1719, 2075
  and election of *1900,* 1005
  and election of *1902,* 1008
  factions
    silverites vs. elastic currency, 1721
  and fusion issue, 1719-20, 1722, 1725
  and Greenback party, 1565-66
  L. D. Lewelling address, 1787-88
  and Prohibition party, 1577-78
  St. Louis Demands, 1737-39
  T. E. Watson on slavery, 1779-86
  J. B. Weaver, 1769-78
  see also National Farmer's Alliance and
    Industrial Union; Grand State
    Farmers Alliance
People's Party Paper, 1714
Pepper, Claude, 1949, 2685, 2689, 2692
Percy, Charles H., 2997, 2999, 3028, 3029,
  3030, 3043
Perez, Leander, 3429
Perkins, Daniel, 152-53
Perkins, Frances, 1942, 1947
Perkins, George W., 2549, 2550, 2554, 2556,
  2557, 2558, 2563, 2564, 2566,
  2567
Perlman, Selig, 2403, 2411, 2412
Perry, Lewis, 746
Perry, Pettis, 3188
Pershing, John J., 2098
Person, Thomas, 164
Persons, Wilton B., 2995
Peters, Thomas M., 427
Philadelphia and Trenton Railroad, 334
Philadelphia *Aurora,* 260
Philanthropist, The, 749
Philippines, 2094-96, 2157-58
Phillips, Kevin, 3006, 3040, 3042-48

Phillips, Wendell, 744
Pickering, John, 22
Pickering, Thomas, 4
Pickering, Timothy, 14, 23
Pierce, Franklin, 524, 1142, 1144
    and election of *1852,* 359, 360, 525
    as president, 525, 526, 527, 531
    and David Wilmot correspondence, 523
Pinchot, Amos, 2550, 2554, 2556, 2557, 2563
Pinchot, Gifford, 1812, 1962, 2080, 2089,
        2113, 2543, 2554, 2556, 2564
Pinckney, Charles Cotesworth, 13, 14, 21, 25
    Constitution defended by, 58-63
    and election of *1800,* 254, 257
    and election of *1808,* 265
Pinckney, Thomas, 13, 247
Pinckney Treaty, 18
Pincus, Walter, 3013
Pingree, Hazen S., 2074
Platt, Orville H., 2079
Platt, Zephaniah, 163
Plumb Plan, 1817
Plumer, William, 20, 24
Poindexter, Miles, 2551, 2553, 2562
Poland, Luke P., 1290-91
Pole, J. R., 7, 20
Political Action Committee (P.A.C.-C.I.O.),
        1957, 1961, 2282, 2423, 2676,
        2678, 2682-83
political parties
    balance of strength of, 1549
    Democratic-Republican coalition, 2112-
        14, 2120, 2275, 2287, 2833, 3315
    image of, 2072, 2092, 2986
    management firms, 2862
Political Text-Book for 1860, A, 1229-38
Polk, James K.
    and election of *1844,* 353, 518-19, 746
    and Mexican War, 1142
    as president, 355, 519, 520, 522, 753
    and slavery, 353, 520, 521, 1142
Polk, L. L., 993, 1711, 1716, 1746-57
Pomeroy, S. C., 1257-58
Pomeroy Circular, 1170
Pontiac's Revolt, 144
Pope, John, 1165
Populism, 1712, 2858, 3440
    and American Independent party,
        3437-39
    analysis of, 1725-31
    and Communist party, 3185
    organizations, 1706-11, 1735-36
Populist party *see* People's party
postal service, 588, 591
Post-Dispatch, 2110
Potter, Clarkson M., 902-3
Potter, David M., 1162
Potter, John F., 1156
Powderly, Terrence V., 1426, 2408
Pre-Emption Act, 1702

Prentice, George D., 351-52
press
    and Antimasonic party, 580
    and Democratic party (*1828-1860*), 503,
        506, 519
    and Federalist party, 242, 243, 259, 260
    and Jeffersonian Republican party, 242,
        243, 269-70, 261, 271
    and Republican party, 618
    and Whig party, 351, 610
Prince, Carl E., 20
Progressive Bulletin, The, 2563
Progressive Citizens of America, 3312, 3313
Progressive Farmer, 1710, 1716
Progressive party (Bull Moose party), 746,
        1948
    beginnings, 2541-51
    Committee of Forty-Eight (post-T. Roose-
        velt), 2567-68
    and election of *1912,* 2557-61
    and election of *1914,* 2564
    and election of *1916,* 2100, 2566-67
    factions, 2555-57
    and Robert LaFollette, 2568-69
    New Nationalism, 1016, 2558, 2564, 2567,
        2570
    Pinchot-Perkins Affair, 2562-64
    racial policy, 2553-56
    reform, move from, 2564-65
Progressive party of Illinois, 3312, 3313
Progressive party of *1948,* 2286, 2434, 2684,
        2687, 3309-14, 3319-28
    campaign funds, 3323-24, 3391-95
    and Communism, 2687, 3190, 3191-93,
        3194, 3195, 3320-22, 3326
    constituent groups, 3319, 3324
    convention of *1948,* 3319-21
    Vermont resolution, 3321
    Wallace speech, 3333-38
progressivism, 1820, 1826, 2072, 2079, 2081,
        2085-88, 2089-91
    W. A. White on, 2178-80
prohibition, 1663-64, 1822-23, 1830
    as campaign issue of *1884,* 989
    and Democrats, 1820, 1831, 2090
    and election of *1930,* 2120-21
    First National Prohibition Convention and
        Platform (*1869*), 1617-18
    legislation, 897, 1551, 1568, 1572, 1575
    Methodist Church on, 1653-55
    National Woman's Christian Temperance
        Union, 1639-44
    and Republican party, 2089-90, 2114
    and Alfred E. Smith, 1821, 1826-28
    "Temperance and Politicians" editorial,
        1615-16
    see also Prohibition party; temperance
        movement
Prohibition party, 1566-81, 1686-87
    background, social-economic, 1549-51

Prohibition party *(cont.)*
  conventions and platforms, national
    1869, 1569-70, 1617-18
    1872, 1571, 1619-20
    1876, 1625-26
    1888, 1645-46
    1896, 1658
    1900, 1659-62
    1920, 1665-69
    1928, 1670-71
    1940, 1672-73
    1952, 1674-77
    1960, 1678-85
    1968, 1688-96
  conventions and platforms, state
    Connecticut *1872,* 1622-24
    New Hampshire *1872,* 1621
    Maine *1877,* 1627
    Massachusetts *1877,* 1628-29
  factions, 1571, 1576-78
  as Prohibition Home Protection party,
    1575
  referenda campaign, 1575, 1577
  strength, 1572, 1576, 1578-79
Proxmire, William, 2703, 2847
Pryor, Roger, 1156
Public Credit Act, 1553
Public Interest, The, 3050
Puerto Rico, 2097
Pulitzer, Joseph, 990, 1015
Pyle, Ernie, 1947

Q

Quakers, 22, 136, 137, 146, 147, 505, 587
Quay, Matthew Stanley, 1414
Quill, Michael, 3191
Quincy, Edmund, 760
Quincy, Josiah, 25, 904
Quint, Howard H., 2410, 2411

R

racism, 889, 891, 1289
  see also blacks; civil rights; Reconstruction
radicalism, 1575, 1577, 1940, 1943-44, 1963,
    2269, 2403, 2425
  see also Communism; Socialism
Rafferty, Max, 3040
Railroad Age, 2069

Railroad Brotherhoods, 1817, 2567, 2568
railroads, 498, 499, 527, 528, 598-99, 898,
    1007, 1013, 1424, 1715, 1817, 1818,
    2082
  and depression, 1556, 2069-70
  expansion effect on economy, 1143, 1702-
    03
  and farmers, 1550-51, 1555, 1703
  and labor, 1559-60, 2416, 2679
  legislation, 1167, 1424, 1718, 2079, 2084,
    2093, 2113, 2543
  and subsidies, 1424, 2073
Randall, Samuel J., 903, 991, 1417
Randolph, A. Philip, 2435, 2437, 2438
Randolph, Edmund, 11, 154
Randolph, John, 21, 23, 264, 265
Rankin, John, 1961, 2682
Raskob, John J., 1827, 1830, 1831, 1942
Rayburn, Sam, 1953, 1963, 2695, 2699, 2701,
    2996, 3000
Rayner, John B., 1728
Rayner, Kenneth, 609, 610, 611, 615
Reader's Digest, 3036
Reagan, Ronald, 2999, 3021, 3024, 3028-29,
    3032-37, 3051
Real Majority, The, 3044
Reconstruction, 362, 892-94, 1282-83, 1287,
    1289, 1292-94, 3171
  and Republican party, 1169-70, 1284,
    1288, 1291, 1293, 1294
Reconstruction Finance Corporation (R.F.C.),
    2122-23, 2124, 2690
Red Scare, 1818, 1820, 3312
  see also McCarthyism
Reed, Daniel, 2994
Reed, John, 2424, 3206-10
Reed, Thomas B., 1416, 1426, 1430
Reform party, 1707
reforms *see* economy, anti-depression legislation;
    land policy; New Deal
Reid, Ogden, 3042, 3048
relief, 1830, 2123, 2271, 2273
Relief party, 499, 504
religious interests, 136-37, 514, 529-30, 587,
    588, 896-97, 1820, 1822, 2071, 2095
  Baptists, 513, 529, 580, 587, 588
  Congregationalists, 513, 514, 587, 588
  and Democrats, 1947, 1958, 2269
  and election of *1880,* 903
  and election of *1894,* 2075
  and election of *1896,* 2078
  and election of *1928,* 1826, 1828-29, 2117
  and election of *1948,* 2987
  and election of *1956,* 2700, 2705
  and election of *1960,* 3006
  Jewish, 1947, 2072
  Methodists, 505, 513, 529, 580, 587, 1653-
    55, 2153-56
  Presbyterians, 137, 580, 587, 590-91

and prohibition, 1567, 1573-74, 1578-80, 1653-55
and Republicans, 1288, 2072, 2987
Roman Catholics, 528, 609, 1820, 1822, 2422
  anti-Catholicism, 1822, 1828, 2113-14
  and Antimasonic party, 587, 591, 597, 605
  and Democratic party, 504, 513, 514, 515, 528, 529, 530, 531, 595, 597, 601, 897-98, 1947
  and elections, 903, 1826, 2075, 2831, 2833, 2876-78, 3006
  and Know Nothing party, 529, 530, 531, 576, 593, 594, 596, 599, 600, 602, 604, 605, 606, 609, 610-11, 620, 680, 701
  and Know Something party, 607, 611
  opposition to, 504, 513, 514, 528-29, 530, 587, 593, 594, 596-601 *passim*, 607, 609, 618
  parochial schools, 514, 528, 597
  party loyalties, 896, 904, 988
  and Republican party, 616, 617, 618, 620
  and Whig party, 591, 595, 600, 601, 602
and Socialism, 2408, 2411-12, 2414, 2422
Republican Establishment, The, 3028
Republican Looks at His Party, A, 2991, 3069-72
Republican Opportunity, The, 3045
Republican party, 361, 362, 523, 527, 529, 530, 533, 594, 606-07, 608, 615, 616, 617-18, 620, 1717, 1719, 1821, 2839
  on banking and monetary policy, 894, 993, 1000, 1003, 1167, 1418-20, 1425, 1430, 1557, 1772
  and "Bull Moose" party, 2090-91, 2093, 2562, 2566-67, 2569, 2993
  campaign funds, 2077, 2083
  and Civil War, 885-86, 890-91, 1162, 1164-67, 1170-71
  coalition with Democrats, 1168, 1283, 1962, 2090, 2099, 2112-14, 2120, 2275, 2287, 2833, 2990, 2996, 3315
  and Congress, 993, 1283-85, 3008
  constituent groups, 896-97, 1158, 1287, 1414, 1415, 1819, 1957, 2070-71, 2073, 2086, 2099, 2108, 2118, 2261-62, 2837, 2857, 2987, 2990, 2992, 2998, 3044-46, 3049-50
  and Democratic party *(1828-1860),* 530, 535, 536, 617, 757
  early development, 1141, 1413-15
  editorials on, 1479-80, 1503-04, 1507-11
  election campaigns *see* elections
  and ethnic groups, 1570, 2076, 2859
  factions, 899-900, 1157, 1811-12, 1820,

2995, 2997, 2998, 3002, 3008-10, 3018-21, 3023-29, 3035-37
  conservatives, 2084-87, 2109, 2270, 2276, 2289, 2541-43, 2996-98, 3003, 3010-15
  East-West, 2260-61, 2985, 3042, 3049-50
  half-breeds, 904, 988
  and H. Hoover, 2267-68, 2270, 2274-75
  insurgents, 1016, 1017, 2080
  moderates, 1292, 2270-73, 2276, 2990
  Mugwumps, 988, 992, 1420-21, 1426, 2080-81, 2095
  progressives, 1812, 2085-86, 2089, 2093, 2100, 2101, 2103, 2104, 2108-09, 2119, 2123
  radicals, 892, 893, 1261-62, 1282, 1292
  Stalwarts, 904, 988
  failures analyzed, 904, 993, 1006, 1533-34, 2089, 2101, 2261-64, 2274, 2998-3000, 3021-23
  foreign policy, 1427, 1941-42, 1958, 2094-98, 2102, 2104-08, 2276-84
    isolationism, 2076, 2099, 2100, 2101-03, 2260-61, 2277-78
  and Free Soil party, 617, 741, 1141, 1148
  and Know Nothing party, 529, 530, 594, 595, 606, 607, 611-19 *passim*, 731
  lack of unity, 2997, 2986, 3008-21
  and leaders, 1147-50, 1150-51, 1285, 1429, 1819, 1942, 2073, 2079, 2082-85, 2088, 2270, 2272, 2275, 2284-85, 2990-93, 3009-15, 3073-78
  and Liberty League, 1141, 2317-26, 2333-37
  and McCarthyism, 2293, 2995
  machines, 886, 2081, 2083, 2264, 2276, 2993, 3001, 3012, 3023
  organizations, 3014, 3018, 3024-27
    Ripon Society, 3014, 3027, 3028, 3050
    Wednesday Group, 3027, 3049
    Young Republicans, 3025-26, 3034
  and patronage, 1284, 1285, 1263, 2269, 2545-46
  philosophies, 1151, 1157-58, 2071-72, 2083, 2091, 2096, 3045
  and prohibition, 1147, 1568, 1570-74
  and racial issue, 1147, 1289, 1412, 1425, 2703, 3003, 3006, 3013, 3022
  and reconstruction, 1169-70, 1282-94
  reforms, 1141, 1417, 1420-22, 1430
  and slavery, 1141, 1145-48, 1151-54, 1156, 1158, 1165-66, 1292
  and South, 1425, 2557, 2703, 2987, 3013, 3022, 3047-48
  structure, 1285-87, 2562
    National Committee, 1259-60, 2266, 2267, 2282, 2312-16, 2989, 3024, 3025, 3026, 3027, 3051

Republican party *(cont.)*
    successes analyzed, 885-87, 904, 1006,
        1172, 2075, 2077-78, 2291, 2987-
        88, 3039-44, 3051-53
    unity of *1968*, 3037-39, 3050-51
    voters, 2086-88, 2109-10, 2270
    voting record, 2072, 2073-74, 2079, 2093,
        2103, 2270, 2285
    and Whig party, 617, 759, 1148
Republican party, Jeffersonian *see* Jeffersonian
        Republican party
Republican party, National *see* National Re-
        publican party
Reston, James, 3009
Resumption Act *see* Specie Resumption Act of
    1875
Reuther, Walter, 2430, 2698, 2706, 3191
Revercomb, Chapman, 2282
Review of Reviews, 2129-33
Rhodes, James Ford, 892
Ribicoff, Abraham, 2697, 2706
Richmond *Enquirer*, 264-65
Rieve, Emil, 2430
Riis, Jacob, 2086
Ripley, William Z., 2112
Ripon Forum, 3027
Ripon Society, 3014, 3027, 3028, 3050
Ritchie, Thomas, 264-65, 500, 501, 502, 516,
        522, 539-40
Ritner, Joseph, 342, 590, 591
Rives, William C., 341, 363, 602, 609, 610, 611
roads, 140-41, 144, 498, 499, 505, 2069
Roane, Spencer, 162
Robeson, Paul, 3320
Robins, Raymond, 2564, 2567
Robinson, Joseph, 1827, 2122
Rockefeller, Nelson, 2704, 2999, 3010, 3026,
        3028-31, 3036, 3037, 3049, 3441
    and election of *1960*, 3001-03, 3073-78
    and election of *1964*, 3015-19, 3095-99
    and election of *1968*, 3031-33
    Fourteen-Point Compact of Fifth Avenue,
        3002, 3079-82
    and B. Goldwater, 3009-10, 3020
Rockefeller, Winthrop, 2847, 3022
Roe, Dudley G., 2680
Rogers, William, 3001
Romney, George, 2999, 3009, 3011, 3017,
        3028, 3037, 3043, 3441
    background, 3029-30
    and election of *1964*, 3016, 3018, 3019
    and election of *1968*, 3029-31
Roosevelt, Eleanor, 1947, 2001-02, 2702, 2831
Roosevelt, Franklin D., 1819, 1827, 2124,
        2430, 2567, 2673, 2676, 2829, 2993
    and "Economic Bill of Rights," 1955, 2048-
        55
    and election of *1932*, 1831, 1940-41, 2264-
        65
    and election of *1936*, 1945, 1947-48

and election of *1938*, 1951
and election of *1940*, 1951-53
and election of *1942*, 1954
and election of *1944*, 1956-57
and foreign policy, 2277
as governor, 1815, 1830, 1831
and the left, 2418, 2422, 2432-33, 3181-83
as party leader, 1824-25, 1940-41, 1942,
        1943, 1945, 1947-51, 1955, 1961-63
and patronage, 1960, 1962
personality, 1947, 2264
popularity, 1943, 1944-45, 1949, 2266
as president, 1941-45, 1947-51, 1953-56,
        2268-70
and Progressive party of *1948*, 3309, 3311
and Second World War, 1954-55, 2281
speeches, 1948, 1971-89, 1997-2005, 2012-
        30, 2042-55, 2060-66, 2268
Roosevelt, James, 1949, 2685, 2690, 2692
Roosevelt, Theodore, 1006, 1013, 1414, 1816,
        2070, 2082, 2117, 2555
    and "Bull Moose" party, 746, 2541-67,
        2573-83, 2596-2643, 2993
    "Confession of Faith" speech, 2554, 2557,
        2596-2602
    and election of *1900*, 1005
    and election of *1904*, 1012, 2082, 2083
    and election of *1908*, 1014, 1015
    and election of *1910*, 2089, 2543
    and election of *1912*, 594, 1813, 1814,
        2090, 2545-52, 2554, 2557-58, 3049
    and election of *1914*, 2564
    and election of *1916*, 2100, 2566-67, 2637-
        43
    and election of *1918*, 2103
    feud with William Taft, 2541, 2543, 2546-
        48, 2550
    and foreign policy, 2094, 2096-99, 2102,
        2103, 2157-68, 2565
    as governor, 2073, 2080, 2081
    Osawatomie address, 1016, 2543, 2546,
        2554, 2573-83
    as party leader, 2082, 2083, 2084-85,
        2265
    as president, 1007, 2080, 2082-86
    on public lands, 2171-74
    reforms, 1012, 1016, 1904, 2564-65
    and trusts, 2082, 2544-46
    Booker T. Washington lunch, 1007, 2083,
        2555
    writings, 2159-68, 2603-34
Roosevelt, Theodore, Jr., 2111
Roosevelt Non-Partisan League, 2566
Root, Elihu, 2074, 2090, 2093, 2095, 2098,
        2099, 2102, 2103, 2105, 2175-76,
        2548, 2566
Root-Takahira Agreement, 2175-76
Roper, Elmo, 3005
Ross, C. Ben, 2272
Rossiter, Clinton, 2400, 2411

Rowell, Chester, 2564, 2567
Rubinow, Isaac Max, 2086
Ruffin, Edmund, 162
rural interests, 1580, 1706, 1831, 2094, 2100
    and agricultural legislation, 1143, 1167,
        1555, 1712, 1820-22, 2087, 2119,
        2271
    and Democrats, 1816, 1818, 1825-26, 1830,
        1942, 1946, 2076
    and economy, 1420, 1703-05, 1941, 1953
    and political organizations, 1555, 2421,
        2569-70, 2833
        see also Populism, organizations
    and railroads, 1550-51, 1555, 1702-03
    and Republicans, 2086, 2110, 2113, 2119,
        2124, 2262-64, 2271, 2677
    and Socialism, 2405, 2414
    and tariffs, 1416-17, 1703-04
        see also individual rural organizations; Mid-
            west, the
Rush, Benjamin, 245
Rusher, William, 3011, 3012, 3013, 3032, 3048
Rushton, Marion, 3325
Rusling, James F., 2153-56
Russell, John, 1571
Russell, Richard, 2685, 2691, 2695, 3317,
    3434
Russell, William E., 1001
Russia see U.S.S.R.
Rustin, Bayard, 2436, 2437, 2438
Ruthenberg, Charles, 3178
Rutland, Robert Allen, 8
Rutledge, Edward, 56-58
Rutledge, John, Jr., 21
Ryan, Mary P., 10
Ryan, Thomas Fortune, 994, 1010

S .

Sabath, Adolph J., 2695
Sabbatarians, 514, 529, 587, 588, 590, 591,
    592, 596
Sacco-Vanzetti case, 1822
St. Clair, Arthur, 18
St. Louis Manifesto, 2419, 2494-97
Saloman, Edward S., 1168
Sanders, Everett, 2266, 2267
Sanford, Edward T., 2112
Santo Domingo, 2097
Savannah Republican, 351
Sawyer, Philetus, 1423
Scammon, Richard, 3044-45, 3046
scandals
    Communist infiltration, 2287-89, 2686
    Credit Mobilier revelations, 901
    Democratic party, income tax, 2690

    in Eisenhower administration, 2703
    8 per centers, 2689-90
    Goldfine-Adams, 2703
    Harding administration, 1822, 2111-12
    Pendergast corruption, 2674
    R.F.C. Loans, 2690
    Tea Pot dome, 2568
    Truman administration, 2287, 2689
    Tweed ring, 899
    Whiskey ring, 901
Schapp, Milton, 2847
Schenk, John, 163
Schevitch, Serge, 2460-66
Schiff, Jacob, 1814
Schimmelfennig, Alexander, 1165
Schlafly, Phyllis, 3013, 3016
Schlesinger, Arthur, jr., 2122, 2429-30, 2693,
    2841
Schmitz, John, 3430, 3444
Schuckers, J. W., 1175-80
Schurz, Carl, 530, 900, 904, 989, 1158, 1165,
    1418
Schuyler, Philip, 18, 149
Schwab, Charles, 2111
Schwarz, Jordan, 2123
Schwellenbach, Lewis, 3189
Scopes trial, 1822
Scott, Hugh, 3000, 3028, 3033, 3049
Scott, John, 270
Scott, John Morin, 149
Scranton, William, 2999, 3001, 3009, 3014,
    3017
    and election of 1964, 3016, 3018-19
    and B. Goldwater, 3020, 3100-01
Seabury, Samuel, 1831
secession, 535, 536, 1161, 1162, 1163
Second World War, 1952-54, 1961, 2277-78,
    2281, 2433, 3182-87
    W. Willkie on, 2352-60
Sedgwick, Theodore, 13, 14, 20
Seeger, Pete, 3320
Selznick, Philip, 3176
Severance, Rollin N., 1686-87
Sewall, Arthur, 1002, 1722, 1723
Sewall, Samuel E., 744
Seward, William H., 362, 606, 607, 609, 1146,
    1148, 1150, 1152, 1155, 1156, 1157,
    1159, 1160, 1163, 1164, 1426
    addresses to New York State legislature,
        379-83, 654-61
    and Antimasonic party, 338, 585, 586, 589
    congressional attempt at removal of, 1167
    and election of 1860, 618
    as governor, 346, 352
    Irrepressible Conflict speech, 1229-38
    "Six Million Dollar Loan" speech, 369-78
    and slavery, 346, 352, 357
    and Whig party, 338, 342, 344, 346, 347,
        348, 349, 352, 357, 359, 360, 361,
        363, 591, 592, 595, 601, 602

Seyd, Ernest, 1726
Seymour, Horatio, 887, 888, 895, 1290
Shachtman, Max, 2428, 2431, 2435, 2437
Shannon, David, 2415, 2427, 2431, 2436
Shannon, Wilson, 512
Shaver, Clem, 1824, 1825, 1826
Shaw, Albert, 2129-33
Shay's Rebellion, 8, 148, 153, 159
Sheredan, Philip H., 891
Sherman, James ("Sunny Jim"), 2550
Sherman, John, 1157, 1412, 1415, 1419, 1425-26, 1557, 1720
Sherman, Roger, 145
Sherman, William Tecumseh, 891, 1171, 1172
Sherman Anti-Trust Act, 993, 999, 1000
Sherman Silver Purchase Act of 1890, 993, 995, 997, 998, 1002, 1720, 2074
Shivers, Allan, 2693, 2694
Shouse, Jouett, 2317-26
Shriver, Sargent, 2853-54, 2864
Sickles, Daniel, 1164
Sigel, Franz, 1165
Sillers, Walter, 3318
Silvermaster, Nathan Gregory, 2686
Silver party, 1717
Silver Republicans, 1003
Simon, Paul, 2863
Simons, A. M., 2420
Simpson, "Sockless" Jerry, 993, 1712
Sinclair, Upton, 2086, 2419
Single Taxers, 2568
Six Crises (R. Nixon), 3085-89
Skidmore, Thomas, 2402-03
Skinner, Harry, 1712
Skinner, Thompson J., 166
slavery
    Alabama Platform, 522
    American Anti-Slavery Society (A.A.S.S.), 742-48 passim, 751, 784-91
    American and Foreign Anti-Slavery Society, 746
    Compromise of 1850, 358, 359, 447-74, 524, 525, 609, 758, 1142-43
    Constitutional Union party, 359
    Crittenden Compromise, 1249-51
    and Democratic party (1828-1860), 502, 520-25 passim, 530-36 passim, 563-70, 610, 611, 758
        Freeport Doctrine, 533, 562, 563
        Jackson, 504, 508, 514, 515, 584
        Pierce, 361, 526-27
        Polk, 353, 520, 521
    Van Buren, 335, 340, 342, 500, 507, 508, 511, 514-15, 517, 518, 519, 520, 527, 550, 755, 760
    District of Columbia, 340, 341, 357, 358, 514, 515, 524, 742, 755
    Dred Scott decision, 531, 562
    Emancipation Proclamation, 1166, 1255-56
    and Federalist party, 22, 24, 26
    and Free Soil party, 755-56, 758, 759, 760, 1142
    Fugitive Slave Law, 359, 524, 607, 614, 701, 1143
    Jeffersonian Republican party, 341, 500, 504
    Kansas-Nebraska Act, 361, 526, 527, 529, 530, 556, 595, 602, 607, 611, 612, 613, 617, 701, 759, 1143-44
    Know Nothing party, 361-62, 595, 607, 608, 611, 612, 699, 701, 706
    Know Something party, 607, 611, 706
    Lecompton Constitution, 532, 533, 562, 563, 1153-54
    Liberty League, 750
    Liberty party, 344, 353, 741, 744, 747, 748, 751-52, 754, 759, 760, 1141
        see also Liberty party
    Mexican Cession, 521, 524, 527
    Missouri, admission of, 24, 498, 500
    Missouri Compromise
        repeal, 361, 526, 527, 556, 611
        restoration, 612, 613, 614, 706, 709
    Preliminary Emancipation Proclamation, 1252-54
    and Republican party, 536, 594, 608, 620, 1185-88
    Seward speech on, 1229-38
    and southern opposition to reform, 1143
    Texas, admission of, 351, 353, 358, 515-21 passim, 526, 550, 752, 753
    Uncle Tom's Cabin, 1143
    and Whig party, 340-41, 344, 346, 348, 352-61 passim, 515, 519, 521, 524, 592, 595, 1142
    Wilmot Proviso, 355, 357, 432, 520-24 passim, 526, 553, 752, 753, 755-56, 758, 1142
        see also abolitionists; The Emancipator; The Liberator
Slidell, John, 534
Smathers, George A., 2689, 2701
Smith, Alfred E., 1822, 1824-25, 1828-29, 2114
    articles on, 1873, 1928-30
    background, 1821-22, 1826-28, 2116
    and election of 1924, 1823
    and election of 1928, 1826-30, 2116-17, 2262
    as governor, 2104, 2115
    and Charles C. Marshall correspondence, 1894-1904, 1905-13
    and prohibition, 1580, 1821, 2115
    and F.D.R., 1831, 1942
Smith, Caleb B., 1160, 1165
Smith, "Cotton Ed," 1950, 1951
Smith, Gerald L. K., 3318
Smith, Gerrit, 746, 748, 749, 750, 754, 758, 759, 821-23, 832-34, 1141, 1144, 1175-80

Smith, James, 1008, 1814
Smith, John, 248
Smith, Melancton, 154, 156, 245
Smith, Samuel Harrison, 260, 269
Smith, S. M., 1558
Smith, Vern, 3178
Smith, William Henry, 1418
Smith, Willis, 2689
Smith Act, 3187, 3189, 3190
Smylie, Robert, 3027
Social Democratic Federation, 2428, 2435
Social Democratic party, 2416, 2428, 2435
    Socialism, 2404-05, 2406, 2407, 3171,
        3173
    British model, 2410-11, 2414, 2420, 2421,
        2423, 2429
    German model, 2410, 2420
    Kautsky's theory, 2422, 2428
    Lassalean dogma, 2410
    "Political Programme" of *1893,* 2410, 2412
    and Progressive party of *1948,* 3320, 3321-
        23
    United Labor party, 2409
    "Voluntarist" philosophy, 2418, 2423
Socialism (M. Harrington), 2440
Socialism, Utopian, 2401-02, 2406
    Brook Farm, 2403
    Brotherhood of the Co-Operative Life, 2416
    New Harmony, 2401, 2403, 2404
    Zoar, Ohio, 2404
Socialist International, First, 2407, 2408
Socialist International, Second, 2410, 2423,
    3173
Socialist Labor party (S.L P.), 1563, 1728,
    2405, 2406-09, 2412, 2414, 2435,
    2439
    article on, Heatter, 2509-10
    and Communists, 2423, 2425, 2432, 3178
    constituency groups, 2415, 2427
    conventions and platforms
        1901, 2416
        1912, 2486-92
        1917, 2494-97
        1921, 2421
        1928, 2498-2503
        1932, 2504-08
        1934, 2428
        1936, 2428
        1960, 2437, 2513-18
        1964, 2437
        1966, 2438
        1968, 2438, 2519-37
    E. Debs speech, 2476-82
    Debsian, 2400, 2415-26
        membership, 2417-18, 2424, 2427,
            2428
    and election of *1917,* 2419
    and election of *1924,* 2423
    founding of, 2414-16
    future forecast, 2439-40

and labor, 2421, 2430, 2476-82, 2491-92
    March on the Convention Movement, *1968,*
        2437
    on New Deal, 2422, 2429, 2511-12
    and Progressive party, 2567, 2568
    St. Louis Manifesto, 2419, 2494-97
    Thomas, 2426-36
Socialist Trade and Labor Alliance, 2412
Socialist Workers party, 2435, 2439
Sorge, F. A., 2406, 2407, 2412
Soulé, Pierre, 526
South, the
    agriculture, 1704, 1706
    and blacks, 1425, 1949, 2697, 2857
    and Congress, 902, 903, 1170
    and Democrats, 892, 988, 1423, 1812,
        1817, 1820, 1825, 1830, 1948, 1959,
        1960-61, 2275, 2683, 2691, 2846,
        3409-17
    economy, 1417, 1701, 1707, 3438
    and election of *1908,* 1811
    and election of *1916,* 1817, 1829
    and election of *1928,* 1827, 1829, 2115
    and election of *1950,* 2689
    and election of *1960,* 1829, 2832
    and election of *1964,* 3022
    and Greenback party, 1561
    and People's party, 1716-18
    and Prohibition party, 1576
    and Reconstruction, 892-94, 1291-92
    and Republicans, 1412, 1425, 2083-84,
        2262, 2263, 2546, 2857
    and Whigs, 1145
    see also Democratic party
Southard, Samuel, 337
Southern Alliance *see* National Farmer's Alli-
    ance and Industrial Union
Southern Mercury, 1710, 1722
Southern Rights parties, 522, 524, 525, 526,
    609
    see also state rights and State Rights parties
Southwick, Solomon, 579
Sovereign, John R., 1724
Soviet Union *see* U.S.S.R.
Spaight, Richard Dobbs, 270
Spangler, Harrison, 2282
Spanish-American War, 1004, 2094-95
    dispatches from Minister to Spain, 2139-41
    McKinley War Message to Congress, 2142-
        46
Sparkman, John J., 2693
Special Committee to Investigate Organized
    Crime—Interstate Commerce,
    (Kefauver), 2691
Specie Resumption Act, 895-96, 901, 998,
    1551, 1556, 1557, 1585-86, 1705,
    1708, 1720
Spector, Arlen, 3028
Spencer, Herbert, 2413
Spooner, John C., 2079, 2095

Spooner, Lysander, 759
Sprague, William, 592
Stachel, Jack, 3188
Staebler, C. Neil, 2706
Stalin, Joseph, 2431-32, 2433, 2435, 3174,
    3175-76, 3183, 3185-86, 3192,
    3194, 3213-19
Stampp, Kenneth, 892
Standard, The, 2460-66
Standard Oil Company, 2563
Stanton, Edwin M., 1163, 1165, 1286
Stanton, Henry B., 743, 744, 748
Star of the West, 1163
Stassen, Harold, 2283, 2290, 3000, 3018
State and the Church, The, 1828
state rights and State Rights parties, 334, 336,
    337, 340-41, 508, 512
    and Democratic party (*1828-1860*), 335,
        336, 502, 505, 508, 514, 525
    and Jeffersonian Republican party, 166,
        498, 500
    and Whig party, 340-41
    see also Nullifiers and nullification; slavery
States' Rights parties of *1948* (Dixiecrats),
    2286, 3309-10, 3314-19, 3399-3425
    Birmingham Conference of *1948,* 3317-19,
        3415-21
    and business interests, 3310, 3324-25
    defeat analyzed, 3327-28
    platform of *1948,* 3422-25
Stedman, Seymour, 2421
Steed, Tom, 2686
Steffen, Lincoln, 2087
Stephens, Alexander H., 344, 345, 346, 355,
    357, 358, 360, 362, 363, 610, 1162,
    1292
    *A Constitutional View of the Late War
        Between the States,* 362
Stetson, Francis L., 994
Steuben, John, 3178
Stevens, Thaddeus, 581-82, 595, 893, 1116,
    1156, 1282, 1285, 1293
Stevenson, Adlai E., 1725
Stevenson, Adlai E., II, 990, 996, 1005, 2291,
    2691, 3043
    background, 2687, 2692
    and election of *1952,* 2693
    and election of *1956,* 2698, 2699
    and election of *1960,* 2706, 2831
    and McCarthyism, 2995
    as party leader, 2696, 2693, 2702, 2828,
        2829
    speeches, 2757, 2772, 2814
Stevenson, Adlai E., III, 2843, 2847
Stewart, Alvan, 748
Stewart, William, 1293, 1426
Stimson, Henry L., 2107, 2121, 2279, 2544
Stockholm Pledge, 3196
Stocking, William, 1185-88
Stockton, Robert F., 615

Stone, William J., 1723
Stowe, Harriet Beecher, 1143
Strauss, Oscar, 995
Strauss, Robert, 2864
Strong, Caleb, 20, 153
Stubbs, William R., 2552, 2560
Student Non-Violent Coordinating Committee
    (S.N.C.C.), 2437
Students for a Democratic Society (S.D.S.),
    2436
suburbia, 2830
    and election of *1960,* 2833, 3007
    and election of *1964,* 2837
    voting patterns, 2987
suffrage, 503, 582
    immigrants (and naturalization), 528, 593,
        596-97, 617
    and Liberty party, 748, 749
    and Whig party, 348
    see also civil rights; feminism
Suite 3505, 3011
Sullivan, Gael, 2692
Sullivan, Roger, 1013, 1813
Sulzer, William, 1814, 1815
Sumner, Charles, 524, 602, 616, 752, 1144,
    1145, 1150, 1151, 1156, 1157,
    1166, 1169, 1175-80, 1282, 1290-93
Sumter, Thomas, 162
Supreme Court
    Brown v. *the Board of Education of Topeka,*
        2697
    and Democratic party, 338, 991
    Dred Scott decision, 531, 562
    Marbury v. *Madison,* 22
    National Republican party, 336, 338
    and F.D.R., 1016, 1949, 2275
    school desegregation, 2697
    and Sherman Anti-Trust Act, 1000
    and H. Spencer theories, 2413
Sutherland, George, 2112
Sydnor, Charles S., 354
Sylvis, William, 2405-06
Symington, Stuart, 2695, 2696, 2704, 2705,
    2831
syndicalists, 3171, 3173, 3179, 3184, 3185

T

Taber, John, 2994
Taft, Charles, 2542
Taft, Phillip, 2412, 2423
Taft, Robert A., 2289, 2988, 3002, 3013
    analysis of Republican convention, 2391-95
    and election of *1940,* 2279
    and election of *1948,* 2286
    and election of *1950,* 2288, 2690

and election of *1952,* 2289-91
NATO speech, 2377-90
as Republican party leader, 2282-83, 3049
as senator, 2270, 2285-86, 3049
Taft, Robert, Jr., 3001, 3024, 3043, 3049
Taft, William Howard, 988, 2084, 2103, 2177, 2544-45
  animosity toward T. Roosevelt, 2541-45, 2547-48, 2550
  and election of *1908,* 1013-15
  and election of *1912,* 1814, 2090, 2091, 2547-52, 2557, 3049
  and election of *1920,* 2105
  foreign policy, 2096-98, 2099, 2102
  Literacy Test Veto Message, 2187-91
  popularity, 1016, 1812, 2070
  as president, 2088-90
  tariff speech, 2181-86
Taft-Hartley Act (Labor-Management Relations Act of *1947*), 2684-85, 2688, 3312
Taggert, Thomas, 1008, 1013, 1818
Tallmadge, Nathaniel P., 510, 511
Tammany Hall, 899, 903, 904, 1004, 1006, 1414, 1814, 1815, 1821, 1831, 2081, 2859-60
  and election of *1904,* 1009-11
  and election of *1908,* 1014-15
  and election of *1912,* 1813
  and election of *1926,* 1826
  and election of *1960,* 2706
  The Nation, editorial on Boss Murphy, 1877-79
Taney, Roger Brooke, 339, 348, 1152
Tappan, Lewis, 744, 758, 784-91, 818-20
tariffs, 590, 748-50 *passim,* 756, 1143
  bills
    Fordney-McCumber Tariff, 2110
    Hawley-Smoot Bill, 2119
    Mills Bill, 992
    Morrill, 894, 1167
    Payne-Aldrich, 1812, 2089, 2543
    Underwood Tariff, 2093
    Wilson-Gorman Tariff, 998, 1000, 1430, 1730, 2074
  and Democratic party, 335, 343, 502-03, 506, 507-08, 512, 519, 531, 756, 991, 992, 997, 1538-40, 1814, 1816
  as issue, 898, 989, 992, 1016, 2075, 2101
  and Jeffersonian Republican party, 269, 500
  and National Republican party, 335, 337
  protectionist, 1415-17, 2073
  and Republican party, 993, 1429, 1507-09, 1538-40, 2079, 2082, 2088, 2108, 2119, 2124, 2181-86
  Tariff Commission, 1816, 2112
  and Whig party, 340, 343, 345, 350, 351, 352, 353, 355, 516-17, 756
  see also nullification
Tariff of *1824,* 502

Tariff of *1828* (Tariff of Abominations), 335, 503, 506, 507
Tariff of *1832,* 335, 507
Tariff of *1833* (Compromise Tariff of *1833*), 335, 340, 343, 345, 508
Tariff of *1842,* 350, 516-17
Tariff of *1846* (Walker Tariff), 353, 520
Tariff of *1890,* 2078
Tariff of *1897* (Dingley), 2088
Tarrance, V. Lance, 2999
T.A.S.S., 3186
Taubeneck, Herman E., 1714, 1719, 1723
taxation, 7, 11, 12, 141, 152, 154, 156-57, 1830
  and Congress, 154, 997, 1825
  and Democrats, 1000, 1538-40, 2103
  income, 997, 1000, 2079, 2093, 2547
  and Jeffersonian Republican party, 166, 254, 259
  and Republicans, 1538-40, 2074, 2079, 2093, 2113, 2123
  and F. D. Roosevelt, 1944, 1945, 1949, 1955
Taylor, Glen, 3322, 3328
Taylor, John W., 241, 269
Taylor, Zachary, 357
  and election of *1848,* 356, 523, 524, 755, 757
Tazewell, Littleton W., 335
Tea Pot Dome Affair, 2568
Teheran conference, 3182, 3184, 3186, 3253
Teller, Henry M., 1001, 1005, 1722
temperance movement, 600, 749, 1567, 1568, 1570-72, 1663-64
  constituent groups, 587, 1579-80
  conventions and platforms
    national (fifth and sixth), 1569
    state, 1569, 1571, 1621-24, 1627-29
  and immigrants, 529, 596, 1568
  and Know Nothing party, 529, 530, 595, 606, 609
  National Protective Association, 1630-38
  organizations, 1567, 1569-70, 1574, 1579
  political activity, 1568, 1569-70, 1615-16
  and Whig party, 514, 525, 592, 594-95, 600
Temperance parties *see* Prohibition party
Templars *see* Independent Order of Good Templars
Ten Men of Money Island (S. F. Norton), 1721
Tennessee Coal and Iron Company, 2544
Tennessee Valley Authority (TVA), 1941, 1949, 1961
  see also Muscle Shoals
Terrell, Ben, 1716
Thelen, David P., 2077, 2081
Theory of the Labor Movement (S. Perlman), 2411
Thomas, Elbert D., 2690
Thomas, Elmer, 1950

Thomas, Norman, 2426-36
  articles, 2509-12
  and election of *1932,* 2399, 2400, 2432
  and election of *1935,* 1946
  and election of *1944, 1948,* 2434
  and election of *1960,* 2437
  and Vietnam War, 2438-39
Thompson, Dorothy, 3321
Thompson, Robert, 3178, 3188, 3196
Three-Fifths Compromise, 22, 24
Thurman, Allen G., 895
Thurmond, J. Strom, 2286-87, 2987, 3028,
    3036, 3038, 3041, 3048, 3316-19,
    3324, 3441-42
  at Southern Governor's Conference, 3409-
    14
Tibbles, T. H., 1725
Ticknor, George, 345
Tilden, Samuel J., 895, 988, 1427, 1428
  as Democratic party leader, 887, 898, 899
  and election of *1876,* 888, 901-03, 956-
    57, 1283
  speech at Cooper Institute, 940-45
Tillman, Benjamin R., 1001 1003, 1713, 1719
Tilton, Elizabeth, 1663-64
Timber Culture Act of *1873,* 1702
Time Magazine, 2997, 3321, 3323
Times-Star, 2089
Tito, Marshal, 3175, 3194
Tobin, Daniel, 2118
Tocqueville, Alexis de, 363, 581, 584
Tod, David, 1168
Toombs, A., 344, 345-46, 348, 354, 355, 357-
    60 *passim,* 362, 363, 610, 1156
Topeka Constitution, 1149
Tories (in America), 6, 18, 137, 138, 142, 143
Toward a Democratic Left (M. Harrington),
    2438
Tower, John, 2999, 3013, 3023, 3028, 3034,
    3036, 3048
Towne, Charles A., 1005, 1725
Townsend, Francis E., 1943-44, 1946, 2269
Townsend Plan, 2430
Tracy, B. F., 1427
trade
  and Antifederalist party, 152, 157
  Embargo (*1807*), 21, 23, 101-05, 265
  Great Britain, 12, 13, 17, 18
  Jay Treaty, 10, 12-13, 17, 18, 19, 246-47
  Jeffersonian Republican party, 246-47, 254
  see also tariffs
Trade Union Educational League (T.U.E.L.),
    2432, 3170-71
Trade Union Unity League (T.U.U.L.), 3171
transportation, 498, 499, 890, 1550
  see also canals; railroads; rivers and harbors;
    roads
Transport Workers Union, 3191
Treaty of Paris (*1783*), 12, 18
Tredwell, Thomas, 154, 163

Trotsky, Leon, 2428, 2431-32
Trotskyism, 2428-29, 2431, 2435, 2439, 3178
Trumbull, Lyman, 999, 1145, 1156, 1157,
    1162, 1166
trusts, 1000, 1014, 1016, 1814, 1945
  anti-trust legislation, 2084, 2093
    Sherman Anti-trust Law, 2079, 2544-
      45, 2546-47
  and T. Roosevelt, 1007, 1014, 1814, 2082,
      2084, 2544-45
  see also Anti-Monopoly party
Truman, Harry S., 2076-77, 2693, 2696, 2725,
    3000, 3183, 3186
  background, 2674-75
  and civil rights, 2685, 3314-15, 3402-08
  and election of *1944,* 1956
  and election of *1948,* 2434, 2685-87, 3309-
    10, 3327
  and election of *1952,* 2691-92, 2693
  and election of *1956,* 2700
  and labor, 2679, 2684
  and MacArthur dismissal, 2289
  move to left (Clifford strategy), 2683-85
  as party leader, 2673, 2677-85, 2702
  as president, first term, 2284, 2676-85
  as president, second term, 2287, 2688-91
  as senator, 2674-75
  and H. A. Wallace dismissal, 2682
Tucker, Raymond, 2702
Tucker, Thomas Tudor, 162
Tugwell, Rexford G., 1942, 1956, 1963, 3320
Tumulty, Joe, 1815, 1827
Tunney, John, 2847, 3043
Turnverein, 2407
Tweed ring scandals, 899
Tweed, William M., 899
Tydings, Millard, 1950, 1951, 2288, 2690,
    2696
Tyler, John, 162, 335, 339, 343, 747
  and Henry Clay, 350-51, 353
  as president, 350, 351, 411-19, 515-20
    passim, 752

U

Udall, Stewart L., 2706
Ullman, Daniel, 605, 612, 616
Uncle Tom's Cabin (H.B. Stowe), 1143
Under the Oaks, 1185-88
Underwood, Oscar, 1812, 1813, 2109, 2553
Unger, Irwin, 1558
Union and Northern Pacific Bills of *1862* and
    1864, 1167
Unionist party, 1162-63, 1168-69
Union Labor party, 1565, 1708-09
Union of Soviet Socialist Republics (U.S.S.R.)

actions, effect on election of *1948,* 3327
and American Communist party, 2425,
    2431, 3173, 3174, 3192
and Hitler, 2432
Revolution, 2423
Union parties, 524, 525, 526, 609, 610, 615,
    616, 891, 1171, 1946
unions *see* individual unions
United Automobile Workers Union (C.I.O.),
    2430, 3191
United Electrical Workers Union (C.I.O.),
    2682
United Labor party, convention and platform
    of *1877,* 1596-98
United Mine Workers Union, 2111, 2113,
    2423, 2429
United Nations, 2366-76
United States Brewers' Association, 1568,
    1569, 1572
United States Steel Corporation, 2544-45,
    2563
United States Telegraph, 502, 506
University of Michigan Survey Research
    Center, 3006
Untermeyer, Samuel, 1814
Uprooted, The (Oscar Handlin), 1827
Upshur, Abel P., 335, 516, 517
urban interests, 897-98, 904, 1714, 1715,
    2085, 2086, 2676-77
    and Democratic party, 1811, 1830, 1959,
        2071, 2829
    and elections, 1820, 1831, 2118-19
    and ethnic groups, 2829, 2859
    and legislation during Johnson administra-
        tion, 2838
    malapportionment, 2086-87, 2290
    racial tension, 2857-58
    and F.D.R., 1946, 1947
    vs. rural, 1820-21, 1822

V

Vallandigham, Clement L., 887, 889-91, 898-
    99, 909-13, 936-39, 1168
Van Buren, Martin, 268, 352-53, 506, 535,
    579, 753
    Autobiography, 348
    and election of *1824,* 501
    and election of *1828,* 502, 503-04
    and election of *1832,* 507
    and election of *1836,* 336, 337, 339, 340,
        349, 511, 592
    and election of *1840,* 343, 512, 517, 591,
        746
    and election of *1844,* 516, 517, 550

and election of *1848,* 356, 523, 754, 755,
    757, 1142
and Andrew Jackson, 334, 337, 338, 340,
    348, 502-07 *passim,* 578
as president, 341, 343, 511-12, 514, 517,
    544-49
Thomas Ritchie, letter to, 502, 539-40
slavery, 335, 340, 342, 343, 500, 507, 508,
    511, 514-15, 517, 518, 519, 520,
    527, 550, 755, 760, 1142
Vandenberg, Arthur H., 2286, 2366-76, 2682
Van Renselaer, Stephen, 18
Van Zandt, Charles C., 1287
Vardaman, James K., 2689
Vaughan, Harry, 2689
Veblen, Thorstein, 3173
Velde, Harold H., 2696
Versailles, Treaty of, 1818-20
Vietnam, South, 2834
Vietnam War, 2439, 2440, 2838, 2917-21,
    2945-51, 3147-55
Vilas, William F., 989, 990, 995, 1001
Villard, Henry, 995
Vinson, Fred M., 2689
Virginia Resolutions, 89-93, 253, 525
Volpe, John, 3028, 3032, 3037, 3043
Voorhis Act, 3175
voting interests, 1421, 1424-25, 2290, 2439
    black registration, 2694, 2697

W

Wade, Benjamin F., 1145, 1156, 1157, 1165,
    1170, 1282, 1293
Wade, Edward, 1175-80
Wade-Davis Bill, 1170, 1268-71
    veto, 1166, 1272
Wade-Davis Manifesto, 1171, 1273-74
Wagner, Robert F., 1947, 2121, 2122, 2123,
    2269, 2430, 2859
Wagner Labor Act, 1945, 2688, 3171
Waite, Davis H., 1718
Walker, Daniel, 2863
Walker, Francis A., 991, 2076
Walker, Frank, 1956, 2675
Walker, Gilbert C., 1293
Walker, Jimmy, 1831
Walker, Robert J., 516, 517, 518, 519
Walker Tariff of *1846,* 353, 520
Wallace, George C., 2854, 2986, 3040, 3047,
    3048, 3051, 3431-32, 3433-34
    and American Independent party, 3429-44
    appeal, 2850, 2859, 3041, 3430-31, 3441
    assassination attempt, 2850, 3443
    and election of *1948,* 3433
    and election of *1964,* 3435

Wallace, George C. (*cont.*)
  and election of *1968*, 2842, 3038
  and election of *1972*, 2850, 2855, 3443
  as governor, 3432, 3433, 3434, 3438
Wallace, Henry A., 1951, 2673, 2678
  background and character, 3310-11,
    3322-23
  and Communist party, 3183, 3186, 3189,
    3190, 3194, 3313, 3321-22, 3351-55
  dismissal as Secretary of Commerce, 1947,
    2681-82, 3194, 3311
  and domestic issues, 2681, 3312
  and election of *1948*, 2286, 2287, 2434,
    2684, 2686, 3312, 3313, 3322-23,
    3339-42, 3343-50
  and foreign policy, 2681, 3311
  as Progressive party leader, 3326-28
  speeches, 2681, 3311, 3322, 3333-38,
    3343-50, 3375-83, 3383-88
  as vice-president, 1952, 1956, 1963
Wallace, Henry C., 2110
Walling, William English, 2420, 2422
Walsh, David I., 2114
Walsh, Thomas, 1822, 1823, 1825, 2104
Warehouse Act of *1916*, 1730
Warner, Sam Bass, 599
War of *1812*, 20, 21, 23, 24, 106-15, 266
Warren, Earl, 2286, 2290
Warren, Frances E., 2102
Warren, Joseph, 1148
Washburn, Israel, 1146
Washburne, Elihu B., 1162, 1248
Washington, Booker T., 1007, 2083, 2555
Washington, George, 7, 155, 158, 576
  Farewell Address, 4, 13, 241
  and Federalist party, 11-12, 15
  Thomas Jefferson, correspondence with,
    243, 284-88
  as president, 11-12, 13, 243, 244, 245, 250
Washington Federalist, 260
Washington Globe, 506, 517, 519
Washingtonian movement, 1567
Washington *National Intelligencer,* 260, 293-95,
  304-05, 324-29, 351, 429-31
Washington Post, 3034
Washington Republican, 269, 322, 323-24
Washington Union, 519, 522
water transportation *see* canals; rivers and
  harbors
Watson, Albert, 3048
Watson, "Pa" (Edwin), 1956
Watson, Thomas B., 1717, 1719, 1723, 1725,
  1728
Watson, Thomas E., 993, 1002, 1714, 1779-86
  2082
Wattenberg, Ben J., 3044-45, 3046
Watterson, Henry, 990, 1008, 1009, 1013, 1417
W.C.T.U. *see* Woman's Christian Temperance
  Union

Wealth against Commonwealth, Henry
  Demarest Lloyd, 999
Weaver, James B., 747, 993, 994, 996, 1562,
  1563, 1708, 1714, 1716, 1723,
  1769-78
Weber, Max, 3181
Webster, Daniel, 24, 335-36, 340, 342, 345,
  348, 351
  on Compromise of *1850*, 461-74
  and election of *1836*, 339-40
  and election of *1852*, 359, 360
  as Secretary of State, 350, 516
  and Whig party, 342, 344, 345, 347, 350,
    352
Webster, Noah, 25
Webster-Ashburton Treaty, 350
Weed, Thurlow, 1146, 1148, 1159
  Albany Evening Journal, 586, 591
  Antimasonic Enquirer, 579
  and Antimasonic party, 338, 578, 579,
    585-86, 589, 590-91, 623-36
  and Know Nothing party, 606
  and Republican party, 607
  and Whig party, 338, 339, 342, 343, 344,
    346, 347, 349, 352, 361, 591, 592,
    602, 604
Weekly People, The, 2435
Weeks, John W., 2104, 2562
Weinstein, James, 2419, 2421, 2422, 2424,
  2427
Weitling, William, 2407
welfare, 2074-75, 2122, 2286, 2416
Welker, Herman, 2288
Welles, Gideon, 519, 527, 602, 1165
Wells, David A., 991
Wells, Rolla, 1008
Werth, Alexander, 3194
West, the, 1820, 1825, 2104, 2120
  and election of *1916*, 1817
  and election of *1928*, 1827
  and populism, 1701, 1716-18
  and progressivism, 2086, 2108, 2543
  and Republican party, 1423, 2091, 2262,
    2546
  and socialism, 2420
Western Federation of Miners, 1719
Western Rural, 1709
Westwood, Jean, 2859, 2863-64
Wheeler, Burton K., 1960, 2275, 2568, 2569,
  2649-61
Wherry, Kenneth S., 2282
Whig party (U.S.), 25, 333-493, 508, 511, 513,
  514, 516, 519, 524, 525, 527, 587,
  591, 592, 594-95, 595-96, 600-01,
  602, 609-10, 749, 750, 751, 752,
  756, 1142, 1145, 1147, 1161, 1291,
  1570
  and Antimasonic party, 338, 341, 342, 346,
    576, 578, 579, 590, 591, 592, 623

Conscience Whigs, 356, 523, 752, 754, 756, 757
and Constitutional Union party, 358-59, 1161
and Democratic party (*1828-60*), 336-44 *passim*, 348, 349-50, 352-53, 356, 357, 359-60, 363, 508, 509, 510, 511, 513-14, 518, 520, 521, 524, 525, 531, 595, 610, 619, 620
factions, 1142, 1145
and Federalist party, 348
and Free Soil party, 757, 758-59, 1142
and Know Nothing party, 576, 595, 600, 602, 605, 608, 610, 614, 616, 1161
and Republican party, 617, 759
Whigs (in America), 17, 18, 137, 138, 143, 144, 148, 149, 150, 153, 154, 155, 157, 162, 165, 894
Whiskey Rebellion, 11, 12, 25
White, Byron, 2706
White, Clifton, 3011, 3012, 3014, 3017, 3019-20, 3025, 3026, 3034, 3036
White, George, 1824
White, Harry Dexter, 2686
White, Horace, 1721
White, Hugh Lawson, 339, 340, 510
White, Theodore, 2999, 3007, 3018, 3021, 3036
White, William Allen, 2077, 2090, 2101, 2178-80, 2560, 2561, 2564
White Man's Committee, 1289
Whitney, Alexander F., 2674, 2679
Whitney, Thomas R., *A Defense of the American Policy . . .,* 680-98
Whitney, William C., 989, 990, 995, 1000
Wiener, Myron, 25
Willard, Frances, 1574-75, 1577
Williams, G. Mennon, 2695, 2702, 2704-06
Williams, Harrison, 2847
Williams, Harrison A., Jr., 2704
Williams, John Sharp, 997
Williams, Samuel W., 1725
Williams, William, 159
Willkie, Wendell L., 1962, 3016
background, 2279-80
and election of *1940*, 1952, 2279
campaign speech, 2344-51
as party leader, 2280-83
testimony before Senate, 2352-60
Wills, Gary, 3000, 3033
Wilmot, David, 355, 520, 523, 527, 753, 1142
Wilmot Proviso, 355, 357, 432, 520-24 *passim*, 526, 553, 752, 753, 755-56, 758, 1142
Wilson, Edmund, 2432
Wilson, Henry, 605, 606, 607, 608, 611, 706, 1148, 1157, 1166, 1199-203
Wilson, William B., 1816, 1817
Wilson, William L., 997-98

Wilson, Woodrow, 1820, 2084, 2099, 2194, 2419, 2422-23, 2561, 2567, 2993
background, 1812
and election of *1908*, 1013
and election, gubernatorial of *1910*, 1017, 2542
and election of *1912*, 1812-14, 2098, 2553, 2557-58
and election of *1916*, 1816
and election of *1920*, 1819
and foreign affairs, 1818, 2098
as party leader, 1813-14, 2561
as president
first term, 1814-16
second term, 1817-18
speech, 1846-55
and World War I, 2102
League of Nations, 2104
Wilson-Gorman Tariff Act of *1894*, 998, 1000, 1730, 2074
Winchell, Walter, 1961
Wing, Simon, 2412
Winston, Henry, 3178, 3189
Winthrop, James, 154
Winthrop, Robert C., 355, 357, 362
Wirt, William, and election of *1832*, 333-34, 589, 662-68
Wirtz, W. Willard, 2693
Wise, Henry, 516, 517
Wittenmyer, Annie, 1574
Wolcott, Alexander, 301-03
Wolcott, Oliver, 11, 14, 23, 24
Wolfe, Berstram, 3178
Woman's Christian Temperance Union (W.C.T.U.), 1574, 1577-78, 1579, 1639-44, 1651-52
Woman's Crusade of *1873-74*, 1574
women's suffrage *see* feminism
Wood, Leonard, 2108
Woodbury, Levi, 503
Woodford, Steward L., 2139-41
Woodhull, Victoria, 2406
Woods, Arthur, 2121
Woodward, George W., 1168
Workers' party, 2428
working class *see* socialism
Workingmen and Labor Reformers' Association *see* United Labor party
Workingmen's parties, 334, 350, 586
Working Men's party (Socialist Labor party), 2402, 2404
Workman, Benjamin, 158
Work Projects Administration (W.P.A.), 1955, 1958
World Court, 1686-87, 2111, 2220-21
World Federation of Trade Unions, 3185
World Tomorrow, The, 2511-12
World War I *see* First World War
World War II *see* Second World War

Wright, Elizur, 752
Wright, Fielding, 3316-19, 3399-401
Wright, Frances, 2402-03
Wright, Silas, 517, 521
Wright, Wallace, 3325
Wyatt, Wilson, 2681, 2693
Wyatt-Brown, Bertram, 746
Wythe, George, 256

X

XYZ affair, 14, 15, 253

Y

Yalta accords, 3186
Yancey, William Lowndes, 522-23, 525
Yarborough, Ralph, 2704
Yates, Robert, 166
Young, Alfred, 16
Young, Milton, 3023
Young, Owen D., 2107
Young Americans for Freedom (Y.A.F.), 3012,
      3025
Young People's Socialist League, 2429

Z

Zeidler, Frank, 2434
Zimmerman, Charles, 2437
Zinoviev, 2432